BROADWAY

BROADWAY

ITS HISTORY, PEOPLE, AND PLACES
AN ENCYCLOPEDIA
Second Edition

Ken Bloom

Routledge
New York and London

Published in 2004 by
Routledge
29 West 35th Street
New York, NY 10001
www.routledge-ny.com

Published in Great Britain by
Routledge
11 New Fetter Lane
London EC4P 4EE
www.routledge.co.uk

Routledge is an imprint of the Taylor & Francis Group.
Printed in the United States of America on acid-free paper.

10 9 8 7 6 5 4 3 2 1

ISBN 0-4159-3704-3 (hbk)
Cataloging-in-Publication Data

Bloom, Ken, 1949–
    Broadway: its history, people, and places: an encyclopedia / Ken Bloom.—2nd ed.
        p. cm.
Includes bibliographical references (p.   ) and index.
    ISBN 0-415-93704-3 (alk. paper)
    1. Times Square (New York, N.Y.)—Encyclopedias. 2. Broadway (New York, N.Y.)
—Encyclopedias. 3. Broadway (New York, N.Y.)—Biography—Encyclopedias. 4. Theater—New
York (State)—New York—Encyclopedias. 5. Historic sites—New York (State)—New York—
Encyclopedias. 6. New York (N.Y.)—Encyclopedias. I. Title.
    F128.65.TB56   2003
    974.7′1—dc21
                                                                        2003002692

CONTENTS

ACKNOWLEDGMENTS

The story of Broadway is replete with the history of many different factors—the theaters, the impresarios, the gangsters, the performers, and so on. This broad scope demanded a huge amount of research. In its two editions, this book required the assistance of a wide range of people and institutions. Thanks to the Billy Rose Theater Collection of the New York Public Library at Lincoln Center. For the first edition, Dorothy Swerdlove and her staff were all patient and professional in answering my many questions. Information on theaters also came in part from Save the Theaters. I also thank Michael Kerker in ASCAP for his patience and for the loan of many photos included in the first edition of this book.

Thanks to Nancy Andrews, Clive Barnes, Joey Bishop, Robert F. Byrnes, Dolly Dawn, Jack Goldstein, Hilary Knight, Bob Larkin, Duke Niles, Robert L. Riddell, Mel Starr, and everyone else who graciously agreed to be interviewed for the first edition.

I especially thank Ellen Zeisler of Susan Bloch and Company, publicists, who was generous in her support both professionally and personally. Ellen made the daunting task of putting this book together much easier. And thanks, too, to Katherine Zeisler for her patience and superior organizational abilities.

David Laskin, my copy editor on the first edition, had perhaps the hardest job of all, deciphering my early drafts and helping me make them understandable and readable. Much of the credit for whatever success this book receives should go to David.

Barry Kleinbort, Berthe Schuchat, Vicki Gold Levi, and Craig Jacobs proofread the first-edition galleys with an unerring sense of history and journalism.

Thanks to David Rose, a friend who patiently tried to get me over the hurdles of dealing with a computer. He tried his hardest to explain exactly what was going on inside the machine.

Tama Starr was terrific in taking time out of her schedule to clear up many misconceptions, supply me with irreplaceable photographs, and give me the benefit of her unique view of Times Square and Broadway. She stepped up to the plate again with humor, intelligence, and generosity for the second edition.

Vicki Gold Levi also selflessly helped me on the first edition with photo acquisitions through her extensive knowledge of both Times Square and photo research. Also on the first edition, Debby Humphreys generously opened her private collection of Times Square and Broadway to me and loaned me many materials that I couldn't find elsewhere.

Louis Botto of *Playbill* was kind enough to supply the information on *Playbill*'s history. Also his excellent book *At This Theatre* was invaluable for the theater history entries.

ACKNOWLEDGMENTS

Times Square, New Year's Eve, 1941.

Thanks to Lucy Stille and Heide Lange of Greenburger Associates for their assistance on the first edition and to the editors of that book, John Thornton and Doug Schulkind. Deb Brody also helped see the first volume come to life and became a friend along the way.

For the second edition, Richard Carlin, a favorite editor of mine, has been patient, inspirational, funny, and supportive as well as being a visionary—all the requisites of a great editor.

I'd like to thank Jean-Marie Derquer, who spent many hours with computer and scanner preparing the manuscript for updating. Florian Suldinger scanned many of the photos included herein.

The second edition was proofread by Barry Kleinbort and Berthe Schuchat two friends who caught many of my errors.

I've tried to include many photos never before published. Many of these came from two excellent private collections. Special thanks to two friends (and performers), Frank Vlastnik and Ken Kantor, for the use of these remarkable images.

Additional help and support for both editions came from Amy Asch, Mike Bowden, Adrian Bryan-Brown, Hap Erstein, Michael Feinstein, Peter Filichia, Jean-Marie Flaguel, Jerry Herman, Karen Hopkins, Edward Jablonski, Richard Norton, Pascal Paioli, Cory Plowman, Pat Plowman, Guy Riddick, Bill Rudman, David Schmittou, Bob Sixsmith, Carl Weaver, Joseph Weiss, and Max Woodward.

I am sure I have forgotten to thank many individuals who helped me compile the enormous amount of research and who gave me moral support. If I have forgotten to thank you, please accept my apologies and send your name to me care of the publisher.

INTRODUCTION

"Broadway may only be a street to some people, but to some of the rest of us it's a religion." So claimed Eddie Foy, Sr. onstage at the Palace Theater, and thousands of people have proved his statement true.

Broadway is the only spot where the hundreds of different worlds that constitute New York City meet face-to-face. The result has been funny, dramatic, and sometimes deadly. Broadway mixes hookers, Broadway stars, gangsters, newspapermen, schnorrers, and bon vivants, rubberneckers, and passersby. These worlds all coexist in 10 blocks of Broadway.

Surprisingly, there has been no comprehensive history of the Times Square area. There have been short books with chatty rundowns on the nightclubs and theaters, but they have tended to be very vague and broad in scope. Few facts enter into the pages of those books. This book is meant to be an informal guidebook to the mercurial history of Broadway. Partly scholarly and partly anecdotal, the book, like Broadway itself, can be used by those who have an exact destination in mind or those who wish to wander aimlessly, browsing up and down the boulevard.

For those hardy souls who are purposeful in their quest, major entries are arranged alphabetically. Subjects not covered in their own separate entries are listed in the index. My hope is that the referrals in the index will lead the interested reader to a somewhat complete idea of a person's career or a place's importance in Times Square history.

Those who would rather take a more lighthearted browse through the history can pick an entry at random and follow the cross-references to additional entries. This method might eventually take one through the entire book.

Since Broadway and Times Square have been the center of the American entertainment industry, many entries are devoted to performers, writers, and theaters. But the electric atmosphere of the area also attracted many ancillary industries and individuals from other walks of life. I have tried to balance the entries accordingly.

Setting the criteria for which entries to include and which to exclude was difficult. I could have made the book more complete with shorter entries, but I felt this would result in a dry book with little room for anecdote. And it is often the stories about the individuals and locations that give Times Square its unique flavor. Also, I decided to include those individuals and institutions that might stand as symbols of their type and that are important in their own right as well. For example, Rector's is the only "lobster palace" included in this book. However, it didn't differ that much in ambiance from Shanley's or the dozens of other haute cuisine restaurants that dotted Broadway in the early years of the century.

Neil Simon, Joseph Fields, Arthur Miller, Eugene O'Neill, and Tennessee Williams are the only playwrights accorded their own entries. However, briefer discussion of many more authors can be discovered through use of the index.

Far more composers and lyricists are represented than are playwrights. This is because I feel that they had greater impact on American theatrical history than their legitimate-theater brethren. After all, the musical theater is Broadway's lifeblood. Its popular songs are known throughout the world, and amateur productions have influenced many Americans beyond the boundaries of Broadway. Because the book was limited in size, not every theater or playwright or restaurant could be covered.

I also tried to focus on those individuals who have had a lasting influence on the area and the art of Broadway beyond their own times. For example, John Golden was a well-known producer, director, playwright, and sometime songwriter, but today his name is practically unknown. This does not mean he didn't make real contributions to Broadway, but he didn't merit an individual entry. Instead, a good description of his professional life can be found through index references. On the other hand, many figures who never received much fame are included simply because they seemed to illustrate a certain ambiance in Times Square at a particular time.

Biographical entries cover actors, gangsters, critics, entrepreneurs, and many incidental but colorful characters. The biographies cover their subjects' lives and careers as they related to Broadway and Times Square.

Entries on Broadway theaters contain the opening dates of the houses, architects, and opening attractions. Additional details are provided by tracing the histories of major productions and their stars.

I have tried to keep my own judgments apart from the factual entries, but Times Square is as much a subjective feeling as an actual location, and the choices of who and what were included obviously reflect my personal consideration of their importance.

The history of Times Square goes back to before the founding of the United States. In 1776 the English general William Howe attacked Manhattan from the East River, near what is today 37th Street. This later became the subject of Robert E. Sherwood's play *Small War on Murray Hill* and the Rodgers and Hart musical *Dearest Enemy*. When news of Howe's landing reached General George Washington, he immediately brought his troops down from Harlem, where they were headquartered. From downtown came the American general Israel Putnam (who later had a Times Square building named after him). Putnam's guide was Aaron Burr.

Washington and Putnam occupied sites on what are now Bryant Park, behind the New York Public Library on 42nd Street between 5th and 6th Avenues, and the area near the present-day Broadway between 43rd and 44th Streets. Years later, Washington would enjoy taking his wife, Martha, on a carriage ride through the area.

During the 1800s this area was the home of squatters who settled along the creek known as Great Kill. The stream was later filled in and became 42nd Street. The area was known for its goat farms and as the site of manure dumping, a big business given the importance of the horse in the 18th century. Dutch farmers began settling the area and developing farms.

John Jacob Astor and William Cutting purchased a 70-acre plot of land between Broadway and the Hudson River, bounded by 42nd Street to the south and 46th Street to the north, for $25,000 and established Medref Eden farm. Astor had arrived in the country in 1784 from Waldorf, Germany. He began a fur trade called the American Fur Company (the Astor Place subway station features a beaver in its tile decoration as a tribute to Astor). Astor built a series of forts in Oregon to protect his fur business and began trading with China from the Pacific Coast. He also dealt in English pianofortes.

John J. Norton owned a large farm on the west side of 42nd Street. On September 28, 1825, he ceded a part of his farm, the Hermitage, to the city so that it could construct 42nd Street. The city paid Norton $10 for the rights of passage.

In 1829 a local paper carried an advertisement that read in part: "To let—large and commodious house and garden spot situated on Forty-second and Forty-third Streets, and 100 feet from Eighth Avenue. Well calculated for boarding school, summer retreat or private family—being pleasantly situated on high ground with view of North River. House has 25 rooms, good well and pump in cellar. Garden is laid out and at present planted for spring vegetables."

The streetcar line finally reached the summer homes around East 42nd Street in 1839. The 42nd Street thoroughfare was used to drive cattle from the docks to slaughter houses on the East Side. The cattle arrived at 42nd Street on the Weehawken ferry from New Jersey. Horsecar lines from the ferry also took passengers downtown.

Houses, stores, schools, and churches were built in the area. Bloomingdale's Baptist Church (1841), the 42nd Street Presbyterian Church (1868), and the Methodist-Episcopal Asylum for the Aged and Infirm (c. 1855) all opened on 42nd Street. The Bloomingdale's Baptist Church became the Central Baptist Church in 1868, the 42nd Street Presbyterian Church became St. Luke's Evangelical Lutheran Church in 1875, and the asylum closed its doors in 1883 and was converted into the Clinton Apartment House. In 1878 St. Louis College, "for Catholic boys of refined families," occupied 224 West 58th Street. The Church of St. Mary the Virgin at 228 West 45th Street was an Episcopal church with 600 members. In 1866 the Sisterhood of St. John the Baptist opened the Midnight Mission "For the reclamation of fallen women, who are here given homes, and, if found worthy, aided in obtaining permanent homes or employment." The mission was at 208 West 46th Street. The George Bruce Memorial Circulating Library was situated at 226 West 42nd Street beginning in 1883.

The area, named after London's Long Acre, became the center of the carriage industry. Where the Winter Garden Theatre now stands was Tattersall's American Horse Exchange. Harness shops and stables made up the majority of the businesses on Longacre Square. As the theater industry moved into the area the carriage shops moved northward along Broadway and were transformed into garages and automobile showrooms when the horse became passé.

Slowly but surely, the New York theater industry came uptown from the City Hall area to 14th Street and Union Square, to 23rd Street and Madison Square, to 34th Street and Herald Square. The theaters followed the diagonal swath that Broadway cut through the city.

Little by little new theaters began nearing Longacre Square. Among the first theaters in the Longacre Square area was the Metropolitan Concert Hall at 41st and Broadway. Built in May 1880, the concert hall was never a success. It became the Metropolitan Casino, Alcazar, Cosmopolitan Theatre, a roller-skating rink, and an exhibition hall. It was demolished in 1887 to make way for the Broadway Theatre, a very successful venture.

T. Henry French and two partners built the Broadway, which opened on March 3, 1888, with a production of *La Tosca* starring Fanny Davenport. French was the son of Samuel French, whose name graces the still popular play-publishing business he founded. The new Romanesque building seated 1,776 patrons and had a 75-foot-wide stage. Like many theaters of the time, the Broadway was the home to acting companies, in this case led by De Wolf Hopper and Francis Wilson. Both companies specialized in comic operas. The Broadway Theatre left the legitimate field in 1908 when vaudeville and movies took over its stage. The theater was torn down in 1929 and replaced with a garment center building.

The Casino Theatre, built in 1882 at the corner of 39th Street and Broadway, was a favorite of audiences and performers. In 1900, the same year that Macy's moved from the "Ladies' Mile" on 6th Avenue in the 20s to Herald Square, the Casino had a roof garden built over its auditorium, the first of a popular breed of theaters around the turn of the century.

One year after the construction of the Casino, the Metropolitan Opera House opened on Broadway between 39th and 40th Streets. The arrival of the distinguished opera company gave the area a new cachet, and soon society began to look at the West Side as an attractive area. The opera house suffered a major fire in 1892 but was rebuilt and lasted until 1966, when a new (and inferior) Metropolitan Opera House was constructed in Lincoln Center.

By 1893 New Yorkers were spending $6 million a year on entertainment. That same year (the year of the World's Columbian Exposition and Grover Cleveland's inauguration as President) landowner Robert Goelet built a theater on his plot of land on 38th Street and Broadway and called it Abbey's Theatre after producer Henry Abbey. *King's Handbook of New York* (1893) predicted that Abbey would occupy "a prominent and worthy place among the most notable theatres of the New York and the world." But this was not to be. Abbey left the theater in 1896, and the name was changed to the Knickerbocker Theatre under the auspices of Al Hayman. The Knickerbocker was torn down in 1930.

The first theater on 42nd Street was the AMERICAN THEATRE, built in 1893, the year of a great stock market panic. After a successful opening with *The Prodigal Daughter*, the theatre's fortunes quickly fell. It became a vaudeville house, a motion picture house, and finally a burlesque theater. It was demolished in 1932.

In 1895, in the area known as "Thieves' Lair" by locals, OSCAR HAMMERSTEIN I built his OLYMPIA theater complex. Electric lights had just been installed in the Longacre area. The theaters that made up the Olympia complex on Broadway between 44th and 45th Streets were not a success, although they managed to draw attention to the square as an entertainment center.

Site of the Time's Tower, 1898.

The area along Broadway from 37th Street to 42nd Street was dubbed "the Rialto." Soon the Longacre theater district would also be called "the Rialto." In the 1950s and 1960s Sam Zolotow wrote a popular theater column in the *New York Times* called "News of the Rialto."

Almost 80 theaters were constructed in the Times Square area. Many were built by producers and actor-managers who headed their own stock companies. They leased the land from the original owners, who were intelligent enough not to let go of their land holdings. More and more producers such as DAVID BELASCO and Daniel Frohman had their own houses built. Later, just before and during the 1920s, impresarios such as FLORENZ ZIEGFELD and EARL CARROLL would build theaters to house their productions.

Most of the successful theaters in the area were owned by the 6 members of the Theatrical Syndicate, a trust that was happy to force out its competition. The syndicate was put out of business in 1916 and replaced by another equally powerful group, the SHUBERT BROTHERS. The Shuberts' power cannot be overestimated. During the Depression, when breadlines snaked around Duffy Square at Broadway and 47th Street, it was the Shuberts who kept American theater alive. The Shuberts were forced to break up their near monopoly in the 1950s.

The square's preeminence was solidified in 1904 when the *New York Times* (founded in 1851) tore down the Pabst Hotel and built its new headquarters, the TIMES TOWER. It is telling that the entrance of the Pabst Hotel faced downtown, while that of the new Times Tower faced uptown.

The move by the *New York Times* to the square led to the City Council's voting to rename Longacre Square, Times Square. In April 1904 the mayor signed the designation.

The Times Tower gained prominence in the square when the MOTOGRAM electric zipper sign was wrapped around the building. The Motogram gave the latest news, and thousands of New Yorkers, in the years before the widespread use of radio, would gather in the square to see the latest reports on modern technology. Even during radio's and, later, television's prominence in timely news reporting, the Times Tower remained a focal point. New Yorkers gathered to see election results, news of the Japanese surrender in World War II (and the resultant V-J day celebration), and sports finals.

The square was also used for mass rallies to sell war bonds, for publicity stunts (see STUNTS), for political demonstrations, and for the annual New Year's Eve celebration. Parades, including Macy's annual Thanksgiving Day parade, marched down Broadway through the square.

On October 27, 1904, the West Side Subway was opened from 4th Avenue to 42nd Street on the East Side, then across the thoroughfare to Broadway and up to 125th Street. Within one year the Times Square subway stop had been used by over 5 million people. The laying of the new subway lines through the city, the consolidation of many train lines into Grand Central Terminal at 42nd Street and Vanderbilt Avenue in 1878, and the completion of the 3rd and 6th Avenue elevated trains also in that year helped the burgeoning area of Times Square.

In 1905 gasoline-driven buses replaced the horse-drawn streetcars. The city saw its first metered taxicabs in 1907. Unfortunately, many of the theaters were not built to screen the increased noise from the traffic. Patrons sitting in the last rows of the orchestra at the REPUBLIC THEATRE could not hear Mrs. Patrick Campbell in *Magda*. Press agent A. Toxen Worm had a brainstorm when George Tyler facetiously suggested that the problem could be solved if 42nd Street were covered in tanbark. Worm thought the idea was the ideal publicity stunt and ordered the street so covered.

John C. Van Dyke described Times Square in his book *The New New York*. He wrote: "At eight in the evening there is the incessant come and go of trolleys, the rattle of cabs, the shuffle and push of many feet along the street, the insistent voice of ticket speculators, and the unintelligible shout of men and boys hawking night editions of newspapers."

The construction of Madison Square Garden at 50th Street between 8th and 9th Avenues brought many sports enthusiasts to the area. The money to be made in area nightclubs and later speakeasies, not to mention the money being laundered through Broadway investments, led to an influx of gangsters (see GANGSTERS).

The opening of such hotels as the ASTOR, the Metropole at 41st Street between Broadway and 7th Avenue (the home of GEORGE M. COHAN and Enrico Caruso), the Vendome at Broadway and 41st Street, the Claridge, and the KNICKERBOCKER brought tourists and travelers to the area. The docks, only four avenues away, hosted the arrivals and departures of the giant luxury liners making port in New York. The Times Square hotels were the nearest deluxe accommodations for these travelers and were halfway between the ports and the rail lines. Fancy restuarants such as RECTOR'S, Shanley's, MURRAY'S ROMAN GARDENS, and Churchill's served such upper-class patrons as ANNA HELD and DIAMOND JIM BRADY. The years following World War I were boom years for Times Square. Money was plentiful and New York was the richest American city. This wealth led to changes along the Great White Way. The theatrical unions, such as ACTORS' EQUITY, gained power and demanded increases in pay. Inflation, spurred by the success of the stock market, raised production costs, and ticket prices reflected the increased costs and increased taxes needed to support the growing metropolis.

The boom era culminated both financially and artistically with the theatrical season of 1927–28, when 257 plays opened in the 71 theaters around Times Square. Shortly after this, however, the industry suffered three major blows, one financial and two artistic. The first was the stock market crash of 1929, which forced many producers and their backers into receivership. Even the powerful Shuberts lost many theaters. The second was the acceptance of sound pictures by the public. Great movie palaces were built along Broadway in the late 1920s. The construction of these massive halls culminated with the greatest of all, the ROXY THEATER, under the auspices of S. L. ("ROXY") ROTHAFEL, the man most responsible for the development of the movie palace. The third big effect on the industry was the emergence of radio as a mass entertainment force.

During the 1930s many theaters were darkened by the sudden drop-off of theatrical ventures. Many of the houses were converted to radio (and later television) studios or burlesque houses. Still more were demolished or left empty. The FEDERAL THEATRE PROJECT managed to keep some of the theaters lit. The burlesque houses slowly led to the eventual decline of the 42nd Street area. When Mayor LaGuardia outlawed burlesque, the theatres became grind movie houses and attracted an even lower class of clientele. Soon low entertainments such as Ripley's Odditorium and Hubert's Museum and Flea Circus attracted a decidedly less ritzy crowd to the Great White Way.

World War II brought a new prosperity to the area, but it was a middle-class and lower-class area. Still, the theater remained the center of the nation's entertainment industry. Due to its vigor and unique signage, especially that of DOUGLAS LEIGH and the ARTKRAFT STRAUSS Sign Company, Times Square itself became a great attraction.

The 1960s and 1970s saw a worsening of the area and a drop in the number of legitimate shows produced on Broadway. Many of the 42nd Street theaters fell into further disrepair and showed kung fu or porno films round the clock. The opening of the Port Authority Bus Terminal brought runaways and vagrants into the area, and 8th Avenue became known as one of New York's most undesirable locations. Hustlers of three-card monte and other scams mixed with pickpockets. Peddlers selling fake Gucci bags and $10 imitation Rolex watches crowded the sidewalks. As drugs and prostitution flourished around 42nd Street and Eighth Avenue, numerous plans, all discarded, promised to clean up the area.

Many New York landmarks, including LINDY'S restaurant, the Astor Hotel, the PARAMOUNT THEATER, and the Roxy Theater, were demolished to make way for high-rise office buildings, which increased land values and destroyed the low-rise ambiance

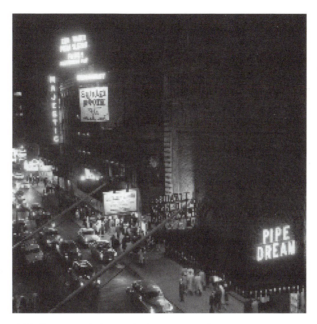

44th Street at Night in 1955.

of the area. Many of the great spectacular signs were taken down and replaced by simple illuminated billboards.

During the 1980s there was a resurgence of activity around the area. Zoning changes made it more profitable to build in the area, and more and more skyscrapers were built, pushing out still more of the ancillary businesses that served the theater industry. Preservationists waged an unsuccessful battle to save the HELEN HAYES and MOROSCO theaters. This led to an increased determination to save the remaining theaters, and by late 1987 most of the remaining theaters enjoyed landmark status (over the objections of their owners). A major redevelopment of 42nd Street was announced by Mayor Edward Koch's administration, but condemnation of buildings in the area and new construction were stalled by a series of lawsuits. A stock market crash in October 1987 made new construction less attractive. Many of the individuals involved in the redevelopment plan were indicted, and the entire plan came under increased criticism. The Koch administration, astoundingly in favor of redevelopment over preservation, insisted in pursuing the plan even after it seemed unwise and unfair to do so.

The Walt Disney Corporation's refurbishment of the NEW AMSTERDAM THEATRE proved to be the most important catalyst in the renovation of 42nd Street. Together with the renovation of the VICTORY THEATER and a flourishing economy under a Democratic president, 42nd Street was finally on its way toward cleanup. The results were impressive even as die-hard New Yorkers mourned the loss of historic theaters and the introduction of generic national chains. The new Times Square was largely an economic success, if not a cultural one. Sidewalks were incredibly crowded with moviegoers, theater patrons, and tourists.

When Edward Arlington Robinson, on his way to a Broadway show, wrote "The White Lights, Broadway 1906," he could not have realized just how prophetic his poem would be:

Here, where the white lights have begun
To seethe the way for something fair,
No prophet knew, from what was done,
That there was triumph in the air.

AARONS AND FREEDLEY. Broadway producers of the 1920s and '30s noted for their association with the Gershwins, and builders of the Alvin Theater; Alex A. Aarons, b. Philadelphia, 1891; d. Beverly Hills, California, March 14, 1943; Vinton Freedley, b. Philadelphia, November 5, 1891, d. New York City, June 5, 1969.

Today the SHUBERT BROTHERS, Jujamcyns, and Nederlanders are the theater owners of note, but prior to the Depression, most producers owned their own theaters. This was a logical outgrowth of the 19th-century tradition of the great actor-managers. These actor-managers produced their own shows in which they starred with their stock companies. That tradition faded in the late 1920s as a new generation of producers came on the scene. Other circumstances leading to the end of the actor-managers were the creation of ACTORS' EQUITY and the increased costs of producing theater, which precluded keeping large companies on salary throughout the year.

Also, as American playwrights came into their own, their plays often replaced the European and British repertoire preferred by the old school. This change in drama led to a change in acting style, a change that was hastened by the new popularity of the movies. As the theater district moved to Times Square, producers rushed to build theaters for their own productions. Owning their own theaters allowed producers to reduce costs and to avoid the control of competitors. Producers Alex Aarons and Vinton Freedley were no exception.

Aarons, the son of composer-producer Alfred E. Aarons, produced the GEORGE GERSHWIN and B. G. DE SYLVA (*see* DE SYLVA, BROWN, AND HENDERSON) show *La-La-Lucille* in 1919 and *For Goodness Sake* in 1922 with a score by the Gershwins, among others. Freedley acted in Aarons' production of *For Goodness*

Sake in 1922 and *Elsie* in 1923. Later that year, Aarons and Freedley teamed up and produced *Lady, Be Good!* (12/1/24; 330 performances) at the LIBERTY THEATRE. FRED AND ADELE ASTAIRE starred in the show, introducing such numbers as "Fascinating Rhythm" and "Oh, Lady Be Good!"

Aarons next produced *Tell Me More!* (4/13/25; 100 performances), also with a score by the Gershwins and B. G. De Sylva. They teamed up again with *Tip-Toes* (12/28/25; 194 performances). Queenie Smith and Jeanette MacDonald starred, and the score included "Looking for a Boy," "That Certain Feeling," and "Sweet and Low Down."

Their next Gershwin show was a smash hit. *Oh, Kay!* (11/8/26; 256 performances) opened at the IMPERIAL THEATRE with Gertrude Lawrence, Oscar Shaw, Victor Moore, and Betty Compton. The superior score

Adele Astaire presents Alex Aarons with a "good luck" brick for his next theatre, while Vinton Freedley and brother Fred Astaire look on.

yielded such tunes as "Maybe," "Clap Yo' Hands," "Do Do Do," and "Someone to Watch over Me." The success of *Oh, Kay!* led the two producers to follow in the path of others and build their own theater. The name Alvin was arrived at by combining the first letters of each producer's first name. The Alvin Theater (*see* NEIL SIMON THEATER) opened with the premiere of *Funny Face* on November 22, 1927. The production of *Funny Face* (250 performances) boasted a score by GEORGE AND IRA GERSHWIN and starred the Astaires. The score introduced such standards as "Funny Face," " 'S Wonderful," and "My One and Only."

Next came *Here's Howe!* (5/1/28; 71 performances), remembered today, if at all, for the pop song "Crazy Rhythm." Next, Aarons and Freedley presented *Hold Everything!* (10/10/28; 413 performances) at the BROADHURST THEATER. Their third premiere in 1928 was the Gershwins' *Treasure Girl* (11/8/28; 68 performances) at the Alvin Theater. The show opened with Gertrude Lawrence, Clifton Webb, and Walter Catlett starring. The score featured such gems as "I've Got a Crush on You," "Oh, So Nice," "I Don't Think I'll Fall in Love Today," and "Feeling I'm Falling."

Spring Is Here (3/11/29; 104 performances) came hard on the heels of the closing of *Treasure Girl*. This time RODGERS AND HART provided a score, including the now well-known "With a Song in My Heart." *Heads Up!* (11/11/29; 144 performances), another Rodgers and Hart show, opened with Ray Bolger and Victor Moore.

The stock market crash slowed the producing team's output, and *Girl Crazy* (10/14/30; 272 performances), their next production, would not open until almost a year after *Heads Up!* It might have played longer if the country's problems hadn't caused theater business to fall off. The score was one of the Gershwins' best. It featured "Bidin' My Time," "Embraceable You," "But Not for Me," and "I Got Rhythm." The cast included Willie Howard, Ginger Rogers, and, making her Broadway debut, ETHEL MERMAN. *Girl Crazy* was the last show to play the Alvin Theater under Aarons and Freedley's management. They lost their theater to the mortgage holders, as did many other theater owners during the Depression.

Aarons and Freedley continued their partnership both at the Alvin and at other Broadway houses after the loss of the Alvin. Following *Girl Crazy* came *Pardon My English* (1/20/33; 43 performances), George Gershwin's ninth and final score for Aarons and Freedley and Alex Aarons' last Broadway show. It premiered at the MAJESTIC THEATRE.

After Aarons' retirement in 1933, Freedley continued on his own, producing *Anything Goes!* (11/21/34; 415 performances) at the Alvin. *Anything Goes!* starred Ethel Merman and featured an excellent COLE PORTER score including "You're the Top," "I Get a Kick out of You," "Anything Goes," and "All Through the Night." The show reestablished Freedley as a top Broadway producer. Freedley's production of Cole Porter's *Red, Hot and Blue!* (10/29/36; 181 performances) at the Alvin starred Ethel Merman, Bob Hope, and Jimmy Durante. The standout song was "It's Delovely."

Freedley next presented Porter's *Leave It to Me!* (11/9/38; 291 performances) at the Imperial Theatre, marking the Broadway debut of MARY MARTIN. She became a star when, in this show, she introduced the Porter song "My Heart Belongs to Daddy." The other notable Porter songs featured in the score were "Most Gentlemen Don't Like Love" and "Get out of Town." VERNON DUKE and John Latouche's *Cabin in the Sky* (10/25/40; 156 performances) was Freedley's next production, opening at the MARTIN BECK THEATRE. Freedley co-produced the show with Albert Lewis. The exceptional score featured "Taking a Chance on Love," which was introduced in the show by Ethel Waters and became an instant success. Freedley produced one more show boasting a Cole Porter score, *Let's Face It!* (10/29/41; 547 performances). The show starred Danny Kaye, Eve Arden, Benny Baker, Mary Jane Walsh, and Vivian Vance.

Jackpot (1/13/44; 44 performances), a Vernon Duke and Howard Dietz (*see* DIETZ AND SCHWARTZ) failure,

Vinton Freedley and Mary Martin in 1938 during the run of *Leave It to Me!*.

returned Freedley to the Alvin. Nanette Fabray, Allan Jones, and Betty Garrett starred. Jacqueline Susann, later to receive fame as an author, played a small role. Freedley's production of *Memphis Bound!* (5/24/45; 36 performances) at the BROADWAY THEATRE was also a failure. Freedley's last Broadway show, *Great to Be Alive!* (3/23/50; 52 performances) at the WINTER GARDEN THEATRE, was another failure.

Aarons and Freedley had their greatest successes when presenting shows by inspired talents. They were not the sort of creative producers who could save weak shows though their own talents. But their long list of hits proves that they recognized talent and could put together attractive packages that enabled the artists to work to their best advantage. The team had seven shows by the Gershwins to their credit. Four of these shows featured libretti by Fred Thompson in collaboration with a series of talents, including GUY BOLTON, who was also responsible for four scripts. Five of the shows featured the duopianists Phil Ohman and Vic Arden. Freedley alone produced 4 Cole Porter shows. Ethel Merman appeared in 3 of their shows. The shows Aarons and Freedley produced were not necessarily the most artistic endeavors of the people they worked with, but they were among the most popular.

George Abbott rehearsing *New Girl in Town* in 1957.

ABBOTT, GEORGE. Noted Broadway playwright, producer, director, actor, and play doctor, with a long career; b. Forestville, New York, June 25, 1887; d. Miami Beach, Florida, January 31, 1995.

George Abbott, or Mr. Abbott as he was known by his contemporaries, enjoyed what is probably the most creative and certainly the longest career in the American theater. He was involved with 122 productions as playwright, producer, director, actor, or play doctor; often he held more than 1 role in the same show. Abbott was responsible for giving many people their first break in the theater. Among those who scored their first successes with George Abbott productions were LEONARD BERNSTEIN, Garson Kanin, John Kander and Fred Ebb, Betty Comden and Adolph Green (*see* COMDEN AND GREEN), Jerome Robbins, FRANK LOESSER, Jean and WALTER KERR, HAROLD PRINCE, Richard Bissell, Jerome Weidman, Jerry Bock and Sheldon Harnick (*see* BOCK AND HARNICK), and Bob Merrill, as well as hundreds of performers, including Carol Burnett, Desi Arnaz, and Nancy Walker.

Abbott's early jobs included Western Union messenger, cowboy, steelworker, swimming instructor, basketball coach, and salesman. His first play, *The Head of the Family*, a one-act, was presented by the Harvard Dramatic Club in 1912. He first appeared on Broadway as an actor in *The Misleading Lady* (11/25/13) at the Fulton Theater (*see* HELEN HAYES THEATER). Other early performances were in *Daddies* (9/5/18), *The Broken Wing* (11/29/20), *Zander the Great* (4/9/23), *White Desert* (10/18/23), *Hellbent for Heaven* (1/4/24), *Lazybones* (9/22/24), and *Processional* (1/12/25).

Abbott's first writing assignment was in collaboration with James Gleason. They wrote *The Fall Guy* (3/10/25), which premiered at the Eltinge Theater (*see* EMPIRE THEATER (2)). He collaborated with Winchell Smith on *A Holy Terror* (9/28/25), which opened at GEORGE M. COHAN'S THEATRE with Abbott in a leading role. With John V. A. Weaver, he wrote and directed *Love 'Em and Leave 'Em* (2/3/26). Abbott's first great success, *Broadway* (9/16/26; 603 performances), was written with Philip Dunning. The melodrama of gangsters and show biz opened at the BROADHURST THEATER under Abbott's direction. He would direct it again as his last Broadway project, opening on his 100th birthday.

Abbott's next assignment was as director of *Chicago* (12/30/26; 172 performances). That show was also a success following its opening at the MUSIC BOX THEATER. It was turned into a successful film and subsequently a very successful stage and film musical with music by John Kander and Fred Ebb.

Coquette (11/8/27; 366 performances) was also a hit under Abbott's direction. With Philip Dunning co-producing, Abbott directed *Twentieth Century* (12/29/ 32; 154 performances). It opened at the Broadhurst Theater. This too was successfully translated into a musical titled *On the Twentieth Century* with a score by Cy Coleman and the team of Betty Comden and Adolph Green.

With John Cecil Holm, he co-authored one of the great hits of the 1930s, *Three Men on a Horse* (1/30/ 35; 812 performances). The fast-paced farce opened at THE PLAYHOUSE THEATRE. It also served as the basis of the musicals, *Banjo Eyes* with Eddie Cantor and, *Let It Ride*, with a score by Jay Livingston and Ray Evans. *Three Men on a Horse* became one of the most produced plays in both commercial and professional theaters.

Abbott's first musical theater assignment was directing the RODGERS AND HART musical extravaganza *Jumbo* (11/16/35; 221 performances). The BILLY ROSE production played the old HIPPODROME on Sixth Avenue. *Jumbo* was followed by a bona fide smash, *Boy Meets Girl* (11/27/35; 669 performances). Abbott produced and directed the farce at the CORT THEATRE.

Abbott and Rodgers and Hart coauthored the script of *On Your Toes* (4/11/36; 318 performances), a musical comedy that opened at the IMPERIAL THEATRE. *On Your Toes* starred Ray Bolger and Tamara Geva and boasted choreography by George Balanchine. Abbott, unlike many directors, was not afraid of surrounding himself with the best talent available.

Abbott produced and directed *Brother Rat* (12/16/ 36; 575 performances), followed by another great hit, *Room Service* (5/19/37; 496 performances), at the Cort Theatre. Both these plays were successfully adapted as Hollywood films. His next musical was Rodgers and Hart's *The Boys from Syracuse* (11/23/38; 235 performances). Abbott wrote the book and produced and directed the musical, which opened at the Alvin Theater (*see* NEIL SIMON THEATER). One of the few true musical farces (*A Funny Thing Happened on the Way to the Forum*, also directed by Abbott, is another). *The Boys from Syracuse* was the first musical to be adapted from a play by William Shakespeare.

He produced and directed the same team's *Too Many Girls* (10/18/39; 249 performances), which starred a young Desi Arnaz. Another Rodgers and Hart show followed, the controversial *Pal Joey* (12/25/40; 374 performances). Gene Kelly opened in the title role at the ETHEL BARRYMORE THEATRE. *Pal Joey* would later be rediscovered in an acclaimed revival in the 1950s.

The next year Abbott gave a break to a pair of new songwriters, Hugh Martin and Ralph Blane. Their show, *Best Foot Forward* (10/1/41; 326 performances), which Abbott directed, produced, and co-authored with John Cecil Holm, opened at the Ethel Barrymore Theatre. It contained such great songs as "Buckle Down Winsocki," "Ev'ry Time," and "Just a Little Joint with a Juke Box." The show starred June Allyson, Danny Daniels, Stanley Donen, Rosemary Lane, and Nancy Walker.

Abbott continued to herald new Broadway talents. *On the Town* (12/28/44; 462 performances) marked the Broadway debuts of composer LEONARD BERNSTEIN, lyricists Betty Comden and Adolph Green, and choreographer Jerome Robbins. They were ably taught under the firm hand of director Abbott. Abbott's next directorial hit, *High Button Shoes* (10/ 9/47; 727 performances), again introduced a new composer and lyricist to Broadway. JULE STYNE and Sammy Cahn provided the songs for the Phil Silvers and Nanette Fabray show.

Another Broadway neophyte, Frank Loesser, was the songwriter who provided the score for Abbott's next hit, *Where's Charley?* (10/11/48; 792 performances). Abbott's musicalization of Brandon Thomas' farce opened at the ST. JAMES THEATRE. Abbott directed Ray Bolger and Allyn Ann McLerie in the leads; "Once in Love with Amy" was the big hit from the show.

Broadway veteran IRVING BERLIN's *Call Me Madam* (10/12/50; 644 performances) opened with ETHEL MERMAN in the leading role. The show, inspired by real-life ambassador and hostess Perle Mesta, was Abbott's next hit as a director. Composer Arthur Schwartz (*see* DIETZ AND SCHWARTZ) and lyricist Dorothy Fields (*see* FIELDS FAMILY) collaborated with George Abbott on *A Tree Grows in Brooklyn* (4/19/51; 267 performances), the musical version of Betty Smith's beloved novel. Abbott wrote the libretto as well as provided direction for the musical; Johnny Johnson and Shirley Booth starred at the Alvin Theater. *Wonderful Town* (2/25/53; 559 performances), Bernstein, Comden, and Green's next collaboration, was directed by Abbott. The show, based on Ruth McKinney's stories in the *New Yorker*, opened at the WINTER GARDEN THEATRE with Rosalind Russell in the lead.

The team of Richard Rodgers and Oscar Hammerstein II (*see* RODGERS AND HAMMERSTEIN) seemed like a sure bet for Abbott treatment. But the result, *Me and Juliet* (5/28/53; 358 performances), was one of the team's few failures. Abbott had greater success with *The Pajama Game* (5/13/54; 1,061 performances), the effort of another team of newcomers. Jerry Ross and Richard Adler wrote the score, and Abbott collaborated with Richard Bissell on the libretto; Bob Fosse made his choreographic debut with the show. "Hernando's Hideaway" and "Hey There" were the two standouts in the score.

After directing a revival of *On Your Toes* (10/11/ 54), Abbott took on directing duties and coauthored the libretto for the second and last collaboration between Adler and Ross, *Damn Yankees* (5/5/55; 1,019 performances). It opened at the 46th Street Theatre (*see* RICHARD ROGERS THEATER) with Gwen Verdon in her first starring role. Her song, "Whatever Lola Wants," became one of the hits of the show. Having had a failure with Richard Rodgers, Abbott did much better with the composer's daughter, Mary. She and Marshall Barer wrote the score to the hit *Once upon a Mattress* (5/11/59; 460 performances). It opened at the Phoenix Theater, and a new star was born, Carol Burnett.

Abbott directed and collaborated on the book for the Pulitzer prize–winning musical *Fiorello!* (11/23/59; 796 performances). The show was the first hit for the team of Jerry Bock and Sheldon Harnick (*see* BOCK AND HARNICK). Their loving portrait of Fiorello LaGuardia starred Tom Bosley in the title role. The same team, Bock and Harnick, and book writers Abbott and Jerome Weidman couldn't repeat their success with *Tenderloin* (10/17/60; 216 performances), which opened at the 46th Street Theatre. Maurice Evans was the unlikely star. Abbott's direction of a comedy, *Take Her, She's Mine* (12/21/61; 404 performances), proved to be one of his only nonmusical successes in the latter part of his career. The show opened at the BILTMORE THEATER.

STEPHEN SONDHEIM's first produced attempt as both composer and lyricist, *A Funny Thing Happened on the Way to the Forum* (5/8/62; 965 performances), opened at the Alvin Theater with Zero Mostel; Abbott directed. Sumner Arthur Long's *Never Too Late* (11/27/62; 1,007 performances) was another comedy success for Abbott. It opened at THE PLAYHOUSE THEATRE with Paul Ford, Maureen O'Sullivan, and Orson Bean.

Abbott's career continued through the 1960s, '70s, and '80s, although he had progressively fewer successes. Among his later productions were *Fade Out—Fade In* (5/26/64; 271 performances), which reunited the director and Carol Burnett; *Flora, the Red Menace* (5/11/65; 87 performances), John Kander and Fred Ebb's first Broadway score and Liza Minnelli's Broadway debut; and *How Now, Dow Jones* (12/7/67; 220 performances), with a score by Elmer Bernstein and Carolyn Leigh.

A major revival of *On Your Toes*, which opened at the VIRGINIA THEATER on March 6, 1983, was Abbott's last Broadway success. A production of *Broadway* opened at the ROYALE THEATRE on June 25, 1987, Abbott's 100th birthday; unfortunately, it played for only 4 performances.

Abbott continued actively pursuing his interests by directing at small theaters and continuing to write for the theater until his death. For exercise, he enjoyed his lifelong interests in golf and ballroom dancing.

Zero Mostel and George Abbott during the run of *A Funny Thing Happened on the Way to the Forum*, 1962.

ACTORS' EQUITY. Actors' Equity was founded on December 22, 1912, by 112 actors as the American Federation of Actors, but it took until May 26, 1913, for the constitution and bylaws to be adopted. It is the labor union of all professional actors in the American theater. The organization has jurisdiction over all Broadway, off-Broadway, and League of Resident Theaters performers. It represents these actors in all negotiations. Actors may join Equity by being cast in an Equity production or by amassing points in smaller regional and summer stock theaters. Given the sorry state of the theater industry, 4 out of 5 Equity members are unemployed. In the Times Square area, Equity members can often be found as waiters in theatrical restaurants and handing out flyers at the TKTS BOOTH.

At the turn of the century the exploitation of actors was rife throughout the theater industry. Poor working and traveling conditions, as well as exploitative employers, made actors' professional lives difficult and precarious. This lack of basic amenities worked to the advantage of unscrupulous producers, who capitalized on the bad communications and great distances between them and their employees. The producers were following in the footsteps of the many captains of industry who exploited workers as a basic economic practice.

While not all producers were untrustworthy, the standard theatrical practices often left the actors stranded in cities far from their home base of New York. Often producers put shows into rehearsal without the capitalization necessary to open. Rehearsals (for which the actors were not paid) could last months or until the producer raised the money. Performers were often expected to provide their own costumes and keep them in reasonable shape. These hardships may have made for many amusing anecdotes in future biographies, but being stranded in the middle of nowhere with hostile locals and no money wasn't something the actors enjoyed.

The Pabst Grand Circle Hotel in New York was the scene of the first meeting to create the organization. Francis Wilson was elected as the first president. The original members of the committee were Albert Bruning, Charles D. Coburn, Frank Gillmore, William Harcourt, Milton Sills, and Grant Stewart. The preamble to the constitution of Actors' Equity states that the organization will do what it can to "advance, promote, foster and benefit the profession." It spells out the conditions under which an actor may be employed, elaborates on several benefits to membership, and instructs the association to work for improved legislation on behalf of the profession.

The producers didn't take the fledgling organization seriously. Problems were exacerbated by the producers' unwillingness to discuss problems with actors' representatives. Clearly, a strong action was necessary by the organization. Its first important action, the ACTORS' STRIKE OF 1919, lasted 30 days; it closed 37 plays in 8 cities, prevented the opening of 16 others, and was estimated to cost the industry $3 million, a huge sum at the time. During the strike, GEORGE M. COHAN sided with management. He had come up through the ranks of performers and felt he had good relationships with both actors and producers. His attitude was more sentimental than logical. Marie Dressler, who remembered her days as an $8-a-week chorus girl, helped bring the chorus girls into the strike. She became the first president of the Chorus Equity Association, which later merged with Actors' Equity. This strike resulted in Equity being recognized as the official trade union of the acting profession.

In 1960 Broadway was again disrupted by a second strike. Contractual negotiations were undertaken between the association and the League of New York Theaters, the producers' organization. An agreement was reached under which actors received higher rehearsal salaries, higher minimum salaries, provisions for a pension plan, and welfare benefits. In 1961 the two organizations agreed that no member of Equity would be required to work in a theater "where discrimination is practiced against any actor or patron by reason of his race, creed or color."

In 2002 Equity Members honored a strike by the musicians union shuttering Broadway for a long weekend.

Equity has a reputation for wariness and distrust of producers. Its newsletter, *Equity News*, reflects the bureaucracy of the main organization and echoes the attitude of its staff and many of its more radical members. To its credit, beginning in the late 1990s Equity began trying to represent the needs of actors outside the Broadway arena. But too often Equity seems to operate without an understanding of the legitimate problems producers and other theatrical professionals face. Critics accuse Equity of operating with too much rigidity, preferring to close shows and lose jobs rather than bend rules to allow for special exceptions.

Unfortunately, the current state of the theater industry encourages producers to cut corners and save money at the expense of others. Shows are now "produced" by pharmaceutical heirs, washed-up television actors, and purveyors of ladies' lingerie as well as big corporations beholden to stockholders. Where once there was 1 name above a show title, there are now often 5 or 6 or more, most of whom have no theatrical experience. Equity can hardly be blamed for being confused as to who exactly is in charge.

It would seem time for all participants, including Actors' Equity, to make concessions in order to control ticket prices and encourage investment. Like all the other theatrical trade unions, Actors' Equity must share part of the blame for the current depressed state of theater.

ACTORS' STRIKE OF 1919. The American Federation of Actors, the precursor of ACTORS' EQUITY, called a strike on August 6, 1919. One hundred actors closed 12 Broadway productions. The 2,700 members of Equity didn't represent all the performers on the legitimate stage. Producers wooed nonunion actors, and many shows were ready to reopen with replacements. But the stagehands and musicians, already members of the American Federation of Labor (AFL), joined the strike, and the shows were closed for the duration of the strike. On September 6, 1919, the strike was resolved to Equity's advantage, and Equity was recognized as the legal bargaining agent for stage performers. The strike lasted 30 days and closed 37 plays in 8 cities, prevented the opening of 16 other shows, and was estimated to cost the industry $3 million.

The only financial demand made on the producers was that performers be paid for extra matinees. It wasn't until 1933 that minimum pay for actors was written into the Equity contract. Rehearsal minimums weren't set until 1935. But the strike did establish Equity and led the way for additional bargaining. Membership in Equity increased from 2,700 to 14,000 following the strike.

The producers themselves laid part of the foundation of the strike, oddly enough. Prior to the strike, producer John Golden met with F. Ray Comstock, J. Fred Zimmerman, Arch Selwyn, FLORENZ ZIEGFELD, Winchell Smith, and L. Lawrence Weber. Golden's goal was to stop the constant warfare between producers, address the problems of censorship and rampant ticket speculation, set up a permanent dialogue

Actors Equity Strike of 1919.

among the different producing organizations in order to facilitate the sharing of ideas, and, most important, stop rival producing organizations from stealing each other's stars. Although not much came out of this first meeting, it wasn't too painful for the parties involved, and it solidified the feelings of community among the producers. Later, at a luncheon at the Claridge Hotel, 40 managers organized the Producing Managers Association. This organization helped convince others in the theatrical community that organization was a workable idea. It also provided a convenient entity for receiving complaints from the producers' employees, including actors. It wasn't long before Francis Wilson, as president of ACTORS' EQUITY, made demands of the producers.

The actors, considering themselves artists, not laborers, sought to limit the amount of free rehearsal time and be paid for added matinees. They also wanted continuation of salary during layoffs in production. Prior to this, managers had stopped tours, no matter where in the country, and laid off the actors without pay until new bookings came up weeks or months later. Whether Equity's demands had merit wasn't considered by the producers. They weren't used to having

their practices questioned. When they rejected the demands, the actors went on strike. The actors were not prepared for the strike they called, but once it was announced, they tried to solidify their stand. There were many different parties and factions. GEORGE M. COHAN, Louis Mann, Janet Beecher, Lenore Ulric, Francis Starr, Minnie Maddern Fiske, William Collier, and others wanted no part of the strike or the American Federation of Actors. These performers split off and formed the Actors' Fidelity League.

Made bold by the apparent dissension between the two actor organizations and among factions within each group, the producers felt no need to arbitrate. They were content to socialize at their meetings and wait for the expected apology from the actors. Weeks went by, and millions of dollars were lost by the theater industry as well as the restaurant, hotel, and transportation interests dependent on the theater business. Finally, the producers agreed to meet with the actors. Attending the meeting in the library of the St. Regis Hotel were Frank Gillmore, Francis Wilson, Ethel Barrymore (see BARRYMORE FAMILY), Lillian Russell, and others for the actors, and Al Woods, Arthur Hopkins, Sam Harris, DAVID BELASCO, WILLIAM A. BRADY,

Henry Savage, and the producer responsible for the meeting, John Golden. Augustus Thomas served as the mediator.

With box office receipts shrinking and the actors showing no sign of capitulation, the strike was soon settled once the producers started taking the actors seriously. The actors did not strike again until 1960.

ADAMS, MAUDE. The favorite actress of a generation of theatergoers from the turn of the century until the 1920s, best known for her interpretations of the characters of James M. Barrie; b. Maude Kiskadden, Salt Lake City, Utah, November 11, 1872; d. Tannersville, New York, July 17, 1953.

Born to businessman James Kiskadden and actress Annie Adams, Maude made her first appearance in her hometown of Salt Lake City in her mother's arms in the show *The Lost Child*; she was only 9 months old. The family moved to San Francisco in 1875, and a year after arriving in California, she became known as "La Petite Maude." On October 17, 1877, she made her debut in the play *Fritz*. In 1882 Maude attended a little over a year of school at the Collegiate Institute in Salt Lake City. It was to be her only formal schooling.

The next year Maude joined a traveling stock company in the company of her now widowed mother. They arrived in New York City in 1888, and the young actress made her debut in *The Paymaster*. A series of roles with the E. H. Sothern stock company followed, and in 1890 she was taken under the wing of producer Charles Frohman. Frohman paired her with John Drew (*see* BARRYMORE FAMILY) in October 1892 in an attempt to make them stars. They first appeared together in the French farce *The Masked Ball*, adapted by Clyde Fitch. Drew and Adams acted together for 4 years. Among the shows that Drew and Adams appeared in was 1894's *The Bauble Shop*. During that time author James M. Barrie caught her performance and was inspired to adopt his novel *The Little Minister* as a vehicle for her. Maude opened in the play in 1897, already manager of her own company. Her performance as Barbie in Barrie's play ensured her fame and began the love affair between her and her audiences.

Through her career Adams became forever associated as the premier interpreter of Barrie's plays. In addition to *The Little Minister*, she also appeared in *Quality Street* (11/11/01; 64 performances) at the Knickerbocker Theatre, *What Every Woman Knows* (12/23/08; 198 performances), *The Legend of Lenora* (1/5/14; 146 performances), and *A Kiss for Cinderella* (12/25/16; 152 performances). The last three plays were all produced at the EMPIRE THEATRE.

But Adams' greatest success was in Barrie's *Peter Pan* (11/6/05). The production was an immense success, playing 223 performances—an amazing run for its time. It proved to be so popular that Adams made 2 return engagements on the Empire's stage as the boy who wouldn't grow up. Her subsequent New York appearances were in 1912 and 1915.

Of course, Adams also appeared in non-Barrie productions. These included 2 of Rostand's plays, *L'Aiglon* in 1910 and *Chantecler* (1/23/11; 96 performances). She was such a success in the latter show, playing a rooster who thought his crowing makes the sun come up, that on one occasion she received 22 curtain calls.

In 1918, while touring in *A Kiss for Cinderella*, Maude was caught in the great influenza epidemic. Though she recovered, she decided to retire from the stage. She did make a few more appearances, notably touring in 1931–32 opposite the great Otis Skinner's Shylock in *The Merchant of Venice*. Her Portia was well reviewed, which wasn't always the case with her attempts at Shakespeare. She appeared as Juliet in 1899 but her performance was not a success. She also played Viola in *Twelfth Night* for 2 performances in 1908 and 1 performance as Rosalind in *As You Like It* in 1910. She again played in *Twelfth Night* in 1934 as part of a summer stock tour, but this time she played Maria. Later that year, having retired once and for all from the stage, she re-created some of her best-loved roles for radio to great success.

Maude Adams (right) as *Peter Pan*, 1905.

Acting wasn't Adams' only interest; she was also an avid lighting designer. She lighted all her tours and designed the lighting bridge of Frohman's Empire Theatre. Her interest in lighting led to her invention of an incandescent bulb used for color film. However, she didn't patent it and refused to sue when others stole her ideas. From 1921 to 1923 she worked in Schenectady, New York, partnering with General Electric Company engineers.

Adams' interest in the theater continued after her retirement from performing. In 1937 she founded the drama department at Stephens College in Columbia, Missouri, where she remained as a full-time teacher for a decade. Following 3 more years of part-time teaching, she retired for good. Adams died at her farm in Tannersville, New York, at age 70 following a heart attack.

ADELPHI THEATER. *See* **George Abbott Theater.**

ALBEE, E. F. Reviled vaudeville theater owner and booking agent; b. Edward Franklin Albee, Machlas, Maine, October 8, 1857; d. Palm Beach, Florida, March 11, 1930.

E. F. Albee was among the most disliked men in show business. With his partner B[enjamin]. F. Keith (1846–1914), Albee owned most of the great vaudeville theaters between Chicago and the East Coast. Keith and Albee tied up bookings for their houses with their United Booking Office. The UBO gave franchises free to agents, provided the agents didn't deal with any of Keith and Albee's competitors. This empire of over 1,500 theaters expanded to include the entire country when Martin Beck's West Coast–based Orpheum Circuit agreed to book through the United Booking Office.

Albee's power and influence were immense. To incur the wrath of Albee was to be practically blacklisted from vaudeville. Smaller chains such as the Gus Sun circuit couldn't provide enough work for top names. Acts played the smaller, less prestigious houses until they improved and, step by step, worked their way up to the apex of the vaudeville performers' art, the PALACE THEATER. Albee had a greater impact on the quality of the nation's entertainment than anyone at the time simply because every major vaudeville star had to please Albee first. With his partner, Albee helped make vaudeville the most successful entertainment of its time. And, due to his greed, he helped kill the goose that laid the golden eggs.

At the end of his life, in the late 1920s, an elderly Albee was speechless when Marcus Heiman of the United Booking Office accused him of killing vaudeville. Heiman told Albee how his 5-shows-a-day policy

Edward F. Albee

broke the backs of actors and audiences alike. But vaudeville was dying anyway. The newer entertainments, talking pictures and radio, had far less demanding schedules and were much more lucrative. For the odd performer who insisted on a live audience, there was always musical comedy and revue. Audiences too grew tired of the same old acts when they could get superior talent free on radio, broadcast from the capitals of the entertainment world: New York and Hollywood. The 5-a-day policy had made Albee a lot of money, but without his lifelong partner, B. F. Keith, to provide the showmanship, the empire crumbled.

Albee's policies of squeezing the market dry originated early in his career. He got his start while still in his teens, as an "outside ticket" or "60-cent" man with the circus. Albee would park a ticket wagon outside the gates to the midway. Customers would arrive at Albee's operation before they got to the main windows and would buy tickets for more than the going rate. Albee was also able to trick customers while counting change and could make a tidy profit off the hicks and rubes. His disregard for the suckers stayed with him his whole life.

It was Albee's teaming up with showman extraordinaire B. F. Keith that got him out of the sawdust and into the spotlight. Keith was also a ruthless businessman, but he provided the partnership with élan and whatever heart it possessed. Keith and Albee began by producing tab versions of Gilbert and Sullivan shows, which were in the public domain in the United States. Tab versions of plays were cut-down adaptations that would usually play for an hour or less. These tab productions were ideally suited to vaudeville since they took up only one part of an evening's entertainment. Keith and Albee would advertise these shows by proclaiming: "Why pay $1.50 when you can see our show for 25 cents?"

The profits from their production of *The Mikado* allowed them to buy the Bijou Theatre in Boston. At 10 A.M. on July 6, 1885, they offered their first vaudeville bill. The team made profits by charging a nickel or a dime for admission. Later they raised the price to 20 cents. The partners expanded the empire, eventually convincing women that the theater was not for men only by offering clean shows in good taste. Backstage, every theater posted a notice to the performers that stated:

> Don't say "slob" or "son-of-a-gun" or "hully gee" on this stage unless you want to be cancelled peremptorily. Do not address anyone in the audience in any manner. If you have not the ability to entertain Mr. Keith's audiences without risk of offending them, do the best you can. Lack of talent will less open you to censure than would be an insult to a patron. If you are in doubt as to the character of your act, consult the local manager before you go on the stage, for if you are guilty of uttering anything sacrilegious or even suggestive you will be immediately closed and will never again be allowed in a theater where Mr. Keith is in authority.

After Keith's death in 1914, the machine went on, but it was clear that years of bad feelings from artists and an inability to change with the times proved Albee's downfall. In 1928 the head of the Film Booking Office, Joseph P. Kennedy, convinced Albee to sell out. Kennedy, patriarch of the influential Massachusetts family and father of future president John F. Kennedy and his brothers Edward and Robert, sold a "substantial interest" in FBO to David Sarnoff's Radio Corporation of America. In October 1928 RCA and FBO acquired the Keith-Albee-Orpheum chain of theaters. The new company was called Radio-Keith-Orpheum (RKO). Kennedy promised to make Albee president of the new company and told him he wouldn't have to worry about the day-to-day problems of the dying vaudeville business.

When Albee sold out, the price of stock was quoted at 16. Kennedy offered Albee 21, and greed and exhaustion convinced Albee to sell. In 3 months the stock was selling for 50. Kennedy dismantled the vaudeville empire and transformed the more profitable theaters into motion picture houses for RKO product. Those that were unprofitable were unloaded or knocked down, and office buildings were erected on their sites. Albee continued as titular head of the company until Kennedy lost all patience with him. The story is that Albee entered Kennedy's office one day to make a suggestion, and Kennedy informed Albee that he was through and had been for years.

Albee had come a long way from his birthplace in Maine. As head of the largest chain of vaudeville theaters in America and the United Booking Office, his impact on American entertainment was immense. His Keith-Orpheum circuit tied the nation together. It enabled acts to hone their art and continue working without layoffs for long periods of time. But the toll his policies took on the acts and the business proved too great. Perhaps Albee's greatest legacy is as adoptive father to playwright Edward Albee.

ALGONQUIN ROUND TABLE. Legend has it that the Algonquin Round Table was the wittiest, most urbane group of people ever to eat in one place at one time. The bon mots that were ascribed to the diners could fill 20 books, yet according to some of its members, the Round Table wasn't anything much. Maybe so, but the legend lives on through the autobiographies of other table members.

It all started with ALEXANDER WOOLLCOTT, columnist, radio personality, and acerbic wit. He lived at the City Club and enjoyed eating nearby at the well-known hotel on West 44th Street. ROBERT BENCHLEY, the humorist and sometime actor, also had a long relationship with the Algonquin. His mother took him into New York when he was a child, and invariably they lunched at Frank Case's Algonquin Hotel. The one time his mother took him to another restaurant, in the ASTOR HOTEL, the young Benchley was said to exclaim, "My, they've changed the Algonquin." So it seemed natural that when he was established in New York, Benchley would make the Algonquin his base. (For a time Benchley lived upstairs, but he moved across the street to the Royalton when the distraction of the Round Table interfered with his writing.)

In 1919, when the table was informally inaugurated, most of its members were just starting their careers. They were as old as the century and hell-bent on changing the course of literature and the arts. Woollcott invited newspapermen Franklin P. Adams and Heywood Broun to join him for lunch, and the clubhouse was born. The group originally met in the Pergola Room (now the Oak Room). But manager Frank Case thought their celebrity would provide a draw to tourists and New Yorkers alike. So he moved the club to a round table in the Rose Room, where the members could be viewed from the lobby. The informal lunch group was originally called the Board. But cartoonist Ed Duffy showed the group as knights in armor, and the name was changed to the Round Table. Other names were used to describe the group, one of which was the Vicious Circle.

Adams, who was the unofficial head of the table, given the popularity of his column, "The Conning Tower," was respected by playwright George S. Kaufman (*see* KAUFMAN and HART). Kaufman joined and brought in his sometime collaborator Marc Connelly. Benchley wandered downstairs, and with him came author and critic Dorothy Parker. Kaufman introduced novelist and playwright Edna Ferber to the group. Playwright Robert Sherwood, critic and author Deems Taylor, and illustrator Neysa McMein rounded out the regular group.

If Adams was the majordomo because of his position in the world of letters, then Woollcott was the social director simply because he said so. The remainder of the group didn't particularly care to take charge. They were content to carp and try to top each other's witticisms. The main contribution made by the Round Table was the reporting of the previous day's bright remarks. Another was the revue *No Siree!* On the night of April 30, 1922, Robert Benchley made his acting debut at the 49TH STREET THEATRE. He recited his Treasurer's Report, a monologue he repeated in the *Music Box Revue*.

Admission to the club was strictly by invitation. Edna Ferber, a great novelist and playwright, wrote a note: "Could I maybe lunch at the Round Table once?" Ferber was accepted as an equal, but others were scorned as too boorish, pseudointellectual, or not witty enough.

Other members at one time or another included press agents Murdock Pemberton and John Peter Toohey; Jane Grant, a writer for the *New York Times*, and her husband, Harold Ross, founder of *The New Yorker*; writer Heywood Broun and his wife, Ruth Hale; Art Samuels of *Harper's Bazaar*; and author Donald Ogden Stewart. Performers who dropped in once in a while include Douglas Fairbanks Jr., Alfred Lunt and Lynn Fontanne (*see* LUNT AND FONTANNE), Ina Claire, Harpo Marx, Tallulah Bankhead, and Margalo Gilmore. Playwrights Charles MacArthur and Noël Coward also dropped in, as did novelist Alice Duer Miller, violinist Jascha Heifetz, and screenwriter Herman Mankiewicz.

Little by little the gang broke up; some went to Hollywood, and some were simply tired of the effort. By the early 1930s the table was completely disbanded. Dorothy Parker, in an Associated Press interview toward the end of her life, discounted the Round Table:

> People romanticize it. It was no Mermaid Tavern, I promise you, these were no giants. Think of who was writing in those days—Lardner, Fitzgerald, Faulkner, and Hemingway. Those were the real giants. The Round Table was just a lot of people telling jokes and telling each other how good they were. Just a bunch of loudmouths showing off, saving their gags for days, waiting for a chance to spring them. It was not legendary. I don't mean that—but it wasn't all that good. There was no truth in anything they said. It was the terrible day of the wisecrack, so there didn't have to be any truth, you know. There's nothing memorable about them. About any of them. So many of them died. My Lord, how people die.

Maybe she was right, or maybe she was just bitter, but the truth is probably somewhere in the middle. These were witty people who did affect their era. Lardner, Fitzgerald, and the others were chroniclers of their time, but the Round Table members were the court jesters who entertained people with their plays, columns, books, and wit.

ALLEN, KELCEY. Critic; b. Eugene Kuttner, Brooklyn, New York, November 11, 1875; d. New York, New York, July 23, 1951.

Caricature of Kelcey Allen, 1928.

"Like all boys," Kelcey Allen once wrote, "I wanted to be an actor. Maybe a star, with my own company." He would never make it as an actor in the theater; but he remained stagestruck for the rest of his life.

Eugene Kuttner (Allen's birth name) joined the staff of the *Tammany Times*, a political weekly, when he was only 16. He then moved to the *New York Recorder*, where he began as a copy boy. In those days, theaters had special rooms reserved for critics so they could write their reviews on the spot.

Allen wrote about his early entree into the theater: "I was enabled to frequent the theatres, usually securing admission by pretending to be a special messenger boy assigned to carry the reviews of a critic to his newspaper office. Finally, in fear of exposure, I decided to become legitimate and offered my services to Nym Crinckle (A. C. Wheeler) of the *Morning World*, Franklin Fyles of the *Morning Sun*, and Hillary Bell of the *New York Press*. These papers were published in what was then known as Newspaper Row—all within a few blocks of each other—and I could cover them all in less than ten minutes. I got either twenty-five or fifty cents from each paper." John R. Stevenson of the old *New York News* and John Carbox Harrington of the *Dispatch* were among Kuttner's other clients.

He joined the editorial staff of the *New York Clipper* at the tender age of 18. Kuttner had run reviews for the *Clipper* critic, Dr. Hartley. The paper was a theatrical trade periodical and a forerunner of *Zits*, BILLBOARD, and VARIETY. Hartley got the teenager a job as an office boy for the salary of $7 per week. Kuttner stayed at the *Clipper* on and off for 20 years (his salary rose to a less than munificent $20 a week), also contributing articles to the *New York Recorder* and sometimes serving as a press agent for Broadway shows. He also served as an advertising solicitor as well as a backstage reporter.

Ever the fan of theater, Allen devised a way to meet the notables he admired so much. The *Clipper* maintained a service of forwarding mail to actors and actresses. Instead of putting the letters in envelopes addressed to the performers, Allen would hand-carry each missive to his idols, and thereby got to know and become friendly with most of the great performers of his day.

In 1910 Eugene Kuttner changed his name. As he told Norton Mockridge, "I borrowed it. I thought that Eugene Kuttner didn't sound glamorous enough, so I made up my name. It wasn't that I didn't want a Jewish name. It was just that I thought I ought to have something that sounded right for professional purposes. So, one day when I was standing in front of the Knickerbocker Theatre, Herbert Kelcey, the actor, came up and stopped and he had with him the actress, Viola Allen. Now both of these charming people were somebody in the theatre and I admired them and I asked Mr. Kelcey if he minded if I used his name. He said sure, go ahead, and then Miss Allen said why don't I use her name too, so I made up my name—Eugene Kelcey Allen. Then later I dropped the Eugene because the name was too long."

In 1915 he noticed that the Fairchild paper *Women's Wear Daily* didn't have a drama critic. He convinced the editors that since the paper's readers came to New York on business, the paper should inform them about goings-on in the theater. For the first few months Allen restricted himself to selling theatrical advertising. Little by little he introduced theatrical news and finally criticism.

In his negotiations with *Women's Wear Daily* Allen conceived a unique formula for his salary. Instead of receiving a set fee, Allen worked for a percentage of the advertising revenue brought into the paper from theatrical concerns.

Getting on the first-night lists was not so easy, as they were extremely selective, with the top reviewers and high society making up the bulk of the audience. So Allen devised a scheme that would ensure his joining the reviewers of the leading papers at premieres. He typed up a list of the critics, their addresses, and their affiliations. On this list he put his own name. The list was sent to press agents, who Allen bet would be too lazy to peruse the list before handing it whole to their secretaries. The trick worked, and though at first he was invited mainly to flops, within 3 years his credentials were established. At first his seats were not well situated in the theaters. But Allen became friends with the box office personnel and could upgrade a poor seat assigned by the press agent to a better location given by the treasurer. Allen published his list of critics, addresses, and affiliations for the rest of his life. In his long career Allen attended over 6,800 first nights.

Allen was picky about which seats he was assigned. Allen was the only critic in New York who regularly sent Christmas presents to box office personnel. In fact, Allen was an inverterate gift giver. RICHARD MANEY recalled that in addition to whiskey and cigarettes he had been presented with enough potato peelers, can openers, and other useful mechanisms to stock a restaurant.

But Allen's priority was good seats at opening nights. When he was given a tour of the newly constructed MUSIC BOX THEATER by its co-owner, Sam H. Harris, the producer asked the critic where he would like to sit on opening nights. Allen dropped his hand on an aisle seat, and for the rest of his career seats C-2 and C-4 belonged to Allen on opening nights.

Allen was known as a particularly kind reviewer. He seldom showboated with vitriolic harangues. He was, to many, the "best-loved scribe on Broadway."

However, Allen did have a sense of humor, and it was said that he never wrote an outright pan. When friends were associated with sure failures, Allen would often choose to go to the prizefights instead of writing a negative review. He would write of a flop: "I hear Cain's horses champing in the alley." Cain's was a stage warehouse for theatrical props and furniture to which the sets of failures were lugged away and stored.

At the opening of one terrible show he was asked how long he thought the play would run. "Until two o'clock in the morning" was his reply.

When Elmer Rice's play *See Naples and Die* opened to dire reviews across the street from the theater that held his hit *Street Scene*, Allen quipped to friends, "Rice won the Pulitzer Prize on that side of the street and lost it on this side."

Although he admitted that "the writing has always been incidental to me," his reviews were mainly written as a stagestruck fan, one who saw his mission as boosterism of the theater. After all, Allen had been around longer than anyone else and, as Woolcott Gibbs wrote in his profile of Allen in *The New Yorker*:

He was a little offhand about cultivated reference (*Amphitryon 38* for instance, has a way of turning up in his conversation as *Amferon 56*). However, he loved the theatre, especially in its more elegant moments, and since he had been hanging around it for almost a quarter of a century, he was a profound expert on what everything in a show cost, who had done exactly what in the past, and all the insanely complicated loves, hatreds, and general chicaneries of social life backstage. In his field, he was as specialized as Sherlock Holmes, who could identify fifty-seven varieties of cigar ash but wasn't aware that the earth went around the sun.

Since Allen wasn't comfortable with negative criticism, he often relied on recounting the play's plot—sometimes in ridiculous detail. He also loved to use quotation marks around words in his reviews, often to comical effect. For example, he wrote, "The act needs 'fixing up,'" "He can 'put a song over,'" and "The airplane breaks a plane, or 'wing,' and crashes to the earth." Allen would also go to extremes of obscure language for simple words. He would describe dancing as "terpsichorean effort" and an elephant as "pachydermatous beasts."

Allen also would assume—perhaps correctly given that the readership of his paper was all garment center professionals—that readers knew nothing of the theater. He wrote things like "The stars are followed by a stage horse (cleverly impersonated by two chorusmen," "Adam and Eve lived, as we all know, in the Garden of Eden," and "The ''Ole' in the title of the play is the Cockney pronounciation of the world 'hole.'"

Because of his vast knowledge of what might be termed the gossip of Broadway, he sometimes brought this knowledge to his reviews. For example, he wrote, "Hilda Spong contented herself with a very small role (she played it as a personal favor to Mr. Miller)." On writing about an actress who made love to her current husband in a play directed by her first husband, Allen wrote, "Surely here is a situation never conceived by the dramatist or novelist, or even the writer of moving pictures but it is with the play that we have to deal."

Allen also utilized the same descriptive words repeatedly. As Gibbs observed, "To him almost every first night is 'large and fashionable' 'the supporting roles' are always 'in good hands,' 'if you are looking for risqué or suggestive lines, the play will not disappoint,' and 'the production' is invariably 'tasteful,' or 'elegant,' or 'brilliant,' or any one of fifty other words expressing rapture."

In accepting the KELCEY ALLEN AWARD (posthumously named after the critic), Rosamond Gilder opined that Allen was noted for his "helpful advice to directors, players and playwrights, as well as for his pithy remarks and incisive drama reviews." But she didn't know Allen. Norton Mockridge in *Variety* took umbrage with Gilder's descriptions:

I knew Kelsey Allen quite well for 20 years and I assure you "pithy" he was not. Tersely cogent, he couldn't be. As for "incisive drama reviews," most of his prosy reports were as trenchant, penetrating and colorful as the Congressional Record.

And the only helpful advice I ever heard him give a director, player or playwright was the eye-squinting admonition: "Don't take any wooden nickels."

I do not wish to detract from Kelcey's reputation, but only to fix it accurately, Kelcey needs no false glory. He was eminently satisfied with his image, and he never got over the happy wonderment that a man of his limited attainments had risen so high. He had a thousand friends and no enemies, and he was closer to heaven right there on Broadway than any man I've known.

Like many critics, Allen sometimes fell asleep during his watch. He once ran into a performer at a restaurant and was kidded that he hadn't fallen asleep yet. Allen replied, "You are not onstage yet."

Later in his career some of the reviews bearing his name were the work of Thomas R. Dash, an associate editor of the newspaper. Dash would often accompany Allen to the theater, and when the play was classical or foreign, it was often Dash who would actually write the reviews. Allen himself said of Dash, "He's a very brilliant author. Uses words that long."

Jack Gould profiled Allen for the *New York Times* in the issue of November 26, 1939. He wrote about Allen:

He is Seventh Avenue's ambassador to Broadway. His avoirdupois has joggled through the theatre district until he is known by more denizens of the mazda midway than any other stalwart of the Drama Critics' Circle.

If he is one of the least read of critics, it is of small account, for Kelcey's fame rests on no such common claim to distinction. His is the essence of the paradoxical: a gourmet and a guy who eats a holiday dinner at a drugstore counter, a liberal and a frugal, a host and a moocher, a gadgeteer from the hinterland general store and a man-about-town from the metropolis, a wit of consequence and a connoisseur of the unimportant. Few are more beloved . . .

Kelcey arrives on Broadway at about 11 o'clock each morning with what Rennold Wolf, one of the first and considered by many the best of the Broadway columnists, described in *The Morning Telegraph* as "six million dollars' worth of useless information." Smoking his inevitable cigar, he holds court on the pavements of the Forties until nightfall, chatting endlessly and often telling the same story he told the week before. His chief headquarters are an office which he has with Bide Dudley, who reviews the drama for WHN and writes a column for *The Sunday Enquirer* at 1476 Broadway.

Wolf further described Allen:

Wherever there is a box office Eugene Kelcey Allen has an acquaintance. He is said to know every theatrical treasurer and door-tender in America, and of him it has been written that in a dream he declined to pay a nominal admission fee of ten cents to Paradise because of his possession of a pass to the other place.

His regular occupation is that of advertising solicitor for a weekly theatrical publication. He is cherubic of face, rotund and formidable as to girth, wears a handkerchief tucked inside of his collar in both summer and winter, and declares that he can out-perspire any man of his weight this side of the Equator. That these pretensions are not the vagaries of excessive ambition and conceit was attested last summer when in a contest with Frank Tannehill, Jr.—weight in condition 270 pounds—Kelcey out-perspired him by two shirts and an alpaca waistcoat.

Playwright John Golden eulogized Allen by remarking on his "sweet character." He continued, "He was more loved and respected than any other person in his line along Broadway. He succeeded to keep more friends than any other critic. He was a very decent creature who commanded a deep, strong affection among men and women of the theatre."

Abel Green of *Variety* called him the "dean of metropolitan New York critics." JOHN CHAPMAN, critic of the *Daily News*, said of Allen, "When I first learned of Kelcey's death, I first thought of some of the many funny stories that were told about him through the years. He really was one of the most generous guys I ever knew. Opening nights without Kelcey standing in the back of the house and greeting everybody will be different from now on. To many of us who have

been associated with him over so many years, the theatre will be empty without him."

ALVIN THEATER. *See* **Neil Simon Theater**

AMBASSADOR THEATRE. 215 W. 49th Street. Architect: Herbert J. Krapp. Opening: February 11, 1921; *The Rose Girl.* The Ambassador was the first of the Shubert Brothers' 6 theaters built on 48th and 49th Streets. They saw the 49th Street block as having the potential of 42nd Street.

The Ambassador Theatre is built in brick Romanesque Revival style with the exterior ornamented through elaborate brickwork patterns. The theater was built diagonally across its lot. This allowed greater seating and a closer relationship between the rear wall and the stage. In 1985 the New York City Landmarks Preservation Commission accorded landmark status to the Ambassador's interior, though it refused to so designate the exterior.

The Ambassador's opening production, *The Rose Girl*, was an undistinguished operetta by Anselm Goetzl and William Cary Duncan that played for 99 performances. The story was so bad that Jake Shubert (*see* SHUBERT BROTHERS) wondered whether it would

Interior of the Ambassador Theatre.

help to switch Act 1 with Act 3. Although well located in the district, the Ambassador has never had great success.

Its next production, *Blossom Time* (9/28/21; 516 performances), proved to be its longest-running show until almost 50 years later. The SIGMUND ROMBERG and Dorothy Donnelly operetta would again play the Ambassador on March 4, 1931, for 29 performances, and once more starting September 4, 1943, for only 47 performances—its last Broadway appearance. *Blossom Time* played a total of 8 times on Broadway. Whenever the Shuberts were strapped for money or found themselves with a dark theater, out would come *Blossom Time*. This musicalization of Franz Schubert's (no relation) life would invariably bring Jake Shubert to tears. The schmaltzy story told of Schubert's unrequited love, which drove him to pen what became the "Unfinished Symphony."

Next came *The Lady in Ermine* (10/2/22; 238 performances). Another operetta, *The Dream Girl* (8/20/24; 118 performances), did even worse even though its score was by the great VICTOR HERBERT. This was Herbert's last operetta; in fact, he died prior to the Broadway opening. Even with additional tunes supplied by Romberg, the score couldn't redeem a shoddy book. The respectable run was more a tribute to Herbert's career and reputation than a result of the merits of the show.

The 1930s were bleak times for the Ambassador. The Shuberts, like many other producers, had trouble holding on to their theaters. They sold the Ambassador in 1935. The new owners' policy of staging only dramatic works afforded the theater few opportunities for success. The only two productions of this period to achieve any notice were an 8-performance run of the Abbey Theater production of *Juno and the Paycock* by Sean O'Casey, and a small musical revue, *The Straw Hat Revue* (9/29/39; 75 performances). This revue, which grew out of Catskill hotel revues, was most notable for newcomers Imogene Coca, Alfred Drake, and Danny Kaye.

Radio, movies, and television occupied the Ambassador until 1956, when the Shuberts regained control of the theater. But later productions, with one exception, proved no more successful than those mounted in the past. These included Lawrence and Lee's *The Gang's All Here* (10/1/59; 132 performances), with E. G. Marshall and Melvyn Douglas, and Ira Wallach's *The Absence of a Cello* (9/21/64; 120 performances), with Ruth White, Fred Clark, Murray Hamilton, Mala Powers, and Charles Grodin.

The theater's greatest success came with Robert Anderson's 4 one-act comedies, *You Know I Can't Hear You When the Water's Running* (3/13/67; 755 performances). Eileen Heckart, George Grizzard,

Martin Balsam, and Melinda Dillon were featured in the comedy.

After that success, the Ambassador resumed its revolving-door policy. *We Bombed in New Haven* (10/16/68; 85 performances), by Joseph Heller, was followed by the Tom Jones and Harvey Schmidt musical *Celebration* (1/22/69; 109 performances); a revival of Sandy Wilson's *The Boy Friend* (4/14/70; 119 performances), starring Judy Carne; *Paul Sill's Story Theater* (10/26/70); Melvin Van Peebles' *Ain't Supposed to Die a Natural Death* (11/17/71); *The Secret Affairs of Mildred Wilde* (11/14/72), by Paul Zindel; and *Scapino* (9/27/74), with Jim Dale, which all had short runs. Three one-person shows next played for a time at the Ambassador: Linda Hopkins in *Me and Bessie* (10/22/75); Billy Dee Williams in *I Have a Dream* (9/20/76); and Estelle Parsons in *Miss Margarida's Way* (10/27/77). *Me and Bessie* marked a change in the Ambassador's history. The theater increasingly became home to shows featuring black performers.

A lame musical revue, *Eubie!* (9/20/78), ran for 439 performances due primarily to the talented cast and the publicity surrounding composer Eubie Blake's 100th birthday.

Next the theater found itself with a new production, *Goodbye Fidel* (4/23/80), and a new name: the New Ambassador Theatre. But the new name stayed as long as the production, 6 performances.

Back as simply the Ambassador Theatre, the theater saw a revival of Alex Bradford's black revue *Your Arms Too Short to Box with God* (6/2/80; 429 performances) and a new play by Steve Tesich, *Division Street* (10/8/80; 21 performances).

Finally the theater had a hit with Bob Fosse's dance revue, appropriately named *Dancin'*. The show was a transfer from the BROADHURST THEATER where it began its 1,774 performance run on March 27, 1978. After it closed at the Ambassador on June 27, 1982, the theater had a fallow period for the next couple of years.

The next notable booking at the Ambassador was another musical revue, *Leader of the Pack* (4/8/85), a celebration of the songs of Ellie Greenwich, a BRILL BUILDING habitué. Despite mostly positive reviews and a talented cast including Darlene Love, Annie Golden, Jasmine Guy, Dinah Manoff, Patrick Cassidy, and Ellie Greenwich herself, the show managed only 120 performances.

Revivals of *Dreamgirls* (1/28/87) and *Ain't Misbehavin'* (8/15/88) garnered little interest among Broadwayites. W. Somerset Maugham's play *The Circle* (11/20/1989) marked the theatrical farewell of Rex Harrison. He was supported through the 208-performance run by Glynis Johns and Stewart Granger. After *The Circle* closed, the theater was dark for almost 6 years. It reopened for a limited engagement of Red Buttons' one-man show, *Buttons on Broadway* (1/8/95; 33 performances).

The theater finally had a success with the opening of the revue *Bring in 'Da Noise, Bring in 'Da Funk*, a transfer from the Public Theater downtown. The show eventually achieved an impressive 1,135-performance run following its April 25, 1996, opening at the Ambassador. The star of the show, Savion Glover, was also its choreographer. It was conceived and directed by the Public's artistic director, George C. Wolfe. Unfortunately, it would prove to be the theater's last success.

A revival of *You're a Good Man, Charlie Brown* (2/4/99; 149 performances) boasted a cast featuring Kristen Chenoweth, Roger Bart, B. D. Wong, and Anthony Rapp. But uninspired direction by Michael Mayer and the inclusion of unnecessary additional numbers by Andrew Lippa all served to undermine the simplicity and drolly understated quality of Clark Gesner's original score.

It Ain't Nothin' but the Blues (9/9/99) was a hit uptown at the Lincoln Center Theater. But transferred to the Ambassador's decidedly nonintimate stage, it only managed to eke out 284 performances. Arthur Miller's play *The Ride down Mt. Morgan* (4/9/2000; 121 performances) suffered from negative publicity surrounding a fight between its star, Patrick Stewart, and its producers, the Shubert Organization, over publicity and promotion.

Another transfer, *A Class Act* (3/11/2001), this time from the Manhattan Theatre Club, was a musical biography of Edward Kleban, the lyricist of *A Chorus Line*. Although buoyed with money from the Kleban estate, the show only managed a run of 105 performances. Lonny Price directed the evening and starred as Kleban. The show was peppered with many of Kleban's songs, including those for which he also wrote the music. Unfortunately, despite excellent performances by Randy Graff and others in the cast, the show failed to move audiences sufficiently.

Ibsen's *Hedda Gabler* opened at the theater on October 4, 2001. Starring Kate Burton, the show received mostly excellent reviews and a mostly ho-hum response from audiences. It managed to run 117 performances.

Suzan-Lori Parks' Pulitzer prize–winning play *Topdog/Underdog* (4/7/2002), featured impressive performances by Mos Def and Philip Wright. Mixed reviews and a plot that struck many as obvious (two characters named Booth and Lincoln, and Booth brandishes a gun in the first scene—how do you think the play will end?) greeted the play at its opening. It closed after 144 performances.

Broadway historians blame the Ambassador's relatively lackluster career on the extreme width of the theater due to its odd placement on the lot and its relatively bland facade.

AMERICAN AIRLINES THEATRE. Original name: The Selwyn. 229 W. 42nd Street. Architect: George Keister. Opening: October 2, 1918; *Information Please.*

Arch Selwyn and his brother Edgar came to New York from Cincinnati and conquered Broadway. They performed, produced, and acted as agents and landlords. The brothers found the opportunity to purchase a portion of 42nd Street and decided to erect 3 theaters on the land. The first was The Selwyn, an Italian Renaissance-style building with a terra-cotta facade covering both the theater and the accompanying 6-story Selwyn office building.

The 1,180-seat theater was designed in a fan shape, making the farthest seat seem close to the stage. The Selwyn had separate smoking rooms for men and women and a large lounge that stood between the hustle and bustle of 42nd Street and the auditorium. The stage was lower than most, allowing for improved sight lines. The pink and blue auditorium's lighting system could be changed from white to pink, rose, or purple.

On the occasion of the theater's opening night performance, a critic wrote:

> The Selwyn, one of the handsomest theatres in New York, opened its doors for the first time last night. This large and commodious theatre, which seats 1,180 persons, is Italian Renaissance in design and has the system of concealed lighting, a large lounge room, comfortable seats and other luxuries of the really modern theatre.... Wherever the guest might come into contact with the walls, pillars, or balustrades of the building there is polished, green-veined marble wainscot, and this same stone, Florentine in the carved examples and Langeloc in the columns and slabs, is extensively used throughout the entire structure. The lighting scheme of the auditorium, dome, balcony and foyer is all of the indirect and evenly distributed sort, with the added novelty of changing color graduations of white, pink, rose and purple being at the disposal of the operator.

The Selwyn opened with the play *Information Please*, which ran only 46 performances. The first hit for the theater was the RUDOLF FRIML and OTTO HARBACH musical *Tumble Inn* (3/24/19; 128 performances). The show starred Charles Ruggles, Zelda Sears, Herbert Corthell, Peggy O'Neill, and Johnny Ford. *Tumble Inn* was produced by ARTHUR HAMMERSTEIN.

The Selwyn's next booking had the delightful title *Helen of Troy, New York* (6/19/23; 193 performances). Harry Ruby and Bert Kalmar contributed the songs, with the libretto credited to George S. Kaufman (*see* KAUFMAN and HART) and Marc Connelly. It was the first musical for the librettists. The show was produced by Rufus LeMaire and actor George Jessel. LeMaire was an important agent and an inveterate gambler; he was also constantly broke. Most of the front money for the show came from bootleggers. Although the play ended its run losing money, the reviews were good. LeMaire used the positive notices to sell his rights and move to California, where he became an executive at Universal.

The opening night program contained the following notice: "Owing to the utter unimportance of the plot, latecomers will positively be seated at all times during the play." The critics were generous. Percy Hammond, writing in the *Tribune*, exclaimed, "It seems improbable that I shall ever again be asked if there exists in New York any musical plays in which bare legs and barer jokes do not abound." *The Constant Nymph* (12/9/26; 148 performances), by Basil Dean and Margaret Kennedy, was The Selwyn's next attraction.

The Selwyn brothers sold the theater in 1927. A huge success was George S. Kaufman and Edna Ferber's *The Royal Family* (12/28/27; 345 performances), a slightly disguised play about the BARRYMORE FAMILY. Kaufman and Ferber denied the play was about the famous theatrical family, insisting it was a composite and mainly about the Davenport family. The playwrights worked so hard and so well together that their first draft turned out to be exactly what was seen on opening night. The reviews were raves, but producer Jed Harris announced that any show that received those kinds of reviews without selling out every performance deserved to be closed. Kaufman threatened to murder Harris, and *The Royal Family* went on to a long run.

Noël Coward's revue *This Year of Grace!* (10/7/28; 158 performances) opened at The Selwyn with Coward, Beatrice Lillie, Florence Desmond, and Queenie Leonard. The show contained two of Coward's biggest hits: "World Weary" and "A Room with a View." English impresario Charles B. Cochran served as producer. Sonnie Hale had played Coward's part in London because the author felt uncomfortable with the juvenile lead. After singing "A Room with a View," Coward announced to Cochran, "It's more than I can bear and more than one should expect of the audience!" The song was given to Billy Milton. Cochran also produced COLE PORTER's *Wake Up and Dream* (12/30/29; 127 performances). The score included the standard "What Is This Thing Called Love?"

Songwriters Arthur Schwartz and Howard Dietz (*see* DIETZ AND SCHWARTZ) had their revue *Three's a Crowd* (10/15/30; 272 performances) open at the Selwyn. It was to be the theater's last success. The revue contained two of the greatest songs of the 1930s: "Something to Remember You By" and the Johnny Green, Edward Heyman, Robert Sour, Frank Eyton,

Haidee Wright and Ann Andrews in *The Royal Family*, 1927.

and Howard Dietz classic "Body and Soul." Fred Allen and his wife, Portland Hoffa, starred along with Libby Holman, Clifton Webb, and Tamara Geva. The show also presented a band, the California Collegians, which included a young Fred MacMurray. Eight flops followed, the most notable being the last, *The Great Magoo* (12/2/32; 11 performances), a play by Gene Fowler and Ben Hecht. The show is notable solely because it contains the song "It's Only a Paper Moon," by HAROLD ARLEN and E. Y. HARBURG. The theater's last legitimate show as The Selwyn was *Ragged Army*, which opened on February 26, 1934, and closed the next day after only 2 performances.

The Depression forced the American theater into a decline, and the 42nd Street theaters suffered particularly. The Selwyn was not spared with 11 failures in a row. Most of the 42nd Street houses were converted to BURLESQUE, but in 1934 The Selwyn became a movie theater. It remained a movie theater until it was decided to make it part of the 42nd Street redevelopment. One respite from the grind (24-hour-a-day) film policy was in the 1950–51 season when an hourlong version of *The Respectful Prostitute* was shoehorned in 5 times a day between film showings. It was followed by a similar presentation of the play *Ladies Night in a Turkish Bath*.

The Roundabout Theatre Company was given the theater and its name was changed to the American

Airlines Theater (for an $8.5 million payment). The Roundabout did an excellent and respectful job in renovating the theater at a cost of $25 million. However, as the theater was being modified, the terra-cotta clad Selwyn Building and lobby fell into an adjacent hole and was destroyed.

The renamed theater opened on July 27, 2000, with Nathan Lane starring in a production of Kaufman and Hart's *The Man Who Came to Dinner*. The subscription series continued with productions of Pinter's *Betrayal* (11/14/2000), Noël Coward's *Design for Living* (3/15/2001), and Shaw's *Major Barbara* (7/12/2001). The Roundabout's second season opened with *The Women* (11/8/2001) and Kevin Bacon starring in the one-person show *An Almost Holy Picture* (2/7/2002).

AMERICAN NATIONAL THEATRE AND ACADEMY (ANTA).

The American National Theatre and Academy (ANTA) was created by an act of Congress on July 5, 1935. President Franklin Delano Roosevelt signed the charter, which grew out of the same idea that fostered the FEDERAL THEATRE PROJECT. ANTA was meant to be a national theater that would be able to operate apart from the commercial theater atmosphere. ANTA's productions would be financed from outside contributions and would not depend on commercial success. In addition, ANTA would encourage new playwrights through readings and workshops. Actors for these productions would rise through the ranks, starting at the ANTA theater school.

As part of the WPA, the Federal Theater Project had achieved commercial success, but the politics expressed in the plays aroused opposition in Congress and eventually the plug was pulled in 1939. The founders of ANTA were determined to limit government control. To avoid any problems with censorship, ANTA was structured to receive no government funds. The founders knew that such an undertaking would be expensive and could never show a profit. So the organization was made nonprofit, enabling it to solicit funds from individuals and corporations. It was also set up to be nonsectarian and, as a reflection of the times, not to have any honorary members. The preamble to its charter stated, "A national theater should bring to the people throughout the country their heritage of the great drama of the past and the best of the present, which has been too frequently unavailable to them under existing conditions."

Although it was created in 1935, ANTA had problems actually getting off the ground. The Depression was the first obstacle in its path. The United States' entry into World War II further delayed the implementation of ANTA. Finally in 1945 a reorganized board of directors formed from theater professionals was ready to implement the charter. The board set up a membership structure and began to produce shows.

ANTA began its producing on a limited level on February 9, 1947. The small PRINCESS THEATER was chosen, and ANTA presented 5 plays for 5 performances each. These early showcases won the Sidney Howard Award as the season's most important development in the theater. But surely no one could foresee the impact of the series on the history of the American theater, because this was among the first examples of a legitimate off-Broadway show, one that was not simply theater produced by amateur clubs for their own amusement.

Emboldened by the successes in a small arena, and dismayed by what seemed a lack of new, quality works, ANTA brought a West Coast production of Bertolt Brecht's *Galileo* to MAXINE ELLIOTT'S THEATRE for 6 performances at the end of 1947. The production starred Charles Laughton and was directed by Joseph Losey. Next came a production of *Skipper Next to God* by Jan de Hartog, featuring the Hollywood star John Garfield under Lee Strasberg's direction. It opened January 4, 1948, and was picked up for a commercial run by Blevins Davis, a member of ANTA's board. In keeping with ANTA's charter, Laughton received the princely sum of $8 a week, but for Garfield, the salary was raised to $10 a week. Jerome Moross and John Latouche's *Ballet Ballads* was next on ANTA's schedule. This amalgam of dance, text, and song was also picked up for commercial production. On March 31, 1950, the former Guild Theater was acquired by two ANTA board members, Robert Dowling and Roger L. Stevens, and renamed the ANTA Playhouse. The first season at the new space was directed by Cheryl Crawford and Robert Breen, the man who originally worked so hard to get the charter passed by Congress.

On November 26, 1950, *Tower Beyond Tragedy* by Robinson Jeffers premiered, starring Judith Anderson. Critics were enthusiastic about the star but were mixed in their reactions to the play. Theatergoers kept the show running for 32 performances. A planned tour was dropped because of the lack of audience response. After that Crawford and Breen presented Paul Green's reworking of *Peer Gynt* with John Garfield. This play, too, proved a failure. The next 3 productions, including *A Temporary Island* by Halsted Welles and starring Vera Zorina, all also were unsuccessful. ANTA soon found itself chronically short of funds.

During the second season in the ANTA Playhouse, Robert Whitehead, one of the theater's most respected producers, became the managing director. He presented more productions, but even though there were successes, the money just wasn't there to support as large and far-reaching a project as ANTA, and Whitehead departed. During these years ANTA presented productions of John Finch's *The Wanhope Building* (2/9/47), Arnold Sundgaard's *The Great Campaign* (3/30/47), Ben Hecht and Charles MacArthur's *Twentieth Century* (12/24/50) with Gloria Swanson and Jose Ferrer, Garcia-Lorca's *The House of Bernarda Alba* (1/7/51), Mary Chase's *Mrs. McThing* (2/20/52) with HELEN HAYES, EUGENE O'NEILL's *Desire Under the Elms* (1/16/52), Clifford Odets' *Golden Boy* (3/12/52), and Virgil Thomson and Gertrude Stein's *Four Saints in Three Acts* (4/16/52), as well as imported regional theater and dance companies. The organization also concentrated on a series of benefit performances. Called the ANTA Album, the benefits featured stars performing scenes from current shows and past successes as well as new scenes performed just for the benefits. The ANTA Albums ran from 1948 through 1951 and again in 1955. Decca Records released selections from the benefits on discs, which helped spread the idea of an American national theater.

Lucille Lortel produced the ANTA Matinee Series at her Theater De Lys in Greenwich Village. There she concentrated on avant-garde and first-time works by such playwrights as Eugène Ionesco, Eugene O'Neill, Paul Shyre, Jean Giraudoux, Garcia-Lorca, TENNESSEE WILLIAMS, William Inge, Samuel Beckett, and Edward Albee. In addition, many poets, writers, and other nontheater types premiered their works there. These writers included Katharine Ann Porter, W. H. Auden, e.e. cummings, Edna St. Vincent Millay, Robert Frost, Langston Hughes, and Paul Vincent Carroll.

In the late 1970s ANTA joined with the John F. Kennedy Center for the Performing Arts as a coproducer of the new National Theater company under the direction of Peter Sellars. The company concentrated on epic (in length and theme) productions staged with Sellars' usual disregard for the author's intent and audience patience. The company was a dismal failure and faded without a trace after wasting millions of dollars. The ANTA Theater, never regarded as a good house, is now owned and operated by the Jujamcyn organization, which renamed it the Virginia Theater.

AMERICAN THEATRE. 260 West 42nd Street. Architect: Charles C. Haight. Opening: May 22, 1893; *The Prodigal Daughter.*

The first theater on 42nd Street was the American Theatre, built in 1893, the year of a great stock market panic. The parcel of land included property on 41st Street, 42nd Street, and 8th Avenue, and was purchased for producer T. Henry French by theatrical real estate agent Hartie I. Phillips from 17 different owners. French was the son of play publisher Samuel French and was the lessee and manager of the Grand Opera house at 23rd Street and 8th Avenue. His success there led him to consider building another theater further uptown.

The American Theatre was built next to the Franklin Savings Bank directly on the corner and across the street from J. Wieland's Pharmacy, which stood on the northeast corner. Although the theater proper was built on land bounded by 41st Street and 8th Avenue, the entrance, due to the plot's odd makeup, was on 42nd Street. Later theaters such as the LYRIC, wanting a 42nd Street facade, copied the example set by the American architect Charles C. Haight. There was another general entrance on 41st Street, but the 42nd Street doors admitted only orchestra seat holders.

French promised that the 1,900-seat (plus 200 standees) Spanish Renaissance–style theater would be "the largest and the handsomest combination theatre in the United States." The *New York Times* said that "the first impression one gets of it is not of great size; its lines are such that every spectator, even those in the upper gallery, is brought in close relation with the stage." Those seated in the balcony or visiting the roof garden could take the elevator, the first in any theater.

The main auditorium's opening production was *The Prodigal Daughter*, an import from London. The production, however, featured a host of great stage stars of the day, including Jefferson de Angelis, Thomas Terris, Julia Arthur, and Helen Dauvray. The show was a spectacle with a cast of almost 200, along with 9 racehorses, which actually ran a steeplechase course complete with water hazard and hurdles constructed on a moving treadmill. It also had a full complement of hounds for the hunt. All did not always go well in the difficult scene. George Odell wrote in *Annals of the New York Stage*: "In the race scene, on May 26th, . . . the horse, Columbus, fell, in jumping over the hurdles, and rolled upon his rider, Guttenberg Billy. The fiery steed, Rochefort, ridden by Leonard Boyne, attempted to climb over the iron balcony. The panic was completed when Julia Arthur employed the leading lady's privilege of fainting. . . . Thenceforth, so far as I know, the horses behaved according to the script of the play."

Typically, the show closed for the summer and the American's entertainment roster continued in its rooftop theater. *The Prodigal Daughter* reopened in September with Maxine Elliot and Adelaide Prince in the company. The show was a great success, and the New York *Dramatic Mirror* exclaimed: "No midsummer theatrical performances in this city have ever met with the phenomenal success of those at Mr. French's American Theatre."

French ran his theater in the same style as his Grand Opera House downtown. Popular entertainments played the theater for anywhere from 1 to 4 weeks. And almost every type of entertainment was represented on its stage, including grand opera, light opera, drama, and comedy. The season of 1899–1900 was devoted entirely to opera. Among the operas that played that season were *Romeo and Juliet* with Grace Golden and Joseph Sheehan, *Cavalleria Rusticana, Il Trovatore, Lucia di Lammermoor, The Bohemian Girl, Faust,* and *The Mikado.*

Another success at the theater was *The Great Diamond Robbery,* which starred William H. Thompson, Odell Williams, Madame Janauschek, Katherine Grey, Orrin Johnson, and Blanche Walsh. The 1896 season saw revivals of two of Dion Boucicault's plays, *The Shaughran* and *The Colleen Bawn.* The latter featured Aubrey Boucicault as Myles-na Coppaleen, Emmet Corrigan as Danny Mann, Amelia Bingham as Ann Chute, and Sadie Martinot as Eily.

In 1897 French terminated his lease and in October of that year the theater was foreclosed. It was purchased by Elliott Zborowski, and in December the new owner and producer Henry T. Savage took over its management. Their opening show was *The Queen's Lace Handkerchief* with Lizzie MacNicol and Grace Golden. The next two seasons were devoted to opera.

In September 1900 a stock company took residence at the American and opened their first season with *The Great Ruby.* This was followed by productions of such favorites as *The Three Musketeers, Charity Ball, The Lost Paradise, The Two Orphans, The Sporting Duchess, Monte Cristo, Rosedale,* and many others. But these offerings were not successful in drawing audiences; the American suffered losses and finally became a vaudeville house, and in 1908 agent William Morris leased the theater and its name was changed to the American Music Hall.

Marcus Loew took over the theater and presented vaudeville on the theater's 2 stages. It briefly presented motion pictures. Loew died in 1927, and the Loew's Corporation sold the theater in 1929. That year it turned to BURLESQUE. The theater couldn't weather the Depression and plans were made for a 30-story office building on the site. But the Depression took its toll on those plans also. On December 8, 1930, a fire burned down the auditorium, and the theater was closed for good. The 8th Avenue facade with its dressing rooms was not affected by the fire, and that part of the building was converted into bachelor apartments. The American was demolished in 1932. A circus played the empty lot in 1933, and afterward a one-story building was erected on the spot. The Franklin Savings Bank was finally built on the theater's plot. Today the land is a parking lot.

Of the American Theatre's rooftop theater, where VAUDEVILLE acts were presented, the *New York Times* reported: "The main garden is 90 feet square, and is brilliantly lighted by arches and trefoils or powerful electric lights. It will accommodate 650 persons, who, in case of rain, can take refuge in two large roofed apartments, where free air is a feature and shelter is perfect. The stage is large, and some say it is the largest among the roof garden stages."

William Morris took over the lease of the theater, and in 1909 architect Thomas Lamb was hired to build a new, enclosed roof theater to replace the open-air roof garden. This was Lamb's first double-decker theater. The new theater seated about 1,400 patrons, and the stage was twice as large as the auditorium downstairs. It opened in July 1909. The *New York Times* wrote: "Trunks of imitation trees form the proscenium supports to the stage, and the roof, studded with tiny twinkling electric lights, is designed to carry out the impression of being under the stars . . . tree-entwined and foliage-hung walks lead to two open-air gardens where patrons may sit at rustic tables for refreshments. . . . The woodwork is disguised with real birch bark, and scores of palms and shrubs add to the attractiveness of the outdoor setting."

American Builder magazine further described the theater's "Adirondack lodge" style:

> The supporting columns at the sides are encased in plaster, a very good imitation of large trees, which seemingly rise from the floor through the balcony and branch out into the ceiling at the lower web of the trusses. At this level a screen of leafy foliage breaks the view of the ceiling above. All the upper part of the trusses, which are unprotected, and the under surface of the roof, are painted a deep blue. Suspended from this, about two feet down are tiny, half-candle power electric bulbs, the flickering illumination of which gives the effect of the night sky. Thus, although the roof garden is entirely enclosed and the patrons are protected from a chance shower, the nearest approach to the outside air is given.

AMERICAN THEATRE WING. The American Theatre Wing is one of the oldest service organizations benefiting the Broadway community. In recent years, it has been closely associated with the Tony Awards, which it administers. The Tony Awards are the most visible of the Wing's projects, which include grants and special entertainments. Critics have condemned the organization as existing merely to serve itself; supporters claim it renders real service to Broadwayites. The truth is probably somewhere in the middle.

The Stage Women's War Relief was the first organization in what later became the American Theatre Wing. A committee of 7 women led by Rachel Crothers organized the War Relief in 1917, and they held their first meeting in the HUDSON THEATRE. The women—Louise Closser Hale, Josephine Hull, Minnie Dupree, Dorothy Donnelly, Bessie Tryee, Louise Drew, and Rachel Crothers—set up a canteen for servicemen and sent entertainers to the front to perform for the troops. The organization also sewed 1,863,645 articles of clothing for the fighting men and raised over $10 million in Liberty Bonds. A men's committee was formed in 1920 to deal with problems of the returning veterans.

In 1940 the American Theatre Wing War Service, an affiliate of the British War Relief Society, began operations in New York. President Rachel Crothers, vice presidents HELEN HAYES and Gertrude Lawrence, treasurer Josephine Hull, and secretary Antoinette Perry oversaw the women's committee. Other members of the committee included Minnie Dupree (a member of the first committee), Vera Allen, Lucile Watson, Theresa Helburn, and Edith Atwater. The men's committee was led by critic Brooks Atkinson, George S. Kaufman (see KAUFMAN AND HART), and Gilbert Miller. Other members of the committee were Raymond Massey, Vinton Freedley (see AARONS AND FREEDLEY) Brock Pemberton, Billy Rose, Lee Shubert (see SHUBERT BROTHERS), and Max Gordon. Co-chairs were Jane Cowl and Selena Royle. Miller organized a benefit to aid British air raid victims. The benefit earned more than $40,000.

When America entered the war, the Wing, by now an independent organization, sold war bonds, did relief work, and, most important, operated Stage Door Canteens in 8 locations. The canteens were set up in many foreign cities, including London and Paris. The New York Stage Door Canteen was opened behind the Paramount Theater in a space underneath SARDI'S RESTAURANT and the 44TH STREET THEATRE. The Shubert brothers donated the space. The canteen served food and provided entertainment to soldiers returning from the front or on the way to battle.

The canteen opened on March 1, 1942, operating from 6 P.M. to midnight seven days a week until the war was over. Over 1,700 Broadwayites ran the canteen, usually committed to one 3½-hour stint per week. The actors, designers, directors, and production staffers were the canteen's entire staff. They hosted the visiting soldiers and sailors, did custodial duties, served meals, and kept the place operating as a restaurant, nightclub, and social hall.

The canteen catered to as many as 4,000 servicemen a night, not only Americans but also visiting foreign troops. Stars entertaining at the canteen included most of the musical theater legends of the day. Dramatic stars such as Alfred Lunt and Lynn Fontanne (see LUNT AND FONTANNE) did their part by waiting tables and dancing with the troops. "Killer Joe," an especially energetic jitterbugger, achieved notoriety. The canteen was an important feather in the cap of the Wing.

The American Theatre Wing also produced USO shows for entertaining the troops overseas. The Wing

donated $75,000 to the USO for entertainment. The *Barretts of Wimpole Street*, starring KATHARINE CORNELL, was the first play sent overseas. Money for the USO was earned through proceeds from the movie *Stage Door Canteen* and the weekly radio program of the same name. IRVING BERLIN's show *This Is the Army* (7/4/42) featured the song "I Left My Heart at the Stage Door Canteen." Proceeds from the show went to the Army Emergency Relief.

Over 40,000 volunteers entertained for the Wing, many in veterans' hospitals and service hospitals. *Lunchtime Follies* was a touring show that entertained factory workers. The head of the production was composer KURT WEILL, and producer Kermit Bloomgarden was the general manager. Among the cast members of the various editions of *Lunchtime Follies* were Jack Albertson, Milton Berle, Shirley Booth, David Burns, Howard Da Silva, Joey Faye, Arlene Francis, Sam Jaffe, Rosetta LeNoire, Fredric March, Zero Mostel, Vivienne Segal, Helen Tamaris, and Benay Venuta. Songs for the revues were written by HAROLD ROME, Weill, and others; sketches were contributed by George S. Kaufman, Moss Hart, Maxwell Anderson, Groucho Marx, Nat Hiken, Joseph Fields, (see FIELDS FAMILY) Billy Rose, S. J. Perelman, Lillian Hellman, and Langston Hughes. During the war and in the 8 months following its conclusion, the Wing produced almost 1,500 auditorium shows, 350 full-length plays, and over 6,700 hospital shows, all in the New York area. Washington, D.C., and Boston also had their branches of the Wing.

On September 13, 1945, members of the Wing received a letter announcing the first postwar planning meeting. A year later, on July 8, 1946, that meeting bore its first fruit when the Wing began a highly regarded Professional Training School for veterans who wanted to pursue theatrical careers. A prestigious faculty offered 50 courses. Sir Cedric Hardwicke, Alfred Lunt, Jose Ferrer, Maureen Stapleton, Cyril Ritchard, and Eva Le Gallienne were the acting teachers. José Limón was a dance instructor along with Martha Graham, Charles Weidman, Katharine Dunham, Ray Bolger, and Hanya Holm. Delbert Mann and Ezra Stone held workshops in television. Leon Barzin and Joseph Rosenstock handled budding conductors. Richard Rodgers and Oscar Hammerstein II (see RODGERS AND HAMMERSTEIN) and HAROLD PRINCE taught music for actors and directors. Oliver Smith explained the intricacies of set design, and he and Kermit Bloomgarden instructed future producers. At each session, 1,200 students attended the unique school. Most of these students studied under the GI Bill. Illustrious alumni of the school included Marge and Gower Champion, Russell Nype, Tony Randall, William Warfield, Gordon MacRae, Pat Hingle, Charleton Heston, and James

Kate Smith performing at the New York Stage Door Canteen.

Whitmore. The school remained a project of the Wing for 10 years.

In 1947 the Wing sent teams of specially trained actors for an intensive 3⅓-month internship at neuropsychiatric hospitals. The actors worked with veterans who had experienced mental problems following their discharge from the services. Families of veterans were also in need of the Wing's services. The actors helped veterans and their families work out problems through short plays that dramatized their plight. Discussion sessions were held after the performances. That same year, the Wing established the Antoinette Perry (TONY) AWARDS. The purpose of the awards was to honor the most distinguished members of the theatrical community.

Currently, in addition to the Tony Awards, the Wing also makes grants to off-Broadway theaters, theater schools, and regional companies. The Wing hosts a Saturday Theater for Children in the public school system and sends tab (cut-down) versions of Broadway shows to hospitals and nursing homes. The Wing's

April and October seminars on the theater are shown on local cable television. In 1983 the Wing received a grant from the Clarence Ross Foundation to establish a master class for American actors at the Eugene O'Neill Center in Waterford, Connecticut. The class is taught by directors from England's Bristol Old Vic.

ANCO THEATER. Original name: Lew M. Fields Theater. 254 West 42nd Street. Architects: J. M. McElfatrick & Co. Opening: December 5, 1904; *It Happened In Nordland.*

The Lew M. Fields Theater was built by OSCAR HAMMERSTEIN I as his eighth (and final) Broadway house. It was leased by producer Lew Fields (*see* FIELDS FAMILY), who promptly named it in honor of himself. The theater was designed by Hammerstein, who invented for it the first fire-control system in any New York theater. A series of pipes led from the rooftop water tank to the stage. This early sprinkler system is still being used in concept by modern theater builders. The *New York Dramatic Mirror* described the system: "The hundreds of pipes composing the gridiron are converted into an immense system of flood pipes which from their height of seventy feet above the stage floor can be made to liberate a deluge of water in which no flame can live. Simply by pulling a chain on the stage the valves of the two roof tanks, each containing 5,000 gallons of water, are opened and the flood pours down the side walls of the house and thoroughly drenches every other portion of the stage." Despite the advanced system, the auditorium was small (770 seats), ugly, and uncomfortable.

The opening production, VICTOR HERBERT and Glen MacDonough's *It Happened in Nordland*, was a hit for the new theater. Fields starred in the show, which also featured Marie Cahill, Bessie Clayton, Joseph W. Herbert, and May Robson, as well as the hit song "Absinthe Frappe." Hammerstein had a way of losing most of the theaters he built, and he lost this one in 1906. Producer James K. Hackett bought the theater and promptly named it in honor of himself. The theater reopened on August 27, 1906, with *The Little Stranger*. Three of the few successful shows produced at the Hackett were *The Witching Hour* (11/18/07; 212 performances), *Salvation Nell* (11/17/08; 71 performances), and *A Woman's Way* (2/22/09; 112 performances), the latter two starring Mrs. Fiske.

In 1910 Hackett lost the theater to William B. Harris, a leading producer. Harris too named the theater in honor of himself. The city widened 42nd Street, causing the theater's box office and balcony entrance to be moved. Since he had to redesign the exterior, Harris hired architects HERTS & TALLANT to alter the interior. The team removed 14 proscenium boxes (the theater originally boasted 20 boxes) and a few rows of seats. Harris reopened a remodeled theater with *Maggie Pepper* (8/31/11; 147 performances).

The Harris Theater was seldom successful. The Selwyn Brothers assumed control of the theater in 1914 and used the house as a secondary theater, moving productions from their more successful theaters to the Harris, where they would complete their runs. New productions included *The Lie* (12/24/14; 172 performances) and *Rolling Stones* (8/17/15; 115 performances).

Producer H. H. Frazee leased the theater and installed his production *Wedding Bells* (11/10/19; 168 performances). In 1920 he bought the theater and renamed it after himself. His first production there was *The Woman of Bronze* (9/7/20; 249 performances). Under Frazee's leadership, the theater was home to *Dulcy* (8/13/21; 246 performances), with Lynn Fontanne (*see* LUNT AND FONTANNE) in her first starring role. But when that hit closed there were no further successes and Frazee lost the theater.

Producer John Cort was the next to try producing at the theater. He reopened the theater, which he renamed Wallack's Theater, with *Shipwrecked* (11/12/24; 28 performances) as the initial production. *Laff That Off* (11/2/25; 390 performances), by Don Mullally, was his biggest success at the theater. It was produced by EARL CARROLL and featured a young Shirley Booth. *She Got What She Wanted* (3/4/29; 118 performances), by George Rosener, was among its most popular productions.

The Depression marked the end of the theater's legitimate policy. Beginning in 1930, the theater showed films exclusively. In 1940, it was remodeled (read gutted of all decoration) and renamed the Anco. The theater showed movies until it was razed in 1997 as part of the new Times Square redevelopment plan.

ANDERSON, JOHN. Critic; b. October 18, 1896, Pensacola, Florida; d. New York, New York, July 16, 1943. John Anderson was a reporter on the staff of the *New York Evening Post* in 1918. In 1924 he was appointed drama critic for the *Evening Post*. Four years later he moved to the *New York Journal*, which later became the *New York Journal-American*. Anderson was also the author of many books on the theater.

ANDERSON, JOHN MURRAY. Noted Broadway revue and musical director of the 1920s to '50s; b. St. John's, Newfoundland, Canada, September 20, 1886; d. New York, New York, January 30, 1954.

John Murray Anderson was among Broadway's earliest jacks-of-all-trades. Anderson was the director of 33 revues and musicals, including 2 popular series, the *Greenwich Village Follies* and *John Murray Anderson's Almanac*. He also directed 7 editions of the Ringling Brothers Circus and 24 shows for nightclubs, including Billy Rose's Diamond Horseshoe (*see* CENTURY THEATER [1]); wrote popular songs; staged 4 Aquacades (including the famous one for the 1939 New York World's Fair), 11 pageants, and 61 stage presentations for movie houses; and directed one of the earliest Hollywood film musicals, *The King of Jazz*, and parts of the Esther Williams film musical *Bathing Beauty*. Anderson himself compared his career with "the piecing together of a jigsaw puzzle."

Anderson's parents were scions of Newfoundland society. His mother, Amelia Murray, came from a long line of Newfoundlanders. His father, John Anderson, was of Scottish birth, immigrating to Newfoundland in 1875. He was an important politician and businessman who is best remembered as the person who convinced the Newfoundland legislature to adopt Daylight Saving Time in 1917.

John Murray Anderson with a very young Bette Davis and Pauline Potter.

Their son attended Bishop Feild College in Newfoundland and then, like many others at the time, went to Europe for higher education and "finishing." He continued his studies in Scotland at the Edinburgh Academy and went on to Lausanne University in Switzerland. Then it was on to London to pursue a career in the theater. He studied acting with Sir Herbert Beerbohm Tree and singing with Sir Charles Santley. His career in England failed to take off, and he returned to Canada in 1909. He earned his living trading in antiques but the stage was calling and he moved to New York City soon after.

In New York his first job was as a dance instructor. That introduction to the theater led to more important jobs, and his first play, *The World Mother*, opened in 1918 and starred Blanche Bates. But he continued operating his school of theater and dance in partnership with Robert Milton throughout the 1920s. The school, located on East 58th Street, saw many future stars enroll in its program. Among these were Bette Davis, Paul Muni, Joan Blondell, and Lucille Ball.

Anderson had a keen eye for color and design and an intimate knowledge of the technical possibilities of modern stagecraft. He specialized in revues and directed many of the greatest. His Broadway output as a director includes *Greenwich Village Follies* (7/15/19; 232 performances; also librettist and lyricist); *What's in a Name?* (3/19/20; 87 performances; also lyricist, librettist, and producer); *Greenwich Village Follies* (8/30/20; 217 performances; also lyricist); *Greenwich Village Follies* (8/31/21; 167 performances; also lyricist, librettist, and producer); *Greenwich Village Follies* (9/12/22; 209 performances; also lyricist); *Jack and Jill* (3/22/23; 92 performances); *Greenwich Village Follies* (9/20/23; 131 performances; also lyricist and librettist); *Greenwich Village Follies* (9/16/24; 131 performances); *Music Box Revue* (12/1/24; 184 performances); and RODGERS AND HART's early musical comedy *Dearest Enemy* (9/18/25; 286 performances).

He took a break from his Broadway assignments as a contract director for Paramount Famous Players Theatres. During the late 1920s and early '30s movie shows in major cities boasted stage shows as accompaniment to the main feature film. Between 1926 and 1929 Anderson produced 57 miniature or "tab" revues for the movie palace market.

His association with Hollywood, albeit as a stage producer and director, led to work on film in the first years of talkies. He convinced Universal Studios to enter the all-talking, all-singing, all-dancing marathon with the 1930 picture *The King of Jazz*. The film was a smash hit, and his contributions didn't go unnoticed back in New York. The *New York Times* review of the film noted, "John Murray Anderson's initial contribution to the audible screen, 'King of Jazz,' with the rotund Paul Whiteman, reveals this director to be a magician of far greater power than one imagined, even from his stage compositions. This Technicolor potpourri of songs, dancing and fun is a marvel of camera wizardy, joyous color schemes, charming costumes and seductive lighting effects." The review for this film might have equally applied to his theatrical skills.

After his stint with Hollywood he returned to the New York stage. Among these later shows were *Hello, Daddy* (12/26/28; 196 performances), *John Murray Anderson's Almanac* (8/4/29; 69 performances; also producer), *Ziegfeld Follies of 1934* (1/4/34; 182 performances), *Life Begins at 8:40* with Ray Bolger and Bert Lahr (8/27/34; 238 performances), *Thumbs Up!* (12/27/34; 156 performances), *Jumbo* (11/16/35; 221 performances), and *Ziegfeld Follies of 1936* (1/30/36; 115 performances).

Anderson was also active in England and worked on the 1937 production *The Coronation Revue*, which celebrated the coronation of King George VI.

Then it was back to Broadway and another series of successes and failures: *One for the Money* (2/4/39; 132 performances), *Two for the Show* (2/8/40; 124 performances), *Sunny River* (12/4/41; 36 performances), *Ziegfeld Follies of 1943* (4/1/43; 553 performances),

Laffing Room Only (12/23/44; 232 performances), *The Firebrand of Florence* (3/22/45; 43 performances), *Three to Make Ready* (3/7/46; 327 performances), and *Heaven on Earth* (9/16/48; 12 performances).

In the 1940s he was also associated with many editions of the Ringling Brothers and Barnum & Bailey Circus as an artistic director. The 1950s began for Anderson with one of his greatest successes, *New Faces of 1952*, which introduced such talents as Paul Lynde, Carol Lawrence, Eartha Kitt, and Ronny Graham (5/16/52; 365 performances), He directed a former student in the musical revue *Two's Company* (12/15/52; 91 performances), which marked Bette Davis' musical-theater debut; and also directed a new edition of *John Murray Anderson's Almanac* (12/10/53; 227 performances).

ANNE NICHOLS' LITTLE THEATER. *See* **Little Theatre.**

ANNIE GET YOUR GUN. Songwriter IRVING BERLIN's masterwork was one of the most successful musicals of its time and has remained a classic of the American musical theatre.

Dorothy Fields (*see* FIELDS FAMILY), after seeing a soldier bragging about the prizes he won at a shooting gallery in Coney Island, came up with the idea of a musical version of sharpshooter Annie Oakley's life. She and her brother Herbert first contacted producer Mike Todd, but he turned them down. They next approached OSCAR HAMMERSTEIN II at an ASCAP meeting and asked if he and his partner Richard Rodgers (*see* RODGERS AND HAMMERSTEIN and RODGERS AND HART) would produce the show. While they wouldn't be writing the show, Hammerstein preferred to provide his own libretti, they suggested JEROME KERN as the show's composer with Dorothy contributing the lyrics. The Fields enthusiastically agreed.

Kern had been toiling in Hollywood and was more than willing to find an excuse to return to Broadway. Rodgers sent him a telegram that read: "It would be one of the greatest honors of my life if you would consent to write the music for this show."

Dorothy Fields had always envisioned ETHEL MERMAN in the lead. Merman later said that Fields drove past Merman's house in Beverly Hills and yelled out the window to the star, "How about you as Annie Oakley?" Merman later met with the Fieldses and agreed to undertake the part.

But before writing could commence in earnest, Kern died and Irving Berlin took his place above the title. The score marked a return by Berlin to the integrated musical. Dorothy Fields had indicated song titles in the script for Kern. When Berlin undertook the project he retained Dorothy's titles. Berlin was nervous about

writing what he perceived as "hillbilly music." But once he realized that show business was the true genre of the show, he enthusiastically began writing the score. And he provided his greatest score. "Doin' What Comes Natur'lly," "I Got the Sun in the Morning," "The Girl That I Marry," "They Say It's Wonderful," "I Got Lost in His Arms," "You Can't Get a Man with a Gun," "I'm an Indian Too," "Anything You Can Do," and "There's No Business Like Show Business" were all high on the hit parade's list of popular songs.

The last of those songs almost didn't make it into the score. After only a week he had written mostly complete versions of 6 songs, among them "Doin' What Comes Natur'lly," "You Can't Get a Man with a Gun," "They Say It's Wonderful," and "There's No Business Like Show Business." He played them for Rodgers, Hammerstein, Dorothy Fields, and the show's director, JOSHUA LOGAN, to enthusiastic response.

At a later run-through he played the finished "There's No Business Like Show Business" for Rodgers and Logan. As the director later wrote, "He would grab me by the collar and sing a lyric into my face the moment I stepped into the room. Only by fixing his eyes on the listener could he sense if the song worked. If one blinked too often or one's eyes glazed for a second, Irving was apt to put the song away."

The next time Berlin played the score, "There's No Business Like Show Business" wasn't included. Rodgers asked what happened to it. Berlin stated that Rodgers and Logan hadn't seemed too enthusiastic the last time it was played. Rodgers insisted he loved it, and Logan backed him up. They wanted the song to be reinserted into the score. But Berlin didn't know where the song was. It was filed away somewhere, in Berlin's words, "in a pile." Rodgers and Logan demanded that the song be found, and after much searching, it finally turned up under a phone book.

The genesis of another of the score's songs was equally astounding. Logan decided that a new song was needed for the second act—specifically, a duet between Annie Oakley and her love interest, Frank Butler. Berlin wasn't sure about writing another song; besides, what could it be? Rodgers suggested some sort of argument or challenge. Berlin picked up on the idea immediately and left the meeting. With Berlin gone, Logan returned to his house to find the phone ringing. It was Berlin on the other line. He began singing the new song, "Anything You Can Do," to Logan.

The director, thunderstruck, asked, "But when did you have time to write it?"

Berlin responded "In the taxicab. I had to, didn't I? We go into rehearsal Monday."

Rehearsals went relatively smoothly and, after engagements in New Haven and Boston, the show moved to the IMPERIAL THEATRE on Broadway. But as the scenery was being hung on the fly lines, bricks began showering on the stage and a steel girder almost snapped.

It was determined that the theater would have to undergo extensive renovation. Rodgers later related, "We couldn't possibly open the show for weeks. Well, this was really disaster. Oscar and I went to see Lee Shubert, whose theatre the Imperial was, and he moved things around. He took a show out of Philadelphia, sent it to New Haven, and got us the Shubert Theatre in Philadelphia."

The show finally opened on May 16, 1946, with Ethel Merman, Ray Middleton, Anne Nyman, and Kenny Bowers. It eventually played 1,147 performances.

The show went over just as well in London, where it opened at the London Coliseum with Dolores Gray, Bill Johnson, Wendy Toye, and Irving Davies headlining the cast. London audiences kept the show on the boards for 1,304 performances.

It was later made into an MGM musical motion picture with Betty Hutton and Howard Keel in the leads. In 1966 Merman herself brought the show back to Broadway in a production that originated at the Music Theatre of Lincoln Center and then moved to Broadway. For that revival, Berlin wrote a new song, "Old Fashioned Wedding."

A second Broadway revival opened at the MINSKOFF THEATRE on March 4, 1999, with Bernadette Peters and Tom Wopat leading the cast. Reba McEntire made a critically hailed Broadway debut opposite Brent Barrett later during the revival's run.

Annie Get Your Gun has become one of the most-performed musicals in Broadway history, and many songs from its old-fashioned score, described by Berlin as "nothing but good old-fashioned hits," became standards.

ANTA. *See* **American National Theatre and Academy.**

ANTA THEATRE. *See* **Virginia Theater.**

ANTOINETTE PERRY AWARD. *See* **Tony Awards.**

ANYTHING GOES! Songwriter COLE PORTER wrote two brilliant Broadway scores, *KISS ME, KATE* and *Anything Goes! Kiss Me, Kate* has the distinction of boasting a superior libretto. But *Anything Goes!* has some of his most recognizable standards as well as a classic performance by the vibrant ETHEL MERMAN.

Anything Goes (*see* NEIL SIMON THEATRE) almost didn't make it to its opening night at the Alvin Theatre.

Producer Vinton Freedley (*see* AARONS AND FREEDLEY) hired librettists GUY BOLTON and P. G. Wodehouse to write a story set aboard an ocean liner that is shipwrecked. Porter wrote his score; Ethel Merman, William Gaxton, Victor Moore, and Bettina Hall were hired as the principals; and playwright Howard Lindsay signed on as director. But *Bon Voyage*, as the show was originally titled, found itself politically incorrect when the U.S.S. Morro Castle burned and sank off the New Jersey coast with many lives lost.

Freedley jettisoned the Bolton and Wodehouse libretto and hired Lindsay to come up with a new book. Lindsay teamed up with THEATER GUILD publicist Russel Crouse, and a new show—and a new writing team—was born. They needed to work fast, and in fact they completed the script while on the train going to Boston for the show's out of town opening.

Russel Crouse recalled the craziness of the out-of-town tryout: "Mr. Porter was equal to all the emergencies we created and I think we hold the record. The show did not even have a name for days and days. . . . Bill Gaxton finally baptized it accidentally. In answer to a question as to whether he would mind making an entrance a minute after the curtain went up, Mr. Gaxton replied, 'In this kind of a spot, anything goes!' We all leaped on the last words and an electrician started spelling them out in electric lights. Mr. Porter dashed off to write a title song. He came in with it the next day."

Anything Goes!, as the new show was named, still took place on an ocean liner, but this time neither the liner nor the script sank. When it opened on November 21, 1934, audiences were taken with the entire proceedings. But it was Merman's performance and Porter's score that received the most accolades. The songwriter wrote a remarkable number of soon-to-be hits including the title song, "I Get a Kick Out of You," "You're the Top," and a perennial Merman favorite, "Blow, Gabriel, Blow."

Anything Goes! eventually played a respectable 420 performances on Broadway and has enjoyed a long life of revivals, film versions, and international productions.

APOLLO THEATRE. 234 W. 43rd Street (originally the Bryant Theatre with entrance at W. 42nd Street). Opening: as a vaudeville and movie house in 1910; as a legitimate theater with *Jimmie*, November 17, 1920.

Like other theaters, and like Times Square itself, the Apollo Theatre has seen its fortunes rise and fall. The house opened as the Bryant Theater in 1910, featuring a combination movie and vaudeville policy. As the 42nd Street corridor established itself as the leading legitimate-theater block in New York, the Bryant's location made it more valuable as a venue for musical comedies, which commanded higher-priced tickets. As a result, the Selwyn brothers, Arch and Edgar, leading producers of their day, bought the theater, renovated it, and renamed it the Apollo. They built a common facade with the TIMES SQUARE THEATER, which they also owned. They christened the theater with the musical *Jimmie* (11/17/20; 69 performances). The show, starring Frances White, unfortunately did not augur well for the future of the theater.

The theater suffered a succession of failures, including SIGMUND ROMBERG's *Love Birds* (3/15/21; 103 performances) and *Daffy Dill* (8/22/22; 69 performances), with a book by GUY BOLTON and OSCAR HAMMERSTEIN II. *Poppy* (9/3/23), starring W. C. Fields, played 346 times at the Apollo, which at that time was the theater's longest run.

The 1920s were a decade of long-running revue series. These included the ZIEGFELD FOLLIES, the SHUBERT BROTHERS' *Passing Shows* at the WINTER GARDEN THEATRE, IRVING BERLIN and Sam Harris's *Music Box Revues*; and *EARL CARROLL'S VANITIES*. The Apollo was home to *GEORGE WHITE'S SCANDALS* for most of their history. The first *Scandals* (6/30/24) at the Apollo, the sixth edition, boasted a score by GEORGE AND IRA GERSHWIN (their last for the series). The hit song "Somebody Loves Me," as sung by Winnie Lightner, and the mugging of comics Tom Patricola and Lester Allen contributed to the respectable 192-performance run.

A straight play, *The Sap* (12/15/24; 15 performances), was soon followed by another edition of the *Scandals* (6/22/25; 169 performances). The team of DE SYLVA, BROWN, AND HENDERSON replaced the Gershwins as the songwriting team and had a modest success with "What a World This Would Be."

Scandals producer GEORGE WHITE took a sublease on the theater and presented the next edition of the annual revue, which opened June 14, 1926. It proved to be the most successful of the series, playing a total of 432 performances. Most of the credit for this outing's success lies with the superior De Sylva, Brown, and Henderson score, which seemed to mirror exactly the youthful exuberance of the Roaring '20s. Three of its songs were among the most successful of 20th-century popular songs: "Lucky Day," with its enthusiastic rendition by Harry Richman; "The Birth of the Blues"; and "The Black Bottom," perhaps the most impressive of the dance crazes to come out of musical comedy. The superior cast of Richman, Ann Pennington, Eugene and Willie Howard, Frances Williams, and Tom Patricola were all *Scandals* regulars.

George White and De Sylva, Brown, and Henderson were also responsible for the next hit at the Apollo, *Manhattan Mary* (9/26/27; 264 performances). White appeared in the show with comedian Ed Wynn and

Ona Munson as a girl whose dream was to appear in the *Scandals*. For the ninth edition of the *Scandals* (7/2/28; 240 performances), the same cast and writers of the last outing came up with another success. The big song hit was "I'm on the Crest of a Wave." But the producer scored a bigger success with a new non-*Scandals* show. *Flying High* (3/3/30; 355 performances) featured a De Sylva, Brown, and Henderson score that, unfortunately, did not equal their earlier offerings. The main reason for the show's success was its star, Bert Lahr, and his supporting cast, including Kate Smith and Oscar Shaw.

The Apollo's bad luck with straight plays continued with its next offering, *The House Beautiful* (3/12/31; 108 performances), which is best remembered for inspiring Dorothy Parker's quip "*The House Beautiful* is the play lousy." The last edition of the *Scandals* to play the Apollo was the third from last in the series. It opened on September 14, 1931, and played for 204 performances. De Sylva had left the team, leaving Brown and Henderson to supply the score, which included the hits "Life Is Just a Bowl of Cherries," belted by ETHEL MERMAN; "This Is the Mrs."; "The Thrill Is Gone"; "That's Why Darkies Were Born," explained by Everett Marshall in blackface; and "My Song," crooned by Rudy Vallee.

The last legitimate theater success at the Apollo was the musical *Take a Chance* (11/26/32; 246 performances). Buddy De Sylva returned to Broadway briefly to co-produce with Laurence Schwab. Most of the songs were by Richard Whiting and Nacio Herb Brown, although some were contributed by VINCENT YOUMANS in his last Broadway assignment before his death. Ethel Merman repeated her previous success on the Apollo stage, supported by Jack Haley, Jack Whiting, June Knight, and Sid Silvers. The songs included "Eadie Was a Lady" and "Rise and Shine."

The last show to play the Apollo was the unsuccessful Bill Robinson revue *Blackbirds of 1933* (12/2/33; 25 performances). The Depression, which had shuttered so many of the Broadway theaters, finally reached the Apollo. A movie policy was initiated, and a year later, the Minsky brothers began presenting BURLESQUE shows on its stage. The burlesque policy remained in effect until Mayor LaGuardia's crackdown on this type of entertainment, and in 1937 the Apollo became a grind (24-hour) movie house.

Forty years later the Broadway theater seemed to be undergoing a slight upsurge in business. There was a lack of available theaters, and the owners of the Apollo, the Brandt Organization, decided to enter the legitimate-theater field. Over $350,000 was spent to restore the Apollo to its former glory. Improvements both in the auditorium and backstage were completed in time for its first legitimate show under its new policy. The New Apollo reopened with *On Golden Pond* (2/28/79; 126 performances), starring Frances Sternhagen and Tom Aldredge. The show received mildly positive reviews. The theater's renovation received much better notices. Although the Brandts changed the entrance to the theater from 42nd to 43rd Street, the New Apollo was still considered somewhat off the beaten track. Also, around this time, the number of independent producers operating on Broadway was severely reduced, and as a result, product grew scarce.

An unsuccessful play, *Bent*, had a short run, followed by a transfer of Lanford Wilson's *The Fifth of July* (1980) from the Circle Repertory Company. *The Fifth of July* proved to be the most successful of the house's bookings, although it hardly paid back its costs. The final offering at the New Apollo was *The Guys in the Truck*, a 1983 failure that starred Elliot Gould and closed after one performance.

The theater briefly returned to its former grind policy before being shuttered. In the fall of 1987 the theater was renamed the Academy, with a short-lived booking of comic Redd Foxx. The theater underwent another transformation, and in September 1988 its name was changed to the Alcazar de Paris. It was remodeled as a dinner-revue theater, featuring Parisian-inspired cabaret acts. It was a quick failure, and the name reverted to Academy. The last production on its stage was *Legends in Concert*, an impersonator show that opened and closed in May of 1989.

When the 42nd Street redevelopment project was announced, the Brandts offered to make the Apollo a cornerstone of the renovation. But the powers that be decided that what the street needed was another large musical theater barn, and took over the Apollo and the Lyric Theatre next door under eminent domain. The two theaters were torn down and replaced by the Ford Center, which incorporated some of the architectural details of the Apollo.

ARLEN, HAROLD. One of America's greatest composers of popular music, equally at home writing for cabaret, motion picture and stage; b. Hyman Arluck, Buffalo, New York, February 15, 1905; d. New York, New York, April 23, 1986.

Harold Arlen (born Hyman Arluck) first sang in the choir of the synagogue in Buffalo, New York, where his father was a cantor. He was also influenced by early jazz recordings, and when still in his teens, he formed his own group, the Snappy Trio. That group soon evolved into the Southbound Shufflers. These bands played local clubs and excursion boats around Buffalo. Then he and his friends formed the Buffalodians, for which Arlen sang and arranged the tunes. The Buffalodians were successful enough to get a small

recording contract, and in 1925 Arlen was encouraged to come to New York. After his move he became a singer, pianist, and arranger with various dance bands before landing a job in Arnold Johnson's pit orchestra for the Broadway revue GEORGE WHITE'S SCANDALS of 1928.

Arlen's unique singing style, influenced by liturgical singing and the techniques of black vocalists, led to jobs in vaudeville. He appeared on the Loew's vaudeville circuit and made it to the venerable PALACE THEATER. Although Arlen would make his greatest mark as a composer, he continued singing, making albums throughout his career. He cut sides with the Red Nichols Orchestra and sang on his own albums for Capitol, Columbia, and Walden Records.

While a rehearsal pianist for the VINCENT YOUMANS show *Great Day*, Arlen was encouraged by songwriter Harry Warren to become a composer. A musical riff Arlen used to call the performers back from their rehearsal breaks was developed into his first hit, "Get Happy" (1930). The success of "Get Happy" led to a job writing the scores for a series of Cotton Club revues with his lyricist, Ted Koehler. In 1933 he and Koehler wrote their greatest hit, "Stormy Weather." Their great success at the Cotton Club included such standards as "Kickin' the Gong Around," "Between the Devil and the Deep Blue Sea," "I Love a Parade," "I've Got the World on a String," "Minnie the Moocher's Wedding Day," "Happy as the Day Is Long," "Ill Wind," "As Long as I Live," "Raisin' the Rent," and "You Gave Me Everything but Love." At the Cotton Club, Arlen cemented his relationships with black performers including Cab Calloway, Lena Horne, and Ethel Waters. He continued providing nonstereotypical scores for black performers throughout his career.

The Cotton Club led back to Broadway and songs for musical revues, including *The Nine Fifteen Revue* (2/11/30; "Get Happy"); EARL CARROLL'S VANITIES (7/1/30; "Hittin' the Bottle"); *Earl Carroll's Vanities of 1932* (9/27/32; I Gotta Right to Sing the Blues," "Rockin' in Rhythm"); *Americana* (10/5/32; "Satan's Li'l Lamb"); *George White's Music Hall Varieties* (11/22/32); *Life Begins at 8:40* (8/27/34; "Fun to Be Fooled," "Let's Take a Walk Around the Block," "You're a Builder Upper"); and *The Show Is On* (12/25/36).

Success in the revue format brought Arlen the opportunity to write for book shows, many of which prominently featured black performers. These shows included *You Said It* (1/19/31; "Sweet and Hot," "You Said It"); *Hooray for What!* (12/1/37; "Down with Love," "In the Shade of the New Apple Tree"); *Bloomer Girl* (10/5/44; "The Eagle and Me," "Right as the Rain"); *St. Louis Woman* (3/30/46; "Any Place I Hang My Hat Is Home," "Come Rain or Come

Shine"); *House of Flowers* (12/30/54; "I Never Has Seen Snow," "A Sleepin' Bee"); *Jamaica* (10/31/57; "Ain't It the Truth," "Napoleon"); *Saratoga* (12/7/59; "Goose Never Be a Peacock," "Love Held Lightly").

While these shows were rarely commercially successful, the scores Arlen wrote, mainly in collaboration with E. Y. HARBURG or Johnny Mercer, were as rich as any on Broadway. His shows featured such greats as Lena Home, Pearl Bailey, Diahann Carroll, Ricardo Montalban, Celeste Holm, Dooley Wilson, Ed Wynn, Bert Lahr, Ray Bolger, the Nicholas Brothers, Ray Walston, Geoffrey Holder, Josephine Premice, Ossie Davis, and Howard Keel.

Arlen also had a long career in Hollywood writing for such films as *The Wizard of Oz* ("Over the Rainbow," Academy Award, 1939); *At the Circus*; *Blues in the Night* ("Blues in the Night," "This Time the Dream's on Me"); *Rio Rita*; *Star Spangled Rhythm* ("Hit the Road to Dreamland," "That Old Black Magic"); *Cabin in the Sky* ("Happiness Is a Thing Called Joe"); *The Sky's the Limit* ("My Shining Hour," "One for My Baby"); *Up in Arms* ("Now I Know"); *Here Come the Waves* ("Ac-cent-tchu-ate the Positive"); *Out of This World* ("Out of This World"); *Casbah* ("For Every Man There's a Woman," "Hooray for Love"); *My Blue Heaven* ("Don't Rock the Boat, Dear"); *The Petty Girl*; *Down Among the Sheltering Palms*; *Mr. Imperium* ("Let Me Look at You"); *The Farmer Takes a Wife* ("Today I Love Everybody"); *A Star Is Born* ("The Man That Got Away"); *The Country Girl* ("Dissertation on the State of Bliss"); and *Gay Purr-ee* ("Paris Is a Lonely Town").

Arlen's total output doesn't match that of the greatest Broadway composers, such as IRVING BERLIN, Richard Rodgers (*see* RODGERS AND HAMMERSTEIN and RODGERS AND HART), or JULE STYNE, and except for *Bloomer Girl*, he never had a major hit show. But his work was consistently brilliant. His range of compositions equals that of the most versatile theater composers, including Styne, FRANK LOESSER, and Cy Cole-

Donald Brooks, Celeste Holm and Margaret Douglass in *Bloomer Girl*.

man. But Arlen's music, be it for a tin woodman, a runaway slave, a madam, or the most innocent of naifs, always reflects Arlen's unique voice. He always wrote with a complete belief in and understanding of the character. He never let the audience know, as so many composers do, that there is a composer behind the character. He always mirrored the character's point of view, and each character's voice is unique yet unmistakably Arlen's.

Few could write as haunting a song as "Ill Wind," as stirring a song as "The Eagle and Me," or as jaunty and carefree a melody as that for "Happy as the Day Is Long." His work was inherently dramatic; even his revue songs were never simply pop songs.

ARTKRAFT STRAUSS. Of all the many companies and individuals who have influenced Times Square and our perceptions of it, none has had more impact than that of Artkraft Strauss, the company primarily responsible for the SIGNAGE that is one of Times Square's most defining features. As of 2002, the company employs almost 100 people, including artists, designers, engineers, carpenters, electricians, electronics technicians, sheet metal workers, sign hangers, and sign painters. Unique among companies in the outdoor advertising field, Artkraft Strauss both leases space to advertisers, and designs and builds the signs that dramatize the advertiser's presence.

The history of Artkraft Strauss, which has designed and built virtually all of Times Square's huge custom outdoor displays over the years, goes back to the turn of the 20th century and the joining of the skills of two men, Benjamin Strauss and Jacob Starr. Times Square was just beginning to be developed, the WINTER GARDEN THEATRE was still the American Horse Exchange, and Benjamin Strauss decided to follow the real-estate boom uptown to 48th Street between Broadway and 7th Avenue and begin making signs for the new theaters constructed along the Rialto.

As it happened, Jacob Starr, a Russian immigrant metalworker and electrician, was working with a wrought-iron company in the same building where Strauss had his business. Incidentally, the wrought-iron company was Frank & Weiss, which made the first New Year's Eve ball. Mel Starr remembered his father relating how the two men met: "Jake used to tell the story of coming to Strauss's workshop around 1907 during the depression with a big sledgehammer and a bag full of tools and saying in Yiddish, "Kenst usen a starker mann?" ("Can you use a strong man?") Jake looked like a 98-pound weakling (he was actually an ironworker so he was pretty strong) and the sledgehammer weighed more than he did. Strauss laughed,

but he hired him. They started making metal and electric signs. It was the perfect joining of skills. Starr was a technician with an instinct for the new technology, and Strauss, a 19th-century artist and craftsman, had a burgeoning sign business. Theater signs at the time were gas lit. The change to electricity was inevitable, but until the electric lines were strung all the way north to Times Square the glow on the Great White Way was from flickering gas flames behind glass lenses set into punched out metal facades. Starr, a highly skilled, European-trained craftsman, modernized Strauss's operation by introducing worker specialization into this primitive industrial area. Henry Ford would later win renown for exactly the same practice. Strauss also specialized in gold leaf and sent teams of gold leafers traveling around the country for two or three years at a stretch.

Starr left Strauss in 1919, and started a company that took burnt-out light bulbs and replaced the filaments. In those days, light bulbs were very expensive and lasted for only a short time. Starr had a factory staffed with young immigrants who gently removed the glass covering and replaced the filaments. The light-bulb companies frowned on Starr's business, because their continued success depended on the short life of their bulbs. They bought Starr out, and he developed an association with the Artkraft Sign Company of Lima, Ohio. Artkraft's main business was in kitchen fixtures, and the company used the same ovens and kilns to make signs. Signs at that time were made out of porcelain-enameled steel, the same material used to make sinks and stoves. Porcelain, which has an impervious finish, is perfect for outdoor use.

Artkraft had one of the American franchises to make neon, which was invented by the Frenchman Georges Claude around 1902. He unveiled the first neon lamp to the Parisians on December 11, 1910. In 1923 the Claude Neon company introduced the first neon signs in America (to a Packard dealership in Los Angeles); prior to this, all electric lights were incandescent including tubes filled with carbon dioxide and manufactured by a man named Moore. The "new light" soon swept the world. Now sign companies went public and began to merge. That same year, Starr started a company called Rainbow Lights, which built electric signs. The introduction of neon marked the first time one could light signs with colors, not just white lights behind colored glass or tinted bulbs. In 1929 the Depression hit, sending the profits of both Strauss and Starr tumbling. The two men decided to join forces. (Starr would later say, "Sometimes zero plus zero makes three.") In 1935 they merged, forming Artkraft Strauss, and moved operations to a warehouse building at 12th Avenue between 57th and 58th Streets. An important client of Artkraft Strauss was Douglas Leigh, a free-lance sign salesman and designer who used Artkraft Strauss to build his creations, which were dubbed Spectaculars.

As Mel Starr remembered:

When the movie business was in its heyday, and Times Square featured first-run limited showings of new movies, palaces like the Capitol, the Astor, the Victoria, the Mayfair and Loew's State would change the theatre's front every time they changed the picture by adding electric letters, thousands of electric light bulbs and miles of neon tubing to the animated electrical displays.

We'd do two or three of those a week. We would do a hundred to a hundred and fifty Spectacular changes a year. Today, most of that is gone. The tendency is for movies to use painted plastic or computer-printed signs. There are fewer movie theater locations now. [When Mel was speaking, there were fewer sign locations than in the past; today there are more sign locations, but fewer movie theaters; and of course, movies are simultaneously released, not first-run on Broadway any more.]

Though there are more movie theatres in the square than before, most are multiplexes without large signage. And today, there are more signs than ever on the square but few are made up of the great spectaculars of the past. Many of the great spectacular locations have been lost. Most notably missing is the Astor/Victoria site where the Marriott Marquis Hotel now stands. Where the ABC Studios are today is where the Kleenex sign was. Above the Brill Building was the Budweiser flying A and eagle. The new office buildings are replacing former sign sites. The new zoning laws mandate electric displays on the new buildings. Due to the leadership of Tama Starr, the New York City Zoning Ordinance specified that signage must be displayed on all new buildings.

Mel died in 1988. His daughter Tama continues the family business. She sees the signs as an integral part of the Square:

The Square itself is the atrium of the theatre district. The Spectacular displays with their surreal components of scale and flash and dazzling color, let you know the minute you get into that environment that you're into a theatre experience. There's a mood of glitter and fun and brightness and fantasy and razzle-dazzle. What makes Times Square unique is the long sight lines and the fact that the rooflines are set way back so even in the middle of a crowded city, and Times Square is one of the most crowded places in a crowded city, you don't feel hemmed in.

Tama continued, "We've been doing this for more than a hundred years, and we hope to be doing it for at least another hundred."

ARTWORK. Thanks to the work of the Public Art Fund and other municipal organizations, artwork has been placed on the islands of Times Square, which separate Broadway and 7th Avenue. There are many more traditional artworks around the Square. These include the SIGNAGE on buildings: commercial artworks designed to be noticed, but which occasionally attract attention for their intrinsic design qualities. Sculpture also abounds in the square. The few older buildings that remain have carved cornices, gargoyles, and other architectural details. Freestanding sculptures include the statues of GEORGE M. COHAN and Father Duffy and those set into the side of the I. Miller Building. The statues on the I. Miller Building (northeast corner of 46th Street and 7th Avenue) were designed by A. Stirling Calder, father of Alexander Calder. They represent Rosa Ponselle, Ethel Barrymore, (see BARRYMORE FAMILY), Marilyn Miller, and Mary Pickford. Since the I. Miller shoe store has ceased operating on the square, the statues have been neglected but have not been destroyed, as have many Broadway landmarks.

The statue of George M. Cohan was designed by George Lober and erected in 1959. Cohan proudly occupies a conspicuous location across from the PALACE THEATER on the island between 47th and 48th Streets and Broadway and 7th Avenue. Father Francis Duffy occupies the same island that is home to the Cohan statue. The northern end of what is usually thought of as Times Square is actually called Duffy Square after the famous "Fighting Chaplain" of New York's 69th Regiment. Father Duffy was later the pastor of Holy Cross Church on West 42nd Street. There he became friends with many Broadway habitués. The statue was sculpted by Charles Keck and placed in the square in 1937.

The longest-lasting of the newer artworks is underneath the street, unseen by passersby. But it has been heard for over a decade. Composer Max Neuhaus convinced the Metropolitan Transportation Authority to allow him the use of an abandoned subway ventilation chamber underneath the island between 45th and 46th Streets. The work, installed in 1977, contains a loudspeaker that resonates to the frequencies generated by several electronic sound generators that pick up the sounds in the ventilation chamber as the chamber resonates in response to street noise and vibration. Electricity for the piece, which cost $100,000 to install, initially came from a nearby light pole; now the artwork has a direct link to the city's electricity. In 1992 homeless men found their way into the chamber and stripped the copper wiring from the piece. Subsequently Neuhaus dismantled the equipment and put it into storage. In 2002 the piece was reinstalled—in its new tamper-proof cage—and, on May 22 the work was turned on again.

ASCAP (THE AMERICAN SOCIETY FOR COMPOSERS, AUTHORS AND PUBLISHERS). The American Society for Composers, Authors and Publishers licenses the right to publicly perform the nondramatic, copyrighted musical compositions of its members. ASCAP's members are the composers and lyricists who write the bulk of America's popular songs. ASCAP collects license fees from 10,000 radio stations, 800 television stations, and over 150,000 other music users, including cabarets, restaurants, nightclubs, Muzak and other background music companies, symphonies, retail stores, colleges, universities, and concerts.

Although it was founded in 1914, ASCAP's history can be traced back to 1910. George Maxwell was the American representative for Ricordi, an Italian publishing company. Puccini was visiting America and asked Maxwell why he was not being reimbursed when he heard his melodies played in hotels and restaurants. (Italy already had a law remunerating composers for performance rights.) Puccini had good grounds for his argument. The United States copyright law of 1909 guaranteed the owners of musical copyrights the exclusive right "to perform the copyrighted work publicly for profit if it be a musical composition."

Nothing was done immediately, but in 1913 unions and other organizations were beginning to be formed. Composer Raymond Hubbell, author of "Poor Butterfly," met with Nathan Burkan, a lawyer, and George Maxwell. They believed songwriters should be paid for performances of their work. The three men approached VICTOR HERBERT, the most important musical-theater composer at that time. Herbert, a prominent fixture on Broadway and the concert stage, agreed to represent the new idea. He called a meeting at Luchow's Restaurant on 14th Street, then the center of the New York theater community. Due to a lack of interest and inclement weather, only 5 people showed up to join the 4 men who had called the meeting: composers Silvio Hein, Louis A. Hirsch, and Gustav Kerker, lyricist Glen MacDonough, and music publisher Jay Witmark. Another meeting was called on February 13, 1914, at the HOTEL CLARIDGE. More than 100 songwriters and publishers attended the second meeting. After much discussion, ASCAP was formally created.

George Maxwell was named president. Nathan Burkan was named general counsel. Victor Herbert, who would not accept the presidency, preferred to hold the position of vice president. John Golden as treasurer, Raymond Hubbell as assistant treasurer, and Glen MacDonough as secretary joined him. There were 17 charter members on the first Board of Directors. IRVING BERLIN was the last surviving member of that first board.

The Fulton Theater (*see* HELEN HAYES THEATER[1]), on 46th Street and Broadway, was the first home of the new organization. An office was rented, and the staff began the difficult task of convincing others to pay for the use of the members' songs. Despite the daunting task, the organization was quite small. The entire payroll was only $15 a week. Dues were $10 for songwriters and $50 for publishers.

Resistance to the organization's goals was strong. RECTOR'S, Broadway's premier restaurant, was the first ASCAP licensee in October of 1914. Rector's fee for that first year was $180. With the influential restaurant behind them, ASCAP found 84 more restaurants and hotels willing to sign an agreement. Unfortunately, the fees paid by these 85 signers, which averaged only $8.23 a year, didn't cover the operating expenses of the organization. Because of the shortfall, royalties were not paid to the membership for years to come.

Widespread opposition to the concept of ASCAP continued. Because music had been free in the past, bandleaders, hotels, and restaurants didn't see a reason to pay for the use of ASCAP members' songs. In the summer of 1914 ASCAP fought its first court battle. John Philip Sousa and his publisher, the John Church Company, brought suit against the Hilliard Hotel Company, owners of the Vanderbilt Hotel. The orchestra in the dining room of the hotel played Sousa's march "From Maine to Oregon" without paying for the rights. Judge Lacombe of the United States District Court for the Southern District of New York ruled in the publisher's favor. But in the Circuit Court of Appeals, Judge Ward overturned the previous court's ruling. The decision handed down on February 9, 1915, stated in part, "Such persons primarily go into the saloon for refreshment and pay for what they order, and not for the music. We are not convinced . . . that the defendants played 'From Maine to Oregon' for profit within the meaning of those words in our copyright act."

Because Judge Ward ruled that performances of music in hotels and restaurants were not for profit, the new organization needed to take another tack. VICTOR HERBERT charged that people had heard a Herbert composition, "Sweethearts," played in Shanley's Restaurant on April 1, 1915. Herbert knew because of the earlier ruling that he could not object to the use of the song as a profit-making venture. Nathan Burkan found another clause in the copyright law that gave to the copyright owner the exclusive right, regardless of profit, to the public performance of a dramatic work. Because Herbert's dramatic work was covered and the song "Sweethearts" was part of the operetta of the same name, ASCAP interpreted the law as stating that any portion of the operetta must also be covered.

Shanley's made four points in its rebuttal. One, there was no cover charge, therefore the music was not a performance. Second, the platform on which the orchestra played was not a stage, therefore no theatrical performance took place. Third, "a young lady who was not an actress, who had never been employed in a theatrical production," sang the song. The last point stated that although "Sweethearts" was a part of a theater piece, the version of the song used by the orchestra was "published as a separate musical composition by G. Schirmer, Inc., in the form ordinarily known as sheet music form, and the song as so published is a complete musical composition of itself."

Judge Learned Hand gave his decision on May 1, 1915. He stated that the previous case's ruling clearly established that performance in a restaurant was not performance for profit. He agreed with Herbert that any part of an operetta was part of a dramatic musical production and that public performance of such a part was an infringement of Herbert's rights. However, because the song was published as a separate song and copyrighted as a unique piece, the plaintiffs had therefore abandoned their dramatic control of the song.

With the first round lost, Herbert appealed the decision, but on January 11, 1916, he lost again. *Musical America*, a popular magazine, stated, "The recent case . . . ended the campaign of the authors and composers to collect royalties from restaurants as far as the courts are concerned, with a complete defeat of the authors." The magazine was wrong. Herbert appealed to the United States Supreme Court. The Court reversed the two lower court rulings in favor of Herbert. Justice Oliver Wendell Holmes stated that whether the work was a piece of a whole or a separate entity was irrelevant. Nor did it matter whether the patrons paid for food only or for a show. Because the restaurant paid the orchestra and the singers a salary, then it followed that the music was an integral part of the restaurant's features. The court explained, "If music did not pay, it would be given up. If it pays, it pays out of the public's pocket. Whether it pays or not, the purpose of employing it is profit, and that is enough." ASCAP would face more legal battles each time a new medium or new technology was introduced. Radio, television, and talking pictures each had their own lawsuits, but through it all, ASCAP has persevered.

Seven years after a 1909 bill was passed by Congress, ASCAP finally collected sufficient royalties to pay its members. ASCAP's first songwriters were primarily composers and lyricists of Broadway shows. Its services eventually made it possible for many of these tunesmiths to control their work and make a living out of their art. Through its licensing agreements, ASCAP has also had an impact on the nightclubs, dance halls, hotels, and restaurants that provide so much of the glitter of the Great White Way. In later years Raymond Hubbell wrote of the early days of the organization:

"Once in a while I close my eyes and in memory I go back to that rainy October night, in 1913, at Luchow's Restaurant. I see that long table with places . . . and vision the little group of which only Jay Witmark and myself remain. Reverently I raise my glass to dear old Victor, Glen, George, Nathan, Lou, Gus and Silvio and whisper, as I think of all the blessings God has showered on ASCAP, if you fellows were here, I know we'd do it all over again!"

ASTAIRE, FRED AND ADELE. The leading dance team of the 1920s and the best-known of all Broadway dance teams, celebrated for their mix of sophistication and humor, combined with their grace and technical virtuosity; b. Adele Austerlitz, Omaha, Nebraska, September 10, 1897; d. Phoenix, January 25, 1981; and Frederick E. Austerlitz Jr., b. Omaha, Nebraska, May 10, 1899; d. Los Angeles, California, June 22, 1987.

In 1904 Ann Geilus Austerlitz, Fred and Adele's mother, packed up herself and her children and brought them from their Nebraska home to New York City. Although Fred was 4½ and Adele was only 6, Mrs. Austerlitz felt that the children might have a career on the stage. Time, of course, proved her right. Yet one wonders what made her believe her children could become successful.

Adele had attended dance schools in Omaha and had become somewhat famous locally. Fred hadn't any lessons, although he did mimic his sister's steps. In New York, the Astaires attended the Alvienne School of the Dance. They followed their lessons with a professional debut in Keyport, New Jersey, in 1906. The engagement paid $50. By this time the children's father had legally changed his name to Astaire. He wrangled a job for the 2 children on the Orpheum Circuit. Another followed that 20-week tour. At the end of the second tour the children found themselves unemployable: they had outgrown their act and were forced to give up the stage. Still, they practiced and took classes at the Ned Wayburn Studio of Stage Dancing. They worked on new material while studying and went to Broadway shows to observe the great dancers on the stage.

Fred and Adele appeared for the first time on Broadway during a benefit at the Broadway Theatre. That led to a booking at Proctor's 5th Avenue Theater on February 19, 1911, in an act called *A Rainy Saturday*. It was stupendously unsuccessful. The Astaires were fired after their opening performance. This failure made them persona non grata on Broadway. They were forced into touring the hinterlands. They slowly improved their technique and worked on their act. After a series of small bookings, they played their last vaudeville booking during the 1915–16 season.

Fred and Adele Astaire.

The Astaires finally received their Broadway break in a SHUBERT BROTHERS production, *Over the Top* (11/28/17; 78 performances), at the 44TH STREET THEATRE. SIGMUND ROMBERG and Herman Timberg contributed the music. The lyrics were by Philip Bartholomae and Harold Atteridge. Justine Johnstone and Mary Baton were the stars of the revue. The Astaires' contributions did not go unnoticed by the CRITICS. Louis Sherwin wrote in the *Globe*, "One of the prettiest features of the show is the dancing of the two Astaires. The girl, a light, spritelike little creature, has really an exquisite floating style in her capering, while the young man combines eccentric agility with humor." Despite positive reviews for the Astaires, the show did not do well. It had a brief tour under the name, *Oh, Justine!*

The Shuberts didn't ignore the Astaires' good reviews, and put them into the next edition of their annual revue, the *Passing Show of 1918* (7/25/18; 124 performances). Sigmund Romberg wrote the score with Jean Schwartz; Harold Atteridge contributed the lyrics. The show also featured Lou Clayton, Frank Fay, Willie and Eugene Howard, Nita Naldi, and Charles Ruggles. The *Passing Show* received mostly favorable reviews. Heywood Broun wrote in the *New York Tribune*:

> In an evening in which there was an abundance of good dancing, Fred Astaire stood out. He and his partner, Adele Astaire, made the show pause early in the evening with a beautiful, careless, loose-limbed dance, in which the right foot never seemed to know just what the left foot was going to do, or cared, either. It almost seemed as if the two young people had been poured into the dance.

Charles Darnton, writing in the *Evening World*, thought that Fred and "Estelle [*sic*] . . . scored the hit of the show." The show undertook a long tour. When Frank Fay dropped out of the show, Fred assumed his part and played in his first sketches.

Apple Blossoms (10/7/19; 256 performances) was the team's next Broadway show. It opened under the auspices of producer Charles Dillingham. Victor Jacobi and Fritz Kreisler wrote the music to William Le Baron's book and lyrics. John Charles Thomas and Wilda Bennett were the leads. The Astaires' roles were interpolated into the proceedings, offering them the opportunity for two numbers. The critics again gave them rave reviews. ALEXANDER WOOLLCOTT, writing about the "Adaires" (*sic*) in the *New York Times*, was especially taken with Fred's dancing: "He is one of those extraordinary persons whose senses of rhythm and humor have been all mixed up, whose very muscles, of which he seems to have an extra supply, are downright facetious." *Apple Blossoms* proved to be among the most successful operettas of its time. But

most of the same team—Jacobi, Dillingham, Thomas, and the Astaires—couldn't repeat their success when they presented *The Love Letter* (10/4/21; 31 performances).

For Goodness Sake (2/20/22; 103 performances) was the pair's next assignment. As usual, the Astaires (although they had only 6th billing) received the best of the notices. ROBERT BENCHLEY, writing in the old *Life* magazine, said there "wasn't much to say about *For Goodness Sake* that you couldn't say about most musicals except that the Astaires (perhaps late of 'Astaire and Down') are in it." Although the Astaires constantly received good reviews, they still weren't well known enough to carry a show by themselves. *The Punch and Judy* (11/28/22; 65 performances) had a score by JEROME KERN and Anne Caldwell, but it contained no hit songs.

Alex Aarons (*see* AARONS AND FREEDLEY) had decided to produce *For Goodness Sake* in London under the title *Stop Flirting*. The Astaires were hired to reprise their performances in the West End. The show opened to rave reviews, especially for the Astaires, and it became one of the longest-running shows at that time, playing a number of theaters for a total of 418 performances. Even with that long a run, the show could have gone on if the Astaires had not wished to return to the New York stage.

While they were appearing in London, Alex Aarons was busy working on their next Broadway show. Aarons had teamed up with Vinton Freedley, and the new producing team hired GEORGE AND IRA GERSHWIN to compose the score. GUY BOLTON and P. G. Wodehouse contributed the libretto, which was built around the talents of the young dance team. The title of the show was originally *Black Eyed Susan*, but it opened on Broadway as *Lady, Be Good!* (12/1/24; 330 performances). The show was an immediate smash hit. Finally, doubts about whether the Astaires could handle the leads of a Broadway musical were put to rest. The Gershwins had provided them with some of their best songs: "Fascinating Rhythm," "Half of It, Dearie Blues," and "Hang on to Me."

Following a national tour and the London production, the Astaires were ready to go into rehearsals for their next Broadway show, *Funny Face* (11/22/27; 250 performances). Aarons and Freedley had again called on the Gershwins for the score, which featured such standards as "Funny Face," "He Loves and She Loves," "High Hat," and "The Babbitt and the Bromide." *Funny Face* was the opening attraction of the new Alvin Theater (*see* NEIL SIMON THEATER). Woollcott enthused, "I do not know whether George Gershwin was born into this world to write rhythms for Fred Astaire's feet or whether Fred Astaire was born into this world to show how the Gershwin music should really be danced. But surely they were written in the same key, those two." *Funny Face* played 263 performances in London. Its success led Paramount to give the Astaires a screen test. Apparently the studio wasn't impressed, because they failed to pick up the team for the movies. A film version with Fred Astaire and Audrey Hepburn was released 30 years later by Paramount.

FLORENZ ZIEGFELD was preparing a musical called *Smiles* (11/18/30; 63 performances) to showcase the talents of Marilyn Miller. He hired the Astaires following their London engagement in *Funny Face*. VINCENT YOUMANS composed the score, which featured what became a standard, "Time on My Hands." Despite the talents involved, *Smiles* turned out to be a flop, "the kind of flop that even made the audience look bad," according to Fred Astaire himself.

With their next Broadway show (which would be their last appearance together), the Astaires had their greatest artistic success. *The Band Wagon* (6/3/31; 262 performances) was a smart, sophisticated revue with just the right amount of silliness. The material by Arthur Schwartz and Howard Dietz (*see* DIETZ AND SCHWARTZ) perfectly suited the Astaires' talents. Their co-stars, Helen Broderick, Frank Morgan, and Tilly Losch, were equally suited to what BROOKS ATKINSON said was "a new era in the artistry of the American revue." *The Band Wagon* opened at the NEW AMSTERDAM THEATRE. The critics raved about the entire production and especially about the Astaires. Richard Lockridge, writing in the *Sun*, stated, "There is something utterly audacious about the two of them; there is a lightness and flexibility and dash in whatever they do, whether it is to chase a plump and bearded Frenchman around the revolving stage or to dance in black and white before an immense encircled drum. They may be chatty and intimate, teasing themselves and the audience. They may be bizarre, tantalizing figures from a modernistic nightmare. They are in any case incomparable."

The Band Wagon went on the road for a brief tour that was marked by Adele's retirement from the stage when she married Lord Charles Cavendish. This left Fred on his own for the first time. His insecurities about performing without his sister did not stand in the way of his signing on to star in a new show. *The Gay Divorce* (11/29/32; 248 performances) was produced by Dwight Deere Wiman with a score by COLE PORTER. The out-of-town reviews were less than favorable. The *Boston Transcript* said, "An Astaire must dance and still does very well—but not for the general good is he now sisterless." Despite good work on the road and a score that contained at least one Porter standard, "Night and Day," the show wasn't well received when it opened in New York. One critic claimed, "Fred Astaire stops every now and then to look off-stage towards the wings as if he were hoping his titled sister, Adele, would come out and rescue him." Some reviewers, however, did enjoy Astaire's performance. WALTER WINCHELL said, "The personable and talented brother of Lady Cavendish never before seemed so refreshing and entertaining."

In his autobiography, *Steps in Time*, Astaire wrote, "I was not upset because they missed my sister. I'd have been disappointed if they hadn't, but at any rate my job was cut out for me and the show had to be put over." Put it over he did. Still, despite the eventual long run, Fred felt the strain of supporting a show. He also realized that as long as he appeared onstage, the critics would comment on the absence of his sister. He was then receiving renewed interest from Hollywood and decided to explore this avenue.

Astaire went on to star in 32 movie musicals with a succession of partners. But despite the brilliance and success of his film career, for many old-timers no movie could match the magic of watching Fred Astaire accompany his sister on the stages of New York. The opening night review of *Lady, Be Good!* in the *Herald Tribune* summed up the audience's enjoyment at watching the greatest dance team in Broadway history:

> Fred and Adele we salute you! Last night at the Liberty Theatre this young couple appeared about 8:30 o'clock and from an audience sophisticated and over-theatered received a cordial greeting. At 8:45 they were applauded enthusiastically and when, at 9:15, they sang and danced "Fascinating Rhythm" the callous Broadwayites cheered them as if their favorite halfback had planted the ball behind the goal posts after an 80-yard run. Seldom has it been our pleasure to witness so heartfelt, spontaneous and so deserved a tribute.

ASTOR HOTEL. Broadway between 44th and 45th Streets. The Astor Hotel was the most celebrated hotel in Times Square and perhaps the most famous in all New York. The plot of land was originally part of the Medref-Eden farm. Around 1830 William B. Astor, Lord Astor's grandfather, purchased the property for $34,000 from the bank that had foreclosed on the farm. Most people felt the investment was a bad one because the site was so far uptown. Lord William Waldorf Astor willed the property to his son, Major John Jacob Astor of the British Horse Guards.

Major Astor, an important New York City real-estate owner, made a lot of money off the Astor Hotel property. He received $500,000 per year from the land lease. When the lease was renegotiated in 1928, the new lease increased the amount to $700,000 per annum, a fee the hotel could afford because the hotel's income was $2 million per year.

The 11-story hotel opened on September 9, 1904. It was an immediate success, and the opening coincided with the burgeoning importance of Longacre Square (as it was then known). In 1907 a group of Japanese diplomats were entertained at the Astor. The Japanese were meeting with American dignitaries to explore improving Japanese-American relations. That same year Andrew Carnegie held a conference on his peace plan at the Astor. Forty years later, the hotel housed United Nations personnel. General Chiang Kai-shek of China complained to the hotel's assistant manager that he would lose sleep because the "Japanese prints on the wall disturb me."

On October 10, 1910, the *New York Herald* announced that the Indian Hall Grill would be reopened for the winter. The Indian Hall, decorated with museum quality artifacts, was one of the Astor's best-known features.

In its more than half century of operation, the Astor had hosted nine presidents and many celebrities. Charles Evans Hughes was staying in Suite 170 when he was running against Woodrow Wilson for the presidency. Hughes went to sleep early, sure that he was to be the next president. When he awoke he learned that the California vote had gone to Wilson. General John D. Pershing stayed at the Astor before setting out for Europe to head the American Expeditionary Force in World War I. General Douglas MacArthur spent his honeymoon night in Suite 386.

By 1921 rumors were already circulating concerning the fate of the hotel. A number of people were sure the "gray lady of Broadway" would be demolished. Instead, the lease was renewed and the lobby and dining rooms were enlarged. Prohibition took its toll on the Astor's profits, so 11 stores, renting for $80 a square foot, were added to the street level. Following Prohibition, the Astor was given hotel liquor license number 1 because of its pristine record during the dry period. In January of 1935, over 6,000 people rang in the New Year at the Astor. This was the largest turnout since Prohibition had been repealed. A local hotel newspaper described the scene at the hotel:

> A few minutes before midnight, the grand ballroom lights were dimmed, a snow scene was enacted and "Father Time" was bombarded with colored balloons thrown by guests in the tier boxes. Simultaneously, a group of Broadway theatrical and screen stars dedicated a new enlarged bar in the Astor's cafe.
>
> Augmented orchestras under the direction of Jack Berger played until dawn. Handsome souvenirs were presented.
>
> Special parties were entertained by Fred A. Muschenheim, proprietor of the Astor, Col. Francis Gorman and William Norbert Nigey of the executive organization, in boxes overlooking the grand ballroom.
>
> Julius Brunner of 527 West 143rd Street (New York, N.Y.) surrounded by relatives and friends, celebrated his 80th birthday anniversary in the hotel's east ballroom at midnight.
>
> In the hotel's roof garden, more than 600 motion picture celebrities, attended the annual New Year's Eve charity ball and supper dance of the Motion Picture Salesmen of New York.

In 1935 the hotel was completely renovated. On January 6, 1936, Robert K. Christenberry succeeded Colonel Gorman as general manager; Gorman had been with the Astor for 25 years. Christenberry sought to upgrade the Astor facilities. By that summer, the rooms were air-conditioned. The Astor became the first fully air-conditioned hotel in the Northeast. By the late 1930s the Astor had 7 public dining rooms: the Astor Roof Garden, the Skywalk Cocktail Lounge, the Bar-Cafe, the Cocktail Terrace, L'Orangerie, the Hunting Room, and the Astor Grill.

With the situation in Europe becoming increasingly uncertain, the Astor introduced, on September 21, 1940, chess and checkers in L'Orangerie: "Many hotel guests wish to indulge in some form of 'homey' pasttime during their leisure. The innovation will provide 'escape' to many guests whose mental burdens have increased during the current international crises." On January 7, 1942, with its male staff drafted for service, 20 women were employed to occupy the previously exclusively male job of elevator operators. The management declared: "Employment requirements call for beauty and intelligence."

In June 1944 Christenberry was named president, treasurer, and a director of the hotel. He ordered another renovation of the hotel in 1949. By 1952 the hotel's public rooms were the Columbia Room, for dining and dancing; the Astor Roof, also a dining and dancing space; the Bar Cafe; the Hunting Room; the Grand Ballroom, which was the largest in New York; the North Garden Lounge, with its Japanese rock garden; the Coral Room; the Yacht Room; the Rose Room; College Hall; the East Ballroom; and the outdoor, roof top Skywalk Cafe.

In 1954 rumors of the hotel's imminent demolition were again circulating up and down Broadway. Instead, William Zeckendorf and two partners bought the hotel. Zeckendorf announced, "The principals are as one in their intention to perpetuate the Astor as a great hotel." On September 1, 1954, the deal was closed. Only 14 days later, on September 15, 1954, the Sheraton Corporation bought the hotel from the new owners. The Sheraton Corporation changed the hotel's name to the Sheraton-Astor. They, in turn, traded the hotel back to the Zeckendorf concern in December 1957. When the deal was completed in March 1958, the name reverted to the Astor.

The Astor's age and the changing hotel trade in New York had dealt a blow to the venerable hotel. In late

1966 Erwin O. Schel, general manager of the hotel, stated that restoration of the hotel was impossible:

> Hotels generally are built to last 35 years. Major things need to be done to it. You simply can't expect a 65 year-old lady to be as spry as a 5 year-old. Arteries harden. Age happens. That's true of a building too.
>
> The jet plane has changed the hotel business more than any other factor. It has shortened the stay. Businessmen from Boston used to come and stay overnight. Now they fly the shuttle in three-quarters of an hour.
>
> Steamship travelers from Europe would spend two or three nights at a hotel before going home. Now they get off the boat, grab a cab, go to Kennedy Airport and wake up in Kansas City.
>
> Our guests fly over our heads. A man from Indianapolis has a 2-week vacation. He used to spend it in New York. Now he goes to Bermuda. The Rotary holds a convention in Japan. New York pales after the marvelous adventure in Tokyo.
>
> The guests used to arrive with six suitcases and stay a week. Now they stay two days with a permanent-pressed suit and shirts they can wash out. The motels did that to the tourist habit.
>
> There used to be a Mexican lady, a grande dame who came here twice a year with her relatives, a maid and six trunks. They expected service and they got it. I would go over their suite with white gloves.
>
> I remember the assistant managers would greet guests while wearing morning dress or tuxedo, depending on the time of day. You would personally escort a guest to his room. Now you have push button elevators.

In 1966 the Astor was finally slated for demolition at the beginning of 1967. The property was sold for $10.5 million. Schel was especially upset over the demolition of the ballroom, which had been remodeled in 1964: "It's a shame to destroy something as beautiful as that. I don't want to be around to see it."

Big-band singer Dolly Dawn remembered her time at the Astor: "I had a two room suite that I kept, even when we were on the road. Bob Christenberry was the finest gentleman that you would ever want to meet— tall and handsome and so gallant and so wonderful. He had been a colonel in the army and lost his arm halfway up to the elbow. Anyway, he had a great respect for performers. He would put us all on the sixth floor, facing Broadway. Anything that happened in Times Square, we had front row seats to it." Jimmy Durante, who rented room 472 for over 20 years, felt that Times Square had changed—for the worse. "It just don't look and feel like New York," Durante said. "When I heard about the Astor, I thought it was a shame. My suite looked up Broadway and you could see the names going up and down on the theaters. Today that's all motion picture theaters. It ain't the same anymore."

In 1967 the Astor was demolished to make way for the MINSKOFF BUILDING.

ASTOR THEATRE. 1537 Broadway at 45th Street. Architect: George Keister. Opening: September 21, 1906; *A Midsummer Night's Dream.*

Producers Wagenhals and Kemper built the Astor directly on Times Square, one of the most prominent locations of any legitimate theater. The theater was built with a 12-story office building above it, an unusual arrangement at the time.

The theater started its life haltingly. The opening of the theater was postponed three times, blamed on faulty water pressure in a fire pipe backstage. Still, when the theater did open, the *New York Dramatic*

The Apollo and Times Square theatres.

Mirror reported, "The walls were still damp and there was a distinct odor of fresh plaster."

Annie Russell starred in the premiere attraction, *A Midsummer Night's Dream*. Russell was joined in the cast by John Bunny (one of the first real movie stars), James Young, and playwright Hubert Osborne. However, the classical inauguration of the theater was not an omen of all things to come.

Shows of this period often had short Broadway runs, depending on New York reviews to sustain long seasons touring the country. On October 22, 1902, came a production of *Cymbeline* featuring Viola Allen, Jefferson Winter, and Alison Skipworth. A month later came Charles Klein's melodrama *The Daughters of Men* (11/19/1906; 59 performances), which included Herbert Kelcey, Effie Shannon, and Dorothy Donnelly among its cast. Although business remained good, it closed on January 5. Among the Astor's other early tenants were Clyde Fitch's *The Straight Road* (1/7/07; 40 performances), with Blanche Walsh and Howard Estabrook; George Broadhurst's *The Mills of the Gods* (3/4/07; 48 performances); Leo Ditrichstein in his plays *The Ambitious Mrs. Alcott* (4/1/07; 24 performances) and *Before and After* (4/25/07; 32 performances); and Marion Fairfax's *The Builders* (5/20/07; 16 performances).

One of the more prominent early tenants of the theater included *A Yankee Tourist* (8/12/07; 103 performances), which starred Raymond Hitchcock and which featured a young Wallace Beery in the cast. It was followed by a musical version of *Tom Jones* (11/11/07; 65 performances), which ran until January 4, 1908, with Louise Gunning, William Norris, Van Renssalaer Wheeler, and Gertrude Quinlan starring. It was followed in quick succession by Channing Pollock's *The Secret Orchard* (12/30/07) and Anthony P. Wharton's *Irene Wycherley* (1/20/08; 39 performances), with Viola Allen.

Three hits followed. The first smash was the drama *Paid in Full* by Eugene Walter. It opened on February 25, 1908, and played until August 15. Audiences flocked to the theater to see Tully Marshall, Lillian Albertson, and Frank Sheridan, and were shocked when the husband broke down his wife's bedroom door. Coming out of the era of melodrama, Broadway audiences were unaccustomed to such realism in the theater. They were aghast at the raw emotion of such a private moment.

The next play would prove to be the longest run in the theater's history. *The Man from Home* (8/17/08) ran until October 30, 1909, 496 performances, an extremely long run at the time. Playwright Harry Leon Wilson and Booth Tarkington's fame was ensured with this production, which boasted a fine cast, including Hassard Short (later one of Broadway greatest direc-

tors and lighting designers), Olive Wyndham, and Ida Vernon. It was followed by the equally long-running *Seven Days* (11/10/09), which played 397 performances. Alan Pollock, Florence Reed, Georgia O'Ramey, and Lucille La Verne acted the leading roles in the Wagenhals and Kemper production.

The next season saw Anthony Mars in Stanislaus Stange's musical *The Girl in the Taxi* (10/24/10; 48 performances), which featured Jessie Milward and Carter de Haven. It only played for six weeks. James Montgomery's play *The Aviator* (12/6/10; 44 performances), with Wallace Eddinger and Jack Devereaux, wasn't much more successful. However, critical raves came with the opening of Edward Sheldon's *The Boss* on January 30, 1911. Howard Estabrook, Emily Stevens, and Holbrook Blinn played for 11 weeks.

The next season began inauspiciously with A. E. Thomas' *What the Doctor Ordered* (9/20/11; 21 performances). *The Red Widow* (11/6/11; 128 performances) had a libretto by Channing Pollock and Rennold Wolf (later a drama critic) and music by Charles J. Gebest (GEORGE M. COHAN's longtime musical director). Raymond Hitchcock and Gertrude Vanderbilt played 16 weeks at the Astor in the show. Next came *The Greyhound* on February 29; Elita Proctor Otis and Jennie Eustace played for 108 performances in the Paul Amstrong–Wilson Mizner play. James B. Fagan's *Hawthorne of the U.S.A.* (11/4/12; 72 performances) only played for 9 weeks with Irene Fenwick, Douglas Fairbanks, Henry Stephenson, and Alan Pollock, but the play's fame endured for years. *Fine Feathers* opened on January 7, 1913, with Wilton Lackaye, Rose Coghlan, and Robert Edeson in the cast. It lasted 79 performances.

George M. Cohan had the first of his productions at the Astor with a huge hit for the time, *Seven Keys to Baldpate* (9/22/13; 320 performances). He returned to the Astor with his adaptation of Frank L. Packard's story *The Miracle Man*. Frank Bacon, Gail Kane, and George Nash were featured in the play, which opened on September 21, 1914, and played for 97 performances. Cohan followed it on Christmas night of 1913 with *Hello, Broadway*, in which he starred alongside Willie Collier, Louise Dresser, Rozsika Dolly, Peggy Wood, and Florence Moore; it ran 123 performances.

Peggy Wood was also in Fred Ballard's *Young America*. She starred with Otto Kruger in the play, which opened on August 28, 1915. The play moved down the block to the GAIETY THEATER to make way for *Hit-the-Trail-Holiday* (11/13/15), which Cohan adapted from a play by George Middleton and GUY BOLTON. The cast was headed by Fred Niblo, Grant Stewart, and Clifford Dempsey for 336 performances. It moved to the Harris to complete its run so that Cohan's *The Cohan Revue of 1916* could open on February 9. It held the Astor stage for 165 performances with Harry Bulger, Richard Carle, Valli Vallie, Miss Juliet, and Charles Winninger in the cast. A little later in the season came Lee Wilson Dodd's adaptation of Harry Leon Wilson's novel, *His Majesty Bunker Bean* (10/2/16), which played for 9 weeks; Taylor Holmes, Jack Devereaux, and Marion Kerby led the cast.

With World War I escalating, *Her Soldier Boy* opened at the Astor on December 6, 1916, for a 9-month run, starring Clifton Crawford, John Charles Thomas, Adele Rowland, Beth Lydy, and Louise Galloway. It moved to the Lyric to make way for a less successful show, *His Little Widows* (4/30/17; 72 performances). The latter featured Carter de Haven and Frances Cameron. August 1917 found William Le Baron's *The Very Idea* (8/9/17; 15 performances) on the Astor stage. It was quickly followed by Selwyn and Company and Roi Cooper Magrue's production of *Why Marry?* (12/25/17; 120 performances) by Jesse Lynch Williams. The play, which featured Nat C. Goodwin, Estelle Winwood, Lotus Robb, Ernest Lawford, Richard Pitman, Edmund Breese, and Shelly Hull, won the first Pulitzer prize for drama.

Beginning in April 1918 and continuing for 118 performances, *Fancy Free* starred Marilyn Miller, Clifton Crawford, Ethel Clayton, and Marjorie Gateson. It was so successful that it moved to the Casino Theatre to make way for the Astor's next tenant. It was the musical *Rock-a-Bye Baby* (5/22/18; 25 performances) with Florence Eldridge, Carl Hyson, Alan Hale, Frank Morgan, Edna Hibbard, Louise Dresser, and Dorothy Dickson (Mrs. Hyson).

The 1918–19 season boasted a number of hits starting with the comedy *Keep Her Smiling* (8/5/18; 104 performances), starring Mr. and Mrs. Sidney Drew and Maidel Turner. It was followed by the musical *Little Simplicity* (11/04/18; 112 performances), which moved to the 44th Street Theatre to end its run and make way for the theater's longest-running hit. Christmas night 1918 saw the opening of *East Is West* by John B. Hymer and Samuel Shipman. The drama ran 680 performances with Fay Bainter, Lester Lonergan, Hassard Short, Ethel Intropodi, Eva Condon, Frank Kemble Cooper, and George Nash. The drama touched a chord with American audiences, who were intrigued by the Orient.

But critical approval of the show was harder to come by. Percy Hammond, writing in the Chicago *Tribune*, said:

> *East Is West* that amazingly popular melodrama about life in China and San Francisco, reeks with its authors' prosperous and beguiling illiteracies. Furthermore, it exhibits Miss Fay Bainter, a wily little actress, as a sort of Tong Topsy, cutting up all over the stage.
>
> Miss Bainter is the apotheosis of cuteness, with crafty eyes, legs like a couple of Cupid's bows, and in posses-

sion of that something which causes stars. Her clipped syllables, excessively distinct, her busy eyes, her quaint phrasings, her shrewdly resonant intonations, are an irresistible battery of artful ingenuousness. . . . Adept in the utterance of precocious twitterings, she is at her best in Mr. Samuel Shipman's and Mr. John B. Hymer's Oriental hippodrome, cunning and therefore can not be criticized.

> Concerning the acting of the other characters, it may be said that in some cases it is not heinous.

Dodson Mitchell's *Cornered* started December 8, 1920, and ran 143 performances. Edward Fielding, Madge Kennedy, and Leslie Austen were in the cast. Owen Davis made a rare foray into drama with his play *The Detour*, which opened in August 1921. Edwin Milton Royle's *The Squaw Man* made a successful revival with its star, William Faversham treading the boards for 50 performances following its opening on December 26, 1921. Percy Hammond wrote of Faversham's demeanor in another play, "So effectively trimmed is he that you feel almost that he has been done by a committee."

Before moving to the 44th Street Theatre to complete its 144-performance run, Sigmund Romberg's musical *The Blushing Bride* (2/6/22; 144 performances), featuring Cecil Lean and Cleo Mayfield, appeared on the Astor stage. It was followed by *The Bronx Express* (4/26/22), which closed when warm weather set in.

Several failures followed before a success, *Sweet Little Devil*, opened in Jaunary 1924. The book was by Frank Mandel and Laurence Schwab and the music was by George Gershwin. It played for 15 weeks with Constance Binney, Irving Beebe, Marjorie Gateson, and William Holbrook before moving to the Central Theater (*see* Movieland). Zoe Akins adapted Hungarian playwright Lajos Biro's *The Moon-Flower* (2/25/24; 48 performances) for Broadway, with Elsie Ferguson, Sidney Blackmer, and Frederick Worlock among the cast. In October of 1924 came the first of 261 performances of Harry Wagstaff Gribble's *Artists and Models*, with music by Sigmund Romberg and J. Fred Coots. The final legitimate offering at the Astor was the musical *June Days* (8/6/25), based on the play *The Charm School*, by Alice Duer Miller and Robert Milton. Roy Royston, Elizabeth Hines, and Jay C. Flippen appeared in its 84 performances.

Between 1913 and 1920, the theater switched back and forth between live theater and motion picture presentations. MGM leased the theater for a first-run showing of its epic *Quo Vadis* in 1913. That engagement of the 12-reeler lasted 22 weeks. By 1925 the theater had turned to a permanent motion-picture policy. Top pictures were frequently premiered at the Astor. Among the other films booked at the Astor were

Billy Wilder's *One Two Three*; Vincente Minnelli's musical *Meet Me in St. Louis*, with Judy Garland; *The Secret Life of Walter Mitty*, with Danny Kaye; *Road to Bali*, with Bing Crosby, Bob Hope, and Dorothy Lamour; *Happy Go Lucky*, with David Niven, Vera-Ellen, and Cesar Romero; *I Wanted Wings*; Alfred Hitchcock's *Spellbound*, with Ingrid Bergman and Gregory Peck; *The Vikings*, with Kirk Douglas; *Gone with the Wind*; and MGM's remake of the film that began the Astor's motion picture policy, *Quo Vadis*.

On May 12, 1935, after the run of *The Gay Divorcee* was concluded, representatives of the City Investing Company foreclosed on the lease of the Astor-Bijou-Morosco Theatres Company, whose principal stockholder was Walter Reade. They were told, "If you don't get out of here, we will kill you." The receivers, B. F. Drew and William Morehead, waited outside the theater until 6 A.M., when they were handed its keys. As the *New York Times* reported, "Inside was devastation. The seats had been ripped up and destroyed. The glass screen behind the orchestra seats had been ripped up and smashed. The $10,000 net screen had been smashed. Fire extinguishers had been sprayed on the walls. The indictment specifies damage of $24,000."

The theater was again renovated in November of 1937 prior to the opening of *The Hurricane* on November 9. On January 25, 1954, it was announced that the Astor/Victoria block would be completely renovated with a huge facade of fluted, frosted aluminum that would curve around both the 45th and 46th Street corners. DOUGLAS LEIGH, it was announced, would design animated lighting effects. The renovation never took place.

In December 1959 the Astor was modernized. The *New York Times* reported that the theater

> features a new sculptured auditorium, designed by theatre architect John J. McNamara. Both the first and second balconies of the old Astor and the protruding side boxes have been replaced by a single, sweeping, cantilevered mezzanine. The proscenium has been set back 20 ft., while the rear of the mezzanine has been extended 20 ft.
>
> An innovation is two giant abstract paintings, each approximately 45 ft. high by 110 ft. long, which grace the sidewalls of the theatre. The canvas murals by Miss Buffie Johnson are said to be among the largest abstract paintings in the world.
>
> Another first is a blue terrazzo sidewalk, from the curb of Broadway through the glass doors and into the lobby. The blue sidewalk is part of the entire design of the theatre.

On May 30, 1972, after the final performance of the film *Hennie Caulder*, the Astor was shuttered. The Walter Reade corporation asked the holders for a new air-conditioning system. When it was announced that the Astor would be demolished along with the VICTORIA, HELEN HAYES, and MOROSCO theaters (*see* BATTLE TO SAVE THE HELEN HAYES, MOROSCO, AND BIJOU THEATERS) Buffie Johnson and some friends began dismantling her murals. The *Daily News* reported:

> To the cheers of admiring hardhats, the artists struggled through a long, zero-degree day to save 50 panels of a giant $3 million mural. . . .
>
> The mural is entitled "A New York Summer Night." First displayed on December 17, 1959, when the refurbished Astor made its debut, it was commissioned by the late Robert W. Dowling, real estate mogul and philanthrophist, to reflect the city's "poetic qualities." Johnson was paid $50,000 for the job.
>
> The mural originally consisted of two sweeping abstract pieces, each approximately 97 feet long and 45 feet high. She painted these parts on 224 canvas sections that were glued to the side walls of the theatre auditorium.
>
> Lost in time, the paintings became hidden behind pegboard in the once-vaunted moviehouse . . .
>
> Gritted by dirt, water seepage and the ugly tears of four-inch bolts, 50 of the 77 panels that Johnson had not previously reclaimed were rescued by the group.
>
> The 77 panels were just a part of what art experts believe was the largest mural in the world, covering more than 9,000 square feet.
>
> More than half of the total 224 panels were recovered six years ago by Johnson, who had them restored and stored—mounted on carpet rollers—in a warehouse near her home in SoHo.

Portions of the mural went to the Boston Museum of Fine Arts, the Cincinnati Art Museum, and the Walker Art Gallery in Baltimore, as well as the Solomon R. Guggenheim Museum and the Whitney Museum of American Art in New York.

The Astor and the Victoria down the block were topped by the fabulous Astor/Victoria sign. This was the largest sign in the world and was best known in the 1960s and 1970s as the site of the Budweiser spectacular. The sign was 270 feet long and over 60 feet high. It and the Astor and Victoria were torn down along with the Helen Hayes and Morosco in 1982.

ATKINSON, BROOKS. Critic and author; b. Melrose, Massachusetts, November 28, 1894; d. Huntsville, Alabama, January 13, 1984. After graduating from Harvard in 1917, Atkinson taught English at Dartmouth, worked for a short time on the *Springfield Daily News*, and joined the *Boston Evening Transcript* as a police reporter and later became the assistant to the drama critic.

In 1922 he found his way to New York and joined the *New York Times* as the *Sunday Book Review* editor. In 1925 the *Times* made him drama critic, a post he retained until 1960. Under Atkinson's tenure, the *Times'* arts reporting became the most respected in the country. At first his byline was J. Brooks Atkinson (he dropped the *J.* the next year), and he retained much of his stolid Bostonian stiffness. But when reviewing the show *East Wind* on October 28, 1931, he concluded his review by writing, "As for the girls they are O.K." That review marked a profound change in Atkinson's writing style. In fact, he tore up his scrapbooks containing his old writing style.

He took a brief hiatus from 1942 to 1944 to serve as a wartime correspondent in China and from 1945 to 1946 in Moscow. After the war he returned to the *Times* and his reviewing post. Billy Rose wrote:

> It's good to have Brooks Atkinson back in an aisle seat, reviewing plays for the *New York Times.* The theatre missed this tweedy and be-spectacled gent while he was foreign-corresponding in Chungking and Moscow. It's nice to know that when the curtain drops on a new play, this discerning gentleman will trot over to the Times Building and tap out ten incisive and witty paragraphs about it. I doubt whether any chunk of journalism is read more avidly in my little world.
>
> The paper hits the street about 3:00 A.M. Actors, authors, directors, backers and producer are generally waiting up for it. When the *Times* truck drives up with the Late City Edition, they swarm around the newsie, help him untie the bundle, snatch a paper, and read it under the nearest lamp-post. When Brooks gives them a good notice, they tell each other they always knew he was a smart fellow. When it's a bad notice, you're likely to hear, "He didn't like *Tobacco Road* either and look how long it ran."

In 1960 he became the *Times'* critic at large. In 1965 he retired for good. Along the way he wrote many excellent books on literature, nature, and the theater, including *Henry Thoreau, the Cosmic Yankee* (1927), *Broadway Scrapbook* (1947), and *Broadway* (1970). A committed naturalist and conservationist, he wrote *This Bright Land: A Personal View* (1972). In 1947 Atkinson won a PULITZER PRIZE for his Moscow reporting.

Atkinson was among the most admired of New York critics. Even those who disagreed with his assessments respected his opinions because he left his personal emotions out of the reviews and made the show the focus of the piece. Atkinson wasn't overly flowery in his praise nor was he exceptionally cute or biting in his criticism. In the August 1956 issue of *THEATRE ARTS MAGAZINE* he wrote, "Good plays drive bad playgoers crazy."

If Atkinson's review was only two or three paragraphs long, it was sure to be a pan. A one-paragraph review was a complete dismissal. The more he wrote on a play, the more he liked it. Atkinson seldom

showed off in his reviews, nor did he revel in the quip. However, while watching Henry Forbes' revival of *The Wild Duck* in 1938, the sound of the *Île de France*'s whistle was heard in the audience. Atkinson remarked in his review, "It proved that something was moving."

For a play titled *Strange Bedfellows*, Atkinson wrote, "The audience laughed uproariously at the parts it regarded as spicy. No doubt an audience would laugh if a brothel-keeper fell down and broke her leg."

He was among the best-read and most sensitive of his colleagues and reviewed shows without the wide-eyed starstruck viewpoints of many of his associates. He would draw upon his general knowledge when reviewing plays. For example, he wrote the following in the *New York Times* when reviewing *Fiddler on the Roof*:

> Since Sholem Aleichem died in poverty he would probably have relished the irony of being the source of a Broadway musical comedy that cost $375,000 to produce and began with an advance sale of $650,000. When he was dying he said, "Let me be buried among the poor, that their graves may shine on mine and mine on theirs." Now a lot of strangers are going to make huge sums of money out of his artful simplicity.

Bosley Crowther wrote an appreciation of Atkinson for *Times Talk*, the paper's employee newsletter. He described why his fellow toilers at the *Times* were reluctant to write a commendation of Atkinson:

> It's not that they're overwhelmed by him or don't recognize his modest faults—including the fact that he *never* shows anger or raises his voice! It's just that they soon discover the flawless competence of the man at his job and the warmness and solidness in him that matches his journalistic skill. They find that he's firm, fair and friendly, without arrogance, conceit or bile, and that he possesses a wonderful abundance of sly, pungent humor and mischievous charm. They are also impressed by the fact that he spends hours talking to kids who are interested in the theatre, writing letters to drama fans and being concerned about the problems of others
>
> To those who only know Brooks as that scholarly looking gentleman with the invariable pipe, the steel-rimmed glasses and the faintly tweedy air, this may sound a little surprising, for I don't think he has ever quite overcome that vague impression of Yankee austerity that he brought to the *Times* from the old *Boston Transcript* and Harvard Yard. And there are still certain things about him and about the way he works that are vestigial of that background and the literary pietism it bred into him.
>
> For one thing, he still does his writing in long-hand on a yellow ruled pad—a practice which I am told he picked up from his revered mentor at the old *Transcript,* the celebrated critic, "H.T.P." [H.T. Parker]. In the old days, when I was in the drama dept. and used to see him come into the office of an evening after catching a play,

go back into the little cubby-hole he had behind the morgue, switch on his desk lamp, stoke his straight brier and settle down to the job to be done, I was always reminded of some student in a quiet library—or some New England quill-writing scribe. And the yellow sheets of copy that he sent out, written ever in a tight, neat hand, had the look of what some call "belles letters." Seemed odd in a modern city room. Not to Brooks, however. He still writes his daily reviews that way, spinning out brilliant critical pieces in amazingly short lengths of time.

ARTHUR MILLER said, "There cannot have been another critic as trusted as Brooks Atkinson was by so large a proportion of the theatergoing public. He is the only one who can be said to have presided over Broadway. For most people, it was probably less his analytical insights that mattered than his common sense and the air of total candor that his reviews carried with them. He followed no bandwagon, viewed each production pragmatically for what it tried to accomplish rather than what he would have preferred it to attempt, and was not at all afraid to be moved."

A measure of the esteem he is held in by the Broadway community is that he was until 1990 the only drama critic to have a theater named after him.

AUTOMAT. 1557 Broadway between 46th and 47th Streets. The Automat was one of Times Square's most enduring landmarks for more than 50 years. The coin-operated cafeteria boasted plain, sturdy food in clean, anonymous surroundings; a good square meal could be bought for less than a dollar. The patron simply walked up to a wall of glass-windowed doors and inserted the price of an item in its accompanying slot. The customer then opened the glass door and *voilà*: a piece of coconut cream pie or baked beans in a crock.

The Automat was born in Germany shortly before the turn of the century. Joseph V. Horn and Frank Hardart brought the first Automat to 818 Chestnut Street in Philadelphia in 1902. Horn & Hardart streamlined the German equipment for Philadelphia, made it sturdier for America's greater population, and gave it some modern touches. The idea—an early form of fast food for a low price—proved popular. The Automat offered a glimpse of the future in which dreams of the industrial revolution had come true. Here was machinery used to help make life easier for humans. It had the virtues of being both easy and anonymous.

The idea was so popular in Philadelphia that plans were made by Horn & Hardart to manufacture new machines and install them in New York. And what better place than the Crossroads of the World, Times Square? That other modern convenience, the subway, had reached the square, theaters were going up on every block, and great, luxurious hotels such as the ASTOR and KNICKERBOCKER served the finest clientele.

Of course, there were risks. Times Square was also known as the culinary center of New York. Nicknamed "Eatinghouse Square" by local wags, it had such restaurants as RECTOR'S, the CAFE DE L'OPERA, the Knickerbocker Grill, and Shanley's. How would the Automat do against these great lobster palaces?

To help combine the best of both culinary worlds, the opening of the Automat on July 2, 1912, was a society bash. Director JOHN MURRAY ANDERSON and Jenny Wren planned the gala opening as a benefit for charity. The top personalities in society and the theatrical world rubbed elbows, strictly by invitation. Beans in a pot, doughnuts, franks, and other Automat favorites weren't in sight that first night. Sherry's, the restaurant beloved of high society, catered the affair in their grandest style. For a nickel, the hoi polloi could receive a plate of caviar from behind the glass door. From the milk spigots flowed not milk but champagne. Meyer Davis' orchestra serenaded the wealthy, who ate, drank, and were generally merry on both levels of the restaurant. Few of the opening-night participants would ever set foot in the Automat again, but the job was done. Word was out, and the Automat had arrived. In fact, it proved so popular that mounted police were posted to keep the crowds away from the huge leaded glass windows. On its first day, the Automat brought in 8,693 nickels.

The Times Square Automat was not only novel but also beautiful. Its most outstanding feature was a stained-glass window 30 feet long and 2 stories high. The designer, Nicola D'Ascenzo, also modeled windows for the Cathedral of St. John the Divine. The name "Automat" was emblazoned across the facade and surrounded by garlands of fruit and flowers. Inside, the dining room featured marble-topped tables on pristine white-tiled floors. The central column was decorated with carvings that reached to the ceiling in a twisting pattern of leaves and vines. Beveled-glass mirrors set into a mahogany framework topped the Automat machinery.

The success of the Times Square Automat led to an expansion of the chain throughout the New York area. By the 1940s the Automat had reached its peak of popularity, with nearly 50 outlets in the city serving over 350,000 customers a day. But the original Automat was still the flagship of the chain. Almost all the food cost a nickel. A hamburger or bacon and eggs were two nickels. Coffee, an Automat staple and considered the best in New York, cost a nickel until 1952, when it was raised to a dime. Immediately sales dropped off.

The success of the Automat reflects the changes occurring in America at the time. There was the novelty of the great machine serving humanity daily bread. Never mind that the food was all made by people in the central kitchens—first located at 47th Street and later at 50th Street and 11th Avenue—or that it was real live people who refilled the slots.

The lower classes of the city were ready for the Automat, and they could get there easily. When the great eating emporiums flourished, only the upper crust could afford transportation. A carriage ride all the way to Times Square could cost as much as a month's rent to a poor family. But the opening of the subway and the growing popularity of the automobile gave people of all classes easy access to all sections of the city. People who couldn't afford Rector's and who didn't have the time to eat a 5-course meal on their lunch hour flocked to the Automat. There was also the new immigrant class. They or the second or third generation were just getting their feet wet in the American experience. A place like the Automat was perfect for their needs. It only cost a couple of nickels, and they didn't have to face anybody. If they were unsure of dress or manners, the Automat ensured invisibility. If they didn't quite have a grasp of the language, that was fine; they didn't have to talk to anyone.

Going to the Automat wasn't like going to a restaurant simply to eat. The neat rows of windows displayed the food like merchandise. Eating at the Automat was like going shopping for lunch. You picked out the product you wanted from among many choices and paid for it. This was the era when self-service was just beginning to be accepted in retailing, and the Automat followed the popular trend and translated it into restaurant terms.

The Automat was among the first hangouts for a new generation of actors, composers, lyricists, and directors. While VICTOR HERBERT ate at Shanley's, IRVING BERLIN was eating at the Automat. In fact, Berlin set one number in his revue *Face the Music* in the Automat. Cast members Katharine Carrington and J. Harold Murray faced the Depression squarely as they dined at the Automat and sang, "Let's Have Another Cup of Coffee."

Robert F. Byrnes, senior executive vice president and secretary of Horn & Hardart, first joined the company at the Automat in Times Square in 1925. In 1988 he commented on the changes he had witnessed during his 50 years with the company:

> It was the Depression and people were starting to think about watching their nickels and dimes. But Broadway at that time was a seething mass of people, a class of people. They wanted to see something for nothing. They could walk down Broadway. The street was the show.
>
> They were getting to eat out for the first time. A different class emerged. These were the people who were offered this inexpensive means of walking in and getting a cup of coffee, nobody says anything to them, and they leave their cup on the table and walk out.

Inevitably people's tastes changed, and the Automat changed too in an attempt to keep up with the times.

At the outset there was no cafeteria; it was all Automat. The initial menu was buns, beans, fish cakes, and coffee. A special window was added later; if you wanted a grill item to order, you'd go to the cashier and buy a token for bacon and eggs and then walk back to a concealed cafeteria and put your token into the slot marked bacon and eggs. The customer still didn't have to face anyone. As the demand for the short-order items grew, the cafeteria was opened to service. Pies, cakes, sandwiches, and desserts all still came from the windows. There was no refrigeration, although there were heating units in the drums so that hot foods such as baked beans in the pot could be served. By 1950 the demands of the customers forced the relationship to become 30 percent Automat and 70 percent cafeteria.

Even with the increased cafeteria service, the management that remained maintained the philosophy that everything would be made in one place. This enabled an absolute uniformity of quality in all stores. Hamburgers were premade, and sent out to the grills to be cooked. All stews and soups were centrally prepared and then warmed over at the Automat. There were 4 deliveries daily from the new commissary, which took up the square block between 49th and 50th Street and 11th and 12th Avenues.

To keep customers coming back, prices were kept low, and the places were kept immaculately clean. But social and economic conditions began to evolve after the Second World War that would kill the Automat. Along with a saturation of the market came an increase in the price of raw materials and a rise in prices. The modes of transportation changed: the trolleys stopped and the elevated trains came down. As more and more neighborhoods were cleaned up, rents increased. The George Washington Bridge went up, the Lincoln and Holland Tunnels were opened, and the population dispersed. The ethnic mix of the population changed, and many of the new immigrants didn't want to eat out. Their food was different from ours, and they weren't in as big a hurry as their predecessors to assimilate American customs.

In 1939 air-conditioning was added to the restaurants. With heat in the winter and now air-conditioning in the summer, the Automats became almost too comfortable. What the company refers to as "undesirables" hung out at the Automats. Originally, there were tables that seated 4 people. When the Automat became crowded, people shared tables. But with a change in the type of patrons, people were loath to share their space. Robert Byrnes remarked, "There were about 200 tables and you would find 200 customers, one at each table, because they didn't want to face each other." At the same time, the counter-restaurant concept arose in inexpensive places such as Chock full o' Nuts. There, the customers could come in and not face anyone and still get out in a hurry. Even if the place was crowded, customers still weren't obliged to sit beside or across from anyone.

As its clientele changed and business slackened off, the Automat began to lose money. There was also a change in people's attitudes toward the machinery. At first the Automat was a symbol of the future. Once the future arrived the Automat seemed dated. With the war effort, technology changed. Transistors and computers made mechanical devices passé. When prices increased, tokens were substituted for coins. That meant the patron had to first go to a cashier for the token. The lunch counter seemed so much easier.

In the old days the Automat was viewed as a family restaurant, but as Times Square deteriorated, fewer and fewer families frequented the neighborhood. With the great movie palaces gone and less and less product on Broadway, there was no reason for parents to take their children to the Automat. For the children brought up in the space age, the appeal of the Automat was short-lived.

The actual turning point for the company came at about 1957, when business radically changed for the worst, but the Automat hung on until 1969. By that time things had gotten so bad that a plan was drafted for the company to go out of business. The plan was implemented through gutting their buildings and renting the space to outside concerns. In 1973 Horn & Hardart bought a mail-order company that became "a phenomenal investment." And then came the new revolution: the fast-food hamburger. The decision was made to convert the Automats to fast-food restaurants. The Broadway Automat was changed over to a Burger King when the company acquired the New York Burger King franchise in 1974. They also operate Arby's in New York, and in 1981 they gained control of Bojangles Fried Chicken. The last Automat in New York was at 3rd Avenue and 42nd Street. It was closed without warning on April 8, 1991, thereby avoiding landmark status.

In the 1940s the Automat system was in its heyday. Robert Byrnes likes to remember this story: "One day an elderly man died in an Automat and on the same day a woman gave birth in the washroom."

AVON THEATER. *See* **Klaw Theater.**

BAER, BUGS. Broadway columnist and celebrated wit; b. Arthur Baer, Philadelphia, Pennsylvania, January 9, 1886; d. Stamford, Connecticut, May 17, 1969.

Arthur "Bugs" Baer was one of Broadway's most colorful characters and greatest humorists. Widely respected for his wit, Baer was a professional columnist who covered the Times Square scene and America at large.

Baer's mother had 14 children, of whom Baer was the seventh. Like many of his contemporaries, he was forced to leave school before graduation to find a job to help support his family. At age 14 Baer left the art school he had been attending, and soon found a job designing lace at $12 a week. Baer next moved on to a job at the *Philadelphia Public Ledger* as an artist. He worked his way up the ladder until he became a sports columnist with the *Washington Times*. At the *Times*, he illustrated his column with cartoons featuring an insect with a body shaped like a baseball. The creature's name was Bugs, and this became Baer's nickname.

Baer left the *Times* to conquer New York, landing a job with the *New York World*. While at the *World*, he penned one of his most quoted quips. Pete Brodie, a member of the Yankees, was thrown out while trying to steal second. Baer wrote: "His head was full of larceny but his feet were too honest." The line captured the fancy of newspaper mogul William Randolph Hearst. The publisher hired Baer for the *New York American*. Baer later moved to the *World Journal Tribune*. His column was syndicated to over 15 million people by the Hearst-owned King Features.

Unbeknownst to Hearst, Baer was also moonlighting for his old paper, the *World*. He wrote the 1921 column under the pseudonym of Graham Wire. The column was called "Wiregrams." DAMON RUNYON, though a difficult man, had helped get Baer hired with

Hearst, and Runyon found out about Baer's moonlighting when he came across the author working on the *World* column at the *American*. Baer begged Runyon not to tell Hearst. "Wiregrams" was so successful that a Hearst executive sent Runyon to woo Graham Wire from the *World*. Runyon didn't know how to handle the situation, finally telling Hearst that Wire had promised his mother he would never work for Hearst.

Baer was a habitué of Toots Shor's watering hole, where many comics sought him out. Baer was flattered that professionals such as Milton Berle would use his quips on radio and television. Baer also appeared as a master of ceremonies and toastmaster at hundreds of dinners and charity shows. He was an active member of the newspapermen's club, the Banshees.

Some of Baer's quips have become widely known. It was he who wrote the famous line, "What would you charge to haunt a house?" He called the Grand Canyon a "great place for old razor blades." He also noted, "Europe is where they name a street after you one day and chase you down it the next one." One of his best-remembered lines is "Paying alimony is like buying oats for a dead horse."

Not all of Baer's remarks were totally humorous. He took his job seriously and found that he couldn't resist putting his own beliefs into his work. "I find that all humorists live in a perpetual state of indignation and are congenital reformers," he remarked. He was against the cancellation of war debts. He stated his position in a typically humorous way: "We must make the world pay for the last war to prevent it from affording the next one." His view on Prohibition was also widely quoted: "Wine, women and song are now wood alcohol, trained nurses, and 'Nearer My God to Thee.'"

Baer wrote about his job: "It's a tough racket being a humorist for once having made yourself a monkey you must continue to pick up coconuts with your feet. However, I'm not complaining. If there is an easier way of making a living than doing the thing you want to, then tell me and I will picket myself for being unfair to my silhouette."

BARNES, CLIVE. Critic and author; b. London, May 13, 1927. Clive Barnes enjoyed an early love for the theater in his native London. His father, an ambulance driver, deserted the family when Clive was only 7. His mother, luckily, found a job as a secretary to a theatrical agent, who would give the young boy free tickets. He recalled:

> I went virtually every night by age 14 and it became a kind of life style. Dance was my great love, but it never occurred to me to be a dancer. It was during the war, 1942, and the male dancer who wasn't drafted had interesting psychological problems. He was so effeminate, so put down, the poor bastard, you just couldn't identify with him.
>
> There were no good dance critics then. Dance was given to music critics or office boys. Reviews in the papers were so stupid! An entire generation of dance critics grew up just because of this.
>
> My original idea was to do criticism as a backup for creative writing, but by 18 I realized I had no creative talent whatsoever. My poetry was a complete copy of either Eliot or Pound. My fiction wasn't bad, but totally without creative impulse. I thought, "Jesus I'm never going to be a creative writer."
>
> But I am amused by people who say the critic is a frustrated artist. He is most often genuinely not. His function, of course, is much less important, entirely parasitic. Sometimes you do get a critic who's a failed something else, and generally speaking he's not too good; carries with him sort of the scars of his failure.

Barnes attended medical school in his native London, where he studied psychiatry—some would say a fine beginning for a life in the theater. He dropped out of medical school, recognizing a complete lack of talent for medicine. After a stint in the Royal Air Force he attended Oxford on a scholarship, read English, and joined the Ballet Club along with a number of men who would later become famous critics. These included John Percival of the London *Times*, Clement Crisp of *The Spectator* and *Financial Times*, Nicholas Dromgoole of *The Sunday Telegraph*, and Oleg Kerensky of the *New Statesman* and *Daily Mail*.

Married at 19, he was forced to find gainful employment. He was employed for a decade as a city planner for the London County Council. During this time he started a small dance magazine and began to write for the British magazine *Plays and Players* as well as other publications. At one time in 1956 he was contributing articles to seven different publications, including the *New York Times* and *Dance Magazine*.

Immediately after the birth of his first son by his second wife, he quit the council job. His career increased its momentum. In England Barnes held several important editorial posts on or contributed articles to such periodicals as *The Spectator*, the *London Daily Express*, and the *New Statesman*. Barnes was also the dance critic for the London *Times* and for four years beginning in 1961 served as executive editor of *Dance and Dancers*, *Music and Musicians*, and *Plays and Players*. In 1965, he came to the United States to assume the position of dance critic for the *New York Times*. "I was planning to come to New York anyway to see Balanchine's *Don Quixote*," Barnes recalls. He also remembers he had no intention of accepting the job. But he was convinced, and in 1967 he also became drama critic. "All the *Times* knew about me was that I wrote quickly—and on deadline." He recalled those days when critics attended opening nights and filed hastily written reviews that evening: "You were at the mercy of your first sentence. I don't know whether I wrote better then or now. . . . I loved the immediacy of it."

In December 1977 Clive Barnes moved (some claim he was pushed out by the *Times*) to the *New York Post*, where he remains. Interestingly, when at the *Times*, Barnes held great power. When he moved to the *Post*, with New York's least-respected arts coverage, he was virtually ignored by theatergoers. He himself knew what would happen if he left the *Times*. In an interview with Ted Townsand in *Avant Garde*, Barnes stated, "I have no illusions. The job makes the man. A Barbary ape on the *Times* would be powerful, and if I got fired I'd have instant oblivion."

Barnes wrote about the necessity of criticism in an article for the *Post*:

> Why "necessary"—except as a way for myself and my cronies to make a few bucks, get free seats and a platform for ego-exposure, possibly shriveled ego-exposure?
>
> Well, even if we just annoy, we give people cause to talk and think about the theatre. By expressing our views, we may serve some risky purpose as a consumer guide and provide some ongoing yardstick of continuing standards. For example, when a New York critic has already seen a Broadway play in London—was it relevant to note the changes? Or to say whether those changes were for the better or worse? I think yes.
>
> When a star returns to Broadway, a critic is apt to ask whether he or she is different now? How? Better or worse? Why? Does this matter? I think yes. Opinions are subjective—even if they come gift-wrapped in the most dogmatic verbiage possible. A few critics imagine they have a direct line to God and can therefore play Moses, but they usually don't even cut the mustard as Charlton Heston.
>
> But while these opinions are subjective, they also need to be informed. . . . The critic should be able to

provide something of a long view in this regard—which is why the aged critic, even with his teeth falling out, his hands trembling and his taste wandering in the wind, will often have a certain usefulness. So bear with us when we mumble on about the past, or compare this adaptation with, say, the original novel, or that performance with this performance. If we do nothing more than remind the reader that the performing arts are a sort of moving tapestry, a shifting mosaic, and that every single performance rests in a magic continuum of past, present and, yes, future, that too is a service.

Of course, he has had his share of critics in the past. DAVID MERRICK reacted to Barnes' initial bad reviews of his productions by wiring the critic: "The honeymoon is over." Barnes wired back: "Had no idea we were married. Did not even imagine you were that type." Merrick was quoted by *Esquire* as saying that, "If I decide to stay around Broadway beyond the current season, it will be for the pleasure of throwing his fat Limey posterior out in the street."

But later, after some good reviews by Barnes, Merrick exclaimed that he was "the most vital force in the American theatre."

William Goldman in his seminal book on the theater, *The Season*, proclaimed Barnes "the most dangerous, the most crippling critic in modern Broadway history . . . the smart assness, the ballet preference, the lack of interest in Broadway, the self-glorification via television—all of this together is less important than one simple fact: the man has a wild English bias."

BARRYMORE FAMILY. The Barrymores were the greatest family in American theater history. During their notable careers (which spanned 5 decades on the stage) their personal lives were as well reported as their distinguished careers. Their exploits were parodied in the George S. Kaufman and Edna Ferber comedy *The Royal Family*.

Georgiana Drew Barrymore

Actor; b. Philadelphia, Pennsylvania, July 11, 1854; d. Santa Barbara, California, July 2, 1893. Georgiana was the daughter of Louise Lane Drew and John Drew. Her mother first appeared onstage at the age of 5 in a melodrama, *Meg Murnock, or the Hag of the Glen*. Louisa Lane specialized in playing adult roles even before she reached her teens. After 2 unsuccessful marriages, Louisa met John Drew, a great Irish comedian. Louisa and John Drew had three children: Louisa, who would not undertake a theatrical career; John Drew Jr., who achieved perfection in drawing-room comedies; and Georgiana.

Her parents barely saw each other because John Drew was often on the road. In fact, they were together

Georgiana Drew Barrymore with her children.

only half the time of their 12-year marriage. While her father was on the road, her mother became the first woman to run an American theater, the Arch Street Theatre in Philadelphia. Georgiana was taken on the road with her father.

She was trained by some of the greatest actors of her time, among them Edwin Booth and Lawrence Barrett, in addition to her own distinguished family. Her debut on the stage was in 1872 in the play *The Ladies' Rattle* at Philadelphia's Arch Street Theatre, which was then managed by her mother. Three years later she went to New York to join Augustin Daly's repertory company. Her first production in New York City was in Bulwer-Lytton's drama *Money*. She continued in repertory, performing in many plays, including *Pique*. It was in that show that she met the English actor Maurice Barrymore. They were married in 1876.

Georgiana co-starred with many of the century's greatest actors, including Edwin Booth, John McCullough, and Lawrence Barrett. She also performed with her good friend Helena Modjeska, one of America's greatest stars. Her greatest success was opposite W. H. Crane in the comedy *The Senator*, which opened in January 1890. In December 1891, after appearing in the play for almost 2 years, sickness forced her to quit the show. The next year brought her to San Francisco as a member of producer Charles Frohman's company. But again sickness caused her to leave that engagement. February of 1893 saw her back on Broadway for the last time. With her condition worsening, in May of that year she tried to recuperate in Santa Barbara, California. She died there a few months later.

Actor Otis Skinner called Georgiana "the funniest comedian I've ever seen; she made you hold your stomach laughing, but she was never distressing." Her legacy extended beyond her life through the talents of her three children, Lionel, Ethel, and John.

Maurice Barrymore

Actor; b. Herbert Arthur Chamberlain Hunter Blyth, Fort Agra, India, September 21, 1847; d. Amityville, New York, March 26, 1905. Instead of following in his family's footsteps in the Indian civil service, Herbert Blyth left India for England, where he became the country's amateur boxing champion before launching an acting career. After two years of touring, he adopted the name Maurice Herbert Blythe and later assumed the surname Barrymore.

Maurice Barrymore in the title role of Haddon Chambers' melodrama *Captain Swift* which opened at the Madison Square Theater, December 24, 1888.

In 1875 Maurice came to America and made his debut in *Under the Gaslight*. Amy Leslie, a drama critic for the *Chicago News*, wrote of him, "He is about as near a desirable man to see across the footlights as the stage shall ever grant us." The young matinee idol made his New York debut in *Hamlet* at the Fifth Avenue Theater. Also featured in the cast were Edwin Booth, making his New York debut, and John Drew. After the run of the play, Drew brought Barrymore home to Philadelphia and introduced him to Georgiana. Their marriage produced three children (Lionel, Ethel, and John), each of whom achieved notable success on the stage.

Lionel Barrymore

Actor; b. Philadelphia, Pennsylvania, April 12, 1878; d. Hollywood, California, November 15, 1954. Lionel first went on the stage at the age of 15 during the 1893–94 season in Philadelphia under the aegis of his grandmother, Louisa Lane Drew. He never really enjoyed performing and, following this engagement, retired from the stage for two years. He joined his uncle John Drew's acting company and made his first real success in *The Mummy and the Hummingbird* during the 1902 season, playing an Italian organ grinder. Lionel preferred character parts, as if seeking to hide his real personality behind the makeup. He specialized in these parts until 1906, when he again left the stage because of ill health. Whether he was actually ill or only looking for an excuse to quit the theater is uncertain.

Lionel next moved to Paris to study painting, with no intention of returning to the theater. Three years later, having achieved little success, he came back to America. In 1909 he appeared in the movies, relieved at not having to face an audience. But even the great director D. W. Griffith couldn't provide Lionel with enough work, so he was forced to return to the stage. He achieved success in *Peter Ibbetson*, *The Jest*, and, in 1918, *The Copperhead*, in which he was first acclaimed a great star. A disastrous production of *Macbeth* followed, but he again achieved fame with *The Claw*.

In 1925 he left for Hollywood, where he remained for the rest of his life. Among his most notable film appearances are *Dinner at Eight* (1933), *You Can't Take It with You* (1938), and 15 films in the Dr. Kildare series. He won an Oscar in 1931 for his performance in the film *A Free Soul*.

During his time in the movies he became confined to a wheelchair (some say he wasn't really sick but decided to just quit walking) and made many films in which he sat in chairs. He also had a notable radio career.

Lionel Barrymore, c. early 1930s.

His interest in art and music led him to create more than 100 musical pieces, all unpublished, and to join the American Society of Etchers. In 1953 he also wrote a novel, *Mr. Cantonwine: A Moral Tale*.

Ethel Barrymore

Actor; b. Philadelphia, Pennsylvania, August 15, 1879; d. Hollywood, California, June 18, 1959. Whereas Lionel fancied himself a painter, his sister Ethel would have preferred to be a concert pianist (she practiced for five hours a day as a youngster). But the power of the family was too great, and Ethel was forced into an acting career. Her mother's ill health brought Ethel to California in 1892. But her mother's illness worsened and she died, leaving her daughter to make all the funeral arrangements. Upon Ethel's arrival in New York, her grandmother informed her that she would have to make her own living. Ethel, then only 14 years old, made her debut as Julia in *The Rivals* in Montreal on January 25, 1894. The production was brought to New York at the EMPIRE THEATER. Also in the cast was the legendary Joseph Jefferson and Ethel's grandmother, Mrs. John Drew. John Drew was appearing with MAUDE ADAMS as part of producer Charles Frohman's stock company at the Empire. Drew arranged for Ethel to appear in basically a walk-on part in *The Bauble*

Shop. In addition to her brief appearance, Ethel understudied the role of Lady Kate, played by Elsie De Wolfe. When the play went on tour, Ethel was given De Wolfe's part. While the play was in Chicago, a critic noted Ethel for the first time. He wrote, "An opalescent dream named Ethel Barrymore . . . came on and played Lady Kate."

Ethel must have also made some impression on the theatrical world, because while she was playing in *Rosemary* again with her uncle, the famed actor and Frohman star William Gillette summoned her to London. He featured her as Miss Kitteredge in his production of *Secret Service* and let her understudy the ingenue part. Laurence Irving, son of Sir Henry Irving, implored his father to cast Ethel in *The Bells*, which also starred Ellen Terry, and in Laurence Irving's play *Peter the Great* also with Henry Irving. In 1900, Ethel returned to America under Charles Frohman's management. She played a small role in *Catherine*. Frohman hired her for the tour of *His Excellency, the Governor* in 1900.

Clyde Fitch, probably the most popular American playwright of his time, had two shows running on Broadway. He had just finished a third play and wanted it to run alongside his other plays in New York. The

Ethel Barrymore in *Mid-Channel*, by Pinero, 1915.

play, *Captain Jinks of the Horse Marines*, concerned a Madame Trentoni who is mistaken as an opera star by New York society. Barrymore was given her first starring role in the lead. However, the play fared poorly in Philadelphia. Still, Fitch was determined to have 3 shows running simultaneously in New York, and so a 2-week limited engagement was arranged at the Garrick Theatre. It was a huge success at its New York premiere on February 4, 1901. The run was extended to three months and then to six months. All the while Ethel Barrymore was enjoying the adulation of New York. In fact, she became a fashion plate, and one writer at the time commented that there existed "a real Barrymore cult among the girls, who model themselves on her."

Ethel's early vehicles included *Carrots*, a one-act play, and *A Country Mouse* (10/6/02; 89 performances), *Cousin Kate* (10/19/03; 44 performances), and *Cynthia* (3/16/03; 32 performances). Frohman took the last of these to London, where Ethel came to the attention of W. S. Gilbert, Sir Arthur Wing Pinero, and James M. Barrie. However, the play was not a hit in either New York or London. Ethel returned to Broadway in *Sunday* (11/15/04; 79 performances), which then toured; *A Doll's House* (5/2/05; 15 performances), which arrived at the Lyceum Theater following a tour; *Alice Sit-by-the-Fire* (12/25/05; 81 performances), which also toured; *The Silver Box*; and revivals of *Captain Jinks of the Horse Marines; His Excellency the Governor*, and *Cousin Kate* (1906–1907). She also appeared in *His Sister* (1907–1908) and *Lady Frederick* (11/9/08; 96 performances). At the end of this period a critic wrote, "Ethel Barrymore now ranks with the most popular stars on the American stage, and, upon the strength of exceptional beauty, a wonderful personality and an acting talent that is constantly growing and developing, she has become one of the most notable stage figures in this country today." Following the engagement of *Lady Frederick* at the Hudson Theatre, Ethel married Russell Griswold Colt, the son of the president of the United States Rubber Company, on March 14, 1909. Their child, Samuel Colt, was born that November.

After a break to enjoy married life and motherhood, Ethel returned in Sir Arthur Wing Pinero's play *Mid-Channel* (1/31/10; 96 performances) in a part that was written for her. Again, she was proclaimed a great star. She followed it with another hit, *The Shadow* (1/25/15; 72 performances), as a wheelchair-bound woman. During her rehearsals of *The Shadow*, Ethel had picked up a book of short stories by Edna Ferber titled *Roast Beef Medium*. She was so taken with the character of Emma McChesney that she asked Ferber and George Hobart to write a play for her based on the stories. The result was *Our Mrs. McChesney* (10/19/15; 191 performances). The triumphant success of the play was

bittersweet for Ethel, because her longtime producer, Charles Frohman, had been killed when the *Lusitania* was sunk earlier that year.

Ethel's next play was also a triumph, but it almost didn't make it to opening night. Zoe Akins, a popular playwright of her day, wrote a new play titled *Declassee*. It was all set to go into rehearsal when in August 1919 the actors went on strike (*see* Actors' Strike of 1919). Ethel was instrumental in leading the strike. After it was over she returned to *Declassee*, which opened on October 16, 1919. Again the press hailed her and the play, and the show went on to play 257 performances. At the 200th performance Ethel broke the house record of the Empire Theatre.

She continued in a variety of plays throughout the next decade, which was most notable for the production of Somerset Maugham's *The Constant Wife* (11/29/26; 295 performances) in which she played Constance Middleton. She toured in the play and returned to New York to see a theater named after her. The Shubert brothers opened the Ethel Barrymore Theatre on West 47th Street on December 17, 1928.

Ethel then briefly joined her brothers in Hollywood for *Rasputin and the Empress*. The film was a success, although she didn't like acting in films. But she was not truly interested in a stage career, nor did she see herself as a great actress. More interested in baseball and boxing than the theater, she would rather have seen her brothers' careers overtake hers. As drama became more and more realistic with the emergence of O'Neill, Ibsen, and their like, Ethel became more disenchanted. She seemed purposely to pick parts that didn't suit her. But the public still adored her, as much for her elegance and bearing offstage as her onstage performances. In 1928 the Shuberts presented her in Martinez Sierra's *The Kingdom of God* in the new Ethel Barrymore Theatre. Her great success as Sister Gracia was not repeated until 1940, when she appeared on stage in *The Corn Is Green*. The *New York Times* enthused, "She plays it forcefully, but she also plays it with compassion and from now on she can wear Miss Moffat as a jewel in her crown." Between Broadway roles, she appeared in motion pictures.

Ethel Barrymore's last stage appearance was in 1950 at a benefit for the American National Theatre and Academy in *The Twelve-Pound Look*.

Ethel's career also encompassed radio, vaudeville, and television in addition to motion pictures. Among her best films are *The Nightingale* (1914), *Rasputin and the Empress* (1933) (the only time she appeared with both her brothers), *The Spiral Staircase* (1946), and *None but the Lonely Heart* (1944), for which she won the Academy Award. She also published her reminiscences in *Memories, an Autobiography* (1955).

John Barrymore, self-portrait showing his conflicted nature, 1920.

John Barrymore

Actor; b. Philadelphia, Pennsylvania, February 15, 1882; d. Los Angeles, California, June 29, 1942. John, too, evinced no desire for a stage career. Determined to pursue a career as an artist, he enrolled in King's College in Wimbledon, England. He received private art training in Paris and finished his art education at the Art Students League of New York. Upon graduation he began a career as a freelance illustrator, placing works in several periodicals, including the *New York Evening Journal*. Still, though somewhat successful as an artist, he found acting to be the easiest way to make money. As the most handsome and talented of his siblings (he was known as "The Great Profile"), John found acting relatively painless, although he became easily bored with long runs and as early as 1914 came onstage drunk.

John made his stage debut on October 31, 1903, at Cleveland's Theater, Chicago, playing Max in *Magda*. He made his New York debut in December of that same year, at the Savoy Theater in *Glad of It*. Later that year, he appeared as a member of William Collier's company in *The Dictator*, which also had a run in London and was made into a silent film starring John. His

sister Ethel arranged for him to appear with her in *Sunday* and *Alice Sit-by-the-Fire*. He then rejoined William Collier in Australia in *The Dictator*. However, it wasn't until 1905 that he finally relented and gave up his career in illustration. In 1906 he again appeared with his sister in *His Excellency the Governor*.

In May 1908 John made his musical comedy debut in the Chicago production of *A Stubborn Cinderella* and then in the Charles Dillingham production of *The Candy Shop*. Although John's musicals were successful, perhaps they proved too much effort for him. He much preferred light comedy, in which he could be suave and debonair. He followed in his father's footsteps as a matinee idol in plays like *The Fortune Hunter* (1909) and Schnitzler's *The Affairs of Anatol* (1910). According to the press, "matinee audiences beat their breasts in admiration."

In 1916 Barrymore, bored with easy roles, found great success in John Galsworthy's *Justice*. The powerfully dramatic role of Falder enabled Barrymore to move the audience to more than breast-beating. This brilliant performance was followed by one in Daphne Du Maurier's *Peter Ibbetson* with his brother Lionel, Constance Collier, Laura Hope Crews, and Madge Evans. This triumph led to another, the part of Fadya in Tolstoy's *The Living Corpse*, retitled *Redemption* for Broadway. Two more great performances followed, *Richard III* (1920) and *Hamlet* (1922). The reviews were astounding; Barrymore was at the peak of his talent and considered the greatest Shakespearean actor of his time.

Following the close of *Hamlet*, Barrymore left for Hollywood (though he had been appearing on film beginning in 1914). Among his notable films were *A Bill of Divorcement*, *Grand Hotel*, *Twentieth Century*, and *Counselor at Law*. He wouldn't return to Broadway until 1940, with a production of *My Dear Children* at the BELASCO THEATRE. By this time, Barrymore was washed up in films, and the parts that came along were mostly parodies of himself. His role in *My Dear Children* was no exception. Ill health forced the closing of the production after only four months.

BARRYMORE THEATRE. *See* **Ethel Barrymore Theatre.**

BATTLE TO SAVE THE HELEN HAYES, MOROSCO, AND BIJOU THEATERS. During the latter part of 1978 and early 1979, a plan to tear down the HELEN HAYES, MOROSCO, and BIJOU theaters and build a high-rise hotel on the site became public. The plan called for not only the destruction of the three theaters but also the leveling of the Piccadilly Hotel and other important structures. Preservationists and others became alarmed about the destruction of two of Broadway's excellent theaters and also about the impact of a massive hotel on the entire theater district. The proposed design of the hotel also received harsh attack because of the large blank walls at street level, which would effectively deaden the surrounding area. Worse, these huge, blank concrete walls would face the monumental blank walls of the MINSKOFF BUILDING across the street.

John Portman, the builder of the proposed hotel, had also built a Marriott Hotel in Washington on Pennsylvania Avenue. In that case, he had wanted to tear down the historic National Theatre (see NEDERLANDER THEATRE). Portman had insisted there, as he would in New York, that the theater could not be saved if the hotel was to be built. Luckily for Washington, a city that has lost all but four of its historic theaters, the National was saved and Portman was proved wrong. In fact, the Marriott Hotel in Washington now boasts of its proximity to the National Theatre.

An advertisement containing a preprinted letter opposing the demolition of the theaters and addressed to government officials appeared in the *New York Times* on September 2, 1981. Over 2,000 people sent it in. A petition was circulated that read, "I am outraged at the planned use of $55.5 million in NYC, NYS and Federal taxpayer dollars for the Portman Hotel Project, as it would destroy the Morosco, Helen Hayes, Bijou, and Embassy 5 theaters and remove no real urban blight. If the Hotel is to truly serve urban renewal and warrant subsidy, it must relocate to an alternate site or be redesigned to include the historic existing theaters." This petition was signed by over 100,000 citizens.

New York Post drama critic CLIVE BARNES wrote that these theaters were

> gems of theater buildings, and represent a type of theater that New York needs. They are both gorgeous to look at . . . these are two of the most handsome theaters, architecturally, in the whole city. If both of them are not protected by the Landmarks Commission to the last drop of its blood then one must question the value of the Landmarks Commission . . . Don't take away these theaters—they are part of Broadway's royal blue lifeblood and cannot ever, ever, be replaced. It would be an act that would diminish our great city, an act of the utmost folly that future generations would rue.

BROOKS ATKINSON, Audrey Wood, Gene Saks, Tony Roberts, Jean Stapleton, Alec McCowen, Frances Sternhagen, Mrs. Richard Rodgers, Oliver Hailey, Beverly Sills, Tony Randall, Elia Kazan, and others wrote letters protesting the planned demolition.

Two letters written by actors stated the case eloquently. Jane White wrote: "There is something that an Actor puts onto his skin when you work in those theaters. A whole history of a tradition of great work that was done in a place, and those ghosts still live. And they live here." Patricia Elliott commented: "[One would be] throwing the baby out with the bathwater by tearing down three of the most beautiful theaters that we have on Broadway . . . if they can give me a good solid reason why we should throw out culture, heritage, art, not to mention all the vibrations of love, and feeling, and the past, and what we are as human beings." Giorgio Cavaglieri, New York State preservation coordinator of the American Institute of Architects, also wrote a letter: "It will be possible to preserve the Morosco, Helen Hayes and Bijou theaters, which happen to be among the most attractive examples of theater architecture of the first quarter of our century. In my opinion, it would be possible and advisable to redesign the lower levels of the hotel building in order to incorporate in it the theaters to be preserved."

The recommendation in that letter made sense to a lot of people, and SAVE THE THEATERS, a nonprofit group formed to save the three theaters, hired Lee Harris Pomeroy to draw up a plan that would make the preservation of the theaters feasible. Pomeroy was a professor at City College, former director of the New York chapter of the American Institute of Architects, and an award-winning architect in his own right. His plan offered the Portman organization many advantages. First, of course, was the retention of the Helen Hayes and Morosco theaters. The saving of these two buildings removed the need for a 1,500-seat musical-theater house to be built on the third floor of the hotel. Two theaters recently built in skyscrapers, the MINSKOFF and Uris (see GERSHWIN THEATER) had proved unwieldy and unsuited to the needs of modern musical theater. These large barns never had successful shows, and audiences and theater professionals alike despised their design and acoustics. Plus the two historic theaters offered 763 more seats than the proposed 1,500-seat theater in the hotel. Second, the hotel in Pomeroy's plan would fit in more harmoniously with the theater district. Instead of the huge blank concrete walls on the sides of the building, there would be the beautiful facades of the theaters.

Portman's design elements and the business features of his plan would be retained, although with some improvement. Shubert Alley, one of the city's most charming thoroughfares, was to be extended another block. A theater gallery lining the walkway and retail space would also replace the blank face of the hotel, allowing more guest rooms to face Broadway. The shops would be lowered one level and brought closer to Broadway and street traffic. The revolving rooftop restaurant, one of the less appealing features of the Portman design, was moved east, affording a better view of downtown Manhattan and Times Square.

Pomeroy probably noted that Portman didn't care about the aesthetic values of his hotel. So Pomeroy presented several financial advantages in his report:

(a) It eliminates significant cost of the proposed new 3rd level theater and over 50,000 square feet of expensive construction. (b) It allows an addition of some 15,000 square feet of space that has commercial value. (c) Portman becomes eligible for tax benefits applicable to those rehabilitating structures listed on the National Register under the Economic Recovery Tax Act of 1981. Those benefits include 25% in investment tax credit available for rehabilitation of National Register properties. The Helen Hayes has already been designated eligible for the Register. The Morosco has received many more recommendations than necessary for designation and should be declared eligible for the National Register.

Perhaps Pomeroy and Save the Theaters were whistling against the wind. Even the environmental impact statement (EIS) came out against the report, but the people behind the EIS hadn't bothered to consider the report fully, and their objections were totally specious. For example, they objected that if the new plan was adopted, the much-needed new theater would not be included. But of course, the retention of the two historic playhouses obviated the need for the new theater. The EIS also stated that the proposal would preclude the atrium, but the atrium was not affected by the new plan.

With their proposal rejected, proponents of saving the theaters turned to the courts. Despite their efforts, demolition of the theaters began in March 1982, and the new hotel was built as planned. What went wrong? Jack Goldstein, Save the Theaters' director of preservation, explains:

There wasn't the inclination on the part of those who could have changed the project. Equity and Save the Theaters never attempted to stop the hotel. But we asked for at least a redesign of the hotel to save the theaters. All those people who said it was too late should have gone to the Department of Housing and Urban Development for an alteration of the grant and an increase in funds. It would have been less expensive than the amount of money it took to tie up that project for as long as we did. And we would have had three theaters; we would still have had an ugly hotel but we would have had the three theaters. So what went wrong was shortsighted thinking on the part of the city and what we felt was a fundamental change in their perception of the historic role of this area of town.

All of a sudden the momentum that had been gathering by development since the economic crisis in the mid-seventies based on the very important role that real estate development played in putting the city back on a firm financial standing was simply being applied to the theater district without much thought. And so we couldn't move that project. We tried to take it to the Supreme Court.

The more unsettling thing was that immediately following the demolition of the Morosco, before the demoli-

tion of the Hayes, the city passed its new zoning ordinance for the entire midtown west area which turned what we thought was a horrible but isolated incident into something which was going to become typical. It was at that point that we decided that we would have to take on the momentum of the real estate development and we would simply have to change the mind of the city about the way it was looking at the area.

Since the building of what became the Marriott Marquis Hotel and the destruction of the theaters, the Landmarks Preservation Committee has granted landmark status to several theaters.

BEACH, THE. The Beach—the concrete island separating Broadway and 7th Avenue across the street from the PALACE THEATRE—was the hangout for out-of-work vaudevillians in the teens and twenties. They would gather on the little island and brag about their recent bookings and hefty contracts. Usually these exploits were greatly exaggerated.

The Beach even had its poet: Philip Stack, a clerk in the Brooklyn Edison Company, who wrote poems under the pseudonym Don Wahn. Stack sent his poems to WALTER WINCHELL and let Winchell print them in his column without charge. These poems soon became an important part of the column. Wahn wrote this paean to the Beach:

They stand nearby the Palace day on day
And talk in low and falsely hopeful tones,
Their snappy clothes, pathetically gay,
    Bespeak ability to wheedle loans;
They swap their gags like children swapping toys,
    And rip their lucky brothers into bits;
Their food and drink is Broadway's blatant noise—
    Their Bible is Variety or Zit's.
So, lolling there, the weeks go swiftly by,
While faded clippings yellow in their hands;
They hum the current hits and watch it die—
And, penniless, they quote their rash demands.
Ah, you, who stand there seven days in seven,
God grant you make the two-a-day in heaven.

BECK, MARTIN. Important early vaudeville producer and theater owner; b. Lipto Szert Miklos, Czechoslovakia, July 30, 1867; d. New York, New York; November 16, 1940.

Martin Beck came to America from Czechoslovakia with a traveling show of German acrobats. He then moved to Chicago and joined the North Clark Street Beer Garden as manager. Beck persuaded the owner to add dressing rooms and a stage, and that was how he started his career as a vaudeville manager. Performers on the Radio-Keith-Orpheum circuit, which Beck

Martin Beck.

later managed, called him "Two Beers Beck" to remind him of his humble roots.

Beck traveled to San Francisco in the early 1890s with the Schiller Vaudeville Company. He became friends with the owner of the prestigious Orpheum circuit, and when in 1899 it was bought by Morris Meyerfield, Beck helped expand the circuit.

During that year Beck perfected the concept of the circuit booking system. By linking together theaters on one chain, he could guarantee bookings for a whole year. This also gave him control of the actors' salaries and the content of their acts. The Orpheum Theater in San Francisco was the first theater in the chain that eventually covered the area between California and Chicago. By 1905 there were 17 theaters in the chain nationwide, and he was running the entire outfit.

The next year Beck came to New York and settled in the Putnam Building, which also housed the Keith-Albee offices and their United Booking Office (*see* E. F. ALBEE). Beck built the PALACE THEATER at Broadway and 47th Street in 1913. This enraged Keith, who saw the eastern half of the country as his domain. He managed to buy out 75 per cent of the ownership

of the Palace from Beck. In 1923 Beck was voted out of the Orpheum chain.

In 1924 he built the MARTIN BECK THEATRE, the first theatre to be constructed without a mortgage. He also built the State Lake Theater in Chicago. Beck returned to vaudeville in 1932, running the RKO booking office. He was responsible for the first appearance in the United States of the D'Oyly Carte Opera Company in 1934. He oversaw bookings in his theaters until his death in 1940.

BELASCO, DAVID. Noted playwright, producer, theater owner, actor, director, and stage manager; b. San Francisco, California, July 25, 1853; d. New York, New York, May 14, 1931.

David Belasco was the total theater man. He was obsessed with the theater and played almost every role possible in the staging of a play. He wrote almost 70 plays, some in collaboration, and produced 121 productions. Belasco was known for the naturalism of his productions as well as their remarkable electrical effects. He also gave Mary Pickford her stage name. However, although there are many anecdotes about Belasco the man, almost nothing is remembered about his work. PERCY HAMMOND, critic for the *Tribune*, said of him, "He is, God love him, as foolish as a fox."

David Belsaco.

Belasco's father Abraham (Humphrey) was a harlequin, acting in London's theaters. But he and his wife Reina Martin Belasco both Jews of Portuguese descent, left their native London for the riches of the California gold rush and from there migrated to Canada. Though they became shopkeepers, they kept their contacts with theater people and introduced their young son to the theatrical profession. He worked a variety of jobs in the theater, eventually moving up to actor.

He played the Duke of York in Charles Kean's production of *Richard III* at the Victoria Theatre in Victoria, British Columbia, 1864. The next year the family returned to California, and the youngster attended the Lincoln Grammar School. He continued his acting career even at this young age, appearing as a supernumerary in local theaters in productions such as Augustin Daly's *Under the Gaslight* at Maguire's Opera House in 1869. He showed an early talent for producing, starting an amateur theater society, and writing plays for his company. By 1872 he had written 15 plays. Among them was *Jim Black; or, The Regulator's Revenge*, which Belasco wrote in 1865 at the ripe old age of 12.

Graduating from grammar school in 1871, he turned to professional performing. His debut was in the play *Help* by F. G. Marsden at the Metropolitan Theatre in San Francisco. Belasco later called himself a "theatrical vagabond" during this rough-and-tumble period of the American stage. While a member of theatrical troupes, he played in mining camps and frontier settlements throughout northern California. During this period he assumed all the different jobs in the theater, including painting and building sets, singing, reciting poetry, selling tickets, and performing a variety of roles, including Fagin in *Oliver Twist*, both the title role and the part of Gertrude in *Hamlet*, and even Topsy in *Uncle Tom's Cabin*.

In 1873 he met Dion Boucicault, the greatest author of melodramas, at Piper's Opera House in Virginia City, Nevada. While Belasco served as the playwright's secretary, Boucicault taught him the value of theatricality and high emotion, as well as an appreciation for scenic realism. With Boucicault's encouragement Belasco began to attempt play writing. He was also influenced by the actors with whom he performed; Edwin Booth and John McCullough performed with him in 1874. That same year he began a friendship with James A. Hearne, a famous American playwright who was inspired by the works of Ibsen. Hearne and Belasco collaborated on several plays, including *Within an Inch of His Life* (1879), *Marriage by Moonlight* (1879), and *Chums* (1879). The latter was renamed *Hearts of Oak*. It afforded Belasco his first success as a playwright. The play, based on an old

melodrama, was first produced in Chicago and toured the country to much success.

Between the years 1876 and 1882 Belasco worked as a stage manager at Baldwin's Academy of Music. While at Baldwin's he also put on productions of hit plays from New York City, acted, and continued his playwriting. In 1877 he began work at the Egyptian Hall, a small theater that specialized in exotic scenery and effects. It was at the Egyptian that he gained experience in the scenic and lighting effects that he would become famous for in later life. During this time he adapted Zola's *L'Assommoir* (1877) into the play *Drink*, which was produced in 1879.

In the spring of 1878 New York's Union Square Theatre Company had an engagement in San Francisco and hired Belasco as its director, a role that was a mix of company manager and producer.

He had a taste of the New York style of production, and, emboldened by the experience, moved to New York to work under the tutelage of theatrical manager Daniel Frohman in the fall of 1882. He became stage manager of the Madison Square Theatre for the next two years. After leaving the Madison Square Theatre, he spent a few years as a freelancer, during which time he had his first directing job in New York. The play was *Young Mrs. Winthrop* by Bronson Howard, the first American to earn a living through playwriting.

With the support of Daniel Frohman and his brothers Charles and Gustave, by 1887 he became a stage manager and producer for Daniel Frohman at the LYCEUM THEATER, a job he would keep for the next four years. While at the Lyceum, his plays included *Lord Chumley* (1888) and *Men and Women* (1890), both written with Henry C. de Mille. Frohman remained good friends with de Mille and mentored his partner's two sons, William C. and Cecil B.

In 1890 the Lyceum also boasted a school of acting, and Belasco was among its most popular teachers. The school eventually evolved into the American Academy of Dramatic Arts. Eventually, though, Belasco left the safety of the Lyceum and struck out on his own.

Belasco's first great success was the Civil War melodrama *The Heart of Maryland* (1895). The show typified Belasco's love for melodrama and the theatrical ingenuity of his staging. The Civil War–era play concerned the heroine Maryland Calvert. At the grand finale of the drama, when Calvert's lover is to be executed at the sound of the ringing of a great bell at the top of a bell tower, according to *Godey's Magazine*, she "dashes up the long, winding stairway. With a gasp of terror she drops the lantern and rushes up the last steps just as the bell begins to swing. One first soft boom has already sounded, when she leaps at the tongue of the bell and with it swings back and forth, silencing the clang with her own soft hands."

The play received dismissive reviews by the critics, but it was a smash in New York, London, and across the country. He wrote it for the first of his "Belasco stars"—Mrs. Leslie Carter, a redheaded society divorcee. Carter and Belasco made headlines—it was rumored that he was her Svengali and that he would drag her by her hair across the stage floor to incite deeper emotion and pathos in her performance. A society woman in Chicago, Mrs. Carter had undergone a very public divorce. With her reputation ruined in society circles, Mrs. Carter decided to become an actress. Her friend Nathaniel K. Fairbank elected himself as her benefactor on her rise to the top of the theatrical profession. Fairbank hired Belasco to train Mrs. Carter, but her debut, in Paul M. Potter's play *The Ugly Duckling* (11/10/1890), was a failure at the BROADWAY THEATRE. Fairbank, chief backer of the play, was not happy at the loss of his money.

Belasco temporarily lost faith in Mrs. Carter but soon starred her in his adaptation of a French play, *Miss Helyett* (1891). Belasco presented Fairbank with a bill for services rendered in the instruction of Mrs. Carter, but Fairbank demurred. Belasco sued and was forced during the three-week trial to describe the unorthodox methods of instruction he employed. The jury awarded Belasco $16,000, and Mrs. Carter's success was hastened.

Belasco and Mrs. Carter worked together for 16 years on such plays as *Zaza* (10/1/00; 42 performances), *DuBarry* (12/25/01; 165 performances), and *Adrea* (1/11/05; 123 performances). The last of these was the third collaboration between Belasco and John Luther Long. But after the show closed in the summer of 1906 Mrs. Carter got married again. Belasco, having a proprietary feeling toward the actress, was incensed. He never spoke to her again, and she never again reached the stardom she attained under Belasco's guidance. Other stars with whom he was associated include Blanche Bates, Ina Claire, David Warfield, Frances Starr, and Lenore Ulric.

Among the other Belasco dramas (usually adaptations) at the Belasco were *The Darling of the Gods*, with John Luther Long (12/3/02; 182 performances); *The Girl of the Golden West* (11/14/05; 248 performances); The *Temperamental Journey* (9/14/13; 124 performances); and *The Return of Peter Grimm* (9/21/21). In addition to Herne and de Mille, his collaborators include Franklyn Fyles, a drama critic for the *New York Sun*, and John Luther Long.

Belasco and Long's first collaboration was an adaptation of a short story by Long that became the play *Madame Butterfly* (3/5/00; 24 performances). The play was a great success among audiences; one of the people who saw it was Giacomo Puccini, who convinced Belasco that the play would make a wonderful libretto for an opera.

Belasco and Puccini would team up again with an opera based on one of Belasco's plays, *The Girl of the Golden West*, for which Belasco served as director, producer, and author. The play was the epitome of the Belasco melodramatic drama. Featuring a realistic blizzard (shades of Boucicault's *The Streets of New York*) that had to be manned by 32 stagehands, the play also employed a melodramatic device that was used as recently as the 2002 film *Spider-Man*: when the wounded hero, Dick Johnson, hides in the loft of a cabin, he is discovered when a drop of his blood falls on the sheriff's hand.

The opera version, *La Fanciulla del West*, opened at the Metropolitan Opera House in New York on December 10, 1910, with Enrico Caruso starring. This time Belasco directed and undertook to teach acting to the great singer: "So I pretended I was Dick Johnson, staggered in with my wound, listened to the approach of the Sheriff's posse, and then climbed up the ladder, singing in a voice that must have made the very walls of the Metropolitan groan with agony."

The opera was a great success, with 14 curtain calls at the end of the first act, 19 at the end of the second, and 20 at the finale. The premiere was conducted by Arturo Toscanini, and he took a curtain call alongside Puccini and Belasco.

Belasco is thought of as the man who introduced realism into the American theater, and who, as a producer, perhaps went too far in his attempts to mimic reality. For Alice Bradley's play *The Governor's Lady* (1912), he reproduced a Childs Restaurant on the stage. And when a boardinghouse set was required for Eugene Walter's *The Easiest Way* (1909), Belasco actually bought a boardinghouse and had it reconstructed on the stage, with its "patched furniture, thread-bare carpet, tarnished and broken gas fixtures, tumble-down cupboards, dingy doors and window casings, and even the faded paper on the walls." This wasn't really art but pure showmanship. Art is in the illusion of reality, but with Belasco there was no illusion.

He once wrote, "The feeling of the scene is always a great factor in determining its arrangement, for symbolism to a certain extent enters the production of every play. For instance, sunlit scenes simply imply happiness, moonlit scenes give a suggestion of romance, while tragedy or sorrow should be played in gloom." However, Belasco's use of realism always was meant to serve the emotion of the work. As he wrote, "I believe in a play that deals with life in its moments of importance, in a crisis of emotion." And toward that goal, Belasco utilized the heightened emotions of melodrama and employed realistic effects to further grab the audience. He was especially concerned with the effect of his dramas on audiences. He never concerned himself with the poetry of writing. "The province of literature," he wrote in *Theatre Magazine* in September 1913, "is entirely outside the province of theatre." He felt that literary drama was impossible to act, noting that many leading writers of his day, including Samuel Clemens, Henry James, and W. D. Howells, never had success with their theatrical endeavors. Furthermore, Belasco called himself a playwright, not a dramatist. As he explained in an interview published in the *Illustrated American* of April 7, 1894, "A wright is a workman. We say wheelwright, shipwright . . . why not playwright? A wright takes the materials he finds to his hand and builds or forms them into a coherent shape. He makes nothing; he only puts them together more or less deftly."

When it came to publishing his plays in 1928, Belasco was uncertain of their success as literature. He explained in the introduction to the volume, "I am aware of a danger in sacrificing the glamour of the stage. My plays are all written to be acted, not to be read."

On his quest for realism on the stage, Belasco did make certain innovations. He pioneered stage lighting, especially at the Stuyvesant Theatre (*see* BELASCO THEATRE), which he built. A favorite effect of his was re-creating a sunset. He was the first to conceal the footlights in order to make the stage even more realistic. He stated, "Lights are to drama what music is to the lyrics of a song. The greatest part of my success in the theatre I attribute to my feeling for colors, translated into effects of light." His theater had the latest in stage equipment, which he used to produce the most astounding effects. The September 1925 issue of *Scientific American* subtitled an article "How David Belasco Produces the Effect of Every Conceivable Sky Color, from Midnight Blue Black, Dusk and Moonrise Shadings to the White Light of Early Dawn." But these were effects without emotion. The plays he produced were simply more modern versions of the melodramas with which he achieved his first fame.

Among his innovations of staging were the first use of a thrust stage for his production in 1889 of Sophocles' *Electra*. And he also was the first to take out the footlights from the lip of the stage. For *The Girl I Left Behind Me* (1893), written in collaboration with Franklyn Fyles, Belasco staged a grand ball by having the ball take place offstage. When, in an adjoining room, army officers hear of an impending attack by Indians, the sound of the ball—laughter, music, talk, and the clinking of glasses—is heard offstage in juxtaposition to the drama unfolding in front of the audience.

His impact extended beyond his plays and direction. He was among the producers who sought to break from the control of the Syndicate, a group of six producers, Sam Nixon, Fred Zimmerman, Charles Frohman, Al Hayman, Marc Klaw, and Abe Erlanger. The Syndicate was successful in controlling a majority of the theaters in the country. When Belasco would send out a touring company of his plays, the Syndicate would send out a company of the same play to the same cities, booking their productions the week before Belasco's was due to hit town. Likewise, the Syndicate's actors were banned from performing in Belasco's plays, and Belasco could not book the group's theaters for his tours.

Belasco tried to sue the Syndicate over the distribution of royalties for Lee Arthur and Charles Klein's play *The Auctioneer*, which Belasco directed. But the real reason for the 1905 lawsuit was Belasco's attempt to shut down the monopolistic practices of the Syndicate. The methods of the group came out in testimony, but Belasco lost the case and was forced to reveal some of his less-than-respectable business practices.

In 1907 Belasco again sued the Syndicate along with Lee Shubert of the SHUBERT BROTHERS. They accused the group of restraint of trade. This trial dealt a further blow to the Trust, but Belasco got no satisfaction. Realizing that the Shuberts were not the perfect ally—in fact they attempted to break the trust only to set up one of their own—Belasco formed a partnership with Klaw and Erlanger. "If you can't beat them, join them" was his philosophy.

Like the Shubert brothers, Belasco realized that in order to break the trust's near-monopoly he must control his own theaters. And so he became an integral figure in the development of Times Square and Broadway. In 1902 he leased the Theatre Republic (*see* NEW VICTORY THEATRE) from OSCAR HAMMERSTEIN I. He renovated the theater and renamed it after himself. In 1906 he built the Stuyvesant Theatre to his specifications. At its opening in 1907 it was technically the most modern theater in the world.

Belasco wore a priest's collar and robes, although he was not particularly religious. He concentrated on his image and built his personality for its effect, just as he produced his plays. His ego enabled him to understand the importance of the director in the shaping of the drama. He might not have believed a director was necessary for others, but he could extend his control as producer by directing the actors also. But his direction relied on tricks and facade, as did his producing. A favorite ruse was the temper tantrum he would throw to make the actors work harder. After lambasting the cast, he would throw his pocket watch onto the floor and crush it with his foot. This astounding action would galvanize the cast. Belasco never told them that he had a trunk full of dollar pocket watches in his office.

Most of Belasco's plays were melodramas that were popular for a time and then forgotten; as new playwrights changed the style of theater in Europe and America, melodramas like Belasco's fell by the wayside. These new masters of the drama—Ibsen, Strindberg, Wilde, Shaw, Zola—brought realism to the stage, but with an emphasis on subtext and psychology. Belasco, realizing that tastes were changing, was entranced with the possibilities that these playwrights opened up, but he could not make the transition himself.

By the 1920s Belasco's style of drama and stagecraft were hopelessly out of date. Designers such as Norman Bel Geddes and Robert Edmond Jones forswore realism for more impressionistic settings. However, his staging of *The Merchant of Venice* in 1922 was considered brilliant, and even the Russian director Constantin Stanislavsky applauded his efforts. In fact, in 1927 the Moscow Art Theatre elected him to an honorary membership. During the last years of his life Belasco received many awards, but time was passing him by. His wife died in 1925, by which time he had directed 355 plays. Actors with whom he had worked were also passing away, and he was increasingly alone as a relic of 19th-century theatre. He retired in 1930.

Belasco's legacy is in his legend. All that is left of the artist is the Belasco Theatre (the second; his first was built in 1902) and Puccini's adaptations of *Madame Butterfly* and *The Girl of the Golden West*. After Belasco died, his ghost was said to have shown up at every opening night at his theater—until that of *Oh! Calcutta!*

BELASCO THEATRE. 111 W. 44th Street. Architect: George Keister. Opening: October 16, 1907; *A Grand Army Man.*

The theater today known as the Belasco was called the Stuyvesant when producer, director, and playwright DAVID BELASCO built it in 1907. The Stuyvesant took the name Belasco in 1910, when the original Belasco Theatre reverted to *its* original name, the REPUBLIC. When it was built, the Belasco was the best-equipped theater of its era. The $750,000 theater boasted a huge elevator stage, areas for scene shops, and the most complete lighting setup (designed by Louis Hartman) of any theater. The technical innovations introduced by Belasco made possible all the realistic effects he doted on. Above the east wing of the theater was Belasco's 10-room duplex apartment, accessible by private elevator. Unfortunately, for all the hits the Belasco housed, it was never considered a prime Broadway theater. Lee Shubert said it was on "the wrong side of the right street." Closer to 6th Avenue than Times Square, the theater was somewhat off the beaten path.

Ferenc Molnár's *The Devil* was presented both at the Belasco with Edwin Stevens (350 performances) and at the Garden Theater with George Arliss (87 performances). Both productions opened on August 18, 1908, and were immediate hits. This must be the only time a play has opened in two theaters on the same day. *The Devil* was followed by *The Fighting Hope* (9/22/08; 231 performances) and *The Easiest Way* (1/19/09; 157 performances).

Belasco's love of feminine pulchritude and melodrama led to a sort of stock company of Belasco heroines, among them Blanche Bates, Lenore Ulric, Ina Claire, Jeanne Eagels, and KATHARINE CORNELL. Plays featuring these actresses included *Polly with a Past* (9/6/17; 315 performances), *Daddies* (9/5/18; 340 performances), *The Son-Daughter* (11/19/19; 223 performances), *Kiki* (11/29/21; 600 performances), *The Harem* (12/2/24; 183 performances), *Lulu Belle* (2/9/26; 461 performances), and *Mima* (12/12/28; 180 performances). VINCENT YOUMANS' *Hit the Deck* sailed into the Belasco on April 25, 1927. The musical featured "Hallelujah" as its big number and ran for 352 performances.

The innovative lighting board installed at the Belasco Theatre.

Humphrey Bogart starred in *It's a Wise Child* (8/6/29; 378 performances), and Belasco's last production, *Tonight or Never* (11/18/30; 232 performances), starred Melvyn Douglas and Helen Gahagan. After Belasco's death on May 14, 1931, the theater was leased to Katharine Cornell. She appeared in *Lucrece* (12/20/32; 31 performances) and Sidney Howard's *Alien Corn* (2/20/33; 98 performances). The theater was then leased to Hazel L. Rice, wife of playwright Elmer Rice of *Street Scene* fame.

The GROUP THEATER inhabited the theater in late 1934, when *Gold Eagle Guy* moved from the MOROSCO. On February 19, 1935, Clifford Odets's *Awake and Sing* opened at the Belasco under the Group Theater's umbrella. These two plays, a flop and a hit, were both part of the reason for the failure of the Group. During the mounting of the first play, major rifts opened in the already strained relationship between actors and Group leader Lee Strasberg. Ruth Nelson actually tried to assault Strasberg because of his handling of Stella Adler during a rehearsal. The second play was produced over Strasberg's vigorous objections. It turned out to be a smash hit and one of the most influential plays of the 1930s.

On October 28, 1935, Sidney Kingsley's *Dead End* opened to rave reviews. The production harked back to the days of Belasco's ultrarealism. The set by Norman Bel Geddes (also the producer) showed a dead-end street and wharf with the orchestra pit standing in for the East River. The Group Theater presented other notable plays at the Belasco in the 1930s: Frances Farmer, Luther Adler, and Elia Kazan featured in Clifford Odets' *Golden Boy* (11/4/37; 250 performances), Odets' *Rocket to the Moon* (11/24/38; 131 performances), and Irwin Shaw's *The Gentle People* (1/5/39; 141 performances).

The 1940s began with an appearance by John Barrymore (*see* BARRYMORE FAMILY) acting a parody of himself in *My Dear Children* (1/31/40; 117 performances). The $50,000 advance sale was one of the largest in Broadway history to that time. It seemed that everyone wanted to catch a glimpse of the Great Profile on his way down the ladder of success. BROOKS ATKINSON wrote that the audience "looked as if they hoped to be present at the final degradation of Icarus. The crowds that watched the tumbrels pass in the French Revolution could not have been more pitiless or morbid."

Later that year, Helen Craig played the deaf-mute in *Johnny Belinda*. The play, which opened on September 18, 1940 (321 performances), later became a hit movie, as did *Mr. and Mrs. North* (1/12/41; 163 performances). December 29, 1944 (67 performances), was the opening of *Trio*, a frank but tasteful treatment of lesbianism. Unfortunately, the management of the

theater refused to let the play run more than two months. Judy Holliday first made her mark at the Belasco in *Kiss Them for Me* (3/20/45; 110 performances); Richard Widmark and Jayne Cotter (later Meadows) were the other stars in the cast.

The 1940s continued with Arthur Laurents' *Home of the Brave* (12/27/45; 69 performances); Gertrude Berg as Molly Goldberg in *Me and Molly* (2/26/48; 156 performances); and *The Madwoman of Chaillot*, with Martita Hunt and Estelle Winwood (12/27/48; 368 performances). In 1949 the Belasco became an NBC radio theater, returning to legitimate use on November 5, 1953, with the hit comedy *The Solid Gold Cadillac*. Another big hit at the theater, George Axelrod's *Will Success Spoil Rock Hunter?* opened on October 13, 1955 (444 performances), with Jayne Mansfield in a leading role.

The PULITZER PRIZE was awarded to the Belasco's next hit, Tad Mosel's *All the Way Home* (11/30/60; 333 performances), starring Arthur Hill, Lillian Gish, Aline MacMahon, and Colleen Dewhurst. The British invasion of the 1960s came to the Belasco in the form of *Inadmissible Evidence* (11/30/65; 167 performances), with Nicol Williamson. Frank Marcus' *The Killing of Sister George* (10/5/66) was the second British play presented at the theater; it played 205 performances. Al Pacino made his Broadway debut at the Belasco in *Does a Tiger Wear a Necktie?* (2/25/69; 39 performances), which also starred Hal Holbrook.

As Broadway's fortunes fell in the late 1960s, so did those of the Belasco. *Oh! Calcutta!* moved to the Belasco from the off-Broadway Eden Theater on February 26, 1971, and caused a sensation with critics and audiences. It also caused a sensation with the ghost of David Belasco, who was often said to be seen in his private box on opening nights; after *Oh! Calcutta!* Belasco never reappeared. Perhaps he realized that there were to be no more successes at the theater. The Shubert Organization used the theater as a final home for musicals on their last legs, like *Ain't Misbehavin'*. It also leased the space to a succession of shows that had little chance for success. These included *The Rocky Horror Show* (3/10/75; 45 performances) (which later became a cult movie), *An Almost Perfect Person* 1/27/77; 108 performances), and *Hide and Seek* (5/4/80; 8 performances). These plays quickly came and went. The 1986–1987 season was devoted to the works of Shakespeare presented to the city's schoolchildren by the New York Shakespeare Festival. In 1991 Tony Randall's National Actors Theatre began operations at the Belasco. But, with few exceptions, their offerings were failures. In 1992 they presented 2 shows at the Belasco, *The Master Builder* (3/19/92; 44 performances) and *A Little Hotel on the Side* (1/26/92; 41 performances). Neither was noteworthy.

There were no bookings at the theater in 1993. In 1994 the sole booking was a magic show, *A Little More Magic* (3/17/94; 19 performances). The theater's first hit in many years was Ralph Fiennes' turn in *Hamlet* (5/2/95; 91 performances). The limited run was followed by the only other booking that year, *Sacrilege* (10/26/95), which lasted only 21 performances. The theater's sole booking in 1996 was *Jack: A Night on the Town with John Barrymore*. Despite Nicol Williamson's turn in the one-man show, the production lasted only 12 performances following its opening on April 6.

1997 saw a successful revival of *A Doll's House* with Janet McTeer, and what should have been a hit show, the irreverent and imaginative *Jackie* (11/10/97; 128 performances), by Gip Hoppe and starring Margaret Colin as Jacqueline Kennedy Onassis. Also receiving much notice was the highly inventive and entertaining setting by David Gallo. The next year the Belasco hosted, *Honour* (4/26/98; 57 performances), starring Jane Alexander, and the Joseph Papp production of the one-woman show *A Mom's Life* (10/19/98), that played alternately with a concert engagement by Mandy Patinkin.

The theater's fortunes rose slightly in 1999 with the Lincoln Center Theater's production of Anouilh's *Ring Round the Moon* (4/28/99; 66 performances), the theater's only booking that season. Things improved when the musical *James Joyce's The Dead* (12/14/99) transferred from Playwrights' Horizons off Broadway. The musical, considered by many to be the best of the year, featured book and lyrics by playwright Richard Nelson and music by Shaun Davey. Though it played only 120 performances, the unconventional musical starred a stellar cast, including Christopher Walken, Blair Brown, Daisy Eagan, Sally Ann Howes, Marni Nixon, Stephen Spinella, Alice Ripley, Emily Skinner, and Brian Davies. Unfortunately, not only did traditional Broadway audiences not respond to the evening's understated charms, but there was no original cast recording to memorialize a fine score.

The following season also saw a single booking, but one that was much anticipated. The Roundabout Theatre Company produced the first Broadway revival of STEPHEN SONDHEIM and James Goldman's *Follies* (4/5/2001). Hopes were high for a production that is considered by many to be the best modern musical ever staged. In addition to its fine score and libretto, *Follies* also offers unique casting opportunities for veteran performers. On that level the production did not disappoint. Featured in the company were such greats as Betty Garrett, Donald Saddler, Polly Bergen, Jane White, Marge Champion, and *Oklahoma!*'s original Laurey, Joan Roberts. The casting of the leads, Blythe Danner, Treat Williams, Gregory Harrison, and Judith

Ivey, left much to be desired, especially as they had so little musical-theater experience and seemed ill at ease throughout the evening. Unfortunately, the production was ill-conceived, with mishandled direction and choreography and a vastly underbudgeted production. It closed ignominiously after only 117 performances. What began as one of the hottest tickets in town limped to its final performances. David Ackroyd's one-man play, *The Mystery of Charles Dickens* (20 performances), starring Simon Callow, opened on April 25, 2002, to mainly enthusiastic notices.

The New York City Landmarks Preservation Commission designated the interior and exterior of the theater a landmark. The commission stated that it was in "an elegant neo-Georgian style reminiscent of town house architecture and specifically intended to suggest the intimate drama presented by Belasco within." The theater's interior "represents an early monument in the development of the 'little theater' movement."

BELMONT THEATER. 123 W. 48th Street. Architect: DeRosa and Periera. Opening: January 18, 1918; *Odds and Ends of 1917*.

The Belmont is one of the least-known of Broadway theaters. The theater opened in the midst of World War I with a transfer from the BIJOU THEATRE of the revue *Odds and Ends of 1917*. Jack Norworth, the composer of "Shine On, Harvest Moon" and a stage performer, built the Norworth Theatre and appeared in the opening production along with Lillian Lorraine and Harry Watson. The theater was called "one of the city's prettiest and most comfortable playhouses." Norworth's reign at the theater lasted only four months. It was then renamed the Belmont. The first show under the new name was Theresa Helburn's *Crops and Croppers* (9/12/18). Helburn, later one of the managers of the THEATER GUILD, didn't have success with this offering. The critics objected to the play as well as its Art Nouveau scenery. The reporter for the *Sun* particularly detested the set's yellow walls with green and violet curtains. Broadwayites only had 20 performances in which to make up their own minds.

The next play at the Belmont was an oddity, a drama based on a film. The film was *The Cheat*, and the play version was titled *I.O.U.* (10/5/18; 10 performances). Producer WILLIAM A. BRADY, though a veteran, made a mistake with this offering, despite its featuring the talents of Mary Nash and José Ruben. One wag opined, "A half a dozen handsome gowns and one thrill do not constitute the modern theatregoing New Yorker's idea of a $2 show."

Further failures followed. One of the more successful was the four-month run of Maurice Maeterlinck's anti-German drama *A Burgomaster of Belgium*, which opened in March 1919. The show featured Claude Cooper, Walter Kingsford, Leonard Willey (father of motion picture actor Alan Marshall), and set designer Raymond Sovey. Why Sovey chose to act in a play is unknown. The show was followed by *Our Pleasant Sins* (4/21/19; 32 performances), with Henrietta Crosman, Vincent Serrano, and Pauline Lord.

The next year, 1920, saw a production of Irvin Cobb's *Boys Will Be Boys* (10/13/19; 45 performances) and *His Chinese Wife* (5/17/20; 16 performances); neither fared well. Two small successes followed, *Little Miss Charity* (9/2/20; 77 performances) and *French Leave* (11/8/20; 56 performances). They were, in turn, followed by a PULITZER PRIZE–winning play of 1920–21, *Miss Lulu Bett* (12/27/20; 198 performances), by Zona Gale. Carroll McComus starred as Miss Lulu, and Catherine Calhoun Doucet and Louise Closser Hale were also in the cast. With a hit finally under its belt, the Belmont began a small roll. Next came another transfer, Arthur Richman's comedy *Ambush*, from the Garrick Theatre. Gilbert Emery's *The Hero* (9/5/21; 80 performances) starred Richard Bennett in what many considered to be his greatest performance. Though it received good reviews from the critics, the play didn't catch on with audiences. A new playwright saw his first Broadway production at the Belmont. Philip Barry came to New York after studying under G. P. Baker at the 47 Workshop with his Harvard Prize play, *You and I* (2/19/23; 136 performances). Emery did better with the next play at the Belmont, *Tarnish* (10/1/23; 248 performances). Ann Harding made a great hit in the play and was soon off to Hollywood.

The theater's good luck continued two years later with John Van Druten's *Young Woodley*, starring Helen Gahagan and Glenn Hunter. The theater's biggest hit came with its next production, the musical revue *Americana* (7/26/26), starring Helen Morgan, Charles Butterworth, Betty Compton, and Roy Atwell. It ran for 224 performances.

The last hit at the Belmont was a bittersweet one. *Stepping Sisters*, a look at a bevy of former burlesque queens, featured Theresa Maxwell Conover, Helen Raymond, and Grace Huff. Critical reviews were excellent, but the Belmont was too small a house for the producer to make money. So he moved it to a larger house, where it completed a 333-performance run.

Renovations of the theater followed, to no avail. From 1933 to 1936, the theater remained dark. On the opening night of *The Puritan* on January 23, 1936, all went well, but the boiler was not working properly and the audience was freezing. Critic GEORGE JEAN NATHAN couldn't take it anymore and started up the aisle and out of the theater. The manager rushed over and asked him what was the trouble. Nathan suppos-

edly replied that the weather was somewhat unseasonable for an al fresco performance.

In 1937 the Belmont was sold in foreclosure and began a foreign-film policy. Jimmy Savo opened in a one-man show, *Mum's the Word* (12/5/40; 12 performances), in the 1940–41 season, but the title seemed to apply equally to word of mouth—audiences stayed away in droves. It was the last legitimate show at the theater. The little theater became a motion picture house until it was finally razed in 1951 to make way for an office building.

BENCHLEY, ROBERT. Drama critic, noted humorist, and monologuist; b. Worcester, Massachusetts, September 15, 1889; d. New York, New York, November 21, 1945.

"Born Isle of Wight, September 15, 1807. Shipped as cabin boy on the *Florence J. Marble*, 1815. Arrested for bigamy and murder in Port Said, 1817. Released, 1820. Wrote *A Tale of Two Cities*. Married Princess Anastacia of Portugal, 1831. Children: Prince Rupprecht and several little girls. Wrote *Uncle Tom's Cabin*, 1850. Editor of *Godey's Lady's Book*, 1851–56. Began *Les Misérables*, 1870, finished by Victor Hugo. Died 1871. Buried in Westminster Abbey." So reads Robert Benchley's autobiography, written in 1930. The truth is almost as amusing.

Robert Benchley.

Broadwayites have never felt much generosity toward their drama critics, so it's all the more amazing that nary a harsh word was ever spoken against Robert Benchley. The Massachusetts native and Harvard graduate was drama editor for the old *Life* magazine for a decade and drama critic for *The New Yorker* magazine. He was also managing editor of *Vanity Fair* magazine, which might seem like a contradiction, since mismanagement was more his style. His curious, bumbling style was best exemplified by his monologue "The Treasurer's Report," which he performed on Broadway in *No, Sirree!* and later in the *Music Box Revue of 1923*. This experience on the stage may have humbled him, for during his years reviewing plays, he seldom had a bad word to say about actors.

Benchley was a man of opposites. On one hand, he was a chary onlooker in the game of life; when he attempted to play the game, he was often a bemused incompetent. On the other hand, he was a deft satirist who honed his skills at the Algonquin Round Table. He numbered among his closest friends Dorothy Parker, she of the rapier wit, and Robert E. Sherwood, journalist and playwright. In truth, he was an optimist whose charm and poise remained unshaken until pushed beyond the breaking point.

Benchley first exhibited his off-center humor at Harvard, where his pranks included introducing a Chinese storekeeper as Professor Soong of the Imperial University of China. Benchley presented Professor Soong at a Harvard victory dinner, where the learned guest lectured on Chinese football, with Benchley providing the translation. Benchley came to New York in 1912 and was hired by Franklin P. Adams to work at the *New York Tribune Sunday Magazine* in 1916 and the *New York Graphic* the following year. After his tenure at the *Tribune*, Benchley evaluated himself as the "worst reporter, even for his age, in New York."

Benchley's move to *Vanity Fair* (his first piece appeared in the magazine in October 1914) as managing director introduced him to Parker and Sherwood. Parker and Benchley became friends with Sherwood through the kind of bizarre event that would befall Benchley throughout his life. The *Vanity Fair* offices were on 44th Street, down from the Hippodrome. Appearing at the time was a troupe of midgets who couldn't resist hectoring the 6'7" Sherwood when they spied him on the street. Sherwood was afraid to go out for lunch alone and employed Benchley and Parker as bodyguards against the midget hordes. At *Vanity Fair*, Benchley, Parker, and Sherwood found themselves at odds with editor Frank Crowninshield. When Crowninshield fired Parker, Benchley and Sherwood resigned in protest. As Benchley put it, "I was getting in a rut."

Benchley was amazed to find himself on Broadway in *No, Sirree!* in which he performed "The Treasurer's Report." This show was a collaboration by members of the Round Table, and its success led to Benchley's repeating his monologue in the *Music Box Revue of 1923* and later in vaudeville. Benchley followed his Broadway appearance in over 40 short films and features for MGM, in which he was portrayed as a somewhat bumbling drunk, which he was not. True, he was one of the great drinkers, but it never seemed to affect him. It simply softened the edges of an already well-rounded personality. Beginning in 1919 Benchley lived in the Algonquin Hotel, site of the Round Table. He later moved across the street to the Royalton Hotel, where he maintained a suite for 24 years.

After walking out on his *Vanity Fair* job, Benchley shared an office with Dorothy Parker and took freelance work. He contributed a column, "Books and Things," to the *New York World* and also contributed drama criticism to the old *Life* magazine and *The New Yorker*. In addition, he compiled his humorous writings in many best-selling books. Benchley's wit was carefully reported by himself. He wrote his many essays with a gentle, if exasperated, wry humor. He usually attributed his more stinging barbs to Dorothy Parker. Among his more famous quips is, "I'd like to get out of this wet suit and into a dry martini."

Benchley's death, from a cerebral hemorrhage, was a shock to his family and friends, but even near death he kept up his characteristic style. The hemorrhaging was brought on by a series of nosebleeds that couldn't be stopped. Benchley had brought a book of essays to the hospital and was making notes in the margins. The last note, at the end of an essay called "Am I Thinking" by James Harvey Robinson, read: "NO. (and supposing you were?)."

Of his career, he once wrote, "It took me fifteen years to discover I had no talent, but I couldn't give it all up because by that time I was too famous." Benchley's son Nathaniel became a well-known author, and his grandson Peter is best known for writing *Jaws*.

BENNETT, ROBERT RUSSELL. Broadway's primary orchestrator of the golden era; b. Kansas City, Missouri, June 15, 1894; d. New York, New York, August 18, 1981.

The influence of the Broadway musical extends beyond Times Square. Robert Russell Bennett was one of its most influential talents, one whose work reached thousands of people. In all, it was estimated that he worked on over 300 Broadway shows, from *Daffydill* (1922) to *The Grass Harp* (1971). The sounds he introduced influenced the way we hear music and the way others interpreted it.

Bennett made his first stage appearance when he was only three years old in a production starring Julia Marlowe. But in spite of this early experience, acting wasn't for him. Music was more his calling, and he

Robert Russell Bennett.

made his professional debut in 1910 playing the piano, violin, and bass. His parents were his first teachers, and he then went on to study with composer-conductor Carl Busch. In 1919 he was commissioned by the T. B. Harms Company to orchestrate several tunes, including "An Old Fashioned Garden" by COLE PORTER. Following that came *Daffydill* and his first Broadway orchestration, *Wildflower* (1923), with a score by VINCENT YOUMANS, OTTO HARBACH, and OSCAR HAMMERSTEIN II. He continued to work with Hammerstein on most of the lyricist's shows, including his last, *The Sound of Music* (1959).

Bennett was awarded a Guggenheim Fellowship and studied with Nadia Boulanger in Paris in 1926. His own compositions include the "Charleston Rhapsody" (1926), "Sights and Sounds" (1929), and several symphonies. He also composed two one-act operas, *Endymion* (1927) and *The Enchanted Kiss* (1935). His full-length opera, *Marie Malibran*, debuted in 1944.

However, Bennett was best known for his Broadway orchestrations. He worked with most of the leading composers, including JEROME KERN (*Show Boat, The Cat and the Fiddle, Sunny*, and *Sweet Adeline*), GEORGE GERSHWIN (*Of Thee I Sing*), Cole Porter (*Kiss Me Kate*), Frederick Loewe (*see* FERNER AND LOEWE) (*My Fair Lady* and *Camelot*, both with Philip J. Lang), BURTON LANE (*Finian's Rainbow* and *On a Clear*

Day), and Arthur Schwartz (*see* DIETZ AND SCHWARTZ) (*Inside U.S.A., By the Beautiful Sea*, and *A Tree Grows in Brooklyn*). His work for Richard Rodgers (*see* RODGERS AND HAMMERSTEIN and RODGERS AND HART) was his best-known. These shows included *Oklahoma!* as well as *Allegro, South Pacific, The King and I, Flower Drum Song*, and *The Sound of Music*. He also orchestrated and arranged Rodgers' themes for the documentary television series *Victory at Sea* (1952). Among his many awards are an Emmy (1963) for original music composed for television and an Academy Award (1955) for *Oklahoma!*

Burton Lane recalled visiting Bennett's office and seeing the great man orchestrating a score while listening to the radio, working a crossword puzzle, and entertaining a girl who was sitting on his lap.

BERLIN, IRVING. Certainly the most successful and prolific songwriter in American history; b. Israel Baline in Mohilev, Russia, May 11, 1888; d. New York, New York, September 22, 1989.

Composer and lyricist Irving Berlin's songs span over 50 years, from his first song, "Marie from Sunny Italy" (1907, lyrics only), to his last performed song, "An Old Fashioned Wedding" (1966), written for a revival of ANNIE GET YOUR GUN. During the six decades of his career, he was the composer most able to chart America's taste in popular song, and he influenced scores of others in his field.

Irving Berlin during rehearsals for *Mr. President*, 1960.

65

When Berlin was five, his family left Russia and settled on the Lower East Side of New York. After the death of his father, when he was eight, he left school and by his teens was singing in Bowery saloons and restaurants. Songwriting was just becoming a big business, and he began writing lyrics for others' tunes and plugging songs for publishers. His first song, "Marie from Sunny Italy," had music by M. Nicholson.

Although he never learned to read music, Berlin was on the way to becoming a professional songwriter. In 1909 he was hired as a staff lyricist by the Ted Snyder Company, and soon Berlin matched his words to his own music. The next year he performed in vaudeville and then musical comedy in *Up and Down Broadway*. His first big success, "Alexander's Ragtime Band," was published in 1911 and catapulted Berlin to the top of his field.

In 1914, having already had songs interpolated into revues and musicals, Berlin saw his first full Broadway score presented. The show was *Watch Your Step* and presented the song "Play a Simple Melody." During World War I Berlin joined the U.S. Army and was inspired to write "Oh, How I Hate to get up in the Morning!" The song appeared in an all-soldier revue, *Yip Yip Yaphank* (8/19/18), which also featured another big hit, "Mandy." Also written for the show but unused was "God Bless America." It wasn't heard until Kate Smith introduced it in 1939.

The young composer was so successful that he was asked to contribute most of the score to the *Ziegfeld Follies of 1919*. For the annual revue, he wrote the theme song of the ZIEGFELD FOLLIES, "A Pretty Girl Is Like a Melody."

Berlin realized the value of his song catalogue, and so in 1919 he dissolved his agreement with the music publishers Waterson, Berlin & Snyder Company and set up his own office, Irving Berlin, Inc. He rented the third floor of 1587 Broadway (at 48th Street) and installed Saul Bornstein as his general manager.

The Berlin offices were described by ALEXANDER WOOLLCOTT in his book *The Story of Irving Berlin*:

Something of the nervousness of the new music, something of the jumpiness and excitement of jazz itself, is in the very air of such a publishing house. This one occupies a loft in a low building of transitory aspect that stands at the corner of 49th Street and Broadway. It is a stone's throw from the vast Capitol Theatre where its new melodies are often heard for the first time and just a step from the Palace, that headquarters of vaudeville where an Elsie Janis or a Nora Bayes may be the first to sing them.

It would be pleasant to be able to report that the new songs are prepared in a marble temple, framed against a bank of black cypresses, that velvet footed servitors lead you respectfully along stately corridors and that the splash of fountains plays a soft accompaniment to the new melodies poised for their first flight into the world. It is necessary, however, to report that Irving Berlin, Inc. is housed in an office building of such ordinary aspect that a passerby would be more likely to look on the signboard by the elevator for the firm name of Potash & Perlmutter.

You no sooner step out of that elevator when it reaches the Berlin floor than you are immediately trampled under foot by something that suggests a crowd in front of a baseball score-board, a mob scene, perhaps, in a William A. Brady melodrama, or a busy day at the gates of Ellis Island—anything, indeed, except a cluster of courtiers in the anteroom of melody.

These are the professionals—these the song-writers with ballads in manuscript, each confident that his unheard opus will sweep the land if the natural jealousy of Berlin himself does not strangle it at birth. These are the minstrels from the two-a-day—drifting in to hear whatever is new in the world of song as stockbrokers drift towards a ticker. Slim-waisted, pasty-faced lads with incredibly nimble feet who stand askew and litter the floor with the nervous butts of their half-consumed cigarettes; small, squeaky actresses of ten or twelve towed by their belligerent mothers—these are the unknowns who rub shoulders with the great folk of minstrelsy in the clamorous outer office. Probably the Al Jolson or the Nora Bayes of tomorrow is somewhere in the group . . .

Back of this, providing a kind of thorough-bass for the composition, is a strange, unending blurr of sound, bits of music seeping out from the supposedly sound-proof studios in which a new Berlin from Chinatown may be eagerly showing what melodies are in his sheaf or a new favorite from vaudeville may be having the latest ballad adjusted to her immovable voice. On the other hand, the voice you hear sifting through the keyhole may be one you recognize fondly as the voice of Grace La Rue. Or the deep boom-boom of Nora Bayes. And, as like as not, that plump and pleasing person elbowing his way through the crowded anteroom will be none other than the Lord of Jazz, Paul Whiteman. In summer time, when the doors and windows of Tin Pan Alley stand open all day long, the sidewalks underneath are clogged with stray listeners to the favorites of the coming season as they leak from the rooms where orchestras and pianos and quartettes are trying them.

It is a ramifying and stupendous business—this farflung enterprise which, in the complicated fashion of modern American life, has come into existence just because that waiter down at Nigger Mike's had so many tunes in his head. Saul Bornstein, the general manager who is also one of the three partners, has charge of some two hundred employees scattered through offices from Boston in Massachusetts to Sydney in Australia. He is the dynamo of the house and it is he who is responsible for seeing that the overhead does not run over $75,000 a month. If, out of the 125 songs the house may publish in a year, four of them prove to be hits, such an overhead can be absorbed and forgotten. No easy job, Mr. Bornstein's, to keep his head when all about him folks are bursting into song, or departing temperamentally for Miami. It must be like keeping books in Bedlam.

Berlin retained control of his publishing empire until his death.

Reacting against the extravagance of the *Follies*, Berlin joined with Sam H. Harris and built the MUSIC BOX THEATER. There, the two partners presented Berlin's *Music Box Revues* (1921, 1922, 1923, 1924), a series of small-scale but lush revues that introduced such songs as "Say It with Music," "Pack Up Your Sins and Go to the Devil," "Learn to Do the Strut," "An Orange Grove in California," "What'll I Do," and "All Alone." The Marx Brothers starred in Berlin's next show, *The Cocoanuts* (12/8/25). The show didn't contain any standout songs but, rather went down in history as a hysterical Marx Brothers film.

Berlin's next smash hit song was contributed to the musical *Betsy* (12/28/26; 39 performances); the song was "Blue Skies." He returned to the *Ziegfeld Follies* in 1927 with a score that included "Shaking the Blues Away," sung by Ruth Etting. Berlin's next score was for *Face the Music* (2/17/32), which featured the songs "Let's Have Another Cup of Coffee" and "Soft Lights and Sweet Music." *As Thousands Cheer* (9/30/33) followed with a cast that included Clifton Webb, Marilyn Miller, and the great Ethel Waters, who introduced one of the most powerful and dramatic of all theater songs, "Supper Time"—one of Berlin's only songs to address a social issue, racism in the South, and quite brave for its day. Other hits from the score were "Easter Parade," "Harlem on My Mind," "Heat Wave," and "How's Chances?"

Berlin spent the remainder of the 1930s in Hollywood writing, primarily for FRED ASTAIRE and Ginger Rogers, such movie scores as *Top Hat* (1935), *Follow the Fleet* (1936), and *Carefree* (1938). He also contributed scores to two Alice Faye vehicles, *On the Avenue* (1937) and *Alexander's Ragtime Band* (1938), as well as other films.

Berlin returned to Broadway on May 28, 1940, with *Louisiana Purchase*, which contained the songs "Fools Fall in Love," "It's a Lovely Day Tomorrow," and the title song. During World War II, Berlin wrote and appeared in another all-soldier show, *This Is the Army* (7/4/42; 113 performances). Berlin reprised his rendition of "Oh, How I Hate to Get up in the Morning" and appeared in the subsequent movie version.

Berlin's greatest show, *Annie Get Your Gun*, starred ETHEL MERMAN and Ray Middleton. The show opened on May 16, 1946, and played for 1,147 performances. The excellent score showed Berlin wasn't merely a Tin Pan Alley tunesmith: each number supported the plot and reflected the character singing it. Furthermore, the songs worked equally well offstage on the hit pa-

rade. "Anything You Can Do," "Doin' What Comes Natur'lly," "The Girl That I Marry," "I Got Lost in His Arms," "I Got the Sun in the Morning," and "They Say It's Wonderful" all achieved lasting success. But the most successful of all the songs was "There's No Business Like Show Business," which has become the unofficial anthem of the entire entertainment world.

Annie Get Your Gun was followed by *Miss Liberty* (7/15/49; 308 performances) and the Ethel Merman starrer *Call Me Madam* (10/12/50; 644 performances). *Miss Liberty* featured "Let's Take an Old Fashioned Walk," and *Call Me Madam* presented "It's a Lovely Day Today" and "You're Just in Love." *Mr. President* (10/20/62) was Berlin's last score and the least successful of his shows, running only 265 performances.

Among the many awards Berlin received are the Medal for Merit for *This Is the Army*, the Legion of Honor, a Congressional Gold Medal for "God Bless America," and an Academy Award for "White Christmas" (1942). Irving Berlin contributed more hits than any of his contemporary Broadway composers. His more than 800 songs captured the spirit of the nation unlike those of any other songwriter.

BERNSTEIN, LEONARD. Famed classical composer and conductor who achieved enormous success as a Broadway songwriter thanks to several classic scores; b. Lawrence, Massachusetts, August 25, 1918; d. New York, New York, October 14, 1990.

Bernstein began his music studies with Helen Coates and Heinrich Gebhard. He was educated at the Boston Latin School and Harvard University. At Harvard he continued his studies with Walter Piston, Edward Burlingame Hill, and Tillman Merritt. He then attended the Curtis Institute in Philadelphia under Randall Thompson, Isabelle Vengerova, and Fritz Reiner. Next, he became assistant to the famous Boston Symphony conductor Serge Koussevitzky, after an apprenticeship. In 1943, he assisted Artur Rodzinski as conductor of the New York Philharmonic. When guest conductor Bruno Walter became ill, Bernstein, in the best show-business tradition, took over the baton and became a star.

Bernstein's first show, *On the Town* (12/28/44), was based on a Jerome Robbins ballet for which Bernstein had written the music. The ballet, *Fancy Free* (1944), was adapted into a musical play by Robbins, Bernstein, and lyricist/librettists Betty Comden and Adolph Green (*see* COMDEN AND GREEN). The exceptional production opened December 28, 1944, and ran for 462 performances. Comden and Green also starred in the production, which featured Cris Alexander, John Battles, Ray Harrison, Alice Pearce, Nancy Walker,

On the Town with Adolph Green and Betty Comden (standing in rear), John Battles, Cris Alexander, Nancy Walker and Frances Cassard.

and ballet star Sono Osato. The success of *On the Town* led to another collaboration with lyricists Comden and Green, resulting in another great show, *Wonderful Town* (2/25/53). GEORGE ABBOTT directed the cast, which included Rosalind Russell and Edith Adams as two sisters from Ohio out to conquer New York. This production ran for 559 performances.

In 1950 Bernstein contributed incidental songs to a production of *Peter Pan* starring Jean Arthur. Bernstein supplied the lyrics as well as the music for the songs in *Peter Pan*, a task he repeated in 1955 for a show called *All in One*. It featured TENNESSEE WILLIAMS' one-act play *27 Wagons Full of Cotton* and Bernstein's one-act opera *Trouble in Tahiti*, which was written in 1952. The show was not a success and ran only for 47 performances.

Bernstein's next show, *Candide* (12/1/56), was a failure, but the album, recorded by Goddard Lieberson for Columbia Records, made the show a cult favorite. It was revived in 1971 in a production that closed out of town. It wasn't until 1974, when the show was revised for Broadway with HAROLD PRINCE producing and directing, that *Candide* achieved success, running for 740 performances. The show then entered the rep-

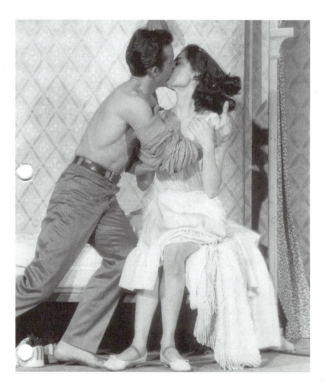

Larry Kert and Carol Lawrence in *West Side Story*.

ertory of the New York City Opera, with Harold Prince again directing.

The year after the original production of *Candide*, Bernstein's most popular musical, *West Side Story*, premiered. Arthur Laurents provided the book and STEPHEN SONDHEIM the lyrics to the retelling of Shakespeare's *Romeo and Juliet* as a love story of two New York City teenagers from different ethnic backgrounds. Larry Kert and Carol Lawrence played the lovers and introduced some of the musical theater's most enduring songs: "Somewhere," "Maria," "I Feel Pretty," and "Tonight." Jerome Robbins directed the production, which opened September 26, 1957, and ran for 732 performances.

Bernstein's heavy conducting and composing schedule prevented him from pursuing a steady career writing for Broadway. His next show, *1600 Pennsylvania Avenue*, opened on May 4, 1976, almost 20 years after *West Side Story*. Alan Jay Lerner (*see* LERNER AND LOEWE) contributed the libretto and lyrics. The show underwent an especially difficult gestation and arrived on Broadway before its many problems could be addressed satisfactorily. The show played only 7 performances on Broadway. It did contain, however, a wonderfully theatrical score that, in part due to a misguided semioperatic recording under the title *White House Cantata*, is sadly underappreciated.

Though Bernstein did not write as much as some of the other songwriting greats, such as KERN, Rodgers (*see* RODGERS AND HAMMERSTEIN and RODGERS AND HART), or BERLIN, the quality of his scores is unsurpassed.

BIJOU THEATRE. 209 W. 45th Street. Architect: Herbert J. Krapp. Opening: April 12, 1917; *The Knife*.

The Bijou was built by the SHUBERT BROTHERS, but because of its small size, 603 seats, it never achieved much success. In 1918 Tallulah Bankhead made her first Broadway appearance here in *The Squab Farm*.

Bijou Theatre marquee in 1919 with *His Honor Abe Potash* and at the Morosco Theatre, next door, *Civilian Clothes*.

During the Depression, while other theaters were transformed to movies or radio use, the Bijou was shuttered. In 1935 the Bijou became a cartoon-only movie house. There was the occasional film booking during the 1940s and '50s, such as the American premiere of *The Red Shoes*.

The theater reopened as a legit house in 1957. The first production of EUGENE O'NEILL's *A Moon for the Misbegotten* reinstated the short-lived legitimate policy. When the ASTOR THEATRE, next door, expanded in 1959, the Bijou's stage left wing and half of the house right audience were given over to the Astor. In 1962 the theater reopened as the D. W. Griffith Theater, a movie theater. Its first presentation, *The Connection*, opened October 3, 1962. The next year the theater was sold again and became a Japanese cinema house called the Toho. The film *Yojimbo* opened there on January 22, 1963, as the first attraction.

In 1965 the theater was again named the Bijou, and in 1970 a gay play, *Foreplay* (12/11/70; 38 performances), had a brief run, temporarily returning the theater to a legitimate policy.

In 1973 the Bijou again became a legitimate theater under its original name. However, because of its small size and the high operating costs of Broadway productions, the theater could be used only for small, intimate shows without stars or big production values. *Mummenschanz* (3/30/77), a mime theater, was the most notable tenant. It played at the Bijou for 1,326 performances. The Bijou ended its spotted history when it was demolished along with the HELEN HAYES and MOROSCO theaters to make way for the Marriott Marquis Hotel (*see* BATTLE TO SAVE THE HELEN HAYES AND MOROSCO THEATERS).

BILLBOARD. *Billboard* is the oldest of all amusement trade papers. It was once the most widely read of the trades, until *VARIETY* usurped its place. W. H. Donaldson and his partner James F. Hennegan founded the paper in 1894. The first issue came out on November 1, 1894, under the name *Billboard Advertising*. The monthly covered traveling shows, circuses, and vaudeville only as a sideline and from the viewpoint of their use of outdoor billboard advertising. In 1897 *Billboard Advertising* became *Billboard*, and in 1900 Donaldson bought out Hennegan's interests. Donaldson expanded the publication to include more entertainment news and in May of that year made *Billboard* a weekly. By the next year *Billboard* was regularly covering dramatic, stock and repertory theater, music, operas, minstrel shows, vaudeville, burlesque, circuses, carnivals, street fairs, and amusement parks. Along with the news of the entertainment world, *Billboard* provided many services for performers. The

paper forwarded letters to performers on the road who listed their addresses as simply "Billboard." *Billboard* also published complete schedules of acts and their locations.

As the years went by, *Billboard* marked the passing of vaudeville, variety, BURLESQUE and other forms of entertainment. Television, movies, and music became the dominant entertainment media, and *Billboard* reflected this change. In 1946 it began regularly charting the top pop artists and their record sales. By the 1960s *VARIETY* had surpassed *Billboard* as the premier entertainment weekly, and *Billboard* concentrated on music news and statistics. The magazine was sold in 1984 to private investors for approximately $40 million. In 1987 it was bought by Affiliated Publishers for $100 million. The magazine is currently part of VNU Business Publications.

BILLY ROSE MUSIC HALL. *See* **Ed Sullivan Theater.**

BILLY ROSE THEATER. *See* **Nederlander Theatre.**

BILLY ROSE'S DIAMOND HORSESHOE. *See* **Century Theater (1).**

BILTMORE THEATER. 261 W. 47th Street. Architect: Herbert J. Krapp. Opening: December 7, 1925; *Easy Come, Easy Go* (moved from George M. Cohan's Theatre).

The Biltmore Theater has had a spotty history. Despite its prime location, the theater has had few long runs. It was built by the Chanin brothers, who would eventually build, and lose, six theaters in Times Square. The Biltmore was the second of the Chanins' Broadway theaters. With 1,000 seats, it was an ideal size to serve plays and musicals equally well. The theater was the first built on the north side of 47th Street.

In its first years the Biltmore's offerings were, for the most part, unexceptional. They included such moderate hits as *Kongo* (3/30/26; 135 performances), *Loose Ankles* (8/16/26; 161 performances), *The Barker* (1/18/27; 225 performances), and *Jimmie's Women* (9/26/27; 217 performances). Later in the 1920s, the Biltmore was host to a controversial play, *The Pleasure Man* (10/1/28), by Mae West. The show was closed by the police only two days after its premiere. Among the shocking proceedings on the stage was a party of female impersonators. A long dry spell hit the Biltmore in the midst of the Depression. It didn't have a hit until January 1, 1934, with the opening of *Big Hearted*

1

1

1

1

1

1

1

1

1

1

1

1

1

0

0

0

Herbert, which played for 154 performances. But the modest success wasn't enough to keep the theater profitable. The Chanins lost the Biltmore as well as their other holdings.

To the rescue came the FEDERAL THEATRE PROJECT with its Living Newspapers, a series of shows that dramatized current events on the stage. *Triple-A Plowed Under* (3/14/36; 85 performances), the first Living Newspaper, urged farmers and consumers to join in a common goal of better incomes for the farmers and more inexpensive food for the consumer. *Injunction Granted* (7/24/36) played to full houses until October 20, 1936. The play traced the history of the American labor movement and proved to be quite controversial. Like many of the Living Newspapers, *Injunction Granted* did not hide its point of view, which was resolutely pro-labor. Hallie Flanagan, head of the Federal Theatre Project, wrote a memo to the show's creators after the opening night. In part it stated, "The production seems to me special pleading, biased, an editorial, not a news issue. Whatever my personal sympathies are I cannot, as custodian of federal funds, have such funds used as a party tool."

Among the only businesses showing a profit during the Depression were the movie studios. Warner Brothers bought the Biltmore and installed GEORGE ABBOTT as its principal producer. His first production there was the John Monks Jr. and Fred Finklehoffe comedy *Brother Rat* (12/16/36; 575 performances), starring José Ferrer, Eddie Albert, Ezra Stone, and Frank Albertson. It was the theater's first big hit. After two failures, *Brown Sugar* and *All That Glitters*, Abbott again struck gold with his production of *What a Life* (4/13/38; 538 performances). The main character of Clifford Goldsmith's comedy, Henry Aldrich, is fondly recalled by generations of radio listeners. Ezra Stone played Henry, and also in the cast were Eddie Albert, Betty Field, and Butterfly McQueen.

The next big hit at the Biltmore was the terrifically successful *My Sister Eileen* (12/26/40; 866 performances), by Jerome Chodorov and Joseph Fields (*see* FIELDS FAMILY) (they later adapted their hit play into the musical *Wonderful Town*). The play starred Shirley Booth, JoAnn Sayers, and Morris Carnovsky under George S. Kaufman's (*see* KAUFMAN AND HART) direction. Tragically, the real Eileen was killed in an auto accident while driving to New York to attend the opening-night performance.

Abbott gave the Biltmore another hit (which would later be adapted to radio and movies) with *Kiss and Tell* (3/17/43; 962 performances) by F. Hugh Herbert. It was a comedy with the unlikely subject of teenage pregnancy. The production starred Richard Widmark, Joan Caulfield, and Jessie Royce Landis in the leads. Fred Finklehoffe, one of the authors of *Brother Rat*, produced the Biltmore's next hit, *The Heiress* (9/29/47; 410 performances), a dramatization by Ruth and Augustus Goetz of Henry James' *Washington Square*. It was directed by the brilliant but much-hated Jed Harris and starred Basil Rathbone, Patricia Collinge, Peter Cookson, and Wendy Hiller. DAVID MERRICK's first producing effort, *Clutterbuck*, opened at the Biltmore on December 3, 1949. It played 218 performances, primarily through the aggressive public-relations STUNTS ordered by Merrick.

Beginning in 1952 the theater was leased to CBS. David Cogan purchased the theater in 1958 and booked another George Abbott–directed production, reinaugurating its legitimate policy. *Take Her, She's Mine* (12/21/61; 404 performances), by Phoebe and Henry Ephron, starred Art Carney, Phyllis Thaxter, and Elizabeth Ashley and was produced by HAROLD PRINCE. Elizabeth Ashley also appeared in the next attraction at the Biltmore, NEIL SIMON's *Barefoot in the Park* (10/23/63; 1,530 performances). Mike Nichols directed the play, which also starred Robert Redford, Kurt Kasznar, and Mildred Natwick.

The biggest hit in the Biltmore's history was *Hair* (4/29/68; 1,750 performances), by Galt MacDermot, James Rado, and Gerome Ragni. The musical included such hits as "Aquarius," "Good Morning Starshine," and the title number. *Hair* was more than just a rock musical. It was one of the last of the truly influential Broadway musicals. The staging and loose construction of the script as well as the unconventional score influenced both theater professionals and audiences. Many audiences came to *Hair* in search of vicarious thrills while they viewed the counterculture from the safety of an orchestra seat. But *Hair* was a phenomenon of its time; a later revival presented at the Biltmore in 1977 was a failure.

Mildred Natwick and Robert Redford in *Barefoot in the Park*, 1963.

On December 10, 1987, the Biltmore suffered a fire of mysterious origins. The stage area and front of house was damaged by the fire, but luckily no structural damage occurred, although the theater's ornate plasterwork was damaged. The police said that vagrants had been using the theater as a drug haven.

On February 16, 1988, the theater was auctioned off for $5.35 million to Morris Gluck, a businessman who promised to retain the building's function as a theater. Gluck purchased the building from Sam Pfeiffer, who had bought the building two years before from David Cogan. The Nederlanders in association with producer Stewart Lane purchased the Biltmore in 1993. The Biltmore went through several other owners who all defaulted on loans before being able to restore and reopen the theater. Following the lead of the Roundabout Theatre's occupancy of the old Selwyn Theatre on 42nd Street (renamed the AMERICAN AIRLINES THEATRE), the Biltmore is to be occupied by the Manhattan Theater Club with the auditorium surrounded by a hotel situated on 8th Avenue.

On November 10, 1987, the New York City Landmarks Preservation Commission designated the interior of the theater a landmark. The commission stated that the theater's auditorium is "a fine example" of the Adamesque style.

Lyricist Sheldon Harnick (standing) and composer Jerry Bock in 1966, just prior to the opening of *The Apple Tree*.

BOCK AND HARNICK. Preeminent musical theater composing team of the 1960s, best remembered for their score for *Fiddler on the Roof*; Jerry Bock, b. New Haven, Connecticut, November 23, 1928; Sheldon Harnick, b. Chicago, Illinois, April 30, 1924.

Songwriters Bock and Harnick showed an almost sweet regard for their characters' humanity and displayed an ability to universalize the problems and dreams of these characters in such shows as *Fiddler on the Roof* and *The Rothschilds*. But their work could also be satirical and sophisticated, especially in their shows *The Apple Tree* and *Fiorello!*

Composer Jerry Bock's early musical-comedy successes included the Sammy Davis Jr. vehicle *Mr. Wonderful* (3/22/56), which ran for 383 performances. Lyricist Sheldon Harnick, after writing for the Northwestern University Waa-Mu shows, achieved his first professional success as a contributor to revues, including Leonard Sillman's *New Faces of 1952* (5/16/52; 365 performances) and Ben Bagley's *Shoestring Revue* (3/2/57; 96 performances).

The two songwriters collaborated for the first time on a book musical, *The Body Beautiful*, which premiered on January 23, 1958. Unfortunately, the show ran only 60 performances, but the score was well received and appreciated by Bock and Harnick's contemporaries. Their second outing, *Fiorello!*, astounded

Broadway when it won the coveted PULITZER PRIZE for drama. *Fiorello!* opened on November 23, 1959, with Tom Bosley as the feisty mayor Fiorello LaGuardia. Supporting him were Ellen Hanley, Pat Stanley, Patricia Wilson, Eileen Rodgers, and Nathaniel Frey. *Fiorello!* played 796 performances and established Bock and Harnick as a top-grade songwriting team. Their next effort was also a period piece. *Tenderloin* (10/17/60) starred Maurice Evans as a righteous minister who took it upon himself to clean up the notorious Tenderloin section of Manhattan. Although the show was not entirely successful, it did have a well-crafted, solid score. *Tenderloin* played 216 performances.

She Loves Me (4/23/63), a major effort for the team, was based on the Ernst Lubitsch classic film *The Shop Around the Corner*. There were 23 songs in the superior score (a typical Broadway score contains only 12–16 songs). The title song achieved some fame. The underappreciated show was produced and directed by HAROLD PRINCE and starred Jack Cassidy, Barbara Cook, Barbara Baxley, Nathaniel Frey, and Daniel Massey. *She Loves Me* managed to run 302 performances.

Their next Broadway assignment was their masterwork, *Fiddler on the Roof*, one of the greatest musicals ever written. *Fiddler on the Roof* opened on September

Zero Mostel in the original production of *Fiddler on the Roof*, 1964.

22, 1964. It had a superior book by Joseph Stein and brilliant direction and choreography by Jerome Robbins. Some people feel that *Fiddler on the Roof* represents the finest achievement in musical comedy. Although only "Sunrise, Sunset" achieved success outside of the show, the entire score is masterfully integrated into the script. Zero Mostel triumphed in the role of Tevye. Other cast members included Maria Karnilova, Joanna Merlin, Julia Migenes, Austin Pendleton, Beatrice Arthur, and Bert Convy. *Fiddler on the Roof* played 3,242 performances, making it, for a while, Broadway's longest-running musical.

The team followed *Fiddler on the Roof* with *The Apple Tree* (10/18/66). Consisting of three one-act musicals, *The Apple Tree* featured a superb performance by Barbara Harris. She was joined by Alan Alda and Larry Blyden. The stories included Mark Twain's "The Diary of Adam and Eve," Jules Feiffer's "Passionella," and Frank R. Stockton's "The Lady or the Tiger." The score was marvelously playful, with a wide range of emotion and humor. The show played 463 performances.

Bock and Harnick's last Broadway musical as a team was *The Rothschilds*. The show opened on October 19, 1970, and although it ran 505 performances, it was not a financial success. The show and especially the score were not light enough for most audiences. However, though unappreciated at the time, the show (or at least the score) is now considered an artistic success. *The Rothschilds* starred Hal Linden, Paul Hecht, Christopher Sarandon, Robby Benson, Keene Curtis, and Jill Clayburgh.

After the team's breakup, Jerry Bock retired from the musical theater. Sheldon Harnick went on to provide lyrics to Richard Rodgers' (*see* RODGERS AND HAMMERSTEIN and RODGERS AND HART) music for *Rex* (4/25/76). Unfortunately, that show, Harnick's last Broadway offering, was a failure. His later attempts to mount a Broadway production included musicalizations of the movie *It's a Wonderful Life* and Dickens'

Barbara Harris as Passionella in *The Apple Tree*, 1966.

A Christmas Carol. Neither made it to New York. He also provided the English lyrics to Peter Brook's *Le Tragedie de Carmen* and *The Umbrellas of Cherbourg.* He also provided libretti to several operas and provided additional lyrics to the Dutch musical *Cyrano* on Broadway.

BOLTON, GUY. British playwright and novelist best remembered for the famed "Princess Theater shows" of P. G. Wodehouse and Jerome Kern; b. Broxbourne, England, November 23, 1884; d. London, England, September 5, 1979.

Though he was born in England, Bolton's parents were American, and the family soon returned to the United States. He was educated at the Pratt Institute in Brooklyn and the Ecole des Beaux-Arts, Paris.

Bolton was one of the most prolific playwrights and librettists of the 20th century. He wrote for productions in both New York and London in a career spanning more than 50 years. He wrote 57 musical libretti. His first play, *The Drone*, was written in collaboration with Douglas J. Wood and premiered on December 30, 1912, at Daly's Theater, London. His last work was the musical *Anya*, which opened at the Ziegfeld on November 29, 1965. In between he collaborated with many authors, among them George Middleton (*Hit-the-Trail-Holiday*, 1915; *Thought*, 1916; *Polly with a*

Past, 1917; *Adam and Eva*, 1919; *The Light of the World*, 1920; *The Cave Girl*, 1920; *Polly*, 1929), Philip Bartholomae (*Very Good Eddie*, 1915; *Tangerine*, 1925), and Fred Thompson (*Lady, Be Good!*, 1924; *Tip Toes*, 1925; *Rio Rita*, 1927; *The Five o'Clock Girl*, 1927; *Song of the Drum*, London, 1931; *Seeing Stars*, London, 1935; *Swing Along*, London, 1936; *This'll Make You Whistle*, London, 1936; *Going Places*, London, 1936; *Going Greek*, London, 1937; *Hide and Seek*, London, 1937; *The Fleet's Lit Up*, London, 1938; *Bobby Get Your Gun*, London, 1938; *Magyar Melody*, London, 1939; *Follow the Girls*, 1944).

His most successful collaboration was with P. G. Wodehouse. The team of Wodehouse, Bolton, and JEROME KERN created the PRINCESS THEATER shows. These were considered the first successful intimate musicals, a dramatic response to the opulent revues and musicals then on Broadway. The Princess Theater shows were smart and sophisticated for their time, and they were the first attempts to link songs to characterization. Bolton's collaboration with Wodehouse included *Have a Heart*, 1917; *Oh, Boy!*, 1917; *Leave It to Jane*, 1917; *The Riviera Girl*, 1917; *Miss 1917*, 1917; *Oh, Lady! Lady!!*, 1918; *The Girl Behind the Gun*, 1918; *Oh, My Dear!*, 1918; *The Rose of China*, 1919; *Sitting Pretty*, 1924; *Oh, Kay!*, 1926; *The Nightingale*, 1927; and *Anything Goes!*, 1934.

Among the composers and lyricists who contributed scores to Bolton librettos were COLE PORTER, Jerome Kern, GEORGE and IRA GERSHWIN, RODGERS and HART, Wright and Forrest, Harry Tierney, VERNON DUKE, Howard Dietz (*see* DIETZ AND SCHWARTZ), BURTON LANE, and E. Y. HARBURG.

BOLTON, WHITNEY. Critic; b. Spartenburg, South Carolina, July 23, 1900; d. New York, New York, November 4, 1969.

Bolton's father, Henry S. Bolton, was a mining engineer. His mother, Elizabeth, was a debutante and free thinker originally from Washington, D.C. His parents moved the family to Mexico, where they became friendly with the revolutionary Pancho Villa. After his father's mining work was completed in Mexico, the family returned to the United States.

Bolton was a graduate of the Staunton Military Institute in Virginia and the University of Virginia. In 1925 he came to New York and began his career as a reporter with the *New York Herald Tribune*. The young writer covered such events as the Valentino funeral and the Snyder-Gray execution. In addition, he wrote features on theater for the *Sunday Herald Tribune*. Those articles came to the attention of Gene Fowler, managing editor of the *New York Morning Telegraph*. In 1928 Bolton joined the paper as a Broadway columnist and later assumed the role of drama critic.

While at the *Morning Telegraph* he became friends with Texas Guinan and nightclub impresario Barny Gallant. He also wrote a theatrical anecdote column under the heading "Beau Broadway."

He left the *Telegraph* in 1938, moving to a career as publicity director for RKO Pictures, Columbia Pictures, and Warner Brothers from 1941 to 1946. Bolton also served as an assistant to movie producer David O. Selznick from 1943 to 1946 (where he was responsible for coming up with the name Jennifer Jones). He rejoined the staff of the *Morning Telegram* in 1949. He scripted the play *Save the Pieces* (1932) as well as several screenplays and wrote a biography of Conrad Hilton titled *The Silver Spade*.

Bolton was the one of the founders of the New York Drama Critics Circle and wrote the group's constitution along with Brooks Atkinson. He served two terms as the organization's president, in 1955 and 1958. He was also a newscaster, drama critic, and commentator for Mutual Broadcasting, and his column was syndicated by the McNaught Syndicate.

BOOTH THEATRE. 222 W. 45th Street. Architect: Henry B. Herts. Opening: October 16. 1913; *The Great Adventure*.

The Sam S. Shubert Theater and the Booth Theatre were designed together as one building. The combination of the Booth and Shubert's shared facade forms Times Square's most famous pedestrian thoroughfare: Shubert Alley. The architectural firm responsible for the design of the theaters was Herts & Tallant, the firm that also designed the Helen Hayes, Longacre, New Amsterdam, Liberty, and Lyceum theaters.

The Venetian Renaissance building was built by producers Winthrop Ames and Lee Shubert (*see* Shubert Brothers). The two men had built the New Theater on Central Park West, the northernmost location for a Broadway theater. That theater failed, and the impresarios decided to locate their next theater in a more traditional spot off Times Square. When their theater was finally finished in 1913, they named it after the noted 19th-century actor Edwin Booth. Because building laws prohibited protruding ornamentation, the

The Booth Theatre with its opening production, Arnold Bennett's *The Great Adventure*, 1913.

theater was decorated with polychromed stucco. The theater's intimacy is due to both its fine design and its small capacity (it has room for 808 people, including standees).

The first production to find success at the Booth was *Experience* (10/27/14; 255 performances), starring William Elliott. The next play, *The Bubble* (4/5/15; 176 performances), was also a hit. Another success, Clare Kummer's *A Successful Calamity* (2/5/17; 144 performances), starred William Gillette, Estelle Winwood, William Devereaux, and Roland Young. Although these were all hits, none had the impact of *Seventeen* (1/22/18; 225 performances), based on the story by Booth Tarkington. Ruth Gordon, Paul Kelly, and Gregory Kelly starred in the comedy. At once a celebration of small-town America's values and a loving look at the younger generation, *Seventeen* caught the imagination of theatergoers just as America was entering the First World War.

Seventeen was followed by many now-forgotten hits, including the George Arliss vehicle *The Green Goddess* (1/18/21; 440 performances). *Seventh Heaven* (10/30/22; 683 performances), starring Helen Menken and George Gaul, was an enormous hit by Austin Strong. HELEN HAYES played a flapper in *Dancing Mothers* (8/11/24; 311 performances), with Mary Young as her mother; it was the mother who turned out to be the real hellion. James Cagney was a dancer in two editions of the *Grand Street Follies*. The first premiered in 1928 with Cagney as choreographer; the second premiered a year later.

During the 1930s hits were scarce at the Booth. The theater's location kept it booked, but the plays did not enjoy long runs. Only when the decade was half over did the theater finally have a hit, George S. Kaufman and Moss Hart's (*see* KAUFMAN AND HART) great comedy *You Can't Take It with You* (12/14/36; 837 performances). The zany comedy won the PULITZER PRIZE, as did the next great hit at the Booth, *The Time of Your Life* (10/25/39; 185 performances). William Saroyan's play starred Eddie Dowling, Gene Kelly, William Bendix, Celeste Holm, Edward Andrews, and Julie Haydon.

Rose Franken's *Claudia* (2/12/41; 453 performances), starring Dorothy McGuire and Frances Starr, was the first big hit of the 1940s. Elisabeth Bergner, Vera Allen, Irene Worth, and Victor Jory starred in *The Two Mrs. Carrolls* (8/14/44), which eventually ran 585 performances. Another 1940s hit was Norman Krasna's *John Loves Mary* (2/4/47; 423 performances), starring Nina Foch in her Broadway debut.

Come Back Little Sheba (2/15/50; 190 performances), William Inge's first Broadway play, starred Shirley Booth and Sidney Blackmer. British comedienne Beatrice Lillie held forth in *An Evening with Beatrice Lillie* (10/2/52; 278 performances). Another Britisher, Cyril Ritchard, starred along with Eddie Meyehoff in Gore Vidal's sardonic comedy *Visit to a Small Planet* (2/7/57; 388 performances). Henry Fonda and Anne Bancroft starred in William Gibson's *Two for the Seesaw* (1/16/58; 754 performances). Paddy Chayefsky's spiritualistic comedy/drama *The Tenth Man* (11/5/59; 623 performances) was the last hit that the Booth enjoyed in the 1950s. Tyrone Guthrie directed Broadway veterans Jack Gilford, Lou Jacobi, Jacob Ben-Ami, George Voskovec, and future director Gene Saks.

In the 1960s Julie Harris triumphed in *A Shot in the Dark* (10/18/61; 389 performances), appearing on the stage along with Walter Matthau, Gene Saks, Diana van der Vlis, and William Shatner. Mike Nichols directed Alan Arkin, Eli Wallach, and Anne Jackson in Murray Schisgal's *Luv* (11/11/64; 902 performances). The decade ended with a production of Leonard Gershe's *Butterflies Are Free* (10/21/69; 1,133 performances). *That Championship Season* (9/14/72; 844 performances), was written by Jason Miller, who won a Pulitzer prize for his efforts. The play transferred from the Public Theater to the Booth. The next hit at the Booth was also a transfer from the Public Theater: Ntozake Shange's *For Colored Girls Who Have Considered Suicide When the Rainbow Is Enuf* (8/29/76; 742 performances).

Bernard Pomerance's *The Elephant Man* continued in the growing trend of plays opening in nonprofit theaters and then transferring to Broadway. The nonprofit arena took the place of the long out-of-town tryout tour. *The Elephant Man* (4/19/79; 916 performances), first produced by the theater at St. Peter's Church, starred a series of leading men, including Philip Anglim, David Bowie, and Mark Hamill. That same year saw a restoration/redesign of the theater's interior by designer Melanie Kahane.

STEPHEN SONDHEIM's *Sunday in the Park with George* (5/2/84; 604 performances), with book and direction by James Lapine, starred Bernadette Peters and Mandy Patinkin and won the Pulitzer prize. Herb Gardner's *I'm Not Rappaport* (11/19/85; 1,070 performances), starring Judd Hirsch and Cleavon Little, was a long-run tenant.

Among the other notable productions at the Booth Theatre were two one-person shows: Willy Russell's *Shirley Valentine* (2/16/89; 324 performances), starring Pauline Collins as an English housewife who dreams of escaping to the Greek Isles; and Jay Presson Allen's *Tru* (12/14/89), in which Robert Morse portrayed Truman Capote for 287 performances.

Two musical transfers followed at the Booth. The first, from Playwrights Horizons off Broadway, *Once on This Island* (10/18/90; 469 performances), marked the Broadway debuts of composer/lyricist team Stephen Flaherty and Lynn Ahrens. The second began life at the Goodspeed Opera House. Frank Loesser's *The Most Happy Fella* (2/13/92) enjoyed its second Broadway revival. Neither was successful, the latter playing 229 performances in spite of its greatly reduced budget (the accompaniment consisted of two pianos).

Emily Mann's biography of the Delaney sisters, two real-life senior citizens, opened at the Booth with Gloria Foster and Mary Alice comprising the entire cast. *Having Our Say* opened on April 6, 1995, and managed to enchant audiences for 317 performances.

Continuing with a small-cast trend on Broadway and especially at the Booth, the theater's next two inhabitants were stand-up comics. The first, Jackie Mason, opened his one-man show *Love Thy Neighbor* on March 24, 1996, and played for 234 performances. Rob Becker, an equally unsubtle comedian, transferred his *Defending the Caveman* from the HELEN HAYES THEATER. It opened at the Booth on January 29, 1997, and lasted six months, finally closing after a grand total of 674 Broadway performances.

The next production at the Booth had a cast of five: David Mamet's *The Old Neighborhood* (11/19/97; 197 performances) starred Patti LuPone and Peter Riegert for its brief run. There was one fewer performer in the next offering at the Booth. *An Evening with Jerry Herman*, featured Jerry Herman himself along with LeRoy Reems and Florence Lacey. Bassist Jared Egan rounded out the "cast." Audiences were less than enchanted to pay Broadway prices for essentially a cabaret show, and the show closed after only 28 performances following its July 28 opening. It was followed by a stint by Sandra Bernhard in the overly ambitiously titled *I'm Still Here . . . Damn It!* (11/5/98), which lasted all of 51 performances.

More one-person performances followed. David Hare himself starred in his own play, *Via Dolorosa* (3/18/99; 99 performances), a fascinating, thought-provoking, and sometimes moving lecture on the playwright's recent visit to Israel. Barry Humphries took over the star dressing room, emerging as his irrepressible character Dame Edna Everage in *Dame Edna: The Royal Tour* (10/17/99). Audiences were convulsed in one of the funniest, most irreverent, and intelligent shows for 297 performances. Dame Edna was accompanied by two showgirls, the Gorgeous Ednaette #1 and the Equally Gorgeous Ednaette #2, as well as an onstage pianist.

The sole booking for the year 2000 was a revival of Lily Tomlin's one-woman play, *The Search for Signs of Intelligent Life in the Universe*, written by Jane Wagner. It opened on November 16 and ran for 184 performances.

Bea Arthur, who, accompanied by Billy Goldenberg at the piano, appeared in *Bea Arthur on Broadway* (2/

17/2002; 65 performances). Her abridged run was due, most likely, to bad timing—Elaine Stritch had her own much-acclaimed one-person autobiographical show uptown at the NEIL SIMON THEATER.

On November 4, 1987, the New York City Landmarks Preservation Commission designated the interior and exterior of the theater a landmark. The commission stated: "The Venetian-inspired design by Henry B. Herts is particularly distinguished and responsive to its prominent site" on Shubert Alley. Its interior "is especially notable for its wood paneling, which enhances the acoustical qualities of the space."

BRADY, DIAMOND JIM. Financier and philanthropist, the most flamboyant of the Broadway characters at the turn of the 20th century; b. New York, New York, August 12, 1856; d. Baltimore, Maryland, April 13, 1917.

Diamond Jim Brady, dubbed "King of the Great White Way," is the symbol of the Gay 1990s. A constant companion to singer and actress Lillian Russell and a great gourmand, Brady was known for his largesse and largeness. Brady frequented the great lobster palaces of Broadway with a different woman on his arm nightly. It was rumored that Brady gave extravagant presents to his dates, but apparently the stories were just hype. Brady reportedly only lent the jewelry to his paramours for as long as the evening lasted. Once the lady was escorted home, her jewelry would stay with Brady.

He certainly would not have missed a brooch or two. Word on the Rialto had it that Brady owned 26,000 diamonds. He acquired his wealth from the sale of railroad equipment. At that time, before income taxes, conglomerates, and foreign imports, barons of industry such as Rockefeller, Carnegie, and Brady could acquire vast fortunes. Brady was said to have amassed a personal fortune of $12 million.

Brady encouraged his reputation. He had a sense of humor about himself, as indicated in an interview of 1909. Brady proclaimed:

> The trouble with our American men is that they over dress. They do not understand that beauty unadorned is adorned the most. Now, I take it that I am considered a handsome man and one who would be called well dressed. Never by any chance do I permit more than seventeen colors to creep into the pattern of my waistcoat. Moreover, I consider that twenty-eight rings are enough for any man to wear at one time. The others may be carried in the pocket and exhibited as occasion requires. A similar rule applies to the cuff and shirt studs. My favorite stud is a petrified prune. Three of them may be worn without entirely covering the shirt bosom. Diamonds larger than door knobs should never be worn except in the evening.

No one could have made that much money and still been the bon vivant the newspapers made him out to be. In fact, Brady was a serious businessman who had excesses but never ones that affected his acumen. He was born in New York City, the son of a saloon owner on Manhattan's West Side. A series of odd jobs led to a sales position with the New York Central Railroad in 1879, selling portable rail-cutting saws. He was such a natural salesman his income sometimes reached $1 million a year.

Brady liked to indulge himself, and he could afford to. He arrived at restaurants sporting diamonds on his cuffs, his watch chain, and his stickpin. His diamonds were large yellow, chunky stones, and it was reported in the *New York Herald* that his stickpin "lit up the road ahead of him like the headlight of a locomotive." But most of the stories and depictions of Brady were grossly exaggerated. Apparently he never wore more than a few stones at a time and then with as much reserve as a man of his size could.

Brady did live up to at least one of the legends surrounding him: he could eat vast quantities of food. The owners of RECTOR's reputedly called him "the twenty-five best customers we had." According to Morris Lloyd in his book *Incredible New York*, Brady boasted, "Whenever I sit down to a meal, I always make it a point to leave four inches between my stummick and the edge of the table. And then, when I can feel 'em rubbin' together pretty hard, I know I've had enough." Playwright and newspaperman Channing Pollock remembered Brady eating 36 oysters as an appetizer to lunch. But for all his culinary excesses, Brady was a teetotaler. He more than made up for it with his eating habits and could sometimes down several quarts of orange juice to quench his thirst. Once FLORENZ ZIEGFELD accompanied Brady to dinner and ordered exactly what Brady ordered. While Brady enthusiastically cleaned his plate, Ziegfeld emptied his plate into a nearby wine bucket. At the end of the meal Ziegfeld presented the overflowing container to Brady and informed him that all that food was in his stomach. But Brady was unfazed.

Perhaps he should have listened: Brady died of an intestinal ailment at Johns Hopkins University Hospital at the age of 60.

BRADY, WILLIAM A. Producer of melodramas, motion picture producer, and boxing promoter; b. San Francisco, California, June 19, 1863; d. New York, New York, June 6, 1950.

Producer William A. Brady is perhaps best remembered as a presenter of melodramatic plays like *Trilby* and Barrie's *Alice Sit-By-the-Fire*. He always mounted

William A. Brady, producer of *A Free Soul*, 1928.

his productions with the utmost taste, regardless of the cost, featuring performers under his management such as HELEN HAYES, Douglas Fairbanks, Grace George (his second wife), Alice Brady (his daughter), and Helen Gahagan.

Brady began his theatrical career in San Francisco in 1882. Following a move to New York, he leased the original MANHATTAN THEATER starting in 1896 and then built The PLAYHOUSE THEATRE in 1911 for his own productions. The next year he also became manager of the 48TH STREET THEATRE. Brady was one of the few producers—FLORENZ ZIEGFELD was another—who foresaw the powers of the new art of motion pictures. Brady owned a film distribution company, the World Film Corporation, in the late teens. He was president of the National Association of the Motion Picture Industry for five years beginning in 1915. President Woodrow Wilson appointed him chairman of a committee to organize the movie industry in 1917.

Brady was also renowned as a boxing promoter. Brady is the only man to manage two undisputed world heavyweight champions, James J. Corbett and James J. Jeffries (both of whom would, as champions, appear in Brady productions). Brady handled Corbett when the pugilist faced down John L. Sullivan. After splitting with Corbett, Brady began an association with Jeffries, Corbett's sometime sparring partner. The producer realized that Jeffries would never become a great boxer unless he had quality opponents and better training. So Brady arranged to hire Tommy Ryan, probably the greatest trainer of his time, and Jeffries was on his way to the title. Brady also managed Youssuf Ishmaelo, the "Terrible Turk," a world-renowned wrestler.

Eventually Brady gave up boxing. Among the plays he produced on Broadway were *Uncle Tom's Cabin* (3/4/01; 88 performances), *Foxy Grandpa* (2/17/02; 120 performances), *Way Down East* (12/14/03; 48 performances), *The Pit* (2/10/04; 27 performances), *Trilby* (5/8/05; 24 performances), *Baby Mine* (8/23/10; 287 performances), *Bought and Paid For* (9/26/11; 431 performances), *Bunty Pulls the Strings* (10/10/11; 381 performances), and *The White Feather* (2/4/15; 140 performances).

Way Down East was a particular triumph for Brady. The show was first seen in Newport, Rhode Island, on September 3, 1897. The play made little impression on its audience. The playwright, Lottie Blair Parker, acknowledging her inexperience, brought the play to Brady, who immediately saw its potential. Brady, Parker, and actor-manager Joseph R. Grismer reworked the play, and it soon became one of the most-performed plays of its day. Brady's belief in the play was further rewarded when he sold the film rights to D. W. Griffith for $175,000.

In April 1915 Brady produced, in partnership with the authors, a repertory season of Gilbert and Sullivan operettas. Among the company was the young GEORGE ABBOTT and DeWolf Hopper. Later productions produced by Brady include *The Ruined Lady* (1/19/20; 176 performances), *The Skin Game* (10/20/20; 176 performances), *Street Scene* (PULITZER PRIZE) (1/10/29; 601 performances), and *A Church Mouse* (10/12/31; 164 performances).

Brady employed the young Humphrey Bogart, the son of his doctor, as an office boy and, later, assistant company manager and production manager in Brady's Peerless Film Studio. Bogart was subsequently employed by the World Film Corporation, a movie production studio of which Brady was a major investor. The corporation was founded in February 1915 by Brady, the SHUBERT BROTHERS, Arthur Spiegel, head of the Spiegel catalogue company, and Lewis J. Selznick, a former jeweler and soon-to-be major Hollywood figure. Brady's film ventures began in 1913 and continued until 1920.

Brady wasn't viewed by all of his fellow Broadwayites in flattering terms. Franklin P. Adams wrote to Brady's onetime press agent (and literary lion) ROBERT BENCHLEY, "While some of my best friends are of the Semitic race, none of them is what you and I would call high-class, let alone Mr. Brady." This assessment of Brady's character might have more to do with his being Jewish than his manners.

Although Brady produced many of the most successful shows in Broadway history, he was often broke. In fact, in 1922 he admitted being broke 10 times in the preceding 20 years. VARIETY commented: "That carries no real news to Broadway, which knows that the line between solvency and stringency among Broadway producers is proverbially thin at most times. Being Broadway broke is a condition that has no equivalent in any other business save that, perhaps, of the racecourse. The purseless producer of today may be the prospective bonanza king of tomorrow."

Brady was an inverterate gambler, whether in the ring or on Broadway. He once said, "The Lord is always good to the honest gambler." Among the many stories illustrating Brady's disregard for the almighty dollar, Brady cut cards against gangster Arnold Rothstein, (*see* GANGSTERS) and won $15,000 with a single cut.

Brady also ran ship's pools, where people would gamble on the daily mileage of transatlantic steamships. Lucius Beebe wrote of Brady:

> Perhaps the most celebrated of all pool auctioneers in the early 1920's was William A. Brady, the Broadway producer, father of Alice Brady and married to Grace George, a brilliant comedienne. An inflammable Celt with a bottomless capacity for liquor, Brady was also a student of parliamentary law and a witty orator, in short the ideal man to auction a ship's pool in those affluent and uninhibited days.
>
> On occasion, when carried away with his own eloquence, not to mention ample potations as he labored, Brady would order wine for the entire smoke room out of his own pocket in order to beguile his audience into even higher bidding. Daily pools well in excess of 1,000 pounds ($5,000 in those times) were not uncommon when Brady sold them, and on one memorable occasion when his wife bid what turned out to be the winning number, it seemed wise for her to spend the entire sum next evening on drinks for everybody—to refute loudly voiced charges of collusion. A lot of drinks could be had for $5,000 in those days.

Brady was broke before and would be broke again (he lost another fortune in the 1929 Wall Street crash), but for all the ups and downs of his career he will be remembered as a smart entrepreneur who was able to adjust to the immense changes in popular culture as the century turned. The range of Brady's remarkable output of 260 productions, from *Way Down East* to *Street Scene*, was not that wide, but it demonstrates an ability to adapt to the changes in popular taste, an ability not shared by many of his contemporaries.

BRICE, FANNY. Among the most beloved of all Broadway performers of the first half of the 20th century; b. Fanny Borach, New York, New York, October 29, 1891; d. Hollywood, California, May 29, 1951.

Fanny Brice was one of the most versatile and popular actors on the Broadway stage in her heyday. Her range of characterization was incredible. She could be the broad, physical comedienne telling her Jewish-accented stories of Becky in the ballet and Mrs. Cohen at the beach as well as the lonely, soulful torch singer who introduced "My Man" to America. Later in her career she added still another facet to her stage personality, that of the irrepressible brat Baby Snooks.

Early on she recognized that the stage was the natural outlet for her flamboyant personality. At the age of 13, looking for a way to get into Keeney's Theatre in Brooklyn for free, she entered an amateur night contest. She sang "When You Know You're Not Forgotten by the Girl You Can't Forget" and won first prize, a $5 gold piece. Seeing how easy show business was, she continued to enter and win amateur contests. During this time she changed her name to Brice. Her

Fanny Brice sings "I'm an Indian" in the *Ziegfield Follies of 1920.*

mother, estranged from "Pinochle Charlie" Borach, also adopted the name Brice, as did her three other siblings.

Brice almost made it to Broadway when GEORGE M. COHAN cast her in a musical, but her inability to dance caused her to be fired. She took dancing lessons and joined the Traveling Burlesque Company. When the leading lady dropped out of an evening performance, Fanny was summoned in her stead. Unable to play the number straight, Brice turned it into a comic tour de force. It was then she decided to become a comedian. The next year she was cast by producer Max Speigel for his musical *College Girls.* She needed a number for her specialty turn and went to the young IRVING BERLIN, who wrote "Sadie Salome" for her to perform with a Yiddish accent.

Brice soon drew the attention of FLORENZ ZIEGFELD, who starred her in seven editions of his *Follies,* in 1910, 1911, 1916, 1917, 1920, 1921, and 1923. She later appeared in two more ZIEGFELD FOLLIES, this time presented by the SHUBERT BROTHERS, in 1934 and 1936. Her other stage appearances were in *The Honeymoon Express* (2/6/13; 156 performances), *Music Box Revue* (12/1/24; 184 performances), *Fioretta* (2/5/29; 111 performances), and two for her husband, producer Billy Rose: *Sweet and Low* (11/17/30; 184 performance), and *Crazy Quilt* (5/19/31; 79 performances). Among the songs she introduced are "My Man," "Rose of Washington Square," "Second Hand Rose," and "I Found a Million Dollar Baby in a Five and Ten Cent Store."

After leaving the theater, Brice had a successful career on radio, mostly portraying Baby Snooks. She made a few movies and recordings, but they didn't reflect her importance as a star. Brice's life provided the material for the Broadway musical *Funny Girl* (3/26/64), which was later transferred to the screen. The sequel, *Funny Lady,* also became a hit movie. Barbra Streisand portrayed Fanny Brice in all three projects.

BRILL BUILDING. 1619 Broadway. Architect: Victor Bork Jr. Completed in 1930.

The Brill Building has long been the nexus of popular music in New York. The 10-story building at the corner of 49th Street and Broadway was the embodiment of Tin Pan Alley (or, as it was dubbed in the 1950s, Teen Pan Alley). The building was named after the Brill Brothers, who owned a clothing store on the ground floor. They bought the building from its owners, who went bankrupt in the worsening Depression.

With a depressed real estate market, soon music publishers began renting office space in the building. The first three were Southern Music, Mills Music, and Famous Music. Shortly thereafter others followed, and by 1962 there were 165 music businesses in the Brill Building.

The building's success was due in large part to what would eventually become known as vertical integration. A song could be written in the building, arranged by musicians renting space there, copied in the duplication office, sung by singers and musicians who prowled the halls, and made into a demo record in one of the building's studios. The demo could then be peddled to one of the building's publishers, who could approach managers and radio promoters—all in one spot.

Songwriter Ellie Greenwich described life in the Brill Building to music historian/producer Alan Betrock: "We used to write songs in the morning, then record a demo and go around playing it for different people later in the day. If they liked it, they'd pay for an hour or hour and a half at a demo studio . . . and we'd go cut it. If we sold the song we'd get an advance, usually something like thirty-five or fifty dollars—maybe seventy-five or a hundred dollars, if you were really lucky—and then we'd go back and write some more."

Greenwich worked there with her then-husband, Jeff Berry. They wrote songs and produced hits for many artists. Among their hit songs written at the Brill Building are "Da Doo Ron Ron," "Why Do Lovers Break Each Other's Hearts," "Baby I Love You," "Chapel of Love," "Be My Baby," "River Deep, Mountain High," "Then He Kissed Me," "I Have a Boyfriend," and "I Can Hear Music." "Chapel of Love" was issued on the Red Bird label, which was owned by two other denizens of the Brill Building, Jerry Lieber and Mike Stoller.

Songwriters Lieber and Stoller, in addition to owning Red Bird, wrote many hits at the Brill Building and also ran Red Bird's recording studio there. Phil Spector, later to become a legendary record producer, slept on the songwriters' couch and learned how to engineer recordings from Lieber and Stoller. In fact, Spector's group, the Ronettes, recorded "Chapel of Love" right after Red Wing's release hit the stores. Spector's "Wall of Sound" was perfected in the Brill Building studios.

Among the great songwriters who worked out of the Brill Building were Barry Mann and Cythia Weil ("You've Lost That Lovin' Feeling," "On Broadway," "Soul and Inspiration," "We Gotta Get Out of This Place"), Doc Pomus and Mort Shuman ("A Teenager in Love," "Turn Me Loose," "Little Sister"), Neil Diamond, Lesley Gore, Burt Bacharach and Hal David, Gerry Coffin and Carole King, Toni Wine, Richard Gottehrer ("I Want Candy," "My Boyfriend's Back"), Neil Sedaka and Howie Greenfield, and in the 1990s, Paul Simon.

Alan Freed had his music publishing business in the Brill Building, and producer Gus Sharkey also had offices there.

The Brill Building was also home to many Broadway songwriters. Richard Adler recalled meeting his partner, Jerry Ross, for the first time outside the Brill Building. "The Brill Building *was* Tin Pan Alley. Every morning, about noon, all these songwriters would pour onto the street in front of the Brill Building and hob-nob, saying 'Let's write a song together' or whatever. The music business was fun in those days. That's where I met Jerry. Al Hoffmann introduced me to him. Al was a title man. He gave Bob Merrill the title of some of his big songs. Al didn't ever do anything for you but give you a title."

BROADHURST THEATER. 235 W. 44th Street. Architect: Herbert J. Krapp. Opening: September 27, 1917; *Misalliance*.

The Broadhurst Theater was built by the Shuberts and playwright/producer George H. Broadhurst as a companion for the PLYMOUTH THEATER. They were located next to another two linked theaters, the BOOTH and the Shubert (*see* SAM S. SHUBERT THEATRE). The land for all four theaters had been leased from the Astor estate to the Shuberts. Like the two earlier theaters, the Broadhurst and Plymouth had a pedestrian alley adjacent to their side exits. The alley, now closed off, was parallel to the more famous Shubert Alley.

The 1,155-seat theater has been among the most popular Broadway theaters, housing major hits in almost every decade since its opening. It opened with William Faversham's production of George Bernard Shaw's *Misalliance* (9/27/17; 52 performances). However, this New York run gave little indication of the play's later renown. The Broadhurst was equally suitable for musicals. The first hit musical was the Nora Bayes vehicle *Ladies First* (10/24/18; 164 performances). Rachel Crothers' *39 East* (3/31/19; 160 performances) starred Alison Skipworth. *Smilin' Through* (12/30/19; 175 performances), later a successful movie, starred Jane Cowl, who co-authored the play with Allan Langdon Martin.

During the 1920s, there were many hits at the theater, including George S. Kaufman (*see* KAUFMAN AND HART) and Marc Connelly's *Beggar on Horseback* (2/12/24; 224 performances); Michael Arlen's *The Green Hat* (9/15/25), starring KATHARINE CORNELL as the bride whose husband commits suicide on their wedding night; and Jed Harris' production of *Broadway* (9/16/26; 603 performances), by Philip Dunning and GEORGE ABBOTT. Almost as successful was the DE SYLVA, BROWN, AND HENDERSON musical *Hold Everything* (10/10/28; 413 performances). The hit song was

"You're the Cream in My Coffee." George S. Kaufman returned to the Broadhurst with *June Moon* (10/9/29; 272 performances), written in collaboration with Ring Lardner. Beginning in 1929, the Shuberts assumed full control of the theater.

George Abbott and Philip Dunning produced another hit at the Broadhurst, Ben Hecht and Charles MacArthur's screwball comedy *Twentieth Century* (12/29/32; 154 performances). Another play first presented at the Broadhurst became a hit movie. The gangster drama *The Petrified Forest* (1/7/35; 194 performances) featured Leslie Howard and Humphrey Bogart in the leads. Later that year HELEN HAYES turned in an astounding performance in Gilbert Miller's production of *Victoria Regina* (12/26/35; 204 performances); the drama also starred Vincent Price.

The 1940s were marked by a series of now forgotten musicals, including *Boys and Girls Together* (10/1/40), with Bert Lahr; *High Kickers* (10/31/41), with George Jessel and Sophie Tucker; and *Early to Bed* (6/17/43), with an exceptional Fats Waller score. Helen Hayes starred in Anita Loos' comedy *Happy Birthday* (10/31/46; 564 performances), one of the few nonmusicals produced by RODGERS AND HAMMERSTEIN.

The 1950s was a decade of great successes at the Broadhurst. The revival of RODGERS AND HART'S sardonic musical *Pal Joey* (12/25/50; 540 performances), starring Harold Lang and Vivienne Segal, actually played longer than the original production. Rosalind Russell gave a tremendous performance in a role that will be forever linked with her, *Auntie Mame* (10/31/56; 639 performances). *The World of Suzie Wong* (10/14/58; 508 performances) starred William Shatner and France Nuyen. The decade closed with a huge hit, the Pulitzer prize–winning musical *Fiorello!* (11/23/59; 796 performances). Jerry Bock and Sheldon Harnick (*see* BOCK AND HARNICK) wrote the score, and George Abbott and Jerome Weidman contributed the book with Abbott also directing; Robert E. Griffith and HAROLD PRINCE produced. Tom Bosley achieved fame portraying the larger-than-life-size Mayor Fiorello LaGuardia.

Tommy Steele starred at the Broadhurst in *Half a Sixpence* (4/25/65; 512 performances), a musicalization of H. G. Wells' novel *Kipps*. Among the outstanding elements in the production was Hilary Knight's beautiful POSTER. Woody Allen's comedy *Play It Again, Sam* (2/12/69; 453 performances) starred the comic along with Tony Roberts and Diane Keaton. *Twigs* (11/14/71; 289 performances), by George Furth, featured a song by STEPHEN SONDHEIM; Sada Thompson starred.

A huge hit (for a while it was the longest-running musical in Broadway history) was *Grease*. It originated off Broadway and moved to the Broadhurst on June 7, 1972. After skipping around to other theaters, it eventually tallied 3,388 performances. NEIL SIMON'S *The Sunshine Boys* (12/20/72; 538 performances) followed. *Godspell*, another long-running off Broadway musical, moved to the Broadhurst, eventually managing 2,118 performances. Bob Fosse's choreographic *Dancin'* (3/27/78; 1,774 performances) was another hit at the popular theater. During the 1980s, the theater hosted Peter Shaffer's smash *Amadeus* (12/17/80; 1,181 performances), with Ian McKellen and Tim Curry in the leads.

The Tap Dance Kid (12/21/83; 669 performances) was the next show at the Broadhurst. *Dreamgirls* composer Henry Krieger wrote the music, and Richard Lorick provided the lyrics. The show starred Alfonso Ribeiro, Samuel E. Wright, Hinton Battle, and Hattie Winston.

Neil Simon's plays occupied the Broadhurst stage for most of the last half of the decade. First, Rita Moreno and Sally Struthers headed up the "female version" of Neil Simon's play *The Odd Couple* (6/11/85; 295 performances). The show marked the first time in Broadway history that the sex of the lead characters in a previously produced play would be changed for a subsequent production. Following revivals of EUGENE O'NEILL'S *Long Day's Journey into Night* and *The Life and Adventures of Nicholas Nickleby*, two more Simon plays premiered at the Broadhurst. *Broadway Bound* (12/4/86; 756 performances) completed Simon's autobiographical trilogy, begun with *Brighton Beach Memoirs* and *Biloxi Blues*. This time Jonathan Silverman played the young Eugene. He was ably supported by Linda Lavin, Phyllis Newman, and Jason Alexander. *Biloxi Blues* was followed at the Broadhurst with Simon's next offering, *Rumors* (11/17/88; 535 performances). The play received mixed reviews from the critics and would prove to be Simon's last Broadway success until *The Dinner Party* in 2001.

One of ANDREW LLOYD WEBBER's rare Broadway failures followed. *Aspects of Love* (4/8/90; 377 performances) had lyrics by Charles Hart and Don Black. Lloyd Webber adapted the libretto himself. At the time of its closing, *Aspects of Love*, despite being a relatively modest production, was the costliest flop in Broadway history.

Following a series of short-lived offerings, the Broadhurst hosted a huge hit, John Kander and Fred Ebb's *The Kiss of the Spider Woman* (5/3/93; 906 performances). Terrance McNally contributed the book based on Manuel Puig's novel. Chita Rivera, Brent Carver, and Anthony Crivello shone under Harold Prince's exemplary direction.

George Furth and Stephen Sondheim, who had last collaborated on the musicals *Company* and *Merrily We*

Helen Hayes in *Victoria Regina*, 1935.

Roll Along, teamed up on a "comedy thriller," *Getting Away with Murder* (3/17/96). Even Sondheim fans couldn't keep the play open more than 17 performances.

Neil Simon returned to the Broadhurst following Sarah Jessica Parker's appearance in an ill-conceived revival of *Once upon a Mattress* (12/19/96; 188 performances) that failed in every respect. Simon's play *Proposals* opened on November 6, 1997, and only managed to run 77 performances.

The Broadhurst's next hit was the musical retrospective of the career of Bob Fosse, logically named *Fosse* (1/14/99). Chet Walker conceived the evening, aided by Ann Reinking, Richard Maltby Jr., and Gwen Verdon. Although there were no "names" in the cast (possibly excepting Scott Wise), the choreography was only sometimes based on Fosse's original, and the numbers were taken out of context, the evening entertained audiences for 1,093 performances.

The theater hosted a revival of Stephen Sondheim and James Lapine's *Into the Woods* (4/2/2002; 279 performances), starring Vanessa Williams.

The Broadhurst is one of Broadway's most successful theaters. Although the shows it houses are not always hits, the theater is usually booked and always popular with producers and audiences alike. On November 10, 1987, the New York City Landmarks Preservation commission designated the exterior of the theater a landmark. The Commission stated that the Broadhurst was important because "the facade of the theater is a response to its Shubert Alley location and the earlier Shubert-Booth pair."

BROADWAY THEATRE (1). 1445 Broadway. Architect: J. B. McElfatrick. Opening: March 3, 1888; *La Tosca.*

As the theater district approached Longacre Square, one of the first theatre buildings was the Metropolitan Concert Hall at 41st and Broadway. Built in May 1880, the concert hall was never a success. It became the Metropolitan Casino, the Alcazar, the Cosmopolitan Theatre, a roller-skating rink, and an exhibition hall. It was demolished in 1887 to make way for the Broadway Theatre, a very successful venture.

James Bailey of Barnum and Bailey Circus fame purchased the Cosmopolitan Skating Rink and hired J. B. McElfatrick to transform the interior. Before the theater was completed, Bailey sold his interest to T. Henry French, Frank Sanger, and Elliot Zborowski. French was the son of Samuel French, whose name graces the still popular play-publishing business he founded. Sanger was the owner of a national chain of theaters. The new theater was immense for the time, seating 1,776 patrons plus standing room for an additional 500, and it had a 75-foot-wide stage. The Broad-

way had a Romanesque exterior and inside was decorated in a vaguely Near Eastern style with tapestries, copper and glass chandeliers, and Persian lamps. Electric lights provided illumination and also were used architecturally in the design. The fronts of the Broadway's two balconies were less concave than the usual horseshoe shape, thus improving the sight lines

The Broadway opened on March 3, 1888, with a production of Victorien Sardou's *La Tosca*, starring Fanny Davenport. Like many theaters of the time, the Broadway was the home to acting companies, in this case ones led by De Wolf Hopper and Francis Wilson. Both companies specialized in comic operas. The opening of *La Tosca*, starring Fanny Davenport, Frank Mordaunt as Scarpia, Melbourne Macdowell as Mario Cavaradossi, and Judith Berolde as Reine Marie Carolina, was auspicious, signaling a great future for the theatre. But just a week later came the great blizzard of 1888. Life in New York, and particularly the theater, came to an abrupt halt. Following the blizzard, which began on Sunday night, March 11, all theaters in New York closed. By the end of the week, life began to return to normal, but the damage was done. *La Tosca* closed on March 28 at a great loss.

A classic theater piece, *Little Lord Fauntleroy*, premiered at the theater with the title role played alternately by Elsie Leslie and Tommy Russell. Also appearing at the opening were J. H. Gilmour as the Earl of Dorincourt, Kathryn Kidder as Mrs. Errol, and Alice Fischer portraying Minna. At the 100th performance, Elsie Leslie played the first act and Tommy Russell the second. The fall of 1889 saw a remarkable joint appearance by Madame Modjeska and Edwin Booth at the Broadway, appearing in repertory performing *Much Ado About Nothing, The Merchant of Venice, Hamlet, Macbeth*, and *Richelieu*. The great Otis Skinner was also in the rep; they were his last stage performances. Another great performer, De Wolf Hopper, achieved star status (in an era when one had to earn having one's name above the title) in *Castles in the Air*. He was joined on stage by Della Fox, Marion Manola, Anna O'Keefe, and Thomas Q. Seabrooke.

Another historic event occurred onstage at the Broadway. In 1890 Mrs. Leslie Carter made her acting debut in *The Ugly Duckling*. Her debut went largely unnoticed because the play opened on November 10 and closed on the 22nd of the month. She would achieve her great fame with her appearance later in *The Heart of Maryland*. The next year Edwin Booth made his final New York stage appearance at the Broadway in *Hamlet*. Lawrence Barrett appeared in a variety of productions at the Broadway, including William Young's *Ganelon, Much Ado About Nothing, Romeo and Juliet*, and *Francesca da Rimini*. Unfortunately, Barrett contracted pneumonia during this repertory season and died on March 20, 1891. In 1903, Sir

The first Broadway Theatre, January 29, 1928.

Henry Irving made his final stage appearance in *Dante* (10/26/03; 14 performances) on the Broadways stage.

The greatest production to play the Broadway is undoubtedly *Ben Hur* (11/29/1899; 194 performances). The cast included Frank Mordaunt, Emmett Corrigan, Frederick Perry, Corona Riccardo, Mabel Bert, and Mary Shaw. Real horses were used on treadmills in the chariot race, to the amazement of audiences. *Ben Hur* was certainly the most spectacular production of the turn of the century.

From 1903 on the Broadway almost exclusively hosted musicals. Among the rare exceptions were two seasons of Shakepeare's plays in repertory. Beginning on December 5, 1910, the Broadway hosted E. H. Southern and Julia Marlowe starring with their company in *Macbeth, As You Like It, Romeo and Juliet,* and *Hamlet.* Southern and Marlowe returned on July 3, 1911, with a repertoire that included productions of *Hamlet, The Merchant of Venice, Romeo and Juliet,* and *Twelfth Night.*

Librettist/lyricist Glen MacDonough, best remembered as collaborator with VICTOR HERBERT on *Babes in Toyland*, had 3 musicals in a row at the Broadway. Two, *The Midnight Sons* (5/22/09; 257 performances) and *The Jolly Bachelors* (1/6/10; 84 performances), had music by Raymond Hubbell. The next,

The Summer Widowers (6/4/10; 140 performances), boasted music by the prolific A. Baldwin Sloane. Sloane and Hubbell (along with lyricist E. Ray Goetz) would return to the Broadway with *The Hen-Pecks* (2/4/11; 137 performances) and *The Never Homes* (10/5/11; 92 performances). Sloane and Goetz would continue their collaboration at the Broadway with three shows in one season. These were the BURLESQUE *Hokey Pokey* and *Bunty Bulls and Strings* (a burlesque on the play *Bunty Pulls the Strings*) (2/8/12; 108 performances), *Hanky Panky* (8/5/12; 10 performances), and *The Sun Dodgers* (11/30/12; 29 performances).

The Broadway Theatre left the legitimate field in 1913 after the musical *The American Maid* (3/13/13; 16 performances), which boasted music and lyrics by John Philip Sousa. Following its legitimate policy, vaudeville and movies took over its stage. The theater finally closed on January 2nd, 1929, with the final performance of the vaudeville show *Broadway Fever.* The theater was torn down in 1929 and replaced with a garment center building.

BROADWAY THEATRE (2). 1681 Broadway. Architect: Eugene DeRosa. Opening: As the Colony motion picture theater, December 25, 1924. As a legitimate theater, December 8, 1930; *The New Yorkers.*

Vaudeville theater owner B. S. Moss opened Universal's Colony Theater as a premier motion picture house on Christmas Day 1924 with a showing of the Douglas Fairbanks silent film *The Thief of Bagdad*. Five years later, after the introduction of sound pictures, the theater adapted a legitimate policy. Its name was changed to B. S. Moss' Broadway Theatre with the opening performance of its first show, COLE PORTER's *The New Yorkers* (12/8/30; 158 performances). (There was a previous Broadway Theatre at Broadway and 41st Street, but that theater was razed in 1929; *see* BROADWAY THEATRE [1].) The 1,765-seat theater was suited only for large musicals. *The New Yorkers* filled the bill. The show, which starred Jimmy Durante, Fred Waring and His Pennsylvanians, and Ann Pennington, is best remembered for the song "Love for Sale," which caused enormous controversy. In fact, the song, sung by a prostitute under a streetlight, was banned from radio broadcast.

The name of the theater was slightly altered to Earl Carroll's Broadway Theatre with the opening of EARL CARROLL's VANITIES (9/27/32; 87 performances), starring Milton Berle, Helen Broderick, Robert Cummings, and Patsy Kelly. Even the great HAROLD ARLEN and Ted Koehler song "I've Gotta Right to Sing the Blues" couldn't help the box office. The failure of the first shows at the theater was a symptom of the general malaise that afflicted Broadway during the early years of the Depression. In 1932 the theater began a vaudeville policy, but it too failed. Another unsuccessful musical, *The O'Flynn* (12/27/34; 11 performances), opened at the theater and quickly closed. The theater's name reverted to B. S. Moss' Broadway Theatre on October 12, 1935, when it again showed films. The name was changed yet again to the Cine Roma on February 25, 1937, with the showing of *Lealta di Donna*. The name was changed for the last time to simply Broadway on November 13, 1940, when Walt Disney's cartoon feature *Fantasia* opened.

Fantasia was not a success for Disney or the theater, and again the Broadway housed live theater. A number of musicals that had opened at other houses moved to the Broadway to finish their runs. The first musical to originate at the theater under the new policy was IRVING BERLIN's *This Is the Army*, which opened, significantly, on July 4, 1942 (113 performances). *This Is the Army* starred armed-services members Burl Ives, Gary Merrill, Ezra Stone, and Philip Truex. Composer Irving Berlin also starred, and he reprised "Oh, How I Hate to Get up in the Morning," which he first sang in *Yip Yip Yaphank* (8/19/18). OSCAR HAMMERSTEIN II based his all-black production of *Carmen Jones* (12/2/43; 582 performances) on Bizet's *Carmen*. Another classic, *The Beggar's Opera*, was transformed by Duke Ellington and John Latouche into *Beggar's Holiday*

(12/26/46; 111 performances), with Alfred Drake, Zero Mostel, Avon Long, and Herbert Ross in the cast.

During the 1950s a series of unsuccessful productions were staged at the Broadway until Sammy Davis Jr. held forth in *Mr. Wonderful* (3/22/56; 383 performances). The show introduced a hit song, "Too Close for Comfort." A short period of Cinerama films followed before the theater hosted its finest show: DAVID MERRICK and Leland Heyward's production of *Gypsy* (5/21/59; 702 performances). ETHEL MERMAN had the greatest role of her career, singing brilliant JULE STYNE and STEPHEN SONDHEIM standards.

The 1960s were lean years for Broadway and for the Broadway Theatre. It was treated to an ill-conceived remodeling that removed most of its detailing and character. Merman returned to the theater in its next genuine hit, the 1966 revival of ANNIE GET YOUR GUN; the revival moved to the Broadway from Lincoln Center. Robert Goulet and David Wayne appeared in *The Happy Time* (1/18/68; 286 performances) with a fine John Kander and Fred Ebb score.

Director HAROLD PRINCE brought his reinterpretation of the musical *Candide* (3/10/74), by John Latouche, LEONARD BERNSTEIN, Lillian Hellman, Dorothy Parker, and Richard Wilbur, to the Broadway. Another revival, a black version of *Guys and Dolls*, was less successful two years later. The 1970s closed with Harold Prince directing Patti LuPone in the ANDREW LLOYD WEBBER and Tim Rice musical *Evita* (9/25/79; 1,568 performances).

The Broadway had another huge hit with *Les Misérables* (3/12/87; 6,680 performances), which received mixed reviews in London and New York but conquered American audiences. After that show moved to the IMPERIAL THEATRE, the Broadway was surrounded by a remarkably soulless 35-story skyscraper (designed by Fox & Fowle) covered in polished granite and cantilevered over the auditorium. Broadwayites commended the developers for sparing the historic theater from destruction.

Cameron Mackintosh, one of the most successful of London's producers, followed his production of *Les Misérables* with another smash hit, *Miss Saigon* (4/11/91). The show equaled its London success, eventually playing 4,092 performances. *Miss Saigon* was followed by something altogether different, *Blast* (4/17/2001), a celebration of marching band halftime festivities with an "up with people" attitude. Amazingly, it ran for 180 performances.

On November 17, 1987, the New York City Landmarks Preservation Commission denied landmark status to the theater.

BROOKS ATKINSON THEATER. 256 W. 47th Street. Architect: Herbert J. Krapp. Original name: The

Mansfield. Opening: February 15, 1926; *The Night Duel.*

The Brooks Atkinson Theater was originally owned by the Chanin brothers, who named it after actor Richard Mansfield. The Mansfield was the third theater built by the Chanins, but they lost them all in the Depression. The 999-seat house proved perfect for intimate dramas and small revues. In its early years, when production costs were lower and musicals did not have to occupy huge, barnlike theaters, some book shows held forth from the Mansfield's stage.

The Mansfield had its first hit with a now-forgotten drama, *The Ladder* (10/22/26; 794 performances). Antoinette Perry, for whom the TONY AWARDS are named, made her second appearance at the Mansfield in this show. Despite negative reviews, millionaire Edgar B. Davis liked the show and poured over $500,000 into it to keep it running. With *The Ladder*, the theater's only success in its first years, and unprofitable at that,

the Chanins' booking policy was clearly amiss. Lew Fields (*see* FIELDS FAMILY) took over booking the house and renamed it Lew Fields' Mansfield Theater. He opened his new theater on October 26, 1928, with RODGERS AND HART's *Present Arms* (10/26/28; 147 performances), and followed it with the same team's *Chee-Chee* (9/25/28; 32 performances). Fields next produced and starred in the aptly titled *Hello Daddy!* (12/26/28; 196 performances). He hired his children Herbert and Dorothy (*see* FIELDS FAMILY) to supply the book and lyrics, respectively; Jimmy McHugh wrote the music.

The theater was then renamed the Mansfield Theater, and *Indiscretion*, a failure, opened on March 4, 1929. The theater's next show, *The Green Pastures* (2/26/30; 640 performances), was Marc Connelly's adaptation of Roark Bradford's *Ol' Man Adam an' His Chillun*, a retelling of Old Testament stories. Connelly won the Pulitzer prize for his efforts.

Mansfield Theatre featuring *The Ladder* and Biltmore Theatre with *Loose Ankles* on the marquee, 1926.

When the Chanins lost the theater in 1933, the Mansfield went dark. From March to December of 1932 there were no bookings at the theater. The Depression continued to take its toll, and the theater did not house a hit until *Behind Red Lights* (1/13/37; 176 performances), a play about prostitution on the fashionable East Side of Manhattan. A revue, *Meet the People* (12/25/40; 160 performances), introduced Nanette Fabray to Broadway audiences. *Anna Lucasta* (8/30/44; 957 performances) arrived direct from the American Negro Theater in Harlem. Hilda Simms, Canada Lee, and Earle Hyman starred. Actress Ruth Gordon's autobiographical play *Years Ago* (12/3/46; 206 performances) starred Bethel Leslie.

After a series of failures, the Mansfield spent the 1950s as a television theater. On September 12, 1960, owner Michael Myerberg, who had bought the theater in 1945, renovated the auditorium and renamed the theater after critic Brooks Atkinson. The opening show was a lively musical revue *Vintage '60* (9/13/60). Despite songs by such future greats as Sheldon Harnick (*see* BOCK AND HARNICK) and Fred Ebb, and cast members Bert Convy and Michele Lee, the show ran only 8 performances.

The first hit under the theater's new name was also NEIL SIMON's Broadway debut. *Come Blow Your Horn* opened on February 22, 1961, and ran for 677 performances. The success of *Come Blow Your Horn* proved to be the theater's only long-running hit in the 1960s, forcing Meyerberg to take the Nederlanders as partners in 1967. The next hit was Peter Nichols' brilliant *A Day in the Death of Joe Egg* (2/1/68; 154 performances). Bravura performances by Albert Finney and Zena Walker kept the play running until the actors' strike of 1968 (June 17–19) forced it to close.

The first hit of the 1970s was Julian Barry's biographical play *Lenny* (5/26/71; 453 performances). Cliff Gorman electrified audiences as comic Lenny Bruce. Upon Myerberg's death in 1974 the Nederlanders purchased his share in the theater. The theater's next success was the two-character comedy *Same Time, Next Year* (3/13/75; 1,453 performances), with Ellen Burstyn and Charles Grodin. Lanford Wilson's play *Talley's Folly* moved from off Broadway on February 20, 1980. Judd Hirsch starred with Trish Hawkins. There would not be another hit at the Brooks Atkinson until *Noises Off* (12/11/83; 553 performances), Michael Frayn's knockabout farce, starring Dorothy Loudon, Brian Murray, and Victor Garber. Then comedian Jackie Mason in his one-man show *The World According to Me* scored a surprise hit. Borschtbelt comic Mason opened on December 22, 1986, to rave reviews and sold-out houses.

The theater's next notable production was Ariel Dorfman's *Death and the Maiden* (3/17/92; 159 performances). Glenn Close, Richard Dreyfuss, and Gene Hackman were the cast. Seven years would pass before the theater would again have a hit. Again, a Hollywood star brought in the crowds. Kevin Spacey starred in a revival of Eugene O'Neill's *The Iceman Cometh* (4/8/99; 102 performances).

On November 4, 1987, the New York City Landmarks Preservation Commission designated the interior and exterior of the theater a landmark. The commission stated: "Its facade is an excellent example of the romantic, eclectic 'modern Spanish' style. Its interior, reflecting the supervision of Roman Melzer, formerly architect to Czar Nicholas II of Russia, is an unusually handsome design."

BROWN, JOHN MASON. Critic; b. Louisville, Kentucky, July 3, 1900, d. New York, New York, March 16, 1969.

After graduating from Harvard University, Brown joined THEATRE ARTS MAGAZINE as an associate editor and drama critic. He remained with *Theatre Arts* from 1924 to 1928. He also lectured at the American Laboratory Theater from 1924 through 1931. Brown was drama critic for the *New York Evening Post* from 1929 to 1941. He then moved to the *New York World-Telegram* for one season. During the war, Brown was on the staff of Vice Admiral Alan G. Kirk and found himself at the Sicily and Normandy landings. In 1944 he became drama critic of the *Saturday Review of Literature*, a post he held until 1955. He also had a successful academic career as a dramatic arts teacher at the University of Montana (1923, 1929, 1931), Yale (1932), Middlebury College (1935–1936), and Harvard (1937–1940). Brown wrote many books on the theater, including *The Modern Theatre in Revolt* (1929), *Upstage: The American Theatre in Performance* (1930), *The Art of Playgoing* (1936), *Two on the Aisle* (1938), *Broadway in Review* (1940), *Seeing Things* (1950), *Seeing More Things* (1948), and *Still Seeing Things* (1950). Brown also became America's best-known lecturer on the American theater.

John Mason Brown.

BROWN, LEW. *See* **De Sylva, Brown, and Henderson.**

BRYANT THEATER. *See* **Apollo Theatre.**

BURLESQUE. The term *burlesque* conjures up images of strippers strutting down a runway before an audience of cigar-chewing, dirty old men. But there were really two kinds of burlesque in America. Of course, by the time of the strip acts, the burlesque shows of the first type were long gone. The original burlesque was broad parodies of popular plays and entertainments of the turn of the century. These burlesques were performed as afterpieces or during act breaks. The company would lampoon current hits using titles like *Bad Breath, The Crane of Chowder; Hamlet and Egglet; Much Ado About a Merchant of Venice*; *Julius the Siezes; Roman Nose and Suet*; and *The Charge of the Hash Brigade*. Popular performers weren't sacred either. Jenny Lind became Jenny Leatherlungs, as portrayed by Lotta Crabtree, and Sarah Bernhardt became Sarah Heartburn. Harrigan and Hart were among the best-loved presenters of burlesques. In the early 1870s they presented *The Two Awfuls*, a satire on *The Two Orphans*.

The other burlesque was one that started with lower-class entertainments. Saloons, beer gardens, and honky-tonks were poor man's vaudeville, with boxing matches staged between the coarse acts. In 1886 Niblo's Gardens in New York presented *The Black Crook*. The formation of the show was entirely accidental. A French ballet troupe was due to perform at the Academy of Music in downtown New York. However, the theater burned down, and the company was stranded. At the same time, a melodrama, *The Black Crook*, was due to open at Niblo's Garden. The play was a weak reworking of the Faust legend, and William Wheatley, manager of Niblo's, brought in the ballet company to upgrade the entertainment. The show ran over five hours, but the audience was transfixed at the sight of lightly clothed ballerinas.

But burlesque had an even earlier precursor. Two decades before *The Black Crook* astonished audiences in New York and around the country, Lydia Thompson arrived on our shores with her British Blondes. She opened under the management of Samuel Colville and Alexander Henderson at Wood's Theatre, New York, on September 28 in Burnand's burlesque *Ixion*. The show was similar to our own lady minstrel shows, with double-entendre songs and artfully posed beauties clad in gauzy material. The success of these two entertainments was unique in American theater history. *The Black Crook* played for over 16 months in Manhattan and made over a million dollars. Lydia Thompson toured America for six years in such shows as *Ixion*, *Sinbad, The Forty Thieves, Aladdin, La Sonnambula, Ivanhoe*, and others.

A Chicago newspaper critic hit the nail on the head when he observed that the girls "really had nothing to offer but their persons." These two phenomena: the Lydia Thompson troupe and *The Black Crook*, and their common denominator, "girls, girls, girls," didn't escape the notice of showmen.

Soon small circuits or "wheels" were set up, like vaudeville's Orpheum circuit and United Booking Office. Lawrence Weber was the biggest manager, and the most extensive wheels were the Columbia and Mutual. Sam T. Jack opened the most prestigious of these theaters, the New York Theater. T. E. Miaco, Samuel Scribner, and the Minskys were other moguls of the "art." The Minskys' WINTER GARDEN THEATRE on Houston Street in downtown Manhattan was their flagship, which also included the APOLLO and Republic (*see* NEW VICTORY THEATRE) in midtown.

While there were also comic sketches, illustrated songs, and boxing demonstrations, it was the girls whom people came to see. Burlesque was not for the faint of heart or the prudish. While vaudeville had a strict sense of morals, burlesque had none at all. The Empire circuit gave orders to "give it as raw as it will come." This, of course, brought trouble in the form of the local constabulary. There were often secret exits that could be used in case of a raid. Comedian Joey Bishop remembers red bulbs in the footlights that would warn a stripper not to go too far because there were police on the premises. Local jails often had a revolving-door policy. When the fine was paid, the performers went back to the theaters, then back to jail, and so on.

Later, comic sketches and dances were introduced. Comedians were classified in four basic groups: the straight man, the Dutch comic, the blackface comic, and the rube or pansy. They performed off-color sketches or bits that utilized essential props: the bladder, the slapstick, the blush detector, the dentist's chair, and the gun. Sketches and blackouts were named by their subjects: "The Butcher Bit," "In the Haystack," "The Schoolroom," "Meet Me Round the Corner," "Pick Up My Old Hat," "Fireman Save My Wife," etc. The top banana or lead comedian had his own favorite sketches. Comedian Bobby Clark originated the often-imitated courtroom sketch wherein he played the judge. Joey Bishop recalls the attitude of the burlesque comics: "Every burlesque comic felt like burlesque was the end of the road for him. If he flopped, he had no place else to go. So he adopted an attitude that would get him through life and he did his humor that way also. There's an attitude about burlesque that you cannot teach someone . . . that's a feeling. The burlesque comic always looked like he'd rather be somewhere else besides where he was. You can't try to be

Caricature of Harrigan and Hart.

funny in burlesque. You can't come out with a funny costume and then try to be funny on top of it. You must play seriously on top of it." Cuckolded husbands and disreputable doctors were forever doomed to run in and out of closets and doors, jump out windows, hide under beds, and be humiliated in court.

The burlesque sketch had a rural attitude about it. It always had the farmer topping the city slicker, usually a traveling salesman. Another typical burlesque stereotype was the rube or hick. The hick was always the stupidest human imaginable. Joey Bishop recollects a sketch called "Elmer" that illustrates this: "Elmer, the hick, is lost and must go to sleep in a farmhouse. The only room available is the farmer's daughter's room. The hick and the daughter are lying in bed and she says, 'Why don't you do something to amuse me?' And he takes out a harmonica and plays it."

Joey Bishop remembers his years in burlesque as a young comic: "I worked for Izzy Herst on the Herst circuit. We could never say 'hell' or 'damn' in burlesque, we could never take the Lord's name in vain. So we used to say, 'Cheeeese and crackers' or 'What the hey.' I don't ever remember seeing any burlesque sketch, and I've seen them all, that was in bad taste or that was vulgar."

The dancers were direct descendants of Lydia Thompson and Little Egypt. They often had exotic names like Fatima and Mazeppa and specialties like Sally Rand's fan dance. These women shimmied, hootchy-cootched, belly danced, and twirled their tassels across the stage in less and less clothing as time went on. In the 1890s "leg shows" were in vogue. Then came quick-change artists who undressed and dressed in full view of the audience, who could catch a glimpse of undergarment. Then around 1917 came strippers who kept their bras and panties on. These acts were usually saved as the "extra added attraction" at the end of the bill. Later, if the customer hadn't had his fill, he could often meet the teaser at the stage door. By the 1920s the public demanded more; after all, they could see legs on any flapper. So the girls showed their breasts and later disrobed down to pasties and G-strings, but they often put material under their strings to simulate pubic hair. Soon tradition was thrown to the wind, and instead of closing the bill, striptease became the raison d'être of burlesque. In 1923 VARIETY noted that burlesque was "ninety nine per cent strip with the other just to pad out the show."

Naturally the lead comics saw greener pastures in vaudeville, musical comedy, radio, and the movies. If they were any good, they honed their craft and got out. Leon Errol, Rags Ragland, Danny Thomas, Phil Silvers, Jackie Gleason, Red Buttons, Abbott and Costello, Zero Mostel, Herbie Faye, Jack Pearl, W. C. Fields, Red Skelton, Joe E. Brown, FANNY BRICE, Bert Lahr, Clark and McCullough, and others all starred in burlesque but achieved fame elsewhere.

As its talent left (even Gypsy Rose Lee, its most famous stripper, gave it up), burlesque became more and more vulgar. During Prohibition, outlawed entertainments moved into saloons, where women like TEXAS GUINAN could be seen for free with only a small charge for bootlegged hooch. Movies, too, made inroads on the burlesque audience, and soon motion pictures came to be shown between burlesque acts. Mayor LaGuardia cracked down on New York burlesque theaters, and in 1942 the city refused to renew the licenses of the burlesque houses; the end was near.

Today burlesque is confined to seedy flophouses in a few cities, and often live sex acts are featured. Old-time burlesque has been glorified in Broadway shows like *Grind* and the enormously successful *Sugar Babies*, showing that good burlesque never goes out of fashion.

CADILLAC WINTER GARDEN THEATRE. *See* **Winter Garden Theatre.**

CAFE DE L'OPERA. Southeast corner of 42nd Street and Seventh Avenue. The Cafe de l'Opera was the American equivalent of Paris's Cafe de Paris. This was one of the first successful cabarets in America in the years before World War I.

Louis Martin was the proprietor of the club, where guests could partake of a "bottle and bird" (champagne and pheasant under glass) and dance to the latest rage, the fox-trot. At midnight a drumroll would clear the dance floor, and a show would begin featuring dance teams like Maurice and Florence Walton and VERNON AND IRENE CASTLE. The headwaiter was Jules Ensaldi. He was almost as powerful as Martin himself; Ensaldi, the guardian of the velvet rope, decided who was seated and who wasn't, as well as (more importantly) *where* they were seated. It is thought that Ensaldi made more money than anyone else at the restaurant. The more prominent patrons wanted the best tables if only to keep their social standing, and Ensaldi was the key to the best locations. Louis Martin had the sense to keep his club intimate. Once it achieved success, Martin resisted the temptation to expand. Keeping the club small and exclusive only encouraged attempts by patrons to get reservations.

Looking down on the guests enjoying their meal was a balcony with a mural picturing the fall of Babylon. A floor above that were the private party rooms, and on the fourth floor were the apartments for the stars of the show. It was at the Cafe de l'Opera that many dance steps were born. After a private party for Elsie Janis on the third floor, Vernon and Irene Castle and their guests enjoyed their own band in a private ballroom upstairs. While fooling around on the dance floor, the Castles tried a new step. They went up on the beat rather than down and invented the Castle Walk. This skipping dance soon swept the country. The Castles left the Cafe de l'Opera to open the Sans Souci with their partner Jules Ensaldi. Their new venture was a mixed blessing, and the place was soon closed by the fire department because it had no fire exits.

The Cafe de l'Opera lasted until World War I turned the country's thoughts to more serious matters, and the society hangouts of the early part of the century gave way to more proletarian locales like the AUTOMAT.

CANDLER BUILDING. 220 W. 42nd Street. Architect: Willauer, Shape & Brady.

The 24-story Candler Building, built by Coca-Cola salesman Asa Candler, was completed in 1914. At the time, it was the tallest building in Manhattan north of 14th Street. It was also one of the last skyscrapers constructed prior to the 1916 Zoning Resolution, which limited the height of buildings on streets (as opposed to avenues) and made mandatory setbacks on taller buildings in order to maximize light. The handsome terra-cotta skyscraper (one of the few still extant in Manhattan) with late Gothic and Renaissance ornaments has a 24-story tower gracing 42nd Street and a 17-story structure fronting 41st Street. White terra-cotta was chosen by the original architects to combat a trend toward dark-hued buildings. The Candler Building has remained a visual landmark since its completion. During the 42nd Street redevelopment, the building, which is listed on the National Register of Historic Places, underwent a complete restoration by the firm of Swanke Hayden Connell Architects, and the street level was developed into a huge McDonald's fast-food restaurant.

CANDLER THEATRE. *See* **Harris Theatre.**

CAPITOL THEATER. 1645 Broadway, southwest corner of 51st Street. Architect: Thomas Lamb. Opening: October 24, 1919.

The Capitol Theater was, at the time of its construction, the largest theater in New York. The movie palace was another step in the career of S. L. ("Roxy") Rothafel, the leading manager of Broadway's motion picture theaters.

Before it became the city's entertainment hub, Times Square was an area that consisted mostly of shops catering to the carriage industry. As the motorcar gained popularity, the stables and carriage factories evolved into filling stations and garages. A livery stable, a blacksmith shop, and a gas station occupied the site of the Capitol Theater. The land was owned by the Jacob Wendell estate, which was bound by somewhat puritanical restrictions. The terms of the lease forbade the manufacture of corsets or cosmetics.

Builder Messmore Kendall recognized the importance of the underdeveloped site and leased it from the Wendell estate. He hired Thomas Lamb, a great theater architect who had already designed the Rialto and Rivoli. Lamb's favorite architectural style was that of the Adam brothers. He used that and the Empire style for the auditorium, which seated 5,300 patrons. Sherry's Restaurant, formerly on Fifth Avenue, was the source of three enormous rock-crystal chandeliers. Artist William Cotton Rose painted beautiful murals for the auditorium walls. Because the theater was built during World War I, construction materials, especially steel, were in short supply. Luckily, the city was constructing the IRT subway system northward from Times Square at the time. As the tunnels were completed, their trusses were sold to Kendall for use in the building of the Capitol.

When completed, the building was hailed as a masterpiece. Kendall had his own apartment at the top of the 6-story building. In the apartment, Kendall could

Capitol Theater.

see the action on the stage by peering through a secret window. From Kendall's window above the balcony level, the stage was almost a full city block away. The stage area was the domain of managing director Major Edward Bowes, who had an apartment suite below Kendall's. He was later known for his *Major Bowes Amateur Hour* radio show. Bowes was a part owner of the CORT THEATRE and had invested heavily in San Francisco real estate. However, Bowes had a hard time developing a viable entertainment policy for the Capitol.

The theater was beset with problems from the beginning. Just before the opening, the theater's bricklayers decided to go on strike. Left with a huge hole in the rear stage wall after the workers broke off negotiations, Kendall was forced to take drastic action. He called a meeting of the board, and when they were assembled he passed out aprons and trowels. The board members, realizing their investment was at stake, pitched in and mended the hole. The opening was further postponed because the lobby boasted mahogany paneling and the New York City Building Department was concerned that the theater wasn't fireproofed; they went over the entire building with blowtorches, torching the mahogany to check the theater's safety.

The opening night's program consisted of a live stage show, which preceded the feature film. The stage show was titled *Demi-Tasse*, and in the cast were Paul Frawley and Mae West. Arthur Pryor's band played for the opening night revels. The evening began with an overture by the Capitol Symphony, a short color film, a travelogue, another short subject that starred a pack of talented dogs, a film of director Ned Wayburn rehearsing the evening's show, and finally the revue proper. About the only notable aspect of the revue was a song written by GEORGE GERSHWIN and Irving Caesar. The song was "Swanee," and, surprisingly, it received little attention. Gershwin's other contribution, "Come to the Moon" (written with Ned Wayburn and Lou Paley), also went unnoticed, despite its elaborate setting. The female chorus, dressed as the Twinkle Star Girls, had electric lights in their ballet slippers that lit up the darkened stage. By the time the opening film, *His Majesty, the American* with Douglas Fairbanks, hit the screen, the battle was lost. The show received lukewarm to negative reviews. Mae West developed a sudden case of tonsilitis after reviewers carped at her "rude way of singing." Pryor's band was also dismissed.

Although changes were made in the show, they didn't halt the theater's troubles. On October 28, 1919, four days after the grand opening, Prohibition went into effect. And at the beginning of the next week's bill, the ushers went on strike demanding the right to accept tips. The *New York Times* reported on the dis-

agreement: "Their actions attracted the attention of the audience many of whom found the strike of more interest than the screen. The boys were ordered to leave, but they refused. Several policemen were sent from the West 47th Street Station House; they arrested Herman Ingberg, one of the strikers, upon his refusal to leave, and charged him with disorderly conduct." The negative publicity surrounding the Capitol kept audiences away in droves. The operation was losing Kendall thousands of dollars a week, money he could ill afford to lose. Kendall sold the theater to a shady character named F. J. Godsol. Godsol was owner of Goldwyn Pictures. He was also briefly jailed for selling what he claimed were horses to the French during World War I; unfortunately, what the French bought were really mules.

Godsol's first problem was what to do with Major Bowes. He decided to make the showman a vice president of Goldwyn Pictures at $25,000 a year. As managing director of the Capitol, Bowes received a similar salary. Bowes' new responsibilities at Goldwyn kept him busy, so he wasn't too upset when Godsol hired S. L. Rothafel to spruce up the theater's operation. June 4, 1920, was the date set for the reopening of the Capitol. An advertisement boasted:

TRIUMPHAL RE-OPENING The Capitol The World's Largest, Coolest, Most Beautiful Theater, Newest, Latest, Rothafel Motion Picture-and-Music Entertainment, under the Personal Supervision of S. L. Rothafel. Edward Bowes, Managing Director. Prices 40 cents—50 cents—75 cents—$1—No Higher (including War Tax)—Matinees, 30 cents—40 cents—No Reservations! First Come First Served!

Roxy was busy whipping together a new gala show in his grand tradition. When directing the show, Roxy sat in the middle of the auditorium and shouted at the action onstage through a megaphone. The Bell Telephone Corporation's scientists were working on a new idea: the public-address system. Roxy, always ready for a new invention, gladly agreed to try their experimental microphones and speaker systems. The public address system was a huge success, saving Roxy his voice and making it unnecessary for him to run constantly from audience to stage and back. Roxy liked the idea so much that he arranged for the entire theater to be wired. Now when people wanted to call the performers in their dressing rooms, they simply paged them over the system.

At the same time, radio station WEAF was begun in Manhattan. This early, experimental radio station even boasted sponsors such as Macy's and Gimbel's. WEAF wasn't content to simply broadcast from their studio. They began taking their microphones around New York and presenting live remote broadcasts. On

November 11, 1922, they broadcast for the first time the Metropolitan Opera's production of *Aïda* from the Kingsbridge Armory in the Bronx. Ironically, Major Bowes was against radio for the same reason that the movies were against pay television in the 1950s. He figured that people wouldn't pay for their entertainment in theaters if it was coming into their homes for free. But Roxy saw the possibilities of the new medium and agreed to allow a broadcast from the Capitol.

On November 19, 1922, the Grand Orchestra, led by Erno Rapee, struck up "Ein Heldenleben," by Richard Strauss, on the Capitol stage. It was the first time any of Strauss' music had been performed in the United States. Throughout New York and as far as WEAF's powerful signal would reach, audiences listened to the proceedings at the Capitol. Roxy was at a microphone in the wings explaining the stage action and what it meant to be in the Capitol amid all the splendor. Of course, this made the listeners feel they were missing the action and led them to the Capitol to see for themselves the elaborate stage shows and the motion pictures. The Capitol radio shows became so successful that it was decided to repeat the program weekly on Sunday evenings. WEAF was also part of a small network, which meant its broadcasts were carried in Providence, Rhode Island, and Washington, D.C., as well.

Every Sunday, audiences heard Roxy's voice over the airwaves opening his show with the words "Hello, everybody. This is Roxy speaking." And every show ended with Roxy signing off with these familiar words: "Good night . . . pleasant dreams . . . God bless you." Supporting Roxy was his "gang," which included soprano Florence Mulholland, basso profundo "Daddy" Jim Coombs, and audience favorite Beatrice Belkin. The concertmaster of the Capitol Grand Orchestra was the young Eugene Ormandy.

As time went on, the radio audience grew. The NBC Blue Network carried the Capitol shows throughout the country starring Roxy. Now the Capitol was the best-known theater in America, and Roxy was equally famous as America's greatest showman. The December 1925 issue of *American Business Record* exclaimed:

> Roxy—here is a name to conjure with! Who has not heard it—and more, who has not heard Roxy, for his is the stellar god of a new force a "Big Timer" of the ether. When science shot lilting melodies through the air and called it radio, Roxy was born in the first pink blush of radio's morning. Before that he was S. L. Rothafel. Then came this new force. They placed a microphone before his lips, he spoke into it, and his words clutched a million hearts though the miles between were many.

Bowes wasn't happy with Roxy's success and grew increasingly miserable when people claimed they didn't even know he was associated with the Capitol.

Bowes became more and more antagonistic toward Roxy. The situation was getting worse; clearly, something had to happen to resolve the problem. The solution came not within the Capitol Building but from without. Roxy was hired to oversee a new theater, one that would be the greatest in the world and would also, incidentally, be named after him.

On July 26, 1925, Major Bowes took over the operation of the Capitol radio show and began his own career on the air. Bowes continued to present the Capitol in classy terms. He created the *Capitol Family Hour*, and the show continued on the NBC Blue Network. Paul Morris in the *New York Evening World* described a typical Bowes high-class show:

> Last night I went to the Capitol Theatre, where one of the most elaborate of musical entertainments garnishes the feature film. It is really extraordinary the amount of pains that are taken here to put over the music. The Capitol Orchestra is admirable. It is as large as any of the regular symphonic organizations and better than many of them. But movie fans come to be shown, not merely to be told. So there are dancers to interpret the music and good ones, too. This week the overture was *Die Fledermaus*, and then they introduced Carlo Ferretti who gave us "Lolita's Serenade" by Buzzi-Peccia. Julia Glass, an excellent pianist, performed Rubenstein's Concerto in "Bal Masque" featuring Mlle. Desha, Miss Doris Niles and Miss Alice Wynne, and Mr. Chester Hale, the Capitol's ballet master, can be justly proud of the product of the ballet school he conducts backstage. After the feature film, a frivolous item called *Soul Mates*—one of those Elinor Glyn things—had been given a delightful scoring by the Capitol Orchestra, D. Melchiorre Mauro-Cottone, at the console of the Capitol's truly grand organ, rendered "Impressions of Cesar Franck" in a most admirable fashion.

Bowes realized that he needed a good assistant to help him produce Capitol revues. He found one in Chester Hale, a successful Broadway choreographer. The Chester Hale Girls, in the spirit of the later Rockettes, were terrifically popular and a great draw for the theater.

By now the Capitol was a member of the Loew's chain. Loew's owned a huge chain of theaters and needed shows to fill their stages. The Capitol became the flagship of the Loew's circuit. Louis K. Sidney, who took a more egalitarian approach to the Capitol's shows, was brought in to head the work. David Mendoza and his associate, Eugene Ormandy, headed the Capitol Grand Orchestra. Walter Roesner and his Capitolians augmented it. Loew's made the Chester Hale Girls into the Chesterettes, and Henry Murtaugh was hired to play the newly refurbished Capitol organ. The entire stage area was overhauled, including the addition of a lift in the orchestra pit. The Capitol was now well suited to stand up to the new Roxy Theater.

Sidney changed the Capitol's shows further by introducing variety acts. One program in October 1927 featured a 55-member chorus and 40 ballet dancers in a show entitled *The Spirit of Syncopation*. Also on the bill were performers Nora Bayes, Morton Downey, Lester Allen, Ben Bernie, Anna Case, and Bobbie Arnst. Other stars to appear on the Capitol stage were Van and Schenck, Winnie Lightner, Vincent Lopez, Georgie Tapps, James Barton, Percy Grainger, diva Mary Garden, and even Sister Aimee Semple McPherson. The Capitol stage policy lasted longer than that of many of its rivals. Although in 1932 the theater claimed that 100,000 paying customers visited the theater weekly, the Depression finally took its toll and in 1935 an "all the show on the screen" policy was inaugurated.

The Capitol continued as just another movie palace, albeit a spectacular one, into the 1960s. With the advent of television (a word banned on the Capitol's stage) and the flight to the suburbs, the Capitol's fortunes dwindled. The land was soon more valuable than the theater. Already the lobby had been renovated and an escalator ran up the once glorious marble staircase. The Capitol was razed in the mid-1960s to make way for an office block.

CARROLL, EARL. One of the greatest producers of extravagant musical revues in the first three decades of the century; b. Pittsburgh, Pennsylvania, September 21, 1892, or September 16, 1893; d. Mt. Carmel, Pennsylvania, June 17, 1948.

Earl Carroll rivaled FLORENZ ZIEGFELD and GEORGE WHITE in presenting Broadway's most popular revues during the opening decades of the 20th century. Carroll's revues stressed the female form and celebrated it with bawdy good humor. His shows were the closest to the BURLESQUE tradition, and, in fact, many of his stars first achieved fame in burlesque. These included Milton Berle, Joe Cook, Sophie Tucker, and Jimmy Savo as well as Ted Healy, Jessie Matthews, W. C. Fields, Jack Benny, Helen Broderick, and Patsy Kelly.

Carroll was a staff writer for a music publisher from 1912 to 1917. He wrote lyrics and music for a succession of Broadway shows, although none of his songs are played today. Among the shows he wrote for are *Pretty Mrs. Smith*, written with Alfred G. Robyn and Henry James (1914), *So Long Letty* (1916), *The Love Mill* (1916), and two editions of *EARL CARROLL'S VANITIES* in 1923 and 1924.

The *Vanities* were the naughtiest of the great revues. Where Ziegfeld would make sure he had the best-dressed showgirls, Carroll would make sure that girls he hired were the best-undressed. The *Vanities* featured forgettable songs and sketches and mostly second-rate stars. The main attraction was always the girls, reflecting the producer's main interest: sex. Not everyone was amused. The *Brooklyn Eagle* wrote that "Carroll's showmanship consisted in selling gutter humor and naked female flesh to morons." Carroll desired to be a producer and director not because he felt he could contribute something to the art, but so he could capitalize on his position to meet girls. His affairs made headlines, thereby boosting ticket sales.

During Prohibition, Carroll threw a party in the EARL CARROLL THEATRE during which Joyce Hawley took a bath in champagne. The press exploited the party on their front pages, and the *Graphic* published a phony photo. The authorities couldn't let an event such as this go unchallenged, and Carroll was hauled before a jury. He was found guilty of perjury after having stated there was no liquor at the party. Carroll served a little over half a year in jail, and again the publicity for the *Vanities* was enormous.

If anything rivaled Carroll's obsession with sex, it was his love of aviation. Carroll was a flyer during World War I and was sent on many reconnaissance missions in France. After the war he established a flying school in China. In 1925 Carroll became the first person to land a plane in Central Park. He received permission for the publicity stunt because he was carrying Santa Claus, who would distribute presents to children waiting in the Sheep Meadow. Joe Cook grudgingly acted as Santa Claus. Unfortunately, the weather was atrocious, with visibility next to zero and sleet beginning to fall. When Carroll attempted to land, he caught a wing of the plane on a tree. Much to the delight of the children, the plane went into a ground loop before coming to rest. Carroll and Cook were unhurt, but the plane was demolished.

The Depression brought bankruptcy and hard times to Broadway. Carroll was no exception, and he left New York to open the Earl Carroll Restaurant in Hollywood in December 1938. Carroll died in a plane crash on June 17, 1948. When the wreckage was located on Mt. Carmel, Pennsylvania, it was discovered that Carroll, his companion, Beryl Wallace, and the crew had died before the plane hit the ground; carbon dioxide had escaped from the fire extinguishers, killing all aboard.

In an interview with *Family Circle* magazine entitled "Your Last Day on Earth," Carroll reflected on his life:

It has been my lifework to stage and produce shows built around beautiful girls. To many people this work of mine may seem insignificant; I deal in beauty, it's true. But we are all starved and hungry for beauty; there is too little of it in the world. A hundred years from now I hope the parade of young American girls will still be walking under the sign of my theater ... which reads: "THROUGH THESE PORTALS PASS THE MOST BEAUTIFUL GIRLS IN THE WORLD."

Even the hands of his dancing girls are important to Earl Carroll, whose summer revue, *Who Cares?* opens in June at the Earl Carroll Theatre, 1930.

CASA MANANA. *See* **Earl Carroll Theatre.**

CASINO DE PARIS. *See* **New Yorker Theater.**

CASINO THEATRE (1). Broadway and 39th Street. Architects: Francis Kimball and Thomas Wisedell.

Opening: October 21, 1882; *The Queen's Lace Handkerchief.*

The Casino, which stood at the southeast corner of Broadway and 39th Street, was one of the best-loved 19th-century houses until it was demolished in 1930. Much farther uptown than most theaters, it was dubbed "Aronson's Folly" after producer Rudolph Aronson.

The Moorish-style theater opened on a stormy night with a leaky roof, unfinished auditorium, and nonfunctioning heating systems. The paneless windows were covered with paper, and unbleached muslin acted as walls.

Seven days after its opening, the theater was closed to permit the completion of its construction. Meanwhile, *The Queen's Lace Handkerchief* went on a national tour. In December the theater was finally reopened with a continuation of the run of its opening production. Finally ready for its audience, the theater was hailed as the finest example of Moorish architecture outside of Spain.

Aronson presented his light opera company at the theater for its first years. A year after it opened, a watchman patrolling the theater found a burning candle set into a box of pine shavings. The stage carpenter was arrested for attempted arson. It seems that Aronson had recently fired him, and so he attempted to burn down the theater.

Nell Gwynne was presented at the theater in 1884. Mathilde Cotrelly had the title role. Others in the cast included Digby Bell as King Charles and Billie Barlow as Rochester. In 1887 Gilbert and Sullivan's operetta *The Yeoman of the Guard* had its American premiere at the Casino. Lillian Russell portrayed Fiorella and Isabelle Urqhart played the Princess.

In 1890 Aronson added New York's first roof garden on top of the Casino. Productions in the 1,300-seat auditorium continued the same year with the return of Lillian Russell in *The Brigands*. That year also saw productions of *La Fille de Mme. Angot* with Camille d'Arville making her American debut alongside Grace Golden, Eva Davenport, and Fred Solomon. In October, *Poor Jonathan* with Jefferson de Angelis as Jonathan Tripp was presented for the first time in America.

On Thursday, October 1, 1890, a matinee performance of *Cavalleria Rusticana* was performed at the Casino. Impresario OSCAR HAMMERSTEIN I objected to the performance, insisting that he alone had the sole right of presenting the opera in America. In fact, he announced a performance of the same opera that evening at the Lenox Lyceum. Faced with the lawsuit, Aronson decided to give a free performance in the matinee, thus negating Hammerstein's objections. Although he lost money, he did go on record as having presented the American premiere of the opera. There was still one more show to premiere in 1890 at the Casino: *The Tyrolean* opened with Marie Tempest as Adam and Louise Beaudet as Christel.

Lillian Russell, always a favorite of Casino audiences, returned singing in *Girofle-Girofla*, assisted by Digby Bell, Marie Dressler, Lucy Daly, and Marie Celeste. Some of the greatest stars of the Gay Nineties appeared at the Casino in the 1894 production, *The Passing Show*, including Jefferson de Angelis, Adele Ritchie, Grace Filkins, and Lucy Daly. Two years later Edna May appeared on the Casino stage in the hit show *The Belle of New York*. Her appearance as a Salvation Army girl and her song "Follow On" were highlights of the season and helped make *The Belle of New York* into one of the favorite musicals at the turn of the century. Another great hit of the late 1800s was *Erminie*, and a revival at the Casino in May 1899 was a great success. Lillian Russell played the title role along with Lulu Glaser as Javotte and Francis Wilson and Thomas Q. Seabrooke as two escaped convicts. This was an all-star cast at the time.

However, the theater's most famous show was *Florodora*, which opened November 10, 1900, with a spectacular line of chorus girls. The original Florodora Sextette comprised Daisy Greene, Marjorie Relyea, Vaughn Texsmith, Margaret Walker, Agnes Wayburn, and Marie L. Wilson. The Sextette elevated the chorus girl to star status. The chorus became an attraction in its own right. FLORENZ ZIEGFELD took the concept of the Florodora Sextette and improved on it.

The show's beginnings were rocky. In fact, it almost closed after the first two weeks of its run. But *Florodora*'s publicist, Anna Marble, the wife of playwright Channing Pollock, saw that the Sextette was touted across the nation. She also pushed the show's hit song, "Tell Me Pretty Maiden," written by Leslie Stuart. The show ran for over 500 performances, one of the longest runs of the early 1900s.

Following *Florodora*'s run, in 1902 the theater was involved in a lawsuit concerning its legal ownership. Lee Shubert (*see* SHUBERT BROTHERS) bought the theater from the Bixby family, who owned it as an investment. The Bixbys had leased it to the Sire brothers, who in turn leased it to Charles Lederer. The affair started when Lee Shubert bought out Lederer's sublease. Lederer was happy to sell, because he was remiss in paying his rent and was about to be kicked out of the theater anyway. Shubert discovered that all the subleases were up at the same time, avoided the Sires by going directly to the Bixbys, and thereby gained control of the theater.

A Chinese Honeymoon (6/02/02; over 300 performances) was the Shuberts' first big hit in New York and established their reputation. Then came a succession of moderate hits: *The Runaways* (5/11/03; 167 performances), *Winsome Winnie* (12/01/03; 56 performances), *Lady Teazle* (12/24/04; 57 performances), and *The Earl and the Girl* (12/04/05; 148 performances). It was while *Lady Teazle* was playing the Casino that a fire broke out in the balcony and, because the theater's water pumps were frozen, the fire quickly spread, destroying the theater and cafe.

The remainder of the century's first decade saw a succession of failures at the Casino. *The Social Whirl, The Blue Moon, The Gay White Way, Nearly a Hero, The Mimic World, Marcelle, Mr. Hamlet of Broadway, Havana,* and *The Girl and the Wizard* were mostly imports of English operettas with some American songs interpolated.

The Shuberts continued to keep the theater occupied with many other modest successes as well as downright flops. *The Mikado,* which had premiered at the Madison Square Roof Garden in 1902, played the Casino three times, in 1910, 1912, and 1913, but none of these engagements was successful. *Up and Down Broadway* (7/18/10; 72 performances) contained the hit song "Chinatown, My Chinatown," by Jean Schwartz and William Jerome. *The Blue Paradise* (08/05/13; 356 performances) broke the long succession of failures with its score by SIGMUND ROMBERG, Edmund Eysler, and Herbert Reynolds. However, the next hit at the Casino wasn't until 1922 with the production *Sally, Irene and Mary,* which ran for 318 performances.

The theater stayed dark for most of its last decade. In 1930 the Depression as well as the constant move uptown of the theater district sealed its fate, and the Casino was torn down to make way for garment district workshops. What was once the northernmost theater in New York ended its life as the southernmost.

CASINO THEATER (2). *See* **Earl Carroll Theatre.**

CASTLE, VERNON AND IRENE. The premier dance team in the United States in the years preceding World War I; Vernon Castle, b. Vernon Blyth, Norwich, England, May 2, 1887; d. Fort Worth, Texas, February 15, 1918; Irene Castle, b. Irene Foote, New Rochelle, New York, April 17, 1893; d. Eureka Springs, Arkansas, January 25, 1969.

Besides popularizing many long-lasting social dances, Vernon and Irene Castle were also influential in many areas outside dancing. Irene's fashions and habits were copied by thousands of young women who were just beginning to break free of the restraints of the Victorian and Edwardian eras. The couple played the major theaters in the country as well as appeared in Broadway shows and made an occasional foray into vaudeville.

Vernon Blyth graduated with an engineering degree from Birmingham University. His sister, Coralie Blyth, was married to actor Lawrence Grossmith, who was preparing to open his new show at the Herald Square Theatre in New York on April 8, 1907. Vernon was given a small part in the show and proved adept enough

to be cast in other shows. He appeared in *The Girl Behind the Counter* (10/1/07; 260 performances), *The Midnight Sons* (5/22/09; 257 performances), *Old Dutch* (11/22/09; 88 performances), and *The Summer Widowers* (6/4/10; 140 performances). It was during the run of the latter play that he met his future wife, Irene Foote.

Irene, born in 1893, was the daughter of the first woman to make a balloon ascension in the United States and the first man to load a Civil War cannon. She met her future husband and dance partner through social contacts and begged him to get her an audition with producer Lew Fields (*see* FIELDS FAMILY). The audition was less than successful, but her friendship with Vernon eventually led to her replacing a minor character in *The Summer Widowers.* Also in the cast of that early show was a very young HELEN HAYES.

The couple was married following the closing of the show and before the opening on August 7, 1911, of their next Broadway show, *The Hen Pecks* (137 performances). When *The Hen Pecks* closed, Vernon was invited to perform in a revue in Paris. His engagement was not a success; they were short of cash, and so they decided to try their luck as a dance team in the famous Cafe de Paris. Surprisingly, they were a big hit. The French were used to rough-and-tumble Apache dancing, and the Castles' more romantic style took the city by storm. On their return to the United States they were quickly hired by Louis Martin, owner of the prestigious CAFE DE L'OPERA. The restaurant was a "bottle and bird" club—wealthy patrons dined on pheasant under glass and a bottle of champagne while the Castles entertained. They were hired for the unheard-of salary of $300 a week, which was soon raised to $600 a week.

While at the Cafe de l'Opera, the Castles moonlighted in Broadway shows. The first was *The Sunshine Girl* (2/3/13; 160 performances) at the Knickerbocker Theatre. They were also playing private parties for huge sums of money. Society discovered the Castles, and soon no soiree was complete without the Castles there to entertain the guests. One night the team was fooling around at a birthday party for Elsie Janis. The party was in the Castles' private apartment above the nightclub. While they skipped around the dance floor, instead of coming down on the beat they went up, and a dance craze was born. The Castle Walk became the newest sensation.

The year 1913 was a year of dance crazes. There was the Turkey Trot, the Grizzly Bear, the Bunny Hug, the Lame Duck, and the Camel Walk. Then came the tango, and never had America seen such a suggestive and romantic a dance. The Castles excelled at them all and were at the height of their fame. A prominent CRITIC, Gilbert Seldes, wrote, "That these two, years ago, determined the course dancing should take is incontestable. They were decisive characters, like Boileau in French poetry and Berlin in ragtime; for they understood, absorbed, and transformed everything known of dancing up to that time and out of it made something beautiful and new."

With everyone dancing, it seemed only natural that the Castles should open Castle House, a dignified dance hall in the Ritz-Carlton Hotel. Society was taken with the Castles and saw fit to copy not only their dance steps but their style as well. It seemed that whenever Irene changed her clothes, fashion changed also. But Irene was concerned less with changing styles than with wearing comfortable clothes that were easy to move in. At the beginning of her Paris trip, she was unable to afford jewelry, so she didn't wear any, and soon other women were copying her. When she received a Dutch bonnet as a present and wore it onstage, she found more and more women in the audience sporting Dutch bonnets. By the summer of 1913 her "Castle frock" became all the rage. A newspaper article of the time described the metamorphosis: "At first, people thought she looked like a French poster and a Revolutionary heroine, and they did not think of imitating the gown. Then a young June bride had the gown copied for her trousseau. This was the beginning of several gowns a la Castle. Now the fashion has become settled as more or less artistic at smart parties." The next year, Irene wore jodhpurs while riding and found them more comfortable than skirts. From then on, women wore jodhpurs. That same year she had her appendix removed, and she cut her hair into a bob in order to make it easier to handle while she was laid up. The effect was devastating. A Connecticut paper headlined the story, "Irene Castle Cuts Hair." Cecil Beaton wrote in *The Book of Beauty*, "If any one person is responsible for the appearance of the modern young lady of fashion whom we admire so much today, it is certainly Mrs. Vernon Castle."

The Castles next opened at the NEW AMSTERDAM THEATRE in the IRVING BERLIN show *Watch Your Step* (12/8/14; 175 performances). In it Irene first wore a gown designed for her by Lady Duff-Gordon, known professionally as Lucile. The dress was an even bigger success than the show, and the Metropolitan Museum acquired it for its permanent collection. Meanwhile, the Castles were very much in the news. They played in the roof theater of the 44TH STREET THEATRE called Castles in the Air. They also played the basement, which was called the Castle Club. They performed there from 1:30 to 4:00 in the morning.

Vernon left to fight in World War I, and Irene continued her career. She made a few successful movies and appeared in a huge failure, FLORENZ ZIEGFELD's revue *Miss 1917*. Vernon Castle died in 1918 when his plane crashed during a training flight in Texas. Irene tried to continue her career but without much

enthusiasm. She eventually married again and retired from the stage.

Through their sense of fun and style, the Castles had influenced a generation of Americans. Arthur Murray explained why they had become such a sensation: "The Castles became all the rage by introducing elegance in modern dancing. They took long, graceful steps and danced apart, in contrast to the awkward bouncing and suggestive clinches of the animal dances. The Castles did more to make dancing acceptable in polite mixed company than any other influence."

CATS. This unlikely musical proved to be the biggest hit in Broadway history. Based on T. S. Eliot's poems from his *Old Possum's Book of Practical Cats*, the show originated in a series of presentations of individual songs at composer Andrew Lloyd Webber's home at Sydmonton.

The songs were gathered together along with other Eliot writings, and with input from director Trevor Nunn and producer Cameron Mackintosh, *Cats* opened at the unpopular New London Theatre behind the Drury Lane Theatre in London on May 11, 1981. The show boasted no libretto but a lot of choreography by Gillian Lynne.

A smash hit from its inception (despite critical carping), *Cats* was a natural for Broadway, where theatergoers from all over the world come to see a big, splashy musical. And what better show for them than one where knowledge of English is unnecessary? The Broadway production opened to the usual mixed reviews and sold out houses. Betty Buckley, Ken Page, Harry Groener, Terence V. Mann, and Stephen Hanan headed the cast. Broadwayites were astounded when the late T. S. Eliot won a TONY AWARD for his "libretto."

Having entertained millions of prepubescent girls and countless Japanese tourists, *Cats* finally closed on Broadway after 7,393 performances.

CENTRAL THEATER. *See* **Movieland.**

CENTURY THEATER (1). 235 W. 46th Street, basement of the Paramount Hotel. Designer: Albert Johnson. Original name: Billy Rose's Horseshoe. Opening 1938; *Billy Rose's Diamond Horseshoe*.

The Century Theater was known as Billy Rose's Diamond Horseshoe for most of its life. Impresario Billy Rose brought his show to the new theater from the Pioneer Palace of the Fort Worth Fair in 1938. Albert Johnson designed the theater with a patriotic color scheme in red, white, and blue. The Diamond Horseshoe initially re-created an evening in the Gay Nineties as seen through the eyes of Lillian Russell and DIAMOND JIM BRADY, and Rose cast it with a number of former stars, including operatic star Fritzi Scheff, minstrel Eddie Leonard, the shimmy dancer Gilda Gray, showgirl Ann Pennington, and a spry 70-year-old who performed handsprings, Emma Francis. Also appearing were Joe Howard, composer of "I Wonder Who's Kissing Her Now," early talkie star Charles King, and Harry Armstrong, the man who wrote "Sweet Adeline."

There was also a group of leggy chorines featuring the famous 6'2" Stuttering Sam. The four Rosebud girls joined her and the other beautiful chorus girls. The Rosebuds, nearly as big around as they were tall, taken together weighed almost 1,200 pounds. About halfway through the show's 12-year run Rose hired Nicky Blair as manager. Blair ran other nightclubs in his career, including the Paradise, the House of (Helen) Morgan, and TEXAS GUINAN's club. Blair later opened the Carnival across the street from Madison Square Garden.

When the Diamond Horseshoe finally closed in 1951, the theater became the Mayfair. It was later renamed the Stairway (for the run of the play *The Castro Complex*, which opened on November 18, 1970, and played for 14 performances) and then again the Mayfair. Finally, it became the Century with the opening of Jack Heifner's play *Patio/Porch* (4/13/78; 21 performances).

Among the shows that played the Century were *Lone Star & Pvt. Wars* (1/7/79; 69 performances), *Are You Now or Have You Ever Been . . .* (2/6/79; 32 performances), *On Golden Pond* (9/12/79; 424 performances), and *Banjo Dancing* (10/21/80; 38 performances). In the mid-1980s the theater was devoted to the Chaiken CPA Review, a course designed to help students pass the test enabling them to become certified public accountants. On November 17, 1987, the New York City Landmarks Preservation Commission denied landmark status for the theater's interior in a move that puzzled preservationists.

In January 1988 the theater was converted back to its nightclub origins. The onetime owners of Studio 54 announced that they would open the space as New York's newest club, but it was not to be and the space remained dark.

CENTURY THEATER (2). *See* **Jolson's 59th Street Theater.**

CHANIN'S 46TH STREET THEATER. *See* **Richard Rodgers Theater.**

CHAPMAN, JOHN. Critic; b. Denver, Colorado, June 25, 1900; d. Westport, Connecticut, January 17, 1972.

John Chapman. Photo by Harold Stein.

Chapman began his journalistic career as a reporter for the *Denver Times* in 1917. He moved to New York, where he worked for the *Daily News* from 1920 to 1923 and from 1926 to 1929. That year he became the drama editor for the *Daily News*. He remained in that position until 1943, when he was appointed drama critic. He once said of a melodrama, "It is enough to make your flesh crawl right out of the theatre."

Chapman succeeded Burns Mantle as editor of the annual *Best Plays* in 1947 and filled the post until 1952. He then became editor of *Theater '53*, the beginning of a short-lived annual on the theater.

CHARLES HOPKINS THEATER. 153 W. 49th Street. Architects: Murphy and Dana. Original name: The Punch and Judy Theatre. Opening: November 10, 1914; *The Marriage of Columbine*.

Producer Charles Hopkins built the Punch and Judy Theatre on a small parcel of land directly off Times Square in 1914. Like the BIJOU, which followed it three years later, the Punch and Judy was an intimate house built for small-cast, single-set plays with a decidedly experimental bent. The interior was modeled after the Shakespearian-era Blackfriars Theatre in London. The theater was unique in one respect: when it was time for the show to begin, a medieval-style musician would play a trumpet fanfare from the roof of the building. The house never achieved any great success, mainly because its small size made profits difficult for even the biggest hits. Unfortunately, producers weren't interested in the limited grosses of small theaters and instead opted for medium-size houses for their productions.

Punch and Judy Theatre before its opening in 1914.

As the Punch and Judy, the 299-seat theater housed few hits. In 1921 it hosted *March Hares*, a transfer from the Bijou by the SHUBERT BROTHERS. The play, a romantic satire, managed only 60 performances between both houses. In 1926, in an attempt to change the theater's luck, Hopkins changed the name to the Charles Hopkins Theater. But the theater fared little better with its new name. Productions included those on the level of *Devil in the Cheese* (12/29/26), a "fantastic comedy" that starred Fredric March and Bela Lugosi. This improbable tale concerns an archeologist who disapproves of a suitor for his daughter's hand. The hapless father eats a piece of ancient cheese discovered in the archeological dig, and the "Spirit of the Cheese" takes him inside his daughter's head, where the father discovers how much she loves her boyfriend. As if this weren't enough, the would-be husband saves everyone from bandits in the third act. Audiences were curious enough to keep the show running for 157 performances. The next season Hopkins presented the A. A. Milne play *The Ivory Door* (10/18/27). Henry Hull, Louise Closser Hale, and Donald Meek starred in this medieval fantasy. It ran for 310 performances.

Hopkins was building a small following for what *Best Plays* editor Burns Mantle called "Charles Hopkins' funny little theater." Hopkins presented another A. A. Milne play on March 4, 1931. The play was entitled *Success* when first presented in England, but the title belied its fate on Broadway. Despite the talents of Louis Calhern, Jane Wyatt, Eric Blore, Montague Shaw, and Nancy Kelly, the play closed after only 72 performances. The cast would be far luckier than the play; all later achieved stardom in Hollywood.

The Depression took its toll on all Broadway theaters, and even the Charles Hopkins with its low overhead couldn't escape. Milne, one of Hopkins' favorite writers, was presented again in the theater's last legitimate season. *They Don't Mean Any Harm* opened February 23, 1932, but played for only 15 performances. Hopkins' checkbook convinced him that the future of his theater was dim, and so in 1933, unlike many producers who couldn't accept the realities of Broadway in the Depression, Hopkins changed his theater to a movie policy.

In 1935 the theater's name was changed to the World Theater, and in the 1960s it presented X-rated films. One of its most successful engagements came in 1972 with the film *Deep Throat*. It was then made a member of the Embassy Theater chain, called the Embassy 49th Street Theatre. It specialized in second-run and children's fare. The theater was razed to make way for a new building in June 1987.

CIRCLE IN THE SQUARE THEATRE. 1633 Broadway on 50th Street. Architect: Allen Sayles.

Opening: November 15, 1972; *Mourning Becomes Electra*.

The Circle in the Square organization moved on November 15, 1972, to this new location in a then-new office building, which also houses the GERSHWIN THEATER. As New York's premier classic theater group, Circle in the Square brought to Times Square exactly the sort of play that is usually abhorred by legitimate producers.

Under the artistic direction of Theodore Mann and with the expertise of managing director Paul Libin, Circle in the Square proved to be an important part of the Broadway theater scene. Its first full season included productions of *Medea* with Irene Papas; Siobhan McKenna in *Here Are Ladies*; a star-studded revival of Chekhov's *Uncle Vanya* with George C. Scott, Lillian Gish, Nicol Williamson, Julie Christie, and Barnard Hughes; Anne Jackson and Eli Wallach in *The Waltz of the Toreadors*; and EUGENE O'NEILL's *The Iceman Cometh*, starring James Earl Jones.

As a not-for-profit theater, the group could afford to present the kinds of shows that would be impossible to produce under normal circumstances. Other notable productions include Jim Dale's athletic performance in *Scapino* in 1974, George C. Scott's staging of O'Neill's *All God's Chillun Got Wings* in 1975, and later that season, an exemplary revival of O'Neill's *Ah, Wilderness!* starring Geraldine Fitzgerald, as well as an incendiary production of *The Glass Menagerie* with Maureen Stapleton and Rip Torn. In 1976 Richard Chamberlain and Dorothy McGuire starred in TENNESSEE WILLIAMS' *The Night of the Iguana*. The next year's highlight was a revival of Moliére's *Tartuffe* with John Wood, Tammy Grimes, and Mildred Dunnock.

New plays have also premiered at the theater, including *Spokesong* by Stewart Parker and *Loose Ends* by Michael Weller, both in 1979, and *Eminent Domain* by Percy Granger, starring Philip Bosco and Betty Miller. Musicals have been represented only twice, with mixed results. In 1975 Raul Julia starred in FRANK LOESSER's *Where's Charley?* and Christopher Chadman and Joan Copeland were featured in a revival of RODGERS AND HART's *Pal Joey* the next year.

Other seasons have included productions of *Once in a Lifetime*, with John Lithgow and Treat Williams (1978); *The Man Who Came to Dinner*, with Ellis Rabb (1980); *Present Laughter*, starring George C. Scott (1982); *The Caine Mutiny Court-Martial*, with John Rubinstein, Michael Moriarty, and William Atherton (1983); *Heartbreak House*, starring Rex Harrison and Amy Irving (1983); *Arms and the Man* (1985); *You Never Can Tell*, with Philip Bosco, Uta Hagen, and Amanda Plummer (1986); and Tina Howe's *Coastal*

Disturbances, with Timothy Daly and Annette Bening (1987).

The Circle in the Square continued to produce, but the early part of the 1990s saw a precipitous decline in quality, and subscriptions plummeted. In 1994 the organization hired Josephine Abady as co-artistic director with Theodore Mann. One production was mounted that year (*The Shadow Box*), but it was a failure. The next season saw four productions that opened to little response from audiences or critics. The last production under the Mann/Abady reign was a revival of Eugene O'Neill's early drama *Hughie* (8/22/96), which starred and was directed by Al Pacino. It received good reviews, but its limited run of 56 performances couldn't save the organization.

The board then hired the Lincoln Center Theater's Gregory Mosher as producing director and M. Edgar Rosenblum as executive producer. They imported the Royal National Theatre's production of *Stanley* (2/20/97) from London, but it was not well received, and Mosher and Rosenblum were out. With the dissolution of the Circle in the Square as a producing company (it remained an eminent theater school) an important era in Broadway history came to a close. Although the Roundabout Theatre Company has attempted to fill the gap with a similar schedule of revivals interspersed with a few new productions, they could not equal the excellence of Mann and Libin in their heyday.

Given the failure of *Stanley*, it was ironic that the next booking at the theater was again from the Royal National Theatre. Tennessee Williams' *Not About Nightingales* was the first production under the theater's new booking policy. The production, under the brilliant direction of Trevor Nunn, opened on February 25, 1999. Despite the excellence of the production, including electrifying performances by Corin Redgrave, James Black, and Sherri Parker Lee, the show only managed a 125-performance run.

The theater next hosted a heralded production of Sam Shepard's drama *True West* (3/2/2000). Philip Seymour Hoffman (who had recently become a well-regarded Hollywood actor) and John C. Reilly played the two warring brothers. In an interesting casting experiment, the two switched roles at alternate performances. Robert LuPone and Celia Weston completed the cast. When the cast replacements, Josh Brolin and Elias Koteas, arrived, the show quickly folded, after a total of 154 performances.

Richard O'Brien's *The Rocky Horror Show* (11/15/2000) featured Dick Cavett, Lea DeLaria (as Dr. Smith and Eddie), Jarrod Emick, Alice Ripley, Tom Hewett, and other Broadway regulars in its cast. Also appearing was rock star Joan Jett. Critical notices were mostly positive and were especially enthusiastic about the high standards of producer Jordan Roth's opulent pro-

duction. The September 11, 2001, attack on the World Trade Center caused the show to close on September 23, but it reopened on October 30. However, the momentum had been lost, and the show closed for good on January 6, 2002, after 437 performances.

The theater then hosted a transfer of the Second Stage Theatre's production of *Metamorphosis* (3/4/2002), Mary Zimmerman's take on the myths of Ovid.

The theater itself has a unique shape—a long oval with the audience surrounding the stage in bleacher-style seating. The tongue-shaped stage has had its detractors, but for the most part it has worked out surprisingly well. The theater, slightly smaller than the smallest commercial houses, seats 648 patrons. Because of its arena setting and steeply raked seating, no one in the audience is ever more than 10 rows from the stage.

CLARENCE DERWENT AWARD. In 1945 actor Clarence Derwent (1884–1959) founded the award that bears his name; it is given for the best actor and actress in a nonfeatured role. Each year two awards are made in New York and, since 1948, two in London. The award consists of a $500 stipend to the American winners and £50 to the British winners.

Past American winners of the award have included Judy Holliday, Barbara Bel Geddes, Tom Ewell, Lou Gilbert, Ray Walston, Fritz Weaver, Frances Sternhagen, George C. Scott, William Daniels, Rosemary Murphy, Gene Wilder, and Gene Hackman.

CLARIDGE HOTEL. Southeast corner of Broadway and 44th Street. Architect: John L. Pope.

In February 1909 Charles E. Rector, owner of RECTOR'S, bought a 5-story building around the corner from his famous restaurant. He hired John L. Pope to design a new hotel for the site. Unfortunately, Rector was unable to purchase the corner plot that connected his restaurant and his new purchase. The land belonged to Henry Schwarzwalder, who steadfastly refused to sell. Rector was forced to lease the land from Schwarzwalder for 20 years. Looking ahead, Rector worried that in 20 years he might be unable to renew the lease with Schwarzwalder, requiring him to divide the lot back into three segments. Rector had Pope design the new building so that the placement of columns and girders required the addition of only interior walls to separate the building's three sections. The Hotel Rector opened on New Year's Eve 1910. It was immediately successful and became a worthy rival to the ASTOR HOTEL across the street. Although the hotel was successful, Charles Rector went into receivership in July 1913 and the hotel was sold.

The new owners changed the name to Claridge when they assumed control. However, their reign was short-lived. In November 1916 the hotel changed hands again, and then in 1922 the Claridge was sold once more. Owner Maximillian Zipkes renovated the building, added the Cadillac Restaurant, and designed a 2-story arcade containing stores. As Prohibition had gone into effect, a soda fountain and candy store replaced the hotel's bar. The hotel was sold again in May 1923, June 1923, and February 1925. In 1928 the name was changed to the Broadway Claridge. With the Depression, the hotel's fortunes sank even lower. It was sold once more in 1930, and in 1932 it went into foreclosure.

The hotel had one last hurrah in 1940. A sign affixed to the hotel announcing the candidacy of Earl Browder, the Communist Party nominee for president, was painted over. The Communist Party took the case to the Supreme Court. Although Justice Collins ordered the 60-by-20-foot sign repainted, the order was never carried out. The Duke of Roxburghe owned the Cadillac Hotel next to the Claridge. The scaffolding needed to repaint the sign would have blocked his hotel, and his permission was needed. Because he was unavailable, the Claridge paid the Communist Party $1,187. The Claridge was torn down in the 1980s to make way for the National movie theater building.

COHAN, GEORGE M. The embodiment of the Broadway song-and-dance man during the opening decades of the 20th century; b. Providence, Rhode Island, July 3, 1878; d. New York, New York, November 5, 1942.

George M. Cohan was known as "the man who owned Broadway." This actor, singer, dancer, producer, director, composer, lyricist, and soft touch was truly the complete performer. Through the Warner Brothers picture *Yankee Doodle Dandy* (1942), new generations have discovered the legend of George M. Cohan.

Though Cohan was born on July 3, 1878, as far as he was concerned, the Fourth of July was his natal day, and he made a career out of it. His shows waved the flag harder than anyone else's. Cohan wrote the most successful patriotic numbers of all time (with the possible exception of IRVING BERLIN's "God Bless America"). The best-known of these was "You're a Grand Old Flag." He wrote the supreme war song, "Over There," and even starred as a sitting president of the United States in musical comedy.

Cohan might have been the supreme egotist, but he also knew his limitations. He wrote:

As a dancer, I could never do over three steps. As a composer, I could never find use for over four or five notes in my musical numbers. As a violinist, I could never learn to play above the first position. I'm a one-key piano

player, and as a playwright, most of my plays have been presented in two acts for the simple reason that I could seldom think of an idea for a third act. I remember hearing Marcus Loew say one night that he left school as soon as he had learned how to count ten—he claimed that any learning beyond that was altogether unnecessary. And mind you that was before he ever became a big moving picture magnate.

Soon after his birth, Cohan joined his family's vaudeville team, the Four Cohans. George, father Jerry, mother Helen, and sister Josephine covered the country with their song-and-dance act. At the age of 15 George, not exactly a shrinking violet, began contributing skits and songs to the family's act. His ego, aggressive personality, and unlimited energy made him continuously test himself and his fellow human beings. Nothing was ever good enough for George. He was a man of the theater, and he was determined to succeed in it as no man had ever succeeded before. As for his family, they would just have to keep up as best they could.

Cohan wasn't just an ambitious youngster. He was smart enough to know what he didn't know and was an avid theatergoer. As he wrote in *The Call Board* magazine, the "official organ of the Catholic Actors Guild":

When I was a youngster in the late Eighties and the early Nineties I was quite a theatregoer. Playing variety engagements we (the family) had many idle weeks throughout the season, which gave me the opportunity to take in most of the shows playing currently in whatever city we happened to be resting. I would walk up to any box office in the world in those days, present my card and ask, "Do you recognize the profession?" The box office boy would invariably refer me to the company manager, who usually stood at the front door with the ticket-taker. If this company manager happened to be a good-natured chap and business would permit, he would as a rule okay my card. On the other hand, if he turned out to be one of the hardboiled babies (as company managers were nine times out of ten in those days), he would glance at the card, hand it back to me, give me a hard look, and walk away without a word. That was my cue to rush out of the lobby, into the street, and around the corner to the gallery entrance, purchase a nice hard twenty-five cent ticket, climb the usual long flight of stairs and witness the play from the top shelf.

George M. Cohan made his first New York engagement at the Union Square Theatre in 1893. Later that year the family made their New York debut at Keith's vaudeville theater in a skit titled "Goggle's Doll House." The act was not a success, at least not with Keith. A telegram was received from the company's headquarters in Boston directing them to change the act to include the parents in a sketch, Josie Cohan in a dance, and George in a number called "The Lively

The Four Cohans on stage: George, Josephine, Jerry, and Helen.

Bootblack." Later in that engagement, Josie Cohan had an offer to appear at Keith's rival's theater, Koster and Bial's Music Hall. Koster and Bial offered Josie a salary twice as much as the entire family was getting combined, so Josie briefly left the act. In 1896 the Four Cohans were appearing at Tony Pastor's in an hour-long sketch titled "Money to Burn." Pastor's theater, on the north side of 14th Street near Third Avenue, was high-class vaudeville. But George wasn't content to remain in vaudeville; he wanted to conquer Broadway.

George made good on his first goal, Broadway, with his show *The Governor's Son* (2/25/01; 32 performances), which opened at the Savoy Theater. The theater was located on the south side of 34th Street, west of Broadway. It had originally been built by George Kraus with the financial assistance of Timothy D. Sullivan and was named the Schley Music Hall. Alfred A. Aarons (*see* AARONS AND FREEDLEY) leased the house and changed the name to the Savoy. Then Hyde

and Berman took over the lease and opened their reign with Cohan's musical. Cohan's next outing, *Running for Office* (4/27/03; 48 performances), also starred the Four Cohans. The show was based on a vaudeville skit he had written with the same title. The show played at the 14th Street Theatre to increasing acclaim for the young performer.

Already George was the only Broadway author, composer, and lyricist who worked in the vernacular and whose shows weren't rehashings of the same formula operettas. Cohan was the only composer whose work was 100 percent American in style and tone. Not for Cohan were the staid drawing-room comedies imported from England. He translated his own brand of speed and exuberance to the stage and broke new ground by planting the seeds of American farce.

Although Cohan offstage was the gregarious Irish upstart, his stage persona was more genteel and sophisticated. In fact, this character showed Americans that they need not be European to possess class and élan.

His stage persona took the best of European sophistication and added to it the totally American qualities of enthusiasm and precocity. As OSCAR HAMMERSTEIN II wrote in the *New York Times*, "Never was a plant more indigenous to a particular part of the earth than was George M. Cohan to the United States of his day. The whole nation was confident of its superiority, its moral virtue, and its happy isolation from the intrigues of the 'old country,' from which many of our fathers and grandfathers had immigrated."

For his next show, *Little Johnny Jones* (11/7/04; 52 performances), Cohan again starred with his parents and wife, Ethel Levey, and he wrote the book and composed the score. But for this outing he added another job: director. He also began at the same time his lifelong friendship and collaboration with producer Sam H. Harris. Cohan used the show to further refine his formula, mixing a healthy dose of patriotism with a strong dash of farce and a liberal sprinkling of good old American corn. It also contained Cohan's first hit songs, "Life's a Funny Proposition After All," "The Yankee Doodle Boy," "I'm Mighty Glad I'm Living That's All," and perhaps his most famous tune, "Give My Regards to Broadway." After a profitable stretch on the road, *Little Johnny Jones* returned to Broadway for a run of almost four months.

Cohan's next Broadway venture, *Forty-Five Minutes from Broadway* (1/1/06; 90 performances), starred Fay Templeton, Victor Moore, and Donald Brian. This score contained more Cohan standards, "Mary's a Grand Old Name," "So Long, Mary," and the title song. One month later Cohan, his parents, his wife, and Truly Shattuck opened in *George Washington, Jr.* (2/12/06; 81 performances). This show contained Cohan's first great patriotic hit, "You're a Grand Old Flag." The original title of the song, the less reverent "You're a Grand Old Rag," was changed at the urging of patriotic groups.

Cohan's attempts at playwriting were not quite as successful. His first was titled *Popularity* (10/1/06; 24 performances). The next year Cohan, never wanting to let a good idea go to waste, rewrote *Running for Office* as *The Honeymooners* (6/3/07; 167 performances). With his next show, *The Talk of New York* (12/3/07; 157 performances), Cohan officially became the co-producer with Sam H. Harris. This time, Victor Moore, Gertrude Vanderbilt, and Emma Littlefield starred. The hit Cohan songs included "When We Are M-A-Double R-I-E-D," "When a Fellow's on the Level with a Girl That's on the Square," and "Under Any Old Flag at All."

Fifty Miles from Boston (2/3/08; 32 performances) contained only one hit song, albeit the great Cohan hit "Harrigan." Perhaps George was saving his energy for his next, which opened two months later. That was *The Yankee Prince* (4/20/08; 128 performances), a title

that seemed to describe Cohan himself. In fact, all of Cohan's shows were semiautobiographical in spirit if not fact. *The Yankee Prince*'s run wasn't due to the score or its hits (there were none); rather, it was popular because, for the first time since *Running for Office* in 1903, the Four Cohans were back together again on Broadway. Cohan premiered a third show in 1908. The fun of *The American Idea* (10/5/08; 64 performances) was due more to the success of *The Yankee Prince* than its own merits.

Broadway was discovering the revue at the end of the first decade of the century. *The Cohan and Harris Minstrels* (8/16/09; 16 performances) was among the first revues seen on Broadway. Cohan and Harris next presented a straight play version of Winchell Smith's *The Fortune Hunter* (9/4/09; 345 performances), which starred John Barrymore. This first non-Cohan production presented by the team turned into a great success. Cohan's next success was again autobiographical in title. *The Man Who Owns Broadway* (10/11/609) opened nearly a year after *The American Idea*. Cohan's next offering was a straight play, *Get-Rich-Quick Wallingford* (9/19/10; 424 performances). Hale Hamilton and Edward Ellis starred in this huge success. Cohan and Harris' next straight offering, *The Aviator* (12/6/10; 44 performances), by James Montgomery, was later adapted into the musical *Going Up* and presented to great success by the producers.

A year later the next Cohan musical opened, *The Little Millionaire* (9/25/11; 192 performances). Cohan, his parents, and Donald Crisp kept the show running for the longest run of his career. Exactly a month later he co-produced the musical *The Red Widow* (11/6/11; 128 performances). In between, Cohan and Harris presented another play by Winchell Smith, *The Only Son* (10/16/11; 32 performances). The star of *The Only Son*, Wallace Eddinger, would have better luck in another Cohan and Harris production, the straight play *Officer 666* (1/29/12; 192 performances), by Augustin Mac-Hugh. Two months later Cohan presented and starred in a revival of his 1906 hit *Forty-Five Minutes from Broadway*. Cohan's next Broadway outing was as author of the straight play *Broadway Jones* (9/23/12; 176 performances), starring Cohan and his parents. Four more straight plays followed: J. B. Fagan's *Hawthorne of the U.S.A.* (11/4/12; 72 performances), with Douglas Fairbanks in the lead; *Stop Thief* (12/25/12; 149 performances); Edgar Selwyn's *Nearly Married* (9/5/13; 123 performances); and finally Cohan's own *Seven Keys to Baldpate* (9/22/13; 320 performances), which starred Wallace Eddinger.

Cohan and Harris next offered the musical *The Beauty Shop* (4/13/14; 88 performances). This modest success had a score by Charles Gebest, best known as Cohan's musical director. Roi Cooper Magrue and

Walter Hackett's play *It Pays to Advertise* (9/8/14; 399 performances) ran under Cohan and Harris auspices. Cohan's next play, *The Miracle Man*, opened 13 days later and ran 97 performances.

Hello, Broadway! (12/25/14; 123 performances) was the first show to have an original Cohan score since *The Little Millionaire* more than 3 years earlier. Fred Ballard's comedy *Young America* (8/28/15; 105 performances) starred Otto Kruger and Peggy Wood. Cohan collaborated with Max Marcin on *The House of Glass* (9/1/15; 245 performances). Cohan alone wrote *Hit-the-Trail-Holiday* (9/13/15; 336 performances), which opened only 12 days later with Fred Niblo headlining. Then Cohan contributed another new score to Broadway, this time for *The Cohan Revue of 1916* (2/9/16; 165 performances). More straight plays followed: *The Intruder* (9/26/16; 31 performances), by Cyril Harcourt; *Captain Kidd, Jr.* (11/13/16; 128 performances), by Rida Johnson Young and starring Otto Kruger; *The Willow Tree* (3/6/17; 103 performances), an English import by J. H. Benrimo and Harrison Rhodes; *A Tailor-Made Man* (8/27/17; 398 performances), by Harry James Smith; and another import, *The King* (11/20/17), by G. A. Caillavet, Robert de Flers, and Emmanuel Arene.

Cohan and Harris then presented Louis Hirsch's musical *Going Up* (12/25/17; 351 performances). This was followed by the *Cohan Revue of 1918* (12/31/17; 96 performances). Its author called it "a hit-and-run play batted out by George M. Cohan." The young Irving Berlin contributed half the score to the show. Seven plays followed, the most notable being *Three Faces East* (8/13/18; 335 performances), by Anthony Paul Kelly, and Cohan's *A Prince There Was* (12/24/18; 159 performances) in which he starred.

Cohan's next musical was *The Royal Vagabond* (2/17/19; 208 performances). Cohan was responsible for doctoring this European operetta while it was still on the road. He called it a "Cohanized opera comique." During the run of *The Royal Vagabond* came the ACTORS' STRIKE OF 1919. Cohan was the most vocal of the managers who fought the actors. He considered the strike a personal affront and refused to join ACTORS' EQUITY, the new union, for the remainder of his career. Cohan's immovable stance led to a break with his longtime friend and producing partner, Sam Harris. The strike was symbolic to Cohan of the increasingly less freewheeling atmosphere of Broadway. He grew increasingly embittered and longed for the happier days when shows could be mounted with limited budgets and limitless enthusiasm. Cohan viewed the theater as a community, especially because his earliest memories were of trouping with his family. He couldn't understand why a strike was necessary at all, and why "the show must go on" wasn't the most important credo to

everyone in the theater. Cohan and Harris' last co-production for 17 years was *The Acquittal* (1/5/20; 138 performances), by Rita Weiman and Cohan.

Cohan was barred from performing because he refused to join Actors' Equity, but he continued his producing activities. His play *The Tavern* (9/27/20; 252 performances) is still produced around the country. Following a production of Augustin MacHugh's *The Meanest Man in the World* (10/12/20; 202 performances), Cohan produced and co-directed the musical comedy *Mary* (10/18/20; 220 performances). His next success was a production of *The O'Brien Girl* (10/3/21; 164 performances), a musical. He then produced *So This Is London* (8/30/22; 343 performances), by Arthur Goodrich.

Cohan's next musical, for which he supplied his usual book, music, and lyrics, was *Little Nellie Kelly* (11/13/22; 276 performances), which he also produced and directed. The show starred Elizabeth Hines, Georgia Caine, and Charles King. Nellie was a name Cohan always liked because it was his mother's nickname. Cohan's score again contained some popular successes, including "You Remind Me of My Mother" and "Nellie Kelly, I Love You." *Little Nellie Kelly* proved to be Cohan's biggest hit. Cohan's next musical was *The Rise of Rosie O'Reilly* (12/25/23; 87 performances). Virginia O'Brien, Georgie Hale, and a young Ruby Keeler appeared in the show. His next three productions were of his own plays, *The Song and Dance Man* (12/31/23; 96 performances), *American Born* (10/5/25; 88 performances), and *The Home Towners* (8/23/26; 64 performances). Cohan's friends and associates banded together to force Actors' Equity to give him special dispensation to appear on Broadway; he appeared in *The Song and Dance Man* and *American Born*.

He then produced Margaret Vernon's play *Yellow* (9/21/26; 135 performances), which starred a young Spencer Tracy, a Cohan discovery. Tracy turned up a year later in Cohan's next production, *The Baby Cyclone* (9/12/27; 184 performances). Cohan himself appeared in his play *The Merry Malones* (9/26/27; 208 performances), and although he produced the show, he did not direct it. Four more straight play productions followed, including his own *Whispering Friends* (2/20/28; 112 performances).

The last show for which he would author the book and score was *Billie* (10/1/28; 112 performances). For his last Broadway score Cohan contributed a big hit, the title song. Nine more straight play productions (including three revivals) followed, but they were all failures. Cohan became increasingly bitter about the Broadway scene and retired over and over again during his last years.

Cohan produced one last show, *Fulton of Oak Falls* (2/10/37; 37 performances), with his old partner Sam Harris. Cohan wrote and starred in the show. In 1933 the THEATER GUILD had convinced him to appear in EUGENE O'NEILL's only comedy, *Ah, Wilderness!*, and Cohan's last musical appearance on Broadway came in a Sam Harris production, the RODGERS AND HART musical *I'd Rather Be Right* (11/2/37). In it Cohan portrayed President Franklin Roosevelt. Cohan's last appearance was in the poorly received play *The Return of the Vagabond* (5/17/40; 7 performances), which Cohan produced, starred in, and wrote. At the time of his death, he was working on a new show, *The Musical Comedy Man*.

Gene Buck, one of Cohan's best friends wrote:

A part of our nation died when George made his final exit. The Song and Dance Man (as he loved to refer to himself), our First Actor and the greatest single figure the American Theatre ever developed in its history has gone to his eternal rest.

As I knew George I believe he would not have us feel sorry he is gone but feel glad that he had lived.

So long, George. God rest your sweet and noble soul.

Another friend, Sam Forrest, remembered Cohan this way:

He was tragic—he was humorous. He had the courage of a lion—he had the gentleness of a child. There were so many elements gathered in the makeup of this man a book might be written of any one of them. The general public think of him as a great figure in the American Theatre. They think of him as the man who wrote the songs that a generation of Americans sang throughout their life-time. They think of him as the man who represented the spirit of America. They think of him as a philanthropist ever ready to help one in distress. All this is true—but oh, so much more. When you live in close association with a man for more than thirty years—as I did with George M. Cohan—you see a side of his life that was not on public view. The kindliness of the man was manifest in a thousand different ways. In the small things of life that go to make up the stature of a man. I once wrote a cablegram to an American actor who was in Europe, offering him a part in a new play. Because of high cable charges I reduced the message to the fewest possible words. George read it and shook his head. "It's too cold," he said. Then he wrote a longer message full of warmth. I remonstrated that his message would cost a lot of money. George said, "Well, isn't it worth the money to send a friendly message to an actor who is thousands of miles from home?" It seems such a small thing but it was characteristic of the man.

Once when he was playing in Boston, he was a very sick man. I begged him to close the theater for a few nights. "You don't need the money," I said—"Why go on?" I'll never forget the surprised look he gave me. "It is not a matter of money," he said. "A lot of people come to the theater to see a play—to send them away is a

disappointment—their evening has been spoiled. I can't be a party to that. I'll go on and give the best that is in me." Saturday night I figured he would have Sunday and Monday to rest. But that day the wife of a friend in New York died. George, sick as he was, took the midnight train out of Boston to be at his friend's side in his sorrow. He was back in Boston Monday night to keep his show going. Every day of his life was punctuated with just such kindly acts. While he was lying desperately ill in a hospital fighting for his life, a friend was lying in another hospital. Every day George, from his sick bed, called his friend on the telephone to give him a word of courage and good cheer. Yes, they seem small things in themselves—but they make up the pattern of the man.

On the other side of his life, he was a vigorous antagonist. He would fight to the bitter end for what he thought was right—but he was never an enemy. An enemy implies doing an injury to someone—and George never knowingly hurt a human being. He had a very definite code of life and lived up to it religiously.

The great affection that existed between him and his father and mother and his sister, Josephine, was the keynote to his insistence on clean plays. He would never be associated with a play that he would be ashamed to associate with his father and mother and sister. The Four Cohans was an institution loved by all America. George M. Cohan was a great gentleman in many ways and he will live in the memory of America for many years.

COHAN AND HARRIS THEATRE. *See* **Harris Theater.**

COLONY THEATER. *See* **Broadway Theatre.**

COMDEN AND GREEN. The preeminent lyricist team in the history of musical theater; Betty Comden, b. New York, New York, May 3, 1915; Adolph Green, b. New York, New York, December 2, 1915; d. New York, New York, October 24, 2002.

Adolph Green and Betty Comden contributed to the development of the art of the musical both in the theater and on the screen. They were the longest-running writing team in Broadway history, yet because their subjects tended to be comedic rather than dramatic, they have not received their due by critics and historians.

Their over-50-year collaboration was remarkable. Betty Comden wrote of her partner:

Adolph is a man who reads while crossing streets. It is no uncommon sight to see him weaving his way across Broadway at Forty-Fifth Street in the crush of matinee traffic, all the daily papers bunched under one arm, the *Saturday Review, Atlantic Monthly, Life,* and *Paris-Match* slipping from under the other, an ash-trailing cigarette drooping from his lips, head deep in some book or periodical as brakes screech and drivers swear. Oblivious, he shuffles across engaged in leisurely perusal of anything from "A Skeleton Key" to "Finnegan's Wake" to this week's grosses in *Variety*.

In her 1995 memoir, *Off Stage*, she wrote, "It seems to me he must have sprung full-blown from his own head. There is no other head quite capable of having done the job. Only his head has the antic, manic imagination and off-beat creative erudite-plus-childlike originality to conceive of such a person."

They both began their careers as members of the Revuers, a nightclub act, which also included Judy Holliday (then named Judith Tuvim), for which they both wrote and performed. Their early collaborations for the Revuers was a success in the Greenwich Village club the Village Vanguard, but less than a success in the swankier environs of the Rainbow Room. They went to Hollywood to star in the movie *Greenwich Village* but were mostly cut from the picture.

LEONARD BERNSTEIN, a former co-camper and roommate of Adolph Green, caught their new act at the Blue Angel and convinced them to write the book and lyrics for the new musical adaptation of his ballet *Fancy Free. On the Town* (12/28/44; 462 performances) was a smash hit and contained such standards as "New York, New York" and "Lucky to Be Me." The show starred Nancy Walker, Sono Osato, Cris Alexander, John Battles, and Alice Pearce, as well as Comden and Green. This auspicious Broadway debut was under the direction of GEORGE ABBOTT, who had led many other neophytes to Broadway success.

Unfortunately, their next outing was not as successful. *Billion Dollar Baby* (12/21/45; 220 performances), for which they teamed up with composer Morton Gould, was a failure; IRVING HOFFMAN headed his review "Inflation." And their subsequent outing with composer Saul Chaplin, 1947's *Bonanza Bound*, closed in Philadelphia. Discouraged by their flops, the team went to Hollywood, where they joined MGM for a series of successful film musicals. They wrote the screenplay for *Good News* (1947), penned lyrics for *Take Me Out to the Ball Game* (1949), adapted their Broadway success *On the Town* to the screen that same year, and contributed a screenplay to the last pairing of FRED ASTAIRE and Ginger Rogers: *The Barkleys of Broadway* (1949).

In 1951 the team made another attempt at Broadway and met their next collaborator, JULE STYNE. The initial entry in the Styne, Comden, and Green canon was *Two on the Aisle* (7/19/51; 279 performances), a musical revue featuring Bert Lahr and Dolores Gray. Following that success, Comden and Green returned to Hollywood to write the screenplay for their best movie and perhaps the greatest movie musical of all time, *Singin'*

in the Rain (1952). They followed that with another huge success for MGM, *The Band Wagon* (1953). The film was released after their next Broadway assignment, *Wonderful Town*, opened on February 25, 1953. For this tribute to New York City, Comden and Green were reunited with Leonard Bernstein. Rosalind Russell and Edith Adams starred in this modern classic, which ran for 559 performances.

They next contributed songs in collaboration with Jule Styne for the legendary MARY MARTIN version of *Peter Pan* (10/20/54; 154 performances). Their songs, "Never Never Land" and "Distant Melody," among others, perfectly captured the mood of the J. M. Barrie classic. *Peter Pan* was followed by the movie musical *It's Always Fair Weather* (1955).

In 1956 they teamed up again with their partner from the Revuers, Judy Holliday, and had a smash hit. The show, *Bells Are Ringing* (11/29/56), also starred Charlie Chaplin's son Sydney. The Styne, Comden, and Green score yielded such gems as "Just in Time" and "The Party's Over." This resulted in their longest run to date, 924 performances. *Say, Darling* (4/3/58; 332 performances), a modest hit with a Jule Styne score and book by Richard Bissell, Marion Bissell, and Abe Burrows, followed. It was a roman à clef about the making of the Broadway musical *The Pajama Game*. Robert Morse first achieved fame in the show, which also featured Vivian Blaine, Johnny Desmond, and David Wayne. "Dance Only with Me" is the best-known of the largely forgotten songs.

While Jule Styne worked on *Gypsy*, Comden and Green returned to Hollywood for the screen adaptation of *Bells Are Ringing*. The threesome reunited for the Phil Silvers–Nancy Walker musical *Do Re Mi* (1/26/60; 400 performances). "Make Someone Happy" was the big hit from that score, which complemented Garson Kanin's tale of a small-time hustler in the jukebox racket. DAVID MERRICK, producer of *Do Re Mi*, hired the trio for *Subways Are for Sleeping* (12/27/61), which presented Sydney Chaplin, Carol Lawrence, and Phyllis Newman to good advantage. Despite a better-than-average score, which featured "Comes Once in a Lifetime," the show played only 205 performances.

Styne went on to write the smash *Funny Girl* with Bob Merrill, and Comden and Green went to Hollywood again for the all-star comedy *What a Way to Go* (1964). The three saw their next show, *Fade Out—Fade In*, premiere on May 26, 1964. The young Carol Burnett followed her success in *Once Upon a Mattress* in this show, which settled in for a long run at the MARK HELLINGER THEATER. But Burnett claimed to have a bad back, and the show was closed while the star and creators met in court. The show reopened with Burnett, but the damage was done and it closed after only 271 performances.

Betty Comden and Adolph Green in the museum scene from *On the Town*, 1944.

The team produced what is possibly their best score with Styne for their next show, *Hallelujah, Baby!* (4/26/67; 293 performances). Leslie Uggams and Robert Hooks starred in this saga of the black experience, which had a cumbersome libretto by Arthur Laurents. Comden and Green wrote only one more score with Styne, for the television musical *Getting Married* later that year.

The pair next collaborated on the STROUSE AND ADAMS musical *Applause* (3/30/70; 896 performances), starring Lauren Bacall. Comden and Green supplied the libretto for this musicalization of *All About Eve*. The show was a great success, but it was eight years before Comden and Green again had a show on Broadway. In 1978 they collaborated with Cy Coleman for the remarkable *On the Twentieth Century* (2/19/78; 460 performances). This wonderfully theatrical production opened with Madeline Kahn starring, along with John Cullum and Imogene Coca. Judy Kaye, who might have become a star overnight had

the sorry state of the Broadway theater at this time not deprived her of suitable vehicles for her great talents, soon replaced Kahn. Kevin Kline also made his first big impression in this show. Robin Wagner's outstanding scenic design helped the glorious proceedings in what is probably the last great musical comedy.

Their next Broadway assignment was for the failure *A Doll's Life* (9/23/82; 5 performances), with a score by Larry Grossman. This musical sequel to *A Doll's House* was pretentious and ponderous, surely a first for Comden and Green. Between Broadway assignments, Comden and Green themselves starred in a two-person retrospective called *A Party with Betty Comden and Adolph Green*.

Comden and Green's last Broadway show was a reteaming with Cy Coleman for *The Will Rogers Follies* (5/1/91; 963 performances), which was also tremendously successful.

Green called their collaboration "an unconscious give-and-take"; Betty Comden called it "mental radar."

Comden and Green attending the rehearsals for *Applause*, 1970.

Whatever it was, it has resulted in some of the most joyfully enthusiastic moments in the musical theater. Their shows, especially if they contributed librettos too, are marked by a smart, urbane innocence perfectly captured in the personality of Judy Holliday. Their characters are plain people who express their feelings with an exuberance and joie de vivre. Comden and Green's wit, humor, and slightly wry look at the world have resulted in one of the finest catalogues of productions in Broadway history. Harold Clurman wrote in *The Nation* of Adolph Green's "ebullient nature," which is "disciplined by Betty Comden's decorous wit." Brendan Gill, in *The New Yorker*, wrote of their "acute, affectionately bantering view of human frailty ... [They] have never lost their freshness, and it is plainly their intention, growing older, never to grow old." Their virtuosity is remarkable. They are the perfect collaborators both with each other and with those who have supplied the music for their shows.

COMEDY THEATER. 108 W. 41st Street. Architect: D. G. Malcolm. Opening: September 6, 1909; *The Melting Pot.*

The Comedy Theater, among the first Shubert theaters in New York (see SHUBERT BROTHERS), was not especially successful. It was built between Broadway and 6th Avenue, the only theater east of Broadway and south of 43rd Street. Among its noteworthy early productions were *The Affinity* (1/3/10; 24 performances), *A Man's World* (2/9/10; 71 performances), *The Three Daughters of Monsieur Dupont* (4/13/10; 21 performances), and *The Family* (10/11/10; 7 performances). The theater became William Collier's Comedy Theater with the opening of *I'll Be Hanged If I Do* (11/28/10; 80 performances). Shows produced during that period included *Bunty Pulls the Strings* (10/10/11; 391 performances) and *Fanny's First Play* (9/16/12). The name was changed back to the Comedy with the opening of *Her Own Money* on September 1, 1913. *Gentlemen from Number 19* (5/1/13) and *Consequences* (10/1/14) were other productions during this period.

As the theater district moved northward into Times Square the Shuberts gave their less promising productions to the Comedy, left behind below 42nd Street. In 1916 the Washington Square Players took over the Comedy. As a member of that company, KATHARINE CORNELL made her Broadway debut in their production of *Bushido* (8/30/16). The following year Ruth Draper made her debut at this theater.

The Depression hit the theater hard. The Comedy, by now well off the beaten track, was closed from 1931 to 1935. It was leased by an amateur theater group from Newark named the Metropolitan Players. Later

in the 1930s, boy genius Orson Welles directed and performed at the Comedy as part of the FEDERAL THEATRE PROJECT. The theater was known as the Mercury, named after Welles' theater company. Welles presented enormously successful productions of *Doctor Faustus* and *Julius Caesar*, which opened on November 11 and 12, 1937. The Mercury Theater productions were controversial. Welles described his *Julius Caesar*:

> Our *Julius Caesar* gives a picture of the same kind of hysteria that exists in certain dictator-ruled countries of today. We see the bitter resentment of freeborn men against the imposition of a dictatorship. We see a political assassination, such as that of Huey Long. We see the hope on the part of Brutus for a more democratic government vanish with the rise of a demagogue (Antony) who succeeds the dictator. Our moral, if you will, is that not assassination, but education of the masses, permanently removes dictatorships.

Welles' productions were the great successes in the theater's history. On December 29, 1939, the theater's name and policy changed again. It became the Artef Theater, a Yiddish theater, during the run of the Yiddish drama *Uriel Acosta*. The Yiddish policy continued until the theater was razed in 1942.

CONCERT THEATER. *See* **John Golden Theater.**

CORNELL, KATHARINE. Considered among the 20th century's greatest stage actors; b. Berlin, Germany, c. February 16, 1898; d. Vineyard Haven, Massachusetts, June 9, 1974.

Katharine Cornell, Laurette Taylor, HELEN HAYES, and Lynn Fontanne (*see* LUNT AND FONTANNE) were the great actresses of their time. ALEXANDER WOOLLCOTT dubbed Katharine Cornell "the First Lady of the American Theater." (He disliked her husband, Guthrie McClintic, and titled a *New Yorker* profile of him "The Tyranny of the Tantrum.") At her death, critic BROOKS ATKINSON wrote in the *New York Times*, "If she had a great reputation it was not because she had manufactured it. It was because—in addition to that personal magnetism—she had the integrity and taste of a lady."

Katharine Cornell was born into a family with theatrical interests. Her grandfather and father were in love with the theater. In fact, her grandfather had a small stage in his home where he and his friends put on amateur productions. Her father, a doctor, was doing postgraduate work in Germany when she was born. Her parents returned to Buffalo and his father gave up medicine to become manager and part owner of the Star Theatre. There is some mystery about the year of her birth. She once claimed her birthday to be February 16, 1898.

When she reached her seventies she moved the year back to 1893. She explained the discrepancy this way: "When an actress is younger she likes to lower her age, but when she is older she likes to add to her years."

Cornell's early background sparked her interest in the theater. While at boarding school at Oaksmere School in Mamaroneck, New York, she produced and acted in the classics. After graduation she stayed on for two years to teach drama. She assumed all jobs in the theater, including that of playwright. Edward Goodman, the director of the Washington Square Players, came to the school to direct one of Cornell's plays and invited her to come to New York. With an inheritance to fall back on, she accepted, and in 1916 appeared with the company in *Bushido*. Her only line was, "My son, my son." She then joined the Jessie Bonstelle Stock Company in Detroit and Buffalo, remaining with the company for three seasons. The company performed a new play every week for 10 performances. Jessie Bonstelle recognized the young actor's talents and brought her to London, where the company performed *Little Women*. Cornell played Jo, a leading role.

While still in London, Cornell was noticed by two women who recommended her to actor-producer Allen Pollock. He was casting Clemence Dane's drama *A Bill of Divorcement* and chose the young actor to open in the play on Broadway with himself in a leading role. Before *A Bill of Divorcement* opened, Cornell made her Broadway debut at the KLAW THEATER in Rachel Crothers' *Nice People* (3/2/21; 120 performance). No one took notice except casting director Guthrie McClintic. He wrote in his notebook, "Interesting. Monotonous. Watch." They were married by the following fall.

Producer Charles Dillingham opened *A Bill of Divorcement* (10/10/21) at GEORGE M. COHAN'S THEATRE on a particularly busy week, back in the days when Broadway might see more than one opening on a single night. Most of the leading critics attended the opening of Booth Tarkington's *The Wren* at the GAIETY THEATER. However, the second-string critics were enthusiastic in their response to the drama. Their positive reviews caused the leading critics to attend the show, and they offered their opinions in Sunday editions. However, despite this acclaim, the show was floundering. The closing notice was put up, and another attraction was booked for the theater. Luckily, business began to improve, and the show was moved to the TIMES SQUARE THEATER, where it enjoyed a healthy run, enabling audiences to discover Katharine Cornell.

Several minor roles followed, until Cornell took on the title role in George Bernard Shaw's *Candida*, which opened at the 48TH STREET THEATRE (12/12/24; 143 performances). She was again acclaimed for her acting. One reviewer raved, "The tenderness, the poetry, the supreme womanliness of Katharine Cornell's impersonation of the title part puts this actress a notch ahead of anything she has yet attempted. It is an impersonation touched by the wand of genius." Actresses did not easily amuse Shaw, although he was forever falling in love with those whom he admired. Shaw wrote to Cornell:

> I don't think I was ever so astonished by a picture as I was by your photograph. Your success as Candida, and something blonde and expansive about your name, had created an ideal suburban British Candida in my imagination.
>
> Fancy my feelings on seeing in your photograph a gorgeous dark lady from the cradle of the human race— wherever that was—Ceylon, Sumatra, Hilo, or the southernmost corner of the Garden of Eden!

Candida led to *The Green Hat* (9/15/25; 231 performances), which guaranteed Cornell stardom. However, a series of undistinguished plays followed, including *The Letter* (9/26/27; 104 performances), *The Age of Innocence* (11/27/28; 207 performances), and *Dishonored Lady* (2/4/30; 127 performances).

Cornell made one of her best-loved appearances as Elizabeth Barrett in Rudolf Besier's *The Barretts of Wimpole Street* (2/9/31) at the EMPIRE THEATER with Brian Aherne. Brooks Atkinson wrote in the *New York Times* that the play

> introduces us to Katharine Cornell as an actress of the first order. Here the disciplined fury she has been squandering on catchpenny plays becomes the vibrant beauty of finely wrought character.
>
> By the crescendo of her playing, by the wild sensitivity that lurks behind her ardent gestures and her piercing stares across the footlights, she charges the drama with a meaning beyond the facts it records. Her acting is quite as remarkable for the carefulness of its design as for the fire of her presence.

The play was a great triumph for Cornell. After 372 performances on Broadway, she took it on a 20,853-mile tour of the country that covered 77 cities. The company also performed *Romeo and Juliet* and *Candida*.

One measure of the tour's popularity may be seen in an incident that occurred in the state of Washington. The train carrying the troupe was delayed by floods. The company finally arrived in Seattle at 11:15 P.M. The actors were surprised to find that the audience had waited at the theater, determined to see the show. Alexander Woollcott, reporting the unusual event, described the audience's enthusiasm: "The excitement, the heady compliment paid by the audience in having waited at all, acted like wine on the spirits of the troupe and they gave the kind of performance one hopes for on great occasions and never gets."

Katherine Cornell and Kent Smith in the *Candida* revival, 1937.

The actress explained the way the tour worked:

We opened up the road. We made "The Barretts" and "Candida" pay for Shakespeare. "The Barretts" never played to an empty house—the receipts would be something like $33,000, then about $28,000 for "Candida" and for "Juliet" about $18,000 to $19,000, so that we came back having more than broken even. We really felt prideful.

We continued like that for many years, alternating New York with the road, paying for ourselves with Sidney Howard's "Alien Corn," Shaw's "St. Joan" and "The Doctor's Dilemma" and some of the others—until later on, when costs got too high with "Antony and Cleopatra," we had to call in angels.

Cornell appeared in her only Chekhov play, *The Three Sisters* (12/21/42; 123 performances), with Judith Anderson and Ruth Gordon at the ETHEL BARRYMORE THEATRE. She seldom performed the classics, although she made a memorable Antigone. "Guthrie persuaded me to do Shakespeare, and I was very frightened of Shakespeare," Cornell once said. "If not for Guthrie, I think I would have continued just drifting. He wanted to be an actor and my career was a sublimation of his desire, because he could pour his talents through me and that was a great advantage to me."

In fact, her husband chose her roles and bolstered her confidence. From the beginning of their marriage, he directed many of her performances and controlled her career. Cornell recalled, "I continued in the theater buoyed up mostly by his enthusiasm for it. He was one of those people who fascinated you always. You were never bored, sometimes upset, but never bored." She was always an insecure, nervous performer and had to relate to her characters before she felt she could assay the role: "I was nervous from the very beginning, and it got worse as the years went on. I was conscientious and wanted to do more, always, than I was able. I don't think, when I was playing, that I was ever happy—beginning at 4 o'clock any afternoon."

Cornell starred in S. N. Behrman's *No Time for Comedy* opposite Laurence Olivier (4/17/39; 139 performances) at the Ethel Barrymore Theatre, following the run with a 6-month tour. The play was the third presentation by the PLAYWRIGHTS' COMPANY. Of the play she said, "The audience enjoyed it but I was never, not from the beginning, happy about my own performance. I have never been happy about my own performance—not in anything."

By the 1950s Cornell's output began to slow down and her successes grew less frequent. Her last appearance was in *Dear Liar*, which toured cross-country from October 1959 to March 1960. It opened in New York at the Billy Rose Theater (*see* NEDERLANDER THEATRE) on March 17, 1960. After her husband's death, on October 29, 1961, she retired from the stage.

She seldom appeared on radio or television and appeared only in one movie, *Stage Door Canteen*. Her autobiographies, *I Wanted to Be an Actress* (1939) and *Curtain Going Up* (1943), were successful books.

After her death, S. N. Behrman called her "the most popular star in the country; an emanation of her rich and generous personality, as well as her luminous beauty, had gotten across to the American audience . . . Exhibitionism is taken for granted as the sine qua non ingredient in any acting career; Miss Cornell had less of it than any actress or actor I have ever known. Her position in the theater transcended technique; she was not, like Ina Claire and Lynn Fontanne, a great comedienne. It was something essential in herself, as a person, that the audiences sensed and reached out to."

Brooks Atkinson wrote, "She was not only a great actress but also a great lady. She was honest and considerate. She respected audiences. She worked hard because she believed that audiences of all kinds and everywhere were entitled to the best."

CORONET THEATER. *See* **Eugene O'Neill Theater.**

CORT THEATRE. 148 W. 48th Street. Architect: Thomas W. Lamb. Opening: December 29, 1912; *Peg o' My Heart*.

John Cort, a producer who had done most of his work on the West Coast, built the Cort Theatre. Cort wanted to begin production east of the Mississippi and built the Cort as his East Coast flagship theater. He built the Louis XVI–style theater on the "wrong side" of Broadway. Conventional wisdom had it that theaters east of Broadway, like the HENRY MILLER and LYCEUM, or west of 8th Avenue, like the MARTIN BECK, were too far off the beaten track to draw audiences. However, the Cort, east of Broadway between 6th and 7th Avenues, was an immediate success and was thought a "lucky" theater. Like MAXINE ELLIOTT'S THEATRE, the Cort's facade was an approximation of the Petit Trianon at Versailles. The interior, designed in a vaguely English style, was the only Broadway theater to feature an organ, in this case a Wurlitzer Hope-Jones console placed in the orchestra pit. Although the theater's owner, Edward B. Corey, was listed as architect, Thomas W. Lamb, one of the premiere theater architects in America, actually did the job. With 999 seats, the theater was suited to both plays and musicals.

The theater started its life with a huge hit, J. Hartley Manners' play *Peg O' My Heart*. The show starred Manners' wife Laurette Taylor, considered one of the greatest of all American actors. The play had a remarkable run at the Cort of 607 performances at a time when even 100 performances indicated a hit. The Cort had another hit with its next presentation, *Under Cover* (8/26/14; 349 performances). Its next success, VICTOR HERBERT's operetta *The Princess Pat* (9/29/15; 158 performances), contained one hit song, "Neapolitan Love Song."

A revival of *The Yellow Jacket* (11/9/16) was followed by *Flo Flo* (12/20/17; 220 performances). Silvio Hein, a prolific composer of the time whose songs have not lasted into the present, wrote the musical. *Abraham Lincoln* (12/15/19; 244 performances), John Drinkwater's play, starred Frank McGlyn. Produced at a time when some Americans still remembered the late president and his death, *Abraham Lincoln* struck a chord with audiences.

The 1920s were stellar years for the theater. The first hit was a somewhat unsophisticated offering. The musical *Jim Jam Jems* (10/4/20; 105 performances) featured comics Frank Fay, Harry Langdon, Joe E. Brown, Joe Miller, and Ned Sparks. Producer Harry Cort even contributed some of the show's lyrics. The next hit was *Captain Applejack* (12/30/21; 366 performances). George S. Kaufman (*see* KAUFMAN AND HART) and Marc Connelly provided one of their enduring hits with the Hollywood satire *Merton of the Movies* (11/13/22; 398 performances); Glenn Hunter starred. Eva Le Gallienne appeared in Ferenc Molnár's *The Swan* (11/23/23; 253 performances) with Basil Rathbone.

The Shuberts took over the lease of the theater in 1927 with John Cort's retirement. Katharine Hepburn made her theatrical debut at the Cort in *These Days*, which opened on November 12, 1928, and played 8 performances.

The 1930s began with Jed Harris' brilliant production of Chekhov's *Uncle Vanya* (4/15/30; 80 performances). For the leads, Harris cast Lillian Gish (who almost 50 years later starred in the same play at Circle in the Square), Osgood Perkins (father of Tony Perkins), Walter Connolly, and Eduardo Ciannelli. GEORGE ABBOTT provided two hits at the Cort in the late 1930s. The first was the hilarious *Boy Meets Girl* (11/27/35; 669 performances), by Sam and Bella Spewack, loosely based on the Hollywood adventures of Ben Hecht and Charles MacArthur. Abbott's next play was a knockabout farce of Broadway. *Room Service* (5/19/37; 496 performances), written by John P. Murray and Allen Boretz, starred Sam Levene, Philip Loeb, Teddy Hart, Betty Field, and Eddie Albert.

During the next decade the theater was equally successful. *The Male Animal* (1/9/40; 243 performances), by James Thurber and Elliott Nugent, featured Nugent himself along with Gene Tierney and Don DeFore. Another often-revived play, *A Bell for Adano* (12/6/44; 296 performances), by Paul Osborn, starred Fredric

March. *Lady Windermere's Fan* (10/14/46; 228 performances) had its most successful Broadway revival at the Cort, with Cornelia Otis Skinner and Estelle Winwood featured. Cecil Beaton designed the sets, lighting, and costumes as well as appeared in the play. The decade ended with Grace Kelly's Broadway debut in Strindberg's *The Father* (11/16/49). Also in the cast were Raymond Massey and Mady Christians.

Hepburn returned to the Cort in Shakespeare's *As You Like It* (1/26/50; 145 performes). The next Cort offering was drama critic Wolcott Gibbs' *Season in the Sun* (9/28/50; 367 performances). José Ferrer starred in the PULITZER PRIZE–winning drama *The Shrike* (1/15/52; 161 performances), by Joseph Kramm. Another Pulitzer prize–winning drama, *The Diary of Anne Frank* (10/5/55; 717 performances), starred Susan Strasberg, Jack Gilford, Lou Jacobi, Gusti Huber, and Joseph Schildkraut. The 1950s were concluded with another hit, Dore Schary's drama of Franklin Delano Roosevelt, *Sunrise at Campobello* (1/30/58; 556 performances), with Ralph Bellamy as the late president.

The theater's success continued into the 1960s. The first offering, Brendan Behan's *The Hostage* (9/20/60), was followed by the run of *Advise and Consent* (11/17/60; 212 performances). At the end of the decade the theater was converted to television. Merv Griffin presented his talk show here from 1969 to 1974. The Cort reopened to live theater with the musical *The Magic Show* (5/28/74; 1,920 performances). The chief draw of the show was magician Doug Henning.

In recent years the Cort's luck seems to have run out. As fewer and fewer shows are produced on Broadway, little quality product has been available for the Cort. The Cort joined the LONGACRE and BELASCO theaters as the least desirable houses due to their small size and location on the "wrong side" of Broadway. However, the few successes proved the "wrong side" theory to be mistaken. And booking what are perceived to be second-rate shows at the theaters proves, all too often, to be self-fullfillment.

Ma Rainey's Black Bottom (10/11/84) by August Wilson, managed to run 275 performances. After 3 years, playwright John Pielmeier, whose *Agnes of God* was a success, struck out with *Sleight of Hand* (4/6/1987), which only played 9 performances. The South African musical *Sarafina!* transferred from Lincoln Center on January 28, 1988. The Steppenwolf Theatre Company of Chicago brought its adaptation of John Steinbeck's novel *The Grapes of Wrath* to the Cort beginning on March 22, 1990. The Frank Galati–directed production opened to excellent reviews and played 188 performances.

Two years passed before the Cort's next tenant, Richard Nelson's *Two Shakespearean Actors* (1/16/92; 29 performances), which featured Brian Bedford,

Laurette Taylor in *Peg O' My Heart*, 1912.

Victor Garber, Zeljko Ivanek, Judy Kuhn, and Eric Stoltz. The next production at the Cort, David Henry Hwang's *Face Value*, was closed in previews. From 1994 to 1998 the theater had only one booking each year. The only notable success was the Lincoln Center Theater's production of Ruth and Augustus Goetz's play *The Heiress* (3/9/95; 340 performances). Cherry Jones made an especially strong impression on critics and was ably supported by Philip Bosco and Frances Sternhagen.

Another success followed *The Heiress*. John Leguizamo made a splash off Broadway with his one-man show *Spicorama*. He made his Broadway debut at the Cort in another one-man show, *Freak* (2/12/98; 144 performances).

A Year with Frog and Toad opened at the Cort on April 13, 2003. An exceptional musicalization of Arnold Lobel's children's books, the cast—Mark Linn Baker, Jay Goede, Danielle Ferland, Jennifer Gambatese, and especially Frank Vlastnik—excelled. Robert and Willie Reale wrote the piece.

On November 17, 1987, the New York City Landmarks Preservation Commission designated the interior and exterior of the theater as a landmark. The Commission said: "Its facade is an exceptional example of the neoclassical style" and its interior is "unusually handsome."

CRAIG THEATER. *See* George Abbott Theater.

CRITERION THEATER. *See* Olympia.

CRITICS.

Theater critics have been the bane and blessing of producers, actors, and writers since the dawn of the theater. From the beginnings of Broadway and Times Square, critics have been under the scrutiny of others in the industy.

In his book *The Footlights—Fore and Aft*, publicist and playwright Channing Pollock described the critical scene around 1911:

The New York critics are about a score in number, and, during the past few years there have been many changes in the corps. Its dean, William Winter, resigned from *The Tribune*, where Arthur Warren fills his post. Alan Dale, of *The American*, continues to be the most widely known of our writers on theatrical topics, and we still have with us, as stand-bys, Adolph Klauber, of *The Times*; Louis De Foe, of *The World*; Rennold Wolf, of *The Telegraph*; Acton Davies, of *The Evening Sun*; Charles Darnton, of *The Evening World*; Rankin Towse, of *The Post*, and Robert Gilbert Welsh, of *The Evening Telegram*. The Press has been carrying on a lively theatrical war, and, perhaps for that reason, its reviews manifest not only ignorance but the most bumptious disregard of general and experto-

pinion. Arthur Brisbane having declared against "abuse," *The Evening Journal* finds good in everything; *The Sun* has had no regular critic since it lost Walter Prichard Baton, and *The Herald* boasts that it prints only "reports" of performances. "First nights" are arranged, when that is possible, on different evenings, so that all the critics may be present at each, but, when there is a conflict, every man picks out the opening he considers most important and either lets the others go until later in the week or sends his assistant.

There are thirty or forty reviewers who represent magazines and periodicals, but, for the most part, these are declassé. They flock alone in the lobbies during intermissions, when the men from the daily newspapers congregate in groups to exchange a word or two about the play and to discuss other matters of common interest. These foyer gatherings pronounce a verdict that, as we have seen, is seldom—perhaps too seldom—overruled. Many a manager has leaned against his box office after the third act of a new piece, eavesdropping to learn what intelligence, experience, keen judgment and careful reading and rehearsing have not told him.

For there are two "anxious seats" on a "first night" in New York: One in the author's box and one in the manager's.

Some notable critics have attempted to define, and sometimes defend, their place in the world of the theater. JOHN MCCLAIN in his *New York Journal-American* column of September 6, 1955, "Man About Manhattan," pondered the worth of critics:

The new season will surely revive the age-old queries: "Can critics kill a show?" and "Are critics necessary?" I might as well get my answers in early: Yes, I think critics can kill a show; I think if a production draws unanimously poor reviews its chances of survival are slim. I also believe enough in the judgement of the critics, myself included, that if none of us likes a show it is not a good show.

Yes, I do think critics are necessary, unless you are prepared to say that newspapers are not necessary. The critic is only a reporter, employed to tell the readers whether this current event, this opening of a new entertainment offering, is worth the price of a seat. It is a news event, in the same sense as a ball game or a prizefight, and the thousands of potential theatre-goers have a right to be informed about it.

BROOKS ATKINSON remarked, "Your only hope is to say what you think, and even that is not so simple." Atkinson didn't prefer to be called a critic. He would rather have been named a reviewer whose specialty is theater. He felt that a true critic would have to stress a kind of analysis that would call for a complete immersion in the play: reading the script before the performance, attending rehearsals, and interviewing the major artistic figures to determine their objectives. He actually attempted this for Thornton Wilder's *Our Town* but gave up on the idea. He preferred to attend

Harold Simon's "In Memoriam" caricatured the leading critics of the day.

the play much as his audience of readers would, with as few preconceptions as possible.

Atkinson once wrote, "You can't be objectively right or wrong about a work of art. You can only have a personal reaction to what other people have done. The only mistake you can make is not to say what you think."

Some have attempted to understand the critics through somewhat scientific means. In 1955 *Critical Digest* assembled the following box scores of critical and public reaction:

Critic (Paper)	Pro	Con	% Pro
Hawkins (World-Tel.-Sun)	17	1	95
Watts (Post)	16	2	90
Coleman (Mirror)	16	2	90
Atkinson (Times)	15	3	85
McClain (Journal-American)	15	3	85
Chapman (News)	14	4	78
Kerr (Tribune)	14	4	78

At the same time, *Variety* assembled a critical "toughness report" and a comparison with public acceptance:

Critic (Paper)	Shows Covered	Pro	Con	% Pro
Kerr (Tribune)	62	22	37	.354
Watts (Post)	61	26	30	.426
McClain (Journal-American)	62	33	27	.532
Hawkins (World-Tel.-Sun)	62	34	25	.548
Coleman (Mirror)	60	34	26	.566
Chapman (News)	62	36	22	.580
Atkinson (Times)	51	31	18	.607
Combined Critic Average	431	221	191	.512
Variety Average	62	29	33	.467
Public Acceptance	62	30	32	.483

Variety's graph showed that public acceptance of shows was actually less liberal than the critics.

In 1940 IRVING HOFFMAN of the *Hollywood Reporter* wrote in his column, "Tales of Hoffman," a response to the *Variety* averages:

The legit critics of New York—the home of big league drama—are no less proud of their "batting average" than the Joe DiMaggios and Hank Greenbergs. The ball players like to belt out hits and runs—the critics like to spot hits and long runs on opening nights. Last season, top man in the crystal ball department of the Critics Circle was Richard Lockridge, dramassassin of the *N.Y. Sun*, who guessed right for a score of. 890. We assumed that this was the ultimate in soothsaying—until someone told us about a lad named Jean Stock Goldstone and his almost perfect figure of .965. And to add to our amazement, our informant told us that Goldstone's average for evaluating the boxoffice merits of plays was garnered not from the plush-covered eminence of an aisle seat on

opening night, but from the original playscripts, for which he had written preproduction analysis—in most cases months before opening.

Goldstone's uncanny crystal-gazing was performed under the worst possible conditions, since the producers of the 29 scripts he analyzed knew nothing of Goldstone and the devious methods by which these manuscripts were obtained. Many of the plays were revised after he had analyzed them, and strange things happened to them during rehearsals. In four cases, the critical reaction at opening controverted Goldstone's analysis, and in each instance he was proven right and the critics wrong.

Goldstone uses no "system." He doesn't know astrology and swears it isn't done with mirrors. He has merely acquired an uncanny ability to evaluate plays by perusing the scripts. This skill is the result of Goldstone's having written analyses of some 1200 manuscripts which came to his attention during the past few years while he was seeking contingency—collaborations with playwrights—in return for a piece of the show. He now has part ownership of 23 scripts by ten unknown authors, all available for immediate production. We don't mind risking our own batting average—and it's a pretty high one, too—by suggesting that these scripts would make excellent movie material.

Goldstone is modest enough to point out that his accomplishment is remarkable only by current standards, for the records show that, in the theater of the past generation, leading managers compiled averages as high as .800, as contrasted with the present best mark of .300. The entire theatre of 1910 showed a .500 success, a figure which has steadily declined to .160 for the last three years—and the fact that during that period there has been no success by an unknown author, further indicates the inability of script on its intrinsic merits alone—a feat which Goldstone apparently has well under control. We predict that once Goldstone gets rolling, he'll gather no moss.

Critics seem to vary between apologists and those who are staunchly militant in defense of their views. A few, however, seem to keep perspective on their jobs and effects on the success or failure of shows. Still others feel a need to defend their knowledge of theater history and its artistic merits. CLIVE BARNES, the drama critic for the *New York Post* and one-time critic for the *New York Times*, wrote in a column of April 16, 1988:

The theatre is a street of memories, and it is memories, the past, performance-nostalgia, and perhaps the maintenance of standards that I thought I would talk about this week. Particularly as the past affects myself and my critical fraternity.

All critics have a great deal to remember, and, perhaps, a great deal we would like to forget.

We see an inordinate amount. I have gone to see *Hamlet* more often than most people ever go to the theatre. Over the years I have attended—counting theatre, dance, opera and concerts but leaving out movies—more than 12,000 events.

This provides problems. We need to maintain something called "response," in a way quite removed from civilian audiences.

We can in fact do this—we would go crazy, I mean *really* crazy, if we couldn't—but of course we are still in a special category of consumerism.

No one writes a play in the expectation that it will be seen by someone who has already seen about 20 plays within the past month!

This is odd, but really, when you come to think of it, unavoidable. It is just one of the reasons why criticism must be called a necessary evil.

PERCY HAMMOND of the *Herald Tribune* wrote, "Dramatic criticism is the venom of contented rattlesnakes." At another time he countered Hiram Motherwell's contention in *The Stage* that modern critics lacked the knowledge of the theater that critics of the past had enjoyed. Hammond wrote in rebuttal, "I, myself, am not a drama critic, and even if I wanted to be, I could not. My humble reviewer's job, as I have understood it for many years, is not didactic, teaching playwrights how to write or actors how to act, but to estimate as accurately as possible, in the interest of playgoers, the results of a performance in a theatre. To be, as Archer said, concerned only with the effect produced, not with the phenomena of its production—to appraise values, not to analyze or assay them."

Hammond was also against the fashion of critics naming the ten best plays or performances of the year.

> This pleasant system might be extended. What ten electricians are most adroit in their counterfeits of twilight and the evening glow? What ten ushers are most proficient in showing us to our places, and what ten box office officials deserve the accolade for civility and the yearning to give us all seats in the fourth row, center, on an aisle and near an exit?
>
> Who are the least odious of the ingénues? What ten American managers had the best scholastic record in their universities? The ten critics and reviewers who know most about drama and life ought to make an amusing catalogue, no less so, perhaps, than the ten actors who best can utter that stable speech of the theatre, "Won't you be seated?"

DANIEL BLUM THEATRE WORLD AWARD. In 1945 Daniel Blum, editor of *Theatre World*, originated this award to recognize "promising personalities" who appear in the New York theater. There is no set number of awards given each season, but there are usually at least 10 names cited by the current *Theatre World* editor.

The *Theatre World* Award has cited many newcomers who went on to become stars. These include Judy Holliday, Betty Comden (*see* COMDEN AND GREEN), Marlon Brando, Barbara Bel Geddes, Burt Lancaster, Wendell Corey, David Wayne, Patricia Neal, James Whitmore, Carol Channing, Gene Nelson, Julie Harris, Charlton Heston, Grace Kelly, Audrey Hepburn, Richard Burton, Nancy Andrews, Geraldine Page, Paul Newman, Gwen Verdon, James Dean, Eva Marie Saint, Jack Lord, Julie Andrews, Barbara Cook, Andy Griffith, Laurence Harvey, Jason Robards Jr., Alan Alda, Carol Burnett, Jane Fonda, Robert Goulet, and Larry Hagman.

DELIA AUSTRIAN MEDAL. This award is given by the Drama League of New York for "the most distinguished performance of the season." It has been awarded since 1935, when KATHARINE CORNELL won for her performance in *Romeo and Juliet*. Other recipients have been HELEN HAYES, Maurice Evans, Paul Muni, Alfred Lunt and Lynn Fontanne (*see* LUNT AND FONTANNE), Ingrid Bergman, Judith Anderson, Julie Harris, Josephine Hull, Charles Boyer, and Alec Guinness.

DE MILLE, AGNES. Influential choreographer of several major Broadway shows and noted modern dancer; b. New York, New York, September 18, 1905; d. New York, New York, October 7, 1993.

Agnes de Mille was instrumental in raising the art of Broadway choreography to new heights of sophistication and psychology. She was not content simply to have her dancers perform until the music stopped. Rather, her ballet-inspired choreography revealed characterization and motivation and was often narrative in form. Her dance was more expressive than the usual Broadway hoofing, though she could incorporate that style into her choreography as needed. Her stress on motivational gestures revolutionized Broadway. She consistently continued the narrative flow of the musical's story instead of just stopping the action for a dance interlude. She wasn't beholden to strict classical style; rather, she coached her dancers to make their movements expressions of their characters' feelings rather than a series of classic steps. She incorporated elements of modern dance, classical ballet, folk dance, and social dance into her works, layering a depth of feeling by utilizing any dance element that would best serve the necessities of the plot. But first and foremost in a de Mille dance was the dramatic situation in which the dances fit and the expression of emotion and character within her dancers.

She associated herself with great Broadway choreographers, including Jerome Robbins and Michael Kidd. Of the three of them she wrote, "To the classic base we have accordingly added colloquialism. We have come down to earth; we have put out feet on the ground."

De Mille had her greatest successes with the composing team of RODGERS AND HAMMERSTEIN. Their constant attempts to stretch the conventions of musical comedy and operetta allowed de Mille to rise to the occasion time and time again.

She was born to a resolutely theatrical family. Her father, William C. de Mille, was a Broadway playwright and screenwriter. Her uncle was the noted film

Katharine Sergova and Marc Platt in the original production of *Oklahoma!*

director and producer Cecil B. DeMille (he altered the styling of the family name). Her mother, Anna George de Mille, was a strong woman, the daughter of Henry George, the social reformer, economist, and single-tax advocate. She instilled in her daughter a sense of self and importance along with a firm regard for the betterment of the human race and the equality of women.

After spending her early childhood in New York City, Agnes moved with her family to Hollywood in 1914. While there, Agnes was brought to performances by Ruth St. Denis and Anna Pavlova, two of the greatest dancers of their time and two of the most revolutionary. Agnes immediately decided to become a dancer and, with her sister Margaret, took ballet classes.

At the insistence of her father she studied English at UCLA, graduating cum laude. However, her mother recognized Agnes' artistic yearnings and brought her and Margaret back to New York to pursue a career in dance. While Margaret attended college, Agnes continued her studies in dance and in 1928 made her choreo-

graphic debut in a solo program. The reviews were good, the *New York Times* critic John Martin stating that like Charlie Chaplin, the young dancer "sees tragedy through a lens of comedy."

De Mille's first and only appearance as a dancer in a Broadway show came with the *Grand Street Follies* (5/28/28; 144 performances). In 1931 she appeared with some of the best up-and-coming modern choreographers of the time, Martha Graham, Doris Humphrey, Helen Tamiris, and Charles Weidman, in a series of programs sponsored by the Dance Repertory Theatre.

She then went to Europe, where she performed in Paris, Copenhagen, and London. While in London she got her first theatrical commission, to choreograph the COLE PORTER musical *Nymph Errant* (10/6/33). The show, starring Gertrude Lawrence, was mildly successful but did not cross the Atlantic. After another London assignment *(Why Not Tonight?)* she made her Broadway choreographic debut with *Hooray for What!* The show opened on December 1, 1937, with a score by HAROLD ARLEN and E. Y. HARBURG. It ran for 200 performances. Robert Alton, also a distinguished Broadway choreographer, shared the credit for staging the dances. Next, a jazz version of *A Midsummer Night's Dream* called *Swingin' the Dream* opened on November 29, 1939, with an impressive cast, including Louis Armstrong, Maxine Sullivan, Benny Goodman and his sextet, Bud Freeman's Summa Cum Laude Band, Dorothy Dandridge, Jackie "Moms" Mabley, Butterfly McQueen, and Muriel Rahn. De Mille shared the choreographic assignment with Herbert White.

De Mille's first solo venture on Broadway was for the landmark musical *Oklahoma!* She received ecstatic reviews from the CRITICS; Lewis Nichols in the *New York Times* announced that these were her "most inspired dances." Howard Barnes, writing in the *New York Herald Tribune*, said that she "worked small miracles." Olin Downes of the *New York Times* wrote,

"The dancing . . . is so original and so expressive of genuine things that lie deep in the people and the soil."

De Mille's other choreographed works for the stage, with her ballets indicated in quotes, were "Venus in Ozone Heights" and "Forty Five Minutes for Lunch" for *One Touch of Venus* (10/7/43; 567 performances); "Civil War Ballet" for *Bloomer Girl* (10/5/44; 657 performances); "Carousel Waltz" for *Carousel* (4/19/45; 890 performances); "The Chase" for *Brigadoon* (3/13/47; 581 performances); *Allegro* (10/10/47; 315 performances), for which she was also director; *Gentlemen Prefer Blondes* (12/8/49; 740 performances); *Out of This World* (12/21/50; 157 performances), for which she was director only; *Paint Your Wagon* (11/12/51; 289 performances); "Pas de Deux" for *The Girl in Pink Tights* (3/5/54; 115 performances); "Huckleberry Island Ballet" and "The Town House Maxixe" for *Goldilocks* (10/11/58; 161 perfor-

Agnes de Mille rehearsing dancers for the original production of *Allegro*, 1947.

mances); "Dublin Night Ballet" for *Juno* (3/9/59; 16 performances); *Kwamina* (10/23/61; 32 performances); *110 in the Shade* (10/24/63; 330 performances); and *Come Summer* (2/18/69; 7 performances), for which she was also director.

Her works for the American Ballet Theater include "Rodeo" (1942), "Tally-Ho" (1944), "Fall River Legend" (1948), "The Harvest According" (1952), "Rib of Eve" (1956), "Sebastian" (1957), "The Wind in the Mountains" and "The Four Marys" (1965), "A Rose for Miss Emily" (1971), and "Texas Fourth" (1976).

In 1973 she established the Heritage Dance Theatre, which toured the country for two years. She was also the author of many well-received books including several volumes of memoirs: *Dance to the Piper, And Promenade Home, Speak to Me, Dance with Me, Where the Wings Grow*, and *Reprieve*. Among her other books were *To a Young Dancer, The Book of the Dance, Dance in America*, and *America Dances*.

She was the recipient of more than 15 honorary degrees and was elected to the Theater Hall of Fame. She was awarded the Handel Medallion, New York City's highest award for achievement in the arts. She was also given the Kennedy Center Career Achievement Award in 1980 and the National Medal of the Arts in 1986.

An early proponent of government subsidy of the arts, she was an original member of the National Council on the Arts and the first chair of its Dance Panel in 1965. She also became, that same year, the first president of the Society of Stage Directors and Choreographers.

DE SYLVA, BROWN, AND HENDERSON.
Among the most popular of Broadway composers in the 1920s and '30s; B. G. "Buddy" DeSylva, b. George G. De Sylva, New York, New York, January 27, 1895; d. Hollywood, California, July 11, 1950; Lew Brown, b. Louis Brounstein, Odessa, Russia, December 10, 1893; d. New York City, New York, February 5, 1958; Ray Henderson, b. Raymond Brost, Buffalo, New York, December 1, 1896; d. Greenwich, Connecticut, December 31, 1970.

The upbeat numbers of lyricists B. G. De Sylva and Lew Brown and composer Ray Henderson seemed to exactly define the bubbly insouciance of the 1920s. Though none of their shows has lasted, they wrote some of the most endearing songs in the American popular song canon.

Although most famous as a trio, each member also worked with others. De Sylva collaborated with GEORGE GERSHWIN, VICTOR HERBERT, JEROME KERN, Emmerich Kalman, and Lewis Gensler; Brown also wrote with Harry Akst, Charles Tobias, and Sam Stept; Henderson also collaborated with lyricists Ted Koehler, Jack Yellen, and Irving Caesar.

Lew Brown

Brown's parents moved from Odessa to New Haven and finally New York City, where Lew began his songwriting career. He was lucky enough to meet up with successful composer Albert Von Tilzer, and the pair had some early successes in musicals in both New York and London. Among their hits were "Give Me the Moonlight, Give Me the Girl" (*Hullo, America*), "Oh, by Jingo, Oh by Gee" (*Linger Longer Letty*), and "Dapper Dan" (*A to Z*).

Brown hooked up with Ray Henderson but continued to have song hits with a variety of other composers. These included "Last Night on the Back Porch" (with Carl Schraubstader), "Shine" (with Cecil Mack and Ford Dabney), "Then I'll Be Happy" (with Cliff Friend), and "Collegiate" (with Moe Jaffe and Nathan A. Bonx).

Friend was a major collaborator with Brown, and together they worked on Brown's first complete musical comedy score. The show was *Piggy*, which opened at the ROYALE THEATRE on January 11, 1927.

B. G. De Sylva

Buddy De Sylva came from a vaudeville family, and his early songs were incorporated into AL JOLSON's Broadway shows (often with Jolson taking a co-writer credit). De Sylva found himself writing for the prestigious Remick music publishing company, the leading publisher of Broadway scores at the time. Remick paired De Sylva with the young George Gershwin and lyricist Arthur Jackson, and the result was *La La Lucille* (5/26/19; 104 performances), the team's first full Broadway score (De Sylva had already had a show close out of town, *Dodo*).

With the success of *La La Lucille*, De Sylva was put together with veteran composer Jerome Kern, and the result was a mixed blessing. Though *Zip Goes a Million* never made it to Broadway, it did contain "Look for the Silver Lining," which became a standard when interpolated in their next show, *Sally*. He had better success with Kern on the show *Sally* (12/21/20; 570 performances), which boasted the hit song "Whippoor-will." Jolson took two more De Sylva numbers and incorporated them into his hit show *Bombo* (10/6/21; 218 performances). Both "April Showers" (with Louis Silvers) and "California Here I Come" (with Joseph Meyer) were smash hits. Jolson and De Sylva had another hit show with *Big Boy* (1/7/25; 48 performances), in which was "If You Knew Susie" and "Keep Smilin' at Trouble," the latter with Joseph Meyer.

De Sylva was now an important force in songwriting, and his next show, *Orange Blossoms* (9/19/22;

B. G. ("Buddy") De Sylva.

95 performances), was written with the great Victor Herbert. The hit song from the show was "A Kiss in the Dark." He was hired along with Gershwin to supply the scores for three editions of the GEORGE WHITE'S SCANDALS (*see also* GEORGE WHITE), which contained "I'll Build a Stairway to Paradise" and "Somebody Loves Me," and with Joseph Meyer he worked on another *Scandal*. When Gershwin moved on to write with his brother, Ira, De Sylva continued with George White as partner of the new team of De Sylva, Brown, and Henderson.

Ray Henderson

The son of a musician who played several instruments, the young Ray Henderson composed his first songs at age eight. He held several jobs in the music industry, including church organist, piano teacher, vaudeville accompanist, pianist in a dance band, and arranger for a music publisher. His first published song was "Humming," written in collaboration with lyricist Louis Breau.

That song found its way into the Broadway show *Tip Top*, which starred the Duncan sisters. With Lew Brown he wrote "Georgette," which was in *Greenwich Village Follies*. The team of Brown and Henderson wrote several songs that would come to be standards, the best-known of which is "Don't Bring Lulu."

Brown continued to collaborate with others as well and found success with "That Old Gang of Mine," written with Billy Rose and Mort Dixon, and "Five Foot Two, Eyes of Blue" and "I'm Sitting on Top of the World," both with Joe Young, and Sam Lewis. Lewis, Young, and Brown were a very successful team in their own right.

Brown first collaborated with Buddy De Sylva in 1925 on the hit song "Alabamy Bound" (written also with Bud Green). Having worked with both De Sylva and Henderson, it was only natural that the three writers would team up to make Broadway's most successful songwriting trio.

The threesome's shows exemplified the roaring Twenties with its emphasis on speed and rhythm. Their songs incorporated jazz and blues into the Broadway idiom. Optimistic and energetic, the team provided a remarkable number of standards in only five years of collaboration.

De Sylva, Brown, and Henderson were responsible for the following revues and musicals, with their famous songs in quotes: *George White's Scandals* (6/22/25; 169 performances); *George White's Scandals* (6/14/26; 432 performances), "Birth of the Blues," "The Black Bottom," "This Is My Lucky Day"; *Good News!* (9/6/27; 551 performances), "The Best Things

in Life Are Free," "Good News," "Just Imagine," "Lucky in Love"; *Manhattan Mary* (9/26/27; 264 performances); *George White's Scandals* (7/2/28; 230 performances), "I'm on the Crest of a Wave"; *Hold Everything!* (10/10/28; 413 performances), De Sylva also as co-librettist, "You're the Cream in My Coffee"; *Follow Thru* (1/9/29; 401 performances), De Sylva also as co-librettist, "Button Up Your Overcoat," "Then I'll Have Time for You"; *Flying High* (3/3/30; 355 performances), Brown and De Sylva also co-librettists; *George White's Scandals* (9/14/31; 204 performances), Henderson and Brown only, "Ladies and Gentlemen, That's Love," "Life Is Just a Bowl of Cherries," "That's Why Darkies Were Born," "This Is the Missus," "The Thrill Is Gone."

Following De Sylva's leaving the team, Ray Henderson and Lew Brown continued their collaboration. They wrote *Hot-Cha!* (3/8/32; 118 performances), with Henderson as co-librettist, and *Strike Me Pink* (3/4/33; 122 performances), with Brown and Henderson also as co-librettists, co-producers, and co-directors.

Ray Henderson went on to write alone, and on *Say When* (11/8/34; 76 performances), written in collaboration with Ted Koehler, he also acted as co-producer. He continued with *George White's Scandals* (12/25/35; 110 performances) and the *Ziegfeld Follies of 1943* (4/1/43; 553 performances) (*see* ZIEGFELD FOLLIES).

Lew Brown, along with Harry Akst, wrote *Calling All Stars* (12/13/34; 35 performances), for which he was also co-librettist, producer, and co-director, and also *Yokel Boy* (7/6/39; 208 performances), on which he was librettist, producer, and director. He occasionally worked in Hollywood before retiring.

De Sylva, meanwhile, was co-librettist and wrote lyrics for *Take a Chance* (11/26/32; 243 performances), "Eadie Was a Lady," "Rise and Shine," "You're an Old Smoothie"; co-wrote the libretto for and produced COLE PORTER's *Du Barry Was a Lady* (12/6/39; 408 performances); produced IRVING BERLIN's *Louisiana Purchase* (5/28/40; 444 performances) and Porter's *Panama Hattie* (10/30/40; 501 performances), on which he was co-librettist. His songwriting days over, De Sylva worked sporadically in pictures as a producer before retiring.

DIAMOND HORSESHOE. *see* **Century Theater.**

DIETZ AND SCHWARTZ. Perhaps the greatest songwriters for Broadway revues, with a 30-year career; Howard Dietz, b. New York, New York, September 8, 1896; d. New York, New York, July 30, 1983; Arthur Schwartz, b. Brooklyn, New York, November 25, 1900; d. London, England, September 3, 1984.

Howard Dietz.

The songwriting team of composer Arthur Schwartz and lyricist Howard Dietz elevated the art of revue writing to new heights. They collaborated on what is considered the greatest of all revues, *The Band Wagon*. Their long career spanned 30 years and resulted in the creation of many standards. Schwartz and Dietz were among the most successful writers of ballads; their hits included "Dancing in the Dark," "I Guess I'll Have to Change My Plan," "You and the Night and the Music," and "Alone Together." Their comedy and upbeat songs were equally well constructed, such as "New Sun in the Sky," "Triplets," and "That's Entertainment."

Howard Dietz was born in New York and attended Townsend Harris Hall and Columbia University. While at Columbia he frequently contributed to Franklin P. Adams' column, "The Conning Tower." His early interest in language landed him a position as a copywriter in the Philip Goodman ad agency. He obtained the position by writing a contest-winning advertisement for Fatima Cigarettes. After his discharge from the navy, Dietz obtained a job with Samuel Goldwyn, the motion picture producer. The publicity post led to a long career with what eventually became Metro-Goldwyn-Mayer. Dietz wrote for the stage as a sideline to his publicity work for the movies. It's ironic that he felt his retirement income would come from his MGM pension. In fact, it was his ASCAP royalties that allowed him to live in comfort.

Dietz's first Broadway lyric was for *Poppy* (9/13/23; 346 performances), a W. C. Fields vehicle and the first time Fields played a legitimate role on Broadway. Dietz also contributed the dialogue for Fields' character. Dietz's lyrics for this show and his contributions to "The Conning Tower" did not go unnoticed. Philip Goodman, who was involved in advertising as well as the theater, suggested to JEROME KERN that he might use Dietz as lyricist on his next show. Kern took Goodman's advice, and the result was *Dear Sir* (9/23/24; 15 performances). This start, though inauspicious, did bring Dietz to the attention of Arthur Schwartz, a lawyer.

Like IRVING BERLIN and others, Schwartz taught himself to play the piano. While at school, Schwartz played piano in neighborhood movie houses. He attended New York University and Columbia University. After graduation he taught English in the New York public school system. Forsaking the teaching profession, he entered legal practice in 1924. Four years later he wrote to Howard Dietz on the advice of publisher Bennett Cerf. Schwartz had already had one of his songs published, "Baltimore M.D., You're the Only Doctor for Me," with lyrics by Eli Dawson. Schwartz wrote to Dietz, complimenting the lyricist by saying that Dietz was the most like Lorenz Hart

(*see* RODGERS AND HART) in style. Dietz was unimpressed, however, and responded by suggesting that Schwartz team up with an established lyric writer to gain from the education, as he himself had done with Jerome Kern. Then when they both became famous they could write together. The musical *Queen High* (11/8/26) provided Schwartz with his first job. Schwartz collaborated on two songs with fellow composer Ralph Rainger and lyricist E. Y. HARBURG: "Brother Just Laugh It Off" and "I'm Afraid of You." Unfortunately, by the time the show opened on Broadway, the Schwartz songs were cut.

Meanwhile, GEORGE AND IRA GERSHWIN were hard at work on their score for *Oh, Kay!* (11/8/26) when Ira had to have his appendix removed. George chose Dietz to work on the score during Ira's recuperation. Dietz wrote the title song's lyrics, "Heaven on Earth," and the verse to "Clap Yo' Hands." Dietz's next assignment, *Hoopla*, was probably the first show in history to close out of town after only one act. Dietz's life as a publicist was turning out to be much more successful than his theater career. Metro-Goldwyn-Mayer had been formed in 1924, and Dietz was made director of advertising and publicity because of his creation of the Leo the Lion trademark and the "*Ars gratia artis*" motto for Goldwyn Pictures. Nonetheless, Jay Gorney and Dietz had better luck with *Merry-Go-Round* (5/31/27; 135 performances), their next collaboration, than they did with *Hoopla*. Henry Souvaine contributed some of the music, with Morrie Ryskind also writing lyrics.

At the end of the 1920s Tom Weatherly, a producer and Broadway bon vivant, decided to put on a revue called *The Little Show*. Dwight Deere Wiman was brought in to help produce the venture, and Dietz was called in to write the lyrics. *The Little Show* was conceived as an answer to the big revues such as the ZIEGFELD FOLLIES, the *Passing Shows*, and EARL CARROLL'S VANITIES. *The Little Show* would be an intimate revue in the manner of *The Garrick Gaieties*. Weatherly had already hired performers Clifton Webb, Fred Allen, and Libby Holman; all that was needed was a composer. Weatherly believed that he had a line on one, however. He asked Dietz whether the name Arthur Schwartz rang any bells. Dietz showed him the correspondence between Schwartz and himself, and Weatherly promptly labeled the coincidence fate. Dietz and Schwartz's first song together was a satire on the movie title songs that were being foisted on the public. The new team's answer to the fad was "Hammacher Schlemmer, I Love You," a paean to the noted New York hardware company. *The Little Show* (4/20/29; 321 performances) opened to immediate acclaim. Dietz and Schwartz's score was especially well received.

Their first great hit from the show and a subsequent standard was "I Guess I'll Have to Change My Plan."

While Dietz was attending to his motion picture duties, Schwartz collaborated with other lyricists. Less than a month after the opening of *The Little Show*, Arthur Schwartz wrote music to Agnes Morgan's lyrics for some of the tunes in *The Grand Street Follies* (5/1/29; 85 performances). Schwartz's next assignment was writing the music for two London musical comedies. The first, *Here Comes the Bride* (2/20/30; 175 performances), had two Dietz lyrics. The second, *The Co-Optimist* (4/4/30), was written in collaboration with Greatrex Newman.

Dietz and Schwartz were reunited for *The Second Little Show* (9/2/30; 63 performances), this time on Broadway. However, the hit song wasn't by Dietz and Schwartz. It was "Sing Something Simple," with words and music by Herman Hupfeld. After a failed collaboration with composer Arthur Swanstrom on *Princess Charming* (10/13/30; 56 performances), Schwartz re-teamed with Dietz for *Three's a Crowd* (10/15/30; 272 performances), the first of the great Dietz and Schwartz Broadway revues. Fred Allen, Clifton Webb, and Libby Holman, all from the first *Little Show*, starred along with ballerina Tamara Geva, Amy Revere, the California Collegians a band that included the young Fred MacMurray in its ranks. The sketches were written by some of the top comedy writers of the time: Corey Ford, Fred Allen, Arthur Sheekman, Groucho Marx, Laurence Schwab, and others. The producer was the great Max Gordon, and the director was Hassard Short in the first of his collaborations with Dietz and Schwartz. The score, written by a number of writers, contained the classic Dietz and Schwartz ballad "Something to Remember You By." Another standard, "Body and Soul," by John Green, Edward Heyman, Robert Sour, Frank Eyton, and Dietz, was also introduced.

The Band Wagon (6/3/31; 262 performances), which opened at the NEW AMSTERDAM THEATRE, was produced by Max Gordon and directed by Hassard Short. The sketches for the revue were by Dietz and George S. Kaufman (*see* KAUFMAN AND HART). The cast featured FRED AND ADELE ASTAIRE, Helen Broderick, Frank Morgan, and modern dancer Tilly Losch. *The Band Wagon* was the first American revue with real sophistication. The score contained the team's greatest song, "Dancing in the Dark." The rest of the score was equally good, especially the upbeat "New Sun in the Sky" and the charming "I Love Louisa." The closing of *The Band Wagon* after 262 performances marked the end of the career of Adele Astaire, who retired following a brief tour.

The next year brought another fine Dietz and Schwartz revue, *Flying Colors* (9/15/32; 181 perfor-

mances). It was again produced by Max Gordon, and this time Dietz directed. Dietz, Kaufman, Charles Sherman, and Corey Ford wrote the sketches. The big hit ballad was "Alone Together." Other successful numbers were "Louisiana Hayride," "Fatal Fascination," and "A Shine on Your Shoes." Buddy and Vilma Ebsen, performers very different in style from the Astaires, were the featured dance team. Also in the cast were harmonica virtuoso Larry Adler, dancer Tamara Geva, comedians Imogene Coca and Patsy Kelly, and the sophisticated Clifton Webb.

After Schwartz contributed music to a London show, *Nice Goings On*, he and Dietz presented their first book musical, *Revenge with Music* (11/28/34; 158 performances). Dietz directed a fine cast, including Libby Holman, Ilka Chase, Joseph Macaulay, Georges Metaxa, and Charles Winninger. The score contained two distinguished ballads: "You and the Night and the Music" and "If There Is Someone Lovelier than You."

The team returned to the revue format with *At Home Abroad* (9/19/35; 198 performances), although the new show had a slight plot and was billed as a musical comedy. The plot, which followed a family on an around-the-world cruise, required a large number of librettists, including Dietz, Marc Connelly, Dion Titheradge, Raymond Knight, and Reginald Gardiner. Gardiner wrote his own monologues for the show. His fellow cast members included Ethel Waters, Eleanor Powell, Eddie Foy Jr., Beatrice Lillie, and Herb Williams. For the first time a Dietz and Schwartz score didn't yield a hit ballad, although "Got a Bran' New Suit," "Hottentot Potentate," "Love Is a Dancing Thing," "O What a Wonderful World," and "Thief in the Night" were all terrific numbers.

Schwartz composed a couple of shows with other lyricists before teaming up with Dietz again for *Between the Devil* (12/23/37; 93 performances). The SHUBERT BROTHERS produced the show at the IMPERIAL THEATRE. It starred Jack Buchanan, Vilma Ebsen, Evelyn Laye, and Eric Brotherson. The Dietz and Schwartz score contained their requisite hit ballad, "I See Your Face Before Me." It also boasted such fine tunes as "By Myself" and "Triplets." Schwartz then collaborated with Dorothy Fields (*see* FIELDS FAMILY) on the ETHEL MERMAN vehicle *Stars in Your Eyes* (2/9/39; 127 performances). Despite a fine score, it was a failure. The composer then collaborated with OSCAR HAMMERSTEIN II on *American Jubilee*, a show at the New York World's Fair. Dietz, meanwhile, joined forces with VERNON DUKE on *Jackpot* (1/13/44; 67 performances), produced by Vinton Freedley (*see* AARONS AND FREEDLEY). Duke and Dietz collaborated again on *Sadie Thompson* (11/16/44; 60 performances), starring June Havoc. Both shows had good scores but were failures. Schwartz tried his luck with Ira Gershwin on *Park*

Mary Martin hangs from the waterfall in *Jennie*, 1963.

Avenue (11/11/46; 72 performances), and despite a fine score, it too was a failure. *Park Avenue* was the last Broadway score for Ira Gershwin.

In 1948 Dietz and Schwartz joined forces again for the revue *Inside U.S.A.* (4/30/48; 399 performances). Schwartz also produced the venture, which starred Beatrice Lillie and Jack Haley, along with Thelma Carpenter, Herb Shriner, Louis Nye, and Carl Reiner. Arnold Auerbach, Moss Hart, and Arnold B. Horwitt provided the sketches. *Inside U.S.A.* had Dietz and Schwartz's last great score. The ballads "Blue Grass" and "Haunted Heart" received their share of fame, but the upbeat numbers "Rhode Island Is Famous for You," "First Prize at the Fair," and "Protect Me" are the best remembered. This show, which was produced at the CENTURY THEATER, was the last of the great Broadway revues. Television, the medium in which much of the cast would achieve their fame, was the death knell of the Broadway revue.

In 1950 Dietz made an excursion, rare for a Broadway lyricist, into the world of opera. He provided the English lyrics to the Metropolitan Opera's production of *Die Fledermaus*. He repeated the job for the Metropolitan in 1952 when he wrote the English lyrics for Puccini's *La Bohème*.

For *A Tree Grows in Brooklyn* (4/19/51; 270 performances), Schwartz teamed up again with Dorothy Fields. Betty Smith, the author of the novel, and GEORGE ABBOTT wrote the libretto. Abbott and Robert Fryer produced it. Shirley Booth, Johnny Johnston, and Marcia Van Dyke helped inspire the songwriters to pen some of their best numbers, including "Make the Man Love Me," "I'm Like a New Broom," "Look Who's Dancing," "Love Is the Reason," "I'll Buy You a Star," and "Growing Pains."

By the Beautiful Sea (4/8/54; 268 performances) also starred Shirley Booth, and Schwartz and Dorothy Fields again supplied the score. Herbert and Dorothy Fields wrote the book, with Robert Fryer producing with his longtime partner Lawrence Carr. The score wasn't up to the team's previous show, but it did contain many good numbers, including "Alone Too Long," "More Love than Your Love," and "The Sea Song." *The Gay Life* (11/18/61; 113 performances), based on Arthur Schnitzler's play *The Affairs of Anatol*, starred Barbara Cook and Walter Chiari along with supporting players Elizabeth Allen and Jules Munshin. The score contained two beautiful ballads, "Magic Moment" and "Something You Never Had Before." The team's last Broadway show, *Jennie* (10/17/63; 82 performances), was a vehicle for MARY MARTIN. Their final score contained another standout ballad, "Before I Kiss the World Goodbye." Personal conflicts among the creative staff and Dietz's poor health (he was suffering from Parkinson's disease) caused impossible obstacles to the show's success. Following that disappointment, the team attempted other projects, notably a musical version of *Mrs. Arris Goes to Paris*, but none would reach the stage.

DONALDSON AWARD. From 1943 to 1955 *BILLBOARD* gave out the Donaldson Award, named for the magazine's founder, W. H. Donaldson (1864–1925). In addition to the usual awards for best actor and actress in a play or musical and supporting actor and actress, the Donaldsons were awarded to the best first play, best debut performance (male and female), and best dancer. There were also prizes awarded to the music and libretto of musicals and theater sets and costumes for both plays and musicals.

DRAMATISTS GUILD. The Dramatists Guild is the official guild of Broadway's playwrights. Prior to its inception, playwrights had no security or safeguards written into their contracts. Now the Dramatists Guild acts in a union capacity, representing professional playwrights.

Like many of its fellow guilds and unions, the Dramatists Guild had a difficult birth. The fight for playwrights' rights began in 1878 when Steele MacKay and Clay M. Greene started the American Dramatic Authors Society "to secure protection of their work." The society didn't make much headway, however, and members of the profession regarded it in a poor light. In 1891 another attempt was made to organize. Thirty-three authors started the Society of American Dramatists and Composers. Bronson Howard was the director of the organization. Again the results were inconclusive.

The first enduring organization was the Authors League of America, which was founded on December 27, 1911. Although the league was made up mainly of novelists, playwrights were included in the ranks. Following that first meeting, the league had its constitution and bylaws accepted on December 13, 1912. When the constitution was ratified, the organization elected its first officers. The American writer Winston Churchill was president and Theodore Roosevelt was chosen as vice president. Although playwrights were allowed to join, they had little representation. There were no playwrights on the executive committee and only three on the council. This situation began to improve in 1914 when a subcommittee was appointed to develop "the standardization of a dramatic contract." The subcommittee drew up a contract the next year, but it had little effect on the theater scene. Two years later another contract was written, but it, too, received little notice.

In 1917 producers had complete power over the theater, and they were very much against sharing that power or compromising their position. However, the union movement in the United States was gaining momentum, and the successful ACTORS' STRIKE OF 1919 resulted in the creation of ACTORS' EQUITY. The success of the performers didn't go unnoticed by the playwrights. Producer and playwright Channing Pollock went to the executive committee of the Authors League and asked that the dramatists be allowed to form an "autonomous committee." The committee agreed with Pollock's request, and 112 playwrights formed a dramatists' committee. The Authors League acted as an overseer or holding company for the dramatists' group.

The group was the beginning of the present-day Dramatists Guild. The first president was playwright Owen Davis. The guild's first challenge came in an action against the practices of the Fox Film Corporation. Fox, looking to Broadway as a source for movie ideas, had an agreement with seven producers whereby Fox would back the plays in return for film rights. They would, as co-producers, also receive half the receipts. The guild opposed the agreement, arguing that bidding on the film rights should be competitive, thereby ensuring a higher price for the playwright. A group of 30 playwrights met in secret on December 7, 1925. Exactly one month later, during a meeting at the Hotel Roosevelt, playwright George Kelly revealed the planned manifesto to 121 members of the guild. This mobilized and inspired the playwrights, and a group was formed to write up a producer-dramatist agreement that would cover all pertinent points. The committee included Rachel Crothers, EUGENE O'NEILL, John Emerson, Gene Buck, OTTO HARBACH, George Kelly, George S. Kaufman (*see* KAUFMAN AND HART), Channing Pollock, J. Hartley Manners, Le Roi Clemons, and George Middleton acting as chair.

The completed Minimum Basic Agreement was presented to the membership and approved. The members all agreed to insist on the signing of the agreement on all future works. If the producers did not sign the agreement, then the plays would not be produced. A conference between the playwrights and producers was set for March 11, 1926. Surprisingly, all of the invited managers agreed to abide by the contract. Some of them actually agreed with the authors that change was necessary. Several of the points raised in the contract were important to the playwright-producer relationship. The film rights were to be negotiated through competitive bidding. There was a minimum basic royalty, which protected first-time playwrights. Established playwrights were covered by the rule that stated there would be no ceiling to royalty agreements. The producers could not make changes in the script without the permission of the playwright. The guild ensured

its future with two rules: no member of the guild would be allowed to sign with any producer who was not a signatory to the guild contract, and no manager who agreed to the guild's terms could sign any playwright who was not a member of the guild. Many producers challenged the strength of the guild by attempting to sign playwrights to the old contracts. The playwrights stood firm and refused to sign anything but the Minimum Basic Agreement. They acted together, and in six months the Dramatists Guild was firmly established.

On April 27, 1927, the five-year Minimum Basic Agreement was signed. Another step forward was taken on July 16, 1927, when members of the British Authors Society agreed to abide by the agreement when their plays were presented on Broadway. Subsequent revisions of the contract came in 1931, 1936, 1941, and 1946. On June 14, 1955, a new agreement was signed incorporating the previous amendments and allowing for advances in technology, which included television.

In October 1964 the Dramatists Guild and the Authors Guild became two separate corporations, under the umbrella of the Authors League. The Dramatists Guild today still serves its members by fighting for acceptance of the agreement, presenting seminars and workshops for its memberships, and, perhaps most important, representing its members in Washington. This political arm of the organization seeks to improve laws protecting authors' rights and freedom of speech. The guild has successfully fought off legal battles by producers and has worked on behalf of playwrights from many foreign countries who have no voice in their homelands.

DUKE, VERNON. One of Broadway's master songwriters and also a classically trained musician; b. Vladimir Dukelsky, Parfianovka, Russia, October 10, 1903; d. Santa Monica, California, January 16, 1969.

One of the classic Broadway composers, Duke escaped from Russia during the revolution and went to Europe. While there, he composed ballets for Diaghilev's Ballet Russe. Although his training under such greats as Reinhold Gliere and Marian Dombrovsky seemed to promise him a distinguished classical career, Duke achieved his greatest success as a musical-theater composer.

Duke arrived in New York in 1929 after trying his hand at several musicals in London, including *Yvonne* (1926) (dubbed "Yvonne the Terrible" by Noël Coward), *The Yellow Mask* (1928), and *Open Your Eyes* (1930). His London lyricists, Percy Greenbank, Desmond Carter, and Collie Knox, didn't sufficiently inspire him. In New York, Duke contributed songs to *The Garrick Gaieties* (6/4/30) before attempting a

Katharine Dunham and Dooley Wilson in *Cabin in the Sky*, 1940.

complete score. His first American score, *Walk a Little Faster* (12/7/32), written with E. Y. HARBURG, included Duke's first hit song, "April in Paris." He then continued his collaboration with Harburg for the *Ziegfeld Follies of 1934* (1/4/34) and another hit, "I Like the Likes of You." He next contributed both music and lyrics to the standard "Autumn in New York," written for the revue *Thumbs Up!* (12/27/34). The next edition of the *Follies* in 1936 saw Duke teamed with IRA GERSHWIN, and they wrote another standard, "I Can't Get Started." Duke and Ted Fetter contributed some songs to the musical revue *The Show Is On*, which opened on Christmas Day, 1936.

Duke's first American book show followed in 1940. This was the classic *Cabin in the Sky* (10/25/40), with lyrics by John Latouche and starring Ethel Waters. The show featured a superior score that contained 3 hits: the title song, "Honey in the Honeycomb," and perhaps Duke's greatest song, "Taking a Chance on Love,"

which had lyrics by Latouche and Ted Fetter. However, this proved to be the last major success of Duke's career. Latouche and Harold Adamson teamed with Duke for an Eddie Cantor vehicle, *Banjo Eyes* (12/25/41). Apart from a Cantoresque song, "We're Having a Baby (My Baby and Me)," there was little in the score that would last. *It Happens on Ice* (7/15/41) contained some forgettable Duke songs. The collaboration with Latouche continued with *The Lady Comes Across* (1/9/42), which played only 3 performances on Broadway.

Howard Dietz (*see* DIETZ AND SCHWARTZ) supplied the lyrics to two of Duke's shows in 1944, *Jackpot* (1/13/44) and *Sadie Thompson* (11/16/44). Neither was a success. Duke's last Broadway show introduced Bette Davis to the musical theater. *Two's Company* (12/15/52) had lyrics by poet Ogden Nash. This show, too, closed quickly when its star became ill and had to withdraw.

Duke found his next assignment off Broadway. Impresario and director Ben Bagley brought Duke and Ogden Nash to the Phoenix Theater to contribute a score for Bagley's *The Littlest Revue* (5/22/56). Duke composed a score for the United States Coast Guard, *Tars and Spars*, and also contributed incidental music to the play *Time Remembered*. His last show, *Zenda* (8/5/63), closed in Los Angeles.

Duke's songs are models of cohesive melody and great emotion. They sound very simple and easy to hum, but when studied they reveal their intricacies, and they're difficult to play. Now, through the help of Bagley and singer Bobby Short, Duke's work is reaching a wider audience, and his songs are being rediscovered and appreciated by a new generation of music lovers.

EARL CARROLL THEATRE. Southeast corner of 7th Avenue and 50th Street. Architect: George Keister. Opening: February 25, 1922; *Bavu*.

The Earl Carroll Theatre had two lives in two theaters on the same site. The first Earl Carroll Theatre was built by the producer with money supplied by Texas oil baron William Edrington, Carroll's principal backer.

Among the theater's technical innovations was the "horizant," a permanent cyclorama painted on the curved back wall of the stage house. Directly in front of the horizant was a trench allowing actors to cross the stage without being seen by the audience.

The theater opened with a three-act melodrama, *Bavu*, written and directed by EARL CARROLL. The author, director, producer, composer, and lyricist was best-known as the producer of the annual revue series, *EARL CARROLL'S VANITIES*. *Bavu* closed after 25 performances. The show is completely forgettable save for the fact that in the cast was the future movie star William Powell. The second and third productions at the theater were also flops. *Just Because*, a musical comedy, opened on March 22 and ran for only 46 performances. *Raymond Hitchcock's Pinwheel* was an even bigger failure. It opened on June 15 and closed after 35 performances.

Finally the theater had a hit with producer Laurence Schwab's *The Gingham Girl* (8/28/22). The show ran 322 performances. The next hit in the theater was the first edition of *Earl Carroll's Vanities*. The show opened on July 5, 1923, with music and lyrics by Carroll. He also produced and directed the show. The revue series was planned as a rival to FLORENZ ZIEGFELD's *Follies* (see ZIEGFELD FOLLIES).

With the advent of the Depression, Carroll's fortunes floundered and he was forced to rent the theater to Radio Pictures for $12,750 a month plus half the taxes. The company was going to use the theater to premiere its film production of *Rio Rita*, originally a show produced by Ziegfeld. As if in reaction to their plans, Carroll leased Ziegfeld's old stomping ground, the NEW AMSTERDAM THEATRE, for his next edition of the *Vanities*.

The old Earl Carroll Theatre seated only 1,000 people, making it unsuitable for the large productions to which Carroll aspired. When Ziegfeld built his own new theater in 1927, Carroll, unfazed by his financial problems, set about to build a new space of his own. Edrington remained Carroll's chief backer. They bought the land east of the original theater for $1 million and leveled the building on that site. The builders retained the office building atop the old theater but tore out the theater itself.

Columnist ED SULLIVAN wrote about the plans for the new theater:

> If you have walked along 49th or 50th Streets just east of Seventh Avenue you have seen in skeleton form the temple that will house the Earl Carroll "wonder works" this coming season on the same site where the former Earl Carroll Theater stood for nine years. The theater is in the "strictly modern" style in the "straight and setback" lines of the new skyscrapers.
>
> If you've happened to notice a man hurrying here and there in an old smock "riding the whole horse," watching the builders, experimenting with costumes and colors and listening to the boys from Tin Pan Alley as they chanted their melodies, it was the indefatigable Mr. Carroll. It is hard work but he can stand it because he grew up in theaters.
>
> In dwelling on the impending innovations of this, his latest and greatest project, he said, "What I want to be remembered for are the changes I have made in the theater, even if they are quickly forgotten."
>
> A very canny showman is Mr. Carroll, and a student of the public. So he has thought it all out. He took time

out to say, "All that is wrong with show business today is the prices that are charged." The way around high prices, he intimated, is by mass production, and "The form to which mass production best adapts itself is the big revue."

So Mr. Carroll, a logician for all his persistent elegance, will concentrate on big revues, and his new edifice will seat 3,000 people with a $3 top, even for opening night.

Next Thursday evening, therefore, Earl Carroll—who knows how to make an entrance—will submit that a new $4,500,000 theater, bearing his name, will be opened and ready with the ninth *Vanities* to do business. It will be a milestone. One has Mr. Carroll's word for this.

Carroll spent $4.5 million of Edrington's money on his new theater. Architect William Keister and interior designer Joseph Babolnay created an Art Deco masterpiece. The new lobby was 3 times as large as the old one. Remarkably, the new theater's seating capacity was also tripled. There were seats for 1,500 patrons in the orchestra alone. The boxes seated 200 people, and the loge and balcony areas seated 1,300. To utilize the space to its maximum, the 60-by-100-foot space under the balcony was given to lounge areas. The theater was the first to be completely air-conditioned backstage, in the auditorium, and in the public areas.

The interior of the building was a classic Art Deco design. The walls were covered with black velvet. Brushed aluminum accented the interior. The lobby area was covered in polished black vitrolite, streaked with brown. The carpeting was in 3 shades of green and the seats covered in plush coral-colored fabric. The orchestra seats were equipped with little lights so patrons could refer to the program during the show. The dressing rooms, decorated in chrome, silk, and satin, were as well appointed as the audience area. The performers had their own tables with triple mirrors. There was also a complete intercom system as well as a gymnasium, showers, a safe for valuables, a refrigerator, and, by the stage, a mirror room for last-minute checks on makeup and costumes.

The stage area boasted two elevator platforms, like those in Radio City Music Hall, which enabled the orchestra to be raised from the basement to stage level while playing. Sixty stagehands were required to operate the stage machinery. Five thousand Berliner acoustical discs were put into the walls to control the acoustics. Six speakers were placed in the auditorium to boost the stage sound, and 20 more were placed in the lounges and lobby. Because of the highly polished and reflective surfaces throughout the theater, lighting became very important. In true Art Deco style, the lighting was concealed. A console in the orchestra pit controlled the indirect lighting effects. Each fixture had four colored circuits: red, blue, white, and green. Radio

City Music Hall later copied this idea. Carroll finished off the theater by hanging a now-famous sign over the stage door: "Through These Portals Pass the Most Beautiful Girls in the World."

The theater's premiere attraction was *Earl Carroll's Vanities of 1931* (8/27/31), which opened with the Depression in full swing. There was a staff of 84 men in the house. They were all at least 6 feet tall and dressed in dark uniforms with chrome highlights to match the inside of the theater. There was no box office, but rather a long table with 8 attendants in front of the ticket racks. During intermission the ushers wheeled a huge chrome-plated tank down the aisles and dispensed free ice water to the audience.

Despite (or perhaps because of) its opulence, Carroll couldn't make the theater a success. The show was especially lavish and could not recoup its cost on the low ticket prices. It also was expensive to operate the giant theater and maintain its lavish interior. Within 6 months Carroll lost the theater. He was sued by the Seven Fifty-five Corporation for $366,632.90. Carroll also owed $64,952.20 for 3 months' back rent, taxes, and interest.

Ziegfeld decided to take it over. He changed its name to the Casino and reopened the space with a revival of his great hit *Show Boat* (5/19/32; 181 performances). During the run of *Show Boat* Ziegfeld died and the show closed. GEORGE WHITE, the third big producer of an annual revue series, used the theater for *Melody* (2/14/33; 80 performances), one of the last Broadway operettas. It was written by SIGMUND ROMBERG and Irving Caesar.

A vaudeville show entitled *Casino Varieties* opened next. In an attempt to counter the effect of the Depression on the box office, its top ticket price was $1.50. This was the theater's last legitimate show. The theater closed only four years after its opening. Clifford Fischer, a former agent for the Orpheum circuit, took up the theater's lease. He took out the seating and put tiers in the balcony and orchestra, upon which he installed tables. Fischer, responding to a wave of enthusiasm for all things French that was sweeping over New York, called the new theater-restaurant the French Casino. It was the second such conversion, following the lead of the Casino de Paris (*see* NEW YORKER THEATRE, which had been the Gallo Theater. Later, the Manhattan Casino was made out of Hammerstein's Theater (*see* ED SULLIVAN THEATER) on Broadway at 53rd Street. Of all the Manhattan casinos, the French Casino was the most successful. The theater opened on Christmas Day 1934, featuring a show modeled on the Folies Bergère—an ironic touch, because this was Earl Carroll's inspiration also. The revues at the French Casino were very successful. The glamorous theater was perfectly suited to the spectacular shows on the stage.

The French Casino prospered until showman Billy Rose, owner of the Casino de Paris, bought the building. He redecorated the interior in a more Latin manner and extended the stage out from the proscenium. He renamed the space the Casa Mañana, featuring a $2.50 price for dinner, dancing, and the show. It opened on January 10, 1938, and closed by the end of the year.

In 1939 the 6-story office building fronting 7th Avenue was razed. The auditorium and stage house still stood, but the interiors were replaced with retail space. A Whelan's drugstore and then a Woolworth's took the place of the magnificent theater. When the Woolworth's was torn down in 1990, the theater was discovered above the store's false ceilings. Unfortunately, it was too late to save any of the theater itself.

EARL CARROLL'S VANITIES. There were three great revue series that graced Broadway in the early years of the century: the ZIEGFELD FOLLIES, GEORGE WHITE'S SCANDALS, and *Earl Carroll's Vanities*. Each of the three had its own trademark, the special stamp of its producer. FLORENZ ZIEGFELD relied on star-filled extravaganzas featuring top talents performing material by some of America's greatest composers. GEORGE WHITE produced jazzy, fast-moving revues with flappers and sheiks and a hint of bawdiness. EARL CARROLL, on the other hand, employed few great stars, relied on mostly second-rate material, but surpassed his competitors with vulgarity, BURLESQUE-inspired humor, and ample nudity. Carroll was author of the famous sign that hung over his stage door, "Through These Portals Pass the Most Beautiful Girls in the World." It was a direct challenge to Ziegfeld, whose aim was "Glorifying the American Girl."

There were 11 editions of the *Vanities* and 2 *Earl Carroll Sketchbooks*. Among the stars that appeared in the series were Patsy Kelly, Peggy Hopkins Joyce, Joe Cook, W. C. Fields, Milton Berle, Ray Dooley, Jack Benny, Helen Broderick, Lillian Roth, and Jimmy Savo. The first edition of the *Vanities* (7/5/23; 204 performances) was the EARL CARROLL THEATRE's premiere production. Carroll himself supplied the music and lyrics. The revue's first number was entitled "The Birth of a New Revue." Showgirls came out representing the other revue series on Broadway: the *Cohan Revue*, the WINTER GARDEN THEATRE's *Passing Shows*, the *Scandals*, the *Music Box Revue*, the *Greenwich Village Follies*, and the *Ziegfeld Follies*. Once these lovelies had paraded across the footlights, out came the loveliest of all, Alice Weaver, representing the *Vanities*.

Like Ziegfeld, Carroll himself handpicked the girls in his revue. He stated, "The Ziegfeld clotheshorse is passé. It's not enough for a girl to be beautiful and dumb. Today vivacity must be a girl's outstanding characteristic, for vivacity means youth and the speed of modernity. And the girl must be intelligent." Carroll's girls were certainly not clotheshorses. So much of them was exposed that Carroll's barber personally shaved every inch of their bodies.

The next edition of the *Vanities* (10/10/24) opened at the MUSIC BOX THEATER. For this edition, Carroll expanded his role, directing and supplying the libretto in addition to producing and writing the songs. The show featured a scene in which, to the rhythms of Ravel's *Bolero*, a bevy of showgirls paraded in King Solomon's court wearing nothing but peacock headdresses. Each girl was armed with a fan and what was called "Carroll's chastity belt," a thin strip covering her privates. This came to the attention of the local authorities, who assigned patrolmen to a performance. When, in the opening number, Kathryn Ray swung nude on a giant pendulum, the police made their move. The showgirl was pulled from her upside-down position and covered with a blanket. She tore the blanket off and, to the amusement of the audience, was chased by a phalanx of cops. The audience thought the incident was part of the show. Then Carroll stepped before the footlights and asked the audience which it preferred, the show as presented on opening night or a bowdlerized version that would pass the censors' criticisms. The audience, of course, demanded the original version, and the show continued. The police realized an attack on the show itself might not succeed. After all, the members of the audience were well aware of what they were getting when they purchased their tickets.

So the authorities cooked up another scheme. Carroll was arrested for exhibiting lewd and indecent pictures of his showgirls in the front of the theater. The police charged that minors might be badly affected if they happened to see the pictures. The judge refused to allow testimony by artists as to the artistic merits of the pictures, which were painted by George Maillard Kesslere. Even the prestigious *New York Times* felt obliged to print an editorial in Carroll's defense. Carroll went to jail instead of posting the modest bond. He proclaimed, "I'm going to jail not for publicity but to focus attention on these self-appointed censors. If I gave the bail of $300 set by the judge, this case would be merely one of many. I want it to stand out so the real people of New York, who are against fanatical censorship, will see what is being done. It is all a very serious affair to me, for conviction could mean the end of my career."

Immediately the box office improved and continued to do so each day the producer remained in the can. Finally, Carroll's brother Jim, his business manager, persuaded him to post bail. The trial commenced with

Carroll pointing to the nude marble statues on the facade of the New York Public Library. The showman won his case, and the *Vanities* were allowed to continue, treading a fine line between titillation and indecency.

The 1925 edition of the *Vanities* was the most successful to date, although none of its elements was especially notable. Its long run, 440 performances, might again be explained by the strength of publicity. On February 22, 1926, Carroll held a joint birthday party for George Washington and William R. Edrington, a Texas oilman and the chief backer of Carroll's productions. To add spice to the proceedings, Carroll arranged for showgirl Joyce Hawley to frolic in a bathtub filled with champagne. Phil Payne, a reporter on the *New York Daily Mirror*, broke the story in the next day's edition, much to the consternation of his rival dailies. *The Graphic*, one of the sleaziest of New York's dailies, printed a picture of the incident on its front page. The photo was one of the *Graphic*'s infamous composite shots, that is, faked. This came to the attention of the federal government, which charged Carroll with breaking the laws of Prohibition.

Carroll, remembering his last brush with the law and its succeeding impact at the box office, refused to settle for a plea of disorderly conduct and a small fine. He insisted that no crime had been committed because the bathtub actually contained no champagne but mostly ginger ale with a dash of sherry for color. The fact that it wasn't illegal to bathe in ginger ale was immaterial; Carroll had clearly lied when he testified before a grand jury that no one had gotten in the bathtub, and perjury was against the law. Carroll was sentenced to a year and a day in prison. After the opening of the 1927 edition of the *Vanities*, he was sent to the penitentiary in Atlanta, where he remained for 4 months and 11 days.

That edition of the *Vanities* evolved into *Earl Carroll's Vanities Featuring the New Charlot Revue*. That show, in turn, further changed into *Earl Carroll's Vanities of 1927*. Although the edition was not a success by any title, Carroll was not fazed. He made plans to expand his empire by building a new theater on the site of the original Earl Carroll Theatre.

In the *New York Times*, Sidney Skolsky described the making of the next *Vanities*, the 1928 edition:

> There were the days when Earl Carroll started to assemble the girls. Then came nights of rehearsal. Carroll standing out in the orchestra in a lemon-colored smock watching Busby Berkeley put the girls through a dance routine until two in the morning.
>
> Then more nights of rehearsal. Warm nights. Hot nights. Everybody sweating. Chorus girls and stars. Legs dancing; gags cracked without feeling funny. Carroll giv-
> ing every girl a brand new silver dollar for learning a new routine.
>
> Then came more days and nights of rehearsal, from eleven in the morning until five the next morning. Soon no one knows, and it doesn't matter, whether it is day or night. A final dress rehearsal and everything moves laboriously and seems to be wrong. A tryout in Atlantic City. This is merely a rehearsal with an audience looking on. After the audience goes, the players work on.
>
> A week at Atlantic City and not one member of the Vanities was on the beach. Atlantic City. It's just another theater. Days and nights and weeks of this, and then finally, the little item: Tomorrow evening at the Earl Carroll Theater the seventh edition of the Earl Carroll Vanities starring W. C. Fields.

That 1928 edition of the *Vanities* marked Carroll's return to the theater. He hadn't lost his touch. The *New York Times* stated, "Considering Mr. Carroll's past achievements in the theater and out, it is conceivably not too foolhardy a procedure to come out here with the unqualified statement that this is the best Vanities of them all." The show ran 200 performances.

Florenz Ziegfeld had just opened his luxurious ZIEGFELD THEATER on 6th Avenue at 54th Street. Carroll was determined to outdo the legendary showman with his own Art Deco palace. While it was being constructed, Carroll mounted his next edition of the *Vanities* (there was no 1929 edition) in the theater that Ziegfeld made famous, the NEW AMSTERDAM. A young Vincente Minnelli, just coming off his success at Radio City Music Hall, designed the costumes. The score, for once, contained some hit songs, notably those of HAROLD ARLEN and Ted Koehler, including "Contagious Rhythm" and "Hittin' the Bottle." Jack Benny made his Broadway debut in the production. In the show Carroll featured a number called "Modes—Window at Merl's." He placed five chorus girls in the window of a store. Comedian Jimmy Savo entered the window and on the pretext of changing the mannequins' outfits completely undressed them. At the first matinee the show was raided, and again Carroll was in front of a court. He won the case, foiling the censors again. The show ran 215 performances.

The new Earl Carroll Theatre was opened on August 27, 1931, with the *Earl Carroll's Vanities of 1931*. The show and theater building together cost $4.5 million. Ziegfeld was known for his tableaux, designed by Ben Ali Haggin, which featured women in skin-colored tights arranged artfully in dramatic poses. Carroll emulated this Ziegfeld trademark with his "living curtains," only Carroll usually left out the tights. The living curtains were based on similar routines performed at the Folies Bergère. In this edition, Carroll had two living curtains: a perfume curtain with the girls posed on a drapery that sent gusts of Odor de la Noche through the audience, and a dinosaur curtain staged to the music of "Dance of the Dinosaur" (composed by Hyman Grossman).

PERCY HAMMOND, writing in the *Herald Tribune*, reviewed the show thusly:

> The theme of the ninth *Vanities* is similar to that of its predecessors, mingling mire with beauty, filth with elegance. Its ballets are picturesque and lovely, its comedy ugly and degrading. Scores of unashamed female beauties unscreen their sacred charms at one moment and at the next a hideous obscenity is performed by some man in the cast. . . .
>
> The *Vanities* is so doltish in its indecencies that it could not have been the deliberate product of a nasty mind. As Mr. Carroll was summoned, wan from the evening's ecstasies he appeared to be neither scamp nor satyr but a rapt and startled poet, awakened from his dreams upon Parnassus. Had I not known better, I would have expected him to recite an ode for us, celebrating the lark, or the morning star. So I am sure he is unknowing rather than vicious and that his next show will be even fouler than this one. I am not one of those who wish to tar and feather Mr. Carroll. His exhibitions revolt but do not anger me, and I suspect his revues are no worse than his audiences. When George Sodom makes one of his less idyllic remarks to a chorus lady during one of the sketches and William Gomorrah joins in the sprightly repartee they inspire the sophisticates to expressions of rapture.

This last great edition of the annual series (and the only edition to play the new theater) closed after 300 performances.

The next *Vanities* opened on September 27, 1932, at the BROADWAY THEATRE. It played only 87 performances, yet it contained one of the greatest songs to come out of any Broadway show, "I Gotta Right to Sing the Blues," by Harold Arlen and Ted Koehler. With the country suffering from the hardships of the Depression, the face of Broadway was changing. Carroll himself had troubles with capital, and Carroll's chief backer, William R. Edrington, went bankrupt. Carroll was forced to give up his theater after the premiere production. It was later a home to others' productions, including, ironically, a revival of Ziegfeld's greatest success, *Show Boat*.

The final *Vanities* opened at the ST. JAMES THEATRE 8 years later, on January 13, 1940. The 1932 edition had suffered from the nation's preoccupation with the Depression. This one was a victim of the coming of World War II. It proved a sad finale to the once-popular series, lasting only 25 performances. Carroll was killed with showgirl Beryl Wallace in a plane accident in 1947.

EDISON THEATER. 240 W. 47th Street, in the Edison Hotel. Opening: March 5, 1970; *Show Me Where the Good Times Are*.

Producer Norman Kean built the Edison Theater for those shows that were too small for ordinary Broadway houses. The Edison didn't achieve much success despite the quality of some of its offerings, which included *Happy Birthday, Wanda June*; *Don't Bother Me, I Can't Cope*; *Sizwe Banzi Is Dead*; *The Island*; and *Me and Bessie*. However, the theater finally hit pay dirt when it presented *Oh! Calcutta!* The show had previously played at the Eden Theater off Broadway, where it opened on January 17, 1969. Its audiences were mostly made up of Japanese tourists. Kean committed suicide in January 1988, and *Oh! Calcutta!* finally closed in 1989, making it then the second longest-running show in Broadway history.

ED SULLIVAN THEATER. 1697 Broadway between 53rd and 54th Streets. Architect: Herbert J. Krapp. Original name: Hammerstein Theater. Opening: November 30, 1927; *The Golden Dawn*.

In 1910 ARTHUR HAMMERSTEIN was determined not to ever speak to his father, OSCAR HAMMERSTEIN I, again. By 1927, eight years after Oscar's death, Arthur was left to run the Hammerstein empire on his own. By then, OSCAR HAMMERSTEIN II had made a name for himself on Broadway. Arthur decided to build the Hammerstein Theater on Broadway as a tribute to his father, using his profits from the Rudolf Friml/Herbert Stothart operetta *Rose-Marie* to finance the project.

In the opening night program, Arthur wrote:

> In making public my reasons for building Hammerstein's, I am literally laying bare my heart so that all may know the glory, the pride, the rejoicing that is mine tonight.
>
> Any article dealing with the reasons which may have prompted me in this undertaking, if it is written at all, must, to a large extent, embody personal references to both my father and myself. It cannot be otherwise. The sacred memory of my father's name—a name which embellished theatrical history for more than a score of years, and the fine things in the theatre for which that name stood, have been a perpetual source of pride and inspiration to me. In the few things I have done in the world of the theatre, I have tried in my humble way, to make the illustrious name to which I have fallen heir, stand for the same ideals that were always the inspiration of my father. If I have succeeded, then I can truthfully say that the training I received under my father during his eventful reign as impresario, has been largely instrumental in any success which has been mine.
>
> For many years past, friends and admirers in particular, and the world of the theatre in general, have been nursing the idea of building a monument to the memory of my father. Statues of varying descriptions with Times Square and the Metropolitan Museum of Art as the locales for the unveiling of such memorials have been suggested. The naming of one of the important thoroughfares in the theatrical district after my father has been proposed

Marquee of the Hammerstein Theatre.

from time to time. And quite often—with indifferent success—the founding of a theatre to be known as Hammerstein's has been broached along Broadway. None of these projects, I am sorry to say ever crystallized, although I understand, subscriptions amounting to many thousands of dollars were collected by various groups for this very purpose.

Quite some years ago I conceived the idea of building a theatre—one which would exemplify the undaunted spirit of my father—and one which would stand as a towering memorial to a man who did so much to improve the conduct and widen the influence of the theatre. It may be indiscreet to mention the fact, but even while others were planning the erection of a monument to the memory of my father, I was secretly formulating plans of my own for the theatre whose doors are opened to the public tonight. That I wanted Hammerstein's to be the only theatre of its kind, the finest theatre of its kind, the best of its kind, is obvious. But more than that, I hoped to make it the home of the finest type of musical entertainment consistent with public demand in the world. I hope that in *Golden Dawn* I have achieved that ambition.

The theater was described in the opening program:

A trip through Hammerstein's is a fascinating stroll through a modern fairyland. From the moment one enters its portals on Broadway where a façade done in modernized Gothic and treated in color with mosaics greets you—to the large lettered glass windows containing art panels in which each of the ten operas created by the late Oscar Hammerstein are pictorially described, its manifold beauties, comforts and conveniences command the interest of the theatregoers. From its orchestra pit which may be raised or lowered to suit the mood of the play—to its revolutionary lighting arrangements, the theatre discloses a blending of the finest concepts of theatrical engineering, architecture, science and art yet brought together in the erection of a modern theater.

. . . On entering the lobby of the theatre which opens on Broadway, one passes through a large and commodious vestibule which is designed to accommodate the crowds of theatregoers in quest of Hammerstein entertainment. The entire interior of the lobby is done in cast stone, and the general effect is one of massiveness and solidity.

A bronze statue of the late Oscar Hammerstein, done with marvelous fidelity, is set on a marble pedestal in the foyer. The statue is the work of Pompeo Coppini, a sculptor who enjoys a wide reputation in American and European art circles. Friends of the late impresario who have been privileged to view the finished work, declare that Coppini has captured the personality as well as the likeness of the maestro in whose memory Hammerstein's has been erected.

The brush of Joseph Cummings Chase, renowned American artist, has also decorated the foyer. He has painted eleven of the principal characters in "Golden Dawn," and the work is on display in the foyer.

The foyer opens on a spacious promenade located at the rear of the orchestra, and here patrons may meet before and after performances. The promenade, though a veritable part of the auditorium, is sufficiently cloistered to enable persons to converse freely during the performance without disturbance to those seated.

Here it is well worth considering the decorative treatment of the theatre proper as it impresses the beholder from a point of vantage in the foyer. One observes that the interior, done in Free Gothic, takes on an aspect of complete simplicity, the choice of design and color being principally induced by a maximum use of restraint and negation. Beautifully designed frieze work and ornate hangings, blending harmoniously with the decorative scheme of the theatre, enhance its transcendant beauty. Light fixtures throughout the theatre which glow without being too obstructive, evenly illuminate the domes so that the rays of light are delicately transfused to the entire auditorium.

Cozy seats, conveniently arranged and easy of accessibility, are a permanent and prominent feature of the new theatre. One sinks into a richly upholstered seat to which he has been directed through a new system of seat-indicator lights which successfully eliminates delay and avoids confusion. One then realizes that the comfort of the patron has been made a very important consideration in the construction of Hammerstein's.

We then come to the stage. Here the colorful musical presentations will be seen; here they will be spawned under the vigilant eye of Arthur Hammerstein. An immense curtain, imported from Paris, together with a score of rich draperies bewilder the beholder with their shimmering beauty. A giant switchboard whose insulated arteries feed the lights to the stage is located nearby, and its operation, it is declared, will prove a revelation.

An orchestra pit in which fifty musicians will sit and interpret the musical coloring of the play—capable of being raised and lowered at will—is yet another feature of Hammerstein's. In this pit is located the console of the first organ ever installed in a "legitimate" theater. The Welte Mignon Company furnished the instrument.

A large dome, which besides forming the ceiling, also forms the upper part of the side walls, adds a coloring to the interior which makes for beauty as well as utility. Large, penetrated niches decorated with actrofoils which frame the mosaic glass windows on both sides of the theatre breathe a decorative treatment into the audito-

rium which is in keeping with the architectural beauty throughout. To relieve the severity of the stone work, the impanelling effects formed by ribs of stone are decorated with mosaics. In each of these panels is the head of a well-known composer.

Opening from the promenade—before entering the theatre proper—are stairways covered with high-pile carpets and Czecho-Slovakian rugs, which lead to the mezzanine and balcony as well as to the lounge, Ladies' and Smoking rooms. The lounge is located directly beneath the auditorium, and is for the use of both ladies and gentlemen. Smoking is permitted here. Off the lounge on the right is the Ladies' Room which has been outfitted with the most approved accessories of milady's toilette.

In the basement of the theatre is the machinery of one of the greatest ventilating systems ever installed in a theatre. This elaborate air conditioning system honeycombs the entire structure, purifying the very air you breathe and keeping the temperature—whether in winter or summer—always normal. Through a suction process the air is drawn from the roof, laundered, and then transferred to the auditorium where it is circulated to the best possible advantage. On the hottest day of the year, the theatre can be cooled to a temperature of 60 degrees. A heating system has been installed so that on the coldest days a warmth can be generated into the theatre that will make the theatregoer forget the wintry blasts outside.

Herbert J. Krapp is the architect who designed Hammerstein's and personally supervised its construction. That he did a commendable job is vouchsafed by the enthusiasm which a preview of the theater occasioned among a group of theatre builders and architects recently. The theatre was built by the O'Day Construction Company.

The story of the wonders of Aladdin's Lamp records no stranger magic than that wrought here by the mind and brain of man. A year ago today the foundation for Hammerstein's was dug deep into the bowels of the Earth on the site of which Hammerstein's now stands. A complete transformation has taken place. A magnificent edifice, rearing its head thirteen stories above the Broadway street level now exists, a shrine to the memory of Oscar Hammerstein, resplendent in the exquisite form and color conceived by genius.

For the first show, *Golden Dawn* (11/30/27; 200 performances), Arthur Hammerstein hired Oscar II, Emmerich Kalman, Herbert Stothart, and OTTO HARBACH to write the libretto and score. Oscar II's brother Reginald directed the proceedings. The next success at the theater was the JEROME KERN and Oscar Hammerstein II show *Sweet Adeline* (9/3/29; 233 performances), with Arthur producing and Reginald directing. The cast included Charles Butterworth, Irene Franklin, and Gus Salzer. Torch singer Helen Morgan stopped the show with "Why Was I Born?" and "Don't Ever Leave Me."

Arthur, a heavy investor in the stock market, lost most of his fortune in the crash. He badly needed a hit show. Unfortunately, his next production, *Luana* (9/17/30; 21 performances) was not it. RUDOLF FRIML and J. Keirn Brennan wrote the operetta's score. But by the 1930s the operetta was going out of favor. With his theater dark, no prospective show in the wings, and the neighboring office building almost empty, Arthur was forced to sell. Later that year, after one more producing attempt, he declared bankruptcy. The young producing team of Frank Mandel and Laurence Schwab bought the theater. They joined with Oscar II to present shows in what was renamed the Manhattan Theater.

The first production in the Manhattan was *Free for All* (9/8/31; 15 performances). Richard Whiting provided the music, and Oscar II and Laurence Schwab (who was also the director) wrote the libretto. In the cast were Jack Haley, Tamara, and Benny Goodman's orchestra. Schwab, Mandel, and Hammerstein's next offering at the Manhattan Theater was *East Wind* (10/27/31; 23 performances). SIGMUND ROMBERG composed the score, and this time Frank Mandel collaborated with Oscar on the libretto. Composer VINCENT YOUMANS produced the next show at the Manhattan Theater, *Through the Years* (1/28/31; 20 performances). The musical, with music by Youmans and lyrics by Edward Heyman, was also a failure; however, the title song and "Drums in My Heart" were hit songs.

The theater remained dark until Billy Rose bought it and renamed it the Billy Rose Music Hall. Rose opened it on June 21, 1934, as a theater restaurant. Rose's luck was no better than that of his predecessors, and he sold it. On November 27, 1934, the theater reopened as the Manhattan Music Hall. However, this new venture was also a failure, and on February 14, 1936, it reverted to the name Manhattan Theater. The FEDERAL THEATRE PROJECT presented a play by Edwin and Albert Barker in the theater, *American Holiday* (2/21/36; 20 performances). But the closing of *American Holiday* marked the end of the theater as a live venue.

CBS bought the theater and made it a CBS Radio Playhouse in September 1936. When television took over the airwaves, CBS converted the space into a

"Reminiscent of the pre-Prohibition era, we see the return of the singing waiters—moustaches, shirt sleeves, and all—at the new Billy Rose Music Hall. They are singing the old favorites from the stage of the Music Hall, formerly the old Hammerstein Theatre which has been converted into what might be called a theatre restaurant where the customers wine and dine as they see the show."

television studio. Its most famous tenant was the *Ed Sullivan Show*. In 1967 the theater was renamed, in the emcee's honor, the Ed Sullivan Theater. In the 1980s the theater was used by the Reeves Communications Company to tape their television production *Kate and Allie*. The *David Letterman Show* now occupies the theater.

ELLIS, ABRAHAM. The man who established the modern hatcheck business in New York clubs; b. January 30, 1901; d. July 1985.

Abraham Ellis was known as the "Hatcheck King." He was one of the many poorly educated men who made their fortunes on Broadway by using their brains. He was born in a tenement on the Lower East Side of Manhattan. His father tried to support the family by pressing pants. Young Abraham helped support the family through a series of odd jobs. He was a delivery boy at 11, and at 14 he was a candy butcher (a candy seller in the theater) in Oscar Hammerstein I's Manhattan Opera House. Twenty-three years later Ellis would buy the building for $750,000.

Ellis moved from selling candy to checking hats and coats at Webster Hall in Greenwich Village. He was promoted when his boss left to fight in World War I. He paid $500 to take over the concession and made the first of many improvements. When the *Lusitania* sank, among the passengers to perish was a Yiddish actor who had willed his money to his daughter. This daughter, Yetta Samuel, married Ellis, and her inheritance went to buy the hatcheck concession at the Brooklyn Elks Club for her new husband. Ellis wasn't content to stay at the Elks Club. By the 1940s he held the concessions at the Latin Quarter, the Algonquin, the Copacabana, and the St. Regis. At these and other clubs, he introduced the first hatcheck girls and numbered claim checks. In these same nightspots he also operated concessions for photographs, washroom towels, and cigars.

In 1951 *The New Yorker* profiled him as a man who "squirms, slouches, slumps and bounces up and down." He divorced his first wife and agreed to pay her $1,000 a week and give her custody of their children after she accused him of raising the children at nightclubs and prizefights. The trial was right out of Damon Runyon's *Little Miss Marker*.

ELTINGE THEATRE. *See* **Empire Theater (2)**.

ELYSEE. *See* **John Golden Theater**.

EMBASSY 49TH STREET THEATER. *See* **Charles Hopkins Theater**.

EMPIRE THEATER (1). 1430 Broadway at 40th Street. Architect: J. B. McElfatrick. Opening: January 25, 1893; *The Girl I Left Behind Me*.

Frank Sanger and Al Hayman (the owner of a vacant lot on Broadway at 40th Street) built producer Charles Frohman and his partner William Harris what was to become the most beloved theater in New York history. Frohman hired J. B. McElfatrick as architect of the Empire, the first of seven theaters that the architect designed.

The Empire building was 5 stories tall and achieved many firsts. It was the first theater to have electricity, although it also had a backup gas system in case the electricity went out. The theater was also the first to be built entirely on the first floor. Other theaters, following the example of English predecessors, were built with the balcony at ground level and the orchestra underground. The Empire was probably the first theater to have an electric sign. It was also the first theater to follow the 1892 building code, which provided greater fire prevention measures. Finally, the Empire hosted 3 companies in their initial engagements: those of John Drew, Maude Adams, and owner Charles Frohman.

Frohman's initial attraction, *The Girl I Left Behind*, by David Belasco, was an immediate success, as was the new theater. The 1,099-seat auditorium was reached through a narrow lobby fronting on Broadway. Patrons who held balcony seats entered on 40th Street. Ticket takers wore formal wear and silk top hats. The *New York Times* exclaimed: "Every spectator is near enough the stage to be in sympathy with the actors." The critic's only reservation was that "the rows of seats are entirely too close for complete comfort, but that is a fault common to most theaters." According to the critic, the "decorations of the interior are handsome and tasteful. The prevailing tints are subdued red, terra cotta, cream and dull green."

Surprisingly, although reviews of the theater were favorable, when his lease came up for renewal, Frohman decided to gut the interior and hire John M. Carrere and Thomas Hastings to redo it. The New Empire Theater opened on October 13, 1903, with John Drew starring in *Captain of Dieppe*. Again the *Times* was enthusiastic: "The elimination of all columns in the rear of the house and the introduction of broad promenades at the rear on each floor are features which add to the practical conveniences of the house. Another advantage that will be appreciated is the installation of seats modeled after a pattern designed by Mr. Frohman. These are roomy and have exactly the right shape, with pneumatic air cushions." *Architectural Record* exclaimed, "It is not too much to say that this room is one of the most consistent, most appropriate, and cleverest pieces of interior decoration in this country. No better example could be desired of the proper way to translate a classic style into a sufficiently modern equivalent."

The first years of the Empire's history saw many classic productions. Among them were Dumas' *Lady of the Camellias* (1895) with Olga Nethersole; Oscar Wilde's *The Importance of Being Earnest* (14/22/1895), with Henry Miller, Viola Allen, and William Faversham; and *When Knighthood Was in Flower* (5/2/04), with Julia Marlowe and Tyrone Power Sr. Among the most famous of all productions at the Empire was the J. M. Barrie classic *Peter Pan* (11/6/05; 223 performances), starring Maude Adams. By most accounts the greatest of all Pans, Adams returned to the Empire as Peter Pan in special holiday attractions in 1906, 1912, and 1915. Adams had previously appeared at the Empire with leading man Robert Edeson in Barrie's *The Little Minister* (9/27/1898). Later she also appeared at the Empire in another Barrie play, *Quality Street* (1/6/08; 7 performances). Another success at the Empire for Adams was *The Pretty Sister of Jose* (11/10/03; 58 performances). On February 6, 1905, she opened 2 plays in repertory, *'Op o' My Thumb* and a revival of *The Little Minister*. On January 15, 1908, she appeared at the Empire in *The Jesters*

(53 performances). J. M. Barrie had other productions at the theater without star Maude Adams. Among them were *Dear Brutus* (12/23/18; 184 performances), with HELEN HAYES and William Gillette, and *Mary Rose* (12/22/20; 127 performances), with Ruth Chatterton.

Other notable productions at the theater in its earliest years were *The Good Hope* (1/28/07; 8 performances), with Dame Ellen Terry, Edith Craig, and Beatrice Forbes-Robinson; George Bernard Shaw's *Captain Brassbound's Conversion* (1/28/07; 14 performances), with Dame Ellen Terry; and Sir Arthur Wing Pinero's *Trelawny of the "Wells"* (1/1/11; 48 performances) with Ethel Barrymore, Louise Drew, Constance Collier, and Edward Arnold.

Frohman, one of the greatest producers of his time, died on May 7, 1915, when a German submarine sank the *Lusitania*. Frohman's brother Daniel, a legend in his own right, was an executive of the film company Paramount Famous Lasky Corporation. The corporation was brought in by Hayman's family and took over management of the Empire, but it was both unsuccessful and insensitive to the Empire's artists. In 1920 producer Gilbert Miller took over the management. Notable productions of the 1920s included *Blood and*

The Empire Theatre featuring John Drew in W. Somerset Maugham's *Jack Straw*, 1908.

Sand (9/20/21), with Otis Skinner and Cornelia Otis Skinner; *The Dove* (2/11/25; 101 performances), with Judith Anderson, Holbrook Blinn, Sidney Toler, and William Harrigan; and Noël Coward's *Easy Virtue* (12/7/25; 147 performances), with Jane Cowl and Joyce Cary.

For his production of *The Captive* (9/29/26; 160 performances), with Helen Menken and Basil Rathbone, Miller spent a night in jail. The show had run 160 performances when the police decided it was obscene. After his arrest Miller was forced to close the show.

Other fine productions of the 1920s were *Her Cardboard Lover* (3/21/27; 152 performances), with Jeanne Eagels and Leslie Howard; and P. G. Wodehouse's *Candle-Light* (9/30/29; 128 performances), with Gertrude Lawrence and Leslie Howard.

Maude Adams wasn't the only star associated with the Empire. KATHARINE CORNELL opened in the *Wingless Victory* (12/23/26; 108 performances). Her subsequent appearances at the Empire include *Age of Innocence* (11/27/28; 207 performances), the classic play *The Barretts of Wimpole Street* (2/9/31; 372 performances), and *Candida* (3/10/37; 50 performances).

John Gielgud starred on the Empire stage in *Hamlet*. The production opened on October 8, 1936, and played 132 performances, the longest-running *Hamlet* in New York history until the 1964 production starring Richard Burton, which played only 5 more performances. Assisting Gielgud were fellow cast members Lillian Gish, Judith Anderson, and Malcolm Keen West.

Gilbert Miller's reign at the Empire drew to a close in 1931. The theater was sold to the 1432 Broadway Corporation. Luckily, they were adept at booking the theater. During the 1930s the theater hosted the American premiere of KURT WEILL and Bertolt Brecht's *The Threepenny Opera*, which opened on April 13, 1933. Unfortunately, the show wasn't a success and played only 12 performances. Elmer Rice's *We the People* (1/20/33) fared little better, running just 50 performances. In 1934 Gertrude Stein and Virgil Thomson's brilliant *Four Saints in Three Acts* (4/2/34) was revived for 18 performances. Zoe Akin's *The Old Maid* (1/7/35) did better, with Judith Anderson, Helen Menken, and Margaret Dale starring. The Edith Wharton story played for 298 performances. The great Ethel Waters played the Empire in Dorothy and DuBose Heyward's *Mamba's Daughters*. The play opened January 3, 1939, and ran 162 performances.

The Empire's most famous tenant was *Life with Father*. Howard Lindsay and Russel Crouse wrote the classic comedy. Dorothy Stickney (Mrs. Lindsay) starred in the play along with her husband. *Life with Father* opened on November 8, 1939, and ran eight years, for 3,224 performances, the longest-running play in theater history. One of the many children who played in *Life with Father* was John Drew Devereaux, who originated the role of Clarence. The boy's grandfather was John Drew, one of the most popular actors of his time.

The Empire changed hands again on July 31, 1946, when real-estate operator Jacob Freidus purchased it. The new owner was, unfortunately, not interested in theater and bought the Empire for its development possibilities. Then playing at the Empire were Alfred Lunt and Lynn Fontanne (*see* LUNT AND FONTANNE) in Terrence Rattigan's comedy *O Mistress Mine*. The comedy opened on January 23, 1946, and proved to be the Lunts' longest-running hit, eventually playing 451 performances. Next, Howard Lindsay, Dorothy Stickney, and John Drew Deveraux returned to the theater in the Lindsay and Crouse play *Life with Mother*. The comedy opened October 20, 1948, and ran 265 performances.

Two years after he purchased the theater Freidus sold the property to the Astor family. On October 11, 1952, Viscount Astor II died. The family hurriedly sold their properties to raise capital. A textile firm, M. Lowenstein & Sons, purchased the theater.

Three other hits were to play the Empire. In Carson McCullers' great play *The Member of the Wedding*, Ethel Waters returned to the Empire's stage. She was joined by Julie Harris and Brandon de Wilde, both giving wonderful performances. *The Member of the Wedding* opened on January 5, 1950, and played 501 performances. John Van Druten's drama *I Am a Camera*, based on Christopher Isherwood's *Berlin Stories*, also starred Julie Harris. It opened on November 28, 1951, and ran 262 performances. Shirley Booth opened in the Empire's last tenant, *The Time of the Cuckoo*, by Arthur Laurents, on October 15, 1952. After 263 performances, on May 30, 1953, the play closed. On that date Shirley Booth led the audience in singing "Auld Lang Syne," and the curtain came down for the last time.

BROOKS ATKINSON wrote of the Empire: "It had the finest auditorium of any theater in its time, the largest and most hospitable lobby and all the comforts of a cultivated institution. The ticket-taker wore full dress and silk hat. The Empire retained its prestige long after Charles Frohman died. He built so well that the pride and luster of his theater outlived him."

Cornelia Otis Skinner led a benefit for the AMERICAN NATIONAL THEATRE AND ACADEMY on Sunday, May 24, 1953, at the Empire. The benefit's theme was "Highlights of the Empire." At the performance, which commemorated the Empire's 60 years of drama, Edna Wallace Hopper re-created a scene from the 1893 comedy *The Girl I Left Behind Me*, the theater's first attraction. Skinner described the theater as "that beloved

Howard Lindsay in *Life With Father*, 1939.

gilt-prosceniumed and red-plush theater which really *is* theater. It was a lovely and exciting temple."

The Empire was the last of the New York theaters south of 41st Street. It was the direct descendant of the theaters of Union Square and Herald Square. Pieces of the Empire went to fans, and the stage equipment and curtains were sent to the Barter Theatre in Abingdon, Virginia.

Julie Harris, who had played in both *The Member of the Wedding* and *I Am a Camera* at the Empire, wrote, "There was something special about acting on the Empire stage, knowing you had to reach the last row in the second balcony. The Victorian splendor gave such a sense of history, knowing the theatre greats had been on that stage. . . . it was a glorious theatre— beautiful wood, damask silk walls, great theatre portraits. A tragedy that we lost it."

The Empire was replaced by an office building.

EMPIRE THEATER (2). 236 W. 42nd Street. Architect: Thomas W. Lamb. Original name: Eltinge Theatre. Opening: September 11, 1912; *Within the Law*.

Producer A. H. Woods hired Thomas W. Lamb, who would become one of the preeminent motion picture theater architects in the 1920s and '30s, to design the Eltinge Theatre, named after famed female impersonator Julian Eltinge. Lamb came up with a distinguished Beaux Arts design for his theater. A critic at the time reported:

> The little Eltinge, named after Mr. Woods' favorite star, is a gem of liveliness and comfort. The seating capacity is about 1,000, and every one of that number is able to witness the performance on the stage from a spacious seat and with unobstructed view. The decorations are both rich and in excellent taste, an Egyptian effect predominating in the friezes and ornamentation. The general color scheme is of gold, light blue, and mauve and the whole gives the atmosphere of brightness, gaiety and comfort. The mask of Drama, embossed in gilt, is conspicuous in the decorations, and the mural paintings are of a high order of excelance.

Another reviewer wrote, "The interior is artistic. The dome and sounding board contain Egyptian paintings. The color scheme of the auditorium is Egyptian, and the walls are of a gold brown. The curtain is of gold plush and the seats are a pretty light blue."

But the *Times* asked, "What the designer intended when he decorated the boxes with bacchantic figures wearing Egyptian headdresses and playing pipes can only be imagined."

The theater was successful with a variety of productions, most notably the opening production *Within the Law* (9/11/12; 541 performances), starring Jane Cowl. John Barrymore (*see* BARRYMORE FAMILY) appeared

Exterior of Eltinge Theatre with Burlesque replacing legitimate theatre.

in *The Yellow Ticket* (1/20/14; 183 performances), and the farce *Fair and Warmer* (11/6/15; 377 performances) was another hit. But Woods, like other producers, fell on hard times when the Depression hit. He lost the theater, and in 1931 it became a BURLESQUE house. When Mayor Fiorello LaGuardia cracked down on burlesque in 1941, the theater was converted to a movie policy as the Laff-Movie. In 1954 it became the Empire Theater.

Because the Empire contained only 759 seats, which were spread over 2 balconies and an orchestra, the 42nd Street Redevelopment Project did not recommend that the Empire be saved. Only the facade would be incorporated into the plan. True to its word, the Empire was destined to serve as the lobby of the AMC movie complex with the central elevators rising through the proscenium to the backstage area. In order to save the facade, the 7.4-million-pound theater was put on rollers and moved 168 feet down 42nd Street. The theater's proscenium and mural were saved in part. Nonetheless, this "preservation" was truly a desecration of art.

ETHEL BARRYMORE THEATRE. 243–49 W. 47th St., between 7th and 8th Avenues. Architect: Herbert J. Krapp. Opened: December 20, 1928; *The Kingdom of God*.

Ethel Barrymore (*see* BARRYMORE FAMILY) was, in the 1920s, considered one of the top Broadway actors. The SHUBERT BROTHERS admired her artistry and wanted to put her under contract. They offered to build a theater in her name if she would join the Shubert fold. She agreed, and the Shuberts hired Herbert J. Krapp, noted theater architect, to design the building.

On December 20, 1928, the new theater opened with the eponymous star in G. Martinez Sierra's *The Kingdom of God* (92 performances). The theater was hailed as ideal. It would also prove to be popular, housing successes in every decade. Of Ethel Barrymore's performance in *The Kingdom of God*, CRITIC Heywood Broun wrote: "Miss Barrymore's performance is the most moving piece of acting I have ever seen in the theater." *The Kingdom of God* and the theater's next attraction, *The Love Duel* (4/15/29; 88 performances), were directed by E. M. Blythe. Blythe was in reality Barrymore herself. Subsequently several plays were presented at the theater without Barrymore, among them *Death Takes a Holiday* (12/26/29; 180 performances). The play, written by Walter Ferris, was adapted from the original Italian play written by Alberto Casella. Death decides to come to earth, where he falls in love with a mortal who willingly agrees to return with him to the other side. The play was originally a comedy but when adapted by Ferris became a drama. Ethel Barrymore returned to the theater in her next play, *Scarlet Sister Mary* (11/25/30). Its 23-performance run wasn't exactly a surprise, given that Barrymore appeared in the play in blackface.

Next, British author Ivor Novello's drawing-room comedy, *The Truth Game* (12/29/30; 105 performances), marked Billie Burke's return to the stage following the death of her husband, FLORENZ ZIEGFELD.

The star for whom the theater was named returned in a revival of *The School for Scandal* (11/10/31). The production introduced her son, John Drew Colt, to Broadway. Her daughter, Ethel Barrymore Colt, had been introduced in her mother's production of the short-lived *Scarlet Sister Mary*. In 1932 Ethel Barrymore severed her relationship with the Shuberts. They retaliated by removing her first name from the marquee of the theater.

The Barrymore was a perfect midsize house for the production of musicals. Its first, COLE PORTER's *The Gay Divorce* (11/29/32; 248 performances), opened with FRED ASTAIRE (his first appearance without his sister, Adele), Claire Luce, Eric Blore, Betty Starbuck, Erik Rhodes, and G. P. Huntley. The show included such Porter hits as "After You, Who?" "I've Got You

on My Mind," and "Night and Day." After *The Gay Divorcee* moved to the SHUBERT THEATER another sophisticate premiered his work at the Barrymore. Noël Coward's sparkling *Design for Living* (1/24/33; 135 performances) starred Alfred Lunt, Lynn Fontanne (*see* LUNT AND FONTANNE) and the playwright.

The next success on the Barrymore stage did not come until Clare Boothe's comedy drama *The Women* (12/26/36; 657 performances). The play starred Ilka Chase, Margalo Gilmore, Betty Lawford, Audrey Christie, Marjorie Main, and Arlene Francis. The next musical to play the theater, *Knickerbocker Holiday* (10/19/38; 168 performances), starred Walter Huston. The KURT WEILL and Maxwell Anderson score is best remembered for "September Song." It was followed by S. N. Behrman's *No Time for Comedy* (4/17/39; 185 performances), starring KATHARINE CORNELL, Laurence Olivier, and Margalo Gilmore.

Ethel Barrymore appeared for the last time in the theater in *An International Incident* (4/2/40). Unfortunately, it ran a scant 15 performances. Its failure was deserved. But the relative failure of its next tenant was not. *Pal Joey* (12/25/40; 374 performances), with a score by RODGERS AND HART, opened with Gene Kelly, Vivienne Segal, and June Havoc starring. "Bewitched, Bothered and Bewildered" and "I Could Write a Book" were the standouts in an exceptional score. But an antihero was unheard of as the lead in a musical, and audiences and critics found the conceit difficult to accept. In a now-famous review, Brooks Atkinson wrote in the *New York Times*: "Although it is expertly done, can you draw sweet water from a foul well?" When the show was revived in 1952 at the BROADHURST THEATER, times had changed and Atkinson and his colleagues raved.

The next production at the theater, *Best Foot Forward* (10/1/41; 326 performances), had a sparkling score by Hugh Martin and Ralph Blane, which included "Buckle Down Winsocki" and "Ev'ry Time." Nancy Walker, Rosemary Lane, June Allyson, and Maureen Cannon starred. GEORGE ABBOTT produced and directed. A series of successful transfers and revivals followed. Its next great tenant was TENNESSEE WILLIAMS' classic *A Streetcar Named Desire* (12/3/47; 855 performances). The Pulitzer prize–winning drama toplined Jessica Tandy, Kim Hunter, and Karl Malden, and it made a star of Marion Brando, whose performance as Stanley Kowalski electrified theatergoers.

During the 1950s husband and wife Rex Harrison and Lilli Palmer starred in John Van Druten's *Bell, Book and Candle* (11/14/50; 233 performances). Another husband-and-wife team, Hume Cronyn and Jessica Tandy, starred in the theater's next big hit, *The Fourposter* (10/24/51; 632 performances). Jan de Hartog's comedy was directed by José Ferrer, who had

Ethel Barrymore Theatre in 1933 with Anthony Armstrong's *Ten Minute Alibi* playing on the
stage.

Jessica Tandy and Marlon Brando in the original production of *A Streetcar Named Desire*, 1947.

previously appeared at the theater in a transfer of his classic performance in *Cyrano de Bergerac* (1946). The theater's next hit was the drama *Tea and Sympathy* (9/30/53; 712 performances), which marked Robert Anderson's Broadway debut as a playwright. Its plot concerned charges of homosexuality leveled against a student of a private school. The play explored the themes of responsibility, loneliness, and society's ability to define morality by judging individuals without prejudice. Deborah Kerr, John Kerr, and Leif Erickson starred.

The Desperate Hours (2/10/55; 212 performances) by Joseph Hayes, starred Nancy Coleman, Patricia Peardon, George Grizzard, Mary Orr, James Gregory, Paul Newman, and Karl Malden. Enid Bagnold's *The Chalk Garden* (10/26/55; 182 performances) was produced by Irene Mayer Selznick, who had previously produced *A Streetcar Named Desire* and *Bell, Book and Candle* at the Barrymore. The show starred Fritz Weaver, Gladys Cooper, Siobhan McKenna, and Betsy von Furstenberg.

Next, Leonard Sillman produced a sequel to his series of *New Faces* (6/14/56; 220 performances) revues at the Barrymore in 1956. The series introduced new talents to Broadway. Among the new faces that year were T. C. Jones, Maggie Smith, Jane Connell, John Reardon, Virginia Martin, and Inga Swenson.

The Barrymore premiered another Pulitzer prize–winning attraction with Ketti Frings' play *Look Homeward Angel* (11/28/57; 564 performances). Anthony Perkins, Arthur Hill, Jo Van Fleet, and Rosemary Murphy opened in the show. *A Raisin in the Sun* (3/11/59; 530 performances), by Lorraine Hansberry, opened at the Barrymore with Sidney Poitier, Diana Sands, Ruby Dee, Louis Gossett, and Claudia McNeil. The production, the first play written by a black woman to be produced on Broadway, was a risk for producer Philip Rose.

Irene Mayer Selznick produced one last show at the Barrymore, *The Complaisant Lover* (11/1/61; 101 performances). Michael Redgrave, Googie Withers, and Sandy Dennis headlined the Graham Greene play. Another British playwright, Peter Shaffer, had a hit production later in the 1960s, *Black Comedy/White Lies* (2/12/67; 337 performances).

As the number and quality of shows produced on Broadway declined in the 1970s and '80s, the theater suffered from a scarcity of first-rate material. The Barrymore had a hit in the Michael Stewart and Cy Coleman musical *I Love My Wife* (4/17/77; 857 performances). However, the musical *Baby* (12/4/83; 231 performances), by Richard Maltby Jr. and David Shire, was not a success. Other productions at the theater included David Rabe's *Hurly Burly* (8/7/84; 343

performances), which featured William Hurt, Sigourney Weaver, Judith Ivey, Harvey Keitel, Jerry Stiller, Ron Silver, and Cynthia Nixon.

August Wilson, the only black playwright regularly produced on Broadway in the 1980s and '90s, authored *Joe Turner's Come and Gone* (3/27/88; 105 performances), which featured Angela Bassett and Delroy Lindo.

It was followed by two London transfers. The first, Stephen Berkoff's *Metamorphosis* (3/6/89), only managed a 96-performance run despite the Broadway debut of Mikhail Baryshnikov. David Rabe's *The Secret Rapture* (10/26/89) never found an audience on Broadway and closed after a disappointing 12 performances.

Neil Simon, whose star had been descending on Broadway, had a hit with his farce *Rumors* (12/13/89; 535 performances). Critics were mostly lukewarm, but audiences flocked to see a bevy of theater stalwarts, including Ken Howard, Christine Baranski, Ron Leibman, and Joyce Van Patten.

Another London hit arrived at the Barrymore on March 25, 1990. But this time the show was a hit. Peter Shaffer's *Lettuce and Lovage* starred Maggie Smith, who was ably supported by her original London co-star Margaret Tyzak. The play ran 286 performances, closing only due to the departure of its star.

Alec Baldwin and Jessica Lange held forth on the Barrymore stage in a revival of Tennessee Williams' *A Streetcar Named Desire* (4/12/92; 137 performances). It was followed by a big hit for its time (plays didn't seem to run as long as they used to), Wendy Wasserstein's *The Sisters Rosensweig* (3/18/93; 556 performances). The Lincoln Center Theater production starred Jane Alexander, Madeline Kahn, Robert Klein, Christine Estabrook, and John Cunningham.

Two more transfer London shows arrived at the Barrymore, but though they achieved moderate runs, they didn't equal their original British successes. The Royal National Theatre's production of Jean Cocteau's *Les Parents Terribles* was renamed *Indiscretions* (4/27/95). It ran only 220 performances despite winning performances by Eileen Atkins, Roger Rees, Kathleen Turner, Jude Law, and Cynthia Nixon. A production of Oscar Wilde's *An Ideal Husband* (5/1/96) ran a respectable 307 performances.

Cy Coleman's new musical, *The Life*, was next at the Barrymore. The show, written with David Newman and Ira Gasman, looked at the lives of some New York street whores. It opened on April 26, 1997, and managed a fair 466-performance run, not enough to put it into the hit category.

A surprising hit at the Barrymore was the McCarter Theatre of Princeton's production of *Electra* (12/3/98; 116 performances), starring Zoe Wanamaker and Claire Bloom.

The Barrymore was increasingly becoming the home for hit English productions. David Hare's *Amy's View* (4/15/99) closed after a limited engagement of 103 performances. Judi Dench starred in the Royal National Theatre's production.

A critical failure off Broadway with Julie Andrews, the Stephen Sondheim revue *Putting It Together* (11/21/99; 101 performances) was also a flop on Broadway. Badly directed and misconceived, the show failed despite the talents of Carol Burnett and George Hearn.

The British influence continued with a revival of Tom Stoppard's comedy *The Real Thing* (4/17/2000; 136 performances) from London's Donmar Warehouse. Stephen Dillane and Jennifer Ehle starred.

Charles Busch's comedy *The Tale of the Allergist's Wife* (11/2/2000; 777 performances) was a transfer from the Manhattan Theatre Club. The show opened with an exemplary cast including Linda Lavin, Tony Roberts, and Michele Lee.

The Barrymore has proven itself to be an ideal and highly versatile Broadway theater, suited to musicals, dramas, comedies, revues, and even one-person shows. The theater, owned by the Shubert Organization, remains an integral part of the Broadway theater scene.

On November 4, 1987, the New York City Landmarks Preservation Commission designated the exterior of the theater a landmark. The commission stated: "Its facade is an exceptionally handsome design, featuring an unusual giant terra-cotta grillework screen and fine beaux-arts style ornament." On November 10, 1987, the commission designated the interior of the theater a landmark, noting the plasterwork ornamentation of its ceiling and the ornamental treatment of its boxes.

EUGENE O'NEILL THEATER. 230 W. 49th Street. Architect: Herbert J. Krapp. Original name: Forrest Theater. Opening: November 24, 1925; *Mayflowers*.

The SHUBERT BROTHERS built this theater as the Forrest, named after the great American actor Edwin Forrest. It was part of the Shuberts' plan to build six theaters on 48th and 49th Streets in an attempt to emulate the success of 42nd Street. The brothers arranged for the Forrest Theater to be built along with an accompanying hotel.

The theater's 1,200 seats (later reduced to 1,101) meant that the stage could accommodate both musicals and straight plays. But the early years of the Forrest were marked with failure. An exception was James Cagney, Mary Boland, and Osgood Perkins starring in *Women Go on Forever* (9/7/27; 118 performances), which was a hit despite critical drubbing.

Another series of failures followed until Edgar Wallace's play *On the Spot* (10/29/30; 167 performances) opened at the theater, then dubbed Wallace's Forrest Theater. The crime melodrama starred Anna May Wong and Glenda Farrell. Another bleak period followed, which was relieved by only the modest success of Rachel Crothers' *As Husbands Go* (1/19/33; 144 performances).

After 7 more flops, the Shuberts lost control of the Forrest as part of their bankruptcy settlement. Although the Shuberts regained some of their theaters at bargain prices, buying them back at the foreclosure sales, they decided not to try for control of the Forrest. It was a mistake they would regret, for only a few months later the Forrest hosted one of the American theater's longest running successes, *Tobacco Road*. Jack Kirkland's play, based on the Erskine Caldwell novel, opened at the Masque Theater on December 5, 1933. It soon moved to the Forrest, where it enjoyed an enormous run, playing from September 1934 to May 1941. The show finally totaled a run of 3,224 performances, making it the second longest-running play in Broadway history.

The Forrest went from feast to famine after *Tobacco Road*, and another four years of failure followed. Finally in 1945 the theater was sold and redecorated, and on October 25, 1945, it reopened as the Coronet with *Beggars Are Coming to Town*. The Coronet had better luck than the Forrest. Its second offering was Elmer Rice's hit *Dream Girl* (12/14/45; 348 performances). Rice's wife, Betty Field, starred along with Wendell Corey and Evelyn Varden.

The theater's success continued with ARTHUR MILLER's Broadway debut. *All My Sons* (1/29/47; 328 performances) starred Ed Begley, Arthur Kennedy, Lois Wheeler, and Karl Malden. A lightweight musical revue, *Angel in the Wings* (12/11/47; 308 performances), followed with stars Elaine Stritch and Grace and Paul Hartman introducing such hits as "Big Brass Band from Brazil" and "Bongo, Bongo, Bongo." The success of one revue led to another. *Small Wonder* (9/15/48; 134 performances) opened with Jack Cassidy, Joan Diener, Tom Ewell, Mort Marshall, Mary McCarty, Alice Pearce, and Tommy Rall. A revival of *Diamond Lil* (2/5/49; 181 performances) followed, starring the play's author, Mae West. Another hit revue with the Hartmans, *Tickets Please* (4/27/50; 245 performances), came next, which also featured Larry Kert, Roger Price, and Dorothy Jarnac.

The theater changed names again with the opening of William Inge's *A Loss of Roses* (11/11/59; 25 performances). It was then dubbed the Eugene O'Neill Theater. The first hit at the O'Neill was *Show Girl* (1/12/61; 100 performances), a revue with Carol Channing that was the first Broadway show broadcast on pay television. Herb Gardner's comedy *A Thousand*

Clowns (4/5/62; 428 performances) starred Sandy Dennis and Jason Robards Jr. BOCK AND HARNICK's under-appreciated musical *She Loves Me* (4/23/63; 302 performances) was directed by HAROLD PRINCE. The exceptional cast included Barbara Cook, Daniel Massey, Jack Cassidy, Barbara Baxley, and Nathaniel Frey.

Playwright NEIL SIMON bought the theater at the end of the 1960s and installed a number of his own productions there. The first was *Last of the Red Hot Lovers* (12/28/69; 706 performances), which starred James Coco and Linda Lavin. Then Peter Falk, Vincent Gardenia, and Lee Grant starred in Simon's *The Prisoner of Second Avenue* (11/11/71; 780 performances). Two less-successful Simon shows opened next at the O'Neill: *The Good Doctor* (11/27/73; 208 performances) and *God's Favorite* (12/11/74; 119 performances). Nonetheless, with some unexceptional interludes, the Simon reign continued. Simon's *California Suite* (7/2/77; 445 performances) starred Tammy Grimes, George Grizzard, and Jack Weston. *I Ought*

to Be in Pictures (4/3/80; 324 performances) was another hit for Simon, but Simon's next offering, *Fools* (46/81; 40 performances), was not a success. A revival of the Neil Simon, Cy Coleman, and Carolyn Leigh musical *Little Me* (1982) met with poor reviews and closed quickly.

The Jujamcyn Theaters organization bought the O'Neill from Simon and installed a string of failures. Finally they struck gold with *Big River* (4/25/85; 1,005 performances), Roger Miller's tepid musicalization of *Huckleberry Finn*.

The theater's next booking, *M. Butterfly* (3/20/88; 777 performances), by David Henry Hwang, starred John Lithgow and B. D. Wong. The story of an English official living with a Chinese woman who turns out to be a man had audiences enthralled, if not a little incredulous. But it was based on a true story.

March 21, 1990, saw a revival of TENNESSEE WILLIAMS' *Cat on a Hot Tin Roof*, 149 performances. Kathleen Turner played Maggie beside fellow cast members

Harold Prince (right) directing Daniel Massey and Barbara Cook in *She Loves Me*, 1963.

Charles Durning, Polly Holliday, and Daniel Hugh Kelly as Brick.

The musical revue *Five Guys Named Moe* (4/8/92; 445 performances) incorporated songs sung by Louis Jordan. A hit in England, the show was less of one in New York. A revival of *Grease* (5/11/94) followed at the O'Neill. Producers Fran and Barry Weissler kept this second-rate offering going for 1,505 performances with such casting as Rosie O'Donnell and later Brooke Shields.

A revival by Chicago's Goodman Theatre of Arthur Miller's classic drama *Death of a Salesman* (2/10/99; 274 performances) featured Brian Dennehy as Willy Loman.

The theater's next success was the musical *The Full Monty* (10/26/2000; 777 performances). David Yazbek made his Broadway songwriting debut with a well-constructed libretto supplied by Terrence McNally. It was followed by a revival of Maury Yeston and Arthur Kopit's musical *Nine*. It opened on April 10, 2003, with Antonio Banderas and Chita Rivera.

On December 8, 1987, the New York City Landmarks Preservation Commission designated the interior of the theater a landmark. The exterior was denied designation. The commission stated that the interior had "elaborate cameo like ornamental work including profiles, theatrical masks and panels with classical scenes."

FALLON, WILLIAM J. One of Broadway's great criminal lawyers; b. 1886; d. 1927.

William J. Fallon represented all types of Broadway denizens and saw to it that they were either acquitted or spent a long time in getting to jail. Gene Fowler's biography of Fallon was titled *The Great Mouthpiece*; Fallon was also dubbed "the Jail Robber" by author Donald Henderson Clarke. He is not to be confused with another William J. Fallon, a "bag man" and one-time owner of Tyson's Ticket Agency, who died in 1943.

During Fallon's 10-year tenure as a member of the New York bar, he never saw one of his 126 clients get the chair. Fallon depended on both legal and illegal means for his success in court. He would often pick out one member of the jury to whom he made his case. This resulted in many hung juries. He was also inclined to bribe members of the jury when the need arose. Fallon was indicted himself on bribery charges in 1924, based on a story in the *New York American*. He denied bribing the jury and decided to represent himself, going so far as to put himself on the stand. Fallon turned the case around by accusing William Randolph Hearst, publisher of the *American*, of carrying out a personal vendetta against him. Naturally the jury acquitted Fallon.

Fallon was the son of an Irish contractor. He was quoted in the *Brooklyn Eagle* that he attended Fordham College and its law school because "it seemed easier than the other courses." He became an assistant district attorney in Weschester (1914–1916), then moved to Manhattan and set up a private law practice. His clients included gamblers and gangsters Nicky Arnstein (husband of Fanny Brice), Charles Fuller, Arnold Rothstein, Broadway performers, and famous athletes. For entertainment, Fallon pursued singer Texas Guinan around town, wherever she was currently entertaining.

Fallon said about his law practice:

The law is like putting money in the bank. You get just as much out as you put in and no more unless you know an official, and then you are lucky. The bank of Legal Learning has a very tough set of officials.

I didn't know being a lawyer was in my head yet; a lot of people would seriously dispute that. I just entered the profession casually without a thought—the way I do everything, without thinking. If I stopped to think I'd get into trouble.

The lawyer was dubbed "Slippery Bill" in 1924, when he was being sought for bribing a jury that acquitted 37 of Fallon's clients. Fallon hid for three weeks in an apartment building until police, trailing Gertrude Vanderbilt, were led to the hideout. Fallon, in true form, escaped prosecution on that case also. Once regarded as one of Broadway's most colorful playboys, Fallon enjoyed his liquor, and it eventually did him in. He died at the age of 41 of alcoholism and heart disease.

At his death, Mark Hellinger wrote, "Bill Fallon is dead. And in those four words rests the greatest sob story that Broadway ever knew. He played Broadway until Broadway finally got him. When he tried to pull out, it was too late. It always is. And so Fallon, who was still a young man, is dead. Perhaps, after all, he was satisfied to go. For his early days had been filled with love and happiness and fame. And when the future holds hope for none of these, it is then time to go."

FEDERAL MUSIC THEATRE. *See* **Studio 54.**

FEDERAL THEATRE PROJECT. The Federal Theatre Project (FTP) was an arm of the Works Progress Administration (WPA) during the Depression. It provided federal subsidy of the theater in order to increase employment and stimulate the nation's economy. Broadway was hard hit by the Depression. Fewer shows were produced as angels (Broadway investors) found their resources wiped out by the stock market crash. Audiences, too, forsook the theater as an unnecessary luxury. Without product or audience, many theater owners went into receivership, and the map of Broadway was changed forever. Theaters were demolished, turned into BURLESQUE houses or radio studios, or simply left abandoned. Actors, ill suited for other jobs, which didn't exist anyway, had nowhere to turn.

Relief administrator Harry Hopkins realized the needs of artists, including actors. He oversaw the establishment of the Federal Music Project, Federal Art Project, and Federal Writers' Project. Hallie Flanagan of Vassar College was hired by the government to oversee the fourth such program, dubbed the Federal Theatre Project. Altogether the WPA employed 40,000 artists by the end of 1936.

Hopkins explained the project to Flanagan:

This is a non-commercial theater. It's got to be run by a person who sees right from the start that the profits won't be money profits. It's got to be run by a person who isn't interested just in the commercial type of show. I know something about the plays you've been doing for ten years, plays about American life. This is an American job, not just a New York job. I want someone who knows and cares about other parts of the country. It's a job just down your alley.

He also advised Flanagan that "whatever happens, you'll be wrong."

Of the thousands of performers and stage technicians who found employment in the FTP were such later luminaries as John Houseman, Orson Welles, Arlene Francis, E. G. Marshall, Arthur Kennedy, Will Geer, and Joseph Cotten. Composers Marc Blitzstein and Virgil Thomson and playwrights ARTHUR MILLER and Dale Wasserman also worked on the experimental project. Future directors John Huston and Nicholas Ray received training on the project. Scenic and costume designers such as Howard Bay and Fred Stover were joined by such lighting designers as George Izenour.

The project officially began on August 27, 1935, inaugurated by Hopkins as a "free, adult, uncensored" federal theater. Its first production, *Black Empire*, opened at Los Angeles' Mayan Theater on March 26, 1936. The first New York production was *Injunction Granted*, which opened at the BILTMORE THEATER on July 24, 1936. Other productions by the Broadway contingent of the project included *Horse Eats Hat* (9/26/36; 61 performances) at the MAXINE ELLIOTT'S THEATRE; *It Can't Happen Here*, which opened at 22 theaters around the country on October 27, 1936; *Doc-*

tor Faustus (1/8/37; 128 performances), at the Maxine Elliott's Theatre; *Revolt of the Beavers* (5/20/37); *Processional* (10/13/37; 81 performances), at the Maxine Elliott's Theatre; *S.S. Glencairn* (10/29/37), including *Moon of the Caribbees, In the Zone, Bound East for Cardiff*, and *The Long Voyage Home*, at the Lafayette Theater; *One-Third of a Nation* (1/17/38; 238 performances), at the Adelphi Theater (*see* GEORGE ABBOTT THEATER); *Haiti* (3/2/38; 168 performances), at the Lafayette Theater; *Big Blow* (10/1/38; 157 performances), at Maxine Elliott's Theatre; *Sing for Your Supper* (4/24/39; 44 performances), at Adelphi Theater; and *Life and Death of an American* (5/19/39; 29 performances), at the Maxine Elliott's Theatre.

The project wasn't limited to only traditional plays. Flanagan, seeking to build a national theater out of the Federal Theatre Project, encouraged all kinds of theater, including circuses, marionette and children's shows, vaudeville, and variety. Emmet Lavery, head of the National Service Bureau of the project, stated:

If the Federal Theater could have survived for six months more, the second emergency, the actuality of war in Europe, would have perhaps extended the base of the first theater operation. . . . This start on theater, which was justified by the first emergency—the necessity of feeding hungry actors—could be held together on a more limited but very professional basis as a necessary arm of entertainment with the army. And if that had happened, we would have the national theater.

But the Federal Theatre Project, which vowed to be "uncensored," proved to be a problem for conservatives. The shows couldn't help being controversial because they reflected the state of the country and its politics. One of the more criticized parts of the project was the series "Living Newspapers," experimental theater pieces that took subjects from the headlines and created plays around the issues. These shows personalized the facts of the news stories and brought them home to the project's surprisingly mixed audience. Audiences were reflective of the entire range of societal makeup. The stories were documentary in form, and after exploring the breadth of the problem asked the government and industry to take action.

The government canceled the first Living Newspaper production, about the Ethiopian war. *Triple A Plowed Under* was the second and dealt with the agriculture problems of the country. Others dealt with problems such as housing, cooperatives, health care, labor unions, race relations, industry, movies, natural resources, and public utilities. The newspaper's most famous editions included *Power*, produced at the RITZ THEATRE. *Power* was an examination of a power failure and solutions to the problem. As the play progressed, the audience followed a typical consumer, Angus K.

Hallie Flanagan, director of the Federal Theatre Project, 1935.

Buttonkooper, as he learned how electricity got to the consumer and the problems of monopolistic utilities.

Historical dramas received their due, with five revolving around the character of Abraham Lincoln. Two of these were called *Abraham Lincoln*, one written by John Drinkwater and another by Ralph Kettering. *Mrs. Lincoln* was written by Ramon Romero, and Howard Koch scripted *The Lonely Man*. But the most successful drama about Lincoln was *Prologue to Glory*, by E. P. Conkle. After almost a year's run in New York, the production moved to the New York World's Fair in Flushing Meadows. There were also productions throughout the country for hundreds of thousands of theatergoers. In New York, Lincoln was played by Erford Gage, an actor who might have become a big star were it not for his untimely death. Lincoln's love, Ann Rutledge, was played by an actress of the same name who was actually her great-grand-niece.

Burns Mantle, editor of the *Best Plays* series, stated, "If the Federal Theater had produced no other single drama, this production of *Prologue to Glory* would doubly justify its history and all its struggles." However, like most Federal Theatre Project productions, *Prologue to Glory* also received its share of criticism. Republican congressman J. Parnell Thomas labeled it "a propaganda play to prove that all politicians are crooked." He thought it was simply "Communist talk."

With the government on the lookout for Communists behind every proscenium, the Federal Theatre Project was doomed to be censored and, finally, disbanded. The most famous case of censorship involved the production of the Marc Blitzstein musical *The Cradle Will Rock*, a pro-union exposé of the steel industry. Orson Welles and John Houseman were the producers of the controversial piece. It was scheduled to open on June 16, 1937. Because the nation was then going through deadly strikes, the subject was especially timely and controversial—so controversial that the government sent a memo to Flanagan ordering that "no openings of new productions shall take place until after the beginning of the coming fiscal year." Actually, *The Cradle Will Rock* was the only opening scheduled.

With the opening canceled, the company was doubly intent on presenting the show. ACTORS' EQUITY, always distrustful of the WPA, had ruled that its members could not perform onstage in a Federal Theatre Project play. The musicians' union also disliked the project and forbade its members from playing in the show, despite its pro-union slant. So on opening night, Houseman and Welles told the audience assembled outside the theater about their problems and marched the entire group to the little Venice Theater. Marc Blitzstein was seated at his piano, alone onstage. The actors, forbidden to appear on the stage, simply took

seats around the audience and stood up to say their lines. The result was tremendously exciting, and *The Cradle Will Rock* is remembered as one of the greatest triumphs of the 1930s. It ended up playing 104 performances.

The House Un-American Activities Committee was quick to identify the Federal Theatre Project as one of its targets when it began its inquiries in August 1938. Congressman J. Parnell Thomas (later jailed for defrauding the government) blasted the project: "It is apparent from the startling evidence received thus far that the Federal Theater Project not only is serving as a branch of the Communistic organization but is also one more link in the vast and unparalleled New Deal propaganda machine."

The Federal Theatre Project couldn't survive the storms of controversy. On June 30, 1939, the project was disbanded. Hallie Flanagan described her vision of theater, a vision that the Federal Theatre Project had fulfilled:

> We live in a changing world; man is whispering through space, soaring to the stars in ships, flinging miles of steel and glass into the air. Shall the theater continue to huddle in the confines of a painted box set? The movies, in their kaleidoscopic speed and juxtaposition of external objects and internal emotions are seeking to find visible and audible expression for the tempo and the psychology of our time. The stage too must experiment with ideas, with psychological relationships of men and women, with speech and rhythm forms, with dance and movement, with color and light—or it must and should become a museum product. In an age of terrific implications as to wealth and poverty, as to the function of government, as to peace and war, as to the relation of the artist to all these forces, the theater must grow up. The theater must become conscious of the implications of the changing social order, or the changing social order will ignore, and rightly, the implications of the theater.

FIELDS FAMILY. The Fields family spanned almost a century of the American theater and spread their talents over a wide variety of roles, particularly in musical theater.

Lew Fields

Producer, director, performer; b. New York, New York, January 1, 1867; d. Beverly Hills, California, July 20, 1941. Lew Fields, the patriarch of the Fields family, is credited with giving the young songwriting team of RODGERS AND HART their first important professional commissions to write Broadway musicals. He also enjoyed a long career as partner of Joseph Weber, with whom he presented many popular BURLESQUES on Broadway hits of the time.

Lew Fields, Dorothy Fields (standing), and Helen Hayes.

Herbert Fields

Librettist; b. New York, New York, July 26, 1897; d. New York, New York, March 24, 1958. Herbert Fields enjoyed long collaborations as librettist to many of Broadway's preeminent songwriters. He began his career with Rodgers and Hart and then wrote a number of musical comedies with COLE PORTER. He collaborated on eight shows with his sister Dorothy, who was also a lyricist.

Dorothy Fields

Librettist, lyricist; b. Allenhurst, New Jersey, July 15, 1901; d. New York, New York, March 28, 1974. The baby of the family, Dorothy overcame much sexism to become one of Broadway's top lyricists. One strength lay in her ability to utilize current slang in her lyrics. Throughout her long career she remained in the vanguard of the musical theater, always up-to-date and able to change along with popular taste. She was the only member of her family to make a successful transition to film, writing with such great composers as JEROME KERN.

Joseph Fields

Librettist, playwright; b. New York, New York, February 21, 1895; d. Beverly Hills, California, March 3, 1966. Joseph Fields wrote many successful comic plays, usually in collaboration with Jerome Chodorov. He also collaborated with OSCAR HAMMERSTEIN II and Anita Loos on musicals and plays. He pursued his career apart from his father and siblings. His sweet and somewhat sentimental works are discussed after those of the rest of his illustrious family.

The saga of the Fields family started when Lew Fields began his more than 50 years in the American theater as the boyhood partner of Joseph Weber. Weber and Fields were "Dutch comics" in early musical comedies,

Herbert Fields writes while the chorus girls watch.

basing their characters on stereotypes of New York's Dutch population. They were the most popular comedy team of their time, and the partners billed themselves as the Dutch Senators. By 1885 they were able to put together their own company of performers. On March 27, 1896, they took a lease on the Broadway Music Hall at Broadway and 29th Street and soon renamed it Weber and Fields' Music Hall. The team wrote and performed burlesques of other theater productions and presented well-known vaudeville performers. The theater opened with its first burlesque, *The Geezer*, on September 5, 1896. *The Geezer*'s company members included Sam Bernard, John T. Kelly, Josephine Allen, and Lillian Swain. Other popular burlesques were *Pousse Cafe* (1897), *Hurly Burly* (1898), *Whirl-I-Gig* (1899), *Fiddle Dee Dee* (1900), *Hoity Toity* (1901), *Twirly Whirly* (1902), and *Whoop-Dee-Doo* (1903). On May 28, 1904, the team broke up following a performance at the NEW AMSTERDAM THEATRE. Weber continued his management of the theater on his own under the name Weber's Theater.

On December 5, 1904, along with two partners, Henry Hamlin and Julian Mitchell, Lew Fields opened the Lew Fields Theater on 42nd Street. Marie Cahill was the chief member of Fields' new company, which presented the VICTOR HERBERT and Glen MacDonough musical *It Happened in Nordland*. OSCAR HAMMERSTEIN I was the owner of the theater who leased the venue to Fields and his partners. Fields' name was taken off the theater in 1906 when it was renamed the Hackett Theater. Fields then leased the Herald Square Theater downtown, beginning operations on August 30, 1906. When Weber lost his theater in 1912, he reteamed with Fields. They built their own theater on 44th Street and named it Weber and Fields' New Music Hall (*see* 44TH STREET THEATRE). But, the team didn't hold on to the theater's lease for long, because in late 1913 the SHUBERT BROTHERS took over the theater's operation. On June 5, 1913, Fields moved his operation to the space above and called it the LEW FIELDS 44TH STREET ROOF GARDEN. The Shuberts also owned this roof garden theater. Typically, Fields lost the space by the end of the year. The last theater named for Fields was the Lew Fields Mansfield Theater, which bore his name from April 26, 1928, to March 4, 1929. Today the theater is known as the BROOKS ATKINSON THEATER.

As he got older, Fields turned increasingly to producing rather than performing. Like most producers, he had his favorite performers. These included VERNON CASTLE, Nora Bayes, Fay Templeton, Lillian Russell, DeWolf Hopper, Marie Dressler, and HELEN HAYES. Fields hit his stride in the 1920s with the production of a series of musicals by Rodgers and Hart. Fields produced the shows, many of which had a libretto by his son Herbert.

Lew Fields was the librettist and producer of *A Lonely Romeo* (6/10/19; 87 performances). On August 26, 1919, Lew Fields added a song, "Any Old Place with You," by Rodgers and Hart. This was their first Broadway song and their first professionally written song. Fields continued his support of the young team with *Poor Little Ritz Girl* (7/27/20; 93 performances). Unfortunately, much of the team's score was cut when the show was in its out-of-town tryouts, and new songs by SIGMUND ROMBERG and Alex Gerber were added. Richard Rodgers was just 18 when the show opened on Broadway.

Blue Eyes (2/21/21; 48 performances) starred Fields and Delyle Alda. They repeated their teaming with the Fields production *Snapshots of 1921* (6/2/21; 44 performances) that same year. Fields next directed two successful editions of the popular revue series *The Greenwich Village Follies* in 1923 and 1924. His production of *The Melody Man* (5/13/24; 56 performances) was not a hit. Rodgers and Hart, the authors of the score, were still practically unknown on Broadway.

Herbert Fields made his Broadway debut choreographing the THEATER GUILD production *The Garrick Gaieties* (5/17/25; 231 performances), the revue that catapulted Rodgers and Hart to fame. The team's hit song from the show was "Manhattan," one of their most enduring standards. While it was running, Herbert saw his first book musical, *Dearest Enemy* (9/18/25; 286 performances), open. Rodgers and Hart provided the score, and it was one of their best. The American Revolution was the scene, and Herbert's book told the story of Mrs. Robert Murray, a woman who stalled the British general William Howe while the American troops got into position for a surprise attack. *Dearest Enemy*, actually written before *The Garrick Gaieties*, starred Helen Ford, Charles Purcell, Flavia Arcaro, and Andrew Lawlor Jr. Writing in the *New York Evening World*, E. W. Osborn said that the book was "wise and truly witty and genuinely romantic."

Herbert Fields wrote the libretto to his father's production of Rodgers and Hart's *The Girl Friend* (3/17/26; 301 performances), a typical 1920s musical. The title tune was a big hit. Abel Green, writing in VARIETY, claimed, "The book is the best libretto Fields has contributed so far and is only paired by the songs with ultra smart lyrics and oddly rhythmed and fetching tunes." Next, Herbert choreographed the second edition of the *The Garrick Gaieties* (5/10/26) with its Rodgers and Hart score. The big hit of this edition was "Mountain Greenery." Herbert's third Rodgers and Hart show of 1926 was *Peggy-Ann* (12/27/26; 354 performances). His father, Lew, produced in association with Lyle D. Andrews. *Peggy-Ann* was a strange musical with surrealistic overtones. The majority of the show illustrated Peggy-Ann's dreams. In one dream, a yachting

The American Theatre featuring *4 Corners of the Earth* and the Hackett Theatre with Rose Stahl in *The Chorus Lady*, 1906.

trip, Peggy-Ann meets a talking fish. The *New York Times* commended Herbert's libretto with its "frequent flights of imagination." ALEXANDER WOOLLCOTT, then writing for the *New York World*, admired the songs, "but it is the libretto which arrests attention. . . . It was all like a chapter out of *Alice in Wonderland*."

Herbert Fields was clearly becoming a major talent in the American musical theater. His next two shows, both produced by his father, were among the biggest successes of the 1920s. The first was *Hit the Deck* (4/25/27; 352 performances), which opened at the BE-

LASCO THEATRE. VINCENT YOUMANS, Leo Robin, and Clifford Grey wrote the score, which contained two huge hits, "Sometimes I'm Happy" and "Hallelujah." Lew Fields co-directed with Alexander Leftwich as well as co-producing with Youmans. The second smash hit of 1927 for Herbert and Lew was *A Connecticut Yankee* (11/3/27; 421 performances), with a score by Rodgers and Hart. Herbert's libretto received mixed notices. Alexander Woollcott wrote: "The libretto did not seem to me quite as funny as it set out to be." But Alan Dale, in the *New York American*, said the show had "a poignantly amusing book . . . lovely, quaint, deliciously droll."

Lew wrote three libretti in 1928 with moderate success. *Present Arms* (4/26/28; 147 performances) had a Rodgers and Hart score and a production mounted by Lew. *Chee-Chee* (9/25/28; 32 performances) was a downright failure for Rodgers, Hart, and the two Fieldses. Herbert's source, *The Son of the Grand Eunuch*, a novel by Charles Petit, had a protagonist whose physical state was unique in Broadway history. Audiences did not warm to the subject. For *Hello Daddy!* (12/26/28; 196 performances), Herbert wrote the libretto, father Lew produced and starred (in his last appearance on Broadway), and Dorothy acted as lyricist to Jimmy McHugh's music. She had previously made a splash with her lyrics to Jimmy McHugh's music for *Blackbirds of 1928* (5/9/28; 519 performances). The team's hit song for the Lew Leslie revue was "I Can't Give You Anything But Love." Lew Fields' last Broadway show was the *Vanderbilt Revue* (11/5/30; 13 performances). He co-produced and co-directed the proceedings, which boasted a score by a variety of writers, including his daughter Dorothy and Jimmy McHugh. After that Lew Fields decided to retire rather than buck the declining opportunities of Broadway during the Depression.

Herbert began his long collaboration with Cole Porter in 1929 with the show *Fifty Million Frenchmen* (11/27/29; 254 performances). The opening-night performance almost didn't happen as planned. Singer Betty Compton complained that her dressing room at the LYRIC THEATER didn't suit her stature as a star. She rectified the situation by calling her boyfriend, Mayor James J. Walker. The theater was hit with 6 code violations, and the show's opening was threatened. Luckily, Helen Broderick, also starring in the show, agreed to switch dressing rooms.

Dorothy had her final Broadway collaboration with Jimmy McHugh in *The International Revue* (2/25/30; 95 performances). They contributed one smash hit, "On the Sunny Side of the Street," to the Lew Leslie production. Dorothy and Jimmy McHugh's *Clowns in Clover*, closed out of town in 1933. They went out with a bang, as the score contained another standard, "Don't Blame Me."

Herbert continued his collaboration with Porter with *The New Yorkers* (12/8/30; 158 performances). Herbert then collaborated for the last time with Rodgers and Hart on their show *America's Sweetheart* (2/10/31; 135 performances). The show, a gentle satire on Hollywood, starred Inez Courtney, Jack Whiting, and Harriette Lake (later better known as Ann Sothern). Most of the reviews were positive, except Dorothy Parker, writing in *The New Yorker*, who acerbically stated: "Mr. Fields has, apparently, compiled his libretto with

a pair of scissors and his poor thumb must be awfully sore after all that clipping of jokes." Herbert's next assignment was a collaboration with GEORGE AND IRA GERSHWIN on *Pardon My English* (1/28/33; 43 performances), produced by AARONS AND FREEDLEY. *Pardon My English*, despite an excellent score, was the least successful of all the Gershwin brothers' musicals.

Both Herbert and Dorothy took a long break from Broadway in the late 1930s and both returned, with different shows, in 1939. Dorothy made her return to the theater after 6 years with *Stars in Your Eyes* (2/9/39; 127 performances), starring ETHEL MERMAN, with music by Arthur Schwartz (*see* DIETZ AND SCHWARTZ) and book by J. P. McEvoy. The show was meant to be a somewhat leftish look at Hollywood, but under JOSHUA LOGAN's direction it turned into a simple satire. The songwriters wrote a very good score, although none of the songs achieved lasting fame. *Stars in Your Eyes* closed just in time for Merman to join the cast of Herbert's next show.

For Herbert, it was back to Cole Porter. The show was *Du Barry Was a Lady* (12/6/39; 408 performances), and Herbert collaborated with producer B. G. De Sylva (*see* DE SYLVA, BROWN, AND HENDERSON) on the hilarious book. The story was about a washroom attendant (Bert Lahr) at a popular nightclub who hits his head against a sink and dreams he is King Louis XV. In his dream, Ethel Merman, in real life a singer at the Club Petite, is Madame Du Barry. John Mason Brown called the show "a rowdy, boisterous, high-spirited extravaganza which stops at just this side of nothing and makes much of little." The show was a change from the polite comedies Herbert had written for Rodgers and Hart.

Herbert, Porter, De Sylva, and Merman were reteamed for *Panama Hattie* (10/30/40; 501 performances), a formula musical that nevertheless gave Merman an attractive vehicle. *Panama Hattie* was Herbert's last libretto written without his sister, Dorothy. She joined Herbert at book writing while still contributing occasional lyrics to shows. Their first project as a team was Porter's *Let's Face It!* (10/29/41; 547 performances), a wartime musical with Eve Arden, Danny Kaye, Nanette Fabray, Mary Jane Walsh, and Vivian Vance. The Fieldses supplied a mischievous script to match Porter's equally sassy music and lyrics.

Another Porter show, *Something for the Boys* (1/7/43; 422 performances) followed. The scene was a military base in Texas, and Ethel Merman was the star. Michael Todd produced, and Herbert, in addition to co-authoring the libretto with Dorothy, co-directed with Hassard Short. *Something for the Boys* wasn't top-notch Porter or Fields. Porter, Herbert and Dorothy, Hassard Short, and Mike Todd repeated their assignments (although Herbert did not direct) for *Mexican Hayride* (1/28/44; 479 performances). It, too, was a crowd pleaser but not especially notable, save for the hit song, "I Love You." June Havoc, Bobby Clark, and Wilbur Evans were the leads.

European-style operetta, pronounced dead at the end of the 1920s, made a surprisingly successful return to the Broadway stage with *Up in Central Park* (1/27/45; 504 performances). Sigmund Romberg wrote the music, and Dorothy returned to lyric writing for the show. She also collaborated with Herbert on the book. To everyone's surprise, the Mike Todd production enjoyed a long run. The songwriters wrote a lovely, melodious score with "Close as Pages in a Book" the hit.

Herbert and Dorothy's entertaining but minor efforts for Porter didn't prepare Broadwayites for the genius of their next show, ANNIE GET YOUR GUN (5/16/46; 1,147 performances). IRVING BERLIN'S score was his finest, and the book by the Fields siblings was their masterwork. Ethel Merman perfectly adapted the role of sharpshooter Annie Oakley to her talents, with Ray Middleton playing her chief rival and chief love, Frank Butler. RODGERS AND HAMMERSTEIN produced and Joshua Logan directed. *Annie Get Your Gun* proved to be one of the top Broadway musicals of all time.

Surprisingly, the team's next show, *Arms and the Girl* (2/2/50; 134 performances), showed little of the talents they exhibited in *Annie Get Your Gun*. The Theater Guild along with Anthony Brady Farrell produced the show, which was based on a play by Theater Guild managers Armina Marshall and Lawrence Langner. Dorothy wrote lyrics to Morton Gould's music and collaborated with Herbert and director Rouben Mamoulian on the script.

While Herbert took a break, Dorothy collaborated again with composer Arthur Schwartz. The show, *A Tree Grows in Brooklyn* (4/19/51; 267 performances), became a vehicle for the great Shirley Booth. GEORGE ABBOTT produced and directed in his usual charming style and collaborated on the book with the novel's author, Betty Smith. Fields and Schwartz came up with a score that had real emotional power. "Make the Man Love Me" became a hit and a standard of pop singers. Nonetheless, the show, about a ne'er-do-well, was not upbeat enough for Broadway audiences. The songwriting team, who brought out the best in each other, collaborated on their next show, *By the Beautiful Sea* (4/8/54; 268 performances). This time Herbert joined Dorothy on the script, but the results were weak. The show was simply too much a vehicle for Shirley Booth, playing the same sort of character she undertook in *A Tree Grows in Brooklyn*.

Herbert's last show was *Redhead* (2/5/59; 452 performances). He collaborated again with his sister on the book. Additional librettists were David Shaw and Sidney Sheldon (later to be a major novelist). Albert Hague (later to play the music teacher in the television show *Fame*) collaborated with Dorothy on the score, but only one song, "Merely Marvelous," was heard after the show closed. Gwen Verdon, one of the musical theater's greatest performers, co-starred with Richard Kiley.

Herbert Fields died in 1958. After a 7-year break, Dorothy resumed her career without her brother, in a show that was another vehicle for Gwen Verdon, *Sweet Charity* (1/29/66; 608 performances). Cy Coleman collaborated with Dorothy on the score, and NEIL SIMON wrote the libretto. The direction and choreography were by a truly unique talent, Bob Fosse. Dorothy's lyrics perfectly matched Coleman's jazzy rhythms, providing exactly the right tone for the alternately romantic, vulgar, and sentimental score. "Big Spender" was the big hit, but the rest of the score was much more sophisticated and entirely more worthy of public acclaim.

Dorothy Fields' last Broadway show, *Seesaw* (3/18/73; 296 performances), was also written in collaboration with Cy Coleman. But the result on opening night wasn't as satisfactory as *Sweet Charity*. The libretto, based on William Gibson's play *Two for the Seesaw*, was attempted by a number of authors with director/choreographer Michael Bennett finally taking book credit. The attempt to open up a two-character play into a full-blown Broadway musical was not successful; the show simply rang false.

Of all the Broadway lyricists, Dorothy Fields was most able to keep abreast of her times. She utilized slang and idiomatic phrases without sounding forced or trendy. Her more poetic lyrics never become cloying, and her imagery remains sharp, fresh, and hip. It's to her credit that she could collaborate with composers as widely divergent in style as Arthur Schwartz, Jerome Kern (in the movies), and Cy Coleman. In a field largely dominated by men, she held her own and was never forced into a "feminine" viewpoint.

Joseph Fields' first Broadway production was *Schoolhouse on the Lot* (3/22/38; 55 performances), written in collaboration with his longtime partner Jerome Chodorov. The two had met while working in Hollywood at Republic Pictures. The team's next collaboration, *My Sister Eileen* (12/26/40; 865 performances), was decidedly more popular. The comedy, based on a series of stories by Ruth McKenney published in *The New Yorker*, starred Shirley Booth and Jo Ann Sayers as the two girls from Ohio who try to make it in the big city. Max Gordon produced and George S. Kaufman directed. Kaufman was an expert play doctor and supervised the young playwrights' rewrites. Though he didn't mind working on the play, Kaufman thought the candy in the writers' hotel room terrible. "In the ensuing weeks they did valiant work with the script," Kaufman admitted. "The candy, however got no better." Kaufman estimated that the writers wrote no less than 6 scripts' worth of words: "It was a rare day, in the weeks preceding rehearsals, that they did not come along with eight or ten new scenes."

Chodorov and Fields repeated the success of *My Sister Eileen* the following season with *Junior Miss* (11/18/41; 246 performances), again produced by Max Gordon. Following the model of their first success, the authors picked a series of stories from *The New Yorker* as their source. The stories, written by Sally Benson, were more simple and tender than those of Ruth McKenney. The director was Kaufman's sometime partner, Moss Hart. Patricia Peardon starred as the 14-year-old title character; Lenore Lonergan co-starred.

Fields went it alone with his next play, *The Doughgirls* (12/30/42; 671 performances). Pearl Harbor had been bombed three weeks after the opening of *Junior Miss*, and wartime comedies became very popular. Again, George S. Kaufman directed and instructed Fields in rewrites. Out of town the show was in trouble, but Kaufman managed to whip Fields' script into shape for the opening at the LYCEUM THEATER. Virginia Field, Doris Nolan, and Arleen Whelan were the stars, but Arlene Francis, playing a Russian guerilla fighter, got the notices. The critical reception was mixed, with most crediting Kaufman for keeping the play proceeding rapidly. John Anderson wrote, "If Mr. Fields' little story is as flimsy as a piece of tissue paper at least Mr. Kaufman blows it around in some gusty patterns and keeps it dancing."

Fields next directed *The Man Who Had All the Luck* (11/23/44; 4 performances) at the FORREST THEATER (*see* EUGENE O'NEILL THEATER). It was ARTHUR MILLER's first Broadway play. He teamed up with Ben Sher to write the play *I Gotta Get Out* (9/25/47; 4 performances), which opened at the CORT THEATRE. These two flops were followed by two of his biggest hits, the musicals *Gentlemen Prefer Blondes* and *Wonderful Town*. He wrote *Blondes* with Anita Loos and *Wonderful Town* with Chodorov. *Gentlemen Prefer Blondes* (12/8/49; 740 performances) opened at the ZIEGFELD THEATER with Carol Channing and Yvonne Adair in the leads. JULE STYNE and Leo Robin wrote the score. *Wonderful Town* (2/25/53; 559 performances) was based on Chodorov and Fields' play *My Sister Eileen*. The score was by LEONARD BERNSTEIN and COMDEN AND GREEN. Rosalind Russell and Edith Adams starred, and George Abbott directed. According to Ab-

bott, Comden and Green and Bernstein shocked Fields and Chodorov when they heard the sophisticated, satirical score. In their minds, they saw the show taking shape in the same warmly humorous vein as their play. The authors lost control of their emotions and cursed the entire production and all the creative staff. Luckily, the show was a smash hit at its opening. Ironically, the writers won the DONALDSON AWARD, the Tony Award, and the NEW YORK DRAMA CRITICS' CIRCLE AWARD for *Wonderful Town*, their only major awards.

The team's next musical, *The Girl in Pink Tights* (3/5/54; 115 performances), opened at the MARK HELLINGER THEATER with a score by Sigmund Romberg, the same composer who had collaborated with Joseph's brother and sister on *Up in Central Park*. Romberg had died three years before the opening of *The Girl in Pink Tights*, and orchestrator Don Walker put together the songs from Romberg's jottings and unfinished songs; Leo Robin added lyrics. The resulting score turned out, surprisingly, to be one of the best of the decade.

The team's next play, *Anniversary Waltz* (4/7/54; 615 performances), opened at the BROADHURST THEATER. Fields next directed the play *The Desk Set* (10/24/55; 296 performances) at the Broadhurst. Chodorov and Fields were back with *The Ponder Heart* (2/16/56; 149 performances) at the MUSIC BOX THEATER. Fields collaborated with humorist Peter DeVries on *The Tunnel of Love* (2/13/57; 417 performances) at the ROYALE THEATRE.

Fields tried his hand in collaboration with Hammerstein at supplying a libretto for the Rodgers and Hammerstein musical *The Flower Drum Song* (12/1/58; 600 performances), a lightweight examination of the clash of cultures between older Chinese immigrants and the younger generation, at the ST. JAMES THEATRE. Fields also co-produced the show with the songwriters. Next Fields co-produced William and James Goldman's *Blood, Sweat and Stanley Poole* (10/5/61; 84 performances) at the MOROSCO THEATRE.

Joseph Fields' work was solid and skillful, with a rich humanity and a sentimental side. He was a witty man whose plays took everyday occurrences and extracted the comedy inherent in the situations in a warm, loving manner.

58TH STREET THEATER. *See* **John Golden Theater**.

51ST STREET THEATER. *See* **Mark Hellinger Theater**.

54TH STREET THEATER. *See* **George Abbott Theater**.

FILMARTE. *See* **John Golden Theater**.

FINE ARTS THEATER. *See* **John Golden Theater**.

FOLIES BERGÈRE. *See* **Helen Hayes Theater**.

FORD CENTER FOR THE PERFORMING ARTS. When Canadian producer Garth Drabinsky was looking for a theater to house his Broadway productions, he met with the 42nd Street Redevelopment contingent and was given free rein to knock down the Apollo Theatre and Lyric Theatre. He also made a deal that forbade any theatrical usage for the Times Square Theater next door. A press conference was held on the stage of the derelict Apollo Theatre that, along with the Lyric Theatre, had been allowed to fall into disrepair by the 42nd Street Redevelopment committee. He announced plans to knock down both theaters (saving their facades) and build a huge, huge auditorium in the place of their more intimate surroundings. He got the Ford Motor Company to pay to put their name on the new theater. It would be named the Ford Center for the Performing Arts, a name many felt was more suited to a theater in the Midwest. Indeed, many other cities, including Chicago, had Ford Centers.

Drabinsky promised to keep much of the Apollo's interior decor in the new theater. He kept his word, but the resulting theater was more barnlike than the Apollo and suffered from shoddy workmanship. In keeping with the new Broadway management style, a gift shop was built just off the lobby, and frames for posters, in the style of a movie theater, were also in the inner lobby—perhaps reflecting Drabinsky's start with the Cineplex Odeon cinema chain.

The premiere production at the new theater was *Ragtime* (1/19/98), with music by Stephen Flaherty, lyrics by Lynn Ahrens, and a book by Terrence McNally. The musicalization of the sprawling E. L. Doctorow novel was mostly well received by critics and managed to run 834 performances. Among the large cast were Brian Stokes Mitchell, Marin Mazzie, Audra McDonald, and Judy Kaye.

Following *Ragtime*, the theater hosted a poorly received revival of *Jesus Christ Superstar* (4/16/2000; 161 performances). It was quickly followed by a spectacular revival of the 1980s smash hit *42nd Street* (5/2/2001). Easily eclipsing even the lavishness of David Merrick's original (though inspired by it), the physical production was beautifully designed by Douglas W. Schmidt (settings), Roger Kirk (costumes), and Paul Gallo (lighting).

FORREST THEATER. *See* **Eugene O'Neill Theater**.

48TH STREET THEATRE. 157 W. 48th Street. Architect: William A. Swasey. Opening: August 12, 1912; *Just Like John*.

The 48th Street Theatre was built by producer William A. Brady on the site of an apartment building. Although it housed many successes, his theater was not to have an especially notable history. The theater's first successes were *Never Say Die* (11/12/12; 151 performances); *Today* (10/6/13; 280 performances); *The Midnight Girl* (2/23/14; 104 performances); *Just a Woman* (1/17/16; 136 performances); and *The Man Who Stayed at Home* (4/3/18; 109 performances).

The Storm (10/2/19; 282 performances) was a melodrama of the Canadian woods. Edward Arnold appeared as Burr Winton, a dashing prospector. Winton competes for the hand of Manette with cultured Englishman David Stewart. The girl just can't make up her mind. The two men are best friends, and at the end of the play they successfully battle a forest fire. Finally Manette decides to marry the prospector. *Opportunity* (7/30/20; 135 performances) was another hit play at the 48th Street Theatre. Owen Davis wrote the comedy, which featured Nita Naldi, later to become a Hollywood movie star.

The theater was renamed the Equity 48th Street Theatre on October 2, 1922, with the opening of *Malvaloca* (48 performances). A successful revival of Ibsen's *The Wild Duck* (2/24/25; 110 performances) was the theater's next success. The name was changed back to the 48th Street Theatre on June 1, 1925, with the play *Spooks* (18 performances). A series of plays with improbable but all-too-typical plots followed. The comedy *Puppy Love* (1/27/26; 112 performances) starred Spring Byington. It concerned a young man who, hopelessly in love with an unattainable young woman, decides to become her chauffeur to get closer to her. To nobody's surprise, the boy gets the girl in the end.

Jean Bart's drama *The Squall* (11/11/26; 262 performances) opened with a cast headed by Blanche Yurka, Romney Brent, and Dorothy Stickney. Also featured was Suzanne Caubet, who played Nubi, a Gypsy woman who blows into the play along with the title storm. Her chief is following her, and she begs the Mendez family to hide her. The family does as she asks. In the meantime, Nubi is kept busy. She seduces the Mendezes' son Juan, moves on to Juan's father, José, and then to Pedro, the hired hand. Finally El Moro, the Gypsy leader, arrives to bring her back.

Unexpected Husband (6/2/31; 120 performances) starred Josephine Hull. The comedy unfolded an incredible tale: Dorothy Atwater, a bored and restless Texan, runs away to New York in order to pursue Broadway playboy Willie Van Loan. Her adventures on the way land her in a hotel bed with a stranger and, after Dorothy's father and a tabloid reporter in pursuit of dirt discover them, there is nothing for the couple to do but get married. They do, and everyone lives happily ever after.

The Pagan Lady (12/27/30; 152 performances) was a drama starring Lenore Ulric as a woman who is tempted by the son of an evangelist. Although she is living with another man, she and the evangelist's son swim away to an island, where they spend the night. The would-be evangelist is depressed and returns to the church. Lenore Ulric's character is happy that he will now be more tolerant of sinners because he has sinned himself.

In the 1930s the Depression forced the sale of the theater. In 1937 the Labor Stage, an arm of the International Ladies' Garment Workers' Union, used the space for plays, lectures, and meetings. Four of the boxes were removed, and the theater would sometimes be used for movies. It was called the Windsor Theater during this period, which began with the production of *Work Is for Horses* (11/20/37; 9 performances). The union's other theater, also called the Labor Stage, was originally the PRINCESS THEATER.

One of the most historic openings in Broadway history occurred on the stage of the Windsor Theatre. Marc Blitzstein's *The Cradle Will Rock*, a production of the FEDERAL THEATRE PROJECT, had its funding stripped by right-wing forces in the government. Even ACTORS' EQUITY forbade its members from appearing on the stage of the Windsor. So the actors performed their roles in the audience while an orchestra of one—Marc Blitzstein on piano—played from the stage. The show opened on January 3, 1938, against great odds and managed to run 108 performances.

On September 1, 1943, the Windsor became the 48th Street Theatre again. Its biggest hit was Mary Chase's classic comedy *Harvey* (11/1/44; 1,775 performances). Frank Fay starred in the fantastic play as the pixilated Elwood Dowd. Another big hit at the theater that was transferred successfully to Hollywood was *Stalag 17* (5/8/51; 472 performances).

On August 24, 1955, steel beams on the roof rusted through, causing the water tower on the roof to collapse into the building and flood the theater with over 10,000 gallons of water. The damage was extensive, and the theater was razed.

44TH STREET THEATRE. 216 West 44th Street. Architect: William A. Swasey. Original name: Weber and Fields' Music Hall. Opening: November 21, 1912; *Roly Poly/Without the Law.*

The SHUBERT BROTHERS planned to name their new theater the Palace Music Hall. But Martin Beck soon announced his intention of opening the leading vaudeville house of its day, also named the PALACE. So the theater was built as Weber and Fields' Music Hall, named after the venerable musical comedy team Joseph Weber and Lew Fields (*see* FIELDS FAMILY) on a plot of land owned, like most of Times Square, by Vincent Astor.

The first show starred the eponymous comedy team, but it ran only 60 performances and the team broke up. Following the first show, the Shuberts realized that the team wouldn't appear together at the theater, and so they renamed it the 44th Street Theatre. The basement of the theater was home to the Little Club, a speakeasy. Later the basement was used as the Stagedoor Canteen. The building's roof was utilized for a rooftop theater, which went through many names and managements; the best-known was the Nora Bayes (*see* LEW FIELDS' 44TH STREET ROOF GARDEN). In 1917 the Shuberts built a conventional theater on the roof.

The first musical presented at the theater, *The Girl on the Film* (12/29/13; 64 performances), was a modest success. Like many of its contemporaries, it was based on a European operetta. The operetta *The Midnight Girl* (2/23/14; 104 performances) was another successful European transplant. Yet another European operetta was *The Lilac Domino* (10/28/14; 109 performances). *Katinka* (12/23/15; 220 performances) was an even bigger success for the theater. RUDOLF FRIML and Otto Harbach wrote the operetta, now forgotten but at the time an enormous hit. ARTHUR HAMMERSTEIN produced the show.

The Shuberts made a stab at an annual series of revues with their production of the *Shubert Gaieties of 1919* (7/17/19). The fine cast included Gilda Gray, George Jessel, and Ed Wynn. The show was a modest success with 87 performances, but the Shuberts decided not to present another edition.

The producers had one of their biggest hits in another operetta, *Blossom Time*. The 44th Street hosted the first revival of *Blossom Time* (5/21/23; 16 performances) (there were eventually seven further revivals). The short run was not the failure it seemed, for the Shuberts never had any intention of running *Blossom Time*—they just wanted to be able to advertise the ensuing tour as "direct from Broadway."

Betty Lee (12/25/24; 98 performances) starred Joe E. Brown, Gloria Foy, and Hal Skelly. The score was by Louis A. Hirsch, Con Conrad, OTTO HARBACH, and Irving Caesar. An unlikely success was Arthur Hammerstein's operetta *Song of the Flame* (12/30/25; 214 performances), which had a strange grouping of songwriters. There was music written in the operetta style by Herbert Stothart and more modern melodies written by GEORGE GERSHWIN. The lyrics were by Otto Harbach and OSCAR HAMMERSTEIN II. The musical was set in Russia. An English operetta, *Katja, the Dancer* (10/18/26; 113 performances), was brought to the theater and was a success. *A Night in Spain* (5/3/27; 174 performances) was a popular revue, which bore only a passing resemblance to anything Spanish.

By the end of the 1920s, operettas were going out of favor with audiences. The 44th Street Theatre followed the trends and hosted one of the new jazz-influenced musicals, Bert Kalmar and Harry Ruby's *The 5 o'Clock Girl* (10/10/27; 278 performances), starring Mary Eaton, Pert Kelton, Oscar Shaw, and Danny Dare. The hit song was "Thinking of You."

The most famous tenant of the 44th Street Theatre was another Kalmar and Ruby show, the Marx Brothers classic *Animal Crackers* (10/23/28; 213 performances). Joining Groucho, Harpo, Zeppo, and Chico was Marx regular Margaret Dumont. The score featured what would become Groucho's theme, "Hooray for Captain Spalding!" Unfortunately, *Animal Crackers* was just about the only successful presentation at the theater in this period. The next offering, *Broadway Nights* (7/15/29; 40 performances), was a flop. Producer Billy Rose presented *Billy Rose's Crazy Quilt* (5/19/31; 67 performances), with a terrific score by Harry Warren, Mort Dixon, and himself. Despite a big hit song, "I Found a Million Dollar Baby (in a Five and Ten Cent Store)" and the efforts of cast member FANNY BRICE, then Mrs. Rose, the show failed.

A Little Racketeer (1/18/32; 48 performances) is notable only because composer Dimitri Tiomkin contributed several melodies. The E. Y. HARBURG and Lewis E. Gensler revue *Ballyhoo of 1932* (9/6/32; 94 performances) didn't catch on, despite the talents of Grace and Paul Hartman, Bob Hope, Willie and Eugene Howard, and Lulu McConnell.

The theater housed two shows in 1934, which were appreciated only after they closed. The first was Virgil Thomson and Gertrude Stein's opera *Four Saints in Three Acts* (2/20/34; 32 performances). The second was Noël Coward's musical *Conversation Piece* (10/23/34; 55 performances). Coward wrote the book, music, and lyrics, including the now famous "I'll Follow My Secret Heart." Yvonne Printemps and George Sanders starred.

Marc Connelly's Pulitzer prize–winning play *Green Pastures* (2/26/35; 71 performances) enjoyed a revival at the theater. Kurt Weill's antiwar musical *Johnny Johnson* (11/19/36; 68 performances) featured Luther Adler, Morris Carnovsky, Lee J. Cobb, John Garfield, Elia Kazan, Robert Lewis, Sanford Meisner, and Art Smith. The GROUP THEATER production had a book and lyrics by Paul Green. Two more failures

followed, both revues: *Crazy with the Heat* (1/30/41; 92 performances), featuring music and lyrics by Dana Suesse, and *Keep 'Em Laughing* (4/24/42; 77 performances).

The theater hosted a few straight plays. One of these, *Winged Victory* (11/20/43; 212 performances), was produced by the U.S. Army Air Forces. The two-act drama was written by Moss Hart and starred Private Red Buttons, Sergeant Kevin McCarthy, Private Barry Nelson, Private First Class Edmond O'Brien, Private Whitney Bissell, Private Grant Richards, Staff Sergeant Daniel Scholl, Corporal Gary Merrill, Private First Class Edward McMahon, Private Philip Bourneuf, Sergeant George Reeves, Sergeant Ray Middleton, Private Karl Malden, Staff Sergeant Peter Lind Hayes, Private First Class Martin Ritt, and Private Lee J. Cobb. The show was as large in scale as a musical and, in fact, had original music composed by David Rose.

The 44th Street Theatre's short life ended when the Astor estate, which owned the theater's land, sold the property to the *New York Times*. The newspaper kept the theater in operation for five years before tearing it down in 1945 to make way for an addition to its printing plant.

49TH STREET THEATRE. 235 W. 49th Street. Architect: Herbert J. Krapp. Opening: December 26, 1921; *Face Value.*

The SHUBERT BROTHERS built the 49th Street Theatre, but it wasn't one of their more successful houses. An early hit was the revue *Chauve-Souris* (2/1/22; 544 performances). Despite the Russian theme, the show was, typically, ersatz Russian. American composers, including L. Wolfe Gilbert and Abel Baer, wrote a number of tunes in a slightly Russian manner. Hit songs from the show included "Dark Eyes" by A. Salami, "Two Guitars," and the "Volga Boat Song." The show was so popular that it eventually had four revivals and a new edition in 1943. The second revival opened at the 49th Street Theatre on January 14, 1925, and ran 69 performances.

The theater was the home for a number of hit plays with somewhat thin plots. *Whispering Wires* (8/7/22; 356 performances) was an early mystery thriller. *Give and Take* (1/15/23; 188 performances), a farce by Aaron Hoffman, concerned John Bauer (played by Louis Mann), whose son comes back from college full of the fire of Communism. He convinces his father to turn his fruit-canning factory over to the employees. The factory fails, but a millionaire industrialist with a new selling scheme arrives on the scene, and, despite the fact that he has just been released from a mental institution, his ideas save the factory. *The Judge's Hus-*

band (9/27/26; 120 performances) was another success, but the plot was no less incredible than that of *Give and Take*. Joe Kirby teaches his wife the law, and his wife is later elected a judge, while Joe becomes a househusband. When Joe disappears for two days, his wife assumes that Joe had an amorous affair with one of the maids. She brings suit against Joe for divorce and tries the case herself. As it turns out, Joe was actually helping their daughter through a nasty time, and all is forgiven.

The Shuberts lost the 49th Street Theatre when the Depression hit. The FEDERAL THEATRE PROJECT leased it for a time. In 1938 it became a movie house, Cinema 49, and in December 1940 it was torn down.

46TH STREET THEATRE. *See* **Richard Rodgers Theatre.**

FORUM THEATER. *See* **Movieland.**

FRAZEE THEATER. *See* **Anco Theater.**

FREEDLEY, VINTON. *See* **Aarons and Freedley.**

FREEMAN, DON. Noted illustrator who often portrayed the Broadway scene; b. San Diego, California, August 11, 1908; d. New York, New York, February 1, 1978.

Artist Don Freeman often used Times Square as the backdrop for many of his highly regarded works. He was also a famed author who won many awards for his children's books and contributed poster art to plays and musicals.

Freeman was born in San Diego on August 11, 1908. At the age of 9 he received a box of paints and began his first artistic endeavors. His father worked in a clothing store that catered to sailors who docked at the large port. Freeman would sketch the servicemen when the fleet was in town.

He received his early schooling at the San Diego School of Fine Arts. After graduation he earned passage to New York by playing the cornet with a ship's orchestra as it came through the Panama Canal. He began studies at the Art Students League under John Sloan and Harry Wickey. Freeman's work was influenced by that of John Sloan, but he soon became fascinated with the caricatures of Honoré Daumier. In his spare time and to make some money, Freeman played trumpet in a succession of jazz clubs and Italian wedding receptions. Freeman had to choose between pursuing a career in music and becoming a professional artist. The decision was made by fate. While riding

the subway with his sketchpad and trumpet, Freeman decided to sketch his fellow passengers. He became so immersed in the drawing he almost missed his stop. Just in time he jumped from the car. Unfortunately, his trumpet remained on the train.

Freeman began submitting his drawings of scenes from New York life to the *Herald Tribune*. He also found a publisher for his works in the *New York Times*. His drawings pictured a Times Square that was rambunctious, turbulent, and exciting. He was the artist who, more than any contemporary, captured the feeling of Broadway in the 1930s and 1940s.

Columnist Lucius Beebe called him "Stage Door Johnny No. 1." Freeman loved to frequent the backstage areas of theaters. He would enter carrying a red book titled *Through Woman's Eyes*, only Freeman blacked out the *Wo*. Inside the covers were pads of drawing papers.

Freeman explained, "People think I'm reading. They get self-concious if they know you are sketching.

"I'd do the best landscapes you've ever seen if I'd ever lived in the country but I've never lived there. Anyway, there is plenty of beauty in bricks."

Freeman was a good friend of William Saroyan. He told a friend he'd like to meet the writer, and a meeting was soon set up. The result was Freeman's illustration of Saroyan's book *My Name Is Aram*. When Saroyan wrote the play *The Beautiful People* he brought it to Freeman's apartment for the artist's feedback. During that evening Freeman played the cornet following along with recordings.

Saroyan was elated and exclaimed, "Say, you have to do that in my show!"

"There isn't any cornet player in your play," observed Freeman.

"There is now," was Saroyan's answer.

The next day the two met at the Broadway AUTOMAT and Freeman was handed a script with the newly written part of a cornet-playing son.

"You see, I'd gotten myself involved and that's how I became an actor," explained Freeman.

He played the part in the Broadway production at the LYCEUM THEATRE during the 1940–1942 season. In the show Freeman played "Wonderful One" on the cornet and had two lines of dialogue. For an earlier, offstage performance of the number Freeman hired a musical stand-in so he had one less cue to worry about. Freeman decided to give up acting following the closing of *The Beautiful People*. As he himself put it, "I never realized before what a privilege it is to be an artist. There is no time element to art. . . . You don't have to be places at certain times."

Freeman also illustrated more than 50 books. Among the best-known are William Saroyan's *The Human Comedy*, Brooks Atkinson's *Once Around the*

Sun, and James Thurber's *The White Deer*. Freeman's children's books included *Norman the Doorman, Pet of the Met, The Circus in Peter's Closet*, and *Mop Top*. Among his theater works are poster illustrations for the ETHEL MERMAN musical *Stars in Your Eyes, A Streetcar Named Desire, Orpheus Descending, Finian's Rainbow*, and *The Skin of Our Teeth*.

FRENCH CASINO. *See* **Earl Carroll Theatre.**

FRIML, RUDOLF. Master of the European operetta; b. Prague, Bohemia (now Czech Republic), December 7, 1879; d. Hollywood, California, November 12, 1972.

In the early part of the century the musical theater took two separate paths: the homegrown American musical comedy, represented by the works of GEORGE M. COHAN, IRVING BERLIN, and JEROME KERN, and the European operetta, represented by VICTOR HERBERT, SIGMUND ROMBERG, and Rudolf Friml. Friml was one of the great composers of this now outmoded form. From his operettas came some of the best-loved melodies of the early years of American popular song.

At the age of 11, one year after composing a barcarolle, Friml began attending the Prague Conservatory, where he studied under the tutelage of Dvořák and Jiránek. He completed the normal 6-year course in half the allotted time and soon began touring Europe with violinist Jan Kubelik. He made his first appearance in the United States in 1901. He returned to play solo piano at Carnegie Hall in 1904 and again in 1906 to perform his own work, "Piano Concerto in B-Major," with Walter Damrosch conducting the New York Symphony Society.

When diva Emma Trentini broke relations with Victor Herbert, producer ARTHUR HAMMERSTEIN was forced to find a composer to write a score for his production of *The Firefly* (12/2/12; 120 performances). Trentini was a major star who had just triumphed in Herbert's *Naughty Marietta*, and finding a composer equal to her volatile temperament was not easy. Through music publisher Max Dreyfus, Hammerstein found Friml and commissioned him to write the score with librettist OTTO HARBACH. The score contained three Friml standards, "Giannina Mia," "Love Is Like a Firefly," and "Sympathy."

The success of *The Firefly* led Hammerstein to sign Friml for additional projects. The first, *High Jinks* (12/10/13; 213 performances), got its title from the name of a perfume that, when sprayed on its target, produced uncontrolled mirth. Of course, this led to many humorous complications in the plot. As an added fillip, the perfume was sprayed on the audience during the proceedings.

The SHUBERT BROTHERS borrowed Friml's talents from Hammerstein for *The Peasant Girl* (3/2/15; 111 performances). Friml contributed additional numbers to the Oscar Nedbal score. Although Friml was reunited with Trentini, he wasn't sufficiently inspired to contribute any standards.

Back with Hammerstein, Friml and Harbach came up with *Katinka* (12/23/15; 220 performances) starring Adele Rowland. *You're in Love* (2/6/17; 167 performances) starred Marie Flynn as the sleepwalking heroine who took an impressive stroll on a ship's boom hanging over the audience. The play is notable today for giving OSCAR HAMMERSTEIN II his first Broadway assignment, that of assistant stage manager. Surprisingly, the next Harbach/Friml partnership resulted in a quick flop, *Kitty Darlin'* (11/7/17; 14 performances). Maybe Arthur Hammerstein's astute producing was the missing element. In the next Friml show Hammerstein paired him with Rida Johnson Young, one of the few women lyricists on Broadway. The result, *Sometime* (10/4/18; 283 performances), featured popular comedian Ed Wynn and the sultry Mae West in an early Broadway appearance. She played Mayme, a vamp who used "Theda Bara tricks" to get her men.

Gloriana (10/28/18; 96 performances), the next Friml offering, opened only 22 days after *Sometime*. For it Friml teamed up with another female lyricist, Catherine Chisholm Cushing. Harbach, Hammerstein, and Friml were successful again with *Tumble Inn* (3/24/19; 128 performances), a minor musical. *The Little Whopper* (10/13/19; 224 performances) starred Vivienne Segal and was based on a silent movie, *Miss George Washington, Jr.* Friml's next score came more than 2 years later. Unfortunately, *June Love* (4/25/21; 50 performances) proved less endearing than its predecessor.

Friml had his songs interpolated into the 15th edition of the *ZIEGFELD FOLLIES* (6/21/21). His next full score under the Hammerstein banner was *The Blue Kitten* (1/13/22; 140 performances). Friml was again teamed with Harbach, who was joined by William Cary Duncan as co-lyricist. *The Blue Kitten* was followed by the premiere of *Cinders* (4/3/23; 31 performances). The failure of *Cinders* and Friml's sporadic output in the early 1920s led many people to believe that he was washed up as a composer, but his next show proved to be his most popular.

Hammerstein, who still believed in Friml, paired him with his nephew Oscar for *Rose-Marie* (9/2/24; 581 performances). Herbert Stothart also contributed music to the operetta. Mary Ellis played the title role, and operetta favorite Dennis King played her lover. The score yielded three giant hits: "Indian Love Call" remains the best known, albeit often parodied with its "oo-oo-oo" lyrics. The title song shows little of the

Rudolf Friml.

European influence of earlier Friml melodies, and the "Song of the Mounties" (with music by Friml and Stothart) was the rousing male chorus number necessary in any good operetta. Hammerstein revealed his yearnings for a truly integrated score, one in which all songs related to the action onstage instead of being just vaudeville turns stuck into the plot to relieve boredom. Hammerstein wrote in the program that the individual songs would not be listed because "the musical numbers of this play are such an integral part of the action that we do not think we should list them as separate episodes. The songs, which stand out independent of their dramatic associations, are 'Rose-Marie,' 'Indian Love Call,' 'Totem Tom-Tom,' and 'Why Shouldn't We?' in the first act, and 'Door of Her Dreams' in the second act." *Rose-Marie* wasn't an entirely integrated work—Hammerstein's later *Show Boat* came much closer to this ideal—but it was another step on the road to a truly American operetta, a form that had its greatest success with *Oklahoma!*

The critics didn't fully agree with Hammerstein when he wrote, "The revolution in musical comedy which *Rose-Marie* has wrought was not accidental. It was a carefully directed attack at the Cinderella show in favor of operatic musical comedy." The *New York Times* called the plot "slightly less banally put forward than has been customary." Surprisingly, the song the critics most singled out for praise was "Totem Tom-Tom."

Rose-Marie also became the greatest financial success in Broadway history until RODGERS AND HAMMERSTEIN's *Oklahoma!* in 1943. The Broadway production had a $4.40 top ticket price. Seven tours crisscrossed America beginning in February 1925 and ending in September 1928. The London production opened at the Theater Royal, Drury Lane, on March 20, 1925, and played even longer than the Broadway production, for a total of 851 performances. Both of those productions were dwarfed by the Paris production, which premiered April 9, 1927, and lasted 1,250 performances. Productions in Berlin, Stockholm, and Moscow were mounted, and the show returned to London for an additional 100 performances in September 1929. Movie versions were produced in 1928, 1936, and 1954. The first was a silent version, which starred Joan Crawford as Rose-Marie, and the second was the MGM classic with Jeanette MacDonald and Nelson Eddy, which opened in 1936. The third starred Ann Blyth and Howard Keel to little effect.

Friml's next Broadway show, *The Vagabond King* (10/21/25; 511 performances), proved almost as successful as *Rose-Marie*, with Friml returning to his European roots. The production, with lyrics by Brian Hooker, starred Dennis King and Carolyn Thomson. Friml again supplied an exceptional score, with the numbers "Only a Rose," "Song of the Vagabonds," "Some Day," and "Huguette Waltz" achieving the longest-lasting fame. FLORENZ ZIEGFELD used Friml songs in his next revue, *No Foolin'*. (It was also called *Ziegfeld's American Revue of 1926*.) Friml's songs included "Florida, the Moon and You," which celebrated the state's current vogue on Broadway. (Irving Berlin's *Cocoanuts* also featured the new vacationland.) Friml's next show, *The White Eagle* (12/26/27; 48 performances), was not a success. In his last Broadway success, *The Three Musketeers* (3/13/28; 319 performances), Friml worked in familiar territory, musicalizing a classic European work as he had done with *The Vagabond King*, based on Justin Huntley McCarthy's novel, *If I Were King*. Dennis King repeated his prior successes in Friml shows. P. G. Wodehouse and Clifford Grey created the lyrics for the spectacular score. Among the best songs were the tremendously popular "March of the Musketeers," "Ma Belle," "My Sword and I," and "Your Eyes" and "One Kiss." The opening night's performance lasted well past midnight, causing ALEXANDER WOOLLCOTT to comment, "I did greatly enjoy the first few years of Act I."

During the 1930s Broadway audiences' tastes were changing. New American songwriters such as RODGERS AND HART and DE SYLVA, BROWN, AND HENDERSON were capturing Broadway's fancy. Operetta was

Dennis King in *The Vagabond King*, 1925.

seen as more and more passé. Friml's last two shows, *Luana* (9/17/30; 21 performances) and *Music Hath Charms* (12/29/34; 29 performances), were failures.

Because Friml could not change his writing style, his career languished for the remainder of his life. He wrote an occasional song for film adaptations of his stage shows. Friml also concentrated on recordings, featuring him at the piano leading orchestras through his repertoire. In 1956 he worked with lyricist Johnny Burke on new songs for the remake of *The Vagabond King*. This was his last assignment. He was saluted by ASCAP on his 90th birthday.

FULTON THEATER. *See* **Helen Hayes Theater.**

GABRIEL, GILBERT WOLF. Critic; b. New York, New York, January 18, 1890; d. Mt. Kisco, New York, September 3, 1952.

Gabriel began his career as a reporter for the *New York Evening Sun* in 1912. From 1917 to 1924 he held the post of music critic and from 1925 to 1929 was drama critic. He assumed the same responsibilities on the *New York American* from 1929 to 1937. At the same time he lectured on dramatic criticism for New York University. At *The New Yorker* magazine he created the "profile" feature. Like many of his contemporaries, Gabriel tried his hand at playwriting. The result, *Clap Hands*, premiered in 1934, never making it to Broadway. He also wrote several books and magazine articles. Gabriel became drama critic for *Cue* magazine from 1949 until his death in 1952. At the time of his death, he was president of the New York Drama Critics' Circle.

GAIETY THEATER. 1547 Broadway, between 45th and 46th Streets. Architects: HERTS & TALLANT. Opening: September 4, 1909; *The Fortune Hunter*.

Klaw and Erlanger built the Gaiety for GEORGE M. COHAN, who shared in its management. The theater was noted for several architectural features. The audience area was built in what was known as the "mushroom" design, which reflected its configuration. The theater was also noted for the absence of pillars holding up the balcony, which in earlier theaters had drastically hampered sightlines. With cantilevered balconies, pillars became unnecessary. Another innovation featured in the new house was the orchestra pit. Prior to this, most orchestras were on the audience level and stages were raised accordingly. This "invisible orchestra" allowed the stage height to be lowered and the sight lines of the first rows to be improved and brought forward.

Surprisingly, although the house was known for its orchestra pit, it seldom housed a musical comedy.

Before the theater officially opened, Cohan's *The Yankee Prince* played a few performances there prior to opening in Washington, D.C., on September 20, 1909. This served as a dress rehearsal for both the new theater and the touring cast of the show.

The New York Telegraph reported on the theater's opening:

> To begin with the Gaiety is not pretentious except in quality. The auditorium is small, as the auditorium in every comedy house should be, according to an expert who gives his opinion on the programme. A joke or a clever line goes twice as well when delivered at short range as when delivered at a distance.
>
> The decorations of the little playhouse which is to become the home of comedy are in Louis XV style, and there is an imposing entrance on the 46th Street side as well as one on Broadway. A broad foyer on the 46th Street side contributes to the convenience and comfort of patrons.
>
> The color scheme is a delight to the eye, being beautiful and soft in Sevres blue, French gray, and old gold effectively blended. The side walls, covered with delicate gray silk, are embossed with a comic mask, surmounted with the laurelled monogram, "G.T."—Gaiety Theatre.
>
> The same blue-gray and old gold prevail in the frescoing of the proscenium arch and the two large proscenium boxes. The boxes are roomy, and off one of them themselves is a reception parlor, where a theater party may retire between acts and enjoy themselves in an atmosphere as exclusive as that of their own homes. Exquisite tapestries are used throughout the house for mural effects. The orchestra chairs, covered with steel-gray leather, are pleasing to the eye and they are arranged with a view to comfort rather than with a view to the utilization of every square inch of space. The dome chandelier is a huge twelve-pointed star, surrounded with circular lamps studded with electric lights.

The first full production at the theater came with the opening of *The Fortune Hunter* (9/4/09; 345 performances). Other productions in the Gaiety's first decade included *First Lady of the Land* (12/4/11; 64 performances), *Officer 666* (1/29/12; 192 performances), *Stop Thief* (12/25/12; 149 performances), *Nearly Married* (9/5/13; 123 performances), *Erstwhile Susan* (1/18/16; 167 performances), *Turn to the Right!* (8/18/16; 435 performances), and *Sick-a-Bed* (2/25/18; 80 performances).

The huge success of *Turn to the Right!* did not prepare the theater owners for the Gaiety's greatest hit, *Lightnin'* (8/26/18; 1,291 performances). The show, written by Frank Bacon and Winchell Smith, was the story of Lightin' Bill Jones, a landlord whose hotel conveniently straddles the border of Nevada and California. When the constabulary came after him, Lightin' simply crosses the border into another jurisdiction. Frank Bacon also starred in the comedy, which ran for three years. This made *Lightnin'* the longest-running play in Broadway history, a position it held until *Abie's Irish Rose* overtook it in the mid-1920s. When *Lightnin'* closed, there was a spectacular parade down Broadway. Mayor John F. Hylan, Commissioner Grover Whalen, Winchell Smith, Frank Bacon, and producer John Golden led the march to Pennsylvania Station, where the cast embarked on a nationwide tour. The great LIGHTNIN' PARADE was one of the first events that was not totally manufactured by an overly avid press agent.

Following *Lightnin'*, Erlanger purchased the Gaiety, but it then housed a string of failures: *The Wheel* (8/29/21; 49 performances), a revival of *Alias Jimmy Valentine* (12/8/21; 46 performances), and *Madeleine and the Movies* (3/6/22; 80 performances). The next hit was *Loyalties* (9/27/22; 220 performances), by John Galsworthy, chosen as a best play by Burns Mantle, editor of the *Best Plays* series. The next play, *If Winter Comes* (4/2/23; 40 performances), was a failure, but the theater's fortunes picked up with a production of Frederick Lonsdale's comedy *Aren't We All?* (5/21/23; 284 performances), with Leslie Howard, Jack Whiting, Cyril Maude, and Marguerite St. John.

The Youngest (12/22/24; 100 performances) was followed by *Loggerheads*, which moved to the Gaiety from the Cherry Lane Theater off Broadway. GEORGE GERSHWIN's modern musical *Tell Me More!* opened at the Gaiety on April 13, 1925, and ran for 100 performances. *These Charming People* (10/6/25; 97 performances) was followed by *By the Way* (12/28/25; 177 performances). The theater's last year of operation as a legitimate house was 1926. Its last show was the modest hit *Love in a Mist* (4/12/26; 120 performances).

Following the run of *Love in a Mist*, the theater was closed and soon reopened as a motion picture house.

In 1932 legitimate theater made a short-lived return to the Gaiety. *Peter Flies High*, a play by Myron C. Fagan, opened on November 9, 1931, with Brian Donlevy in the cast. It closed after only 8 performances. The next show at the Gaiety, the theater's last, was *Collision* (2/16/32). It didn't even do as well as *Peter Flies High*, closing after only 7 performances.

In 1932 the theater was converted to a Minsky's BURLESQUE house. Among the performers who walked the boards at Minsky's were Ann Corio, Abbott and Costello, and Gypsy Rose Lee. In 1943, after Mayor LaGuardia's crackdown on burlesque the previous year, the name was changed to the Victoria and a vaudeville policy was instituted. Film star Stepin Fetchit played the Victoria in *Harlem on Broadway*.

The first movie to play the Victoria was *The City That Stopped Hitler—Heroic Stalingrad*, which opened on September 4, 1943. In 1944 United Artists leased the theater. The auditorium was remodeled by designer Edward Durell Stone in 1949; gone was the Louis XV decor, in its place a dropped ceiling and walls covered in aluminum mesh. Also, the auditorium was enlarged to 1,050 seats. City Investing Company, who had bought the theater following Erlanger's death, sold the property to Peter Sharp, Inc., in 1967 for the proposed Portman Hotel project. In 1980 the theater was renamed the Embassy 5 when Guild Enterprises took over the lease.

The Victoria and its next-door neighbor the ASTOR THEATRE had the world's longest sign positioned on their shared roofs. The SIGNAGE location above the two theaters was used primarily as an advertisement for their current movie attractions. The most spectacular of these was for *The Vikings*. When the theaters ceased to show first-run features, the sign was put to more prosaic uses. The huge Budweiser billboard was perhaps the best-known of these.

The Embassy 5 was demolished along with the Astor, MOROSCO, BIJOU, and HELEN HAYES theaters on March 22, 1982. Its destruction and that of the other theaters led to the establishment of SAVE THE THEATERS and a renewed interest in historic preservation, although the movement did little during the 42nd Street Redevelopment Project.

GAIETY THEATER BUILDING. 1547 Broadway at 47th Street. The Gaiety Theater had an office building built above the lobby areas. It soon became known as the Black Tin Pan Alley because of the many black music publishers who rented offices there. Unable to rent in the BRILL BUILDING because of racist policies by the owners, these publishers concentrated around the Gaiety. It didn't hurt that the Gaiety was across the street from the PALACE THEATER, the temple of

American vaudeville. Black composers uptown in Harlem nicknamed the Gaiety "Uncle Tom's Cabin."

Among the black publishers renting offices in the Gaiety Theater Building were Pace and Handy, who moved into the Gaiety in 1917. The firm consisted of Harry Pace, the money and business side of the enterprise, and W. C. Handy, composer of such standards as "The St. Louis Blues" and "Memphis Blues." They moved into the Gaiety Building from Chicago, and once in New York their business took off. The firm left the Gaiety Building in August of 1920.

Another black publisher to rent space in the building was the Clarence Williams Music Publishing Company. Composer Clarence Williams also moved from Chicago to the Gaiety. Upon his arrival in 1921 business soared. In 1922, his first full year in New York, he published "I Wish I Could Shimmy Like My Sister Kate," "Got to Cool My Doggies Now," "That Da-Da Strain," and "Tain't Nobody's Biz-Ness if I Do." The next year Williams wrote another great hit, "Sugar Blues." Though successful, Williams was known as an unscrupulous publisher, treating his black writers as badly as the white publishers they avoided. Among the composers whom Williams cheated was Thomas "Fats" Waller.

Perry Bradford was another publisher of Waller's songs located in the Gaiety building. But Bradford was honest, unlike Williams. After moving to the Gaiety around 1919 or 1920, he had his first million-selling smash, "Crazy Blues." Among his other songs are the popular "You Can't Keep a Good Man Down" and "He May Be Your Man, But He Comes to See Me Sometimes." Bradford's offices were the unofficial clubhouse of a variety of writers and performers who would converge every afternoon after a hard day of plugging songs and prior to carousing in Harlem through the night.

Bradford's office soon got the nickname "Joy Club." Its motto was "Whenever business mess up with pleasure, then cut out the business and let the pleasure roll on."

Bert Williams & William Vodery Publishers, longtime Gaiety tenants, founded their company on the fame of Williams, Broadway's first black star.

Andy Razaf, lyricist of such classics as "Ain't Misbehavin'," "Honeysuckle Rose," "The Joint Is Jumpin'," "Memories of You," and "Stompin' at the Savoy" didn't have his office at the Gaiety—he preferred the Greyhound bus station on 50th Street between Broadway and 8th Avenue, but he did receive his mail at the Gaiety. Besides, he was there many afternoons at Perry Bradford's Joy Club visiting his friends.

The Gaiety Building was torn down along with the Gaiety Theater in 1982.

GANGSTERS. Broadway and Times Square have long been the turf of gangsters and hoodlums. In the 1930s, during Prohibition, the area was known for its nightclubs and speakeasies, which afforded the bootleggers ample opportunities to sell their wares and the crime syndicates opportunities to launder money. In more recent times, with the social disintegration of the area, prostitutes and drugs have taken hold, though the redevelopment of Times Square has cleaned up the 42nd Street and 8th Avenue neighborhood. And throughout its history the Broadway musical has been a perfect money-laundering device.

The Prohibition years were the most fruitful for gangsters. Because the era roughly coincided with the Depression, legitimate operators had been wiped out, and gangsters moved in to take control of New York's entertainment areas. Mob-associated hoodlums had cash to spare and, in addition to backing Broadway shows and running nightclubs, laundered their money through real-estate holdings. They bought up a lot of prime midtown property, and their families still control many choice plots of land in Times Square. The exploits of notorious hoodlums were duly recorded by journalists such as DAMON RUNYON and WALTER WINCHELL. Their favorite subjects were Legs Diamond, Lucky Luciano, Arnold Rothstein, and Herman Rosenthal. The supporting cast included Gyp the Blood, Whitey Lewis, and Lefty Louis.

Legs Diamond (1896–1931) operated the Hotsy Totsy Club, a front for criminals, on Broadway between 54th and 55th Streets. The manager of the club was ostensibly Hymie Cohen. Diamond used the club as his headquarters. Many men met their end in the back room and were then carried out "drunk" through the bar. The murders reached their apex in July 1929. A fight erupted, supposedly over whether prizefighter Ruby Goldstein was a capable fighter. The argument turned into a full-fledged gun battle with Charlie Entratta (Green) and Legs Diamond in the middle. They both disappeared after shooting gangster Red Cassidy. A bystander, Simon Walker, was also killed, as were a waiter and bartender. The hatcheck girl and cashier were never found, and three other witnesses were later found dead; Hymie Cohen was also missing. Because there were no witnesses, Diamond and Entratta got off scot-free. The club closed soon after the murders.

Diamond, much hated, was the target of many attempts on his life. However, each time he recovered and set about to control an ever larger piece of the Broadway pie. He was finally killed by two unknown assailants on December 18, 1931, in Albany, New York.

One of Diamond's chief rivals was Waxey Gordon (1888–1952), a bootlegger and nightclub owner. Gordon made almost $2 million a year in his bootlegging industry. However, he claimed only $8,125 on his income tax declaration, and that resulted in his downfall. He was probably lucky. If he had stayed out of jail, Gordon's feuds with Lucky Luciano and Meyer Lansky would have certainly resulted in his death. When Gordon got out of Leavenworth in 1940, he announced the death of Waxey Gordon and the birth of Irving Wexler, salesman. He took a suite of offices at Broadway and 42nd Street and dabbled in drug dealing. Gordon was also a backer of many Broadway shows. Those he had a stake in always featured his current flame somewhere in the chorus.

Lucky Luciano (1897–1962), Gordon's enemy, was another of the gangsters who enjoyed fame on The Great White Way. He was a leading member of the syndicate and perhaps its most important figure. Luciano operated out of several speakeasies and clubs as a board member of the Broadway Mob. The group of rumrunners was headed by Joe Adonis (1902–1972), with Frank Costello (1891–1973) also on the board. The Broadway mob, which controlled all liquor distribution in the Times Square area, supplied Jack and Charlie's 21 Club, the Stork Club, the Silver Slipper, and other, smaller outlets. Meyer Lansky and Bugsy Siegel were made members of the club so their gangs could provide protection for the mob.

Arnold Rothstein (1882–1928) was called, variously, "the banker for racketeers," "the Big Bankroll," "the Fixer," "the Man Uptown," and "Mr. Big"; Damon Runyon dubbed him "The Brain." Runyon wrote, "Nobody knows how much dough The Brain has, except that he must have plenty because no matter how much dough is around, The Brain sooner or later gets hold of all of it." Rothstein was a fixer, one who could bribe almost any official no matter how high the office. He was an inveterate gambler who also bankrolled such biggies as Legs Diamond and Waxey Gordon. Rothstein had almost $3 million in real estate investments as well as his own personal wealth, made when he sold his liquor importing business in the mid-1920s.

While at LINDY's restaurant on November 4, 1928, Rothstein made about $600,000 in bets on the presidential election. Rothstein supported Hoover over Al Smith and Franklin Roosevelt as New York's next governor. He would have made a lot of money had he lived to see the election. A few days earlier he had lost heavily to racketeer George McManus. Rothstein claimed the poker game was fixed and tore up over $300,000 in IOUs. McManus called Rothstein at Lindy's and suggested that Rothstein meet him at the Park Central Hotel. That night Rothstein was found dead at the hotel's servants' exit on 56th Street. Though there were no indictments, it was clear to Broadwayites that Nigger Nate Raymond and Titanic Thompson, Rothstein's poker partners, authorized the hit.

Damon Runyon's character The Brain also had some characteristics of Herman Rosenthal. Rosenthal, a Times Square gambler and club owner, is best known as the man who stood up to Lieutenant Charles Becker (1869–1915). Becker was a New York City policeman who wanted to muscle in on Rosenthal's territory through "legitimate" police protection. When Rosenthal refused to play ball and threatened to turn Becker in to the newspapers, he was murdered in front of the Metropole Cafe at 43rd Street and Broadway on July 16, 1912. Gyp the Blood, Dago Frank, Whitey Lewis, and Lefty Louie were the hit men. They were hired by Big Jack Zelig, whom Becker arranged to have released from jail to undertake the job. Becker's boss, police Commissioner Rhinelander Waldo, protected him from prosecution. Waldo saw to it that important leads were "lost," and a witness was locked up in jail away from the police's search. Becker, called "the crookedest cop who ever stood behind a shield," was eventually sentenced to death along with the hit men. District Attorney Whitman was instrumental in bringing Becker to the electric chair.

Becker wasn't the only public official who was in on the graft and crime surrounding Times Square. New York Supreme Court Judge Joseph Force Crater (b. 1889) disappeared off the streets of Times Square on August 6, 1930. Crater had previously bought tickets to a musical and had exited Billy Haas' restaurant at 332 West 45th Street, where he had lunched with theatrical lawyer William Klein and showgirl Sally Lou Ritz. A little after 9:00 P.M. Crater got in a cab and disappeared. Despite hundreds of leads, he was never found. Frederic Johnson, Crater's law clerk, claimed that he knew why Crater disappeared: "He died because he knew too much."

However, not all the law enforcers on the city payroll were crooked. Among the most honest, and toughest, was police officer Johnny Broderick (1894–1966). To "broderick" someone meant to deck him or her with a powerful punch, a SLANG term that described Broderick's rough method of justice. Broderick seldom used his gun; usually he used his fists or any useful object that was close at hand. For example, once Broderick found a criminal he was searching for in a Broadway cafeteria. He strode up to the man and knocked him out with a sugar bowl. Broderick announced to the amazed gathering, "Case closed."

Broderick's most famous exploit concerned Legs Diamond. The two were experts at their respective jobs, and neither held the other in much regard. Diamond, fed up with Broderick, announced that he was taking the cop on and was going to teach him a lesson. Diamond and his boys hit all the spots that Broderick frequented: Lindy's, Toots Shor's, the ASTOR HOTEL bar, and Leone's. Broderick wasn't one to avoid confrontation, so he set out on his own search for Diamond. The two men met on Broadway at 46th Street. When confronted with the 5'10", 170-pound Broderick, Diamond's henchmen ran away. Without his body-guards, Diamond was less brave. He asked Broderick whether he could take a joke, to which Broderick responded by picking Diamond up and depositing him headfirst into a trash can. Mayor James J. Walker later commented, "Broderick as good as killed Diamond with that garbage can stunt. It finished him as a leader." Walker was right. Diamond was later rubbed out while hiding out in an Albany hotel room. Broderick went on to enjoy a 24-year career patrolling Times Square before his retirement in 1947.

Today's criminals along the Great White Way have none of the flash or panache of Diamond or Rothstein. Crooks today deal in the distribution of crack and co-caine and in prostitution. Other petty criminals deal in three-card monte rackets set up on cardboard boxes not far from the Metropole site on 43rd Street, where three-card monte was invented, or sell copies of de-signer clothing and accessories from card tables on the street. But the era of the flashy gangster has faded away, leaving Times Square less rambunctious and colorful.

GASSNER, JOHN. Critic; b. Marmaros-Sziget, Hun-gary, January 30, 1903; d. New Haven, Connecticut, April 2, 1967.

John Gassner.

Gassner was a teacher at Hunter College beginning in 1928. He became a play reader for the THEATER GUILD in 1930. From 1935 to 1937 he served as drama critic for *New Theatre* magazine. He then moved from magazine to magazine: *Forum* (1937–1938), *Time* (1938), and *Direction* (1939–1943). He also taught drama at many universities, including Columbia, Bryn Mawr, and Queens College, and was Sterling Professor of Playwriting at Yale. Gassner, also an editor of the annual *Best Plays* series, wrote or edited many other theater books, including *Masters of the Drama* (1940), *Best American Plays* (1939–1963), *Treasury of the Theater* (1935–1960), and *Theater at the Crossroads* (1960).

GAVER, JACK. Critic; b. Tolono, Illinois, 1902; d. New York, New York, December 16, 1974.

Gaver spent his entire Broadway career as drama critic for United Press International (UPI). Both before and after his studies at the University of Illinois, he worked for the *Champaign News-Gazette*, the *Illinois State Register* in Springfield, and United Press in Chi-cago and Columbus. He began with UPI in 1929 cover-ing the night desk and Broadway. The next year he was appointed theater critic and amusement columnist. He remained with UPI for over 30 years. He also wrote many books, including *Curtain Calls* (1949), *Critics' Choice* (1954), and *Season In—Season Out* (1967).

GEORGE ABBOTT THEATER. 152 W. 54th Street. Architect: R. E. Hall & Co. Original name: Craig Theater. Opening: December 24, 1928; *Poti-phar's Wife.*

The Craig Theater couldn't have opened at a worse time, just as the Depression was changing the face of Broadway. Producers lost millions in the market as well as their theater holdings. The theater's location north of the theater district proper sealed its fate. From the beginning, the Craig was a disaster. The popular actor William Gaxton called the theater "the dump of dumps."

On November 27, 1934, the original owners, the Houston Properties Corporation, lost the theater, when it was renamed the Adelphi for the opening of *The Lord Blesses the Bishop*. It didn't bode well for the success of the new venture when it closed after only 7 performances. The theater remained a failure, and it was taken over by the FEDERAL THEATRE PROJECT. Under the new management, the theater became suc-cessful for the first time. *It Can't Happen Here* (95 performances) was an enormous hit for the theater and the Federal Theatre Project. The show was written by Sinclair Lewis and was unique in that it opened on October 27, 1936, in 18 cities. New York alone had four productions. The show was the story of a fascist

The Craig Theatre, at the time of its opening, 1928.

politician who becomes president of the United States. Hallie Flanagan, director of the Federal Theatre Project, commented: "The play says that when dictatorship comes to threaten such a democracy, it comes in an apparently harmless guise, with parades and promises; but that when such dictatorship arrives, the promises are not kept and the parade grounds become encampments."

Playwright Arthur Arent's *One-Third of a Nation* (1/17/38; 237 performances) was part of the Federal Theatre Project's "Living Newspapers" series. The show was the best-known of all the project's presentations, seen by over 2,000 people in New York alone. Ten other cities later presented the show. The theme of *One-Third of a Nation* was the problems of the nation's slums. The title of the piece was taken from Franklin Roosevelt's second inaugural address. The last significant production at the Adelphi by the Federal Theatre Project was *Sing for Your Supper* (4/24/39; 60 performances). Its best-known song was "Ballad for Americans," by Earl Robinson and John Latouche.

With the end of the Federal Theatre Project, the Adelphi was taken over by the Royal Fraternity of Master Metaphysicians. In December 1940 they changed the name of the theater to the Radiant Center. Three years later, on October 18, 1943, the theater became the Yiddish Art Theater. Its opening production was *The Family Carnovsky*. But it wasn't successful as a Yiddish theater either.

On April 20, 1944, the theater became the Adelphi again. The musical *Allah Be Praised!* opened at the Adelphi but ran only 20 performances. When out-of-town producer Alfred Bloomingdale asked play doctor Cy Howard what to do, Howard suggested to Bloomingdale that he "close the show and keep the store open nights."

Finally, the theater's luck changed with the opening of *On the Town* (12/28/44; 462 performances). The show was directed by GEORGE ABBOTT, who gave LEONARD BERNSTEIN and COMDEN AND GREEN their first Broadway break. It starred such young up-and-comers as Nancy Walker, Sono Osato, Cris Alexander, John Battles, Alice Pearce, and Comden and Green. The big song was "New York, New York."

Unfortunately, *On the Town* led the way to another series of flops. *Carib Song* (9/27/45; 36 performances) starred the great choreographer and dancer Katharine Dunham. *Nellie Bly* (1/21/46; 16 performances), with a score by Johnny Burke and James Van Heusen, starred William Gaxton, Marilyn Maxwell, and Victor Moore. *Three to Make Ready* (3/7/46; 327 performances) was the third in a series by Morgan Lewis and Nancy Hamilton. It moved to the ST. JAMES THEATRE to make way for the next tenant, another failure about world travelers, but a spectacular one.

Around the World in Eighty Days (5/31/46; 75 performances) was the brainchild of Orson Welles, who wrote the extravaganza's book and directed the show. In addition, Welles became producer when Michael Todd decamped while the show was in tryouts. COLE PORTER wrote music and lyrics to the show, but none of the songs achieved any success. Broadway wags called the show "Wellesapoppin'" after Olsen and Johnson's hit *Hellzapoppin'*. When it opened on Broadway, the 36 scene changes required 55 stagehands. (At the time the Adelphi was not air-conditioned.) Welles also starred in the show after taking over for an actor while the show was out of town. Welles' contract with CBS Radio had him committed to a Friday night radio show. Therefore, the musical could not play Friday nights. All in all, the show lost almost half a million dollars.

KURT WEILL saw his musical version of Elmer Rice's play *Street Scene* open at the Adelphi (1/9/47; 148 performances). Anne Jeffreys, Polyna Stoska, Brian Sullivan, Sheila Bond, and Danny Daniels ably rendered the wonderful score, with lyrics by Langston Hughes. *Music in My Heart* (10/2/47; 124 performances), a musical with melodies by Tchaikovsky, was not a success. *Look Ma I'm Dancin'* (1/29/48; 188 performances) probably should have been a bigger hit than it was. Hugh Martin wrote the catchy score, and

Jerome Lawrence and Robert E. Lee contributed the libretto. George Abbott produced and directed in association with Jerome Robbins. Robbins also choreographed the musical, which starred Nancy Walker, Harold Lang, Tommy Rall, and Alice Pearce. *Hilarities* (9/9/48; 14 performances) was apparently a misnomer for a revue that closed quickly.

The DuMont television network used the theater for a decade beginning in 1948. Jackie Gleason's popular television show *The Honeymooners* was filmed there. It was renamed the 54th Street Theater on October 8, 1958, with the opening of *Drink to Me Only* (77 performances). Richard Adler and Jerry Ross' hit *Damn Yankees* transferred to the theater in 1958; another hit, *Bye Bye Birdie*, also ended its run there. Adler, without his late partner Jerry Ross, tried his hand at both music and lyrics for *Kwamina* (10/23/61; 32 performances), starring Robert Guillaume and Sally Ann Howes.

Richard Rodgers opened his first show without either Lorenz Hart or OSCAR HAMMERSTEIN II with *No Strings* (3/15/62; 580 performances). Rodgers provided both music and lyrics. The show starred Diahann Carroll, Richard Kiley, Noelle Adam, Alvin Epstein, and Don Chastain. The wonderful score contained the hit "The Sweetest Sounds." *What Makes Sammy Run?* (2/27/64; 541 performances) was a musicalization of the famous novel by Budd Schulberg. Ervin Drake composed the score and wrote the lyrics which included the popular "A Room Without Windows." Steve Lawrence, Robert Alda, Sally Ann Howes, and Bernice Massi starred in the show. *La Grosse Valise* (12/14/65; 7 performances) had music by Gerard Calvi and lyrics by HAROLD ROME. This was the last show to play the theater before it was renamed the George Abbott Theater.

Darling of the Day (1/27/68; 32 performances) was a failure by the usually reliable JULE STYNE and E. Y. HARBURG, although the score is much admired. *Buck White* (12/2/69; 7 performances) was a musical failure, most notable for the Broadway debut of Cassius Clay (Muhammad Ali). The theater's last show did even worse. *Gantry* (2/14/70), with Robert Shaw and Rita Moreno, opened and closed in one day. The theater had already been sold to the Hilton Corporation.

The George Abbott Theater was demolished in 1970 to make way for the New York Hilton.

GEORGE JEAN NATHAN AWARD. Famed critic George Jean Nathan (1882–1958) founded the award "to encourage and assist in developing the art of drama criticism and the stimulation of intelligent theater going." A committee of English-department chairs from Cornell, Princeton, and Yale decides the award

winner. The award comes with a $4,000 stipend and is given to the author of "the best piece of drama criticism published during the previous year, whether an article, treatise, or book."

GEORGE M. COHAN'S THEATRE. 1482 Broadway, at southeast corner of 43rd Street; main entrance on 43rd Street. Architect: George Keister. Opening: February 13, 1911; *Get-Rich-Quick Wallingford*.

George M. Cohan's Theatre was built by the team of GEORGE M. COHAN and Sam H. Harris, among the busiest producers of the late teens. They also managed the HARRIS THEATER, the Grand Opera House, the ASTOR THEATRE, the GAIETY THEATER, and the Bronx Opera House, as well as Cohan's Grand Opera House in Chicago. Cohan, one of Broadway's biggest egotists, thought of the theater as a tribute to his career. The marble lobby (in the FitzGerald Building) featured exhibits on the history of the Four Cohans. The theater's boxes were topped by murals depicting Cohan's many stage successes.

The first great hit at Cohan's Theatre was *The Little Millionaire* (9/25/11; 192 performances). It featured Cohan as composer, lyricist, librettist, director, co-producer, and star. The musical also starred Cohan's par-

The lavish interior of George M. Cohan's Theatre.

ents and Donald Crisp. In *Broadway Jones* (9/23/12; 176 performances), Cohan played a Broadwayite who finds himself in the sticks. *Theatre* magazine said that the plot "is so simple that it is almost juvenile. But Mr. Cohan is a true observer of men and conditions, and applies the little comic and pathetic touches of life in a way which makes his completed fabric something distinctly vital and real." The show marked the end of an era, the last time the Four Cohans appeared together on Broadway. During its subsequent tour, Cohan's parents retired from the stage. The comedy *Potash and Perlmutter* (7/16/13; 441 performances) was a huge hit. Roi Cooper Megrue and Walter Hackett's play *It Pays to Advertise* (9/8/14; 399 performances) starred Grant Mitchell.

In 1915 Cohan and Harris sold their theater to Joe Leblang. The discount ticket seller knew his limitations and allowed A. L. Erlanger to manage the property. *Pom-Pom* (2/28/16; 128 performances) had music by Hugo Felix and book and lyrics by one of Broadway's few female lyricists, Anne Caldwell; Mitzi Hajos had the lead. Later that year *Seven Chances* (8/8/16; 151 performances) opened to acclaim. Another of the theater's early successes was *Come Out of the Kitchen* (10/23/16; 224 performances). *The Kiss Burglar* (5/9/18; 100 performances) was a minor musical by Raymond Hubbell and Glen MacDonough. *Head over Heels* (8/29/18; 100 performances) was an early musical by JEROME KERN. *A Prince There Was* (12/24/18; 159 performances) had as its author Robert Hilliard, who also starred; Cohan rewrote the play and made it a success. *Elsie Janis and Her Gang* (12/1/19; 55 performances) featured the talented actress Eva Le Gallienne; Charles Dillingham and FLORENZ ZIEGFELD produced the show. *The Genius and the Crowd* (9/6/20; 24 performances), a comedy by John T. McIntyre and Francis Hill, was significant because it was the first show Cohan produced on his own following a split with Harris.

Cohan had a great hit with his melodrama *The Tavern* (9/27/20; 252 performances). The story was meant by Cohan to be an affectionate travesty, but opening-night critics took it seriously and panned the proceedings. However, ROBERT BENCHLEY, Dorothy Parker, and Robert E. Sherwood appreciated the play in the spirit in which it was presented and gave it rave reviews. Benchley noted, "There can no longer be any doubt that George M. Cohan is the greatest man in the world. Anyone who can write *The Tavern* and produce it as *The Tavern* is produced places himself automatically in the class with the gods who sit on Olympus and emit Jovian (or is it Shavian?) laughter at the tiny tots below on earth. In fact, George M. Cohan's laughter is much more intelligent than that of any god I ever heard of." It was revived five times on Broadway and countless times across the country. It was followed by

Two Little Girls in Blue (5/3/21; 135 performances), with music by VINCENT YOUMANS and lyrics by Arthur Francis, better known as IRA GERSHWIN. The musical starred Madeleine and Marion Fairbanks.

One of the theater's biggest successes was Clemence Dane's drama *A Bill of Divorcement* (10/10/21; 173 performances); KATHARINE CORNELL starred. *A Bill of Divorcement* moved on to make way for the opening of Ed Wynn's musical, *The Perfect Fool* (11/7/21; 275 performances); GEORGE GERSHWIN composed two of the numbers in the show. *The Love Child* (11/14/22; 169 performances) starred Janet Beecher and Sidney Blackmer. In between theatrical engagements, the theater presented silent films. Among the most notable of these were Cecil B. DeMille's *The Ten Commandments* (1923) and MGM's *Ben-Hur* (1925), starring Ramon Novarro.

Adrienne (5/28/23; 235 performances), a musical with a score by popular favorites Albert Von Tilzer and A. Seymour Brown, had as its musical director Max Steiner, who would make a name for himself as one of Hollywood's greatest composers. Owen Davis' farce *The Haunted House* (9/2/24; 103 performances) starred Wallace Edinger as an author who lives his life in the style of the book he is writing. While writing about a haunted house, he scares everyone he is in contact with. Another farce by Davis to play Cohan's Theatre was *Easy Come, Easy Go* (10/26/25; 180 performances). The show starred Edward Arnold, Otto Kruger, Victor Moore, and Betty Garde. A Frank Craven play, *The 19th Hole* (10/11/27; 119 performances), followed the downward path of a golf addict. Craven himself played the inveterate golfer whose compulsion ends only when his livelihood and marriage are threatened by the game. Milton Ager and Jack Yellen wrote the score to *Rain or Shine* (2/9/28; 360 performances).

At the beginning of the Depression Heywood Broun organized a show to give out-of-work actors some employment. The result, *Shoot the Works* (7/21/31; 87 performances), had as contributors to the score and sketches Peter Arno, Broun himself, Dorothy Parker, Nunnally Johnson, Sig Herzig, E. B. White, Ira Gershwin, IRVING BERLIN, Leo Robin, Dorothy Fields (*see* FIELDS FAMILY), Jimmy McHugh, Jay Gorney, E. Y. HARBURG, and VERNON DUKE. Among the performers the show helped out were Imogene Coca, Jack Hazzard, George Murphy, and Broun.

There You Are (5/16/32; 8 performances) was a short-lived musical that marked an end to the theater's legitimate policy. Along with many other Broadway houses, during the Depression the theater adopted a movie policy. In 1938, with Leblang defaulting on his mortgage, the theater was torn down along with the FitzGerald Building, which shared its facade.

GEORGE WHITE'S SCANDALS. *George White's Scandals* were a long-running (1919–1939) annual series of revues produced and sometimes written by GEORGE WHITE.

The *Scandals* were one of the most important of the revue series, a popular genre in the first part of the century. Other important revues were the ZIEGFELD, FOLLIES, EARL CARROLL'S VANITIES, the SHUBERT BROTHERS' *Passing Shows*, and IRVING BERLIN's *Music Box Revues*. The *Follies* were distinguished for their elaborate production numbers and big stars. The *Vanities* were notorious for their risqué numbers featuring scantily clad chorines. The *Passing Shows* were simple entertainments without much to distinguish them, and the *Music Box Revues* were intimate shows featuring Irving Berlin's songs. What made the *Scandals* noteworthy was the high quality of their material. They were the first revues to assign complete scores to songwriting teams. Until the *Scandals*, songs were submitted to producers, who would pick and choose the best. White also put an emphasis on dance, because he was

a former hoofer in the *Ziegfeld Follies* and other Broadway shows.

White came up with the idea for the *Scandals* while he was in the *Follies*. He realized Ziegfeld was immersed in the producing styles of the teens and earlier, and White was sure he could move the revue into a more modern fashion in his own series. His revues were much faster-paced than Ziegfeld's, reflecting a new trend in jazzy entertainment.

The first *George White's Scandals* was the 1919 edition (6/2/19; 128 performances). White contributed some sketches and lyrics in addition to starring in the revue. He hired Ann Pennington, a dancer who had also appeared as his partner in the *Follies*. Pennington would become a *Scandals* regular, appearing in 5 editions. White hired up-and-coming composers Richard Whiting and Herbert Spencer for the tunes; Arthur Jackson and White himself handled lyric chores.

White certainly had a knack for finding other young talents. His next edition featured a score by the young GEORGE GERSHWIN and Arthur Jackson. Ann Penning-

Showgirls from the 1925 edition of *The George White's Scandals*.

ton, Lou Holtz, and White reappeared as headliners. The 1920 edition (6/7/20; 134 performances) introduced a new dance step to Broadway, the scandal walk. For this edition White co-directed with William Collier.

White again co-directed, co-authored, produced, and starred in his next *Scandals* (7/11/21; 97 performances). Gershwin and Jackson had a hit with their score, which featured "Drifting Along with the Tide." Pennington was back as was Lester Allen, who had made his first appearance in the previous edition. Rounding out the cast were Tess Gardella (also known as Aunt Jemima), Bert Gordon, and Charles King.

For the fourth edition (8/28/22), White assumed his usual roles with an assist on the libretto by Andy Rice and Ziegfeld star W. C. Fields. This time B. G. De Sylva and E. Ray Goetz provided lyrics to Gershwin's tunes. The hit song of this edition was "I'll Build a Stairway to Paradise," with lyrics by De Sylva and Arthur Francis (a pseudonym of Ira Gershwin). Lester Allen, Delores Costello, W. C. Fields, Winnie Lightner, Paul Whiteman and His Orchestra, and White were featured.

In the next *Scandals* (6/18/23; 168 performances), the De Sylva and Goetz lyrics were augmented by Ballard Macdonald's contributions to Gershwin's tunes. The score was undistinguished, resulting in no lasting hits. Allen and Lightner reappeared with an assist by Olive Vaughn and Tom Patricola. The latter would join the list of *Scandals* regulars. For the first time White wasn't in the cast of his annual revue; he wouldn't return to the stage until the 1929 edition.

The 1924 edition (198 performances) opened on June 30 with Costello, Lightner, Patricola, and the Williams Sisters starring. The Gershwin and De Sylva score presented one great standard, "Somebody Loves Me," which featured additional lyrics by Ballard Macdonald. For the next edition (6/22/25; 169 performances), George Gershwin, who had abandoned the revue field to concentrate on book musicals, was replaced by the songwriting team of DE SYLVA, BROWN, AND HENDERSON. This was the first uniting of the noted team, who would provide some of their greatest hits for future *Scandals*, but this show did not contain any big hits. Tom Patricola was the only *Scandals* regular to appear in the cast. Helen Morgan, Harry Fox, Gordon Dooley, and the successful black performers Flournoy Miller and Aubrey Lyles joined him.

In the 1926 edition (6/14/26; 432 performances), the De Sylva, Brown, and Henderson team was in top form. The trio presented White with three smash hit songs. "The Birth of the Blues" was the most highly regarded, especially as energetically presented by Harry Richman. "The Black Bottom" was the next big

dance craze to come out of the *Scandals*. These were the days when many of the dance steps that swept the nation originated on Broadway. The last big song was "Lucky Day," an enthusiastically upbeat number typical of De Sylva, Brown, and Henderson. Former *Scandals* contributor George Gershwin returned with an interpolation of his "Rhapsody in Blue." The show was a reunion of sorts for other former *Scandals* stars. Ann Pennington was back along with Tom Patricola and Frances Williams, who had appeared in the 1924 *Scandals* as one of the Williams Sisters. Several sibling groups also appeared: Willie and Eugene Howard, the Fairbanks Twins, and the McCarthy Sisters. White charged $55 a ticket for seats in the front of the orchestra on opening night. He was right to do so, because the show was a huge success.

Because of the long run of the 1926 edition, there was no 1927 show. The next *Scandals* (7/2/28) didn't have a particularly good score; in fact, one song was titled "Not As Good As Last Year." The Howards, Tom Patricola, Ann Pennington, Harry Richman, and Frances Williams all returned, but the show wasn't as successful as the previous edition. However, it did manage a 230-performance run, mostly because of the previous edition's success.

Willie and Eugene Howard and four-legged friends in *The George White's Scandals*, 8th edition.

For the next edition (9/23/29; 159 performances), George White contributed songs to one of his own shows; his lyricist was Irving Caesar. Cliff Friend wrote the rest of the unmemorable score. White seemed to enjoy performing teams, and this edition featured the Abbott Dancers, the Elm City Four, Willie and Eugene Howard, Mitchell and Durant, and the Scott Sisters. White rejoined the cast of his series. Frances Williams was practically the only other cast member unrelated to another performer on the bill.

In 1930 White was producer and director of a book show, *Flying High*. He returned to his *Scandals* the next year. The 1931 edition (9/14/31; 204 performances) boasted a score by Brown and Henderson, but this time without De Sylva. The duo didn't seem to miss their former collaborator, because the score contained five huge hits: "Ladies and Gentlemen That's Love," "Life Is Just a Bowl of Cherries," "That's Why Darkies Were Born," "This Is the Missus," and "The Thrill Is Gone." The cast, too, was the greatest in *Scandals* history. ETHEL MERMAN, Rudy Vallee, Alice Faye, Ethel Barrymore Colt, Ray Bolger, Everett Marshall, and Willie and Eugene Howard were the stars. However, the country was in the middle of the Depression, and theater was suffering. So despite the excellent cast and material, the show didn't run as long as it might have in better times.

There was no *Scandals* the next year, although White did present a revue, *George White's Music Hall Varieties* (11/22/32). The Depression took its toll, and the next *Scandals* was not produced until Christmas Day 1935 (110 performances) at the NEW AMSTERDAM THEATRE, site of most of the *Ziegfeld Follies*. Ray Henderson was the only one of the songwriting trio left; his lyricist was Jack Yellen. The cast included Rudy Vallee, Bert Lahr, Cliff Edwards, Hal Forde, and Willie and Eugene Howard.

The last *Scandals* was the 1939 edition (8/28/39; 120 performances). The score was mostly by Sammy Fain and Jack Yellen. They supplied the standard "Are You Havin' Any Fun?" which was introduced by singer Ella Logan. The two other hits were by Yellen and Herb Magidson, "Something I Dreamed Last Night" and "The Mexiconga." Additional cast members included the Three Stooges, Ben Blue, Ray Middleton, Ann Miller, and Willie and Eugene Howard.

The last *Scandals* was White's last Broadway show. He retired from the stage, leaving behind a wealth of great songs and the satisfaction of knowing that he helped boost the careers of many newcomers. The *Scandals* were certainly the revue series most in step with the times, and it was the vision of George White, their producer, director, writer, composer, choreographer, and star, that created them.

GERSHWIN, GEORGE AND IRA. Perhaps the greatest popular songwriters of the "Golden Age" of Broadway theater; George Gershwin, b. Jacob Gershvin, Brooklyn, New York, September 26, 1898; d. Hollywood, California, July 11, 1937; Ira Gershwin, b. Israel Gershvin, New York, New York, December 6, 1896; d. Hollywood, California, August 17, 1983.

George Gershwin was born into a poor family of first-generation immigrants. In 1912 his parents purchased a piano so that his older brother, Ira, could take lessons. But it was George who showed the natural predilection for music. He amazed his family when he sat down at the new piano and played simple tunes. In fact, George had begun his "studies" at a neighbor's house, where he taught himself the basics of piano playing. He went on to more structured schooling with Charles Hambitzer. Hambitzer in turn urged George to study theory, orchestration, and harmony with Edward Kilenyi.

George had ambitions to become a concert pianist, but his teachers convinced him that such a dream was impractical. Luckily, he had an interest in the burgeoning field of American popular song. Like most of his contemporaries, he idolized JEROME KERN and IRVING BERLIN, two composers who, with GEORGE M. COHAN, were most responsible for bringing an American sensibility to what had been a predominantly European art. "When You Want 'Em, You Can't Get 'Em (When You Got 'Em, You Don't Want 'Em)" was the title of George's first published song, copyrighted in 1916 with lyrics by Murray Roth. George's first Broadway song, "The Making of a Girl," was written for *The Passing Show of 1916* (6/22/16; 140 performances) in collaboration with SIGMUND ROMBERG, with lyrics by Harold Atteridge.

George created his first important song, "Swanee," which was written for the CAPITOL THEATER's revue *Demi-Tasse* (10/24/19) and was later incorporated into the AL JOLSON show *Sinbad* (2/14/18; 164 performances) after its opening. "Swanee," written with Irving Caesar, was an enormous hit as a result of its exposure in *Sinbad* and led to composing offers by Broadway producers.

La, La, Lucille (5/26/19; 104 performances), George's first Broadway show, opened at the HENRY MILLER'S THEATRE with a libretto by Fred Jackson and lyrics by Arthur J. Jackson and B. G. De Sylva (*see* DE SYLVA, BROWN, AND HENDERSON). *Morris Gest's Midnight Whirl* (12/27/19; 110 performances), with lyrics by B. G. De Sylva, followed. The annual revue *George White's Scandals of 1920* (6/7/20; 134 performances) was Gershwin's next Broadway assignment. GEORGE WHITE had the foresight to hire George Gershwin when the composer was just beginning to make a name for himself; Arthur Jackson contributed the lyrics.

George's next Broadway attempt, *A Dangerous Maid*, closed out of town in Pittsburgh. The show is notable as the first for which Ira Gershwin wrote all the lyrics. Ira was concerned that it would appear he was hired only because he was George's brother, so he assumed the pen name Arthur Francis, the first names of their brother and sister.

Ira was always interested in language, having written light verse all through school. Ira successfully submitted his early work to Franklin P. Adams for publication in Adams' newspaper column, "The Conning Tower." Other lyricists whose work appeared in "The Conning Tower" included Howard Dietz (*see* DIETZ AND SCHWARTZ) and E. Y. HARBURG.

The first song with lyrics by Ira and music by George to appear in a Broadway show was "The Real American Folk Song Is a Rag." It was put into *Ladies First* (10/24/18; 164 performances), where it received little notice and wasn't published until years later. The first published song with music by George and lyrics by Ira was "Waiting for the Sun to Come Up," which was written for *The Sweetheart Shop* (8/31/20; 55 performances). Their next Broadway show was *Two Little Girls in Blue* (5/3/21; 135 performances), which opened at GEORGE M. COHAN'S THEATRE. VINCENT YOUMANS and Paul Lanin also wrote some of the music for the score. The show starred Madeline and Marion Fairbanks, who were known as the Fairbanks Twins.

George White's Scandals of 1921 (7/11/21; 97 performances) had lyrics by Arthur Jackson and music by George. The only semisuccess in the score was "Drifting Along with the Tide." The following year's edition of the *Scandals* (8/28/22; 88 performances) contained the Gershwins' first standards as a team. The show opened with lyrics also supplied by B. G. De Sylva and E. Ray Goetz. The biggest hit was "I'll Build a Stairway to Paradise," with lyrics by De Sylva and Ira.

For a while it seemed that George was destined to compose minor scores for minor musicals. These included *Our Nell* (12/4/22; 40 performances), with interpolated songs by George; *The Rainbow* (4/3/23; 113 performances); the 1923 edition of the *Scandals* (6/18/23; 168 performances) at the Globe Theatre (*see* LUNT-FONTANNE THEATER); and *Sweet Little Devil* (1/21/24; 120 performances) at the ASTOR THEATRE.

George was already an established popular composer when *Rhapsody in Blue* premiered at Aeolian Hall on February 12, 1924. The first show of that year for George was another edition of the *Scandals* (6/30/24; 192 performances) at the APOLLO THEATRE. The show's lyrics were by B. G. De Sylva, who contributed the lyrics to the show's big hit, "Somebody Loves Me,"

with Ballard Macdonald. The song has remained a standard more than 60 years after the show's premiere. George and Ira reunited for *Primrose* (9/11/24; 255 performances), which opened at the Winter Garden Theatre in London with lyrics by Ira and Desmond Carter. The libretto was written by George Grossmith and GUY BOLTON. It was the Gershwins' biggest hit to date, and it paved the way to a successful return to America.

The brothers' next show, with Ira writing under his own name, was a huge hit. *Lady, Be Good!* (12/1/24; 330 performances) opened at the LIBERTY THEATRE on 42nd Street, produced by AARONS AND FREEDLEY with a book by Guy Bolton and Fred Thompson. The stars were FRED AND ADELE ASTAIRE, Walter Catlett, and Cliff Edwards. *Lady, Be Good!*'s jaunty score contained at least two standards: the title song and "Fascinating Rhythm." The show was subsequently produced in London on April 14, 1926, with the Astaires. *Lady, Be Good!* established the brothers as a successful team.

Tell Me More! (4/13/25; 100 performances) wasn't as big a success as *Lady, Be Good!* The lyrics by Ira and B. G. De Sylva accompanied one moderately successful song, "Kickin' the Clouds Away." Another song had an interesting title, "My Fair Lady," originally the show's title song. The show was conducted by Max Steiner, who later achieved renown as a composer of Hollywood epics like *Gone with the Wind*. *Tip-Toes* (12/28/25; 194 performances), at the Liberty Theatre, was twice as successful. Alex A. Aarons, who produced *Tell Me More!*, produced this show too, this time with Vinton Freedley. The Gershwin brothers' score contained several hits, including "Looking for a Boy," "That Certain Feeling," and "Sweet and Low Down." George continued his more serious composing with his "Concerto in F," which premiered at Carnegie Hall on December 3, 1925. Seven days later *Song of the Flame* opened, George's third Broadway show of the year. It was an old-fashioned operetta with music also by Herbert Stothart; OTTO HARBACH and OSCAR HAMMERSTEIN II wrote the lyrics.

Reunited with his brother Ira, George wrote some of his best tunes for the Aarons and Freedley musical *Oh, Kay!* (11/8/26; 257 performances) at the IMPERIAL THEATRE. The book was by Guy Bolton and P. G. Wodehouse. The cast included Gertrude Lawrence, Victor Moore, Oscar Shaw, Betty Compton, and Harland Dixon. The score was one of the brothers' best. "Maybe," "Clap Yo' Hands," and "Do, Do, Do" were all hits, but they were overshadowed by "Someone to Watch over Me."

The Gershwins' next show, *Strike up the Band*, closed in Philadelphia in September 1927. That temporary setback was partially compensated for by their next smash hit, *Funny Face* (11/22/27; 250 performances), the show that Aarons and Freedley used to open their new Alvin Theater (*see* NEIL SIMON THEATER). The theater and the show were an immediate success. Fred Thompson and Paul Gerard Smith provided the book, which was mainly an excuse for the great Gershwin songs. The conductor was Alfred Newman, who, like Max Steiner, found greater fame as one of Hollywood's top composers. The show subsequently opened a successful engagement in London on November 8, 1928.

FLORENZ ZIEGFELD commissioned George and Sigmund Romberg to compose the score of *Rosalie* (1/10/29; 335 performances); P. G. Wodehouse and Ira supplied the lyrics to the hit show. It opened at the NEW AMSTERDAM THEATRE and starred Marilyn Miller, Frank Morgan, and Jack Donahue. The most famous of the Gershwin brothers' songs was "How Long Has This Been Going On?" The Gershwins' next show was equally successful. *That's a Good Girl* (6/5/28; 365 performances), their third show to premiere in London, opened at the London Hippodrome.

For *Treasure Girl* (11/8/28; 68 performances), the brothers were back at the Alvin Theater under the auspices of Aarons and Freedley. Gertrude Lawrence, Clifton Webb, and Mary Hay introduced a fine score, including "I've Got a Crush on You," "I Don't Think I'll Fall in Love Today," and "Feeling I'm Falling." At year's end George's *An American in Paris* premiered at Carnegie Hall on December 13, 1928. Walter Damrosch conducted the Philharmonic Symphony Society of New York.

Ziegfeld used the Gershwins' talents for his production *Show Girl* (712/29; 111 performances); Gus Kahn collaborated on the lyrics. Ruby Keeler, Eddie Foy Jr., Frank McHugh and Clayton, Jackson, and Durante starred with Duke Ellington's Orchestra in the pit. However, as with many shows of the same period, *Show Girl*'s run was cut short by the Depression. Nonetheless, Ziegfeld again commissioned a Gershwin score, this time for *Ming Toy*. But the Depression hit Ziegfeld hard, and the show was never produced. In the score was a Gershwin song that became an enduring standard, "Embraceable You," later used in the hit *Girl Crazy*.

The 1930s began for the Gershwins with a revival of *Strike up the Band* (1/14/30; 191 performances). The revised version opened at the TIMES SQUARE THEATER. Bobby Clark, Paul McCullough, Blanche Ring, and Dudley Clements starred in the early satire. The score included "Soon," "Strike up the Band," and "I've Got a Crush on You" (previously in *Treasure Girl*).

The Gershwins' next score accompanied another great success. Aarons and Freedley opened *Girl Crazy* (10/14/30; 272 performances) at their Alvin Theater;

Guy Bolton and John McGowan devised the libretto. The cast included Ginger Rogers, Allen Kearns, William Kent, Willie Howard, and, making her Broadway debut, ETHEL MERMAN. The show's orchestra was equally luminous. Among its members were Benny Goodman, Glenn Miller, Red Nichols, Jimmy Dorsey, Jack Teagarden, and Gene Krupa. The show contained five standards: "Bidin' My Time," "Embraceable You," "I Got Rhythm," "But Not for Me," and "Boy! What Love Has Done to Me." Though Ginger Rogers was the nominal star of the show, when Ethel Merman first sang "I Got Rhythm" a superstar was born.

The Gershwins took a brief sojourn in Hollywood to write the score for *Delicious*, released by the Fox Film Corporation on December 3, 1931. Five days later the Gershwins' *Of Thee I Sing* (441 performances) opened at the MUSIC BOX THEATER under the leadership of producer Sam Harris. George S. Kaufman (*see* KAUFMAN AND HART), who had written the first book of *Strike up the Band*, collaborated with Morrie Ryskind, the coauthor of the revised *Strike up the Band*. William Gaxton starred as President John P. Wintergreen in the mildly satirical show. Victor Moore created one of his most successful characters in Alexander Throttlebottom, the hapless Vice President. Lois Moran, Grace Brinkley, and future United States senator George Murphy completed the leads. The score included three standards, the title song, "Love Is Sweeping the Country," and "Who Cares." *Of Thee I Sing* proved to be an enormous success and won the PULITZER PRIZE, the first musical to do so. It played 441 performances.

Following the premieres of George's *Second Rhapsody* on January 29, 1932, and his *Cuban Overture* on August 16, 1932, George and Ira saw *Pardon My English* (1/20/33; 46 performances) open at the MAJESTIC THEATRE with Aarons and Freedley producing. The score contained several hit songs, "My Cousin in Milwaukee," "The Lorelei," and "Isn't It a Pity." *Let 'Em Eat Cake* (10/21/33; 90 performances) was a sequel to *Of Thee I Sing*. The song "Mine" was the big hit from the score. William Gaxton, Victor Moore, and Lois Moran repeated their roles from the earlier show.

While George was working on his monumental opera *Porgy and Bess*, Ira worked on his first collaboration with another composer. The SHUBERT BROTHERS presented *Life Begins at 8:40* (8/27/34; 227 performances) at their WINTER GARDEN THEATRE. The music was written by HAROLD ARLEN and the lyrics by Ira and E. Y. HARBURG. Bert Lahr, Ray Bolger, Luella Gear, and Frances Williams starred in the show. The hit songs included "You're a Builder Upper," "Fun to Be Fooled," and "Let's Take a Walk Around the Block."

George Gershwin's last Broadway score—and what most people consider his masterpiece—was *Porgy and Bess* (10/10/35; 124 performances). The show was presented by the THEATER GUILD at the Alvin Theater. The lyrics were written by Ira and Du Bose Heyward. Todd Duncan, Anne Brown, John W. Bubbles, and Ruby Elzy starred. The show contained George's richest melodies and most theatrical ballads. "Summertime," "My Man's Gone Now," "I Got Plenty o' Nuthin'," "Bess, You Is My Woman Now," and "It Ain't Necessarily So" are among the greatest songs written for the American musical theater.

However, the show received a surprisingly mixed reaction from critics. They couldn't understand whether the piece was opera or musical theater. This inability to place the show in a convenient pigeonhole seemed to throw off their critical acumen. Other performers and the team's close friends knew that the work was a masterpiece, but George in particular was distraught at the critical reaction.

Next Ira again collaborated with another composer, this time VERNON DUKE. The show was the *Ziegfeld Follies of 1936* (1/30/36; 227 performances), which was presented by Ziegfeld's widow, Billie Burke, and the Shuberts. It opened at the Winter Garden Theatre and starred FANNY BRICE, Bob Hope, Eve Arden, Gertrude Niesen, and Josephine Baker. The only hit to emerge from the score was "I Can't Get Started."

George and Ira went to Hollywood to script the songs for three movies. RKO released *Shall We Dance* in May 1937 and *A Damsel in Distress* that November; Goldwyn released *the Goldwyn Follies* in February 1938. While in Hollywood, George began having frequent headaches. At first doctors were unable to find anything wrong. As the illness progressed, it was discovered that he had a brain tumor. After an unsuccessful operation, George Gershwin died. *The Goldwyn Follies* was completed after George's death by Vernon Duke and Kay Swift, who used George's notes. Ira was devastated by the loss of his brother.

Porgy and Bess in rehearsal under the direction of Rouben Mamoulian.

Ira returned to Broadway in a collaboration with KURT WEILL for the score to *Lady in the Dark* (1/23/41; 467 performances), which boasted a book by Moss Hart and opened at the Alvin Theater. The show starred Gertrude Lawrence, Danny Kaye, Victor Mature, and Macdonald Carey. *Lady in the Dark* was one of the first shows to examine psychoanalysis. The subject lent itself to several magnificent dream sequences.

Then Ira wrote a score for the movie *The North Star*, released by RKO in October 1943. He was teamed with an unlikely partner, Aaron Copland; the screenplay was written by Lillian Hellman. A more lighthearted assignment followed when Ira teamed up with Jerome Kern for the movie *Cover Girl*. It was produced by composer Arthur Schwartz (see DIETZ AND SCHWARTZ) for Columbia, which released it in April 1944.

Kurt Weill was again Ira's collaborator for *The Firebrand of Florence* (3/23/45; 43 performances) based on the life of Benvenuto Cellini. The show was a failure, opening at the Alvin Theater. Weill and Gershwin went to Hollywood to supply the score to *Where Do We Go from Here?* The movie was released by 20th Century-Fox in May 1945. Ira returned to New York for his last Broadway show, *Park Avenue* (11/4/46; 72 performances). Arthur Schwartz, producer of *Cover Girl*, was Ira's collaborator. The show was presented by Max Gordon at the Shubert Theatre (see SAM S. SHUBERT THEATRE). The score was a bright spot in an otherwise unsuccessful show.

Following *Where Do We Go From Here?* Ira settled permanently in Hollywood, where he supplied the lyrics to a succession of film musicals. The score for *The Shocking Miss Pilgrim* (20th Century-Fox, 1947) was built around jottings George had left at his death. Ira wrote the *Barkleys of Broadway* (MGM, 1949) with Harry Warren. It would prove to be the last film featuring the team of Fred Astaire and Ginger Rogers. A minor effort, *Give a Girl a Break*, was an MGM film released in 1953. It had music by BURTON LANE. Harold Arlen was the composer of one of Ira's biggest movie hits, *A Star Is Born*. Warner Brothers released the movie, starring Judy Garland and James Mason, in October 1954. Ira's last score was written for Paramount Pictures' *The Country Girl*, with music by Harold Arlen. It was released in December 1954. *Kiss Me, Stupid*, a Billy Wilder film, contained three previously unpublished songs by the Gershwin brothers. It was released by United Artists in December 1964.

The Gershwins' songs live on, though their shows, with the exception of *Porgy and Bess*, are seldom revived. But their songs are still heard in new shows built around the Gershwin brothers' catalogue. Shows such as *My One and Only* and *Crazy for You* have enjoyed long runs with Gershwin songs (especially those written for *Oh, Kay!*) as their basis.

GERSHWIN THEATER. 1633 Broadway, between 50th and 51st Streets. Designer: Ralph Alswang. Original name: Uris Theater. Opening: November 28, 1972; *Via Galactica*.

This theater, originally named the Uris, was the first new Broadway theater built in New York since the EARL CARROLL THEATRE went up in 1931. Scenic designer Ralph Alswang described his theater: "The Uris represents what I think is the total philosophy of a modern musical comedy house—seating, sight lines, acoustics—the economy and aesthetics for this kind of theater." Critics disagreed, calling the theater an ugly barn with poor acoustics and too deep an auditorium. The 1,900-seat theater was built on the site originally occupied by the CAPITOL THEATER, a huge movie palace that critics thought would have served the same purpose as the Uris with more style. However, the Uris was definitely an afterthought. The first priority was to build a massive office building on the site. This was one of the first giant offices in Times Square and was criticized for ruining the low-rise area. Critics at the time prophesied correctly that the Uris was only one of the first of many skyscrapers that would forever change the special qualities of Times Square. Included in the theater is what is referred to as the Theater Hall of Fame. This consists of names of theater greats tacked up on a huge side wall. There is no explanation of who the people are, nor are there any exhibits. There are just the names on the wall. It should also be noted that some of the names are misspelled.

The Uris opened with a short-lived musical, *Via Galactica*, which had music by Galt MacDermot, composer of *Hair*, and lyrics by Christopher Gore. The show ran for only 7 performances. Cy Coleman and Dorothy Fields (see FIELDS FAMILY) wrote the score to *Seesaw* (3/18/73; 296 performances), the next offering at the Uris. *Seesaw*, under Michael Bennett's direction, was not successful. More failures followed in the Uris' early years. A revival of *Desert Song* opened in late 1973 and lasted only 15 performances, and a stage adaptation of LERNER AND LOEWE's film *Gigi* played 103 performances.

In 1975 the theater found no legitimate bookings. Instead the Uris presented a series of concerts by pop stars. The next year, with the short-lived exception of *Treemonisha* (10/21/75; 64 performances), a previously unproduced opera by ragtime great Scott Joplin, the theater hosted more pop concerts and ballet companies. The Houston Grand Opera, which had been responsible for the production of *Treemonisha*, revived *Porgy and Bess* in 1976. It was followed by still more concerts.

Finally the theater had a success with a revival of RODGERS AND HAMMERSTEIN's *The King and I* (5/2/77; 719 performances). The musical featured original cast member Yul Brynner and Constance Towers. Angela Lansbury assumed the role of Anna with Michael Kermoyan as the King while Brynner was on vacation. Lansbury returned in another long-running show, *Sweeney Todd* (3/1/79; 557 performances), which was the Uris' next tenant. The musical had a score by Stephen Sondheim and book by Hugh Wheeler. Len Cariou co-starred as the demon barber of Fleet Street. Todd murdered his enemies, and Mrs. Lovett, the Lansbury character, baked the victims' remains into meat pies. *Sweeney Todd* ran an impressive 557 performances but was not a financial success. Blame was put on the huge theater with its large weekly operating cost and the overblown production necessary to fill its cavernous stage.

Following some bookings of ballet companies, the Uris hosted Joseph Papp's Public Theater production of Gilbert and Sullivan's *The Pirates of Penzance* (1/1/81; 772 performances). The operetta opened with Linda Ronstadt, Kevin Kline, and Rex Smith headlining the cast. Another musical revival, *My Fair Lady* (8/18/81; 124 performances), opened with Rex Harrison repeating his starring role as Henry Higgins and Nancy Ringham playing Eliza Doolittle. Next came *Annie*, which moved from the Eugene O'Neill Theater to end its 2,377-performance run.

The Houston Grand Opera opened a production of Jerome Kern and Oscar Hammerstein II's musical *Show Boat* (4/24/83; 73 performances). On June 5, 1983, during *Show Boat*'s run, the name of the theater was changed to the Gershwin, after composer George Gershwin. The announcement was made during the Tony Awards ceremony. Critics felt that the songwriter would have been embarrassed to have such a poor theater named after him. They also pointed out that the Alvin (*see* Neil Simon Theater) was really the theater that should have been renamed the Gershwin, since both Gershwin brothers had such great successes there.

A lackluster revival of *Mame* (7/24/83; 41 performances), Lansbury's third appearance at the theater, quickly closed. The Royal Shakespeare Company presented two fine productions, *Cyrano de Bergerac* and *Much Ado About Nothing*, in repertory at the Gershwin beginning October 14, 1984. The limited run was extremely successful. Another classic Hollywood musical adaptation, *Singing in the Rain*, opened at the Gershwin in 1985 but was a failure. The theater finally had a long run with Andrew Lloyd Webber's musical *Starlight Express* (3/15/87; 761 performances) though it closed a failure.

The theater, which had long been used for concert presentations of everyone from Frank Sinatra to Barry Manilow to Bugs Bunny, had a difficult time finding a long-term tenant. Jule Styne's final show, *The Red Shoes* (12/16/93; 5 performances) was an ignominious end to a stellar career.

The Gershwin's next show, another revival of Jerome Kern and Oscar Hammerstein II's *Show Boat* (10/2/94; 947 performances) was an altogether happier experience. Director Harold Prince's lavish production ably filled the Gershwin's vast stage.

The revival of *Show Boat* was followed by a series of lackluster revivals including *Candide* (4/29/97; 104 performances) directed by Harold Prince, *1776* (12/3/97; 33 performances), *On the Town* (11/19/98; 69 performances), *Peter Pan* (4/7/99; 166 performances) with Cathy Rigby, and *Tango Argentino* (11/16/99; 63 performances).

The theater finally had somewhat of a success with *Riverdance on Broadway* (3/16/2000; 605 performances). The Gershwin was next occupied by a revival of Rodgers and Hammerstein's *Oklahoma!* (3/21/2002), a transfer from London's National Theatre.

GILDER, ROSAMOND. Critic; b. Marion, Massachusetts, July 17, 1891; d. Tyringham, Massachusetts, September 5, 1986.

Rosamond Gilder's father, Richard Watson Gilder, was editor of *Century* magazine and a well-respected poet. He instilled in his daughter a love for the arts and encouraged her penchant for writing. Her first important work was *Letters of Richard Watson Gilder* in 1916. She was editorial secretary for the National Theater Conference (1933–1936); director of the Playwrights Bureau of the Federal Theatre Project (1935–1936) under the supervision of her close friend Hallie Flanagan; and drama critic and associate editor of *Theatre Arts Magazine* (1925–1948). Gilder sat on the editorial committee of *World Theatre* and was associated with ANTA (*see* American National Theatre and Academy) beginning in 1946. She was also made an honorary member of the London Drama Critics Circle.

In 1947, along with J. B. Priestley, Julian Huxley, Tyrone Guthrie, Jean-Louis Barrault, and Lillian Helman, she founded the International Theatre Institute (ITI). She was the first president of the organization, a post she retained until 1975. At the time of her death, at age 95, she was the honorary president. Under her direction, the organization eventually boasted 65 national centers.

In 1948 she received a special Tony Award, and in 1964 she was admitted to the French Order of Arts and Letters.

Ruth Mayleas wrote in the *Village Voice*:

Gilder was an indefatigable world traveler, leading ITI delegations to over 50 international congresses and conference. Her vitality, intelligence, and acute diplomatic skills helped make ITI the major network of communication for theater professionals in six continents. She brought to the theater she loved a tough mind and high standards, along with the belief that, as the ITI charter states, "Theatrical art is a universal expression of mankind and possesses the influence and power to link large groups of the world's people in the service of peace."

She had the reserve of her class and generation, yet she was also a person of great feeling and warmth. She will be remembered by the many whose lives she touched in her long and exceedingly rich career.

GLOBE THEATRE. *See* **Lunt-Fontanne Theater**.

GOLDEN THEATER. *See* **John Golden Theater; Royale Theatre**.

GOLDSTONE, JEAN STOCK. *See* **Critics**.

GOODMAN, ALFRED. Noted conductor of cast albums of Broadway musicals; b. Nikopol, Russia, April 12, 1890; d. New York, New York, January 10, 1972.

Al Goodman was an important Broadway conductor who occasionally composed for Broadway shows but without much success. He is best known for the recordings of studio cast albums of Broadway shows, which he made primarily for RCA Victor.

After arriving in the United States, Goodman attended Peabody Conservatory on scholarship. In 1907 he made his theatrical debut playing piano in a nickelodeon in Baltimore, Maryland. Following this inauspicious beginning, he joined the Aborn Opera Company as a singer. Apparently his singing wasn't as good as his conducting, and he soon became the company's musical director. The Aborn Opera Company was one of many small opera companies that produced original operas and revivals. Goodman received valuable training with the short runs and many productions that the Aborn company produced every year.

Goodman's talents were brought to the attention of the SHUBERT BROTHERS, who hired him as a staff conductor for the WINTER GARDEN THEATRE. He made his Broadway debut conducting *The Passing Show of 1912*, which opened July 22. This was the first in a series of *Passing Shows* that were the Shuberts' entry in the revue field. The Shuberts, operating under the title Winter Garden Theatre Company, had many artists and performers under exclusive contract. In addition to Goodman, these included composer SIGMUND ROMBERG, lyricist and librettist Harold Atteridge, director J. C. Huffman, choreographer Allan K. Foster, and musical director Oscar Radin. These men worked on almost all the *Passing Shows*. Goodman took over the baton from Radin when Radin was called to conduct another Shubert show. In all, Goodman conducted 14 *Passing Shows* each year from 1912 through 1926, except for the 1919 edition. Among the stars he accom-

Al Goodman conducting for a radio broadcast.

panied were Charlotte Greenwood, Willie and Eugene Howard, Marilyn Miller, John Boles, Ed Wynn, FRED AND ADELE ASTAIRE, George Raft, Blanche Ring, Fred Allen, George Jessel, and Nat Nazzarro Jr. All these stars and more appeared in the yearly series. Unfortunately, no famous songs emerged from the *Passing Shows*. In between Goodman's annual assignments at the Winter Garden, the Shuberts called on him to conduct other shows. These included *So Long Letty* (10/23/16) and *Sinbad* (2/14/18), with AL JOLSON.

Goodman also convinced the Shuberts to give him a chance writing original musicals. The first was *Linger Longer Letty* (11/10/19; 69 performances), one in a series of musicals starring Charlotte Greenwood as the popular Letty. Bernard Grossman supplied the lyrics. Goodman's second composing job was with Bert Grant for *Cinderella on Broadway* (6/24/20; 126 performances). Harold Atteridge provided the lyrics. KELCEY ALLEN wrote in his review for *Women's Wear Daily*, "Haver Dickenson and Walter Brower were engaged as comedians but were not found guilty of the charge."

With Lew Pollock and Gustave Kerker, Goodman wrote *The Whirl of New York* (6/13/21; 124 performances). The modest success of these outings led to more assignments by the Shuberts, including collaborations with Jean Gilbert on *The Lady in Ermine* (10/2/22; 238 performances) and with Edward Ridemus on *Caroline* (1/31/23; 151 performances). He also contributed songs to the *Passing Show of 1922* (9/20/22) and the score to *Dew Drop Inn* (5/17/23; 37 performances). Goodman contributed songs to *Artists and Models* in 1923, 1924, and 1925. This was a short-lived series of annual revues presented by the Shuberts. He also had songs added to the score of *Sky High* (3/2/25) and the score of *Gay Paree* (8/18/25). Although some of these shows were successful, none of Goodman's songs were; he made his mark as conductor, rather than as composer, of some of the greatest Broadway shows.

Meanwhile, Goodman was still conducting for Shubert productions. He was musical director for one of the Shuberts' biggest successes, *Blossom Time* (9/28/21; 516 performances); again, Goodman replaced Radin as conductor of the long-running hit. He worked again with Al Jolson in *Bombo* (10/6/21; 218 performances), which played at JOLSON' 59TH STREET THEATER. In *Sinbad* and *Bombo* Goodman helped Jolson in presenting many of his greatest hits, including "April Showers," "Avalon," "Toot, Toot, Tootsie," "My Mammy," "Swanee," and "Rock-a-Bye Your Baby to a Dixie Melody."

Goodman was musical director for the smash hit *Rio Rita* (2/2/27; 494 performances), with a score by Harry Tierney and Joseph McCarthy. He also conducted *Good News* (9/6/27; 551 performances), with its up-to-date score by DE SYLVA, BROWN, AND HENDERSON. The *New Moon* (9/19/28; 519 performances) boasted a score by Sigmund Romberg and OSCAR HAMMERSTEIN II. Goodman continued his lucky streak with De Sylva, Brown, and Henderson's *Follow Thru* (1/9/29; 401 performances). The last show of the 1920s with musical direction by Al Goodman was *Sons o' Guns* (11/26/29; 297 performances).

During the 1930s Goodman, in the pit of the NEW AMSTERDAM THEATRE, conducted what is probably the greatest revue of all time, *The Band Wagon* (6/3/31; 262 performances). The DIETZ AND SCHWARTZ show starred Fred and Adele Astaire, Tilly Losch, Helen Broderick, and Frank Morgan. Goodman conducted such songs as "I Love Louisa" and "Dancing in the Dark." JEROME KERN and OTTO HARBACH's *The Cat and the Fiddle* (10/15/31; 395 performances) was next. Under Goodman's direction, Bettina Hall, Georges Metaxa, and Odette Myrtil sang such Kern and Harbach standards as "Try to Forget," "She Didn't Say 'Yes,'" and "The Night Was Made for Love."

By now Goodman was considered the top Broadway conductor. Released from his Shubert contract in 1927, he was able to pick and choose his assignments. He chose to work with only the top composers on shows that looked like hits or that had interesting scores. After *The Cat and the Fiddle*, he worked with songwriters Howard Dietz and Arthur Schwartz on *Flying Colors* (9/15/32; 181 performances), which introduced such standards as "Louisiana Hayride" and

"Alone Together." He worked again with Ray Henderson and Lew Brown on *Strike Me Pink* (3/4/33; 122 performances) at the MAJESTIC THEATRE. A revue, *Life Begins at 8:40* (8/27/34; 238 performances), was next with its jaunty score by HAROLD ARLEN, E. Y. HARBURG, and IRA GERSHWIN. The show introduced "Let's Take a Walk Around the Block." *Calling All Stars* (12/13/34; 35 performances) was one of Goodman's few flops on Broadway. His next show, *Music Hath Charms*, was also a flop, opening only 16 days after *Calling All Stars*. Despite a RUDOLF FRIML score, the show played only 25 performances.

Goodman was on the upswing again when conducting more Dietz and Schwartz tunes for *At Home Abroad* (9/19/35; 198 performances). The loosely constructed musical opened with Eddie Foy Jr., Beatrice Lillie, Eleanor Powell, Ethel Waters, and Reginald Gardiner. The score included "Love Is a Dancing Thing," "O What a Wonderful World," and "Thief in the Night." Arthur Schwartz also composed Goodman's next assignment, *Stars in Your Eyes* (2/9/39; 127 performances). This time Dorothy Fields (*see* FIELDS FAMILY) supplied the lyrics for the ETHEL MERMAN starrer. Goodman's last Broadway show was the RODGERS AND HART musical *Higher and Higher* (4/4/40; 84 performances), one of their less-successful shows.

Goodman was a workaholic who often moonlighted on national radio shows. He began his radio work in 1932 and continued after leaving his Broadway conducting chores. Among the shows for which he conducted were *Ziegfeld Follies of the Air, Your Hit Parade, The Fred Allen Show, Millions for Defense, The Family Hour, Star Theater, Show Boat Hour, Your Hollywood Hit Parade*, and *Al Goodman's Musical Album*. He moved to television conducting in 1949. He also continued working on records, conducting 42 studio cast recordings and original cast recordings. His last recording of a show score was for *Fiddler on the Roof* in 1964.

Goodman affected the history of Times Square and Broadway as few others have. Through his conducting of Broadway scores, he helped introduce and set the sound of hundreds of standards. He popularized many of these shows and others through his national radio programs. His records reached still more Americans who might never have heard a Broadway show. In this way he helped carry the spirit of Broadway to thousands of people for almost 50 years.

GREEN, ADOLPH. *See* **Comden and Green.**

GROUP THEATER. The Group Theater, described by itself as "an organization of actors and directors formed with the ultimate aim of creating a permanent acting company to maintain regular New York seasons," was an outgrowth of the THEATER GUILD. The group was determined to follow the tenants of Method acting espoused by Konstantin Stanislavsky and practiced at the Moscow Art Theater. During its decade-long existence during the 1930s, the Group changed the course of American theater.

The Group originated as the Theater Guild Studio, which tried to present somewhat experimental plays for "the masses." Therefore its offerings, while experimental in technique, were easily accessible to mainstream audiences. They began in Brookfield Center, Connecticut, at a summer workshop. Twenty-eight actors took part in the workshop.

The first New York production, *Red Rust* (12/17/ 29; 65 performances), was presented at the MARTIN BECK THEATRE. Other early productions were Waldo Frank's play *New Year's Eve* and Padraic Colum's *Balloon*. However, the breakthrough production was Paul Green's *House of Connelly* (9/23/31; 91 perfor-

mances), which opened at the Martin Beck Theater. The Group organization was led by Cheryl Crawford, Harold Clurman, and Lee Strasberg. With the success of *House of Connelly*, the Group Theater was officially launched as a separate entity from the Guild.

Toward its goal of forming a permanent company, the Group gathered a strong core of actors, including Luther Adler, Ruth Nelson, Morris Carnovsky, Margaret Becker, Art Smith, Phoebe Brand, Elia Kazan, Lee J. Cobb, and Roman Bohnen. The core was augmented by such Hollywood stars as Frances Farmer, Jane Wyatt, and Sylvia Sydney. Conversely, some of the Group's actors went on to earn fame in Hollywood. These included Franchot Tone, J. Edward Bromberg, and John (then Jules) Garfield. Boris Aronson was the preferred set designer.

The Group also had its favorite playwrights. The most frequently produced was Clifford Odets, a one-time actor who decided to pursue playwriting when his one-act play *Waiting for Lefty* won an award from *New Theatre* magazine for plays of social significance.

Odets' first full-length play, *Awake and Sing* (2/19/ 35; 104 performances), was produced at the BELASCO THEATRE. The opening night of *Waiting for Lefty* (based on the 1934 taxi drivers' strike; 1/6/35) at the Civic Repertory Theater was so powerful, the audience rose to its feet shouting, "Strike! Strike!" The play was so well received that the Group found itself presenting it to leftish groups all over the country as well as in London, where it was rapturously received.

Another of Odets' successes was *Till the Day I Die* (3/26/35; 135 performances), which was presented with *Lefty* at the LONGACRE THEATER. Other hits of Odets and the Group were *Paradise Lost* (12/9/35; 72 performances), which opened at the Longacre Theater; *Rocket to the Moon* (11/24/38; 131 performances); and the most successful of all, *Golden Boy* (11/4/37; 248 performances). The Group also had success with the work of other modem dramatists. These included Dawn Powell's *Big Night* (1/17/33; 7 performances), Maxwell Anderson's *Night over Taos* (3/9/32; 13 performances), John Howard Lawson's *Success Story* (9/ 26/32; 121 performances), Sidney Kingsley's PULITZER PRIZE–winning drama *Men in White* (9/26/33; 351 performances), Irwin Shaw's *The Gentle People* (1/5/39; 141 performances), and William Saroyan's *My Heart's in the Highlands* (4/13/39; 44 performances).

The Group was an energetic proponent of a socialistic system. All the members were paid equally regardless of whether they were onstage or not and no matter how large their part was. During the 1932–33 season the Group put up its needier actors in a 10-room brownstone on West 57th Street. In 1933 Stella Adler returned from Paris, where she studied with Stanislavsky, to the group's summer workshop in Ellenville, New York. Adler felt that Strasberg had misinterpreted Stanislavsky's Method, and a rift was created within the company. In 1937 the disagreements grew so strong that Crawford and Strasberg quit, their dissatisfaction increased by recent defections to Hollywood by Tone, Garfield, Odets, Clurman, and others. Robert Lewis assumed control of the Group Theater School for the 1937–38 season. Clurman returned from Hollywood, but although the company was still producing hits, it disbanded in 1941.

In 1947 Robert Lewis, Elia Kazan, and Cheryl Crawford, all members of the Group Theater, founded the Actors Studio. Lee Strasberg became its artistic director in 1951 and brought with him the Method, an acting style that derived from the performer's life experiences. Upon Strasberg's death in 1982 his post was taken over by Ellen Burstyn and Al Pacino. In 1988 Frank Cosaro became the Studio's artistic director.

GUDE, O. J. The leading pioneer of the electric sign; b. New York, New York, March 29, 1862; d. Bad Nauheim, Germany, August 15, 1925.

Gude was nicknamed the "Creator of the Great White Way" after his early experiments in SIGNAGE. He was forced to leave school at 17 because of the death of his father. Gude entered the advertising field and spent the following years with a variety of companies. In 1889 he began his own firm, the O. J. Gude Company. It was a steady success, growing into one of the largest advertising firms in the country. He specialized in representing various food-processing companies.

Gude made history around 1900 when he erected the first electric advertising sign on the site of what is now the Flatiron Building. The sign was an immediate success, although it was modest in size by today's standards. As Manhattan's population moved uptown, so did Gude's sign locations. His most famous sign was the Wrigley's Gum spectacular at Seventh Avenue and 43rd Street above the Putnam Building. It's said that in 1901 Gude coined the term "Great White Way" for Broadway. Gude retired from the business in 1918 because of ill health. He went to Europe for sightseeing and to take the cure, and died there in 1925.

At the time of his death, Gude was chair of the board of directors of the O. J. Gude Company, an outdoor advertising specialist. He also was a director of the Poster Advertising Company and the Van Buren New York Bill Posting Company.

GUILD THEATER. *See* **Virginia Theater**.

GUINAN, TEXAS. Owner of or principal attraction at many speakeasies during Prohibition; b. Mary Louise Cecilia Guinan, Waco, Texas, January 12, 1884; d. Vancouver, British Columbia, November 5, 1933.

Born on a small ranch near Waco, Texas, to Irish immigrants Michael and Bessie Guinan, Mary Guinan learned to ride horses and handle a lariat, and when she was older she enjoyed a brief career as a bronco-buster and received the nickname "Texas." In 1898 she traveled to Chicago for music lessons. Two years later she returned home and joined the companies of Wild West shows. Stricken by the acting bug, she traveled to New York to seek her fame on the stage—but not before she had a two-year marriage.

By 1906 Guinan had found employment in a Gibson girl act on the vaudeville circuit. She then found roles in such early musical comedies as *Miss Bob White, The Hoyden*, and *The Gay Musician*. She also worked for the SHUBERT BROTHERS in their *Passing Show* series at the WINTER GARDEN THEATRE.

A scout from the Balboa Amusement Producing Company "discovered" her and convinced her she could be a screen star in silent westerns. Her first picture was the 1917 release *The Wildcat*. But the picture's opening was overshadowed by America's entrance into World War I.

Guinan claimed she joined the war effort entertaining troops in France. She wrote that she spent the time

> driving an ambulance and working as an entertainer in spare time. I met Albert, King of Belgium—was saluted and entertained by Clemenceau, did social service work with Queen Marie of Roumania. I toured the trenches along with an all-star cast which included Elsie Janis, Mme. Ernestine Schumann-Heink and Elizabeth Brice. Maybe they sang better but I sang louder.

Whether she ever went to Europe is unknown, but it is known that she was in Hollywood in the fall of 1917 and appeared in some more two-reel movie westerns, for which she was publicized as "The Female Two-Gun Bill Hart." (Hart was one of the best-known stars of early westerns.) She often played strong, self-reliant women who were fully the equal of their male co-stars. Some of her many other films were *The Hellcat, The She Wolf, The Gun Woman* (all 1918), and *Little Miss Deputy* (1919)—all descriptive of the characters she played.

She began her own film production company, Texas Guinan Productions, in 1921. But the company was not a success, and a year later she was back in New York. Within the year she was hired as a singer at the club in the Beaux Arts Hotel on West 40th Street. She was no shrinking violet and soon became known for her salty demeanor and brash personality. She had the ability to excite an audience, bantering back and forth with them in a good-natured manner. She soon graduated to emcee, and sales of liquor increased with her newfound position.

The hostess made her fame as the originator of such lines as "Let's give the li'l girl a great big hand" and "Hello, sucker." Other quips ascribed to Guinan are "Never give a sucker an even break"; "Her brain is as good as new"; "It's having the same man around the house all the time that ruins matrimony"; "A guy who would cheat on his wife would cheat at cards"; and "I'm a country girl who came to Broadway to make enough money to go back and live in the country." Once at the El Fay Club a rich (and drunk) patron was throwing around $50 bills. When asked by Guinan where he got his money, he replied, "Dairy produce." Guinan quipped, "Give a big hand to the big butter-and-egg man." George S. Kaufman (*see* KAUFMAN AND HART) took the line and made it the name of one of his plays.

Joe Pani, owner of the King Cole Room at the KNICKERBOCKER HOTEL, took Guinan away from the Beaux Arts. Among the celebrities who visited were Rudolf Valentino, Peggy Hopkins Joyce, and Mrs. W. K. Vanderbilt.

Although Guinan herself was a teetotaler, she reigned over some of the most popular speakeasies in Manhattan. Her acquaintances ranged from mobsters such as Al Capone to clergymen and even the mayor of New York, James Walker. Her oversized personality enabled Guinan to relate as easily to the business executives who were her customers as to the GANGSTERS who were her bosses. The gangster with whom she mainly associated was Larry Fay, a one-time cab driver who used his wiles to gain control of an entire fleet of cabs. In 1924 Fay stole Guinan away from the Knickerbocker so she could oversee his new El Fay Club. The El Fay was in the Parisian style, although Guinan was all-American. Guinan's renown soon spread, and the club did a booming business as a popular hangout for the denizens of Times Square.

When police padlocked the El Fay club, Guinan opened Texas Guinan's at 117 W. 48th Street with Fay as a partner. After the same fate befell that club the Del Fay opened in the same location as the El Fay. When that was closed she raised money on her own and opened the 300 Club at 151 W. 48th Street. Among those discovered by Guinan as performers in her clubs were Lon Chaney, Jack Oakie, Clare Luce, Ruby Keeler, Barbara Stanwyck, and Rudolph Valentino.

On July 4, 1926, Guinan threw a party for golfer Bobby Jones, who had just won the British Open. There were 400 partygoers, including the captain of the *Aquitania*, the former president of Cuba, Jones' friend Walter Hagen (the two golfers did a lively Charleston), and two senators. At 3:00 A.M. two policemen disguised as flappers set off a raid.

After a few days the club reopened and was raided again for the sixth time. On February 16, 1927, police broke up the club. A detective quipped, "Give the little girl a great big handcuff." At the 47th Street police station Guinan gave a show for the photographers, policemen, reporters, Treasury agents, and her patrons. The show went on for 9 hours, finally ending when bail was posted.

Three days later the club was visited by Aimee Semple McPherson, the publicity-hungry evangelist. Guinan asked the audience for "a hand for the brave little woman." Photographers snapped pictures of the two women, opposites in every way. McPherson announced, "This is an experience such as I never had in all my life." She invited Guinan and her troupe to the Glad Tidings Tabernacle on West 33rd Street later that morning. Presumably there would be no rest for the wicked.

Texas Guinan in *The Two Gun Gal*, one of her many films.

Guinan and her girls surprised everyone by showing up at the service, praying and singing along with the congregation. But after more photo opportunities, Guinan exhorted her unrepentant group, "Come on, my chicks, let's get on to the club."

The 300 Club was padlocked by the police for 6 months in 1927. Guinan followed that club with others—the Club Intime, the Salon Royale, the Argonaut—but they were all shuttered by the authorities.

Guinan also made appearances in Chicago clubs on occasion. Although she was hounded by agents, in 1926 she still managed to earn $700,000 in 10 months (over $6 million in 2003 dollars). The next year, notoriety intact, she appeared at the Shubert Theater (*see* SAM S. SHUBERT THEATRE) in the Broadway revue *Padlocks of 1927*—an obvious reference to her run-ins with the law. It ran for 95 performances.

Although her clubs were raided, there was never enough proof that she actually owned the clubs, so she was never prosecuted. And the resultant publicity only heightened the public's awareness and curiosity. But the stock market crash of 1929 put the country in a different mood. Suddenly life was serious and money was scarce. Patrons stopped coming to speakeasies and the entertainment business suffered.

She returned to Hollywood for appearances in somewhat autobiographical roles in two talkies, *Queen of the Night Clubs* (1930) and *Broadway Through a Keyhole* (1933). Between her Hollywood appearances she concentrated on her nightclub-hosting duties. She also appeared in FLORENZ ZIEGFELD's lavish film *Glorifying the American Girl*.

In 1931 she took a stab at a European tour. But France was also in a depression and didn't need an American troupe taking jobs away from French performers. Guinan was angry at her reception: "There's no more liberty here than in Russia. I understand why the French shipped the Statue of Liberty to New York—they don't need her anymore."

She returned to the States and parlayed her experience into a revue titled *Too Hot for Paris*. In many towns she received the same cold shoulder that she was given by the Europeans. The show was banned by several communities, but perhaps they needn't have bothered. Guinan and the world she represented were increasingly passé.

While touring with her show, just a few months before the end of Prohibition, Guinan developed ulcerated colitis. After an unsuccessful emergency operation, as she lay on her deathbed, she proclaimed, "I would rather have a square inch of New York than all the rest of the world."

Before her death Guinan left instructions that she be taken to Campbell's Funeral Home, where she wanted an open casket so "the suckers can get a good look at me without a cover charge." She got her wish—over 12,000 "suckers" viewed her body. The pallbearers at her funeral included O. O. McIntyre, MARK HELLINGER, ED SULLIVAN, Louis Sobol, Paul Yawitz, and Heywood Broun. The journalists were among Guinan's greatest admirers. The funeral cortege went down Broadway and passed the RIVOLI THEATER, where Guinan's name was in lights as star of the motion picture *Broadway Through a Keyhole*. At the cemetery Guinan had a grand, if unruly, send-off. As she herself put it a few days before her death, "I've broken box-office records most of my life. Don't let me flop in death." She didn't; the 2,000 onlookers rioted and ran for the vault. The flowers topping Guinan's casket were stolen, and the vault was damaged by the hysterical crowd.

The *New York Herald Tribune* editorialized: "She was a master showman, and accomplished psychologist. . . . She had ability too, and would have been successful in any one of a dozen more conventional fields. To New York and the rest of the country Texas was a flaming leader of a period which was a lot of fun while it lasted."

The "Queen of Whoopee," as Guinan was dubbed, gave Prohibition some of its livelier moments.

HACKETT THEATER. *See* **Anco Theater**.

HAMMERSTEIN, ARTHUR. Noted producer of operettas on Broadway, and a part of one of America's best-known theatrical clans; b. New York, New York, December 21, 1872; d. Palm Beach, Florida, October 12, 1955.

Arthur Hammerstein, the least flamboyant of the Hammerstein family, is the least remembered. But of all of OSCAR HAMMERSTEIN I's sons, it was Arthur who would have the strongest influence on the American theater. Arthur was one of the most successful Broadway producers of his time. Many of his productions were operettas, primarily by RUDOLF FRIML and OTTO HARBACH. Arthur, unlike such producers as FLORENZ ZIEGFELD, DAVID BELASCO, and GEORGE WHITE, did not put his own stamp on productions, but they were marked by an emphasis on strong production values. His settings, lighting, and costumes were all exquisitely designed and executed.

His father, Oscar Hammerstein I, was Broadway's most important pioneer. Arthur was the second son of the impresario, and it was always assumed that he would enter the family's profession. He began his working life as a building contractor, a job well suited to the needs of his father, who was always planning to build a new legitimate theater or opera house. The Victoria Theater (*see* GAIETY THEATER) on Broadway was the younger Hammerstein's first important job. He supervised the construction of his father's architectural plans. Naturally the Victoria, like many of Oscar Hammerstein's productions, was ready only at the very last minute on March 2, 1899.

In 1905 Arthur was hired by his father to build the Manhattan Opera House down the street from its rival, the Metropolitan Opera House. He inherited his father's interest in opera, and in 1908 he took his first steps toward becoming a producer. The younger Hammerstein's first major move was to sign the great opera singer Luisa Tetrazzini. She repeated her triumphant London success with her American debut at the Manhattan Opera House. Hammerstein's success led to his assisting his father in managing the opera house. He entered into negotiations with financier Otto Kahn, a noted member of the Metropolitan Opera board. The rivalry of the two operations was hurting both institutions. The result of the meetings was that the Hammersteins agreed not to produce opera in New York, Philadelphia, Boston, or Chicago for the decade beginning in 1910. In return, the Metropolitan agreed to pay the Hammersteins more than $1 million.

Later, in 1910, Oscar, looking for new horizons, wanted to go to London. Arthur took a loan on his life insurance to finance his father's trip. When Oscar announced plans to build a new opera house in London, Arthur, fed up with Oscar's money-losing schemes, was so incensed that he vowed never to speak to his father again.

Arthur decided to become a producer himself. His first production, under his father's auspices, was VICTOR HERBERT's newest operetta, *Naughty Marietta* (11/7/10; 136 performances). The show, presented at the New York Theatre, drew heavily on the Manhattan Opera House's talents, including soprano Emma Trentini, Orville Harrold, the chorus, most of the orchestra, and the conductor. The show was an immediate success and contained one of Broadway's finest scores, including " 'Neath the Southern Moon," "Ah! Sweet Mystery of Life," "I'm Falling in Love with Someone," "Tramp! Tramp! Tramp!," and the "Italian Street Song."

Arthur's first solo production and the first of 10 collaborations with composer Rudolf Friml was *The Firefly* (12/2/12; 120 performances), with book and

Arthur Hammerstein (left) and Oscar Hammerstein II with their wives, aboard the ocean liner *Mauritania*.

lyrics by Otto Harbach. Emma Trentini repeated her great success in *Naughty Marietta* with the new show. The songs included "Giannina Mia," "Love Is Like a Firefly," and "Sympathy." The next year Arthur produced another Friml and Harbach show, *High Jinks* (12/10/13; 213 performances). Surprisingly, although the show was a huge hit, the score contained no standards.

In 1914 three of Oscar's sons died. The loss of Abe, Harry, and Willie was an immense blow to their father and caused Arthur, the surviving brother, to forgo his own productions that year. He took over the Victoria, but it was already suffering from the success of the new PALACE THEATER, the opening of which was facilitated by Oscar selling his exclusive right to present vaudeville in Times Square. In 1915 Oscar sold the Victoria as well as the Lexington Opera House and was forced into retirement.

Free to produce on his own again, Arthur presented another Friml and Harbach musical, *Katinka* (12/23/15; 220 performances). He produced two shows in 1917, *You're in Love* and *Furs and Frills*. *You're in Love* (2/6/17; 167 performances) boasted a Friml score with book by Edward Clark and Harbach and lyrics by Clark. *Furs and Frills* (10/9/17; 32 performances) was Arthur's first failure. It had a score by Clark and Silvio Hein, a minor composer. The show did contain an important song, "Make Yourself at Home." It was his nephew OSCAR HAMMERSTEIN II's first professional song.

Arthur also produced two shows in 1918. The first, *Sometime* (10/4/18; 283 performances), had music by Friml and lyrics and libretto by the author of *Naughty Marietta*, Rida Johnson Young. The cast, an unusual blend of talents, featured Francine Larrimore, Mae West, and Ed Wynn. The second was *Somebody's Sweetheart* (12/23/18; 234 performances), with music by Anthony Bafunno and libretto and lyrics by Alonzo Price. In 1919 Arthur produced only one show, *Tumble Inn* (3/24/19; 128 performances). It featured a Friml and Harbach score.

Always You (1/5/20; 66 performances) was Arthur's first show of 1920. It was also the first complete score written by Oscar Hammerstein II. *Tickle Me* (8/17/20; 207 performances), the second of Arthur's 1920 shows, had music composed by Herbert Stothart and book and lyrics by Harbach and Oscar Hammerstein II; Frank Mandel also collaborated on the libretto. A gimmick in *Tickle Me* almost landed Arthur in jail. During the song "We've Got Something," the chorus girls went into the audience and distributed bottles labeled, "Compliments of Arthur Hammerstein, a Tickle from *Tickle* McCarstair's Whiskey." When the Federal Prohibition Enforcement Bureau heard of the STUNT, it dispatched agents to the theater and the next day arrested Arthur in his office. Arthur informed them that the bottles contained only iced tea. *Jimmie* (10/17/20; 71 performances) was the third show presented by Arthur that year. It had the same authors as *Tickle Me*.

Another Friml and Harbach operetta, *The Blue Kitten* (1/13/22; 140 performances), started the new year for Arthur. William Cary Duncan helped on the libretto and lyrics. *Daffy Dill* (8/22/22; 69 performances), a Stothart, Oscar Hammerstein II, and Bolton musical, was the second 1922 show.

For Arthur 1923 was a banner year. The first of his three shows that year, *Wildflower* (2/7/23; 477 performances), was Arthur's first show with VINCENT YOUMANS; Harbach and Oscar Hammerstein II supplied the libretto and lyrics, and Herbert Stothart contributed to the music. It was followed by Arthur's first and last foray into the revue field, *Hammerstein's Nine o'Clock Revue* (10/4/23; 12 performances). The third 1923 show, *Mary Jane McKane* (12/25/23; 151 performances), was written by Youmans, Stothart, Duncan, and Oscar Hammerstein II.

Arthur's sole 1924 production was also his biggest success: *Rose-Marie* (9/2/24; 581 performances). The Friml, Stothart, Harbach, and Oscar Hammerstein II show contained such fine songs as "Indian Love Call," "Only a Kiss," "Pretty Things," "Rose-Marie," and "Totem Tom-Tom." The show broke box office records and earned Arthur $2.5 million. GEORGE GERSHWIN's only operetta, *Song of the Flame* (12/30/25; 214 performances), had additional music by Stothart with book and lyrics by Oscar Hammerstein II and Harbach.

Next Arthur produced *The Wild Rose* (10/20/26; 62 performances), one of the few Friml, Harbach, and Oscar Hammerstein II flops. *Golden Dawn* (11/30/27; 200 performances), an Emmerich Kalman, Stothart, Harbach, and Oscar Hammerstein II musical, might have been a greater success, but by this time operetta was losing its vogue. *Golden Dawn* did contain two Broadway firsts: the first topless chorus girl and the Broadway debut of Archie Leach, who would later become better known in Hollywood as Cary Grant.

Arthur's production of *Good Boy* (9/5/28; 253 performances) was a collaboration among Oscar Hammerstein II, Harbach, Bert Kalmar, and Harry Ruby. It featured Helen Kane, Charles Butterworth, and Borrah Minevitch. One of Arthur's rare forays into musical comedy, *Polly* (1/8/29; 15 performances), was written by Philip Charig and Irving Caesar. *Sweet Adeline* (9/3/29; 233 performances) was Arthur's only production of a JEROME KERN show; Oscar Hammerstein II provided the book and lyrics. Helen Morgan, Irene Franklin, and Gus Salzer starred.

With operettas out of vogue and the Depression hurting Broadway's business, Arthur moved to Hollywood to produce movies. His daughter Elaine had already enjoyed a successful acting career on the screen. But his only production, *The Lottery Bride* (1930), made for United Artists, was a failure. He returned to Broadway.

Arthur's last year of producing included two productions on Broadway that were both failures. A Rudolf Friml and J. Keirn Brennan score was featured at the opening of *Luana* (9/17/30; 21 performances). Arthur's last Broadway show, *Ballyhoo* (12/22/30; 68 performances), had a score by Louis Alter, Harry Ruskin, Leighton K. Brill, and Oscar Hammerstein II. The show starred W. C. Fields.

The failures of Arthur's Hollywood foray and his last two Broadway shows forced him into bankruptcy. At the courthouse he was quoted as saying, "When Mayor Walker comes back into the city I will ask him to take the statue of my father and put it in some public place—possibly around Times Square. It is a curious thing that when he was exactly my age, my father went through the same thing. In 1897 he lost under foreclosure the OLYMPIA THEATER. In a couple of years, when conditions improve, I'll be back again, bigger than ever." But unlike his father, Arthur didn't bounce back. His producing days over, Arthur led a quiet retirement. He dabbled in inventions and even collaborated on a number one song on the hit parade, "Because of You." The 1950–51 hit was certainly a surprise to the family.

HAMMERSTEIN, OSCAR, I. Among New York's greatest theater builders and producers, father of Arthur, and grandfather of Oscar II; b. Stettin, Germany, May 8, 1847; d. New York, New York, August 1, 1919.

Of all the individuals responsible for the emergence of Times Square as the entertainment center of New York, producer and developer Oscar Hammerstein I was the most important. As the 20th century opened, Hammerstein changed the face of opera and theater in America. He produced a range of shows from opera to vaudeville and built more than a dozen theaters in New York, Philadelphia, and London. A born publicist, Hammerstein was arguably the most famous person of his era, with the sole exception of Teddy Roosevelt. "The Father of Times Square" was also the founder of the greatest theatrical family in the history of the American theater. The 5′4″ producer was a striking figure as he sauntered down Broadway. He sported a pointed Van Dyke beard and always carried a cigar. His favorite dress was a Prince Albert coat, striped trousers, and an ever-present hat, which he designed himself. Even today he is the epitome of what people think of as the consummate impresario.

Biographer Carl Van Vechten wrote of Hammerstein, "Surely no adventurer, however gifted or successful, gets half the fun out of his adventuring unless he is able to watch himself all the time and smile and marvel at the tricks and turns of destiny. Hammerstein had this quality." This self-awareness and understanding of the powers of publicity belied the person within. Hammerstein wasn't concerned with personal wealth; he made and lost a number of fortunes without blinking an eye. He lived simply in a small, two-room apartment over the Victoria Theater (see GAIETY THEATER). He once said, "I try to do everything no one ever did before and differently."

Hammerstein was born in Germany on May 8, 1847. He entered a Berlin music conservatory when he was 12. Although he worked hard on the violin, he proved only a fair student. However, he did acquire one thing in the conservatory: his love of grand opera. After the death of his mother, his relationship with his father deteriorated. With the army in his future and an unhappy life at home, the 15-year-old Hammerstein ran away and arrived in New York City in 1863, penniless and unable to speak the language. Like many immigrants before him, he found piecework in a cigar factory at $2 dollars a week. Hammerstein's intelligence allowed him to prosper in the cigar works. He invented many gadgets that he gave to his bosses before he learned of the patent system.

In 1868 Hammerstein married Rose Blau, and they had their first son, Harry, the following year. Harry would, like his siblings, be brought into his father's theatrical business. However, Hammerstein had a distant relationship with his family. His grandson, OSCAR HAMMERSTEIN II, met his grandfather for the first time when he was 7. He expected his sons to become his co-workers, and they did.

Hammerstein quit his job in 1871 against his wife's wishes. He took their savings and invested it in a producer friend's scheme to present opera in German. The opening night proved successful, but the undertaking failed when audiences fell off during the run. The entire investment was lost (the first of many bankruptcies), but Hammerstein was unconcerned. He had a marvelous time and was bitten by the theatrical bug. Although he returned to the cigar business, he now had a new goal: to become a producer himself.

Hammerstein's second son, Arthur (see ARTHUR HAMMERSTEIN), was born in 1872. That same year Hammerstein became an American citizen and patented his first invention: a multiple cigar mold. He received $1,500 from the sale of the patent. The success of his patent sale gave Hammerstein courage. In 1874 he established the *United States Tobacco Journal* with $50. The highly successful journal became a leading voice in the business. Hammerstein followed the lead of other publishers of the day and indulged in a little yellow journalism to drum up advertising revenue. The magazine is still published today.

Also in 1874 Hammerstein acted as guarantor for the opening of his producer friend's Germania Theater. Hammerstein decided that he could write plays and had five premieres at the theater. He even had his incidental music performed at the Germania. The theater survived somewhat longer than the two men's previous theatrical outing. The Germania closed 3½ years later when it became Tony Pastor's.

Hammerstein's third son, William (see WILLIAM HAMMERSTEIN), was born in 1874; another son, Abraham Lincoln Hammerstein, came along two years later. Their mother, Rose, died, and Hammerstein's younger sister Anna was brought from Germany to help him raise his four sons. Two years later, in 1878, Anna left to marry Harry Rosenberg. Their son Walter, Hammerstein's nephew, would also enter the theater business. (He owned the BROADWAY THEATRE, and later established a chain of movie theaters under the Walter Reade name.) After Anna's departure, Hammerstein married Malvina Jacobi. They would later have two daughters of their own, Rose and Stella.

Hammerstein still had the urge to embark on a theater career, and in 1882 he backed a play called *The Perjured Peasant*. The star was Heinrich Conried, who achieved fame in the role. Hammerstein and Conried would be forever linked as enemies. Their disagreements forced the closing of *The Perjured Peasant*. Later, when Conried became general director of the Metropolitan Opera, the feud intensified. Meanwhile, Hammerstein was still involved in the cigar business. He founded the New York Leaf Tobacco Dealers Protective Association and the New York Leaf Tobacco Board of Trade. In 1884 he invented a pneumatic cigar-making machine, a device that would go on to make $1 million. Unfortunately, Hammerstein sold the patent for $6,000.

In addition to opera and tobacco Hammerstein's interests extended to real estate. In 1888 he took the $6,000 from the pneumatic cigar-making machine and a loan against his interests in the *Tobacco Journal* and built an apartment house, the Kaiser Wilhelm, on 7th Avenue between 136th and 137th Streets. He eventually built 24 apartment buildings and 30 houses.

As Hammerstein's interest in the neighborhood increased, he figured that Harlem, then a place of middle-class residences, needed its own opera house. To finance the theater Hammerstein sold the *Tobacco Journal* for $50,000. His first theater the Harlem Opera House, was built on 125th Street between 7th and 8th Avenues. That theater, like all his others, was designed by Hammerstein himself. In what was an amazingly ironic comment on Hammerstein's career, he forgot only one thing in his design: the box office.

The new theater opened in 1889. Among the stars that appeared were Joseph Jefferson, Mme. Modjeska, and Edwin Booth. They insisted on receiving higher salaries because the theater was so far uptown. Jefferson received 90 percent of the gross. The theater was a success, but Hammerstein, typically, lost money. However Hammerstein could always rely on his inventive genius to pull him out of debt. In 1890 he sold another patent that paid him $65,000.

Hammerstein began his lifelong battle with the Metropolitan Opera when its management denied his request to present their stars in Harlem. So he created his own company instead. Soprano Lilli Lehmann was his star and his main draw. The week-long season was a tremendous success, but Hammerstein lost $50,000. Walter Damrosch, conductor for the engagement, remembered Hammerstein's attitude toward the failure: "That didn't faze the indomitable Hammerstein. He ran his hand deep into his trouser pocket, made up the deficit without a murmur, and when everything had been settled, he said to me, 'Someday I will be an impresario.'"

Despite his mixed success with the Harlem Opera House, Hammerstein decided to build another theater in the neighborhood. The Columbus Theater on 125th Street between Lexington and Fourth Avenue opened in October 1890. This time Hammerstein booked vaudeville and minstrel shows into the theater, which ended its first season with 3 weeks of opera. The theater was a success and drew a steady audience.

In 1891 Hammerstein mounted the American premiere of Mascagni's *Cavalleria Rusticana*. Although he held the exclusive rights to the opera, another production was mounted by a competitor taking advantage of a loophole in the copyright laws. Hammerstein's production was a tremendous success and emboldened Hammerstein to increase his empire.

The first Manhattan Opera House was constructed by Hammerstein in Herald Square, on 34th Street between Broadway and 7th Avenue. He offered season subscriptions for $2,500. They were a less than overwhelming success. Without the money to present opera, the theater opened on November 14, 1892, with the play *Lena Despard*. Although it was a tremendous bomb, Hammerstein wasn't particularly concerned. The failure merely proved to him that grand opera was the only thing that would succeed in the new house. He was proven wrong. The opera season was an abject failure. Koster and Bial, successful vaudeville producers, teamed up with Hammerstein to present Koster and Bial's Music Hall in the Manhattan Opera House. It was an immense hit.

Hammerstein hadn't forgotten his foray into writing music for the Germania Theater. He bet $100 that he could write an opera in two days. Hammerstein set to work despite his friends' attempts to distract him by sending cocktails up to his room and placing organ grinders outside his window at the Gilsey House around the clock. The result, *The Koh-I-Noor*, was deemed unproducible, and Hammerstein was refused the $100. Naturally, he mounted the production at Koster and Bial's Music Hall.

Critic James Huneker described the piece: "The first night of *The Kohinoor* was a side-splitting one. The audience, of pure tenderloin variety, laughed themselves blue in the face. I remember that the opening chorus consumed a third of the first act. . . . Two comic Jews, alternatively for half an hour, sang 'Good morning, Mr. Morganstern. Good morning, Mr. Isaacstein,' while the orchestra shifted harmonics to avoid too much monotony." It lost $10,000, but Hammerstein did get his $100.

Hammerstein's show received so much press that on December 22 Frank Dupree presented a burlesque which he titled *Hamm-in-Stein in Distress*.

Hammerstein was never an easy man to get along with, and his relationship with Koster and Bial grew strained; he called the producers "liquor dealers and restaurateurs." George Kessler, a salesman for Moët and Chandon, tried to get Hammerstein to present his girlfriend Marietta diMio at the Manhattan Opera House. Hammerstein disliked both the playboy and the singer. When Hammerstein refused, Kessler approached Koster and Bial. They were only too happy to show Hammerstein who was boss and immediately signed diMio. On opening night Kessler and Hammerstein were seated in the same box. During di Mio's curtain call, Hammerstein stood and booed the singer.

Kessler threw a punch at the producer, and the audience was treated to the sight of the two men fighting. They carried their fight to the street after being forcibly ejected from the theater. The police were called, and both men were arrested.

Koster brought Kessler's bail money but refused to spring Hammerstein. A friend later showed up to post Hammerstein's bail. When the case came to court, the judge ruled that Hammerstein had the right to boo in his own theater. Koster and Bial tried to force him out of the theater, but he sued them and won. In fact Hammerstein proved to be a master of the lawsuit. Once, he had 40 suits pending concurrently. Different accounts report that Koster and Bial paid Hammerstein either $370,000 or $650,000. Hammerstein swore, "When I get through with you, everyone will forget there ever was a Koster & Bial's. I will build a house the like of which has never been seen in the whole world." Hammerstein took his money, and an additional $2 million, and changed history.

In 1895, with his interest in Harlem dwindling, Hammerstein made his most important move. He took an option on a piece of land between 44th and 45th Streets on the east side of Broadway, and on it he built a complex of four theaters, the largest theater group at the time. Although the OLYMPIA created a sensation, it never proved very profitable. The opening was marred by wet paint and a near riot. But the Olympia firmly established Longacre Square, the original name for Times Square, as the new theater district.

Hammerstein featured French music hall star Yvette Guilbert as his star at the Olympia. She drew a large crowd to the theater, and receipts totaled more than $15,000 a week. But in 1896, with his usual penchant for argument, Hammerstein lost Guilbert. He devised an original ballet and put it on in the Olympia. The receipts fell to $4,000 a week. Hammerstein couldn't help but realize his error, and he replaced the ballet with a series of *Living Pictures*. The main attraction of the *Living Pictures* was scantily clad women. Lillian Russell was drawing crowds into the Harlem theaters, and George Bernard Shaw's *Arms and the Man* premiered uptown. Downtown, the less-artistic fare continued. Hammerstein and his sons, now all in the business with their father, were arrested for offending public morals. They were released, and Hammerstein learned the lesson of publicity with the resultant rise in profits at the Olympia.

The success brought on by the publicity didn't last long, however. The president of the New York Life Insurance Company had written Hammerstein that the company would consider co-operating the theater. Hammerstein answered the letter by writing, "I am in receipt of your letter which is now before me, and in a few minutes will be behind me. Respectfully yours,

Oscar Hammerstein." In 1898 the company foreclosed on the Olympia and Hammerstein's two Harlem theaters as well as his 120th Street townhouse. The Olympia was sold at auction to rivals Marc Klaw and Abe Erlanger. Hammerstein was legally barred from the premises. By this time he owed more than $1,000,000.

During this period Hammerstein met a friend on Broadway and gave him a cigar, saying, "I have lost my theaters, my home and everything else. My fortune consists of two cigars. I will share it with you." The story was more than just a humorous anecdote. Hammerstein was by turns despotic and benevolent and seemed unfazed by the roller-coaster quality of his fortunes. He had liquidated his Harlem properties to build the Olympia, and he lost the Harlem Opera House and Columbus when he went bankrupt with the Olympia fiasco. Still, he wouldn't be stopped.

The following year Hammerstein recovered enough to build the VICTORIA THEATER at 7th Avenue and 42nd Street. He raised part of the capital by selling more patents. He announced that he chose the name Victoria because "I have been victorious over mine enemies— those dirty bloodsuckers at New York Life." Ready at the last minute, the Victoria opened as scheduled, and Hammerstein won a suit of clothes on a bet he'd made that the theater would open on time. Hammerstein wore the suit on opening night.

Theater was America's leading form of entertainment. The public followed Hammerstein's rise and fall in the same way current audiences follow the careers of movie stars. Audiences packed the Victoria at its opening, and the theater proved a constant success. Not only did Hammerstein open the path to theater development in Times Square, but his optimism and ability to recover from blows that would have ended the career of a lesser man proved an inspiration to succeeding generations of Hammersteins and other theater professionals. He was once quoted as saying, "I am never discouraged. I don't believe in discouragement. I was not cast down. I merely discovered my inability to do what I thought I could do. That discovery did not fill my heart with tears or regrets, neither did it destroy my self-esteem. To do anything in this world, a man must have full confidence in his own ability. If I haven't confidence in myself, others will not have confidence in me." Hammerstein even appeared on the Victoria stage. When Lew Dockstader, the minstrel man, complained about the difficulty in finding qualified talents, Hammerstein nominated himself. The press was duly informed, and Hammerstein appeared for one performance making his "Debut Extraordinary."

As the century turned, the impresario built the Republic Theater (*see* NEW VICTORY THEATRE) on a plot next to the Victoria. On the shared roof he opened the

Paradise Garden (*see* VICTORY THEATER(1)). The roof garden opened with another of Hammerstein's attempts to write opera, but it was a success nonetheless. The Paradise Gardens featured the Swiss Farm with barnyard animals and New York's first singing waiters. In 1901 Hammerstein leased the Republic to producer DAVID BELASCO, who promptly rechristened it the BELASCO THEATRE. In 1902 Leo Tolstoy's drama *Resurrection*, with Blanche Walsh as the star, became a big hit, running almost two years at the Victoria and netting $100,000 for Hammerstein. However, after the run of *Resurrection* Hammerstein changed the policy of the Victoria to vaudeville. Willie was installed as manager with his father, operating in an office and apartment off the balcony. The Victoria's success led Hammerstein to construct a theater on 42nd Street. When comic Lew Fields (*see* FIELDS FAMILY) leased it, he named it, appropriately, the Lew M. Fields' Theatre (*see* ANCO THEATER). The theater was the first to have a firefighting system in which water was carried from a tank on the roof.

When Macy's moved to 34th Street, the Manhattan Opera House was demolished. Hammerstein decided to take on his old rival the Metropolitan Opera. He built what he declared would be the largest theater in the world, choosing once again the Herald Square area, a few blocks from the Metropolitan Opera House. The New Manhattan Opera House opened on December 3, 1906, on 34th Street west of 8th Avenue. (The theater is now known as the Manhattan Center.) Again, the theater opened just in the nick of time. When asked what he was opening with, Hammerstein responded, "With debts." The 3,100-seat theater's opening was a tremendous success. That success received worldwide notice. Nellie Melba joined the company, and the box office was boosted. The productions were expensive to mount; whenever box office fell off, the debts multiplied. Frank Woolworth, owner of the Woolworth chain, was convinced by Hammerstein to lend $400,000 to the Opera House. Hammerstein secured the talents of Emma Calve and the Opera House turned a profit. Artistically and financially the theater had a successful 1906–7 season—and the Metropolitan suffered its first loss in years. The 1907–8 season began auspiciously with *Tales of Hoffman* and the American premiere of *Thaïs* with Mary Garden singing the lead. In the next few years Hammerstein presented many other notable operas. His son Arthur signed Luisa Tetrazzini to appear in *La Traviata, Rigoletto*, and *Lucia Di Lammermoor*. The American premiere of Debussy's *Pelléas et Mélisande* with Mary Garden in the lead also proved triumphant.

With the Manhattan Opera House a raging success, Hammerstein appointed Arthur to oversee the construction of a new 4,100-seat theater in Philadelphia. Although the Manhattan and Victoria theaters were bringing in profits, the Philadelphia theater's construction costs drained the family's coffers. To raise capital Hammerstein sold the Lew M. Fields' Theatre for $225,000. By the end of 1908 the Philadelphia theater opened to great acclaim. Back in New York Mary Garden opened the Manhattan Opera House in *Le Jongleur de Notre Dame*. She played the boy's role at Hammerstein's insistence and received critical huzzahs. Later that year Richard Strauss' *Salome* was another smash at the 34th Street theater, but the Philadelphia house's fortunes declined.

Part of Hammerstein's reason for opening the Manhattan Opera House was to provide opera for the middle class. He never liked society and hated the snobbish attitude at the Metropolitan. He insulted one of his wealthier backers, and when she withdrew her support, his conductor, Campanini, set sail for Italy. Hammerstein was undisturbed. In 1909 he commenced buying land in Brooklyn, Cleveland, and elsewhere to build opera houses. As his son Arthur observed, "If Father could buy enough plush to make a theater curtain, there would be a theater built around it." A tour of his New York operatic successes to Boston, Pittsburgh, and Chicago proved critically popular but financially draining. In 1910 he mounted the premiere of Strauss' *Elektra*, an immense success. That same season, he presented the debut of singer John McCormack.

The Metropolitan-Manhattan feud wasn't doing either theater any good. Hammerstein met with the Metropolitan's leading backer, Otto Kahn, to arrange some sort of understanding. The result was that the Metropolitan paid Hammerstein $1.25 million to forgo producing opera in New York, Chicago, Boston, and Philadelphia for a period of 10 years. Hammerstein sorely needed the money and accepted the deal. He sold the Philadelphia theater for $400,000, which paid off the mortgage.

Looking for new worlds to conquer, Hammerstein sailed to London on money given to him by his son Arthur. Arthur took a loan on his life insurance to pay the fare. In London Hammerstein bought property where, he announced, the construction of another Hammerstein Opera House would soon take place. As Hammerstein himself commented, "Opera's no business. It's a disease." He kept his promise, and the London Opera House opened on Kingsway in November 1911. The theater appeared at first to be popular, but after seven months, Hammerstein had lost $1 million. In 1913 Hammerstein's fortunes suffered a major blow when he sold the exclusive rights to present vaudeville in Times Square for $250,000. That ended the Victoria's monopoly on the popular art and opened the doors to competition. From that time the Victoria, Hammerstein's sure breadwinner, began its decline. But he had other ideas for the $250,000. He used it to open the

Lexington Opera House, where he intended to present operas in English. Hammerstein felt that the gimmick would get him around his agreement with the Metropolitan. At the Manhattan Opera House he presented comic opera.

The year 1914 proved especially tragic for the impresario. His sons Abe, Harry, and Willie all died. The Metropolitan Opera House sued Hammerstein and won. He was prevented from opening the Lexington Theater as an opera house, and it switched to a movie policy. In 1915, with his fortunes diminished, Hammerstein sold the Victoria and the Lexington. At the age of 68 he bought a home in New Jersey and married Emma Swift. His last years were spent in forced retirement.

On August 1, 1919, the man who, John Philip Sousa said, "has done more for music than any other man in America," died.

Following his death, the *New York Times*' editorial page contained a tribute to the showman:

> In the popular mind Hammerstein's fame rests on the minor aspects of his greatness. . . . His name will always recall the eccentric silk hat of his prime, with a black cigar tilted up beneath it. It will recall his tireless energy, his fertility of resource, his amazing faculty of enlisting the support of men and money, his building of gigantic theater after theater—most of which failed through being located according to ideas of real estate values which were true in themselves but too far ahead of his time. It will recall his cheerful courage in failure and his quick turns of speech at all times. It will recall the amazing publicity expert who used his own eccentricities to their limit for public effect. One sentence reveals vividly the intense workings in his mind, "Nature's greatest mistake is her failure to equip us with a switch to turn off our thought." The restless energy of his mind and his inexhaustible fertility of invention made him, during one brief period, the regenerator of our musical life; but first and always he was a character of almost titanic force and picturesqueness.

HAMMERSTEIN, OSCAR, II. Broadway's preeminent librettist and lyricist, best known today for his successful collaborations with composer Richard Rodgers; b. New York, New York, July 12, 1895; d. Doylestown, Pennsylvania, August 23, 1960.

Oscar Hammerstein II, the son of WILLIAM HAMMERSTEIN, the manager of the Victoria Theater (*see* GAIETY THEATER), grandson of the great theater builder and impresario OSCAR HAMMERSTEIN I, and nephew of noted producer ARTHUR HAMMERSTEIN, was a scion of the greatest theater family of its time. Hammerstein's career as lyricist and librettist was equaled in length and breadth only by that of author, director, and producer GEORGE ABBOTT and by Hammerstein's partner Richard Rodgers (*see* RODGERS AND HAMMERSTEIN). He was among the first authors to attempt a true integration of songs and script in the new American form of musical comedy.

The Right Honorable Earl Attlee, past prime minister of Britain, commented on Hammerstein's career in 1962: "Oscar Hammerstein's vision was not limited by the boundless, yet confined area of the theater. He was deeply aware of the world in which he lived and deeply sensitive equally to human emotion and to human folly. Hatred was his chief abomination. . . . If the world is to be made one, we have to see ourselves as Oscar did, as individual members of a great human family." Attlee caught the thread that ran through all of the writer's works: His concern for understanding among people was his hallmark.

Hammerstein attended Columbia University (1912–1916) and Columbia Law School (1915–1917). It was at Columbia that Hammerstein began writing books and lyrics for his first musicals. In fact, his first collaboration with Richard Rodgers was for a Columbia University show. *Up Stage and Down* (1916) was the show, and the first Rodgers and Hammerstein songs were "Weaknesses," "Can It," and "There's Always Room for One More." A year later Hammerstein had his first song, "Make Yourself at Home," with music by Silvio Hein, interpolated into the Broadway show *Furs and Frills*. His first full score was a collaboration with Herbert Stothart, who would make his mark in Hollywood as an award-winning scorer of motion pictures. Their show, *Always You* (1/5/20; 66 performances), opened at the Central Theater (*see* MOVIELAND). The young lyricist also contributed the libretto for the show, which starred Helen Ford, a future RODGERS AND HART star.

Reviewers were quick to note the young Mr. Hammerstein's talents. The *New York Times* said the "lyrics are more clever than those of the average musical comedy." The *New York World* commented, "Mr. Hammerstein couldn't forget the dear old college days . . . the lyrics are good as a whole, and some of them are keen." The *New York Dramatic Mirror*'s review noted: "Hammerstein appears to be a far better lyricist than librettist. His lyrics have a distinct quality, while his wheezes are rather antiquated. The plot is inconsequential but it is sturdy enough not to be lost, ever."

Hammerstein had greater success with his next show, *Tickle Me* (8/17/21; 207 performances). Herbert Stothart was the composer, and the book was written by Hammerstein in collaboration with OTTO HARBACH and Frank Mandel. Hammerstein and Stothart next came up with *Jimmie* (11/17/20; 71 performances). After *Jimmie* came a play, *Pop*, written with Frank Mandel, but it closed in Atlantic City before opening in New York. Another Stothart show, *Daffy Dill* (8/

22/22; 71 performances), was also a flop. Hammerstein had even less success with *Queen o' Hearts* (10/10/22; 39 performances) at GEORGE M. COHAN'S THEATRE. The music was by Lewis Gensler and Dudley Wilkinson, and additional lyrics were written by Sidney Mitchell.

Hammerstein would have his first big hit in collaboration with Stothart and VINCENT YOUMANS. The show, *Wildflower* (2/7/23; 477 performances), had a book by Hammerstein and Otto Harbach. Its hit song, "Bambalina," had music by Youmans. Hammerstein's *Mary Jane McKane* (12/25/23; 151 performances), with music by Youmans and Stothart, opened at the IMPERIAL THEATRE. Next Hammerstein again attempted playwriting and again found failure with *Gypsy Jim* (1/14/24; 24 performances), written with Milton Herbert Gropper. The two playwrights' next play, *New Toys* (2/18/24; 24 performances), opened and closed quickly at the Fulton Theater (*see* HELEN HAYES THEATER).

Clearly, straight playwriting was not for Hammerstein. He would receive greater acclaim as a librettist and lyricist, and in fact his next show, *Rose-Marie* (9/2/24; 557 performances), proved to be one of his greatest hits. This time RUDOLF FRIML was the composer along with Stothart. Arthur Hammerstein, Oscar's uncle, produced. *Rose-Marie* opened at the Imperial Theatre with Dennis King and Mary Ellis. The title song, "Pretty Things," "Totem Tom-Tom," and Indian Love Call" were all standouts in the score. With *Rose-Marie* Hammerstein had embarked on his quest for the perfect integration between song and story. The program for the show contained the following note: "The musical numbers of this play are such an integral part of the action that we do not think we should list them as separate episodes." In addition to its successful New York run, *Rose-Marie* ran 851 performances in London. The musical proved equally successful on film, with MGM producing three versions, in 1928, 1936, and 1954.

Hammerstein first collaborated with composer JEROME KERN on the show *Sunny* (9/22/25; 517 performances). Harbach worked with Hammerstein on the book and lyrics, and Charles Dillingham produced the musical at the NEW AMSTERDAM THEATRE. *Sunny* starred Marilyn Miller, with Clifton Webb, Joseph Cawthorn, Cliff Edwards, and Jack Donahue. The score was also a hit, with no fewer than three big numbers, the title song, "Who," and "D'Ye Love Me?" achieving fame. *Sunny* played 363 performances in London and was filmed in 1930 and 1941.

Stothart and GEORGE GERSHWIN were the composers on the next Harbach and Hammerstein show, *Song of the Flame* (12/30/25; 219 performances). Perhaps the show's Russian setting was not suited to either Gershwin or Hammerstein. Harbach, Hammerstein, and

Friml's next outing, *The Wild Rose* (10/20/26; 61 performances), was a failure. But Harbach, Hammerstein, and SIGMUND ROMBERG's *Desert Song* (11/30/27; 471 performances) was an immediate and enormous hit. Frank Mandel, co-librettist, was also producer with Laurence Schwab. Vivienne Segal, Robert Halliday, and Lyle Evans sang the exceptional score, which included "The Riff Song," "The Desert Song," "One Alone," and "Romance." The *New York Times* called the score "excellent" and "rather imposing." Hammerstein's book received weaker reviews than his and Harbach's lyrics. The *New York American* reflected the general opinion when it commented, "The book is its weakest point, and even that may 'draw,' for it appeals to those who like silly, sheikish stories, with a dashing He pursuing a shrinking She." The *Desert Song* played 432 performances at the Theatre Royal, Drury Lane, London. Film versions were released by Warner Brothers in 1929, 1943, and 1953.

Hammerstein's next show, *Golden Dawn* (11/30/27; 184 performances), was followed by his first classic musical comedy, the enormously successful *Show Boat* (12/27/27; 572 performances). This legendary musical, with book and lyrics by Hammerstein and music by JEROME KERN, opened at the ZIEGFELD THEATER. *Show Boat* starred Norma Terris, Edna May Oliver, Tess Gardella, Charles Winninger, Howard Marsh, Jules Bledsoe, and Helen Morgan. *Show Boat* was the first show to exhibit Hammerstein's concern with human issues. The show's plot dealt with miscegenation and the problems faced by blacks. The score, including "Bill," "Make Believe," "Can't Help Lovin' Dat Man," "You Are Love," "Why Do I Love You?," and "Ol' Man River," is still considered by many to be the supreme musical theater work. *Show Boat* embarked on a long national tour and then returned to New York in 1932 for an additional 180 performances. *Show Boat* was presented in London for 350 performances and was revived in New York in 1946, 1954, 1961, 1966, 1976, 1983, and 1994. It was filmed in 1929, 1936, and 1951. Hammerstein's next show, *Good Boy* (9/5/28; 253 performances), with music by Herbert Stothart and Harry Ruby, also had lyrics by Bert Kalmar.

The New Moon (9/19/28; 509 performances), with book and lyrics by Hammerstein and music by Sigmund Romberg, opened at the Imperial Theatre. The operetta contained at least six hits, "The Girl on the Prow," "Softly, as in a Morning Sunrise," "Stouthearted Men," "Lover, Come Back to Me," "Wanting You," and "One Kiss." BROOKS ATKINSON stated in the *New York Times*, "It is not merely a good book; it is almost too good." E. W. Osborn, reviewing the show for the *New York Evening World*, called it "a glory, take it for all in all of light opera at its best, as far from the plain musical play as the sun is from the stars."

Hammerstein had another of his flops with *Rainbow* (11/21/28; 29 performances), a collaboration with Youmans. Hammerstein and Kern's *Sweet Adeline* (9/3/29; 234 performances) was a moderate success at Hammerstein's Manhattan Theater (*see* ED SULLIVAN THEATER). It featured Helen Morgan, who introduced the three hits in the score, "Here Am I," "Why Was I Born?," and "Don't Ever Leave Me." In 1931 Hammerstein had a string of failures, including *The Gang's All Here* (2/18/31), *Free for All* (9/8/31), and *East Wind* (10/27/31). None played more than 23 performances. Next, another Hammerstein collaboration with Kern, *Music in the Air* (11/8/32; 275 performances), opened at the Alvin Theater (*see* NEIL SIMON THEATER). "I've Told Ev'ry Little Star," "And Love Was Born," and "The Song Is You" were the hit songs in the score. *Music in the Air* played 275 performances in London and was filmed in 1934.

Hammerstein had two rare London premieres in 1933 and 1934. The first, *Ball at the Savoy* (9/8/33), with Paul Abraham contributing the music, ran 148 performances at the Theater Royal, Drury Lane. The second, *Three Sisters* (4/9/34; 45 performances), was written with Jerome Kern. It also opened at the Theater Royal, Drury Lane.

When Hammerstein returned to the United States, he completed two projects with Romberg. The first was a film, *The Night Is Young*. The second, the musical *May Wine* (12/5/35; 213 performances), opened at the ST. JAMES THEATRE. After that show Hammerstein had more Hollywood assignments. *Give Us This Night* featured music by Erich Wolfgang Korngold. *Swing High, Swing Low* had a screenplay co-written by Hammerstein and Virginia Van Upp. Kern and Hammerstein wrote the score to the 1937 hit film *High, Wide and Handsome*.

Gentlemen Unafraid was Hammerstein and Kern's next stage production. It opened in St. Louis on June 3, 1938, and closed there on June 12. Then it was back to Hollywood for *The Lady Objects* with music by Ben Oakland and lyrics by Hammerstein and Milton Drake; *The Great Waltz*, a film with music by Johann Strauss II; and *The Story of Vernon and Irene Castle*. This teaming of FRED ASTAIRE and Ginger Rogers had a script by Hammerstein and Dorothy Yost.

Hammerstein's bad luck on the stage continued with his next collaboration with Jerome Kern. *Very Warm for May* (11/17/39; 59 performances) at the Alvin Theater contained a fine score, including "All the Things You Are," "That Lucky Fellow," "In the Heart of the Dark," and "All in Fun." Hammerstein had his only collaboration with Arthur Schwartz (*see* DIETZ AND SCHWARTZ) in *American Jubilee*, which premiered at the New York World's Fair of 1940. The Romberg

operetta *Sunny River* (12/4/41; 36 performances) added to his string of failures. Hammerstein was generally thought to be washed up. Aware of the talk along Broadway, he needed a hit to revive his career.

Desperate as he felt for renewal, Hammerstein was nonetheless unprepared for the amazing turnaround he was to enjoy as the lyricist and librettist in the team of Rodgers and Hammerstein, the most successful songwriting partnership in the history of musical theater. The THEATER GUILD approached Hammerstein to collaborate on a new show with Richard Rodgers. Rodgers' longtime partner, Lorenz Hart, was having his own personal problems, and the composer was looking for a new collaborator. The new team's first production changed the course of musical theater and broke most of the commonly held conventions. *Oklahoma!* began a second chapter in Hammerstein's career.

As a retort to all those who said he was washed up artistically, he took out an ad in *VARIETY*, that read:

Holiday Greetings from Oscar Hammerstein 2nd
author of

SUNNY RIVER (6 weeks at the St. James)
VERY WARM FOR MAY (7 weeks at the Alvin)
THREE SISTERS (7 weeks at the Drury Lane)
FREE FOR ALL (3 weeks at the Manhattan)
"I've Done It Before And I Can Do It Again!"

For his next production, Hammerstein chose to adapt Georges Bizet's opera *Carmen*. The show, *Carmen Jones*, opened at the BROADWAY THEATRE on December 2, 1943, to rave reviews. The all-black show was a success, running 502 performances.

Although the team of Rodgers and Hammerstein had their occasional failures, their great successes, *Oklahoma!*, *Carousel*, *South Pacific*, *The King and I*, and *The Sound of Music* introduced a unique voice into the American theater. Rodgers' melodies to Hammerstein's lyrics were more expansive and soaring than those written with Hart. Hammerstein's lyrics and libretti were warm and humane and touched on themes of tolerance and understanding. Critics have accused Hammerstein of resorting to too much sweetness, but his accomplishments with Rodgers should not be underestimated. Rodgers and Hammerstein opened the musical to new forms and formulas.

Oscar Hammerstein died on August 23, 1960. As a tribute, the lights were dimmed on Broadway, and taps was played in Times Square. Dore Schary memorialized him in 1962: "Oscar Hammerstein was a rare man who wrote rare words and accomplished rare deeds. His legacy includes not only the hundreds of lyric words that are part of our lives but also the burning conviction that there can be a better future for us than the atomization of the world."

HAMMERSTEIN, WILLIAM. Son of the great OSCAR HAMMERSTEIN I, father of OSCAR HAMMERSTEIN II, and a legendary impresario in his own right; b. New York, New York, 1874; d. New York, New York, June 10, 1914.

Willie dressed conservatively and was quiet in demeanor, but he was the most outgoing and showy of the turn-of-the-century producers when it came to the theater he managed, the Victoria (*see* GAIETY THEATER). Willie's father was a strict disciplinarian, and his childhood was not an especially happy one. He described it in a letter to his wife: "As a child growing up, I never really had the feeling of belonging. My mother, as you know, died when I was all of four years old, and, although I grew very dependent on my Aunt Anna, she too left to be married very shortly thereafter. When my 'shadow of a father' remarried, I, for one, retreated into myself. More and more I became a loner." Willie raised his own son in the same detached way. His only contact with his son was a kiss good-bye in the morning and hello in the evening. Oscar (*see* OSCAR HAMMERSTEIN II) knew his father loved him, even though he received little affection.

Unlike his father or brother Arthur (*see* ARTHUR HAMMERSTEIN), Willie was not concerned with furthering the theatrical arts or making himself known as an arbiter of taste. He wasn't really interested in the theater. He never attended others' attractions and preferred the quiet life. In contrast with his private home life, his producing style was flamboyant. Willie's chief concern was filling his theaters, which he did in almost any way he could. He booked both typical vaudeville acts and stars of his own making, usually some freak act or personality in the news.

The Victoria was host to the most bizarre performers. The most notorious of these acts was the Cherry Sisters, billed as "America's worst act." The Cherry Sisters more than lived up to their billing; they had to be protected by a net from projectiles tossed from the audience. Willie also made a vaudeville star of Evelyn Nesbitt, the mistress of Stanford White. Nesbitt was billed as "The Girl on the Red Velvet Swing." Nesbitt had no talents, so Willie had a tenor do the singing while Nesbitt did the swinging. After White was murdered by Nesbitt's jealous husband, Harry K. Thaw, and Thaw escaped from prison, Willie arranged for an armed guard to protect Nesbitt. Competitors said that Willie himself had orchestrated Thaw's escape to boost attendance at Nesbitt's performances. Willie even arranged for his own dancers to be arrested for indecent exposure. He was the first producer to use motion pictures between acts, although initially they were used to clear the house. Willie presented freaks, criminals, and wrestlers all in the name of ticket sales.

The onetime Gay Nineties dancer Carmencita made her stage comeback under Willie's auspices, but in fact the real Carmencita had been dead for nine years. Sober Sue was another huge hit at the Victoria Theater. Willie challenged the leading comedians of his day to make her laugh; none ever succeeded. What Willie never explained was that Sober Sue's face was paralyzed. A woman whose acquittal for murdering her husband landed her on the front pages, and subsequently on the stage of the Victoria, asked Willie whether she was being held over. "Not unless you shoot another man," he responded. This led to the theater's being dubbed "the great nut vaudeville house of New York."

Willie managed the Victoria Theater brilliantly. In summer months he would advertise that the temperature inside the theater was 10 degrees cooler than it was outside. To prove it, he showed a thermometer mounted on a hidden block of ice.

Willie's wife, Allie, died in 1910 at the age of 35. The next year Willie married Allie's sister. Also in 1911 Willie expanded the Victoria's repertoire and presented some of the greatest performers of his time: Will Rogers, VERNON AND IRENE CASTLE, FANNY BRICE, Weber and Fields, Buster Keaton, the Dolly Sisters, AL JOLSON, Harry Houdini, Annette Kellerman (the "Million Dollar Mermaid"), and Charlie Chaplin.

Lillian Ross quoted Chaplin's comments on Willie in *The New Yorker*:

> "You know, it was Willie Hammerstein, Oscar's son, who invented pie-throwing. The legend is that Mack Sennett invented it. But when the Karno company worked for Willie Hammerstein, he loved the act, and he gave us a bit of business for the act with the dour drunks." Chaplin lowered his voice a couple of octaves and, putting on a pompous manner, sang, "Hail, morn, smiling morn." He went on, "We had a boy in the box with me, and I used to knock him over. One day, Hammerstein said, 'Why don't you do it with a pie?' So we did. The laughter we got lasted two minutes, which was a long time. Willie Hammerstein had such a sad face. But the *acts* he had. The big time. He had Eva Tanguay. Willie Howard. Acts like that."

When Marie Dressler appeared at the Victoria for a four-month engagement, her accompanist was an unknown musician named JEROME KERN. Willie had discovered Kern and arranged for him to get the job. IRVING BERLIN also appeared at the Victoria as "the composer of the recent hit, 'Alexander's Ragtime Band.'" Willie and Berlin would often shoot craps in the Hermitage Hotel across the street.

Although the Victoria was doing booming business, Willie resigned when he found out that his father planned to sell it. "I left the Victoria Theater because I hoped that by so doing I could save my father from himself," Willie said. Oscar hoped to use the proceeds from the sale of the Victoria to finance a series of opera houses across the country. Oscar decided not to sell the theater after all, and three months later Willie returned. But then Oscar decided to sell the exclusive vaudeville booking rights that belonged to the theater. This enabled the rival PALACE THEATER to thrive, and soon the Victoria's fortunes fell. Ironically, the Victoria was enjoying its most fruitful season when the booking rights were sold.

On June 10, 1914, Willie died at the age of 41. After suffering a mild case of scarlet fever, he entered a hospital and died of Bright's disease. The *New York Times* headlined its notice of Willie's death by writing, "Hammerstein, the Barnum of vaudeville, dead at forty." Just before he died, Willie made his brother Arthur promise not to let his son Oscar II pursue a theatrical career. Luckily, Arthur broke the promise.

HAMMERSTEIN'S MANHATTAN THEATER. *See* **Ed Sullivan Theater**.

HAMMERSTEIN'S ROOF GARDEN. *See* **Victoria Theatre (1)**.

HAMMOND, PERCY. Critic; b. Cadiz, Ohio, March 7, 1873; d. New York, April 25, 1936.

The young Percy Hammond was enraptured with the touring productions coming through his hometown. From the beginning he knew his mind. He ran away from home at age 15 and got as far as Pittsburgh, where he sold papers on the streets and took his earnings to the theaters, sitting high up in the balconies. He then traveled to Washington, D.C., where after almost starving he got a job at the Government Printing Office on the recommendation of Senator John Sherman of Ohio.

After four years with the government, Hammond returned to Ohio and attended Franklin College. He then traveled to a newspaper job with the *Chillicothe News-Advertiser*, eventually becoming the paper's editor. It was there that he met the young George C. Tyler, who was editor of the rival *Chillicothe Gazette*. Hammond wrote of meeting Tyler, "In those days his ambition was to be a showman, mine to be a destroyer of showmen, a protector and avenger of audiences. When in our few friendly moments he would read me extracts from *Spartacus, the Gladiator* or *Richard III*, I would complain that they were neither adequate nor convincing. He went his way, I went mine; he on a freight train with his father's curse, I on a Pullman-palace car paid for gaily by an uncle who was pleased to be rid

Caricature of Percy Hammond, 1927.

of me." Tyler would become renowned as the producer who gave George S. Kaufman (*see* KAUFMAN AND HART) his first play doctor job.

Hammond's train dropped him off in Chicago, where he found work for $8 a week He covered police news for the City Press Association. In 1898 he began a new job as a general reporter on the *Chicago Evening Post*. While at the *Post*, Hammond tried his hand on the stage. He appeared in a bit part opposite Richard Mansfield. After the first performance Mansfield instructed his stage manager that Hammond was "at heart a CRITIC, not an actor. Dispose of him as constructively as you can."

Eugene Field read a particularly florid piece of reporting by Hammond and jokingly suggested that Hammond's editor assign him to the drama desk due to his melodramatic writing style. As Hammond recalled, "The editor took Mr. Field seriously and assigned me to report the sins of the playhouses. I have been doing it ever since."

A year later, in 1909, he moved to the *Chicago Tribune*, where he wrote editorials and dramatic criticism (succeeding Burns Mantle) until 1921. Hammond moonlighted as a press agent for the Grand Opera House. It was there that he learned the backstage ropes of the theater that would color his view of the shows he was reporting.

While at the *Tribune*, Hammond showed his freewheeling style. IRVING HOFFMAN told a story about Hammond and Valeska Suratt, who

> worked in a whorehouse—an elegant and expensive one in San Francisco—run by the Everleight Sisters.
>
> Percy Hammond was a critic for a Chicago paper and knew her at that time. She was a great beauty. Percy was not surprised when she ankled from the whorehouse but he was surprised one night to find her trotting the boards of a Chicago theater as a star of a play he was assigned to cover. He was momentarily taken aback—but he took care of everything when he sat down at his typewriter and wrote "Last night it seemed strange to find Miss Valeska Suratt in a $2.20 house."

Hammond also got into a fight with the SHUBERT BROTHERS and their agent, the remarkably named A. Toxen Worm. Worm barred the critic from their theaters, making it impossible for Hammond to review their plays. In response, the *Tribune* refused to run advertising for Shubert shows. The feud lasted two years, with Hammond winning the dispute.

At the end of the First World War Hammond was sent to France as a war correspondent and returned in 1919. Hammond's last job for the *Tribune* was as a reporter of the Dempsey-Carpentier fight at Boyle's Thirty Acres in Jersey City on July 2, 1921. The piece, a typically excellent piece of writing by Hammond, became his favorite, probably because it wasn't his usual beat.

In 1921 Hammond moved to the *New York Herald Tribune* with the offer of a $25,000 salary to take over the post of drama critic Heywood Broun, who decamped for the *World*. Hammond was held in low regard by many because of his "Chicago reputation." His style was described as

> gracious and pliable without being trivial, learned and leisurely without being pedantic. Where most critics, hounded by deadlines in the small hours of the morning, fell into the habit of making their reviews a report of the play, with the lean, staccato prose of a news reporter, Mr. Hammond made each review an essay. It was invariably concise, whether it was lyrical in praise or acid in denunciation and it was always good reading. He did not always pass judgment on a play; he often damned with faint praise or praised with faint damns, but no one could pass off a mediocre production as gracefully as Mr. Hammond.

Hammond remained at the *Tribune* as drama critic until his death in 1936. Along the way, when there was no show to review, Hammond contributed a column titled "Oddments and Remainders."

Hammond was one of the most influential and respected critics in New York. He wrote his reviews in a small, closet-sized office with a companion bottle of gin. BROOKS ATKINSON quoted Hammond as saying: "Never praise an actress because it will bite you." He was no fan of the use of chorus girls as decoration in shows and once commented about a revue he found risqué, "The producers seem to forget that the female knee is a joint and not an evening's entertainment." Hammond also concluded a review by stating, "I find that I have knocked everything but the chorus girls' knees, and there God anticipated me." He also opined about one production, "The costumes looked as though they had been selected by Helen Keller." This pleased Miss Keller greatly, and she was known to frequently quote Hammond.

In the same vein Hammond wrote of Gaby Deslys, "One bit of apparel came near to disrupting her performance. It was black, and in the back of it were three discomfiting apertures so extensive that they suggested preparedness for a major operation."

Hammond was one of the few critics to admit that their opinions might have been wrong. When he regretted bad reviews for *Ah, Wilderness!* and *Double Door*, he wrote, "In these impressions my judgment, though not my taste, betrayed me. . . . The best I can do now is to admit that I am remorseful, and to withdraw my objections to two of the season's most inexplicable masterpieces."

A profile in *The Stage* began,

> Out of odds and ends of Broadway's chatter you can, if you like, form an image of Percy Hammond. It is a composite gargoyle: something of a bear, who crunches the bones of young actresses in his den; something of a *bon vivant* who, after a good dinner and his third jeroboam, often sits with a chorus girl on each knee and quietly annihilates a room full of New York's smartest and wiliest with his rapier wit. Some of its other fragments are a man who never goes to the office; a grouch who sits glumly on opening nights, glancing neither at royalty on the right nor at Alexander Woollcott on the left; a hard worker who writes his reviews stripped to the waist; a personality who is as difficult to approach as the Pope. There are other items: the actors' enemy, whom Fred Stone once threatened to kill in a Chicago night club; the literary exquisite, who sits alone with his prejudices and his vocabulary, developing the plowman's trade of daily play reviewer into a scimitar-edged art.

Hammond's death from a sudden bout with pneumonia was shrouded in mystery, at least according to John Houseman in his book *Run-Through*. Orson

Welles' so-called voodoo *Macbeth* opened at the Lafayette Theatre in Harlem under the sponsorship of the FEDERAL THEATRE PROJECT. The *Herald Tribune* was a staunchly Republican paper, opposed to Roosevelt and his New Deal policies, including that of the FTP. Hammond began his review, "The Negro Theatre, an offshoot of the Federal Government and one of Uncle Sam's experimental philanthropies, gave us last night an example of de luxe boondoggling."

Houseman writes that some of the African members of the cast, including the witch doctor, showed up in his producer's office with a copy of Hammond's review. They asked, "This review; this is bad?"

"Yes," said Houseman. "This is bad."

The drummer asked, "This man is a bad man?"

"Yes," replied Houseman, with Welles himself adding his agreement: "This is a bad man."

Houseman continues in his book:

> It was reported to us by our distracted stage manager when we arrived at the theatre around noon the next day that the basement [of the theatre] had been filled during the night with unusual drumming and chants more weird and horrible than anything that had been heard on the stage. Orson Welles and I looked at each other, and quickly looked away. For in the afternoon paper, which we had picked up on our way uptown, was a brief item announcing the sudden illness of the well-known critic, Percy Hammond. He died some days later, of pneumonia.

In his obituary in the *Herald Tribune* his manner of writing was explained:

> Mr. Hammond used to write of "my battle with Kronos and the composing room after the plays." The composing room floor was the scene of those battles. He preferred to work there; his office on the editorial floor was dark from one year's end to the next. In recent years he would appear on the fourth floor of the Herald Tribune Building, where the composing room is, and retire to the small private office of Isaiah Bardsley, the superintendent, in a corner, shut off by two stout doors from the hum and bustle of the main room. He would lock the door, open the window, even in coldest winter nights, and set his electric coffee percolator to work.
>
> His habit of brewing coffee in a percolator was acquired in Chicago. He would set the pot at his elbow and empty it while he wrote a review. He couldn't work unless the room was cold and the coffee hot, and he was alone. He would peck away at his typewriter, or as often revert to longhand, oblivious of time and the demands of editions, while the printers fidgeted and wondered how long they would have to hold the presses for him.

Richard Watts Jr. wrote in the same paper,

> Because he was so witty and immaculate a stylist, it was often forgotten that Mr. Hammond was also a critic of unusual sapience. Essentially he belonged to a theatre

that deserved to be more scourged than praised, and so his greatest talent was for pillorying. He was not always completely comfortable with masterpieces and he was a little dubious of earnest aesthetics, but he could scent a fraud a mile away, no matter how beguilingly it might be disguised, and he always smote it magnificently. His greatest praise for something was to say that it was square and his most violent condemnation was to denounce an unworthy play or performance as dishonest. Sham never fooled him, and that is a pretty fine epitaph for any dramatic critic. In the end, though, what fascinated his enthusiasts, chiefly was his devastating scorn. I, for example, will always remember that he said of some players in Chicago who had acted in some work too often, that they had "played it so long they can act it in their sleep which they did yesterday afternoon."

He was a droll, witty man who was missed greatly after his death by both his readers and those he judged, a rare tribute to a drama critic. As proof of his fame, all his co-critics gave tribute in their own newspapers to the excellence and honesty of his writing.

HARBACH, OTTO. Productive Broadway librettist and lyricist of the early 20th century, most famous for his collaborations with composers Rudolf Friml and Jerome Kern; b. Otto Christiansen, then Otto Hauerbach, Salt Lake City, Utah, August 18, 1873; d. New York, New York, January 24, 1963.

In the American theater of the early 20th century there were more than 100 musicals premiering each season. Composers, lyricists, and book writers working at that time often had the opportunity to work on as many as 10 shows a season. Otto Harbach was one such prolific librettist and lyricist. Although much of his work in early operetta and musical comedy has not lasted, several of his songs, particularly those written to music by JEROME KERN, have become classics.

Harbach was born Otto Christiansen of Danish immigrant parents in Salt Lake City, Utah, on August 18, 1873. When Danish citizens were conscripted into the army in the late 1800s, their names were changed to make bookkeeping easier, much as new arrivals to Ellis Island found their names changed. The Christiansens worked on the Hauerbach farm, and their name and their fellow farm workers' names were changed to Hauerbach. After attending Knox College, Otto moved to New York, where he held newspaper jobs from 1902 to 1903. He moved from journalism to advertising for the remainder of the century's first decade.

Hauerbach's first theatrical job brought his first hit song. *Three Twins* (6/15/08), written with composer Karl Hoschna, introduced the favorite "Cuddle up a Little Closer, Lovey Mine." Based on the popularity of the song and the star performance of Bessie McCoy, *Three Twins* ran 288 performances. *Bright Eyes* (2/

Otto Harbach.

28/10; 40 performances) was the next musical by the Hauerbach and Hoschna team. The collaboration after that proved more successful. *Madame Sherry* (8/30/10; 231 performances) was a triumph at the NEW AMSTERDAM THEATRE. For this show, Hauerbach contributed both lyrics and book. The show featured Hauerbach's second hit song, "Every Little Movement." After Broadway the show enjoyed a long tour and many revivals as an early mainstay of the touring circuit. In 1911 the successful team wrote the scores for three shows: *Dr. De Luxe* (4/17/11; 32 performances), *The Girl of My Dreams* (8/17/11; 40 performances), and *The Fascinating Widow* (9/11/11; 56 performances). None of these shows played more than 60 performances, and no standards were to come from their scores. Hoschna died at the age of 34, only five months after the opening of *The Fascinating Widow*, so Hauerbach was forced to find another partner.

Otto found an ideal collaborator in RUDOLF FRIML. Their first show together turned Hauerbach's fortunes around. *The Firefly* (12/2/12; 120 performances) was all the more remarkable for being Friml's first Broadway score and producer ARTHUR HAMMERSTEIN's first producing venture. The show seemed doomed at the start when VICTOR HERBERT, who had signed to com-

pose the score, dropped out due to an argument with star Emma Trentini. Music publishers Max Dreyfus and Rudolf Schirmer encouraged Hammerstein to give the young Friml a chance. Three of the songs—"Giannina Mia," "Love Is Like a Firefly," and "Sympathy"—attained classic status.

The next year, the Hammerstein, Friml, and Hauerbach team contributed *High Jinks* (12/10/13; 213 performances) to Broadway. The score was a superior operetta work, but perhaps because a current, big hit was interpolated ("All Aboard for Dixie," by Jack Yellen and George L. Cobb), it was seldom heard after its initial presentation. In 1914 Hauerbach contributed a libretto only to *The Crinoline Girl* (3/16/14; 88 performances). He then Americanized *Suzi* (11/3/14; 55 performances). Hammerstein, Friml, and Hauerbach teamed up again for *Katinka* (12/13/15; 220 performances). The show had a workmanlike score from which no standards emerged. In 1917 the Hauerbach and Friml team contributed two shows, *You're in Love* (2/6/17; 167 performances) and *Kitty Darlin'* (11/17/17; 14 performances). Also in 1917 Hauerbach, responding to the mounting antagonism toward German-sounding names, changed his surname to Harbach.

Harbach, aware of the public's changing tastes in musical theater, tried his hand at the book and lyrics to a real American musical comedy rather than the American operettas that he had been writing. The result, written in collaboration with Louis Hirsch, was *Going Up* (12/25/17; 350 performances), Harbach's third score and libretto of 1917. Although no lasting songs emerged from the score, the effect of a full-size biplane flying on stage was enough to keep audiences enthralled.

Despite his success in this modern vein, Harbach rejoined Friml for his next two shows, *Tumble Inn* (3/24/19; 128 performances) and *The Little Whopper* (10/13/19; 224 performances). *Tumble Inn* might have achieved a longer run if it weren't for the ACTORS' STRIKE OF 1919. *The Little Whopper* was Friml's first attempt at a more modern style of composing. Arthur Hammerstein produced *Tumble Inn* and also Harbach's next show, *Tickle Me* (8/17/20; 207 performances), with a score by Herbert Stothart. Stothart achieved more fame during his long career on the staff of MGM, where he scored 75 pictures, among them *The Wizard of Oz. Tickle Me* was Harbach's first collaboration on a libretto with OSCAR HAMMERSTEIN II, nephew of Arthur. In all, Oscar collaborated with Harbach on 10 libretti and/or lyrics. Frank Mandel also collaborated on the book. None of the Hammerstein/Harbach/Stothart songs achieved fame.

In 1920 Harbach had another successful collaboration with Louis Hirsch in *Mary* (10/18/20; 220 performances). The show was under the direction of

GEORGE M. COHAN. Its hit song was "The Love Nest." The song later achieved greater fame as the theme song for George Burns and Gracie Allen. Harbach worked on a number of shows during the 1920s, including *Jimmie* (11/17/20; 71 performances), *June Love* (4/25/21), *The O'Brien Girl* (10/3/21; 50 performances), *The Blue Kitten* (1/13/22; 140 performances), and *Molly Darling* (9/1/22; 99 performances). Harbach's next show, *Wildflower* (2/7/23; 477 performances), proved to be one of his biggest successes. Arthur Hammerstein was the producer, and his nephew Oscar collaborated on book and lyrics with Harbach. VINCENT YOUMANS, one of the finest composers of the 1920s, wrote most of the score; Herbert Stothart composed the remainder. Several of the songs became quite popular, and a few became minor standards. The best were "Bambalina" and the title song. Edith Day starred in the show. *Jack and Jill* (3/27/23; 92 performances) featured a young Clifton Webb. *Kid Boots* (12/13/23; 479 performances) had Harbach contributing the libretto in collaboration with William Anthony McGuire.

The team responsible for the success of *Wildflower* was reunited for Harbach's next big hit, *Rose-Marie* (9/9/24; 581 performances), with music by Rudolf Friml and Herbert Stothart. Arthur Hammerstein again produced, and Oscar Hammerstein II collaborated with Harbach on book and lyrics. The score was one of the best of the 1920s, with several songs achieving long-lasting fame, including "Indian Love Call," "The Mounties," the title song, "Pretty Things," and "Totem Tom-Tom." The critics were enthusiastic about the new show, although sometimes in a backhanded way. The *New York Times* admitted that it was "one of the big musical successes of the new season," but it went on to describe the book as "slightly less banally put forward than has been customary." Of the songs the *Times* said, "Several numbers . . . will probably become nuisances before long." The show enjoyed several extensive national tours and international productions in London, Paris, and Berlin. London was an especially enthusiastic city. The show played the Theatre Royal, Drury Lane, for 851 performances. It was revived in London in 1929 for an additional 100 performances, again in 1942 for 149 performances, and yet again in 1960 for 135 performances.

In 1924 Harbach was in the middle of his most productive period. His next show after *Rose-Marie*, *Betty Lee* (12/25/24; 98 performances), had music by Louis Hirsch and Con Conrad and starred Joe E. Brown. Next Vincent Youmans was again tapped for a Harbach show, this time with Irving Caesar collaborating on lyrics with Harbach as he had on *Betty Lee*. The show was *No, No, Nanette* (9/16/25; 329 performances). Almost the direct opposite of *Rose-Marie* in tone, *No, No, Nanette* was the quintessential 1920s musical, with

flappers, fast women, and bobbed hair. The terrific score contained one of the greatest hits of the 1920s, "Tea for Two," with lyrics by Caesar, and "I Want to Be Happy." Louise Groody played Nanette and appeared without her trademark curls. She was also the first star who received a percentage of the box office gross.

Harbach's second show of 1925, *Sunny* (9/22/25; 517 performances), was an even bigger hit than *No, No, Nanette*. It marked Harbach's first collaboration with Jerome Kern; Oscar Hammerstein again collaborated on book and lyrics. Marilyn Miller, one of the biggest stars of the 1920s, headlined as Sunny. Her supporting cast included Clifton Webb, Cliff Edwards, Pert Kelton, and Jack Donahue. The score was one of Kern and Harbach's best and contained many standards, including "D'Ye Love Me?," "Sunny," and "Who?" The show received almost unanimous raves; the sole dissenter was Gilbert Gabriel, who wrote in the *New York Sun*, "Kern's music is spread rather thin. . . . The lyrics are at least workable." Most critics agreed with ROBERT BENCHLEY writing in the old *Life*, "It isn't so much that it is consistently good, but that it has practically no bad spots."

On his next outing, *Song of the Flame* (12/30/25; 219 performances), Harbach collaborated with Hammerstein, Stothart, and a young new composer, GEORGE GERSHWIN; Arthur Hammerstein produced. The show opened to excellent reviews for the sets and costumes and only fair reviews for the score and libretto. It contributed a hit song, "The Cossack Love Song."

The year 1926 started slowly but ended with a bang for Harbach. His fourth show of the year, after *Kitty's Kisses* (5/6/26; 170 performances), *Criss-Cross* (10/12/26; 206 performances), and *The Wild Rose* (10/20/26; 61 performances), was the very popular *The Desert Song* (11/30/26; 465 performances), another Hammerstein and Harbach operetta. SIGMUND ROMBERG supplied the rousing music, with Frank Mandel helping on the book. The score included such standards as "The Riff Song" and "One Alone." A mark of its lasting qualities is the fact that it was filmed three times, in 1929, 1943, and 1953. Amazingly, Harbach had a fifth show open in 1926. *Oh, Please!* (12/17/26; 79 performances) had a book by Harbach and Anne Caldwell and music by Vincent Youmans.

Harbach's first show of 1927, *Lucky* (3/22/27; 71 performances), was followed by *Golden Dawn* (11/30/27; 184 performances). In *Golden Dawn*, Stothart, Harbach, and the Hammersteins were teamed with composer Emmerich Kalman to little effect. The show concerned an English girl captured by an African tribe and saved by an American prisoner of war. The story didn't play much better than it reads, although the score received some nice notices. *Golden Dawn* was notable on two counts, however. It was the debut production at Hammerstein's Theatre (*see* ED SULLIVAN THEATER), and it featured Archie Leach in a supporting role. Leach received more renown later in his career as Cary Grant.

Harbach's output began to slow as the 1920s drew to a close. In 1928 Harbach had only one show, *Good Boy* (9/5/28; 253 performances). Hammerstein produced, and Stothart conducted and composed the score with Harry Ruby. Oscar Hammerstein II and Harbach collaborated with Henry Myers on the script, and Bert Kalmar contributed the lyrics. Two years passed before Harbach's next show, *Nina Rosa* (9/20/30; 129 performances). Harbach contributed the libretto to the Romberg/Caesar score. Broadway's output had fallen off with the advent of the Depression, and Harbach's career suffered accordingly. Royalties assured him a comfortable life, so he was not inclined to work too hard to get projects on.

His next Broadway show was a success with critics and audiences. *The Cat and the Fiddle* (10/15/31; 395 performances) paired Harbach with Jerome Kern. The fine score boasted such standards as "Try to Forget," "She Didn't Say Yes," and "The Night Was Made for Love." The following year saw Kern and Harbach's *Roberta* (11/18/33; 294 performances). Bob Hope, Sydney Greenstreet, George Murphy, Tamara, Lyda Roberti, and Fay Templeton starred along with the California Collegians, whose membership included Fred MacMurray. The score was one of Kern and Harbach's finest, featuring "Smoke Gets in Your Eyes," "Don't Ask Me Not to Sing," "I'll Be Hard to Handle" (with lyrics by Bernard Dougall), "Let's Begin," "The Touch of Your Hand," "Yesterdays," and "You're Devastating."

Harbach's last Broadway show, *Forbidden Melody* (11/21/36; 32 performances), featured a score by Romberg and was one of the last European-style operettas. The show was a disappointing end to a remarkable career. Harbach was a craftsman whose writing certainly inspired others to do their best work.

HARBURG, EDGAR YIPSEL, (E. Y., "YIP"). Famed and witty Broadway lyricist of the Golden Era who contributed to many of musical theater's most popular songs; b. New York, New York, April 8, 1896; d. Los Angeles, California, March 5, 1981.

E. Y. "Yip" Harburg was perhaps Broadway's most complex lyricist. At once outspoken, liberal, and uncompromising, Harburg was also sentimental, romantic, and humorous. He was a man of strong moral and political beliefs who felt tolerance for those whose politics differed from his own. He believed in the power of lyrics and used that power to move audiences both emotionally and artistically in such shows as *Finian's Rainbow* and *Bloomer Girl*.

Yip began as a lyricist while still at New York City's Townsend Harris Hall High School along with schoolmate IRA GERSHWIN. While at City College, Harburg had his work published in Franklin P. Adams influential column, "The Conning Tower." After graduating, Harburg followed in the footsteps of Gershwin and became a lyricist. Harburg's first partner was composer Jay Gorney. After contributing songs to a succession of musical revues, the team struck gold with "Brother Can You Spare a Dime?" which was practically the official anthem of the Depression. The show was *Americana* (10/5/32; 77 performances). Along the way Harburg also collaborated with HAROLD ARLEN, BURTON LANE, and VERNON DUKE. Harburg's wit and social consciousness shone through in all his lyrics.

Three early revues contained hit songs by Harburg. *Walk a Little Faster* (12/17/32; 121 performances) featured Duke and Harburg's classic "April in Paris." People couldn't believe that Harburg had never actually visited Paris but that his inspiration came from a travel brochure. Bobby Clark, Beatrice Lillie, and Evelyn Hoey appeared in the revue. The *Ziegfeld Follies of 1934* (1/4/34; 182 performances) also had a Harburg and Duke score, although it included many songs by other songwriters. The show featured the Harburg and Duke success "What Is There to Say?" *Life Begins at 8:40* (8/27/34; 238 performances) had music by Harold Arlen, and Harburg teamed with his old friend Ira Gershwin. The three songwriters came up with such hits as "Let's Take a Walk Around the Block," "You're a Builder Upper," and "Fun to Be Fooled."

Hooray for What! (12/1/37; 199 performances) was Harburg's first book show, written in collaboration with Arlen. The show starred June Clyde, Vivian Vance, Jack Whiting, and Ed Wynn. Songs included "Down with Love," "Moanin' in the Mornin'," and "In the Shade of the New Apple Tree." The antiwar musical gave Harburg ample opportunity to express his pacifist leanings.

Harburg explored both race relations and women's rights with the show *Bloomer Girl* (10/5/44; 657 performances). The brilliant musical opened with Celeste Holm, David Brooks, Joan McCracken, and Dooley Wilson singing such Arlen and Harburg hits as "Right as the Rain," "The Eagle and Me," "T'morra' T'morra'," and "Evelina." Harburg was professional enough to make sure that he not only made his points but also entertained the audience. Harburg co-directed *Bloomer Girl* with William Schorr.

Harburg's greatest success was certainly *Finian's Rainbow* (1/10/47; 725 performances), written in collaboration with Burton Lane. Harburg also contributed the libretto along with Fred Saidy. *Finian's Rainbow* contained one of the theater's finest scores, including such brilliant songs as "How Are Things in Glocca Morra," "Look to the Rainbow," "Old Devil Moon," and "When I'm Not Near the Girl I Love." His associates felt that Harburg, who at times could be magical and mischievous himself, was closely reflected in the character of Og the leprechaun. *Finian's Rainbow* starred an exceptional cast, including David Wayne, Ella Logan, Donald Richards, and Albert Sharpe.

Flahooley (5/14/51; 40 performances) was a rare failure for Harburg. However, the score, with music by Sammy Fain, featured some excellent songs, including "He's Only Wonderful," "The World Is Your Balloon," and "Here's to Your Illusions." Artistically, *Jamaica* (10/31/57; 555 performances) suffered because it was too often just a vehicle for its star, the singer Lena Horne. The terrific score by Arlen and Harburg included such fine songs as "Ain't It the Truth," "I Don't Think I'll End It All Today," and "Napoleon."

Harburg tackled the Lysistrata legend for his Broadway show *The Happiest Girl in the World* (4/3/61; 96 performances). The music was adapted from the works of Jacques Offenbach, to which he added lyrics that perfectly reflected the Harburg view of the world. Although some thought Harburg's unofficial theme song was "When I'm Not Near the Girl I Love (I Love the Girl I'm Near)" from *Finian's Rainbow*, those who knew him best felt his theme might be "Adrift on a Star" from this show.

Harburg's last Broadway show, *Darling of the Day* (1/27/68; 32 performances), was written with Jule Styne. The show starred Vincent Price and Patricia Routledge. Although the show was a failure, Harburg considered it his *My Fair Lady*. Perhaps not as wonderful as the Lerner and Loewe show, *Darling of the Day* does have an excellent but sadly unappreciated score.

Harburg is also known for his many movie songs, most notably the lyrics for *The Wizard of Oz*.

HARNICK, SHELDON. *See* Bock and Harnick.

HARRIS THEATRE (1). 226 W. 42nd Street. Architect: Thomas W. Lamb. Original name: The Candler Theatre. Opening as a movie theater, May 14, 1914, *Antony and Cleopatra*; as a legitimate theater, August 19, 1914, *On Trial*.

The Candler family, who had made their money from Coca-Cola, built the Candler Theatre on 42nd Street next to the Candler office building, which had been constructed two years earlier. They built the theater for movies but had architect Thomas Lamb design the house so that it could also serve as a fully equipped legitimate theater. The theater proper fronted on 41st Street, but the entrance was on the well-traveled 42nd Street. Its theatrical policy began with the show *On Trial* (8/19/14; 365 performances).

The *Dramatic News* described the theater's architecture:

Entering from the street, one passes through a marble vestibule, the ceiling of which is beautifully stenciled in gold. This leads to a foyer, and from here you pass into a tapestry hall, the walls of which are covered with six loom tapestries by Albert Herter depicting different Shakespearean scenes. The two larger ones represent scenes from *The Merchant of Venice* and *Othello*. The smaller ones are from the comedies. The lobby is exquisitely ornamented with flower panels characteristic of the 18th century school. The whole is carried out in Caen stone and conveys an air of dignity and purity. The passageways and staircases are of a magnitude that shows no attempt at economizing in space.

The auditorium of the Candler, while comparatively small—or, to use the more fitting term, intimate—makes an impression of vastness quite beyond its actual dimensions. The reason of this is its perfection in design and the beauty of its lines and curves. The house is one of the handsomest and most magnificently appointed theatres in New York. The first floor contains 625 seats, while the one balcony, of the cantilever type, seats 575. The architecture is Italian Renaissance; the prevailing tone is mouse color and orange. Carpets and seats are in harmonious keeping with the general scheme, the latter with tapestry backs of twelve different designs, giving an unusual effect to the lower floor. Generous promenades are provided here as well as on the balcony. A feature which cannot fail to create general interest is the very beautiful mural panel which covers the wall of the lower promenade. The subject is a "Fete Champetre," painted in oil by Herter. It is, in the truest sense of the word, a work of art which leaves a most pleasing impression.

The producing team of GEORGE M. COHAN and Sam Harris along with movie magnate George Kleine and his partner Sol Bloom took over the theater's operation. Soon thereafter Kleine and Bloom dropped out, and the two producing partners renamed the Candler Theatre the Cohan and Harris Theatre. They opened their first production, *Object—Matrimony* (10/25/16; 30 performances). After a brief sojourn by *The Intruder* (9/6/16; 128 performances), the theater had a hit with *Captain Kidd, Jr.* (11/13/16; 28 performances) written by operetta librettist Rida Johnson Young. The show starred Otto Kruger.

The theater hosted three offerings in 1917. The first, *The Willow Tree* (3/6/17; 103 performances) by J. H. Benrimo and Harrison Rhodes, had Fay Bainter in the lead. The musical revue *Hitchy-Koo* (6/7/17; 220 performances), the first in a continuing series, starred comedian Raymond Hitchcock, Irene Bordoni, Leon Errol, Grace LaRue, and Frances White. Bordoni was an immediate sensation. The French singer's message,

The producing team of Sam Harris and George M. Cohan.

that sex could be light and fun and gay, shocked Broadway's audiences. An even bigger hit was *A Tailor-Made Man* (8/27/17; 398 performances), by Harry James Smith. The play opened with Grant Mitchell achieving stardom in the leading role. Another long run at the Cohan and Harris Theatre was Anthony Paul Kelly's *Three Faces East* (8/13/18; 335 performances). Violet Heming and Emmett Corrigan opened in the play.

Cohan himself appeared at the theater in *The Royal Vagabond* (2/17/19; 208 performances). The musical was originally written by Anselm Goetzl, William Cary Duncan, and Stephen Ivor Szinngey. Music publisher Isadore Witmark had approached Cohan with the original script. Cohan loved it, but for the wrong reasons. He thought it was a brilliant parody of Ruritanian operettas, or at least would be with a little rewriting. Cohan remembered that Witmark had rewritten his first song's lyrics, so Cohan found it amusing to be able to turn the tables on the publisher. Cohan told Witmark that he and Harris would produce it if Cohan could rewrite it. Witmark agreed, and Cohan opened the "Cohanized Opera Comique" to rave reviews. Cohan contributed music to the show, and songs were also written by Harry Tierney, Joseph McCarthy, and IRVING BERLIN.

Rita Weiman's drama *The Acquittal* (1/5/20; 138 performances) was also "Cohanized." Unfortunately, the show marked the end of the Cohan and Harris producing relationship. Following *The Acquittal*, the musical *Honey Girl* (5/3/20; 142 performances) opened at the theater with a score by popular songwriter Albert Von Tilzer and Neville Fleeson.

When the partnership with Cohan dissolved, Harris took over the operation of the theater. He changed the name to the Sam H. Harris Theatre. There had previously been a Harris Theater (*see* ANCO THEATER), but its name was changed to the Frazee in 1920. *Welcome Stranger* (2/21/21; 307 performances) was the first offering under the banner of the Sam H. Harris Theatre. Next, *Six-Cylinder Love* (8/25/21; 430 performances), William Anthony McGuire's comedy, starred Donald Meek, June Walker, Ernest Truex, and Hedda Hopper in the days before she became one of the most powerful columnists in Hollywood.

The theater hosted one of its most notable attractions when John Barrymore (*see* BARRYMORE FAMILY) starred in *Hamlet* (11/16/22; 101 performances). Producer Arthur Hopkins presented the play at the Harris because his own PLYMOUTH THEATER was occupied with Don Marquis's comedy *The Old Soak*. Hopkins was also producing *Rose Bernd*, featuring Barrymore's sister Ethel. Franklin Adams wrote in his column "The

Sam H. Harris Theatre, 1933.

Conning Tower" on November 18, 1922: "All day at my desk and so in the evening to see Hamlet and J. Barrymore's acting of it the finest I ever saw, and all about it as close to perfection as ever I hope to see, and when my grandchildren say to me, 'This or that is a great Hamlet,' I shall say, 'Ay, but not so fine as Barrymore's.' And I will disinherit those babes." Other critics were equally enthusiastic. Barrymore's portrayal of Hamlet set a Broadway record for the tragedy until Richard Burton's production played for 137 performances in 1964. Barrymore might have played longer, but he was exhausted by the role. On its closing night more than 1,000 people were turned away from the box office.

Edna May Oliver, Eva Condon, and Andrew Lawlor starred in Owen Davis' PULITZER PRIZE–winning drama *Icebound* (2/10/23; 170 performances). Although Davis had a big success with this drama, he was best known as a writer of farce. His *The Nervous Wreck* (10/9/23; 271 performances) was an immediate hit with Otto Kruger, Edward Arnold, June Walker, and William Holden in the cast. The play was later adapted into the musical *Whoopee. One Helluva Night* lived up to its name. The play opened on June 4, 1924, and closed the same evening. *Topsy and Eva* (12/23/24; 165 performances) was a hit musical for the theater. *Alias the Deacon* (11/24/25; 277 performances) was a comedy by John B. Hymer and Le Roy Clemens. The comedy *Love 'Em and Leave 'Em* (2/3/26; 152 performances) was written by GEORGE ABBOTT and John V. A. Weaver. *We Americans* (10/12/26; 120 performances) was a drama starring Muni Weisenfreund, better known later as Hollywood star Paul Muni.

In 1926 Harris sold his interests to the SHUBERT BROTHERS, who booked the theater with film attractions in addition to theater events. The theater wasn't lucky enough to host the hit musical *No, No, Nanette*, but it did host *Yes, Yes, Yvette* (10/3/27; 40 performances). The show had lyrics by *Nanette*'s lyricist, Irving Caesar, and starred Jeanette MacDonald and Charles Winninger. *Congai* (11/27/28; 135 performances), a play by Harry Hervey and Carleton Hildrith, was staged by Rouben Mamoulian and starred Helen Menken. *Mendel, Inc.* (11/25/29; 216 performances), about an eccentric inventor whose wife has to go to work to support the family, starred Alexander Carr and the sometime vaudeville team of Smith and Dale. *Rhapsody in Black* (5/4/31; 80 performances), an all-black revue, had an impressive cast, including Ethel Waters, Valaida Snow, and Eloise Uggams. Songs included "Till the Real Thing Comes Along," by Alberta Nichols and Mann Holiner, and also GEORGE GERSHWIN's "Rhapsody in Blue." The following play, *Sing High, Sing Low* (11/12/31; 70 performances), was a failure, as was *The Black Tower* (1/11/32; 72 performances). Its plot con-

John Barrymore in *Hamlet*, 1922.

cerns Dr. Eugene Ludlow, who attempts to create the perfect statue by using his own special embalming method on real humans. When he tries to subject the heroine to his nefarious scheme, the police arrive in the nick of time.

The Shuberts, like many of their rivals, lost many of their holdings because of the Depression, and the Harris was no exception. The Harris became one of the city's grind movie houses. At first the Nederlanders planned to renovate the theater and make it a Broadway legit house. Then the 994-seat theater was planned to become a twin movie theater under the Times Square Redevelopment Plan; instead it was demolished.

HARRIS THEATER (2). *See* **Anco Theater**.

HART, MOSS. *See* **Kaufman and Hart**.

HAYES, HELEN. One of the greatest Broadway actors of the 20th century; b. Washington, D.C., October 10, 1900; d. Nyack, New York, March 17, 1993.

Playwright Robert Emmett Sherwood once commented that Helen Hayes "seems to regard the theater much as a champion mountain climber regards Everest: it is a challenge to her remarkable determination and courage and skill." Sherwood, writing in the theater magazine *The Stage* was referring to Hayes' reluctance to settle for one stage persona. Rather, she insisted on tackling a wide variety of roles. Most of her characters were genteel and seemingly civilized, but they all had an inner strength and maturity. They were marked by a sort of sly, mischievous twinkle in the eye with a promise of sexuality beneath their refined exterior.

PERCY HAMMOND, writing in the *Tribune*, reported that she was "one of those artists, apparently, who can dare extravagance, and by her charm and her deft obviousness blur the line between acting and an exhibition."

"The First Lady of the American Theater" evinced a talent for acting at an early age, first appearing as Prince Charles in the Columbia Players' production of *The Royal Family* in 1905 at the National Theatre. In 1908, when she was 8 years old, she appeared in three more productions in her hometown: *Little Lord Fauntleroy*, *The Prince Chap*, and the lead in *The Prince and the Pauper*. Her New York debut was in the *Victor Herbert* musical *Old Dutch* (11/22/09; 88 performances), which premiered at the Herald Square Theater. The Gerry Society did not allow children to sing in Broadway shows, so Herbert had Hayes and another actor mime the leading couple's actions as they sang their love duet. Critics said the two children "stole the show." The *New York Herald*'s critic observed that "Miss Helen Hayes, a wee miss, won the favor of the audience by a bit of acting that was refreshing."

Hayes made many appearances on Broadway, and she scored a great success in the role of Cora Wheeler in Booth Tarkington's comedy *Clarence* (9/20/19) at the HUDSON THEATRE. Also in the cast were Glenn Hunter, Mary Boland, and Alfred Lunt (*see* LUNT AND FONTANNE) in the title role. *Clarence* was an immense success and closed after 300 performances. Of Hayes' performance in *Quarantine* (12/16/24; 163 performances), critic Heywood Broun reported that a woman sitting behind him exclaimed, "Isn't she just too cute?" no fewer than 21 times.

The young Hayes desperately wanted to present a more grown-up image when she attacked the part of Cleopatra in George Bernard Shaw's *Caesar and Cleopatra* (4/13/25; 128 performances) at the Guild Theater (*see* VIRGINIA THEATER) under the auspices of the THEATER GUILD. Lionel Atwell played the Roman general. However, the critics seemed to feel that Hayes was more suited to play an ingénue than the Queen of Egypt. Broun stated: "Helen Hayes is probably the most carefully trained and expert of all the younger actresses in America, but I wish she would forget some of her tricks. Her Cleopatra is certainly a half-sister of the little girl in Clarence who would not wash her face."

Hayes' crack at maturity would finally come with WILLIAM A. BRADY's revival of James Barrie's *What Every Woman Knows* (4/13/26; 268 performances). Brady had a lease on the little BIJOU THEATRE and still had 4 weeks left to use it. He approached Hayes to try the role best remembered for Maude Adams' striking interpretation. Despite her nervousness at stepping into Adams' shoes, Hayes took the job, and it proved to be a turning point in her career. JOHN MASON BROWN was among the CRITICS who noticed a change in Hayes' abilities: "In Maggie Wylie [her character in *What Every Woman Knows*] Miss Hayes has grown up, and has recaptured the grace, the charm, and, though I be excommunicated for saying it, the wistfulness of a Barrie heroine. It lights up the whole play and brings out of it the enchantments of pure magic." The play and Hayes were a big hit, playing well beyond the initial 4-week engagement; it later went on tour.

While *What Every Woman Knows* was playing at the Bijou, performances were constantly interrupted by the sound effects accompanying the silent picture *The Big Parade*, playing next door at the ASTOR THEATRE. The cast was relieved when their play closed and went on tour. However, they were disappointed to find that the movie was also playing next door to their theater in Boston!

Coquette (11/8/27; 366 performances), at MAXINE ELLIOTT'S THEATRE, was another success for Hayes. The play marked her emergence as a star of the first order. Her role, written by GEORGE ABBOTT and Ann Preston Bridgers, proved perfect for her talents. George Cukor was the original director of the play, but he was replaced by co-author Abbott. Producer Jed Harris, one of the most hated men in the New York theater, fired Abbott and directed the play himself. Critic Howard Taubman described the character Hayes played as full of sugared malice. Hayes' portrayal served as the basis for hundreds of similar Southern belles in movies and stage plays. Noel Coward announced that "Helen Hayes gave an astonishingly perfect performance. She ripped our emotions to shreds." Hayes toured in the production for 2 years.

Ferenc Molnár's *The Good Fairy* (11/24/31; 154 performances) marked Hayes' return to Broadway after a visit to Hollywood to make several pictures, which received mixed reviews. In *The Good Fairy* Hayes played an almost too-good-to-be-true character, but she managed to make the play enchanting rather than saccharine. Following her return to Hollywood and a starring role opposite Gary Cooper in *A Farewell to Arms*, Hayes received an Academy Award for *The Sin of Madelon Claudet*. Her next great success on Broadway was in Maxwell Anderson's *Mary of Scotland*. Anderson had seen Hayes in *Mr. Gilhooley* (9/30/30; 31 performances). Although it was a failure (audiences would not accept their favorite little actress as a prostitute), Hayes herself received good notices, and Anderson was determined to write her a play. The result was *Mary of Scotland* (11/27/33; 236 performances) in which Hayes played the title role of Mary Queen of Scots. The Theater Guild production opened at the Alvin Theater (*see* NEIL SIMON THEATER). Hayes and the playwright imbued Mary with a bittersweet character. Especially in her scenes with her cousin Elizabeth, she was simply a vulnerable woman forced to assume her role as queen. Burns Mantle wrote:

> Never in a career that began with her childhood and has included many successes has this actress approached the quality of this particular performance. And the answer is not entirely that never before has she had so fine a chance. She has in these last few years been gaining in poise and force and understanding. . . . Here she stands, definitely planted near the top of her profession not, I suspect, to be again shaken from that eminence.

The production enjoyed a long run, although Hayes had to return to her contract with MGM. She was replaced by Margalo Gilmore on June 1, 1934.

In her next stage appearance, Hayes again portrayed a member of British royalty. *Victoria Regina* (12/26/35), by Laurence Housman, opened at the BROADHURST THEATER with Vincent Price costarring. The original script consisted of 32 short scenes. A third of them had been used in the London production. The play spanned Victoria's life from age 17 to 60 and finally to 80. To achieve the effect of age, she had costume designer Rex Whistler make specially padded costumes. She was advised by Charles Laughton to fill her cheeks with apple slices, but when the apples proved too tasty, she replaced them with cotton wool. The final effect was not cosmetic but came from inside Hayes. She patterned her speech and carriage after her paternal grandmother. In her last scene many audience members did not believe it was still Helen Hayes onstage. For her performances as Queen Victoria, she was hailed as the greatest American actress of her generation. After 204 performances, the play closed. It reopened at the Broadhurst on August 31, 1936, for an additional 311 performances. It was then launched on a 10-month tour of the country. While on tour Hayes assembled the company and announced that they would perform special matinees of Shakespeare's *The Merchant of Venice*. Shakespeare would also provide her next Broadway success as Viola in *Twelfth Night* (11/19/40; 129 performances). Maurice Evans played Malvolio in the production at the ST. JAMES THEATRE

Hayes had another moderate run in Maxwell Anderson's *Candle in the Wind* (10/22/41; 95 performances) at the Shubert Theater (*see* SAM S. SHUBERT THEATRE) Alfred Lunt directed Hayes as an actress who attempts to win the freedom of a French journalist from a Nazi concentration camp.

In 1909 the young Helen Hayes was forbidden to sing onstage; in 1946 she was finally given the chance. The occasion was *Happy Birthday* (10/31/46; 564 performances), a play by Anita Loos that opened at the Broadhurst Theater under the auspices of producers RICHARD RODGERS AND OSCAR HAMMERSTEIN. The team wrote a song for the play, "I Haven't Got a Worry in the World." The Hayes character is a frustrated old woman who one day takes her first drink of liquor, then her second, and third, and ends up discovering the human behind the stern facade. The play proved a pleasure to watch and perform. For her performance in *Happy Birthday*, Hayes won the TONY AWARD for best actress; it was the first time the award had been given.

Hayes' first appearance in London's West End came next. The opportunity arose when the great American actor Laurette Taylor died. Before her death, Taylor asked that Helen Hayes be given the opportunity to play Amanda in TENNESSEE WILLIAMS' *Glass Menagerie* if she herself could not. Helen Hayes opened at the Theater Royal, Haymarket, on July 28, 1948.

Hayes had considered retirement, and the death of her daughter Mary in 1949 convinced her to give up performing. But JOSHUA LOGAN enticed her back to the stage with his adaptation of *The Cherry Orchard* entitled *The Wisteria Trees* (3/29/50; 165 performances) at the MARTIN BECK THEATRE. Mary Chase, the author of *Harvey*, had her play *Mrs. McThing* (2/20/52; 350 performances) optioned by the AMERICAN NATIONAL THEATRE AND ACADEMY (ANTA). They convinced Hayes to undertake the title role. Brandon de Wilde was her co-star.

In November 1955 the Fulton Theater was renamed the HELEN HAYES THEATER in her honor. She told George Oppenheimer about her reaction to the news of the theater's renaming:

> I got the news by phone and it seems I was overcome and cried a bit. Then I called Charlie [MacArthur, her husband] and asked him how he felt about being married to a building. He didn't seem to mind. In fact, he paid me a great tribute. He was on the way out and he had on his hat, but when I told him about it, he took it off. It's a pretty important occasion when Charlie takes off his hat.

During the run of *Mrs. McThing*, Hayes' mother, Brownie, died. She received another blow when, on April 21, 1956, her husband, playwright Charles MacArthur, died.

After an appearance in the movie *Anastasia* Hayes returned to Broadway in Jean Anouilh's *Time Remem-*

bered (11/12/57; 248 performances) at the MOROSCO THEATRE. Her co-stars were Susan Strasberg and Richard Burton. Although they had no scenes together, Burton and Hayes immediately took a dislike to each other. The show, however, was a success, winning a second Tony Award for Hayes. Then she played her first role in the Helen Hayes Theater in EUGENE O'NEILL's *A Touch of the Poet* (10/2/58; 284 performances). She played Norah Melody, the bedraggled wife of a disheveled, drunken innkeeper. Eric Portman played the down-at-the-heels Irishman, and Kim Stanley played their daughter. Whitney Brown summed up the critical opinion when he wrote, "Miss Hayes plays the pseudo gentleman's low-born Irish wife with lovely perception and a gift for using tiny and seemingly inconsequential things to build a creature of dimension and earthy grandeur."

In 1966 Hayes joined the repertory company APA Phoenix. Not all her roles were starring ones, but she enjoyed flexing her theatrical muscles and also being away from the pressures of a normal Broadway run. While at APA Phoenix she appeared in *The School for Scandal*, *Right You Are If You Think You Are*, *We, Comrades Three*, and *You Can't Take It with You*. During the next season she was in George Kelly's *The Show Off* (12/5/67; 69 performances). She also appeared in her husband and Ben Hecht's classic, *The Front Page*, at the ETHEL BARRYMORE THEATRE in October 1969, replacing another actress for six weeks.

After her Oscar-winning performance in the movie *Airplane*, Hayes opened opposite James Stewart in Mary Chase's *Harvey* (2/24/70) at the ANTA Theater (*see* VIRGINIA THEATER). Clive Barnes enthused, "She is one of those actors—Laurence Olivier is another, for she keeps the grandest company—where to watch how she is doing something is almost as pleasurable as what she is doing. Her technique is so close to the surface of her acting that it gives it a special blush."

Helen Hayes and Kim Stanley in *A Touch of the Poet*, 1958. Photo by Fred Fehl.

Harvey was her last Broadway appearance and her next-to-last stage appearance.

After 65 years of professional service, Hayes retired from the stage after a 1971 production of O'Neill's *Long Day's Journey into Night* at Catholic University in Washington, D.C. Critics raved about her performance as Mary Tyrone in the harrowing drama. WALTER KERR wrote: "By first creating the facade and by making it halfway plausible, Miss Hayes gained suspense to begin with and a heart-sinking sympathy when, inevitably, the foundation gave way. . . . The standing ovation she received was in order and not simply because she had spent a lifetime being Helen Hayes. It was Eugene O'Neill she was working for, first to last."

HELD, ANNA. Early, famed Broadway beauty; b. Warsaw, Poland, March 18, 1873; d. New York, New York, August 13, 1918.

Anna Held was the first and most famous of the performers in what was called the Broadway Beauty

The comely Anna Held.

Trust. The Beauty Trust referred to all the beautiful women employed on the stages of the Great White Way. Anna Held was the first great star who owed her fame as much to publicity as to talent.

Debate raged as to whether she was born in Warsaw, Poland, or Paris, France; some even speculated that she was actually reared in Illinois. Although the mists created by a great publicity machine obscured her earliest days, her later career is certainly well documented. At 8 she was singing for coins in Montmartre. When she was 12 and an orphan, she found a chorus job at Prince's Theatre in London. The pay was only five shillings, but the dainty chorine rose quickly through the ranks. She soon played throughout the continent, in the Netherlands, Hungary, Germany, and Scandinavia. At 15 she was already featured in Parisian revues.

Like Lillian Russell, Anna Held used her obvious assets to overcome limitations. She certainly looked the part of a Parisian chanteuse. Her 18-inch waist gave her the hourglass form so admired by both sexes. Her first turning point came when she sang what became her theme song, "Won't You Come and Play Wiz Me." The song was adapted from "Die Kleine Schrecke" ("The Little Teaser"). Later in her career, one critic remarked, "It was not an invitation; it was a demand."

Held's second big break came when she was seen by FLORENZ ZIEGFELD at the Palace Music Hall, London. Ziegfeld brought her to the United States, where she made her debut at the Herald Square Theater on September 21, 1896. The play was *A Parlor Match*, by Charles Hoyt. She certainly earned her salary, said to be $1,500 per week. Of her debut the *New York Times* observed, "As a spectacle Mlle. Held is a success, absolute and complete. Her eyes are long, narrow and heavily circled; her nose is straight; her mouth perfect; and as for her chin, people might go some ways to see it without regretting the experience." The *Times* realized that she was not a particularly strong singer and remarked that "she would not be a 'sensation' at all if the idea had not been ingeniously forced on the public that she is naughty."

For her second production, *Papa's Wife* (11/13/1899; 147 performances), Ziegfeld ingeniously forced some more ideas on her public. The most famous publicity STUNT concerned her celebrated milk baths. Ziegfeld was given the idea by playwright Max Marcin who had heard a story about a French woman's daily bath in asses' milk. Ziegfeld adapted the idea for his star by arranging for a New Jersey milkman to deliver 40 gallons of milk to her apartment at the Netherland every day. Newspaper reporters were willing to print almost anything, but at this they balked. So the great impresario brought them up to Miss Held's boudoir, where they could observe her in the bath. She exclaimed, "It is, you see, to take the beauty bath. In

Paris I ate some fish and it brought out a pimple on my wrist. The milk she preserve the creamy complexion." The reporters were convinced, and milk baths became the rage across the country. Ziegfeld kept the story alive by having the milkman sue him for nonpayment.

In *Papa's Wife* Held introduced the second of her great numbers, "I Just Can't Make My Eyes Behave." In this production Ziegfeld again made headlines by decking out his star with $40,000 worth of costumes. One dress, a yellow crepe de chine with poppies embroidered on its skirt, cost $20,000. Around this time it was announced that Held and Ziegfeld had been married in Paris before she came to this country. This wasn't true, but newspapers seemed indulgent and didn't push the issue. She was recognized as his common-law wife when divorce papers were served on him in 1912.

Flo stepped up the publicity campaign as Anna brought in the money. It was reported that she saved the life of a city judge when she overtook his runaway horse with her bicycle. A special railroad car was outfitted in an Oriental style, and Ziegfeld took his breadwinner on the road in two plays, *The Cat and the Cherub* and *A Gay Deceiver*. The provinces were not so liberal as the big city of New York, as witnessed in this article in the *Pittsburgh Post*:

> Police censorship has caused the removal of portraits of Anna Held from the lobby of the Nixon Theater. The piece, which Inspector McQuade especially frowned on, was in a frame almost six feet square and showed a scene in an artistic studio in the second act of *The Parisian Model*. The police refused to countenance the exhibition of her bare shoulders and feet in the theater lobby, and there is speculation and fear as to what will happen to the production when it comes here next week.

Ziegfeld's advance man, under orders from his boss, probably coerced the police to remove the offending poster.

Miss Held made a splash in other musicals: *The Little Duchess* (10/14/01; 136 performances), *Higgledy Piggledy* (10/20/04; 185 performances), and *Miss Innocence* (11/30/08; 176 performances). It was in *The Little Duchess* that Ziegfeld surrounded his petite beauty for the first time with tall, stately showgirls. One critic exclaimed, "The nymphic Anna of the amber eyes pitted her beauty against a dozen others." Of course she held her own magnificently and, in fact, looked all the more rare and beautiful when compared with the long-legged opposition.

Late in her career the SHUBERT BROTHERS managed her while Ziegfeld was concentrating on his Follies (*see* ZIEGFELD FOLLIES). Though she never had as great a success without Ziegfeld as with him, Anna Held remained a top draw at the box office. By this time

Ziegfeld had alienated her affections through his affair with showgirl Lillian Lorraine. After their divorce Ziegfeld married another of his stars, Billie Burke. Anna Held became ill following a road tour of *Follow Me* for the Shuberts. She was diagnosed with myeloma. The constant dieting, which kept her weight around 90 pounds, and her tightly laced corsets hastened the progress of the disease. Her estate was settled at $257,859. Most of this was jewels, including a $100,000 necklace. When her body left Campbell's Funeral Home, 5,000 people watched along Broadway. Ziegfeld was not there, although he sent a huge wreath of orchids for her coffin.

HELEN HAYES THEATER (1). 210–14 W. 46th Street. Architects: Herts & Tallant. Opening: as theater/restaurant Folies Bergère, April 27, 1911; as Fulton Theater, October 20, 1911, *The Cave Man*; as Helen Hayes Theater, November 21, 1955, *Tiger at the Gates*.

Producers Henry B. Harris and former musician (and later head of Famous Players-Lasky) Jesse Lasky opened a Broadway branch of the Parisian nightclub Folies Bergère on April 27, 1911. They hired the architectural firm of HERTS & TALLANT, then the premiere theater architects in New York, to design the nightclub. It would prove to be the architects' last theater design. Herts & Tallant designed a Louis XVI–style auditorium with tables and chairs on the orchestra level and front mezzanine. The back of the first balcony and the second balcony contained conventional theater seating. The kitchen was located in the theater's basement.

The space was designed as a theater/restaurant where patrons could enjoy a meal followed by a three-act show, usually three different comedies. The club, which some consider the first American nightclub, was not successful enough to continue as a cabaret largely because of its small 636-seat capacity and because fewer than half the seats were given over to table dining. The owners renovated the space into a legitimate theater and called it the Fulton.

The theater was a moderate success from the beginning. *Linger Longer Letty* (11/20/19; 69 performances) was written by AL GOODMAN, Bernard Grossman, and Anne Nichols. Charlotte Greenwood starred in this production, an installment in one of the first musical comedy series to be based on one character. Letty Pepper, played by Greenwood, was a favorite of audiences, especially when she kicked her legs high over her head. *Linger Longer Letty*'s one big hit song, "Oh by Jingo, Oh by Gee," was written by Albert Von Tilzer and Lew Brown (*see* DE SYLVA, BROWN AND HENDERSON).

In 1921 A. L. Erlanger took over the theater and hired Joseph Urban to remodel the interior. Urban

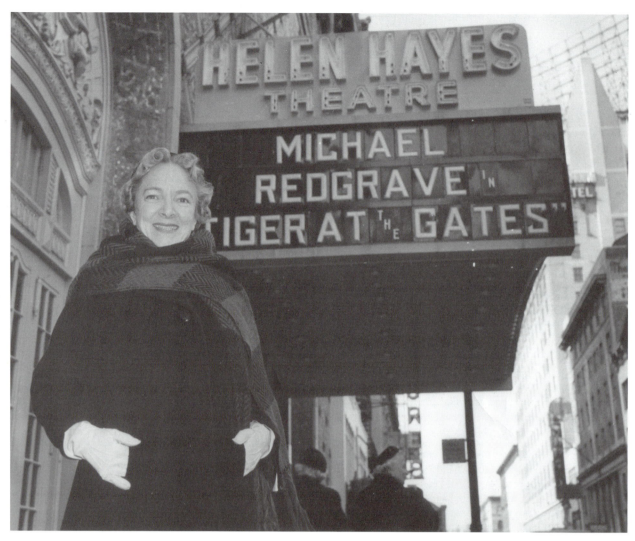

Helen Hayes standing outside the newly renamed Helen Hayes Theatre in 1955.

painted over William DeLeftwich Dodge's murals, including "Vaudeville Paying Homage to Les Folies-Bergeres," which topped the proscenium. The first production under the new management was Anne Nichols' *Abie's Irish Rose* (5/23/1922; 2,237 performances). Today the play is seen as hopelessly dated, but at the time it was produced it struck a chord with audiences. Though most critics saw it as the sitcom it was, it soon became the longest running play in Broadway history, a record it retained until *Tobacco Road* passed it in the 1930s. *Abie's Irish Rose* is currently the third longest-running play in Broadway history (surpassed by *Life with Father* and *Tobacco Road*). Nichols' play moved to several theaters before completing its run.

In *Orange Blossoms* (9/19/22; 95 performances) was VICTOR HERBERT's last musical comedy produced in his lifetime. Edith Day introduced a great Herbert standard, "A Kiss in the Dark." Despite many pluses, the show received mixed reviews. Ticket prices were cut from $4.00 to $3.50 to help attract audiences, but it didn't help, and the show closed.

Nifties of 1923 (9/25/23; 47 performances) was a failure despite a score by such contributors as Eubie Blake, Noble Sissle (*see* SISSLE AND BLAKE), GEORGE AND IRA GERSHWIN, Irving Caesar, Harry Ruby, and Bert Kalmar. However, Ira Gershwin (writing under his pseudonym Arthur Francis) wrote lyrics to music by Raymond Hubbell, not for his brother; Irving Caesar provided the lyrics to the song by George Gershwin. Gus Van and Joe Schenck headed the cast.

Sitting Pretty (4/8/24; 95 performances) was a JEROME KERN, P. G. Wodehouse, and GUY BOLTON musical in the same vein as their Princess Theater shows: small, intimate, American-themed productions. The musical director was Max Steiner. It might have run longer had composer Kern not banned others from performing the show's songs on radio, in clubs, or on records. The composer was distraught over the treatment his tunes had received by modern orchestrators and arrangers. As he put it:

None of our music now reaches the public as we wrote it, except in the theater. It is so distorted by jazz orchestras as to be almost unrecognizable. A composer should be able to protect his score just as an author does his manuscripts. No author would permit pirated editions of his work in which his phraseology and punctuation were changed, thereby giving to his work a meaning entirely different from which he intended.

Kern went on to further lambaste the new American jazz.

There is no such thing as jazz music per se, at least nothing that may honestly be called original and characteristically American. The Gypsy orchestra of Hungary knew and used similar methods years ago, but they were artists and knew how and when to apply these methods.

A drama that would, in another medium, change the history of entertainment opened at the Fulton. The play was *The Jazz Singer* (9/14/25; 315 performances), which was later made into the revolutionary talking picture by Warner Brothers, with stage great AL JOLSON in the lead. The original play was written by Samson Raphaelson and starred George Jessel as the cantor's son who wants a life in the theater rather than a life devoted to religion.

Beatrice Lillie appeared in her first American book musical, *Oh, Please!* (12/12/26; 79 performances) at the Fulton. The hit song was "Like She Loves Me." The VINCENT YOUMANS score had lyrics by OTTO HARBACH and Anne Caldwell. Next Hamilton Deane and John Balderston were the playwrights responsible for scaring the wits out of audiences at the Fulton Theater with their play *Dracula* (10/5/27; 265 performances), based on Bram Stoker's novel. The play starred Nedda Harrigan (daughter of Ned Harrigan and wife of JOSHUA LOGAN) and Dorothy Peterson as Lucy Harker. The Count was played by Bela Lugosi, who later replayed the character in many motion pictures. Lugosi became a star with *Dracula*, but despite his excellence as a classical actor, he became typecast in the role. The first of Leonard Sillman's *New Faces* (3/15/34; 148 performances) revues introduced actors Imogene Coca, Hildegard Halliday, and James Shelton to New York audiences—but by far the greatest new face was that of Henry Fonda. The score's hit songs, written by a variety of composers, were "My Last Affair" and "The Gutter Song."

Another long running comedy, *Arsenic and Old Lace* (1/10/41; 1,444 performances), was the next attraction at the Fulton. The comedy, by Joseph Kesselring with an assist by Howard Lindsay and Russel Crouse, starred Josephine Hull and Jean Adair as two maiden aunts who bury a number of lonely old men

Jean Adair, Josephine Hull, and Boris Karloff in *Arsenic and Old Lace*, 1941.

in their basement. Also featured were Allyn Joslyn, John Alexander, Edgar Stehli, and Boris Karloff.

Lillian Hellman's play *The Searching Wind* (4/12/44; 326 performances) starred Montgomery Clift and Dudley Diggs in the drama, which showed how too much sentimentality can disguise true feelings and lead to ruin. IRVING HOFFMAN, writing in the *Hollywood Reporter*, decided that the play "was all wind." Arnaud D'Usseau and James Gow's play *Deep Are the Roots* (9/26/45; 477 performances) explored the problems of black veterans returning from World War II. The drama starred Barbara Bel Geddes, Gordon Heath, and Helen Martin. Then Lillian Hellman had her second Fulton Theater premiere with *Another Part of the Forest* (11/20/46; 182 performances). Patricia Neal starred in the leading role. William Wister Haines' *Command Decision* (10/1/47; 409 performances) starred James Whitmore, Paul Kelly, and Paul Ford.

The 1950s opened with a production of Anita Loos' adaptation of Colette's story *Gigi* (11/24/51; 217 performances) for the stage with Audrey Hepburn, Mel Ferrer, and Marian Seldes in the leads. *The Seven Year Itch* (11/20/52; 1,141 performances), George Axelrod's comedy about the male libido, starred Tom Ewell and Vanessa Brown. It was later made into a very successful movie with Ewell and Marilyn Monroe.

Then the theater underwent one last renovation. A marquee was added to the facade, and many of the theater's decorations were removed. Finally the entire auditorium was painted a pinkish beige. On November 21, 1955, with the opening of *Tiger at the Gates*, the theater was renamed to honor HELEN HAYES. José Quintero directed Fredric March, Florence Eldridge, and Jason Robards in EUGENE O'NEILL's autobiographical drama *Long Day's Journey into Night* (11/7/56; 390 performances) in its world premiere production. It won the PULITZER PRIZE for Drama that year. Another O'Neill play, *A Touch of the Poet* (10/2/58; 284 performances), directed by Harold Clurman, had its Broadway premiere at the Helen Hayes. The drama starred Hayes, Eric Portman, Kim Stanley, and Betty Field.

The 1960s saw a string of successes at the theater. Jean Kerr's comedy *Mary, Mary* (3/8/61; 1,572 per-

formances) starred Barbara Bel Geddes and Michael Rennie. Another Jean Kerr play was the Helen Hayes Theater's next tenant. *Poor Richard* (12/2/64; 118 performances) starred Gene Hackman and Alan Bates. Brian Friel's comedy *Philadelphia Here I Come* (2/16/66; 326 performances) was a hit in the 1965–66 season. *The Prime of Miss Jean Brodie* (1/16/68; 378 performances) had Zoe Caldwell in the lead; Jay Presson Allen's play was later successfully transferred to the screen. Alec McCowen also had a tour de force in his portrayal of Frederick Rolfe/Baron Corvo in Peter Luke's play *Hadrian VII* (1/8/69; 359 performances).

The 1970s opened with *The Me Nobody Knows* (12/18/70; 378 performances), which moved after a successful run off Broadway. The Gary William Friedman and Will Holt revue, based on children's poetry and writing, featured a cast of youngsters that included Irene Cara. The theater's next hit was a light comedy, Bob Randall's *6 Rms Riv Vu* (10/17/72; 247 perfor-

Kathryn Baumann, Zoe Caldwell and Joseph Maher in *The Prime of Miss Jean Brodie*, 1968.

mances), starring F. Murray Abraham, Jerry Orbach, Jane Alexander, and Jennifer Warren. The next notable show at the Helen Hayes was *Rodgers and Hart* (5/13/75; 111 performances), a revue based on the songs of the great composing team. An all-star revival of George S. Kaufman (*see* KAUFMAN AND HART) and Edna Ferber's comedy satire of the Barrymores (*see* BARRYMORE FAMILY), *The Royal Family* (12/30/75; 233 performances), followed. Among the cast members were Rosetta LeNoire, Joseph Maher, Mary Louise Wilson, Eva Le Gallienne, Sam Levene, Rosemary Harris, and George Grizzard.

After Anthony Shaffer's *Equus* transferred from the Plymouth and a brief stay by *The Night of the Tribades* (10/13/77; 12 performances) came the classic O'Neill drama *A Touch of the Poet* (12/28/77; 141 performances). The revival opened at the same theater in which it had premiered in 1958. This production starred Milo O'Shea, Geraldine Fitzgerald, Jason Robards, Kathryn Walker, and George Ede under the direction of José Quintero.

The Crucifer of Blood (9/28/78; 236 performances) was a Sherlock Holmes mystery starring Paxton Whitehead as the intrepid deducer and Timothy Landfield as his assistant, John Watson, M.D. Glenn Close also starred in the mystery. *The Crucifer of Blood* was the last semisuccess to play the Helen Hayes Theater. *Perfectly Frank* (11/30/80; 16 performances) was another revue that focused on the career of a major Broadway composer: FRANK LOESSER.

Following Erlanger's death in 1930 the Helen Hayes had been sold to the City Investing Company. They resold the theater to Peter Sharp, Inc., in 1967 as part of the Portman Hotel project, which would eventually become the Marriott Marquis Hotel. A long battle to save the Helen Hayes, MOROSCO, and BIJOU theaters and the ASTOR and Victoria (*see* GAIETY THEATER) movie theaters was fought in the late 1970s (*see* BATTLE TO SAVE THE HELEN HAYES, MOROSCO, AND BIJOU THEATERS). Despite the best efforts of preservationists, architects, theater people, and audiences, the pro-developer city government and the builders won the battle, and in 1982 the theaters were torn down to make way for the Marriott Marquis Hotel.

HELEN HAYES THEATER (2). *See* **Little Theatre.**

HELLINGER, MARK. Producer, critic, and the first reporter to cover the Broadway scene exclusively; b. New York, New York, March 21, 1903; d. Hollywood, California, December 21, 1947.

Hellinger's "About Broadway" column in the *Daily News* was the first to cover the Broadway scene as its only subject. His compatriots were WALTER WIN-CHELL, the first Broadway columnist, and DAMON RUNYON, the author of many stories that captured the spirit of "the Main Stem." In addition to his work as a reporter, Hellinger wrote thinly disguised fictional stories about the men and women who inhabited Times Square. Like Damon Runyon, Hellinger loved the eccentric characters he discovered and found their stories to be more fascinating than fiction could ever be. Hellinger was a prolific writer, and it is said that he wrote more than 4,500 short stories.

Hellinger had several favorite Broadway hangouts. Billy LaHiff's tavern was the home of several journalists, including Runyon and ED SULLIVAN, sports figures like Jack Dempsey, humorist BUGS BAER, and restaurateur Toots Shor. Author Gene Fowler set his typewriter up next to the butcher block in the basement and wrote his first novel, *Trumpet in the Dust*, in 21 days at LaHiff's. Another favorite hangout (for its underworld element) was Bob Murphy's Cellar. It was located a few steps down the stairs at Broadway and 50th Street. A special on the menu was "eggs on a platter." However, when newcomers asked for the dish, the waiter always informed them that they had the platter but were fresh out of eggs. The Cellar was not a nice place; it wasn't frequented by a high-class clientele, which was perfect for Hellinger because his columns featured tales of shady characters. Murphy's was a mother lode of material. However, one day the proprietor went outside for a second and was shot. After his recovery, Murphy sold the Cellar and moved to a farm in New Hampshire.

After covering Broadway for the short-lived VARIETY competitor *Zit's*, Hellinger was hired by *Daily News* owner Captain Joseph Patterson. Hellinger was only too happy to leave *Zit's*, which was a somewhat sleazy paper. He began his coverage of Broadway for the *News* in 1923 and used the time to solidify his contacts. One year later Winchell was given his first daily column in the *News*. Hellinger was awarded a Sunday column beginning on July 12, 1925. He called it "About Town," soon after amended to "About Broadway." Hellinger's column often opened and closed with the phrase: "Episodes, Roscoe, Episodes."

Hellinger didn't write in the florid, sometimes sentimental style of Runyon, nor did he employ the language of Broadway or revel in the SLANG of the streets. He made his sentences terse and delivered them in a staccato fashion. He loved irony and sprinkled his writing with puns. He also loved sentence fragments and the modified repeat sentence. For example, he would write: "She was pretty. Very pretty. A good girl too. But sad. Very sad. She was broke. And out of a job. And despondent. Life was harsh. Then one day she met Bill. Bill wasn't good-looking. But he was honest. And noble." The Hellinger style of writing was

Mark Hellinger.

often imitated by screenwriters, playwrights, and less-talented columnists who wanted to evoke the image of a hard-boiled reporter.

On January 16, 1928, Hellinger began writing a daily column called "Behind the News." He hired an assistant, Jimmy Burbridge, who handled all correspondence, answered the phone, and tracked down leads. Burbridge was continually being fired by his boss, then rehired soon thereafter. It has been suggested that Burbridge was hired and fired more than any other employee in the history of journalism.

Hellinger, known as a soft touch, was often the first person visited by convicts after they had served their sentences. Hellinger always had a few dollars to help them. In this way Hellinger heard some of his favorite stories, stories that would later make their way into his columns and his books. Perhaps his most famous and controversial short story concerned a husband sent to Sing Sing for 20 years for murdering his wife. The husband is taken away protesting his innocence, but the police have discovered a skeleton (identified as his wife through dental records) buried in the back yard. At the end of his prison term, the man is released and

returns to his old neighborhood. A few months later, he discovers his wife walking down the street. The wrongly convicted husband runs over to his wife's side and strangles her. The police cannot touch him, for he has already been convicted for the crime and has paid his debt to society. Because of the laws preventing double jeopardy, he remains a free man.

Hellinger, Runyon, and Winchell all cultivated contacts with members of the underworld. Hellinger liked and admired many of the miscreants, and they in turn trusted him. They made Hellinger the official arbiter of any arguments. Hellinger's rulings didn't hold much water, but it seemed to suit everyone's purposes to at least make the effort.

Hellinger was wooed away from the *News* by Albert J. Kobler, publisher of the *Daily Mirror*. Kobler thought Hellinger would bring 10,000 readers to the *Mirror*; in fact, Hellinger brought 25,000. Obviously Hellinger wielded much power, and he demanded a $500-a-week salary, 50 percent of his syndication profits, his picture at the top of the column, a private office, a full-blown promotional campaign, and the help of Jimmy Burbridge at $45 a week.

Hellinger's move from the *News* created a merry-go-round of Broadway columnists. Sidney Skolsky took over Hellinger's job at the *News*. Louis Sobol moved to Skolsky's vacated post at the *New York Journal*. Sobol's column at the *Graphic* was filled by Ed Sullivan, a former sports writer. Soon after, Sullivan replaced Skolsky on Hellinger's old column at the *News*.

Hellinger's *Daily Mirror* column was titled "All in a Day." He solidified his style and arranged his columns under several headings. One heading was "People I've Met," which covered celebrities; under the heading "Unsung Broadwayites," he covered those who were unknown to the general public. Hellinger expanded his domain by collecting his columns into books, including *The Ten Million* (a title inspired by O. Henry's collection entitled *The Four Million*); *Broadway Bill*; *Moon over Broadway*; and *Six Girls and Death*. Hellinger also wrote sketches for Broadway shows including the *ZIEGFELD FOLLIES* (7/1/31; 165 performances) and *Hot-Cha!* (3/8/32; 119 performances). Hellinger also played the Loew's vaudeville circuit in 1930 with his wife, Gladys Glad. Hellinger later moved into radio and color commentary of sports events.

Clearly the newspaper column wasn't enough for the writer. He quit the *Mirror*, publishing his last column on November 13, 1937. Hellinger then moved to Hollywood, where he became a successful screenwriter and producer. Hellinger often returned to his haunts on Broadway, confirming what one journalist wrote: "The man was born and bred a newspaperman and he only went to Hollywood to get some sucker money." Hellinger did truly love Broadway. He once wrote:

This morning being this morning we will take you on another personally conducted tour of Broadway. People in every walk of life have told us that they would give anything to pace the Broadway beat as we do. And there are others who shudder and swear that they would not adopt our life for all the money in the world. Both classes are right, depending totally on the point of view. Every hour in the night life of Broadway brings sadness, gladness, love, romance, hate, joy, laughter and sorrow. Sometimes bitterness. Sometimes happiness. And again. And again. And again . . .

Hellinger had once participated in a phony feud with his fellow *News* columnist Paul Gallico. Gallico wrote after Hellinger's death:

They wrote him up as a big tipper and a picker-up of tabs and dinner checks. It was true enough, but there were so many more things to say of Mark Hellinger. . . . He was sweet. He was kind. He was gentle. He was honest, and he was good. He worked hard. He never double-crossed his friends. He was rich in talent, and with his talent he enriched his times—when he died, he left too large a hole to fill in the hearts of many, including my own.

When tycoon Anthony B. Farrell bought the Warner Brothers Theater on West 51st Street, he rechristened it the MARK HELLINGER THEATER in the writer's honor.

HENDERSON, RAY. *See* **De Sylva, Brown and Henderson.**

HENRY MILLER'S THEATRE. 124 W. 43rd Street. Architects: Harry Creighton Ingalls and Paul R. Allen. Opening: April 1, 1918; *The Fountain of Youth*.

Henry Miller's Theatre, home of distinguished straight plays, especially those from London, saw its fortunes fall along with Broadway's. The theater was built by English actor/manager Henry Miller and his partners in the real estate firm of William A. White to house Miller's productions. Miller made sure that his architects included a balcony in their designs, because he remembered his youth and the years when he only had enough money for the balcony seats. He wanted other young people of small means to be able to enjoy the theater, too.

The first production at the theater, *The Fountain of Youth*, was a failure and closed after only 32 perfor-

Interior of Henry Miller's Theatre.

mances. The second offering, *A Marriage of Convenience*, opened on May 1, 1918, with Billie Burke starring. It played for only 53 performances. The first hit to play the theater was *Mis' Nelly of New Orleans* (2/4/19), which played 127 performances.

On May 26, 1919, the theater housed a musical, GEORGE GERSHWIN's *La, La, Lucille*. Alex Aarons (*see* AARONS AND FREEDLEY) and George B. Seitz produced the show, which was one of the few musicals produced on the Henry Miller stage. The "New Up-to-the-Minute Musical Comedy of Class and Distinction" was Gershwin's first complete score for a Broadway production. The show was well received by critics and would have run longer than 104 performances but for the ACTORS' STRIKE OF 1919.

The teens ended with a successful production of *The Famous Mrs. Fair* (12/22/19), which ran 343 performances, well into the 1920s. Also in the early 1920s were the openings for *Wake Up, Jonathan* (1/17/21; 105 performances), Booth Tarkington's *Intimate Strangers* (11/7/21; 91 performances) with Alfred Lunt (*see* LUNT AND FONTANNE) and Billie Burke, *The Awful Truth* (9/18/22; 146 performances) starring Ina Claire, and *Romeo and Juliet* (1/24/23; 161 performances), with Jane Cowl and Dennis King. Next, HELEN HAYES starred in *Quarantine* (12/16/24) along with Sidney Blackmer. The play ran 163 performances, but wasn't a hit with the Broadway crowd. When Hayes' friends asked where she had been because they hadn't seen her lately, she explained, "I've been in *Quarantine*."

Noël Coward's *The Vortex* opened on September 16, 1925, and ran 157 performances. It was followed by Ferenc Molnár's *The Play's the Thing* (11/3/26; 313 performances) and GEORGE M. COHAN's play *The Baby Cyclone* (9/12/27). The title character Cyclone was a tiny Pekingese sold by a henpecked husband. His wife makes sure he regrets his action. *Theatre Magazine* said the play had "a not very subtle plot . . . [that] you would not believe could possibly fill any stage from 8:45 to 11:00. But Mr. Cohan is a master of padding." *The Baby Cyclone* ran 187 performances. The house long-run record was set with *Journey's End* (3/22/29), which ran 485 performances.

In 1930 the theater was bought by manager-producer Gilbert Miller. During the 1930s the theater's success continued. Philip Barry's *Tomorrow and Tomorrow* opened on January 13, 1931, and ran 206 performances. Helen Hayes returned to the theater in *The Good Fairy* (11/24/31; 154 performances) by Molnár. It was followed by Sidney Howard's *The Late Christopher Bean* (10/31/32; 211 performances); EUGENE O'NEILL's *Days without End* (1/8/34; 57 performances); Lawrence Riley's *Personal Appearance* (10/17/34; 501 performances), with Gladys George; Edward Woolf's *Libel* (12/20/35; 104 performances),

which marked the emergence of director Otto Preminger as a major talent; and Terence Rattigan's *French Without Tears* (9/28/37; 111 performances).

Next the theater presented an American classic, Thornton Wilder's *Our Town*. It opened on February 4, 1938, with little advance word. The play received mixed reviews in Boston before coming to New York. In fact, the Boston run was canceled before its scheduled closing. The show was booked into Henry Miller's, but the theater gave it only a limited guarantee, believing the show would be a sure failure. The reviews at its Broadway opening were mixed, and audiences stayed away. However, when the play won the PULITZER PRIZE, business picked up. By this time the play had to make room for the theater's next booking, Clare Boothe's *Kiss the Boys Good-bye* (9/28/38; 286 performances), so it was transferred to the MOROSCO THEATRE, where it concluded its 336-performance run.

The theater's first play of the 1940s was *Ladies in Retirement* (3/26/40; 151 performances). *Harriet* (3/3/43; 377 performances) followed, starring Helen Hayes as Harriet Beecher Stowe. Julius J. and Philip G. Epstein's comedy *Chicken Every Sunday* (4/5/44; 317 performances) followed. Norman Krasna, a popular writer of light comedies, had a major success with *Dear Ruth* (12/13/44; 683 performances). Moss Hart (*see* KAUFMAN AND HART) staged the play, which starred Virginia Gilmore and Lenore Lonergan. June Lockhart, best known as the mother in the television series *Lassie* and the daughter of Gene Lockhart, starred in *For Love or Money* (11/4/47); F. Hugh Herbert's play ran 263 performances.

The 1950s started with a hit for the theater, T. S. Eliot's *The Cocktail Party* (1/21/50). The play starred Alec Guinness, Irene Worth, and Cathleen Nesbitt. Although some critics said the play was indecipherable, it kept audiences happy for 409 performances. *The Cocktail Party* was the first big British hit to play the theater, which enjoyed a reputation as the American home of English shows.

F. Hugh Herbert had another success at the theater with *The Moon Is Blue* (3/8/51; 924 performances). Barbara Bel Geddes and Barry Nelson starred in the long-running play. Edward Chodorov's hit comedy *Oh, Men! Oh, Women!* opened on December 17, 1953, and ran for 382 performances. Another English offering, Graham Greene's *The Living Room*, opened on November 17, 1954, with Barbara Bel Geddes, but lasted only 22 performances. It was quickly replaced with another import, Agatha Christie's *Witness for the Prosecution* (12/16/54), which did considerably better with its 645-performance run.

The "British invasion" continued with the October 10, 1956, opening of *The Reluctant Debutante* by William Douglas Home. The show pleased audiences for

Frank (left) and John (right) Craven with Martha Scott in *Our Town*, 1938.

134 performances. A hilarious production of Fey-deau's comedy, *Hotel Paradiso* opened at the theater on April 11, 1957. The play starred Bert Lahr and, making her stage debut, Angela Lansbury. Harold Clurman wrote in *The Nation* that the production was "louder, faster, closer to burlesque. The changes . . . helped our audience which can more readily accept departures from realism when they are unmistakable." Audiences were thrilled for 107 performances. Elmer Rice's last play, *Cue for Passion*, opened on November 25, 1958, with Robert Lansing. Unfortunately, it was a failure and closed after 39 performances. Another failure by a great dramatist, Noël Coward's *Look After Lulu*, opened on March 3, 1959. Tammy Grimes starred in the play for 39 performances. The next hit at the theater was Saul Levitt's courtroom drama, *The Andersonville Trial*. The play opened on December 29, 1959, with George C. Scott and Albert Dekker; it ran 179 performances. Movie star Bette Davis opened on

September 14, 1960, in the short-lived *The World of Carl Sandburg*. It closed after 29 performances. A much bigger hit was Lawrence Roman's *Under the Yum-Yum Tree* (11/16/60; 173 performances), starring Gig Young.

Joseph Stein's play *Enter Laughing* opened on March 13, 1963, with Alan Arkin and Vivian Blaine. The comedy enjoyed a long run of 419 performances. However, a series of flop plays followed. Lawrence Roman's *P.S. I Love You* (10/19/64) starred Geraldine Page and Lee Patterson; it closed after 12 performances. Jerome Lawrence and Robert E. Lee's *Diamond Orchid*, a drama about Eva Peron, opened on February 10, 1965, and closed after five performances. Other plays at the theater included *The Promise*, with Ian McKellen; Jack Gelber's *The Cuban Thing*, with Rip Torn, Jane White, and Raul Julia; *Morning, Noon and Night*; and Julius J. Epstein's *But, Seriously*, with Richard Dreyfuss and Tom Poston. Epstein's play opened on February 27, 1969, and closed on March 1, 1969, after 4 performances, the last production to play the theater until the 1990s.

After Henry Miller's death on April 9, 1926, the theater remained in his family's hands. His son, Gilbert Miller, a noted producer in his own right, oversaw the theater's operation. In 1966 Gilbert Miller's widow sold the theater, and it became the Park-Miller Theatre which showed male porno films. The theater's name was changed again to the Avon-on-the-Hudson in 1972. It continued its X-rated policy.

From 1978 through 1984 the theater was the disco Xenon. While the theater was serving as a disco, a legit production opened there, against all odds. On May 2, 1983, Terrence McNally's comedy *The Ritz* opened with Warhol favorite Holly Woodlawn and gay porno star Casey Donovan. A ticket to the play allowed one to stay and dance in the disco following the final curtain. *The Ritz* closed on opening night. The theater then became a dance hall, Shout!!, which featured 1950s rock 'n' roll.

The Roundabout Theatre Company opened an American version of the acclaimed British revival of *Cabaret* (3/19/1998) at the theater, which was renamed the Kit Kat Klub. When *Cabaret* moved to another theater that was once a disco, STUDIO 54, the theater returned to its original name, Henry Miller's.

The off-off-Broadway hit *Urinetown* (9/20/2001) transferred to the theater, where it remains at press time.

On November 8, 1987, the Henry Miller's exterior was designated a New York City landmark. The Landmarks Preservation Commission said: "Its facade is a handsome example of the neo-Georgian style [used to] express the concept of intimate productions being presented."

HERBERT, VICTOR. The most important and prolific of the early composers of musical comedy and operetta; b. Dublin, Ireland, February 1, 1859; d. New York, New York, May 26, 1924.

The Irish-born composer and conductor Victor Herbert was a major influence on an entire generation of musicians and composers. His 30-year career included many triumphs on the stage and off. Among his best known shows are *Babes in Toyland*, *The Red Mill*, *Naughty Marietta*, *Mlle. Modiste*, *Sweethearts*, *Eileen*, and *Orange Blossoms*. Herbert wrote 44 complete scores for the stage. In addition he composed 2 operas, *Natoma* in 1911 and *Madeleine* in 1913. They were not successful, although their music has won greater appreciation today. Herbert wrote many orchestral works, including "A Suite of Serenades," written for the Paul Whiteman Aeolian Hall concert at which

GEORGE GERSHWIN's "Rhapsody in Blue" also appeared. He was a portly figure known for his generosity, business sense, appreciation of fine food and drink, and love for Ireland. His 1892 work "Irish Rhapsody" contains some of his most heartfelt melodies. He was also a staunch supporter of composers' rights. His suit against Shanley's Restaurant set the stage for the establishment of the American Society for Composers, Authors and Publishers (*see* ASCAP).

Herbert was born in Dublin on February 1, 1859. When his father died, his mother remarried and the family moved to Stuttgart. He attended Stuttgart Conservatory and studied with Bernhard Cossman and Max Seifriz. He spent many years as a cellist with German and Austrian symphony orchestras, including five years with the Court Orchestra of Stuttgart. After emigrating to the United States in October 1886, Herbert became a cello soloist at the Metropolitan Opera House. He also played in the symphony orchestras of Anton Seidl and Theodore Thomas. He soon graduated to conductor, first with the 22nd National Guard Band, and then from 1898 to 1904 with the Pittsburgh Symphony. In 1898 he performed his own work, the "Concerto No. 2 for Cello and Orchestra, Op. 30," with the New York Philharmonic.

In 1894 Herbert was commissioned by the Bostonians to compose the score for the operetta *Prince Ananias*. This group was founded in 1879 as the Boston Ideal Opera Company to present Gilbert and Sullivan operettas. After its success the composer collaborated with HARRY B. SMITH on the hit *The Wizard of the Nile*. Herbert would write 13 scores with Smith, who matched Herbert's prolificacy but not his talent. Many critics felt that Herbert never had a collaborator worthy of his talents. Although many of his scores are famous today, their libretti and lyrics are dated or second-rate.

The Wizard of the Nile was followed by a dazzling succession of operettas that featured lush melodies, stirring ballads, and delightful character songs. In 1896 Herbert premiered *The Gold Bug* (9/14/1896; 28 performances) with lyrics by Glen MacDonough. The next year two shows written with Smith premiered: *The Serenade* (3/16/1897; 79 performances) and *The Idol's Eye* (10/25/1897; 56 performances). In 1898 Herbert and Smith presented *The Fortune Teller*. The following year three Herbert shows made their debuts: *Cyrano de Bergerac* (Smith; 9/18/1899; 28 performances), *The Singing Girl* (Smith; 10/23/1899; 80 performances), and *The Ameer* (Frederic Rankin and Kirke La Shelle; 12/4/1899; 51 performances). In 1900 Herbert and Smith's *The Viceroy* opened (4/9/00; 28 performances).

In 1903 the first of Herbert's masterpieces opened. *Babes in Toyland* (10/13/03; 192 performances), with book and lyrics by MacDonough, remains a favorite more than 80 years after its opening. The songs "March of the Toys," "Toyland," and "I Can't Do The Sum" are still played in pops concerts and occasional revivals. The *Dramatic Mirror* predicted, "It will prove a perfect dream of delight to the children, and will recall the happy days of childhood to those who are facing the stern realities of life." Those words are just as true today as when they were written.

Herbert followed the triumph of *Babes in Toyland* with *Babette* (11/16/03; 59 performances), written with Smith. A critic for the *Evening Post* rejoiced over Herbert's work:

> Mr. Herbert is, like Johann Strauss, a high-class musician, who can adapt his style to popular taste without ever becoming vulgar; and underlying his pretty tunes there are orchestra touches which rejoice the heart of lovers of the best in music. Some of the choruses, too, are excellent; but the gem of the whole score is a quartet in the last act, which got two encores and deserved a hundred. There is nothing more admirable in the whole range of operatic concerted music, and it deserves to become as famous as the quartet in "Rigoletto," to which, in fact, it is far superior.

MacDonough and Herbert's next show was *It Happened in Nordland* (12/5/04; 154 performances). During the run Blanche Ring assumed the role usually played by Marie Cahill. Cahill's temperamental replacement proved just as high-strung. Ring, insulted by Lew Fields (*see* FIELDS FAMILY), the star of the show, walked out without warning taking her costumes. A minor player who knew the role took over the part on October 16, 1905, saved the show, and established herself as a top Broadway star. Her name was Pauline Frederick, and she became one of the great Broadway actors of her time. Ironically after the run of *It Happened in Nordland*, she lost her singing voice and never again appeared in a musical.

Miss Dolly Dollars (9/4/05; 72 performances), with words by Smith, had a number with an enduring title: "A Woman Is Only a Woman but a Good Cigar Is a Smoke." Though Rudyard Kipling originated the phrase, it entered the language through the popularity of the song. In the same year were the premieres of *Wonderland* (10/24/05; 73 performances), written with MacDonough, and one of the composer's greatest successes, *Mlle. Modiste* (12/25/05; 202 performances). The latter opened with Fritzi Scheff in the lead. Also in the cast in a chorus role was movie pioneer Mack Sennett. *Mlle. Modiste* contained two of Herbert's classics, "Kiss Me Again" and the rousing "I Want What I Want When I Want It." Henry Blossom supplied the words to that score and to Herbert's next hit, *The Red Mill* (9/24/06; 274 performances). It contained four Herbert standards: "When You're Pretty and the World

Is Fair," "Moonbeams," "Every Day Is Ladies' Day with Me," and "The Streets of New York." Largely because of its four hit songs, the show is still revived today.

Three months after the opening of *The Red Mill*, Herbert and Edgar Smith saw their *Dream City and the Magic Knight* open on Broadway. The show had a plot that was ridiculous even for the time. A program note described the somewhat unusual plot:

> Elsa and her brother Godfrey have been left orphans under the guardianship of their uncle and aunt, Frederick and Ortrud, and the latter conspire to defraud them of their estates.
>
> The brother has disappeared, and Elsa is accused before the King of having made away with little Godfrey, and is about to be condemned when, as a last resource, she demands to have the herald ask for some knight errant to appear and champion her cause against her uncle.
>
> Lohengrin appears, sailing down the river in a boat drawn by a swan, and in answer to Elsa's appeal, fights and defeats Frederick, whereupon Ortrud confesses that she used her magic arts to change little Godfrey into a swan, and Lohengrin, being something of a magician himself, changes him back again and returns to Fairyland. If the audience will listen intently it is possible that the shade of Richard Wagner may be heard to turn over.

Herbert's sole 1907 offering, *The Tattooed Man* (2/18/07; 59 performances) was a minor effort by the composer and Harry B. Smith. *Algeria* (8/31/08; 48 performances), written with MacDonough, fared little better. *Little Nemo* (10/20/08; 111 performances), based on the comic strip *Little Nemo in Slumberland* by Winsor McKay, was an elaborate fantasy. It was among the most expensive musicals ever mounted on Broadway. The average Broadway musical in that period cost between $20,000 and $30,000. Those were the preunion days when dollars bought more. Producers Klaw and Erlanger spent an astounding $60,000 on *Little Nemo*.

The Prima Donna (11/30/08; 72 performances) was written with Henry Blossom. The program of the Fritzi Scheff vehicle carried a brief statement by producer Charles Dillingham: "Made in America." The producer meant to imply that the current spate of foreign operettas didn't come up to the standards of the homegrown product. *Old Dutch* (11/22/09; 88 performances) was written in collaboration with George V. Hobart. The show starred Lew Fields, Vernon Castle (*see* VERNON AND IRENE CASTLE), John Bunny, Ada Lewis, and Alice Dovey, but it is best remembered today for marking the Broadway debut of the girl who played Little Mime: HELEN HAYES.

In 1910 another Herbert classic premiered: *Naughty Marietta* (11/7/10; 136 performances). Herbert wrote the show with Rida Johnson Young. Together they came up with what some consider Herbert's finest score. Among the songs were the hits "Tramp! Tramp! Tramp!" "'Neath the Southern Moon," "Italian Street Song," "I'm Falling in Love with Someone," and "Ah! Sweet Mystery of Life." The show was produced by OSCAR HAMMERSTEIN I under the direction of his son Arthur (*see* ARTHUR HAMMERSTEIN). The popularity of *Naughty Marietta* is indicated by its financial success. The show had a $2 top ticket price, yet it averaged $20,000 a week. The property was revived twice on Broadway and was even presented in 1964 in the Dutch Coffee House of the ASTOR HOTEL. It has also been presented thousands of times in summer theaters and stock companies throughout the world. MGM filmed it with great success in 1935; Jeanette MacDonald and Nelson Eddy starred. Herbert followed the triumph of *Naughty Marietta* with a minor effort, *When Sweet Sixteen* (9/14/11; 12 performances), in collaboration with George V. Hobart. The composer next attempted two grand opera productions. They were nowhere near as successful as his operettas.

Herbert returned to the Broadway stage with a SHUBERT BROTHERS production, *The Duchess* (10/16/11; 24 performances). The lyrics were by Joseph W. Herbert and Harry B. Smith. Smith worked on Victor Herbert's next show, *The Enchantress* (10/19/11; 72 performances). It was, remarkably, Herbert's third show to open in little more than a month. The librettist, listed as Fred de Gresac, was actually Mme. Victor Maurel, the wife of a famous French baritone. *The Enchantress* starred the English actor Kitty Gordon, whose primary attribute was her beautiful back. She was talented enough, though, to carry off the title role.

During the run of *The Enchantress*, Herbert wrote of the need for an American school of light opera composition. It may come as a surprise to modern students of the musical to note that Herbert, whose work was associated with the European tradition of operetta, knew that the musical would have to evolve and that part of that evolution would be the increasing importance of American music styles. He wrote:

> We need an American School of Music in order to give our young composers a chance to develop and drive out the quacks. Our young composers are too prone to get their ideas from the old world, and their work naturally will fall into the style of foreign composition. They do not get into their music that freshness and vitality so characteristic of this country. And yet on the other hand American musical taste has developed to a point where it demands something that is native. I believe that one reason why "The Enchantress" has had so huge a success in New York, and wherever it has played, is that I determined, when I started its composition, to disregard absolutely every foreign impulse and to write in a frank, free American style.

In fact, Herbert's successor, JEROME KERN successfully adapted an American style to musical comedy.

The Lady of the Slipper (10/28/12; 232 performances) boasted a star-studded cast that included Vernon Castle, Elsie Janis, David C. Montgomery, Fred Stone, and Peggy Wood. James O'Dea supplied the lyrics. According to local wags, producer Charles Dillingham was stuck on the idea for a new show. He then remembered producer Charles Frohman's byword: "When in doubt, do Cinderella."

Sweethearts (9/8/13; 136 performances) was another of Herbert's shows with a celebrated score. It had lyrics by Robert B. Smith and book by Harry B. Smith and Fred de Gresac. Two songs were standouts, "Sweethearts" and "Every Lover Must Meet His Fate." Surprisingly, a later Broadway revival, which opened on January 21, 1947, surpassed the run of the original. The Bobby Clark vehicle ran 288 performances. *The Madcap Duchess* (11/11/13; 71 performances) had book and lyrics by Justin Henry McCarthy and David Stevens. McCarthy was best known for his novel *If I Were King*, which later became the source of *The Vagabond King*. *The Madcap Duchess* wasn't quite as successful, but the reviews were quite positive.

The Only Girl (11/2/14; 240 performances) was "a musical farcical comedy." It had one somewhat popular song, "When You're Away." When the musical was revived in 1934, Robert Benchley, writing in *The New Yorker*, put his finger on the problem with reviving Herbert shows: "The Herbert music is, of course, perennially lovely, but those Henry Blossom librettos need a cold winter's night and an attendant air of excitement in the theatrical district to make them bearable. Even in its heyday, the book to 'The Only Girl' was not so hot, and in the not-so-very-merry month of May, 1934, you could go clamming in it."

Herbert's *The Debutante* (12/7/14; 48 performances) had Robert B. Smith lyrics. The day after its opening, *Watch Your Step* opened with IRVING BERLIN's jazzy score and pointed the way to the future of the American musical theater. As time went on more shows were written in the newer musical styles, and Herbert was soon considered an old-fashioned composer. Ironically, just what Herbert proposed must happen to the American musical did happen, and the popular acceptance of the new style American musical made his work less popular. Still, at the time, Herbert was considered America's greatest composer.

Henry Blossom penned the book and lyrics for Herbert's next venture, *The Princess Pat* (9/29/15; 158 performances), which was a success. The song that has lasted the longest is "Neapolitan Love Song," a favorite of sopranos since its introduction. Herbert's next show featured both the musical theater's past, represented by Herbert, and its future, represented by Berlin. Both composers created the score for the revue *The Century Girl* (11/6/16; 200 performances); Blossom supplied Herbert's lyrics. The show was the idea of producers Charles Dillingham and FLORENZ ZIEGFELD. With Ziegfeld at the helm, it was inevitable that the show would be a lavish extravaganza. In one scene entitled "The Music Lesson," both Herbert and Berlin were portrayed onstage. Herbert's hit "Kiss Me Again" was played for the scene, and Berlin wrote a countermelody to the tune.

Blossom also collaborated on Herbert's next show, *Eileen* (3/19/17; 64 performances), with the great Herbert song, "Thine Alone." Ziegfeld tapped Herbert's talents for another revue, the legendary *Miss 1917* (11/5/17; 40 performances). The show opened without a chance of making back Ziegfeld's investment. Although it played to sold-out houses with a cast featuring Elizabeth Brice, Marion Davies, Lew Fields, Bessie McCoy, Vivienne Segal, Ann Pennington, Savoy and Brennan, Van and Schenck, and GEORGE WHITE, the show lost money due to its huge weekly operating expenses. The revue had a few Herbert songs, but the majority of the score was written by Jerome Kern, whose star was rising as fast as that of Irving Berlin. As Kern and Berlin had greater and greater successes, Herbert found his shows increasingly less popular.

Her Regiment (11/12/17; 40 performances) had book and lyrics by William Le Baron. Ziegfeld hired Herbert to compose a few numbers for the ZIEGFELD FOLLIES *of 1917* (6/12/17; 111 performances). His next operetta, *The Velvet Lady* (2/3/19; 136 performances), again featured Blossom's words. *Angel Face* (12/29/19; 57 performances), with Robert B. Smith lyrics, introduced an enduring standard, "I Might Be Your Once-in-a-While." *My Golden Girl* (2/2/20; 105 performances) had book and lyrics by Frederic Arnold Kummer. It contained one interesting number, "Ragtime Terpsichore," in which Herbert attempted to write in the jazz idiom. However, the show was still basically a romantic operetta. Herbert next composed a few numbers for the *Ziegfeld Follies of 1920*. His next operetta, *The Girl in the Spotlight* (7/12/20; 54 performances), teamed him with Robert B. Smith.

Herbert's fortunes fell even further with his next show, *Oui Madame*. It was his last collaboration with Robert B. Smith and closed out of town in 1920. The composer's output then slowed even further. He contributed to the *Ziegfeld Follies of 1921* and *1922*. His next-to-last show, *Orange Blossoms* (9/19/22; 95 performances), had lyrics by B. G. De Sylva (*see* DE SYLVA, BROWN, AND HENDERSON) and a book by Fred de Gresac. Herbert proved that, although his output had slowed, he still had much to offer and could still write a superior score, composing a beautiful song, "A Kiss in the Dark." He completed his usual assignment for the *Ziegfeld Follies of 1923* and followed it with

a concert work, "Suite of Serenades," commissioned by Paul Whiteman for his famous Aeolian Hall concert. The suite was a major success and reemphasized Herbert's preeminence in American music.

For the composer's final operetta, *The Dream Girl* (8/20/24; 118 performances), Rida Johnson Young supplied the lyrics and collaborated on the book with Harold Atteridge. SIGMUND ROMBERG, another top operetta composer, also composed songs for the score. The Shubert production wasn't quite up to Herbert's usual standard but was a great public success. Herbert's last Broadway assignment was for the 1924 edition of the *Ziegfeld Follies*. He composed three instrumental numbers for the revue. After Herbert's death Ziegfeld interpolated a medley of the composer's greatest songs.

After Victor Herbert's death, the *New York World* published a reflection on his by noted musicologist Deems Taylor:

> Losing Victor Herbert, the musical world loses someone it will never quite replace. He was the last of the troubadours. His musical ancestor was Mozart and the family of which he was so brilliant a younger son numbered Offenbach, Delibes, Bizet, the Strausses and Arthur Sullivan among its elders.
>
> What he had was what they all had, the gift of song. His music bubbled and sparkled and charmed, and he brought the precious gift of gayety to an art that so often suffers from the pretentiousness and self-consciousness of its practitioners.
>
> The thirty years of his too short career have left us two grand operas and over forty operettas and musical comedies, all distinguished by an unending flow of melodic invention, harmonic and rhythmic individuality and brilliant instrumentation.
>
> Above all he had perfect taste. Herbert's music could be trivial at times but he never wrote a vulgar line in his life. Now that he is gone there is no one left who has quite his combination of effortless spontaneity and endearing light heartedness.
>
> He is not dead, of course. The composer of "Babes in Toyland," "The Fortune Teller," "The Red Mill," "Nordland," and "Mlle. Modiste" cannot be held as dead by a world so heavily in his debt.

HERMAN, JERRY. A tunesmith in the old-fashioned sense whose smash hit successes are the definition of musical comedy; b. New York, New York, July 10, 1932.

Herman may be the only contemporary Broadway songwriter whose name is recognized by the general public, with the possible exception of ANDREW LLOYD WEBBER. Surprisingly, this fame is due to the success of only three shows: *Hello, Dolly!, Mame,* and *La Cage Aux Folles*. The hallmark of Herman's works is smart, sophisticated women, whose characters drive them to sing a rousing, optimistic number before the curtain falls. His work defines what most people think of when asked to describe the Broadway musical: glitzy, upbeat extravaganzas, long on energy and catchy tunes that the audience is sure to hum while leaving the theater.

Herman was educated at the University of Miami and the Parsons School of Design. His first score was for *I Feel Wonderful* (10/18/54; 49 performances), a college revue that moved to off-Broadway. Herman followed with another revue, *Nightcap* (5/18/58), which enjoyed a 400-performance run in the Showplace nightclub off Broadway. Another off-Broadway show, *Parade*, followed in January 1960.

The modest success that Herman had thus far enjoyed didn't portend the enormous successes of his Broadway book shows. The first was *Milk and Honey* (10/10/61). Molly Picon, Robert Weede, and Mimi

Benzell starred in the show, which was set in Israel. The production ran for 543 performances, a long run by Broadway standards, yet the young songwriter didn't receive much notice, because most critics attributed the show's success to the large Jewish audience for Broadway musicals. His next show, *Madame Aphrodite* (12/29/61), played only 13 performances off Broadway. Two years later Herman would have his biggest success when DAVID MERRICK hired him to write the score to Michael Stewart's musicalization of Thornton Wilder's *The Matchmaker*. The show was *Hello, Dolly!* and this time Herman was definitely considered a major talent.

Hello, Dolly! opened on January 16, 1964, with Carol Channing in the lead. It became one of the most successful musicals in Broadway history, achieving 2,844 performances. After it passed the record number of performances held by *My Fair Lady, Hello, Dolly!*

Angela Lansbury and Kurt Peterson in *Dear World*, 1969.

was for a time the longest running show in Broadway history. It was shortly thereafter overtaken by *Fiddler on the Roof*, which opened nine months later.

Herman's next show proved almost as popular as *Hello, Dolly! Mame* opened on May 24, 1966, with Angela Lansbury portraying Patrick Dennis' zany character. *Mame* contained another first-rate score by Herman. Most popular were the title tune and "It's Today." Other songs that received notice were "If He Walked into My Life" and "Open a New Window." *Mame* also gave a boost to the careers of Lansbury's co-stars, Beatrice Arthur and Jane Connell. It played a total of 1,508 performances on Broadway.

Lansbury, Herman, and *Mame* librettists Lawrence and Lee teamed up again for *Dear World* (2/6/69), a musical version of Jean Giradoux's *The Madwoman of Chaillot*. The show did not repeat the success of *Mame* and lasted only 132 performances. *Mack and Mabel* (10/6/74) followed, and, despite having what some fans consider Herman's most mature score, as well as the contributions of Bernadette Peters and Robert Preston, the show played only 65 performances. Although the failure of the show meant that few people were exposed to the score, two songs, "I Won't Send Roses" and "Time Heals Everything," have achieved minor success. Herman's next show performed slightly worse than even *Mack and Mabel*. *The Grand Tour* (1/11/79) starred Joel Grey in an unsuccessful musicalization of S. N. Behrman's play *Jacobowsky and the Colonel* based on a play by Franz Werfel.

With three failures in a row, critics proclaimed Jerry Herman's career finished. Skeptics pointed to the success of *Hello, Dolly!* and *Mame* as flukes and suggested that Herman's style wasn't suited to the supposedly more sophisticated Broadway of the 1980s. But on August 21, 1983, Herman surprised Broadway with *La Cage aux Folles*, a huge hit in the style of his previous extravaganzas. George Hearn and Gene Barry played homosexual lovers in the musical adaptation of the French screen hit. The most popular of the songs, "I Am What I Am," even had the rare distinction of hitting the charts in a disco version. *La Cage* was a huge hit, with all the Broadway pizzazz and slick professionalism associated with Herman's name. Formerly blasé Broadwayites took notice when *La Cage aux Folles* was nominated for a TONY AWARD for best musical, competing against STEPHEN SONDHEIM's *Sunday in the Park with George*. Herman's success and the relative failure of the Sondheim show polarized theater goers. Although both men were respected for their skills, they represented opposite ends of the musical comedy spectrum. Herman's jubilant, melodic scores and cotton-candy productions contrast sharply with Sondheim's dark, intricate music featured in shows long on concept.

In 1996 Herman wrote a television score, *Mrs. Santa Claus*, for Angela Lansbury. He also wrote another stage score, *Miss Spectacular*, for a casino in Las Vegas.

HERTS & TALLANT. Architectural firm responsible for many of the finest theaters in New York; Henry Beaumont Herts, b. New York, New York, January 23, 1871; d. New York, New York, March 27, 1933; Hugh Tallant, b. Boston, Massachusetts, September 15, 1869; d. Savannah, Georgia, December 8, 1952.

The theater designs of the firm Herts and Tallant successfully bridged the gap from the old style theaters of the 19th century to the much improved theater designs of the early 20th century. Their Beaux Arts masterpieces remain some of the best loved theaters in New York.

Henry Beaumont Herts was born in New York into a design oriented family. His father ran Herts Brothers, a famous interior design and furnishings firm. Herts apprenticed for Bruce Price, a notable New York City architect. He dropped out of both City College of New York and Columbia University despite showing an aptitude for art and architecture; during his four years at Columbia he even won a competition for the design of the Columbus Arch. He then traveled to Paris, where he attended the Ecole des Beaux-Arts in 1894. He did not graduate from there either, but Herts did meet his future partner, Hugh Tallant.

Unlike Herts, Tallant excelled in academia. A student at Harvard, where he was a sportsman and editor of the *Harvard Lampoon*, he graduated Phi Beta Kappa in 1891 with both bachelor's and master's degrees in art. After spending a year with a local architectural firm, he was awarded Harvard's Kirkland Fellowship, which led him too to Paris and the Ecole des Beaux-Arts. In Paris he won more than a dozen prizes, including the 1896 Grande Medaille d'Honneur for graduating first in his class.

In 1900 the new partners opened offices in both Paris and New York, with Herts concentrating on the business end, technology, and engineering and Tallant in charge of the architecture and decorative design proper.

After a few nondescript commissions, mainly houses and libraries, Herts and Tallant were hired to design what would eventually become the most beautiful theater in New York, the NEW AMSTERDAM THEATRE. The producing team of Klaw and Erlanger hired the firm to design their flagship theater and allowed them a remarkable $500,000 budget. Not only did they design the theater proper, they were also responsible for the office building next door as well as a roof theater. The New Amsterdam Theatre was a remarkable achievement, a nearly perfectly imagined theater with excellent acoustics and sight lines as well as a beautiful design mixing Beaux Arts and Art Nouveau elements.

The team soon developed a reputation for excellence in theater design, especially for advancements in fireproofing and stage engineering. The remarkable success of the New Amsterdam job soon made them the premier theater architects in New York.

The team's next commission was for the LYCEUM THEATER, built for Daniel and Charles Frohman and William B. Harris. Daniel Frohman envisioned a year-round repertory company for the theater, and Herts and Tallant offered a beautifully appointed modern theater with an attached seven-story building suitable for production shops and dressing rooms. In 1904 Klaw and Erlanger hired the firm for another 42nd Street project, the LIBERTY THEATER. This time the producers held tight to their purse strings. But the theater was still deemed a success even if it was sparsely decorated.

Another auspicious commission was to follow. The Brooklyn Academy of Music had been destroyed by fire in 1903. Two years later a competition was announced to design a new building that would house a 1,400-seat concert hall, a 2,200-seat opera house, a 5,000-square-foot ballroom, banquet hall, and offices for the Brooklyn Institute of Arts and Sciences. Herts and Tallant won the competition with an imaginative design, one that pushed them further into the forefront of New York theater designers. Next, Klaw and Erlanger hired the company for a third commission, that of the GAIETY THEATER. Their projects doubled with the almost concurrent job of designing the New German Theatre at Madison Avenue and 59th Street.

In 1911 the partnership began their last theater commission as partners. The Folies Bergère Theatre (see HELEN HAYES THEATER [1]) was a theater-restaurant meant to house both a dining area and a stage area. The design was resplendent, with cream, red, and blue terra-cotta tiles set in a diamond pattern over the facade. The roof of the theater held two electric signs that were modeled after banners. Unfortunately, the theater-restaurant concept was almost immediately a failure. Later that year Herts was called in to redesign the space as a traditional theater to be named the Fulton.

Between the opening of the Folies Bergère and its reimagining as the Fulton, in May 1911, the team of Herts and Tallant broke up. Herts a suspected alcoholic and possible morphine addict, set up his own office of along with two of his assistants, Harry Arnold and Herbert Krapp. They designed the BOOTH THEATRE, the Shubert (see SAM S. SHUBERT THEATRE), and the

LONGACRE theaters. But with Herbert Krapp's departure in 1915, their theater design work was over. Herts' office stayed open until illness forced him to close in 1928. Five years later he was dead. Hugh Tallant became a partner in the firm of Lord and Hewlett, adding his name to those of his partners. He retired in 1931 and moved to Savannah, Georgia, where he died.

Along with their associates, Harry Arnold, Herbert Krapp, J. B. McElfatrick, Frank Nute, and Edwin Denby, Herts and Tallant were the preeminent theater architects of their time. They provided New York with theaters that excelled in all technical respects, incorporated the latest in technology, and put an emphasis on both the theater's interior as well as its exterior design.

HEWES, HENRY. Critic; b. Boston, Massachusetts, April 9, 1917.

Hewes spent his early career at the *New York Times*, beginning as a copy boy and eventually achieving the post of staff writer (1949–1951). He edited the *Best Plays* series and adapted and directed many plays for regional theaters. He began his career in theater journalism as drama editor of the *Saturday Review* in 1952, two years later becoming its critic. Hewes was the first critic to regularly review Broadway, off-Broadway, stock, and regional productions with equal emphasis.

Henry Hewes with Rosemary Harris.

When he was president of the Drama Desk from 1958 to 1976, he saw to it that the awards recognized excellence on both Broadway and off-Broadway.

In 2001 the American Theatre Wing Design Awards, once named the Maharam Awards, were renamed the Hewes Design Awards. The 36-year-old awards honor Broadway and off-Broadway designers.

The Outer Critics Circle gave him a 1984–85 special award. In 1993 he was awarded the Margo Jones Award. In 2001 he was inducted into the Theatre Hall of Fame and was critic emeritus at the *Saturday Review*.

HIGH SCHOOL OF PERFORMING ARTS. 120 W. 46th Street. Architect: Charles B. J. Snyder.

The Romanesque revival building was designed in 1893 as P.S. 67. Charles B. J. Snyder, the Superintendent of Buildings for the New York City Board of Education, made sure the building was the most up-to-date at the time. It had improved ventilation and fire protection, unilateral lighting, and small, intimate classrooms. The school was best known as the School of Performing Arts, or P.A., as it was nicknamed.

In 1937 Dr. Franklin Keller, principal of the Metropolitan Vocational High School, found some boys skipping classes to rehearse with a band in the boiler room. Dr. Keller was quoted as saying, "I thought if we gave them music, they wouldn't have to sneak in." So New York City founded the High School of Performing Arts. Thousands of students passed rigorous auditions to gain entry to the school's programs. Among the most famous alumni are Liza Minnelli, Barbra Streisand, Ben Vereen, Al Pacino, Melissa Manchester, and Suzanne Pleshette. The school was featured as the background for the movie and subsequent television series *Fame*.

The school's programs were transferred to 108 Amsterdam Avenue, across from Lincoln Center, in 1985. The 46th Street building was then dubbed Liberty High School and was devoted to classes for immigrants learning English. In February 1988 the school suffered a five-alarm fire that destroyed the roof and most of the interior. It was restored and rebuilt and is today used for government offices.

HIPPODROME. 6th Avenue between 43rd and 44th Streets. Architect: J. H. Morgan. Opening: April 12, 1905; *A Yankee Circus on Mars*.

For most Broadwayites, the Hippodrome is synonymous with spectacle, just as the ROXY connotes lavishness. The theater, the largest in the world, certainly lived up to its reputation. It presented the biggest shows ever seen in New York or anywhere else.

The Hippodrome was the brainchild of Elmer S. Dundy and Frederic Thompson, the builders and operators of Coney Island's Luna Park. Their backer, John W. Bates, urged the team to conquer Broadway at his expense. They set to work to build the biggest and most sophisticated theater of its time. Thompson envisioned a stage big enough to hold 600 people. It was 110 feet deep and 200 feet wide and was divided into 12 sections. Each section could be raised or lowered by hydraulics. The Hippodrome also had a huge tank that could hold a lake big enough to float boats in or take the spill from a huge waterfall. The water pumps could handle 150,000 gallons of water. Because of the huge machinery required to run these devices, the stage weighed 460,000 pounds. The roof and balcony of the building used 15,000 tons of steel. The roof itself was constructed from four giant steel trusses, the largest in any American building.

One of the most important elements of the Hippodrome's design was the lighting system. More than 25,000 light bulbs were used to illuminate the theater and stage. The stage used 9,000, and another 5,000 were arranged in a stunning sunburst pattern in the auditorium. Under the stage was a complete menagerie area where the famous Hippodrome elephants were kept. The theater also had a full complement of offices, costume shops, property houses, and scenery shops. The elaborate scenery itself was changed by a unique system of cranes that carried the equipment up to the fly area high above the stage.

The Hippodrome and its shows were a publicist's dream. On March 12, 1905, a month before it opened, the theater received its first great publicity coup when Police Commissioner William McAdoo had the building surrounded by 100 police officers. They were sent because of a complaint by the Sabbath Association that construction workers were putting in long hours on Sunday. Construction had started in July 1904, almost a year earlier, so it seems strange that action was taken only then. Nonetheless, when the next shift of workers showed up, they were stopped by the police. Thompson and Dundy took matters in hand, giving each of the workers a card that invited him into the theater as a sightseer. The police were powerless to stop the men from entering as guests of the management. After they had entered the auditorium, they were instructed to put material over the windows so that the police couldn't see what was happening inside.

The excitement rose as the building neared completion. Thompson and Dundy walked their menagerie all the way from Luna Park in Coney Island to Manhattan. A herd of elephants led the parade, followed by camels, 175 horses, and even a team of bloodhounds. They marched, on foot and in vans, over the Brooklyn Bridge, up Broadway, and across 42nd Street to the theater.

Hippodrome exterior, at the time of the production of *Cheer Up*, 1917.

By opening night the stage was set for what was certainly the largest opening in theater history, one that had cost $4 million. The ticket prices ranged from 25¢ for the cheapest seats to $2 for the boxes. The theater seated 5,200 patrons. The *New York Clipper* described the theater as "remarkable for its grandeur and magnitude, a place of magnificent distances." The opening show was *A Yankee Circus on Mars*. The play was written by George V. Hobart; Jean Schwartz and Manuel Klein composed the music, and, along with Harry Williams, contributed the lyrics. The settings were designed by the brilliant Arthur Voegtlin, who created most of the great special effects that helped make the Hippodrome's fame.

The star was one of Broadway's favorite actresses, Bessie McCoy, who made her entrance in a gold chariot driven by two white horses. A 30-foot airship landed on the stage and disgorged a Martian who asked the Americans to bring a circus to his planet. At one point in the proceedings, Barlow's Magnificent Hippodrome Elephants appeared behind the steering wheels of autos. The pachyderms drove 10 chorus girls around the Hippodrome's huge stage. The show also featured 280 chorus girls.

Apart from the Hippodrome elephants, the only other regular star of Hippodrome shows was Marceline the Spanish clown. He appeared in every Hippodrome show for a decade. Marceline became as big an attraction as the Hippodrome itself. Gretchen Finletter wrote in her autobiography, *From the Top of the Stairs*, about Marceline's pranks onstage:

When the men appeared to set up the ring, Marceline pulled each peg out as it was hammered down and ran ahead with it to the man in front. . . . The men never caught on and they would have to set up the ring three times. When the carpet was unrolled for the ponies, Marceline rolled it up again just before the ponies appeared. Marceline pulled a net out from under the highest trapeze artist as he was preparing to drop down, and folded it neatly away, thinking the act was over.

The manager appeared in a red coat and high hat and protested in a loud voice. He gesticulated, he pointed up at the trapeze. Did Marceline understand! This was the Dip Of Death! He must leave the net alone! Marceline looked at the manager's gestures, pointed at the figure above, pointed at himself, shook his head, then nodded and smiled. Yes, he understood.

The drums rolled again. The Dip Artist started swinging and then at the very moment he was about to plunge, Marceline jumped forward, pulled at a rope, and net and all fell on the manager in a wild tangle, knocking him over, while the trapezist by a lucky chance caught another swing.

The *Yankee Circus* was only the first part of the opening night program. Next came the *Dance of the Hours*, which featured 150 dancing girls. That piece was in turn followed by *Andersonville, or a Story of Wilson's Raiders*. This spectacular pageant traces the story of a Union officer and a Southern belle. The first scene takes place during a West Point ball. Then we are whisked to the Andersonville prison. Our hero digs a tunnel out of the prison but is spotted by the guards, who chase him to a Southern mansion. Inside, the heroine gives the soldier a horse, and he gallops away, with bloodhounds in hot pursuit. The scene then changes to Rocky Ford Bridge over what appeared to the audience to be a real lake. Four hundred and eighty soldiers meet at the bridge and fight to the death. A team of horses pulling a caisson charges across the stage while the soldiers fight on the bridge and in the water. After the battle the scene changes to the McLean House at Appomattox. The Civil War ends as the hero is united with the heroine.

The *Clipper* called the evening "probably the most unique and remarkable entertainment ever seen in New York." The *Evening World* exclaimed, "Even our skyscrapers will have to bow to it." The rest of the reviews all agreed that the Hippodrome show was the greatest seen on any stage. *A Yankee Circus on Mars* played for 120 performances. The run was long by the standards of the day and even more remarkable when one considers the number of patrons that the theater held.

Thompson and Dundy realized that their next offering would have to surpass the premiere attraction. They decided to mount another show with a circus theme. *A Society Circus* (12/13/05; 596 performances) was indeed bigger and better than the previous show. The spectacular presentation lasted four hours. Sydney Rosenfeld wrote the book, and Manuel Klein wrote the lyrics. Its many elaborate set pieces included: a Gypsy camp complete with a Gypsy wedding; a circus featuring the famous elephants, this time bowling; a ballet of lions and monkeys; a thunderstorm; the ele-

phants performing as a marching band; *The Song of the Flowers* with 144 ballerinas; and, finally, a stupendous wedding ceremony around the Hippodrome pool, which was dotted with fountains and colored lights.

The reviewers were ecstatic. The *Evening Telegram* raved, "Six thousand blasé New Yorkers sat from eight o'clock until nearly midnight, and then got up and cheered. Could anything more be said to show just what this new spectacle is? In every way it is the biggest and best thing of its kind ever presented in America." Despite the rave reviews, audiences were strangely unsatisfied with the show. True, it was bigger than *A Yankee Circus on Mars*, but it was not substantially different. With business falling off, Thompson and Dundy were in trouble. They simply couldn't afford to keep the theater open without a sizable audience.

The July 1906 issue of *Theatre Magazine* reported the current state of the Hippodrome.

> The announcement that Messrs. Thompson and Dundy had retired from the management of the New York Hippodrome came as a surprise to everyone, for it was generally believed that the enterprise had proved a veritable gold mine to its founders. The truth, however, was that the receipts fell off considerably this last season, and with a concern of that magnitude, when enough money does not come in at the front door to furnish the avalanche of dollars that goes out the back door, the situation soon becomes critical. One reason given for the decreased patronage was that the prices of the seats had been advanced against the judgment of Messrs. Thompson and Dundy. A more likely reason is that the novelty of the place had worn off and that its further popularity had to depend solely on the character of the entertainment provided. The show given this last season was not nearly so good. . . . We said that the splendid auditorium and vast stage of the Hippodrome presented magnificent opportunities, which were not taken full advantage of. An enormous amount of money was spent on the stage for costumes, scenery, and performers, but it was not well spent. It was all light and tinsel; there was not art in it. The ballets were poor and the gipsy camp, made a star feature of the last bill, was positively tiresome. Give a good show at moderate prices, and there will be no trouble about crowding the Hippodrome.

The only producers with enough nerve to take over the Hippodrome were the SHUBERT BROTHERS. They reopened a fixed-up version of *A Society Circus* on September 2, 1906, and made a popular success of the show. It ended up running 596 performances with a reduced top price of $1.50.

The next show, *Pioneer Days* and *Neptune's Daughter* (11/28/06), amassed an astonishing $91,000 advance at the box office. The first half of the evening's bill was a Wild West story of bad guys, good guys, and Indians. Everyone is fighting each other, and stagecoaches are forever running in and out. The end of the show is a climactic battle between the Indians, the settlers, and the cavalry. More than 600 performers took part in the melee. The second act, *Neptune's Daughter*, featured a violent storm complete with huge waves and lightning flashes. A ship capsizes, and only one passenger survives: a baby. He grows up and prays to the gods of the sea. Then, as if by magic, Neptune himself surrounded by mermaids appears from the waters of the tank. The audience was thrilled. How could he have risen from the sea? The show began an hour before; surely no one could hold his breath that long. So how did he do it?

During the finale a troupe of mermaids and mermen accompanied by seahorses walked down a broad flight of steps that led into the pool. Down they went into the pool never to be seen again. They simply disappeared into the waters. The audience was astonished at the trick. Word got around the city of the marvelous finale to the Hippodrome show. It swelled the box office to $60,000 a week. Considering the Shuberts needed only one-tenth that amount to break even, the show was a great success. The water tank trick remained a mystery for years, although reports of how it worked sometimes leaked out to the press. Under the water tank was the top half of a tube that trapped air. When the chorus descended into the tank, they walked to the tube, able to breathe normally, then ascended stairs to the backstage.

However, Shubert publicist Will Page knew he had to keep beating the drums to keep the huge theater full. He devised a series of STUNTS that kept the Hippodrome in the public eye. He arranged for a carriage to be drawn through the streets by an ostrich. Alongside ran a dog with a sweater that had *Hippodrome* on it. Page took the Hippodrome's Sioux tribe, which appeared in the show, around the city in an open truck. In the winter he also arranged for a team of elephants to draw a sleigh through the streets. Little Hip, the baby elephant mascot of the Hippodrome, was on view daily in the theater's lobby, where he would nuzzle children and hand out flyers. Page's gimmicks worked, and *Pioneer Days* ran 288 performances.

Next came *The Auto Race* (11/25/07; 312 performances). It also had on the bill *The Battle of Port Arthur* and *Circus Days*. The names described what occurred on stage. Drama critic and playwright George Oppenheimer remembered his experience as a child watching *The Battle of Port Arthur*: "At the first bombardment—I was ultra-gun-shy—my screams of childish fright mingled with the groans of the wounded, adding to the din but not to the realism. My parents hastily removed me from the scene of battle to the relative peace of Sixth Avenue. It was not peaceful for long. My fear of the shell and shot was as nothing compared to my rage at having been removed from them."

The next Hippodrome show, *Sporting Days* (9/5/08), was accompanied by *The Land of Birds Ballet* and *Battle of the Skies*. *Sporting Days* featured a depiction of a real baseball game on what was surely the only indoor stage large enough to hold one. It also featured a rowing match on the Hippodrome's pool, which stood in for the Hudson River, and a horse race. For *The Land of Birds Ballet*, 400 dancers enacted beautiful avian delights. But it was the *Battle of the Skies* that most captured the audience's attention. It portrayed a huge battle over the streets of New York in the far away year of 1950. Above the roofs of the great metropolis slide graceful monorails. The roofs serve as landing docks for giant blimps. Between the buildings, high over the streets, are walkways. Across them march small children dressed as adults. Their size helps sustain the illusion in the forced perspective of the scene. In the window of a newspaper office is a giant screen on which flashes pictures of the latest news events with commentary by a megaphone-wielding announcer. In a museum stands the last living horse in the world.

But all is not well in the future. A group of spies plans to steal America's radium gun. The spies carry flashlight-sized guns that emits beams of light that disintegrate people in a puff of smoke. The second act was a full-scale war between hundreds of balloons and blimps. Some were equipped with the radium gun. Its deadly light beam spares neither man nor machine. A great storm breaks out, full of thunder and lightning, and from the Hippodrome's tank comes two submarines. One is sunk by the radium gun; on the other is the heroine. When her craft is hit, it begins to sink. She climbs to the tower of the great ship just in time to see a balloon coming to her rescue. A line is dropped, and as her submarine slips beneath the waves, she is hoisted into the air. Behind her, also on the rope ladder, comes the villain. She climbs the swaying rope and reaches the airship's perch just in time. The ladder is cut loose, and the villain falls into the sea. This battle is fought twice a day for 448 performances.

A Trip to Japan (9/4/09) was next. Along with the title show was *Inside the Earth* and *The Ballet of Jewels*. The climax of the opening melodrama was a fire atop a tall building. Luckily, the hero is also a tightrope walker. To save his girlfriend he walks across telephone wires. Another highlight of the first act was the stunt performed by Desperado. He jumped off a high platform through 40 feet of air and then hit a giant slide, which deposited him on his feet on the stage floor. *Inside the Earth* actually featured an entire tribe of Maori natives who played a tribe of Incas who lived in a cave in New Zealand. The heroine is kidnapped and taken to an island in the center of the Hippo-drome's great pool. The island sinks with its inhabit-ants, and the heroine sinks beneath the waters. Despite the spectacular effects, the show was not a critical suc-cess. However, audiences kept it open for 447 perfor-mances.

The International Cup (9/3/10; 333 performances) was accompanied by *The Ballet of Niagara* and *The Earthquake. The International Cup* had planes landing on the Hippodrome's stage. Its exciting finale featured a shipwreck at sea in a perilous storm. *The Earthquake* took place in a Central American country that con-tained the fabled Valley of the Moon, inhabited by aliens from outer space. Naturally, there was the earth-quake of the title, abetted by the mighty hydraulics beneath the stage. Islands bearing golden moon girls rose from the Hippodrome tank. The reviews were fa-vorable for the melodrama, ballet, and special effects of the Hippodrome shows. The *New York Dramatic Mirror* stated, "To see and to enjoy everything requires an able bodied person in prime health. Others will droop before the end."

A topic ripe for the Hippodrome treatment was *Around the World* (9/2/11; 445 performances), paired with *The Ballet of the Butterflies, The Fairies Glen,* and *The Golden Barge.* The show followed its cast from New York State to the Swiss Alps and a race on the slippery peaks and then to a battle with Bedouins on the sands of Egypt. It led to a sandstorm that gave way to the slave markets of Constantinople. A circus was the entertainment at a coronation in India, and then there was a midnight gondola ride in Venice. A runaway bull highlighted the action in Spain, which led, surprisingly, to Hawaii and hula dancers. From Hawaii, the intrepid travelers somehow ended up in Ireland.

Under Many Flags (5/31/12; 445 performances) was the optimistic story of how world peace was brought about through the invention of a machine of destruction. A man invents a blimp that could travel 200 miles an hour and carry a payload of explosives. Another man steals the airship and travels around the world with it to Brittany, Holland, Scotland, Arizona, and Persia. As a result of the flight, the world's leaders sign the Treaty of Universal Peace.

The next Hippodrome extravaganza, *America* (8/30/13; 360 performances) was followed by an atypical offering. Opening on April 19, 1914, Gilbert and Sulli-van's *H.M.S. Pinafore,* ran 89 performances. *Wars of the Worlds* (9/5/14; 229 performances), the next offer-ing, was described in *Theatre Magazine*: "Breath-lessly, we are whisked through the centuries as man's struggle against man is depicted in a series of magnifi-cent stage pictures." *Wars of the Worlds* was somewhat topical, because Europe was involved in the begin-

nings of World War I. The Shuberts then put in the *Mammoth Midwinter Circus Supreme.* It also featured a film, *The Heart of Maryland,* a cartoon, a medley of Southern songs, and a dancing-waters ballet. The show wasn't successful, and the Shuberts began to get cold feet. They put in a series of films and vaudeville acts that did little to attract audiences. The Shuberts owed $100,000 in back rental, and the sum was mounting daily.

Following the Shuberts' failures came Charles B. Dillingham, an up-to-date producer of the time, who decided to clean up the Hippodrome. Instead of the customary old-fashioned extravagant melodrama, he presented a fast-paced Broadway-style revue. The dif-ference was that the Hippodrome enabled Dillingham to give the show a spectacular production. Dillingham opened *Hip-Hip-Hooray* (9/30/15; 425 performances) in a newly scrubbed Hippodrome. For the show he hired Broadway composer Raymond Hubbell and John Golden, a noted lyricist and producer. R. H. Burnside wrote the libretto and directed the proceedings. Band-master John Philip Sousa composed a new work, "The New York Hippodrome March." Sousa even appeared in the show along with comic Nat Wills and Toto, a clown who replaced Marceline.

The critics were enthusiastic about the new show. *Theatre Magazine* wrote, "The name fits the show. The astonished and delighted spectator feels like cheering all the way through the really wonderful program. A spectacle of marvelous beauty and varied interest, with a host of star performers, tableaux of surpassing splen-dor, and no end of novel surprises—such a show has never been seen in New York!" The show heralded a new successful era at the Hippodrome. Dillingham celebrated the theater's success with a huge parade composed of 1,274 performers.

Dillingham next presented *The Big Show* (8/31/16; 425 performances), a lavish revue that created a num-ber of firsts in Hippodrome history. It was the first Hippodrome show to feature a genuine superstar, dan-cer Anna Pavlova. It was also the first to contain a smash hit song, "Poor Butterfly." Between editions of the Hippodrome shows and on its dark nights, Dilling-ham filled the theater with concerts and benefits. These featured such stars as Pavlova, Paul Whiteman's Or-chestra, John McCormack, Carmella Ponselle, AL JOL-SON, DeWolf Hopper, W. C. Fields, Harry Houdini, Weber and Fields, VERNON AND IRENE CASTLE, Babe Ruth, GEORGE M. COHAN, Gus Edwards, Amelita Galli-Curci, Feodor Chaliapin, Tito Ruffo, Leon Errol, and Mme. Ernestine Shumann-Heink. VERNON CASTLE made his last stage appearance at a Hippodrome ben-efit.

With the war raging in Europe it seemed appropriate for Dillingham to call his next show *Cheer Up* (8/23/

17; 456 performances). The finale of the show was a resplendent version of Coney Island in all its gaudy fame. At the end the Disappearing Diving Girls dove into the Hippodrome tank and vanished beneath the waters. The number was constructed around the talents of swimmer Annette Kellerman, who had become a Hippodrome regular after the run of *The Big Show*. Dillingham's next show was aptly titled *Everything* (8/22/18; 461 performances). This revue had some music and lyrics contributed by IRVING BERLIN. It starred Houdini, Hopper, and Belle Story.

With America now fighting World War I and Prohibition about to go into effect, Dillingham had the nerve—or optimism—to title the next Hippodrome show *Happy Days* (8/23/19; 452 performances). The *New York Dramatic Mirror* said, "Perhaps it is Mr. Dillingham's little joke." The title proved even more ironic when the actors struck the Broadway theaters in the ACTORS' STRIKE OF 1919. Dillingham, though sympathetic to the actors, remained a member of the Producing Managers' Association, which opposed ACTORS' EQUITY. When the Hippodrome's 412 stagehands walked out, Dillingham quit as manager of the Hippodrome. The stagehands went back on the job, and when the strike was settled Dillingham returned to the theater.

With the war over, Dillingham titled his next show *Good Times* (8/9/20; 455 performances). The show featured Abdullah's Arabs, Nanette Flack, the Poodles Hanneford Family of trick horsemen, Joe Jackson, Joseph Parsons, and Belle Story. *Get Together* (8/3/21; 397 performances) was heavy on ballet. It featured *The Thunder Bird Ballet* by Vera Fokine, directed by Russian choreographer Michel Fokine. There was also an ice ballet based on *The Red Shoes*. *Get Together* was followed by *Better Times* (9/2/22). Most critics and the public felt *Better Times* was the best of all the Hippodrome spectaculars. Unfortunately, it was also the last. The show ran for 405 performances, after which Charles Dillingham left the theater. Production costs were rising as the theater struggled to maintain a cast of 1,000 people as well as a massive physical plant.

Because the Hippodrome occupied a large chunk of prime property, the site was viewed with interest by a number of real estate developers. The U.S. Realty and Improvement Company owned the theater and its land and tendered offers. But the theater was saved when E. F. ALBEE decided to take it over and present vaudeville in the huge hall. Albee took out all the complex stage mechanics and replaced the stage with a small wooden platform. The proscenium was brought to a more manageable size, and the Hippodrome became just another vaudeville theater. The theater reopened on December 17, 1923, with an undistinguished vaude-

ville bill. The Hippodrome presented what might be called high-class vaudeville with movies thrown in for good measure. However, by 1929 vaudeville was all but dead, and so was the Hippodrome. Morris Gest leased the theater to present *The Passion Play*, but it closed after five weeks with a $250,000 loss. In July 1930 the theater was closed tight.

RKO had inherited the theater from Albee and subsequently sold it to Frederick Brown, a real estate investor. Brown then sold it to the Fred T. French Operators for $7.5 million. The French company announced that they would tear the theater down and construct an 83-story office building on the site. Unfortunately, the country was in the depths of the Depression, and construction was at a standstill. The Hippodrome sat empty until master showman Billy Rose decided to rent the theater to present a new musical, *Jumbo*.

Rose cleaned up the exterior of the theater and renovated the interior to resemble a huge circus arena. The seating area was altered so that it sloped in one continuous line from the far reaches of the balcony to the stage floor. Albert Johnson designed the new interior as well as the production. RODGERS AND HART were assigned the task of writing the score for the mammoth show. Rose hired Ben Hecht and Charles MacArthur to script the proceedings and Jimmy Durante, Gloria Grafton, Paul Whiteman and his orchestra, Poodles Hanneford, Donald Novis, and Arthur Sinclair to head the cast. Then he chose 1,200 animals to appear in the circus setting. The show was so big that it needed two directors, JOHN MURRAY ANDERSON and GEORGE ABBOTT. They whipped the show into shape amid countless delays. MacArthur once quipped that opening night was postponed because there were a few people who hadn't seen the show yet.

Jumbo finally opened on November 16, 1933 (221 performances). The critics were unanimous in their praise. PERCY HAMMOND, in the *New York Herald Tribune*, called the show "a sane and exciting compound of opera, animal show, folk drama, harlequinade, carnival, circus, extravaganza and spectacle." GILBERT W. GABRIEL agreed, writing in the *New York American* that it was "chockfull of so many thrills, musical, scenic, gymnastic and humanitarian, it deserves endowment as an institution." These reviews might have applied equally well to the early Hippodrome extravaganzas. The theater itself also got good notices. Richard Lockridge, writing in the *New York Sun*, stated, "It all adds up to a fairly superlative entertainment. This is largely due to what Albert Johnson has done in designing the show and, above all, the theater."

Jumbo was a huge hit, but it cost so much to run that it was forced to close. The Hippodrome was closed again. In 1939 it was used briefly as a basketball court.

Then in September of that year crews came and knocked down the theater. Ironically, development plans for the site continued to fall through. Twelve years passed before the site was finally utilized. In 1952 a garage, appropriately named the Hippodrome Garage, and an office building opened.

HOFFMAN, IRVING. Caricaturist, columnist, and humorist during the 1940s and '50s; b. New York, New York, 1909; d. New York, New York, December 9, 1968.

Irving Hoffman influenced the careers of many stars and became a confidant of many of the personalities on the Rialto. Because Hoffman was born in 1909 on the anniversary of the invention of the steamboat, his parents gave him the middle name Fulton, after its inventor. He dropped out of DeWitt Clinton High School a year before graduation because he found his teachers boring. In 1924 he went to the Democratic National Convention. While there, the industrious 14-year-old made caricatures of the leading lights: William Jennings Bryan, Franklin Delano Roosevelt, Alfred E. Smith, and others. He sold the drawings to the *New York Evening World* and thus started his professional career. One of his trademarks was the incorporation of the subject's initials into the drawing. For George Bernard Shaw the "G" was used to form the nose, the "B" became his mouth, and Shaw's beard was defined by a flourished "S." He later became a reporter for *The Morning Telegraph* under the moniker Beau Broadway.

The caricatures opened doors for Hoffman, and his offbeat sense of humor ingratiated him to many theatrical personages. Hoffman might not have always meant to be funny. Often the cue for his unexpected quips was his poor eyesight. Hoffman himself was aware of his unintended gaffes. As he remarked about himself

Self-portrait by Irving Hoffman.

in the *New York Times*, "I shake all the wrong hands, I offer smokers trays with olives because I think they're ash trays. I put salt on leaves of the table decorations and eat the flowers. The dinner table is lighted by candles, and I don't say a thing. People laugh and say I'm a great wit, but I feel a constricted feeling in the back of my head and wish I were at LINDY'S."

Hoffman's wit got him into many elegant parties where guests viewed him with much amusement. He turned the tables somewhat by selling gossip to such friends as columnist WALTER WINCHELL, ED SULLIVAN, and DAMON RUNYON. In fact, Hoffman shared a two-room apartment at 156 West 48th Street with the three columnists. They were happy to have Hoffman as a source of material, and when he was unable to come up with a tidbit they could always write about the source himself. Other friends who passed through the portals above Duffy's Tavern were BUGS BAER, who lived in the flat occasionally, IRVING BERLIN, Peter Lorre, Edward G. Robinson, and countless others. At the same time Hoffman actually lived with his parents on Riverside Drive.

Hoffman was for a time a press agent for Coney Island. It was there that he got the break that propelled his career forward. Franklin D. Roosevelt had invited King George VI and Queen Elizabeth to America, and the royals took a trip to Coney Island. Hoffman arranged to have them photographed eating a Nathan's hot dog at the resort. The picture ran throughout the world, resulting in free publicity for the beach community and the hot dog company.

In 1936 Hoffman became the drama critic for the *Hollywood Reporter*. He also started writing a column on Broadway life for the paper. Like many of his contemporaries, Hoffman used the pen to deal satirical blows at his subjects. He explained the practice by asking, "Why should I be as dull as the play?" Hoffman's column was called "Tales of Hoffman." In it he would often promote new personalities and up-and-coming talents. Among these were the young Shirley MacLaine, Lauren Bacall, and Judy Garland. Irving Berlin had a fondness for Hoffman and often used him as a sounding board for his newest tunes. Darryl F. Zanuck, head of Twentieth Century-Fox, also sat in on these tryouts.

The column was not a source of income for Hoffman. He originally received $65 a week for the column, which took him 10 hours a day to produce. When television's popularity caused a reduction in the coffers of the big studios, the result was a loss of advertising for the *Reporter*. Hoffman's salary was reduced to $50 per week. Since it cost him $48.50 a week to have the column researched and typed, he made a grand profit of $1.50.

In addition to his daily column Hoffman wrote regularly for *Coronet* magazine and several others. He edited a page of anecdotes and snappy sayings that was syndicated by King Features under the title "Celebriteehees."

Hoffman acted as the go-between when the notorious GANGSTER Louis Lepke surrendered to Walter Winchell. In his autobiography Winchell failed to credit Hoffman's role. Perhaps it was because Hoffman was the only person who could tell Winchell to shut up when Winchell droned on, bragging about the incident. Hoffman not only helped Winchell get scoops but also helped the young columnist develop his style. Hoffman called gossip columnists "the carpet sweepers in the Hall of Fame," but as a publicist, he recognized their power. Hoffman would even make changes in the proofs of Winchell's column.

The clients Hoffman handled as a press agent never got a break in Hoffman's own column; he felt it would be unethical. But the fact that Hoffman had the ear of Winchell helped persuade these clients to pay him hefty retainers. His friendship with the powerful Winchell also made Hoffman wealthy through the movies. Several studios paid Hoffman a retainer of $25,000 per year to keep Winchell abreast of the latest in motion pictures. However, Hoffman's close relationship with Winchell sometimes backfired on the studios. Ernest Lehman, later a noted screenwriter himself, was on Hoffman's staff. Hoffman was on retainer for Hollywood producer David O. Selznick. Lehman concocted a story about Joan Fontanne being so upset over losing the Oscar for best actress in *Rebecca* that Selznick gave her one himself. Hoffman placed the item in Winchell's column, and Selznick hit the roof. Hoffman rejoined, "We're through. I don't tell you how to make pictures; don't tell me how to write publicity." Hoffman served as a movie reviewer, book reviewer, and talent scout for Winchell. Hoffman was much better read than his friend, and many of Winchell's opinions were based solely on Hoffman's say-so.

Hoffman had many friends in the industry who stood by him. One example is the showgirl Mary Dowell, who traipsed the boards for Billy Rose. She was dubbed "Stuttering Sam" by Broadway wags because of her speech impediment. But she entered into a long correspondence with Hoffman, who occasionally reprinted her letters in his column. When Warner Brothers was seeking a female writer, Hoffman got Dowell the job. Needless to say, she was one of Hoffman's biggest boosters. "People love to exist for Irving. When you're in Irving's circle your soul is no longer your own! It belongs to him! But you give it voluntarily, gladly—and that's the way you want it to be!"

Others decamped from the Hoffman group when they received bad reviews. Fredric March, once a fan, seceded after Hoffman's review of *A Bell for Adano*. (Hoffman had proclaimed that March acted more like Thomas E. Dewey than Major Joppolo.) And Rouben Mamoulian dropped out after a pan of *Sadie Thompson*. But Hoffman didn't enjoy cutting down his friends. For the review of *The Ryan Girl*, the first half of the column illuminated the warm, sentimental relationship Hoffman enjoyed with the film's author and producer, Edmund Goulding. Then he proceeded to eviscerate the film. Hoffman defended his vituperative reviews, "Dramatic critics who write pleasant obituaries are in a class with sanctimonious preachers."

Many felt the idea of Hoffman reviewing movies was ludicrous, since they believed he was unable to see the screen. He began reviewing plays for the *Hollywood Reporter* in 1931. When Hoffman wrote an unfavorable review of the play *Ethan Frome*, Max Gordon complained that "Hoffman can't see." "Yes," replied Hoffman, "but there's nothing wrong with my nose." Hoffman was proud of his critical acumen. He wrote the poet Walter Benton, "Oh yes—I write dramatic criticism too. I do that best, I believe, because I do it with integrity and imagination. In the theatre on a bright night I can see past the four walls and view the horizon of a better theatre—and a better world."

Both the *New Yorker* and the *Saturday Review of Literature* wanted Hoffman to come over as a film critic, but he turned them down.

Once Hoffman entered a fancy party with a date on his arm and literally bumped into an acquaintance; he inquired, "Tell me. Is she pretty?"

After Hoffman died Damon Runyon described Hoffman thus:

> Now there is a great document. He is a tall, loose-jointed New York fellow, a man-about-tables, a squire of dames, a bon vivant, a raconteur, and all that truck. He should be one of the greatest writers of these times. He is a good caricaturist. A man can make a neat living with either accomplishment nowadays. Hoffman neglects them both in favor of press agentry.
>
> Maybe the mug fancies money. He is said to have some fat publicity accounts. He knows his Manhattan Island better than a detective. He is constantly digging up unusual places to eat. . . .
>
> Hoffman made himself solid with me by keeping his hellos up big and strong all the way through, though, to tell the truth, I suspect that in his nearsightedness he may have mistaken me for Winchell.

HOLIDAY THEATER. *See* **Movieland.**

HOLLYWOOD THEATER. *See* **Mark Hellinger Theater.**

HUBERT'S FLEA CIRCUS. *See* **Murray's Roman Gardens.**

HUDSON THEATRE. 139 W. 44th Street. Architect: J. B. McElfatrick & Co. Opening: October 19, 1903; *Cousin Kate.*

After OSCAR HAMMERSTEIN I's pioneering efforts in the new theater district growing up around Times Square at the turn of the century, the best-regarded theater locations were on 42nd Street. Producer Henry B. Harris chose to build his Hudson Theatre on 44th Street following the lead of Daniel Frohman's LYCEUM THEATER, built the year before on 45th Street. Harris hired J. B. McElfatrick to design his theater, but for some unknown reason McElfatrick dropped out of the job and the theater was finished by Israels and Harder. Unfortunately, this rocky beginning proved to be the norm for the theater. The Hudson has had a spotty career ever since its inception.

The 1,006-seat theater, considered one of the more modern of its time, seemed to have a bright future.

Henry B. Harris.

However, some critics preferred more overtly decorated playhouses. The *Architectural Record* reported, "One wishes for a few notes of virility and for some big, strong masses of color somewhere in the ensemble. The theater is pretty but it is very tame."

Harris presented *Cousin Kate* (10/19/03; 44 performances), with Ethel Barrymore (*see* BARRYMORE FAMILY) in the lead, and Shaw's masterpiece *Man and Superman* (9/5/05; 192 performances). For the latter play Harris put his reputation on the line. Police Magistrate McAdoo announced that he was aghast at the thought of a play that ridiculed marriage. McAdoo quoted Theodore Roosevelt, who proclaimed that marriage was the basis of a healthy civilization. The leading critic of the day, William Winter, avowed that he held Shaw in little regard, adding, "I do not waste thought on him." The public library made sure that juveniles could not come across the play on its shelves. The script was put on the library's restricted list.

Harris lost his life on the *Titanic,* and his widow Rene, did not have much luck in producing plays (though otherwise she was lucky, as she was the last person to leave the *Titanic* before it sank). She presented a few successes including Sean O'Casey's *The Plough and the Stars* (11/28/27; 48 performances). One of the only musical successes at the Hudson was the black show *Hot Chocolates* (219 performances), which opened June 20, 1929. It had an above-average score by Fats Waller, Harry Brooks, and Andy Razaf. The songs included "Black and Blue" and the smash hit, "Ain't Misbehavin'." Cab Calloway and Edith Wilson were featured, and Duke Ellington contributed two tunes.

It seemed that Mrs. Harris had used up her luck on the *Titanic.* In 1929 she was offered $1 million for the theater. She turned down the offer. Events would prove that to be a very, very bad decision. Like many of the other Broadway houses, the Hudson ceased legitimate use with the Depression. Mrs. Harris lost the playhouse to foreclosure. The Emigrant Industrial Savings Bank bought the theater for $100,000 and leased it to CBS. It reopened as the CBS Radio Playhouse Number 1 on February 3, 1934. Three years later the theater returned to its original use with a production of *An Enemy of the People,* which opened February 15, 1937 and ran for 16 performances.

The writing team of Howard Lindsay and Russel Crouse bought the theater in 1944. Their play *State of the Union* opened at the Hudson on November 14, 1945, and ran for 765 performances. This enormous run was capped when the play won the PULITZER PRIZE. On March 23, 1949, Sidney Kingsley's *Detective Story* opened at the Hudson and ran an estimable 581 performances.

This return to live theater lasted just over a decade until NBC bought the theater for $595,000 and converted it for television in 1950. Among the television shows presented from the theater were *Broadway Open House* (1950–1954) and *The Tonight Show* (1954–1959). In 1960, with *The Tonight Show* having moved to Los Angeles the previous year, the theater again became a stage house. NBC spent $100,000 restoring the theater to legitimate use.

At the same time NBC discovered that the theater had a tenant, producer Robert Breen. It seems that Breen, later noted for bringing *Porgy and Bess* to Russia, had lived in the building since 1942 in a nine-room apartment on the third and fourth floors. He and his family had heat and hot water only when the theater was booked. NBC wanted Breen out so they could make the apartment into office space. But Breen refused and the parties went to court. The judge ruled that the Breens could remain in their apartment, so members of the Breen family stayed in the Hudson until at least the 1990s.

The theater reopened with a one-person show featuring Dorothy Stickney performing Edna St. Vincent Millay's poetry. Titled *A Lovely Light* (2/8/60; 17 performances), the show was produced by Sol Hurok and directed by Stickney's husband, Howard Lindsay, former owner of the Hudson. Among the few successes during NBC's tenancy was Lillian Hellman's *Toys in the Attic* (2/25/60; 556 performances). Mostly the theater remained dark.

NBC decided to sell the Hudson in 1961. The plan was to sell the theater to a garage owner who planned to turn the site into a parking lot. When this came to light, there was an uproar. NBC decided to postpone a sale of the theater. In 1962 NBC was finally successful in selling the auditorium with the proviso that it remain a theater.

The theater remained dark for the next two years until stripper Ann Corio decided to bring her show *This Was Burlesque* (3/16/65; 124 performances) to Broadway where it received great acclaim. The theater was again up for sale, this time with the idea of making the theater itself into a parking garage. That plan fell through when the city came to the rescue. Another owner purchased the lot and planned to tear down the theater for an office building. But the market was soft, and the theater was saved again.

Molly Picon and Godfrey Cambridge opened at the Hudson in the musical *How to Be a Jewish Mother* (12/28/67; 20 performances). Madhur Jaffrey, known for her Indian recipes and work on art films, appeared with Michael Kermoyan in *The Guide*. The play opened on March 6, 1968, and closed after only 5 performances. The last play to appear on the Hudson's historic stage was *Mike Downstairs* (4/18/68; 4 performances). It was an ignoble end to a noble theater.

In 1968 the theater was renamed the Avon-Hudson, with porno films the featured attractions and a new entrance on 45th Street. That policy was stopped in 1975 when second-run double features were presented.

A succession of uses followed. In 1981 the theater became the Savoy, a disco and concert venue under the auspices of promoter Ron Delsener. After the Savoy closed in 1983 a nearby condo used the stage of the Hudson to erect a model apartment.

Finally, in the late 1990s, instead of being destroyed as planned, the theater was restored and incorporated into the Hotel Macklowe to be used for meetings and conferences.

On November 17, 1987, the New York City Landmarks Preservation Commission gave the interior and exterior of the Hudson Theatre landmark status. The commission stated that the facade is a "restrained but handsome version of Beaux-Arts classicism," and it has "unusually handsome auditorium and lobby spaces."

IATSE (INTERNATIONAL ALLIANCE OF THEATRICAL STAGE EMPLOYEES).

This union of stage workers was organized by 11 local unions in New York City on July 17, 1893. Originally called the National Alliance of Theatrical Stage Employees, the word *National* was changed to *International* in 1898, although the union did not actually become international until October 1, 1902. In 1914 the American Federation of Labor added movie projectionists to the union, and the name of the union became what it is today: International Alliance of Theatrical Stage Employees and Moving Picture Machine Operators of the United States. The union currently represents press agents; stagehands; sound technicians; hair stylists; wardrobe handlers and dressers; makeup artists; set, costume, and lighting designers; and projectionists.

IATSE has been blamed for high production costs with the resultant high ticket prices, loss of audience, and reduction in quantity and quality of productions on both Broadway and the road. While the exorbitant fees and featherbedding associated with the union have had an effect on Broadway, IATSE is not totally to blame. Like its sister unions, the American Federation of Musicians and ACTORS' EQUITY, IATSE has its share of illogical work rules and arcane practices, but the producers who negotiated the contracts are equally to blame. Broadway's precarious future will be assured only if the unions and producers create reasonable production contracts.

IMPERIAL THEATRE.

249 W. 45th Street. Architect: Herbert J. Krapp. Opening: December 25, 1923; *Mary Jane McKane*.

The 1,650-seat Imperial Theatre has proved to be among the most successful of all musical comedy houses. Its ideal location across from the Golden (*see* JOHN GOLDEN THEATER) and ROYALE theaters and down the block from the MUSIC BOX and now demolished MOROSCO and BIJOU theaters gave the SHUBERT BROTHERS, its owners, a prime musical theater.

The Shuberts wanted a replacement for their aging LYRIC THEATRE on 42nd Street. They chose a lot running between 45th and 46th Streets. The land fronting 46th Street was less expensive, but 45th Street was a more desirable location. Thus the thin entrance was erected on the 45th Street side of the lot, and the theater

Imperial Theatre featuring *Let 'Em Eat Cake*, 1933.

proper was built on the cheaper land on 46th Street. The theater opened on Christmas Day 1923 with *Mary Jane McKane* (115 performances), a musical with music by VINCENT YOUMANS and Herbert Stothart and book and lyrics by William Cary Duncan and OSCAR HAMMERSTEIN II. The producer was Oscar's uncle, ARTHUR HAMMERSTEIN. Among the biggest hits was the Youmans song "Come on and Pet Me." *Mary Jane McKane* starred Mary Hay, Hal Skelly, and Eva Clark.

Rose-Marie (9/2/24; 518 performances) opened at the Imperial with Hammerstein as book and lyric writer in conjunction with OTTO HARBACH. Herbert Stothart and RUDOLF FRIML composed the stirring melodies; Arthur Hammerstein again produced. *Rose-Marie* had several hit songs, including "Indian Love Call," "Rose-Marie," "Pretty Things," and "The Song of the Mounties."

A decidedly more modern musical, *Oh, Kay!* (11/8/26; 257 performances), boasted a superior score by GEORGE AND IRA GERSHWIN and Howard Dietz (*see*

DIETZ AND SCHWARTZ) and a serviceable book by GUY BOLTON and P. G. Wodehouse. Among the hit songs introduced by stars Constance Carpenter, Betty Compton, Gertrude Lawrence, Victor Moore, and Oscar Shaw were "Someone to Watch Over Me," "Maybe," and "Do, Do, Do." *Oh, Kay!*'s exuberant score and superior production by Alex A. Aarons and Vinton Freedley (*see* AARONS AND FREEDLEY) were responsible for its success.

Operetta returned to the Imperial with SIGMUND ROMBERG's *The New Moon* (9/19/28; 519 performances). It had lyrics by Hammerstein, who collaborated on the book with Frank Mandel and Laurence Schwab. The three librettists were also credited with the show's direction, and Schwab and Mandel handled producing chores. The songs "The Girl on the Prow," "Wanting You," "Gorgeous Alexander," and "Marianne" were minor hits from the lush score. More popular were the classic songs "Softly, as in a Morning Sunrise," "Lover, Come Back to Me," and "Stout-

The cast of *Oh, Kay!*, Victor Moore (at left with tea cup) and Gertrude Lawrence (at left with mop), 1926.

hearted Men." *The New Moon* was among the last successful operettas mounted on Broadway.

Popular songwriters J. Fred Coots, Arthur Swanstrom, and Benny Davis contributed the score to the theater's next hit, *Sons o' Guns* (11/26/29; 297 performances). Although none of the songs achieved great success ("Why?" and "Cross Your Fingers" did attain slight renown), the show was a big hit with audiences, despite the stock market crash and the onset of the Depression.

The Depression changed the fortunes of many Broadway producers. Some, like the Chanins, lost all their holdings. The Shuberts also had some setbacks. Some of their theaters were sold to the burgeoning radio industry, and some simply went dark. But the Imperial managed to house a series of highly successful shows. Ed Wynn was coauthor, producer, and director as well as star of *The Laugh Parade* (11/2/31; 243 performances). Harry Warren, better known for his later Hollywood scores, contributed music with accompanying lyrics by Mort Dixon and Joe Young. The big hit from the score was "You're My Everything."

Broadway's preeminent revue writers, Howard Dietz and Arthur Schwartz had another success with their revue *Flying Colors* (9/15/32; 181 performances). Their score included such wonderful tunes as "Alone Together," "Fatal Fascination," "Louisiana Hayride," and "A Shine on Your Shoes." *Flying Colors* had skits by George S. Kaufman (*see* KAUFMAN AND HART), Charles Sherman, Corey Ford, and Howard Dietz. Dietz also directed the show, whose cast included Clifton Webb, Larry Adler, Patsy Kelly, Charles Butterworth, Imogene Coca, Vilma and Buddy Ebsen, Tamara Geva, Jean Sargent, and Philip Loeb.

The Gershwins returned with *Let 'Em Eat Cake* (10/21/33; 89 performances), a sequel to their satirical musical comedy *Of Thee I Sing*. Kaufman directed the show and wrote the book with Morrie Ryskind. The show contained one of the Gershwins' most consistent scores, including the hit song "Mine." William Gaxton, Victor Moore, and Lois Moran all repeated their roles from its predecessor. The show was surprisingly sophisticated by Broadway standards and is only now receiving its due. *Let 'Em Eat Cake* perhaps hit too close to home for Depression audiences.

Say When (11/8/34; 76 performances) was also not a hit, although its creators received fame later. The show had music by Ray Henderson (*see* DE SYLVA, BROWN, AND HENDERSON) and lyrics by Ted Koehler. Bob Hope, Harry Richman, and Prince Michael Romanoff, later of restaurant fame, starred. One of the greatest of all musical comedy songs, "Begin the Beguine," graced the Imperial tenant *Jubilee* (10/12/35; 169 performances). Moss Hart (*see* KAUFMAN, AND HART) wrote the book while sailing the seas with composer/lyricist COLE PORTER. The show was very funny

and sophisticated in its story of a royal family given a few days of freedom to taste the pleasures enjoyed by commoners. The show starred Mary Boland, Melville Cooper, June Knight, and Charles Walters. Also included in the cast was Montgomery Clift. Another hit song, "Just One of Those Things," came from the playful Porter score.

RODGERS AND HART's *On Your Toes* (4/11/36; 318 performances) was the Imperial's next musical offering. The songwriters wrote the book in collaboration with GEORGE ABBOTT, who also co-directed with Worthington Miner. A major contribution to the show was George Balanchine's choreography, especially for the now classic "Slaughter on Tenth Avenue." The score was brimming with great standards. These included "On Your Toes" and "There's a Small Hotel." Those songs that didn't achieve renown, such as "Quiet Night" and "The Heart Is Quicker Than the Eye," are nevertheless noteworthy.

The theater hosted a rare nonmusical production with Leslie Howard's ill-conceived version of *Hamlet*. It ran only 39 performances. The operetta form was almost totally dead, but the Shuberts opened the Franz Lehar operetta *Frederika* (2/4/37; 94 performances) at the Imperial. Despite an excellent cast and production, the public was not interested. Dietz and Schwartz fared as badly with a book show, *Between the Devil* (12/23/37; 93 performances). Again, the elements were all top-notch. Vilma Ebsen, Jack Buchanan, and Evelyn Laye starred, and the score included "I See Your Face before Me" and "By Myself."

The Imperial finally had another big hit with the return of Cole Porter. He wrote the score to *Leave It to Me!* (11/9/38; 291 performances), which accompanied a libretto by Bella and Samuel Spewack. The score contained the usual complement of hit songs, including "Get out of Town," "Most Gentlemen Don't Like Love," and "My Heart Belongs to Daddy." The last song was introduced by a newcomer, MARY MARTIN. It launched her career. Also in the cast were William Gaxton, Adele Jergens, Victor Moore, Sophie Tucker, and Tamara. Another newcomer included in the cast of *Leave It to Me!* was Gene Kelly, who was relegated to a part in the chorus.

Rodgers and Hart had another hit at the Imperial with their college musical *Too Many Girls* (10/18/39; 249 performances). The show had a lightweight book by George Marion Jr. As producer and director, George Abbott kept the production moving briskly. The score included the classic "I Didn't Know What Time It Was" as well as "I Like to Recognize the Tune," "Give It Back to the Indians," and "She Could Shake the Maracas." The show starred Mary Jane Walsh, Richard Kollmar, Hal Le Roy, Marcy Wescott, and Eddie

The cast of *Leave It to Me* (l to r) April, Ruth Daye, Audrey Palmer, Mildred Chernaval, Victor Moore, Sophie Tucker and unknown porters, 1938.

Bracken, along with newcomer Desi Arnaz. It also had a future star, Van Johnson, in the chorus.

The 1940s were even more successful than the 1930s at the Imperial. In 1940 IRVING BERLIN's production of *Louisiana Purchase* (5/28/40; 444 performances) opened. Morrie Ryskind, of *Let 'Em Eat Cake* fame, wrote the book. Vera Zorina, of *On Your Toes*, Irene Bordoni, and Carol Bruce starred along with two Imperial regulars, William Gaxton and Victor Moore. Also in the cast were two future songwriting stars, Hugh Martin and Ralph Blane. The Berlin score contained such enduring hits as "Fools Fall in Love" and "It's a Lovely Day Tomorrow."

Let's Face It! (10/29/41; 547 performances) was another Cole Porter vehicle to play the Imperial. The Porter score yielded no standards, but "Farming," "A Little Rhumba Numba," "I Hate You Darling," "A Lady Needs a Rest," "Everything I Love," and "Ace in the Hole" are top-drawer Porter tunes. The librettists were Herbert and Dorothy Fields (*see* FIELDS FAMILY). The show's wonderful cast included Eve Arden, Nanette Fabray, Benny Baker, Edith Meiser, Vivian Vance, Mary Jane Walsh, Frances and Jack Williams, and newcomer Danny Kaye in his first starring role on Broadway.

Mary Martin returned to the Imperial in *One Touch of Venus* (10/7/43; 567 performances), the KURT WEILL–Ogden Nash musical. She perfectly personified a mortal's view of Venus. The offbeat book was by the somewhat dyspeptic humorist S. J. Perelman and Nash. The show was directed by Elia Kazan. Despite Nash's inexperience at lyrics, he and Weill came up with a delightful score, including the hits "Foolish Heart," "I'm a Stranger Here Myself," "That's Him," and "Speak Low." Kenny Baker, John Boles, Teddy Hart, Paula Laurence, and Sono Osato completed the cast.

After a continuation of the run of the ZIEGFELD FOLLIES, from the WINTER GARDEN THEATRE, came one of the Imperial's greatest successes. Irving Berlin's ANNIE GET YOUR GUN (5/16/46; 1,147 performances) toplined ETHEL MERMAN as Annie Oakley. *Let's Face It*'s librettists Herbert and Dorothy Fields repeated the task for this show. The entire show proved to be one of the classics of the American musical theater. RODGERS AND HAMMERSTEIN produced, with JOSHUA LOGAN directing. The Berlin score was the tunesmith's finest. The hits included "They Say It's Wonderful," "Anything You Can Do," "Doin' What Comes Natur'lly," "I Got the Sun in the Morning," "You Can't Get a Man with a Gun," and the show business anthem "There's No Business Like Show Business."

After a minor effort, *Along Fifth Avenue* (1/13/49; 180 performances), another offering came from Berlin. *Miss Liberty* (7/7/49; 308 performances), the story of the Statue of Liberty, was not as successful as *Annie Get Your Gun*, although the score was delightful. The hit song was "Let's Take an Old-Fashioned Walk." Eddie Albert and Allyn Ann McLerie starred. The LEONARD BERNSTEIN version of *Peter Pan* (4/4/50; 321 performances) followed, with Jean Arthur and Boris Karloff. Then Ethel Merman was tapped again by Berlin to star in *Call Me Madam* (10/12/50; 644 performances), a slightly disguised story about Washington socialite Perle Mesta. Howard Lindsay and Russel Crouse wrote the book, and George Abbott directed. Also featured in the cast were Pat Harrington, Russell Nype, Tommy Rall, and Paul Lukas. "The Best Thing for You," "It's a Lovely Day Today," and "You're Just in Love" were the big hits.

Joshua Logan, director of *Annie Get Your Gun*, also directed the Imperial's next tenant, *Wish You Were Here* (6/25/52; 598 performances). He coauthored the libretto and coproduced as well. HAROLD ROME's show was not a success at first, but producers Leland Hayward and Logan worked on improving the show after it opened. The popularity of the title song also contributed to the show's long run. The Imperial had a swimming pool installed into its stage for the production.

John Murray Anderson's Almanac (10/12/53; 227 performances) was one of the last large revues on Broadway. Hermione Gingold, Polly Bergen, Carleton Carpenter, Harry Belafonte, Orson Bean, Billy De Wolfe, and Kay Medford starred. Then, Cole Porter's last Broadway show, *Silk Stockings* (2/24/55; 477 performances), opened at the Imperial with Don Ameche and Hildegarde Neff in the leads. "All of You" was the hit in the score. FRANK LOESSER's ambitious musical version of *They Knew What They Wanted* was titled *The Most Happy Fella* (5/3/56; 676 performances). Metropolitan Opera star Robert Weede and Jo Sullivan had the leads. Also in the cast were Susan Johnson, Lee Cass, and Mona Paulee. The musical epic contained some of the most sweeping melodies heard on any Broadway stage in addition to traditional musical comedy songs, semioperatic arias, and sung narrative. The show's musical comedy numbers "Big D" and "Standing on the Corner" were the big hits, but the other numbers were what made this score so unique.

Audiences loved the DAVID MERRICK production *Jamaica* (10/31/57; 555 performances) and its star, Lena Horne. But the show was a far cry from what its authors contemplated. Composer HAROLD ARLEN and lyricist E. Y. HARBURG didn't think they were writing the *Lena Horne Show*, but that's how it turned out. Luckily the score was first-rate even if it contained no major hits. Ricardo Montalban, Josephine Premice, Adelaide Hall, Ossie Davis, and Erik Rhodes played second fiddle to Ms. Horne.

Harold Rome had another hit at the Imperial with *Destry Rides Again* (4/23/59; 472 performances), starring Andy Griffith and Dolores Gray. Everyone thought a western musical would not be a hit on sophisticated Broadway, but Rome and librettist Leonard Gershe proved them wrong with this David Merrick production. Then Merrick moved *Gypsy* to the Imperial from the BROADWAY THEATRE, with Ethel Merman continuing in the starring role. He then premiered Bob Merrill's musical *Carnival!* (4/13/61; 719 performances) at the Imperial with Anna Maria Alberghetti and Jerry Orbach starring. Gower Champion directed the proceedings, and the hit song was "Love Makes the World Go Round." Merrick retained his lease on the theater with the next attraction, a transfer of the London success, *Oliver!* (1/6/63; 774 performances). Lionel Bart's musical contained several big hit songs, including "As Long as He Needs Me," "Consider Yourself," and "Where Is Love?" Bruce Prochnik starred in the title role, ably assisted by Georgia Brown, Alice Playten, Clive Revill, and Danny Sewell.

The Imperial Theatre's greatest success came next: *Fiddler on the Roof* (9/22/63; 3,242 performances), claimed by some to be the greatest of all musicals. BOCK AND HARNICK provided the score, and Joseph Stein wrote a strong libretto. Zero Mostel had the role of his career as Tevye the milkman. Also featured were Beatrice Arthur, Bert Convy, Maria Karnilova, Julia Migenes, and Austin Pendleton. The best-known song was "Sunrise, Sunset." *Fiddler on the Roof* was produced by HAROLD PRINCE and directed by Jerome Robbins, to whom much of the credit for its success was given.

Cabaret moved to the Imperial from the BROADHURST THEATER in 1967. It was followed by another John Kander and Fred Ebb show, *Zorba* (11/17/68; 305 performances). Joseph Stein, author of the book to *Fiddler on the Roof*, wrote the libretto to *Zorba*. Harold Prince produced and directed the show. *Minnie's Boys* (3/26/70; 76 performances) was a musicalization of the early career of the Marx Brothers and starred Shelley Winters. Richard Rodgers and Martin Charnin chose the story of Noah as the basis for their musical *Two by Two* (11/10/70; 343 performances). Danny Kaye starred in the show. A greater success, although its material was weak, was *Pippin* (10/3/72; 1,944 performances). The show, with score by Stephen Schwartz and book by Roger O. Hirson, owed its success to the direction and choreography of Bob Fosse.

In the 1970s Broadway saw fewer and fewer musicals mounted because of the high cost of production. The Imperial hosted a revival of EUGENE O'NEILL's *Anna Christie,* with Liv Ullmann, and Victor Borge's *Comedy with Music.* NEIL SIMON's comedy hit *Chapter Two* (12/4/77; 857 performances) was a long-running

Sheila Bond and Roslynd Lowe help dig a swimming pool under the stage of the Imperial Theatre for *Wish You Were Here*, 1952.

tenant of the theater and starred Judd Hirsch, Anita Gillette, Cliff Gorman, and Ann Wedgeworth. Neil Simon also provided the script to the Imperial's next production, the musical *They're Playing Our Song* (2/11/79; 1,082 performances), a decidedly minor effort with its Marvin Hamlisch and Carole Bayer Sager score.

Another long-running musical occupied the Imperial's stage next. *Dreamgirls* (12/20/81; 1,522 performances) owed much of its success to Michael Bennett's brilliant staging. Henry Krieger provided the music and Tom Eyen the book and lyrics. The show made a star of Jennifer Holliday, who scored on the pop music charts (rare for Broadway scores in the 1970s and '80s) with "And I Am Telling You I'm Not Going." Other notable cast members included Obba Babatunde, Deborah Burrell, Vondie Curtis-Hall, Cleavant Derricks, Loretta Devine, Ben Harney, and Sheryl Lee Ralph. After *Dreamgirls* closed on August 11, 1985, the Imperial hosted another long-running hit, *The Mystery of Edwin Drood* (12/2/85; 680 performances) with book, music, and lyrics by Rupert Holmes. George Rose, Howard McGillin, Betty Buckley, Patti Cohenour, and Cleo Laine starred in the Joseph Papp production. Shortly before closing, the show officially changed its name to *Drood*. The name change did put it further up the alphabet in the *New York Times*' theatrical listings but did little else.

The most recent tenant is *Les Miserables*, which transferred to the Imperial from the Broadway Theatre in 1990 and closed in March, 2003.

INTERNATIONAL ALLIANCE OF THEATRICAL STAGE EMPLOYEES AND MOVING PICTURE MACHINE OPERATORS OF THE UNITED STATES OF AMERICA. *See* **IATSE.**

INTERNATIONAL CASINO. East side of Broadway between 44th and 45th Streets.

The International Casino building occupied the site of Hammerstein's OLYMPIA complex. The plot of land was huge by New York standards: 44,000 square feet, about half the size of the base of the Empire State Building. Noted theater architects Thomas Lamb and Eugene De Rosa designed the building, which also included a new Criterion movie theater. The rooftop was utilized as a premier location for spectacular SIGNAGE, most notably the Pepsi Cola waterfall.

The casino was opened in 1937 and continued operating until 1940 when the Bond's clothing store opened on the 45th Street side. Bond's erected a famous sign on the building's facade and remained on the scene for 40 years, a stalwart of Times Square. In 1980 Bond's opened the Bond's International Casino on the site. It remained in operation for two years. In 1988 the Bond's International Casino space was subdivided into two theater spaces (Stage Left and Stage Right), one devoted to off-Broadway-size plays and the other to a cabaret policy as part of the Criterion Center. The Criterion movie theater was also split into six smaller theaters as part of the new arrangement. However, the theater/cabaret spaces were not successful, and in 1991 the Roundabout Theatre Company took over both spaces for their operations. In 1995 the Stage Left theater became the Laura Pels Theatre. The Roundabout remained at the Criterion Center until the year 2000, when they moved to the renovated Selwyn Theater (*see* AMERICAN AIRLINES THEATRE) on 42nd Street. The Criterion movie theaters were shuttered at the same time. The interior of the building was then gutted, and in the fall of 2001 part of the space was reopened as the largest Toys "R" Us store in the world.

JACOBS, MIKE. Ticket seller, fight promoter, and one of Broadway's most colorful characters; b. New York, New York, March 10, 1880; d. New York, New York, January 21, 1953.

Jacob's domain was the world of boxing, but he also had an important influence on theater and journalism. He was born in New York City on March 10, 1880. Like most residents of the Lower East Side, his family was poor, and the children had to help out with part-time jobs. Jacobs left school after the sixth grade and began selling papers outside Tammany Hall. Joe Bannon, a circulation manager for the Hearst empire, tipped him a pair of tickets to the Terry McGovern–George Dixon featherweight fight; the tickets changed the young newsboy's life dramatically. Jacobs didn't attend the fight. Instead he took the $1 tickets and sold them at twice the price. Jacobs discovered the joys of ticket scalping. It was certainly easier to buy lots of tickets and scalp them than to stand outside in inclement weather to make a few cents selling newspapers. By the time he was 16 Jacobs had built up quite a business reselling tickets to sports events. He was proud to have saved $1,000 from his speculations, and later bragged, "I have never been broke since."

Jacobs' business grew under his astute leadership. His ability to gauge the popularity of an attraction was uncanny. By 1907 he had to open a storefront ticket agency to handle all his business. The office was in the lobby of the Normandie Hotel in Times Square. The location of his business made selling theater tickets a natural, so Jacobs began augmenting the money made from sports events with theater tickets. He even found time to indulge in several other occupations, some related to his main business, some not. He backed theater projects, basketball teams, and wrestling bouts. He was a concessionaire on steamboats and even owned a circus. As a personal manager he

booked great artists of the day on concert tours. Enrico Caruso was one of his clients. Caruso was booked by Jacobs on a string of 10 one-night stands. The great tenor was guaranteed $1,000 a concert; Jacobs still made an $80,000 profit.

Jacobs also backed many fighters. Walter St. Denis, sports editor of the *Globe*, introduced Jacobs to George L. "Tex" Rickard, the greatest fight promoter of his time. Rickard was promoting the Jess Willard–Frank Moran bout for the heavyweight title. Jacobs became a pupil of Rickard, and after Rickard's death in 1929 he took his place as New York's preeminent boxing promoter and speculator. Jacobs also bought "shares" in up-and-coming fighters' careers by lending their managers money in times of need. When the fighters became successful, Jacobs often owned a substantial piece of their winnings. On the odd occasion when a fighter didn't live up to Jacobs' ambitions, the promoter would chalk up the losses to development costs.

Jacobs' proximity to the theater district and his ticket office brought him in touch with many of the leading producers of the time. It seemed that Jacobs' appraisal of a new show's chances on the Great White Way was infallible. Many would-be angels consulted Jacobs on whether the show looked like a hit or a flop. In cases in which Jacobs believed a show to be a sure thing, he himself would invest heavily.

Several of the producers who Jacobs helped also became interested in boxing; WILLIAM A. BRADY was one. He and English impresario Charles Cochran formed a partnership with Rickard to sponsor the Dempsey-Carpentier fight. Both fighters were guaranteed a purse of $200,000 regardless of the outcome of the bout. Brady and Cochran balked at the high fees and felt they could never recover their investment. They withdrew from the partnership and lived to regret it. Rickard turned to Jacobs, who proposed a plan: Jacobs would agree to invest $20,000 of his own money if Rickard would raise a $200,000 fund from other speculators. They plowed that investment and the money from advance ticket sales into building their own arena: Boyle's Thirty Acres Arena in Jersey City. The fight was an enormous success, grossing $1,798,238—enough to return handsome profits to its investors and pay the boxers their substantial fees. Rickard and Jacobs also found themselves the owners of the arena.

The Dempsey-Carpentier fight was the first to break the $1 million mark. That 1921 fight led Jacobs into other partnerships on future bouts. In 1933 his associates were journalists DAMON RUNYON, Bill Farnsworth, and sports editor of the *American* Ed Frayne. But this time the profits went to charity. Mrs. William Randolph Hearst used the proceeds for her celebrated Milk Fund. Jacobs, flush with success, decided to challenge the biggest arena in New York, Madison Square Garden. In 1934 he began the Twentieth Century Sporting Club with his Milk Fund partners and installed himself as president. The first bout was the Barney Ross–Billy Petrolle match, held in the Bronx Coliseum.

By 1935 Jacobs had a controlling interest in Joe Louis. His investment began to pay off as Louis began rising in the rankings. With Louis firmly under contract Jacobs could really put pressure on Madison Square Garden. The arena held a contract for a fight between heavyweight champion James J. Braddock and Max Schmelling. Jacobs approached Braddock's manager, Joe Gould, and convinced him that a Braddock-Louis fight would make more money. So Braddock canceled his agreement with Madison Square Garden and went on to fight Louis in Chicago for 20 percent of the gross. Louis won the fight and with it the championship. Because Jacobs owned Louis' services, he could call the shots. As manager of the champion, Jacobs was at the top of his field. Louis went on to defend his title 23 times; each fight was produced by Jacobs. For Jacobs money was important, but he also did his share for others. In one of the many fights that he arranged for armed service charities, he sold $36 million in war bonds. He broke another record with his $100 charge for ringside seats in the Louis-Conn fight. That bout grossed $1,925,564 and an additional $50,000 for the movie rights.

On December 3, 1946, Jacobs suffered a brain hemorrhage that nearly proved fatal. He retired from promotions and three years later sold the Twentieth Century Sporting Club to his old nemesis Madison Square Garden for $110,000. Jacobs achieved a further degree of fame when the block of 49th Street between Eighth Avenue and Broadway became known as Jacobs' Beach. Out-of-work pugilists would gather on the Beach in much the same way as out-of-work vaude-

villians gathered on the BEACH in front of the PALACE THEATER. Jacobs went into a part-time retirement until his death on January 21, 1953.

JOHN GOLDEN THEATER (1). 202 W. 58th Street. Architect: Harrison G. Wiseman. Opening: November 1, 1926; *Two Girls Wanted* (transfer from THE LITTLE THEATRE).

There were two theaters named for John Golden, the noted Broadway producer. The first opened at 202 W. 58th Street between Broadway and 7th Avenue on November 1, 1926, with the play *Two Girls Wanted* (324 performances). Harrison G. Wiseman was the architect for this theater. On September 17, 1935, the theater's name was changed to the 58th Street Theater with the play *Few Are Chosen* (15 performances). The name was changed again to the Filmarte on September 20, 1936, with the movie *La Kermess Heroique*. On April 2, 1940, with the movie *The Life of Giuseppe Verdi*, the name was changed again to the Fine Arts Theater. On February 14, 1942, the theater briefly returned to a legitimate policy under the name the Concert Theater with the musical revue *Of V We Sing*. The show starred Betty Garrett and Phil Leeds, but if only lasted 76 performances. The Concert Theater became

John Golden donates his theatre sign to the wartime scrap drive.

the Rock Church in 1943. It became a theater again on January 15, 1946, when it was renamed the 58th Street Theater. In April 1946 the theater became the ABC Radio Theater. On January 28, 1948, now named the Elysee, returned to a film policy. The theater was finally taken over by ABC as a television studio.

JOHN GOLDEN THEATER (2). 252 W. 45th Street. Architect: Herbert J. Krapp. Original name: Theater Masque. Opening: February 24, 1927; *Puppets of Passion*.

The Chanin brothers built the current John Golden Theater as their fifth theater in the Times Square area. Brooks Atkinson described the new theater, originally called the Theater Masque, in the *New York Times* on the occasion of its opening night: "Like all the Chanin houses the Theater Masque is pleasing and comfortable. The architecture is modern Spanish in character, and the interior of the house is decorated in pastel shades, trimmed in grayish blues and reds."

The 800-seat theater's first tenant, *Puppets of Passion*, closed after only 12 performances. In 1927 and 1928 there were other bookings, but none proved successful. Finally the first success at the Theater Masque

came with Patrick Hamilton's drama *Rope's End* (9/19/29; 100 performances). The show later became the basis for the Alfred Hitchcock movie *Rope*.

As the Chanins' fortunes declined during the Depression, the theater did not fare well. Productions included the Albert Hackett and Frances Goodrich play *Up Pops the Devil* (9/1/30; 146 performances), starring Sally Bates and Brian Donlevy; the Norman Krasna comedy *Louder, Please!* (11/12/31; 68 performances) directed by George Abbott; the comedy *Goodbye Again* (12/28/32; 212 performances); and *Post Road* (12/4/34; 210 performances), which starred Percy Kilbride (later famous as Pa Kettle) and Lucile Watson. A series of failures followed, and the Chanins lost the Theater Masque along with their other theaters.

The first success under the new name, the John Golden Theater, was *Shadow and Substance* (1/26/38; 206 performances) by Paul Vincent Carroll, starring Julie Haydon and Sir Cedric Hardwicke. A bona fide, long-running hit, the thriller *Angel Street* (12/5/41; 1,293 performances), was produced by Shepard Traube and starred Judith Evelyn, Vincent Price, and Leo G. Carroll. The play had begun in London as *Gaslight*. It had been successful there, and a few summer theater productions followed. A production in Hollywood

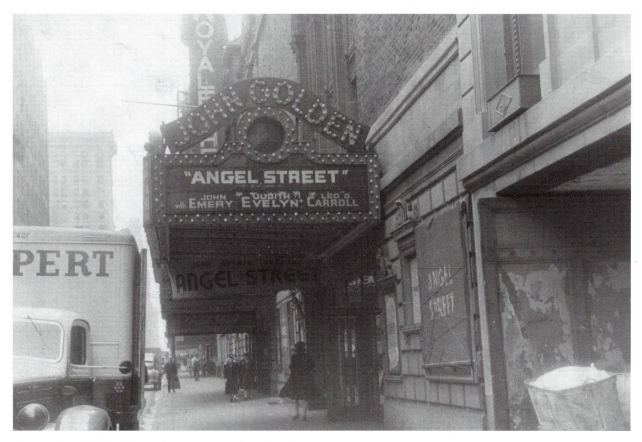

The new John Golden Theatre featuring *Angel Street* in 1941.

under its original title was moderately received, so when the show opened at the John Golden under its new name it was understandable that nobody expected it to be a hit. Even the lessees of the theater, the SHUBERT BROTHERS, had expected the play to be a quick failure. They ordered tickets printed for only the first three performances. Even Traube was not going to put his own money into the show; he had raised money by selling $15,000 shares to 15 angels. But the reviews were raves, and audiences began telling friends about the surprise hit at the John Golden Theater.

Unfortunately, *Angel Street* was not an omen for things to come. A modest comedy, *The Soldier's Wife* (10/4/44; 255 performances), by Rose Franken, played at the John Golden and starred Martha Scott, Glenn Anders, and Myron McCormick. A few more modest successes and a few failures followed, and in the middle of 1946 the theater was changed to a motion picture policy. It reverted to a legitimate policy on February 29, 1948, with the production of a one-man show featuring Maurice Chevalier. He was the first of a series of performers to present one-person shows at the theater, including Emlyn Williams, Cornelia Otis Skinner, and Victor Borge. The last opened his show *Comedy in Music* on October 2, 1953, and played 849 performances at the theater.

An acclaimed production of Samuel Beckett's *Waiting for Godot* (4/19/56; 59 performances) was not a hit, despite raves for Bert Lahr's performance. After this, in the late 1950s and '60s, the theater housed a series of two-person revues. First came *A Party with Betty Comden and Adolph Green*. COMDEN AND GREEN were two of Broadway's most cherished lyricists, and they held their audiences in thrall for a 38-performance run commencing on December 23, 1958, and again for 44 performances commencing on April 16, 1959. The next two performers to hold forth on the John Golden stage were the English songwriters and humorists Michael Flanders and Donald Swann with their delightful show *At the Drop of a Hat* (10/8/59; 215 performances). Then came *An Evening with Mike Nichols and Elaine May* (10/8/60; 306 performances), followed by a concert by Yves Montand (10/24/61; 55 performances).

The next hit was a small revue from London called *Beyond the Fringe* (10/27/62; 673 performances), with its cast of Peter Cook, Dudley Moore, Jonathan Miller, and Alan Bennett. In 1964 Victor Borge returned with his show, which had a 192-performance run. Another hit revue, twice as large as *Beyond the Fringe*, was *Wait a Minim* (3/7/66; 457 performances), which featured the traditional music of South Africa.

After a series of failures came the celebrated American comedy team of Bob Elliot and Ray Goulding with their hilarious show *Bob and Ray the Two and Only* (9/24/70; 158 performances). In 1972 David Rabe's Vietnam-era drama *Sticks and Bones* (3/1/72; 366 performances) came to the John Golden Theater via Joseph Papp's Public Theater, with Elizabeth Wilson and Tom Aldredge in the leads. Lyricist Sammy Cahn's revue *Words and Music* (4/16/74; 127 performances) was followed by a PULITZER PRIZE winner, *The Gin Game* (12/31/77; 517 performances), the two-person drama that starred Hume Cronyn and Jessica Tandy. Another success was the English import *A Day in Hollywood, a Night in the Ukraine* (5/1/80; 588 performances), with Priscilla Lopez, Peggy Hewett, Frank Lazarus, and David Garrison. Frank Lazarus and Dick Vosburgh supplied the score, and Tommy Tune provided the imaginative direction and choreography. Composer JERRY HERMAN even contributed a few songs to beef up the show.

The 1980s saw a series of distinguished dramas at the theater. An off-Broadway transfer, Beth Henley's Pulitzer prize-winning *Crimes of the Heart* (11/4/81; 535 performances), gave way to David Mamet's exposé of the real estate industry, *Glengarry Glen Ross* (3/25/84; 378 performances). Another Pulitzer prize winner, Marsha Norman's *'Night Mother* (4/18/84; 434 performances), starred Anne Pitoniak and Kathy Bates. Athol Fugard's powerful play *Blood Knot* (12/10/85; 96 performances) was revived at the theater with Zakes Mokae and Fugard starring.

A decade would pass before the theater's next hit show, *Master Class* (11/5/95; 598 performances) by Terrence McNally. It starred Zoe Caldwell as Maria Callas. *Side Man* moved to the Golden from off Broadway on October 20, 1998. The Warren Leight play concluded its 517-performance run at the Golden. Edward Albee's *The Goat, or Who Is Sylvia*? (3/10/2002) perplexed audiences for 309 performances.

On November 17, 1987, the New York City Landmarks Preservation Commission designated the interior and exterior of the John Golden Theater a landmark. The commission stated: "It was designed as a small 'intimate' theater seating only 800. Its facade is a fine example of the romantic 'modern Spanish' style."

JOLSON, AL. Larger-than-life early star of Broadway musicals, films, radio, and television; b. Asa Yoelson, St. Petersburg, Russia, March 26, 1886; d. San Francisco, October 23, 1950.

Jolson is considered to be the greatest performer of all time by those who were lucky enough to see him in action. A little of his dynamic personality comes through in his movie performances, which offer a hint of indication of his prodigious energy. Jolson was defined by his energy and humor. He introduced more hit songs than any other performer, with the possible exception of Bing Crosby. He was a unique link with America's entertainment heritage, for it was Jolson who brought the minstrel tradition into musical comedy, movies, radio, and finally television. He was the one performer who embodied the complete range of the American popular arts.

Critic George Jean Nathan said of Jolson:

> The power of Jolson over an audience I have seldom seen equaled. There are actors who, backed by great dramatists, can clutch an audience in their hands and squeeze out its emotion as they choose.
>
> There are singers who, backed by great composers, can do the same. And there are performers who, aided by external means of one kind or another can do the same.
>
> But I know of none like this Jolson—Or at best very few who, with lines of prewar vintage and melodies of the cheapest tin piano variety, can lay hold of an audience the moment he comes on the stage and never let go for a second thereafter.
>
> Possessed of an immensely electric personality, a rare sense of comedy, considerable histrionic ability, a most unusual music show versatility in the way of song and dance, and, above all, a gift for delivering lines for the full of their effect, he so far outdistances his rivals that they seem like the wrong ends of so many opera glasses.

When Jolson's family came to the United States, Jolson's father found work as a cantor in a Washington, D.C. synagogue. Jolson left home on several occasions to make a name for himself on the stage, only to return beaten. At a Washington vaudeville theater, Jolson was in the audience while the singer-comedian Eddie Leonard performed onstage. Jolson sang along with his big voice, and Leonard, after his initial shock, was impressed. Leonard teamed with Jolson in an act that repeated their first meeting. Jolson would pretend to be a paying customer who just couldn't help joining in from the balcony.

Jolson appeared as an extra on Broadway in *The Children of the Ghetto* (10/16/1899; 49 performances) at the Herald Square Theater. Jolson joined Lew Dockstader's Minstrels in 1908 while both acts were appearing in Little Rock, Arkansas. Will Oakland, a producer and songwriter, recommended Jolson to Dockstader, who hired the young performer. Jolson adopted the blackface makeup, which became a trademark for him when he was part of an early act, Jolson, Palmer, and Palmer. To Jolson the blackface was simply another gimmick for what would otherwise be simply another singing act. Somewhat shy, he also found it easier to portray a character rather than himself. Jolson was never the kind of performer who adopted blackface in order to make fun of blacks. He never assumed the stereotypes most often connected with the blackface comic. Jolson simply used the conceit as a means to make himself stand out from other singers. Later, when he was inextricably linked to the character, he used the makeup to signal that a highlight of the performance was coming up. Other blackface performers kept their Jewish identities and characterizations even when in blackface.

But the minstrel tradition was quickly dying. Jolson realized that he would have to move on to other more sophisticated entertainments if his career was to proceed. The SHUBERTS BROTHERS opened their new WINTER GARDEN THEATRE with *La Belle Paree* (3/20/11; 104 performances). The show was a typical early mishmash of styles. Its subtitle, *The Cook's Tour Through Vaudeville with a Parisian Landscape*, left room for just about anything. Jolson appeared in the last scene as Erastus Sparkler and sang "Paris Is a Paradise for Coons" to little effect. However, the *New York Times* singled Jolson out, and the Shuberts moved him up in the show to better effect. Another of his songs, "He Had to Get out and Get Under," was interpolated in the score, and in it Jolson introduced what became another trademark. In the second chorus, instead of singing the lyrics, Jolson whistled the tune.

Jolson's second Broadway success was *Vera Violetta* (11/20/11; 112 performances). This time he was top-billed with the French star Gaby Deslys. Jolson was the smash hit of the show, and he introduced another gimmick in his performances. While singing his numbers "Rum Tum Tiddle" and "That Haunting Melody," Jolson jumped off the stage and continued performing up and down the aisles. The *New York Times* enthused, "There was Al Jolson in the role of a colored waiter who succeeded in rousing the audience into its first enthusiasm in the early part of the evening and kept them enthusiastic much of the time afterwards." Solidly established as a Broadway star, Jolson began behaving in a way that earned him a reputation as Broadway's supreme egotist. He took out an ad in *Variety* stating, "Everybody likes me. Those who don't are jealous. Anyhow, here's wishing those that do and those that don't, a Merry Christmas and a Happy New Year—Al Jolson."

The Whirl of Society (3/5/12; 136 performances) was the third Jolson show at the Winter Garden. It opened with Stella Mayhew and Jose Collins as Jolson's co-stars. In it he created the character Gus, one he would play 5 more times on Broadway and also in the movies. Under New York's blue laws, performances on Sunday were illegal. But Jolson got around it by performing for show people only, without sets, props, or his blackface. These Jolson concerts electrified members of the Broadway community who were otherwise unable to witness Jolson in action because their own shows were running the same nights as his.

The Honeymoon Express (2/6/13; 156 performances), again at the Winter Garden, gave Jolson his first song success. "My Yellow Jacket Girl" isn't remembered today, but at the time it was a big hit. Supporting Jolson were Gaby Deslys and Harry Pilcer. FANNY BRICE was also in the cast in her third Broadway appearance. The show featured a special effect depicting a race between a locomotive and an automobile. Jolson created another sensation by stopping the show midstream and asking the audience, "Would you rather see the rest of the show or just hear me sing?" The answer was self-evident, and for the next few hours Jolson dismissed the cast and performed an impromptu concert. During the run Jolson had trouble with an ingrown toenail. While singing "Down Where the Tennessee Flows," he sought to relieve the pressure on his foot by going down on one knee; this stance became another trademark for the performer.

Jolson's next production, *Dancing Around* (10/10/14; 145 performances), was mostly undistinguished. The more successful *Robinson Crusoe, Jr.* (2/17/16; 139 performances) followed. This time Jolson was given a SIGMUND ROMBERG score, which took more and more of a backseat to Jolson's interpolations as the fun continued. Jolson added several songs that he made into big successes. "Yacka Hula Hickey Dula" was another in the current wave of Hawaiian-inspired songs. "Where Did Robinson Crusoe Go with Friday on Saturday Night?" was in the same spirit as "Who Paid the Rent for Mrs. Rip Van Winkle? (When Rip Van Winkle Was Away)," which Jolson introduced in *The Honeymoon Express*. "Where the Black-Eyed Susans Grow" would also become a Jolson perennial, one he would sing for the rest of his career.

Jolson then opened in *Sinbad* (2/14/18; 164 performances), another excuse to do his usual shtick. This time he put a ramp from the stage into the audience. Jolson discovered what became three of his most famous songs and added them to the score of *Sinbad*. "Rock-a-Bye Your Baby with a Dixie Melody" was Jolson's favorite song of all time; "Swanee," by GEORGE GERSHWIN and Irving Caesar, was inserted into the show while it was on the road; and perhaps the most famous of all, "My Mammy," was introduced when the show reopened after a brief vacation for Jolson.

After the armistice was signed a huge concert was scheduled on November 18, 1918 at the Metropolitan Opera House for the benefit of the returning soldiers. After Enrico Caruso finished singing "Vesti la Giubba," Jolson ran on to the stage before the applause was over for the great tenor. "Folks, you ain't heard nothin' yet," exclaimed Jolson, and so another piece was added to Jolson legend. Shortly after came the

ACTORS' STRIKE of 1919, which led to the formation of ACTORS' EQUITY. Jolson and GEORGE M. COHAN were the biggest opponents of the new union. But Jolson loved performing too much, and so to avoid being blacklisted, he gave in to the union. Cohan never joined Actors' Equity and only performed on Broadway with special permission.

For Jolson's next show, *Bombo* (10/6/21; 218 performances), the Shuberts built him a new theater and named it, unsurprisingly, JOLSON'S 59TH STREET THEATER. Jolson had previously had a success with two songs by B. G. De Sylva (*see* DE SYLVA, BROWN, AND HENDERSON) and Gus Kahn, "'N' Everything" and "I'll Say She Does," both written for *Sinbad*. Also credited on the sheet music was Al Jolson, although it was doubtful that Jolson did anything more than introduce the songs. But those songs were nowhere near as popular as the songs written for *Bombo*. *Bombo's* conductor, Lou Silvers, and De Sylva wrote "April Showers." De Sylva also wrote "California, Here I Come," another huge hit for Jolson. Gus Kahn contributed "Toot Toot Tootsie." *Bombo* was brought back to Broadway to the Winter Garden for an additional 32 performances on May 14, 1923.

Jolson not only took credit for songs he didn't write, but also took jokes from other shows and incorporated them into his own. Jolson would go to the popular nightclubs or vaudeville houses in the city and hear the great comics. He would then write down the jokes that got the biggest laughs and insert them into whatever show he was starring in. He would then instruct his lawyers to contact the comic and threaten to sue unless the comic removed the joke from his act!

Big Boy (1/7/25; 48 performances) had everything going for it. For one thing, it co-starred Eddie Cantor, who introduced one of his greatest hits, "If You Knew Susie." It also featured a horse race with real horses running on hidden treadmills on the stage floor. Jolson introduced more great songs into the score; "California, Here I Come" was reintroduced, as well as "Keep Smiling at Trouble." *Big Boy's* run was prematurely halted when Jolson came down with strep throat. When Jolson left a show, that was it; there was no discussion of replacing him or having an understudy go on. Jolson knew as well as anyone else that you could never replace the World's Greatest Performer.

On occasion Jolson would show up late and go onstage to apologize to the audience. He would tell them about the delicious dinner he'd had next door to the theater and how he just hadn't been able to rush through it. He would then ask whether the audience minded if he put on his makeup onstage, and instructed his dresser, Louis Shreiber, to bring on the burnt cork. He would ask the ushers to go out and buy dozens of

Al Jolson in *Robinson Crusoe Jr.* in 1916.

boxes of candy, which he then passed out to the audience while he sang. After the concert he would inform the audience that he was going back to the restaurant for dessert and if the audience would give him a half hour, they could join him there for more songs around the piano.

Jolson next appeared as a late addition to the cast of *Artists and Models*, a revue series produced by the Shuberts. He played the show for only 4 weeks and then took it on the road, where it achieved the then highest gross in history, more than $60,000. After the *Artists and Models* tour Jolson went to Hollywood and made one of the most important pictures in the history of Hollywood, *The Jazz Singer*. Contrary to popular legend there had been other talking pictures, but before this none achieved any success. With Jolson *The Jazz Singer* changed the future of movies forever. Before *The Jazz Singer*'s release, Jolson was hired by the Shuberts for $10,000 a week to star in the road tour of *A Night in Spain. The Jazz Singer* opened on October 7,

1927, and for a while, at least, Jolson became the property of Hollywood.

However, by 1931 Jolson's movie career was stalled. His pictures were successes (*The Singing Fool* [1928] was the biggest money-making picture in Hollywood history until *Gone with the Wind* surpassed it), but his roles became more and more alike, and the vehicles were mostly unmemorable. While Jolson onstage could stop the show and just give a concert, in the movies he was forced to stick to the script no matter how bad it was. Following his hit films there were the disappointing *Say It with Songs* and the equally clichéd *Mammy* (1930) and *Hallelujah I'm a Bum* (1933) with a RODGERS AND HART score. Later that year he made a movie of his stage show *Big Boy*, but it wasn't much of a success.

Jolson opened on Broadway in *The Wonder Bar* (3/17/31; 86 performances). Unfortunately, the show wasn't tailored to Jolson's talents, and none of the usual Jolson interpolations caught fire.

The 1930s were Jolson's darkest period. He had trouble finding work except for occasional radio appearances. Jolson's last appearance on Broadway was in a book show, *Hold on to Your Hats* (9/11/40; 158 performances) with a score by BURTON LANE and E. Y. HARBURG. Jolson had committed to doing the show because his wife, Ruby Keeler, was to be given a part. But Keeler departed both the show and the marriage during the Chicago run, and Jolson was left in what to him was an increasingly alien Broadway. Jolson could no longer control the show. He had to stick to the script. There were no more Jolson interpolations, although the script allowed him a medley of his hits. He shared billing with Martha Raye, Bert Gordon, and Jack Whiting. Although Jolson and the show had received rave reviews, he lost interest. Claiming that he couldn't stand the cold of New York's winter, Jolson left the production, and it closed. It was revived briefly in July 1941 in Atlantic City. Once more Jolson seemed unsatisfied and felt he would lose his voice if he continued.

Jolson's career continued to decline, with radio appearances and touring for the USO taking up most of his time. More and more he was considered a nostalgic figure. Then the Columbia picture *The Jolson Story* (1946), starring Larry Parks as Jolson, reawakened interest in the singer. The film was followed by a new recording contract for Decca Records and a continuing radio series for Kraft. Then came *Jolson Sings Again* (1949), another big hit. Television was the new medium, and Jolson approached it warily. A final USO tour of Korea in 1950 left Jolson exhausted and sick, and he died, shortly after his return home from overseas.

ROBERT BENCHLEY, writing in the old *Life* magazine of Jolson's performance in *Big Boy*, captured Jolson's unique effect on audiences:

> The word "personality" isn't quite strong enough for the thing that Jolson has. Unimpressive as the comparison may be to Mr. Jolson, we should say that John the Baptist was the last man to have such a power. There is something supernatural at the back of it, or we miss our guess. When Jolson enters, it is as if an electric current has been run along the wires under the seats where the hats are stuck. The house comes to a tumultuous attention. He speaks, rolls his eyes, compresses his lips, and it is all over. You are a member of the Al Jolson Association.
>
> He trembles his underlip, and your heart breaks with a loud snap. He sings a banal song and you totter out to send a night letter to your mother. Such a giving-off of vitality, personality, charm, and whatever all those words are, results from a Jolson performance.

JOLSON'S 59TH STREET THEATER. 932 7th Avenue between 58th and 59th Streets. Architect: Herbert J. Krapp. Opening: October 6, 1921; *Bombo*.

This theater had an especially difficult history. The site was originally the Central Park Gardens, which were replaced by the Central Park Riding Academy. The horses left in 1916, and then the SHUBERT BROTHERS purchased the land. They built the theater as the Imperial but soon found that one of their biggest stars, AL JOLSON, wanted the theater for his own. They quickly named the theater after him and saved the name "Imperial" for another time. He opened his successful musical *Bombo* (10/6/21; 218 performances) there. *Bombo*'s score was written by SIGMUND ROMBERG and Harold Atteridge, but as usual the hit songs were written by others and interpolated into the score. The most famous of these was "April Showers" by Louis Silvers and B. G. De Sylva (*see* DE SYLVA, BROWN, AND HENDERSON). Other hit songs that received their first hearing in *Bombo* were "Dirty Hands, Dirty Face" by James V. Monaco, Jolson, and Edgar Leslie; "My Mammy" by Walter Donaldson and B. G. De Sylva; and "Toot Toot Tootsie" by Gus Kahn, Ernie Erdman, and Dan Russo. These were all enormous successes for Jolson. Unfortunately, *Bombo* was one of the theater's few successes, and Jolson never again appeared at the theater.

A revolution hit the Broadway theater in 1923 with the arrival of Constantin Stanislavsky and his Moscow Art Theater. The 3-month booking introduced such future stars as Maria Ouspenskaya and Akim Tamiroff. Once America got wind of Stanislavsky's acting techniques, including the much-misinterpreted Method system, American acting was never the same.

After a series of failures another huge hit opened: *The Student Prince* (12/2/24; 608 performances). This time Romberg, along with lyricist and librettist Dorothy Donnelly, came up with a smashing score. "Deep in My Heart, Dear," "Drinking Song," "Golden Days," "Students' Life," and "Serenade" were all big hits at the time. Sixty years after its creation, *The Student Prince* is still much performed. A couple of moderate successes followed, including a revival of the Shuberts' warhorse, *Blossom Time*. Romberg and Donnelly saw the curtain rise on *My Maryland* (9/12/27; 312 performances), another success.

The last 3 months of 1929 and the early months of 1930 were taken up by some halfhearted revivals of past operettas (*Robin Hood, Sweethearts, The Fortune Teller, The Merry Widow, Babes in Toyland, The Count of Luxembourg, The Serenade,* and *Mlle. Modiste*). This series of revivals marked the end of Shubert ownership. The Depression hit the Shuberts hard, and they were forced to sell the theater. It would never again have a success. The theater, renamed Shakespeare's Theater, reopened with Sothern and Marlowe's Shakespearean troupe presenting *A Midsummer Night's Dream* (11/12/32; 27 performances). Two years later the theater reopened as the Venice Theater with *Africana* (11/26/34; 3 performances), a new edition of the popular revue, which had opened originally in 1927.

Maurice Schwartz took over operation of the theater and named it after his theatrical troupe, the Yiddish Art Theater. It opened with a production of *The Brothers Ashkenazi* (9/20/37). It was again renamed the Jolson Theater with *Comes the Revolution* (5/26/42; 2 performances). Yiddish theater returned, and the theater was renamed the Molly Picon Theater with the opening of *Oy Is Das a Leben* (10/12/42).

The Shuberts returned to the theater, which they renovated and renamed the Century. *Follow the Girls* (4/8/44; 882 performances), a musical with music by Philip Charig and lyrics by Dan Shapiro and Milton Pascal, was a surprising success. It starred Jackie Gleason, Gertrude Niesen, and Irina Baranova. But the success did not transfer to other shows.

The last musical show to play the theater was the musical *Carnival in Flanders* (9/8/53; 6 performances), which starred John Raitt and Dolores Gray. Despite having the hit song "Here's That Rainy Day" in its Johnny Burke and James Van Heusen score, the show folded after only 6 performances. Ouida Rathbone wrote the drama *Sherlock Holmes* to feature the talents of her husband, Basil Rathbone. The show opened on October 30, 1953, and closed 3 performances later. Mary Orr, author of the smash hit *Harvey*, was among its cast members. It would be the last legitimate show at the theater. But the Japanese Consulate did present a dance company, the Azuma Kabuki Dancers and Musicians, at the New Century beginning on February 22, 1954, for 32 performances. On March 21, 1954, the curtain came down for good on Jolson's 59th Street Theater.

On March 29, 1954, the theater was dubbed the NBC Theater with the inside adapted to television. In the fall of 1959 it became the Video Tape Center. The Shuberts sold the theater in 1962, and it was demolished and replaced by an apartment building.

KAUFMAN AND HART. Famed playwrighting duo of the 1930s and '40s, noted for their light comic work; Moss Hart, b. New York, New York, October 24, 1904; d. Palm Springs, California, December 20, 1961; George S. Kaufman, b. Pittsburgh, Pennsylvania, November 16, 1899; d. New York, New York, June 2, 1961.

George S. Kaufman was one of the theater's most versatile participants. He was equally adept at playwriting and directing, but his greatest asset was as a play doctor.

He contributed occasional witticisms to Franklin P. Adams' column, "The Conning Tower," in the *Evening Mail*. In fact Kaufman arbitrarily chose the middle initial "S" out of respect for Adams. Years later he would claim that the letter stood for Simon, his grandfather's first name, but it was simply not true. At 18 Kaufman found employment as a surveyor, a job at which he was spectacularly inept. In 1909 his father found him a job as a salesman for the Columbia Ribbon Company. Incredibly, he held that job for 3 years.

In 1912 Adams started Kaufman off on his journalistic career, recommending him for a post at the *Washington Times*. A year later the owner of the paper, Frank Munsey, walked into the press room, noticed Kaufman at his desk, and bellowed, "What is that Jew doing in my city room?" Kaufman was immediately fired.

In 1914 he moved from Washington to New York, where he served on the drama staffs of the *New York Tribune* (for 1 year), the *Mail* (6 months), and, beginning on September 17, 1917, the *New York Times*. At the *Times* he was drama editor and second-string critic. A contemporary called his reviews "crisp, curt, and to the point." He could also be as vitriolic as other critics. About one play he wrote, "There was laughter in the back of the theatre, leading to the belief that someone was telling jokes back there." A famous quote of his is, "I saw the play at a disadvantage. The curtain was up." Kaufman preferred to cast his lot with the *Times*, content to be the secondary critic. He valued the job so much that even though he was a successfully produced playwright, he kept his job at the *Times* as insurance. Critic BROOKS ATKINSON wrote that Kaufman "trusted the *Times* more than he trusted the theatre. There was nobody less sure of himself as a theatrical genius. . . . He felt that if everything else blew up, he could always come back to the *Times*."

Another article in the *Times* concurred, "It took years of soul-searching before he would commit his future to anything as transient as the theatre. The *Times* was real. It came out late each night. It had presses and newsprint and friends and a check each week. . . . In the end it was the Depression which forced him to leave the *Times*. There they were, so many editors and reporters out of work, and there he was keeping one of them from a salary while his royalty checks piled up week after week. So, being a fair man, he left to make room for someone else."

When ALEXANDER WOOLLCOTT stepped down as chief drama critic of the *Times*, he offered Kaufman the job. But Kaufman had been bitten by the playwriting bug and the job went to Atkinson.

Kaufman found playwriting a distinct change from the structure of newspaper work. He wrote Sam Zolotow, "The playwriting business is not like putting up a building. In my case, a big hole is often dug and then nothing happens."

There was no better play editor in the theater. He was often called on by producers to fix ailing productions. In 1917, at the urging of Burns Mantle, Kaufman wrote a farce for Henry Stern, who was going to open an agency for untested playwrights. The farce, *Going Up*, was not accepted by any producer to whom it was

George S. Kaufman and Moss Hart.

submitted. But one of these men, George C. Tyler, kept a note of Kaufman's name. Later that year Tyler had a production that needed writing help. He had other playwrights try to fix the show's problems, but he was not happy with their submissions. So he called in Kaufman.

The result was *Someone in the House* (9/9/18; 32 performances) by Larry Evans and Walter Percival and, in his first credited production, George S. Kaufman. Although Kaufman couldn't save the play, he did contribute an ad for the show at the behest of Tyler. It read:

Beware of Flu
Avoid Crowds
See "Someone in the House"

Someone in the House, although a failure, would prove to be a success of sorts for Kaufman. Tyler had instructed the play doctor to beef up the part of Helene Glendenning, played by Lynn Fontanne (*see* LUNT AND FONTANNE). He based his rewriting of the character on one invented by Franklin Price Adams named Dulcinea. The character spoke in clichés, but she had a rare sweetness and optimism. Tyler was entranced with this character and urged Kaufman to write a play around her. Kaufman agreed but only if he could collaborate with a fellow newspaperman, Marc Connelly.

After trying to fix another of Tyler's plays, *Jacques Deval*, which closed out of town, Kaufman and Connelly began work on what would become *Dulcy* (8/13/21; 246 performances). The show was a decided hit, and the team of Kaufman and Connelly was on its way.

Kaufman, a shy man, nevertheless had many followers who thrived on his presence, for Kaufman was one of the great humorists. He used his wit constructively to teach, scold, and show his affection. Kaufman's shyness was but one aspect of his insecurity. He always preferred to write with collaborators and did so in all but two cases. Among Kaufman's playwriting partners in addition to Hart and Connelly were Edna

Ferber, Ring Lardner, J. P. Marquand, Morrie Ryskind, Abe Burrows, Alexander Woollcott, Herman Mankie-wicz, Howard Teichman, and Howard Dietz (*see* DIETZ AND SCHWARTZ). Kaufman would say, "It's nice to have company when you come face to face with a blank page."

Howard Teichman, Kaufman's collaborator on *The Solid Gold Cadillac*, recalled,

> Dig a layer or two deep into Kaufman's nature and it is easily seen that he had need for an instantaneous re-sponse to a line, a situation, or a scene. Kaufman would bounce a line off a collaborator. If it worked, keep it. If it didn't, Kaufman was the most ruthless of editors. He would throw away two dozen, three dozen lines in an attempt to come up with what he thought was the right one. For the discards he had a wastebasket 2 feet wide and fully 4½ feet high.
>
> To the collaborative process, Kaufman brought the theme (or asked that his collaborator bring a theme ac-ceptable to him). In return, Kaufman would bring dra-matic discipline. From his collaborators, Kaufman would expect a rather large amount of the characterization; if there was a love scene, he could barely participate with-out making it maudlin. As a good tennis player may vol-ley, Kaufman would slam the lines back to his partner almost endlessly, hoping to trim, change, sharpen, and achieve the economy of words which is so necessary to the Kaufman type of play.

Kaufman wrote a letter to critic Howard Teichman in which he wrote:

> A thought on collaboration. It is marriage without sex, and subject to many vexations. But pay no attention to them, because in one respect at least it is wonderful. The total result is frequently far more than the combined abilities of two people might give you—one person feeds the other, and in some way something absolutely great comes out of it—much better than the two talents added together. . . . The two people fly far above their talents, and if I don't know about collaboration who the hell does?

Alexander Woollcott, profiling Kaufman in the *New Yorker*, wrote that the playwright and director was someone who,

> rather than let a fresh vegetable soil his lips, subsists on a severe diet of meat, bread, and chocolate peppermints; who, in the laboratory work any dramatist must do, limits his studies of human nature and the American scene as far as possible to the moments when he is dummy at the New York Bridge Club; who, while walking hatless and alone down our avenues, talks continuously to himself in what appears to terrified passersby as a low, confidential snarl; and who, during the seven or eight years in which he has been one of the most competent, fertile, and suc-cessfully productive of American playwrights, has hung on with puzzling tenacity to the same newspaper job with which he was, by a narrow margin, keeping body

and soul apart when his first play was accepted for pro-duction. There is Mr. Kaufman for you in a nutshell.

Kaufman was one of the wittiest men on the Broad-way scene, and many of his quips have achieved leg-endary status. During the run of *Of Thee I Sing*, Kauf-man was appalled by the overacting of William Gaxton. He sent the actor a telegram, "I am watching your performance from the rear of the theatre. Wish you were here." Once he attended, unannounced, a performance of a play of his. When the actors came offstage, they found a note on the call board: "11 A.M. rehearsal tomorrow morning to remove all improve-ments to the play inserted since the last rehearsal." Kaufman, in observing two understudies tearing up the scenery, remarked, "They're not understudies, they're overstudies."

Prior to his collaboration with Moss Hart, Kaufman enjoyed many successes. Among his most notable plays, with his collaborators noted in parentheses, were *Dulcy* (Marc Connelly; 8/13/21; 246 performances); *To the Ladies* (Marc Connelly; 2/20/22; 128 perfor-mances); *Merton of the Movies* (Marc Connelly; 11/13/22; 248 performances); the musical *Helen of Troy New York* (Marc Connelly; 6/19/23; 191 perfor-mances); *Beggar on Horseback* (Marc Connelly; 2/12/24; 144 performances); *The Butter and Egg Man* (9/23/25; 243 performances); the musical *The Cocoanuts* (Morrie Ryskind; 12/8/25; 218 performances); *The Royal Family* (Edna Ferber; 12/28/27; 345 perfor-mances); the musical *Animal Crackers* (Morrie Rys-kind; 10/23/28; 191 performances); *June Moon* (Ring Lardner; 10/9/29; 273 performances); and the musical *Strike up the Band* (Morrie Ryskind; 1/14/30; 191 per-formances).

Kaufman hated his opening nights. He was always convinced that the evening would go drastically wrong and that his contributions were less than satisfactory. Woollcott remembered Kaufman: "Pale, distraught, he weaves about the balcony, and is occasionally so af-flicted that angry drama-lovers have been compelled to rebuke him for getting up in the middle of a scene to take a long, frantic ramble in the aisle."

In the theater, Kaufman could be the epitome of patience, but outside the theater he was a hellion. George S. Oppenheimer recalled working with Kauf-man on the play *Here Today*:

> The outstanding virtue that I found in George, both in the planning and directing of the play was his amazing patience. Patience, outside his work, was not one of George's more noticeable qualities. He was the scourge of incompetents, whether it was a maid at a dinner table or a partner at a bridge table. I once heard him say to a particularly inept player, as he peered fiercely over his glasses and his hair seemed to bristle, "I know that you only learned to play bridge today, but what *time* today?"

Moss Hart, stagestruck as a youth, worked for the producer-director Augustus Pitou, a specialist in plays featuring Irish tenors and dubbed "the King of the One Night Stands." While working for the producer, Hart was given the additional job of reading scripts and judging their worth. After reading scripts for 6 months, Hart decided he could write as well or better than the authors of the scripts he had rejected. Hart set upon writing his first play, which Pitou produced. *The Hold-up Man or the Beloved Bandit* closed out of town in 1923, losing Pitou $45,000.

Pitou let Hart go, and the young man undertook a series of odd jobs, including social director in the Catskills in the summer and director of little theater groups in the winter. Hart had a brief acting career when, in 1923, he was cast as Smithers in EUGENE O'NEILL's *The Emperor Jones*. Hart achieved good reviews for his acting, but he soon returned to the world of the Catskills and little theater groups.

Agent Richard J. Madden of the American Play Company suggested to Hart that he give up on writing dramas and concentrate on comedies. Hart was shocked. He equated being a serious playwright with writing dramatic plays. Comedies were simple little plays that were knocked off in a week or two and existed only to please the masses. But Madden explained that the lighter portions of Hart's dramas were the most successful parts—in fact, the only successful parts.

As Hart said, "I grumpily removed the mantle of Shaw and O'Neill from my shoulders and regarded the yellow pad of paper in my lap." Hart had admired a certain kind of satirical comedy, like that written by George S. Kaufman and Marc Connelly. In fact while watching the team's comedy *Dulcy*, Hart conceived an idea concerning a zany family of performers.

Hart was inspired by the idea of Hollywood performers made redundant by the coming of sound to motion pictures. He had read an article in *VARIETY* about exactly that subject, and he was intrigued by the dramatic possibilities. In only three weeks he wrote the first draft of *Once in a Lifetime*. With the script finished, Hart began showing it around. His friend Dore Schary arranged for another friend to give the play to the notorious (but successful) producer Jed Harris. He was mildly interested but kept putting Hart off. So a second copy went to producer Sam H. Harris (no relation to Jed Harris).

Harris later wrote, "Back in 1930, Moss Hart was a name that was familiar to a small circle of his relatives. Certainly I hadn't ever heard it till Max Siegel, who was my general manager in those days, came into my office one day with a script in his hand and a rather excited look." Harris took the script home and read it, believing it to have been penned by a writer who had worked in the maelstrom of Hollywood "and devel-

oped a disgust for the mad things that used to go on there." Harris believed that "it was authentic satire but I felt it needed work. It needed pointing up and a general reconstruction which would give it polish and a finish."

Harris advised Hart to collaborate with a more seasoned professional. Hart didn't warm to the idea. Harris went ahead and sent the script to Kaufman, who immediately read it and sent a note back to Harris: "I'd love to be mixed up with it." Harris again broached the subject of collaboration with Hart, who asked, "But who would you suggest?"

"I never saw a face change so suddenly as when I said George Kaufman," Harris remembered. "First a look of incredulity came over it, then this melted into a thin smile which spread until he was beaming like a little child who had just been presented with a toy he never fancied he could own. Later he told me that he felt I had passed a miracle for him, that Kaufman had been his ideal since boyhood, and that he had never dreamed that his play would enable him to sit down at the same typewriter with Kaufman."

"There's one point that should be mentioned," Harris warned Hart. "Kaufman has never been to Hollywood and hasn't your background and experience there. You'll have to provide the source material."

"That's no problem," Hart replied. "You see, I've never been to Hollywood either. I picked up my dope from the fan magazines and Hollywood columns."

However, it seemed for a time that the team of Kaufman and Hart would not outlive *Once in a Lifetime*. During tryouts in Atlantic City the first act went over gangbusters with audiences. But from that point on there were diminishing returns, and by the end of the third act the audience that remained sat on their hands. The team tackled the problems in the play but to no avail, and Kaufman withdrew from the project. Hart, though, believed in his work and undertook a major revision of the comedy. These changes convinced Kaufman to return to the collaboration, and on the evening of September 24, 1930, the new writing team found themselves at opening night at the MUSIC BOX THEATER.

The play was an immediate success, and, seemingly overnight, Hart was catapulted from insolvency to riches and from obscurity to fame. He went home to his family in Brooklyn and told them to leave the apartment and all its contents immediately. They abandoned their possessions and were moved into a luxurious apartment in the Ansonia Hotel.

Kaufman's collaborations with Hart include *Once in a Lifetime* (9/24/30; 305 performances); *Merrily We Roll Along* (9/29/34; 155 performances); *You Can't Take It with You* (12/14/36; 837 performances); the musical *I'd Rather Be Right* (11/2/37; 266 performances); *The Fabulous Invalid* (10/8/38; 65 performances); *The American Way* (1/21/39; 244 performances); *The Man Who Came to Dinner* (10/16/39; 739 performances); *George Washington Slept Here* (10/18/40; 173 performances); and *Dream on, Soldier*, a special production for the American Red Cross (4/5/43; 1 performance).

Though still stagestruck even years into his success, Hart was not blinded by the glamorous world of the theater. As he once commented, "Charity in the theatre begins and ends with those who have a play opening within a week of one's own."

Hart finally broke the partnership with Kaufman on the urging of his psychiatrist. Subject to bouts of depression, Hart would never get over the feeling that people ascribed his success to the talents of his partner. In spite of evidence to the contrary, his great successes on his own and with other collaborators, Hart felt he needed to sever the ties with Kaufman that fueled these feelings. Not surprisingly, Hart's next theatrical en-

deavor was a musical comedy that used psychiatry as the catalyst for its major themes. *Lady in the Dark* (1/23/41; 467 performances) boasted music by KURT WEILL and lyrics by IRA GERSHWIN. Gertrude Lawrence starred as magazine editor Liza Elliott, a woman who makes thousands of decisions a day in her professional life but in her personal life is paralyzed and unable to make any choices. She goes to a psychiatrist to help resolve her problems of self-doubt and to explore her dreams. All the musical numbers in the show took place within the dream sequences. Slowly she begins to identify the roots of her personal insecurities, and by the time the curtain falls she is on her way to being cured.

During and after his collaboration with Hart, Kaufman collaborated on the following plays and musicals: the revue *The Band Wagon* (Howard Dietz; 6/3/31; 260 performances); the PULITZER PRIZE–winning musical *Of Thee I Sing* (Morrie Ryskind; 12/26/31; 441

Alan J. Lerner, Moss Hart, and Frederick Loewe discussing their production of *Camelot*, 1960.

performances); *Dinner at Eight* (Edna Ferber; 10/22/32; 232 performances); the musical *Let 'Em Eat Cake* (Morrie Ryskind; 10/21/33; 90 performances); *First Lady* (Katharine Dayton; 11/26/35; 238 performances); *Stage Door* (Edna Ferber; 10/22/36; 169 performances); *The Late George Apley* (John P. Marquand; 11/21/44; 357 performances); *The Solid Gold Cadillac* (Howard Teichman; 11/5/53; 526 performances); and the musical *Silk Stockings* (Leueen MacGrath and Abe Burrows; 2/24/55; 478 performances).

Hart also enjoyed a successful career, mainly in musical theater, apart from his collaboration with Kaufman. Among his successes were an IRVING BERLIN revue, *Face the Music* (2/17/32; 166 performances); the musical *The Great Waltz* (9/22/34; 297 performances); the COLE PORTER musical *Jubilee* (10/12/35; 169 performances); a David Freedman revue, *The Show Is On* (12/25/36; 236 performances); *Winged Victory* (11/20/43; 212 performances), for which Hart was also co-director; *Christopher Blake* (11/30/46; 114 performances); *Light up the Sky* (11/18/48; 214 performances); and *The Climate of Eden* (11/13/52; 20 performances). Hart also directed the musicals *My Fair Lady* (3/15/56; 2,717 performances) and *Camelot* (12/3/60; 873 performances).

KELCEY ALLEN AWARD. Kelcey Allen (1875–1951) was the founder of the New York Drama Critics Circle and drama editor of *Women's Wear Daily* from 1915 until 1951. The award named for him was given each year to an individual who made a significant contribution to the American theater. The first recipient, in 1955, was Vincent Sardi Sr., owner of SARDI'S RESTAURANT.

KERN, JEROME. Broadway composer who introduced a distinctly American style and sound; b. New York, New York, January 27, 1885; d. New York, New York, November, 11, 1945.

Along with GEORGE M. COHAN, Kern was the first composer for the Broadway stage to give the musical an American feeling. Although Cohan brought vaudeville and music hall influences into the musical, Kern was more in touch with the musical's European roots, giving the European operetta a real American sound. Thereby, Kern had a greater impact than Cohan on the transition from operetta to a truly American musical theater.

Kern attended the New York College of Music, where he studied piano with Alexander Lambert and Paolo Gallico and harmony with Dr. Austin Pierce. Kern was introduced to the great operetta traditions when he went to England and Germany. When he returned to the United States in 1904, Kern found work

at T. B. Harms, a leading music publisher. While at Harms, Kern became acquainted with most of the leading artists and producers of early musical comedy.

Kern began interpolating songs into American versions of foreign musicals. As an American, Kern was influenced by the harmonies and rhythms employed by America's classical and popular writers. In 1904 Kern contributed songs into *Mr. Wix of Wickham*, an English show transplanted to America with female impersonator Julian Eltinge as the star. More important to Kern was his next interpolation, "How'd You Like to Spoon with Me?" with lyrics by Edward Laska. The song was included in the show *The Earl and the Girl* (11/04/05). It became the first hit for Kern, and soon Broadway producers were demanding his talents. Kern had songs interpolated into many shows that opened during the early 20th century, including *The Catch of the Season* (8/28/05), *The Little Cherub* (8/6/06), *My Lady's Maid* (9/20/06), *The Rich Mr. Hogenheimer* (10/22/06), *The Orchid* (4/8/07), *The Dairymaids* (8/26/07), *Fascinating Flora* (5/20/07), *The Great White Way* (10/7/07), *A Waltz Dream* (1/27/08), *The Girls of Gottenberg* (9/2/08), *Fluffy Ruffles* (9/7/08), *The Dollar Princess* (9/6/09), *The Gay Hussars* (7/29/09), and *The Kiss Waltz* (9/18/11).

Kern finally had his first full score commissioned for *The Red Petticoat* (11/13/12; 61 performances). Paul West supplied the lyrics to the Kern songs. The next year Kern wrote his second full score for *Oh, I Say!* (10/30/13; 68 performances). HARRY B. SMITH wrote the lyrics for the show. In 1914 Kern and Smith wrote "You're Here and I'm Here" for *The Laughing Husband*, and Kern saw a great early hit, "They Didn't Believe Me," premiere in *The Girl from Utah* (8/24/14; 120 performances), with a lyric by Herbert Reynolds.

Kern had a banner year in 1915. He had five shows open that year, including one of his most enduring hits, *Very Good Eddie*. The first was *90 in the Shade* (1/25/15; 40 performances). Smith again provided lyrics, and the libretto was written by GUY BOLTON, who would become an important player in Kern's career. The second show was *Rosy Rapture*, a J. M. Barrie play produced in London. For *Nobody Home* (4/20/15; 135 performances), Bolton again supplied the book with most of the lyrics by Schuyler Greene. Elsie Janis was the star and lyricist of *Miss Information* (10/5/15; 47 performances). The final Kern musical of the year was *Very Good Eddie* (12/23/15; 341 performances). Schuyler Greene was the lyricist along with Herbert Reynolds. Guy Bolton and Philip Bartholomae contributed the libretto. Elisabeth Marbury and F. Ray Comstock produced the show, which was an immediate hit.

Nobody's Home and *Very Good Eddie* were the first two of what are now known as the PRINCESS THEATER shows. Elisabeth Marbury was a well-known literary agent of the day. She had the idea that a kind of permanent company devoted to the American musical should be established, similar to several companies that were at that time devoted to American drama. Producer Comstock owned the Princess Theater, which, with only 299 seats, had difficulty finding tenants. Marbury's idea was a perfect long-term solution to his problem. Kern and Bolton were the first writers hired as the core of the new company. The Princess Theater shows are generally acknowledged as the first of the modern musical comedies. Because of the small size of the theater, they were necessarily intimate shows that broke away from the general operatic tradition. The songs were better integrated into the story than in the old-style shows, and the plots revolved around American characters in American settings. The shows were less overtly romantic than the typical musical comedy, and they were more in tune with current trends and feelings.

Nonetheless, Kern's next show, produced in London, was more traditional. *Theodore and Co.* (9/19/16; 503 performances) had lyrics by Adrian Ross and Clifford Grey. Kern was back in the United States for his next show, *Have a Heart* (1/11/17; 76 performances), the first Kern show to boast lyrics by P. G. Wodehouse and the first of 5 written by him in 1917. Bolton and Wodehouse contributed the book. "And I Am All Alone" was a mild success from the score. Harry B. Smith was the lyricist for *Love O' Mike* (1/15/17; 192 performances). *Oh, Boy!* (2/20/17; 463 performances), another Bolton, Wodehouse, and Kern production, contained several wonderful songs: "The Land Where the Good Songs Go," cut prior to the opening; "Nesting Time in Flatbush," probably the funniest song in the show; and the enduring classic " 'Till the Clouds Roll By," one of the greatest of all American popular songs.

Leave It to Jane (8/28/17; 167 performances) was the third show by the successful trio. The score was one of the team's most consistent. "Cleopatterer," "The Crickets Are Calling," "The Siren's Song," and the title song all received a measure of success. The songs are enchanting and written with the humorous innocence that hallmarked the team's work. *Miss 1917* (11/5/17; 40 performances) was hailed by reviewers. It played to sold-out houses and yet closed prematurely. Produced by Charles B. Dillingham and FLORENZ ZIEGFELD, the show's running costs were greater than the ticket prices could cover. The Kern, Wodehouse, and Bolton show starred Elizabeth Brice, Marion Davies, Lew Fields (*see* FIELDS FAMILY), Ann Pennington, Vivienne Segal, Van and Schenck, GEORGE WHITE, and Bessie McCoy.

Jerome Kern.

In 1918 Kern was busy with another 5 shows on the boards. *Oh, Lady! Lady!!* (2/1/18; 219 performances) was the first of the year's Kern, Bolton, and Wodehouse shows. None of the songs achieved great fame, but a song that was cut from the show, "Bill," would later become one of the hits from *Show Boat*. Kern's other 1918 efforts with a variety of lyricists were all rather minor: *Toot-Toot!* (3/11/18; 40 performances), *Rock-a-Bye Baby* (5/22/18; 80 performances), and *Head over Heels* (8/29/18; 100 performances).

In 1919 Kern wrote only one musical, *She's a Good Fellow* (5/5/19; 120 performances). It is most noteworthy as the first Kern show for which Anne Caldwell supplied the book and lyrics. Caldwell was one of the only women working in what was then a male-dominated field. Her success led to slightly greater acceptance for women in the ranks of composers, lyricists, and librettists. Caldwell worked on a total of nine shows with Kern. Her second, *The Night Boat* (2/2/20; 313 performances) was the first of three shows written by Kern in 1920. Two of the songs, "Left All Alone Again Blues" and "Whose Baby Are You?" achieved some success. Anne Caldwell also contributed lyrics to Kern's next show, *Hitchy-Koo of 1920* (10/19/20; 71 performances). The annual revue starred popular comedian Raymond Hitchcock.

Kern's last show of 1920 was one of his greatest successes. *Sally* (12/21/20; 570 performances) had a book by Guy Bolton and lyrics by Clifford Grey, Anne Caldwell, P. G. Wodehouse, and B. G. De Sylva (*see* DE SYLVA, BROWN AND HENDERSON). The show's great success was due to the excellence of the score and Florenz Ziegfeld's lavish production. The star was one of the most beloved performers on the American stage, Marilyn Miller. Leon Errol, Walter Catlett, Irving Fisher, and Mary Hay also appeared. The score contained many great Kern melodies, including the title song, "Wild Rose," and "Whip-Poor-Will." The best song, however, was one of Kern's most enduring standards, "Look for the Silver Lining." The De Sylva lyric was perfectly married to Kern's simple melody.

Kern's next show, *Good Morning, Dearie* (11/21/21; 347 performances), also had a long run, in part because of the success of *Sally*. It boasted a book and lyrics by Anne Caldwell. "Ka-lu-a," "Blue Danube Blues," and the title song are still remembered by Kern fans. FRED AND ADELE ASTAIRE were the stars of Kern's next show, *The Bunch and Judy* (11/28/22; 63 performances), which was followed by *Stepping Stones* (11/6/23; 241 performances). *Sitting Pretty* (4/8/24; 95 performances), at the Fulton Theater (*see* HELEN HAYES THEATER [1]), was the last of the Bolton, Wodehouse, and Kern shows. The musical starred Queenie Smith and Frank McIntyre. Kern provided his only score in collaboration with Howard Dietz (*see* DIETZ AND SCHWARTZ) for *Dear Sir* (9/23/24; 15 performances). Dietz had contributed to Franklin P. Adams' column, "The Conning Tower," under the pseudonym "Freckles." Like most of his contemporaries he was in awe of Kern and was amazed that the master had called on him for his musical. *Dear Sir* was not a success, but it did give Dietz his start in musical comedy.

Kern's next show, *Sunny* (9/22/25; 517 performances), another great success, reunited the composer with his star of *Sally*, Marilyn Miller. OTTO HARBACH

Frank McIntyre *Sitting Pretty* among the chorines from the 1924 show.

and OSCAR HAMMERSTEIN II provided the book and lyrics. *Sunny* contained such big hits as "Who?" "D'ye Love Me?" and the title song. Critic PERCY HAMMOND called the score "comparatively aristocratic." However, critic Alan Dale found the music "not remarkable." He said, "It had some effective harmonies, however, and it was at least scholarly, and it wasn't treacle." Burns Mantle in the *New York Daily News* proclaimed the score "excellent."

For *The City Chap* (10/26/25; 72 performances), which opened at the LIBERTY THEATRE, Kern teamed with lyricist Anne Caldwell. For *Criss-Cross* (10/12/26; 210 performances), Caldwell and Kern worked together for the last time; Otto Harbach also contributed to the lyrics. Fred Stone made his second appearance in a Kern show supported by his daughter, Dorothy, and Oscar ("Rags") Ragland. Stone played an aviator who made his entrance from the top of the proscenium dangling from a parachute. As soon as he hit the stage a spring action catapulted him back into the flies. Stone kept up his trademarked brand of physical humor throughout the show. In one scene he rescued his daughter by hanging by his knees from a trapeze that was attached to the body of an airplane. As he swung over the stage he grabbed two handles attached to the back of his daughter's costume and lofted her into the wings. *Lucky* (3/22/27; 71 performances), Kern's next show, proved less strenuous for its cast. Bert Kalmar and Harry Ruby provided the lyrics and coauthored the libretto with Otto Harbach.

Around this time Kern began the most important phase of his career. His last 6 shows, written with either Hammerstein or Harbach, contain some of the finest songs of the American musical theater. Although some of these shows may not be well remembered today, their songs have endured for more than half a century. *Show Boat* (12/27/27; 575 performances) is generally considered to be Kern's masterpiece. *Show Boat* was presented by Florenz Ziegfeld at the ZIEGFELD THEATER. The cast, Charles Winninger, Howard Marsh, Norma Terris, Helen Morgan, Edna Mae Oliver, and Jules Bledsoe perfectly personified Edna Ferber's fas-

"Morris Gest, P.G. Wodehouse, Guy Bolton, F. Ray Comstock and Jerome Kern in Detroit for the opening of Sitting Pretty, the seventh and most recent of the Princess Theatre Intimate Musical Comedies, April 8, 1924."

cinating characters. The score was equally brilliant, containing such standards as "Can't Help Lovin' Dat Man," "Life upon the Wicked Stage," "You Are Love," "Why Do I Love You?" and "Bill." John Byram in the *New York Times* stated that the show had "an exceptionally tuneful score—the most lilting and satisfactory that the wily Jerome Kern has evolved in several seasons." Richard Watts Jr., in the *New York Herald Tribune*, said that Kern "came out of the proceedings with the highest credit." Abel Green stated in VARIETY that "the music is typically Kernian, titillating, infectious, refreshing and never tiring." *Show Boat* has been revived numerous times on Broadway and around the world.

Sweet Adeline (9/3/29; 234 performances), at Hammerstein's Theater (*see* ED SULLIVAN THEATER), was a vehicle written for one of the stars of *Show Boat* and one of the greatest Broadway stars: Helen Morgan. The torch singer was the lead character in the new show. Oscar Hammerstein II repeated his lyric and libretto duties. Two of Morgan's numbers, "Why Was I

Born?" and "Don't Ever Leave Me," are among Kern and Hammerstein's most dramatic songs. Nearly all the reviews were favorable. Gilbert Seldes echoed the majority opinion when he commented in the *New Republic*, "The music is more of a concentration of the spirit of the 1890's than a reminiscence of its tunes. Kern is a master of many styles and handled the charm and rather awkward grace of the time perfectly."

Otto Harbach provided the book and lyrics to *The Cat and the Fiddle* (10/15/31; 395 performances) at the Globe Theater (*see* LUNT-FONTANNE THEATER). The score was filled with beautiful Kern melodies, and Harbach's lyrics fitted the show's European ambiance perfectly. "The Night Was Made for Love," "She Didn't Say Yes," "Try to Forget," and "One Moment Alone" have all become standards. *Music in the Air* (11/8/32; 342 performances) retained *The Cat and the Fiddle*'s European feeling. Oscar Hammerstein II provided the book and lyrics for the show. Walter Slezak, Natalie Hall, Vivian Vance, Marjorie Main, and Al Shean starred at the Alvin Theater (*see* NEIL SIMON

Bob Hope tickles the ivories while Fay Templeton (seated) listens approvingly in *Roberta*, 1933.

THEATER). "I've Told Every Little Star" was the best received song in the score, which also included "There's a Hill beyond a Hill," "And Love Was Born," and "The Song Is You." Most of the reviews were favorable, with all the critics agreeing on the merits of the Kern' and Hammerstein score. JOHN MASON BROWN, in the *New York Post*, said that *Music in the Air* "abounds in the sort of soft, insinuating melodies which rarely are heard along Broadway and of which Mr. Kern is a past master. It is subtle, captivating music." That opinion was typical of the critical raves the score received.

Roberta (11/18/33; 295 performances) is one of Kern's most recognizable titles, mostly due to the successful movie version with Fred Astaire and Irene Dunne. The stage version starred Lyda Roberti, Bob Hope, Tamara, Sydney Greenstreet, Fay Templeton, and George Murphy. Otto Harbach supplied the libretto and lyrics. Among the songs featured in the show (and mostly cut from the movie version) were "The Touch of Your Hand," "You're Devastating," "Yesterdays," "Let's Begin," "I'll Be Hard to Handle," and the classic "Smoke Gets in Your Eyes."

Kern's last show was *Very Warm for May* (11/17/39; 59 performances) at the Alvin Theater. Jack Whiting, Eve Arden, Hiram Sherman, and Donald Brian were the stars. Oscar Hammerstein II provided the lyrics and libretto and also co-directed the show with Vincente Minnelli. The wonderful score featured "In Other Words, Seventeen," "All in Fun," "In the Heart of the Dark," "Heaven in My Arms," and the timeless "All the Things You Are." Reviews of the show, especially the book, were harsh, but Kern's score was well received. BROOKS ATKINSON, in the *New York Times*, said that Kern's work was "rich in variety and feeling and a testament to honest composing."

Following *Very Warm for May*, Kern composed the classic song "The Last Time I Saw Paris" with Hammerstein. He wrote scores to films, including *One Night in the Tropics*, *Swing Time*, *You Were Never Lovelier*, *Can't Help Singing*, and *Cover Girl*. After a successful sojourn in Hollywood, Kern returned to New York to work on a new musical with Dorothy Fields. It was to be produced by RODGERS AND HAMMERSTEIN and was based on the life of Annie Oakley. However, before work commenced on the show, on November 5, 1945, Kern collapsed on Park Avenue at 57th Street. Because he had no identification on him, Kern was taken to the City Hospital on Welfare Island. Hospital personnel found Kern's ASCAP membership card. The organization informed Hammerstein, and he arranged for doctors to examine Kern. The composer was diagnosed as having a cerebral hemorrhage. He was moved to Doctors' Hospital on November 7. Kern intermittently regained consciousness, but his condition steadily worsened. On the last day of Kern's life,

Hammerstein sat at his bedside and gently sang "I've Told Every Little Star," hoping to rouse him. After finishing the song, Hammerstein looked at his friend and realized that he had died.

KERR, WALTER. Critic, author and playwright; b. Evanston, Illinois, July 8, 1913; d. Larchmont, New York, October 9, 1996.

Kerr was on the drama faculty of Catholic University during its heyday from 1938 to 1949. While there, he collaborated with Leo Brady and Nancy Hamilton in the revue *Count Me In* (61 performances). It opened at the ETHEL BARRYMORE THEATRE on October 8, 1942. Kerr also wrote and directed the folk-music revue *Sing Out Sweet Land* (12/27/44; 102 performances) and the revue *Touch and Go* (10/13/49; 176 performances), the latter with his wife, playwright Jean Kerr.

In 1949 Kerr left Catholic University and became drama CRITIC for *Commonweal* for 2 years beginning in 1950. He became drama critic for the *New York Herald Tribune* in 1951 and remained at that post until the paper folded in 1966. Meanwhile, he continued his occasional activities as a theater director and writer. Kerr directed *King of Hearts* (4/1/54; 279 performances), which his wife wrote with Eleanor Brooke. Mr. and Mrs. Kerr collaborated with composer Leroy Anderson on *Goldilocks* (161 performances), a musical that opened at the LUNT-FONTANNE THEATER on October 11, 1958; Kerr also directed the production.

After the *Tribune* closed Kerr moved to the *New York Times* and briefly became drama critic. In 1967 he stopped reviewing plays on a daily basis and concentrated on writing pieces on the theater for the Sunday *Times*. Although retired, Kerr continued to contribute occasional pieces to the *Times*. In early 1990 the RITZ THEATRE was renamed the Walter Kerr.

When reviewing, Kerr would take hundreds of notes during opening night. His wife once asked jokingly if he had ever "seen" a play. Kerr is well respected for a series of books on playwriting and criticism that are considered classics. These include *How Not to Write a Play* (1955), *Pieces at Eight* (1957), *The Decline of Pleasure* (1962), and *Theater in Spite of Itself* (1963).

KISS ME, KATE. The Broadway community knew that COLE PORTER could write witty, sophisticated, urbane songs with an elevated sense of silliness or, conversely, deep emotion. But the libretti for Porter's shows were always secondary to the songs. In *Kiss Me, Kate* Porter proved he could write a mature score to a perfectly integrated libretto.

Bella and Sam Spewack, who had already collaborated with Porter on the wartime musical *Leave It to Me*, based their new project on Shakespeare's *The*

Taming of the Shrew. What gave the show an added boost was the outer story of a troupe of players performing Shakespeare's plays onstage while their offstage antics rivaled and complemented the Bard's work. The quarreling leads of the backstage story were loosely patterned on the Lunts (*see* LUNT AND FONTANNE). *Kate*'s producer, Arnold Saint Subber, had served as an apprentice to the Lunts while they performed in the Shakespeare classic.

Saint Subber convinced an initially doubting Bella Spewack that the idea was a good one. He had foreseen a straightforward musicalization of the original play. But Spewack, who admitted she was largely unfamiliar with the background work and was, in any event, no Shakespearean scholar, thought up the idea of having the bulk of the musical happen backstage.

Alfred Drake and Patricia Morison were the stars, ably supported by Lisa Kirk and Harold Lang. Porter's score contained some of his greatest songs, including "Another Op'nin', Another Show," "So in Love," and "Wunderbar." The latter song was a surprise hit, as it was intended as a parody of Viennese operetta. Its lyrics, such as "gazing down on the Jungfrau" (the tallest mountain in the Alps), were strictly tongue in cheek. But audiences either didn't care or didn't get the joke, and the song soon became a standard.

Kiss Me, Kate had the longest run of Porter's career, 1,077 performances. It went on to conquer London, Sydney, Frankfurt (as the first postwar musical to play continental Europe), and beyond.

KIT KAT KLUB. *See* **Henry Miller's Theatre.**

KLAW THEATER. 251–57 W. 45th Street between Broadway and 8th Avenue. Architect: Eugene De Rosa. Opening: March 2, 1921; *Nice People.*

The Klaw Theater led an unimpressive existence. It was built by Marcus Klaw of the Klaw and Erlanger partnership, members of the dreaded Theatrical Syndicate. Sam H. Harris produced the first play, *Nice People* (3/2/21; 120 performances), by Rachel Crothers. It featured a stellar cast headed by Tallulah Bankhead, Katharine Cornell, and Francine Larrimore. The second play at the Klaw was also a success. *Lilies of the Field* (10/4/21; 169 performances), by William J. Hurlbut, starred Marie Doro, Alison Skipworth, and Cora Witherspoon. But these early successes were not to be repeated for the majority of bookings in the house.

Lynn Starling's *Meet the Wife* (11/26/23) starred Humphrey Bogart, Clifton Webb, and Mary Boland and ran for 232 performances. The theater's next offering, *Hell-Bent for Heaven* (1/4/24; 122 performances), featured a performance by the young GEORGE ABBOTT.

On September 18, 1929, it reopened as the Avon Theater with Preston Sturges' comedy *Strictly Dishonorable* (557 performances). There would be no more hits at the theater until the next-to-last play to open at the Avon, *The Pursuit of Happiness* (10/9/33; 252 performances). The play was written by Alan Child and Isabelle Louden. They were pseudonyms for Mr. and Mrs. Lawrence Langner, heads of the THEATER GUILD.

In September 1934 CBS took it over as a radio playhouse, naming it CBS Radio Playhouse No. 2. The network bought the theater outright 3 years later. In 1953 the theater was sold by CBS to Abraham and Frederick Dreier, two developers. The theater was razed in 1954.

KNICKERBOCKER HOTEL. 142 W. 42nd Street. Architects: Marvin & Davis, Bruce Price, consultant.

Construction on the Beaux Arts Knickerbocker Hotel began in 1901, but because of the original owner's default on rent, construction stopped in 1904. The hotel was finally completed in 1906.

The Knickerbocker was planned as a rival to the ASTOR HOTEL. No expense was spared to make the 15-story hotel as luxurious as possible. Advertisements featured its $10,000 gold service for 60. Trowbridge and Livingston, architects of the St. Regis Hotel, designed the interior. Their designs were a great success, especially the important artworks they commissioned. Maxfield Parrish's mural *Old King Cole and His Fiddlers Three* was the most prominent. Frederick Remington's painting *The United States Cavalry Charge* was hung in the basement bar. A bas-relief of Aphrodite by John Flanagen graced the Flower Room. Also in the Flower Room was a scene painted by James Wall Finn.

Concerning the design and decoration of the Knickerbocker, the 1906 *Architectural Record* stated:

> There are few hotels in the country in the appearance of which such uniform good taste has been displayed; and there is certainly no hotel which will owe so much of its success to its aesthetic distinction. Its architecture is, unfortunately, not as successful as its decorative scheme. Certain architectural errors have been made, of which the failure to insert a partition between the restaurant and the Flower Room is one of the worst, because it seriously hurts the architectural effect of both these rooms. But even after all deductions have been made, the hotel marks a real advance in the art of making that sort of a building legitimately entertaining to its patrons.

Society took to the Knickerbocker and made its early years successful. The hotel, dubbed the "42nd Street Country Club," numbered among its tenants GEORGE M. COHAN and Enrico Caruso. It was so successful that on October 18, 1911, the Knickerbocker acquired the Ryan Hotel next door. The two spaces were merged, and the Knickerbocker added 100 extra rooms. However, with the onset of Prohibition the Knickerbocker, like many other hotels, lost money. Liquor sales at bars and restaurants accounted for much of the hotel's profits. The Astor Hotel was able to add stores on the ground floor to offset the loss in revenue.

On June 14, 1920, Vincent Astor, Nicholas Biddle, and S. B. Thorn bought the hotel and converted most of it to office space. The Knickerbocker's two lower floors were transformed into retail space, but the Grill was retained. Many of the interior appointments were saved in the transformation. The King Cole mural was transferred to the St. Regis Hotel. In February 1921 the National Drug Stores chain was the first lessee. The company took nearly the entire first floor retail space. It leased the space for $3.5 million over a 21-year period. The building's last major tenant was the *Newsweek* organization. In October 1956 *Newsweek* moved to new offices on the East Side.

The mansard-roofed building still retains much of its turn-of-the-century splendor. With the rampant development in the area, the Knickerbocker remains the last vestige of bygone Times Square. A relic of the past can be viewed in the front of the Times Square shuttle's track number one. A small door is still topped by a sign reading "Knickerbocker," a forgotten memento of the great hotel.

LABOR STAGE. *See* **48th Street Theatre.**

LAFF-MOVIE. *See* **Empire Theatre (2).**

LANE, BURTON. Noted Broadway composer, best remembered for his scores for *Finian's Rainbow* and *On a Clear Day You Can See Forever*; b. New York, New York, February 2, 1912; d. New York, New York, January 5, 1997.

Composer Burton Lane did not have as many of his shows produced as his contemporaries, but his shows all contained superior scores. When not writing for Broadway, Lane had a successful career in Hollywood. Each of Lane's Broadway scores—written with such greats as Harold Adamson, E. Y. Harburg, Alan Jay Lerner (*see* Lerner and Loewe), and Al Dubin—were full of rich, inventive melodies.

Lane showed an early predilection for music; he took his first piano lessons at age 3. He returned to the piano after his parents imposed a 6-year break so that he could concentrate on his school studies. Amazingly, Lane was so good that he was given an audience with J. J. Shubert, one of the Shubert brothers, the two most powerful men on Broadway. Lane, only 14 at the time, was assigned the score for a new Shubert show. The show was not produced because the star was not available, but had it been, Lane would have been the youngest songwriter in Broadway history.

When Lane was only 15, he went to Remick Publishing Company, where he was given a job plugging songs. While at Remick's, Lane was befriended by George Gershwin. He also met lyricist Howard Dietz (*see* Dietz and Schwartz) who was working on the revue *Three's a Crowd* (10/15/30; 272 performances) with his partner Arthur Schwartz. When the show

opened, it contained two Dietz and Lane songs, "Out in the Open Air" and "Forget All Your Books." Lane next had one song put in *The Third Little Show* (6/1/ 31; 136 performances) and nine in the 1931 edition of *Earl Carroll's Vanities,* (8/27/31; 556 performances) with lyrics by Harold Adamson. The *Vanities* score led to Hollywood and his first film score, *Dancing Lady*, in 1933. The movie contained the first hit song by the 21-year-old composer, "Everything I Have Is Yours," and also marked the film debut of Fred Astaire.

In 1940, after a series of successful films, Lane wrote the score to *Hold On to Your Hats* (9/11/40; 158 performances). The show marked the return to Broadway from Hollywood of Al Jolson, who costarred with Martha Raye. The great Jolson left the show after supposedly catching pneumonia, and the show quickly closed. Lane's score, written with lyricist Harburg, contained the hits "The World Is in My Arms" and "There's a Great Day Comin' Manana."

Laffing Room Only (12/23/44; 232 performances), a vehicle for comedians Olsen and Johnson, was produced by the Shuberts at the Winter Garden Theatre. Lane tried his hand at writing his own lyrics for the show, which included one big hit, "Feudin' and Fightin'." The song had lyrics ascribed to Al Dubin, but they were actually written by Lane and Frank Loesser. The Shuberts, used to challenging any and all comers, were fighting the American Society for Composers Authors and Publishers (*see* ASCAP), the licensing agents for songwriters and publishers. The producers decided to withhold the right to broadcast songs from their productions on radio. They started their own Performing Acts Society of the Theater to defy ASCAP. Broadcasters had formed their own challenge to ASCAP, Broadcast Music Incorporated (BMI), and the Shuberts sided with BMI. Unfortunately, Lane was caught in the middle, unable to receive royalties from "Feudin' and Fightin'" because the Shuberts refused to allow it to be broadcast. In 1947, after the ASCAP ban was lifted, the song received its due.

Lane's next score was written with Harburg for one of the best Broadway musicals, *Finian's Rainbow* (1/10/47; 725 performances). The show opened at the 46th Street Theater (*see* RICHARD RODGERS THEATER) with Ella Logan, David Wayne, Donald Richards, and the Lyn Murray Singers. Lane collaborated with Harburg on the excellent score, which included "How Are Things in Glocca Morra?" "When I'm Not Near the Girl I Love," "If This Isn't Love," "Old Devil Moon," and "Look to the Rainbow."

Almost 20 years passed before the next Broadway score by Burton Lane. He spent much of his time in Hollywood writing for MGM and also began and abandoned several theater projects.

On a Clear Day You Can See Forever (10/17/65; 280 performances) starred Barbara Harris, John Cullum, and William Daniels. The show proved Lane had not lost his touch. With lyricist and librettist Alan Jay Lerner (*see* LERNER AND LOEWE), Lane composed a winning score. Lane and Lerner contributed more fine work to their next show, *Carmelina* (4/8/79; 17 per-

John Cullum and Barbara Harris in *On A Clear Day You Can See Forever*, 1965.

formances). Unfortunately, the show had many troubles and never recovered in time for its opening. The show marked Lane's last Broadway assignment.

Although Lane's Broadway output was not extensive, the quality of his work is impressive. His songs have a depth rarely seen on Broadway. They are not just pop songs; they are true theatrical statements that help define their characters, advance the plots, and express true emotions.

LATIN QUARTER. Between Broadway and 7th Avenue on 48th Street.

The Palais Royal was the first of the famous nightclubs to operate out of the building that would later house the Cotton Club and the highly successful Latin Quarter. Paul Salvin, dubbed the King of Nightclubs, owned and ran the Palais Royal from its inception in the latter part of the 1910s. Salvin made the club a fashionable hangout for East Siders, insisting that his patrons wear evening dress. Soon the Palais Royal rivaled Sherry's and Delmonico's. The club sometimes grossed $20,000 a week, a huge sum at the time.

Helping Salvin were his assistants Gil Boag and James Thompson. Salvin's maîtres d'hôtel were Pierre and Borgo. Each left Salvin and became successful in his own right. Pierre later built the famous Fifth Avenue hotel that bears his name.

Salvin's other operations were the Pavilion Royal, RECTOR'S RESTAURANT, and the Montmartre, which was atop the WINTER GARDEN THEATRE. He was a man of simple tastes who had a knack for making people feel comfortable. Salvin had a way of growing fond of certain words that he would use over and over again. For a period, his favorite word was *environment*. When performer Fritzi Scheff hit a sour note on the stage of the Palais Royal, Salvin told director JOHN MURRAY ANDERSON, "She has lost her environment. She can't do a thing like that in a respectable place like this." It was Scheff who had appeared in the Palais Royal's first production, which was staged by her husband, silent film cowboy Bronco Billy Anderson. She sang her great hit "Kiss Me Again," written for her by composer VICTOR HERBERT for her appearance in his operetta *Mlle. Modiste*. Anderson staged later shows in the club that were the first true nightclub shows. Anderson supplied the lyrics to music by A. Baldwin Sloane and Frank Harling.

The building housed the downtown version of Connie's Inn from 1933 to 1934. The Immerman brothers, owners of Connie's Inn, changed the name to the Harlem Club and made it a blacks-only club. However, blacks seldom frequented Times Square, and the club quickly closed. The Ubangi Club followed, with a floor show featuring male and female impersonators.

Among the performers was Gladys Bentley, who sang in a man's full evening dress. After a year the Ubangi Club moved farther downtown.

On September 24, 1936, Harlem's renowned Cotton Club moved downtown to this location. The Cotton Club opened under Herman Stark's direction, assisted by Big Frenchy DeMange. Columnist Louis Sobol remembered sitting in the Cotton Club and playing pinochle with DeMange, "one of the formidable chieftains of gangdom."

The first show at the club's new location starred Bill "Bojangles" Robinson and Cab Calloway. The songs for that first edition of the downtown Cotton Club were by J. Fred Coots and Benny Davis. The show was an immediate success. By its third week the club was grossing $45,000. In the first 3 months the club averaged a weekly gross of $30,000. The large earnings were due to the number of shows given, not to high prices. A steak sandwich was $2.25. Scrambled eggs and sausage cost only $1.50, and a lobster cocktail cost $1.50. Filet mignon and french fries cost $3. The club offered Chinese selections also. Moo goo gai pan cost $2.25. The cover charge for a complete table d'hôte was $1.50 to $2 for dinner. Otherwise, there was no cover charge.

The Cotton Club's success continued with its second revue, which was mounted in the spring of 1937. The songs were written by Duke Ellington, Andy Razaf, and others. Ellington's band appeared in the show along with Ethel Waters, Ivy Anderson, George Dewey Washington, and the Nicholas Brothers. The show was titled the *Cotton Club Express*. Columnist ED SULLIVAN called it "easily the most elegant colored show Broadway has ever applauded," and said that it "would corner the hi-de-ho and ho-de-ho market." The show was an even bigger success than the club's first downtown revue. In one month more than 50,000 people attended. Opening nights at the Cotton Club could easily rival those of Broadway shows. Among the opening night patrons were actress Sylvia Sidney, comedian Lou Holtz, and Dr. Leo Michel, nicknamed Dr. Broadway.

The Cotton Club continued its success through the 1930s. But as the Depression dragged on, Stark began to have money problems. The government was watching the club closely because of its ties to organized crime. The cost of doing such lavish shows also rose, and the club's fortunes suddenly began to fall. Audience tastes were changing, and more luxurious, sophisticated clubs were gaining favor. Featured in the final Cotton Club show were Louis Armstrong and Maxine Sullivan, fresh from their star turns in the Hollywood movie *Going Places*. Also appearing were Stepin Fetchit, Midge Williams, Stump and Stumpy, and

Andy Kirk's Orchestra. Finally, on June 10, 1940, the Cotton Club closed.

The Latin Quarter, one of the greatest New York nightclubs for almost a quarter of a century, opened on the premises on April 1, 1942. Some New Yorkers preferred the more sophisticated East Side clubs like El Morocco and the Copacabana. But Times Square clubs like Billy Rose's Diamond Horseshoe (*see* CENTURY THEATER [1]) and the Latin Quarter entertained more than their share of native New Yorkers. By 1945 the Latin Quarter was grossing $45,000 a week. In its first 10 years the club grossed $10 million and served more than 5 million patrons. New Yorkers came here to mingle with the tourists who paid to see such stars as Ted Lewis, Sophie Tucker, Mae West, Harry Richman, Milton Berle, and Willie and Eugene Howard. Columnist Earl Wilson wrote of the Latin Quarter: "the show was long, with acrobats, Apache dancers, jugglers, harmonica wizards—but you got a lot for your money and the chorus girls did their best to show you their breasts although they usually had to wear pasties over their nipples (sometimes the pasties came unpasted, however, or the girls forgot to apply them)." The club was run by LOU WALTERS, the father of television personality Barbara Walters, in partnership with E. M. Loew of Boston.

The Quarter, like other Broadway clubs, survived a number of calamities. In the 1930s the rule in New York was that bare-breasted women were allowed as long as they stood still. When police tried to enforce the law, the Latin Quarter girls threatened to hold a topless strike outside the club. In 1944 the government announced a 30 percent amusement tax. Many nightclubs went out of business when patrons stopped coming. The government later apologized and reduced the tax to 20 percent. During World War II the club took another blow. War mobilization director Jimmy Byrnes announced that although he "regretted the inconvenience," there would be a midnight curfew for all amusements. The clubs were up in arms. However, Toots Shor, one of the greatest club owners, calmed everyone down when he stated, "Any crum-bum what can't get plastered by midnight just ain't tryin'." The curfew led to a resurgence of the speakeasy. These secret bottle clubs were thought to be permanently dead when Prohibition was repealed. Mayor LaGuardia proclaimed that "New York is still New York; I don't like the curfew law." He extended the curfew to 1 A.M. That was late enough for most people, and the speakeasies disappeared.

Walters saw the handwriting on the wall for the Latin Quarter and sold out his interest in 1958, but he rejoined the enterprise as manager in 1965. He remained until he retired to Florida in 1967, 2 years before the club closed. The chorus girls brought on the downfall of the club. Their union, the American Guild of Variety Artists, decided the chorus was not paid enough. The union's vice president, Penny Singleton (Blondie in the movies), called for a strike. What neither she nor her union appreciated was that times had changed, and the clubs were quickly disappearing. Loew, also the owner of several profitable drive-ins, was not intimidated at the threat of a strike. He offered the girls $130 a week, a raise of $8. Each week the girls performed in 13 shows.

The previous January, Jules Podell, operator of the Copacabana, had fired his chorus line. Loew felt he could do the same. However, Loew was also having trouble renewing his lease. On February 20, 1969, the club was closed. Loew planned to reopen the club (sans chorus) elsewhere, but the death knell for New York nightclubs was already sounding, and he abandoned the idea. The closing of the Latin Quarter marked the end of the nightclub era in New York.

With the Latin Quarter closed, the building remained empty. Several attempts to inaugurate a legitimate theater policy in the space failed. One of the building's names during this period was the 22 Steps Theater, so called because of the 22 steps that the patrons had to walk up to reach the theater. Among the failures in the space during its various incarnations were *My Old Friends* (4/12/79; 54 performances), starring Cotton Club headliner Maxine Sullivan, and *The Madwoman of Central Park West* (6/13/79; 86 performances), starring Phyllis Newman. The name was then changed to the Princess Theater, and here *Censored Scenes from King Kong* (3/6/80; 5 performances) and *Fearless Frank* (6/15/80; 12 performances) played. One big hit at the Princess Theater was *Pump Boys and Dinettes*, which moved from a 132-performance run off Broadway on February 4, 1982. *Pump Boys* eventually ran a total of 685 performances, making it the only success in the space in 20 years. The name reverted to the Latin Quarter when the room was refurbished in November 1984. It reopened with the show *Haarlem Nocturne*, which quickly closed. The space remained empty until the entire block was demolished in 1990 to make room for another office tower.

LEAGUE OF AMERICAN THEATRES AND PRODUCERS. Born as the League of New York Theatres and Producers in 1930, this organization is the voice of the producers and theater owners. The organization was founded to fight ticket speculation. The League's charter stated its purpose: to "protect the general public patrons of the theater, owners of theatrical entertainments, operators of theaters and reputable theater ticket brokers against the evils of speculation of

theater tickets." The campaign against speculators worked. The League and ACTORS' EQUITY wrote a Theater Ticket Code of Fair Practice that limited the premiums on tickets sold through speculators. In 1940 the code was revised and made a state law.

The League expanded its charter in 1931 and again in 1933. In 1938 it further expanded its role by becoming the official bargaining group for producers in negotiations with craft unions and Actors' Equity. The League's goals at that time were announced as "1. To effectuate and bring about amicable adjustment of labor disputes in the theatrical industry in the City of New York. 2. To make on behalf of its members all agreements with other organizations, to carry out one or more purposes of the League. 3. To procure and effect uniformity and certainty in the customs and usages of the theatrical industry; and those having an interest therein. 4. To effect economy in the conduct of the business of its members. And 5. To eliminate unfair and unjust practices."

Since then the organization has spearheaded campaigns for the cleanup of Times Square. The group also commissions studies on audience composition and marketing techniques. One of the League's most visible efforts has been the "I Love New York" tourism campaign. The League also administers the TONY AWARDS for the AMERICAN THEATRE WING. The League expanded its domain when Broadway fortunes fell in the 1970s and '80s by becoming the League of American Theatres and Producers. The League publishes what many consider a propaganda column in each month's issue of *PLAYBILL*, given to each theater patron.

LEIGH, DOUGLAS. Designer of spectacular signs; b. May 24, 1907, Anniston, Alabama; d. New York, New York, December 14, 1999.

Times Square is defined as much by its look as by its events. Leigh's signs, as much as anything else, gave Times Square its distinctive look. Leigh also had a successful career as a specialist in lighting some of New York's most impressive skyscrapers.

After attending the University of Florida, Leigh took a sales job with an outdoor advertising company that had offices in Alabama and New York. At age 22 Leigh came to New York, and after a brief relationship with an outdoor advertising office, he decided to start his own advertising sales firm. E. J. Kahn, in a profile of Leigh in *The New Yorker*, called him "perhaps the only person in the United States besides President Roosevelt who is now in charge of a going business that officially got under way on March 4, 1933." Leigh's firm's first account was the sale of billboard space in the Bronx to the St. Moritz Hotel. Because this was the Depression, Leigh was not paid cash for the sale. Instead, he took meals and a place to stay from the St. Moritz.

Leigh's next assignment put him on the map and changed the look of Times Square forever. When he arrived on the scene, there were only four moving electric signs on the square. The Atlantic and Pacific Tea Company asked him to design a sign for them on Times Square. Leigh wasn't content to settle for the usual illuminated billboard. Instead, he designed a 25-foot-tall steaming coffee cup. Leigh dubbed the new type of sign a "spectacular." The A&P sign signaled the start of an era. There was no holding back either Leigh or the history of SIGNAGE on Broadway.

Leigh went on to design some of Broadway's most incredible spectaculars, usually in collaboration with the artisans at ARTKRAFT STRAUSS. His work included the Kool Cigarettes winking penguin, which stood atop a giant cake of ice and winked 100,000 times a day. For Ballantine Beer he designed an effect of clowns pitching quoits to form the beer's 3-ring trademark. He created the Bromo Seltzer sign, which bubbled over Times Square, and the Pepsi Cola spectacular, which featured a 120-foot waterfall that pumped 50,000 gallons of water a minute.

Leigh also imported and perfected EPOK from the Swiss. EPOK was a huge billboard covered in light bulbs. Images were projected onto photoelectric cells that then sent the signal to the light bulbs. The wonderful thing about EPOK was that the images could move, and New Yorkers were thrilled to see images of Charlie Chaplin, FRED ASTAIRE, and Ray Bolger scamper across the skyline. Old Gold Cigarettes, Wilson Whiskies, and others sponsored the sign.

During a 46-year period, Leigh designed about 78 different spectaculars, each unique and individual. When World War II brought nightly blackouts, Leigh built a different kind of spectacular, the Camel smoke-ring sign, which endured on Broadway for 27 years. Leigh also affected Times Square in his 13 years as president and chairman of the Broadway Association, a group created to help solve Times Square's many problems. During his tenure he pushed for a redeveloped Times Square and enhanced its streets by putting concrete planters along Broadway from 43rd Street to 46th Street. Leigh was also instrumental in the war bond drive. He created a bomb-burst effect and a waving flag of lights in Grand Central Terminal. He also designed a war bond show at Madison Square Garden, which raised $100 million in bonds. Later he entered the U.S. Navy's Special Services Division, where he developed a one-lens system for gunnery training, replacing seven projectors with one. After the war Leigh leased the fleet of surplus dirigibles owned by the navy. He put lights on the blimps and sent them out over the city on behalf of Ford, Tydol, Wonder Bread, and Mobil. The first went out for MGM, which used the airships to advertise its newest feature, *National Velvet*.

In Grand Central Station, Leigh designed the giant clock (removed in February 1988) and an indoor spectacular for Salem cigarettes. On a larger scale, he was appointed city decorator for the Bicentennial and Democratic Convention in 1976 and for the convention again in 1980. Next he undertook some of his most important assignments: the relighting of the Empire State Building, the Helmsley Building, the St. Moritz Hotel Tower (his first client), the Citicorp Building, the Waldorf-Astoria Hotel, Grand Central Terminal, and the arch in Washington Square.

Leigh owned the franchise for bus advertising for New York, and in less than 3 years, he doubled the city's take of the revenue. One of his most visible designs was the giant pole of lights above the MONY building, which predicted the next day's weather.

Douglas Leigh received 5 New York City awards plus the most prestigious New York award: the Bronze Medallion. He also received 2 first-prize Lumen Awards from the Illumination Society of America, the key to the city, the Applause Award from the New York Sales Executives Club, and the Broadway Association's award for 13 years as its president and chairman. Leigh continued his urban design work, constantly traveling around the world, until his death.

Paul Goldberger of the *New York Times* wrote, "When Douglas Leigh was in the business of creating Times Square (a business I wish he could continue along with his present one since those great signs are a much-missed part of the cityscape) he gave nighttime New York its visual identity for a whole period of our history."

LERNER AND LOEWE. Famed lyricist-composer team who created some of Broadway's most popular musicals; Alan Jay Lerner, b. New York, New York, August 31, 1918; d. New York, New York, June 14, 1986; Frederick Loewe, b. Berlin, Germany, June 10, 1904; d. Palm Springs, California, February 14, 1988.

Alan Jay Lerner was born in New York, the scion of a family with a fortune built on the Lerner Shops chain of women's clothing stores. Lerner was sent to the best schools in England and the United States. It was during this exceptional schooling that Lerner developed his love of the English language. He graduated from Harvard in 1940.

During college Lerner lost sight in one eye during a boxing match. That injury kept him out of World

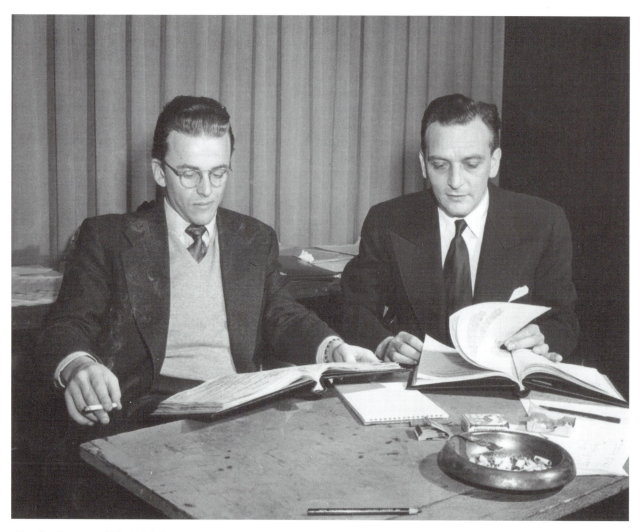

Alan Jay Lerner and Frederick Loewe.

War II and enabled him to pursue his writing career after graduation. He began in radio as a scriptwriter. The career lasted 2 years, during which time Lerner wrote hundreds of scripts. But during his years at Harvard Lerner had caught the theater bug. He contributed to a couple of Hasty Pudding shows, *So Proudly We Hail* and *Fair Enough*. Lerner was a member of the Lambs Club and contributed some lyrics to *The Lambs Gambols*, a small revue.

Frederick Loewe was born in Berlin, Germany, to Austrian parents. His father, Edmund, a leading vocalist, encouraged his son in music, and Frederick became a child prodigy on the piano. The young Loewe studied with well-known contemporary composers Eugène d'Albert and Ferrucio Busoni. At the age of 13 he became the youngest soloist to appear with the Berlin Symphony. When only 15 he wrote the song "Katrina," which was a huge hit in Europe. The family emigrated to the United States in 1924 so that the elder Loewe could appear in operetta. Unfortunately, Edmund

Loewe died shortly after the family arrived in New York. Left virtually penniless, the young Loewe had to make his own way.

Time and popular taste in music worked against the young composer. Operetta was being replaced by a more distinctive American style on the nation's stages and in its clubs. Composers such as RUDOLF FRIML and SIGMUND ROMBERG soon found their European style of composition out of favor, replaced by the syncopated rhythms of IRVING BERLIN, GEORGE GERSHWIN, and COLE PORTER. Loewe found work in Greenwich Village as a piano player. A series of odd jobs followed, including work as a busboy in a cafeteria and a short career as a riding instructor in New Hampshire. After returning to New York, Loewe tried his luck as a boxer in Brooklyn. The unfortunate loss of several teeth to an opponent led to another change in career. This time Loewe tried his hand as a cowboy out West. Then Loewe returned to the East Coast and took a job on a ferry, plying the international waters between Miami and Havana, Cuba. Prohibition had been passed, and cruises to Havana suddenly became very popular. Loewe became a shipboard pianist until the end of Prohibition marked the end of his job. Loewe then returned to New York, where he took a job in a beer garden in the Yorkville section of Manhattan.

Loewe finally broke into the theater as a rehearsal pianist for one of the last operettas, *Champagne Sec* (10/14/33; 113 performances). The job only whetted his appetite for a composing career. Like Lerner, he joined the Lambs Club in order to meet people working in the theater. The scheme worked beyond his wildest expectations. While at the Lambs, Loewe became friends with actor Dennis King. King was set to appear with Oscar Shaw in the play *Petticoat Fever* (3/4/35) at the RITZ THEATRE. He was taken with a song, "Love Tiptoed through My Heart," which Loewe had written in collaboration with Irene Alexander. King decided to interpolate the song into the play. For the first time a Frederick Loewe song was heard on Broadway.

Next Loewe had another song interpolated into a revue, *The Illustrators' Show* (1/22/36; 5 performances). The song was "A Waltz Was Born in Vienna," written in collaboration with Earle Crooker. The popularity of the song lasted longer than *The Illustrators' Show*. Crooker, a script writer and sometime lyricist, collaborated with Loewe on a full-length score to a new musical, *Salute to Spring* (7/12/37), which premiered in St. Louis. The show was a great success, but it did not transfer to New York. However, producer Dwight Deere Wiman enjoyed the team's work and commissioned them to compose the songs for his next Broadway show, *Great Lady* (12/1/38; 20 performances). The operetta was produced at the MAJESTIC THEATRE. In the cast were Norma Terris, of *Show Boat* fame, Irene Bordoni, a saucy French chanteuse, and Helen Ford, star of many RODGERS AND HART shows. In the dance chorus were such future stars as Nora Kaye, Alicia Alonso, and Jerome Robbins.

After the failure of *Great Lady* Loewe resumed his piano playing in restaurants and clubs and continued going to the Lambs Club. But for a time his Broadway activities stopped. Then in 1942 producer Henry Duffy was looking for a team to write shows for his theater in Detroit. Duffy approached Loewe, asking to use the score to *Salute to Spring*. Earle Crooker had written the lyrics to the score, which Loewe felt could use some improvement. Loewe told Duffy that a new lyricist would have to be found. A few days later Loewe came across Lerner playing cards in the club. Loewe approached Lerner, and two days later the two of them found themselves bound for Detroit. The first Lerner and Loewe collaboration, *Life of the Party* (10/8/42),

premiered in Detroit with Dorothy Stone, Margaret Dumont, Charlie Ruggles, and Charles Collins starring.

Although not the best of friends, the two men got on well enough. Lerner was notoriously unreliable, although remarkably talented, and Loewe was disliked as an extremely mean person. However, their talents certainly meshed, and they decided to team up for another show. The result was *What's Up?* (11/11/43; 63 performances). The directors were Robert H. Gordon and George Balanchine. The show starred Jimmy Savo, Larry Douglas, and Lynn Gardner. Despite the talents on hand, the show wasn't a hit. For their next project, the team wrote *The Day before Spring* (11/22/45; 165 performances), which opened at the National Theatre (*see* NEDERLANDER THEATER). In spite of some favorable reviews and what is regarded as a good score, the show never caught on with audiences.

However, *The Day before Spring* was Lerner and Loewe's last failure together. From then on each of their shows achieved great success. The first was *Brigadoon* (3/13/41; 581 performances), a story of the power of love and faith, which opened at the ZIEGFELD THEATER. It starred David Brooks and Lee Sullivan as two jaded Americans who stumble upon the Scottish town that appears only one day each century. Marion Bell and Pamela Britton were the two lassies who found their loves in the two strangers from the 20th century. The score was a lyrical evocation of the Scottish Highlands. "Come to Me, Bend to Me," "The Heather on the Hill," and "Almost Like Being in Love" all became hits. The other songs, more traditional musical comedy numbers, such as "My Mother's Wedding Day," were equally expert. *Brigadoon* was directed by Robert Lewis and produced by Cheryl Crawford. AGNES DE MILLE choreographed the proceedings. *Brigadoon* became an even bigger success in London, where it played His Majesty's Theater for 685 performances after its April 14, 1949, opening.

Lerner next undertook a project with KURT WEILL. *Love Life* (10/7/48; 252 performances) was the result. It opened at the 46th Street Theater with (*see* RICHARD RODGERS THEATER) with Nanette Fabray and Ray Middleton. It was produced by Cheryl Crawford and directed by Elia Kazan.

Lerner returned to his partnership with Frederick Loewe for *Paint Your Wagon* (11/12/51; 289 performances). The show was a lighthearted adventure set against the backdrop of the California Gold Rush. Cheryl Crawford produced, Agnes de Mille choreographed, and Daniel Mann directed. The show starred Olga San Juan, James Barton, and Tony Bavaar. Lerner and Loewe's score was, according to the reviewers, much more entertaining than the book. "They Call the Wind Maria" was a huge hit as was another of the show's ballads, "I Talk to the Trees."

Their next Broadway offering was their biggest success, but it took 6 years for it to reach the stage. The musicalization of George Bernard Shaw's *Pygmalion* was turned down by most of Broadway's veteran composers and lyricists. E. Y. HARBURG, DIETZ AND SCHWARTZ, Noel Coward, Cole Porter, and RODGERS AND HAMMERSTEIN all passed on the project. Lerner and Loewe attempted it and worked on the project for two years before giving up. After the aborted attempt both Lerner and Loewe split to pursue projects that never reached fruition. In 1954 the two songwriters reunited to tackle the project again. This time the work seemed to come together more easily, and *My Fair Lady* (3/15/56; 2,717 performances) opened at the MARK HELLINGER THEATER.

My Fair Lady starred Julie Andrews as Eliza Doolittle and Rex Harrison as her mentor, Henry Higgins. The supporting cast was equally excellent: Robert Coote, Stanley Holloway, Cathleen Nesbitt, Michael King, and Christopher Hewitt. The show was produced by Herman Levin and directed by Moss Hart (*see* KAUFMAN AND HART). The illustrious score contained many hits. Perhaps the most successful was "I Could Have Danced All Night." But "On the Street Where You Live," "I've Grown Accustomed to Her Face," "Wouldn't It Be Loverly?" and "The Rain in Spain" all became standards. *My Fair Lady*'s run was a Broadway record until 1971, when it was overtaken by *Hello, Dolly!*

After the success of *My Fair Lady* there was tremendous pressure put on Lerner and Loewe. The result was bound to be a disappointment, and *Camelot* (12/3/60; 873 performances) was considered so by most of the critics. Prior to its opening at the Majestic Theater, *Camelot* had a stormy tryout period; director Moss Hart suffered a heart attack, and Lerner was also hospi-

Rex Harrison and Julie Andrews in *My Fair Lady*, 1956.

talized. The songwriters and Hart produced the story of King Arthur and Guinevere. The stars were Richard Burton in his only musical theater appearance, Robert Goulet in his Broadway debut, and Julie Andrews following her great success in *My Fair Lady*. Despite mostly unfavorable reviews, the show went on to become one of the most-produced Broadway musicals. This is due in large part to the superior score by Lerner and Loewe. "I Wonder What the King Is Doing Tonight," "If Ever I Would Leave You," and "How to Handle a Woman" all won a fair amount of success on records and television. The Kennedy administration was called Camelot after the title and spirit of the show. *Camelot* was presented in London with Laurence Harvey and Elizabeth Larner in the leads. It was subsequently revived in a long national tour with Richard Harris starring. Harris also starred in the movie version (Warner Brothers, 1967) alongside Vanessa Redgrave.

The difficulties that accompanied *Camelot*'s birth and Loewe's heart problems led to the composer's decision to retire. It was a decision he adhered to with the exception of brief collaborations with Lerner on a movie version of Antoine de Saint-Exupéry's *The Little Prince* (Paramount, 1975) and the stage adaptation of *Gigi*, their hugely successful film musical.

Lerner was not ready for retirement and searched for other collaborators. His first choice was Richard Rodgers, who also lost his collaborator, OSCAR HAMMERSTEIN II, around the same time Lerner and Loewe broke up. The announced project was a musical dealing with E.S.P., having a proposed title of *I Picked a Daisy*. But the Rodgers and Lerner collaboration did not occur. The two professionals found they had divergent working styles, and the project was dropped. Lerner took the idea to BURTON LANE, with whom he had collaborated on the movie *Royal Wedding* (MGM, 1951). The working relationship with Lane proved slightly more successful than that with Rodgers. The result was *On a Clear Day You Can See Forever* (10/17/65; 280 performances). Barbara Harris, John Cullum, William Daniels, and Byron Webster starred in the show, which was eventually made into an unsuccessful film (Paramount, 1970) starring Barbra Streisand and Yves Montand.

Lerner turned to composer Andre Previn for the music of *Coco* (12/18/69; 332 performances), a musicalization of the life of fashion designer Coco Chanel,

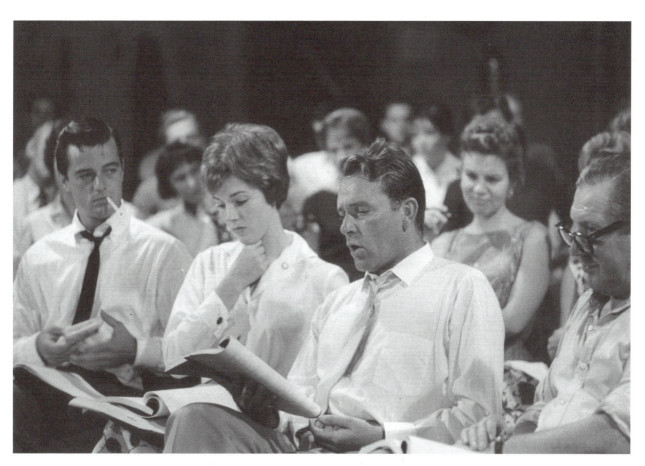

Robert Goulet, Julie Andrews, and Richard Burton at the first reading for *Camelot*, 1960.

Katharine Hepburn (left) takes care of business in *Coco*, 1969.

with Katharine Hepburn in the leading role. *Coco*'s score was unappreciated though excellent. However, soon after Hepburn left the show, it closed.

Failure was to dog Lerner's heels till the end of his career. *Lolita, My Love*, by Lerner and John Barry, closed out of town in 1971. *Music! Music!* (4/11/74; 37 performances), a revue that contained no original songs, had Lerner's book. Lerner's collaboration with LEONARD BERNSTEIN, *1600 Pennsylvania Avenue* (5/4/76; 7 performances), was written to commemorate the American Bicentennial. The show proved to be a legendary failure. In spite of its very good score, the libretto and production were sadly lacking. Despite many changes in personnel, the show could not find an audience, and the score has remained frustratingly unappreciated.

Lerner and Lane collaborated again in 1979 with worse results than their first outing, although the score is also topnotch. *Carmelina* (4/8/79; 17 performances) was based on the film *Buona Sera, Mrs. Campbell* and

starred Georgia Brown, Virginia Martin, and Cesare Siepe. Lerner's last Broadway outing was *Dance a Little Closer* (5/11/83; 1 performance), written with Charles Strouse (*see* STROUSE AND ADAMS). The show was based on Robert E. Sherwood's play *Idiot's Delight*. Like Lerner's other work, even this failure contained great lyrics.

During their heyday the team of Lerner and Loewe produced some of the most enduring of all American musicals. The Lerner and Loewe hallmark was witty, sophisticated, and emotionally complex lyrics married to lively, passionate music that enthralled a generation of theatergoers. Their songs were sometimes sentimental, sometimes satirical, but always professional.

LEW FIELDS' 44TH STREET ROOF GARDEN.
216–230 W. 44th Street, between Broadway and 8th Avenue. Architect: William Albert Swansey. Opening: June 5, 1913; *All Aboard*.

Fields' theater was one of many rooftop theaters built in the days before air-conditioning and stringent fire codes. The auditorium had an erratic career as a number of different ventures. Soon after its premiere, it was reopened as the Folies Marigny in January 1914. A little more than a year later, it was rechristened Castles-in-the-Air. The theater was named for VERNON AND IRENE CASTLE and was used for their shows. They opened the theater on June 14, 1915, with a show called *Look Who's Here*. On December 1, 1917, the date of the opening of the wartime revue *Over the Top*, the theater was renamed the 44th Street Roof Theater. The theater was renovated and walls and roof were added, making the roof theater a traditional house. *Over the Top* had a score in part by SIGMUND ROMBERG. FRED AND ADELE ASTAIRE, the successors to the Castles as Broadway's top dance team, starred.

Popular comedienne, singer, and songwriter Nora Bayes had the theater named after her on December 30, 1918, with her vehicle *Ladies First*. Although Hayes and Seymour Simon wrote most of the score along with A. Baldwin Sloane and HARRY B. SMITH, the hit songs "The Real American Folk Song Is a Rag" and "Some Wonderful Sort of Someone" had music by GEORGE GERSHWIN and lyrics by IRA GERSHWIN and Schuyler Greene, respectively. *Ladies First* was a hit, running 164 performances.

The Nora Bayes Theater became simply the Bayes Theater on September 11, 1922, with *East Side West Side*. Yiddish theater was presented beginning with the opening of *The Three Little Business Men* on September 3, 1923. The theater was renamed Thomashefsky's Broadway Theater, after actor Boris Thomashefsky. Nora Bayes again took over on May 12, 1924, with *Two Strangers from Nowhere*, and the theater again became the Bayes Theater. The theater was renamed Giglio's Radio Theater on August 28, 1937, with *La Figlia Brutta*. The theater's name changed for the last time with *Fickle Women* on December 15, 1937, when it was again christened the Nora Bayes Theater. When the theater below was razed in July 1945, so too was the roof theater. Today one of the *New York Times* printing plants occupies the site.

LEW FIELDS' MANSFIELD THEATER. *See* **Brooks Atkinson Theater.**

LEW M. FIELDS' THEATRE. *See* **Anco Theater.**

LIBERTY THEATRE. 234 W. 42nd Street. Architects: Herts & Tallant. Opening: October 5, 1904; *The Rogers Brothers in Paris*.

Marc Klaw and Abraham Erlanger of the Theatrical Syndicate hired HERTS & TALLANT to design an inexpensive theater down the street from their NEW AMSTERDAM THEATRE. Whereas the New Amsterdam was lavish in every regard, the producers and architects scaled down their expectations for the new theater. Like the New Amsterdam, the Liberty had a small lobby entrance on 42nd Street with the theater proper built on 41st Street reflecting the higher real estate costs on 42nd Street. The main decorations in the Liberty auditorium were on the boxes and the proscenium arch. Later, in 1917, Ziegfeld's favorite scenic artist, Joseph Urban, created murals over the boxes and on the asbestos curtain.

The *New York World* reported at the opening:

> The house is a compact beauty in amber, old gold and ivory mural decorations, carpets, hangings, and upholstery. The house is 70 feet wide, while it is only sixty feet from the footlights to the rear wall, and the standee in the foyer could almost shake hands with the effervescent comedians in their more exuberant moments, while Josephine Cohan's facile toe might have lifted the standees' high hats.

The *Evening Post* writer opined, "Every seat on the three floors has a direct view of the stage, and one feels—no matter where one is sitting—that there is no

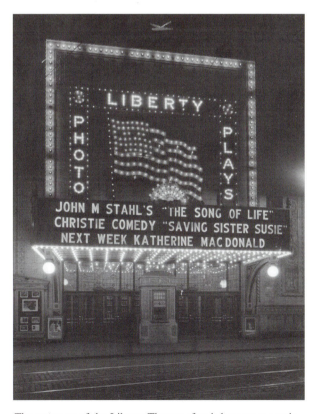

The marquee of the Liberty Theatre after it became a movie house, 1922.

great distance between himself and the people back of the footlights."

Klaw and Erlanger built the Liberty for the Rogers Brothers, a couple of Dutch comics. The comedy team had previously opened the Victoria Theater (*see* GAIETY THEATER) up the block and were popular enough to ensure success to the new theater's premiere, *The Rogers Brothers in Paris* (72 performances). They would return to the Liberty in *The Rogers Brothers in Ireland* (9/4/05; 106 performances). During its heyday as one of Broadway's most successful musical houses, the Liberty presented some of the best talents on the Great White Way. GEORGE M. COHAN had two productions play the Liberty. The first was *Little Johnny Jones* (11/7/04; 52 performances), which marked Cohan's emergence as the top musical comedy talent of his time. Cohan wrote, directed, produced, and starred in the show, which also featured his father and mother and his wife, Ethel Levey. The score contained some of Cohan's most enduring hits, including "The Yankee Doodle Boy" and "Give My Regards to Broadway." Today's audiences remember James Cagney as George M. Cohan singing songs from this show in the picture *Yankee Doodle Dandy.* Cohan's next hit at the Liberty was *Little Nellie Kelly* (11/13/22; 276 performances). The score included "You Remind Me of My Mother" and "Nellie Kelly, I Love You." However, by the 1920s, Cohan saw his fame begin to wind down as newer talents entered the scene. One was JEROME KERN.

Kern had several musicals premiere at the Liberty. The first, *Have a Heart* (1/11/17; 76 performances), was a minor show with a GUY BOLTON and P. G. Wodehouse libretto and Wodehouse lyrics. Though none of the songs achieved standard status, "You Said Something" had a brief vogue. Kern's next show at the Liberty, *The Night Boat* (2/2/20; 318 performances), isn't well remembered today, but the score he wrote with Anne Caldwell did contain two popular songs, "Whose Baby Are You?" and "Left All Alone Again Blues." Charles Dillingham's production of *The City Chap* (10/26/25; 72 performances) also had a Kern/Caldwell score, but none of the songs outlasted the show's run. George Raft, Irene Dunne, and Jimmy Walker's mistress, Betty Compton, all played secondary characters.

Two annual revues played the Liberty. The first was *Hitchy-Koo of 1919* (10/6/19; 56 performances). Raymond Hitchcock, a popular comic and monologist, served as master of ceremonies in this revue's only stop at the Liberty. The score was by the young COLE PORTER and introduced one of his earliest hits, "An Old Fashioned Garden." But the production was a flop, and Porter didn't return to Broadway for 5 years.

GEORGE WHITE'S SCANDALS (6/2/19; 128 performances) began one of its two yearly editions at the Liberty with the 1919 version. The score, by Richard Whiting and Arthur Jackson, didn't have any hits, so for the next edition White enlisted GEORGE GERSHWIN to contribute tunes. The *Scandals of 1920* (6/7/20; 134 performances) introduced the "Scandal Walk," and the *Scandals of 1921* (7/11/21; 97 performances) contained "Drifting Along with the Tide." Gershwin would create better scores in two other productions that opened at the Liberty.

The first is one of Gershwin's greatest hits, *Lady, Be Good!* (12/1/24; 330 performances). The score, written with his brother Ira, boasted many of the Gershwins' most enduring standards, "Fascinating Rhythm," "The Half of It Dearie Blues," and the title song. FRED AND ADELE ASTAIRE starred in the show along with Cliff Edwards and Walter Catlett. The libretto was by Guy Bolton and Fred Thompson. The other Gershwin show to play the Liberty was *Tip Toes* (12/28/25; 194 performances). AARONS AND FREEDLEY repeated their roles as producers, as did the librettists and songwriters of *Lady Be Good!* Again the Gershwins provided an exceptional score, including "Sweet and Low Down," "Looking for a Boy," "These Charming People," and "That Certain Feeling."

Black shows were big successes during the late 1920s and early '30s. The last big hit to play the Liberty, *Blackbirds of 1928* (5/9/28; 519 performances) was one of the most successful. It featured a stellar cast, including Adelaide Hall, Mantan Moreland, Aida Ward, Elisabeth Welch, and Bill Robinson. The score by Dorothy Fields (*see* FIELDS FAMILY) and Jimmy McHugh included "Doin' the New Low-Down," "I Can't Give You Anything but Love," and "Porgy." Three years later Fields and McHugh again contributed two songs for an all-black show at the Liberty, *Singin' the Blues* (9/16/31; 46 performances), but it was not a hit.

The Liberty was one of the most successful theaters on 42nd Street. But in 1932, due to the Depression, the theater began a vaudeville policy. The poor economy took a further toll, and the theater, like its neighbors, became a grind movie house. In 1989 the Seymour Durst Organization bought the Liberty from the Brandts and planned to turn it into a legitimate house again.

The Liberty's orchestra and two balconies held 1,054 patrons. The Times Square Redevelopment Plan called for the theater to be used for nonprofit theater productions from around the country, as well as dance and small musical programs. Forest City Ratner, a development company, leased the property in the late 1990s. Today the lobby area is demolished, and the

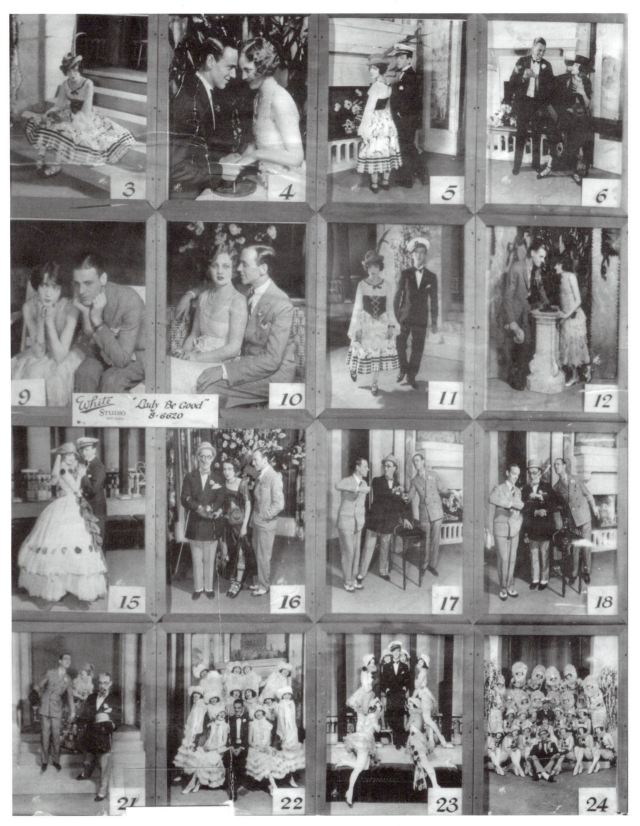

Contact sheet showing scenes from the original production of *Lady, Be Good!*, 1924. Examples of cast: #3 Adele Astaire; #4 Fred Astaire and Kathlene Martyn; #5 Fred and Adele Astaire; #6 Alan Edwards and unknown woman; #8 unknown woman and Walter Catlett.

stage house sits forlornly behind a wall of the Empire 25 movie complex.

LIEBLING, ABBOTT JOSEPH (A. J.). Noted Broadway chronicler whose interests ranged from gastronomy to prize fighting, and a well known watchdog of the journalism field; b. New York, New York, October 18, 1904; d. New York, New York, December 28, 1963.

According to Liebling, his father embodied all the traits of the Horatio Alger legend, only in reverse. It seems his father, a furrier, started wealthy and found himself penniless at his death. Liebling himself enjoyed a checkered career in the halls of academe. After refusing to attend chapel he was expelled from Dartmouth. He ended up at Columbia University's School of Journalism. He commented that Columbia had "all the intellectual status of a training school for future employees of the A&P."

Liebling received his first break shortly after graduation. He obtained a job at the *New York Times* in the sports department but was soon fired for his somewhat cavalier disregard for facts. After the 8-month stint at the *Times*, he took a step backward to the *Providence Journal and Evening Bulletin*. His first job was translating part of "a book about the history of the Italian immigration to America" for two reporters working on "a series of articles on the different colonies of foreign-born Americans in New York."

His sojourn in Rhode Island was more successful. He spent almost 5 years at the paper, with a year off to study ancient history at the Sorbonne.

In 1930 Liebling decided to make another attempt to break into the New York newspaper world. Toward that end he employed a picketer to carry a sign outside the offices of the *World* reading, "Hire Joe Liebling." Liebling did not realize that the city editor never used the front entrance, preferring instead to go in the back way. By the time Liebling caught the attention of the managers, the *World* had expired.

But Liebling had made an impression and was hired at the newly formed *World-Telegram*. This was the beginning of Liebling's love affair with the more unusual segments of the New York population, especially those of Broadway. His writing celebrated the misfits and colorful characters of the Big Apple. He remained at the *World-Telegram* for 5 years.

In 1935 Liebling joined the staff of the *New Yorker*. His fame increased when he served as the magazine's Paris correspondent at the start of World War II. After the war Liebling resumed his more freewheeling style. In 1946 he replaced ROBERT BENCHLEY on the "Wayward Press" column, devoted to criticism of the field of journalism. His more notable columns concerned the journalism community's handling of the Alger Hiss

trial as well as rebuttals to various editorials and policies of the papers. Liebling was against the large newspaper chains, which he saw as a threat to free enterprise and competition. In one of his most memorable quotes Liebling stated, "Freedom of the press is guaranteed only to those who own one."

He would wake up promptly at 9:00 and spend the next three hours poring over the daily newspapers. If he found an interesting story, he would tear it out and put it into his pocket. His wife, Jean Stafford, remembered, "From time to time he laughed, now in amusement and now in disbelief; often, wrathful, he used rude language." Another of Liebling's famous quotes is "People everywhere confuse what they read in the newspapers with news."

Liebling also covered the prizefighters who inhabited the old Madison Square Garden on 50th Street. Liebling, who had been an amateur boxer, was always happy to point out his lack of success in the ring. He compared himself unfavorably with the young Ernest Hemingway, who, Liebling allowed, was both a better pugilist and a better writer.

In the latter part of the 1940s Liebling moved to Chicago. His book *Chicago: The Second City* aroused ire on both sides of the Appalachians and gave Chicago its permanent nickname. His boxing articles were collected in 1956 to make the book *The Sweet Science*. In 1953 Liebling profiled James A. Macdonald, better known as Lord Stingo, Broadway habitué and racing columnist for the *New York Enquirer*. Liebling's profile was published as a book under the title *The Honest Rainmaker*. He also had a collection of essays entitled *Between Meals*, which was an autobiography of his early life. The title alluded to Liebling's long attraction to things gastronomical. He once wrote, "I used to be shy about ordering a steak after I had eaten a steak sandwich but I got used to it."

Eating was one of Liebling's prime activities. James Thurber wrote, "Liebling is the only fast-writing fat man I know." Liebling himself celebrated the quickness at which he wrote. He said, "I can write better than anybody who can write faster, and I can write faster than anybody who can write better."

Liebling continued with *The New Yorker* until his death.

LIGHTNIN' PARADE. *Lightnin'* was a play by Frank Bacon (also its star) and Winthrop Ames that opened at the GAIETY THEATER on August 26, 1918. John Golden was the producer of what was to become at that time the longest-running play in Broadway history. Its run of 1,291 performances was not surpassed until *Abie's Irish Rose* ran 2,327 performances in the early 1930s.

When *Lightnin'* closed, the event was marked by a huge celebration at the Gaiety Theater. The idea for the ceremony and subsequent parade came from songwriter Silvio Hein. He suggested to John Golden that a small celebration might make the papers and help box office receipts in Chicago, the show's next stop. Golden devised a plan whereby a demonstration could be arranged. He called ACTORS' EQUITY to "inform" them that the Lambs Club was planning a small reception at the Gaiety. Naturally, the actors' union asked to be invited, and Golden opined that it might be all right with the Lambs. Next the producer contacted the Lambs Club president. He was told of Equity's plans to hold a small gathering in tribute to the show and its star. The Lambs politely asked if they might attend the festivities. Soon other groups were signing up to attend the ceremonies. Golden went to Grover Whalen, then police commissioner, and inquired whether Whalen would speak to New York Mayor John F. Hylan about a parade. Hylan was more than happy to oblige; in fact, he would lead the entourage. As an added bonus he would throw in the New York Police Band to augment the festivities.

Friends and admirers of star and co-author Frank Bacon attended the reception at the theater. Bacon and his wife were seated onstage with the cast as playwright Augustus Thomas presided over the ceremonies. They were joined on the stage by Commissioner Whalen, Secretary of Labor James J. Davis, and later by Mayor Hylan. DeWolf Hopper, one of the greatest actors of his generation, spoke of the effect of *Lightnin'* on the morale of the theater community and specifically on the contributions of Frank Bacon to the survival of the fledgling Actors' Equity. Thomas read a speech appropriately titled "Lightnin'," written by Bliss Carman. Letters in tribute to Bacon written by Postmaster General Will Hays and Mayor Hylan were read aloud to the cheering audience. Secretary Davis read a letter from President Harding and presented Bacon, actor-producer Winchell Smith, and Golden with gold-buckled championship belts in tribute to "the champion long-distance actor, the champion writer of American successes, and the champion producer of wholesome, American plays."

After the presentation by Secretary Davis, the audience stormed the stage. Included were stars of past and present Broadway shows. They brought Bacon, Smith, Golden, and the assembled celebrities outside to Broadway and 46th Street, where thousands of well-wishers jammed Longacre Square. The show was due to open in Chicago, and the troupe was packed and ready to go to their train. As they and their fans made their way down Broadway, additional celebrities and plain citizens joined the impromptu celebration. The Police Band struck up a march, as did another band

led by composer and conductor VICTOR HERBERT. John Golden later wrote, "The sidewalks from Broadway to Eighth Avenue were impassable. Longacre Square presented the appearance of a riot."

Although the parade was unannounced, passersby became curious at the sight of police stationed on the sides of the parade route. The growing crowds were barely controlled by mounted police. Thomas observed to Bacon that although Bacon had "slipped into Broadway in gumshoes three years before, he was going out with a brass band—three or four, in fact." More than 10,000 people joined the happy mob, stopping traffic as they made their way to Pennsylvania Station. Police estimated that more than 100,000 more lined the pavement, and countless thousands watched from windows along the route. On reaching the station, the cast found the gates and cars plastered with signs wishing the company good fortune. The band began "Auld Lang Syne," and as the company entered the train, they heard the huge station echoing with thousands of voices singing the refrain.

This was certainly the greatest moment in Frank Bacon's life. It was made all the more poignant when the actor died in Chicago during the run of *Lightnin'*. He had played the part of Bill more than 2,000 times. Broadway would not see another such outpouring of emotion until the Valentino funeral.

LINDY'S. 1626 Broadway, at the northwest corner of Broadway and 51st Street.

Lindy's was the best known and greatest of the Broadway delicatessens. Leo Lindemann and his wife Clara met when Lindy was a busboy in Clara's father's restaurant, the Palace Cafe, at 47th Street and Broadway. They opened Lindy's on August 20, 1921. "Broadway's lighting was all gold and silvery then," Leo recalled. "But mostly silvery—more like a Great White Way."

The deli was a minor success, no better than a host of other Jewish delis in the neighborhood, but Lindy's was situated in an advantageous location. Directly across Broadway was the CAPITOL THEATER, and also across the street and down the block was the BRILL BUILDING. On the same side was the WINTER GARDEN THEATRE, home of the SHUBERT BROTHERS' productions, including a series of shows starring AL JOLSON. Jolson, a regular patron of Lindy's, suggested that Lindy put seats in the deli and turn it into a restaurant. Lindy took Jolson's advice, and soon it was the gathering place of the stars of Broadway and vaudeville.

The deli was best-known for its cheesecake, apple pancakes, and enormous combination sandwiches. Another draw were the wisecracking waiters who sometimes treated the customers rudely—and the customers loved it. Lindy was an easy mark and often ran tabs for performers who were temporarily out of luck. The restaurateur, who used to listen patiently to his clients' sad stories, was dubbed "the Magnificent Ear." Lindy gave special treatment to celebrities who brought in crowds. Lyricist Irving Caesar made up a rhyme about Lindy's while strolling down Broadway with GEORGE GERSHWIN:

> We take our tea at Lindy's
> We find much pleasure in this
> As we look through the windows
> To watching people pass
> With Lindy we're a trio
> Just Georgie, me and Leo
> He never takes what we owe
> He wants us for the class!

Lindy sometimes went to extremes to keep his steady customers happy. One day three comics—Jack Benny, Eddie Cantor, and Jesse Block—and their wives discussed where to have dinner. They had dined as usual at Lindy's all week, and Benny said he wanted to go to the nearby Ruby Foo's (not the same Ruby Foo's now occupying 49th and Broadway) for Chinese food. Eddie Cantor insisted on having his usual cornflakes and milk for dinner. After a coin toss the party went to Lindy's. Benny told Lindy about the argument, and when Cantor was brought his cornflakes, the rest were served Chinese food by a battalion of waiters from Foo's.

Lindy wasn't so proud of all his patrons. Moe "the Gimp" Snyder, a small time hood, demanded that Lindy serve only female lobsters. Snyder, married to Ruth Etting, was arrested for shooting his wife's piano player. The regulars at Lindy's sent their regards to the incarcerated Gimp, who urged them to hold a rally in his defense at Madison Square Garden. Lindy regular Chuck Green, a jewelry salesman whom DAMON RUNYON called the Doorway Tiffany, wisecracked, "The Gimp must think he's Sacco and Vanzetti." Another infamous patron of Lindy's was GANGSTER Arnold Rothstein. Clara Lindemann didn't like Rothstein and told him so. Lindy instructed his cashier to stop taking messages for Rothstein. The cashier was understandably afraid of Rothstein and took one last message—that the gangster was wanted at the Park Central Hotel. Later Rothstein was found murdered behind the hotel, and Damon Runyon helped take the heat off Lindy's by saying that the same might have happened to a man who left a church.

Runyon was one of Lindy's champions. He put the restaurant in his stories, thinly disguised as Mindy's. Runyon began one of his most famous stories, *Little Miss Marker*, with the line, "One evening, along toward seven o'clock, many citizens are standing out on Broadway in front of Mindy's restaurant." His story *Butch Minds the Baby* begins, "One evening along about seven o'clock, I am sitting in Mindy's restaurant putting on some gefilte fish." Lindy returned the favor by putting Runyon's latest books in the Broadway window of his restaurant. Runyon's stories were read throughout the country and were made into Hollywood movies, thereby spreading Lindy's fame.

Another reason for Lindy's early success was the EUGENE O'NEILL play *Strange Interlude* (1/30/28; 426 performances). The play was more than twice as long as usual plays and included a dinner break. Patrons of the JOHN GOLDEN THEATER on West 58th Street found Lindy's to be a convenient restaurant. When the same show was banned in Boston and opened in the suburbs, the audience patronized a nearby restaurant owned by a struggling restaurateur named Howard Johnson.

Lindy's best patrons had their own special tables. Broadway and radio's most famous comedians had their tables, as did mobsters. Songwriters sat in their own area, and political figures like Bernard Baruch, J. Edgar Hoover, and Clyde Tolson sat in theirs. Singer Dolly Dawn, who as a teenager appeared with George Hall's orchestra at the Taft Hotel, remembered some of the Lindy's regulars and where they sat:

> When you came in to the left there was a bar where all the song pluggers would stand, their foot upon the rail and one elbow crooked, and they'd be watching for what celebrities would come in. They'd pounce on them and go right into their pitch. Whether it was working hours or not they were always on.
>
> To the right you had all the newspapermen—Walter Winchell, Damon Runyon, Jack O'Brian and Ben Gross. You would see a stream of celebrities coming from one side of the room to greet the newsmen. Everybody was table-hopping. It was back and forth and in and out and kissing and hugging.
>
> In another part of the restaurant would be all the comics. The big stars would be seated wherever they wanted to be seated. And in the middle of it all Mr. and Mrs. Lindy were greeting everybody. If you ordered a piece of cheesecake—which was supposed to be the best in the world—Mr. Lindy would come over and look down over your shoulder and say, "Do you know that cheesecake killed more Jews than Hitler?" And then he would laugh and say, "Go on, eat it, it won't hurtcha."
>
> The waiters would come and sit down with you. There was a waiter there named Jacobs. He'd sit down and say, "Dolly! How are you? What can I get for you?" And he'd say, "Did I have a day today! I had a bad day in the market!—I couldn't get a chicken!" He would do all the gags that he heard from the comics. The waiters were hilarious. They were so cute and so lovable and wonderful.
>
> If you wanted to avoid all the turmoil and all the commotion and all the people coming and going and have dinner quietly and get out quick you went to the "old

[original] Lindy's." You know, you say you never look back, but you wish sometimes those days would come back again. They were so precious.

Lindy had a disagreement with his partner and opened a second Lindy's across the street in 1930. The new Lindy's was enlarged in 1939. By that time the restaurant was earning $20,000 a week. Soon the "little" or "original" Lindy's patrons left to join the Lindemanns. Both restaurants prospered until July 27, 1957, when the original Lindy's closed its doors. When the second Lindy's closed in 1969, some time after Lindemann's death, fellow restaurateur Toots Shor commented, "It's a shame to see a place like this turned into a whatsiz."

The current chain of restaurants using the Lindy's name has no relation to the original restaurants.

THE LITTLE THEATRE.

238 W. 44th Street. Architects: H. C. Ingalls and F. B. Hoffman Jr. Opening: March 12, 1912; *The Pigeon.*

Producer-director Winthrop Ames specialized in the mounting of small, intimate plays in the first decades of the twentieth century. He had trouble placing these small shows in the average Broadway house, which contained about 800 seats, so Ames built his own theater with only 299 seats. (Ames was also involved in the construction of the BOOTH THEATRE, which he built with the SHUBERT BROTHERS.) Ames wanted to give the marginally commercial plays he presented a chance, because there was no off-Broadway alternative at the time. As he himself put it, he wished to produce "the clever, the unusual drama that has a chance of becoming a library classic." Ames had his architects design a neo-Federal building with such homey amenities as a working fireplace in the lobby. The sparsely adorned auditorium contained no boxes or balcony, just a gently sloping orchestra section. BROOKS ATKINSON called it "a gem of a theater." Above the theater proper, Ames had his offices.

The first production at the theater was John Galsworthy's comedy *The Pigeon.* The show was moderately successful with a 64-performance run. Arthur Schnitzler's *The Affairs of Anatol* (10/14/12; 72 performances) opened with John Barrymore (*see* BARRYMORE FAMILY) and Doris Keane in the leads. Barrymore returned to the stage of The Little in George Bernard Shaw's *The Philanderer* (12/30/15; 103 performances).

By this time Ames had realized his plan wasn't working. Even with sellout business Ames could barely support a salary for a star like Barrymore. Just as he couldn't lose much money on the small productions, he also couldn't make much if the plays were hits. He announced his intention of refurbishing the house by increasing the number of seats to 1,000 by adding a balcony and enlarging the auditorium. However, Ames' plan didn't reach fruition, because the cost of remodeling would have amounted to as much as he was losing in ticket sales. So instead, in 1917, he opted to increase the seating to 450 seats with reconfigured seating and the added balcony. The first long run at The Little was Rachel Crothers' comedy *A Little Journey* (12/26/18; 252 performances). The next offering, *Please Get Married* (2/10/19; 160 performances), starred Ernest Truex.

In 1920 the theater was renovated by architect Herbert Krapp who again increased the seating capacity as well as improving the acoustics. *The First* (10/20/20; 725 performances) was written by actor Frank Craven. Broadway was a more freewheeling arena in those days. When Craven told producer John Golden that acting jobs had dried up, Golden suggested that Craven write a play and stated that he would produce it sight unseen. Craven took Golden up on the offer, and 8 weeks later the play was in rehearsal. Craven and Golden's attempt to repeat their success resulted in the play *Spite Corner* (9/25/22; 124 performances). By now Ames' family fortune was being depleted quickly. By 1922 he had lost $504,372 on the operation of The Little, despite its many successes. Luckily the Booth Theatre offset some but not all of the losses.

GUY BOLTON, best known for his collaborations with P. G. Wodehouse and JEROME KERN, had his straight play *Polly Preferred* (1/11/23; 202 performances) produced at the theater. Bolton's straight plays were exactly like his musical libretti, only without any songs. Bolton's next offering at The Little, *Chicken Feed* (924/23; 146 performances), was produced by John Golden, who took the lease on the theater with F. Ray Comstock and L. Lawrence Weber. Burns Mantle described *Chicken Feed* as a play that inspired "as much laughter as a farce without losing too completely its hold upon its theme, which is fundamentally both sound and serious." The play concerned a woman, Nell Bailey, who convinces her fellow wives and girlfriends to strike against their husbands and boyfriends for a share in the men's net income. The play, based on *Lysistrata*, ran to good houses, but it was forced to close because Weber wanted to move his production of *Little Jesse James* to the theater from the LONGACRE THEATER.

John Golden presented another hit play, *Pigs* (9/1/24; 347 performances), at The Little. *Pigs* was written by Anne Morrison and Patterson McNutt and directed by Frank Craven. The play was originally entitled *Johnny Jones, Jr.*, but since GEORGE M. COHAN had already written a musical *Little Johnny Jones*, Golden decided another title was in order. The authors and Golden puzzled over what would make a good title.

The Little Theatre featuring *Tambourines to Glory*, 1963.

Golden observed that because the play was about pigs, they should simply call it *Pigs*. Morrison wanted to call the show *A Pig Tale*. But Golden won because he was set on the subtitle: *A Litter of Laughs*. Word of mouth and Golden's elaborate publicity STUNTS drew attention to the show.

Winchell Smith fell in love with Marc Connelly's comedy *The Wisdom Tooth* and planned to open it at The Little Theatre on February 15, 1926. However, the out-of-town tryouts in Washington, D.C., and Hartford were complete failures. The show, starring Thomas Mitchell, almost closed out of town, but Golden wired Smith: "We have had plenty of successes. Let's have a failure for a change. The Little Theatre needs a tenant. Try it out for a week or two there." Golden congratulated himself later, for *The Wisdom Tooth* proved to be a great success, with a 160-performance run; critics compared Connelly with James M. Barrie. A bigger hit was *Two Girls Wanted* (9/19/26; 324 performances). Rachel Crothers returned to The Little Theatre as playwright and director of *Let Us Be Gay* (2/21/ 29; 132 performances). Another hit was Elmer Rice's *The Left Bank* (10/5/31; 241 performances).

By 1931 Ames had left the theater business. His last activity in the theater was the production of his own play *Mr. Samuel* (11/10/30; 8 performances) with Edward G. Robinson. The play marked the end of Ames' theater career. Ames died on November 3, 1937. Brooks Atkinson called Ames "the pioneer of the modern theater" and "the greatest stage director of the time." At his death his estate was reduced to $77,000.

In February 1935 CBS took over the theater as the CBS Radio Playhouse, but the theater returned to legitimate use on September 28, 1936, with the production of *Pre-Honeymoon*, which moved from the LYCEUM THEATER. Anne Nichols, best known as the author of *Abie's Irish Rose*, wrote the play, and the theater was renamed Anne Nichols' Little Theater. The theater's name was changed back to The Little Theatre with the opening of *Edna His Wife* (12/7/37; 32 performances), a one-woman show starring Cornelia Otis Skinner.

Then the *New York Times* took over operation of the theater in January 1942 and renamed it New York Times Hall. They used the space as a conference hall and permitted an occasional concert. The theater became an ABC television studio in 1959.

The theater returned to legitimate use with the black revue *Tambourines to Glory* (10/26/63; 24 performances) and a reversion to its original name. The show, by Langston Hughes and Jobe Huntley, didn't catch on. Black plays mostly disappeared from the Broadway theater after the heyday of the black musical in the 1910s and '20s. A substantial amount of time passed before an all-black show could succeed on Broadway. When Frank D. Gilroy's PULITZER PRIZE–winning play *The Subject Was Roses* moved from the ROYALE THEATRE on September 7, 1964, The Little was renamed the Winthrop Ames Theater. In March 1965 the theater resumed its original name and again became a television studio, this time for the Westinghouse network. Among the television shows that were broadcast from the stage of the theater were the *Merv Griffin Show* and the *David Frost Show*. Griffin's show made the theater famous, because at the beginning of every show announcer Arthur Treacher said it was coming from "The Little Theatre off Broadway."

The theater again housed live performances with the opening of *My Sister, My Sister* (4/30/74; 119 performances), by Ray Aranha. Three years later the theater saw the opening of its greatest hit, Albert Innaurato's comedy *Gemini* (5/21/77; 1,788 performances). The long run was abetted by a popular television advertisement. The Little was given special status by ACTORS' EQUITY and other unions to permit plays to run profitably in its small auditorium.

In 1981 Adcadesign redesigned the theater for its new owners, The Little Theatre Group. The next hit was Harvey Fierstein's three one-act plays, *Torch Song Trilogy* (6/10/83; 1,222 performances). Fierstein's popular play dealt with gay themes in a sometimes frank way. In July 1983, shortly after the opening of *Torch Song Trilogy*, the name of The Little was changed again. It was renamed the Helen Hayes Theater as a tribute to the "First Lady of the American theater" (*see* HELEN HAYES). The previous HELEN HAYES THEATER (1) had been demolished after a particularly bitter fight to save it and the MOROSCO THEATRE. Those citizens who took part in the battle to save the theaters (*see* BATTLE TO SAVE THE HELEN HAYES, MOROSCO, AND BIJOU THEATERS) were not appeased by the renaming of The Little Theatre.

Martin Markinson and Donald Tick bought the theater from Westinghouse for $800,000 in 1979. They in turn decided to sell it at auction on March 24, 1988. The owners said there would be a $5 million minimum value put on the theater. Rocco Landesman, president of the Jujamcyn Theater chain, said he was thinking of purchasing the theater. Apparently the owners forbade the Shuberts or Nederlanders from buying the house. However, the auction was a failure, and the theater was not sold.

The renaming of The Little Theatre didn't change its track record. The first show to win any recognition after the name change was *Romance/Romance* (5/1/88; 297 performances). Comprised of two one-act musicals, the Barry Harman and Keith Herrmann show is best remembered today as having starred Scott Bakula before his television career took off.

Craig Lucas' play *Prelude to a Kiss* (5/1/90; 440 performances) received good reviews, especially for the cast, which featured Timothy Hutton, Mary-Louise Parker, and Barnard Hughes.

Lynn Redgrave appeared in a one-woman tribute to her father, Michael Redgrave, titled *Shakespeare for My Father* (4/26/93; 266 performances). The theater's next show premiered almost a year later. *Sally Marr . . . and Her Escorts* (5/5/94; 50 performances) starred Joan Rivers as Lenny Bruce's mother. But despite a good performance, the unfocused script and direction kept audiences at bay.

The Helen Hayes had its first hit in a long time with the one-man stand-up comedy act *Defending the Caveman* (3/26/95). Audiences, especially those from out of town, were convulsed at the admittedly chauvinistic comedy of writer-performer Rob Becker. The show played 674 performances on Broadway and enjoyed a long national tour despite being largely ignored by veteran theatergoers.

Alfred Uhry's *The Last Night of Ballyhoo* (2/27/97; 556 performances) was next at the Helen Hayes. It proved to be Uhry's biggest Broadway success. The much-admired production featured Paul Rudd and Dana Ivey.

A series of short-lived bookings followed until the opening of Claudia Shear's examination of fame, *Dirty Blonde* (5/1/2000; 352 performances). Shear played two characters, including an elderly Mae West. She was ably supported by Kevin Chamberlin and Bob Stillman, who played a variety of offbeat characters. The evening was adroitly directed by James Lapine.

ANDREW LLOYD WEBBER had yet another Broadway flop with his and Alan Ayckbourn's musical *By Jeeves* (10/28/2001; 73 performances). The show had originally been performed as just *Jeeves* in London decades earlier. It was revived by the Goodspeed Opera House and then enjoyed an additional run at the Pittsburgh Public Theatre. But audiences found the evening too twee and a little self-satisfied with its humor.

The Helen Hayes found Claudia Shear back on stage in the feminist comedy, *The Smell of the Kill* (3/26/2002). Three women find their husbands locked in a walk-in freezer. Should they let them out or let them freeze to death? Audiences gave it the cold shoulder, and it closed after 40 performances.

On November 17, 1987, the New York City Landmarks Preservation Commission gave the interior and exterior of the building landmark status. The commission stated that the theater was "an elegant neo-federal style" exterior with an "unusual" interior "intended to suggest intimate drama."

LOESSER, FRANK. Among the most versatile of all the Broadway composers; b. New York, New York, June 29, 1910; d. New York, New York, July 26, 1969.

Loesser wrote lyrics to his own tunes, and all of his Broadway shows but one were hits. (Another, *Pleasures and Palaces*, closed out of town.) His output on Broadway was small compared to that of his contemporaries, but each of his shows was a unique contribution to the art of the musical theater.

Loesser was born in New York and educated at Townsend Harris Hall. He dropped out of City College. While holding various odd jobs, Loesser began writing song parodies to popular tunes of the day. RKO Radio Pictures hired Loesser as a staff lyricist after he published his first song, "In Love with a Memory of You," with music by William Schuman. None of Loesser's work at RKO reached the screen, and he returned to New York. He later worked at Universal Pictures. As a contract writer for Paramount Pictures, he wrote the lyrics to hundreds of songs, a high percentage of which became standards. When writing for the movies, Loesser was primarily a lyricist. He collaborated with such greats as BURTON LANE, JULE STYNE, Hoagy Carmichael, Jimmy McHugh, Arthur Schwartz (*see* DIETZ AND SCHWARTZ), and Victor Schertzinger.

His film titles include *College Swing*, *Destry Rides Again*, *Thank Your Lucky Stars*, *The Perils of Pauline*, *Let's Dance*, *Happy-Go-Lucky*, *Seven Days Leave*, and *Hans Christian Andersen*.

Frank and Lynn Loesser at rehearsals of *The Most Happy Fella*.

Among his movie songs are "The Moon of Manakoora," "Moments Like This," "Says My Heart," "Small Fry," "Heart and Soul," "Two Sleepy People," "The Lady's in Love with You," "Hey, Good Lookin'," "See What the Boys in the Back Room Will Have," "I Hear Music," "Dolores," "I Said No," "I Don't Want to Walk without You," "Sand in My Shoes," and "Kiss the Boys Goodbye." Other Loesser greats are "Can't Get Out of This Mood," "What Do You Do in the Infantry?" "Murder, He Says," "Leave Us Face It We're in Love," "Spring Will Be a Little Late This Year," "Rumble, Rumble, Rumble," "Poppa, Don't Preach to Me," "I Wish I Didn't Love You So," "Tallahassee," "What Are You Doing New Year's Eve?" "That Feathery Feeling," "On a Slow Boat to China," "Baby, It's Cold Outside" (Academy Award, 1949), "No Two People," "Thumbelina," "Inchworm," "Anywhere I Wander," and "A Woman in Love."

Loesser's first Broadway assignment was a revue, *The Illustrator's Show* (1/22/36; 5 performances). He then spent the next 12 years toiling in Hollywood. His next Broadway show was a musicalization of Brandon Thomas' farce *Charley's Aunt*, entitled *Where's Charley?* (10/11/48; 792 performances), for which he contributed both music and lyrics. It starred Ray Bolger and Allyn Ann McLerie. Many hits emerged from the show, including "Once in Love with Amy," "The New Ashmolean Marching Society and Student Conservatory Band," "My Darling, My Darling," and "Make a Miracle." GEORGE ABBOTT, known for giving many Broadway neophytes their first break, directed and wrote the libretto to Loesser's score. George Balanchine contributed the dances.

Two years later audiences at the 46th Street Theatre (*see* RICHARD RODGERS THEATER) were treated to the definitive Broadway depiction of Times Square when

Left to right: Rudy Vallee (in back), Charles Nelson Reilly, Ruth Kobart, Paul Reed, Robert Morse, and Sammy Smith in the "Brotherhood of Man" number from *How to Succeed in Business without Really Trying*, 1961.

the curtain went up on *Guys and Dolls* (11/24/50; 1,200 performances). Abe Burrows wrote the libretto, with Jo Swerling, the original librettist, also credited; George S. Kaufman (*see* KAUFMAN AND HART) directed. The show starred Robert Alda, Vivian Blaine, Sam Levene, Isabel Bigley, Pat Rooney, and Stubby Kaye. It was full of great Loesser tunes, including "If I Were a Bell," "Sit Down You're Rockin' the Boat," "I've Never Been in Love Before," "My Time of Day," "A Bushel and a Peck," "I'll Know," and the hilarious "Adelaide's Lament." *Guys and Dolls*, based on the stories of DAMON RUNYON, was one of the most popular musicals in Broadway history.

With musicals based on an English farce and the New York underworld behind him, Loesser next tackled the Italian winemaking community of Napa, California, with *The Most Happy Fella* (5/3/56; 676 performances). The show was based on Sidney Howard's drama, *They Knew What They Wanted*. It tells the story of an old grape grower who uses the picture of his handsome ranch hand to send for a mail-order bride. When the woman shows up, she is so repulsed by the old man that she flees to the ranch hand's bed. The grower, Tony, suffers injuries in a car accident, and while nursing him back to health, the bride learns to love him. The Loesser score ably mastered the difficult material with a wealth of melody. The show was almost entirely sung; in fact, some thought it closer to opera than to traditional musical comedy. Loesser himself wrote the book so that the songs and story would be truly integrated. Despite the operatic overtones of the score, several of the numbers achieved success on the hit parade. The most popular were "Standing on the Corner," "Joey, Joey, Joey," and "Big D." Other hits were "Warm All Over" and "My Heart Is So Full of You." The score was considered so exceptional that Columbia Records issued the entire show on a 3-record set, a first for a Broadway musical. *The Most Happy Fella* featured opera star Robert Weede, Susan Johnson, Jo Sullivan (later Mrs. Loesser), and Art Lund.

Loesser's next challenge was the quiet, bucolic *Greenwillow* (3/8/60; 95 performances), based on a novel by B. J. Chute. Anthony Perkins made his musical comedy debut in a cast that also included Cecil Kellaway and Pert Kelton. The one big hit from the show was "Never Will I Marry," made popular through a recording by Barbra Streisand.

Loesser's last Broadway show won him the PULITZER PRIZE. *How to Succeed in Business without Really Trying* (10/14/61; 1,417 performances) was a broad satire of the American workplace. Robert Morse attained stardom through his portrayal of a ruthless worker on his way to the top. Rudy Vallee, Bonnie Scott, Virginia Martin, Charles Nelson Reilly, and Claudette Sutherland all turned in first-rate performances under Abe Burrows' direction. Among the songs, "I Believe in You" achieved standard status, although people unfamiliar with the show never realized the love song was sung by the hero to his own reflection. Loesser's next attempt at Broadway, *Pleasures and Palaces*, closed out of town in 1965.

Loesser affected Broadway in other ways besides his scores. Through his publishing company, Frank Music, he encouraged the careers of many Broadway newcomers. Loesser convinced George Abbott to hire Jerry Ross and Richard Adler to write the score of *The Pajama Game*. He also gave Meredith Willson the encouragement needed to start him on what eventually became *The Music Man*. Loesser later co-produced the show along with Kermit Bloomgarden. Loesser also encouraged composer Moose Charlap and lyricist Norman Gimbel, among others.

LOEW'S STATE THEATER. 1540 Broadway at W. 45th Street. Architect: Thomas Lamb.

The Loew's Corporation, distributors of MGM films, built their offices and flagship theater across Times Square from the Paramount Corporation's headquarters. Thomas Lamb, favorite architect of the Loew's chain, designed the theater in 1922. Just two years later, when Loew's Corporation purchased the Goldwyn Pictures theaters, the deal included the CAPITOL THEATER at Broadway and 50th Street, and Loew's State lost its flagship status. Still, "1540" as the theater was called by insiders, remained a top showcase as well as the Loew's corporate offices. The north wall of the theater, which towered over its neighboring 5-story buildings, was usually used as a 100-foot-tall advertising sign for shows at the theater. Among the hits to play the theater were *ANNIE GET YOUR GUN*, *The Barkeleys of Broadway*, *Easter Parade*, *Thunder Bay*, and *Ben-Hur*.

In 1959 the theater was renovated to a relentlessly modern style. The renovation of the facade was described by Loew's publicity department:

"Slab" type marquee with double soffit has been erected on the "New" Loew's State Theatre in New York. Round panels in soffit are down lights. Oblong panels are flashing fluorescent lights. 12″ deep show cases make possible dimensional displays on current attractions. Side box office has one ticket-selling position with space for a second. Black-and-white herringbone sidewalk patterns serve as directional reminder.

Specially-designed top-of-marquee displays will be created for each new attraction. Being designed at this moment is an animated display for MGM's "Ben-Hur" which will have its world premiere at LOEW'S STATE in late 1959.

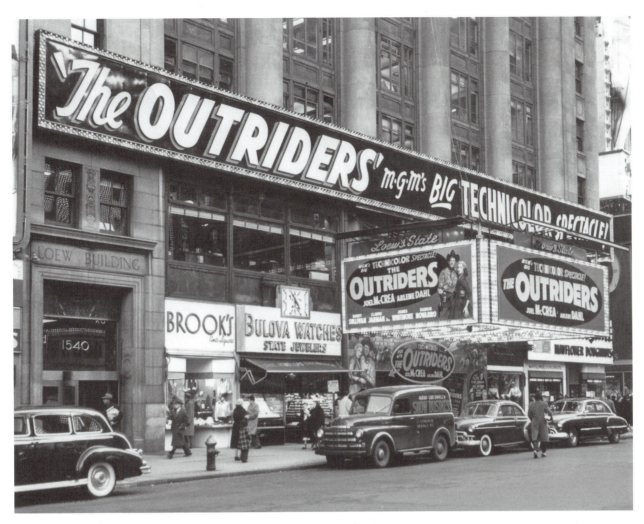

The Loew's State Theater, 1950.

Marquee features built-in loudspeakers and vents through which warm air is forced down during the winter and cool air in the summer.

The projection booth was moved from the rear of the balcony to the front of the balcony for the showing of 70 mm or CinemaScope pictures. Included in the booth were three Todd-AO-Phillips "All Purpose" projectors, Ampex stereo sound installation, tape recorder, record pick-up, toilet facilities, rewind room, and rectifier room. On March 30, 1959, the newly refurbished theater opened with an engagement of *Some Like It Hot* with Marilyn Monroe, Tony Curtis, and Jack Lemmon. In 1968 the auditorium was twinned, following the rage of the day.

The final shows at Loew's State occurred on February 19, 1987, and the next day demolition of the 16-story building was begun. On its site a 44-story building was erected with 850,000 square feet of office space, a shopping mall, and four movie theaters.

LOEWE, FREDERICK. *See* **Lerner and loewe.**

LOGAN, JOSHUA. One of Broadway's preeminent directors, who also sometimes assumed the role of playwright; b. Joshua Lockwood Logan III, Texarkana, Texas, October 5, 1908; d. New York, New York, July 12, 1988.

Legendary director Josh Logan's main strengths lay in his vibrant staging of musical comedies, including some of the greatest in the genre. Logan was partially responsible for the success of such landmark musicals as *South Pacific* and ANNIE GET YOUR GUN. His successes on Broadway led to an equally successful career as a film director. He worked with such songwriters as Richard Rodgers (teamed with both Lorenz Hart [*see* RODGERS AND HART] and Oscar Hammerstein II [*see* RODGERS AND HAMMERSTEIN]), IRVING BERLIN, and HAROLD ROME.

Josh Logan (third from left), directing *Wish You Were Here*, 1952.

Logan's interest in the theater was solidified when he enrolled at Princeton University in 1927. He chose Princeton because of its famous Triangle Club, a touring drama troupe. He enjoyed acting and writing for the Triangle shows for the next 3 years. During his stay there Logan and Bretaigne Windust (also a future Broadway director) founded the University Players, a summer stock company situated on Cape Cod. Among its members were fellow Princetonites Jimmy Stewart, Henry Fonda, and Margaret Sullavan. In 1930 he left Princeton without graduating and began studying with Stanislavsky and the Moscow Art Theatre. Upon his return from Moscow he again joined the University players, then playing a season of repertory in Baltimore. Logan directed *Lysistrata* and *Mary Rose* for the company.

In 1932 the company decided to tackle Broadway and premiered Frank McGrath's play *Carry Nation* at the BILTMORE THEATER. The play, in which Logan made his Broadway acting debut, lasted only 30 performances and led to the breakup of the University Players.

Logan continued his Broadway career as the sixth assistant stage manager on Howard Lindsay's play *She*

Loves Me Not (11/20/33; 360 performances) at the 46th Street Theatre (*see* RICHARD RODGERS THEATER). After a series of jobs that moved him up the professional ladder, he made his Broadway directorial debut (also co-producing) with the play *To See Ourselves* (4/30/ 35; 23 performances) at the ETHEL BARRYMORE THEATRE. The production was a flop. His next play, *Hell Freezes Over* (12/28/35; 25 performances) was also a failure, as was his next, *It's You I Want* (2/5/35; 15 performances), and Logan left Broadway for Hollywood. His brief sojourn there as a dialogue director was interrupted by an acting job in a revival of *What Price Glory*. Then it was back to Hollywood.

But he soon returned to Broadway and a very prolific period fueled by his manic personality. He achieved much notice for his direction of Paul Osborn's *On Borrowed Time* (2/3/38; 321 performances) at the LONGACRE THEATER. Logan's first musical assignment was for the Rodgers and Hart show *I Married an Angel* (5/11/38; 338 performances) during which he began a long working relationship with Richard Rodgers. He went on to direct many of Broadway's top musicals, including KURT WEILL and Maxwell Anderson's *Knickerbocker Holiday* (10/19/38; 168 performances); Arthur Schwartz (*see* DIETZ AND SCHWARTZ) and Dorothy Fields' (*see* FIELDS FAMILY) *Stars in Your Eyes* (2/9/39; 127 performances), starring ETHEL MERMAN; *Two for the Show* (2/8/40; 124 performances); and Rodgers and Hart's *Higher and Higher* (4/4/40; 84 performances), for which he was also co-librettist.

Logan experienced his first nervous breakdown in 1940. Initially, he was ashamed of his health problem, although he later admitted, "Without my illness . . . I would have missed the sharpest, rarest and, yes, the sweetest moments of my existence."

After a hiatus from his career, for service as a public relations and intelligence officer in World War II, he returned to the theater and another manic period. He directed Ray Bolger in Rodgers and Hart's *By Jupiter* (6/3/42; 427 performances), and Irving Berlin's all-soldier revue *This Is the Army* (7/4/42; 113 performances).

Producers Rodgers and Hammerstein hired Logan to direct Ethel Merman in Irving Berlin and Herbert and Dorothy Fields' musical *Annie Get Your Gun* (5/16/46; 1,147 performances). He co-authored, with Thomas Heggen, and directed his first hit play, *Mister Roberts* (2/18/48; 1,157 performances), in which he was reunited with Henry Fonda.

Josh Logan, Richard Rodgers and Oscar Hammerstein II in a stunt evening celebrating the fifth anniversary of *South Pacific*.

South Pacific (4/7/49; 1,925 performances), for which he was also co-librettist, choreographer, and co-producer, was a bittersweet experience. While the play was a smash hit, because of Rodgers and Hammerstein's fame, he wasn't given the credit he was due. The *New York Times* neglected to mention him as co-author in their review, and the PULITZER PRIZE committee neglected to include him with his collaborators when awarding the musical their award. Subsequently both organizations corrected their errors. Logan also had his first fights with the songwriting team, who treated him as a hired hand rather than as an equal. Since they were also producing the show, they felt they had all the power, and Logan had to fight to receive proper credit and proper royalties.

Logan went on to direct many other stage musicals, most of them hits. Among them are *Wish You Were Here* (6/25/52; 598 performances), for which he was also co-librettist and co-producer; *Fanny* (114/54; 888 performances), for which he was also co-librettist and co-producer; *All American* (2/19/62; 80 performances); *Mr. President* (10/20/62; 265 performances); and *Look to the Lilies* (3/29/70; 25 performances).

Logan also worked on many straight plays, although for the most part they weren't as noteworthy as his musical projects. Among the straight plays he directed were *Mornings at Seven* (11/30/39; 44 performances); *Charley's Aunt* (10/17/40; 233 performances); *Happy Birthday* (10/31/46; 564 performances); *John Loves Mary* (2/4/47; 423 performances); *The Wisteria Trees* (3/29/50; 165 performances), which he also adapted and produced; *Picnic* (2/19/53; 477 performances), which he also produced; *Kind Sir* (11/4/53; 165 performances), which he also produced; *Middle of the Night* (2/8/56; 477 performances), which he also produced; *Blue Denim* (2/27/58; 166 performances); *The World of Suzie Wong* (10/14/58; 508 performances); *Tiger Tiger Burning Bright* (12/22/62; 33 performances); and *Ready When You Are C.B.!* (12/7/64; 80 performances).

Logan's movie career included the film version of *Picnic* (1955); *Bus Stop* (1956), with Marilyn Monroe; and *Sayonara* (1957). His film musicals, *South Pacific* (1958), *Camelot* (1967), and *Paint Your Wagon* (1969), were much less successful artistically than his stage musicals.

LONGACRE THEATER. 220 W. 48th Street. Architect: Henry B. Herts. Opening: May 1, 1913; *Are You a Crook?*

Many Broadway producers made their fortunes in industry or business and with their profits turned to the colorful world of the theater. One of these was H. H. Frazee, owner of the Boston Red Sox. Frazee hired

Longacre Theatre featuring the play *Three And One*, 1933.

architect Henry B. Herts to design his Longacre Theater. Herts had recently broken up with his partner, Hugh Tallant (*see* HERTS & TALLANT), and was anxious to prove that he could go it alone. For the Longacre Theater, Herts chose an Italian Renaissance design and employed limestone and terra-cotta as the building materials. Frazee was delighted with Herts' sophisticated design and made plans to produce musicals in the 1,400-seat auditorium.

Surprisingly, Frazee's first offering was a straight play, *Are You a Crook?* Perhaps he should have stuck to his original notion of presenting only musical comedy, because *Are You a Crook?* closed after 12 performances. His next offering was a musical, *Adele* (8/28/13; 196 performances), by Jean Briquet and Adolf Philipp. The show was a hit, with Georgia Caine, William Danforth, Alice Yorke, and Hal Forde in the leads. The production was taken to the Gaiety Theater in London but failed to capture English audiences. It closed there after only 2 weeks.

John Barrymore (*see* BARRYMORE FAMILY) was the next star to command the Longacre's stage in a melodrama entitled *Kick In* (10/15/14; 188 performances). It was followed by another success, *A Pair of Sixes* (3/17/14; 207 performances). *The Great Lover* (11/10/15; 245 performances), starring Leo Ditrichstein, spoofed the world of opera. *Nothing but the Truth* (9/

14/16; 332 performances) was a comedy whose main character bets he can go an entire day without telling a lie; William Collier starred.

Leave It to Jane (8/28/17; 167 performances) was a musical by JEROME KERN, P. G. Wodehouse, and GUY BOLTON, the trio known for their small, intimate musicals with integrated libretti and scores. The show contained Jerome Kern's sprightliest score and included some of his most charming tunes, among them "Sir Galahad," "Cleopatterer," "The Crickets Are Calling," "It's a Great Big Land," and one of the most enchanting and innocent songs written for the American musical theater, "The Siren's Song."

Guy Bolton, in collaboration with George Middleton, was also responsible for the next hit at the Longacre, *Adam and Eva* (9/13/19; 312 performances). The William B. Friedlander musical *Pitter Patter* (9/28/20; 111 performances) starred William Kent, Jack Squire, and John Price Jones. Also in the cast was future Hollywood star James Cagney. *The Champion* (1/3/21; 176 performances) starred Grant Mitchell.

Little Jessie James (8/15/23; 385 performances) was a charming musical with a score by Harry Archer and Harlan Thompson. It introduced the hit song "I Love You." Allen Kearns, Nan Halperin, and Jay Velie were featured along with the young Miriam Hopkins. *Moonlight* (1/30/24; 174 performances), also a small musical, boasted a score by Con Conrad and William B. Friedlander. Conrad and Friedlander had another musical presented at the Longacre, *Mercenary Mary* (4/13/25; 136 performances). George S. Kaufman (*see* KAUFMAN AND HART) had a big success with his play *The Butter and Egg Man* (9/23/25; 241 performances). The show starred Gregory Kelly as an out-of-towner who decides to invest $20,000 in a Broadway show. The comedy, one of Kaufman's best, is notable as the only play he wrote without the aid of a collaborator.

Miriam Hopkins had appeared at the Longacre in the musical *Little Jessie James*. She returned to its stage in a decidedly different kind of show, an adaptation of Theodore Dreiser's *An American Tragedy* (10/11/26; 216 performances). Also featured were Morgan Farley and Katherine Wilson. The play made almost as much of a splash as the novel originally had. It was among 6 shows that District Attorney Jacob H. Banton regarded as morally unacceptable. (The others were *The Captive*, Mae West's *Sex*, *Lulu Belle*, *The Virgin Man*, and *Night Hawk*.) Philip Kearney's drama remained open, despite the government's displeasure.

Roger Pryor appeared as a WALTER WINCHELL type of reporter in *Blessed Event* (2/12/32; 124 performances). The title referred to one of Winchell's favorite SLANG phrases. The Winchellian reporter was portrayed as an unscrupulous wise guy, and audiences at the opening watched the real Winchell's reaction as much as the play. A reviewer stated the next day that Winchell appeared uncomfortable. ALEXANDER WOOLLCOTT, in his column, disagreed:

> Nonsense! Winchell's emotions at *Blessed Event* if any were probably an ingenuous and gratified surprise on finding himself at thirty-five, already recognized as enough of a national institution to be made the subject of a play. If he squirmed and blanched, it was because he, and he alone, knew that the two large and unsmiling men occupying the seats behind his own were Central Office plainclothesmen, assigned by an uneasy Police Commissioner to see that Winchell should come to no bodily harm.

The Depression hurt the Broadway theater, because less money became available for risky investments. The Longacre suffered along with many other theaters. A high point of the 1930s was the series of productions the GROUP THEATER presented at the Longacre. The first was a double bill of Clifford Odets' two one-act plays, *Waiting for Lefty* and *Till the Day I Die* (3/26/35; 168 performances). *Waiting for Lefty* had been given a single performance at the Civic Repertory Theater on January 5, 1935, and it caused an immediate sensation. It was an incendiary play based on an actual strike of New York taxi drivers. In the play the members of the union meet to decide whether to strike. Moderate members of the union want to wait until their leader, Lefty, arrives, but labor racketeers and unscrupulous union leaders urge the meeting to begin. The audience at the Longacre was treated as the union members, and speeches were directed to them. As different members of the union addressed their brethren, the evening became more and more explosive. Elia Kazan, as the most vocal of the pro-strike members, whipped the audience into a frenzy. At the end of the play word comes that Lefty has been killed, and the meeting explodes. The cast, on the stage and in the theater's aisles, takes up the chant, "Strike! Strike! Strike!"

The second play, *Till the Day I Die*, told of a German Communist who is tortured by police. His only recourse is to commit suicide. The cast of the two plays included Elia Kazan, Lee J. Cobb, Robert Lewis, Russell Collins, Alexander Kirkland, Roman Bohnen, and Odets himself. *Lefty* remained a classic of the American theater. After its closing at the Longacre, it toured union halls around the country.

Odets and the Group Theater returned to the Longacre with the show *Paradise Lost* (12/9/35; 73 performances), the story of a mild-mannered businessman and his radical partner. *Paradise Lost* traced what Odets considered the continuing decline of the American middle class.

Another playwright, almost diametrically opposed to Odets in style and substance, also had two plays performed at the Longacre in the 1930s. Paul Osborn's *On Borrowed Time* (2/3/38; 321 performances) told of a grandfather who keeps Death at bay up a tree so that he can enjoy a few more moments with his grandson. JOSHUA LOGAN directed the cast, which included Peter Holden, Dorothy Stickney, and Dudley Digges. Osborn's other production at the Longacre, *Morning's at Seven* (11/30/39; 44 performances), was a gentle comedy of three sisters and their families. A later revival in 1980 was a hit and ran 564 performances at the LYCEUM THEATER.

Three's a Family (5/5/43; 497 performances), by Phoebe and Henry Ephron, was produced by John Golden. The farce had what CRITIC Burns Mantle called a "confused but possible ending." It was the last play presented at the Longacre until 1953. The theater was used for radio and television productions in the interim.

The Dorothy Parker and Arnaud d'Usseau play *The Ladies of the Corridor* (11/21/53; 45 performances) was the first play after the Longacre returned to a legitimate policy. Jean Anouilh's play *Colombe* was adapted by Louis Kronenberger as *Mademoiselle Colombe* (1/6/54; 61 performances) and starred Julie Harris as Colombe, a young innocent who discovers her own strengths in the backstage world of a Paris theater. The play was Anouilh's seventh successive failure on Broadway. But his next play, *The Lark* (11/17/55; 229 performances), changed his luck. Julie Harris starred as Joan of Arc, with Boris Karloff as Cauchon, and Theodore Bikel, Sam Jaffe, Christopher Plummer, and Joseph Wiseman rounded out the cast. Samuel Taylor's *The Pleasure of His Company* (10/22/58; 474 performances) opened with Cornelia Otis Skinner, Cyril Ritchard, George Peppard, Charlie Ruggles, and Walter Abel.

The 1960s began with Eugène Ionesco's anticonformist play *Rhinoceros* (1/9/61; 240 performances), which opened with Zero Mostel (as the man who becomes the title animal), Eli Wallach, Jean Stapleton, Anne Jackson, and Morris Carnovsky. It was the only Broadway production for the Romanian-born playwright. *Rhinoceros* received rave reviews for Mostel's performance. The play was later revived at the Longacre on September 18, 1961, for an additional 16 performances.

A Case of Libel (10/10/63; 242 performances), by Henry Denker, opened with Van Heflin, Larry Gates, M'el Dowd, Sidney Blackmer, and Philip Borneuf in the cast. The play was based on Quentin Reynolds' libel suit against Westbrook Pegler as reported by Louis Nizer in his book *My Life in Court*. Lorraine Hansberry's drama *The Sign in Sidney Brustein's Window* (10/15/64; 101 performances) starred Gabriel Dell, Rita Moreno, and Alice Ghostley. The play later found more appreciative audiences, and it has enjoyed many productions throughout the country. Unfortunately, Hansberry died on January 12, 1965, and never witnessed her play's success.

Robert Anderson's *I Never Sang for My Father* (1/25/68; 124 performances) explored the relationship between an estranged father and his son, two frightened people who feel they should love each other but bury their emotions under the protection of selfishness. *I Never Sang for My Father* starred Teresa Wright, Lillian Gish, Hal Holbrook, and Alan Webb.

Terrence McNally's rollicking comedy set in a homosexual bathhouse, *The Ritz* (1/20/75; 400 performances), starred Jack Weston, Rita Moreno, F. Murray Abraham, Stephen Collins, and Jerry Stiller.

The Fats Waller retrospective *Ain't Misbehavin'* moved from the Manhattan Theater Club to the Longacre on May 9, 1978. It made stars of its cast members Armelia McQueen, Ken Page, Nell Carter, Charlene Woodard, and Andre De Shields. *Ain't Misbehavin'* was the best of all the revues that attempted to examine a composer's career. The credit for its success goes to director Richard Maltby Jr., who gave each of the cast members an individual character and kept the proceedings humming at a rapid clip. *Ain't Misbehavin'* ran 1,604 performances, making it one of the biggest hits of the 1970s.

Deaf actress Phyllis Frelich electrified audiences in the Mark Medoff play *Children of a Lesser God* (3/30/80; 887 performances). John Rubinstein co-starred in the production, which won a TONY AWARD and was the Longacre's last success.

A number of well known authors saw decidedly lesser plays of theirs premiere at the Longacre in the 1980s and '90s. These included Lanford Wilson's *Angel's Fall* (1/22/83; 57 performances); Peter Nichols' *Passion* (5/15/83; 97 performances); George Furth's *Precious Sons* (5/20/86; 93 performances); Frank D. Gilroy's *Any Given Day* (11/16/93; 32 performances); Horton Foote's *Young Man from Atlanta* (3/27/97; 84 performances); David Henry Hwang's *Golden Child* (4/2/98; 69 performances); and John Pielmeier's *Voices in the Dark* (8/12/99; 64 performances).

A revival of Vernal Bagneris' off-Broadway revue, *One Mo' Time* (3/6/2002) closed after only 21 performances.

On December 8, 1987, the New York City Landmarks Preservation Commission designated the interior and exterior of the theater a landmark. The commission called the theater's Neoclassical facade "exceptionally handsome"; it has 5 bays formed by stylized Corinthian pilasters, "adorned with elaborate ornament."

LUNT AND FONTANNE. Husband-and-wife team, considered the greatest acting couple in American history; Alfred Davis Lunt Jr., b. Milwaukee, Wisconsin, August 12, 1892; d. Chicago, Illinois, August 3, 1977; Lynn Fontanne, b. Lynn Woodford, Essex, England, December 6, 1887; d. Genesee Depot, Wisconsin, July 30, 1983.

Alfred Lunt and Lynn Fontanne enjoyed long careers on the Broadway stage, both together and separately, from the first decade of the 20th century until their retirement in 1960. The team was responsible for many of the great hits of the THEATER GUILD, and they certainly accounted for the Guild's long preeminence.

Lunt was born in Milwaukee, Wisconsin, to a family that had deep roots in New England. His early love for the theater launched his stage career before his 20th birthday. The year was 1912, and Lunt was in Boston ostensibly to attend the Emerson School of Oratory. He made it to only one session of one class before passing the Castle Square Theater and inquiring about employment. School was forgotten, and Lunt was hired to play small parts at $5 a week. After a month he worked his way up to the generous salary of $20 a week. Lunt's stage debut was in the play *The Aviator*, which opened on October 7, 1912. Lunt remained at the Castle Square Theater for three years. In 1914 he joined Margaret Anglin's touring company and remained with the company for two years. He then found work in vaudeville, supporting Lily Langtry. Later that same year, 1916, he rejoined the Anglin company.

Lunt moved to New York and made his Broadway debut at the HARRIS THEATRE (1) in *Romance and Arabella* (10/17/17). Two years later he met Lynn Fontanne in a Chicago production of *A Young Man's Fancy*. He returned to New York and had his first great success with the title role in *Clarence*. Booth Tarkington wrote the play expressly for Lunt. *Clarence* (9/20/19) opened at the HUDSON THEATRE. The CRITIC for the *Sun* wrote, "Alfred Lunt gave a most amusing performance of the entomologist, making the physical manifestations of the character broadly grotesque. He seemed at times to adopt the dramatic method of the experienced Bert Williams, even in his gait and his furtive and worried look."

After two years with *Clarence* Lunt opened in another Tarkington play, *The Intimate Strangers* (11/27/21; 97 performances). Alan Dale, writing in the *New York American*, was relieved to find Lunt back on the stage. "A better and more satisfactory leading man could never have been secured. I had been wondering if Mr. Lunt was too good an actor to be in demand, and it was a pleasure to meet him again. Sometimes the actors who have achieved one success vanish curiously."

British-born Lynn Fontanne made her stage debut in J. M. Barrie's *Alice-Sit-by-the-Fire* in 1905. The touring production starred Ellen Terry, Fontanne's idol. The great actor taught the newcomer posture, interpretation, and other skills. Terry gave her pupil a letter of introduction to the successful London producer Arthur Collins, manager of the Theatre Royal, Drury Lane. He cast Fontanne in one of his Christmas pantomimes, *Cinderella*, which began a long tour at the end of 1905. After other touring plays she made her West End debut in *Billy's Bargain* in June 1910.

Laurette Taylor, who had seen Fontanne in the London production of Edward Knoblock's *My Lady's Dress* in 1914, prompted Fontanne's move to America. Taylor convinced Fontanne to come to New York to act in *The Harp of Life* (12/27/16; 24 performances), a play by Taylor's husband, J. Hartley Manners. The play opened at the Globe Theatre (*see* LUNT-FONTANNE THEATER). Fontanne had already appeared on Broadway in a short-lived production of *Mr. Preedy and the Countess* at the 39th Street Theatre on November 7, 1910. The critics noticed her performance in *The Harp of Life*. The reviewer for the *New York Times* wrote, "In Lynn Fontanne, an appallingly gowned young woman who wore plum colored shoes during all the evening, the audience found a character to regard with the warmest applause. In all that she said and did she was one of the few recognizable humans on the stage." A reviewer for the *Sun* exclaimed, "One of the delights of the performance is the exquisite acting of a newcomer, Lynn Fontanne, who established a reputation for uncommon ability overnight. Miss Fontanne comes from England, and it is earnestly hoped that she never returns." The uncredited reviewer's wishes were answered, for she seldom returned to England's stages.

The biggest hit of Fontanne's early career came in Marc Connelly and George S. Kaufman's (*see* KAUFMAN AND HART) *Dulcy* (8/13/21; 246 performances) that opened at the Frazee Theater (*see* ANCO THEATER). *Dulcy* was a modern Mrs. Malaprop. Fontanne received glowing notices in what many critics felt was her first appearance out of the shadow of Laurette Taylor.

Lunt and Fontanne kept in touch following their first meeting in Chicago. They became more and more involved and finally decided to get married at New York's City Hall on May 26, 1922. The marriage took place with no fanfare. Two strangers were asked to be witnesses and were called upon to front the couple a few dollars for the license fee. This humble ceremony was the beginning of a long and successful collaboration on stage and in marriage.

After their marriage the couple appeared separately in many productions. Notable was Lunt's first dramatic appearance in Sutton Vane's *Outward Bound* (1/7/24; 144 performances) at the RITZ THEATRE (1). John Corbin, writing in the *New York Times*, was pleased to discover the new facet to Lunt's talents. "Mr. Lunt," he wrote, "finds large scope for his acting powers as a comedian and finally does a bit of emotional acting of the first order."

The couple's first appearance together was in *Sweet Nell of Old Drury*, a production mounted at the 48th Street Theatre (5/16/23; 51 performances). There followed one of their greatest triumphs and the beginning of their long association with the Theater Guild. Ferenc Molnár's play *The Guardsman* was a failure when first produced on Broadway in 1913. But the Guild's offer was too good to refuse, and the acting team opened in a revival of *The Guardsman* (10/13/24; 274 performances) at the Garrick Theater. The play was a huge success, with Dudley Digges and Helen Westley completing the cast. The team played two jealous actors. Lunt's character disguises himself as a guardsman and makes love to his unknowing wife. She claims to have known it was he all along. E. W. Osborn, writing in the *New York Evening World*, was among the first to recognize the couple's special powers when sharing the stage:

> Alfred Lunt as the jealous actor and Lynn Fontanne as the wife who is too keen for his masquerading self are a comedy pair who need fear no compare. Their swift transition from the spats and dissension of an afternoon in their dear little home to the flirtatious byplay of the evening at the opera is wonderfully smooth and complete, and they rise most happily to the moment of confounding revelations in the third act.

A revival of George Bernard Shaw's *Arms and the Man* (9/14/25; 181 performances) presented by the Theater Guild at the Guild Theater (*see* VIRGINIA THEATER) was the Lunts' next production. They gave many other performances in Guild productions, both as a team and separately, though sometimes the productions and plays were not nearly up to the level of the team's performances.

Among the most highly acclaimed shows of their careers were EUGENE O'NEILL's nine-act marathon *Strange Interlude* (1/30/28; 426 performances) with Lynn Fontanne alone; Maxwell Anderson's *Elizabeth the Queen* (11/3/30; 145 performances); Robert E. Sherwood's *Reunion in Vienna* (11/16/31; 280 performances); Noel Coward's sophisticated comedy *Design for Living* (1/24/33; 135 performances in a limited engagement); *Idiot's Delight* (3/24/36; 299 performances), the PULITZER PRIZE winner by Robert E. Sherwood; Jean Giraudoux and S. N. Behrman's *Amphitryon 38* (2/15/37; 152 performances); Robert E. Sherwood's *There Shall Be No Night* (9/29/40; 115 performances) at the Alvin Theater (*see* NEIL SIMON THEATER); S. N. Behrman's comedy *The Pirate* (11/25/42; 176 performances); and *The Great Sebastians*

(1/4/56; 174 performances) by Howard Lindsay and Russel Crouse.

Friedrich Dürrenmatt's *The Visit* (5/5/58; 189 performances) was the duo's final Broadway assignment that opened as the inaugural production in the newly renamed Lunt-Fontanne Theater. BROOKS ATKINSON, writing in the *New York Times*, heralded the two performers. "After squandering their time on polite trivialities for a number of years, Alfred Lunt and Lynn Fontanne are appearing in a devastating drama, *The Visit*, which opened, appropriately enough, at the Lunt-Fontanne Theatre last evening.

"When Friedrich Duerrenmatt, the author, gets seriously down to work in the savage last act, our two most gifted comic actors look like our two most gifted dramatic actors. Under Peter Brook's ingenious direction, they give an unforgettable performance."

Their last New York appearance was in a return of *The Visit*, which played City Center on March 8, 1960.

Lunt served as director for the play *First Love* (12/25/61; 24 performances), which opened at the MOROSCO THEATRE.

Many authors have attempted to pinpoint the couple's unique acting style. Playwrights who had written for the Lunts were effusive in their praise. Robert Emmett Sherwood once wrote a poem about their box office appeal:

> If you want a play to run many a munt
> Get Lynn Fontanne and Alfred Lunt.

S. N. Behrman claimed that the Lunts were insulated and lived in their own fantasy world. One day Lynn Fontanne rushed to the singer Alma Gluck and insisted that Gluck introduce her to Rachmaninoff. It seemed that Fontanne had seen the composer on Fifth Avenue and was so struck by his mien that she followed him around all day. When Gluck arranged for Fontanne to meet the composer (who played bridge

Lynn Fontanne and Alfred Lunt in *The Visit*, 1958.

with Gluck's husband, Efrem Zimbalist Sr.), the actress was taken aback. "That's not Rachmaninoff," she exclaimed. Gluck assured her that it was indeed Rachmaninoff in the other room. It was then that Fontanne realized she had followed a stranger around Manhattan.

Brooks Atkinson, in his book *Broadway*, said of the Lunts, "Brilliant actors with mischievous personalities and an insatiable appetite for the stage, they were the most exhilarating and enviable couple on Broadway." Lynn Fontanne told theater historian George Freedley that people accused them of being "all tricks. What we do is exactly the opposite. We search for the truth and try to express it. We do the natural thing."

LUNT-FONTANNE THEATER. 205 W. 46th Street. Architects: Carriere and Hastings. Original name: Globe Theatre. Opening: January 10, 1910; *The Old Town*.

In 1909 producer Charles Dillingham hired the high-class architecture firm of Carriere and Hastings to design the Globe Theatre, which later became the Lunt-Fontanne. Carriere and Hastings are best known for their designs for the New York Public Library (1898–1911), the Frick Collection (1913–1914), and the Manhattan Bridge approach (1912–1915).

Dillingham was described by Fred Stone, one of his stars, as "a swell. Dapper, meticulously dressed, his hat always tilted a little over one eye, he was a unique figure in the theater. He knew more of the important society people than any other producer, but he preferred the company of prize fighters." Dillingham's lifestyle was as flamboyant as his personality, and he spared little expense on his new theater. He wanted to cater to the carriage trade, so he made sure that the interior and exterior of the building were lavishly decorated. An additional entrance on West 46th Street, which was designed for patrons who wanted to make

Globe Theatre prior to its opening, 1910.

grand entrances, supplanted the theater's original entrance at 1555 Broadway. Above the 46th Street doors was a balcony from which audience members could view arrivals.

Inside, the theater proper was decorated in hues of gold, blue, and ivory. Above the auditorium was a dome that could be opened to the sky in good weather. Upstairs, the theater contained private apartments for Dillingham and his retinue. The six-story Renaissance revival–style building presented an awesome facade to passersby and theatergoers.

Dillingham was primarily a producer of musicals, so the early years of the theater were spent hosting musicals and revues almost exclusively. Dillingham's initial offering at the Globe was a Gustave Luders and George Ade musical, *The Old Town*. The main draw of the show was the popular team of Dave Montgomery and Fred Stone; Peggy Wood was also featured. Montgomery and Stone were riding high on the popularity of their last two musicals, *The Wizard of Oz* and VICTOR HERBERT's *The Red Mill*. For *The Old Town*, Stone worked up a specialty act in which he twirled a lasso and danced with it. He also walked a high wire in the show. As might be evident, the plot was of little importance, and by the end of the show's Broadway run it had been completely discarded. A reviewer noted that the authors had removed "the grass that was growing in the streets of *The Old Town*." *The Old Town*'s 171-performance run was an auspicious success for the new theater.

Dillingham's next show, *The Slim Princess* (1/2/11; 104 performances), also included popular American humorist George Ade on the creative staff. This time Ade's original story was the basis for the book. Leslie Stuart and Henry Blossom were responsible for the score. The cast of *The Slim Princess* included popular musical comedy stars Queenie Vassar, Charles King, Elizabeth Brice, and Joseph Cawthorn. But the biggest star in the show, and one of the biggest in the early part of this century, was Elsie Janis. *The Slim Princess* was about a country where obesity was looked on as beauty. The slim plot gave Janis plenty of opportunities to demonstrate her well known impressions.

Producer Charles Frohman's advice to fellow producers was "When in doubt, do Cinderella." Dillingham took Frohman's advice in his next offering at the Globe, *The Lady of the Slipper* (10/28/12; 232 performances). Elsie Janis returned to the Globe's stage, as did Montgomery and Stone and Peggy Wood. The cast also featured dancer Vernon Castle (*see* VERNON AND IRENE CASTLE). The songs were by Victor Herbert, who had contributed uncredited music to *The Slim Princess*, and lyricist James O'Dea. *The Lady and the Slipper* also had troubles while out of town. IRENE CASTLE had been to Paris the previous summer, where she

had discovered a new style in brief underwear. She took pride in her discovery and decided to introduce the style to America. As described by Elsie Janis, during the dress rehearsal in Philadelphia, Castle "suddenly pulled up her skirts like a naughty little girl, showing her 'complete understanding,' Charley (Dillingham) groaned, Fred Stone looked the other way, and Mother's gasp of dismay must have been heard in Trenton!" Dillingham begged the dancer to put on her Dutch bonnet and chiffon skirts, but she refused, and she was out of the show.

If the 232-performance run of *The Lady of the Slipper* was remarkable, then the 295-performance run of Dillingham's next production, *Chin-Chin*, was almost a miracle. *Chin-Chin* (10/20/14) opened with Dillingham favorites Montgomery and Stone in the leads. The music was by Englishman Ivan Caryll, and lyrics were by Anne Caldwell and James O'Dea. Montgomery and Stone played two slaves of Aladdin's lamp. Stone impersonated Paderewski. He accomplished the amazing feat of duplicating the pianist's great technique by sitting in front of a player piano on stage. Paderewski even came to one performance and complimented Stone on his playing. Stone also performed a horseback riding trick. He was suspended by a wire while riding the horse. As he circled the stage, he slipped further and further back until, hanging in the air, he was holding on to only the horse's tail. The trick ended when the tail appeared to come off in Stone's hand, and the actor crashed to the ground.

Dillingham was smart enough to realize that tastes in popular music were changing, and the old-fashioned operettas and comic operas were becoming dated. The producer hired the young IRVING BERLIN to write the score to the next production at the Globe, *Stop! Look! Listen!* (12/25/15; 105 performances). The show boasted a libretto by the prolific HARRY B. SMITH. Berlin's score contained two classics: "The Girl on the Magazine Cover" and the ragtime-inspired "I Love a Piano." The fine cast included future film star Marion Davies, Gaby Deslys, Blossom Seeley, and Joseph Santley. The Globe's first straight play presentation was *The Harp of Life* (11/27/16; 136 performances). Laurette Taylor starred in the play, which was written by her husband, J. Hartley Manners. *The Harp of Life* marked Taylor's return to New York after a period in England.

In the second year of touring *Chin-Chin*, Dave Montgomery died. Fred Stone went on to appear at the Globe in *Jack o'Lantern* (10/16/17; 265 performances). The musical had music and lyrics by Ivan Caryll and Anne Caldwell. The hit song from the show was an interpolation by Irving Berlin, "I'll Take You Back to Italy." For *Jack o'Lantern*, Fred Stone learned to ice skate. He described another of his stunts in his

Charles Frohman and Charles Dillingham.

Dave Montgomery and Fred Stone in *The Lady and the Slipper*, 1912.

autobiography: "I jumped up and down on a hay wagon which was a trampoline, pursued by the police, then ran two steps up a tree, turned a back somersault over the heads of the police, leaped on a bicycle and somersaulted with it through the window of a house." At the time Stone was 41 years old.

Dillingham's production *The Canary* (11/4/18; 152 performances) had songs by Ivan Caryll, Irving Berlin, Anne Caldwell, P. G. Wodehouse, Harry Tierney, Harry B. Smith, Benjamin Hapgood Burt, and others. Despite the large number of composers and lyricists, the show was a musical comedy, not a revue. Of course, at the time there was sometimes little difference between the two forms. Dillingham's production of *She's a Good Fellow* (5/5/19; 120 performances) boasted a score by JEROME KERN and Anne Caldwell. Joseph Santley (in drag), the Duncan Sisters, Olin Howland, and Ivy Sawyer starred. The show's run was cut short by the ACTOR'S STRIKE of 1919, which helped establish ACTORS' EQUITY.

Along with Irving Berlin and Jerome Kern, GEORGE GERSHWIN was responsible for the new direction of Broadway musicals. Gershwin finally had a show of his produced at the Globe with the second edition of *GEORGE WHITE'S SCANDALS* (6/7/20; 134 performances). Arthur Jackson was Gershwin's collaborator on the score. *Scandals* regulars Ann Pennington, Lou Holtz, Lester Allen, and GEORGE WHITE himself starred in the show. The *Scandals* was the first show presented in the Globe that was not produced by Dillingham.

Dillingham returned to producing at the Globe with *Tip Top* (10/5/20; 241 performances). Ivan Caryll and Anne Caldwell provided the score for the show, which starred Fred Stone, the Duncan Sisters, and Rags Ragland. *Tip Top* featured Stone up to some new tricks. He opened the show by shooting up through a trap door in the stage with his hair covered with foam. Stone told the audience that he had added too many raisins to the bootleg hooch that he was brewing in the basement. He had also learned the art of Australian whip cracking, and he removed a cigarette from the mouth of an assistant with the whip. Stone's pièce de résistance was breaking resin balls with shots fired from a. 22 rifle. While he shot at the airborne balls, he danced.

George White's chief rival, FLORENZ ZIEGFELD, presented the 1921 version of the ZIEGFELD FOLLIES (6/21/21; 119 performances) at the Globe. Performers included W. C. Fields, Raymond Hitchcock, Ray Dooley, and Vera Michelena. FANNY BRICE was given the two best songs: "My Man" and "Second Hand Rose." Then Jerome Kern had another show open at the Globe, *Good Morning, Dearie* (11/1/21; 347 performances). Anne Caldwell wrote the book and lyrics. Among the best songs in the score were the title tune and "Blue Danube Blues." The biggest hit in the show was "Ka-Lu-a."

George White's Scandals returned to the Globe (8/28/22; 89 performances) with music by George Gershwin and lyrics by B. G. De Sylva (*see* DE SYLVA, BROWN, AND HENDERSON), E. Ray Goetz, and Arthur Francis. Francis was a pseudonym for George's talented brother, Ira. The cast included Lester Allen, Winnie Lightner, George White, and W. C. Fields; Paul Whiteman and his Orchestra also appeared onstage. The most famous of the Gershwin songs was "I'll Build a Stairway to Paradise."

Fred Stone appeared along with his wife, Allene, and daughter Dorothy in the aptly titled *Stepping Stones* (1/16/23; 241 performances). Jerome Kern and Anne Caldwell wrote the score, which included the beautiful ballad "Once in a Blue Moon." On opening night producer Charles Dillingham had a surprise for the cast. After the performance Dillingham took Dorothy outside the theater to show her where he had put her name up in lights on the marquee. Next the *Scandals* returned to the Globe (6/18/23; 168 performances), with Gershwin again supplying the score along with lyricists B. G. De Sylva, E. Ray Goetz, and Ballard Macdonald. However, none of the songs achieved success.

Ed Wynn was composer, lyricist, librettist, producer, and star of *The Grab Bag* (10/6/24; 184 performances). The show and Wynn's hijinks proved to be a huge hit. It was followed by one of the Globe's biggest hits, *No, No, Nanette* (9/16/25; 329 performances). The show's tremendous success was due mostly to the great VINCENT YOUMANS and Irving Caesar score. The hit songs included "Tea for Two" and "I Want to Be Happy." Another factor in the success of the show was its star Louise Groody. Groody was the first star to receive a salary plus a percentage of the box-office receipts. As a result, she was the first musical comedy star to earn more than $1 million dollars. The actress shocked audiences when she appeared on the stage of the Globe Theatre shorn of her trademark curls. Luckily, audiences cheered her performance despite her tonsorial change.

Ziegfeld produced his revue *No Foolin'* (6/24/26; 108 performances) at the Globe. Ziegfeld planned the show as the 1926 edition of his *Follies*, but because of a breakup with his former partners and owners of the New Amsterdam Theatre, Marc Klaw and A. L. Erlanger, he was refused the right to the *Follies* name. Out of town the show was titled *Ziegfeld's Palm Beach Nights, Ziegfeld's Palm Beach Girl*, and *Ziegfeld's American Revue of 1926*. After its Broadway opening as *No Foolin'*, Ziegfeld retitled the show *Ziegfeld's American Revue*. When the show toured following its Broadway run, Ziegfeld, having settled his argument with Klaw and Erlanger, could at last call the show the *Ziegfeld Follies of 1926*.

Jerome Kern, OTTO HARBACH, and Anne Caldwell were responsible for the Dillingham production of *Criss Cross* (10/12/26; 210 performances). Fred Stone and his daughter Dorothy appeared in the show with Fred dropping onto the stage from the fly system above. When he reached the stage floor, a rubber contraption he was linked to jerked him back above the proscenium arch. Stone also swung 40 feet from the wings by his knees. At the bottom of his swing he picked up his daughter Dorothy and, continuing to swing from side to side, carried her to the opposite side of the stage.

Vincent Youmans' second production at the Globe, *Oh, Please!* (12/17/26; 79 performances), had a hit song, "I Know That You Know," and a talented cast, including Beatrice Lillie, Charles Winninger, Helen Broderick, and Charles Purcell. *Three Cheers* (10/15/28; 218 performances) was to star Fred Stone and his daughter Dorothy, but prior to the opening Stone, who had taken up flying, crashed the plane he was piloting. His injuries prevented him from appearing, and Will Rogers, Stone's closest friend, replaced him in the show. On the opening night Rogers told the audience, "I don't know one thing that Fred does that I can do." Rogers was smart enough not to try duplicating Stone's acrobatics, and he got laughs by admitting it. "You know, folks," Rogers would tell the audience, "if Fred Stone were here, he'd be making a standing jump up there. But I think I'll just stay where I am." Future Hollywood comedian Patsy Kelly was also in the cast. Ray Henderson and B. G. De Sylva wrote the score, but none of the songs achieved any success. If Stone had been able to perform, the show would have been the first Globe musical featuring Stone that was not produced by Dillingham. The great producer's luck was running out.

The last show to play the Globe was the Jerome Kern and Otto Harbach musical *The Cat and the Fiddle* (10/15/31; 395 performances). The brilliantly tuneful score featured such hits as "I Watch the Love Parade," "She Didn't Say Yes," "The Night Was Made for Love," and "Try to Forget." The show starred Odette Myrtil, Georges Metaxa, Bettina Hall, and George Meader.

The stock market crash wiped out Dillingham's savings, and the producer was forced to sell his beloved theater. Beginning in 1932 the Globe showed motion pictures. Twenty-five years later, in 1957, Roger L. Stevens (of City Playhouses Group) and Robert W. Dowling bought the theater and had the interior completely refurbished by Roche & Roche. The Broadway entrance was closed, the box office was added to the 46th Street lobby, the second balcony was removed, and a mezzanine was added. The refurbished interior was also redecorated with an 18th-century motif. The theater was renamed for the greatest of all American acting teams, LUNT AND FONTANNE.

The theater's second opening took place on May 5, 1958, with the stars who gave it their names in the leading roles of Friedrich Dürrenmatt's explosive drama *The Visit* (189 performances). BROOKS ATKINSON described the play as "a horrifying indictment of a cruel and greedy culture, staged with ingenuity and bravado by a gifted heretic and acted with subtlety, insight, and coolness by America's greatest actors." However, the unrelenting drama of the play kept many theatergoers away. Sadly, it marked the end of the team's career on Broadway.

The theater's greatest hit, *The Sound of Music* (11/16/59; 1,443 performances), marked the end of another team's Broadway career. It would be the last collaboration for RODGERS AND HAMMERSTEIN. The MARY MARTIN vehicle received decidedly mixed reviews but was an enormously popular hit with the public. Critics cited the operetta's sentimentality as its biggest fault. The score also received mixed notices, although many of the songs, chiefly "Climb Ev'ry Mountain," "Sixteen Going on Seventeen," "Do Re Mi," "My Favorite Things," and the title song, became standards.

One of Broadway's funniest musicals, *Little Me* (11/17/62; 257 performances), followed *The Sound of Music* at the Lunt-Fontanne. The Cy Coleman and Carolyn Leigh score was perhaps the wittiest and brashest ever to play on Broadway. It was perfectly complemented by NEIL SIMON's hilarious libretto. The hit songs from the score were "I've Got Your Number" and "Real Live Girl." The play was the story of Belle Poitrine, a not-so-dumb blonde, and her succession of husbands. Two actors played Belle: Nancy Andrews

The Lunt-Fontaine Theater just prior to opening, 1958.

played the older Belle, and Virginia Martin the younger. Master comic Sid Caesar played all the husbands. The reviews were excellent, but a newspaper strike hurt the musical's business.

Richard Burton opened in William Shakespeare's *Hamlet* on April 9, 1964. His performance was generally hailed, and the production enjoyed a 137-performance run, a record for the play on Broadway. However, a series of middling musicals followed Hamlet. By now, 500 performances were usually necessary for a show to recoup its investment. Julie Harris was allowed to sing in the James Van Heusen and Sammy Cahn musical *Skyscraper* (11/13/65; 248 performances). "Everybody Has the Right to Be Wrong" was the most popular song in the otherwise undistinguished score. The same songwriting team was responsible for the next attraction at the Lunt-Fontanne, *Walking Happy* (11/26/66; 161 performances). The title tune and Norman Wisdom's performance were the chief draw. Lyricist Carolyn Leigh teamed up with film composer Elmer Bernstein for the DAVID MERRICK production *How Now, Dow Jones* (12/7/67; 220 performances). The score contained a bona-fide hit, "Step to the Rear." Max Shulman's book was considered the biggest flaw in the show, which starred Marlyn Mason, Anthony Roberts, and Brenda Vaccaro.

Hal Linden, Jill Clayburgh, Keene Curtis, and Paul Hecht starred in BOCK AND HARNICK's story of the celebrated banking family, *The Rothschilds* (10/19/70; 505 performances). During the 1970s, there was a series of revivals at the Lunt-Fontanne. These included STEPHEN SONDHEIM's *A Funny Thing Happened on the Way to the Forum* with Phil Silvers and Larry Blyden; the Richard Adler and Jerry Ross hit *The Pajama Game* with Hal Linden and Barbara McNair; and *Hello, Dolly!* with a return performance by Carol Channing. One new production in the 1970s was the Richard Rodgers and Sheldon Harnick musical *Rex* (4/25/76; 49 performances). The show, a retelling of the life of Henry VIII, starred Nicol Williamson, Penny Fuller, and Barbara Andres.

A big hit for the theater was the Duke Ellington revue *Sophisticated Ladies* (3/1/81; 767 performances) with Gregory Hines, Phyllis Hyman, Judith Jamison, and Hinton Battle. *Sophisticated Ladies* covered the best known songs in the Ellington canon.

Songstress Peggy Lee had an inauspicious Broadway debut trying for an autobiographical show like the recent *Lena Horne: A Lady and Her Music*. But Lee's show, which included a harrowing song, "One Beating a Day," made audiences uncomfortable, and *Peg* (12/14/83) closed after only 5 performances.

Jason Robards reprised his acclaimed performance as Hickey in a revival of EUGENE O'NEILL's *The Iceman Cometh* (9/29/85), but it failed to find an audience and closed after a meager 55 performances.

The 1980s were lean years on Broadway. In order to keep their theater's lit, owners booked in concert performances for a few nights. The Lunt-Fontanne hosted its share of concerts, featuring an amazingly wide range of performers. The first was French singer Charles Aznavour (3/14/83; 14 performances). He was followed by magician Doug Henning (12/11/84; 60 performances), Jerry Garcia (10/15/87), Joan Jett (3/1/89; 5 performances), Freddie Jackson (9/12/89), Bobby McFerrin (11/5/90; 8 performances), and Harry Connick Jr. (11/23/90; 13 performances).

In between, the theater was booked by a succession of shows that sounded good in theory but failed to materialize artistically. Marvin Hamlisch, composer of *A Chorus Line*, and Howard Ashman, lyricist and librettist of *Little Shop of Horrors*, joined forces for *Smile* (11/24/86; 48 performances). Based on a hit film that took swipes at local beauty pageants, the show began life as a collaboration between Hamlisch and Carolyn Leigh. When Leigh died, her biting lyrics were replaced by Ashman's more benign satire. *Smile* would be remembered as the first show that boasted corporate sponsorship. The song "Disneyland" was underwritten by the Walt Disney Company, and a backdrop depicting an overhead view of Santa Rosa, California, had local McDonald's restaurants prominently marked.

The Gospel at Colonus (3/11/88) was a brilliant retelling of three Sophocles plays transplanted to a concert atmosphere with a decidedly R&B slant. First produced by the Brooklyn Academy of Music, the show featured a dynamic score by Bob Telson and Lee Breuer. Also directed by Breuer, it featured the talents of some of the greatest black talents in America, including Morgan Freeman, Sam Butler Jr., Clarence Fountain and the Five Blind Boys of Alabama, the Institutional Radio Choir, J. J. Farley and the Soul Stirrers, Robert Earl Jones (father of James), and the J. D. Steele Singers. Unfortunately, despite the powerhouse lineup and superb production, white suburban middle-class audiences, black inner-city audiences, and hardcore Broadwayites all found something to dissuade them from attending. *The Gospel at Colonus*, a true leap ahead in the development of the Broadway musical, closed after only 61 performances.

Rock 'n' roll superstar Sting made his Broadway debut not in a concert but as MacHeath in a revival of KURT WEILL and Bertolt Brecht's classic, *3 Penny Opera* (11/5/89). Georgia Brown, Alvin Epstein, and Maureen McGovern, all major musical talents, were supported by additional wonderful talents including Larry Marshall, Suzzanne Douglas, Kim Criswell, Josh Mostel, MacIntyre Dixon, Anne Kerry Ford, and K. T. Sullivan. But John Dexter's staging left audiences cold, and the show closed after only 65 performances. A great opportunity was wasted.

A surprise hit with critics and audiences was the evening of standup comedy *Catskills on Broadway* (12/5/91). Dick Capri, Marilyn Michaels, Mal Z. Lawrence, and Freddie Roman, not exactly household names in the 1990s, had audiences convulsed for a well-deserved 453-performance run—a smash by any yardstick.

Mitch Leigh (of *Man of La Mancha* renown), Lee Adams (of *Bye Bye Birdie* fame), and Thomas Meehan (librettist of *Annie*) all failed to come up with a successful biomusical of Mike Todd's life titled *Ain't Broadway Grand*. It closed after 25 disappointing performances.

The flops kept on coming with the next booking at the Lunt-Fontanne, *The Best Little Whorehouse Goes Public* (5/10/94), an offensive sequel to the surprisingly sweet and touching *The Best Little Whorehouse in Texas*. Collaborators Carol Hall (songs) and Larry L. King and Peter Masterson (book) failed to come up with the goods, and the whole mess closed after 16 performances.

Lightning again failed to strike twice with another variety evening inspired by *Catskills*. This time Dorothy Loudon, Joy Behar, Michael Davis, and Mort Sahl, all tops in their fields, failed to make an impression as a group. *Comedy Tonight* (12/18/94) closed on Christmas Day after 9 performances.

Carol Channing made what was promised as her last Broadway appearance in *Hello, Dolly!* at the Lunt-Fontanne beginning on October 19, 1995. Channing showed exactly why she deserved to be a star for a total of 116 performances.

The next musical at the theater was also its next hit. *Titanic* (4/23/97; 804 performances) had an unlikely subject for a musical. But despite so-so reviews, Maury Yeston's score and Peter Stone's book managed to interest audiences for a sufficient period until the show won the TONY AWARD for Best Musical, and the run was extended. Astute marketing by the producers, Dodgers Endemol Theatricals, and equally astute PR by Boneau-Bryan-Brown ensured a long run.

The theater was subsequently occupied by the Disney musical *Beauty and the Beast*, a transfer from the PALACE THEATER.

On December 14, 1987, the New York City Landmarks Preservation Commission designated the exterior of the theater a landmark. The interior was denied status. The commission stated that the theater's facade is an "exceptional example" of Beaux Arts style, with a five-bay arcade of double-height Ionic columns, a smaller version of the Century Theater that once stood on Central Park West.

LYCEUM THEATER. 149 W. 45th Street. Architects: HERTS & TALLANT. Opening: November 2, 1903; *The Proud Prince*.

When producer Daniel Frohman opened his new Lyceum Theater on 45th Street, it was the first of the Times Square theaters north of 42nd Street. Other theaters had opened around Columbus Circle, and there was a healthy theater district in Harlem, but the success of the Lyceum and the other theaters surrounding it firmly established the Times Square area as the hub of legitimate theater. Frohman recognized Times Square's importance as the center of the new theater world. His previous Lyceum Theatre was located downtown on 14th Street. He joined with his brother Charles and producer William B. Harris in ownership of the theater.

The theater was considered quite modern for its time. There were no balcony supports to block the audience's view. In addition, it contained carpentry and costume shops, scene painting studios, and 14 dressing rooms in a 7-story building to the rear of the theater proper. The Neo-Baroque interior style and beautiful facade made the Lyceum one of the most attractive Broadway houses. It was the first theater building to receive landmark status and is the oldest continuously

operating legitimate theater in New York. Frohman's private apartments contained a window from which he could view the performances below. This was a common practice in theaters whose managements liked to keep a tight rein on their companies. When Frohman's wife, Margaret Illington, acted on the Lyceum stage, her husband would signal her from his window if she was overacting.

The theater has had a distinguished past, starting with its first offering, *The Proud Prince* starring E. H. Sothern, a favorite of Frohman. Soon after, William Gillette starred in J. M. Barrie's *The Admirable Crichton* (11/17/03; 144 performances). The biggest hit of the early years of the Lyceum was *The Lion and the Mouse* (11/20/05; 686 performances) by Charles Klein.

Great women graced the Lyceum stage in a number of mostly forgotten plays. Billie Burke, Ethel Barrymore (*see* BARRYMORE FAMILY), Lenore Ulric, and Ina Claire all had great success at the theater. Daniel's brother, Charles, was responsible for most of the bookings in the early years of the theater. Charles Frohman died in the sinking of the *Lusitania* in 1915; at the time, Charles Frohman, Inc., owned 60 percent of the theater and DAVID BELASCO owned 40 percent. Daniel Frohman teamed with Belasco for a string of popular successes. These included *The Gold Diggers* (9/30/19; 720 performances) and *Berkeley Square* (11/4/29) by John L. Balderston, starring Leslie Howard and Margalo Gilmore. In 1919 Famous Players–Lasky bought a controlling interest in Charles Frohman, Inc., as a way to obtain stage properties for its films. They let Daniel and Belasco continue running the theater.

Belasco died in 1930, and during the ensuing decade and the Depression, Daniel Frohman's fortunes declined, but the theater still housed a number of interesting shows. Charles Laughton and Elsa Lanchester starred in *Payment Deferred* (9/30/31; 70 performances). *Sailor, Beware!* was a big hit beginning on September 28, 1933 (500 performances), and Ina Claire, who had previously starred at the Lyceum in *The Gold Diggers*, returned to the Lyceum in *Ode to Liberty* (12/21/34; 66 performances). *Having Wonderful Time* (2/20/37; 310 performances), Arthur Kober's affectionate view of a summer camp for adults in the Catskills, would later be made into the musical *Wish You Were Here*. J. B. Priestley's delightful farce *When We Are Married* (12/25/39; 156 performances) closed out the 1930s.

However successful the plays staged at the Lyceum were, Frohman's career was suffering. The theater was faced with destruction. A group of investors, however, led by George S. Kaufman, Moss Hart (*see* KAUFMAN AND HART), and Max Gordon bought the theater and allowed Frohman to live in his apartment for $1 a year. It was natural that the first show of the 1940s would be Kaufman and Hart's riotous comedy *George Washington Slept Here* (10/18/40; 176 performances), but it did not prove as successful as their other outings. Moss Hart then staged Jerome Chodorov and Joseph Fields' (*see* FIELDS FAMILY) *Junior Miss* (11/18/41; 710 performances). It would later make a successful movie and a television musical. Joseph Fields provided the theater with its next hit, *The Doughgirls* (12/30/42; 671 performances); Kaufman directed the Arlene Francis vehicle. Kaufman then cowrote with John P. Marquand and directed *The Late George Apley* (11/21/44; 384 performances). At the end of that play's run, the Kaufman/Hart/Gordon group sold the Lyceum. Garson Kanin's *Born Yesterday* (2/4/46; 1,642 performances) was the Lyceum's next smash hit. It made stars of Judy Holliday and Paul Douglas.

In 1949 the Lyceum became a part of the SHUBERT BROTHERS empire. The 1950s were also rich years for the Lyceum. Clifford Odets' *The Country Girl* (11/10/50; 236 performances) starred Uta Hagen, Paul Kelly, and Steven Hill. Melvyn Douglas starred in *Glad Tidings* (10/11/51; 100 performances) and followed it with *Time Out for Ginger* (11/26/52; 248 performances), one of the most successful plays in the amateur market, receiving countless productions in summer stock and schools. Jean Kerr and Eleanor Brooke continued the comedy tradition at the Lyceum with *King of Hearts* (4/1/54; 279 performances); drama CRITIC and Kerr's husband WALTER KERR directed Jackie Cooper and Donald Cook in the hit comedy. Viveca Lindfors portrayed the title role in *Anastasia* (12/29/54; 272 performances), written by Broadway veteran GUY BOLTON. Eugenie Leontovich played the dowager empress in the production. Another drama followed, the harrowing *A Hatful of Rain* (11/9/55; 389 performances), starring Ben Gazzara, Shelley Winters, and Harry Guardino. During the second half of the 1950s, Walter Pidgeon starred in a production of *The Happiest Millionaire* (11/20/56; 271 performances). The next hit was John Osborne's *Look Back in Anger* (10/1/57; 407 performances) with Kenneth Haigh, Alan Bates, and Mary Ure. It reopened at the 41st Street Theatre for an additional 116 performances.

The 1960s began with Shelagh Delaney's *A Taste of Honey* (10/4/60; 376 performances), starring Angela Lansbury. The third hit at the Lyceum, a British import, was a production of Harold Pinter's *The Caretaker* (10/4/61; 165 performances) with Alan Bates, Robert Shaw, and Donald Pleasance. Ellis Rabb, artistic director of the APA Phoenix company, took over the theater for the rest of the decade. During this period of 1965 to 1969, such plays as *War and Peace*, *The Cherry Orchard*, *The Cocktail Party*, and George Kelly's *The*

Show Off, starring Helen Hayes, appeared on the Lyceum stage.

The 1970s proved to be lean years for the Lyceum as well as Broadway in general. The best play of the decade at the Lyceum was Arthur Kopit's brilliant drama *Wings* (1/28/79; 113 performances), starring Constance Cummings. In 1980 an all-star revival of *Morning's at Seven* (4/10/80; 564 performances) opened at the Lyceum. In the cast were Nancy Marchand, Maureen O'Sullivan, Teresa Wright, Elizabeth Wilson, and David Rounds. Paul Osborn's forgotten play was hailed as a modern classic.

The next hit at the Lyceum was Athol Fugard's *'MASTER HAROLD' . . . and the Boys* (5/4/82; 344 performances). The play, set against South Africa's apartheid society, starred Danny Glover, Zakes Mokae, and Lonny Price. Whoopi Goldberg made her New York debut with her one-person standup show, which opened on October 24, 1984, and ran for 156 performances under the supervision of Mike Nichols.

William M. Hoffman's politically charged play, *As Is* (5/1/85) was an early look at the then unacknowledged AIDS epidemic. The show ran for 284 performances and helped change public attitudes toward the disease. The next play at the Lyceum also dealt with the AIDS epidemic but in a more surrealistic style.

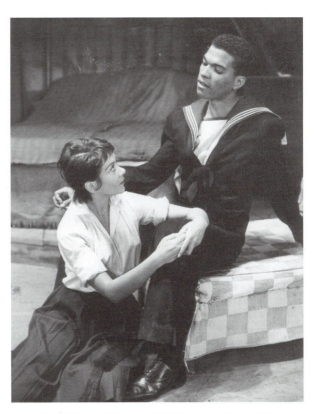

Joan Plowright and Billy Dee Williams in *A Taste of Honey*, 1960.

Harvey Fierstein's *Safe Sex* (4/5/87) failed to engage either audiences or critics and closed after only 9 performances.

Tony Randall's stab at a resident theater company on Broadway, the National Actors Theatre, held forth on the Lyceum stage for the next few shows. The first was Anton Chekhov's *The Seagull* (11/29/92; 49 performances). It was followed by productions of *Saint Joan* (1/31/93; 48 performances); and *Three Men on a Horse* (4/13/93; 39 performances); *Timon of Athens* (11/4/93; 39 performances); *The Government Inspector* (1/6/94; 37 performances); *The Flowering Peach* (3/20/94; 41 performances); *Gentlemen Prefer Blondes* (5/10/95; 24 performances); and *The School for Scandal* (11/19/95; 33 performances).

The National Actors Theatre resumed productions at the Lyceum with Julie Harris and Charles Durning starring in *The Gin Game* (4/20/97; 145 performances). The next offering, *The Sunshine Boys* (12/8/97; 230 performances), marked a reunion of television's *Odd Couple*, Tony Randall and Jack Klugman (recently recovering from cancer surgery). A year and a half later the company presented Matthew Broderick in the thriller *Night Must Fall* (3/8/99; 119 performances). It would be the National Actors Theatre's last presentation at the theatre at the Lyceum.

The theater's saw a revival of a previous hit, *Morning's at Seven* (4/21/02; 112 performances) starring Frances Sternhagen, Elizabeth Franz, Piper Laurie, and Estelle Parsons.

The Shuberts restored the theater and placed their archives upstairs in Frohman's old offices. On December 8, 1987, the New York City Landmarks Preservation Commission designated the interior of the theater a landmark. The exterior had been designated in 1974. The commission stated that the auditorium was in an "unusually handsome Beaux-Arts style design . . . with an elaborate proscenium arch and boxes adorned with elegant French-inspired ornament." The Lyceum was awarded "distressed" status among the theater's unions, enabling it to qualify for reduced minimums and fees.

LYRIC THEATER (1). *See* **Olympia.**

LYRIC THEATRE (2). 213 W. 42nd Street. Architect: V. Hugo Koehler. Opening: October 12, 1903; *Old Heidelberg.*

The Lyric was one of the most beautiful of the 42nd Street theaters. Although the entrance to the Renaissance-style theater was on 42nd Street, the main part of the theater fronted 43rd Street. In most theaters fronting major thoroughfares, the lobbies were on the main streets while the theaters proper were built on the less expensive side streets. The Lyric's 43rd Street side features a beautifully ornamented facade with cartouches inscribed "Music" and "Drama."

The Lyric was built by developer Eugene C. Potter to house composer Reginald DeKoven's American School of Opera. DeKoven had made thousands from his show *Robin Hood*. The school failed before the theater was finished, and Potter leased the unfinished theater to the SHUBERT BROTHERS. Leading man Richard Mansfield opened the house in 1903. DeKoven's troupe didn't last long, and the Shuberts subsequently booked some of the greatest actors and productions of the time. Douglas Fairbanks Sr. and Wilton Lackaye starred in an adaptation of Channing Pollack's *The Pit* (2/10/04; 77 performances); Mrs. Fiske, George Arliss, and Dudley Diggs played in *The New York Idea* (11/19/06; 66 performances); Tyrone Power Sr. and William Faversham appeared in *Julius Caesar* (11/4/12; 32 performances). Musicals included RUDOLF FRIML's *The Firefly* (12/2/12; 120 performances) and *High Jinks* (12/10/13; 213 performances). *The Firefly* had lyrics by OTTO HARBACH and featured the Friml favorite "Giannina Mia."

Following World War I, the theater alternated between first-run film engagements and theatrical offerings. FRED AND ADELE ASTAIRE starred in *For Goodness Sake* (2/20/22; 103 performances). Although the score was by Paul Lannin, William Daly, and Arthur Jackson, newcomers GEORGE AND IRA GERSHWIN contributed the hits "Someone" and "Tra-La-La."

In 1925 the Oppenheimer Brothers assumed management of the theater. IRVING BERLIN supplied the score to the madcap musical comedy *The Cocoanuts* (12/8/25; 375 performances). Along with the Marx Brothers, the show featured the Brox Sisters and the Brothers' constant foil, Margaret Dumont. The show was later made into the brothers' first motion-picture success.

The great showman FLORENZ ZIEGFELD brought his musicalization of *The Three Musketeers* into the Lyric on March 13, 1928. Rudolph Friml again delighted audiences with such songs as "Gascony," "March of the Musketeers," "My Sword," "One Kiss," and "Your Eyes." The show was a smash hit and ran 319 performances. COLE PORTER's *Fifty Million Frenchmen* (11/27/29; 254 performances) was the theater's last success, opening at the dawn of the Depression and during Prohibition. Among its songs were "You Do Something to Me" and "You've Got That Thing." The last legitimate show to play the Lyric was *Run, Little Chillun!* beginning on March 1, 1933.

The Lyric, like other 42nd Street theaters, became a motion-picture house because of the Depression, starting its movie policy in 1933. Luckily, as with most of the 42nd Street theaters, economics did not allow for major renovation. Thus the Lyric survived in almost exactly the same condition as when it opened more than 80 years ago, although when wide-screen movies came in, the nine original boxes were removed. It was cleaned in 1979 by its owners the Brandts, with the expectation of reopening it as a legitimate house. But the effort failed as Broadway continued its most recent decline. The financial plight of the theater district ruled out any reversal of the theater's movie policy.

A huge theater with a double balcony, the Lyric seated 1,256 patrons. Because of its size, the Lyric, under the Times Square Redevelopment Plan, was recommended for legitimate theater productions. The Brandts also wanted to reopen their APOLLO THEATRE next door. The Apollo was reopened but producers could not be found who wanted to book the Lyric. The 42nd Street Redevelopment organization condemned the Lyric and Apollo and gained control of the spaces. In spite of the excellent shape of the Lyric, the heat was turned off, and the theater was allowed to deteriorate.

In 1996 producer Garth Drabinsky of Livent Corporation came from Canada to New York looking for a theater for his productions. He talked the 42nd Street Redevelopment people into allowing him to destroy the Lyric and Apollo theaters to build a new, inferior theater, the FORD CENTER FOR THE PERFORMING ARTS, in their place. He did, however, have the foresight to save the exteriors of both theaters. A year later Drabinsky was out, under the threat of lawsuits by the New York State government and his investors.

MAJESTIC THEATRE. 245 W. 44th Street. Architect: Herbert J. Krapp. Opening: March 28, 1927; *Rufus LeMaire's Affairs*.

With 1,800 seats, the Majestic was the largest legitimate house in Times Square. The Majestic was the last theater commissioned by the Chanin brothers and was built as the flagship of their theater holdings. Unfortunately, the Chanins lost all their theaters during the Depression. Built on the same large plot of land as the Theatre Masque (*see* JOHN GOLDEN THEATER [2]), ROYALE THEATRE, and the Lincoln Hotel (now the Milford Hotel), the Majestic's interior design is similar to the RICHARD RODGERS THEATER with its bleacher-style orchestra. However, the sight lines in the Majestic are much better than that of the earlier theater.

Booked by the SHUBERT BROTHERS, the Majestic did not have an easy time attracting hit shows. The initial attraction, *Rufus LeMaire's Affairs*, closed after only 56 performances. SIGMUND ROMBERG, the great operetta composer, premiered *The Love Call* (10/24/27; 81 performances) with lyrics by the prolific HARRY B. SMITH. Several successful transfers from other theaters held the Majestic's stage, along with a few original failures. Boxer Jack Dempsey actually starred there in a Broadway play aptly titled *The Big Fight* (9/18/28; 31 performances).

The Shuberts then gained control of the Majestic and filled it with their productions. *Pleasure Bound* (2/18/29; 136 performances) was a minor revue that cost the producers little, because most of its cast and creative staff were on the monthly Shubert payroll. They probably used the sets and costumes over again in another of their shows. *A Wonderful Night* (10/31/29; 125 performances) was a retelling of *Le Reveillon*, the story that served as the basis for the opera *Die Fledermaus*. The music was also taken from Johann Strauss composer of the opera. A young cast member

was Archie Leach, who would later achieve fame in Hollywood as Cary Grant.

Impresario Lew Leslie, who had scored a big success with his *Blackbirds of 1928*, thought he had another hit with *The International Revue* (2/25/30; 95 performances). He poured $200,000 into the show and hired the *Blackbirds*' songwriters Jimmy McHugh and Dorothy Fields (*see* FIELDS FAMILY). They came up with a couple of big hit songs, "Exactly Like You" and "On the Sunny Side of the Street." Leslie hired a wonderful cast including Americans Harry Richman and Jack Pearl, the British star Gertrude Lawrence, and the Spanish dancer Argentinita. But despite their talents the show was one of the first victims of the Depression. Then Romberg returned with another operetta, *Nina Rosa* (9/20/30; 129 performances). OTTO HARBACH wrote the book, and Irving Caesar wrote the lyrics. However, stars Ethelind Terry, Guy Robertson, and George Kirk couldn't overcome the audience's antipathy toward operetta.

After a long, dark period the Majestic presented what seemed a sure hit. Instead of a dated operetta, the Shuberts booked the modern-style musical *Pardon My English* (1/20/33; 43 performances). AARONS AND FREEDLEY, two of Broadway's most successful producers, presented GEORGE AND IRA GERSHWIN and librettist Herbert Fields' (*see* FIELDS FAMILY) newest creation. The score contained several standards, including "Isn't It a Pity?" and "The Lorelei." Lyda Roberti's comic song "My Cousin in Milwaukee" also achieved a bit of fame. But the production failed to catch on in the depths of the Depression.

Ray Henderson and Lew Brown (*see* DE SYLVA, BROWN AND HENDERSON tried to buck the Depression with their production *Strike Me Pink* (3/4/33; 122 performances). Henderson and Brown contributed the score as well as co-authored the libretto, co-produced

"Chanin's Majestic Theatre, a revue house of 1800 seats, located in West Forty-fourth Street, which opens tomorrow night (Monday, March 28th). Occupying 140 feet of frontage on West Forty-fourth Street, on a plot 100 feet deep, the Majestic, which is built in stadium style, is the largest legitimate theatre in the Times Square district. It is the third unit to reach completion in the Chanin's West Side $12,000,000 development which in its entirety includes the Royale Theatre, opened in January, the Threatre Masque, opened in February, and the Lincoln Hotel, a thirty-story structure of 1400 rooms, to be completed in the late summer."

the show with silent partner Waxey Gordon, a notorious GANGSTER, and co-directed with Jack McGowan. However, none of their songs caught on with the public. The show starred Hal LeRoy, Jimmy Durante, Lupe Velez, and Hope Williams. *Strike Me Pink*'s opening night tickets cost $25, around 3 times the normal ticket price.

Murder at the Vanities (9/12/33; 298 performances) was a backstage musical mystery show produced by EARL CARROLL. Carroll set the show during a performance of his *EARL CARROLL'S VANITIES*, thus advertising his long-running revue series. The show contained a typical "Carrollian" number called "Virgins Wrapped in Cellophane." Carroll later moved his *Earl Carroll Sketch Book* to the Majestic, where it concluded its 207-performance run.

In 1936 the theater was occupied with revivals of Gilbert and Sullivan operettas produced by S. M.

Chartok. Casts of relative unknowns assayed *The Mikado*, *The Pirates of Penzance*, *Trial by Jury*, *HMS Pinafore*, and *Iolanthe*. None were successes, playing for a week or two each.

A stellar cast was featured in the musical *Stars in Your Eyes* (2/9/39; 127 performances). ETHEL MERMAN played the lead role, and the company also featured Richard Carlson, Jimmy Durante, Mildred Natwick, and Mary Wickes. Dancers Jerome Robbins, Alicia Alonzo, and Nora Kaye were all in the chorus. Arthur Schwartz (*see* DIETZ AND SCHWARTZ) and Dorothy Fields provided the fine score, and JOSH LOGAN directed.

Six years after *Strike Me Pink* struck out, Lew Brown returned to the Majestic with *Yokel Boy* (7/6/39; 208 performances). Brown collaborated on the lyrics with Charles Tobias, provided the libretto, and produced and directed the proceedings. Sam H. Stept wrote the music and was responsible for the one hit song, "Comes Love." Buddy Ebsen, Judy Canova, Dixie Dunbar, and Phil Silvers starred.

In 1942 Cheryl Crawford revived the Gershwin opera *Porgy and Bess*. Although it was not a success when first produced in 1935, the show scored this time around. In the cast were many of the original cast members, including Todd Duncan, Anne Brown, Ruby Elzy, J. Rosamond Johnson, and Warren Coleman. Another major revival, Franz Lehar's *The Merry Widow* (8/4/43; 321 performances), starred Jan Kiepura, Marta Eggerth, David Wayne, Melville Cooper, Gene Barry, and Ruth Matteson. Audiences were ready to forget the troubles in Europe and lose themselves in the Lehar music.

RODGERS AND HAMMERSTEIN opened what many people consider their greatest achievement, *Carousel* (4/19/45; 890 performances), starring Jan Clayton, John Raitt, Mervyn Vye, and Jean Darling. The THEATER GUILD production, under the brilliant direction of Rouben Mamoulian, proved to be the Majestic's biggest hit up to that time. *Carousel* contained such standards as "You'll Never Walk Alone," "If I Loved You," and "June Is Bustin' out All Over."

HAROLD ROME's *Call Me Mister*, an affectionate tribute to wartime America, moved from the National Theatre (*see* NEDERLANDER THEATRE), with Betty Garrett, Maria Karnilova, Jules Munshin, and Lawrence Winters leading the cast. Among the hit songs were "South America, Take It Away," "The Face on the Dime," and "The Red Ball Express." *Call Me Mister* struck a responsive chord and amassed a deserved 734-performance run.

Rodgers and Hammerstein struck out with their next offering, *Allegro* (10/10/47; 315 performances). The show was probably not as bad as critics thought, but they and the public expected more after *Carousel*. It featured John Battles, John Conte, and Annamary Dickey. Lisa Kirk scored big with her rendition of "The Gentleman Is a Dope." The songwriting team redeemed their reputation with a huge hit, *South Pacific* (4/7/49; 1,925 performances). MARY MARTIN, Ezio Pinza, Juanita Hall, William Tabbert, and the supporting company were given the opportunity to introduce such songs as "Dites-moi," "A Cockeyed Optimist," "Happy Talk," "I'm Gonna Wash That Man Right outa My Hair," "Some Enchanted Evening," "There Is Nothin' Like a Dame," "A Wonderful Guy," and "Younger than Springtime." Under Joshua Logan's direction the show was an immense hit, erasing the memory of the less-than-successful *Allegro*. The musical won many awards including the PULITZER PRIZE. However, Rodgers and Hammerstein's next production at the Majestic was another disappointment. *Me and Ju-*

liet (5/28/53; 358 performances) opened with Isabel Bigley, Mark Dawson, Bill Hayes, and Joan McCracken in the leads. The show made money, but critics considered it uninspired. "No Other Love" was the only hit tune in the otherwise second-rate score.

Shirley Booth was the star of the moderate success *By the Beautiful Sea* (4/8/54; 268 performances), along with Wilbur Evans, Mae Barnes, Cameron Prud'homme, and Libi Staiger. The show's score, by Arthur Schwartz and Dorothy Fields, didn't set off any fireworks, although it was entertaining and tuneful. An even bigger hit was DAVID MERRICK's production of *Fanny* (11/4/54; 888 performances) with wonderful songs by Harold Rome. Ezio Pinza returned to the Majestic in the show, ably supported by Walter Slezak, Florence Henderson, and, also returning to the Majestic, William Tabbert. *Fanny* was not an immediate success, but with a boost from some imaginative publicity STUNTS by Merrick and his press agent RICHARD MANEY, the show became a hit.

Next came Meredith Willson's masterwork, *The Music Man* (12/19/57; 1,375 performances) with Robert Preston, Barbara Cook, Pert Kelton, Eddie Hodges, and David Burns. The big hit tunes were "Till There Was You," "Seventy-Six Trombones," and "Ya Got Trouble." Songs like "Lida Rose" and "Sincere" became barbershop quartet standards after the Buffalo Bills introduced them. *The Music Man* accurately pictured the naive America of 1912. Later shows that attempted to cover the same territory often proved too treacly or condescending to their subjects.

In *Camelot* (12/3/60; 873 performances) LERNER AND LOEWE nearly equaled the brilliant score of *My Fair Lady*, and director Moss Hart (*see* KAUFMAN AND HART) gave the proceedings his usual polish. Julie Andrews was also a success, as was Richard Burton in his musical comedy debut. But the libretto by Lerner seldom caught fire, and the show fell short of the brilliance of *My Fair Lady*.

A series of failures followed *Camelot*. These included Judy Holliday's return to Broadway in *Hot Spot* (4/19/63; 43 performances); Mary Martin in the Dietz and Schwartz musical *Jennie* (10/17/63; 82 performances); and Arthur Laurents and STEPHEN SONDHEIM's *Anyone Can Whistle* (4/4/64; 9 performances), with Angela Lansbury, Lee Remick, and Harry Guardino. Finally a hit came when Sammy Davis Jr. starred in a musical version of the Clifford Odets drama *Golden Boy* (10/20/64; 569 performances). It boasted an impressive score by STROUSE AND ADAMS and a mostly successful book by Odets and William Gibson.

The remainder of the 1960s was inauspicious. *Funny Girl* transferred from the WINTER GARDEN THEATRE in March 1966 and remained until it transferred to the BROADWAY THEATRE in November to make room for the opening of Bob Merrill's musical, *Breakfast at Tiffany's*, due to open that December. But producer David Merrick closed the Richard Chamberlain and Mary Tyler Moore vehicle after four previews.

Since he already held the lease on the theater, Merrick filled in at the Majestic with a revival of *The Persecution and Assassination of Jean-Paul Marat as Performed by the Inmates of the Asylum of Charenton under the Direction of the Marquis de Sade*, which opened on January 3, 1967, and ran for 55 performances. Another transfer followed with *Fiddler on the Roof*, which moved from the IMPERIAL THEATRE on its way to the Broadway Theatre. *Fiddler* spent almost the entire year at the Majestic following its March opening.

The 1970s were dominated by musicals, opening with a musical version of *The Teahouse of the August Moon* entitled *Lovely Ladies, Kind Gentlemen* (12/28/70; 16 performances), which quickly failed. David Merrick's production of JULE STYNE and Bob Merrill's musical version of *Some Like It Hot*, called *Sugar* (4/9/72; 505 performances), was more successful. It starred Tony Roberts, Cyril Ritchard, and Robert Morse; Gower Champion directed. JERRY HERMAN's musical set in the silent film era, *Mack and Mabel* (10/6/74; 66 performances), starred Bernadette Peters and, returning to the Majestic, Robert Preston. The all-black musical version of *The Wizard of Oz*, entitled *The Wiz* (1/5/75; 1,672 performances), was supposed to be a quick flop, but it caught on with audiences and was a tremendous hit. John Kander and Fred Ebb wrote the Liza Minnelli vehicle, *The Act* (10/29/77; 233 performances), but it failed to catch on with audiences or critics. *Ballroom* (12/14/78; 116 performances) was Michael Bennett's first musical following the remarkable success of *A Chorus Line*, but the material was thirdrate and even Bennett couldn't make *Ballroom* come alive. It was fitting that Richard Rodgers' last show, a musical version of *I Remember Mama* (5/31/79; 108 performances), opened at the Majestic, where he had enjoyed some of his greatest successes. However, *I Remember Mama*, starring Liv Ullmann, was a quick failure.

In 1981 David Merrick's *42nd Street* moved to the Majestic from the Winter Garden Theatre, and remained there until 1987, when it moved across the street to the ST. JAMES THEATRE, *42nd Street* was forced to move so that the Majestic could be made ready for what is its most financially successful show, *The Phantom of the Opera* (1/26/88). The ANDREW LLOYD WEBBER musical was an enormous hit in London, and prior to opening on Broadway it had almost $20 million in advance sales.

On December 8, 1987, the New York City Landmarks Preservation Commission designated the interior and exterior of the theater a landmark. The commission stated that the theater was a "fine example of the romantic 'modern Spanish' style."

MAMMA LEONE'S RISTORANTE. 261 W. 44th Street, at 8th Avenue.

Mamma Leone's, New York City's largest restaurant, employed more than 400 people. It was primarily a tourist-oriented restaurant that catered to large groups who arrived in buses or on package tours from Times Square hotels. Leone's served huge amounts of Italian food.

The original Mamma Leone's Ristorante opened on April 27, 1906, in the Leone family's living room on West 34th Street. It seated only 20 diners, a far cry from the 1,250 patrons the restaurant seated at 239 W. 48th Street. The restaurant was opened at the urging of Enrico Caruso, who was present at the opening night dinner. That meal, featuring seven courses, cost only 50¢; Luisa ("Mamma") Leone was the chef. Her husband, Gerome, was against the idea of his wife working, but Caruso convinced him to let her open the restaurant.

In 1926 the restaurant moved to the 48th Street location and slowly expanded down the block, taking over the President Theater. It occupied 35,000 square feet with 11 dining rooms. The interior was decorated in a vibrant, kitschy manner with every square inch covered by paintings, plastic plants, flowers, and statuary. Developers purchased the Leone's site, and the restaurant's last meal on 48th Street was served on October 3, 1987. In April 1988 the restaurant relocated to the former Kippy's Restaurant in the Milford Plaza Hotel at Eighth Avenue and 44th Street, next door to the MAJESTIC THEATRE. However, the move was not successful, and the restaurant soon closed. The hotel space remains empty due to a battle over jurisdiction between the restaurant employees and hotel employees unions.

MANEY, RICHARD. Press agent known as "the Boswell of Broadway" and "The Homer of the Great White Way"; b. June 11, 1891, Chinook, Montana; d. Norwalk, Connecticut, June 30, 1968.

Famed press agent Richard Maney plugged away for more than 300 shows in his time. Playwright Russel Crouse wrote in 1945: "The hands that feed Maney include those of practically every producer of standing on Broadway and they are practically porous with Maney's teeth marks. He has corrected Gilbert Miller's English, questioned Orson Welles' veracity, blithely deflated Jed Harris and publicly derided Billy Rose—all the while being paid by them. There must be a reason for this. Foremost, I should think, is Maney's vicious, vituperative, almost sadistic honesty. There isn't any question of Maney's talking behind your back unless you turn it." Maney was probably the best PR man in his field and he knew it, but his attitude toward his compatriots in the theater was somewhat disdainful. Maney himself described his job as "a fusion of midwife, clairvoyant, public address system and hypnotist."

Maney graduated from the University of Washington in 1912. The next year he began working as a press agent for the national tour of actress ANNA HELD and her All-Star Jubilee. Maney didn't immediately take to the job, nor did he stay with it very long. His next position was as associate editor and then editor for the *American Angler* magazine. He put out the monthly for five years. But the theater somehow still called to him. In 1920 he was hired as press agent for the Broadway revue *Frivolities of 1920*. The show ran only 61 performances on Broadway, but it was enough to give Maney a foothold. He never left.

Among the biggest hits that Maney represented in the ensuing decades were *My Fair Lady, Camelot,* ANNIE GET YOUR GUN, *The Corn Is Green, The Male Animal, Arsenic and Old Lace, Private Lives, The Front Page,* and *Dial M for Murder.* He was the agent for all of Tallulah Bankhead's Broadway shows, including *The Little Foxes* and *The Skin of Our Teeth.* In fact, Bankhead had two things written into her contract: that Pete Smith be her stage manager and that Richard Maney be her publicist.

Bankhead was one of Maney's few close friends. They could drink for hours, arguing over sports, theater, and politics. The saloon of choice was Bleeck's Artist and Writers Club on 40th Street near the old *Herald Tribune* plant. Maney was ghostwriter on Bankhead's autobiography, and she in turn wrote a tribute to Maney in the *New York Times* after his death.

Maney, like many in his profession, preferred the company of journalists to that of theatrical types. However, Maney did defend actors by saying, "Despite the pettiness, the egomania and the persecution complex of stage folk, they are more amusing, more generous and more stimulating than any other professional group." He didn't hold the same regard for producers. "Producing is the Mardi Gras of the professions," he averred. "Anyone with a mask and enthusiasm can bounce into it." Wolcott Gibbs writing in *The New Yorker* commented that Maney treated his clients (the producers) with a healthy disdain: "There are a good many press agents in New York who operate on a sort of man-to-man basis. [Mr. Maney] is the only one who persistently treats them with the genial condescension of an Irish cop addressing a Fifth Avenue doorman." One producer asked Maney what he should wear on

opening night—a black or white tie. Maney answered, "A track suit."

Maney had little truck with most of the offerings presented by producers. He hated the theater and its audiences and their "notorious affair with mediocrity." He insisted that CRITICS should "bat the ears off" cheap and vulgar plays: "The statutes covering indecent exposure have been teached long enough." Maney said that one of the shows he represented "flew shut like a door."

Maney's first office was in the EMPIRE THEATER building. When that was razed, he moved to the 48TH STREET THEATRE. On his retirement in 1966 he celebrated the occasion by stating,

> Richard Maney, reformed altar boy, who entered this vale of tears in Chinook, Mont. in 1891 to the obbligato of coyote yelps, after 50 years of inflating and/or deflating the theater's famous and infamous, slapped the cover over his Underwood for the last time today.
>
> "Press agentry is an exciting profession," says Mr. Maney, "for one who can tolerate the pranks and prattle of children.
>
> "What is Mr. Maney going to do? Retire to my Connecticut estate and contemplate my navel."

MANHATTAN THEATER. *See* **Ed Sullivan Theater.**

MANSFIELD THEATER. *See* **Brooks Atkinson Theater.**

MARK HELLINGER THEATER. 237 W. 51st Street. Architect: Thomas Lamb. Opening: movie, Hollywood Theater, April 22, 1930, *Hold Everything*; legitimate theater, December 13, 1934, *Calling All Stars.*

The 1,600-seat Mark Hellinger is one of Broadway's most beautiful theaters and the last surviving Times Square movie palace. Thomas Lamb, designer of the theater was one of the greatest theater architects, responsible for such other former Times Square landmarks as the STRAND, RIALTO, and RIVOLI. The spectacular interior was designed by Lamb and Leif Neandross, chief designer of the Rambusch Decorating Studios.

Originally called the Hollywood, the theater was one of the last of the great movie houses built in America. The Depression, which hurt both the movie business and Broadway, brought theater construction to a standstill. In fact, the outer lobby of the Hollywood was built to support a much taller building, but the Depression forced the abandonment of that idea. Only in the mid-1980s did the building, which originally

Interior of the Mark Hellinger Theater.

housed the outer lobby, have a structure built over it; the Novotel Hotel occupies the site.

The Hollywood, which originally had its entrance on Broadway, began in 1930 as a flagship house for its owners, Warner Brothers. Four years later it housed its first legitimate production, *Calling All Stars*. Lyricist Lew Brown (*see* DE SYLVA, BROWN AND HENDERSON) produced the show and contributed lyrics to Harry Akst's tunes. Brown also wrote sketches and co-directed the show, which starred Judy Canova, Lou Holtz, Jack Whiting, Martha Raye, Gertrude Niesen, and Phil Baker. However, *Calling All Stars* lasted only 35 performances, and the theater reverted to showing movies.

Two years later, on October 28, 1936, the theater was renamed the 51st Street Theater, and for a time the theater's entrance was on 51st Street. The new entrance boasted an Art Deco design inspired by Frank Lloyd Wright. GEORGE ABBOTT's musical adaptation of *Uncle Tom's Cabin*, entitled *Sweet River*, opened in the renamed house but closed after only five performances. The theater's name reverted to the Hollywood on August 11, 1937, and beginning with *The Life of Emile Zola*, movies were again presented in the ornate auditorium.

In November 1939 the last of the *GEORGE WHITE'S SCANDALS* moved from the Alvin Theater (*see* NEIL SIMON THEATER) to finish its run at the Hollywood. Then the theater again became the 51st Street Theater with what everyone thought was a surefire hit: Laurence Olivier's production of Shakespeare's *Romeo and Juliet* (11/5/40; 35 performances). The audience was enthusiastic when the curtain rose, but by the end of the evening it was clear the production was not a success. The show featured Olivier's design and direction as well as a star turn as Romeo. Vivien Leigh as Juliet, Dame May Whitty, Edmond O'Brien, Wesley Addy, Cornel Wilde, and Halliwell Hobbes supported him.

The theater again presented motion pictures under its alternative name, the Hollywood. A new musical, *Banjo Eyes* (12/25/41; 126 performances), starred Eddie Cantor as the title character, with Audrey Christie, June Clyde, Lionel Stander, and Bill Johnson in supporting roles. Jacqueline Susann, who later went on to become a best-selling novelist, also appeared in the cast. The show, a musical version of *Three Men on a Horse*, boasted a score by VERNON DUKE and John Latouche. The hit song, "We're Having a Baby, My Baby and Me," had lyrics by Harold Adamson. The show promised to be the Hollywood's first hit and a much-needed success for composer Duke. Unfortunately, Cantor became ill, and the show closed prematurely.

The theater again reverted to movies. On August 15, 1947, while the film version of *Life with Father* was filling the seats, it was renamed the Warner Brothers Theater. The theater's name was changed again when Anthony B. Farrell bought it from Warner Brothers for more than $1.5 million in 1948. Farrell renamed the theater after Broadway columnist MARK HELLINGER, who had died on December 21, 1947. His first production at the theater was *All for Love* (1/22/49; 121 performances), a revue starring Grace and Paul Hartman and Bert Wheeler. It lost half a million dollars.

For a while at the end of 1949 Farrell booked the theater with Gilbert and Sullivan. He then mounted his second show, a musical called *Texas Li'l Darlin'* (11/25/49; 293 performances). The musical starred Kenny Delmar, Mary Hatcher, Danny Scholl, and Loring Smith. The score by Robert Emmett Dolan and Johnny Mercer was a letdown. Surprisingly, the show was a hit, the first for the theater since its opening almost 20 years before.

The success of *Texas Li'l Darlin'* seemed to reverse the theater's fortunes. Despite the lukewarm reception accorded the Hartmans in *All for Love*, they had a hit with the revue *Tickets, Please!* which moved from the Coronet Theater (*see* EUGENE O'NEILL THEATER) Jack Albertson, Larry Kert, Roger Price, and Dorothy Jarnac appeared with the Hartmans. Another revue, *Bless You All* (12/14/50; 84 performances), had a score by HAROLD ROME and featured Pearl Bailey, Jules Munshin, Mary McCarty, and Gene Barry. The theater's next hit, *Two on the Aisle* (7/19/51; 279 performances), headlined Bert Lahr and Dolores Gray. The revue marked the first collaboration between composer JULE STYNE and lyricists COMDEN AND GREEN. *Two on the Aisle* contained many fine revue songs, including "If You Hadn't but You Did" and "Give a Little, Get a Little Love."

Hazel Flagg (2/11/53; 190 performances), a new Jule Styne musical, had lyrics by Bob Hilliard and a libretto by Ben Hecht based on his screenplay *Nothing Sacred*. Styne produced the show himself, and Helen Gallagher, John Howard, Thomas Mitchell, and Sheree North starred. Jack Whiting made a comeback of sorts as the mayor of New York. He was given the show's big hit, "Every Street's a Boulevard." Another song, "How Do You Speak to an Angel," was a minor success.

The Girl in Pink Tights (3/5/54; 115 performances), SIGMUND ROMBERG's last Broadway show, was posthumously produced at the Mark Hellinger. It proved a surprisingly successful cap to an amazing career. Don Walker adapted Romberg's melodies and sketches into songs that were set to lyrics by Leo Robin. As Walker noted at the time, no one simply develops a score without doing a great deal of original writing. The show starred Jeanmaire, David Atkinson, and Charles Goldner. It contained Romberg's last hit song, "Lost in Loveliness."

The next original musical to play the Mark Hellinger was *Plain and Fancy* (1/27/55; 461 performances), which had an Amish setting. The show opened with Barbara Cook, Nancy Andrews, Shirl Conway, David Daniels, and Richard Derr starring. The Albert Hague and Arnold B. Horwitt score contained a bona-fide hit, "Young and Foolish," as well as a host of other good songs. The next offering was one of the greatest Broadway shows of all time. *My Fair Lady* (3/15/56; 2,717 performances) opened with Julie Andrews, Rex Harrison, Robert Coote, Stanley Holloway, John Michael King, and Cathleen Nesbitt starring. Alan Jay Lerner provided the witty, sophisticated lyrics and libretto, and Frederick Loewe provided the enchanting music (*see* LERNER AND LOEWE). Moss Hart (*see* KAUFMAN AND HART) directed, and Herman Levin produced. The score contained such standards as "On the Street Where You Live," "I've Grown Accustomed to Her Face," "Get Me to the Church on Time," "I Could Have Danced All Night," "With a Little Bit of Luck," and "Wouldn't It Be Loverly." *My Fair Lady* became the longest-running show in Broadway history, a record it held for more than a decade.

After a seven-month stay by RODGERS AND HAMMERSTEIN's last show, *The Sound of Music*, an Italian musical, *Rugantino* (2/6/64; 28 performances), opened at the Mark Hellinger. One of producer Alexander Cohen's most misbegotten ventures, *Rugantino* played in the original Italian with subtitles. The show was one of the most expensive flops at the time, although it was actually not a bad show. Then Jule Styne and Comden and Green returned to the Mark Hellinger with their gentle satire of Hollywood, *Fade Out—Fade In* (5/26/64; 271 performances). The Carol Burnett vehicle opened to mostly favorable reviews and settled in for a projected long run. Other cast members included Jack Cassidy, Lou Jacobi, Tiger Haynes, and Tina Louise. Some say the star got bored with her role, so she claimed she was injured. In any case, the show closed, reopened, and closed again. It was followed by *On a Clear Day You Can See Forever* (10/17/65; 280 performances), which boasted a superior score by BURTON LANE and Alan Jay Lerner. There were also exceptional performances by Barbara Harris and John Cullum. Lerner's libretto, however, didn't work as well, and it brought down the proceedings.

Three musicals opened and closed at the Mark Hellinger without much success: *A Joyful Noise* (12/15/66; 12 performances), starring John Raitt, Susan Watson, and Karen Morrow, with choreography by Michael Bennett; *Illya Darling* (4/11/67; 320 performances), based on the hit film *Never on Sunday*, with the film's star Melina Mercouri and director Jules Dassin; and *I'm Solomon* (4/23/68; 7 performances) with Dick Shawn and Karen Morrow in the leads.

Two major names saw their next productions at the Hellinger, but neither was a major success. JERRY HERMAN followed his string of hits—*Milk and Honey*, *Hello, Dolly!* and *Mame*—with a failure, *Dear World* (2/6/69; 112 performances). Based on Jean Giraudoux's play *The Madwoman of Chaillot*, the Alexander Cohen production featured the stars of *Mame*, Angela Lansbury and Jane Connell, as well as Milo O'Shea, Kurt Peterson, and Miguel Godreau. Alan Jay Lerner presented *Coco* (12/18/69; 332 performances), based on the life of designer Coco Chanel. Andre Previn provided the music for the underappreciated score. The show's draw was its star, Katharine Hepburn, making her musical comedy debut.

After a horrible attempt to convert the book and movie *Exodus* to a Broadway musical entitled *Ari* (1/15/71; 19 performances) and a visit by *Man of La Mancha*, came a big hit, *Jesus Christ Superstar* (10/12/71; 711 performances). The production, ANDREW LLOYD WEBBER and Tim Rice's first Broadway hit, was a rock musical based on the life of Christ. The director of *Hair*, Tom O'Horgan, repeated his somewhat unconventional style of staging with this show. Jeff Fenholt starred as Jesus, and future Broadway star Ben Vereen made an impression as Judas. "I Don't Know How to Love Him" was the hit song from the score.

After a potpourri of offerings the Hellinger hosted another Alan Jay Lerner show, the much-awaited *1600 Pennsylvania Avenue* (5/4/76; 7 performances), written in collaboration with LEONARD BERNSTEIN. The show followed the staffs and families who inhabited the White House in its early years. The Bicentennial tribute was a tremendous flop despite another underappreciated score. More failures followed: a reworking of *Kismet* entitled *Timbuktu!* (3/1/78; 243 performances), starring Eartha Kitt; Alexis Smith in *Platinum* (11/12/78; 33 performances); the Brazilian-inspired musical *Sarava* (2/23/79; 140 performances), produced by Eugene V. Wolsk with music by Mitch Leigh; and Clark Gesner's musical comedy *The Utter Glory of Morrisey Hall* (5/13/79), starring Celeste Holm, which closed on opening night.

Finally another success opened at the theater; the raucous, exuberant salute to BURLESQUE, *Sugar Babies* (10/9/79; 1,208 performances), which had former movie greats Ann Miller and Mickey Rooney in the leads. Producers Terry Allen Kramer and Harry Rigby and Ralph Allen, the show's conceiver, put together the best of burlesque and made sure that director Rudy Tronto and the entire creative staff presented the hoary old burlesque bits in a classy, imaginative setting.

Doug Henning, a superior magician, had a big hit in his first Broadway musical, *The Magic Show*. He tried to repeat his success with *Merlin* (2/13/83; 199 performances), which co-starred Chita Rivera, but he couldn't transform the material. Ben Vereen returned to the Mark Hellinger in *Grind* (4/16/85; 79 performances). The show opened with a score by Larry Grossman and Ellen Fitzhugh; Harold Prince directed the proceedings. A musical revue, *Tango Argentino* (10/9/85; 198 performances), followed *Grind*. The show featured seven pairs of tango dancers, four singers, and a band.

A series of one-person shows and industrial bookings followed at the Mark Hellinger. Peter Allen's musical *Legs Diamond* was the last legitimate show to play the theater. In 1989 the theater was leased for five years to the same church that occupied the NEDERLANDER THEATRE. Over the objections of many in the Broadway community, the theater was sold in 1992 to the church for a reported $17 million. Despite repeated attempts to buy it (Cameron Mackintosh wanted it for *The Phantom of the Opera*), the theater remains a church.

On November 17, 1987, the New York City Landmarks Preservation Commission gave the theater's interior landmark status. The commission called the theater "the last surviving grand movie palace in midtown Manhattan." The spaces are "an extraordinary adaptation of Baroque sources." The church has altered the facade.

MARQUIS THEATER. Marriott Marquis Hotel, Broadway between 45th and 46th Streets. Architect: John C. Portman. Opening: July 9, 1986.

The Marquis Theater was built in the new Marriott Marquis Hotel, one of the most controversial buildings in Times Square history. The hotel took the place of the MOROSCO, BIJOU, and HELEN HAYES theaters, and the ASTOR and VICTORIA movie theaters. The Broadway community did not think the trade was worth it. Louis Botto's excellent column in *PLAYBILL*, quoted architect/designer John Portman as claiming, "Our dream was to create a new theater for the Broadway of today that could handle any type of production, any kind of light and sound equipment, provide maximum comfort for audience and actors and still convey a feeling of intimacy." Portman succeeded admirably in many of those areas, although, like all new theaters, the Marquis lacks warmth and ornamentation.

The problems with the 1,600-seat theater are not in the auditorium design but in the theatergoing experience. The box office is located in an especially cramped little room on street level. Patrons must exit the box office area and go outside again to take the escalator to the theater proper. The theater has no real lobby of its own; instead, the hotel's common area is used as the theater lobby. This is a problem at intermission when patrons want to use the rest rooms. Because there are none reserved for theater patrons, audience members must use the hotel's rest rooms and make sure they have kept their ticket stubs to reenter the auditorium. The down escalator is so poorly designed that it requires the supervision of a guard. Patrons tend to bunch up at the bottom of the escalator, so the audience is allowed access to the escalator only in small groups.

Designers and theater technicians lambaste the theater because it contains no freight elevator. All sets must be designed to fit in the small passenger elevators of the hotel. The theater has also proved terribly uncomfortable for its performers. When it first opened, the stage area was sometimes so cold that the cast could actually see their breath; the hotel and theater shared heating and ventilation systems. The Marriott Corporation spent about $500,000 to give the theater its own heating, ventilation, and plumbing systems. The systems were also overhauled because of noxious fumes that were seeping into the backstage areas, causing nausea and dizziness. Among the causes for the fumes were an exterior vent for the sewer system, which was located only 30 feet from the theater's air intake, and ten drains in the floor of the theater spewing sewage that had backed up through the system. ACTORS' EQUITY executive secretary Alan Eisenberg was quoted in the *New York Times* as saying, "We are concerned that there may be damage to the actor. They are representing to us that it will be fixed. We expect a schedule." Equity announced that it would close *Me and My Girl* if the problems were not handled.

The theater's design maddened Broadway professionals, who had noted no such problems in the Helen Hayes or Morosco theaters. They pointed to the problems as another result of uncaring developers who tear down excellent historic theaters and replace them with unwieldy, poorly designed auditoriums.

The theater, run by the Nederlander Organization, opened with a concert by Shirley Bassey and comedian George Kirby. After that dry run, its first production, *Me and My Girl*, opened on August 10, 1986. The show was a smash in London and repeated its success in this country with its original star, Robert Lindsay. It closed after a remarkable 1,420 performances.

Sadly, the show would be the theater's last hit for quite a while.

Oba Oba '90 was the next show to open. The musical revue played 45 performances following its March 15, 1990, opening. It was followed by the musical version of James Clavell's best-selling novel *Shogun*. Perhaps Clavell himself shouldn't have attempted to write the libretto to what was titled *Shogun, the Musical* (11/20/90; 72 performances).

JULE STYNE, STEPHEN SONDHEIM, and Arthur Laurents' classic musical *Gypsy* completed its well-received revival at the Marquis. This, the second Broadway revival of the show, starred television's Tyne Daly as Rose. The production, under Laurents' direction, moved from the ST. JAMES THEATRE to the Marquis on April 18, 1991, where it completed its 476-performance run.

Arthur Laurents returned to the Marquis for its next production, *Nick and Nora*. But a fractious collaboration between composer Charles Strouse (*see* STROUSE AND ADAMS) and lyricist Richard Maltby Jr. didn't help the show, which forsook the customary out-of-town tryout. The talented cast, including Barry Bostwick, Joanna Gleason, Christine Baranski, and Faith Prince, couldn't help matters. The musical opened on December 8, 1991, and closed 9 performances later.

Raul Julia and pop star Sheena Easton opened in a revival of Mitch Leigh, Dale Wasserman, and Joe Darion's perennial hit, *Man of La Mancha*, only this time audiences weren't buying tickets. The production opened on April 24, 1992, and managed to squeeze out 108 performances.

The folks who produced *Oba Oba '90* at the Marquis returned with the overly optimistically titled *Oba Oba '93*. The Brazilian extravaganza opened on October 1, 1992, and closed after 22 performances.

The flops kept coming at the Marquis, albeit with talented people involved. NEIL SIMON adapted his hit play *The Goodbye Girl* into a musical with songs by Marvin Hamlisch and David Zippel. Again there was a strong cast, including Bernadette Peters, Martin Short, Carol Woods, and Scott Wise. But the show opened to negative reviews on March 4, 1993, and managed to use up its advance sale audiences after 188 performances.

March 3, 1994, found another revival, and another flop, on the Marquis stage although it boasted a long run. The production of *Damn Yankees* received mixed reviews but audiences were substantial enough to keep the show running with an excellent cast including Victor Garber, Jarrod Emick, Bebe Neuwirth, and Dick Latessa. The show became a hot ticket when, after a brief hiatus, it reopened with Jerry Lewis making his long-awaited Broadway debut. The revival played 718 performances but was still a financial failure.

Another legend made a rare appearance in the Marquis' next booking. Julie Andrews triumphed over a misbegotten musical version of her film success *Victor/Victoria* (1/25/95). The composer, Henry Mancini, died before the show opened, so lyricist Leslie Bricusse collaborated with Frank Wildhorn on additional songs. Andrews' husband, Blake Edwards, director of the film, repeated his assignment here despite no previous stage directing experience. Edwards also wrote the embarrassing libretto. Andrews vowed to stay with the production until it recouped, but after a long run of 734 performances, audiences dwindled, as did the stamina of the star. *Victor/Victoria* closed without recouping its investment.

One of America's greatest songwriters, Paul Simon, made his Broadway composing debut with the controversial musical *The Capeman* (1/29/98). The story of a Hispanic murderer riled the community, resulting in halfhearted picketing of the theater. Audiences were not drawn to the production, which was put together by Broadway neophytes including director-choreographer Mark Morris and librettists-lyricists Simon and Derek Walcott. By the time the overproduced show opened, the excellent cast featuring Marc Anthony, Ruben Blades, and Ednita Nazario didn't stand a chance. Simon's score was excellent (perhaps more suited to an oratorio), but the cast album, recorded on the Warner Brothers' label, has never been issued. *The Capeman* closed after 68 performances.

Following the transfer from the Walter Kerr Theatre (*see* RITZ THEATRE) of *Forever Tango*, the theater hosted a concert by French legend Charles Aznavour. He held forth on the Marquis stage for 23 performances following his October 21, 1998, opening. A revival of the musical *Peter Pan* (11/23/88) with Cathy Rigby made a brief stop at the Marquis for 48 performances.

The theater finally had another success with its next booking. And, again, a brilliant piece of stunt casting gave legs to a show about to fold its tent. An ill-conceived revival of IRVING BERLIN's masterwork *Annie Get Your Gun* opened at the Marquis on March 4, 1999, with Bernadette Peters in the lead, ably supported by Tom Wopat. The reviews were mixed (especially for Peter Stone's adaptation), but Peters and the score proved a moderate draw. When Peters left, she was replaced with TV actress Cheryl Ladd. The box office plummeted, but the producers, Fran and Barry Weisler, weren't ready to shutter the show. They cast country music star Reba McEntire as Ladd's replacement. McEntire (and her co-star Brent Barrett) received ecstatic reviews. Suddenly, the show became the hottest ticket in town and ran an astounding 1,045 performances.

A holiday season performance of Patrick Stewart's one-man version of Charles Dickens' *A Christmas Carol* played a limited engagement of 8 performances at the Marquis beginning December 24, 2001.

Thoroughly Modern Millie (4/18/2002), opened to decidedly mixed reviews.

The Marquis' auditorium is successful in most respects, but the inconvenient aspects of the theater's construction and the destruction of the Helen Hayes and Morosco theaters still rankle many concerned theatergoers.

MARTIN, MARY. Famed musical theater actor who created many memorable roles; b. Weatherford, Texas, December 1, 1913; d. Rancho Mirage, California, November 3, 1990.

Mary Martin and Ethel Merman—the two queens of the American musical theater—reflect two very different styles of singing and acting. Whereas Merman was a brassy siren, Martin portrayed a series of sly, sexy women with tomboyish enthusiasm and spirit.

Martin's interest in things theatrical seemed to be with her from the beginning. At age five she made her stage debut at a local fireman's ball. She took voice lessons with Helen Fouts Cahoon and sang in a recital when she was 12. For three months in 1930 she went to the Ward Belmont Finishing School in Nashville. When she returned to Weatherford and graduated from high school, she opened a dance academy. But she realized she was too inexperienced to teach and went to Hollywood to attend the Fanchon and Marco School of the Theatre. When she graduated, she returned to Texas, and soon there were three branches of the Mary Hagman School of the Dance (she had married Benjamin Jackson Hagman while in Tennessee).

The next summer she returned to the Fanchon and Marco school for more training. She went to Hollywood and dubbed vocal numbers for Margaret Sullavan and Gypsy Rose Lee. Universal hired her to coach Danielle Darrieux in singing and dancing, but the French star had her fired after Martin demonstrated a number for the film crew. Martin arranged to audition at the Trocadero nightclub during the club's weekly Sunday night talent show. The popular radio comedian Jack Benny was in the audience, and he was bowled over by the singer's interpretation of Arditi's "Il Bacio." Benny took Martin to his table and introduced her to Broadway producer Lawrence Schwab. Schwab invited her to appear in a musical comedy that he was planning. She signed a contract, and in the time before the show was to begin rehearsals, she appeared at the Trocadero.

Schwab meanwhile canceled plans for his musical, but he introduced Martin to playwrights Bella and Samuel Spewack, COLE PORTER, Sophie Tucker, Victor Moore, William Gaxton, and producer Vinton Freedley (*see* AARONS AND FREEDLEY). They were all involved in the production of a new musical entitled *Leave It to Me!* (11/9/38; 291 performances). Martin auditioned and was hired on the spot. She replaced singer June Knight, who had introduced "Begin the Beguine" in Porter's *Jubilee*. Knight's new husband would not let her sing "My Heart Belongs to Daddy" (which proved to be the hit song of *Leave It to Me!*) and forced her out of the show. Martin took over the role; during the number she did a modified striptease and stopped the show. *Leave It to Me!* opened at the Alvin Theater (*see* NEIL SIMON THEATER).

After its run concluded, Paramount Pictures signed Martin to a contract. She appeared in such movies as *The Great Victor Herbert*, *Rhythm on the River*, *Love Thy Neighbor*, *Kiss the Boys Goodbye*, *New York Town*, and *Happy Go Lucky*. The films, and Martin, failed to make much of a splash. Martin still owed six pictures to Paramount when her contract was terminated.

After leaving Paramount Martin returned to musical theater in the 1943 musical *Dancing in the Streets*. The show was written by VERNON DUKE, John Cecil Holm, Howard Dietz (*see* DIETZ AND SCHWARTZ), and Matt Taylor. It closed in Boston before coming to Broadway. After this disappointment came the joy of a starring role in the KURT WEILL and Ogden Nash musical *One Touch of Venus* (10/7/43; 567 performances). Martin appeared in the title role, a statue of the goddess that comes to life. The script was written by S. J. Perelman with Marlene Dietrich in mind. When Dietrich dropped out, Martin replaced her. Today Martin has a pure, wholesome image typified by *The Sound of Music*'s Maria and Peter Pan, but in the 1940s she was considered a star with a lot of sex appeal. Her comely figure and sensuous soprano voice helped make her a convincing Venus. *One Touch of Venus* opened at the IMPERIAL THEATRE with Kenny Baker, John Boles, Paula Laurence, Sono Osato, and Teddy Hart also starring. Martin was given three exemplary songs, "That's Him," "I'm a Stranger Here Myself," and "Speak Low."

Martin's next Broadway show was the musical *Lute Song* (2/6/46; 142 performances), by Bernard Hanighen and Raymond Scott. The only song in the score to achieve much fame was "Mountain High, Valley Low." *Lute Song* opened with Clarence Derwent (who later had an award [see CLARENCE DERWENT AWARD] named in his honor), Mildred Dunnock, and Rex O'Malley. Nancy Davis, who later became Ronald Reagan's second wife, also appeared in the show. After a sojourn in London at the Theatre Royal, Drury Lane, in Noël Coward's *Pacific 1860*, Martin toured the United States in IRVING BERLIN's *Annie Get Your Gun*.

OSCAR HAMMERSTEIN II had seen Martin in *One Touch of Venus* and swore that he would write a show for her. He made good on his promise when he, Richard Rodgers (see RODGERS AND HAMMERSTEIN), and JOSHUA LOGAN wrote *South Pacific*. The show, in which Martin gave her most mature, serious performance, is considered the high point in her career. Rodgers and Hammerstein provided her with great songs, including "A Cockeyed Optimist," "I'm Gonna Wash That Man Right outa My Hair," "A Wonderful Guy," and "Honey Bun." *South Pacific* (4/7/49; 1,925 performances) opened at the MAJESTIC THEATRE with a record $500,000 advance sale. After 2 years Mary Martin left the Broadway company to take the show to London.

Martin's next Broadway assignment was Norman Krasna's play *Kind Sir* (11/4/53; 166 performances), staged by Joshua Logan with Charles Boyer costarring. The cast also included Margalo Gilmore and Dorothy Stickney. It was followed by Martin's favorite role, the title character of *Peter Pan* (10/20/54; 152 performances). Producer Edwin Lester hired Martin to portray the eternally youthful character in a new musical version of the J. M. Barrie classic, written by two songwriting teams. The first, Moose Charlap and Carolyn Leigh, had written an excellent score, but Lester felt more songs were needed. JULE STYNE and lyricists Betty Comden and Adolph Green (see COMDEN AND GREEN) were brought in by Jerome Robbins after negative reviews in San Francisco. *Peter Pan* moved to Los Angeles and finally to Broadway's WINTER GARDEN THEATRE. The New York engagement was planned as a dress rehearsal for a live television broadcast. Cyril Ritchard played Captain Hook and Sondra

Lee played Tiger Lily. The show became a television perennial on NBC.

Martin then toured Europe in *The Skin of Our Teeth*, the classic comedy by Thornton Wilder. She brought the show to the United States and appeared in Washington, D.C., New York, Chicago, and finally a television production. The New York premiere took place at the ANTA Theater (see VIRGINIA THEATER) on August 17, 1955, and played a limited run of 22 performances. *The Skin of Our Teeth* was followed by national tours of *South Pacific* and *Annie Get Your Gun* and a one-person show, *Music with Mary Martin*.

Martin next appeared on Broadway in Rodgers and Hammerstein's last show as a team, *The Sound of Music* (11/16/59; 1,443 performances). Martin opened at the LUNT-FONTANNE THEATER along with Theodore Bikel, Brian Davies, Kurt Kasznar, Marion Marlowe, Patricia Neway, and Lauri Peters. *The Sound of Music* received mixed reviews, although Martin was treated kindly by the CRITICS. The performance and the fine score, including "Climb Every Mountain," "Sixteen Going on Seventeen," "My Favorite Things," "The Sound of Music," and "Do-Re-Mi," ensured the show a long run.

Next came one of Martin's few failures, *Jennie* (10/17/63; 82 performances). The musical, based on the early career of actor Laurette Taylor, had a score by

Mary Martin in *The Sound of Music*, 1959.

Arthur Schwartz and Howard Dietz, but it never jelled, and fights among the creative staff brought on a quick demise. In 1965 Martin played Dolly Gallagher Levi in JERRY HERMAN's *Hello, Dolly!* for the troops in Vietnam following a run in Tokyo. The production was then taken to Okinawa and Korea before closing. After a break it reopened on December 2, 1965, at the Theatre Royal, Drury Lane, in London.

Martin opened in the Tom Jones and Harvey Schmidt musical, *I Do! I Do!* (12/5/66; 560 performances). Gower Champion directed the proceedings, based on Jan de Hartog's play, *The Fourposter*. Martin's co-star, and the only other performer in the show, was Robert Preston. *I Do! I Do!* proved to be a marvelous show as produced by DAVID MERRICK. The production closed soon after the two stars left.

After *I Do! I Do!* it was widely assumed that Martin would retire. Instead she returned to the stage twice more, although the occasions were less than felicitous: *Do You Turn Somersaults?* (1/9/78; 16 performances), co-starring Anthony Quayle, and *Legends* (*1986*), with Carol Channing, closed out of town.

Mary Martin's vivacity and sly sexuality as well as her impressive singing and acting talents endeared her to two generations of theatergoers. Her portrayal of Peter Pan on television ensures her continued fame.

MARTIN BECK THEATRE. 302 W. 45th Street. Architect: G. Albert Lansburgh. Opening: November 11, 1924; *Madame Pompadour.*

Vaudeville impresario MARTIN BECK played out chapter one of his Broadway adventures when he built the PALACE THEATER. When the theater was taken over by the Keith/Albee (*see* E. F. ALBEE) vaudeville interests, Beck returned to his West Coast–based Orpheum Circuit. When he was forced out of the Orpheum Circuit, Beck returned to New York for the second chapter of his life on Broadway. Beck built the theater bearing his name in 1924 on what many people considered the wrong side of Eighth Avenue. However, the 1,200-seat theater proved immensely popular with audiences and theater people.

The first attraction at the Byzantine-style theater was the operetta *Madame Pompadour*, with music by Leo Fall, a favorite of Viennese audiences. Broadway audiences, however, were growing tired of operetta by the end of the 1920s and instead wanted musicals in a more modern vein. *Madame Pompadour* closed after 80 performances. The famous Clyde Fitch play *Captain Jinks of the Horse Marines* was adapted into a musical called simply *Captain Jinks* (9/8/25; 167 performances). It opened with Joe E. Brown, J. Harold Murray, and Marion Sunshine in the leads.

Actress Florence Reed shocked audiences as Mother Goddam in the sensational play *The Shanghai Gesture* (2/1/26; 210 performances). Reed's character kills her own daughter, a dope fiend, when it is discovered that the girl's father was a Britisher who had dumped Mother Goddam and, unbeknownst to himself, slept with his daughter—a coupling her mother had arranged when she found out he had married another woman. The play was laughed at by the CRITICS, but audiences couldn't wait to see the proceedings. Next, actor James Gleason, who would later achieve much success as a character actor in Hollywood, wrote a play, *The Shannons of Broadway* (9/26/27; 288 performances), which opened at the theater. Following this the THEATER GUILD took over the stage of the Martin Beck with a series of plays.

The first Guild play at the theater was *Wings over Europe* (12/10/28; 91 performances) by Robert Nichols and Maurice Browne, directed by the great Rouben Mamoulian. The play, whose subject was the enormous destructive power of atomic energy, proved to be prophetic. The drama was chosen as one of the year's 10 best by the *Best Plays* series. Critics enjoyed the play, although they admitted it was somewhat more intellectual than emotional. Next the Guild presented Dudley Digges, Claudette Colbert, Glenn Anders, and Helen Westley in EUGENE O'NEILL's little-known play *Dynamo* (2/11/29; 66 performances). O'Neill himself described the play's theme as "the passing of the old idea of a Supreme Being and the failure of Science, all-important in this day, to supplant it with something satisfying to the yearning soul of men permeated with the idea that the creations of Science are miraculous as the creations of the Supreme Being." The play was not exactly the prescription for the tired businessperson.

Miriam Hopkins, Claude Rains, Henry Travers, Helen Westley, and Morris Carnovsky starred in the next Guild presentation, *The Camel through the Needle's Eye* (4/15/29; 195 performances). The play was a natural for the Guild, which often presented middle-European light comedies. The play received good reviews from such disparate critics as WALTER WINCHELL and PERCY HAMMOND. Then, Lee Strasberg, Luther Adler, Lionel Stander, George Tobias, Gale Sondergaard, and Franchot Tone starred in *Red Rust* (12/17/29; 65 performances). This was the second Soviet play to appear on Broadway, and it was just as unsuccessful as the first, *The First Law*. It proved to be an important event nonetheless, for it was the first play presented by the Theater Guild Acting Company, which later metamorphosed into the GROUP THEATER.

Philip Barry's drama *Hotel Universe* (4/14/30; 81 performances) followed with Ruth Gordon, Morris Carnovsky, Glenn Anders, and Franchot Tone in the leading roles. It opened to decidedly mixed reviews. The Theater Guild actually printed opposing reviews next to each other in newspapers. Percy Hammond perhaps best expressed the audience's reaction to the play when he wrote: "I felt an embarrassed urge to cry out to Mr. Barry: 'Wait a minute! I didn't quite get that! Pray say it over again.' As it was, the night's pleasure was modified considerably by the feeling that I was but a yokel, astray in the court of Thespis, trying his best to join the proceedings and failing."

Roar China (10/27/30; 72 performances) featured a huge cast of mostly Asian actors. The drama concerned the Chinese rebellion and the British response. A model of a British warship filled the immense stage in a particularly stunning effect. The Lee Simonson set was among the most impressive of any in Broadway's history. Simonson wrote that director Herbert Biberman

> conceived the idea of using sampan sails as a scene curtain. They floated in a tank behind the front stage ramp. The tawny, interlocking sails formed a curtain that almost hid the gunboat; only its topmast was dimly visible. At a cry of "sampan, sampan" they parted, gliding with incredible grace to stage right and left, where their sails in shadow gave the suggestion of a river front harbor. As they opened the warship was dramatically revealed, in towering, menacing silhouette.

Despite the lavish sets, *Roar China* was perhaps too propagandistic for the typical audience member.

The first production of the new Group Theater was *The House of Connelly* (9/28/31; 91 performances) by Paul Green. It was presented at the Martin Beck Theatre under the auspices of the Theater Guild, with Franchot Tone, Art Smith, Stella Adler, Morris Carnovsky, Clifford Odets, and Robert Lewis in the cast. *The House of Connelly* was an auspicious debut for the new theater group.

After moving their successful production of *Elizabeth the Queen* to the Martin Beck, LUNT AND FONTANNE chose the theater for the opening of their next play, Robert E. Sherwood's comedy *Reunion in Vienna* (11/16/31; 264 performances). The cast also included Lloyd Nolan, Henry Travers, Helen Westley, and Eduardo Ciannelli. Richard Lockridge reflected the majority view of critics when he wrote in the *New York Sun*: "It is as light and frisky as one always believes Viennese comedy should be, and as one so seldom finds Viennese comedy is. It needs, apparently, an American to write it—and a couple of Americans to play it." In 1932 another group took over the stage of the Martin Beck Theatre. The Abbey Irish Theater Players presented productions of *Playboy of the Western World*, *Shadow of a Gunman*, *The Far-off Hills*, and *Juno and the Paycock* at the theater.

Next came Katharine Hepburn's return to Broadway after success in Hollywood. The play was *The Lake* (12/26/33; 55 performances), and the director was one of the most hated geniuses in the history of Broadway, Jed Harris. The production was a failure. Soon thereafter Dorothy Parker made her famous quip that in it Hepburn had "run the gamut of emotions from A to B." *Yellow Jack* (3/6/34; 79 performances) was Sidney Howard's dramatization of the yellow fever epidemic in Cuba and the search by Walter Read for its cause. The distinguished cast included James Stewart, Myron McCormick, Edward Acuff, and Sam Levene. *Yellow Jack* was a surprising failure.

In *Romeo and Juliet* (12/23/35; 78 performances), KATHARINE CORNELL received raves as Juliet, as did Basil Rathbone in the role of Romeo. The production also boasted the enormous talents of Orson Welles, Brian Aherne, John Emery, and Edith Evans. It was the second longest-running *Romeo and Juliet* in Broadway history. Cornell kept her dressing room at the Martin Beck with a revival of her classic production of *The Barretts of Wimpole Street* (2/25/35; 24 performances). The story of Robert and Elizabeth Barrett Browning also starred Brian Aherne, Brenda Forbes, and Burgess Meredith. Cornell continued her stay after the run of *The Barretts* with a production of John van Druten's *Flowers of the Forest* (4/8/35; 40 performances).

Maxwell Anderson's *Winterset* (9/25/35; 178 performances) was written entirely in blank verse. Burgess Meredith, who had appeared in the last two Cornell productions, starred in the drama about Sacco and Vanzetti with Richard Bennett, Eduardo Ciannelli, and Margo. A controversial play, *Winterset* was a revision of an earlier play presented by the Theatre Guild, *Gods of the Lightning*. The Guild wanted Anderson's play, but Anderson was committed to a production by the Group Theater. When they decided not to produce it, producer Guthrie McClintic was given the script. Anderson's decision to bypass the Theatre Guild was not unique. More and more playwrights were rejecting it, preferring to have their plays presented by producers more responsive to the needs of their plays. The loss of *Winterset* was a blow to the Theatre Guild. The play won the first NEW YORK DRAMA CRITICS' CIRCLE AWARD.

The Theatre Guild received another blow with Katharine Cornell's revival of George Bernard Shaw's *Saint Joan* (3/9/36; 89 performances). The Guild was Shaw's American representative, but it was not consulted when the playwright gave permission to Guthrie McClintic, Cornell's husband, to produce and direct the show. McClintic had previously produced *Winterset*, the other thorn in the Guild's side. The Guild was afraid that they would lose control of the American licensing of Shaw's work. To make matters worse for the Guild, the production, which also starred Maurice Evans, Brian Aherne, Eduardo Ciannelli, Kent Smith, Arthur Byron, and George Coulouris, was an immediate hit. Tyrone Power Jr., later to achieve fame in Hollywood, was also featured in the cast.

Maxwell Anderson's next play, *High Tor* (1/8/37; 171 performances), won the second Drama Critics' Circle Award. The play starred Burgess Meredith, Hume Cronyn, and Peggy Ashcroft. Surprisingly light after Anderson's *Winterset*, *High Tor* was the story of a man who owns a mountain and must deal with attempts to purchase it against his will. Ghosts of Dutch sailors waft through the play, giving the young man courage to keep his land.

HELEN HAYES appeared twice at the Martin Beck in the late 1930s. First, she revived her acclaimed performance in *Victoria Regina* (10/3/38; 87 performances). She later appeared in the Ben Hecht and Charles MacArthur courtroom drama *Ladies and Gentlemen* (10/17/39; 105 performances). The Martin Beck's next success was Lillian Hellman's anti-fascist drama *A Watch on the Rhine* (4/1/41; 378 performances) with Paul Lukas, Mady Christians, George Coulouris, and Lucile Watson in the leads. The play examines the moral dilemma a man faces when forced to defend his beliefs.

In S. N. Behrman's comedy *The Pirate* (11/25/42; 176 performances), Alfred Lunt played an actor who pretends to be a notorious pirate in order to impress a young innocent, played by Lynn Fontanne. Behrman's next play at the Martin Beck was even more successful. *Jacobowsky and the Colonel* (3/14/44; 415 performances), Franz Werfel's comedy, was adapted by Behrman for the talents of Louis Calhern, Annabella, J. Edward Bromberg, Oscar Karlweis, and E. G. Marshall.

After a transfer of the LEONARD BERNSTEIN, Betty Comden and Adolph Green (*see* COMDEN AND GREEN) musical *On the Town* from the 44TH STREET THEATRE came an original musical, *St. Louis Woman* (3/30/46; 113 performances). The HAROLD ARLEN and Johnny Mercer musical had a libretto by African-American poets Arna Bontemps and Countee Cullen. Rouben Mamoulian directed the proceedings, which featured Pearl Bailey, Rex Ingram, June Hawkins, Ruby Hill, Juanita Hall, and Harold Nicholas. The Arlen and Mercer score was among the greatest for any musical. It boasted such standards as "Any Place I Hang My Hat Is Home" and "Come Rain or Come Shine."

Eugene O'Neill's *The Iceman Cometh* (10/9/46; 136 performances) premiered at the Martin Beck with James Barton, E. G. Marshall, Nicholas Joy, and Dudley Digges in the cast. Katharine Cornell again appeared in a production of a Shakespeare play in *Antony and Cleopatra* (11/26/47; 126 performances). The im-

pressive cast included Godfrey Tearle, Eli Wallach, Kent Smith, Maureen Stapleton, Lenore Ulric, and Charleton Heston. The great actor returned to the Martin Beck stage in *That Lady* (11/22/49; 79 performances). Another well-loved American actor, Helen Hayes, appeared on the Martin Beck's stage in JOSHUA LOGAN's *The Wisteria Trees* (3/29/50; 165 performances), an Americanized version of Chekhov's *The Cherry Orchard*.

TENNESSEE WILLIAMS' drama *The Rose Tattoo* (2/3/51; 300 performances) was the theater's next hit. Maureen Stapleton, Eli Wallach, and Don Murray opened in the passionate drama, one of Williams' many successes in the 1950s. Another great American dramatist, ARTHUR MILLER, had an important play premiere at the Martin Beck, a thinly disguised indictment of the McCarthy hearings, *The Crucible* (1/22/53; 197 performances). Only five years later, the play was revived at the Martinique Theater off Broadway and ran 633 performances. By then the public had turned against McCarthy.

The Teahouse of the August Moon (10/15/53; 1,027 performances), a play by Kentuckian John Patrick, opened with David Wayne, Paul Ford, and John Forsythe. The comedy was an immediate success and became one of the decade's biggest hits. Critics hailed the story of attempts to democratize Okinawa following World War II. JOHN MASON BROWN stated, "No plea for tolerance between peoples, no editorial against superimposing American customs on native tradition has ever been less didactic or more persuasive." Patrick's play won five TONY AWARDS, the New York Drama Critics' Circle Award, and the PULITZER PRIZE.

An all-star revival of George Bernard Shaw's *Major Barbara* (10/30/56; 232 performances) starred Cornelia Otis Skinner, Burgess Meredith, Eli Wallach, and Glynis Johns along with director Charles Laughton. The next offering at the Martin Beck, the operetta satire *Candide* (12/1/56; 73 performances), was also an all-star production. This time the stars were the creative team, which included Leonard Bernstein, Dorothy Parker, Lillian Hellman, Richard Wilbur, and Tyrone Guthrie. *Candide* had an unusually stormy tryout run in Boston prior to New York. Luckily, Columbia Records recorded the show, and the album soon became something of a cult hit. Attempts to revive the show in 1959 (London) and 1971 also met with failure. Finally in 1974 a much-reworked version of the show opened with a brand-new concept by producer/director HAROLD PRINCE. This time *Candide* was a success.

Tennessee Williams had a flop at the Martin Beck when *Orpheus Descending* (3/31/57; 68 performances) opened with Maureen Stapleton. Like *The Crucible*, *Orpheus Descending* fared better in a later off-Broadway run. However, Williams' next offering was a big success. Geraldine Page and Paul Newman starred in *Sweet Bird of Youth* (3/10/59; 375 performances). Williams summed up the play's theme (and a thread that runs through all his works) when he stated: "Desire is rooted in a longing for companionship, a release from the loneliness which haunts every individual."

The 1960s began auspiciously for the Martin Beck with the first Broadway musical by the team of STROUSE AND ADAMS. They kicked off their long, successful Broadway collaboration with *Bye Bye Birdie* (4/14/60; 607 performances). Dick Van Dyke, Chita Rivera, Susan Watson, Dick Gautier, and Paul Lynde starred in the affectionate lampoon of Elvis Presley's induction into the army. Strouse and Adams' light and playful score contained such hit songs as "Kids" and "Put on a Happy Face." Next the Martin Beck hosted the work of another Broadway newcomer who would become one of the most successful writers of the musical theater. JERRY HERMAN's *Milk and Honey* (10/10/61; 543 performances), the story of a group of Americans visiting Israel, starred Robert Weede, Molly Picon, Mimi Benzell, and Tommy Rall.

The theater's offerings during the remainder of the 1960s showed great promise, but somehow none of the shows caught on with Broadway audiences. These included Edward Albee's adaptation of Carson McCullers' *Ballad of the Sad Cafe* (10/30/63; 123 performances), which starred Colleen Dewhurst and Michael Dunn; *I Had a Ball* (12/15/64; 184 performances), a musical with a fun, bright score by Jack Lawrence and Stan Freeman, starred Richard Kiley, Buddy Hackett, and Karen Morrow; the Royal Shakespeare Company's import *The Persecution and Assassination of Paul Marat as Performed by the Inmates of the Asylum of Charenton under the Direction of the Marquis de Sade* (12/27/65; 145 performances), with Glenda Jackson, Ian Richardson, and Patrick Magee; Edward Albee's Pulitzer prize–winning drama *A Delicate Balance* (1/14/67; 132 performances), with Jessica Tandy, Hume Cronyn, and Rosemary Murphy; and *Hallelujah, Baby!* (4/26/67; 293 performances), with a superior score by JULE STYNE, Betty Comden and Adolph Green, and an exceptional cast that included Leslie Uggams, Allen Case, Robert Hooks, and Lilian Hayman.

The Martin Beck estate sold the theater to the Jujamcyn Organization (the third-largest theater owners) in 1968. And finally the Martin Beck housed a hit, *Man of La Mancha*, which moved from off-Broadway on March 19, 1968. Star Richard Kiley was given the show's big song, "The Impossible Dream (The Quest)," with music by Mitch Leigh and lyrics by Joe

"Everything is Rosie" for Chita Rivera and Dick van Dyke in *Bye Bye Birdie*, 1960.

Darion. The show was an enormous success, playing 2,329 performances.

Edward Albee's third production at the Martin Beck, *All Over* (3/28/71; 42 performances), starred Jessica Tandy, Betty Field, Colleen Dewhurst, and George Voskovec. *All Over* was a disappointment in a disappointing decade. The Martin Beck Theatre finally housed a hit show in the 1970s with *Dracula* (10/28/77; 925 performances). Frank Langella starred as the Transylvanian vampire count and was proclaimed one of Broadway's brightest stars. Unfortunately, this would be his only success in the theater to date.

The 1980s proved even more depressing for the Martin Beck than the '70s. John Kander and Fred Ebb, the songwriting team responsible for *Cabaret*, opened their musical *The Rink* (2/9/84; 204 performances) there. The show had all the ingredients for success: a libretto by Terrence McNally and starring roles for Liza Minnelli and Chita Rivera. But the script and score were lackluster, and the show was a failure.

Into the Woods (1/5/87; 764 performances) was the first success at the Martin Beck in almost a decade. The STEPHEN SONDHEIM and James Lapine musical garnered mostly favorable reviews. Bernadette Peters, Chip Zien, Joanna Gleason, Kim Crosby, and Ben Wright starred as various fairy-tale figures for whom "happily ever after" turns to tragedy.

After *Into the Woods* the hit musical *Grand Hotel* (11/12/89; 1,017 performances) opened at the Martin Beck. The piece, based on the Vicki Baum novel, was originally produced by the Los Angeles Civic Light Opera Company as *At the Grand*. That 1958 production starred Paul Muni. But songwriting team George Forrest and Robert Wright of *Kismet* fame did not give up on their project. Finally, thirty years later, the show reached Broadway. Director Tommy Tune supplemented the Wright and Forrest score with additional songs by Maury Yeston, with whom he worked on the musical *Nine*.

A hugely successful revival of *Guys and Dolls* (4/14/92; 1,143 performances) was the next to play the theater. Starring Peter Gallagher, Josie de Guzman, Faith Prince, and Nathan Lane, *Guys and Dolls* inaugurated a new era of revivals on Broadway and at the Martin Beck.

Although the theater's last shows were great successes, it would be some time before a hit again played the Martin Beck. Following a 12-performance run of the play *My Thing of Love* (3/3/95), playwright Ken Ludwig's *Moon over Buffalo* (10/1/95; 301 performances) marked Carol Burnett's return to Broadway. But the poorly written, badly directed comedy couldn't be saved by Burnett or her acting partner, Philip Bosco. A documentary record of the ill-fated production was released on DVD as *Moon over Broadway*; it easily outdoes the original play.

Magician David Copperfield held forth on the Martin Beck stage for 55 performances beginning March 5, 1996. The sold-out engagement was followed by a flop revival of *Annie* (3/26/97; 239 performances) directed by librettist Martin Charnin. Nell Carter was the nominal star of the proceedings, which received major negative press when the girl originally cast as *Annie* was fired just prior to the show's opening.

Following a brief booking of the Moscow Art Theatre's productions of *The Cherry Orchard* and *Eugene Onegin*, the next revival was an ill-conceived remounting of RODGERS AND HAMMERSTEIN's last show, *The Sound of Music* (3/12/98; 533 performances). It was followed by a more successful revival, *Kiss Me, Kate* (11/18/91; 881 performances). Brian Stokes Mitchell and Marin Mazie starred in the COLE PORTER hit under the direction of Michael Blakemore.

Another failure, though a notable one, followed. Marvin Hamlisch and Craig Carnelia wrote a serious score to John Guare's excellent libretto based on the classic film *Sweet Smell of Success*. Although the show had much to recommend it, including standout performances by John Lithgow, Brian d'Arcy James, and their supporting cast, which included Eric Michael Gillett and Frank Vlastnik, critics lambasted the show. The review in the *New York Times* was especially vitriolic, and the *Times* took every opportunity to knock the show.

The next production at the Martin Beck was another revival. Brian Stokes Mitchell starred in *Man of La Mancha* (12/5/2002). During the run of *Man of La Mancha*, on June 23, 2003 the theatre was renamed the Al Hirschfeld after the famed artist.

On November 4, 1987, the New York City Landmarks Preservation Commission designated the interior and exterior of the theater a landmark. The commission stated: "A designer primarily of movie palaces, Lansburgh created for Beck a fantastic Moorish-inspired theater, among the most lavishly decorated in the Broadway area. Its interior is an unusual Moorish design, unlike any other Broadway theater."

MAXINE ELLIOTT'S THEATRE. 109 W. 39th Street, between Broadway and 6th Avenue. Architect: Ben Marshall. Opening: December 30, 1908; *The Chaperon*.

Maxine Elliott selected Ben Marshall, an architect from Marshall and Fox of Chicago, to design a showplace theater. As she wrote in the *Woman's Home Companion*, "For eight years I have cherished consistently—though I am a woman—the dream of building a theatre that should be small and intimate;

that should be beautiful and harmonious to the eye in every last detail; that should be comfortable for the spectators, and, behind the scenes, comfortable and humane for every least player in the company." Marshall designed what was the most expensive theater at that time, modeling the facade after Le Petit Trianon in Versailles. The stage house was clad in custommolded white brick whose pattern created a lattice effect.

Elliott, a supreme beauty, was dubbed "Venus de Milo with arms." Her only drawback was her lack of great talent. However, her theater, rumored to have been built by an admiring financier, outshone its competition. The theater was among the first to have running water and carpeting. Backstage, the five tiers of dressing rooms boasted full-length mirrors, outside windows, and private toilets. On the left side of the backstage was the star's dressing room, a 3-room suite. Elliott's husband, Nat Goodwin, was a popular actor. He didn't seem to mind it when Lee Shubert (*see* SHUBERT BROTHERS) bankrolled the theater's construction.

The theater began inauspiciously. After a string of failures *The Passing of the Third Floor Back* (10/4/09; 216 performances), by Jerome K. Jerome, opened. The next success was *The Gamblers* (10/31/10; 192 performances) by Charles Klein, known for his HIPPODROME extravaganzas and his play *A Milk White Flag*; Jane Cowl had the lead. Edward Sheldon's play *Romance* (2/10/13; 160 performances) starred Doris Keane. Part of its fame was due to Sheldon's plot, which concerned a preacher who was attracted to a loose woman. Audiences were relieved that the parson retained his composure throughout. Musicals also occasionally occupied the Maxine Elliott's stage. COLE PORTER's first attempt at Broadway, *See America First* (3/28/16; 15 performances), was unappreciated. In the cast was future movie star Clifton Webb, then a popular musical comedy performer.

Spanish Love (8/17/20; 307 performances), by Avery Hopwood and Mary Roberts Rinehart, was the first hit of the 1920s. *Spanish Love* set the stage for the theater's biggest hit, Jeanne Eagels in *Rain* (11/7/22; 648 performances) which, only 9 years after the opening of *Romance*, entranced audiences with the story of a minister who loses the battle for his virtue. Noel Coward's *Hay Fever* (10/5/25; 49 performances), about an infuriating but fascinating family led by a grand actress, was revived again and again throughout the world, although it was a failure at its Broadway debut.

Another English playwright, Somerset Maugham, saw a near-classic premiere at the theater, *The Constant Wife* (11/29/26; 295 performances). HELEN HAYES had a great success (later repeated in the movies) with *Coquette* (11/8/27; 366 performances). The GROUP THE-

ATER featured Lew Ayres in *Success Story* (9/26/32; 120 performances) at the Maxine Elliott's.

The last two successes at the theater were Lillian Hellman's *The Children's Hour* (11/20/34; 691 performances) and the drama *Separate Rooms* (3/23/40; 613 performances). In 1936 the Shuberts leased the theater to the Federal Theatre Workshop. In 1941 the Mutual Radio Network took over the theater for WOR. In 1944 CBS brought its radio operations to the theater and dubbed it Radio Playhouse No. 5. CBS then transformed the theater into a television studio where the first few years of *The Ed Sullivan Show*, then known as *The Toast of the Town*, was presented. In 1956 the Elliott estate sold the theater to the Shuberts, and they turned around and sold it to developers. When CBS's lease expired in 1959 the theater closed to make room for a skyscraper. In January 1960 the theater, the last remaining Broadway house south of 41st Street, was torn down.

MAYFAIR THEATER. *See* **Century Theater**.

MCCLAIN, JOHN. Critic; b. Marion, Ohio, 1904; d. London, England, May 3, 1967.

McClain became a columnist for the *New York Sun* in 1918 after graduation from Brown University and then Kenyon College. While at the *Sun* he did it all, from covering the police beat, criminal courts, City Hall, Brooklyn, the Bronx, and shipping news. Of his coverage of the liners arriving in New York he wrote that it was a "merry ball" in those "lovely days when there were no planes and everybody had to arrive in New York harbor, sometime, aboard an ocean liner.

"I would close the Stork Club at 4 A.M. and take a cab to the Battery and lie down aboard the Coast Guard cutter, to be awakened by Capt. John Parker when the cutter came alongside the ship I was to cover in the Narrows between Staten Island and Brooklyn. Making the tottering way aboard the vessel I would proceed to interview Greta Garbo and J. P. Morgan and sundry other luminaries and then retire, usually to the 'children's dining room' where I would be served a stiff beaker and a delicious breakfast. After the ship docked I would repair to the office, write the column and call it a day—usually in early afternoon." He would nap and then travel back to the Stork Club in the evening. He wrote for the *New York American*, and *New York Journal-American* for a decade beginning in 1928. After 3 years in Hollywood as a screenwriter (including the screenplay for *Cairo*), he joined the Naval Reserve as a lieutenant commander. In the service he was assigned to a photographic unit and took battle movies at Iwo Jima, in Africa, and in France.

On returning to New York after the war he rejoined the *Sun*, to write a column titled "Man about Manhattan," and later the *Journal-American*, where he became drama critic in 1951. He was named president of the New York Drama Critics' Circle for 1958 and 1959. But McClain tired of the Broadway beat. On April 24, 1966, he wrote in the *Journal-American*, "After more than 15 years it would be nice to have an evening life of one's own, when you can say with certainty that, sure, you can have dinner with some chums next Wednesday, without the threat that the show originally scheduled to open Tuesday has decided to postpone it a day, or that the one announced to open Friday has found a vacant theater and will move up the premiere to Wednesday."

He continued in another column, "I haven't been on 62nd Street in years and I think I've earned the right to have an evening at home. In any case, it is not fair to all concerned to cover the theatre reluctantly. Once enthusiasm wanes, you owe it to the theater to bow out. I'd like to be a travel editor."

The *Journal-American* ceased publication in 1965, by which time he was a travel editor at the merged *Herald Tribune World Telegram and Sun*, preferring to leave the editing to others and the traveling to himself.

McClain's fever for travel was not only centered on the world at large. McClain boasted that he had lived in more than 23 different apartments in New York City. His first domicile was a 6th-floor walk-up on Morton Street at the corner of Hudson in Greenwich Village. He then moved to an apartment on Gay Street and then a larger one on Christopher Street. He kept moving up the real estate market with flats in the Grosvenor and Fifth Avenue Hotels. He finally left the Village, making his way to the George Washington Hotel on East 23rd Street and then to Tudor City, the Barbizon-Plaza, the Algonquin, the Elysee, the Gotham, the Pierre, and the St. Regis.

But the one he liked best was a brownstone on East 55th Street where he and John O'Hara had ground floor apartments across the hall from each other. O'Hara had just had his novel, *Appointment in Samarra*, published, and McClain was seeing success in the magazine field. So the two authors decided to hire a butler and split his duties between the two apartments. Burton, the butler, quit after 6 months, tired of racing back and forth between the two apartments.

McClain reminisced about "more than 30 years of service in this ink-polluted atmosphere." He was unrepentant about his chosen field. "I think one of the greatest things in the world is to wake up every morning and be able to say, 'If I had my choice of what to do to earn a living I would be doing exactly what I am about to today.' I have been able to say this every day since I started out as a cub reporter on the old *New York Sun* in 1928, and that is a large order. How many men can match it?"

He also relished his role as a drama critic. "A fortune wouldn't reward you for the thrill of being there the night 'My Fair Lady' opened. Or many others—too many to mention—but there are the eight clinkers you have to sit through before you finally come up with 'Death of a Salesman' or 'A Man for All Seasons.'"

MERMAN, ETHEL. Grande dame of the musical theater, whose brassy singing enthralled decades of listeners; b. Ethel Zimmerman, Queens, New York, January 16, 1909; d. New York, New York, February 15, 1984.

Ethel Merman and MARY MARTIN are considered the two greatest actresses in the history of the American musical theater. Merman was the more boisterous of the two. Whereas Martin was a sexy tomboy, Merman was an up-front, no-nonsense dame. In an October 28, 1940, cover story on Merman, *Time* magazine described the singer as:

A dark, bouncy, oval-faced young woman. Ethel Merman can lay no great claim to great beauty, glamor or "legitimate" vocal quality, but she is a dynamic baggage with syncopation in every breath and gesture, and a voice with the hard, clarion, forthrightness of a jazz trumpet. Where most people hum or whistle for their personal pleasure, Ethel Merman imitates (Ta-ta-ta-ta!) the trumpet part.

Merman was the favorite of such songwriters as COLE PORTER, IRVING BERLIN, and GEORGE AND IRA GERSHWIN. Her trademark voice was known for its strength and clarity. Berlin once commented:

To me, her great quality as a singer is her genius at socking the whole meaning across. She's a lyric writer's dream; nobody in show business can project the lyric of a song like Ethel. She times a lyric as carefully and brilliantly as a comedian timing a gag. She sings with feeling for the audience and will space a passage when she gets a laugh.

Ira Gershwin said she had "a no-nonsense voice that could reach not only standees but ticket-takers in the lobby." Cole Porter described watching Merman from the audience's point of view: "It was like watching a train hurtle down the tracks, undeviating, the whole performance radiating zest and spontaneity, and yet you knew that it was exactly the same yesterday, and would be the same the day after." Merman appeared in many of the greatest shows in musical comedy history, chief among them *Gypsy* and *Annie Get Your Gun*. She introduced such standards as "It's Delovely," "I Got Rhythm," "I Get a Kick out of You," "Everything's Coming up Roses," "There's No Business Like Show Business," and "Life Is Just a Bowl of Cherries."

Merman claimed she was born in 1912; musical theater historian Stanley Green puts her birth at January 16, 1909; biographer Bob Thomas claims she was born a year earlier. Born Ethel Zimmerman in Queens, New York, she was discovered by talent agent Lou Irwin while performing in a club called Little Russia on 57th Street. Irwin arranged for her to be signed by Warner Brothers, which in 1929 was trying to conquer the new sound pictures. Warner Brothers signed her at $200 per week but couldn't quite figure out what to do with her. Her contract was not renewed after its 6-month period.

Producer Vinton Freedley (see AARONS AND FREEDLEY) heard Merman sing during an engagement at the Brooklyn Paramount. He arranged for Merman to meet George Gershwin at the composer's apartment at 33 Riverside Drive. George was joined by his brother Ira. Merman sang "Little White Lies" and "Exactly Like You" and impressed the two songwriters. They, in turn, performed two of the songs they had written for their new show, Girl Crazy (10/14/30; 272 performances), which Freedley and his partner Alex Aarons were producing at their Alvin Theater (see NEIL SIMON THEATER). They offered Merman a contract at $375 per week. While she rehearsed Girl Crazy, she was booked by Irwin into the PALACE THEATER. The Palace engagement resulted in her first New York Times review, a rave: "From the night clubs to her Palace debut comes Ethel Merman, a comely ballad singer, accompanied by Al Siegel, who is not so new. Miss Merman's torch singing premiere turns out to be an auspicious event in lyric celebration of the broken Broadway heart, and promises well for her debut later this season on the musical comedy stage."

The CRITICS' enthusiasm over her Palace engagement prepared them for Merman's musical comedy debut. Girl Crazy opened with Willie Howard, Ginger Rogers, and a band that included Glenn Miller, Jack Teagarden, Benny Goodman, Gene Krupa, Red Nichols, and Jimmy Dorsey. Merman was introduced singing "Sam and Delilah." In her next spot she nailed her stardom with a performance of "I Got Rhythm." Critic Robert Coleman enthused, "The big surprise of the evening was Ethel Merman, a young and talented songstress with a peculiar delivery who tied the proceedings up in knots. A graduate of night clubs and motion picture theaters, this girl bids fair to become the toast of Broadway."

After Girl Crazy closed Merman was booked into several clubs and a return to the Palace. GEORGE WHITE was trying out his latest edition of GEORGE WHITE'S SCANDALS in Atlantic City. He wired Merman to come and join the faltering show, and she agreed. White paid Aarons and Freedley $25,000 for Merman's services, as they had an option on her next show. The amount

was well spent. Merman's talents inspired songwriters Lew Brown and Ray Henderson to come up with one of their most enduring standards, "Life Is Just a Bowl of Cherries." The Scandals opened at the APOLLO THEATRE on 42nd Street on September 14, 1931. Merman also sang a duet, "My Song," with Rudy Vallee, and another effective solo, "Ladies and Gentlemen, That's Love." BROOKS ATKINSON caught the Merman style with an especially felicitous turn of phrase. He called her "queen of the singing announcers."

After more club appearances and another run at the Palace, Merman went into a new musical, Humpty Dumpty. Nacio Herb Brown, Richard Whiting, and B. G. De Sylva were the composers. Humpty Dumpty was in trouble on the road, and the show closed in Pittsburgh. The show was reworked and opened on Broadway as Take a Chance (11/26/32; 243 performances). Merman was given the hit tune "Eadie Was a Lady," along with "I Got Religion," VINCENT YOUMANS' "Rise and Shine," and a big hit, "You're an Old Smoothie" in a duet with Jack Haley. Merman's performance of "I Got Religion" was described in the magazine The Stage:

> The fluttering hands; the doubled fist extended toward you, Billy Sunday style, as though to seize your soul and raise it to heaven; the swing of the hips as she walks; the rolling of the shoulders and the accompanying wave of the head; the cocky stride ever so faintly suggestive of the ancient cake walk; the clasping of the quivering hands, imploring the audience to join in glory; the outspread palms, the raised fingers, the hands flinging at you a message of joy; and, at last, the arms stretched up to heaven, and the whole body straining to follow upward, as though one ounce more of faith would give it soaring wings.

Merman's next success also started out with a shaky out-of-town tryout. Cole Porter's Anything Goes originally had a book about a group of shipwrecked passengers. However, the real-life burning of the Morro Castle with 134 lives lost made the P. G. Wodehouse and GUY BOLTON libretto impossible to produce. Producer Vinton Freedley approached Howard Lindsay and Russel Crouse to rewrite the libretto and keep the passengers safely on board their ship. Anything Goes (11/21/34; 415 performances) was produced in the days before photocopiers. Performers received only their "sides," just the scenes they were in. The script was painstakingly typed with carbon copies. With changes in the script arriving daily, Merman's experience as a secretary came in handy. She copied down the changes in shorthand and typed up the corrections for herself and her fellow actors. The opening night at the Alvin Theater was a smash success. Porter had provided a brilliant score with many standards, including "I Get a Kick out of You," "All through the Night," "Blow, Gabriel,

Blow," "You're the Top," and the title tune. The role of Reno Sweeney gave Merman her first opportunity to create a classic musical comedy character.

After this great success Merman spent another unsatisfying stint in Hollywood. She returned to Broadway to appear in *Red, Hot and Blue!* (10/29/36; 181 performances), another hit show with a score by Porter. The Alvin was packed on opening night, with some patrons paying up to $50 for their tickets. They weren't disappointed when Merman, Jimmy Durante, and Bob Hope sang such terrific Porter numbers as "Down in the Depths," "Ridin' High," and "It's Delovely." The title of the show refers to Merman's character "Nails" O'Reilly Duquesne, who sat on a waffle iron as a child, thereby receiving the impression that figures prominently both on her posterior and in the plot. Brooks Atkinson again summed up the Merman manner: "She is still the most commanding minstrel in the business, wearing her costumes like a drum major, swinging to

the music and turning the audience into a congregation of pals for the evening."

Arthur Schwartz (*see* DIETZ AND SCHWARTZ) and Dorothy Fields (*see* FIELDS FAMILY) gave Merman her next Broadway assignment, *Stars in Your Eyes* (2/9/39; 127 performances). J. P. McEvoy's script called for Merman to play Jeanette Adair, a film star who inherits Monotonous Pictures from her late husband. Jimmy Durante, Mary Wickes, Richard Carlson, Tamara Toumanova, and Mildred Natwick joined Merman. Toumanova wasn't the only top dancer in the cast, which also included future greats Jerome Robbins, Alicia Alonso, Dan Dailey Jr., Nora Kaye, and Maria Karnilova.

Du Barry Was a Lady (12/6/39; 408 performances) was the singer's next Broadway outing. Cole Porter supplied the lively score, and La Merm, as she was dubbed, was ably supported by co-stars Bert Lahr and the young Betty Grable. B. G. De Sylva produced and

William Gaxton, Ethel Merman, and Victor Moore in *Anything Goes*, 1934.

collaborated on the libretto with Herbert Fields (*see* FIELDS FAMILY), and the fine and funny Porter score boasted at least one standard, "Friendship." The show was a smash in its out-of-town tour, but on its arrival on Broadway, the critics were not amused. They did, however, rave about Merman. JOHN MASON BROWN exclaimed in the *Post*:

> She needs no vitamins; she has plenty to spare. Her throat houses as beguiling a calliope as Broadway knows. The Midas touch is upon her tonsils because she can turn brass into gold. She can do more than that. She can keep it brass. No one can match her in putting a song across, in trumpeting its lyrics, in personifying its rhythms. All the bright lights of Broadway seem to shine behind her face. Hard-boiled she frankly is, but she makes toughness itself an irresistible virtue. She possesses not only great energy, but a kind of shimmering dignity, too; a dignity born of her poise, her skill, her honesty and her magnificent professionalism.

De Sylva convinced Merman and Porter to reteam for *Panama Hattie* (10/30/40; 501 performances), her first solo starring role. *Panama Hattie* opened at the 46th Street Theatre (*see* RICHARD RODGERS THEATER) with Betty Hutton, Oscar "Rags" Ragland, Joan Carroll, and Arthur Treacher in supporting roles. Porter was also the songwriter on Merman's next show, *Something for the Boys* (1/7/43; 422 performances). Herbert and Dorothy Fields wrote the script, which at one point was titled *Jenny Get Your Gun*. The producer of *Something for the Boys* was the extraordinary showman, Michael Todd. Todd was upset by the New York critics' practice of leaving shows early so they could make deadlines. Todd had his ushers block the aisles, and he himself refused to let Burns Mantle of the *Daily News* and Howard Barnes of the *Herald Tribune* pass. The reviews were mostly favorable, although some critics criticized the lightweight book and hitless score.

Annie Get Your Gun (5/16/46; 1,147 performances), produced by RODGERS AND HAMMERSTEIN, opened with an exceptional score by Irving Berlin. The Boston tryout went brilliantly, but New York had a wait-and-see attitude. It moved from Boston to New York's IMPERIAL THEATRE and was set to open when the heavy scenery broke a supporting beam. The show clearly could not open until the brace was repaired. The SHUBERT BROTHERS arranged for the show to move to Philadelphia while they saw to the repairs. The theater community believed the broken-beam story was just a cover to give the authors more time to fix the show. Word on the Rialto was that *Annie Get Your Gun* was doomed.

On its opening, the show, hailed by some critics as one of the greatest in musical comedy history, also received some less-than-favorable notices. Again, everyone praised Merman. Despite the mixed reviews

the show was an immediate smash hit. Berlin gave Merman a cornucopia of great songs. She introduced no fewer than five standards in *Annie Get Your Gun*: "They Say It's Wonderful," "I Got the Sun in the Morning," "Doin' What Comes Natur'lly," "There's No Business Like Show Business," and "You Can't Get a Man with a Gun."

Berlin was also responsible for the score of her next show, *Call Me Madam* (10/12/50; 644 performances). Lindsay and Crouse wrote the script, which was based loosely on the career of hostess Perle Mesta. *Call Me Madam* presented Merman as still more of a lady—in fact, ambassador to the mythical country of Lichtenburg. The show cost $225,000 to produce. The entire amount was covered by RCA, which bought the rights to the original cast album. RCA was galled later when Decca Records, which held Merman's contract, refused to loan her to RCA for the album. RCA had to substitute Dinah Shore while Decca put out its own album of the show's songs with Merman.

Call Me Madam was in trouble while out of town, and changes were added daily until Merman announced, as she did before every show, that it was frozen. From then on, nothing could be changed. When she announced "Call me Miss Birdseye" (an allusion to the show being frozen like Birdseye foods), the authors and director knew that no amount of cajoling could change her mind. John Chapman, writing in the *Daily News*, summed up the critical opinion: "Miss Merman is her old great self, singin' like a boat whistle and leering like a female Valentino, except when that confounded Graustarkian plot slows her down."

Lindsay and Crouse also wrote the script to Merman's next Broadway show, *Happy Hunting* (12/6/56; 412 performances). The show was not a happy experience for any of the creative staff. Merman constantly argued with her leading man, Fernando Lamas. Although the score by newcomers Harold Karr and Matt Dubey did contain one hit, "Mutual Admiration Society," there was little else of interest musically in the show, and Lindsay and Crouse's book was creaky. The show received more bad publicity when Lamas, after having kissed Merman onstage during a performance, wiped his hand across his mouth. When questioned by Mike Wallace, Lamas described kissing Merman as "somewhere between kissing your uncle and a Sherman tank."

Merman's last Broadway appearance in an original musical was also her greatest triumph. *Gypsy* (5/21/59; 702 performances), with a score by STEPHEN SONDHEIM and JULE STYNE and libretto by Arthur Laurents, was the musical story of Gypsy Rose Lee and her sister June Havoc's adventures in vaudeville and BURLESQUE. It starred Merman as the ultimate stage mother, Rose. Styne and Sondheim provided Merman with great

Ethel Merman in *Annie Get Your Gun*, 1946.

Ethel Merman in *Call Me Madam*, 1950.

in 1966, 1968, and 1969 in small theaters across the country, co-starred in *Dolly*. On December 27, 1970, the curtain fell for the last time on *Hello, Dolly!*—and on the Broadway career of Ethel Merman.

DAVID MERRICK. Legendary Broadway producer; b. David Margulois, St. Louis, Missouri, November 27, 1911; d. London, England, April 25, 2000.

Peter Ustinov called him the greatest producer of the 20th century. Others have called him the "abominable showman." But whether they love him or hate him, all agree that David Merrick was the most fabulous showman of our time, and maybe of all time. No other producer, neither FLORENZ ZIEGFELD nor the SHUBERT BROTHERS, has matched his percentage of hits or his flair for publicity. Even a partial list of his achievements includes some of the greatest shows ever presented: *Gypsy*, *A Taste of Honey*, *Irma La Douce*, *Hello, Dolly!*, *Cactus Flower*, *I Do! I Do!*, *The World of Suzie Wong*, *Stop the World—I Want to Get Off*, *Promises, Promises*, and *42nd Street*. At the height of his career, during the beginning of the 1970–71 season, Merrick presented seven shows on Broadway. At the same time he also had two shows on the road, one show in rehearsal, and four in the planning stages. By this stage in his career he had produced 16 shows on Broadway, of which all but 3 had been hits.

Merrick's musicals have employed most of the great composers and lyricists of our time, including HAROLD ARLEN and E. Y. HARBURG; JERRY HERMAN, Tom Jones, and Harvey Schmidt; JULE STYNE with both STEPHEN SONDHEIM and COMDEN AND GREEN; John Kander and Fred Ebb; and Bob Merrill. Although best known for his big splashy musicals, he also presented some of the most adventurous dramas, like *Look Back in Anger*, *The Entertainer*, *Epitaph for George Dillon*, and *A Taste of Honey*. He introduced such unconventional playwrights as John Osborne and Tom Stoppard to Broadway and American theatergoers.

It was Merrick who single-handedly created the famous "British invasion" of Broadway in the 1960s, when it seemed that only shows by British authors were being produced. In addition to the already mentioned shows, Merrick imported *Oliver!*, *Luther*, *Becket*, *Rattle of a Simple Man*, *Oh What a Lovely War*, and others. American playwrights were also introduced to audiences by Merrick; Woody Allen's first plays, *Don't Drink the Water* and *Play It Again Sam*, were successful David Merrick productions. Merrick introduced audiences to Barbra Streisand in *I Can Get It for You Wholesale*. He presented Thornton Wilder's *The Matchmaker* and later had it musicalized as *Hello, Dolly!* And Merrick led the way to the other black

songs: "Everything's Comin' Up Roses," "Small World," "Together, Wherever We Go," and "You'll Never Get Away from Me." But the greatest of all and the triumphant apex of Merman's career in musical theater was "Rose's Turn." The song came at the end of the spot that is reserved for the "eleven o'clock number," the big song that kicks up the audience's emotions before the curtain falls. "Rose's Turn" found the mother with her nerves exposed, unable to control her frustration over pushing her two daughters to be stars with no applause for herself. Producer DAVID MERRICK repeated the maneuver of Mike Todd, stationing himself at the head of the aisles to stop WALTER KERR from running out of the theater before "Rose's Turn."

In 1966, at the age of 58, Merman returned to New York to appear as Annie Oakley in a revival of *Annie Get Your Gun* for the Music Theatre of Lincoln Center. Irving Berlin even wrote a new song for the occasion, "An Old Fashioned Wedding." Merman's last Broadway appearance came in JERRY HERMAN's *Hello, Dolly!* The show was originally written for Merman, who had vowed after *Gypsy* that she would never appear in another original musical on Broadway. She was the last in a long string of Dollys when she assumed the part in March 1970. Russell Nype, who appeared with Merman in *Call Me Madam* on Broadway and musicals that flooded Broadway in the 1970s and '80s when he presented Pearl Bailey in an all-black version of *Hello, Dolly!* on Broadway and on the road.

Most of the great performers of the latter half of the 20th century appeared at one time or another in Merrick shows. MARY MARTIN, Lena Horne, ETHEL MERMAN, Anthony Newley, Ezio Pinza, Peter Ustinov, Woody Allen, and Jackie Gleason all enjoyed success in shows produced by Merrick. Gleason, shortly after the opening of the musical *Take Me Along*, exclaimed, "Merrick's the most terrific producer I've ever known. What a showman. What a guy!" Later Gleason also said, after many clashes with Merrick, "I can't stand David Merrick." All the arguments with Gleason and others were dutifully reported in the press, but that didn't bother Merrick. He knew it only resulted in greater ticket sales. Merrick did not really mind what was printed about him as long as the title of his current show was spelled correctly.

Merrick maintained an aura of mystery about his beginnings. He told a press-agent friend that he was born in 1946, the year he began his Broadway career. A decade later he claimed he was born on November 4, 1954, the day his first big hit, HAROLD ROME's musical *Fanny*, opened. We do know that he was born in St. Louis, the son of Celia and Samuel Margulois; they divorced when he was 10. He graduated with a law degree from St. Louis University, whereupon he made his way to New York. His arrival in 1940 was greeted with little fanfare, and for a while Merrick was unsure of how to proceed with his theatrical plans.

Merrick looked up producer Herman Shumlin, who was then raising money for *The Male Animal*. Merrick invested $5,000, and the success of the play returned him $20,000 as well as a place on Shumlin's staff. Merrick learned about the theater by working as Shumlin's assistant and later as a stage manager of Broadway shows on the road. He waited until it was the right time

Adolph Green, David Merrick, and Phil Silvers in rehearsal for *Do Re Mi*, 1960.

to break out on his own. From his first solo producing venture, *Clutterbuck*, through his last hit, *42nd Street*, Merrick's life was intertwined with the life of his shows.

Merrick's love-hate relationship with the press began with *Clutterbuck* (12/3/49; 218 performances). The play received less than enthusiastic reviews from the CRITICS, so Merrick conceived of a series of STUNTS to draw public attention to the show, such as having a fictitious Mr. Clutterbuck paged in hotel lobbies. Merrick's pet project was a musicalization of the Marcel Pagnol trilogy *Marius*, *Fanny*, and *Cesar*. He amassed a preproduction fund from one of Herman Shumlin's assistants, and he even threw in a little money of his own. At this time he didn't own the rights nor did he have a script or score or anything but the will to make it happen. As he demonstrated again and again, that was enough for David Merrick. He flew to France and begged Pagnol to assign him the rights. After a long battle, mainly to get Pagnol even to speak to him, the rights were attained.

Merrick wanted JOSHUA LOGAN, director of *South Pacific* and other smash shows, to direct *Fanny*. But Merrick did not know Logan. He did know Edward F. Kook of the Century Lighting Company through his relationship with Shumlin. Kook introduced Merrick to the great set designer Jo Mielziner. Mielziner arranged for Logan to attend a screening of Pagnol's film *Marius*. Logan remembered his first impression of Merrick. "He struck me a little like he strikes everybody," Logan said. "As an undertaker. Not a very happy looking face." Logan was not impressed with the film, and a year passed while Merrick hired and fired book writers. He finally asked Logan back to see the second film of the trilogy. "It was *Fanny* and I thought it was the most marvelous thing I'd ever seen in my life," recalls Logan. "I couldn't wait to do it."

Fanny's opening (11/4/54; 888 performances) might have meant the beginning of his life to Merrick, but the critics were less than inspired. Their reviews were apathetic, and there was no line at the box office window the next morning. But Merrick did not take his defeat lying down. Just as with *Clutterbuck*, Merrick took his fight to the media.

He allowed scenes from *Fanny* to appear on *The Ed Sullivan Show*. He took out the first full-page theatrical ads in the *New York Times* and the *Tribune*. He took out ads in foreign papers, hoping that tourists would see *Fanny* when they came to this country. If they came by ocean liner, they saw ads for *Fanny*; if they came from another city by train, they saw a giant billboard in Penn Station, and they were reminded of the show again when they hailed a taxi. He put ads in more than 40 American cities. When *Fanny* finally closed, the ledger showed a handsome profit of almost $1 million.

Merrick often had highly publicized fights with his stars. During the run of *Carnival!* (4/13/61; 719 performances), Anna Maria Alberghetti had a long-running feud with Merrick. After exiting the stage at one performance, her body mike was left on while she went to the ladies' room. It was shortly after this "accident" that Alberghetti came down with a mysterious malady that prevented her from performing unless her weekly check was increased. Merrick refused to be blackmailed and instead sent Alberghetti a lovely bouquet of plastic flowers. He then fired his star and built an enormous publicity campaign around her understudy, Anita Gillette. Merrick went so far as to invite the critics to Gillette's opening night. When the show was ready to tour, Alberghetti's sister Carla got the part.

But all these stories pale beside the saga of *42nd Street*, which opened in New York on August 25, 1980. Merrick's hit best illustrates his luck, charm, and savvy. Based on Warner Brothers' classic 1932 musical *42nd Street*, the show was planned as the most opulent musical on any stage. Merrick chose as director Gower Champion, the man who delivered Merrick's greatest hit *Hello, Dolly! Dolly*'s book writer, Michael Stewart, was brought on the project with newcomer Mark Bramble. The score was the same as that used for the movie, with other Harry Warren/Al Dubin hits added.

While on the road at the John F. Kennedy Center in Washington, D.C., the show was clearly in trouble. It ran about an hour too long. The costumes were late to arrive at the opening night performance, and when they did finally show up they were judged unbelievably ugly. Merrick's backers balked at putting more money into what was clearly a bomb. Merrick had been away from theater production during a 5-year sojourn in Hollywood, and the talk along the Rialto was that the master had lost his touch. To top it all off, director-choreographer Champion came down with what was reported to be a bad case of the flu.

Unable to raise more money through his investors, Merrick came up with an unheard-of plan; he bought each investor out, saving the investors from certain loss when the show finally reached New York. Merrick then proceeded to whip the show into shape. He threw out all the costumes and ordered a completely new set. By the time the show reached the WINTER GARDEN THEATER, it had been totally renovated. The book was reduced to "lead-ins and crossovers," according to the program. Champion had been in and out of hospitals and hadn't been seen near the theater for several days.

At the end of the opening night performance the audience gave the production a standing ovation. The critics had been asked to stay in their seats following the show, and the local television news teams were asked to send video crews and correspondents. Immediately after the curtain call Merrick strode onstage amidst thunderous applause. He quieted the audience and announced the death that afternoon of Gower Champion. The resulting publicity catapulted *42nd Street* into legendary status.

The momentum that *42nd Street* gained on opening night, plus later publicity and good word-of-mouth, kept the show running for more than 3,000 performances. VARIETY carried a headline reading, "David Merrick Hits a B'way Homer. 42nd Street Owner Grosses 500G Per Week." This $500,000 was pure profit for Merrick.

Merrick was again in the news when he suffered a near-fatal stroke. While he was in the hospital Merrick's current wife and his former wife were locked in a battle over the management of his estate. In a 2-week whirlwind of legal wrangling and its resultant publicity, Merrick divorced his then-current wife and remarried his previous wife. He appeared in court to prove himself competent to manage his own affairs, and to cap it all off, he escaped the hospital in a wheelchair, racing down First Avenue before being caught.

From his first productions through his triumphal return to Broadway, Merrick infuriated, amused, and astounded his public for almost 50 years. The David Merrick story is rich with fact and fiction, and it's anyone's guess as to where to draw the line. Whatever Merrick touched became news; each of his productions had its own story, which is also a reflection of the change in the theater since World War II.

A partial list of Merrick productions includes *The Willow and I* (12/10/42; 28 performances); *Bright Boy* (3/2/44; 16 performances); *Fanny* (11/4/54; 888 performances); *The Matchmaker* (12/5/55; 486 performances); *Look Back in Anger* (10/1/57; 407 performances); *Romanoff and Juliet* (10/10/57; 389 performances); *Jamaica* (10/31/57; 555 performances); *The Entertainer* (2/12/58; 97 performances); *The World of Suzie Wong* (10/14/58; 508 performances); *Epitaph for George Dillon* (11/4/58; 23 performances); *Maria Golovin* (11/5/58; 5 performances); *La Plume de Ma Tante* (11/11/58; 835 performances); *Destry Rides Again* (4/23/59; 472 performances); *Gypsy* (5/21/59; 702 performances); and *Take Me Along* (10/22/59; 448 performances). In the 1960s Merrick produced *The Good Soup* (3/2/60; 21 performances); *Vintage '60* (9/12/60; 8 performances); *Irma La Douce* (9/29/60; 524 performances); *A Taste of Honey* (10/4/60; 376 performances); *Becket* (10/5/60; 193 performances); *Do Re Mi* (12/26/60; 400 performances); *Carnival!* (4/13/61; 719 performances); *Ross* (12/26/61; 159 performances); *Subways Are for Sleeping* (12/27/61; 205 per-

formances); *I Can Get It for You Wholesale* (3/22/62; 300 performances); *Stop the World I Want to Get Off* (10/3/62; 556 performances); *Tchin-Tchin* (10/25/62; 222 performances); *Oliver!* (1/6/63; 744 performances); *Rattle of a Simple Man* (4/17/63; 94 performances); *Luther* (9/25/63; 212 performances); *110 in the Shade* (10/24/63; 330 performances); *Arturo Ui* (11/11/63; 8 performances); *One Flew over the Cuckoo's Nest* (11/11/63; 82 performances); *The Milk Train Doesn't Stop Here Anymore* (1/1/64; 5 performances); *Hello, Dolly!* (1/16/64; 2,844 performances); *Foxy* (2/16/64; 72 performances); *Oh, What a Lovely War* (10/30/64; 125 performances); *A Severed Head* (10/8/64; 29 performances); *I Was Dancing* (11/21/64; 16 performances); *The Roar of the Greasepaint—The Smell of the Crowd* (5/16/65; 231 performances); *Cactus Flower* (12/8/65; 1,234 performances); *We Have Always Lived in the Castle* (10/19/66; 9 performances); *Don't Drink the Water* (11/17/66; 598 performances); *I Do! I Do!* (12/5/66; 584 performances); *The Astrakhan Coat* (1/12/67; 20 performances); *Rosencrantz and Guildenstern Are Dead* (10/16/67; 420 performances); *How Now, Dow Jones* (12/7/67; 213 performances); *The Happy Time* (1/18/68; 286 performances); *Promises, Promises* (12/1/68; 1,281 performances); *Forty Carats* (12/26/68; 780 performances); and *Play It Again, Sam* (2/12/69; 453 performances).

In the 1970s, Merrick's productions include *Child's Play* (2/17/70; 342 performances); *The Philanthropist* (3/15/71; 72 performances); *Vivat! Vivat! Regina!* (1/20/72; 116 performances); *Moonchildren* (2/21/72; 16 performances); *Sugar* (4/9/72; 505 performances); *Mack and Mabel* (10/6/74; 65 performances); *The Misanthrope* (3/12/75; 94 performances); and *Very Good Eddie* (12/21/75; 304 performances); *42nd Street* (8/25/80) ran for 3,486 performances.

MILLER, ARTHUR. One of the greatest American playwrights; b. New York, New York, October 17, 1915.

Arthur Miller is the author of such American classics as *Death of a Salesman*, *A View from the Bridge*, *All My Sons*, and *The Price*. His serious and searching dramas probe the themes of human crises of identity and responsibility in relationships, also exploring the problems that arise when a person does not acknowledge change or current circumstances. Miller believes his plays are lessons for life.

The playwright owes a debt to the realistic theater of Ibsen, though he has benefited from more modern techniques of scene construction. His characters speak in the vernacular of the person on the street, but the language is heightened by Miller's dramatic powers, achieving a poetic quality.

Arthur Kennedy, Lee J. Cobb, and Cameron Mitchell in *Death of a Salesman*, 1949.

Miller began his playwriting career in the early 1940s as the author of radio plays. His first Broadway show, *The Man Who Had All the Luck* (11/23/44), opened at the Forrest Theater (*see* EUGENE O' NEILL THEATER) and played only four performances, but it certainly presaged his great talents. *All My Sons* (1/29/47), his first Broadway hit, was soon followed by what many consider his masterpiece, *Death of a Salesman* (2/10/49). The play, staged by Elia Kazan, starred Lee J. Cobb and Mildred Dunnock. It won the PULITZER PRIZE. *Salesman* told the story of Willy Loman, his wife, and their two sons, Biff and Happy, chronicling Willy's increasing incompetence and Biff's inability to hold a job and disillusionment with his father. Faced with the reality of his lies and the notion that Biff could be a success if only he had money, Willy kills himself so Biff can get the life insurance money. Willy dies a forgotten man with the legacy of a family ill-equipped for the modern world.

Miller's next Broadway outing was an adaptation of Ibsen's *An Enemy of the People* (12/28/50; 36 performances). It was in part a reaction to the wave of McCarthyism that was just beginning to break over the country. Next came another reaction to McCarthy's witch-hunt. The subject, the Salem witch trials of 1692, seemed perfectly analogous to the American political situation in the early 1950s. *The Crucible* (1/22/53), although it originally played only 197 performances, has received countless revivals over the years. The solid cast included E. G. Marshall, Walter Hampden, Arthur Kennedy, Jean Adair, Madeleine Sherwood, Philip Coolidge, Beatrice Straight, and Joseph Sweeney.

Miller changed his tack with his next plays, an evening of two one-acts, *A View from the Bridge* and *A Memory of Two Mondays* (9/29/55; 149 performances). They were sympathetic portrayals of two middle-class Americans. *After the Fall* (1/23/64; 208 performances) was inspired by Miller's marriage to Marilyn Monroe. It was a much better play than initial reaction to it indicates. Critics and audiences could not separate the drama from their feelings about Monroe. That same year Miller's drama *Incident at Vichy* (12/3/64; 99 performances), opened at Lincoln Center. Set against the horrors of Nazi Germany, *Incident at Vichy* portrays a Jewish psychiatrist who tells Prince Von Berg that he must learn to confront his collaboration with the Nazis with his own humanity, a major theme in Miller's plays.

In his next Broadway production, *The Price* (2/7/68; 429 performances), Miller portrays two brothers who are joined by their lack of appreciation of each other's differences. Estranged for years, the brothers know only how to be capitalists, without love or heart to make them human. He followed it with other less successful plays: *The Reason Why* and *Fame* (1970), *The Creation of the World and Other Business* (1972), *Up from Paradise* (1974), *The Archbishop's Ceiling* (1976), *The American Clock* (1984), and *Danger: Memory!* (1987).

Despite his lack of recent success on Broadway, Miller remains a major voice in the American theater. Although solidly rooted in the sensibilities of the 1940s and '50s, his plays have continued to speak to the common person's universal problems. Miller's humanity and compassion shine through his plays along with his profound sense of morality. Miller always believed in the importance of the theater in society. In 1951 he wrote, "The stage is the place for ideas, for philosophies, for the most intense discussion of man's fate."

MINSKOFF BUILDING. 1515 Broadway between 44th and 45th Streets. Architects: Kahn and Jacobs.

Sam Minskoff and Sons erected the Minskoff building in 1969 on the site of the beloved ASTOR HOTEL. The 50-story building was the first of the skyscrapers to blight the theater district. It was also the first to take advantage of the Times Square Theater District zoning bonuses, which allowed developers to build additional stories to their buildings if they included new legitimate theaters in their designs. Unfortunately, the resulting MINSKOFF THEATRE has more in common with a barn than a theater and is unpopular with both theatergoers and theater professionals. The building also includes the Loew's Astor Plaza movie theater, which remains one of the only large-screen movie theaters in Manhattan. (The other is the Ziegfeld.)

On the third floor of the Minskoff Building, overlooking Shubert Alley, were the Minskoff rehearsal rooms, used for rehearsals of Broadway shows. Many theater people considered the rehearsal rooms to be the only saving grace in a building that should never have been allowed. However, they were eventually converted into office space. One architecture critic said that the building's ridiculously designed top made it look like a 1950s-style spaceship that had crashed head first into Times Square.

MINSKOFF THEATRE. 1515 Broadway between 44th and 45th Streets. Architects: Kahn and Jacobs. Opening: March 13, 1973; *Irene*.

The Minskoff Theatre was built in the MINSKOFF BUILDING on the site of the ASTOR HOTEL. Although it contains many technical innovations, the auditorium is uncomfortable, and, with 1,600 seats, it is far too large for optimum viewing. The theater has no ornamentation and is considered one of the coldest looking of the new theaters. The theater's architects were quoted in *PLAYBILL* as claiming, "We think we've created one of the most exciting, three-dimensional processional routes for the theatergoers—a series of forms, changes in ceiling heights, and spatial explosions. The whole processional, from the moment you enter and rise thirty-five feet to the theater level, is a theatrical event in itself."

Although the walk to the auditorium is well designed, the theater is not. The balcony overhangs too far from the front of the stage, and the uppermost seats are also too distant. The orchestra area has what is called continental seating, with no center aisles, only two aisles on either side of the seats. Row T, for example, is 52 seats wide. Patrons who have tickets in the center of the row must cross over the feet of 25 people to get to their seats. On a matinee day, when many audience members have shopping bags, this can be extremely difficult. In its favor, however, the Minskoff was the first New York theater to be fully accessible to handicapped patrons.

The Minskoff has not attracted many successes. Its many critics think that the audience's distance from the stage and the coldness of the theater's design may account for its lack of hits. Architecture, sight lines, and acoustics all play their part in an audience's enjoyment of a show. While the theater can make a lot of money at capacity, most shows do not play to full

houses. The Minskoff's shows might do better in a more intimate house where a full audience might equal half or three-quarters of the Minskoff's capacity.

The first show to play the theater, *Irene* (3/13/73; 604 performances), seemed to promise a bright future for the new theater. A revival of a successful 1919 musical that originally premiered at the Vanderbilt Theater, it starred Debbie Reynolds, Patsy Kelly, Monte Markham, and George S. Irving. However, a series of concerts, ballets, and flop musicals followed *Irene*'s opening. *Rockabye Hamlet* (2/17/76; 7 performances) was directed by the usually reliable Gower Champion, but he made a mistake with this rock version of the Shakespeare classic.

The next original shows to play the Minskoff were *Angel* (5/10/78; 5 performances), a musicalization of Ketti Frings' play *Look Homeward Angel* that in turn was based on Thomas Wolfe's novel; *King of Hearts* (10/22/78; 48 performances), based on the French film; and *Got Tu Go Disco* (6/25/79; 8 performances). A revival of *West Side Story* (2/14/80; 333 performances) did not pay back its investors. Another revival, *Can-Can* (4/30/81), closed after only 5 performances. For one year the theater hosted Joseph Papp's version of Gilbert and Sullivan's *The Pirates of Penzance*, which moved from the Uris Theatre (*see* GERSHWIN THEATER), another huge, modern auditorium.

The theater's failures continued unabated. Charles Strouse (*see* STROUSE AND ADAMS) and Alan Jay Lerner (*see* LERNER AND LOEWE) fell under the theater's curse with their musicalization of Robert Emmett Sherwood's *Idiot's Delight*, which they titled *Dance a Little Closer* (5/11/83; 1 performance). *Marilyn: An American Fable* (12/16/83; 16 performances) was a musical version of the life of Marilyn Monroe that suffered an especially long preview period and became a legendary failure. Following a revival of *Sweet Charity* with Debbie Allen, the next failure at the Minskoff was *Teddy and Alice* (11/12/87; 77 performances), a musical starring Len Cariou.

A terrific revue, *Black and Blue* (1/26/94; 829 performances), occupied the Minskoff. It was a deserved and rare hit for the theater, featuring many top black performers including Ruth Brown, Linda Hopkins, Carrie Smith, Bunny Briggs, and a young Savion Glover. The show was lavishly produced by Mel Howard and Donald K. Donald and was imaginatively directed by Claudio Segovia and Hector Orezzoli and choreographed by Cholly Atkins, Henry LeTang, Frankie Manning, and the legendary Fayard Nicholas.

A couple of flops played the Minskoff, including the odd Polish musical, *Metro* (4/16/1992; 13 performances), before a revival of *Joseph and the Amazing Technicolor Dreamcoat* (11/10/93; 231 performances). The revival, a hit in London, was another failure at the Minskoff. Another London transfer by ANDREW LLOYD WEBBER, *Sunset Boulevard* (11/17/94; 977 performances), opened with Glenn Close, George Hearn, and Alan Campbell in the leads. Glenn Close was replaced by Betty Buckley and Elaine Paige during the long run, but the show closed a financial failure.

Another long-running failure came to the Minskoff, *The Scarlet Pimpernel* (11/9/97; 772 performances), with music by Frank Wildhorn and book and lyrics by Nan Knighton. Wildhorn had several long-running musicals on Broadway—all failures.

Two more flops appeared on the Minskoff stage. *Saturday Night Fever* (10/21/99; 501 performances) and *The Adventures of Tom Sawyer* (4/26/2001; 21 performances) were both met with lukewarm reviews and audience apathy.

MOLLY PICON THEATER. *See* **Jolson's 59th Street Theater.**

MOREHOUSE, WARD. Critic; b. Savannah, Georgia, November 24, 1898; d. New York, New York, December 7, 1966.

Morehouse began his journalistic career as a reporter for the *Savannah Press* in 1915. He moved to the *Atlantic Journal* in 1916 where he remained until 1919. He then moved to the *New York Tribune*, where during the next seven years he assumed the posts of reporter, rewrite man, assistant night editor, and drama columnist. In 1926 he transferred to the *New York Sun* as a reporter and drama columnist. He became drama critic for the *Sun* in 1943. In 1956 Morehouse moved to the S. I. Newhouse newspapers, and he eventually became drama critic and columnist ("Broadway after Dark") for the entire Newhouse chain. He also wrote a number of plays, including *Gentlemen of the Press* (1928), *Miss Quis* (1937), and *U.S. 90* (1941).

MOROSCO THEATRE. 217 W. 45th Street. Architect: Herbert I. Krapp. Opening: February 5, 1917; *Canary Cottage.*

The SHUBERT BROTHERS built the Morosco and named it in honor of Oliver Morosco, a West Coast producer who had helped the Shuberts break Erlanger's Theatrical Trust. The Morosco enjoyed a long history of distinguished productions, including *Death of a Salesman* and *Cat on a Hot Tin Roof*, until it was destroyed to make way for the Marriott Marquis Hotel and the Marquis Theater (*see* BATTLE TO SAVE THE HELEN HAYES, MOROSCO, AND BIJOU THEATERS).

Oliver Morosco's management of the theater only lasted seven years; the end of his tenure, was the result of a particularly confrontational divorce. His first pro-

duction in the new 1,009-seat theater was *Canary Cottage* (2/5/17; 112 performances). EARL CARROLL, famous for EARL CARROLL'S VANITIES, wrote the music and lyrics and co-authored the libretto with Elmer Harris. He also produced and directed the proceedings. Following *Canary Cottage* the theater got onto more serious affairs. EUGENE O'NEILL's *Beyond the Horizon* (2/2/20; 111 performances) and *The Bat* (8/23/20; 878 performances), by Mary Roberts Rinehart, were early successes. The PULITZER PRIZE–winning drama *Craig's Wife* (10/12/25; 360 performances) was written by George Kelly, best known as the author of *The Show-Off*. Crystal Heme played the shrewish wife who drives away her husband and neighbors and ends up an embittered, lonely woman. Also starring in the play were Anne Sutherland, Charles Trowbridge, and the great Josephine Hull.

Novelist Somerset Maugham's play *The Letter* (9/26/27; 105 performances) next opened at the Morosco. *The Warrior's Husband* (3/11/32; 83 performances) is best remembered today as the first good look theatergoers had at the talents of Katharine Hepburn. Next ALEXANDER WOOLLCOTT tried his hand at playwriting in collaboration with George S. Kaufman (*see* KAUFMAN AND HART); the pair produced *The Dark Tower* (11/25/33; 57 performances). Woolcott's fellow journalists slammed the play. Richard Dana Skinner, writing in the *Commonweal*, called it "a comedy of errors in taste and judgment." Woollcott took the reviews personally and was hugely depressed when the play closed.

Although *The Dark Tower* is largely forgotten, one aspect of its opening did make theatrical history and was responsible for a historic change in Broadway tradition. Producer Sam Harris was disgusted with the usual opening night audience, many of whom arrived late and noisily drunk. Harris decided to forgo the custom that offered the elite of New York society free tickets to all openings. Instead Harris democratized his show's opening night by making up a new list of friends, critics, and people he liked. Harris sent out a letter with the invitation that read in part:

> The management of *The Dark Tower* has promised the distinguished players assembled for its cast the unusual luxury of giving a first-night performance before an audience not predominantly composed of Broadwayites. To this end, a list of 500 citizens of this city has been drawn up, and the first call on the opening night seats will be reserved for them. Your name is on this list.

Any tickets not covered by the new list were put on sale at the box office. The press attacked him, but Harris had made his point, and soon all opening nights were handled in the same way.

Ward Morehouse at the *New York Sun* offices, 1945.

The Dark Tower also introduced another theatrical innovation. In the play the character of Max Sarnoff was really another character in disguise. The authors, wishing to fool the audience, felt that the plot twist might be given away if audience members noticed that there was no actor listed in the PLAYBILL as playing Max Sarnoff. So they simply made up the name Anton Stengel. The fictitious thespian even had a fabricated biography printed with the genuine biographies of the rest of the cast.

Tallulah Bankhead and Walter Pidgeon starred in *Something Gay* (4/29/35; 72 performances). Bankhead herself reviewed the play, quipping it was "as misleading a title as ever was hung on two hours of plot and dialogue." Critic Richard Lockridge concentrated his criticism on the author, Adelaide Heilbron: "Miss Heilbron's slight inadequacy as a writer of witty comedies apparently results only from an inability to think up any witty dialogue." *Call It a Day* (1/28/36; 195 per-

formances) starred Gladys Cooper, Frances Williams, and Glenn Anders; the THEATER GUILD produced this Dodie Smith comedy. GEORGE M. COHAN was reunited for a brief time with his former producing partner Sam Harris for *Fulton of Oak Falls* (2/10/37; 37 performances). Cohan extensively revised radio comedian Parker Fennelly's play for himself. Cohan's acting received glorious reviews, but the critics were less tolerant of his old-fashioned writing.

Noel Coward's delightfully wry comedy *Blithe Spirit* (11/5/41; 650 performances) entranced audiences with the performances of Mildred Natwick, Peggy Wood, Leonora Corbett, and Clifton Webb. One of the biggest hits in the Morosco's history was *The Voice of the Turtle* (12/8/43; 1,557 performances). The John van Druten comedy starred Margaret Sullavan, Elliott Nugent, and Audrey Christie. Coward wrote *Blithe Spirit* in five days; Van Druten wrote his even bigger hit in three weeks.

The Morosco Theatre, 1981.

The City Playhouses corporation bought the Morosco from the Shuberts in 1943. ARTHUR MILLER's greatest success, and another Pulitzer prize–winner for the Morosco, was *Death of a Salesman* (2/10/49; 742 performances). Lee J. Cobb created a masterful performance as washed-up salesman Willy Loman; he was ably supported by Mildred Dunnock as his long-suffering wife and Arthur Kennedy as his disillusioned, alienated son.

Another great American writer, TENNESSEE WILLIAMS, won a Pulitzer prize for a play presented at the Morosco: *Cat on a Hot Tin Roof* (3/24/55; 694 performances), the theatrically vibrant drama that starred Burl Ives, Mildred Dunnock, Ben Gazzara, and Barbara Bel Geddes. Elia Kazan staged the proceedings brilliantly. Critic BROOKS ATKINSON wrote in the *New York Times*, "It seems not to have been written. It is the quintessence of life. It is the basic truth."

Ives' character, Big Daddy, is one of Williams' greatest creations. Big Daddy's need to dominate his family and surroundings and his fear of sickness and death clashes with the desires of his equally strong-willed family. Williams used the tortured lives of his characters to work out his own feelings of loneliness and hostility, but try as he might in this searing play and others, Williams never succeeded in exorcising his own ghosts.

HELEN HAYES, Richard Burton, Susan Strasberg, Glenn Anders, and Sig Arno starred in Jean Anouilh's *Time Remembered* (11/12/57; 248 performances). VERNON DUKE composed the incidental music for the play. Patricia Moyes, the translator of the play, described it as "a joyful statement of faith in life, in common sense and in quality."

For the Morosco, the 1960s was a decade of comedies, including *Generation* by William Goodhart (10/

6/65; 299 performances), starring Henry Fonda, and DAVID MERRICK's production of Woody Allen's *Don't Drink the Water* (11/17/66; 598 performances), with Lou Jacobi, Kay Medford, Anita Gillette, Tony Roberts, and Dick Libertini.

In 1968 the theater was sold to a consortium of investors represented by the Bankers Trust Company. Arthur Miller's *The Price* (2/7/68; 429 performances) proved to be an exception from the comedy roster of the 1960s. It starred Pat Hingle, Kate Reid, Harold Gary, and Arthur Kennedy. *The Price* surprised and shocked audiences who were used to Broadway comedies that were more rooted in television than theater and to big empty musicals with catchy title songs and little else. *Forty Carats* (12/26/68; 780 performances), another David Merrick production, returned comedy to the stage of the Morosco. Jay Allen adapted a French play by Pierre Barillet and Jean-Pierre Gredy. Julie Harris starred along with Marco St. John, Polly Rowles, Murray Hamilton, Glenda Farrell, and Nancy Marchand. The story concerned a 40-year-old divorcee and her romance with a young man in his twenties.

The 1970s saw a series of serious dramas at the Morosco. Julie Harris returned to the theater in Paul Zindel's drama *And Miss Reardon Drinks a Little* (2/25/71; 108 performances). The play also starred Nancy Marchand, Virginia Payne, Estelle Parsons, and Rae Allen. Alan Bates came from London with *Butley* (10/31/72; 135 performances), a play by Simon Gray. An acclaimed revival of Eugene O'Neill's *A Moon for the Misbegotten* (12/29/73; 314 performances) opened with Jason Robards, Colleen Dewhurst, and Ed Flanders starring. *The Shadow Box* (3/31/77; 315 performances) was a no-nonsense drama about terminally ill patients and their families. The show boasted steady performances by Laurence Luckinbill, Mandy Patinkin, Josef Sommer, Simon Oakland, Patricia Elliott, and particularly Geraldine Fitzgerald. *The Shadow Box* won the Pulitzer prize. The Theater Guild presented William Gibson's play *Golda* (11/14/77; 108 performances) with Anne Bancroft in an acclaimed performance as Israeli political leader Golda Meir. A year later Hugh Leonard's very popular play *Da* (5/1/78; 697 performances) starred Barnard Hughes, Brian Murray, and Mia Dillon. Leonard's sequel to *Da*, *A Life* (11/2/80; 64 performances), also opened at the Morosco, but it was not a success. Barnard Hughes did not appear in the play; his wife, Helen Stenborg, did. Also appearing in *A Life* was Roy Dotrice and Pat Hingle.

In 1981 the Morosco was locked in a battle for survival along with the HELEN HAYES and BIJOU theaters. Playwright Arthur Miller wrote to James Watt, the Secretary of the Interior, to condemn the plan to destroy the theater. Miller's letter stated in part: "I think it is

the best theater in New York. The relationship of the auditorium to the stage is very nearly perfect; the height of the stage is optimum and the sight lines are superb. Perhaps most vital of all, the acoustical qualities are remarkable for their trueness. All of which is probably unique in a theater that is by no means small."

The Morosco and the people of New York lost, and in March 1982 the theater was demolished.

MOTOGRAM. The Motogram, the world's first "moving sign," has been a prominent Times Square landmark since 1928. The TIMES TOWER (now 1 Times Square) serves as the base for the 360-foot-long sign. The sign's 14,800 bulbs have announced major events in American history as well as the daily news and weather forecast. In 1910 *New York Times* owner Adolph Ochs allowed managing editor Carl Van Anda to post round-by-round results of the Jim Jeffries–Jack Johnson fight from a window on the tower. More than 30,000 people jammed the square to watch the results.

In the days before radio or television, the Times Tower became the focal point of important news and, of course, the annual New Year's Eve celebration. The *Times* realized that any paper that could draw 30,000 people to its windows would soon be recognized as the most important news organization in town. The management of the *Times* installed an electric sign to keep score of the Cincinnati–Chicago World Series of 1919. In 1921 10,000 people gathered at the base of the tower to follow the course of the Jack Dempsey–George Carpentier fight.

Seven years later, in 1928, the Motogram began operation with constant news bulletins. The sign's greatest moment came on V-J DAY when more than 750,000 Americans gathered to wait for news of the Japanese surrender in World War II. At 7:03 the Motogram lit the message. "Official—Truman announces Japanese Surrender."

In 1978 the Motogram was extinguished by the owner of the Times Tower in protest over the decay of Times Square. However, the sign was relit barely 10 years later with *New York Newsday*, a new daily paper, supplying the news.

MOVIELAND. 1567 Broadway at 47th Street. Architect: Herbert I. Krapp. Original name: The Central Theater. Opening: September 9, 1918; *Forever After*.

The SHUBERT BROTHERS built the Central Theater as a rival to the fabulously successful PALACE THEATER across the square. The lobby was built in a 19th-century brick building that was once the Matthushek & Son piano factory. It was one of the few theaters with an entrance actually on Broadway. The Shuberts proved unable to compete, however, and the Central, hosting plays

The Central Theatre, 1933.

and musicals, led a surprisingly unsuccessful life as a legitimate theater. One of its few hits was the Lew Fields (*see* FIELDS FAMILY) production of *Poor Little Ritz Girl* (7/27/20; 93 performances); RODGERS AND HART wrote their first Broadway score for the show. Unfortunately, much of their score was cut when the show was still out of town, and new songs by SIGMUND ROMBERG and Alex Gerber were added.

A film policy was established at the theater when the United Artists company leased the theater to premiere their films in 1921. In 1927 the Central became a movie house. In 1932 *Connie's Inn Revue*, the last show to play the theater, opened. In July 1932 the Minsky brothers leased the house from the Shuberts and made it their flagship BURLESQUE house. Three months later films took over briefly, but in 1934 the theater's name was changed to the Columbia and burlesque returned. Fiorello LaGuardia cracked down on burlesque during his administration, and two months later the

theater reverted to its original name and was returned to a film policy.

In 1942 burlesque type shows called "mirror-girl shows" briefly played the theater, but soon thereafter it reverted to grind film policy. In 1944 the theater's name was changed to the Gotham, and the movie policy continued.

The theater closed in 1951 for renovations and reopened as the Holiday. Once again live shows were presented on its stage; the first was *Bagels and Yox* (9/12/51; 204 performances). In 1952 a burlesque type show, *A Night in Havana*, quickly opened and closed. None of the subsequent shows was successful.

A revival of *Abie's Irish Rose* opened at the theater on November 18, 1954. It held on for 20 performances, not exactly equal to its original run. Christmas Day 1954 saw Harry Kurnitz' *Reclining Figure* open at the Holiday with Martin Gabel, David Opatoshu, Mike Douglas (yes, *that* Mike Douglas), and Nehemiah Persoff. It ran for a respectable (for the Holiday) 116 performances under the direction of Abe Burrows. Eva Le Gallienne, Enid Markey, and Parker Fennelly played in John Cecil Holm's comedy *The Southwest Corner* (2/3/55; 36 performances). On October 11, 1955, the Holiday saw the premiere of *Deadfall* with a cast consisting of Sheila Bond, Clarence Derwent, and John Ireland. The play closed after 20 performances. *The Righteous Are Bold* (11/22/55; 68 performances), by Frank Carney, produced and directed by Eddie Dowling, was the penultimate production at the theater. The last play to run at the Holiday was Mary Drayton's inaptly named *Debut*, which closed 5 performances after its February 22, 1956, opening. On February 26th the Holiday's life as a legit theater was over for good.

By 1957 strippers occupied the Holiday's stage. Shortly thereafter films returned. In 1958 the theater's name was changed to the Odeon; in 1965 it was called the Forum, its name became the Forum 47th Street in 1975. In the early 1980s, the name was changed once again to Movieland. Through all the changes in policy, the Shuberts retained ownership of the building. The theater was sold to a restaurateur in 1989. Soon demolition began, and, the site was replaced by what was supposed to be a Hard Rock Hotel. When the chain experienced financial troubles, the unfinished hotel was sold to the W chain.

MURRAY'S ROMAN GARDENS. 228 W. 42nd Street.

In the 1910s 42nd Street was making a name for itself with polite society. The best-known restaurant on the street was Murray's Roman Gardens, a forerunner to such famed Broadway eateries as MAMMA LEONE'S RISTORANTE. Like Mamma Leone's, Murray's Roman Gardens was decorated at the height of kitsch. The decor was a boldly imagined Roman garden complete with statuary, fountains, and temples. Pseudo-Roman and Egyptian murals decorated the walls. Unlike many Roman gardens, however, the restaurant boasted a revolving floor. In the spirit of later atmospheric movie theaters, Murray's appeared to the uninitiated to actually be outdoors. A moon even traversed the starlit ceiling several times each evening.

The next incarnation of the space at 228 W. 42nd Street was Hubert's Flea Circus. Certainly further down the entertainment scale than Murray's but even more realistic, Hubert's actually did contain a flea circus. Hubert's opened in 1925 and was looked on skeptically by Broadwayites who still considered 42nd Street to be smart and sophisticated. Its 10¢ admission allowed the patron to enter what was essentially a carnival sideshow. The walls were lined with distorting mirrors, such as those found in an amusement park

funhouse. The pitchman at Hubert's was Karoy, "the Man with the Iron Tongue." He bade the patron to plunk down an additional 15¢ to see belly dancers, and if the patron was over 18, another 15¢ would admit the curious to an educational exhibit on human sexuality, direct from the French Academy of Medicine in Paris. Hubert's 42nd Street branch (another was on 14th Street) had such acts as Libera, a contortionist, and Ajax, the sword swallower. Later patrons gaped at Albert-Alberta, half man and half woman, and Chief Amok, a headhunter. Hubert's emulated the notorious Victoria Theater (*see* GAIETY THEATER) presenting the famous as sideshow attractions. Boxer Jack Johnson and baseball great Grover Cleveland Alexander appeared on Hubert's stage. A cleaned-up Hollywood version of Hubert's can be found in the film *The Band Wagon*. FRED ASTAIRE sings the DIETZ AND SCHWARTZ song "Shine on Your Shoes" in a Hubert's-like environment.

Patrons during the 1930s might have been aghast at the degradation of taste Hubert's brought to 42nd Street. Imagine then how surprised they would have been if they could have taken a glimpse into the future to see that Hubert's closed for good in 1975 only to be replaced by a porno house named Peepland. Peepland gave way in the 1990s to the 42nd Street redevelopment, and the building was demolished.

MUSIC BOX THEATER. 239 W. 45th Street. Architect: C. Howard Crane. Opening: September 22, 1921; *Music Box Revue*.

Producer Sam Harris, who was previously GEORGE M. COHAN's partner, built the Music Box Theater with partner IRVING BERLIN at the start of the 1920s. The Adamesque exterior was modeled after Philadelphia's Chestnut Street Theatre. The intimate interior, designed by C. Howard Crane and William Baumgarten in ivory and green, proved ideal for plays and small musicals.

Critical reception of the new house's architecture was unanimous. ALEXANDER WOOLLCOTT, writing in the *New York Times* on September 23rd, 1921, exclaimed, "There's this odd thing about the theatre itself; it is not only costly but beautiful."

On the same date the *Evening Telegram* enthused, "It is an intimate theatre, so beautiful and so satisfying that its like is not to be found here or even in the great Continental centers. Sam Harris and Irving Berlin, its managers, may well be proud in that they have given New York a theatre unparalleled."

Harris and Berlin planned a series of revues for the theater. Revues were the vogue in the 1910, '20s, and '30s. There were the *ZIEGFELD FOLLIES*, *EARL CARROLL'S VANITIES*, *GEORGE WHITE'S SCANDALS*, the *Pass-*

Music Box Theater, October 31, 1949, the day after the opening of *Lost in the Stars* and its long box office line. Note the Hotel Piccadilly next door, demolished to make way for the Marriott Marquee Hotel.

ing Shows, the *Artists and Models* series, the *Greenwich Village Follies*, and others. The other revues stressed their opulence and girls. The big draws of the Music Box's revues were the scores by Irving Berlin and an almost European stylishness and refinement.

The first edition of the *Music Box Revue* (9/22/21; 440 performances) had a cast that included Sam Bernard (who said of the new theater, "It stinks of class"), the Brox Sisters, Florence Moore, Joseph Santley, Ivy Sawyer, Ethelind Terry, and Berlin himself. As planned, it was the score that received the most acclaim. Chief among the songs was "Say It with Music," one of Berlin's most enduring hits. Other popular songs from the score are "Everybody Step" and "The Schoolhouse Blues."

The second edition (10/23/22; 330 performances) of the series opened with much the same creative team:

Berlin wrote the music and lyrics, Sam Harris produced, and Hassard Short directed. This time the cast included John Steel, William Gaxton, Charlotte Greenwood, the Fairbanks Twins, and the comedy team of Clark and McCullough. The songs included "Pack up Your Sins and Go to the Devil," "Bring on the Pepper," "Crinoline Days," "Lady of the Evening," and "Will She Come from the East?"

The third edition (9/22/23; 277 performances) proved only a little less successful than its predecessors. The cast featured a return by the Brox Sisters, Joseph Santley, Ivy Sawyer, John Steel, and Florence Moore. Newcomers included Grace Moore, Frank Tinney, Phil Baker, and ROBERT BENCHLEY. Benchley, a popular CRITIC, humorist, and member of the ALGONQUIN ROUND TABLE, turned to acting with popular acclaim for his droll monologue "The Treasurer's Re-

361

port." Berlin provided his usual hit score, including "What'll I Do?" "Learn to Do the Strut," "The Waltz of Long Ago," and "An Orange Grove in California."

The fourth edition (12/1/24; 184 performances), the last in the series, starred Grace Moore, the Brox Sisters, and Clark and McCullough, alongside newcomers Claire Luce, Carl Randall, Oscar Shaw, and Tamara. The biggest star, however, was FANNY BRICE, borrowed from her home at the *Ziegfeld Follies*. Berlin's big hit from the score was "All Alone." Each edition of the series had done slightly less business than the previous edition.

The first straight play to be presented in the theater was *Cradle Snatchers* (9/7/25; 485 performances), a comedy by Russell Medcraft and Norma Mitchell. Margaret Dale played a woman who suspects her husband of cheating when she sees him lunching with a flapper. She decides to pay her husband back by hiring a college boy to make love to her. The wife's friends, Mary Boland and Edna May Oliver, like the idea. They don't trust their husbands either. A mad party fueled by champagne ensues, and the husbands arrive to find their wives slightly disarrayed. By curtain's end, the couples have come to an agreement, although Dale's character still decides to go to the movies with her college beau. The cast also included two future Hollywood stars, Raymond Guion (he changed his name to Gene Raymond) and Humphrey Bogart (playing the character Jose Vallejo). Another somewhat racy theme was treated in *Chicago* (12/30/26; 173 performances) in which Roxie Hart shoots her lover and, with the help of a lawyer who is more theatrical director than barrister, gets off without a conviction for the crime. Through the power of publicity, not only does she get out of jail, but she also secures a 10-week booking in vaudeville. The Maurine Watkins satirical comedy starred Francine Larrimore, Charles Bickford, Edward Ellis, Dorothy Stickney, and Juliette Crosby. Later the play served as the basis for the musical and movie of the same name.

Philip Barry's comedy *Paris Bound* (12/27/27; 234 performances) was an aptly titled show for the Music Box, because the theater's next offering was COLE PORTER's musical *Paris* (10/8/28; 194 performances). *Paris* was a Roaring Twenties show whose content was summed up by the title of one of its songs, "Let's Misbehave." However, "Let's Misbehave" was cut when the show was still out of town and replaced by the hit song of the show, the equally suggestive "Let's Do It." The star of the evening was the delightful French import Irene Bordoni. Porter received some of his best early reviews with *Paris*. The *New Yorker*'s critic had high praise: "No one else writing words and music knows so exactly the delicate balance between sense, rhyme and tune. His rare and satisfactory talent

makes other lyricists sound as though they'd written their words for a steam whistle."

Howard Dietz and Arthur Schwartz (*see* DIETZ AND SCHWARTZ) made history with *The Little Show* (4/30/29; 321 performances). The songwriting team was warming up for their biggest triumph, *The Band Wagon*. *The Little Show* was one of the first intimate revues that proved to audiences that all the Ziegfeldian trappings were not necessary for the enjoyment of a revue. Dietz and Schwartz contributed a big hit to the show, "I Guess I'll Have to Change My Plan." Herman Hupfeld wrote a novelty number for the show, "A Hut in Hoboken," that won some renown. Kay Swift and her husband, Paul James, had a hit with "Can't We Be Friends," and Ralph Rainger and Dietz wrote the classic "Moanin' Low," both introduced by the torchy Libby Holman. Other cast members included Fred Allen, Romney Brent, and Clifton Webb.

The 1930s began at the theater with *Topaze* (2/12/30; 159 performances). The next offering was one of the great hits of the decade, KAUFMAN AND HART's *Once in a Lifetime* (9/24/30; 305 performances). The comedy marked their first collaboration. Moss Hart had written the play and submitted it to producer Sam Harris. Harris thought it needed work and passed it on to George S. Kaufman. The plot was a satire of Hollywood, although neither author had actually been there. The two lead characters are second-rate vaudevillians, one very shrewd and one very dumb, who decide a fortune is to be made in Hollywood now that talkies are all the rage. They become vocal coaches for movie mogul Sam Glogauer's studio. George, the dumb partner, makes a series of inept mistakes, and naturally they are hailed as geniuses. George is promoted again and again until he rivals Glogauer himself. Following a particularly disastrous tryout, the play closed out of town. Further rewrites were undertaken, and the show was brought out again. This time it clicked and became a smash hit when it opened at the Music Box Theater. The cast included Hugh O'Connell, Jean Dixon, Grant Mills, Spring Byington (as a Louella Parsons character), Charles Halton, and George S. Kaufman himself as Lawrence Vail, a playwright whose sanity is ruined by Hollywood.

The Third Little Show (6/1/31; 136 performances), the last edition of this revue, opened at the Music Box with Edward Arnold, Constance Carpenter, Carl Randall, and Ernest Truex supporting the zany comedy of Beatrice Lillie. Herman Hupfeld's "When Yuba Plays the Rhumba on His Tuba" was the only original song to achieve any success. Noël Coward's "Mad Dogs and Englishmen" was introduced to American audiences in this show.

George S. Kaufman enjoyed two more hits at the Music Box in rapid succession. The first was the

GEORGE AND IRA GERSHWIN satirical musical *Of Thee I Sing* (12/26/31; 446 performances); Kaufman wrote the book with Morrie Ryskind. The brilliant score contained a healthy dose of satire as well as great romantic numbers: "Love Is Sweeping the Country," "Who Cares," and the title song. *Of Thee I Sing* starred William Gaxton, June O'Dea, Lois Moran, future politician George Murphy, and Victor Moore. After seeing the show, critic JOHN MASON BROWN wrote a letter to his wife paraphrasing Lovelace: "I could not love thee, dear, so much, loved I not Victor Moore." The authors, particularly Kaufman, were concerned that the audience would take offense at their swipes at the sacrosanct offices of president and vice president. In the 1930s when the whole country looked to the White House for relief from the Depression, the satire was quite risky. They need not have worried. John Mason Brown wrote in the *Post* that *Of Thee I Sing* "represents not only a new and welcome departure in the world of entertainment, but also in the field of American musical comedy. Here at last is a musical comedy which dodges nearly all the clichés of its kind, which has wit and intelligence behind it, which brings Gilbert and Sullivan to mind without being derived from them." The lone naysayer was the usually reliable *New Yorker* critic Robert Benchley who wrote, "I was definitely disappointed. *Of Thee I Sing* struck me as dull musically, and not particularly fresh satirically. The whole thing, during great stretches, was reminiscent of an old Hasty Pudding 'spoof' in which lese-majeste was considered funny enough in itself without straining for any more mature elements of comedy."

Benchley's review notwithstanding, the musical was a tremendous success, breaking the house record for the Music Box. Further proof of the show's excellence came when Kaufman, Ryskind, and Ira Gershwin were awarded the PULITZER PRIZE. The award was not made to George Gershwin, because the prize went only to writers of words, and he had written the music. Despite this obvious gaffe, the authors appreciated the Pulitzer. After all, it was the first time the prize was awarded to a musical. Ryskind was especially amused, because the person who signed his scroll was Dr. Nicholas Murray Butler of Columbia University. Years before, Dr. Butler had signed a letter to Ryskind expelling him from the university.

Before it closed, the show moved to the 46th Street Theatre (*see* RICHARD RODGERS THEATER) to make way for the next attraction at the Music Box: Kaufman and Edna Ferber's *Dinner at Eight* (10/22/32; 232 performances). Ferber described Kaufman's method of collaboration. As she sat at the typewriter taking down the ideas, Kaufman paced "hither, thither and yon or draped himself over and under or around such pieces of defenseless furniture as happened to be in the room."

When they actually put down some dialogue, they'd "wander all over the place, deciding on positioning, and we'd experiment with the spoken lines. I might add that we didn't spare our voices in the dramatic scenes. One of my maids and the man who cared for my lawn are still, I think, a little suspicious of our sanity."

Musical theater returned to the Music Box with the Irving Berlin and Moss Hart revue *As Thousands Cheer* (9/30/33; 390 performances). Sam Harris, who presented most of the plays in his theater, produced the show, and Hassard Short directed. Berlin's score contained one of his biggest hits, "Easter Parade." Ethel Waters let loose with "Harlem on My Mind" and "Heat Wave." Her big number, though, was the plaintive wail of a woman who must explain to her children that their father would not be coming home because he had been lynched. The song was "Supper Time," and Berlin had his doubts as to its part in a musical-comedy revue. Harris convinced Berlin to leave the song in, and Waters stopped the show with it every night. Clifton Webb sang "Not for All the Rice in China" in his impeccably clipped style. Other cast members included Marilyn Miller, the nominal star of the proceedings, and Helen Broderick.

Kaufman returned with his collaborator Moss Hart and their unconventional play *Merrily We Roll Along* (9/29/34; 155 performances). The play told its story in a reverse chronology. Audiences were not completely confused by the strange construction, but they certainly did not care for any of the cynical, disillusioned characters. Kaufman's next assignment at the Music Box was as play doctor for the Samuel and Bella Spewack drama *Spring Song* (10/1/34; 40 performances), produced by Max Gordon. Unfortunately, Kaufman couldn't save the show.

Kaufman was one of Harris' favorite playwrights, and he returned to the Music Box with *First Lady* (11/26/35; 244 performances), written in collaboration with Katharine Dayton. Reviewers felt that the character played by veteran actor Jane Cowl was fashioned on Alice Roosevelt Longworth. Kaufman was also responsible for the next play at the theater, *Stage Door* (10/22/36; 169 performances). He collaborated with Edna Ferber on the story of the performers at the Foot-Lights Club. Among the cast who played aspiring actresses were Margaret Sullavan and Jean Maitland. When Sullavan became pregnant and had to leave the show, Kaufman and Harris decided to close rather than attempt to replace her. Kaufman directed John Steinbeck's *Of Mice and Men* (11/23/37; 207 performances), the theater's next hit. The drama opened with Wallace Ford and Broderick Crawford in the leads. Kaufman worked on the script as an editor and technician. The dialogue was all by Steinbeck, who had written the original novel with the intent of turning the property into a play or film.

Kaufman and Hart's satirical musical *I'd Rather Be Right* moved from the Alvin Theater (*see* NEIL SIMON THEATER) to finish its run at the Music Box. The team then turned to producing with the revue *Sing Out the News* (9/24/38; 105 performances). HAROLD ROME wrote the music and lyrics and collaborated on the sketches with Charles Friedman, who directed the show. The cast included June Allyson, Mary Jane Walsh, Rex Ingram, Joey Faye, and Will Geer. The show's numbers were satirical in nature as indicated by such titles as "My Heart Is Unemployed" and the "Peace and the Diplomat Ballet." Rome's hit song from the show was the exuberant "Franklin D. Roosevelt Jones." Noël Coward's revue *Set to Music* (1/18/39; 129 performances) featured Beatrice Lillie singing such Coward songs as "I Went to a Marvelous Party" and "Mad about the Boy."

Kaufman and Hart were back at the theater with *The Man Who Came to Dinner* (10/16/39; 739 performances) starring Monty Woolley as Sheridan Whiteside, a character based on Alexander Woollcott. The play was an immediate hit and made Woollcott an even bigger celebrity in the public's eyes. Woollcott begged to play the part, although he had originally refused it. He was finally hired to lead the Pacific coast company.

When Sam Harris died in 1941 his share of the theater went to Berlin who later sold half ownership to the SHUBERT BROTHERS. Michael Todd's production of *Star and Garter* (6/24/42; 605 performances) opened at the Music Box with Gypsy Rose Lee, Bobby Clark, Pat Harrington, and Professor Lamberti. Critics were not kind to the show, which had more in common with BURLESQUE than musical comedy, but audiences loved being able to see burlesque in the safe environs of Broadway.

I Remember Mama (10/19/44; 714 performances) was one of the best-loved comedies of the 1940s. The play, written and directed by John Van Druten, starred Mady Christians, Oscar Homolka, Frances Heflin, and, making his Broadway debut, Marlon Brando. The first-time Broadway producers were the renowned songwriting team RODGERS AND HAMMERSTEIN.

The theater would not have a notable tenant until the opening of TENNESSEE WILLIAMS' *Summer and Smoke* (10/10/48; 102 performances), which was not a success. One problem was that audiences had seen *A Streetcar Named Desire* the previous year and expected more of the same. Williams actually wrote *Summer and Smoke* before *Streetcar* and after *The Glass Menagerie*, to which it is very similar in tone.

KURT WEILL's *Lost in the Stars* (10/30/49; 281 performances) was written with Maxwell Anderson. The PLAYWRIGHTS' COMPANY produced the musical, based on Alan Paton's novel *Cry, the Beloved Country*, which dealt with race relations in South Africa. Weill and Anderson's dramatic score was well served by Inez Matthews, Julian Mayfield, Herbert Coleman, and the original Porgy, Todd Duncan.

William Inge had three plays open at the Music Box in quick succession. The first, *Picnic* (2/19/53; 477 performances), starred Ralph Meeker and Janice Rule under JOSHUA LOGAN's sensitive direction. *Picnic* didn't please all the critics, but they did agree that Inge had the makings of a major American playwright. However, the critics were unanimous in acclaiming Inge's next play, *Bus Stop* (3/2/55; 478 performances). They praised Inge for tempering his themes of loneliness and the longing for dreams to come true. *Bus Stop* starred Kim Stanley, Albert Salmi, Elaine Stritch, Anthony Ross, Lou Polan, and Phyllis Love. Harold Clurman directed brilliantly, helping Inge make the conflicts more human and sometimes even funny. Inge's third play was *The Dark at the Top of the Stairs* (12/5/57; 468 performances). Through the story of a boy's suicide, Inge explored the unbreakable links that bind a family and the search for true freedom and tolerance. Pat Hingle and Teresa Wright starred, and Elia Kazan directed.

Claire Bloom and Rod Steiger were featured in the hit play *Rashomon* (1/27/59; 159 performances) at the Music Box, and at the end of that year Peter Shaffer's first play, *Five Finger Exercise* (12/2/59; 337 performances), opened at the theater with Jessica Tandy and Brian Bedford. Shaffer was hailed for his excellent use of language as well as his incisive understanding of class, society, and sexual tensions. One of the "angry young men" who changed the face of British drama, Shaffer impressed critics as having the artistic and technical means to convey the ideas that less-talented playwrights were addressing.

Following Henry Denker's play about Sigmund Freud, *A Far Country* (4/4/61; 271 performances), with Kim Stanley and Steven Hill, came S. J. Perelman's comedy, *The Beauty Part* (12/26/62; 85 performances). It opened to excellent reviews, but due in part to the NEWSPAPER STRIKE OF 1962–63, it closed a failure. Marilyn Stasio described the play as "a mad show, a happy marriage of the most refined wit with the most insane low-comedy traditions. It was eighteenth-century rococo literary humor laced with pit humor. It was the world of baroque in tandem with the world of burlesque. It was a howl." Bert Lahr and the whole cast gave an inspired performance, or rather a series of inspired performances. There were 17 people in the cast playing 40 to 50 parts. The characters had names like Octavia Weatherwax, Vernon Equinox, April Munkhood, Chenille Schreiber, and Mrs. Lafcadio Mifflin.

The comedy *Any Wednesday* (2/18/64; 983 performances) opened with Don Porter, Sandy Dennis,

The Homecoming, 1967. Back row: Terence Rigby, Michael Craig. Seated: Paul Rogers, John Normington, Ian Holm. Front row: Vivien Merchant.

Gene Hackman, and Rosemary Murphy. The show, Muriel Resnik's first play, suffered a particularly grueling tryout period before its opening. The playwright told the story of her play's difficult birth in one of the great theater books, *Son of Any Wednesday*. After changes in cast and directors, the show opened to rave reviews and ran through 1965. Two undistinguished plays opened at the theater in 1966, and the year was completed with the move to the Music Box of *Wait until Dark*, which completed its long run at the theater.

Harold Pinter's disturbing drama *The Homecoming* (1/5/67; 324 performances) opened direct from the Royal Shakespeare Company. The play concerns a university teacher's wife who decides to become a prostitute and move in with her in-laws. Some critics viewed the play as an indictment of the drawing-room comedy; others felt that the play had no viewpoint. Pinter became one of the most important playwrights of his time in part due to this production.

Following Terrence Frisby's *There's a Girl in My Soup* (10/18/67; 321 performances), with Gig Young,

came Anthony Shaffer's *Sleuth* (11/12/70; 1,222 performances). The two-character mystery thriller opened with Anthony Quayle and Keith Baxter. The British invasion continued with Alan Ayckbourn's *Absurd Person Singular* (10/8/74; 592 performances), produced by the THEATER GUILD and the John F. Kennedy Center. Another English import, *Comedians* (11/28/76; 145 performances) by Trevor Griffiths, was followed by another show developed in England. *Side by Side by Sondheim* (4/18/77; 390 performances), a retrospective of STEPHEN SONDHEIM's works, starred the original English cast: Ned Sherrin, David Kernan, Millicent Martin, and Julia McKenzie. Playwright Ira Levin brought another thriller to the Music Box with *Deathtrap* (2/26/78; 1,793 performances). The play starred John Wood and Marian Seldes. She stayed with the show throughout its run. John Pielmeier's *Agnes of God* (3/30/82; 486 performances) was another hit at the theater. Geraldine Page and Amanda Plummer starred in the mystery/drama.

The next years proved to be dire for the Music Box, with a series of quick flops. Finally in 1987 the theater had a mild success with the London transfer of *Les Liaisons Dangereuses* (4/30/87; 149 performances). Lindsay Duncan and Alan Rickman headlined the Christopher Hampton drama.

More flops followed until the engagement of Aaron Sorkin's drama *A Few Good Men* (11/15/89; 487 performances). The show, already optioned for the movies, was mounted in order to work out the kinks before filming began.

The 1990s proved no more successful at the Music Box. The first semi-success of that decade was Willy Russell's British musical, *Blood Brothers* (4/25/93; 840 performances). Stephanie Lawrence opened the show and was replaced later in the run by Petula Clark, who co-starred with David Cassidy.

There would be no more successes at the Music Box until *Fortune's Fool*, which opened on April 2, 2002, and closed on July 21st after 127 performances. Alan Bates and Frank Langella provided the star power for the limited engagement.

On December 8, 1987, the New York City Landmarks Preservation Commission designated the interior and exterior of the theater a landmark. The commission stated that the theater's Neo-Federal facade was "exceptionally handsome," with a double-height loggia and flanking Palladian windows. Inside are "elegant semi-circular boxes" and "classically inspired plasterwork." The Music Box Theater is still co-owned by the Shubert Organization and the Berlin Estate.

NATHAN, GEORGE JEAN. Critic; b. Fort Wayne, Indiana, February 14, 1882; d. New York, New York, August 8, 1958.

Nathan became one of New York's premier drama critics over the course of a 50-year career. He began his professional reviewing in 1906 at the *New York Herald*. In 1908 he left the *Herald* and became the drama critic and editor of *Bohemian Magazine*. He also wrote for *Smart Set*, becoming editor in 1914, *Harper's Weekly*, *Esquire*, *Scribner's*, *Saturday Review of Liter-*

At the Stork Club: Deems Taylor, Barry Fitzgerald and George Jean Nathan.

ature, *Newsweek, Puck, Judge, Life, New Freeman,* and *Vanity Fair.* He was the founder and editor (with H. L. Mencken) of the *American Mercury* from 1924 to 1930. In 1932 he wrote for the *American Spectator.*

The critic was the president of the New York Drama Critics' Circle from 1936 to 1939. He worked for the *New York Journal American* from 1943. Nathan was the author of several books on the theater, including *Mr. George Jean Nathan Presents* (1917), *The Theater, The Drama, The Girls* (1921), *The Critic on the Drama* (1922), *The Testament of a Critic* (1931), *The Morning after the First Night* (1939), and a series entitled *The Theater Book of the Year* beginning in 1942.

Through his various writings, Nathan exerted an important influence on drama in America. He trumpeted early on the talents of August Strindberg, EUGENE O'NEILL, William Saroyan, and Henrik Ibsen. He did not suffer foolish plays and insisted on the highest standards for both himself and the theater. His review of the play *Tonight or Never* read, "Very well, then, I say, 'Never'."

However, Nathan appreciated farce and musical comedy equally well, simply demanding good craftsmanship, not necessarily seriousness. Nathan was one of the few critics who felt no compunction at leaving during intermission.

NATIONAL THEATRE. *See* **Nederlander Theatre.**

NEDERLANDER THEATRE. 208 W. 41st Street. Architect: William N. Smith. Opening: September 1, 1921; *Swords.*

The theater, built on the site of an indoor tennis court by theatrical agent Walter C. Jordan, opened as the National in 1921. It reputedly cost $950,000 to build and contained 1,200 seats. Although Jordan owned the theater, the SHUBERT BROTHERS booked it. Its first production, *Swords,* was also the first play by Sidney Howard.

The National presented a series of fine plays with great stars. One of the biggest successes was John Willard's *The Cat and the Canary* (2/2/22; 349 performances). The thriller would be revived on Broadway in 1937 and was made into movies on several occasions. Actor/producer Walter Hampden brought a production of *Cyrano de Bergerac* (11/1/23; 250 performances) there and returned to the National in *Hamlet,* which moved from the Hampden Theater. Chester Morris and Spencer Tracy appeared in *Yellow* (9/21/26; 132 performances); magician Harry Houdini brought his magic show, *Houdini Lives,* to the theater in 1926. More great stars appeared on the National's stage in

Billy Rose Theater.

the 1920s: Fredric March in *The Half-Caste* (3/29/26; 63 performances), and Ann Harding in *The Trial of Mary Dugan* (9/19/27; 437 performances).

In 1927 the Shuberts bought the building and solidified their control of Broadway. The 1930s and the Depression, although disastrous for most theaters, proved no problem to the National. Great stars continued to grace its stage: Eugenie Leontovich, Henry Hull, and Sam Jaffe in Vicki Baum's *Grand Hotel* (11/13/30; 444 performances); Pauline Lord, Ruth Gordon, and Raymond Massey in *Ethan Frome* (1/21/36; 119 performances); and *Tonight at 8:30* (11/24/36; 113 performances) by Noel Coward, starring the author and Gertrude Lawrence.

The Mercury Theater under the direction of Orson Welles presented *Julius Caesar* (157 performances) at the National on November 11, 1937, and followed it with Thomas Dekker's *The Shoemaker's Holiday* (1/1/38; 69 performances). Tallulah Bankhead gave her greatest performance in Lillian Hellman's *The Little Foxes* (2/15/39; 410 performances). BROOKS ATKINSON commented on Tallulah's performance: "She plays with superb command of the entire character—sparing of the showy side, constantly aware of the poisonous spirit within." Bankhead herself described the character of Regina Giddens as "soulless and sadistic, an unmitigated murderess." Much of the credit for Bankhead's performance went to her director, Herman Shumlin. He made sure she didn't rely on the tried-and-true gimmicks that had served her in the past.

The 1940s were also good years for the National, beginning with Ethel Barrymore (*see* BARRYMORE FAMILY) in Emlyn Williams' *The Corn Is Green* (11/26/40; 477 performances). Another highlight of this decade was Maurice Evans and Judith Anderson in Shakespeare's *Macbeth* (11/11/41). LERNER AND LOEWE's first musical, *What's Up?* (11/11/43; 63 performances), was a quick failure, but they would return

Billy Rose with tickertape.

with *The Day before Spring* (11/22/45; 165 performances), a moderate success. In between, Eva Le Gallienne and Joseph Schildkraut appeared in Chekhov's *The Cherry Orchard* (1/25/44; 96 performances).

HAROLD ROME's musical revue *Call Me Mister* (4/18/46; 734 performances), with Betty Garrett, introduced the songs "South America, Take It Away," "The Face on the Dime," and "The Red Ball Express." Judith Anderson returned, this time with John Gielgud, in *Medea* (10/20/47; 214 performances). A musical revue, *Lend an Ear* (12/16/48; 460 performances), by Charles Gaynor, followed. John Garfield appeared with Nancy Kelly in *The Big Knife* (2/24/49; 109 performances). The 1940s came to a close with George Bernard Shaw's *Caesar and Cleopatra* (12/21/49), with Sir Cedric Hardwicke, Arthur Treacher, and Lilli Palmer.

The quality of the offerings stayed high through the 1950s. KATHARINE CORNELL, Grace George, and Brian Aherne were featured in a revival of *The Constant Wife* (12/8/51; 138 performances), and Margaret Sullavan and Joseph Cotten followed in *Sabrina Fair* (11/11/53; 318 performances). The next major production at the National was *Inherit the Wind* (4/21/55; 806 performances). This huge hit, a retelling of the Scopes monkey trial, starred Paul Muni, Ed Begley, and Tony Randall. Arlene Francis, Walter Matthau, and Joseph Cotten appeared in *Once More with Feeling* (10/21/58; 263 performances). Harry Kurnitz's light comedy was the National's last success under its original name.

In 1959 the Shuberts were forced to divest themselves of some of their theaters. Seizing the opportunity, showman Billy Rose bought the National and reopened it as the Billy Rose Theater on October 18, 1959, with Shaw's *Heartbreak House* (112 performances). Katharine Cornell made her last Broadway appearance there in Jerome Kilty's *Dear Liar* (3/17/60; 52 performances) with Brian Aherne. Edward Albee's

George Grizzard, Uta Hagen and Arthur Hill in *Who's Afraid of Virginia Woolf?*, 1960.

Who's Afraid of Virginia Woolf? (10/13/62; 664 performances) grabbed audiences with an intensity rarely seen on Broadway. George and Martha, the play's protagonists, cannot live in peace, because they cannot face their own reality. Their fantasies, supposedly their only real communication, actually keep them apart. By the end of the wrenching drama, the couple begins to take the first halting and sincere steps toward relating to each other. George Grizzard, Arthur Hill, Uta Hagen, and Melinda Dillon starred in the drama.

As production on Broadway slowed, the theater had more and more spells when it was dark. Edward Albee's *Tiny Alice* was a failure in 1964 (12/29/64; 167 performances). The play examined the theme of reality through a dialogue on religion. Critics claimed to be confused about the writing, and indeed it was difficult to follow. Tammy Grimes and Brian Bedford appeared in a notable revival of Noel Coward's *Private Lives* (12/4/69; 198 performances) at the end of the 1960s.

The Royal Shakespeare Company came to the Billy Rose in 1971 with Peter Brook's outrageous production of *A Midsummer Night's Dream* (1/20/71; 62 performances). Harold Pinter's *Old Times* (11/16/71; 119 performances) examined a marriage and relationships by having a husband deal simultaneously with his wife and another woman, who is actually his wife at a younger age. The play proved confusing to audiences, because Pinter didn't let the audience in on his conceit. Nonetheless, it is considered to be among the best of the modern plays to grace Broadway. Another English playwright, Tom Stoppard, had his play *Jumpers* presented at the Billy Rose (4/22/74), but it did not translate well to the American stage and closed after 48 performances.

The English influence continued when James and Joseph Nederlander and the British team of Cooney-Marsh bought the theater. In 1979 the name was changed to the Trafalgar and, after a refurbishment, the theater opened with Brian Clark's *Whose Life Is It Anyway?* (4/17/79; 223 performances), starring Tom Conti. Mary Tyler Moore took over the lead role and won an honorary TONY AWARD. It was followed by Harold Pinter's drama, *Betrayal* (1/5/80; 170 performances). Pinter kept up his experiments with dramatic form and constructed his play so that the first scenes took place in the most recent time frame; each succeeding scene went further back in time. *Betrayal* was like one long flashback. The technique was not new; KAUFMAN AND HART tried it with their play *Merrily We Roll Along* in 1934. *Betrayal*, with an excellent 3-person cast (Blythe Danner, Roy Scheider, and Raul Julia), deserved a much longer run.

In late 1980 the theater, renamed again, became the Nederlander. Lena Horne (5/12/81; 333 performances) appeared in a one-person show in 1981. Since then a

string of failures has been presented on its stage: *84 Charing Cross Road* (12/7/82; 96 performances), a musical version of James Baldwin's *Amen Corner* (11/10/83; 28 performances), Peter Ustinov's *Beethoven's Tenth* (4/22/84; 25 performances), a musical based on Kenneth Grahame's children's book *The Wind in the Willows* (12/19/85; 4 performances), a musical version of *Raggedy Ann* (10/16/86; 5 performances), and Frank Langella in *Sherlock's Last Case* (8/20/87; 124 performances) have all seen short runs at the theater.

Following the run of *Sherlock's Last Case* at the end of 1987, the Nederlanders rented the theater to a church group for services. The church moved to the larger Mark Hellinger Theater in 1989.

The 1990s were lean years for the Nederlander. After only 3 productions opened, all failures, the theater finally had a smash hit. *Rent* (4/29/96) by Jonathan Larson transferred from off Broadway.

NEIL SIMON THEATER. 250 W. 52nd Street. Architect: Herbert I. Krapp. Original name: Alvin Theater. Opening: November 20, 1927; *Funny Face.*

The early history of the Neil Simon Theater is also the history of the producing team of AARONS AND FREEDLEY. Like other producers, Aarons and Freedley wanted their own theater. They convinced a builder, real estate mogul Alexander Pincus, to build it in 1927 and chose the name Alvin by combining the first letters of their first names.

The Adamesque theater is best known for the many successful musicals that enjoyed long runs on its stage. This tradition began with the first production, *Funny Face* (11/20/27; 250 performances). It boasted a score by GEORGE AND IRA GERSHWIN and a libretto by Paul Gerard Smith and Fred Thompson. The show starred FRED AND ADELE ASTAIRE, Victor Moore, and Allen Kearns. The score included such standards as "Funny Face," "'S Wonderful," and "My One and Only." Next, a number of short-running musicals played the Alvin: *Here's Howe!* (5/1/28; 71 performances); *Treasure Girl* (11/8/28; 69 performances), a Gershwin show starring Gertrude Lawrence (with an exceptional score, including "Feeling I'm Falling," "I Don't Think I'll Fall in Love Today," "I've Got a Crush on You," "Oh, So Nice," and "Where's the Boy, Here's the Girl"); and *Spring Is Here* (3/11/29; 104 performances) by RODGERS AND HART.

In fall 1930 the Gershwins were back with a major hit, *Girl Crazy* (10/14/30; 272 performances). ETHEL MERMAN, making her Broadway debut, co-starred with Willie Howard and, in her second Broadway appearance, Ginger Rogers. The score included "Bidin' My Time," "But Not for Me," "Embraceable You," "I Got Rhythm," "Sam and Delilah," and "Treat Me Rough."

In the orchestra were Benny Goodman, Glenn Miller, Red Nichols, Jimmy Dorsey, Jack Teagarden, and Gene Krupa.

After *Girl Crazy* the theater's ownership reverted to the real estate firm that built it. The new owners booked the Alvin's first straight play, Maxwell Anderson's *Mary of Scotland* (11/27/33; 236 performances) with HELEN HAYES as the tragic queen, Mary Stuart. Following his partner's death in 1933 Vinton Freedley returned to the Alvin to produce *Anything Goes* (11/21/34; 415 performances). COLE PORTER wrote the score, and Ethel Merman, Victor Moore, and William Gaxton sang such hits as "All Through the Night," "I Get a Kick out of You," "You're the Top," and the title song. For *Red, Hot and Blue!* (10/29/36; 181 performances), Porter, Merman, and Freedley were reunited with other *Anything Goes* alumni Russel Crouse, Howard Lindsay, and Vivian Vance. Merman was aided and abetted by Bob Hope and Jimmy Durante. The big hit song was "It's Delovely."

The Alvin next hosted Rodgers and Hart's *I'd Rather Be Right* (11/2/37; 289 performances). GEORGE M. COHAN made his next-to-last Broadway appearance in this production as Franklin D. Roosevelt, president at the time. The libretto by KAUFMAN AND HART allowed for some gentle ribbing of the current administration as well as room for a good score, which featured "Have You Met Miss Jones?" Rodgers and Hart returned with *The Boys from Syracuse* (11/23/38; 235 performances), based on Shakespeare's *A Comedy of Errors*. The musical featured such great songs as "Falling in Love with Love," "This Can't Be Love," and "Sing for Your Supper." GEORGE ABBOTT produced, directed, and supplied the book. The musical showcased choreography by George Balanchine.

Another straight play next occupied the Alvin's stage. LUNT AND FONTANNE starred in Robert E. Sherwood's *There Shall Be No Night* (4/29/40; 115 performances). After its New York run, the show was taken on tour. It returned September 9 for an additional 66 performances before a second tour was undertaken. The play, which featured the young Montgomery Clift, won Sherwood his third PULITZER PRIZE. Altogether, the Lunts played more than 1,600 performances, including a run in London, cut short when their theater was bombed during the Blitz.

The next occupant of the Alvin was among the first shows to explore psychiatry, *Lady in the Dark* (1/23/41; 467 performances). The musical starred Gertrude Lawrence, returning to the Alvin in a better vehicle than her previous offering, *Treasure Girl*. KURT WEILL and Ira Gershwin supplied the score to a libretto by Moss Hart. Musical comedy continued at the Alvin with Cole Porter providing Ethel Merman with another starring vehicle, *Something for the Boys* (1/7/43; 422

performances). This undistinguished show enjoyed a long run, which was surprising because no hit songs came from the Michael Todd production. *Jackpot* (1/13/44; 44 performances), a VERNON DUKE and Howard Dietz (*see* DIETZ AND SCHWARTZ) show, returned Freedley to the Alvin. In 1946 the Alvin was sold to producer Herman Bernstein.

Through the later 1940s and early '50s the Alvin was home to numerous distinguished performances: Ingrid Bergman in Maxwell Anderson's *Joan of Lorraine* (11/28/46; 199 performances), Maurice Evans in George Bernard Shaw's *Man and Superman* (10/8/47; 294 performances), Henry Fonda and David Wayne in JOSHUA LOGAN and Thomas Heggen's wartime comedy *Mister Roberts* (2/18/48; 1,157 performances), and Claude Rains in Sidney Kingsley's *Darkness at Noon* (1/13/51; 186 performances).

Musical comedy returned to the Alvin with *A Tree Grows in Brooklyn* (4/19/51; 267 performances), starring Shirley Booth. Novelist Betty Smith co-wrote the libretto with George Abbott, who also served as director and producer. Arthur Schwartz (*see* DIETZ AND SCHWARTZ) and Dorothy Fields (*see* FIELDS FAMILY) wrote a beautiful score. Henry Fonda returned to the Alvin in *Point of No Return* (12/13/51; 364 performances), and MARY MARTIN appeared in the comedy *Kind Sir* (1/4/53; 165 performances) with Charles Boyer. Melodies by HAROLD ARLEN next filled the Alvin in *House of Flowers* (12/30/54; 165 performances). Truman Capote was the unlikely author of the book and co-author of the lyrics with Arlen. Pearl Bailey and Juanita Hall starred in the show, but the best songs, "A Sleepin' Bee" and "I Never Has Seen Snow," went to newcomer Diahann Carroll.

Andy Griffith made his Broadway debut in *No Time for Sergeants* (10/20/55; 796 performances) by Ira Levin, also the author of *Rosemary's Baby*. Lucille Ball made her Broadway debut in *Wildcat* (12/16/60; 171 performances). Cy Coleman and Carolyn Leigh provided the score, and N. Richard Nash wrote the book. STEPHEN SONDHEIM's first score for which he provided both music and lyrics, *A Funny Thing Happened on the Way to the Forum* (5/8/62; 965 performances), starred Zero Mostel and Jack Gilford. The show, under the direction of George Abbott, would prove to be one of the few true musical-theater farces. *High Spirits* (5/7/64; 375 performances) top-lined Beatrice Lillie and Tammy Grimes and was based on director Noël Coward's play *Blithe Spirit*. The musical had a fine libretto and excellent score by Hugh Martin and Timothy Gray. Liza Minnelli was the next major star to make her Broadway debut at the Alvin. The vehicle was the John Kander and Fred Ebb musical, *Flora, the Red Menace* (5/11/65; 87 performances). George

George Bernard Shaw and Maurice Evans conferring on the production of *Man and Superman*, c. 1947.

Abbott co-authored the script with Robert Russell and also directed the HAROLD PRINCE production.

Two major productions came to the Alvin in the late 1960s. *Rosencrantz and Guildenstern Are Dead* (10/16/67; 420 performances) was hailed by the London *Observer* as "the most brilliant debut of the sixties." Although it did not prove as successful as expected, the DAVID MERRICK production certainly proved a remarkable introduction to the remarkable talents of English playwright Tom Stoppard. Next James Earl Jones and Jane Alexander brought Howard Sackler's epic drama *The Great White Hope* (10/3/68; 556 performances) to the Alvin. The dramatic retelling of the life of prizefighter Jack Johnson won the Pulitzer prize. The play was originally produced by the Washington, D.C., Arena Stage and was the first important sign that America's resident theaters would play an ever-increasing role in the development of new American plays.

Company (4/26/70; 690 performances), the Stephen Sondheim musical, was next at the Alvin. Sondheim and librettist George Furth's examination of marriage was an important link between musicals of the past and the new style of musical in which the libretto moved in an often nonchronological fashion. The musical *Shenandoah*'s (1/7/75; 1,050 performances) long run was based largely on the success of its television advertisement. The Gary Geld and Peter Udell score had no popular songs, and the show itself received mostly lukewarm reviews.

The next musical at the Alvin became one of the most popular in the theater's history. *Annie* (4/21/77; 2,377 performances), with music by Charles Strouse (*see* STROUSE AND ADAMS) and lyrics by Martin

Lou Gilbert, Jimmy Pelham, James Earl Jones, George Eberung, George Matthews and George Curley in *The Great White Hope*, 1968.

Charnin, was based on the comic strip "Little Orphan Annie." The show introduced a standard, the song "Tomorrow." *Annie* moved from the Alvin on September 13, 1981, and eventually became the biggest musical hit of the 1970s. Its space was filled with what promised to be a huge success. Stephen Sondheim returned to the Alvin with his musical *Merrily We Roll Along* (11/16/81; 16 performances). Librettist George Furth, who had previously collaborated with Sondheim on *Company* (also at the Alvin), based his book on the Kaufman and Hart play of the same name. The play was a flop, and so was the musical version despite an excellent score and fine performances by a number of Broadway unknowns who would later achieve greater fame. These included Jason Alexander, Lonny Price, Ann Morrison, Liz Callaway, Tonya Pinkins, and Jim Walton.

The flops continued with a series of extremely short-lived musicals. The first, *The Little Prince and the Aviator*, began previews the day after Christmas 1981. With a score by John Barry and Don Black, book by Hugh Wheeler, and starring the ill-cast Michael York, the show never had an opening night, closing in

previews on January 17, 1982. It was followed by Donny Osmond starring in a revival of George M. Cohan's *Little Johnny Jones*. The show fared a little better than the Alvin's previous tenant—but just barely. It closed on opening night, March 21, 1982. That run was slightly bested by the next tenant at the Alvin, *Do Black Patent Leather Shoes Really Reflect Up?* The show squeaked out 5 performances after its May 27, 1982, opening. That run was equaled by the Alvin's next tenant, a theatricalization of the MGM movie musical *Seven Brides for Seven Brothers*. It opened on July 8, 1982. The year ended with another failure, a revival of *Your Arms Too Short to Box with God* (9/9/82; 69 performances).

The first play of a trilogy by NEIL SIMON, *Brighton Beach Memoirs* (3/27/83), starring Matthew Broderick, moved to the 46th Street Theatre (*see* RICHARD RODGERS THEATER) to finish out its remarkable 1,299-performance run.

During the show's run, on June 29, 1983, the Alvin was renamed the Neil Simon by its new owners, the Nederlanders. However, the theater community raised a small cry over the Alvin's renaming. It seemed unfair that the Alvin, a historic name and the scene of most of the Gershwins' greatest successes, should be renamed the Neil Simon, while the Uris Theatre (*see* GERSHWIN THEATER) should be rechristened the Gershwin. But the great sign that spelled out A-L-V-I-N (which had been altered to read A-N-N-I-E while that show was in residence) was changed to S-I-M-O-N.

Brighton Beach Memoirs made room for the second play in the Neil Simon trilogy, *Biloxi Blues* (3/28/85; 524 performances). Again, Matthew Broderick starred.

The name change proved no better at improving the luck of the theater's bookings. In fact, the theater would have no hits and no notable failures until the presentation of Jackie Mason's one-person stand-up act, *Jackie Mason: "Brand New"* (10/17/90; 216 performances). Neil Simon then returned to the theater with his new play, *Jake's Women* (3/24/92), but the show, starring Alan Alda, only managed 245 performances.

Following a series of concert performances in the mid-1990s by Basia, Laurie Anderson, and Danny Gans, the theater had a legitimate show with a revival of RODGERS AND HAMMERSTEIN's *The King and I* (4/11/96; 780 performances), with Donna Murphy and Lou Diamond Phillips in the leads.

Choreographer Matthew Bourne brought his reimagining of *Swan Lake* to the Neil Simon on October 8, 1998. The show's limited run of 124 performances preceeded a national tour.

A lackluster and ill-conceived revival of Meredith Willson's *The Music Man* (4/27/2000; 699 performances) was directed and choreographed by Susan Stroman. Craig Bierko and Rebecca Luker were the leads. The show would later make headlines when the national tour was announced with cast members who were not members of ACTORS' EQUITY.

The next production at the theater (following a concert by Mandy Patinkin) was a transfer from the Public Theatre. *Elaine Stritch: At Liberty* (2/21/2002) played 69 performances with the indefatigable Ms. Stritch in a semi-autobiographical show.

The new musical version of the John Waters film *Hairspray* opened at the Neil Simon on August 15, 2002, and should occupy the theater for years to come.

The New York City Landmarks Preservation Commission designated the exterior and interior of the Neil Simon a landmark.

NEW AMBASSADOR THEATRE. *See* **Ambassador Theatre.**

NEW AMSTERDAM THEATRE. 214 W. 42nd Street. Architects: Herts & Tallant. Opening: November 2, 1903; *A Midsummer Night's Dream.*

The renovation of the New Amsterdam was an exceptionally dramatic catalyst in the 42nd Street Redevelopment Project of the later 1990s. It brought back to life one of the great theaters of the early 20th century.

Klaw and Erlanger built their new theater as the flagship of their Theatrical Syndicate. They spent $1.5 million and for their money got a legitimate theater, a 10-story office building and a rooftop theater. When the New Amsterdam opened in 1903, the *New York Times* described it for its eager readers under the headline "The House Beautiful":

> In the New Amsterdam, Art Nouveau, first crystallized in the Paris Exposition of 1900, is typified on a large scale in America. The color scheme is of the most delicate reds and green and dull gold. Such painters as E. Y. Simmons and Robert Blum, sculptors, George Gray, Hugh Tallant and Enid Yandell and such designers as Wenzel and Ostertag have worked in harmony and with inspiration! The allied arts of painting, sculpture and architecture have, through their exponents, combined to produce a result that astonishes and delights, and whose effect and feeling are that of permanence, durability and extreme beauty.

The auditorium, designed in the unusual Art Nouveau style, was described in the *Dramatic Mirror* as "beyond question the most gorgeous playhouse in New York." The architects used three motifs throughout the building: the history of New Amsterdam from Henry Hudson to 1903, the history of theater, and the typical Art Nouveau flora and fauna motifs. Murals and friezes depict scenes from Shakespeare's *Macbeth*, Homer's *Odyssey*, and the operas of Wagner. Busts of Shakespeare and Homer look down from on high above the vaulted ceilings. The theater's color scheme was basically green with mauve accents. No primary colors were used in the design.

The Art Nouveau design was the most remarkable element of the theater's architecture. Considered ultramodern in its day, the style was shockingly avant-garde to audiences.

At the time, the New Amsterdam was the largest theater in New York, with seats for 1,800 patrons. It was among the first nonskyscrapers to use structural steel in its construction. The steel had to perform a unique task: It had to support the huge cantilevered balconies as well as the entire weight of the rooftop theater. The 70-ton main girder over the ceiling was the largest piece of steel in any building, measuring 90 feet in length and 14 feet in height. The huge beam was lifted into place from the office tower platform that was constructed first. The balconies did not have the usual pillars blocking the audience's view. Instead they were cantilevered into the theater's structure. These were the largest cantilevered balconies in the world when they were built.

The orchestra floor was designed to be quickly changed into a ballroom; however, the conversion never took place. The stage was one of the largest in the city, measuring 100 feet wide and 52 feet deep. The stage floor was divided into 4 hydraulic platforms 42 feet by 7 feet. These giant elevators could be raised, lowered to a depth of 33 feet, or inclined independently from each other.

The architects also eliminated dressing rooms on the stage level, instead incorporating them into the 7-story building next door. A special elevator connected the dressing rooms and the stage. Other innovations included a sophisticated system of cooling and heating that constantly circulated and filtered fresh air throughout the auditorium. Fire was an important concern at the turn of the century. HERTS & TALLANT devised double fire walls for the theater as well as an elaborate system of fire escapes. Another innovation was the cleaning system; it relied on a central vacuum, which carried the dirt through hidden pipes into the basement where it was collected and disposed of.

Under Klaw and Erlanger's direction, the New Amsterdam presented many of the great hits of the early 20th century. An early musical comedy success, *Whoop-De-Doo* (9/24/03; 151 performances), had Weber and Fields (*see* FIELDS FAMILY) starring and producing, though it marked the end of their long partnership. They would change their mind years later and reteam briefly.

On June 6, 1904, the producers opened the Aerial Gardens, a different kind of rooftop theater. Most were summer gardens with a small platform acting like a stage. But the New Amsterdam boasted a complete miniature theater on its roof. Although it could be used year-round, it was open only during the summer months. The Gardens boasted double-hung windows that could be raised to let in the summer breezes. However, its auditorium was not nearly as successful as its sister theater below. The rooftop theater had a raked orchestra and small stage. But the balcony was U-shaped, a throwback to the precantilevered past. Side seating in the balcony actually faced the opposite wall. Behind the stage of the Aerial Gardens was an open air Dutch garden with refreshments and café tables, perfectly in keeping with the typical roof garden of the period.

The first show, *A Little Bit of Everything*, was a variety program, a style that was favored throughout the Aerial Gardens' history. While the main auditorium presented its schedule of shows, the rooftop theater had its own schedule. It replaced variety with a series of musicals and operettas but still closed for the winter months.

New Yorkers saw their first production of Oliver Goldsmith's *She Stoops to Conquer* (4/17/05; 24 per-

formances) at the New Amsterdam. The comedy starred Eleanor Robson. Another great American actor, Richard Mansfield, played a limited engagement at the New Amsterdam each season. The music of GEORGE M. COHAN filled the theater when *Forty-Five Minutes from Broadway* (1/1/06; 90 performances) opened. Cohan's *The Governor's Son* was revived upstairs on June 4, 1906, with the Cohan family starring. *The Honeymooners* (6/30/07; 72 performances), which opened at the Aerial Gardens, was a revision of Cohan's musical *Running for Office*.

A smash hit for the New Amsterdam and one of the most influential shows of the early 20th century was Franz Lehar's operetta *The Merry Widow* (10/21/07; 416 performances). Its first American production opened with Ethel Jackson portraying the widow. The play, a smash hit, was also influential on women's fashions. *The Merry Widow* hat became a quick-selling item. To celebrate the 275th performance of the show, producer Henry Savage offered each woman in attendance a free hat. What the *New York Times* referred to as a "hot skirmish" ensued when 1,300 women showed up for the June 13 matinee. Savage had bought only 1,200 hats. The producer promised the extra 100 women their own hats at a later date. *The Merry Widow* survived the STUNT, and moved upstairs to the Aerial Gardens for the summer of 1908. It finally closed after returning to the main auditorium.

European-style operetta continued on the New Amsterdam stage with *The Silver Star* (11/01/09; 80 performances), by Robin Hood Bowers and HARRY B. SMITH. It was followed by a new melodrama, *Madame X* (2/2/10; 125 performances), which has become a sort of camp classic. It concerns a lawyer who prosecutes his mother. Of course, in the melodrama, he doesn't know who the lady is. Despite the critics' scoffing, the show enjoyed a Broadway revival and 3 film versions. There was also a burlesque of the popular hit produced at the Victoria Theater's (*see* GAIETY THEATER) roof garden.

A European operetta, *Madame Sherry* (8/30/10; 231 performances), opened at the theater with a popular Karl Hoschna score. Another European-influenced show that also became a smash hit at the New Amsterdam was Ivan Caryll's *The Pink Lady* (3/13/11; 312 performances); it made a star of Hazel Dawn. A huge success in the 19th century, Reginald DeKoven and Harry B. Smith's operetta *Robin Hood* (5/6/12; 64 performances), did not have a long run in its revival. However, during the revival it did mark more than 6,000 performances since its first presentation. Another perennial favorite, *The Count of Luxembourg* (9/16/12; 120 performances), featured a score by Franz Lehar, the composer of *The Merry Widow*. *Oh! Oh! Delphine* (9/30/12; 248 performances) brought Ivan

Caryll's tunes back to the New Amsterdam. Caryll followed this success with another, *The Little Cafe* (11/10/13; 144 performances).

The next tenant of the New Amsterdam changed its history for almost two decades, and the producer became the most successful in Broadway history. On June 16, 1913, FLORENZ ZIEGFELD moved his ZIEGFELD FOLLIES to the theater from the Moulin Rouge. From that year until he moved to the new ZIEGFELD THEATER in 1927, Ziegfeld presented an annual revue at the New Amsterdam (he missed only one year, 1926, because of a legal problem over the name *Follies*). Ziegfeld brought some of the greatest stars of Broadway to the New Amsterdam. Among them were comedians Leon Errol, Bert Williams (the first black performer to receive star billing), FANNY BRICE, Will Rogers, W. C. Fields (at the time a remarkable juggler and humorist), Eddie Cantor, Van and Schenck, and Joe Frisco. There were also great beauties including Lillian Lorraine, Olive Thomas, Ina Claire, and Marion Davies as well as great dancers like Marilyn Miller, Mae Murray, Ann Pennington, and Carl Randall. Singers included John Steel, Bert and Betty Wheeler, Ethel Shutta, Brooke Johns, Lupino Lane, Vivienne Segal, and musicians such as George Olsen and Paul Whiteman.

During the reign of the *Ziegfeld Follies* at the New Amsterdam, the theater housed other productions between *Follies* editions including the VICTOR HERBERT and Robert B. Smith classic, *Sweethearts* (9/08/13; 136 performances), Herman Finck and C. M. S. McClelland's *Around the Map* (11/01/15; 104 performances), *The Girl Behind the Gun* (9/16/18; 160 performances) with music by Ivan Caryll, and *The Velvet Lady* (2/3/19; 136 performances) with a score by Victor Herbert and Henry Blossom.

Ziegfeld not only produced the annual edition of the *Follies*, but also presented many successful musical comedies and a series of revues on the New Amsterdam's roof. In 1915 he hired John Eberson to redesign the theater with a U-shaped balcony and a 22,000-square-foot dance floor. With its opening attraction, *Ziegfeld Midnight Frolic* on March 29, 1915, the producer renamed the roof theater the Ziegfeld Danse de Follies. Ziegfeld's musical presentations downstairs continued with *Sally* (12/21/20; 570 performances). Marilyn Miller, Walter Catlett, and Ziegfeld favorite Leon Errol starred in the JEROME KERN, P. G. Wodehouse, Clifford Grey, and GUY BOLTON show. The hit songs included the title song and two with lyrics by B. G. De Sylva (*see* DE SYLVA, BROWN, AND HENDERSON). The first was "Whip-Poor-Will," and the other, "Look for the Silver Lining," became one of the greatest of all American popular songs.

In 1923 Ziegfeld and his sometime co-producer Charles Dillingham refurbished the New Amsterdam's roof, renamed it the Dresden, and opened a show called *Cinders* (4/3/23; 31 performances). *Cinders* had a score by RUDOLF FRIML. On September 12, 1923, the roof garden was named the Frolic Theater with a foreign theater troupe's production of *Teatro dei Piccoli*.

Marilyn Miller and Jerome Kern were involved in another hit musical at the New Amsterdam, *Sunny* (9/22/25; 517 performances). This time, OSCAR HAMMERSTEIN II and OTTO HARBACH supplied the book. The cast also included Cliff Edwards, Pert Kelton, Jack Donahue, and Clifton Webb. One of the five choreographers was FRED ASTAIRE. The big songs from this score were the title song and "Who?" another smash hit for the Kern catalog.

After the short-lived run of the RODGERS AND HART musical *Betsy* (12/28/26; 35 performances) the New Amsterdam hosted an all-star production of *Trelawney of the Wells*. The stars included Helen Gahagan, John E. Kellerd, Otto Kruger, Wilton Lackaye, Henrietta Crosman, Rollo Peters, Estelle Winwood, John Drew, Pauline Lord, and Effie Shannon. For one week the Frolic Theater hosted a play called *He Loved the Ladies* (5/10/27). The show's Thursday matinee played for no patrons. Not one audience member was present when the curtain rose. Statisticians disagree whether the play can claim to have run 6 performances or 7, and whether a performance counts as a performance if there is no one there to see it.

Musical comedy triumphed again at the New Amsterdam with Ziegfeld's production of *Rosalie* (1/10/28; 327 performances), boasting a score by GEORGE AND IRA GERSHWIN. SIGMUND ROMBERG and P. G. Wodehouse contributed an equal number of songs, but they took a backseat to such future Gershwin standards as "How Long Has This Been Going On?" "The Man I Love" (cut prior to the show's opening), and "Oh Gee! Oh Joy!" The show starred the New Amsterdam favorite, Marilyn Miller, along with Jack Donahue and Frank Morgan.

Ziegfeld's next offering at the New Amsterdam was the Walter Donaldson and Gus Kahn hit, *Whoopee* (12/4/28; 255 performances). Ruth Etting, George Olsen's Orchestra, Tamara Geva, and Ethel Shutta joined star Eddie Cantor. The better-than-average score yielded such musical comedy gems as "Love Me or Leave Me," "Makin' Whoopee," and "I'm Bringing a Red, Red Rose." The show that followed was the fifth production of William Gillette's American classic *Sherlock Holmes* (11/25/29; 45 performances), but it played only briefly at the New Amsterdam.

The New Amsterdam's survival at the beginning of the Depression was a testament to its good reputation with producers and audiences. The beginning of the 1930s saw only a slight falling off in the number or quality of shows premiering at the theater. However, the rooftop Frolics Theater did not fare so well. Bookings fell off throughout Times Square, and only the theaters with the most advantageous locations could keep lit. As 1930 turned to 1931, VARIETY reported that 31 theaters were dark in what was usually a busy holiday season. A theater on a roof, without a proper marquee, wasn't attractive to those producers still operating. Erlanger announced that the Frolics would undergo another transformation. The proscenium arch was filled in with a movable wall of glass. The soundproofed wall allowed the theater to operate as a legitimate theater, a radio studio, and a feature film studio. Erlanger even predicted that the theater would be used for television. In 1930 the theater became NBC Times Square Studio. Erlanger died on March 7, 1930, but his theater continued to prosper for a time.

The 1930 edition of EARL CARROLL'S VANITIES (7/1/30; 215 performances) featured Jack Benny, Patsy Kelly, Jimmy Savo, and Herb Williams. Hit songs were mainly by HAROLD ARLEN and Ted Koehler, and included "Contagious Rhythm," "Hittin' the Bottle," and "The March of Time." Vanities was followed by probably the greatest revue in musical comedy history, The Band Wagon (6/3/31; 262 performances). Max Gordon produced the new revue, which boasted performances by Fred and Adele Astaire, Helen Broderick, modern dancer Tilly Losch, and Frank Morgan. The exceptional Howard Dietz and Arthur Schwartz (see DIETZ AND SCHWARTZ) score included "High and Low," "I Love Louisa," "New Sun in the Sky," "White Heat," and the classic "Dancing in the Dark." The next New Amsterdam attraction was the IRVING BERLIN and Moss Hart (see KAUFMAN AND HART) revue Face the Music (2/17/32; 166 performances). This sometimes humorous, sometimes trenchant musical revue starred Mary Boland, J. Harold Murray, and Andrew Tombes.

Cast of *The Band Wagon*, Tilly Losch, Fred Astaire, Adele Astaire, Frank Morgan and Helen Broderick, 1931.

The two big song hits from the score were "Let's Have Another Cup of Coffee" and "Soft Lights and Sweet Music."

Following the close of *Face the Music*, the theater had its first shaky season. The 1932–33 season found no musical presentation premiering. Producers simply didn't have enough money to launch a large number of new operettas or musical comedies. *Murder at the Vanities* (9/12/33; 298 performances) was the next hit to play the New Amsterdam. The Earl Carroll production gave audiences both a murder mystery and a full musical revue. One production number, "Virgins Wrapped in Cellophane," gives a clue to the reason for the show's long run.

Roberta (11/18/33; 294 performances), with a score by Jerome Kern and Otto Harbach, starred George Murphy, Lyda Roberti, Bob Hope, Sydney Greenstreet, Tamara, and Fay Templeton, marking her 50th anniversary in the theater. A youthful Fred MacMurray appeared as one of the California Collegians. The score introduced such perennials as "Smoke Gets in Your Eyes," "I'll Be Hard to Handle" (with lyrics by Bernard Dougall), "The Touch of Your Hand," and "Yesterdays." Dietz and Schwartz returned to the New Amsterdam with their new show *Revenge with Music* (11/28/34; 158 performances). The show was the only legitimate theater production on 42nd Street. The rest of the theaters had converted to sub-run motion pictures, were presenting burlesque, or were closed. The musical had a superior score, including "When You Love Only One," "If There Is Someone Lovelier than You," and "You and the Night and the Music."

Having hosted many editions of the *Ziegfeld Follies* and the 1930 *Earl Carroll's Vanities*, the New Amsterdam seemed a natural for George White's Scandals (12/25/35; 120 performances). The *Scandals* were short on material and stars but long on beautiful, seminude chorines. This last edition of the *Scandals* featured the hit songs "Are You Havin' Any Fun?" "The Mexiconga," and "Something I Dreamed Last Night." Sigmund Romberg found his popularity waning when *Forbidden Melody* (11/2/36; 32 performances) opened at the theater. The run reflected the change in taste along Broadway. European operettas were no longer in vogue. New songwriters like the Gershwins and Rodgers and Hart inherited the mantle of popularity from such European stalwarts as Herbert, Friml, and Romberg.

A production of *Othello* (1/6/37; 21 performances) was to be the last live attraction at the New Amsterdam for the next 60 years. It featured Walter Huston in the title role. However, on May 7, 1936, the Dry Dock Savings Institution foreclosed on the New Amsterdam Theatre. There was $1.6 million due in interest and

taxes. Max Cohen, a theater owner who also owned the Harris and Wallack's (*see* Anco Theater) theaters, put up $500,000 to purchase the New Amsterdam. By then, all the owners of the theater—Erlanger, Ziegfeld, and Dillingham—were dead. Cohen was forbidden to present burlesque in the theater.

The New Amsterdam reopened on July 3, 1937, with a showing of the movie *A Midsummer Night's Dream*, the film version of the first play to occupy the New Amsterdam's stage. On September 12, 1937, the rooftop theater was renamed the WOR-Mutual Radio Theater and served as home for the show *Tim and Irene's Fun in Swingtime*. The rooftop theater returned to legitimate use as the New Amsterdam Roof with the production of *The Petrified Forest* (11/1/43; 8 performances). On September 15, 1951, the theater became the NBC Times Square Television Theater.

Downstairs a motion picture policy began in 1937 and remained in effect until the New Amsterdam was shuttered in the early 1980s. In 1982 the Nederlanders purchased the theater for $5 million and proposed to renovate it and open Jerry Herman's musical *La Cage aux Folles* there. Renovations took longer than expected, and suddenly the Broadway theater scene was less healthy, so *La Cage* opened at the far more attractive Palace Theater in the heart of the theater district. Other shows were announced for the theater and then withdrawn. Plans to move the lobby to 41st Street across from the Nederlander Theatre were scrapped, and subsequently major problems were discovered with the main supporting beam. The film *Vanya on 42nd Street* gives an excellent tour of the decrepit theater.

The city and state made the redevelopment of 42nd Street a priority. In 1992 the 42nd Street Development Project bought the theater for $247,000. They brought in the architectural firm of Hardy Holzman Pfeiffer to stabilize the building. This included sealing the building from vagrants, pumping out the water in the basement, and turning the heat back on to stop the loss of plasterwork and halt the spread of fungus.

The city targeted Disney as a prime tenant for the New Amsterdam. The company had just begun Disney Theatricals and had *Beauty and the Beast* in rehearsal. To lure Disney to the site the city renovated the Victory Theatre (*see* New Victory Theatre) as a children's theater.

Disney, seeing the success of the New Victory, agreed in 1995 to take over renovations of the New Amsterdam and sign a long-term lease. The renovation of the theater took 18 months and $36 million.

Disney undertook a dry run of the New Amsterdam with a concert production of a new theater piece, *King David*. Written by Alan Menken and Tim Rice, the production opened on May 18, 1997, and played 3 previews and 6 performances.

With the theater's operations in place, Disney opened their second theatrical venture, *The Lion King*, on November 13, 1997. An adaptation of their popular animated hit, Disney hired songwriters Elton John and Tim Rice to expand the cartoon's score. In a radical move for Disney, avant-garde director Julie Taymor was hired to direct the piece and design the remarkable masks, costumes, and puppets. The results were remarkable, and *The Lion King* immediately became the biggest hit on Broadway.

NEW APOLLO THEATER. *See* **Apollo Theatre.**

NEW VICTORY THEATRE. 207 W. 42nd Street. Architect: J. B. McElfatrick & Co. Original name: Theatre Republic. Opening: September 27, 1900; *Sag Harbor*.

After building the Victoria Theater (*see* GAIETY THEATER) on the corner of 42nd Street and 7th Avenue, OSCAR HAMMERSTEIN I built the Theatre Republic next door on 42nd Street. The Republic thus became the first theater built on 42nd Street. The Republic and Victoria share the same roof, and on it Hammerstein built the Paradise Garden (*see* VICTORIA THEATER [1]).

A reporter described the theater's facade:

The front wall is of brownstone and dark gray brick, surmounted by a row of Doric columns, in the center of which is a carved stone medallion bearing the words "Theatre Republic." From the street a broad double staircase leads to the piazza, where the entrance to the second balcony is located. The stairway and piazza are ornamented with wrought iron lamps of artistic design. The second balcony has its own box-office and is entirely independent of the lower part of the theatre.

The *New York Times* described the theater before its opening:

Through three broad low doors, like Grecian gateways, into a lobby where are situated the box office, check room, information bureau, and cab office. From the lobby two gateways in similar style lead directly to the orchestra floor—which in this case is a misnomer since the orchestra, except during opera engagements, will be located in a gallery over the proscenium arch. On the left and right, respectively, as one enters are seen broad marble stairways with heavy carved and gilded balustrades leading to the first balcony or dress circle. There are only 1,100 large and comfortable loges, six proscenium boxes, plus a number of boxes set in the side walls of the theatre. The proscenium arch is thirty-five feet high from the stage level and is decorated with allegorical figures and classic designs in relief. Immediately above the arch the life-size figures representing Harmony

and Melody, supporting between them a large golden lyre, mask the musician's balcony.

The decorations throughout the house are in harmony with those of the proscenium arch and boxes, the color scheme being green, ivory and old gold. The commanding feature of the theatre is the great dome over the whole auditorium. This dome is gilded, and from it depends an immense chandelier, whose pale incandescents blend in marvelous effects with the upthrown cardinal lights concealed in the broad bottom rim of the dome. This forms an entirely novel scheme of interior decorations and illuminations, being a replica on a slightly smaller scale of the dome at the Capitol in Washington.

The first production at the theater was James A. Herne's *Sag Harbor*. Herne appeared in the show as well, accompanied by his two daughters, Crystal and Julie, and a young Lionel Barrymore (*see* BARRYMORE FAMILY). December 31, 1900, saw an early theatrical favorite, Viola Allen, open in the play *In the Palace of the King* (138 performances). In February 1902 Henrietta Crossman played the Republic in two shows, *As You Like It* and *Mistress Nell*.

Hammerstein wasn't interested in operating his new theater and leased it in 1902 to DAVID BELASCO, who immediately rechristened the house the Belasco. The producer gutted the theater and hired architects Bigelow, Wallis, and Cotton and interior designers Rudolph Allen and William Linde to redesign the interior. With their $125,000 budget, they removed the musician's gallery atop the 35-foot-wide proscenium arch as well as all of architect McElfatrick's stenciling, brocaded walls, decoration on the balcony fronts, and any unnecessary cherubs and their ilk.

Belasco, long known for the excellence and innovation of his electrical effects, outfitted his theater with the latest in electrical technology. The first rheostats on Broadway were among the innovations. A further 20 feet under the stage was excavated to make room for a vast labyrinth of machinery underneath the stage to allow for grand scenic effects. During the excavation workers accidently struck an underground spring, which flooded the theater, thereby doubling the cost of renovation. Belasco also added a handsome iron and glass marquee outside, spelling out his name on frosted glass panels.

Belasco's first production at what was definitely the most technically advanced theater in the world was a transfer from the Criterion Theater (*see* OLYMPIA) of his own play, *Du Barry*, which premiered September 29, 1902, starring Mrs. Leslie Carter. She exclaimed about the remodeled theater, "The stage and the auditorium are so related that one is on confidential terms with the audience." CRITIC Alan Dale of the *New York American* wrote that the theater was "by all odds the most beautiful theater playhouse in the city, bar none."

Other hits at the Belasco were *The Music Master* starring David Warfield, and *The Girl of the Golden West*, later the basis for the Puccini opera.

In 1910 Oscar Hammerstein I turned over control of the theater to his son ARTHUR HAMMERSTEIN, but Belasco was unwilling to let his lease lapse. Oscar took him to court, and Belasco was forced to vacate the theater. He then built the current BELASCO THEATRE. Hammerstein brought in A. H. Woods as producer. Woods changed the name of the theater back to Republic on September 11, 1910, during the production of *Bobby Burnit* (32 performances), which opened August 22, 1910. That same year the city widened 42nd Street, and the theater lost its marquee and staircase. The Republic was host to a variety of presentations for the next decade. Attractions included Mary Pickford and Lillian Gish appearing in 1913's *A Good Little Devil* (1/8/13; 133 performances), *Common Clay* (8/26/15; 316 performances) with Jane Cowl, and the New York premiere of *Peter Ibbetson* (4/17/17; 71 performances). A notable transfer was that of *Abie's Irish Rose* from the Fulton Theater in September of 1922. At its opening at the Republic someone nailed a lucky horseshoe above the stage door. It certainly proved to be lucky; *Abie's Irish Rose* ran, in no small part due to Joe Leblang's half-price ticket stand in Gray's Drugstore, for 2,327 performances, making it the longest-running show of its time. When the play finally closed on October 1, 1927, the lucky horseshoe was taken down. When in 1929 William A. Grew's play *My Girl Friday* was playing the Theatre Republic, the Associated Press reported that a stagehand found the horseshoe and the doorman nailed it in its place above the stage door. That night the theater was raided.

Like most of the 42nd Street theaters, the Republic ceased to stage legitimate productions during the Depression. The Republic became a Minsky's BURLESQUE house in 1931, but after Mayor Fiorello La-Guardia's crackdown on burlesque it was renamed the Victory Theater with a second-run movie policy on May 9, 1942. It continued as such until 1995 when it was renovated at a cost of $11 million and turned into a nonprofit theater devoted to presenting an amazing variety of children's entertainments. The theater (with its exterior staircase restored), now renamed the New Victory, is one of the success stories of the Times Square redevelopment.

NEW YORK DRAMA CRITICS' CIRCLE AWARD.

This award was inaugurated in 1935 as a protest against the awarding of the PULITZER PRIZE to Zoe Akins' play *The Old Maid*. The Circle had been meeting informally since 1927 when CRITIC KELCEY ALLEN called the critics together. Helen Deutsch, press agent for Maxwell Anderson's *Winterset* (one of the overlooked plays), called a meeting at the Algonquin Hotel. On October 22, 1935, the Circle adopted a constitution, and the organization stated its goal as "the fostering and rewarding of merit in the American theater, and the awarding of a prize to be known as the Drama Critics Prize for the best new play by an American playwright produced in New York during the theatrical season." The first award went to Maxwell Anderson for his play *Winterset*. The original award, a plaque featuring a depiction of the John Street Theatre, was designed by sculptor Henry Varnum Poor. After a few years the Circle lost the mold for the plaque, and a scroll was given to winners instead.

The Circle added an award for Best Foreign Play in 1938. In 1946 an award for Best Musical Production was first given. An award in each category is not mandatory, and in many years the Circle makes no award in a particular category. In 1962 the rules were altered to read: "There shall be one ballot cast for the Best Play—drama or musical, regardless of the country of its origin. If a foreign work should win the award, the Circle may if it chooses, name a Best American Play. If an American Play wins, the Circle may choose a Best Foreign Play. The choice of a musical is, as always, left to the discretion of the Circle."

NEW YORK THEATRE. *See* **Olympia.**

NEW YORKER THEATRE. *See* **Studio 54.**

NEW YORK TIMES HALL. *See* **Little Theatre.**

NEWSPAPER GUILD OF NEW YORK (PAGE ONE) AWARD IN THEATER.

This award is given by a board composed of New York journalists. There are no set categories, and past winners have included plays, musicals, critics, authors, and institutions. The awards were initiated in 1945 and have been awarded annually except for 1963 because of a newspaper strike (*see* NEWSPAPER STRIKE OF 1962–1963).

NEWSPAPER STRIKE OF 1962–1963.

The power of the newspapers over the fortunes of Broadway are amply illustrated by the newspaper strike of 1962–1963. The strike forced the early closing of some shows and, incredibly enough, allowed for the run of another. On December 8, 1962, the International Typographical Union, the newspapers' printers' union, called a strike against the New York press. New Yorkers didn't believe that the strike would last long, but it wasn't settled until 114 days later. Because the papers together printed more than 5.5 million copies each day, little news of the Broadway theater was available, except for the occasional television review. The newspaper strike led to a consolidation of the television reviewers' power.

The strike deprived Broadway shows of their two major sources of promotion. The typical PR campaign consists of primary advertising and secondary publicity. Without newspapers, primary advertising was limited to billboards and fliers, because television advertisement was not yet used. Secondary publicity consists of the articles in newspapers that appear after the show's opening and remind the audience that the show is still running. But after the strike there were no feature stories or gossip items to catch the public's eye. In New York, at least, it was as if the theater had simply closed up.

The fate of two shows in particular illustrates the impact of the strike on the Broadway theaters. *The Beauty Part* was a hilarious comedy by S. J. Perelman. It received rave reviews after its opening on December 26, 1962. But the reviews on television and in the major weekly magazines had little impact, because they didn't hit all on one day the way newspaper reviews do. They just kept dribbling in. *The Beauty Part*'s star, Bert Lahr, commented in a *New Yorker* profile on the strike's effect on the play's box office: "It's been murder with this newspaper strike. Normally, with the kind of reviews we got, we'd be sold out for two months in advance, but as it is, we're selling out performance by performance, with a steady line of maybe six customers at the box office all day long." Michael Ellis, *The Beauty Part*'s producer, attempted to offset the lack of publicity through a series of STUNTS and alternative means of advertisements. He arranged for a million bookmarks with reviews of the show to be distributed to cigar stores and bookshops. People in Revolutionary War dress, complete with a bell-ringing town crier, handed out tabloid-sized fliers with the reviews printed on them. Ellis put the fliers in 100,000 packages of laundry, and 100,000 people found fliers

slipped in with the photo prints they picked up from their local film developers. There were countless other promotions and stunts. In all Ellis spent more than $50,000 in attempts to advertise the show. None of these tricks worked. *The Beauty Part* still needed the day-to-day reinforcement that only a newspaper ad could bring. An additional problem for a potential audience member was figuring out where the show was playing. When *The Beauty Part* moved from the MUSIC BOX to the PLYMOUTH THEATER, Ellis had no way to tell the public about the move. When the show had to move from the Plymouth, it was decided simply to close it after only 85 performances. Ellis commented, "Every possible kind of deal that could be made to spread the word about that show was made. But it just isn't the same thing as having that newspaper in your hand."

The Beauty Part never got off the ground without newspapers to spread the word, but Lionel Bart's musical *Oliver!* actually succeeded because of the strike. The musical opened on January 6, 1963, under the watchful eye of producer DAVID MERRICK. Merrick, a master showman and manipulator of the press, knew *Oliver!* wasn't the greatest show. He was just as happy not to have newspaper reviewers telling the public that the show was mediocre. Still, Merrick needed publicity. Luckily, *Oliver!* was a musical and one with an excellent score. Merrick made sure every radio station in town had recordings of the show's hit songs, "Consider Yourself" and "As Long as He Needs Me." The airwaves were inundated with the songs, and they soon became deserved hits. When the newspapers went back to publishing and the mixed reviews were in, they had no effect. There was already solid word of mouth, and the success of the songs made the show a success in the minds of the public. *Oliver!* ran 774 performances.

Of course the strike hurt more shows than it helped. The newspaper industry would further hurt Broadway as more and more papers folded. A few critics became all-powerful, and without a wide range of opinion or outlets for advertising and stories, the entire theater community suffered.

OLYMPIA. 1514–26 Broadway, between 44th and 45th Street. Architect: J. B. McElfatrick & Company.

Music Hall Opening December 17, 1895, Yvette Guilbert; reopened as the New York Theater, April 24, 1899, *The Man in the Moon*; opening as the Moulin Rouge, 1912; reopened as Wonderland, January 1913; renamed the New York Theatre, 1913; opened as Loew's New York, 1915.

Lyric Opening November 25, 1895, *Excelsior, Jr.*; reopened as the Criterion Theater, August 29, 1899, *The Girl from Maxim's*; reopened as the Vitagraph Theater, February 7, 1914, as a movie theater; reopened as the Criterion Theater, September 11, 1916, *Paganini*.

The Olympia complex established Times Square as the city's theater district and served as a cornerstone for development of the whole area. Earlier in the 19th century, the theater district moved from lower Manhattan to the Herald Square area. OSCAR HAMMERSTEIN I began the move northward to Times Square (then Longacre Square) in 1895 with the Olympia Theater complex. Hammerstein realized the potential of the area, already used as a transfer point between streetcar routes. He purchased the entire block of the east side of Broadway between 44th and 45th Streets and decided to build a huge complex called the Olympia. Hammerstein crowed, "My theater will make a place for itself because I will give the public what they have never had before."

In January 1895 ground was broken. When completed, the complex contained a restaurant, a promenade or central lobby, a bowling alley, billiard rooms, a Turkish bath, a smoking room, an Oriental café, three theaters seating more than 6,000 people, and a roof garden (an idea imported from Europe). One admission allowed patrons to explore any of the theater's attractions. In an advertisement in the *New York Times*, Hammerstein bragged about "the grandest amusement temple in the world."

The opening of the complex was planned for November 18, but delays pushed the opening back to November 25. Hammerstein claimed that he had lost $3,000 by postponing the opening. The *Times* accused him of overselling the house to make up the difference. Opening night proved to be an ill omen. The crowds began to arrive in the afternoon, long before the doors were opened. The heavens then opened, and cold rains beat down on the thousands of ticket holders, who began to push and shove to get under the marquee. The *Times* reported that the crowd, "with the strength of a dozen catapults, banged at the doors of the new castle of pleasure and sent them flying open . . . puffed sleeves wilted and crimped hair became hoydenish in the crush and the rain; toes were trampled and patent leathers and trousers were splashed, dresses were torn, and still the crowd pushed on." The staff was unable to control the throng. Hammerstein had oversold the theater by almost 4,000 seats. The police called for reinforcements to try to shut the theater doors. At 10 P.M. more than 5,000 patrons, as the *Times* put it, "slid through the mud and slush of Longacre back into the ranks of Cosmopolis." A band played until 1 A.M. in the concert hall to try to appease the disgruntled crowd. Hammerstein had private rooms for his guests, but unfortunately the paint was still wet and several of the elite found their clothes marked with the wall covering. The next day Hammerstein's troubles continued. A steam pipe burst in the cellar; two workers were killed and others badly scalded.

Yvette Guilbert was to have opened the Music Hall, but she was unavailable until mid-December, and a series of vaudeville acts filled in for her. The Lyric presented Edward E. Rice's *Excelsior Jr.* starring Fay Templeton. "The Cornerstone of Times Square," as the

Hammerstein's Olympia.

Olympia was christened, never overcame the disaster of opening night. In the book *The Planning and Construction of American Theatres* William H. Birkmire described the theater:

> The walls and ceilings are rich in panels of beautiful designs. A massive chandelier decends from a rosette surrounded by dancing cupids. A heroic female figure upholds the forty-eight boxes, which are all different in design.
>
> The proscenium panels, as technically described by decorators, are round form at top and bottom, with a slight square break, with motifs in relief ornamenting the base, the middle and top having a bold cartouche with hanging laurel pendants at either side. The carved and undulating Louis XIV lines are easily recognized in the lyre crossed by two flutes which appear to grow from the top of the cartouche.
>
> The base is decorated with a rich design, a semi bas-relief, consisting of an ornamental pedestal on which rests a vase with dolphin handles. Japanese dragons crouch at each side of the base.
>
> The panel is surmounted with a female head at the top, decidedly "French" in its expression, on whose forehead rests a star, with festoons of flowers hanging at either side. Below this will be found suspended by cupid's chains an emblem, of which a classic shield, cupid's bow, arrows, etc., form its composition. Its alternate strong and low reliefs and soft lines, with plain grounds well distributed, at once betray to the layman the quality of its execution. The main group over the proscenium arch represents Poetry and Prose being crowned by the goddess Fame. Its dimensions are 24 × 10 feet.

A reporter from the *New York Herald* wrote, "In some of our other theaters, there is space to walk about, but you are out of luck if you have not a seat at the Olympia."

Rooftop Theatre

On November 2, 1895, the roof garden hosted a "Bal Champetre" in which the Florenz aerobatic troupe astounded patrons with their triple pirouettes. The roof garden was later renovated and renamed the Jardin de Paris. The first ZIEGFELD FOLLIES was presented there in 1907, and subsequent editions were also produced there through 1911. The 1912 edition moved to the larger New York Theatre, which was renamed the Moulin Rouge.

Music Hall

The Music Hall had a Broadway frontage of 75 feet. It was separated from the concert hall by a 10-foot-wide alley. Then came another 10-foot-wide alley and the theater. Situated on the 45th Street side, the Music Hall had prices of 75¢ to $1.50 for reserved seats. It had 11 tiers of boxes; Hammerstein boasted that it held more boxes than any other theater, 124 in all. The theater resembled a European opera house with its huge proscenium crowned by the goddess Fame crowning Poetry and Prose.

Yvette Guilbert played the Music Hall on December 17, 1895, and by January 27 of the next year had become a star. Later that year Collbri's Midgets, the Aerial Ballet, and Grand Opera in Tableaux were presented. The Cherry Sisters, often referred to as the worst act in vaudeville history, appeared on November 28, lasting through the enmity of audiences to December 14. A paper described their act:

> Those who recall the sisters when they were in their pristine glory say their voices were so harsh and rasping that audiences were moved to rise and howl in anguish. The program was opened when the three sisters marched on the stage. One of them carried a drum which she beat furiously as they executed an awkward drill:
>
> HERE IS THEIR SONG,
>
> Their song was something like this:
>
> Cherries pretty and cherries sweet,
> Cherry sisters hard to beat,
> Cherries pretty and cherries ripe,
> Cherry sisters out of sight.
>
> We're the Cherry sisters, don't you know?
> Come and see the Cherry show,
> Folks laugh with joy where'er we go
> Because we always please them so.
>
> After the first verse or two the rest of the song was always lost in the derisive howls of the audiences. They wore red costumes from their caps to their shoes and all wore long red silk "mitts." There were three, Addie, Effie and Jessie. Addie was tall and thin and Effie was taller and thinner. Jessie was the only one in the leastwise comely. She was rather small, well rounded and had large, half sad eyes that almost made one sympathize with her in the midst of all the uproar. But when she stepped out alone to sing all compassion vanished because, it is alleged, she had the worst voice that was ever inflicted on an audience. There was a peculiar, grating tone to it that enraged all who heard it.

Among the more notable offerings was Fay Templeton appearing in E. E. Rice's BURLESQUE of *Excelsior Jr.* (11/25/1895; 144 performances). Also in the cast were Charles A. Bigelow, Richard Carle, Harry Hearle, Marie Cahill (soon to be married to producer Daniel V. Arthur), and Kitty Connor. It marked Templeton's first Broadway appearance in five years.

Little Egypt, a great star of the World's Columbian Exposition in Chicago, opened at the Music Hall on January 4, 1897. However, more than one act called itself Little Egypt, and which one this was is impossible to determine. Burlesque came again to the theater's stage on March 7 with the *Mrs. Radley Bradley Ball*, a satire of the Bradley Martin Ball, a society sensation that was plastered in headlines across the front pages of newspapers.

Another renowned appearance was ANNA HELD in the musical comedy *La Poupee* (10/21/1897; 46 performances). This was her second season in America and her first speaking role. However, an argument with Hammerstein a week into the run led to her exiting the cast. She was replaced by Louise Hepner on October 30. Also in the cast was vaudeville great Trixie Friganza.

In 1897 the president of New York Life wrote Hammerstein a note apprising him that the mortgage would be foreclosed and that a bank employee would run the theater. Hammerstein responded, "I am in receipt of your letter, which is now before me, and in a few minutes will be behind me." The next year Hammerstein found himself bankrupted by the Olympia. Previously, he had turned down an offer to rent the two corners of the building as a drugstore and haberdashery. The proposed rental was $6,000 annually, but Hammerstein was too proud or optimistic to accept it. New York Life sold the building at auction to producers Henry and M. L. Sire for $967,400. They in turn sold it to Klaw and Erlanger, heads of the Theatrical Syndicate, for almost twice that amount. (In 1920, a department store offered $6 million.)

The Music Hall was gutted by Klaw and Erlanger, who hired architects HERTS & TALLANT to renovate the interior in the style of a Broadway theater. Gone were all but twelve of the boxes, and only two balconies were retained. Klaw and Erlanger renamed the Music Hall the New York Theatre and changed the entrance to 44th Street, permanently severing its ties to the Olympia complex.

New York Theatre

George Lederer became manager of the New York Theatre. Musical comedy was the order of the day there with occasional forays into vaudeville and burlesque. The first attraction to play the New York was *The Man in the Moon* with music by Ludwig Englander, Reginald de Koven, and Gustave Kerker. Starring at the April 24, 1899, opening were Christie MacDonald, Sam Bernard, and Marie Dressler. January 1900 saw the opening of *Broadway to Tokio* (1/23/1900; 88 performances) with Fay Templeton, Otis Harlan, and Josie Sadler. In August came *Quo Vadis* with Richard Buehler, Alice Fischer, and Joseph Haworth. In October the smash hit show *Florodora* moved from the CASINO THEATRE to finish its run. Hagenback's Trained Animals cavorted on the stage in October, and Marie Cahill opened at the theater in Julian Edwards' *Sally in Our Alley* in November.

Composer A. Baldwin Sloane dominated the New York's stage with a series of shows: the aforementioned *Broadway to Tokio*, a spectacular musical with music by Sloane and Reginald De Koven; the musical comedy *A Million Dollars* (9/27/1900; 28 performances); Sloane's burlesque of *Nell Gwynn* titled *Nell Go In* (10/31/1900; 25 performances); *The Giddy Throng* (12/24/1900; 164 performances), a burlesque revue with May Yohe and including the minimusical *After Office Hours*; and finally *The King's Carnival* (5/13/01; 80 performances), another burlesque by Sloane and Sydney Rosenfeld.

After Sloane's reign at the New York Theatre the first show to open was Julian Edwards' *When Johnny Comes Marching Home*. It enjoyed a 71 performance run beginning March 16, 1902, with George Backus in the lead.

The Chaperons (6/5/02; 49 performances) featured musical comedy favorite Eva Tanguay and her rendition of "My Sambo," which would remain a favorite in her repertoire. On June 30 of that year the production would move upstairs to the New York's rooftop theater, which was then named the Cherry Blossom Grove. It was followed by *King Highball* (9/6/02; 33 performances) starring Marie Dressler.

One of the most significant musicals of the decade opened at the New York Theatre on February 18, 1903. *In Dahomey*, (106 performances) was one of the first musical comedies written by black men to play Broadway. Poet Paul Laurence Dunbar contributed the lyrics, with music by Will Marion Cook and libretto by J. A. Shipp. Dunbar and Cook had previously written *Clorindy or the Origin of the Cakewalk* in 1898, the same year that Bob Cole and Billy Johnson produced the first black musical comedy, *A Trip to Coontown*. *In Dahomey*'s cast featured a who's who of black performers including Bert Williams and his partner George W. Walker, Ada Overton Walker, Lottie Williams, and Shipp himself. The show was so successful it was presented in London, where a royal command performance was given.

In September 1903 Henry Woodruff and Annie Irish appeared in the ever popular spectacular *Ben-Hur* (9/21/03; 96 performances). December brought Bertha Galland in Paul Kester's dramatization of Charles Major's novel, *Dorothy Vernon of Haddon Hall* (12/14/03; 40 performances). The 1904 season was not a very auspicious one; however, many stars appeared on the New York's stage, including Chauncey Olcott in *Terence* (1/5/04; 56 performances); Richard Carle in *The Tenderfoot* (2/22/04; 81 performances); Eddie Leonard, Elfie Fay, and Abbie Mitchell in *The Southerners* (5/23/04; 36 performances); *The Maid and the Mummy* (7/25/04; 42 performances) with May Boley and Annie Yeamans; Harry Bulger, Ida Mulle, and Emma Carus in *Woodland* (11/21/04; 83 performances); and on the day after Christmas, C. T. Dazey's *Home Folks* (12/26/04; 34 performances) with William S. Hart, Thomas A. Wise, and Julie Herne.

That same season saw the opening of a beloved American play *The Old Homestead*. A particular favorite of the 19th century, *The Old Homestead* was written by Denman Thompson and George W. Ryer. The origins of this play went back to February 1875 and Harry Martin's Varieties Theatre in Pittsburgh, Pennsylvania, where Thompson's sketch *Joshua Whitcomb* premiered. The piece was so successfully received that Thompson expanded it into a four-act play that premiered at the LYCEUM THEATER in New York on September 2, 1878. Ryer was subsequently brought in to help shape the comedy, and under the title *The Old Homestead* it opened in Boston in 1886 followed by a New York engagement on January 10, 1887, at the 14th Street Theatre. The play opened at the New York Theatre on September 12, 1904, and ran for 61 performances. Thompson played the lead of Joshua Whitcomb in all the various incarnations until his death on April 14, 1911.

One of the highlights of the 1905 season was GEORGE M. COHAN's *Little Johnny Jones*, starring the author along with Donald Brian, William Seymour, and Truly Shattuck. Cohan would have four of his musicals play the New York. Other shows that season were *A Pair of Pinks* with Ward and Vokes, *The Shep-*

herd King (2/20/05; 48 performances) with Wright Lorimer and May Buckley, and the twelfth engagement of *The Prince of Pilsen* to play on Broadway.

Anne Crawford Flexner dramatized one of America's favorite novels, *Mrs. Wiggs of the Cabbage Patch* (24 performances), which opened at the New York on September 17, 1906, with Madge Carr Cook, Edith Taliaferro, and Myrtle Tannehill in it. That season also saw Cohan's *45 Minutes from Broadway* (11/5/06; 32 performances), with Fay Templeton, Donald Brian, and Victor Moore that November. On March 25, 1907, came Edwin Milton Royle's smash hit, *The Squaw Man* (8 performances), starring William Faversham and Julie Opp. That August saw the return of vaudeville to the New York stage.

January 28, 1908, saw a return of legitimate theater with the opening of *The Soul Kiss* (122 performances) starring Cecil Lean and Adeline Genee. It was followed by Richard Carle in *Mary's Lamb* (5/25/08; 16 performances). Another big hit, *Miss Innocence* (176 performances), with Anna Held, Charles A. Bigelow, and Emma Janvier, opened on November 30.

George M. Cohan's *The Man Who Owns Broadway* played for 128 performances at the New York beginning on October 11, 1909, with Raymond Hitchcock and Flora Zabelle in the leads. The house wouldn't have another hit until almost a year later, when VICTOR HERBERT's classic *Naughty Marietta* (11/7/1910; 136 performances) opened with book and lyrics by Rida Johnson Young. Edward Martindell, Emma Trentini, and Orville Harrold starred. The theater's next show boasted an all-star cast including Richard Carle, Jeanne Eagels, Helen Broderick, Ina Claire, Natalie Alt, and Edna Wallace Hopper. Unfortunately, *Jumping Jupiter* (24 performances), opening in March 1911, was not a success. That fall, Victor Herbert had a modest success at the theater with *The Enchantress* (10/19/11; 72 performances) featuring Kitty Gordon and Ralph Riggs; it ran for 9 weeks.

On April 11, 1912, the New York's name was changed to Moulin Rouge with the opening of *A Winsome Widow* (172 performances), which was based on the smash hit play *A Trip to Chinatown*. Raymond Hubbell provided the music. The great FLORENZ ZIEGFELD produced, with a stellar cast including Charles King, Leon Errol, Kathleen Clifford, Emmy Whelen, Frank Tinney, the Dolly Sisters, and Mae West. Its 21-week run was followed by another Ziegfeld show, the *ZIEGFELD FOLLIES of 1912* (10/21/12; 88 performances). Raymond Hubbell again provided some songs for a cast that included Leon Errol, Harry Watson Jr., Bernard Granville, Bert Williams, Josie Sadler, and Lillian Lorraine. It ran for 11 weeks. One of Broadway's favorite playwrights of the time, Owen Davis, saw his play *Big Jim Garrity* play 3 weeks commenc-

ing October 16, 1914, with John Mason and Janet Dunbar in the leads. On November 16 of that year, *The Traffic* by Rachael Marshall and Oliver D. Bailey played for 1 week. It was the final show at the theater before Loew took over the theater on January 15, 1915.

Management of the Music Hall had been acquired by William Morris in 1913. Two years later Marcus Loew took over the Morris organization, and the theater was given over to a movie/vaudeville policy. When Loew took over the New York Theatre, he changed the name to Loew's New York, and it became the flagship of the Loew's chain. It retained that role until the 1922 opening of LOEW'S STATE THEATER.

Lyric Theater

The Lyric Theater opened in September 1897 with Chester Bailey Fernald's play *The Cat and the Cherub*, featuring Holbrook Blinn, Richard Ganthony, and Grace Sheridan. The Lyric soon became the Criterion, named after a famous London music hall in Piccadilly Circus. Under Charles Frohman's direction, the Criterion offered comic opera, musical comedy, variety, and straight plays. Among his many successes there were *The Girl from Maxim's* (8/29/1899; 54 performances), by George Feydeau, starring Josephine Hall and Paul McAllister; *Barbara Frietchie* (10/23/1899; 83 performances), by playwright Clyde Fitch, starring Julia Marlowe in her first nonrepertory appearance; and a revival of DAVID BELASCO's *Zaza* (10/1/1900; 42 performances), starring Leslie Carter, in which modern dancer Ruth St. Denis also appeared in a minor role. *The Gay Lord Quex* (11/12/1900; 67 performances), by Arthur Wing Pinero, was another hit for the theater.

The Pride of Jennico (3/6/1900; 111 performances) marked the New York debut of George W. Barbier. Also in the cast of the Abby Sage Richardson and Grace L. Furniss play were James K. Hackett and Thomas A. Hall. The show returned to the Criterion later that season, opening on September 3 and playing for an additional 32 performances. Margaret Illington first appeared on stage in New York in the revival, billed under her real name of Maude Light. Producer Charles Frohman (also Light's husband) suggested she take a stage name. Because she was from Bloomington, Ill., she fashioned a stage name from those names. She later became a star under that name.

One of the most famous plays of the decade, *When Knighthood Was in Flower* by Paul Kester, opened on January 14, 1901, and played 176 performances with Julia Marlowe in the lead. Her performance was judged as one of the best in the Criterion's history. Marlowe had previously appeared in *Barbara Frietchie* at the Criterion, and, two years after *When Knighthood Was in Flower*, would appear in *The Cavalier*. She would play a total of 43 weeks at the Criterion, a record for any performer. It was followed at the Criterion by the debut of William Faversham as a star in *A Royal Rival* (8/26/01; 112 performances). The play was adapted by Gerald Du Maurier from *Don Caesar de Bazan*, which premiered in New York at the Olympic Theatre on December 9, 1844. During the run on *A Royal Rival* on December 9, no fewer than 3 adaptations were presented in New York; the other 2 being a version by George Henry Trader, presented by the Henry V. Donnelly Stock Company at the Murray Hill Theatre for a 1-week engagement, and another version titled *Don Caesar's Return*, starring James K. Hackett, which premiered on September 3.

David Belasco returned to the Criterion, for the second of his three productions at the theater, with another great hit, *Du Barry* (12/25/01; 165 performances), with the author also producing and directing. Mrs. Leslie Carter, returning from a triumphant stand in London in *Zaza*, starred along with Walter Belasco. The roles of Du Barry and Zaza were so important to Mrs. Carter's career that, for the 17 years ending in 1907, she appeared altogether in only six roles.

Pinero returned with *Iris* (9/23/02; 77 performances), a five-act drama directed by Dion Boucicault. Francis Hodgson Burnett's *The Little Princess* (1/14/03; 34 performances), best remembered for the Shirley Temple film adaptation, was one of the first productions mounted on Broadway specifically for children. The play was performed on matinees only, Sunday through Friday. It later moved to the Savoy Theatre, again only playing matinees. It finally concluded its run at the Madison Square Theatre.

James M. Barrie's *Alice Sit-by-the-Fire* and *Pantaloon* (12/25/05; 81 performances), two one-act plays with Ethel and John Barrymore (*see* BARRYMORE FAMILY), was a legendary production. Johnson Briscoe, theatrical agent and former casting director for Winthrop Ames, recalled, "Ethel Barrymore startled all her admirers by playing the mother of two grown up children . . . while still in her mid-twenties. It was one of her greatest successes. John Barrymore played Stephen Rollo in that play, one of his four appearances at the Criterion."

On August 17, 1908, modern dancer Isadora Duncan made her first appearance as a solo star at the Criterion. *Samson* (10/19/08; 152 performances), a play by Henri Bernstein, opened at the theater on October 19 that year and ran for a more than respectable 152 performances. Making her New York debut was future star Constance Collier. William Gillette and Pauline Frederick also appeared in the cast. Belasco produced the last of his three plays at the Criterion with Roland Burnham Molineux's play *The Man Inside* (11/11/13; 63 performances). The

New York Times prematurely reported the death of legit theater at the Criterion with Belasco's production.

The Criterion lease was acquired by the Vitagraph Company for $50,000 a year in 1914 and was renamed the Vitagraph Theater. This marked the first time a Broadway legitimate theater featured a full evening of cinema. But movies failed to catch on, and the Vitagraph name reverted to the Criterion under the management of matinee idol James K. Hackett. His reign lasted from 1915 to 1919. Hammerstein, Frohman, and Hackett were responsible for almost all the Criterion's legitimate stage career. *Young Wisdom* (1/5/14; 56 performances) featured Mabel and Edith Taliaferro; Mabel had previously appeared at the Criterion as a child actor. *The Melody of Youth* (2/15/16; 111 performances) featured Eva Le Gallienne in the leading role. *On the Hiring Line* (10/20/19; 48 performances) was an unexceptional production, except that it marked the last stage appearance of Josephine Hall, who had appeared at the Criterion 20 years before in *The Girl from Maxim's*. In the latter play she apppeared as a low-comedy servant.

When Hackett's management term ended in 1919, it also marked the end of the Criterion as a legitimate house. In 1920, and until the PARAMOUNT THEATER was built, the Criterion was operated by Paramount-Famous-Lasky. Among the films presented at the Criterion were *The Golem*, *The Covered Wagon*, *Humoresque*, and *The Ten Commandments*.

John Golden, producer, playwright, and press agent, wrote that the Criterion was no more successful than its predecessors: "I shall never forget the sick feeling that came over me every time I walked into the empty lobby of the Criterion Theater and saw no one at the box office except the ticket seller." One day he and Winchell Smith stood in front of the theater and watched thousands of people passing it by. Smith wondered why the theater was called the Criterion. Golden explained, "It's a pretty good name. A criterion is something to go by—and they're certainly going by here."

The entire Olympia complex was razed in 1935. A new building went up in its place housing a nightclub and dance hall named the INTERNATIONAL CASINO.

Oscar Hammerstein's Olympia complex was a remarkably forward-looking achievement. As what would now be dubbed a performing-arts center, the Olympia spurred the development of Times Square, hosted top stars of vaudeville, musical theater, and straight plays, saw the introduction of the *Ziegfeld Follies,* and became an early lynchpin in the emerging Loew's chain of movie theaters.

O'NEILL, EUGENE. Considered by many theater historians to be the father of 20th century American theater; b. New York, New York, October 16, 1888; d. Boston, Massachusetts, November 27, 1953.

Eugene O'Neill pioneered American realism, taking the theater away from the melodramatic and farcical theater that Europe bequeathed to America at the turn of the 20th century. O'Neill was among the earliest playwrights to work in experimental techniques and non-naturalistic styles. He delved into the psyches of his characters as few other playwrights had before him. Although some of his plays may seem overwritten and dated now, O'Neill set the groundwork for a native theater in the new century. Without his leadership, there might not have been a GROUP THEATER, TENNESSEE WILLIAMS, or ARTHUR MILLER. O'Neill, ever the tragedian, won four PULITZER PRIZES and the Nobel prize for literature.

Critic GEORGE JEAN NATHAN hailed O'Neill in the introduction to the published version of *The Moon of the Caribees*, an early O'Neill drama. Nathan wrote of the playwright's impact on the American theater:

In O'Neill, theater has found its first really important dramatist. To it he has brought a sense of splendid color, a sense of vital drama and a sense of throbbing English that no native playwright before him was able to bring. . . . The essential difference between O'Neill and the ma-jority of his contemporaries in the field of American drama lies in the circumstance that where the latter think of life (where they think of it at all) in terms of drama, O'Neill thinks of drama in terms of life.

O'Neill was born on October 16, 1888, to Irish Catholic parents, James O'Neill and Ella Quinlan, at Barrett House, on the northeast side of 43rd Street just off Broadway. Later Barrett House was converted into part of the Cadillac Hotel around the corner from RECTOR'S RESTAURANT. O'Neill's father, a matinee idol best remembered for his performance in the play *Monte Cristo*, rivaled Edwin Booth for acting honors. However, Eugene O'Neill's home life was especially difficult. He wrestled with his upbringing throughout his life. His parents were able to express affection only by tormenting each other, reconciling their love only through alcohol and narcotics. O'Neill worked autobiographical themes into many of his plays including, most importantly, *Long Day's Journey into Night* (completed in 1941) and also *All God's Chillun Got Wings* (1923). In these plays he barely disguised the names of members of his family. O'Neill spent much of the early 1910s on a variety of vessels sailing the world. He assisted his father on two theatrical tours and thereby learned the intricacies of the theater. Ill health forced him into a sanitarium in 1912 after a stint as a reporter in New London, Connecticut.

His first play, *A Wife for a Life*, was written in the spring of 1913 but not produced in his lifetime. The second, also written in 1913 and unproduced during O'Neill's life, was *The Web*. During the next four years the playwright would pen 24 plays.

In 1915 O'Neill joined a group of young writers who were disenchanted with Broadway and had the youthful optimism to believe they could change the status quo. The group met on Cape Cod at a glorified shack, which they dubbed the Provincetown Playhouse, under the direction of George Cram Cook. The next year, emboldened by their efforts, they set up shop on MacDougal Street in Greenwich Village in a new Provincetown Playhouse.

The year 1917 was important for O'Neill. His talents came to the attention of the Washington Square Players, who later evolved into the THEATRE GUILD. The Players leased the Bandbox Theater on West 57th Street. There they presented O'Neill's one-act play *In the Zone* (10/31/17) to critical applause. The *New York Herald* reported that the play "registered so realistically that several spectators laughed awkwardly in its tense moments as a result of the nervous strain of the sustained thrill." The Provincetown Players presented *The Long Voyage Home* (11/17/17) to even more acclaim. O'Neill was slowly getting a name for himself in the theater community and beyond.

Kenneth MacGowan, Eugene O'Neill, and Robert Edmond Jones.

Beyond the Horizon (2/3/20; 111 performances), the playwright's first important full length play and first Broadway production, was produced at the MOROSCO THEATRE. The drama was presented during matinees only. The *New York Times* critic ALEXANDER WOOLL-COTT enthused, "[*Beyond the Horizon* is] an absorbing, significant, and memorable tragedy, so full of meat that it makes most of the remaining fare seem like the merest meringue." When the Morosco's regular tenant, *For the Defense*, closed, *Beyond the Horizon* began a full Broadway schedule. The play was a naturalistic play with no melodramatic overtones. The plot was propelled by its characters, not theatrical contrivance. O'Neill was criticized for overwriting and for taking a literary rather than theatrical approach to structure, but most CRITICS agreed that *Beyond the Horizon* was a major step forward in the direction of a new American theater. The play received the first of O'Neill's four Pulitzer prizes for drama.

O'Neill's career flourished as he called on his past for a seemingly infinite number of variations. He would draw on his experiences, mixing them with New England folk stories passed down in the oral tradition and experimental techniques. Immediately following *Beyond the Horizon* O'Neill undertook a number of tasks all at once. He had plays on and off Broadway, some with out-of-town tryouts and others commissioned or waiting to be produced.

The Emperor Jones (11/1/20; 192 performances) played at the Provincetown Playhouse. Set to the rhythms of tom-toms beaten at exactly the rate of the human heartbeat, *The Emperor Jones* was highly experimental. The play, which was basically a long monologue, also experimented with the use of ghosts appearing onstage as manifestations of the central character's imagination.

Anna Christie (11/2/21; 177 performances) was O'Neill's next success. The play was a rewrite of his play *Chris Christopherson*, a drama starring KATHARINE CORNELL, which folded in Atlantic City. Arthur Hopkins, one of the most adventurous of Broadway producers, presented *Anna Christie*. The drama opened at the Vanderbilt Theater and was an immediate success. Pauline Lord, in the title role, received glowing reviews, as did her leading man, George Marion, and the sets of Robert Edmund Jones. Alexander Woollcott wrote in his review, "Though this *Anna Christie* of his has less directness and more dross and more moments of weak violence than any of its forerunners, it is, nevertheless, a play written with that abundant imagination, that fresh and venturesome mind and that sure instinct for the theater which set this young author apart." The play won a second Pulitzer prize for O'Neill.

Expressionism, explored in *The Emperor Jones*, was again utilized for dramatic impact in *The Hairy*

Ape (3/9/22; 120 performances). Louis Wolheim played the loutish Yank, juxtaposed by O'Neill with the upper-class brat Mildred. The play received decidedly mixed reviews, with the negative outweighing the positive.

All God's Chillun Got Wings ostensibly explored the travails of miscegenation. It actually had many of the overtones of O'Neill's youth. The main characters were named Jim and Ella, after O'Neill's parents. Later in *Long Day's Journey into Night*, O'Neill would name the mother Mary. His mother's actual name was Mary; she changed it to Ellen and later to Ella.

The opening night of *All God's Chillun Got Wings* (5/15/24; 43 performances) ran into problems before the curtain rose. The first scene, almost a prologue, featured several children. Unfortunately the Children's Society of New York refused to issue the Provincetown Playhouse a license allowing the children to perform. The objection was actually a thinly disguised attempt by racists in the government to keep the play from opening. Word had gotten around that a white woman kissed the hand of a black man during the show. Ku Klux Klan members had already sent threatening letters to the leads, Paul Robeson and Mary Blair, as well as director James Light and O'Neill. A bomb threat was phoned in, threatening the theater with destruction if the play proceeded. James Light addressed the defiant audience at the opening, asking them whether the play should proceed or not. After receiving a strong yes from the audience, Light proceeded to read the brief prologue, because the children were legally unable to appear. The rest of the evening continued without incident. Unfortunately, the play was not a success in the critics' eyes. Heywood Broun called it "a very tiresome play." Woollcott, one of O'Neill's chief boosters, wrote, "There is a perceptible chill in the air of the theater of Eugene O'Neill at present. It is the chill of compromise—the compromise with the old realism which results in a kind of halfhearted sublimation of the material world through which his figures move." The play was revived a few months after its closing and ran an additional 62 performances.

Desire under the Elms (11/11/24; 208 performances) was another presentation of the Provincetown Playhouse at the Greenwich Village Theater. Robert Edmund Jones designed the production and also directed the fine cast. Walter Huston, not yet established as a Broadway performer, starred along with Mary Morris. The play was not a success with the critics, who seemed to feel the dramatic construction was clichéd and shopworn. The play later became somewhat of a classic, with many productions throughout the world.

Along with Kenneth Magowan and Robert Edmund Jones, O'Neill presented *The Great God Brown* (1/23/26; 271 performances). O'Neill utilized masks to point up the differences between the characters' true personalities and emotions and how others perceive them. The lead characters let down their masks only when unafraid to bare their innermost souls. After the opening the critics ran to their typewriters to applaud the play. BROOKS ATKINSON, then recently appointed as the *New York Times* drama critic, wrote that O'Neill "has not made himself clear. But he has placed within the reach of the stage finer shades of beauty, more delicate nuances of truth and more passionate qualities of emotion than we can discover in any other single modern play." *The Great God Brown* moved from the Greenwich Village Theater to the Garrick Theater and finally the KLAW THEATER.

Marco Millions (1/9/28; 102 performances) was the first O'Neill play to open on Broadway in four years. His previous Broadway production, *Welded* (3/17/24; 24 performances), was not a success. O'Neill's other plays had previewed at the Greenwich Village Theater, and many had subsequently moved uptown. The Theatre Guild produced *Marco Millions*. The play opened at the Guild Theater (*see* VIRGINIA THEATER) and received mixed to positive notices.

The Guild quickly followed with the opening of *Strange Interlude* (1/30/28; 426 performances). As produced at the JOHN GOLDEN THEATER, *Strange Interlude* was an especially provocative play. The drama actually contained 3 complete 3-act plays. The play was referred to by star Lynn Fontanne (*see* LUNT AND FONTANNE) as a "six day bisexual race." O'Neill put many asides into the dialogue to indicate the characters' inner monologues. Director Philip Moeller solved the problem by having the rest of the action freeze while the aside was given. The 5-hour production (excluding the dinner break) had audiences enthralled. Dudley Nichols, later a successful Hollywood screenwriter, was the critic for the *New York World*. Woollcott was the first-string critic for the paper, but as he had given the play an unfavorable review in *Vanity Fair* (based on a reading of the script), Nichols was assigned opening-night duties. Nichols opened his review by stating, "The Theatre Guild produced Eugene O'Neill's 'Strange Interlude' last night and it needs all the restraint a reporter can muster not to stamp the occasion, without a second thought, the most important event in the present era of the American theater." Nichols went on to state that the play wasn't only "a great American play but the great American novel as well." This was what O'Neill had planned. All through his career he strove to bring the depth and structure of a novel to the stage. *Strange Interlude* was O'Neill's

greatest success to date and won him a third Pulitzer prize.

O'Neill based his next major work, *Mourning Becomes Electra* (10/28/31; 150 performances), on the *Oresteia* of Aeschylus. Again New England was chosen as the background for the tragedy. Alice Brady and Alla Nazimova starred in what was actually 3 plays: *Homecoming*, *The Hunted*, and *The Haunted*. The play opened under the auspices of the Theatre Guild at the Guild Theater. The show ran 7 hours, with the customary break for dinner. Again O'Neill garnered great reviews. JOHN MASON BROWN, writing in the *New York Evening Post*, exclaimed,

> It is a play which towers above the scrubby output of our present-day theater as the Empire State Building soars above the skyline of Manhattan. Most of its fourteen acts, and particularly its earlier and middle sections, are possessed of a strength and majesty which are equal to its scale. . . . It is one of the most distinguished, if not the most distinguished, achievements of Mr. O'Neill's career. . . . It is an experiment in sheer, shuddering, straightforward storytelling which widens the theater's limited horizons at the same time that it is exalting and horrifying its patrons.

PERCY HAMMOND wrote in the *Tribune*, "From four o'clock yesterday afternoon until eleven at night, Eugene O'Neill heckled Life in one of the bitterest and lengthiest of his attacks upon that popular institution." *Mourning Becomes Electra* was considered by many to be O'Neill's greatest achievement.

O'Neill's next success, a major departure in his usual oeuvre, was *Ah Wilderness!* (10/2/33; 285 performances), an affectionate comedy set in the New England of O'Neill's boyhood. GEORGE M. COHAN starred in the sentimental play. Critics were astounded that O'Neill could write such a light, bright comedy. Brooks Atkinson admitted, "As a writer of comedy Mr. O'Neill has a capacity for tenderness that most of us never suspected."

O'Neill had one more play premiere on Broadway, *Days Without End* (1/8/34; 57 performances), before devoting himself to writing a series of plays that he vowed would not be performed until all were finished. He took a break from the play cycle to write *The Iceman Cometh* (10/9/46; 136 performances), which premiered at the MARTIN BECK THEATRE.

During the time he worked on the cycle, he also finished *Long Day's Journey into Night*, *Hughie*, and his last completed play, *A Moon for the Misbegotten*. The latter, now considered a great play, was not well received when it opened at the tiny BIJOU THEATRE (5/2/57; 68 performances).

O'Neill finished drafts of eight of the plays in the cycle, none of which were performed before his death on November 27, 1953. The only play of the cycle to be completed was *A Touch of the Poet*. The remainder were torn up and burned by O'Neill and his wife, Carlotta. With his health declining, O'Neill feared that he would die before the plays could be finished, and he was determined that no one else should work on them after his death. Only a rough, uncut draft of *More Stately Mansions* survived.

Director José Quintero became a leading proponent of O'Neill's plays. He produced and directed a groundbreaking production of *Long Day's Journey into Night* at the HELEN HAYES THEATER, the first Broadway production of the playwright's work following his death. The production opened on November 7, 1956, and ran for 390 performances. It starred Fredric March, Florence Eldridge, Jason Robards, and Bradford Dillman. O'Neill was posthumously awarded a fourth Pulitzer prize for the play. Jason Robards, too, would become an acclaimed interpreter of O'Neill's characters.

Brooks Atkinson wrote in the *New York Times*,

> With the production of *Long Day's Journey into Night* at the Helen Hayes last evening, the American theater acquires size and stature.
>
> The size does not refer to the length of Eugene O'Neill's autobiographical drama, although a play three and three-quarter hours long is worth remarking. The size refers to his conception of theater as a form of epic literature.
>
> *Long Day's Journey into Night* is like a Dostoevsky novel in which Strindberg had written the dialogue. For this saga of the damned is horrifying and devastating in a classical tradition.
>
> The characters are laid bare with pitiless candor. The scenes are big. The dialogue is blunt. Scene by scene the tragedy moves along with a remorseless beat that becomes hypnotic, as though this were life lived on the brink of oblivion.

The world premiere of O'Neill's *A Moon for the Misbegotten* (5/2/57; 68 performances) was produced and directed by Carmen Capalbo with Franchot Tone, Wendy Hiller, and Cyril Cusack in the leads.

Broadway next saw O'Neill's work when *Anna Christie* was adapted into the musical *New Girl in Town* (5/14/57; 431 performances). Bob Merrill provided the score, and GEORGE ABBOTT directed, with Gwen Verdon and Thelma Ritter heading the cast.

Another world premiere followed on Broadway with the opening of *A Touch of the Poet* (10/24/58; 284 performances). Harold Clurman directed an excellent cast including Helen Hayes, Kim Stanley, and Eric Portman.

Following a short-lived revival of *The Great God Brown*, Broadway again found itself with another musicalization of an O'Neill play. His one comedy, *Ah, Wilderness!* was the basis for the musical *Take Me Along* (10/22/59; 448 performances). Again Bob Merrill handled the songwriting chores. DAVID MERRICK

was the producer, and the stars were Jackie Gleason, Walter Pidgeon, Una Merkal, and Eileen Herlie.

A revival of *Strange Interlude* (3/9/63; 97 performances) opened at the HUDSON THEATRE with an exceptional cast including Franchot Tone, Betty Field, Ben Gazzara, Jane Fonda, Pat Hingle, Geraldine Page, and a young Richard Thomas. José Quintero directed, a role he repeated in the next O'Neill production on Broadway, *Marco Millions* (2/20/64; 49 performances), presented at the downtown ANTA Washington Square Theatre. Hal Holbrook, Zohra Lampert, and David Wayne starred.

Quintero continued as the premiere interpreter of O'Neill with his production of *Hughie* (12/22/64; 61 performances) at the ROYALE THEATRE. Jason Robards continued his connection with O'Neill in his acclaimed performance.

Quintero also directed the next O'Neill premiere, *More Stately Mansions* (10/31/67; 142 performances). The stellar cast included Ingrid Bergman, Colleen Dewhurst, and Arthur Hill. Dewhurst also appeared in the next O'Neill production, a revival of *Mourning Becomes Electra* (11/15/72; 55 performances) at the Circle in the Square Theater downtown. Quintero, Dewhurst, and Robards teamed up for a revival of *A Moon for the Misbegotten* (12/29/73; 313 performances) at the Morosco Theatre. This acclaimed production solidified the show as one of O'Neill's masterworks.

Quintero continued his successful interpretations of O'Neill's works with a revival of *Anna Christie* (4/14/77; 124 performances) starring Liv Ullmann and John Lithgow. He also directed the next production of O'Neill's work on Broadway, a revival of *A Touch of the Poet* (12/28/77; 141 performances), again with Robards. Also featured were Geraldine Fitzgerald and Milo O'Shea. Quintero and Robards teamed up again with *The Iceman Cometh* (9/29/85; 55 performances), also featuring Barnard Hughes and Donald Moffat. Quintero, Robards, and Dewhurst were again reunited in a production of *Long Day's Journey into Night* (1/14/88; 28 performances). Campbell Scott, son of George C. Scott and Colleen Dewhurst, was also in the limited engagement, which played in repertory with *Ah, Wilderness!* (1/23/88; 13 performances), also with Dewhurst, Robards, and Scott, though directed by Arvin Brown.

Al Pacino starred in and directed a production of *Hughie* (8/22/96; 56 performances) at the CIRCLE IN THE SQUARE THEATRE uptown. Hollywood actor Kevin Spacey made a splash in the latest revival of *The Iceman Cometh* (4/8/99; 102 performances).

O'Neill brought the American theater into the 20th century. He allowed it to mature until it could stand on its own against any of the European dramatists. O'Neill, Shakespeare, and Shaw are the most performed playwrights throughout the world. His dramas continue to mesmerize audiences with their stark theatricality and raw emotions.

O'NEILL THEATER. *See* **Eugene O'Neill Theater.**

OUTER CIRCLE AWARD. Newspaper and magazine writers who report on the New York theater from outside the New York metropolitan area have given this award since 1950. The judges of the Outer Circle Awards have always been less consistent than the judges of other major awards in adhering to fixed categories. In some years no Best Play or Best Musical has been voted. Other categories that have been selected for awards on an irregular basis are best set design, most effective and imaginative individual contribution to a stage production, best ensemble acting, achievements in staging, and outstanding debut.

PAGE ONE AWARD *See* **Newspaper Guild of New York (Page One) Award in Theater.**

PALACE THEATER. 1564 Broadway, between 46th and 47th Streets. Architects: Kirchoff and Rose. Opening: Vaudeville, March 24, 1913; legitimate theater, January 29, 1966; *Sweet Charity.*

Perhaps the best-known of all American theaters is the Palace. The Palace was to vaudevillians what Carnegie Hall was to classical musicians: a sign that the performer had reached the height of his or her art. West Coast vaudeville impresario MARTIN BECK, head of the Orpheum Circuit, who wanted to conquer the East Coast, built the Palace. Standing in Beck's way was the team of B. F. Keith and E. F. ALBEE, who controlled the East Coast vaudeville circuit. Albee decreed that any act that played the new theater would be banned from the Keith-Albee circuit. Beck didn't underestimate his competition and gave 75 percent ownership to Keith and Albee. However, Beck retained control of the theater's bookings.

The opening program was a matinee on March 24, 1913. The "first-class" vaudeville program was not considered a success by the trade paper *VARIETY*. The headline reporting the event read "Palace $2 Vaudeville a Joke: Double-Crossing Boomerang." The newspaper criticized the program and indulged in a prediction as to the Palace's future prospects:

> The fate of $2 vaudeville at the new Palace, New York, was sealed before the house opened Monday. Since then its doom has become accepted along Broadway. Monday afternoon, following an expenditure of $4,000 for preliminary advertising of the initial variety program the Palace failed to draw capacity, even with the great quantity of "paper" given away. In the evening the Palace held capacity on the orchestra floor but was not filled upstairs. About one-half present received free coupons.
>
> The news of "the Palace flop" pleased the regulars around New Times Square mightily. Whoever arranged the opening program for the Palace presented the poorest big time vaudeville show New York has ever seen. It's also the worst exhibition of showmanship New York has known. A betting book was made up last Friday, $100 to $75 was offered the Palace would be the first big time house in New York to close this season, and $100 even money was offered in any amount that the Palace policy will be altered by April 7.

The Palace appeared to be headed for certain failure, but appearances were deceiving. The theater that would later be referred to as "the home plate of show business" by vaudevillian Pat Rooney Sr. finally made a splash on May 5, 1913. The occasion was an appearance by the almost 70-year-old Sarah Bernhardt. The tragedian appeared on the Palace stage with her partner, Lou Tellegen. Business improved, and the Palace was on its way to becoming the Mecca for vaudeville.

The Palace's success led to changes in Times Square. The Palace office building, surrounding the theater, quickly filled up with agents. Across the street, on what is known as Duffy Square, was a concrete island created by the convergence of Broadway and Seventh Avenue. Today the island holds the TKTS BOOTH and the statues of GEORGE M. COHAN and Father Francis Duffy. Back in the heyday of the Palace, the area was known as the Palace Beach. The BEACH became the gathering place of performers who were between bookings.

WALTER WINCHELL told biographer, Herman Klurfeld, about life on the Beach, in front of the Palace, when he was a young performer:

> I often stood in front of the Palace for hours swapping lies. There were always jobs we turned down because

Palace Theater interior.

the agents were either too stupid to appreciate us or unable to meet our prices. I used to wait at the Palace, hoping to meet a friend rich enough to invite me to join him across the street for a cup of coffee and a sandwich. It was all so damn frustrating and humiliating.

The theater changed its bills every Monday at a matinee performance attended by agents, producers, critics, and fellow actors. The typical Palace bill consisted of 9 acts. The Monday matinee performance was the most important of the week and could make or break a career. It was also considered the toughest audience of the week; if an act failed to go over, it often didn't make it to the evening show.

Most of the Monday afternoon regulars had subscriptions to the theater. In fact, 75 percent of the Palace's business was subscription sales. Business remained good throughout most of the 1920s until new forms of entertainment began to take hold. As radio became increasingly popular, many Palace performers gave up the live stage for the microphone. The arrival of talking pictures also dealt a blow to vaudeville and the Palace. A *Variety* article summed up the Palace's declining fortunes when the paper reported on "a line in front of the Palace Monday matinee—on its way to the Roxy" (see ROXY THEATER). The stock-market crash and the Depression finished off vaudeville.

The theater had some successful acts after the crash, but they were few and far between. Mostly the theater resorted to gimmicks to draw patrons. The first idea was to present celebrities who were not true vaudevillians. It had worked with Sarah Bernhardt when the theater was first starting out, so show business wisdom suggested a repeat performance. Nightclub artists like Paul Whiteman, who appeared with his band at the Palais Royal, were welcomed at the Palace where they were once banned. As talkies gained hold of the public's imagination, washed-up silent-screen stars made personal appearances.

The theater had a strict 9-act vaudeville bill playing 2 shows a day. With the theater's fortunes falling, however, a third daily performance was added in 1929. In the next few years, a fourth and fifth performance was added. The old vaudeville spirit revived briefly when Kate Smith set a record in August 1931, with her *Swanee Revue* and an 11-week run. Musical theater stars William Gaxton, Lyda Roberti, and Lou Holtz remained at the Palace for 8 weeks. But these successes were exceptional bright spots. When E. F. Albee died on March 11, 1930, it seemed to mark the end of vaudeville forever and the end of an era at the Palace. On July 9, 1932, the last week of straight vaudeville was begun at the Palace.

Thereafter, the Palace added movies to its vaudeville offerings. The *New York Times* noted,

After almost twenty years of straight vaudeville, the Palace is saying good-bye to all that with its current show. On Saturday a program combining variety acts and feature motion pictures will take over the stage of what until recently was the proudest and most empurpled of all the country's former big-time music halls, the goal of vaudevillians everywhere.

Over the next few months, the vaudeville portion of the show faded, and the last 2-a-day vaudeville show with a movie accompaniment began on November 12, 1932. The *Times* commented: "Vaudeville is singing its swan song at the Palace this week prior to the defection of the time-honored variety house to motion pictures . . . the Honey Family are swinging the old Palace trapeze for what may be the last time. *Sic transit gloria mundi.*"

The once great theater succumbed to the movies on November 17, 1932, with the first film to play the Palace without an accompanying vaudeville show. The movie was the Samuel Goldwyn production of *The Kid from Spain*, starring Eddie Cantor. Only 10 days later, a major competitor opened its doors for the first time—Radio City Music Hall. A straight movie policy continued for a few months at the Palace, but it didn't draw audiences. The major studios had their own flagship theaters in Times Square, including the Warner Brothers Theater (see MARK HELLINGER THEATER), the LOEW'S STATE THEATER, and the PARAMOUNT THEATER. So the Palace was forced to scramble for product. Most of the top movies went to the major houses.

From January 7 through February 4, 1933, the Palace reinstated its vaudeville and movie schedule, but by February 11, 1933, the vaudeville was out again. The picture that opened on that day was *The Bitter Tea of General Yen*—on a second run after playing Radio City Music Hall. On April 29, 1933, vaudeville was brought back and played in a continuous stage show/movie format, much like the Radio City Music Hall shows of later years. The continuous grind of shows meant the Palace could book only lesser acts who were willing to undergo the torturous regime. That policy also didn't work out, and it ended in the week beginning September 30, 1935.

For the next 14 years the Palace stuck to a movie-only policy. The vaudeville booking office had long since moved from the 6th floor of the Palace office building to the building housing Radio City Music Hall. Yet ex-vaudevillians without much hope of ever working again still hung out on the Beach across from the Palace. The theater itself was renovated in August 1941. *Daily News* reporter Robert Sylvester noted the occasion:

Yesterday they started to tear down and "streamline" the old-fashioned marquee and lobby, with its twinkling little electric bulbs and displays that once were as bitterly contested for as the favors of a great beauty. The marquee still reads B. F. Keith's Palace having ignored the changes and mergers of the years. But inside the 25-year-old theater a double feature film bill was the attraction on the stage where Sarah Bernhardt once played Camille, dragging her wooden leg from stage to dressing room over a long white bearskin rug.

On May 19, 1949, vaudeville acts once more accompanied movies on stage. The idea originated with Sol Schwartz, the president and general manager of RKO Theaters. He was quoted in a *New York Times* interview with J. P. Shanley:

I think the time is ripe for a little change. Many people haven't seen "round" actors perform on a stage for more than fifteen years. Some of the men who were in the service during the war were seeing live talent for the first time when USO shows played for them. They liked it and I think they want more.

Schwartz's idea caught on with the public, who oohed and aahed over the theater's $60,000 renovation.

The theater limped along into the 1950s with an occasional good week, but as the decade progressed television became an increasingly greater threat to its existence. On October 4, 1951, the theater closed for 2 weeks for sprucing up to make ready for its next incarnation. It reopened on October 16, 1951, with an appearance by Judy Garland. By this time, Garland's career in pictures was almost finished; she needed the Palace, and the Palace needed her. She appeared on a 2-a-day policy with such veteran vaudevillians as Smith and Dale, whose "Dr. Kronkhite" act was the inspiration for the NEIL SIMON play *The Sunshine Boys*. Garland was booked for a 4-week run and stayed for 19 weeks. She finished on February 4, 1952, with what everyone conceded was a triumphant engagement. More straight vaudeville followed until April 12, 1952, and an appearance by Betty Hutton, which proved almost as popular as Garland's. Ironically, it was Hutton who replaced Garland in the film version of IRVING BERLIN's stage hit *ANNIE GET YOUR GUN*.

Hutton appeared for 4 weeks, and then it was back to Schwartz's 8-act vaudeville policy. The next great event at the Palace took place on January 18, 1953, with an engagement by Danny Kaye. He played 14 weeks, for a total of 135 performances before 243,250 patrons. A few more imaginative bookings in the 1950s broke the vaudeville monotony. Betty Hutton returned with newcomer Dick Shawn, who was "discovered" and became a star. Phil Spitalny and his All Girl Orchestra held the Palace stage for a week in the summer of 1955, and in November the Grand Ole Opry took over the Palace stage. On November 26, 1956, Judy Garland returned to a triumphant reception at the Palace. This time, comic Alan King was "discovered" at

the Palace. Garland concluded another record-breaking run on January 8, 1957, after 15 weeks at a $7.50 top ticket price. Jerry Lewis convulsed Palace audiences beginning on January 8, 1957, and proved he could make it without his one-time partner Dean Martin. Lewis's 4-week run had an advance sale of $90,000, and that was with a top ticket price of only $6.00. During that run, television singer Eydie Gorme was "discovered." Liberace was the next superstar to appear in the Palace with an acclaimed act. However, although he had been booked for 4 weeks beginning on April 20, 1957, he did poor business and closed after only 2 weeks.

On August 13, 1957, the Palace again gave up its vaudeville policy. Blockbusters were hard to come by, and in the weeks between their appearances the theater did not do well. If Liberace could not pack them in, then who could? The only exception to the theater's all-movie policy was a tremendously successful appearance by Harry Belafonte beginning on December 15, 1957. He was booked for 8 weeks and stayed for a little more than 3 months, playing to sold-out houses.

On August 19, 1965, the theater was sold to producer James Nederlander, who restored the theater under the supervision of Ralph Alswang. In August 1965 the last movie to play the Palace—*Harlow*—premiered. Nederlander began a new era at the Palace, with legitimate theater. The first show, *Sweet Charity* (1/29/66; 608 performances), premiered with an exceptional score by Cy Coleman and Dorothy Fields (see FIELDS FAMILY). Neil Simon was responsible for the libretto, and Bob Fosse directed. Gwen Verdon perfectly captured the title character. The score contained several standout numbers, including "Baby Dream Your Dream," "Where Am I Going?" and "I'm a Brass Band." But the big hit was "Big Spender."

Judy Garland made another appearance at the Palace starting on July 31, 1967, in her show *At Home at the Palace*. She appeared with her children Joey and Lorna Luft, comedian Jackie Vernon, and vaudeville veteran John Bubbles. She played 24 performances. Eddie Fisher and Buddy Hackett opened at the Palace on August 28, 1967, and remained for 42 performances.

The next musical at the Palace, *Henry, Sweet Henry* (10/23/67; 80 performances), was based on the movie *The World of Henry Orient*. Despite the talents of songwriter Bob Merrill, author Nunnally Johnson, and cast members Don Ameche, Carol Bruce, Alice Playten, Neva Small, and Robin Wilson, the show was a failure. Although George M. Cohan never played the Palace, the musical *George M!* (4/10/68; 435 performances), starring Joel Grey as the irrepressible Broadway star, opened there. Joe Layton staged the musical with gusto.

Supporting Grey were Bernadette Peters, Danny Carroll, Jerry Dodge, Betty Ann Grove, and Jill O'Hara.

The next hit to play the Palace was the STROUSE AND ADAMS musical *Applause* (3/30/70; 896 performances). Based on *All About Eve, Applause* starred Lauren Bacall, an unlikely musical comedy star. COMDEN AND GREEN wrote the script, and choreographer Ron Field directed. Bonnie Franklin was hailed as a new Broadway star because of her rendition of the catchy title song. However, Franklin subsequently left Broadway for television and never looked back.

Cyrano (5/13/73; 49 performances) was an especially dismal musicalization of Edmond Rostand's classic *Cyrano de Bergerac. Gentlemen Prefer Blondes*, in which Carol Channing made her first great success, was reworked into the musical *Lorelei* (1/27/74; 320 performances) featuring Channing. Joel Grey returned to the Palace in *Goodtime Charley* (3/3/75; 104 performances) and again in one of JERRY HERMAN's few flops, *The Grand Tour* (1/11/79; 61 performances). Based on the play *Jacobowsky and the Colonel* by S. N. Behrman, the show became less and less successful as rehearsals went on.

Lauren Bacall returned to the Palace in what seemed to be a sure success, *Woman of the Year* (3/29/81; 770 performances) with a fair score by John Kander and Fred Ebb. Despite its long run, *Woman of the Year* never paid back its investors. As a result, the Securities and Exchange Commission revised its rules for investments in Broadway shows. *Woman of the Year*, a forgettable musical, is now chiefly remembered as one of the shows that scared investors away from Broadway. Jerry Herman recovered from the failure of *The Grand Tour* and presented the Palace with his smash hit musical, *La Cage aux Folles* (8/21/83; 1,761 performances). Harvey Fierstein wrote the libretto, based on a hugely popular French movie. George Hearn and Gene Barry starred.

La Cage might have run longer, but plans were announced to build a new 40-story office building with 364,000 square feet of office space around the theater, retaining the theater itself. It was considered too expensive to move the show. The architecture firm of Fox & Fowle redesigned the theater as well as the new Embassy Suites Hotel that replaced the old Palace office building. Today the Palace is barely recognizable from the street, having been entirely subsumed by the hotel.

Still, the Palace hosted hit shows. *The Will Rogers Follies* (5/1/91; 983 performances) starred Keith Carradine. The show, which won the Tony Award for Best Musical, was written by Cy Coleman, Betty Comden, and Adolph Green. Tommy Tune's imaginative direction and choreography, Carradine's charm, and the wonderful set by Tony Walton helped the show achieve its long run.

Disney's stage adaptation of its cartoon hit *Beauty and the Beast* (4/18/94) played the Palace before moving to the LUNT-FONTANNE THEATER on November 11, 1999, *Beauty and the Beast*, a relatively straight retelling of the cartoon, was presented in full operetta style, even down to the painted drops. Still, the success of the film ensured success in its stage transfer.

Liza Minnelli made an ill-conceived comeback with her salute to Vincente Minnelli, her father, with the revue *Minnelli on Minnelli* (12/8/99). The public didn't buy it, and the show closed after only 20 performances.

Disney returned to the Palace with its third theatrical venture and its third smash hit. Elton John and Tim Rice's *Aida* (3/23/2000) pleased few critics, but audiences kept coming, drawn by John's name. Bob Crowley's impressive physical production overwhelmed the lackluster but heavily miked score. In the show's favor were strong performances by its leads Adam Pascal (formerly of *Rent*), the stunning Heather Headley, and Sheri Rene Scott in a classic camp performance.

The interior of the Palace has been given landmark status by the New York City Landmarks Preservation Commission. Gene A. Norman said: "If one theater were to be named the most famous, that privilege would fall to the Palace." This presumably means that future generations of performers can feel what Jack Haley felt when playing the Palace: "Only a performer can describe the anxieties, the joys, the anticipation, and the exultation of a week's engagement at the Palace. The walk through the iron gate on 47th Street, through the courtyard to the stage door, was the cum laude walk to a show business diploma. A feeling of ecstasy came with the knowledge that *this is the Palace*."

PARADISE GARDENS. *See* **Victoria Theatre (1).**

PARAMOUNT BUILDING. 1501 Broadway, between West 43rd and West 44th Streets. Architects: C. W. and George Rapp; constructed 1925–27.

The Paramount Building is one of New York's most recognizable skyscrapers, yet it hasn't had the same acclaim that other New York landmarks have had. Perhaps the reason is its poor upkeep until recently. The 35-story building, though classically inspired, has a decided Art Deco style. As it rises, the building employs a series of setbacks, culminating in a ziggurat upon which stands a magnificent clock tower. The apex of the entire structure is the 20-foot glass globe that has recently been illuminated again. The globe was perhaps inspired by the London Coliseum, which is also topped by a lighted globe, creating a beacon in London's West End.

The Paramount Building had an auspicious opening tied to the opening of the PARAMOUNT THEATER, over which it towered. It was built to house the New York offices of Famous Players–Lasky Corporation, the parent of Paramount Pictures. Shanley's Restaurant, in the Putnam Building, was demolished to make way for the office building. The building also contained an observation tower on its roof from which sightseers could look over Manhattan for only a quarter. After the theater was converted to office space in 1964–65, the Paramount Building went into a decline, as did the rest of the Times Square area. Today it is one of the only original large office buildings to remain on Times Square, serving as the headquarters to many theatrical concerns.

In the late 1990s the clock and globe were renovated and brought to their former glory. Right at 8:00 on theater evenings, as the clock strikes the hour, GEORGE M. COHAN's "Give My Regards to Broadway" echoes through the Times Square area.

PARAMOUNT THEATER. 1501 Broadway between West 43rd and West 44th Streets. Architects: C. W. & George Rapp, constructed 1925–27. Opening: November 19, 1926; *Cavalcade of Motion Pictures.*

The Times Square Paramount Theater was perhaps the best-loved theater on the square. Thousands remember lining up at the theater to hear their favorite band and vocalist. Before adopting a big-band policy, the theater mounted the usual movie palace stage shows, similar to those that later became famous at the ROXY THEATER and other giant theaters. The Paramount is the one that remains in most people's minds as the ultimate Times Square theater.

It was built by the Famous Players–Lasky Corporation, the money behind Paramount Pictures, which constructed the PARAMOUNT BUILDING above it to house their New York headquarters. The opening night program stated, "Thirty years ago Herald Square was the very heart of Broadway. Today it has become only a memory, and ten blocks uptown Times Square now rules as the Capital of the Amusement World. The Paramount Theater stands at the Crossroads of the world."

The opening program, staged by Broadway director JOHN MURRAY ANDERSON, was a typical, if overblown, example of movie palace offerings. The show was titled *Cavalcade of Motion Pictures.* After some specialty numbers and the usual speeches, the program began. The show featured a newsreel and some vaudeville-type specialties, followed by a Paramount picture: *God Gave Me Twenty Cents,* starring Lois Moran. Among the notables present at opening night was a man with his wife on his arm. As the couple took their seats in a special box, the entire audience rose and gave him a standing ovation. The man was unaware of the applause because he was deaf. He was Thomas Alva Edison, the inventor of the motion picture.

Ticket prices ranged from 40 cents to 99 cents. The theater opened at 10:45 A.M. and closed a little more than 12 hours later. An advertisement placed in the *New York Times* on November 23, 1926, boasted of the attendance records set by the new theater,

> 30,222 in Two Days! Into the Paradise of luxury, color and enchantment they came, more than 30,000 in two days. Saturday and Sunday, thrilling with new excitement at every step! The spaciousness of the place! The superb height and dignity of the Grand Hall as they entered! The decoration and equipment throughout, so beautiful that each detail made people halt to admire it alone! And then, a *show* worthy of the *setting!* These thousands are telling more thousands and they are all coming back, week after week, for there is nothing like the Paramount in all New York for sheer luxury and unprecedented entertainment values!

Patrons entered the beautiful ticket lobby and then the low-ceilinged Hall of Nations, which opened into the enormous Grand Hall. The Grand Hall lobby was much larger and more ornate than the lobby of the Paris Opera House, which had inspired it. The theater itself seated 3,664 people. The auditorium was criticized at the time but today is viewed in a kindlier light. The only trouble with the theater was the relatively narrow width of the proscenium arch. Later theaters featured huge stages suitable for spectacular presentations and wide-screen movies. Most shows staged at the Paramount extended a thrust stage into the auditorium over the orchestra pit. When the big-band policy went into effect, the bands played in front of the proscenium. When VistaVision wide-screen films were shown, the sides of the arch were demolished.

The August 1926 issue of *Metronome Magazine* carried an article that described other areas of the Paramount:

> When the Paramount Theater opens this fall, you can meet your friends in any of 25 rooms, foyers or lobbies. Each will have a definite name and luxurious appointments. Entering at the box office lobby, one passes into the intermediate lobby, thence into the grand hall which is lined with Breche Centella marble, imported from Italy at a cost of over a half a million dollars. The main lounge will be known as the Elizabethan room, and is located in the basement where there are also a ladies' lounge, dressing room and ladies' smoking room. The men will also have a smoking room in the basement known as the University Room. Leaving the grand hall and passing upward, one finds the intermediate mezzanine lobby, which gives access to the mezzanine loges. Here also is a men's smoking room and a ladies' rest room.

The most novel rooms ever incorporated into a theater are the period, club and fraternity rooms. Here, you can lounge in luxury and await the arrival of your friends. These rooms are named as follows: Elizabethan, Marie Antoinette, Chinoiserie, College, Jade, Club, The Galleries, Peacock Alley, Grand Hall, Hall of Nations, the Rotunda, Music Room and Fraternity Room. The College Club and Fraternity rooms will be decorated with the insignia and colors of all the clubs, colleges and fraternities, represented.

The Paramount is rapidly nearing completion. It will be one of the great art buildings of the world, with almost 50 percent of the space devoted to promenades, lounges, rest rooms and comfortable conveniences for its patrons.

The theater presented musical revues, featuring stars of the day such as FRED ASTAIRE, Beatrice Lillie, and ETHEL MERMAN, and cut-down versions of Broadway shows. It had a permanent staff, including ballet master Boris Petroff, costume designer Charles LeM-

aire, and conductor of the Paramount Grand Symphony, Nathaniel Finston. Producing directors, in addition to John Murray Anderson, were R. H. Burnside, a Shubert (*see* SHUBERT BROTHERS) contract director, Jack Partington, and Frank Cambria. At the Wurlitzer twin organs (called "our masterpiece" by Fanny Wurlitzer, chairman of the board of the Wurlitzer Company) were Mr. and Mrs. Jesse Crawford.

By 1934, in the middle of the Depression, the stage shows were discontinued. Only the organ concerts remained. Then someone got the idea to present big bands and singers. The most famous appearance was that of Frank Sinatra, who sang with the Tommy Dorsey Orchestra at the height of his popularity.

Big-band singer Dolly Dawn also appeared there. She recalled her experiences:

The people lined up around the block, from Broadway down 43rd and around 8th Avenue. When the doors

Paramount Theater interior.

would open they would pile in. Some people would get in before 1:00 for thirty-five cents and stay in there for six shows.

The crowds at the stage door—you couldn't get out. You just stayed in and had food sent in. You slept between shows because it was just too hectic to try to get out. One hundred people would grab you. It was exciting. I'd say to the kids coming up, if you never played that theater you hadn't really played a theater. The smell in your nose when you opened the backstage door and you'd think, "Oh my God, I'm here!" It was a certain distinct odor; I don't know how to express it.

There was an old doorman who had been an old vaudevillian; he was always called "Pop." He'd say, "If there's anything I can do for you" but you'd have to help him because he was so old.

The big thrill was when they'd ring a buzzer and say "half hour." Then "fifteen minutes." And finally "five minutes." By then whoever was supposed to be on stage had to be in the orchestra pit. When you heard that band strike up, what a thrill! What a thrill it was! You knew the orchestra lift was going to come up and there would be thousands of people applauding you.

The bobby-soxers ruled the theater. But after the big-band era came television and the beginning of the end for the Paramount. Entertainers preferred to host their own television shows for more money, bigger audiences, and less work. They required inflated fees to appear at the Paramount and other theaters.

In the 1960s, with the advent of rock and roll, the theater catered to a younger crowd. When school was not in session, the Paramount would draw the younger set in record numbers, but during the day, and when New Yorkers were out of town during the summers, the theater died.

The Paramount finally closed on August 14, 1965. The great marquee was taken down, and the theater was gutted. Offices were put in the huge space.

An approximation of the marquee was erected in 2001 as part of the World Wrestling Federation restaurant on the site of the original marquee. Dolly Dawn offered one last thought on the Paramount: "These kids have no idea what it was, and they'll never know because there will never be anything like those theaters again. And I am so grateful to the Lord that I was a part of it. And I saw it, I felt it. It's not easily forgotten and I don't want to ever forget it."

PAUL, MAURY. The real name of society columnist Cholly Knickerbocker; b. Philadelphia, Pennsylvania, 1890; d. July 17, 1942.

The majority of Broadwayites do not recognize the name of Maury Paul, but as Cholly Knickerbocker he exerted great influence over their lives. Knickerbocker was the name Paul signed to a society column that was widely syndicated across the country.

Paul was born in Philadelphia to a society family. He attended the University of Pennsylvania, graduating in 1914. After graduation, he joined the staff of the *Philadelphia Times* for a brief period. He soon moved to the *New York Press* as its society editor. When that paper merged with the *Morning Sun*, he left journalism for Wall Street. The brokerage business didn't suit him, and he found employment with the *New York Mail*. At the *Mail* he created a society column, using the pen name Dolley Madison.

In 1917 Paul moved to the *New York American* and took over the Cholly Knickerbocker column. He continued at the *American* through its merger with the *New York Evening Journal*. At the new *New York Journal-American*, Paul thrived. He contributed a daily society column and contributed features to the Sunday edition. Paul was basically a reporter and seldom expressed his own opinions in the column. He almost never reported on society's events, concentrating instead on his subjects' lives and actions. He was known to encourage feuds between himself and the doyens of society. The feuds guaranteed a lively column and a loyal readership. Paul invented the terms "Cafe Society" and "Old Guard," and they soon entered the language. Paul divided the "Old Guard," society's oldest families, into two categories, A and B. The fights and controversies over placement in the two classes contributed to Paul's renown.

Paul enjoyed a remarkably long career. He remained at the *Journal-American* as Cholly Knickerbocker for 25 years until his death on July 17, 1942. Subsequent Cholly Knickerbockers include Igor Cassini (the coiner of the term "jet set") and his assistant Liz Smith and, as Suzy Knickerbocker, Aileen Mehle.

PLAYBILL. *Playbill* is the most consistently recognizable aspect of theatergoing. The theater program lists all-important information about a play including cast lists, technical credits, production staff, musical numbers, and biographies of important contributors. Such theater programs have been a part of the audience experience since the turn of the 20th century.

The 18th century saw the introduction of playbills, listing the cast members and information on the play's locale and scenes. In the 19th century programs expanded to much the same form that they have today, although they had much finer design and usually gave more information on individual productions. The early programs usually consisted of four pages: a cover, which was individualized for the show or theater; a back page, which contained a drawing of the theater layout and exits; and two interior pages with the show's credits.

In 1884 Frank Vance Strauss had the idea of combining the theater program with advertising. The Ohioan established his business the following year, and such companies as Caswell-Massey, Runkel Brothers Cocoa, and Schirmer pianos were among the first advertisers. In early programs the names of set designers and directors were listed in the back, along with names of prop studios and costume houses. Lighting designers were almost never listed. The programs usually stated "Electrical effects by Kleigel Bros." or another lighting-supply house. Individual authorship of songs in revues was usually not indicated, and typographical errors abounded. Programs were printed for individual theaters, and they might be in any format or size.

In 1891 Strauss merged operations with the only competitor left in New York. In 1905, Strauss decided to standardize the design and layout of the programs so that the makeup would be easier and the sizes of advertising space uniform. When the programs became standardized, special features were introduced in the free handout. These included "What the Man Will Wear" (one of the first men's fashion columns), "Beauty Hints," "For Book Lovers," "What the Woman Will Wear," "Doorways to Beauty," short stories, poems, and sometimes biographies of the cast under the title "From Our Stageland Scrapbook." The last page, as in earlier programs, was reserved for diagrams of the orchestra and balcony levels of the theater and their exits. Each cover depicted the particular theater in which the show played. The 4-color designs were especially fanciful and are much in demand today as collector's items.

In 1908 artists F. Earl Christy and John M. Burke drew "The Program Girl." The sketches appeared in the programs and were also sold in groups of three for a dime. Three years later, for the first time the program acquired a name: the *Strauss Theater Magazine Program*. Because many audience members kept their playbills and put them into scrapbooks, Strauss decided to offer for sale binders that could hold the magazine.

Strauss sold the operation in 1918 to his nephew, Richard M. Huber, who promptly renamed the handout *The Magazine Theater Program*. In only 6 years, by 1924, Huber was printing more than 16,000,000 playbills a year for more than 60 theaters. Huber started up operations of *Playbill*'s parent company, the New York Theater Program Corporation, in the 1934–35 season. By this time Huber's programs had completely outstripped those of competitors, and Huber's corporation had a monopoly on programs for the Broadway theater. Max Reinhardt's production of *The Eternal Road*, presented at the 34th Street Manhattan Opera House, was the only legitimate production not to use the company's program service. Even the Metropolitan Opera House handed out the magazine.

That same season a new name appeared on the program's cover, *The Playbill*. By this time advertisements could be placed in individual programs. One advertiser who consistently took advantage of the policy was the clothing chain Rogers Peet Company. They incorporated the titles of individual shows into their advertisements. For example, the program of the revue *Rain or Shine* carried the following ad: "Rain or shine Scotch Mists are fine. Handsome, stylish overcoats that are wetproof too!" And the ad in the program for Preston Sturges' *Strictly Dishonorable* read in part, "It's strictly dishonorable to say that a fabric is wool if there is any trace of cotton." Needless to say, some titles of productions were a challenge to Rogers Peet's advertising firm. Because the number of advertising pages varied from show to show, the size of a *Playbill* could indicate how big a hit the show was. The *Playbill* for *ANYTHING GOES* was 48 pages thick, whereas the one for *Post Road* contained only 12 pages.

During World War II couples were requested to share one *Playbill* to help save paper for the war effort. Space was donated to war bonds just as Frank Strauss had done for liberty bonds during World War I. *Playbill* also became smaller in size to save on paper. Covers had long featured logos or photographs from the shows rather than generic theater logos. In 1948 the cover's color was changed from sepia to ivory. In February 1951 the color was changed again from ivory to white.

The business changed hands in 1956 when Richard Huber sold *The Playbill* to producer and real-estate magnate Roger L. Stevens. Stevens streamlined the design. He changed the name simply to *Playbill* and made a generic cover for all editions of *Playbill*. No longer did the name of the show appear on the cover. Of course, collectors and others railed against the change. Although the cover sketch changed each month, there was no way to tell without flipping through the magazine what show it was covering. Collectors weren't the only ones upset by the change. Stars had in their contracts that their pictures would appear on the cover of *Playbill*. In the fall of 1958 a new design was introduced: a colored band, different for each theater, was placed across the top with a show's logo or photo beneath. Then a standard yellow band was introduced.

Gilman Kraft bought the magazine from Stevens in 1961. Kraft installed Arthur Birsh to head the operation, and Birsh took over as publisher in October 1965. The year before, *Playbill* had become a monthly instead of a weekly. Also, columns and staff were added to give the magazine a new, more modern look. Bernice Peck began her fashion column, "On a Personal Bias," which continued into the 1990s. In 1973 the column was expanded to an entire fashion supplement. The main reason for giving her this section was to attract a wider range of advertising. Also at this time Al Hirschfeld, noted caricaturist, started his feature "Unlikely Casting."

In 1968 Kraft sold the magazine to Metromedia, a small chain of independent television stations that later became the basis of the Fox Television Network. The new editor-in-chief was Joan Alleman. Metromedia could not have picked a worse time to buy the program, because Broadway went into a dangerous slump during the late 1960s and '70s. Fewer shows were being produced; audiences stayed out of the Times Square area, which was becoming increasingly sleazy and unsafe; and ticket prices were quickly rising. As a result, Arthur Birsh was able to reacquire *Playbill* from Metromedia. When Birsh took control again of *Playbill*, Broadway theaters began a small upswing. The success of shows like *A Chorus Line*, *42nd Street*, and *Cats* gave theater as a whole a base on which to build.

Unlike European theaters, Broadway theaters offer free programs to ticket holders. *Playbill* actually pays the theaters for the rights to produce each production's programs. *Playbill* makes money through selling advertisements in the magazine. The system works much like a television network's advertising department. *Playbill* guarantees each advertiser that a certain number of audience members will receive each magazine. Publicists on each production supply the information on the show, cast, production staff, and crew to the *Playbill* editorial staff. Production information takes up the inner pages of the distinctive yellow-and-white magazine. The outer pages contain articles on the theater, interviews, restaurant news, fashion sections, and advertising. The production information includes the title page with all credits, scene information, musical numbers, biographies of the cast and major staff members, listings of producers and production staff, and usually a column called "At This Theater," giving an abbreviated history of the most famous productions that played at the theater. Whereas the outside pages are printed in quantities of more than a million monthly, the inside show pages are produced each week. The quantity of the inner pages depends on estimates derived from past business and advance sales. The two sections are then put together and delivered weekly by *Playbill's* yellow trucks.

In the early years of the magazine, the entire product was printed weekly. As the number of shows has fallen, so has the need for weekly printings. In the old days, a *Playbill* employee named Callahan went from theater to theater and personally checked out each show's business. He then would estimate the needs of each show. After Callahan left the post, Herman Pepper replaced him. Pepper would also make the rounds of the theaters, checking on business and ordering the necessary number of *Playbills* to be delivered the next day. Although Pepper went into thousands of theaters during his time on the job, he sat through only one complete production, *My Fair Lady*. What he thought of the musical is not recorded. When he died, the job was assigned to the truck drivers who deliver the magazines. They check the previous night's leftovers and supply the necessary number of copies of *Playbills*.

Mistakes and typographical errors are almost non-existent today. Many theatergoers are not particularly happy with the magazine's articles, but these critics are only beginning to express their complaints. Still, despite the reservations of some, *Playbill* is a mostly excellent guide to the Broadway theater season. In the 1990s *Playbill* began selling a national edition by subscription and through newsstand sales. They also started Playbill.com, an Internet version of the magazine with many special features.

PLAYERS CLUB. 16 Gramercy Park. The Players Club and the Friars Club are the two performing-arts clubs that cater to those in the Broadway theater. Edwin Booth, one of the greatest actors of the 19th century, founded the Players in 1888, fashioning the club after the Garrick Club in England. Its charter states that the Players Club is a place where "actors and dramatists could mingle in good fellowship with craftsmen of the fine arts as well as those of the performing arts."

In May 1888 Booth purchased the Clarkson Potter house on Gramercy Park for $75,000 and commissioned Stanford White to redesign the brownstone as a private club. The name of the club was the idea of author Thomas Bailey Aldrich after the famous lines in William Shakespeare's *As You Like It*.

Booth lived in an apartment in the club until his death in 1893. Among the other founders of the club were Mark Twain, John Drew, General William Tecumseh Sherman, Albert M. Palmer, Augustin Daly, Lawrence Barrett, and Joseph Jefferson.

The club accepts not only actors but also playwrights, artists, press agents, directors, editors, producers, publishers, cartoonists, musicians, writers, and educators. It holds annual pool, bridge, and backgammon tournaments and dinner theater programs, as well as the club's famous Pipe Nights, Ladies Day, and Founder's Night celebration. Among the notable presidents of the club were Edwin Booth, Joseph Jefferson, John Drew, Walter Hampden, Howard Lindsay, Dennis King, Alfred Drake, Roland Winters, Jose Ferrer, and Michael Allinson.

An important feature of the club is the Walter Hampden Memorial Library. This research library is one of the largest in the country. It fulfills the club's manifest, which called for the creation of "a library relating especially to the history of the American stage, and the preservation of pictures, playbills, photographs and curiosities." The library used Booth's personal library of 1,000 volumes as its nucleus. The collection has since expanded greatly and now numbers more than 20,000 volumes. These deal primarily with 19th-century theater. Since 1957 the library has opened its doors to nonmembers to use for research projects.

The Players presented an annual show from 1922 through 1940. The first production was *The Rivals* at the Empire Theater, June 5–10, 1922. The cast included the leading players of the day, both male and female. These actors donated their services, with 10 percent of the proceeds going to The Actors Fund. The total receipts for the 15 productions were $412,117. Among the stars who graced the stage in these productions were John Drew, Pauline Lord, Mary Shaw, Otis Skinner, Tom Wise, HELEN HAYES, Fay Bainter, Blanche Ring, James T. Powers, Walter Hampden, Laurette Taylor, Elsie Ferguson, Charles Coburn, Ethel Barrymore (*see* BARRYMORE FAMILY), Henry E. Dixey, Philip Merivale, GEORGE M. COHAN, Blanche Ring, Effie Shannon, Dorothy Stickney, and Tyrone Power.

On April 23, 1989, The Players, previously an exclusively male club, admitted women to its membership. Inductees included Helen Hayes, Lauren Bacall, Betty Comden (*see* COMDEN AND GREEN), Mary Tyler Moore, Toni Morrison, Eudora Welty, Beverly Sills, Tharon Musser, Kitty Carlisle Hart, and Gwen Verdon.

THE PLAYHOUSE THEATRE. 137 West 48th Street. Architect: Charles A. Rich. Opening: April 15, 1911; *Sauce for the Goose*.

The Playhouse Theatre was one of the most successful Broadway theaters although it has been almost forgotten in the years since its demolition in 1967. Producer WILLIAM A. BRADY built the theater to hold his productions. He paid particular attention to the architecture of the theater, which was duly noted in the *New York Commercial Advertiser*:

The building is constructed of brick, with stone facings, and is a combination of the French and Colonial styles of architecture. The front of the building is imposing and almost severe, but this severity is relieved by stone carvings of comedy and tragedy set in the wall, marble window medallions, a flowered frieze, and other ornaments of trimmed stone.

The main entrance is under a canopy of steel and glass, and leads through oaken doors, set in diamond glass, into the lobby, which is enclosed in white marble.

The main entrance as well as the entrances leading to the gallery and studios are flanked by brick posts, surmounted with stone urns, and joined by a novel grilled iron fence.

The interior of the house gives the impression of cosy compactness. All parts of the house, including the balcony and gallery, are brought very near to the stage, so that audience and players will be in close sympathy. The loss of depth in obtaining this desirable result is compensated for by the extreme width of the auditorium. The boxes are set back, although they are large and roomy, and there is no interference with the line of vision. There is a free view of the stage from every part of the house. The decorations are in deep red, gold, and brown, with brown carpets and blue draperies.

Brady had his offices on the 4th floor of the theater, with studios above. The first offering of the new playhouse was *Sauce for the Goose* (4/15/11). Although it starred one of the greatest actresses of her time, Grace George, also known as Mrs. Brady, the show played only 2 performances, closing on opening day.

George Broadhurst, namesake of the BROADHURST THEATER, had the first big hit at the theater—his play *Bought and Paid For* (9/26/11; 431 performances), with Frank Craven and Julia Dean in the leads. Brady produced the next offering at the theater, a dramatization of Louisa May Alcott's *Little Women* (10/14/12), featuring his daughter Alice Brady. A success, it played 184 performances, a fine run for the time. The actress would also appear in the theater's next hit, *The Family Cupboard* (8/21/13; 140 performances) by Owen Davis, one of the most successful playwrights of his time. She appeared in the next hit at the theater as well, *The Things That Count* (224 performances), also under Brady's tutelage; this was a transfer to the Playhouse on December 22, 1913, from the MAXINE ELLIOTT'S THEATRE, where it had opened only 14 days before.

On March 29, 1915, Grace George herself produced and starred in George Bernard Shaw's *Captain Brassbound's Conversion* at the Playhouse. She was supported by Ernest Lawford, Mary Nash, Louis Calvert, John Cromwell, Clarence Derwent, Guthrie McClintic, and Conway Tearle. Lawford and Nash would appear in the next hit at the theater, *The Man Who Came Back* (9/2/16; 457 performances), by Jules Eckert Goodman. Many failures followed in quick succession, but the theater was one of the most successfully booked on Broadway.

The theater's next hit was also the first musical to grace its stage. *Up She Goes* (11/6/22; 256 performances) boasted a score by Harry Tierney and Joseph McCarthy, composers of the hit *Irene*. But, although a success, this time the score would yield no hits on the level of "Alice Blue Gown."

One of the biggest hits of the 1920s and a play still revived today, *The Show Off*, by George Kelly, opened at the Playhouse on February 25, 1924, and played 571 performances. Elmer Rice's *Street Scene*, another oft-revived play, began its run at the Playhouse on January 10, 1929, and lasted well into the Depression, closing after 601 performances. Even as the Depression took its toll on theaters, Brady held on to his with a steady stream of bookings, even though he had as many as 16 flops in a row. Just as his luck seemed to run out, a smash hit would book the theater and save the day.

Yet another perennial was the next big hit, GEORGE ABBOTT and John Cecil Holm's comedy *Three Men on a Horse* (1/30/35; 835 performances). Shirley Booth, Teddy Hart, Garson Kanin, Sam Levene, William Lynn, and Joyce Arling headed the cast. Mark Reed's *Yes, My Darling Daughter* (1/9/37; 405 performances) was another hit.

Brady died in 1944, and the theater was sold to the SHUBERT BROTHERS. They "improved" the theater by eliminating the second balcony.

The next notable success at The Playhouse was the premiere of TENNESSEE WILLIAMS' *The Glass Menagerie* (3/31/45; 563 performances). Laurette Taylor's performance as Amanda was hailed as one of the greatest of the 20th century. She was ably supported by Julie Haydon as her daughter, Laura; Anthony Ross as the Gentleman Caller; and Eddie Dowling as her son, Tom. Dowling, in association with Louis J. Singer, produced the play.

Although not a success, *All in One* (4/19/55; 47 performances) was an auspicious and curious booking for the theater. The first act consisted of Tennessee Williams' one-act drama, *27 Wagons Full of Cotton*, with Maureen Stapleton, Myron McCormick, and Felice Orlandi. The first intermission was followed by

Paul Ford and Maureen O'Sullivan in *Never Too Late*, 1962.

Springtime for Hitler in Mel Brooks' film *The Producers* on the stage of the Playhouse Theatre.

Leonard Bernstein's now classic one-act opera *Trouble in Tahiti* with Alice Ghostley and John Tyers. A second intermission led to a dance concert by Paul Draper.

The Playhouse was nearing the end of its life, although, ironically, it was enjoying its biggest successes. Among them was William Gibson's dramatic story of Helen Keller and her teacher Annie Sullivan, *The Miracle Worker* (10/19/59; 719 performances). Anne Bancroft and Patty Duke starred under Arthur Penn's sensitive direction. James Congdon, Patricia Neal, Torin Thatcher, and Beah Richards (making her Broadway debut) were also featured in the exemplary production.

George Abbott returned to the Playhouse to direct its longest-running hit, *Never Too Late* (11/26/62; 1,007 performances). Sumner Arthur Long's comedy starred Paul Ford, Orson Bean, and Maureen O'Sullivan. While *Never Too Late* was in its run, the Shuberts sold the theater to a group of developers who pledged to tear down the building.

The last play at the venerable theater was also a smash hit. *The Impossible Years* (10/13/65; 670 per-

formances), by Robert Fisher and Arthur Marx (Groucho's son), featured Alan King, Scott Glenn, Bert Convy, and Sudie Bond. The Playhouse's legitimate career was finally over when the curtain rang down on the theater on May 27, 1967.

But there was to be one extraordinary event still to come at the Playhouse—one that would lead to a kind of immortality. With demolition near, the owners leased the theater to a film company who were shooting a sleeper named *The Producers*. In a way, the last show to play the Playhouse was *Springtime for Hitler*. Both the exterior and interior of the theater were used in the Mel Brooks film.

And with that ridiculous end, the Playhouse was finally demolished. Today the Time-Life Building occupies part of the Playhouse site.

THE PLAYWRIGHTS' COMPANY. The Playwrights' Company was one of the more successful of the production companies established in the 1930s. Like its brethren, the AMERICAN NATIONAL THEATRE

407

AND ACADEMY (ANTA) and the GROUP THEATER, it proposed to establish a protective environment for the production of plays and with the goal of improving the theater. Playwright Maxwell Anderson stated that the purpose of The Playwrights' Company was "to make a center for ourselves within the theater, and possibly rally the theater as a whole to new levels by setting a high standard of writing and production."

The first members of the company were playwrights Anderson, S. N. Behrman, Sidney Howard, Robert Emmett Sherwood, and Elmer Rice. Later members included composer KURT WEILL, playwright Robert Anderson, lawyer John F. Wharton, and producer Roger L. Stevens. They sought a more socialistic approach to the theater, whereby the group as a whole could share the occasional failure of one member. They also desired more input into the production of their plays and a freer hand in crafting important plays, regardless of the vagaries of the box office.

The first play presented by the new organization was Robert E. Sherwood's *Abe Lincoln in Illinois* (10/15/38; 472 performances). It was an immediate success at the PLYMOUTH THEATER due to the quality of the script and a powerful yet understated performance by Raymond Massey in the title role. Massey won the DELIA AUSTRIAN MEDAL for the best performance of the season. Sherwood won a Theater Club Award for the best play of the season, as well as the PULITZER

The Playwrights' Company members S.N. Behrman, Maxwell Anderson, Robert Sherwood and Elmer Rice.

PRIZE for drama. Sherwood also won in 1936 for *Idiot's Delight* and again for the company's production of *There Shall Be No Night* in 1940.

The company's next outing was a musical with book and lyrics by Maxwell Anderson and music by Kurt Weill. *Knickerbocker Holiday* (10/19/38; 168 performances) opened only 4 days after *Abe Lincoln in Illinois*. It starred Walter Huston, and it introduced the classic ballad "September Song." Other plays quickly followed, including Elmer Rice's *American Landscape* (12/3/38; 43 performances); S. N. Behrman's *No Time for Comedy* (4/17/39; 185 performances); Anderson's *Key Largo* (12/27/39; 105 performances); Rice's *Two on an Island* (1/22/40; 22 performances); Robert E. Sherwood's *There Shall Be No Night* (4/29/40; 115 performances); Anderson's *Journey to Jerusalem* (10/5/40; 17 performances); Rice's *Flight to the West* (12/30/40; 136 performances); Behrman's *The Talley Method* (2/24/41; 56 performances); Anderson's *Candle in the Wind* (10/22/41; 95 performances) and *The Eve of St. Mark* (10/7/42; 307 performances); and Behrman's *The Pirate* (12/25/42; 177 performances).

The 1940s continued with Sidney Kingsley's *The Patriots* (1/29/43; 173 performances), winner of the NEW YORK DRAMA CRITICS' CIRCLE AWARD for Best Play; Rice's *A New Life* (9/15/43; 70 performances); Anderson's *Storm Operation* (1/11/44; 23 performances); Sherwood's *The Rugged Path* (11/10/45; 81 performances); Rice's *Dream Girl* (12/14/45; 348 performances); Anderson's *Truckline Cafe* (2/27/46; 13 performances) and *Joan of Lorraine* (11/18/46; 199 performances); the musical version of *Street Scene* (1/9/47; 148 performances) with book by Elmer Rice, lyrics by Langston Hughes, and music by Kurt Weill; Anderson's *Anne of the Thousand Days* (12/8/48; 288 performances); Garson Kanin's *The Smile of the World* (1/12/49; 5 performances), the first nonmember-produced play; and Weill and Anderson's powerful musical adaptation of Alan Paton's *Cry the Beloved Country*, entitled *Lost in the Stars* (10/30/49; 273 performances).

In the 1950s, the company increased its productions of plays by outside authors. The Playwrights' Company began the 1950s on a sharp note with Sidney Kingsley's *Darkness at Noon* (1/31/51; 186 performances), which won the New York Drama Critics' Circle Award for Best Play. Other productions of the 1950s included Rice's *Not for Children* (2/13/51; 7 performances); Jan de Hartog's *The Fourposter* (10/24/51; 632 performances), winner of the TONY AWARD for Best Play; Maxwell Anderson's *Barefoot in Athens* (10/31/51; 29 performances); Rice's *The Grand Tour* (12/10/51; 8 performances); Stanley Young's *Mr. Pickwick* (9/17/52; 61 performances); George Tabori's *The Emperor's Clothes* (2/9/53; 16 performances);

Robert Anderson's *Tea and Sympathy* (9/30/53; 712 performances); Samuel Taylor's *Sabrina Fair* (11/11/53; 318 performances); Jane Bowles' *In the Summer House* (12/29/53; 55 performances); Rice's *The Winner* (2/17/54; 30 performances); Jean Giraudoux's *Ondine* (2/17/54; 157 performances), winner of the New York Drama Critics' Circle Award for Best Foreign Play; Robert Anderson's *All Summer Long* (9/23/54; 60 performances); Horton Foote's *The Traveling Lady* (10/27/54; 30 performances); and Maxwell Anderson's *The Bad Seed* (12/8/54; 334 performances).

The second half of the decade began with the classic production of TENNESSEE WILLIAMS' *Cat on a Hot Tin Roof* (3/24/55; 694 performances), which opened at the MOROSCO THEATRE. For his efforts, Williams received the Pulitzer prize as well as the New York Drama Critics' Circle Award. Other plays in the company's last decade included Baruch Lumet's *Once upon a Tailor* (5/23/55; 8 performances); Jean Giraudoux's *Tiger at the Gates* (10/3/55; 217 performances); Joseph Fields (*see* FIELDS FAMILY) and Jerome Chodorov's *The Ponder Heart* (2/16/56; 149 performances); Leslie Stevens' *The Lovers* (5/10/56; 4 performances); Robert E. Sherwood's *Small War on Murray Hill* (1/3/57; 12 performances); Jean Anouilh's *Time Remembered* (11/12/57; 248 performances), which marked Richard Burton's American debut; Noël Coward's *Nude with Violin* (11/14/57; 80 performances); Morton Wishengrad's *The Rope Dancers* (11/20/57; 189 performances); a revival of William Wycherly's *The Country Wife* (11/27/57; 45 performances); Ray Lawler's *Summer of the Seventeenth Doll* (1/22/58); Phoebe Ephron's *Howie* (9/17/58); N. Richard Nash's *A Handful of Fire* (10/1/58; 5 performances); Samuel Taylor and Cornelia Otis Skinner's *The Pleasure of His Company* (10/22/58; 474 performances); Milton Geiger's *Edwin Booth* (11/24/58; 24 performances); Elmer Rice's *Cue for Passion* (11/25/58; 39 performances); Alec Coppel's *The Gazebo* (12/12/58; 218 performances); Noël Coward's *Look After Lulu* (3/3/59; 39 performances); *Juno*, Joseph Stein and Marc Blitzstein's musical version of Sean O'Casey's *Juno and the Paycock*, (3/3/59; 16 performances); Anita Loos' *Cheri* (10/12/59; 56 performances); Robert Bolt's *Flowering Cherry* (10/21/59; 5 performances); Peter Shaffer's *Five Finger Exercise* (12/2/59; 337 performances); Robert Anderson's *Silent Night, Lonely Night* (12/3/59; 124 performances); and Gore Vidal's *The Best Man* (3/31/60; 520 performances).

The Best Man was the last production of the Playwrights' Company. By this time Maxwell Anderson, Kurt Weill, Sidney Howard, and Robert E. Sherwood had died. Other members, like Roger L. Stevens, had formed new links to other producing organizations.

Although many of the plays produced by the company were failures, The Playwrights' Company had more than its share of important openings. Moreover, many plays that were ignored in their time have gone on to become parts of the permanent literature of the American theater.

PLYMOUTH THEATER. 236 W. 45th Street. Architect: Herbert J. Krapp. Opening: October 10, 1917; *A Successful Calamity.*

The SHUBERT BROTHERS had leased land from the Astor Estate for the Shubert Theater (*see* SAM S. SHUBERT THEATRE) and the BOOTH THEATRE. The remaining land was split between the BROADHURST and PLYMOUTH THEATERS. The brothers, who already owned every other theater on the same side of 45th Street, were happy to extend their domain. They backed producer Arthur Hopkins in his wish to have his own theater. Hopkins was already the owner of the tiny Punch and Judy Theatre (*see* CHARLES HOPKINS THEATER), and the Plymouth gave him a more positive cash flow. A theater worthy of the best in contemporary drama, the Plymouth fulfilled Hopkins' high-minded goals. A

Plymouth Theater interior.

proponent of serious American drama, he rejected the melodrama and parlor plays that typified the theater's offerings at the turn of the 20th century. Hopkins was a staunch believer in spiritualism, and his kindly demeanor and good taste endeared him to the Broadway community. Even after his successful years had passed, Hopkins retained offices in the Plymouth Theater. He died in 1950.

Architect Herbert Krapp designed the Plymouth (on 45th Street) and the Broadhurst (on 44th Street) as a single unit, like their neighbors the Sam S. Shubert and Booth Theaters. The shared side walls of the Shubert and Booth theaters, together with the back of the old ASTOR HOTEL, formed the famous narrow walkway known as Shubert Alley. Similarly, the Plymouth and Broadhurst formed an alley parallel to Shubert Alley. At the time, zoning regulations demanded a side alley exit from all theaters. However, the Broadhurst and Plymouth alley was almost immediately closed off to foot traffic.

The first booking, Clare Kummer's *A Successful Calamity*, had originally opened at the Booth and finished its run at the Plymouth. The first production to originate at the Plymouth was the John Barrymore (*see* BARRYMORE FAMILY) vehicle *Redemption* (10/3/18; 204 performances). After a run of Shakespeare's *Hamlet* (11/22/18), with Walter Hampden in the title role, Barrymore returned to the Plymouth's stage in *The Jest* (4/9/19; 77 performances). Barrymore was joined by his brother, Lionel, in the Sam Benelli drama. Hopkins produced and directed the venture, and Robert Edmond Jones, the premier set designer of his day, repeated the assignment he had carried out for *Redemption*. The three men, Hopkins, Jones, and Barrymore, were fast becoming Broadway's most formidable artistic team. In France the Barrymore role had been played by Sarah Bernhardt, and in Italy by Mimi Aguiglia. It was the fashion of many female European stars to play men's roles. Clearly, the play was not the thing but the actors who appeared in it were, and the Barrymores took full advantage of the histrionics of the script. After a short hiatus, *The Jest* reopened at the Plymouth on September 19, 1919, for an additional 179 performances. The play was to be presented at the Plymouth once more, on February 4, 1926, with Basil Sydney under Hopkins' direction. Without the Barrymores, the play failed to incite the audiences' passions, and the revival closed after 78 performances.

Rida Johnson Young, best remembered today as lyricist and librettist for a number of VICTOR HERBERT operettas, saw her melodramatic play *Little Old New York* (9/8/20; 311 performances) open at the Plymouth. Genevieve Tobin starred as the girl who masquerades as a boy to win an inheritance rightfully the property of another lad with whom she falls in love. She wins both by the curtain's fall.

Zoe Akins' *Daddy's Gone A-Hunting* (8/31/21; 129 performances) opened with Marjorie Rambeau in the lead. Hopkins produced and directed the comedy *The Old Soak* (8/22/22; 325 performances) by Don Marquis, with Harry Beresford in the title role and Minnie Dupree as his wife. J. P. McEvoy's play *The Potters* (12/8/23; 245 performances) was meant to be a realistic look at American family life. The comedy was essentially a string of episodes without the usual problem or event that is followed through to the play's conclusion.

High drama returned to the Plymouth's stage with Laurence Stallings and Maxwell Anderson's *What Price Glory?* (9/5/24; 435 performances). Hopkins produced and directed the harrowing World War I drama, which starred William Boyd (who later played Hopalong Cassidy in movies), Louis Wolheim, and Brian Donlevy. The play, with its raunchy language and unromantic look at war, shocked audiences. Although the play revived several clichés, including that of comradeship in the trenches, it presented them in a more down-to-earth, no-nonsense way. The play's abundant use of profanity caused much controversy. One story tells of a prim, straitlaced woman who, during intermission, bent over to retrieve something from the floor and announced, "I seem to have dropped my goddam program." Controversy usually sells tickets, as does excellence, and *What Price Glory?* had both.

Philip Barry's first play at the Plymouth, *In a Garden* (11/16/25; 73 performances), starred Laurette Taylor and Louis Calhern, but it failed to catch on. Barry had better luck later. In the aptly titled *Burlesque* (9/1/27; 372 performances), Arthur Hopkins and George Manker Watters treated audiences to what they thought was a realistic view behind the scenes in a burlesque house, letting audiences into the world of cheap theatrics. The play starred Barbara Stanwyck and Hal Skelly. Clark Gable and Zita Johann starred in Sophie Treadwell's reworking of the story of Ruth Snyder, the first woman in America to die in the electric chair, entitled *Machinal* (9/7/28; 93 performances).

Holiday (11/26/28; 230 performances), Philip Barry's sparkling comedy, was produced and directed by Arthur Hopkins and starred Hope Williams and Ben Smith. The play is best remembered for its movie version with Katharine Hepburn, who was Hope Williams' Broadway understudy. The show later toured to enthusiastic response until October 28, 1929, the date of its opening in Boston. This was also the day of the Wall Street crash; the play, which was partly about getting rich without being ready, hardly seemed appropriate any longer. Donald Ogden Stewart, who had a small role, remembered that the play was "received by the Boston mourners with an impressive two and a half hours of silence." Hopkins saw the writing on the wall, and after a commitment in Philadelphia the tour folded. This was lucky for Stewart because he had written a comedy, which Hopkins produced—*Rebound* (2/3/30; 124 performances)—at the Plymouth and with Hope Williams in the lead. Stewart also wrote a small part for himself. The play was a hit. ALEXANDER WOOLLCOTT stated, "The finale of that second act is one of the most exciting things I ever saw in the theater." This was high praise from a difficult critic. *Rebound* was picked by Burns Mantle as one of the year's 10 best plays.

Elmer Rice's *Counselor-at-Law* (11/6/31; 293 performances), starring Paul Muni, reopened on September 12, 1932, for an additional 104 performances. The following year, Clare Kummer had another hit at the Plymouth with *Her Master's Voice* (10/23/33; 220 performances). It starred Laura Hope Crews and Roland Young.

Tallulah Bankhead explored the dramatic possibilities of *Dark Victory* (11/7/34; 55 performances), the story of a woman's emotional triumph over a brain tumor. ROBERT BENCHLEY, a Bankhead aficionado, wrote in *The New Yorker*, "There has always been a feeling among the admirers of Miss Bankhead that she should sometime play Camille. In *Dark Victory*, she makes a step toward this goal, without the unpleasantness of coughing." Benchley liked the George Brewer Jr. and Bertram Block play. He commented, "The sobs and sniffling which rock the Plymouth Theater at the end of the last act ought to testify to her success." Benchley wasn't alone in liking *Dark Victory*, but Bankhead became ill and the play was withdrawn.

The second half of the 1930s saw a string of dramas at the Plymouth. Samson Raphaelson wrote *Accent on Youth* (12/25/34; 229 performances), starring Constance Cummings. Robert E. Sherwood adapted *Tovarich* (10/15/36; 356 performances) for stars Marta Abba and John Halliday. Gertrude Lawrence opened in Rachel Crothers' *Susan and God* (10/7/37; 287 performances). In 1943 the star opened City Center's drama program with the same play at affordable prices. Sherwood followed *Tovarich* with his PULITZER PRIZE–winning play *Abe Lincoln in Illinois* (10/15/38; 472 performances). Raymond Massey as the future president captured the hearts and minds of the audience. The play was the first production of the newly formed PLAYWRIGHTS' COMPANY. Otto Preminger directed himself as a Nazi in Clare Boothe Luce's *Margin for Error* (11/3/39; 264 performances), with Sam Levene co-starring.

Tallulah Bankhead returned in triumph to the Plymouth in Thornton Wilder's *The Skin of Our Teeth* (11/18/42; 355 performances). Wolcott Gibbs, the *New Yorker*'s critic, exclaimed that Bankhead gave "what may be the most brilliant and is certainly the most versatile performance of her career." Elia Kazan directed the Pulitzer prize–winning drama, which also starred Fredric March, Florence Eldridge, Florence Reed, E. G. Marshall, and Montgomery Clift.

Viola Frayne, Gladys George, Larry Hugo, Remo Buffano as the Dinosaur and Andrew Ratousheff as the Mammoth in a scene from *The Skin of Our Teeth*, 1942.

Raymond Scott and Bernard Hanighen contributed the score to an odd bit of orientalia, *Lute Song* (2/6/46; 142 performances), the first musical to play the Plymouth. MARY MARTIN starred along with Clarence Derwent (namesake of the award; *see* CLARENCE DERWENT AWARD), Mildred Dunnock, and Yul Brynner. Nancy Davis, who later married Ronald Reagan and became First Lady, also appeared in the show. Noël Coward's *Present Laughter* (10/29/46; 158 performances) starred Clifton Webb.

Tallulah Bankhead made another brief appearance at the Plymouth later in the 1940s in a considerably lesser play, *The Eagle Has Two Heads* (3/19/47; 29 performances), which wags dubbed *The Turkey Has Two Heads*. Critics were of one mind: they hated the play in spite of the fact that, at each performance, Bankhead fell down a flight of 10 steps. The fall received the most praise. Set designer Donald Oenslager said, "I took care to put a lot of padding under the carpet on those stairs but who except Tallulah would have taken such chances, and not once but night after night?" In his review, John Lardner wrote, "Miss Bankhead spared herself nothing on opening night at the Plymouth. In a plunge that I would hesitate to make with football pads on, she toppled headfirst, majestically and in a pure line, down several stairs. She was fresh as a daisy, however, for her curtain calls, which were up to the standards of the Bankhead public." Bankhead was back at the Plymouth in Noël Coward's *Private Lives* (10/4/48) with costar Donald Cook. The revival played 248 performances, the exact same number of performances as the original production of 1931.

RODGERS AND HAMMERSTEIN produced Samuel Taylor's *The Happy Time* (1/24/50; 614 performances), with Claude Dauphin, Johnny Stewart, Eva Gabor, and Kurt Kasznar. *Dial "M" for Murder* (10/29/52; 552 performances), a thriller by Frederic Knott, starred Maurice Evans, Richard Derr, Gusti Huber, and John

Williams. It would later be made into a well-received film directed by Alfred Hitchcock (in 3-D!).

Herman Wouk adapted his novel *The Caine Mutiny Court Martial* (1/20/54; 405 performances) for the Plymouth stage. Charles Laughton directed Henry Fonda, Lloyd Nolan, and John Hodiak. Again, a well-known film was made from this success. *Three for Tonight* (4/6/55; 85 performances) opened with Marge and Gower Champion, Hiram Sherman, and Harry Belafonte. The singer later created a near riot with his one-man show at the PALACE THEATER.

Peter Ustinov's comedy *Romanoff and Juliet* (10/10/57; 389 performances) opened at the Plymouth with the playwright starring. Romanoff is the son of the Soviet ambassador to a small neutral country that purposely prints its stamps with mistakes to drive up their value on the collectors' market. Juliet is the daughter of the American ambassador. The light comedy *The Marriage-Go-Round*, by Leslie Stevens (10/29/58; 431 performances), followed; it starred Charles Boyer, Claudette Colbert, and Julie Newmar. Elizabeth Seal created a sensation as a whore with a heart of gold in the musical *Irma La Douce* (9/29/60; 527 performances) by Marguerite Monnot, Julian More, David Heneker, and Monty Norman. The musical's big song was "Our Language of Love." Supporting Seal were Keith Michell, Clive Revill, Fred Gwynne, George S. Irving, Elliott Gould, Stuart Damon, and Rudy Tronto, all in producer DAVID MERRICK's production.

The work of NEIL SIMON dominated the Plymouth's stage during the second half of the 1960s. One of the greatest hits of the 1960s was Simon's *The Odd Couple* (3/10/65; 965 performances), starring Art Carney and Walter Matthau. Simon followed that success with *The Star-Spangled Girl* (12/21/66; 261 performances), which starred Anthony Perkins, Richard Benjamin, and Connie Stevens. Simon returned to the Plymouth with a bigger success, *Plaza Suite* (2/14/68; 1,097 performances), an evening of 3 one-acts all taking place in the Plaza Hotel. Each starred George C. Scott and Maureen Stapleton. The playwright had less success with his first noncomedy dramatic attempt, *The Gingerbread Lady* (12/13/70; 193 performances). Maureen Stapleton starred as an alcoholic singer down on her luck. Although not a hit, the play did have its fans, and it was named one of the 10 best plays of the year by the *Best Plays* series.

For the next few years, beginning in 1973, British productions dominated the Plymouth Theater. Peter Cook and Dudley Moore opened in their two-man show *Good Evening* (11/14/73; 438 performances), in the vein of their previous success, *Beyond the Fringe*. *Good Evening* was titled *Behind the Fridge* in England. *Equus* (10/24/74; 781 performances), by the English playwright Peter Shaffer, starred Anthony Hopkins as

the psychiatrist of a boy who has inexplicably blinded several horses; Peter Firth starred as the youth. John Dexter's direction was hailed, as were the performances. *Equus*'s theatricality sometimes overshadowed the script, but critics judged that it was for the better. Briton Simon Gray's play *Otherwise Engaged* (2/2/77; 309 performances) starred Tom Courtenay as a man who could never get a moment's peace.

After a two-year stay by the Fats Waller retrospective *Ain't Misbehavin'*, which moved to the Plymouth from the LONGACRE THEATER, the theater hosted another English import, *Piaf* (2/5/81; 165 performances). Jane Laportaire starred as French singer Edith Piaf, and her performance won more kudos than the script.

The theater's next booking was a true theatrical event—the Royal Shakespeare Company's production of *The Life and Adventures of Nicholas Nickleby* (10/4/81) based on the Charles Dickens novel. Roger Rees played the title role. The play took 8 hours to perform; audiences had a choice of either seeing it in one day with a dinner break or coming to the theater on two successive nights. "Nick Nick" (as it was affectionately dubbed) played to sold-out audiences for a limited engagement of 49 performances.

On January 6, 1983, David Hare's *Plenty* transferred to the Plymouth from the Public Theater, where it premiered on October 21, 1982. Kate Nelligan and Edward Herrmann starred in the drama, which played 92 performances at the Plymouth in addition to the 45 performances it had enjoyed at the Public. *The Real Thing* (1/5/84; 566 performances), by Tom Stoppard, continued the British dominance of the Plymouth's stage. Jeremy Irons became a Broadway heartthrob as a result of his performance. Then Lily Tomlin brought her one-woman show, *The Search for Signs of Intelligent Life in the Universe* (9/26/85; 398 performances), to the Plymouth for a limited engagement. Lanford Wilson's *Burn This* opened on October 14, 1987, with John Malkovich and Joan Allen in the leads.

Wendy Wasserstein, a New York Jewish feminist playwright, had a big success with *The Heidi Chronicles* (3/19/89; 622 performances). She was hailed as a new voice in the theater but didn't live up to her press, though she managed a career far beyond her successes.

Hits and notable productions were in short supply over the next few years. STEPHEN SONDHEIM's musical, *Passion* (5/19/94), was, as usual for Sondheim, a *success d'estime*. After the Sondheim core audience attended the musical, general audiences stayed away from the grim story, and the show managed only 280 performances. Still, as is also usual for Sondheim, the original cast album reveals an excellent, if dense, score.

A revival of E. F. ALBEE's *A Delicate Balance* (4/21/65; 185 performances), presented by the Lincoln Center Theatre at the Plymouth, proved to be an enter-

Fred Gwyunne, Elizabeth Seal, and George S. Irving in producer David Merrick's 1960 production, *Irma La Douce*.

taining and thought-provoking evening. This practically guaranteed a limited run. The revival, starring a stellar cast that included George Grizzard, Rosemary Harris, Elaine Stritch, Elizabeth Wilson, and Mary Beth Hurt, closed after only 185 performances. It would be a few years before Albee would be rediscovered by New York audiences.

Frank Wildhorn and Leslie Bricusse's musical, *Jekyll and Hyde* (4/28/97), had its own set of groupies. They, and a few civilians, managed to keep the show running for an impressive 1,543 performances, in spite

of critical brickbats. Despite its long run, the show still managed to lose money.

Two more flop musicals followed. Faith Prince starred in an ill-conceived revival of the JULE STYNE and COMDEN AND GREEN musical *Bells Are Ringing* (4/12/2001; 68 performances). And the acclaimed director Susan Stroman teamed up with composer Harry Connick Jr. and librettist David Thompson to deliver to Broadway a huge failure, *Thou Shalt Not* (10/25/2001; 85 performances). Lincoln Center Theatre was the producer of this well-intentioned but badly executed musical mess. At least it was an attempt at a serious musical on Broadway, and for that alone it should be applauded. A supporting actor with the unlikely name Norbert Leo Butz got critical raves in this retelling of Emile Zola's novel *Thérèse Raquin*.

Next at the Plymouth was the critically lambasted but audience favorite stage version of the film *The Graduate*. Kathleen Turner played Mrs. Robinson against movie stars Jason Biggs (of *American Pie* fame) and Alicia Silverstone (*Clueless*). The play opened on April 4, 2002, following an equally successful engagement in London.

On December 8, 1987, the New York City Landmarks Preservation Commission designated the exterior of the theater a landmark. The commission stated that the theater's "facade is a response to its Shubert Alley location."

PORTER, COLE. The most urbane and sophisticated of all the composers and lyricists on Broadway; b. Peru, Indiana, June 9, 1891; d. Santa Monica, California, October 15, 1964.

Cole Porter composed some of the best-loved songs of the golden era of the Broadway musical. He was a celebrated wit and bon vivant both at home in the United States and in Europe. His wealth and social contacts made him the spokesperson and satirist of the upper classes. Whether down in the depths on the 90th floor or beginning the beguine, Porter was an important voice in the musical theater. Of course, he also spoke to the average person, as witnessed by the hundreds of popular songs to his credit. In his heyday, during the Depression, he fueled the dreams and fantasies of a generation. People could escape to exotic locales with the upper crust in the comfort of a balcony seat. Porter's facility with rhythms and rhymes masked the hard work he put into the shows. This facility was all the more remarkable when juxtaposed with Porter's own personal torments.

Born in Peru, Indiana, on June 9, 1891, Porter showed an early talent for music and composed his first published song, "The Bobolink Waltz," at the age of 10. Porter set out to become a lawyer. Toward that end, he enrolled in Worcester Academy and then Yale at the direction of his grandfather. But Porter proved more interested in his extracurricular songwriting than in his studies. While at Yale, he wrote two of that school's more enduring standards, "Bingo Eli Yale" and the "Yale Bullfrog Song." After Porter left Yale for Harvard Law School, his dean suggested that the School of Music might suit his temperament better. So Porter switched majors and began to write musical comedies.

Porter's first break came when he met Elisabeth Marbury, the woman who produced many of JEROME KERN's early hits. Their show entitled *See America First* (3/28/16; 15 performances) was written in collaboration with T. Lawrason Riggs. It opened at the MAXINE ELLIOTT'S THEATRE with Clifton Webb in the lead. "I've a Shooting Box in Scotland" became a minor hit. After the failure of *See America First*, Porter abandoned the stage for three years. He didn't need to work, so he spent the time touring the world as well as spending a brief sojourn with the French Foreign Legion. While on board a ship bound for the United States, Porter met Broadway producer and comedian Raymond Hitchcock. Hitchcock hired Porter to compose the score to the third edition of a short-lived revue series, *Hitchy-Koo* (10/6/19; 56 performances). Presented at the LIBERTY THEATRE, it was more successful than Porter's previous outing. Porter's score yielded his first full-scale hit, "Old Fashioned Garden." Comedian Joe Cook, making his Broadway debut, introduced the song. Even early in his career, Porter explored themes familiar to him from his monied and leisured situation. The lyrics of "I've a Shooting Box in Scotland" were a litany of residences around the world owned by the singer. *Hitchy-Koo of 1919* contained "In My Cozy Little Corner of the Ritz" and "I Introduced," the latter a list of all the greats introduced to each other in one social outing or another.

In 1923 Porter was left more than $1 million by his grandfather, which allowed him more time to travel the world. He returned to the Broadway theater with his score for the *Greenwich Village Follies of 1924* (9/16/24; 131 performances). The show introduced "I'm in Love Again," a moderate hit at the time. *Paris* (10/8/28; 195 performances) starred the French performer Irene Bordoni, known for her saucy smile and insinuating air. It was Bordoni who was largely responsible for showing Americans of the 1920s what the French knew about love. Porter provided her with what became one of his best-known songs, "Let's Do It." Through Porter's lyrics, Bordoni introduced Americans to a new concept: sex could be fun. Up to then, sex was either unmentionable or serious and passionate in the manner of Rudolf Valentino. Bordoni and Porter were the perfect matching of talents for bringing sex into musical-comedy productions. The reception to Porter's music was tremendous. He realized that celebrity could not only be fun but could also distinguish him from all the other bored millionaires in his circle of friends. Indeed, his popularity extended to his social strata, and he was in great demand for parties and soirees.

Porter's *Fifty Million Frenchmen* (11/27/29; 254 performances) opened at the LYRIC THEATER. The show was the second one produced by Bordoni's husband, E. Ray Goetz. The book writer was Herbert Fields (see FIELDS FAMILY), who later wrote libretti for six other Porter shows. "You Do Something to Me" was the hit of the show, which starred Helen Broderick, Genevieve Tobin, and William Gaxton. In spite of the stock market crash, the show was a big success, providing Porter with even more fame. Next, several of Porter's songs were used in an English import, *Wake up and Dream!* (12/30/29; 127 performances). The show starred Tilly Losch, Jack Buchanan, and Marjorie Robertson (Anna Neagle). The principal Porter contribution was "What Is This Thing Called Love?" Porter's work gained new depth with each succeeding score. His melodies were uniquely his own, not based on clichéd musical forms currently in vogue. His lyrics, too, showed added layers of emotion. He never relied on the *moon-June-croon* rhymes of his contemporaries, nor did he resort to straightforward and unimaginative contrivances.

Porter's next show, *The New Yorkers* (12/8/30; 158 performances) opened at the BROADWAY THEATRE. E. Ray Goetz was Porter's producer for the third time. Herbert Fields contributed the book, and Monty Woolley directed his second Porter offering. The show starred Jimmy Durante, Hope Williams, Ann Pennington, Frances Williams, Charles King, Richard Carle, Marie Cahill, Oscar "Rags" Ragland, and Fred Waring and His Pennsylvanians. The score contained several of Porter's best songs, including "Where Have You Been?," "Let's Fly Away," and "Take Me Back to Manhattan." The song that became the biggest success and caused the biggest sensation was "Love for Sale." Percy Hammond, writing in the *New York Herald Tribune*, opined, "When and if we ever get a censorship, I will give odds that it will frown upon such an honest thing." Charles Darnton of the *New York Evening World* took the opposite tack, "Love for Sale . . . was in the worst possible taste." It proved too much for some audience members to see the beautiful Katharyn Crawford playing a prostitute on the stage, so the character was given to Elisabeth Welch—brought on especially to sing the song. Because Welch was black, audiences seemed better able to accept her rendition of the song. The number's backdrop pictured a city street. The sign "Park Avenue" was simply changed to "Lenox Avenue", and the show went on.

Porter next produced three classic musicals that included many of his best-remembered songs. *The Gay Divorcée* (11/21/32; 248 performances), at the ETHEL BARRYMORE THEATRE, starred FRED ASTAIRE in his first solo outing away from his sister Adele, as well as Claire Luce, Luella Gear, and Betty Starbuck. *The Gay Divorcée* featured what is considered by many to be Porter's finest song, "Night and Day." ANYTHING GOES

(12/4/34; 420 performances) featured Porter's favorite musical comedy star, ETHEL MERMAN. Supporting her were William Gaxton, Victor Moore, Vivian Vance (later to achieve greater fame on television as Ethel Mertz in *I Love Lucy*), and Bettina Hall. The score was among Porter's best, with no less than four gems. "All Through the Night," "I Get a Kick out of You," "You're the Top," and the title song have all become recognized as classic examples of American popular song. Porter's next offering, *Jubilee* (10/12/35; 169 performances) contained a score almost the equal to that of *Anything Goes*. "Begin the Beguine" and "Just One of Those Things" were the standouts. A young Montgomery Clift made his Broadway debut in the show. It might have run longer had not its star, Mary Boland, left to do a film.

Porter had hit his stride, and next provided the score for a zany musical comedy, *Red, Hot and Blue!* (10/29/36; 183 performances), at the Alvin Theater. The title referred to the fact that the heroine has an identifying mark on her posterior caused when she sat on a waffle iron. The lady in question was Ethel Merman, who was ably abetted by Jimmy Durante and Bob Hope. The score again showed Porter at the top of his class, with such great songs as "It's De-lovely," "Ridin' High," and the title song.

While on vacation in the summer of 1937 Porter suffered a horrible riding accident. His horse threw him and fell on his legs, crushing them and causing extensive damage to his nervous system. Porter spent the remainder of his life in constant pain. Even after 31 operations, he never fully recovered. In 1958 his right leg was amputated. His friends doubted that he would ever write again and blamed his later failures on his great pain. But Porter bounced back creatively from this tragedy.

You Never Know (9/21/38; 78 performances), Porter's first Broadway assignment after the accident, opened at the WINTER GARDEN THEATRE. "At Long Last Love" was the most notable song in an otherwise inconsequential score. MARY MARTIN got the Porter treatment, along with William Gaxton, Victor Moore, and Sophie Tucker in *Leave It to Me!* (11/9/38; 291 performances). Martin introduced the song "My Heart Belongs to Daddy," which made her a star.

Ethel Merman and Bert Lahr were back in *Du Barry Was a Lady* (12/6/39; 408 performances). Betty Grable, Charles Walters, and Benny Baker helped round out the cast in the Porter hit. Herbert Fields and B. G. De Sylva (see DE SYLVA, BROWN, AND HENDERSON) wrote the book, which told the story of a lowly washroom attendant who dreams he is the king of France. "Friendship" was the archetypal Porter song, a genre he elevated to an art form. Merman also appeared in the next Porter musical, *Panama Hattie* (10/

30/40; 501 performances), little remembered today. Arthur Treacher, Rags Ragland, James Dunn, and Betty Hutton also appeared in the production. *Let's Face It!* (10/29/41; 547 performances) was Porter's second show of the 1940s. Danny Kaye made the biggest effect with his songs "Farming" and "Let's Not Talk About Love." Eve Arden, Benny Baker, Mary Jane Walsh, and Vivan Vance were also featured. *Something for the Boys* (1/7/43; 422 performances), at the Alvin Theater, marked Porter's last score written for Ethel Merman. Bill Johnson, Paula Laurence, and Betty Garrett were also in the wartime musical. *Mexican Hayride* (1/28/44; 481 performances) was another hit show for Porter; the show had a less-than-top-notch score, though "I Love You" became a big hit. Bobby Clark and June Havoc starred. This show, like Porter's last four shows, played more than 400 performances, yet none of the scores for these shows achieved the success of Porter's musicals of the 1930s.

Porter's next score was for producer Billy Rose's revue *The Seven Lively Arts* (12/7/44; 183 performances). The cast was superlative: Beatrice Lillie, Bert Lahr, Benny Goodman, Alicia Markova, and Dolores Gray headlined. The revue introduced one hit, "Ev'rytime We Say Goodbye," one of Porter's greatest ballads. Porter's next show, the monumental *Around the World in Eighty Days* (5/31/46; 75 performances), was written for the enormous talents of Orson Welles, who produced, directed, and contributed the book. The young genius also starred in the show, which proved to be an expensive failure. Porter's contributions contained nothing of much interest to his fans.

Word on the Rialto was that Porter was washed up. Although he began the 1940s with long runs, he had few big hit tunes. Porter seemed to have lost touch with the changing scene on Broadway. After World War II, high society and sophistication were decidedly out of fashion. At his lowest ebb, however, Porter came up with his greatest success. Samuel and Bella Spewack (librettists of *Leave It to Me!*) wrote a modern adaptation of William Shakespeare's *The Taming of the Shrew*, a work totally different from the kinds of shows Porter had been writing. Porter and the Spewacks produced a masterpiece, *Kiss Me, Kate* (12/30/48; 1,077 performances). It was a show in the best tradition of what came to be known as the RODGERS AND HAMMERSTEIN–style musical. The songs were not the usual star turns that Porter was so adept at writing. Instead, the songs in *Kiss Me, Kate* defined characters, advanced the plot, and provided an excellent opportunity for Porter to exhibit his characteristically ingenious wordplay. The show opened with Alfred Drake, Patricia Morison, Harold Lang, and Lisa Kirk heading the cast. The score is among Porter's best, with "Another Openin', Another Show," "Wunderbar," and "So

in Love" receiving the greatest airplay. But the rest of the score was as good as, and sometimes better than, the songs that made the hit parade. Porter had proved that reports of the death of his career were premature.

Kiss Me, Kate's producers, Saint Subber and Lemuel Ayers, commissioned Porter's next show, *Out of This World* (12/21/50; 157 performances). Surprisingly, "From This Moment On," the song that became the best known of the score, was dropped from the show during its out-of-town tryout. The remaining songs, sung by Charlotte Greenwood, William Eythe, Priscilla Gillette, and William Redfield, were almost of the same caliber of those for *Kiss Me, Kate*.

Porter's next-to-last show, *Can-Can* (5/7/53; 892 performances), was a much bigger hit. The Parisian locale was better suited to Porter's sensibilities, and the score yielded several hits: "I Love Paris," "C'est Magnifique," and "Can-Can." Lilo, Peter Cookson, and Hans Conried were the advertised stars, but by the end of the opening night at the Shubert Theater (*see* SAM S. SHUBERT THEATRE), another star was born, Gwen Verdon. The production proved to be Porter's second-longest run. Porter's last show, *Silk Stockings* (2/24/55; 478 performances), was based on the film *Ninotchka*. Hildegarde Neff had the Greta Garbo part, with support from Don Ameche and Gretchen Wyler. "All of You" was the hit song of the show, which was later made into a movie musical starring Fred Astaire and Cyd Charisse. The musical proved a successful end to Porter's Broadway career.

Porter wrote two scores for the movies, *High Society* and *Les Girls*, as well as an original television musical, *Aladdin*.

POSTER. Of all the artifacts and mementos from long-forgotten Broadway shows, often it's the poster that gives the best idea of the spirit of a show and provides the most valuable clues to Broadway's past. In contrast, the playbills list names (some recognizable, most not) and give facts that don't mean much unless one was lucky enough to see the show. In looking back, newspaper reviews can be used to judge the critic and the accuracy of his or her opinions, if one is familiar with the show that was reviewed. Old photographs depict actors in exaggerated poses in harsh and unflattering lighting that casts them as unmoving masses in gray costumes. Posters, on the other hand, seem to bring the actors to life. They are dramatically posed against backgrounds that suggest the style and location of the offering. The poster may bear only a passing resemblance to the reality of the show, but the poses, the vibrant colors, and the exciting typography are definitely theatrical.

Posters have always served a commercial purpose in the history of illustration. They represent a show or a show's star in a way that entices the public to come to the theater and buy tickets. The early poster designers of the late 19th century were staff artists working for the lithography houses that serviced the theatrical world. The artist was given photos of the piece and sometimes a script or a written description of what scenes were to be depicted. Louis Prang, a leading printer, explained that the job of the poster artist was "to reproduce, to imitate, not to create." Matt Morgan of Strobridge Lithograph Company of Cincinnati is generally considered to be the first great American poster artist.

However, at the turn of the 20th century, during the heyday of the European art-poster craze led by such fine artists as Toulouse-Lautrec, Mucha, and Beardsley, American posters were just beginning to show imagination and drama. Charles Cochran, the English producer, wrote in 1898,

> When I first visited America, I was struck with the horrors that looked down upon one from the hoardings. The huge theatrical posters, although beautifully printed, were entirely lacking in taste as regards design and colour. The figures were tailors' dummies without life or movement and the backgrounds were the old stereotyped German photographic reproductions of scenes from the play advertised.

Some designs were taken from photographs of the productions, and others were completely fanciful renditions of the onstage action. Taking their cue from the overstated, overblown circus poster, Broadway posters often featured incredible scenes that could obviously never be enacted onstage.

European influences soon changed the look of American posters. During the 1920s, posters reflected the growth of the field of advertising. Publicity posters received their first wide distribution when they were applied to the sides of buildings and buses, and to billboards. Theater posters reflected the changes brought by advertising art. In the 1930s illustration became less important as more names were featured on the posters. Since then, the basic look of the theater poster has not changed. As fashions in art changed, so did the designs of the theater poster. Styles today are as varied as the styles of writing in the thousands of shows whose images have been "sniped" on construction walls throughout Manhattan. Recently the poster has tended to feature the show's logo, an image that will forever define the show in the public's mind. For the most part, the designer of the logo is also the designer of the poster, but not always. Even today advertising agencies put together posters following contractual requirements.

After fitting all the names on the poster, they find whatever place is available and jam in the logo.

Many prominent artists not primarily known for poster work have tried their hands at theater posters. These include Thomas Nast (*The Little Corporal*, 1898), Alexander Calder (*The Glass Slipper*, 1925), Milton Glaser (*The Wiz*, 1975), Lee Simonson (*Porgy*, 1927; *Marco Millions*, 1928), John Held Jr. (*Boy Meets Girl*, 1935), Saul Steinberg (*The Waltz of the Toreadors*, 1957), Leonard Baskin (*The Ballad of the Sad Cafe*, 1963), Ben Shahn (*A View from the Bridge*, 1965), Maurice Sendak (*Stages*, 1978), and Edward Gorey (*Dracula*, 1977).

At its best, the Broadway poster excites the eye and mind and tries to get tickets sold at the box office. The works of great designers like Tom Morrow (*Fiddler on the Roof*, 1964; *Grind*, 1985), Joe Eula (*High Spirits*, 1964; *Legends*, 1985), David Byrd (*Follies*, 1971), James McMullan (*Comedians*, 1976; *Anna Christie*, 1977; *I Remember Mama*, 1979), Paul Davis (N.Y. Shakespeare Festival), and Hilary Knight (*Half a Sixpence*, 1965) help define Broadway and Times Square.

PRESS AGENT. The press agent's job is the most influential of all the jobs in the Broadway area. Nothing reaches the public without first going through the press agent. The agent places stories and interviews in the press, invites the critics, picks the quotes for advertising, and keeps the show in the public's mind.

At the turn of the 20th century, when Times Square became Times Square, the age of ballyhoo and bumbergriff was upon us. The art of flimflammery had reached its apogee with P. T. Barnum and his cohorts. These early flacks realized the power of advertising. They would go to almost any length for valuable newspaper space. They didn't rely on polls or psychological samplings or truth in advertising. Adjectives were flung without care, landing where they may. In other fields, blatant exaggeration had led to censorship or government regulations. The Food and Drug Administration had reined in the overly effusive advertising of Lydia Pinkham and her ilk, but on Broadway it was still anything goes. Behind the hoopla were talented individuals who helped shape the future of the theater: press agents like Will Page, Harry Reichenbach, Walter Kingsley, and Dexter Fellows. They were scorned by the news reporters, even though the reporters depended on the press agents' steady ouput of hype and hyperbole, and even though most flacks had graduated from news writing themselves.

By World War I things had calmed down. The newspapers were warier of incredible stories about the stars, and they were loath to print such features as "Marie Dressler Teaches You How to Hail a Taxicab."

Puffery was out, and a new concept was introduced—journalism. Gone were articles without bylines. Only staff writers were permitted to contribute to the papers, so press agents had to use a different kind of psychology. Instead of fooling just the public, they had to fool the editors and columnists into believing the most outrageous stories. The press agents had to change their methods of grabbing column inches. STUNTS were going out of fashion; so, too, were outright lies and extravagant claims. Some press agents went so far as to change their job titles to publicity director, counselor in public relations, or even propagandist. Although their titles had changed, the nature of the job remained the same.

Many stars emerged from press agentry, including Herman Shumlin, producer of *Grand Hotel*, *Spofford*, *The Children's Hour*, and *The Little Foxes*; Arthur Kober, author of *Having Wonderful Time*; Harry Reichenbach, author of *Phantom Fame*; Bernard Sobel, press agent for FLORENZ ZIEGFELD, A. L. Erlanger, Charles Dillingham, EARL CARROLL, and others; Ben Hecht, playwrighting partner to Charles MacArthur; columnist O. O. McIntyre; Jed Harris, producer of *Broadway* and *Coquette* and director of *Our Town*; and Howard Dietz (*see* DIETZ AND SCHWARTZ) author of *The Band Wagon*, lyricist of "Dancing in the Dark," "Alone Together," and other standards, and vice president of public relations for MGM. The most famous of all Broadway press agents was the great RICHARD MANEY. He brought back some of the flash, glitter, and outrageousness of the old days. He especially excelled when teamed with a born showman like producer DAVID MERRICK.

In the depressed theater atmosphere of the 1980s, press agentry lost its sting. By the 1990s corporations had taken over Broadway, and a field once dominated by free spirits who had chimpanzees drive cars down Broadway and actresses take milk baths for their complexion, and who routinely described shows as "the best," "the most," "the greatest," and "positively the most amazing confluence of music and mirth seen upon any stage," had disappeared forever.

PRINCE, HAROLD. Highly successful producer and director of the second half of the 20th century; b. New York, New York, January 30, 1928.

Prince began as a stage manager for producer, director, and librettist GEORGE ABBOTT. Prince wrote, "[Abbott] did musicals and you don't look a gift horse in the mouth. So I ended up doing musicals." He then became a boy wonder through his partnership with the more experienced producer Robert Griffith. Prince set out on his own when Griffith died in 1961. He is noted for a series of astonishing musicals he produced and sometimes directed in collaboration with songwriter STEPHEN SONDHEIM. After several financially unsuccessful pairings with Sondheim, Prince moved on. The next period was rather fallow. But with his direction of *The Phantom of the Opera*, Prince was again on top.

Some consider Prince to be an important part of the evolution of the American musical. He has an ability to control pacing and structure and a great eye for theatricality and stage pictures. On the negative side are his penchant for overly large productions that overwhelm the humanity of the material and sometimes an inability to work with actors on performance subtleties. Prince is often more concerned with the physical and technical elements of script and production. However, he can be brilliant at casting. Since leaving his partnership with Sondheim, he has tended to work with less-than-adequate writers. It must be said, however, that Prince's record of success is almost unequaled in the history of American theater.

He was thrust onto the Broadway arena as an assistant stage manager on IRVING BERLIN's *Call Me Madam* (10/12/50; 644 performances). He began his Broadway producing career (in association with Frederick Brisson and Robert E. Griffith) with a huge success, librettist Richard Bissell and songwriters Adler and Ross' first smash hit musical, *The Pajama Game* (5/13/54; 1,063 performances). The show, directed by George Abbott, won the Tony Award for Best Musical, an honor six of his subsequent collaborations with Abbott (including *Damn Yankees*, 1955; the PULITZER PRIZE–winning *Fiorello!* 1959; and *A Funny Thing Happened on the Way to the Forum*, 1962) would also receive. A year later, the same producers continued their relationship with Abbott, Adler, and Ross on the musical *Damn Yankees* (5/5/55; 1,019 performances).

Prince, Brisson, and Griffith moved on to produce Bob Merrill's adaptation of EUGENE O'NEILL's *Anna Christie*, titled *New Girl in Town* (5/14/57; 431 performances). Prince and Griffith, along with associate producer Roger L. Stevens, produced a musical-theater masterwork, *West Side Story* (9/26/57; 732 performances). This production began Prince's long association with director-choreographer Jerome Robbins, librettist Arthur Laurents, and composer Stephen Sondheim. The show was a modern-day retelling of William Shakespeare's *Romeo and Juliet*. Although the show received rave reviews, it wasn't considered an American classic until the release of the 1961 film version. The production was remarkable in its integration of music, story, and dance.

Prince, again in association with Griffith, began another long relationship between himself and songwriters Jerry Bock and Sheldon Harnick. Their first collaboration, *Fiorello!* (11/23/59; 795 performances), won the Pulitzer prize for drama. Bock, Harnick, Griffith, and Prince repeated their roles for their next production, *Tenderloin* (10/17/60; 216 performances). The show was not a success.

His next production with Griffith, *A Call on Kuprin* (5/25/61; 12 performances), was his first straight play. Unfortunately, it was a complete failure. Prince's next production was his first to be produced on his own. George Abbott directed Sam and Bella Spewack's hit, *Take Her She's Mine* (12/21/61; 404 performances).

Another long relationship, with composer John Kander (and later also with Fred Ebb), began with the presentation of the musical *A Family Affair* (1/27/62; 65 performances). James and William Goldman, who would also work with Prince again, wrote the book and lyrics respectively. Prince did not produce the failure; it marked his directing debut.

Sondheim, Abbott, Robbins, and Prince reunited for *A Funny Thing Happened on the Way to the Forum* (5/8/62; 964 performances). Zero Mostel and Jack Gilford

starred in the hilarious musical farce. Prince reestablished his association with Bock and Harnick as well as with Joe Masteroff (future librettist of *Cabaret*) with *She Loves Me* (12/23/63; 302 performances). Although the show was not a financial success at the time, it is now considered one of the finest Broadway musicals with an especially excellent score. Barbara Cook and Jack Cassidy toplined the cast.

In spite of the relative failure of *She Loves Me*, Prince continued his loyalty to Bock and Harnick by producing their next show. His continued belief in their talents paid off with one of the biggest hits of his career and the greatest hit of the 1960s—*Fiddler on the Roof* (9/22/64; 3,242 performances). Jerome Robbins, continuing his work with Prince, directed; Zero Mostel starred; and Boris Aronson, another member of the Prince stable, designed a beautiful set with a nod to the talents of Marc Chagall.

Prince took an artistic gamble with his next producing gambit. Jean Anouilh's *Poor Bitos* opened on No-

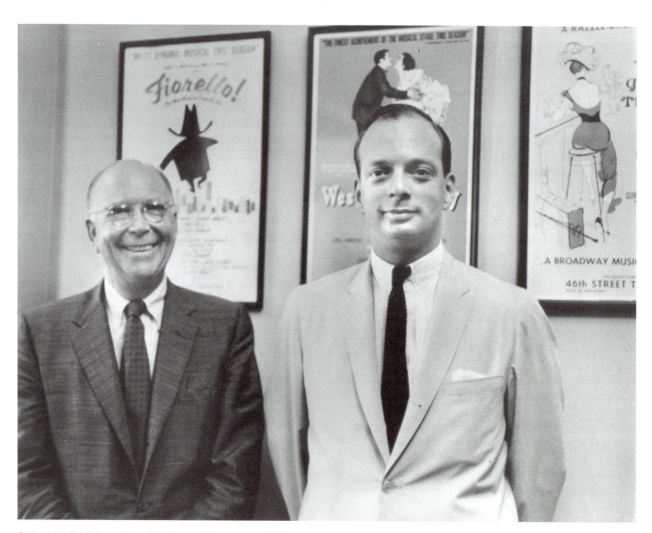

Robert E. Griffith and Harold Prince with posters of their productions.

vember 14, 1964, and closed after only 17 performances. Prince's next show, another directorial assignment (this time for producer Alexander H. Cohen), was also a failure. *Baker Street* (2/16/65; 311 performances) was billed as "The Sherlock Holmes musical." An average score by Raymond Jessel and Marian Grudeff was supplemented with some fine songs by Bock and Harnick. But the show never caught on despite an excellent cast, which included Fritz Weaver and Inga Swenson, and Prince's imaginative direction.

Liza Minnelli made her Broadway debut in Kander and Ebb's *Flora, the Red Menace* (5/11/65; 87 performances). The story of a naive young woman who embraces the Communist Party didn't catch on with theatergoers, although Kander and Ebb provided an above-average score and Minnelli gave a youthfully charming and energetic performance. George Abbott directed the proceedings. Another failure followed. *It's a Bird . . . It's a Plane . . . It's Superman* (3/29/66; 129 performances) marked Prince's first outing as both a director and a producer. The imaginative score was by Broadway veterans STROUSE AND ADAMS. But the idea of a pop musical version of a popular comic strip was, perhaps, ahead of its time. The show's book writers, Robert Benton and David Newman, would later write the screenplay for the film version of the *Superman* comic book.

Kander and Ebb's next show for Prince (which the producer also directed) was a smash hit. By the time he directed *Cabaret* (11/20/66; 1,165 performances), Prince and other directors of his era (especially Arthur Penn in his direction of *Golden Boy*) had begun to bring cinematic techniques to the theater. Prince also began his exploration of including the audience in the show's milieu with *Cabaret*, an idea that reached its fruition in his early environmental staging of the revival of *Candide*. Boris Aronson suggested hanging a huge mirror upstage of the action at the Kit Kat Club, which reflected the BROADHURST THEATER's audience. This conceit, along with revolutionary lighting by Jean Rosenthal, made the theater audience part of the cabaret audience—thereby suggesting their complicity in the actions on stage and making them, perhaps subconsciously, ask themselves the question posed by Lotte Lenya in her song "What Would You Do?"

Prince's direction of *Cabaret* as well as Joseph Masteroff's remarkable libretto were quite daring in its day. It is interesting to recall that in 1966 the Holocaust generation was still alive and active. And the anti-Semitic actions in *Cabaret* brought up uncomfortable memories that were unusual for a Broadway musical. Later revivals of the show, without Prince's staging, emphasized the sexual abnormality of the Weimar Republic at the expense of the human toll and political

tragedy, as well as softened the message of personal responsibility that was a central theme of the original production. In fact, the song that expressed the theme of individual responsibility, "Why Should I Wake Up?" was deleted from later productions in deference to adding the more show-bizzy songs from the film version.

Kander, Ebb, and Prince, along with their *Cabaret* co-conspirators Boris Aronson, orchestrator Don Walker, choreographer Ron Field, and costumer Patricia Zipprodt, came up with another immensely brave and emotional show, *Zorba* (11/16/68; 305 performances). Some audience members felt that the lessons learned in *Cabaret* became fully realized in *Zorba*, but the show never achieved its full potential despite an excellent score, brilliant staging, and rich performances by Herschel Bernardi, Maria Karnilova, Carmen Alvarez, and John Cunningham.

Prince continues to be lionized for his collaboration with Stephen Sondheim. His production of *Company* (4/25/70; 705 performances), which he also directed, marked the beginning of an especially fruitful period in both artists' careers. Playwright George Furth had approached Prince with a number of one-act plays. It was Prince's idea to tie the plays together around the character of Bobby, an emotionally detached bachelor surrounded by his married friends. *Company* is considered the first of the modern revusicals—that is, musicals loosly tied around a central theme without the exegesis of traditional plotting. The idea had been lightly explored with shows like DIETZ AND SCHWARTZ's *At Home Abroad* and *Inside USA*, but those were basically revues with a simple throughline involving a continuing set of characters. There were no underlying subtleties in those shows or emotional themes in their concept. Basically, their concept was how to hang sketches and songs on a simple premise, such as a trip around the world or through the United States. But *Company* had real emotional weight; its new uses of choreography (by Michael Bennett), in which character movement replaced formal choreography, and Boris Aronson's ultramodern unit set, which defined the cold, linear world of haute monde New York, were truly revolutionary, not evolutionary.

Prince, Sondheim, Bennett, and Aronson represented the perfect distillation of their ideas of plot, movement, and stagecraft with their next show, *Follies* (4/4/71; 522 performances). A brilliant, if brittle, look at the road not taken, *Follies* celebrated and damned nostalgia with a potent message of acceptance and self-understanding. Audiences were split between those utterly confused and those "blown away," in the parlance of the times. *Follies* became the rallying point for thousands of young theatergoers who saw it as the greatest musical of its time. Certainly, the production, especially Boris Aronson's magnificent settings and Florence Klotz's exquisite costumes, was the most lavish and spectacular in recent memory (and, in fact, has not been surpassed since). *Follies* remains the perfect intersection of writing, casting, and production; a moment in time that exemplifies the maddeningly ephemeral nature of theater. The show has become a legend, and decades later still had the power to either bring audiences to their feet or make them wonder what all the fuss was about.

In 1972, Prince became involved with the not-for-profit sector of theater as one of the artistic directors of the New Phoenix Repertory Company. Prince directed a number of the Phoenix's productions, including Eugene O'Neill's *The Great God Brown* (12/10/72) and Molière's *Don Juan* (12/11/72), both presented for limited engagements at the LYCEUM THEATER.

Meanwhile, Prince seemed to be concentrating his producing efforts on collaborations with Sondheim. *A Little Night Music* (2/25/73; 601 performances) was the musical version of Ingmar Bergman's film *Smiles of a Summer Night*, as reinterpreted by librettist Harold Wheeler. The score, written almost entirely in waltz time, featured the soon-to-be classic "Send in the Clowns." Glynis Johns, Len Cariou, Hermione Gingold, and Laurence Guittard headed an excellent cast. Scenic designer Boris Aronson won acclaim for his evocative settings.

Following the opening of *Night Music*, Prince directed three shows in repertory for the New Phoenix at the ETHEL BARRYMORE THEATRE: *The Visit* (11/25/73), *Chemin de Fer* (11/26/73), and Philip Barry's *Holiday* (12/26/73). This was the company's first season of true repertory, but American audiences couldn't grasp the concept; the next season saw three separate limited engagements following each other.

Before returning to another limited season with the New Phoenix, Prince teamed up with the Chelsea Theatre Center to co-produce and direct a radical new revival of Leonard Bernstein's *Candide* (3/11/74; 740 performances). Hugh Wheeler was brought in to revise the original libretto, and Stephen Sondheim supplanted the lyrics of Richard Wilbur and John Latouche. For the production, the orchestra seating of the BROADWAY THEATRE was removed and bleacher-style seating was introduced. The audience surrounded the narrow thrust stage and was often drawn into the action. Although *Candide* enjoyed a long, profitable run, the show ended up in the red. Prince blamed the musician's union and their policy of stipulating a minimum number of paid musicians per Broadway house. Since *Candide* employed a smaller number of musicians than the union contact stipulated, Prince was forced to pay additional musicians for not playing. The amount paid to these "walkers" equaled the amount that *Candide* lost.

Then it was back to the final season of the New Phoenix, presented in the original HELEN HAYES THEATER. This time the schedule consisted of revivals of *Love for Love* (11/11/74), *Rules of the Game* (12/12/74), and *The Member of the Wedding* (1/2/75).

Prince and Sondheim next collaborated on a remarkable production, *Pacific Overtures* (1/11/76; 193 performances). The story of the forced opening of Japan to international trade was presented in a staging based on the Noh Theater traditions of Japan. Boris Aronson imagined a brilliant and beautiful set that belied its obvious weight with billowing curtains and exotic materials. The show, a further exploration of the musical-theater form by Sondheim, this time with John Weidman as the librettist, was an unfortunate failure in an increasingly conservative Broadway.

Prince saluted his friend and co-worker Stephen Sondheim with the production of *Side by Side by Sondheim* (4/18/77; 384 performances) at the MUSIC BOX THEATER. Ned Sherrin devised the revue and acted as moderator and narrator of the proceedings. Vocal duties were handled by an excellent cast of British musical-theater stars: David Kernan, Millicent Martin, and Julia McKenzie. The tribute to Sondheim's work was an immediate hit and, following its close on Broadway, toured the country with a succession of narrators including Cyril Ritchard and even Burr Tillstrom's Kukla and Ollie.

Prince was next tapped to direct a play, *Some of My Best Friends* (10/25/97), a quick flop that closed after only 7 performances. He returned to Broadway to direct the Cy Coleman and COMDEN AND GREEN musical *On the Twentieth Century* (2/19/78; 449 performances). The production, one of the most stylish in recent Broadway history, was designed by Robin Wagner in an attenuated Art Deco style. The cast included Madeline Kahn (replaced by Judy Kaye shortly after the opening), John Cullum, Imogene Coca, and Kevin Kline in the role that made him a star. This magnificent show represented Broadway at its best, with a hilarious libretto and an equally imaginative and effective score. Many Broadwayites consider *On the Twentieth Century* to be the last great musical—one that wed all aspects of production in a brilliant whole. This, Prince's next show, *Sweeney Todd*, and Sondheim's later output were the last in a long history of shows that didn't pander to their audiences. They represented the last gasp of a long Broadway tradition of sophistication and ideas mounted in a fully professional, well-conceived production.

Sondheim reteamed with Hugh Wheeler for the Grand Guignol–inspired *Sweeney Todd* (3/1/79; 557 performances), aptly subtitled *The Demon Barber of Fleet Street*. This gruesome horror starred Angela Lansbury as Mrs. Lovett, a poor woman who owns a meat pie shop. She rents a room upstairs to Len Cariou as the title character, a man set on avenging past slights. They soon come to a mutually beneficial agreement in which Todd dispatches his enemies and Mrs. Lovett uses the corpses as the basis for an ever-burgeoning pie business. Sondheim's score married opera and music hall styles in an impressive, effective, and unique manner.

Prince was again hired by an outside producer, in this case Robert Stigwood, to direct a big Broadway musical. The show was *Evita* (9/25/79; 1,567 performances), ANDREW LLOYD WEBBER and Tim Rice's musicalization of the life of Eva Peron. An unlikely idea for a musical turned into a smash hit due in large part to the excellent cast, which included Patti LuPone, Mandy Patinkin, and Bob Gunton. All three became stars on the basis of their performances in this hit show. Prince's staging and directorial ideas brought together his years of experimentation with filmic and multimedia elements in a remarkably fluid and impressive manner.

The Prince-Sondheim collaboration ended with the ill-fated *Merrily We Roll Along* (11/16/81; 16 performances). Reteaming with George Furth, the pair attempted to musicalize a KAUFMAN AND HART comedy about friendship that was told in reverse chronology. Setting the story against a show-biz milieu allowed for some interesting scenes, but there were fundamental difficulties despite Sondheim's most accessible score. The backward time frame was retained, which confused audiences, and Prince opted to cast young, mostly inexperienced actors (including his own daughter Daisy). Following this flawed musical, the Prince-Sondheim professional partnership came to a temporary end.

The ignominious failure of *Merrily* marked an unfortunate turning point in the producer/director's career. Despite his best efforts, Prince's next shows were all flops. He followed *Merrily* with a musical sequel to the Henrik Ibsen play *A Doll's House*. The musical, titled *A Doll's Life* (9/23/82; 5 performances), followed Nora after she slammed the door on her husband Torvald. Betty Comden and Adolph Green supplied the turgid, overwrought book, an unlikely choice for such eternally youthful bon vivants as they. Larry Grossman, a relative unknown, was the composer. *Sweeney Todd*'s George Hearn headed the cast, along with Betsy Joslyn (as Nora) and Peter Gallagher. Prince next was hired to direct Joanna M. Glass' drama *Play Memory* (4/26/84). Like *A Doll's Life*, *Play Memory* lasted only 5 performances. Another play followed, Arthur Kopit's *End of the World* (5/6/84; 30 performances). Larry Grossman provided the incidental music to both plays.

Grossman and lyricist Ellen Fitzhugh provided the score and Fay Kanin the libretto to Prince's next musical, *Grind* (4/16/85; 71 performances), an original musical with burlesque as its background. Ben Vereen, Stubby Kaye (in his final Broadway appearance), and Leilani Jones starred in the ill-fated show. Two years later Prince returned to direct the Gilbert Becaud musical *Roza* (10/1/87; 12 performances). Georgia Brown starred in her final Broadway appearance, ably backed by Bob Gunton in drag. A revival of *Cabaret* (10/22/87; 261 performances) brought Joel Grey back to his star-making role of the Emcee.

Prince's fortunes turned with a vengence for his next assignment. He traveled to London to stage Andrew Lloyd Webber's new musical, *The Phantom of the Opera*. The show was an immediate sensation and catapulted Michael Crawford into superstardom. Lyric duties were assigned to newcomer Charles Hart, and the libretto was written by Lloyd Webber and Richard Stilgoe in an overly dramatic and very apt manner. The production was brought to New York, and it opened at the MAJESTIC THEATRE on January 26, 1988, with Michael Crawford reprising his London performance. The show was equally a smash in New York. *Phantom* allowed Prince to create stunning set pieces in collaboration with set and costume designer Maria Bjornson and lighting designer Andrew Bridge. The show, a throwback to the operettas of the 1920s, looked magnificent, with especially lush draperies and rich-looking fabrics. Cameron Mackintosh and Lloyd Webber's Really Useful Company produced the proceedings on a grand scale. The evening was noted for the falling chandelier effect, which proved somewhat anti-climactic after the hype. But the evening was a triumph for all concerned and deserved to be a great success.

Phantom, the most successful Broadway show of its decade, turned around Prince's career. But Prince's next musical appeared destined to be a complete failure. *Kiss of the Spider Woman* premiered about an hour from New York City at the City University of New York's Purchase campus. It was part of an ambitious new summer program. The program was not meant to be reviewed by Manhattan's critics, but because the university was charging a high ticket price, and as a flexing of their muscle, the press descended on the show. They lambasted it, and it appeared that the world had seen the last of *Spider Woman*.

But Prince and his collaborators, John Kander and Fred Ebb and book writer Terrence McNally, believed in the show. Prince decided to open a completely reconceived *Spider Woman* in London. The revamped show was an immediate success and soon found its way to Broadway, where it opened at the Broadhurst Theatre on May 3, 1993. Chita Rivera was with the show from its beginning in Purchase, and she lent a much-needed energy (both sexual and malevolent) to the proceedings. Anthony Crivello and Brent Carver co-starred. *Spider Woman* eventually played 904 performances on Broadway, although it closed in the red.

Prince directed his first original revival when Livent, Garth Drabinsky's doomed producing organization, decided to present a lavish revival of JEROME KERN and OSCAR HAMMERSTEIN II's classic *Show Boat* at their Toronto headquarters. The show was an immediate success in Canada, and plans were made to open the production on Broadway. The reception at the October 2, 1993, opening was excellent, and the show settled in for a long run at a huge barn of a theater, the GERSHWIN THEATER, where it enjoyed a run of 947 performances.

Prince's next show, also produced by Livent, also a revival, and also at the Gershwin, was of *Candide* (4/29/97; 104 performances). The mostly excellent cast included Jason Danieley in the title role, with Jim Dale, Brent Barrett, Harolyn Blackwell, Andrea Martin, and Arte Johnson rounding out the cast. For this production, Prince did not emulate his staging of 1974 but presented a traditional proscenium-bound production.

Parade (12/17/98; 85 performances), was produced by the Lincoln Center Theater uptown. Prince directed and co-conceived the production, which featured a score by Jason Robert Brown and libretto by Alfred Uhry. Audiences were mixed, and the show completed its limited engagement at the Vivian Beaumont Theatre without transferring to Broadway. Prince reteamed with Sondheim for *Bounce* a new musical that tried out at the Goodman Theatre in Chicago.

In addition to his work on the Broadway stage, Prince's opera productions have been seen at the Chicago Lyric, Metropolitan Opera, New York City Opera, San Francisco Opera, Houston Grand Opera, Dallas Opera, Vienna Staatsoper, and Teatro Colón in Buenos Aires. He directed the films *Something for Everyone* and *A Little Night Music*. He serves as a trustee for the New York Public Library and served on the National Council of the Arts of the NEA for six years. He has received 20 Tony Awards. He was a 1994 Kennedy Center Honoree. In 2000, President Clinton awarded him the National Medal of the Arts.

Harold Prince is the most successful producer/ director of the second half of the 20th century. He expanded the art form of musical theater first as a producer with his collaborations with Jerry Bock and Sheldon Harnick. He continued to refine and improve the art form through highly successful collaborations with John Kander and Fred Ebb and, of course, Stephen Sondheim. He is responsible, as either director or producer, of some of the greatest artistic successes in Broadway history, including *West Side Story, Fiddler*

on the Roof, Company, and *The Phantom of the Opera*. Even his so-called failures, such as *Follies, Sweeney Todd*, and *Zorba*, have become legendary shows and have expanded the world of musical theater.

PRINCESS THEATER. 104 W. 39th Street. Architect: William A. Swasey. Opening: March 14, 1913; one-act plays: *The Switchboard; Fear; Fancy Free; Any Night; A Tragedy of the Future*.

The Princess Theater, long a failure as a legitimate house, played an important role in the history of the American musical. In the 1910s the Princess served as the home of the first great intimate musicals written by JEROME KERN, GUY BOLTON, and P.G. Wodehouse. Later the theater served as the home for the long-running revue *Pins and Needles*.

The Princess, designed by William A. Swasey, was built as a small auditorium by the SHUBERT BROTHERS, William A. Brady, and Arch Selwyn. The site for the 299-seat theater was chosen for its proximity to the Metropolitan Opera. Unlike other theaters uptown, the Princess had a simple design, with 14 rows of seats in the orchestra section and 4 boxes. After several false starts, Holbrook Blinn was named director and F. Ray Comstock the manager of the venue. The theater was to feature the works of new playwrights. Five one-act plays were presented at its opening. The opening bill proved to be unpopular, and Brady and Selwyn gave Comstock their shares in the theater.

Comstock decided that a new policy was necessary and asked a leading agent, Elisabeth Marbury, for her help. She represented many of the best-known playwrights, and her business sense was legendary. She was the first agent to get her playwrights a percentage of the gross receipts of their productions instead of a flat fee. Marbury also helped the career of America's leading dance team, VERNON AND IRENE CASTLE.

Marbury suggested small, intimate musicals for the Princess' stage. Comstock agreed, but it was thought that the leading Broadway composers wouldn't be interested, given the small size of the house. Marbury approached the young Jerome Kern, who in turn suggested librettist Guy Bolton. Comstock meanwhile booked a production of a decade-old English musical, *Mr. Popple of Ippleton*. The show was retitled *Nobody Home* for its American debut.

The *Dramatic Mirror* contained an advertisement about the theater's new policy: "A radical change of policy is impending at the Princess Theater, on West Thirty-ninth Street, where the Barnes South African moving pictures are now being shown." *Nobody Home* (4/20/15; 135 performances) had some new Jerome Kern numbers interpolated into the original Paul Rubens score. During its run, the Shuberts had one of their occasional fights with the *New York Times*. A statement in the program read, "This theater does not advertise in the 'New York Times.'" The producers might have considered themselves lucky that the *Times* didn't send a reviewer, because those who did attend did not like the show. Before the show closed, it was decided to move the production to the MAXINE ELLIOTT'S THEATRE nearby. The Princess' small seating capacity simply didn't allow for a big enough profit.

Kern wrote the score for the second Princess Theater show, *Very Good Eddie* (12/23/15; 341 performances). Philip Bartholomae and Guy Bolton contributed the book, and Herbert Reynolds and Schuyler Greene wrote the lyrics to Kern's tunes. *Very Good Eddie* led the way to a string of successful, intimate musicals at the Princess. The following Princess show, *Go To It* (12/24/16; 23 performances), was an adaptation of Charles Hoyt's 1894 hit, *A Milk White Flag*.

The Princess' next show, *Oh, Boy!* (2/20/17; 463 performances), represented another step forward in the gradual evolution of a truly American musical that was distinct from the European operetta tradition. The Kern, Bolton, and Wodehouse musical was an immediate success. The trio continued their advancement of the musical theater form with the fifth Princess Theater show and their last collaboration, *Oh, Lady! Lady!* (2/1/18; 219 performances), with Vivienne Segal. For *Oh, My Dear!* (11/27/18; 189 performances), Wodehouse and Bolton collaborated with a new composer, Louis A. Hirsch. The last of the Princess Theater musicals was the Richard Whiting and Raymond B. Egan musical *Toot Sweet* (5/7/19; 45 performances).

In 1928 the name of the theater was changed for the first time. Beginning with the opening of *Sun-Up* (10/22/28; 137 performances), the theater was called the Lucille La Verne Theater. The theater was renamed the Princess, however, with *He Walked in Her Sleep* (4/4/29; 20 performances). The old name lasted only a few months. On October 16, 1929, with the opening of the play *Lolly* (29 performances), the Princess became the Assembly Theater.

The Depression took a toll on Broadway theaters, and the Assembly was no exception. In 1933 the theater became a movie house, the Reo. The International Ladies' Garment Workers' Union bought the building and used it as a union hall. They presented a show in their theater, which they renamed the Labor Stage. The result was HAROLD ROME's surprise success, *Pins and Needles* (11/27/37; 1,108 performances). The topical revue starred members of the union, many of whom were making their performing debuts. *Pins and Needles* became a smash hit and played several editions at the Labor Stage. Until *Hellzapoppin, Pins and Needles* was the longest-running Broadway musical. It played the Labor Stage for most of its run, leaving for the Windsor Theater in June 1939.

The theater changed again in 1944 when it became the Theater Workshop. On October 31, 1947, the movie *Lucia di Lammermoor* opened in the theater, which was renamed the Cinema Dante. On April 22, 1948, the movie *Not Guilty* opened; this time, the theater was called the Little Met. Its name was changed one last time on April 16, 1952, with the opening of the movie *La Forza Del Destino*. The theater's last name was Cinema Verdi.

In June 1955 the theater, which had figured so strongly in the history of the musical, was razed to make room for an office building.

PULITZER PRIZE. The controversial Pulitzer prize for drama has been awarded since 1917–18, when the first recipient was *Why Marry?* by Jess Lynch Williams. The prize is given to "the original American play performed in New York which shall best represent the educational value and power of the stage in raising the standard of good morals and good manners." The award choices proved unpopular with members of the critical community in the 1930s and early '40s. The choice of Edith Wharton's *The Old Maid* over such later classics as Lillian Hellman's *The Children's Hour*, Clifford Odets' *Awake and Sing*, and Robert E. Sherwood's *The Petrified Forest* angered the critical community and led to the founding of the NEW YORK DRAMA CRITICS' CIRCLE AWARD.

The first Pulitzer prize for a musical was given to *Of Thee I Sing* in 1931–32. Because the judges felt this was a literary award, however, composer GEORGE GERSHWIN was not included. In some years no Pulitzer prize for drama has been given. On occasion the judges' choices have been rejected by the Pulitzer board, and other plays have been awarded the prize.

PUNCH AND JUDY THEATRE. *See* **Charles Hopkins Theater.**

RADIANT CENTER. *See* **George Abbott Theater.**

RECTOR'S RESTAURANT. Broadway, between 43th and 44th Streets. Rector's was the most lavish and most important of the "lobster palaces" that dotted Broadway at the turn of the 20th century. When its doors were opened on September 23, 1899, a new era of fine dining was born in what was then Longacre Square.

Charles Rector's father was a short-order cook at the Frontier House in Lewiston, New York. He moved to Rockport, a location near the Erie Canal. At his restaurant, The Sign of the Griffin, the elder Rector refined his culinary skills by serving traders and travelers going up the canal. His son Charles was an ambitious teenager. After a term in the Civil War and a subsequent tour of duty driving a 2nd Avenue horsecar, Charles Rector moved to Chicago where he found a job with railroader George Pullman. He managed the first Pullman hotel dining car to cross the continent.

With Pullman, Rector got a taste of society, and he left to open his own restaurant at the corner of Clark and Monroe Streets in Chicago. Rector's Oyster House was the first to serve the upper classes live oysters. Live lobsters were brought in by train from the East Coast. And to complete the innovations, Rector used the only cash register with a bell west of the Appalachian Mountains.

When the Chicago World's fair of 1893 opened, Charles Rector held the only restaurant license for the fairgrounds. At that time, Chicago was an important industrial and theatrical city. The added drawing power of the fair ensured Rector's new Cafe Marine an important clientele. There Rector met DIAMOND JIM BRADY and GEORGE M. COHAN, both of whom implored the restaurateur to try his luck in New York. Jack Dunston and Thomas Healy had erected a building but couldn't afford to finance their operation, so Rector was convinced to take over the building and open an exclusive restaurant.

From the outside, Rector's was a sight to behold. The two-story yellow facade was dominated by the huge griffin standing guard over the first revolving door on Broadway. Legend had it that Gentleman Jim Corbett and his wife were the first patrons to be spun into the $200,000 interior. They were ushered into a green and yellow wonderland of crystal and gold in an exaggerated Louis XIV style. Chandeliers especially commissioned for the restaurant shone over the huge main floor. Floor-to-ceiling mirrors enabled all patrons to see who was entering the revolving door. The ground floor held more than 100 tables, and the second floor an additional 75. The restaurant had four private dining rooms for large private parties and exclusive tête-à-têtes. But most patrons wanted to be noticed; that was part of the fun of dining at what was termed "The Cathedral of Froth" or "The Court of Triviality." The fun and the patrons of Rector's heyday were described in a song written by Raymond Hubbell and Will D. Cobb and sung by comedian Nat Wills in the *Ziegfeld Follies of 1913*.

Rector's was expensive to maintain. The rent on the building was an astronomical $10,000 a year. Hammerstein's OLYMPIA, on the next block, clearly illustrated the future of the area. The mustachioed proprietor realized that in order to pay the rent and make a profit, no expense could be spared. He furnished his new surroundings with $30,000 in linen from Belfast. Only a year later, a third would have to be replaced due to thefts and wear and tear. Each year $20,000 worth of silver was stolen as souvenirs. Nonetheless,

Rector managed to turn a profit, although his prices averaged only $2 for each dinner bill. Still, patrons like Diamond Jim Brady and Commodore Cornelius Vanderbilt might run up tabs of up to $15 for dinner for two. To get patrons to part with such sums, Rector knew the kitchen must be as professional as the front of the house. All the silver and crystal would not keep his clientele if the food was not also exquisite. He sent his son George to France to study the great eating establishments of Paris. George returned a graduate of the Cordon Bleu after studying at Marguery's and the Café de Paris.

Eight captains commanded 60 waiters in full evening dress with divided coattails and white vests. The maître d'hotel received a salary of $150 a month, and he might make an additional $30,000 in tips during the holiday season. The waiters were paid $25 from the captains and received almost $1,000 a month in tips. The coatroom alone brought in $10,000 a year. The orchestra was well versed in the latest song hits; when Lillian Russell or ANNA HELD entered, they were serenaded with the theme songs from their latest Broadway successes. The stars of the Great White Way all flocked to the new restaurant. George Rector is quoted as saying, "While others are forced to pay to see the theatrical stars of the day, the theatrical headliners paid to see Rector's."

By the end of the first decade of the 20th century, the area around Rector's was known as "Eatinghouse Square." Charles Rector once said, "I found Broadway a quiet little lane of ham and eggs and left it a full blown avenue of lobsters and champagne." Surprisingly, it was Rector's fame that eventually led to its demise. Paul Potter, a second-rate dramatist, opened his newest musical comedy at Weber's Theater on February 1, 1909. It was called *The Girl from Rector's* and told the story of a married woman who led a double life. In her own town, she was simply Mrs. Grimes Caperton, but she also kept house in New York as the mistress of Richard Van Arsdale, a playboy of the upper crust. By the end of the play, it was clear that Rector's and other midtown haunts catered to loose women.

The reputation of Rector's was sullied in the public's mind, and attempts to resuscitate the restaurant failed. In 1911 the dining room was remodeled, but the restaurant continued to lose $1,000 a day. George M. Cohan tried, with brief success, to lend his name to the cause. Charles Rector retired, and his son George tried his hand at a new address on 48th Street and Broadway. The final blow came with the imminent passage of the 18th Amendment and Prohibition. On New Year's Day, 1919, Rector's closed forever.

REPUBLIC THEATER. *See* **New Victory Theatre.**

RIALTO THEATER. Northwest corner of 42nd Street and Broadway. Architect: Thomas Lamb. Opening: April 21, 1916.

The Rialto was built on land occupied by OSCAR HAMMERSTEIN I's VICTORIA THEATER. Like its sister theater the RIVOLI, the Rialto was built by Crawford Livingston and Felix Kahn, owners of the Mutual Film Company. This "Temple of the Motion Picture—Shrine of Music and the Allied Arts" was designed by Thomas W. Lamb, one of the greatest architects of motion-picture theaters.

Lamb designed the interior of the theater in his favorite style, that of the Adam brothers. The Rialto, which opened in 1916, was probably the first theater built expressly to show motion pictures, as this was the dawn of feature pictures. The Rialto had no stage area. The screen was mounted directly on the back wall of the theater. On either side of the screen were two platforms on which soloists performed between shorts and while reels were changed. The same policy was later used by S. L. ("ROXY") ROTHAFEL in Livingston and Kahn's Rivoli Theater. In the orchestra pit, Hugo Reisenfeld conducted the symphony orchestra that accompanied the silent films.

Lighting dimmers were just coming into use, and Lamb installed a series of lights throughout the auditorium that could be faded from one color to the next. The Rialto's "color harmonies" were widely imitated and can be seen today at Radio City Music Hall. The Broadway facade was marked by a huge sign in a pinwheel shape with sparks that seemed to shoot out and spelled the word R-I-A-L-T-O. Above the sign, an American eagle beat its electric wings. Atop the eagle, also designed in lights, was the Stars and Stripes. Livingston and Kahn were smart enough to hire "Roxy" Rothafel to manage their new theater for $200 a week. Roxy was the genius behind the operation of the Strand Theater, one of the first motion-picture palaces.

The theater's opening was delayed, in part because of meddling by Hammerstein, who made sure he would have an office in the new Rialto Theater. Hammerstein's impish nature took over, and he plotted his revenge on Livingston and Kahn. First, he refused to leave the Victoria, even as it was being demolished. Then he decided to move into the new Rialto on the date specified on his lease. Naturally, the space wasn't ready yet. Hammerstein insisted on occupying the office. When workmen threw him out, he went to the West 47th Street police station.

Roxy explained the altercation by saying Hammerstein was "politely but firmly refused admission to the building because it was feared that he might make a

The old Rialto Theater, opened in 1916, was designed for motion picture exhibition only.

speech to the workmen and delay the completion of the theater, now months overdue." The *New York Times* quoted Roxy further in an article entitled "Oscar in Three Reels":

> S. L. Rothapfel, director of the Rialto, stole the last scene in the episode. "Mr. Hammerstein's little affair," he said, "is jeopardizing our opening which has been set for a week from Saturday. That is his loss as well as ours, for I had him on the invitation list and was arranging a little complimentary feature in his honor in consideration of his long managerial activities on that corner. If he continues to give an imitation of Mt. Vesuvius in eruption, we may have to withdraw the invitation out of consideration for our other guests on that occasion."

The Rialto opened on April 21, 1916. The opening night was a glorious affair, with Mary Pickford, Adolph Zukor, and Marcus Loew present. Also at the opening was R. A. Rolfe, Roxy's replacement at the Strand. Everyone was curious to see how Roxy could top his achievements there. The *New York Times* called the theater "a new palace of polite pleasure for the thousands." The ads for the Rialto's opening boasted "the World's Largest Grand Organ—Superb Concert Orchestra—Most Wonderful System of Electrical Effects Ever Installed in Any Theater—15 cents—25 cents—50 cents—No Higher."

Roxy outfitted his ushers with his usual pomp and circumstance. Their uniforms were scarlet, and the tunics featured gold piping and tassels. Every usher also carried a swagger stick whose mother-of-pearl tip lit up in the dark. To add to the splendor, the head usher carried a bugle. According to a press release, the ushers were all versed in first aid and knew how to use their swagger sticks in tourniquets. The Rialto was so successful that its owners decided to lease the site of the Palmer-Singer Garage and built the Rivoli Theater in 1917. After taking control of both the Rivoli and the Rialto, Roxy moved on to the CAPITOL THEATER.

The Rialto fell on hard times with Roxy gone and the Mutual Film Corporation unable to make the transition to sound. The Depression hit Broadway hard. The Rialto was sold and razed. In its place was built another Rialto Theater. The new Rialto had an uneventful life. In 1980 the theater was refurbished, and a legitimate-theater policy was attempted. Among the theater's shows (all failures) were *Musical Chairs* (5/14/80) and

The new Rialto Theater.

A Reel American Hero (closed in previews). After this brief period (together, the shows played less than a month), a movie policy was renewed. The entrance reverted to 42nd Street, and kung fu movies were the speciality of the house. In May 1987 the theater was in the process of being twinned, having been bought by the Cineplex Odeon chain. After serving briefly as a television studio, in 1998 the theater was razed and replaced by the new Reuters skyscraper, which opened in 2001.

RICHARD RODGERS THEATER. 226 W. 46th Street. Architect: Herbert J. Krapp. Original name: Chanin's 46th Street Theatre. Opening: December 24, 1924; *Greenwich Village Follies.*

Chanin's 46th Street Theatre was one of the six Broadway theaters built by the Chanin brothers, Irwin and Henry, prominent New York developers. They commissioned theater architect Herbert J. Krapp to build the theater, and he came up with a unique idea. Instead of dividing the theater, into orchestra and balcony, he raked the seats bleacher style to the upper back wall. Unfortunately, patrons sitting in the rear of the orchestra found their sightlines blocked by the overhang of the balcony.

The SHUBERT BROTHERS leased the house from the Chanins and booked the theater. Most of the early shows to play the 46th Street had opened at other theaters and were moved here to end their runs. The opening presentation, *The Greenwich Village Follies of 1924*, was no exception. It had run previously at the Shubert (*see* SAM S. SHUBERT THEATRE) and WINTER GARDEN theaters, and it closed soon after arriving.

The theater had its first big hit with the college musical, *Good News* (9/6/27; 551 performances). DE SYLVA, BROWN, AND HENDERSON contributed an enthusiastic score to the show. The hit songs included "The Best Things in Life Are Free," "Just Imagine," "The Varsity Drag," "Lucky in Love," and the exhilarating

Chanin's 46th Street Theatre where *She Loves Me Not* was playing, 1933.

title song. Zelma O'Neal starred in *Good News* as well
as the theater's next hit, *Follow Thru* (1/9/29; 401 performances). De Sylva, Brown, and Henderson again
provided a superior score, including "Button up Your
Overcoat." In addition to O'Neal, the cast included
Jack Haley and Eleanor Powell. Next, *Top Speed* (12/
25/29; 104 performances) opened with Ginger Rogers
making her Broadway debut.

To begin the new decade, Billy Rose presented a
revue, *Sweet and Low* (11/11/30; 184 performances).
Hit songs included "Cheerful Little Earful," with
music by Harry Warren and lyrics by IRA GERSHWIN
and Billy Rose. An even bigger hit was "Would You
Like to Take a Walk," with music by Warren and lyrics
by Mort Dixon and Rose. Other song titles such as "I
Wonder Who's Keeping Him Now," "Ten Minutes in
Bed," and "When a Pansy Was a Flower" point up
some of the naughtier aspects of the revue. Busby
Berkeley and Danny Dare choreographed the proceedings, which featured FANNY BRICE, George Jessel,
James Barton, Borrah Minevitch, and Arthur Treacher
in the cast.

HAROLD ARLEN and Jack Yellen wrote the score to
You Said It (1/19/31; 192 performances). Benny Baker,
Lyda Roberti, and Lou Holtz starred in the musical.
The Depression hit Broadway hard, and the Chanins
lost their theaters. Later that year, the Shuberts gained
ownership of the theater from the Chanins in a deal
that included the Shuberts giving control of the land
under their CENTURY THEATER to the Chanins. The 46th
Street Theatre continued as one of Broadway's most
successful venues.

Howard Lindsay had a hit comedy at the theater
with *She Loves Me Not* (11/20/33; 367 performances).
Burgess Meredith, John Beal, and Polly Walters
starred in the thriller/comedy. In the show, Walters is
a nightclub singer who sees a murder and has to hide
out in a college. Along the way, she sings two songs
by Arthur Schwartz (*see* DIETZ AND SCHWARTZ) and
Edward Heyman: "After All, You're All I'm After"
and "She Loves Me Not." *The Farmer Takes a Wife*
(10/30/34; 104 performances) was Henry Fonda's
entry to Hollywood. He and Margaret Hamilton appeared in both the Broadway production and the film
version.

One of the biggest hits in Broadway history, *Hellzapoppin'* (9/22/38; 1,404 performances), opened at the
46th Street Theatre to mostly negative reviews. Audiences loved it, however. They were convinced to attend
by columnist WALTER WINCHELL, who used his vast
power to plug the show whenever possible. Ole Olsen
and Chic Johnson were responsible for the craziness
on stage (and sometimes in the audience and lobby)
that ranged from cheap BURLESQUE jokes to cheaper
vaudeville acts. *Hellzapoppin'* might be compared
with the latter-day television hit *Laugh-In*. Actu-

ally, *Laugh-In* was more sophisticated. In November
1938 the revue moved to the larger WINTER GARDEN
THEATRE.

COLE PORTER returned to the 46th Street Theatre
(*ANYTHING GOES* had previously moved there from the
Alvin Theater [*see* NEIL SIMON THEATER]) with a zany
show, *Du Barry Was a Lady* (12/6/39; 408 perfor-
mances). *Du Barry*, the story of a washroom attendant
who falls asleep on the job and dreams he is Louis
XV, starred Bert Lahr and ETHEL MERMAN and fea-
tured Betty Grable, Benny Baker, Ronald Graham,
Adele Jergens, and Charles Walters. Porter's inspired
score included two big hits, "Friendship" and "Do I
Love You." Merman and Porter returned to the 46th
Street with *Panama Hattie* (10/30/40; 501 performances). Porter's score included "Make It Another
Old-Fashioned, Please," and "Let's Be Buddies." Also
in the cast were Arthur Treacher, Pat Harrington Sr.,
Oscar "Rags" Ragland, Joan Carroll, and Betty Hutton.

After the successful run of the eerie play *Dark of
the Moon* (3/14/45; 318 performances) came a revival
of VICTOR HERBERT's operetta *The Red Mill*. Then another classic musical, *Finian's Rainbow* (1/10/47; 725
performances), opened at the 46th Street. BURTON
LANE and E. Y. HARBURG wrote the brilliant score,
and Harburg and Fred Saidy contributed the alternately
fantastic and trenchant book. The superior score included "How Are Things in Glocca Morra?" "If This
Isn't Love," "Old Devil Moon," "Look to the Rainbow," and "When I'm Not Near the Girl I Love." The
delightful cast included David Wayne, Ella Logan, and
Albert Sharpe.

The next three shows at the 46th Street received
mixed reviews. The first, *Love Life* (10/7/48; 252 per-
formances), was an underappreciated gem by Alan Jay
Lerner (*see* LERNER AND LOEWE) and KURT WEILL.
Elia Kazan directed the cast, which included Nanette
Fabray, Ray Middleton, and Lyle Bettger. Producer
Cheryl Crawford presented *Love Life* and also the 46th
Street's next offering, Marc Blitzstein's opera *Regina*
(10/31/49; 56 performances). Based on Lillian Hellman's *The Little Foxes*, *Regina* starred Priscilla Gillette, Brenda Lewis, Russell Nype, Jane Pickens, and
William Warfield. Nanette Fabray returned in *Arms
and the Girl* (2/2/50; 134 performances), with a score
by Morton Gould and Dorothy Fields (*see* FIELDS
FAMILY).

The 1950s reestablished the theater's good fortune
with one of Broadway's greatest hits, FRANK LOES-
SER's masterpiece *Guys and Dolls* (11/24/50; 1,194
performances). The musical boasted a book by Jo
Swerling and Abe Burrows. George S. Kaufman (*see*
KAUFMAN AND HART) directed the exceptional cast,
which included Vivian Blaine, Robert Alda, Isabel
Bigley, Stubby Kaye, and Sam Levene. The score included "Adelaide's Lament," "I'll Know," "I've Never

Been in Love Before," "If I Were a Bell," "Luck Be a Lady," "Sit Down You're Rockin' the Boat," and the title song. Next, Audrey Hepburn starred in *Ondine* (2/18/54; 156 performances) with Mel Ferrer. Maxwell Anderson's *The Bad Seed* (12/8/54; 334 performances) was another hit at the 46th Street. Patty McCormack played the murderous child, and Nancy Kelly played her mother.

Gwen Verdon began a long run at the 46th Street in three different musicals. The first was the Jerry Ross and Richard Adler hit *Damn Yankees* (5/5/55; 1,019 performances). GEORGE ABBOTT directed. Hit songs included "Heart" and "Whatever Lola Wants." Bob Fosse was the brilliant choreographer. Verdon kept her dressing room and opened in Bob Merrill's *New Girl in Town* (5/14/57; 431 performances). The show was also written and directed by George Abbott and choreographed by Bob Fosse. The musical version of EUGENE O'NEILL's *Anna Christie* contained two wonderful songs, "Look at 'Er" and "It's Good to Be Alive." Verdon's co-stars were Eddie Phillips (also of *Damn Yankees)*, Cameron Prud'homme, George Wallace, and Thelma Ritter. Verdon stayed at the theater for *Redhead* (2/5/59; 452 performances). Albert Hague and Dorothy Fields provided the score, including two hits, "Look Who's in Love" and "Merely Marvelous." For *Redhead*, Bob Fosse not only choreographed but also directed. This show ended Gwen Verdon's long reign at the 46th Street Theatre.

BOCK AND HARNICK wrote the score to *Tenderloin* (10/17/60; 216 performances). The book, by Jerome Weidman and George Abbott, is about a priest's attempt to clean up Manhattan's notorious Tenderloin district. The cast included Maurice Evans, Ron Husmann, Rex Everhart, Eileen Rodgers, and the ubiquitous Eddie Phillips. Next, Frank Loesser returned to the 46th Street Theatre with a PULITZER PRIZE–winning musical, *How to Succeed in Business Without Really Trying* (10/14/61; 1,417 performances). The satire made a star of Robert Morse, who co-starred with Rudy Vallee, Claudette Sutherland, Charles Nelson Reilly, Virginia Martin, Bonnie Scott, and Ruth Kobart. Abe Burrows provided the direction, and Bob Fosse and Hugh Lambert choreographed. *How To Succeed*'s big hit song, "I Believe in You," was sung in the show by the hero—to himself.

Next came veteran Richard Rodgers (*see* RODGERS AND HAMMERSTEIN and RODGERS AND HART) and STEPHEN SONDHEIM's *Do I Hear a Waltz?* (3/18/65; 220 performances). Arthur Laurents based the libretto on his own play, *The Time of the Cuckoo*. The show had many assets, including performances by Elizabeth Allen, Sergio Franchi, and Carol Bruce. MARY MARTIN and Robert Preston were the sole cast members of the enchanting *I Do! I Do!* (12/5/66; 560 performances),

a musical version of Jan de Hartog's *The Fourposter*. Tom Jones and Harvey Schmidt wrote the score, DAVID MERRICK produced, and Gower Champion directed and choreographed. The theater's next hit had an unlikely subject for a musical. *1776* (3/16/69; 1,217 performances) traced the founding of the United States. Sherman Edwards's score and Peter Stone's libretto made the proceedings dramatic. *1776* starred William Daniels, Howard Da Silva, Betty Buckley, Ken Howard, and Virginia Vestoff.

In 1971 a revival of the tremendously successful *No, No, Nanette* opened at the theater. Ruby Keeler, Helen Gallagher, Susan Watson, Jack Gilford, and Bobby Van starred. The hit even brought Busby Berkeley back to Broadway. The spirited revival ran for 861 performances. *Raisin* (10/18/73; 847 performances) was a musical version of Lorraine Hansberry's *A Raisin in the Sun*. The theater was again host to Gwen Verdon and Bob Fosse with the John Kander and Fred Ebb musical *Chicago* (6/1/75; 947 performances); it co-starred Chita Rivera and Jerry Orbach. *Chicago* would prove to be a big hit, although a later, scaled-down revival at the same theater would prove to have an even longer run—thus confusing theatergoers into believing that the original production was a failure. In truth, the original was a far better and better-realized production than the subsequent revival.

The next show, *The Best Little Whorehouse in Texas* (4/17/78; 1,584 performances), became the theater's longest-running show to date. Carol Hall provided music and lyrics, and Larry L. King and Peter Masterson wrote the libretto. The show was a popular hit, due in part to Tommy Tune and Peter Masterson's energetic direction.

In 1981 the Shuberts sold the 46th Street Theatre to the Nederlanders. Another offbeat subject, Federico Fellini's *8-1/2*, a movie about an artistically blocked film director, was the basis for the next hit musical at the 46th Street. *Nine* (5/9/82; 729 performances) was another success for director Tommy Tune. *Fences* (3/26/87), by August Wilson, starred James Earl Jones and was awarded the Pulitzer prize.

NEIL SIMON had two hits in the theater now named the Richard Rodgers. The first, *Lost in Yonkers* (2/21/91; 780 performances), featured Mercedes Ruehl, Kevin Spacey, and Irene Worth. It was followed by *Laughter on the 23rd Floor* (11/22/93; 320 performances), a re-creation of the madcap atmosphere of writing for comedian Sid Caesar in the early days of television. Even an especially impressive cast including Nathan Lane, Lewis J. Stadlen, Randy Graff, Ron Orbach, and Mark Linn-Baker couldn't make the show a hit.

An ill-conceived revival of Abe Burrows, Willie Gilbert, Jack Weinstock, and Frank Loesser's Pulitzer prize–winning musical, *How to Succeed in Business Without Really Trying* (2/23/95; 548 performances) starred Matthew Broderick in his musical comedy debut. The production team and artistic team didn't trust the original material and instead made all the obvious and, in the case of the physical production, ugly choices.

City Center's Encores Series presented a semi-staged version of *Chicago* that was a hit with audiences and critics. Then Fran and Barry Weissler picked up the show and moved it to the Richard Rodgers Theater—the same theater that hosted the original production. Stylish and smart, the new production emphasized sex and sleaze at the expense of character development, while totally ignoring the original concept as envisioned by Fosse, Kander, and Ebb. *Chicago* opened on November 14, 1996 and, moved to the Shubert Theatre in February 1997.

Chicago moved to the Shubert to make way for the latest Kander and Ebb musical, *Steel Pier* (4/24/97; 76 performances). Unfortunately, though the musical showed promise, there was no out-of-town tryout, and the producers and director were not up to the difficult task of fixing a show in trouble. So *Steel Pier* became an unnecessary failure.

An overconceived show followed. *Side Show* (10/16/97; 84 performances) became a sort of cult hit—the sort that is followed by fans whose memories of musical theater go all the way back to *Cats*. Badly (and cheaply) produced, with an amateurish score by Henry Kreiger and Bill Russell, *Side Show* nevertheless had touching performances by Alice Ripley and Emily Skinner as conjoined twins.

The failures just kept on coming at the Richard Rodgers. *Footloose* (10/22/98; 709 performances) was next. Based on the film of the same name, *Footloose* enjoyed an extended run due to creative producing and press agentry, but nevertheless it closed after losing millions for its investors.

Seussical (11/30/2000; 198 performances) was meant to be the hit of its season. But what started as an excellent workshop deteriorated through the casting and rehearsal process. The tryout in Boston was a debacle, and many production people were replaced. Nothing could save the show, however, since there was no strong hand on either the production or artistic side. David Shiner starred, although singing, dancing, and acting were not his forte (his only Broadway appearances were as a mime—at which he was excellent). The songs by Lynn Ahrens and Stephen Flaherty of *Ragtime* fame, were better than the book, but barely so. A series of stunt casts including Rosie O'Donnell, Cathy Rigby, and Aaron Carter still couldn't make the show into a success.

Neil Simon's *45 Seconds from Broadway* (11/11/2002; 73 performances) told the story of a bunch of habitués, at the Edison Coffee Shop (in the Edison Hotel) next door to the theater. Audiences and critics were not amused, and the show became one of Simon's biggest failures.

An acclaimed production of Noël Coward's *Private Lives* (4/28/2002; 127 performances) played a limited engagement at the Richard Rodgers. Although not the smash it was in London, the show featured excellent performances by Allan Rickman and Lindsay Duncan. But somehow it never caught on with American theatergoers.

On November 17, 1987, the New York City Landmarks Preservation Commission granted landmark status to the interior and exterior of the theater. The commission stated: "Its facade is an exceptional design based on Renaissance and neo-classical sources," and its interior was "designed in the 'stadium' plan, an innovation." In 1990 the theater was renamed in honor of composer Richard Rodgers.

RIPLEY'S WAX MUSEUM. 1539 Broadway, between 43rd and 44th Streets.

Ripley's Wax Museum was a Times Square landmark for 23 years until it closed just before New Year's 1972, when Ripley's executive vice president called Times Square the "Avenue of Perverts." Attendance at the house of horrors, sometimes called the Odditorium, had been falling steadily as the Times Square area declined in the late 1960s. The last manager of the museum, Richard Carputo, had urged the parent organization—which also owned outlets in Niagara Falls; St. Augustine, Florida; San Francisco; Goodlettsville, Tennessee; and Chicago—to upgrade the Times Square exhibits, but to no avail.

At its high point in 1961, the basement wax museum made $280,000. By the time the decision was made to close the museum after the 1971 Christmas season, however, revenues had dropped by half while the cost of rent and upkeep had increased dramatically. There had also been two suspicious fires in February and May 1971. After the Times Square museum closed, the wax statues and simulated torture devices were packed up and sent to Los Angeles. Ripley's later opened an exhibit in the basement of the Empire State Building.

RITZ THEATRE (1). 223 W. 48th Street. Architect: Herbert J. Krapp. Opening: March 21, 1921; *Mary Stuart*.

The SHUBERT BROTHERS built the Ritz in only 66 days as a sister theater to the AMBASSADOR. The brothers leased their theater to producer William B. Harris of the Theatrical Syndicate.

The opening production at the Ritz was John Drinkwater's *Mary Stuart* (3/21/21; 40 performances). The first hit was *Bluebeard's Eighth Wife* (9/19/21; 155 performances) with Ina Claire and Edmund Breeze. Claire played a woman whom an American buys as his wife. She works up a prenuptial agreement with her future husband for double the alimony he is paying his other 7 wives. After they are married, she refuses to live with him and arranges to be found with another man in her husband's bed. The marriage is annulled and—legally free from each other—the former husband and wife can now wed for love. Other notable dramatic productions of the early 1920s included *In Love with Love* (8/6/23; 122 performances), which starred Lynn Fontanne (*see* LUNT AND FONTANNE); and Sutton Vane's imaginative play, *Outward Bound* (1/7/24; 145 performances), which starred Fontanne's future partner, Alfred Lunt. Vane's play took place on a boat carrying dead passengers to the other side. The drama opened with Leslie Howard and Margalo Gilmore also in the cast.

The first musical production at the theater was *Hassard Short's Ritz Revue* (9/17/24; 109 performances). Short was one of the revue format's greatest directors. He later directed such classics as *The Band Wagon* and IRVING BERLIN's *As Thousands Cheer*. The revue opened with Charlotte Greenwood, Raymond Hitchcock, and Madeleine Fairbanks.

Ina Claire, Lynn Fontanne, and Margalo Gillmore were only the first of a string of great actors to play the Ritz Theatre. Others included Claudette Colbert in *The Kiss in a Taxi* (8/25/25; 103 performances), HELEN HAYES in *Young Blood* (11/24/25; 72 performances), Grace George in *The Legend of Lenora* (3/29/27; 16 performances), Alice Brady in *The Thief* (4/22/27; 86 performances), Miriam Hopkins in *Excess Baggage* (12/26/27; 216 performances), Janet Beecher in *Courage* (10/8/28; 283 performances), and Bette Davis in *Broken Dishes* (11/5/29; 165 performances).

The theater's lack of hits led to the Shubert brothers' taking over its booking in the late 1920s. However, they didn't fare much better than Harris. Nonetheless, the 1930s featured other great performers. Mildred Natwick appeared in *The Wind and the Rain* (2/1/34; 119 performances). Dennis King starred with Leo G. Carroll (television's Topper) in *Petticoat Fever* (3/4/35; 137 performances).

When the Depression changed the face of Broadway, the Ritz found bookings hard to come by. The FEDERAL THEATRE PROJECT took over the stage on February 16, 1938, with the world premiere of T. S. Eliot's *Murder in the Cathedral*. The drama about Thomas Becket, archbishop of Canterbury in 12th-century England, proved to be a huge success, and its 6-week run played to more than 39,000 people. Although the Federal Theatre Project was not wealthy, its productions actually benefited from their tight budgets. The directors and designers were forced to use their imagination to overcome their financial limitations. *Murder in the Cathedral* was designed and directed by Yale professor Halsted Welles. Welles chose to use platforms and minimal set pieces to suggest settings. He deployed his actors and props in geometric patterns that gave shape to the stage. Most of the important effects came from the imaginative use of lighting to create shadows, silhouettes, and stark contrasts in mood. These abstract stage pictures brought the play out of its period and distinguished it from ordinary costume dramas.

One of the Federal Theatre Project's goals was to use theater to communicate to people about the time and place in which they lived. Productions like *Murder in the Cathedral* made audiences conscious of how history was being replayed in their own lives. BILLBOARD attested to the power of the production: "A hardboiled audience of Broadway professionals stood up and cheered, literally stood and cheered as this reporter has seldom if ever heard an audience cheer in the theater."

The project's "Living Newspapers" series dramatized issues from the front pages of the nation's newspapers. *Power* (2/23/37; 142 performances) advocated public ownership and control of utilities. The play was also presented by other project companies in Seattle, Chicago, San Francisco, and Portland, Oregon. *Power* presented a typical American, Angus K. Buttonkooper, as he tours his local power company. Worried that his electric bill is too high, Buttonkooper asks questions about just how and why the power system works. By the end of the first act, he is fighting mad but powerless to change the system. The second act begins with the government's establishment of the Tennessee Valley Authority, a series of dams constructed to provide inexpensive electricity. Some government officials, and the power companies, challenged the right of the government to go into the power business. At the play's end a voice on the public address system asks: "What will the Supreme Court do?"

Power was instructive and entertaining and, as far as the government was concerned, not controversial. Harry Hopkins, one of the prime architects of the New Deal, commented:

> It's fast and funny, it makes you laugh and it makes you cry and it makes you think—I don't know what more anyone can ask of a show. . . . People will say it's propaganda. Well, I say what of it? It's propaganda to educate the consumer who's paying for power. It's about time someone had some propaganda for him. The big power companies have spent millions on propaganda for the utilities. It's about time that the consumer had a mouthpiece. I say more plays like *Power* and more power to you.

Of course, when the project began to explore views that were unpopular with the government, the politicians were not so amused or supportive. Until that happened, the project was riding high and, in the government's opinion, fulfilling its mandate.

Pinocchio (12/23/38; 197 performances) was one of the most popular of all the Federal Theatre Project offerings. The play was developed and directed by Yasha Frank, who developed many of his ideas while working at the ROXY and CAPITOL theaters. Frank even went so far as to scent the theater with perfume during certain scenes. *Pinocchio* was part of a children's theater unit, but it had a grown-up message, which Frank explained as: "One should share his pennies with poorer folk."

Frank also used some unusual staging techniques. As he explained:

> We achieve success because we invite the children in the audience to take part in the performance. They are asked their opinion in critical situations and, afterward, they share in the distribution of goodies that have been used in the play. This creates for them an intensely personal experience and they remember the points that have been driven home.

Surprisingly, almost three-quarters of the audience were adults who returned again and again to see the play. Robert Rice wrote in the *New York Telegraph*, "In it there are sequences which approach more closely the classic works of Walt Disney than anything I have seen the stage produce." In fact, Disney and his staff attended eight performances of the Los Angeles production. They then announced their next cartoon feature—*Pinocchio*.

The Federal Theatre Project was disbanded on June 30, 1939, while *Pinocchio* was still playing to packed houses at the Ritz Theater. At the closing night performance, *Pinocchio* finished the play inside a simple coffin. Children held signs reading, "Who killed Pinocchio?" The curtain remained up after the curtain call, and, with the audience still in the theater, stagehands tore down the fanciful sets.

With the Federal Theatre Project out of the picture, the Ritz went dark. At various times all three broadcast networks used the theater. CBS used the Ritz as a radio studio. ALEXANDER WOOLLCOTT broadcast his "Town Crier" radio show from its stage. The Ritz returned to legitimate theater when Leonard Sillman presented his *New Faces of 1943* (12/22/42; 94 performances). The show starred such new faces as Alice Pearce and John Lund, as well as producer and director Sillman. Next *Tobacco Road* moved to the theater for a brief period. Then in 1943 NBC took control for their radio operations. Later ABC used the theater for radio and television.

On January 12, 1971, the theater reopened for legitimate productions with a rock musical called *Soon*. Peter Allen, Barry Bostwick, Nell Carter, Richard Gere, Marta Heflin, and Marion Ramsey starred. Although the talent was impressive, the show was not; it closed after 3 performances. Viveca Lindfors and Rip Torn played in a short-lived revival of August Strindberg's *Dance of Death* later that season. Later that year, the theater was closed for renovation; it reopened on March 7, 1972, with Gwen Verdon in *Children! Children!* The play opened and closed with the same performance. The theater was again dark until Maureen O'Sullivan opened in *No Sex Please, We're British* (2/20/73; 16 performances). The play, which was a huge hit in England, playing for more than a decade, closed quickly in New York.

The theater closed again, and for a while it was called the Robert F. Kennedy Theater, with plans to make it a national children's theater. But the Kennedy family sued to have the name changed, and the project folded for lack of funds. The theater was thereafter used to store posters. During that time, the roof began leaking, causing major interior damage. The Jujamcyn chain bought the theater from the city and spent $1.5 million on restoration. The interior was redesigned by Karen Rosen and The Roger Morgan Studios to approximate its original splendor. The first production at the restored Ritz was *The Flying Karamazov Brothers* (5/10/83; 47 performances), a juggling act. The Karamazovs later reopened the Vivian Beaumont Theater at Lincoln Center.

Producer Morton Gottlieb reached a unique deal with ACTORS' EQUITY, allowing the Ritz to present plays that might not otherwise have much chance for success. The theater's capacity was reduced by roping off sections of seats. One of the plays presented under this policy was David Wiltse's *Doubles* (5/8/85; 277 performances). A British revue called *Jerome Kern Goes to Hollywood* (1/23/86; 13 performances) had as its only asset a charming performance by the great Elisabeth Welch. Magicians Penn and Teller (12/1/87; 122 performances) worked their magic on the Ritz's stage in the theater's last hit. The limited engagement was extended, and the theater finally had a success.

In late 1989 the Ritz was completely renovated. It reopened as the Walter Kerr Theatre (*see* RITZ THEATRE) in honor of the great theater CRITIC, with August Wilson's *The Piano Lesson* (4/16/90; 328 performances). Wilson returned to the theater with *Two Trains Running* (4/13/92; 160 performances). Wilson presented a series of plays examing the black experience in America, devoting one play to each decade in the 20th century.

Tony Kushner's *Angels in America* was divided into two separate plays running in repertory. The first was titled *Millenium Approaches* (5/4/93; 367 performances), and the second was titled *Peristroika* (11/23/93; 217 performances). The show was a grand spectacle that examined America's attitudes toward religion and sexuality. The play was one of the first on Broadway to examine gay life in the United States; in fact, both evenings were subtitled *A Gay Fantasia on America*. Another gay-themed play followed, Terrence McNally's *Love! Valour! Compassion!* (2/14/95; 248 performances). Though McNally's play failed to reach a broad audience, it was hailed as one of the most honest depictions of human relationships that, in this case, happened to be homosexual.

August Wilson returned to the Walter Kerr with his drama *Seven Guitars* (5/28/96; 188 performances). Two British plays were the next successes at the theater. Martin McDonagh's *The Beauty Queen of Leenane* (4/23/98; 365 performances) was part of his Leenane plays that premiered at London's Royal Court Theatre. It was followed by Conor McPherson's eerie drama *The Weir* (4/1/99; 277 performances), which also originated at the Royal Court Theatre. Both plays received ecstatic reviews but didn't equal their London runs.

Legendary producer Alexander H. Cohen's final Broadway production was an all-star revival of Noel Coward's seldom produced play *Waiting in the Wings* (12/16/99; 186 performances). Featured were Broadway veterans Lauren Bacall, Rosemary Harris, Barnard Hughes, Dana Ivey, Rosemary Murphy, Elizabeth Wilson, and Helen Stenborg.

The Walter Kerr Theatre next hosted David Auburn's play *Proof* (10/24/2000; 917 performances). The show examines the relationship of a brilliant mathematician and his equally brilliant daughter.

RITZ THEATRE (2). *See* **Studio 54.**

RIVOLI THEATER. 1620 Broadway and 720 7th Avenue at W. 49th Street. Architect: Thomas W. Lamb. Opening: 1917.

S. L. ("ROXY") ROTHAFEL was the genius of the movie palace. His fame grew as he moved from new theater to new theater, improving and refining the concept of the movie palace. One of the theaters Roxy put his mark on was the Rivoli at Broadway and 49th Street. According to the December 1917 issue of *Theatre Magazine*, the theater was named after Paris' Rue de Rivoli, which connected "the Louvre, France's home of pictorial art, with the Opera, her home of music."

When the Rivoli was built, Roxy was at the RIALTO THEATER on 42nd Street, which was owned by Crawford Livingston and Felix Kahn. The two builders were

Rivoli Theater featuring Rudolph Valentino in *Blood and Sand*, 1922.

happy with the Rialto's performance and decided to increase their holdings. Six blocks uptown at 49th Street stood the old Palmer-Singer garage, owned by Maurice Heckscher. Livingston and Kahn bought the land and hired Thomas W. Lamb to design their new theater. Lamb was one of the three greatest motion picture theater architects, along with John Eberson and the team of Rapp and Rapp.

Lamb gave the new theater, dubbed the Rivoli, one of Broadway's most imposing facades. The glazed terra-cotta design was based on the Parthenon. Inside, the theater was decorated in Lamb's favored Adamesque style. The Rivoli had no stage and thus it never held large stage shows—presenting, rather, a series of movie shorts that alternated with soloists. The theater had three proscenia, the center for the film entertainment and two side proscenia for solists and the orchestra.

The interior decoration was in the style of the Italian Renaissance, with "colors of dull gold, ivory and black, with carpet of gray and seats upholstered in tapestry," according to the December 29, 1917, issue of the *Dramatic Mirror*.

Livingston and Kahn hired Roxy to run the new theater, which opened on December 19, 1917, featuring the Douglas Fairbanks vehicle *A Modern Muske-*

teer. The audience at the theater's opening saw the screen draped with a "Conservatory of Jewels," or a "dome within a dome, each studded with crystal gems." This "Conservatory of Jewels" was modeled after the Tower of Jewels at the Panama Pacific Exposition of 1915–1916. According to the theater's opening-night program, the "Conservatory of Jewels" was meant to "flash with kaleidoscopic effect when the light plays on them from the front and will glow softly in their several colors when another set of lights is brought into play behind them." The source of the lights was invisible, thereby increasing the illusion of glowing jewels. Also according to the program, the "brightest of jewels" was said to be "the Screen."

The theater consisted of a variety of rooms, including the Gentleman's Smoking Room, the Ladies' Retiring Room, the Lounge, the Writing Room, the Check Room, and the Emergency Hospital. Men would not be admitted without jackets.

Roxy was never one to stint, and the operation of the Rivoli cost Livingston and Kahn dearly. The weekly operating budget was $13,000, which the theater barely met. In fact, few of the Broadway movie palaces made money. Rather, their cachet was that they enabled the producers to advertise that their pictures had come from a triumphant run on the Great White Way.

Although it was built for silent films, the Rivoli had excellent acoustics. Joseph Kelly, former head of the United Artists theater chain, proclaimed that the Rivoli had excellent "dialogue intelligibility." The acoustics were important because the Rothafel Symphony Orchestra, consisting of the combined Rialto and Rivoli orchestras (the Rivoli shared some of its staff with the Rialto), was a weekly feature of the programming. Hugo Reisenfeld was the conductor of the Rialto orchestra and also oversaw that of the Rivoli, but Erno Rapee usually conducted the Rivoli's orchestra. The Hungarian-born Rapee used the Rivoli as a stepping-stone to greater fame when he moved with Roxy to the ROXY THEATER. Soprano Gladys Rice also began her long association with Roxy at the Rivoli. Roxy preferred to keep his "family" with him as he went from triumph to triumph. Roxy presented a program that would become a standard feature at motion-picture palaces. It began with an overture by a symphony orchestra; then the Rialto Male Quartet; a newsreel or educational featurette; and a number sung by Gladys Rice with the accompaniment of Sepp Morscher on harp, William Feder on cello, and Professor Firmin Swinnen on organ. Finally, the feature picture would be presented.

In addition to the large orchestra and soloists, the Rivoli contained what was then the largest organ ever installed in a movie house. Built by the Austin Organ

Company of Hartford, Connecticut, the pipe organ provided accompaniment for those shows in which the orchestra did not appear, as well as augmenting the orchestral programs.

The July 1918 issue of *Motion Pictures* explained another facet of the theater's design: "'Color Symphonies' are literally played by a system of meshed and multi-hued lights whose effects blend chromatically with the symphony orchestra of sixty [*sic*] pieces. A novel feature of the Rivoli is 'olfactory music,' or a system of atomizers which spray perfume—oriental, clover, new-mown hay—and in accord with the orchestra, the screen and the stage settings literally imbue one's senses with the atmosphere of the play." The colored light system would be carried over into each of Roxy's subsequent theaters.

The theater began as an independent, beholden to no studio. Product was hard to come by, however, and in 1919 the theater made a deal with Paramount Pictures to feature their films.

Roxy's mounting extravagances eventually got him in trouble. He made almost $700 a week and had his spacious offices moved to the Rivoli. Livingston and Kahn's theaters were associated with their Mutual Film Company, and they could ill afford the losses that began to quickly mount up. They replaced Roxy with Hugo Reisenfeld as director of operations at both the Rivoli and the Rialto. Roxy moved on to the CAPITOL THEATER a few blocks uptown. With Roxy gone, the owners removed the soloist platforms and replaced them with a full stage. They instituted full-blown productions by Frank Cambria, who came fresh from staging shows for theater owners Balaban and Katz in Chicago.

The Rivoli was the site of many innovations, including the first presentation of Lee De Forest's Phonofilm process. It premiered at the Rivoli on April 15, 1923. Phonofilm was a sound-film process that featured De Forest's audion amplifier. De Forest recorded sound movies of vaudeville's top stars, including Noble Sissle and Eubie Blake (*see* SISSLE AND BLAKE), Eddie Cantor, and Weber and Fields.

In August 1924 De Forest recorded Rivoli conductor Hugo Reisenfeld's score to the silent film *The Covered Wagon* with the Phonofilm process. The score was replayed at the theater during the lunch and supper showings, when the organ ordinarily filled in for the orchestra.

These experiments were somewhat successful and popular with audiences, but De Forest's system never really caught on; the Rivoli returned to a silent-film policy. On February 11, 1927, however, the RCA Photophone system (a.k.a. the Kinegraphophone) was unveiled at the Rivoli. The demonstration included two reels of MGM's *Flesh and the Devil* synchronized to an orchestral score, a clip of the Van Curier Hotel Orchestra of Schenectady, and a medley sung by General Electric employees.

Two years later, the Rivoli made another attempt at presenting sound films. On May 25, 1929, the Rivoli installed the Warner Brothers' Vitaphone sound system, which consisted of soundtrack recordings on disk synchronized to the film.

With only 2,200 seats, the Rivoli was a relatively small movie palace. It never earned the money of its far larger brethren in Times Square. There were many dark weeks during the Depression when suitable films could not be found to bring in a large enough audience to fill its seats. In the late 1930s the theater came under the ownership of United Artists, but they couldn't guarantee the theater a steady flow of first-rate films. In 1941 the theater was closed for the entire summer.

In March 1949, when *The Portrait of Jenny* opened at the Rivoli, additional speakers were placed around the theater for the climactic storm sequence. In 1974, with the premiere of the Sensurround system, the Rivoli presented the film *Earthquake*. Sensurround had special speakers that broadcast both audible and sub-audible frequencies that vibrated the air and gave the impression of a real earthquake.

The Rivoli also boasted one of the largest screens of any New York movie palace. In December 1926 a new projection system, Magnascope, was unveiled at the Rivoli after experiments at the Eastman Theatre in Rochester, New York. The film was *Old Ironsides*, and several sequences were projected in Magnascope. The Rivoli screen measured 15 by 20 feet, but the Magnascope system (using a wide angle, 3.5-inch lens) covered a 30-by-40-foot screen, twice the size of the Rivoli's standard screen. When the Magnascope sequences arrived, the black masking around the screen revealed the larger screen area.

Another experiment in wide-screen format took advantage of the Rivoli's huge screen. In July 1929 Lorenzo del Riccio's 56 mm format, Magnafilm, was given a demonstration at the theater.

In addition to the surround-sound speakers used for the 1949 engagement of *A Portrait of Jenny*, a Magnascope type lens was used to project a larger image for the film's climactic sequence. *New York Times* critic Bosley Crowther described the finale: "a green flash of lightening electrifies the screen, which expands to larger proportions and sound vents around the theater roar with the ultimate and savage fury of a green-tinted hurricane."

When Todd-AO was installed in the 1950s 5 speakers were installed behind the screen (two more than with CinemaScope). An additional 19 speakers were placed around the auditorium, all playing an additional sixth channel of sound. When the film version of *Oklahoma!* played at the Rivoli, a completely separate strip of film contained the magnetic sound tracks.

The interior of the Rivoli had been completely changed through the years. During the changeover to Todd-AO, a giant curved screen was installed that extended past the proscenium. The screen was made of a "plastic-coated fabric with an aluminum surface embossed in a formation of lenticules, or tiny lenses, of depth, shape and disposition to prevent the surface from reflecting light back on itself at the extremities and also to adjust light angles for optimum reflection into the audience area" according to *Motion Picture Daily* of October 7, 1955. There were more than 600 lenticules (reflectors) per square inch of screen surface. The curved screen (13 feet deep at its center) measured an enormous 52 by 26 feet.

Before the opening of *Oklahoma!*, the Rivoli was treated to a $350,000 renovation. A new projection booth was created, and the theater's 2,000 seats (18 inches wide) were replaced with more than 1,600 seats (22 inches wide). A new theater curtain was designed especially for the engagement of *Oklahoma!*. The $12,000, 90-by-40-foot curtain was decorated with symbols associated with the state.

Oklahoma! played the Rivoli for 51 weeks, introducing roadshow distribution. The film was treated much like a legitimate production with advance-sale tickets, reserved seats, and a matinee and evening show each day; Saturday and Sunday had 3 or 4 showings per day. Tickets ranged in price from $3.50 in the orchestra and loge to $1.50 in the balcony seats. Also emulating legitimate theater presentations, there would be no popcorn sold during this important engagement. That policy soon was adopted by the Roxy and other roadshow houses.

After *Oklahoma!*'s year-long run, another roadshow engagement followed. Mike Todd's *Around the World in 80 Days* premiered at the Rivoli on October 17, 1956, and ran for more than a year. During that engagement, Mike Todd Jr. took over as general manager of the Rivoli to make sure the operation of the theater was commensurate with the excellence of the film. Todd himself produced the premiere.

On October 31, 1984, the theater reopened after a $500,000 renovation and refurbishment as the UA Twin. The opening film was Brian De Palma's *Body Double*. At the same time, the stage area behind the screen was turned into shops, which fronted 7th Avenue. Around 1985, scaffolding went up over the theater's facade, and the sculptures on the pediment were removed. Some of the columns were covered over with concrete, probably to avoid the theater's being designated a landmark. Work stopped in late 1986, and the theater was closed. In July 1987 the Rivoli was razed.

ROCK CHURCH. *See* **John Golden Theater.**

RODGERS, RICHARD. *See* **Rodgers and Hammerstein** and **Rodgers and Hart.**

RODGERS AND HAMMERSTEIN. The masters of postwar American musical comedy; Richard Rodgers, b. New York, New York, June 28, 1902, d. New York, New York, December 30, 1979; Oscar Hammerstein II, b. New York, New York, July 12, 1895, d. Doylestown, Pennsylvania, August 23, 1960.

Rodgers and Hammerstein are considered to be among the greatest of all Broadway authors of musical theater. Their formula consisted of well-integrated songs and book, with songs that reflect the characters' personalities in both words and music. This formula or pattern for show construction and writing has been emulated since the years of their first big hit, *Oklahoma!*

The success of *Oklahoma!* came at a crucial point in both their careers and at a crucial point in the history of the THEATER GUILD, its producer. Rodgers had already enjoyed a successful career with his longtime partner Lorenz Hart. The team of RODGERS AND HART was known for sophisticated, witty contributions to a series of mostly playful, lighthearted shows. When Hart's personal problems stood in the way of further collaboration, Rodgers was forced to seek another partner. He turned to Oscar Hammerstein II, the scion of a great theatrical family.

Hammerstein at the time had his own problems. His most recent productions were failures, and it was whispered along Broadway that he was washed up as a creative artist. He had already enjoyed a distinguished career with such offerings as *Show Boat*, *Rose-Marie*, and *The Desert Song* to his credit. He was looking for a new partner, one who would challenge him to achieve new artistic heights.

The Theater Guild was also suffering. Their recent productions had proven unsuccessful at the box office, and the producing organization was close to bankruptcy. Theresa Helburn, co-director of the Guild, had recalled an earlier Guild-produced play, *Green Grow the Lilacs*, and thought that it might work as the basis for a successful musical. The Guild approached Rodgers, who in turn approached Hammerstein. Rodgers had previously helped the Guild when his early musical *The Garrick Gaieties*, written with Hart, proved to be a great success. The revue had put the early Guild on a firm financial footing.

In transforming *Green Grow the Lilacs* into *Oklahoma!* Rodgers and Hammerstein took many liberties with the musical-comedy tradition. There was no opening chorus sung by a bevy of leggy chorines. Instead, the show opened with a lone figure singing "Oh, What a Beautiful Morning." Furthermore, the villain, Jud, was a truly menacing figure, not just a two-dimensional moustache twirler. Another change was that Jud is killed at the end, an uncommon occurrence in musical comedy.

Oklahoma! (5/31/43; 2,248 performances) was somewhat unique in that it dealt with three-dimensional characters in an American locale. Most musicals at the time still featured the operetta conventions of exaggerated lovers in exotic foreign locales. *Oklahoma!* boasted a dream ballet choreographed by the great Agnes de Mille. This was the first important musical-comedy ballet that actually advanced the plot and wasn't simply an excuse for dancing, although George Balanchine's *Slaughter on Tenth Avenue*, choreographed for Rodgers and Hart's *On Your Toes*, was an early attempt at integration of dance and plot.

The show opened at the ST. JAMES THEATRE. The production starred a host of unknowns who would become famous as a result of the success of *Oklahoma!* Alfred Drake, Joan Roberts, Betty Garde, Howard Da Silva, Celeste Holm, and Lee Dixon were the leads. *Oklahoma!* played for five years and nine weeks in New York. That was enough to make it the longest-running musical record holder until July 11, 1961, when *Hello, Dolly!* passed it.

Questions as to whether Rodgers and Hammerstein could repeat their success were answered when *Carousel* (4/19/45; 890 performances) opened at the MAJESTIC THEATRE. The Theater Guild repeated its role as producer. Again Rodgers and Hammerstein broke new ground. Their lead character, Billy Bigelow, a bully and crook, is killed and reappears as a spirit. The show was also unique in that it dealt with serious subjects that the average musical comedy, meant mainly to entertain, rarely attempted. The cast was another talented group of unknowns. John Raitt and Jan Clayton were the star-crossed lovers Billy Bigelow and Julie Jordan. They were given some of the songwriters' greatest songs. "If I Loved You," "Soliloquy," and "What's the Use of Wond'rin'" are all among the finest songs in musical theater. Other hits in the score were "June Is Bustin' out All Over" and "You'll Never Walk Alone." *Carousel* ran until May 24, 1947.

After a stint in Hollywood, where they wrote the movie musical *State Fair*, the team's next Broadway musical was *Allegro* at the Majestic Theater (10/10/47; 315 performances). It was not nearly as successful as their previous works. Many of Rodgers and Ham-

Alfred Drake in *Oklahoma!*, 1943.

merstein's previous collaborators repeated their chores with *Allegro*. The Theater Guild produced, Agnes de Mille choreographed and moved into the director's seat, and ROBERT RUSSELL BENNETT, the noted Broadway orchestrator, also returned. With *Allegro*, the team attempted to break more musical-theater conventions. One idea was to have the musical-comedy chorus act as a Greek chorus, but this and other ideas simply didn't work. *Allegro* closed on July 10, 1948. It did contain a minor hit, "The Gentleman Is a Dope."

The team redeemed themselves with *South Pacific* (4/7/49; 1,925 performances), an immensely successful show. It opened at the Majestic Theater with MARY MARTIN, opera great Ezio Pinza, Juanita Hall, William Tabbert, and Betta St. John. JOSHUA LOGAN co-authored the book with Hammerstein and directed the production. The score contained more songs destined to become standards. "Dites-moi," "A Cockeyed Optimist," "There Is Nothin' Like a Dame," "Bali Ha'i," "I'm Gonna Wash That Man Right Outa My Hair," "Some Enchanted Evening," "Younger than Springtime," and "This Nearly Was Mine" made up one of the greatest scores written for any musical. CRITIC Howard Barnes, writing in the *New York Herald Tribune*, was wide of the mark when he commented, "The Rodgers music is not his finest, but it fits the mood and pace so felicitously that one does not miss a series of hit tunes." *South Pacific* ran until January 16, 1954.

Their next hit, *The King and I* (3/29/51; 1,246 performances), opened at the St. James Theatre. Gertrude Lawrence, Yul Brynner, Doretta Morrow, Dorothy Sarnoff, and Larry Douglas starred. The score was up to Rodgers and Hammerstein's high standards. "I Whistle a Happy Tune," "Hello, Young Lovers," "Getting to Know You," "I Have Dreamed," and "Shall We Dance?" were the standouts. Hobe Morrison in VARIETY especially liked Hammerstein's lyric contributions. He wrote, "Hammerstein's lyrics are another of his characteristic blends of apparently effortless grace, pictorial beauty and irresistible sentiment."

The show followed in the Rodgers and Hammerstein tradition of breaking new ground. Throughout the show, the two leads, Anna and the King, have an adversarial relationship. At the end, they have a grudging respect for each other. Before they have a chance to enter into a typically clichéd musical-comedy romance, the King dies. The music and lyrics also contained the hallmarks of Rodgers and Hammerstein. The songs were perfectly suited to the demands of the script and exactly defined each character's personality and point of view. Typically, the songs propelled the plot forward instead of merely commenting on the themes. *The King and I* played 1,246 performances.

BROOKS ATKINSON got to the essence of Rodgers and Hammerstein in his review of *The King and I.*

> Since Richard Rodgers and Oscar Hammerstein 2d do not have to write a new musical play every two or three years, they must have motives aside from the earning of money. Perhaps it is merely that they have a hospitable attitude toward people. Like *South Pacific, The King and I* is a skillfully written musical drama with a well-designed libretto, a rich score, a memorable performance and a magnificent production.
>
> But there is more to it than that. Note that in both *South Pacific* and *The King and I* there are no villains. There are only human beings, subject to the usual frailties of human nature—people decent at heart, but incompletely heroic. Their impulses are good, but they are not masters of every situation. In the course of the evening, they learn from each other. Being genuine artists, which means that they have an attitude toward life, Mr. Rodgers and Mr. Hammerstein have got way beyond the mechanical formulae on which musical shows are founded and are saying something fundamental about human beings.

Me and Juliet (5/28/53; 358 performances), at the Majestic Theater, was a second failure for Rodgers and Hammerstein. The story was about two backstage romances. Isabel Bigley, Bill Hayes, Ray Walston, George S. Irving, Joan McCracken, Buzz Miller, and Mark Dawson starred in the cast. "No Other Love," based on a theme Rodgers wrote for the television documentary *Victory at Sea*, was the hit song in the show. The critics didn't consider the show a failure, although all agreed it wasn't up to the team's usual standard. Richard Watts Jr., in the *New York Post*, seemed to sum up the critics' opinions:

> . . . if it is far from a peak achievement, it still has its pleasant virtues. For one thing, it isn't a bore. It is lively, vigorous and filled with the showmanlike craftsmanship of its makers. It has a number of attractive songs, its lyrics are bright and intelligent. But for the creative professionalism of the show, there is a curious and surprising air of the commonplace hanging over the evening.

A milestone of sorts was reached on April 5, 1954, when, for the first time since March 31, 1943, no Rodgers and Hammerstein production was playing on Broadway. During the 11 years since the opening of *Oklahoma!*, sometimes as many as four attractions were playing on Broadway with the Rodgers and Hammerstein names associated as either authors or producers.

Pipe Dream (11/30/55; 246 performances), a musicalization of John Steinbeck's novel *Sweet Thursday*, was the next show on the Rodgers and Hammerstein schedule. It opened at the Shubert Theater (*see* SAM S. SHUBERT THEATRE). William Johnson, Mike Kellin, Judy Tyler, and Helen Traubel were featured in the cast. Again the critics were disappointed. Most were

Richard Rodgers and Oscar Hammerstein II working on *South Pacific* in Boston Commons, 1949.

impressed with the professionalism, but as John Chapman of the *Daily News* put it, "for a surprising amount of time, it is dull." Richard Watts Jr. wrote in the *New York Post*, "the show is clearly the work of theater men who know their business. It merely appears oddly lacking in the sense of excitement that had been hoped for." Walter Kerr, writing in the *New York Herald Tribune*, concurred: "The people are capable, the material keeps promising to turn into a party. But someone seems to have forgotten to bring along that gallon jug of good, red wine." The songs "The Man I Used to Be" and "All at Once You Love Her" received the most critical notice. All told, the reviews were mixed, not necessarily pans but not up to the team's usual raves. The audiences were also disappointed, and the show closed after only 246 performances.

Cinderella was the team's next musical, written for television. It played on March 31, 1957, on CBS. Julie Andrews and Jon Cypher were the stars. Another version of the show was broadcast on February 22, 1965, on CBS. It starred Lesley Ann Warren and Stuart Damon.

Gene Kelly was the director of Rodgers and Hammerstein's next outing, *Flower Drum Song* (12/1/58; 600 performances). It opened at the St. James Theatre. *Flower Drum Song* was the story of the Chinese population of San Francisco and conflicts between the immigrant population and native-born Chinese. It starred Juanita Hall, Ed Kenney, Keye Luke, Larry Blyden, Jack Soo, Miyoshi Umeki, and Pat Suzuki. The score received modest praise. "I Enjoy Being a Girl" was the one hit. "Love Look Away" and "Sunday" were also singled out by some reviewers. They noted that although the score wasn't top-quality Rodgers and Hammerstein, it was still better than most Broadway offerings.

The show, although not as well regarded as Rodgers and Hammerstein's greatest hits, was better received than *Allegro, Pipe Dream,* or *Me and Juliet.* Brooks Atkinson, writing in the *New York Times,* said, *"Flower Drum Song* is not one of their master works. It is a pleasant interlude among some most agreeable people." Much praise went to the physical production. John Chapman in the *Daily News* described the show as "lavishly colored, delightfully tuneful and thoroughly sentimental." That sentimentality, along with a certain homogeneity, some critics felt, became more and more of a problem with each succeeding Rodgers and Hammerstein show. The blame was placed at Hammerstein's feet. Louis Kronenberger noted in *Time* that the team "makes Chinatown almost indistinguishable from Broadway." Marya Mannes wrote in the *Reporter,* "The Chinese in San Francisco cannot be quite as quaint as Rodgers and Hammerstein make them."

The team's sentimentality reached its zenith with *The Sound of Music* (11/16/59; 1,443 performances), their last show. Based on the early career of the Trapp Family Singers, the show opened at the LUNT-FONTANNE THEATER. The cast included Mary Martin,

Patrick Adiarte, Keye Luke and Juanita Hall in *Flower Drum Song,* 1958.

Theodore Bikel, Patricia Neway, Nan McFarland, Kurt Kasznar, Marion Marlowe, Lauri Peters, and Brian Davies. The score was in the tradition of the great Rodgers and Hammerstein's shows and yielded the hits "My Favorite Things," "The Sound of Music," "Sixteen Going on Seventeen," "Do-Re-Mi," and "Climb Every Mountain."

This time, the critics were apt to carp at the increasingly cloying aspects of the team's contributions. WALTER KERR, writing in the *New York Herald Tribune,* was among the most critical. He commented that

> before the play is halfway through its promising chores it becomes not only too sweet for words but almost too sweet for music. . . . The people on stage have all melted long before our hearts do. The upshot? What might have been an impressive and moving entertainment will be most admired by people who have always found Sir James Barrie pretty rough stuff.

Louis Kronenberger in *Time* concurred: "In general, the show's virtues are marred by its weaknesses . . . instead of offsetting sweetness with lightness, it turns sticky with sweetness and light . . . ends by making its warmheartedness as cloying as a lollipop, as trying as a lisp." Of course, not all the reviews were as unkind as these, but most critics, even when praising the show and noting that it was bound to be a terrific hit, had reservations about the tone. They were right about its success. The movie version, released by Twentieth Century-Fox on March 2, 1965, was an even greater hit. It became one of the top-grossing pictures of all time.

Oscar Hammerstein II died on August 23, 1960, leaving Richard Rodgers without a partner. Rodgers went on to write a succession of musicals with various partners, to varying success. For his first outing after Hammerstein's death, he contributed the lyrics himself. The show was *No Strings* (3/15/62; 580 performances) at the 54th Street Theater (*see* GEORGE ABBOTT THEATER). Diahann Carroll and Richard Kiley had the leads in the romantic musical. Rodgers again broke new ground with the new show. The book makes no comment on the racial differences in the leads. The score yielded a great hit, "The Sweetest Sounds." Rodgers' surprisingly adept lyrics had more in common with Hart's work than Hammerstein's. Howard Taubman, writing in the *New York Times,* commented, "Richard Rodgers is still a magician of the musical theater . . . a score full of romance and vivacity . . . enchanted music . . . his lines have la touch of the wholesome ease of Hammerstein and a soupçon of the peppery impertinence of Hart." *No Strings* differed from other musicals in another regard. Taking a cue from the show's title, Ralph Burns' orchestrations featured no string instruments save a piano and harp. And director Joe Layton's staging included members of the orchestra strolling through the scenes.

The job of writing both music and lyrics was tough, and Rodgers decided to join up with a new partner for his next show, *Do I Hear a Waltz?* Arthur Laurents adapted his play *The Time of the Cuckoo* as the source for the libretto. For his new partner, Rodgers chose Hammerstein's protégé, STEPHEN SONDHEIM. The two didn't see eye to eye, however, and their collaboration was stormy. Nonetheless, they did produce a good score. *Do I Hear a Waltz?* (3/18/65; 220 performances), starring Elizabeth Allen and Sergio Franchi, opened at the 46th Street Theatre (*see* RICHARD RODGERS THEATER).

Rodgers' next show fared slightly better. *Two By Two* (11/10/70; 343 performances) found him teamed with Martin Charnin. The show, a retelling of the story of Noah, opened at the IMPERIAL THEATRE. It starred Danny Kaye in a return to Broadway after almost 25 years. The show was not one of Rodgers' best, and the score was largely undistinguished. Critics were especially disappointed in the libretto by Peter Stone and the lyrics by Charnin. Rodgers received some glowing notices for his music, but the rest of the production was, as Brendan Gill put it, "as nearly dead as a musical can be." Danny Kaye received enthusiastic notices, but as the run continued he got bored and exhibited some unprofessional hijinks on stage.

Sheldon Harnick (*see* BOCK AND HARNICK) was Rodgers' next choice for a collaborator. *Rex* (4/25/76; 49 performances), at the Lunt-Fontanne Theater, was based on an unlikely subject for Rodgers, the court of King Henry VIII. Clive Barnes, writing in the *New York Times*, reflected the general critical opinion when he stated that the show "has almost everything not going for it." Rodgers' last show, though slightly more successful, was still a failure. *I Remember Mama* (5/31/79; 108 performances) opened at the Majestic Theater; his lyricists were Martin Charnin and Raymond Jessel. The musical was based on the straight-play version of Kathryn Forbes' story, *Mama's Bank Account*, that Rodgers and Hammerstein had produced earlier. Liv Ullmann was the unlikely choice to play Mama but received mostly good notices. Reviews for the show, however, were mostly devastating. Richard Eder in the *New York Times* opined, "the result is not a marriage but a divorce of talents."

RODGERS AND HART. Great songwriting team of the 1920s and '30s; Richard Rodgers, b. New York, New York, June 28, 1902, d. New York, New York, December 30, 1979; Lorenz Hart, b. New York, New York, May 2, 1895, d. New York, New York, November 22, 1943.

Richard Rodgers and Lorenz Hart were the premier collaborators in the early years of the American musical theater. In fact, they were the first team in which the lyricist received equal billing with the composer. Rodgers and Hart were the perfect songwriting team. (Later RODGERS AND HAMMERSTEIN would be equally famous as a team.) Their fame was enduring and well deserved. Their music and lyrics were superbly integrated in a sophisticated whole. Although their personal relationship was somewhat stormy, their songs never reflected the problems they were having.

Lorenz "Larry" Hart's parents, Max and Frieda Hart, were immigrants who instilled in their son a love of language and literature. He attended his first play when he was 7, and was permanently hooked on the theater. Rodgers wrote of their first meeting in *Theatre Arts*: "Neither of us mentioned it, but we evidently knew we'd work together, and I left Hart's house having acquired in one afternoon a career, a partner, a best friend and a source of permanent irritation."

Richard Rodgers showed an early gift for music, and he could play the piano when only 4 years old. Like most aspiring songwriters of his generation, the young Rodgers hoped for a career in musical comedy. At that time, composing for the Broadway theater was considered the top of the art form. There were no movies or radio, and most popular songs were introduced first on the Broadway stage. Like many of his contemporaries, Rodgers sought to realize his aspirations by writing scores for amateur shows.

Richard Rodgers and Lorenz Hart.

Rodgers' first song, for which he supplied the music and lyrics, was "Campfire Days," written while at Camp Wigwam in Maine. His first copyrighted song was "Auto Show Girl," with lyrics by David Dyrenforth. It was registered on June 30, 1917. His first complete score was written for the show *One Minute Please* (12/29/17). It was presented by the Akron Club, of which his brother Mortimer was a member. Rodgers wrote the music and lyrics to the show as well as the next Akron Club presentation. *Up Stage and Down* (3/8/19), also a success, resulted in Rodgers's father paying for five of the songs to be published.

A friend, Philip Leavitt, introduced Rodgers to the young Lorenz Hart. Leavitt believed that the two would make a good songwriting team, so they met and began trying to write together. Leavitt was pleased with the way the two boys got along. He convinced Lew Fields (*see* FIELDS FAMILY) to listen to their songs, and the producer decided to interpolate a Rodgers and Hart number in his Broadway show *A Lonely Romeo* (6/10/19; 87 performances). The song, "Any Old Place with You," was added after the show's opening. Fields was impressed with the team's effort. Rodgers and Hart next contributed songs to another Akron Club show, *You'd Be Surprised* (1920). The show contained 11 Rodgers and Hart songs. Rodgers also collaborated with Herbert L. Fields (*see* FIELDS FAMILY), Robert A. Simon, and his future collaborator Oscar Hammerstein II on three additional songs. In the cast was Dorothy Fields (*see* FIELDS FAMILY), who would become a famous lyricist in her own right.

Rodgers enrolled in Columbia University in 1919. He and Hart supplied the songs for the Columbia University Players' Varsity Show of 1920, *Fly with Me*. The show was presented in the grand ballroom of the ASTOR HOTEL on March 24 through 27, 1920. Oscar Hammerstein also collaborated with Rodgers on two songs for this show. Herbert Fields was the choreographer, so it was natural that his father, Lew Fields, attended the show. The elder Fields was even more impressed than before with Rodgers and Hart's work and decided to incorporate three songs from *Fly with Me* in his next Broadway show, *Poor Little Ritz Girl*. In addition, Fields announced that he would allow the team to write the remainder of the score, their first Broadway musical.

Poor Little Ritz Girl (7/27/20; 93 performances) opened at the Central Theater. By that time, Fields had gotten cold feet and had cut eight of the Rodgers and Hart tunes. He hired SIGMUND ROMBERG and Alex Gerber to supply additional songs. Heywood Broun wrote in the *New York Tribune*, "the more serious songs are from Sigmund Romberg, and they are pleasing, but hardly as striking as the lighter numbers." Both Charles Pike Sawyer in the *New York Post* and Kenneth Macgowan in the *New York Globe* also compared Romberg

and Rodgers' styles. Sawyer wrote about "Romberg being in his best Viennese waltz style, while Rodgers has written some good numbers." Macgowan noted "Rodgers' hard, brisk tunes and Romberg's rich and syrupy melodies." This distinction between the 2 composers' styles reflected the differences in the 2 predominant styles then on Broadway. As time passed, Romberg's operatic scores would lose favor, and Rodgers' all-American style would prove to be the next step in the evolution of American musical theater.

Rodgers and Hart soon found themselves writing another score for the Akron Club. *Say Mama* played in the Plaza Hotel on February 12, 1921. It was followed by another Columbia Varsity Show, *You'll Never Know*. Oscar Hammerstein II directed the outing, which opened on April 20, 1921. Eight more amateur shows followed. Next, "Herbert Richard Lorenz" contributed the script and two songs to *The Melody Man* (5/13/24; 61 performances), a play produced by Lew Fields. Herbert Richard Lorenz was, of course, a nom de plume for Herbert Fields, Richard Rodgers, and Lorenz Hart. It was noteworthy as the first Broadway play for Fredric March.

Rodgers and Hart received their big break in 1925. The show was a revue, *The Garrick Gaieties* (6/8/25; 230 performances). It was produced as a two-performance special fund-raiser. The THEATER GUILD, which was building a new theater on Broadway, had run short of money and needed the benefit to buy curtains and draperies for the new house. The show was also seen as a way for the guild to showcase its lesser-known members such as Sterling Holloway, Libby Holman, Romney Brent, and Lee Strasberg. The show, featuring a virtually unknown composer-lyricist team and an unknown cast, was an immediate hit. Six performances were added, and they, too, sold out. Finally it was decided to run the show indefinitely. It proved a great success for the guild and the cast, and Rodgers and Hart were finally established as a top-rate songwriting team.

For the show, Rodgers and Hart contributed one of their best tunes, "Manhattan." Still one of the most recognizable of their hits, the song has continued as a standard in the jazz repertoire. The *New York Daily News* critic called the "music and lyrics well above the average Broadway output." ALEXANDER WOOLLCOTT, writing in the *New York Sun*, opined that there was "a distinct 'varsity show' character to the lyrics. They are the kind invariably written by those who set out to show up the banal sentiments and meager vocabulary of IRVING BERLIN—rich in sprightly elaborate rhymes and suffering only from the not unimportant qualification that they do not sing well."

The next Rodgers and Hart project was the first in a long line of Broadway musicals with a book by Herbert

Fields. *Dearest Enemy* (9/18/25; 286 performances) opened at the Knickerbocker Theater and was an immediate success. Helen Ford, Flavia Arcaro, and Charles Purcell starred in the show, which was actually written before the *Garrick Gaieties*. "Here in My Arms" was the biggest hit of the show's delightful score. Most of the reviews were highly favorable, with many of the critics calling the show a comic opera.

Frank Vreeland, writing for the *New York Telegram*, singled out Rodgers for praise: "He continues to improve markedly with every score, and he has such a fecund store of catchy tunes and has obviously mastered so well the peculiar technique of arranging them for popular consumption that he will go far as a composer." Of the new team of Rodgers, Hart, and Fields, Vreeland wrote, "We have a glimmering notion that someday they will form the American counterpart of the once great triumvirate of Bolton 'Wodehouse' and Kern." Ed Barry, who reviewed the show for *VARIETY*, went so far as to recommend it as "a good buy at $3.30."

Billy Rose commissioned the team to write a revue called *The Fifth Avenue Follies*. It opened at the Fifth Avenue Club in January 1926. The trio was back on Broadway with *The Girl Friend* (3/17/26; 301 performances), which opened at the Vanderbilt Theater. Lew Fields, having passed on *Dearest Enemy*, saw the error of his ways and produced the new show. The title tune became a hit, as did "The Blue Room," which has enjoyed a somewhat longer life. Next Rodgers and Hart were asked to contribute songs to the second edition of the *Garrick Gaieties* (5/10/26; 174 performances) at the Garrick Theater. "Mountain Greenery" was the hit song. The duo then went to London, contributing the score to *Lido Lady* (12/1/26; 259 performances), which opened at the Gaiety Theater. None of the songs achieved much success.

The team was reunited with librettist Herbert Fields for *Peggy-Ann* (12/27/26; 333 performances). The show was another success for the trio and for Lew Fields, who produced it in association with Lyle D. Andrews. The score was delightful, with "A Tree in the Park" and "Where's That Rainbow?" worthy of additional attention. Helen Ford, star of *Dearest Enemy*, also starred as the title character in *Peggy-Ann*. Somewhat surrealistic, the show was a departure from the usual Cinderella story told in most Broadway shows. There was no opening chorus, which was generally used to set the scene and to allow the audience to settle down before the show actually began, and no songs until almost 20 minutes into the show. Nevertheless, the show was a hit, playing almost 10 times as long as Rodgers and Hart's next show, *Betsy* (12/28/26; 39 performances), a failure produced by FLORENZ ZIEGFELD

The team escaped to London, where they contributed a score to another revue, *One Dam Thing After Another* (5/19/27; 237 performances). Douglas Byng, Jessie Matthews, Sonnie Hale, and Melville Cooper were featured in the London Pavilion show. The hit song was "My Heart Stood Still," which had its American debut in their next outing (with Herbert Fields), *A Connecticut Yankee*, which opened at the Vanderbilt Theater (11/3/27; 418 performances). William Gaxton, Constance Carpenter, June Cochrane, and Paul Everton starred in the retelling of Mark Twain's novel. The top-notch score contained additional hits, including "Thou Swell" and "I Feel at Home with You." Busby Berkeley was the choreographer.

Without Herbert Fields, the songwriters seemed to have difficulty. *She's My Baby* (1/3/28; 71 performances) had a book by GUY BOLTON, Bert Kalmar, and Harry Ruby. It opened at the Globe Theatre (*see* LUNT-FONTANNE THEATER). Herbert Fields rejoined the team for *Present Arms* (4/26/28; 147 performances). Lew Fields produced and Busby Berkeley choreographed. It didn't have any big hits in the score, but the critics seemed almost unanimous in their praise. *Chee-Chee* (9/25/28; 33 performances), the trio's next show, was even more of a failure. In fact, it had the shortest run of any Rodgers and Hart show. The protagonist of the show and title character was a Chinese eunuch. *Spring Is Here* (3/11/29; 104 performances) had a book by Owen Davis. It premiered at the Alvin Theater (*see* NEIL SIMON THEATER). The script was much more traditional and inspired the songwriters to write one of their best tunes, "With a Song in My Heart." They followed it up with two middling productions, *Heads Up!* (11/11/29; 144 performances) and *Simple Simon* (2/18/30; 135 performances), which opened at the ZIEGFELD THEATER. "Ten Cents a Dance" was featured in *Simple Simon*.

London called again for *Ever Green* (10/13/30; 254 performances) with a book by Benn W. Levy. The show was a much-needed hit at the Adelphi Theater (*see* GEORGE ABBOTT THEATER). Jessie Matthews and Joyce Barbour starred. The hit song was "Dancing on the Ceiling." Back in New York, Herbert Fields was brought back into the fold for *America's Sweetheart* (2/10/31; 135 performances). It opened at the BROADHURST THEATER with Harriette Lake (better known today as Ann Sothern) and Jack Whiting. They introduced the hit song from the show, "I've Got Five Dollars."

Like many of their Broadway contemporaries, Rodgers and Hart were wooed to Hollywood in the early 1930s. They completed a series of films (some great, some bad), but they found New York more to their liking and soon returned. Their movies were *The Hot Heiress* (1931), *Love Me Tonight* (1932), *The*

Phantom President (1932), *Hallelujah, I'm a Bum* (1933), *Hollywood Party* (1934), and *Mississippi* (1935).

The duo returned to New York with *Jumbo* (11/16/35; 221 performances), certainly their biggest show and one of the largest shows ever seen in New York. Producer Billy Rose rented Manhattan's enormous theater, the HIPPODROME, for the extravaganza that employed an entire circus. Ben Hecht and Charles MacArthur wrote what book managed to be seen amid the clowns, tumblers, and animals. The show was so big that both JOHN MURRAY ANDERSON and GEORGE ABBOTT shared directorial chores. It featured Gloria Grafton, Donald Novis, Jimmy Durante, and Big Rosie as Jumbo the elephant. Paul Whiteman and his orchestra provided the accompaniment.

The production had been promised for three months before it actually opened, but most critics felt that it was worth the wait. Percy Hammond described *Jumbo* in the *New York Herald Tribune* as "a sane and exciting compound of opera, animal show, folk drama, harlequinade, carnival, circus, extravaganza and spectacle." Despite rave reviews and a score that featured such Rodgers and Hart perennials as "The Most Beautiful Girl in the World," "My Romance," and "Little Girl Blue," the show was a failure. It managed to run 7 months, but it cost an astounding $340,000 to produce, and the weekly operating cost precluded any profit.

After *Jumbo*, Rodgers and Hart entered their most productive and successful decade. It began with the opening of *On Your Toes* (4/11/36; 315 performances) at the IMPERIAL THEATRE. The show was the story of a vaudeville family who get mixed up with gangsters and a Russian ballet company. It starred Ray Bolger, Doris Carson, Tamara Geva, Luella Gear, and Monty Woolley. The score featured such great songs as "There's a Small Hotel," "Glad to Be Unhappy," and the title song. The two ballets, "La Princesse Zenobia" and the classic "Slaughter on Tenth Avenue," were an added bonus. Both were choreographed by the legendary George Balanchine. Nonetheless, the production received surprisingly mixed reviews. Percy Hammond in the *New York Herald Tribune* opined that "the songs are mildly hearable . . . if you do not expect too much you will not be disappointed." Frank Norris in *Time* magazine took the opposite view, calling it "a definite milestone in the musical theater."

Following a largely unsuccessful return to Hollywood with the film *Dancing Pirate* (1936), Rodgers and Hart presented Broadway with one of their most exuberant hits, *Babes in Arms* (4/14/37; 289 performances) at the Shubert Theater (*see* SAM S. SHUBERT THEATRE). They had collaborated on the book to *On Your Toes* with George Abbott. This time they did it all alone. George Balanchine again choreographed. Ray Heatherton, Alfred Drake, Mitzi Green, and the tal-

ented tap-dancing Nicholas Brothers starred. The songs were top-drawer Rodgers and Hart, and almost every song in the score became a standard. They included "Where or When," "I Wish I Were in Love Again," "My Funny Valentine," "Johnny One Note," and "The Lady Is a Tramp."

George S. Kaufman and Moss Hart (*see* KAUFMAN AND HART) contributed one of Rodgers and Hart's most unusual books. The show was *I'd Rather Be Right* (11/2/37; 289 performances), about Peggy and Phil, who want to marry but can't afford to until Phil receives a promised raise. Unfortunately, Phil won't receive his raise until the federal budget is balanced. The hapless couple run into President Franklin Roosevelt in Central Park. This was the first time that a living president was depicted in a musical comedy. For the role, they chose GEORGE M. COHAN. He was certainly one of the most patriotic Americans and one who could give a mature, serious performance even when dancing and singing. The show, although more gently satirical than GEORGE AND IRA GERSHWIN's *Of Thee I Sing*, caused some controversy. George Jean Nathan, writing in *Newsweek*, questioned all the brouhaha:

> Why the idea of calling George M. Cohan Franklin D. Roosevelt should have engendered so intense an interest I can't figure out, unless it was because Franklin D. Roosevelt, on the other hand, has been called everything under the sun but George M. Cohan.

Peggy and Phil got the best song in the show, "Have You Met Miss Jones?" Cohan did have several good numbers, including "I'd Rather Be Right" and "Off the Record." The show is best known today for a scene from it that was included in the James Cagney movie *Yankee Doodle Dandy*.

For their next show, *I Married an Angel* (5/11/38; 338 performances), Rodgers and Hart again supplied the book, and George Balanchine choreographed his third show for the duo; JOSHUA LOGAN was chosen to direct the fantasy. The plot concerned a count who states that only an angel will do as his wife. When she appears, the complications begin. Dennis King, Vivienne Segal, Charles Walters, Walter Slezak, and Audrey Christie led the cast. Ballerina Vera Zorina was chosen to play the part of Angel. The show opened at the Shubert Theater. *I Married an Angel* had a wonderful score, most important of which was "Spring Is Here."

One of the team's greatest successes followed. *The Boys from Syracuse* (11/23/38; 235 performances), at the Alvin Theater, was based on William Shakespeare's *The Comedy of Errors*. George Abbott contributed the book, and he produced and directed the show as well. The songwriters were obviously inspired by the material, because they wrote a terrific score.

Alfred Drake, Mitzi Green, and Ray Heatherton in *Babes in Arms*, 1937.

"Falling in Love with Love" and "This Can't Be Love" were the big hits, and the remainder of the songs were just as well crafted. The show starred Eddie Albert, Teddy Hart (Larry's brother), Burl Ives, Ronald Graham, Jimmy Savo, Wynn Murray, Muriel Angelus, and Marcy Westcott. The reviews were mostly raves, with the score singled out as perhaps the team's best work to date. The book, however, received its share of criticism. *The Boys from Syracuse* was made into a film by Universal in 1940. In 1963, the show was successfully revived off Broadway at the Theater Four, where it ran for 502 performances. That same year it was revived on the West End of London, but it wasn't received well there and ran only 100 performances.

Rodgers and Hart followed *The Boys from Syracuse* with a show that ran longer but is almost forgotten today. *Too Many Girls* (10/18/39; 249 performances) opened at the Imperial Theater. It is noteworthy today as the Broadway debut of Desi Arnaz. Also cast were Eddie Bracken, Hal LeRoy, Marcy Westcott, Mary Jane Walsh, Diosa Costello, and, in a small role, Van Johnson. George Abbott was again responsible for the producing and directing; George Marion Jr. provided the book. The score was sometimes inspired, though it was not as good as their best work. There was, however, one standout song, "I Didn't Know What Time It Was." George Abbott received most of the credit for the show's youthful exuberance and snappy timing. A film version was made in 1940 by RKO. Desi Arnaz repeated his role, as did Eddie Bracken and Hal LeRoy; also starring in the movie was Lucille Ball. The rest is television history.

Higher and Higher (4/4/40; 108 performances), their next Broadway show, at the Shubert Theater, was a disappointment. A standard did emerge, the wistful "It Never Entered My Mind." It was followed by *Pal Joey* (12/25/40; 374 performances), not the typical musical comedy. For one thing, the lead character, the unscrupulous Joey, was a tough character for 1940s audiences to accept. He was a scoundrel: talented and attractive, but a scoundrel. The score was among the team's most sophisticated and adult. In fact, "Bewitched, Bothered, and Bewildered" had to have its lyrics softened before radio stations would play it. The show was not the sort one would expect to open on Christmas Day. The reviews were mixed. The CRITICS wanted to like the show because it was clear superior talents were at work. However, most of them couldn't get past the unsentimental aspects of the show and its cynicism. Brooks Atkinson in the *New York Times* wrote, "If it is possible to make an entertaining musical comedy out of an odious story, *Pal Joey* is it. . . . Although it is expertly done, can you draw sweet water from a foul well?"

Other critics liked the show better than Atkinson did, but audiences seemed to agree with his assessment. *Time* called the show "a profane hymn to the gaudy goddess of metropolitan night life." The score received excellent reviews, although most critics frowned on the "smuttiness" of Hart's lyrics. Gene Kelly as Joey, Vivienne Segal, and Leila Ernst received good notices, but the general public was simply not ready for an adult musical comedy.

Although too strong for the conventional audience, the show did play 374 performances, perhaps an indication that there were sophisticated theatergoers willing to spend an evening at the theater without the usual baggy-pants clowns. The run also indicates that it wasn't quite as big a failure as is generally assumed. In 1952, the show was revived at the Broadhurst Theater by producer Jule Styne to greater acclaim. This time Brooks Atkinson wrote,

> In 1940, there was a minority, including this column, that was not enchanted. But no one is likely now to be impervious to the tight organization of the production, the terseness of the writing, the liveliness and versatility of the score and the easy perfection of the lyrics. It is true that *Pal Joey* was a pioneer in the moving back of musical frontiers, for it tells an integrated story with a knowing point of view.

The revival ran 542 performances, and the show is today considered a classic American musical comedy.

The film musical *They Met in Argentina* (RKO, 1941) was released prior to the opening of the team's last Broadway show, *By Jupiter* (6/3/42; 427 performances), for which they supplied the book, music, and lyrics. The show opened at the Shubert Theater. It might have been their greatest success but for the fact that Ray Bolger, the star, quit to entertain troops overseas. It achieved the longest run of any Rodgers and Hart show until the revival of *Pal Joey*.

Unfortunately, it was the last full-scale collaboration between Rodgers and Hart. Rodgers was a finely disciplined man used to working regular hours with great determination and single-mindedness; Larry Hart was exactly the opposite. Whereas Rodgers knew exactly where he stood in the world, Hart was insecure and unstable, becoming increasingly more difficult as the partnership progressed. Often, Hart would disappear for days, forcing Rodgers to halt production or even write lyrics himself. Hart's insecurities led to heavy drinking and missed deadlines. Rodgers reached the end of his patience during *By Jupiter* and began quietly to inquire about other partnerships.

Theresa Helburn of the Theater Guild wanted Rodgers to adapt the play *Green Grow the Lilacs* into a musical comedy. Rodgers reluctantly approached Hart, who realized he was not up to the role either mentally or physically. Rodgers then turned to his old friend and sometime collaborator from the early days at Columbia University, Oscar Hammerstein. The result was *Oklahoma!* (5/31/43; 2,248 performances). Hart was present at the opening of the milestone musical and congratulated Rodgers on his success. But the show must have been a further blow to Hart's already damaged self-esteem.

The last project that the 2 worked on together was the 1943 revival of *A Connecticut Yankee*. Hart had collaborated with Rodgers on a new song for the show, "To Keep My Love Alive." Following the opening night performance on November 17, Hart disappeared. He remained missing for two days until he was found unconscious in a hotel room. He was taken to Doctors' Hospital, where it was determined he had pneumonia. He died a few days later.

A *New York Times* editorial on November 25, 1943, stated:

> The word most frequently used to describe Lorenz Hart was the word that fitted him best, puckish. He never quite grew up. He was the college boy of the Nineteen Twenties to the end. The peculiarly brittle quality of his humor stemmed from Morningside Heights, and two decades of deep immersion in Broadway never quite soaked it off. Especially when blended with the sure suavity of Richard Rodgers' tunes his lyrics were tinpanablation at its best: sophisticatedly simple, tenderly trite, like "With a Song in My Heart," "Isn't It Romantic," or "My Heart Stood Still"; gaily garrulous like "To Keep My Love Alive."
>
> From his long and memorable list of lyrics, a score or more gave a pleasure of that tingling sort which a vast public instinctively demands. For twenty years the credit line "Music by Richard Rodgers; Lyrics by Lorenz Hart" was a signal of almost sure success. They were a remarkable team. Not the lesser of the two was "Larry" Hart, whose facility with simple words added something felicitous to our lives. That his particular genius will be missed

along the Broadway where his puckish figure was so familiar goes without saying. And since Broadway even today contributes greater than its share to the American culture, his death at the age of 48 is more than a local loss.

ROMBERG, SIGMUND. Broadway's most prolific composer, and a king of the operetta form; b. Nagy Kaniza, Hungary, July 29, 1887; d. New York, New York, November 9, 1951.

Sigmund Romberg had more than 60 musical productions produced in his 40-year career. Although Romberg was proficient in most musical theater styles, he achieved his greatest fame as a composer of operettas. His most enduring shows are still performed. *Blossom Time, The New Moon, The Desert Song*, and *The Student Prince* are all favorites of light opera companies and summer theaters. Romberg's most famous songs are still sung today. These include "Will You Remember?" "Deep in My Heart," "Lover Come Back to Me," "Stouthearted Men," "The Desert Song,"

Sigmund Romberg conducting.

"Close as Pages in a Book," "Softly, as in a Morning Sunrise," and "Serenade." As Romberg said, "I don't care what the form is. But a melody is still a melody. Nothing succeeds like a popular tune—a romantic tune. Romantic music will never die because deep at the roots of all people is the theme of love."

As a young man, Romberg attended school in Vienna to study engineering. Music was his real love, however, and he studied harmony and composition with Victor Heuberger. While in Vienna, Romberg had a job at the Theater-an-der-Wien, well known for its operettas.

In 1909 Romberg came to the United States, where he held a variety of jobs, from work in a pencil factory for $7 a week to pianist in restaurants. While at Bustanoby's restaurant, he met Edward Marks, a prominent music publisher. Marks encouraged the young man to pursue composing, and soon Romberg had his first published song, "Some Smoke (Leg of Mutton)."

The job at Bustanoby's also introduced Romberg to J. J. Shubert, of the great SHUBERT BROTHERS theater empire. The Shuberts needed shows to fill their theaters, including the huge WINTER GARDEN THEATRE, home of the annual revues called the *Passing Shows*. Romberg's talents seemed to fit the bill perfectly. Like many Shubert productions, the *Passing Shows* were low-cost, high-profit productions. Louis A. Hirsch had been the Shubert's house composer for the Winter Garden shows, but he and the Shuberts had had a falling-out. So Romberg was hired to write the score for *The Whirl of the World* (1/10/14; 161 performances). The Shuberts had previously produced *The Whirl of Society*, and this new show was the second in what was hoped to be a series of "Whirls." Romberg's lyricist and librettist was Harold Atteridge, another Shubert contract writer.

As a staff writer, Romberg was not expected to write good songs. The real stars of Shubert revues were the showgirls. The cast and material were simply an excuse to parade a series of women in various stages of undress. Songs were freely interpolated into the shows. The Shuberts felt that if the scores needed any popular hits, they could easily be bought. Publishers were all too happy to provide songs to the revue series just to be able to print on their sheet music, "as sung by___in the Winter Garden show___." Romberg obliged the Shuberts by cranking out a series of good if not exceptional songs.

His next assignments for the Shuberts were a series of mostly forgettable revues and musicals with lyrics by Harold Atteridge. The *Passing Show of 1914* (6/10/14; 133 performances) and *Dancing Around* (10/10/14; 145 performances) were followed by *Maid in America* (2/18/15; 108 performances); *Hands Up* (7/22/15; 52 performances), with lyrics by E. Ray Goetz;

The Blue Paradise (8/5/15; 356 performances), with lyrics by Herbert Reynolds; and *A World of Pleasure* (10/14/15; 116 performances). These shows were all relatively successful, and most made money for the Shuberts. *The Blue Paradise* contained Romberg's first hit song, "Auf Wiedersehen."

Romberg had six shows open in 1916. The first was a vehicle for the great AL JOLSON. *Robinson Crusoe, Jr.* (2/17/16; 139 performances) did contain a hit song, "Yacki Hula Hicki Doola," but unfortunately it wasn't written by Romberg. Pete Wendling, E. Ray Goetz, and Joe Young were the songwriters. It was followed by the *Passing Show of 1916* (6/22/16; 140 performances); *The Girl from Brazil* (8/30/16; 61 performances), with Matthew Woodward lyrics; *The Show of Wonders* (10/26/16; 209 performances); *Follow Me* (11/29/16; 78 performances), with lyrics by Robert B. Smith; and *Her Soldier Boy* (12/6/16; 198 performances), with book and lyrics by Rida Johnson Young. Naturally, with so many shows to churn out, Romberg needed help. On most of these shows Romberg collaborated with other composers.

It is surprising that Romberg could produce anything of quality considering his output. Yet he did manage to create many successful hits. For *Maytime* (8/16/17; 492 performances), Romberg collaborated with Rida Johnson Young, a lyricist and librettist who also wrote hit shows with VICTOR HERBERT *(Naughty Marietta)* and RUDOLF FRIML *(Sometime)*. Young gave Romberg his first long-lasting hit and one of his greatest songs, "Will You Remember (Sweetheart)." Another of *Maytime*'s hit songs was "Road to Paradise." The success of *Maytime* proved to Romberg that he could write a show by himself. He began to resent the Shubert assignments that came his way. But the Shuberts, and many of Romberg's Broadway contemporaries, felt that the success of *Maytime* was a fluke.

Following his work on the *Passing Show of 1919*, Romberg left the Shubert fold. He decided to go out on his own as a composer and to produce his own shows in association with producer Max Wilner. Their two efforts, *The Magic Melody* (11/11/19), with Clare Kummer's lyrics, and *Love Birds* (3/15/21), with Ballard Macdonald, were both failures. Romberg also wrote the music to *Poor Little Ritz Girl* (7/27/20) with Alex Gerber. Richard Rodgers and Lorenz Hart *(see* RODGERS AND HART) had already written a complete score for the show while it was out of town prior to appearing on Broadway. But producer Lew Fields *(see* FIELDS FAMILY) threw out most of their score and added songs by Romberg. Despite the interpolations, the show was a failure.

With three unsuccessful shows to his credit, Romberg found it difficult to get more writing assignments, so he returned to the Shubert fold. The Shuberts had Romberg on a salary, so no matter how successful the

shows were Romberg received the same amount of money. Also, because he was a contract employee in the years before ASCAP (THE AMERICAN SOCIETY FOR COMPOSERS, AUTHORS AND PUBLISHERS) was established, Romberg did not own his songs. The Shuberts received all the rights and royalties from them. Occasionally, Romberg would play the piano for rehearsals as well as conduct the orchestra during previews, all to supplement his salary. The producers sought to placate Romberg by assigning him what eventually became *Blossom Time* (9/28/21; 516 performances). Romberg collaborated with Dorothy Donnelly on the adaptation of *Das Drei Maedelhaus*, a European operetta. The music was based on melodies by Franz Shubert and H. Berte.

George S. Kaufman *(see* KAUFMAN AND HART) wrote in the *New York Times* that Romberg's "songs of passionate longing . . . illuminate *Blossom Time* like pictures in a Christmas book." "Song of Love" was the only hit song to emerge from the score. The Shuberts were overjoyed with the success of *Blossom Time*. They sent out many national companies for years afterward, and the piece became as good as money in the bank. For all the companies of *Blossom Time* that the Shuberts sent out on the road, they never redid the sets or costumes. J. J. ("Jake") Shubert always cried whenever "Song of Love" and "Ave Maria" were played. He would put the touring companies into the AMBASSADOR THEATRE for one night, so he could then send them out on the road with the billing "direct from Broadway." By February 1924, the show had earned the Shuberts an amazing $700,000.

After *Blossom Time*, it was back to the same old grind for Romberg. *Bombo* (10/6/21; 218 performances) was next, another Jolson starrer. The show had many hit songs (none were by Romberg), and it made $445,000 for the Shuberts. Following *Bombo* came *The Blushing Bride* (2/6/22; 144 performances) written with Cyrus Wood; then *The Rose of Stamboul* (3/7/22; 111 performances); *Springtime of Youth* (10/26/22; 68 performances), with Harry B. Smith; and *The Dancing Girl* (1/24/23; 142 performances). Another edition of *The Passing Show* (6/14/23; 4 performances) followed.

In 1924 Romberg had a banner year. He fulfilled his usual assignments for the Shuberts and others with *Innocent Eyes* (5/20/24; 31 performances); *Marjorie* (8/11/24; 144 performances), produced by Rufus Le Maire and Richard W. Krakeur; the *Passing Show of 1924* (9/3/24; 93 performances), the last in the series; *Artists and Models* (10/15/24; 261 performances), the second edition of a new Shubert revue series, with lyrics by Sam Coslow and Clifford Grey; and his first show for producer FLORENZ ZIEGFELD, *Annie Dear* (11/4/24; 103 performances), again with Grey. Romberg's next hit was the biggest of his career. *The Student Prince* (12/2/24; 608 performances) was written in collaboration with Dorothy Donnelly. Its hit songs included "Golden Days," "Deep in My Heart," "The Drinking Song," and "To the Inn We're Marching." The show turned out to be the longest-running of all the Romberg operettas.

The night before *The Student Prince* opened, Broadway saw the premiere of *Lady, Be Good!* The Gershwin brothers' musical was a sign of things to come. Romberg stated his opinion of the new musical style heralded by this show:

> Casting no reflection, you will notice today that there are types of musical comedies which "flop," in the parlance of the theater. On the other hand, you will find one here and there that plays for a seemingly endless time to capacity houses. The latter, if you will observe, is usually the musical comedy which leans toward the operatic rather than the jazz type.

This was more wishful thinking than fact. Unfortunately for Romberg, his style of musical became less and less popular while the so-called jazz style musicals succeeded more and more with audiences. Romberg's oblique criticism of the Gershwins was all the more ironic, because, a few years later, they each contributed half a score to the show *Rosalie*.

The success of *The Student Prince* firmly established Romberg as a top composer who could handle a full score with skill. His next show, *Louis the 14th* (3/3/25; 319 performances), was a Ziegfeld production. It was written by Romberg and Arthur Wimperis, and it starred Leon Errol and Ethel Shutta. His second show of the season was *Princess Flavia* (11/2/25; 152 performances).

With his output slowing, Romberg's successes grew. *The Desert Song* (11/30/26; 471 performances), his next operetta, was another great hit. The lyrics were by Otto Harbach and OSCAR HAMMERSTEIN II, who also wrote the libretto with Frank Mandel. *The Desert Song* opened at the Casino Theatre. The superior score included the hits "Ho! (The Riff Song)," "French Military Marching Song," "Romance," "The Desert Song," "One Flower Grows Alone in Your Garden," and "One Alone." Laurence Schwab and Frank Mandel produced the lavish show, which the *New York Times* called "floridly contrived and executed in the grand, unstinting manner of the more affluent impresarios." Although they lauded the show, most of the reviewers did not see the score as anything special. The *New York American* said that the show had music "of a 'superior' quality. Although some of it sounds like 'left-overs' from *The Student Prince* there are one or two numbers that are delightful." Richard Watts Jr., writing in the *New York Herald Tribune*, admitted, "I am perhaps ungrateful in regretting that, with the exception of one song called It, the lyrics gave indication

that W. S. Gilbert lived and died in vain." The public obviously disagreed with the naysayers. *Desert Song* later had 2 national companies that played a total of 34 cities. It ran almost as long in London as on Broadway, amassing 432 performances at the Theater Royal, Drury Lane. There were three film versions, in 1929, 1943, and 1953.

In 1927, a good year for the musical theater, Romberg contributed music to four productions. *Cherry Blossoms* (3/28/27; 56 performances) was first with book and lyrics by Harry B. Smith. The failure led to his second production, *My Maryland* (9/12/27; 312 performances). Dorothy Donnelly was the author of book and lyrics of the hit show based on the play *Barbara Frietchie* by Clyde Fitch. The hit song of the show was "This Land Is My Land." Claude Greneker, the Shubert publicist, wrote to Representative Emanuel Celler of New York suggesting that the song replace the "Star-Spangled Banner" as the national anthem; it didn't. Donnelly also collaborated on the third Romberg production in 1927, *My Princess* (10/6/27; 20 performances). It, however, didn't repeat the success of the last show. *The Love Call* (10/24/27; 81 performances), written with Smith, did little better.

With *Rosalie* (1/10/28; 327 performances) the composer tried his hand at a show in a more contemporary vein. Romberg and P. G. Wodehouse wrote half the score, and GEORGE AND IRA GERSHWIN contributed the other half of the Ziegfeld production. Romberg's second production in 1928 was even more successful. *The New Moon* (9/19/28; 519 performances), another operetta, had a book by Oscar Hammerstein II, Frank Mandel, and Laurence Schwab. The latter two were also the producers. Hammerstein and Romberg came up with another fine score. The hits include "The Girl on the Prow," "Lover, Come Back to Me," "Marianne," "One Kiss," "Softly, as in a Morning Sunrise," "Stouthearted Men (Liberty Song)," and "Wanting You." The success of *The New Moon* was exceptional, because by the end of the 1920s the operetta was going out of vogue. The reviews were almost unanimous, although at least one reviewer, noting the divergence of the two competing styles of musical theater of the day, wondered whether even a superior operetta could still please the public. Gilbert Gabriel of the *New York Sun* commented,

> Theoretically, romantic musical comedies are all so many brave St. Georges against the dragonfly, jazz. Everyone of us howls for a return to librettos with big overstuffed plots, choral fireworks, grand ululations by heroes in hand-cuffs and heroines in tears, with overtures, reprises, finaletti and all the other earmarks of old-time operetta scores. Then as if in answer, along comes something like "The New Moon"—which is certainly and superlatively as good as they come—and we aren't so sure.

The other reviewers had no reservations about enjoying the operatic form. Brooks Atkinson wrote in the *New York Times*, "Deep, rushing, stirring, it is one of the best scores written for many months." Robert Littell of the *New York Post* was of two minds:

[E]ven if it was long and many of the solo songs were pretty dull, there was something full-measured and gay and brightly colored about it, which was satisfying and a welcome relief from the usual cheap stuff . . . the music, which without giving you anything to take home, filled the air with something for which there is only one word—tuneful.

Although Charles Brackett, writing in *The New Yorker*, called the show "the best of the musical shows I've seen so far this year," he also commented, "the score, I must admit, is the sort which sends into vocalists, who do a great deal of gesturing, palms up and fingers brought to the clench on certain notes." *Nina Rosa* (9/20/30; 129 performances) was Romberg's next show. It had lyrics by Irving Caesar and libretto by Otto Harbach.

The next year found Romberg collaborating again with Hammerstein. The result was *East Wind* (10/27/31), a failure. After a year off, Romberg came up with *Melody* (2/14/33; 80 performances), another show with Irving Caesar. It was produced by GEORGE WHITE, best known for his annual revue series, GEORGE WHITE'S SCANDALS. Hammerstein took his next turn with Romberg, and the result was *May Wine* (12/5/35; 212 performances). Laurence Schwab produced the show, which was a minor success. *Forbidden Melody* (11/2/36; 32 performances) had lyrics and book by Harbach.

The operetta form was practically dead on Broadways, so during the 1930s, Romberg occupied himself with assignments in Hollywood. In the 1940s, Romberg toured the country with an orchestra that featured his music. Five years passed between *Forbidden Melody* and his next Broadway opening, *Sunny River* (12/4/41; 36 performances). The Romberg and Hammerstein show was one of the first to deal with psychoanalysis, opening the same year as *Lady in the Dark*. It was also notable in that it dispensed with a chorus line, but it was still clearly an operetta. Wilella Waldorf in the *New York Post* stated:

Max Gordon made a noble gesture last night at the St. James. Mr. Gordon apparently feels that the time has come to bring operetta back to Broadway. A number of theatergoers, including this reviewer, agree with him heartily. We must admit, however, that if "Sunny River" is the best new operetta he could discover, it is not surprising that few producers these days are inclined to give much attention.

Apparently other producers agreed with Gordon that the operetta was still a valid theatrical form. In 1945 Romberg was teamed up with a decidedly modern lyricist, Dorothy Fields, for *Up in Central Park* (1/27/45; 504 performances). The Michael Todd production's surprise success was probably due as much to the renewed interest in American subjects in musicals, aroused by the success of *Oklahoma!*, as to the piece itself. What was more surprising was the success of the score. The hit, "Close as Pages in a Book," was among Romberg's best compositions.

Although *Up in Central Park* was a hit, it was assumed that its success was unique. While some other lesser operettas were produced, on the whole Broadway ignored the style. Romberg's next-to-last Broadway show was the last he would live to see. *My Romance* (10/29/48; 95 performances), written with Rowland Leigh, was, appropriately, produced by the Shubert brothers. In his review Brooks Atkinson, in the *New York Times*, effectively put the last nail in the coffin of operetta:

Lovers of the dramatic unities should study *My Romance* which was put on at the Shubert last evening. It is standard operetta with standard routines and situations that have not changed through the years. At one time the authors and composers may have believed in those ritualized gestures toward stock romance. But they are pure formula now with high society, passionate love that tears the vocal chords apart and sets the brasses and drums to roaring in the orchestra pit, a theme song of nobility, elegance and boredom.

Jeanmaire and David Atkinson in Romberg's last show, *The Girl in the Pink Tights*, 1954.

On November 10, 1951, Sigmund Romberg died in New York City. But there would be one more Romberg show on Broadway—*The Girl in Pink Tights* (3/5/54; 115 performances). Leo Robin provided the lyrics to the songs that were worked up by orchestrator, Don Walker. The show contained Romberg's last hit song, "Lost in Loveliness."

Romberg's melodies continue to grace theaters all over the world. His shows are even occasionally revived on Broadway and at the New York City Opera. His most successful shows will be performed as long as musical theater is performed.

ROME, HAROLD. Great Broadway songwriter; b. Harold Jacob Rome, Hartford, Connecticut, May 27, 1908; d. New York, New York, October 26, 1993.

Harold Rome's output might not match that of his contemporaries in quantity, but the quality and success of his shows puts him near the top of the list of Broadway songwriters. He contributed both words and music to a variety of themes and characters. His shows exhibited an unusual diversity in subject matter—from the Old West of *Destry Rides Again* to the New York garment district of *I Can Get it for You Wholesale* to the Old South of *Gone with the Wind*. But it was in capturing the archetypal New York urban dweller, usually Jewish, that he first made his mark.

Like other successful songwriters, Rome studied to be a lawyer. He graduated from Yale in 1929, the year of the stock market crash. He worked for a law office and asked for lunch money. The firm refused him, and Rome quit. He began accompanying ballet classes on piano and decided to become a songwriter. His first show, *Pins and Needles*, was his most successful and something of a miraculous success story. The International Ladies' Garment Workers' Union (ILGWU) owned a small theater called the Labor Stage (*see* 48TH STREET THEATRE). In fact, it was originally the Princess Theater, where JEROME KERN, GUY BOLTON, and P. G. Wodehouse first presented their landmark Princess Theater shows. But the ILGWU had other uses for the tiny stage, holding their elections and meetings in the theater. Union leader Louis Schaffer conceived the notion of producing an amateur show featuring members of the union. The show was intended as both an outlet for talent within the union and an entertaining way to present his union's views. Schaffer hired the young Harold Rome to compose the score and play the piano.

The show was scheduled to be performed for a limited run. As it was, the rehearsals took more than a year and a half because they could be held only on the performers' days off or after work. After a long gestation, *Pins and Needles* (11/27/37; 1,108 performances) opened. Rome's song titles illustrate the light-hearted approach the show took to its serious themes: "Sing Me a Song of Social Significance," "It's Better with a Union Man," "One Big Union for Two," "The Red Mikado," and "Doin' the Reactionary." Once the show settled into a long run, additional material was constantly added. Many more contributors were brought in to the production team, and the show evolved as it continued its remarkable run. *Pins and Needles* had become the longest-running musical in Broadway history at the time of its closing.

Rome's next project was another satirical revue, this time on a grander scale than *Pins and Needles*. *Sing Out the News* (9/24/38; 105 performances) opened at the MUSIC BOX THEATER. The show starred Joey Faye, Mary Jane Walsh, Will Geer, Philip Loeb, Rex Ingram, June Allyson, and Christina Lind. Rome's score included one popular hit, "Franklin D. Roosevelt Jones," and another topical hit, "My Heart is Unemployed." Despite the libretto by Rome and Charles Friedman and the producing talents of Max Gordon, George S. Kaufman, and Moss Hart (*see* KAUFMAN AND HART), the show was not a success.

Rome continued in a topical vein with his next show, written while he was in the army. *Call Me Mister* (4/18/46; 734 performances) featured ex-servicemen in the cast, in much the same manner as IRVING BERLIN's *This Is the Army*. *Call Me Mister* starred Betty Garrett, Lawrence Winters, Maria Karnilova, Jules Munshin, and Danny Scholl. The score again contained a topical hit, "The Red Ball Express," and a popular hit, "South America Take It Away." Like *Sing Out the News*, *Call Me Mister* made President Roosevelt the subject of a song. This time, the song, "The Face on the Dime," was more reverent.

Rome's high regard and affection for the middle class were again expressed in his next show, the light-hearted *Wish You Were Here* (6/25/52; 598 performances), which opened at the IMPERIAL THEATRE. Arthur Kober and JOSHUA LOGAN wrote the story of a group of New Yorkers enjoying a brief vacation in an adult camp in the Catskill Mountains. It was based on the hit play by Kober, *Having Wonderful Time*. The show featured an attractive cast, including Jack Cassidy, Sheila Bond, Florence Henderson, Patricia Marand, Larry Blyden, and Sammy Smith. Harold Rome's fresh, youthful score included one major hit, the title song. The initial reviews for the show weren't very positive, but, in an unusual move, the creative staff stayed on the project after the opening, strengthening the book. One gimmick working for the show was the swimming pool constructed in the center of the stage. The swimming pool proved to be a great attraction. The show steadily built an audience through word of mouth, and several critics returned to the theater to

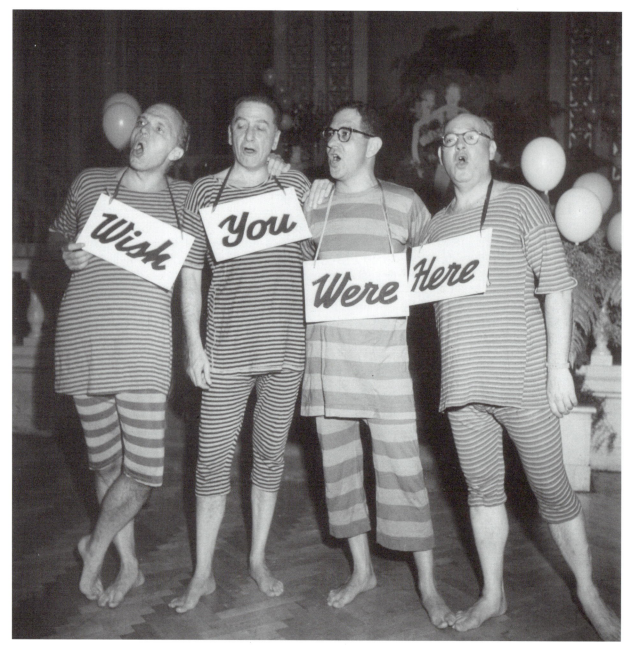

Josh Logan, Leland Hayward, Harold Rome, and Arthur Kober promoting *Wish You Were Here*, c. 1952.

review the new changes in the show. The hard work paid off, and *Wish You Were Here* enjoyed a long run.

Joshua Logan in his capacity of co-librettist, director, and co-producer of *Wish You Were Here* deserved most of the credit for the show's success. He took on the same responsibilities for Rome's next show, *Fanny* (11/4/54; 888 performances). Fanny was the brainchild of producer DAVID MERRICK. Merrick went to great lengths to obtain the rights from playwright Marcel Pagnol. Three years passed before the show finally

opened. Ezio Pinza followed his spectacular musical comedy debut in *South Pacific* with *Fanny*. Florence Henderson, who had had a small part in *Wish You Were Here*, played the title character. Gerald Price, Walter Slezak, and William Tabbert completed the cast. Rome's score for *Fanny* was one of his most haunting, The score yielded another hit, the title song. Like *Wish You Were Here, Fanny* received mixed reviews, but producer Merrick was determined to make the show a success. He and his publicist RICHARD MANEY con-

Wish You Were Here, 1952.

cocted a series of outrageous STUNTS in order to keep the name in the public's eye. The strategy was successful, and *Fanny* became a big hit.

Merrick, overjoyed at the success of *Fanny*, commissioned Rome to tackle what appeared to be an improbable subject for a musical. Merrick bought the stage rights for the Universal picture *Destry Rides Again* (4/23/59; 472 performances) and hired Rome to write the score. Andy Griffith and Dolores Gray headed the cast, and Rosetta LeNoire, Jack Prince, Libi Staiger, Scott Brady, and Marc Breaux were comprised the supporting players. The new hit contained a typically well-crafted score by Rome, although none of the songs achieved a life after the show.

New York's garment district was the setting for Rome's next Broadway musical, *I Can Get It for You Wholesale* (3/22/62; 300 performances). The show was based on a trenchant novel by Jerome Weidman. It is

perhaps best remembered as the Broadway debut of Barbra Streisand in a supporting part. Streisand's biography in PLAYBILL read, "Barbra Streisand is nineteen, was born in Madagascar and reared in Rangoon." El-liott Gould, Marilyn Cooper, Harold Lang, Bambi Linn, Sheree North, and Lillian Roth were also featured.

Rome's final Broadway production was the play with music, *The Zulu and the Zayda* (11/10/65; 179 performances). Louis Gossett and Menasha Skulnik played the lead roles, which combined two of Rome's favorite subjects. The Zayda, an old Jewish man, was a natural character for Rome to write about. The Zulu was equally familiar to Rome because he had collected African art since 1939. (Eventually he assembled one of the most important collections in the world.) Rome was also intrigued with African music and wove a rich score combining the best of Jewish and African music.

Despite its rather unusual subject matter, *The Zulu and the Zayda* deserved a better fate. Its title was confusing to many theatergoers, who couldn't tell exactly what the show was about.

Rome's next subject was again quite unlikely. He originally wrote a musical version of *Gone with the Wind* for a 1970 production in Japan. The show was reworked following its Japanese success, and it opened in 1972 in London. It finally made it to the United States in 1973, but it never reached Broadway.

Rome did not have another show produced on Broadway. In his last years he concentrated on his collection of African art and his painting. Broadway was poorer for the absence of one of its most versatile and creative songwriters.

ROSELAND. 239 W. 52nd Street. Roseland is the sole survivor of the many dance halls and tango palaces that have lined Broadway since the turn of the 20th century. Roseland, with its restaurants, bars, and huge dance floor, was by far the biggest of the halls.

Roseland was the idea of Louis Brecker, who began his entrepreneurial career in Philadelphia, home of the original Roseland. Brecker and his fiancée, Dorothy Faggen, were students at the University of Pennsylvania. He studied business administration by day and danced with his fiancée by night. They had a hard time finding a place that wasn't overrun by ragtime. They longed for ballroom dancing, not the current fads. After receiving his degree in 1917, Brecker convinced Frank Yuengling, a local brewer, to invest $20,000 in a new high-class establishment at 12th and Chestnut Streets in Philadelphia. The new dance hall proved successful beyond anyone's expectations. Despite the Sunday blue laws then in effect, the original Roseland managed to pay back its initial investment in only six months.

Brecker took a trip to New York City and decided to check out the local concerns. He found that more than 6,000 dancers patronized the Grand Central Palace dance hall on Sundays. Brecker decided to move to New York and try his luck. He returned to Yuengling, who was delighted to provide the young entrepreneur with $40,000 to start the new venture. In 1919 the Breckers opened the second Roseland on the site of an old carriage factory at 51st Street and Broadway. The Broadway and Times Square area was just beginning to come into its own as the center of entertainment. Brecker, like OSCAR HAMMERSTEIN I, *New York Times* publisher Adolph Ochs, and others, was a true visionary. These individuals realized the potential of the crossroads and established their businesses in what they believed would become the new center of the city.

The opening night for Roseland took place on New Year's Eve, 1919. The location was an immediate success—a crowd circled the block 4 abreast.

Brecker had firm ideas about how the operation should be run. People had to behave in a respectable fashion at all times. The dance-hall hostesses were to be treated with respect, and customers were not allowed to fraternize with the girls after hours. Jackets and ties were always required, even as dress codes began to relax in other establishments. Brecker would provide ties and jackets for his patrons, if necessary. He believed that Roseland was an experience that should be fun and yet treated with respect. In case anyone got out of line, there were always bouncers (called "housemen" by Brecker) to see that miscreants were promptly evicted from the premises.

In the early days, all the dancing was ballroom dancing. Roseland was the place where many couples practiced, perfected, and even invented variations on the latest dance crazes. These crazes included the Charleston, probably the biggest dance sensation in history. Certainly the fox-trot has lasted longer, but the Charleston took the country by storm in the decade called the Roaring Twenties.

It wasn't easy for the dance hall in its first years. Reformers took umbrage at the Sunday openings. It was bad enough that people were dancing on the Sabbath, but even worse, they were dancing the Charleston. Brecker didn't consider his establishment a dance hall; he preferred to call it a ballroom. His critics called it a "dance hell." The violent negative reaction to the dance halls in the 1920s was just like the violent reaction to rock and roll music in the 1950s. Ironically, Brecker became one of the chief critics of that music when the Twist burst onto the scene in the early 1960s. On June 20, 1923, the *New York Daily News* carried the headline:

YELLOW GOLD LURES GIRLS TO DANCE LAIRS
Many a White Maid, Whirled by Oriental Arms,
Sinks in Trysts of Shame

Dance halls, or ballrooms, were blamed for all the evils of society. Dance hall hostesses were labeled prostitutes, and drugs were supposedly sold in the dim recesses of the huge auditoriums. Actually, the dance hall hostess was a different sort altogether. RODGERS AND HART wrote what is probably the most accurate description of the average hostess's life in their 1930 musical *Simple Simon*. The song was "Ten Cents a Dance," introduced by Ruth Etting. Etting's character never met her hero, but 1 or 2 of Roseland's hostesses did. Claire Patton married millionaire Archibald R. Graustein, the president of International Paper and Power Company, in 1919. Sandra Davis was swept off her feet by a big-time shoe manufacturer from Chicago.

But those were only two of the thousands of hostesses who lugged partners across the floor. When Roseland first opened, 150 taxi dancers were ready, willing, and able to trip the light fantastic. Florence Forder, the chaperone and management's watchdog, didn't let things get out of hand. The women sat on chairs on a platform in a roped-off area. Miss Forder would take the gentleman to the ladies and introduce them. After he made his selection, Miss Forder would release the dance partner from the corral. The woman had to observe several rules. First, there was no trading of phone numbers or making dates for after hours. Second, they had to wear underwear for those times their nether regions might be in view. Third, no gum chewing was allowed; and finally, there was no talking slang.

By 1948 the charge was 35 cents for three spins on the floor with a dancer. The hostesses received 70 percent of the price of a dance. Of course, a man could also pay for dances by the hour; that rate was $2.80. The dancers received about $40 a week in commissions. They also received tips, which usually amounted to another $40. Sometimes a hostess was given an especially large tip. Uncle Joe, a restauranteur, was known to hand out $100 bills as tips, but most often a hostess would be tipped $5 for an hour's work.

The hostess trade began to decline, and the Depression marked the end of the lavish spenders. Fewer and fewer customers could afford to spend their money on dancing, and business faltered. By 1951 there were only four hostesses left on the line. That was the end of hostesses for Roseland. Brecker wasn't sorry to see them go. In an early interview, he stated:

I should have got rid of the hostesses in 1933 when Prohibition was repealed, but I felt a certain loyalty to the girls. Sentimentality cost me a fortune, because I couldn't get a liquor license while I employed hostesses. The hostess is a ghostess. It was the happiest day of my life when I finally got rid of the hostesses. They gave the place an unsavory reputation. Don't misunderstand me. The girls we engaged were perfect ladies, but the mere presence of them suggested a flesh market.

Roseland's clientele was a cross section of the population of the country. As the population changed, so did Roseland. During the World War II, there were always dozens of men in uniform on the dance floor, furiously attempting to return from leave in a totally exhausted state.

Brecker employed two bands that provided continuous music. The house band was usually a Latin band, and another orchestra would fill in their breaks with American rhythms. From time to time, famous guest bands occupied the bandstand, including Paul Whiteman, Guy Lombardo, Benny Goodman, Count Basie, Glenn Miller, Harry James, the Dorseys, Xavier Cugat, and Larry Clinton. There was also an emcee who got the people out on the dance floor and who ran contests and giveaways.

In the early years, the contests were quite physical. On March 6, 1923, across the Atlantic in Sunderland, England, history was made. That was the date of the first marathon dance. A couple managed to dance continuously for nine and a half consecutive hours. The fad swept the United States, and Brecker saw the craze as an opportunity to pack the house. Claims of endurance were made daily but were never officially verified. Brecker decided to remedy the situation by holding the official world championship at Roseland. Nine couples took the floor and proceeded to wear down their heels. Their merriment was halted by the police, who cited a law that restricted continuous activity to 12 hours in length. Brecker was not one to capitulate even in the face of official actions. He pulled up a truck to the back of the auditorium and loaded the dancers and some band members into it. They drove to Sheepshead Bay, where the *Josephine*, a 60-foot sloop, awaited the group. The *Josephine* set sail, heading for the 3-mile limit, out of harms' way. Unfortunately, this grand scheme didn't entirely succeed. After 16 hours, the loyal followers back in Times Square received a missive. The telegram read, "Heavy seas force cancellation of contest. Dancers suffering horribly from seasickness."

Brecker realized the importance of STUNTS in boosting attendance and getting publicity. His second most notorious escapade was the jazz wedding. An ad was placed offering $200 to any couple who would be willing to prove that they were "really in love" by getting married on the dance floor in Roseland. Robert Wagner, an accountant from Jersey City, and Katherine Bott answered the advertisement. The Reverend Dr. William Klett, pastor of the Evangelical Lutheran Church of the Mediator performed the ceremony. He received $50 for his ministrations. The lucky bride and groom found 2,985 well-wishers, who had paid $1.10 each to witness the nuptials. Brecker threw in 20 bridesmaids and groomsmen, who paraded down the aisle to the jazzed-up strains of the "Wedding March" from Lohengrin. Twenty flower girls were followed by a overweight Dan Cupid dressed only in a diaper.

There were also sneezing contests and women's wrestling, but Roseland didn't have to resort to stunts to attract a clientele. Clifton Webb, then a Broadway musical-comedy star, frequented the ballroom, as did Tony DeMarco and Ray Bolger. In fact, most of the great dancers of the 1920s and '30s polished their routines or stayed in shape between engagements by dancing at Roseland. George Raft worked there for $2.50 a night, demonstrating the latest steps. Mayor Jimmy Walker punched Betty Compton at Roseland. AL JOLson met Ruby Keeler at Roseland, and Joan Crawford was also a celebrity regular. Other Roseland regulars included star ballroom dancers Johnny Lucchese, Lillian Kenyon, Joe Nobles, and Rose Gerard, as well as producer-director GEORGE ABBOTT

Roseland survived the Depression, but after the war its clientele began to get older and older. Brecker himself didn't dance with his wife at his own establishment: "Frankly the atmosphere offended me. It held too many memories of cheap publicity stunts. When my wife and I wanted to dance, we went to a hotel or one of the better night clubs. I hate to admit it, but I felt the place was an affront to my wife and children."

In 1956 a new Roseland opened on 52nd Street across from the the Alvin Theater (see NEIL SIMON THEATER) in what was the Gay Blades ice-skating rink. The new ballroom cost $2,750,000. The dance floor is 185 by 64 feet of maple wood over cork padding. The floor holds more than 2,000 dancers, who can retire to the Rose Bar for a refresher. The Terrace Restaurant seats 700, and there are additional facilities downstairs. Another attraction is the Wall of Fame, which displays the dancing shoes of Anna Held, Bill "Bojangles" Robinson, Ruby Keeler, Joel Grey, Sandy Duncan, IRENE CASTLE, Ann Miller, Betty Grable, June Taylor, James Cagney, ADELE ASTAIRE, and Ray Bolger. Near the Wall of Fame is a plaque listing the names of those dancers who met at Roseland and later married.

Nancy Brecker took over the day-to-day operation of the room in the 1960s. She said:

> The only battle I ever had with my father was when I told him he had to put the twist in. Everybody in New York was doing it and he just had to do it. There was no way we could talk him into it, my brother and I both tried. He would not change and he was probably right. Because his dancers really didn't care that much.

In an attempt to bring new blood into the hall, she instituted disco nights. The room filled to capacity during the disco segments, which began at midnight after the regulars had gone: "I called it the metamorphosis of Roseland. The entire place changed over, the lights were all different, everything changed. It was fascinating to watch it. It was great. I set up the atmosphere of the place."

When her father had first started, the admission was about $1.50. By the time Nancy Brecker took over the operations in what she calls "a trial by fire," the entry fee was up to $7, and $10 on special evenings. Private parties were sought, and they added luster to the once-faded ballroom. She noted, "We really tried to improve the image of Roseland, rather than letting it go downhill by having not only prestigious private parties but by making Wednesday night into a buffet night."

Nancy completely redid the interior, including new carpeting and new mirrored walls to give the impression of a larger room. The purpose was to make the room appear bright and new, as well as to add an air of romance to the surroundings. The regular patrons appreciated the renovation: "They would come in around 2:30 and they would stay until ten o'clock at night." But it was still difficult to induce a younger clientele except on the disco nights. Brecker began advertising in the *New York Times*, but the results were mixed. Part of the problem was that Roseland was an institution and taken for granted. Nancy noted, "I have heard more people say, 'I've always been dying to go to Roseland and we just never did it.'"

When both Louis Brecker and his wife died, the family decided to sell Roseland. Al Ginsberg, a real-estate developer, bought the dance hall in 1981. He remodeled again and reinstated the taxi dancers. This time, both men and women were available for $1 a dance. In the 80s dancing at Roseland was discontinued and the hall was used for special events, parties, and rock concerts. There have been rumors of Roseland's demolition in the wild real estate speculation surrounding the Times Square area, although, at publication, Roseland is still going strong. If it does go, hundreds of people, including Nancy Brecker, will be sorry to see its passing: "There's no other dance floor anywhere in the world to rival it. It was always a very wonderful, unique place and it would be a shame to see it torn down but I suppose like everything else things change."

ROTHAFEL, S. L. ("ROXY"). Impresario who created the great movie palaces of the 1920s and '30s; b. Samuel Lionel Rothapfel, Stillwater, Minnesota, July 9, 1882; d. New York, New York, January 13, 1936.

S. L. Rothafel, better known as "Roxy," was the chief architect in the transformation of the movie theater from its humble beginnings as nickleodeon to its heyday as great movie palace. A pioneer impresario, Roxy rose quickly in his career until he became responsible for the creation of the largest and most elaborate movie theaters in history.

Samuel Lionel Rothapfel's (he dropped the *p* when German-sounding names were viewed with unease during World War I) father, Gustave Rothapfel, was a shoemaker. In 1895 the elder Rothapfel uprooted the family and brought them to New York in search of greater economic opportunity. Although the family became somewhat more comfortable financially, the young son still had to find a job. He became a cashier in the John B. Collins department store on 14th Street, where he earned $2 per week. While he was still in his teens, Roxy went from job to job. As he later recalled,

Roxy and Clark Robinson, Art Director, take possession of the New Roxy Theatre.

"Through the next few years I had so many jobs it would take me hours just to name them all. I could not hold one more than two weeks. Usually I left, or was fired, even quicker than that."

Rothapfel lied about his age and enlisted in the Marine Corps at the age of 14. He was sent to Santo Domingo and China, where he fought in the Boxer Rebellion. Rothapfel became a drill sergeant and learned about discipline and training, and he later applied this knowledge when dealing with his staffs. After seven years in the Corps, Rothapfel returned to the United States to find that he had no marketable skills. He became a door-to-door salesman and eventually worked his way to Pennsylvania, where he tried out for the Northeast Pennsylvania League as a baseball player. He didn't get signed, but he did acquire something more valuable, his nickname. A boy in the stands called out, "Slide, Roxy!" when he was running out a two-base hit. From then on he was known as Roxy.

In Forest City, Pennsylvania, Roxy met the woman who became Mrs. Rothapfel. Roxy's father-in-law originally objected to the proposed marriage because of Roxy's precarious financial status. Roxy took a job with his future father-in-law in the family-owned saloon. He tended bar for 18 months, saving his money toward his future married life. Roxy married in 1907,

the same year that he entered the motion picture business. His father-in-law's tavern had a large assembly room in the back, which was occasionally used for sauerkraut dinners and gatherings. Roxy first decided to put a roller rink in the room but soon changed his mind, having noted the success of a new invention, motion pictures. As he told it: "I persuaded my father-in-law to let me turn this dance hall into a motion-picture theater. I bought a second-hand screen and projection machine, hired a pianist and charged 5 cents admission. In that little dance-hall theater I started in a crude way to do what I am doing now."

On Christmas Eve 1908 Roxy put up a sign that announced, "Grand Opening in Vaudeville—Special matinee Xmas afternoon." The screen was a white sheet, the projector was an early hand-cranked Cineograph, and the chairs were borrowed from his father-in-law's funeral parlor. The program consisted of an overture by pianist Professor James Curry, vaudeville, illustrated songs, a one-reel comedy, and films of the "World's Series between the Chicago 'Cubs' and the Detroit 'Tigers,' showing the famous plays and all the favorites in actual motion."

As business grew, Roxy began to demonstrate his penchant for showmanship. He covered the screen with a curtain that drew open at the start of each show, and Professor Curry's piano was augmented with a violin and a baritone singer. A series of colored lights were added, which played on the screen. They cast their magical glow in alternating pink, green, and blue. Roxy's little theater became a success, and his ingenuity caught the attention of several local businessmen. Distributors in New York noticed that Roxy was ordering as many films as the owners of big nickleodeons. B. F. Keith, the owner of an increasingly important chain of vaudeville theaters (*see* E. F. ALBEE), noticed Roxy's imaginative success. Keith hired Roxy to improve the motion-picture portion of his programs. Keith had long considered the movies an insult to his vaudeville presentations, and in the early days he used movies primarily to clear the audience after each vaudeville bill. As the new medium grew, audience members began staying in their seats just to see the pictures. Roxy was then introduced to Herman Fehr, the owner of an ailing vaudeville theater in Milwaukee. Roxy used his talents to upgrade Fehr's Alhambra Theatre into a mini movie palace. The transformation was impressive and unique at the time. The Fehr theater became one of the most profitable in the city.

By 1913 Roxy was ready to conquer New York. He became manager of the Regent Theater at 116th Street and 7th Avenue. The Regent was the first high-class theater in New York built just for showing movies. It had an 8-piece orchestra and a string ensemble to accompany the picture, as well as the city's first movie pipe organ. Roxy improved the auditorium and projection system, and he generally overhauled the entire operation. He had special arrangements written for the musicians. Roxy went on to success after success with a series of motion-picture houses: The RIALTO, the RIVOLI, the CAPITOL, and, finally, his ultimate achievement, the ROXY THEATER.

Roxy's innovations were both artistic and technical. He was considered a genius in the new field of stage lighting. The *Encyclopaedia Britannica* called him an authority in the field. Roxy also realized the importance of music in the program, even after silent pictures were replaced by sound. He was the first to employ 100-piece orchestras and immense pipe organs in his halls. Roxy also conquered radio and realized the great promotional possibilities of the new medium. On November 19, 1922, WEAF broadcast a program live from the Capitol Theater. The two-hour radio show was hosted and designed by Roxy. After the opening of the Roxy Theater, he began a national radio show on the NBC Blue Network.

He took his radio family, known as Roxy's Gang, out of the studio and into many hospitals and charitable functions. In February 1931 Roxy was the first person to receive an award from the New York City Federation of Women's Charities. The *New York Times* stated, "Thousands of those who had heard his cheery 'Hello, everybody!' as master of ceremonies in the great theaters he directed became anxious to come to New York to see the man and his 'gang' and his super-show houses."

While beginning plans to open the new Radio City Music Hall in Rockefeller Center, Roxy suffered a minor heart attack. On the day after the theater's opening, he collapsed again. After recuperating, he attempted to go back to work but found the interim management had taken firm control. Virtually powerless at the Music Hall, Roxy put his efforts toward the RKO Roxy Theater. The owners of the Roxy sued the RKO Roxy owners on the basis of the similarity in names. The RKO Roxy was rechristened the Center Theater. Roxy remained director of the two Rockefeller Center theaters for a year, but it was clear that he was not in control. He resigned in January 1934. Roxy went to London to examine the possibility of repeating his great success in that city, but the plans did not work out.

For the first time in many years, Roxy was without a theater. He went on a tour of the South with his "gang." Following that, he took over control of the Mastbaum Theater in Philadelphia. He changed the name of the huge white elephant to the Roxy-Mastbaum, but even the great showman couldn't help the immense auditorium. It closed on Christmas Day

1934. Roxy was distraught at the problems encountered in his last efforts. Even his once-loyal staff abandoned him, preferring the security of their new jobs at the Music Hall. On January 13, 1936, Roxy died in his suite in the Gotham Hotel.

At the opening of the Roxy Theater, *The New Yorker* printed the following tribute to Roxy:

> Roxy is forty-two, fat and short, and has sentiment. One admirable trait is his great sincerity of purpose. The erection of this handsome old-gold and plush cathedral was done with a magnificent gesture and with a very intimate feeling for his dear public—to him, they say, a very real emotion.

ROXY THEATER. 50th Street at 7th Avenue. Architect: W. W. Alschlager. Art designer: Pietro Ciavarra. Opening: March 1927.

The Roxy Theater, the largest theater in the world at the time of its opening in 1927, was dubbed "The Cathedral of the Motion Picture." It was the grandest of all movie palaces and a popular tourist attraction.

Developer Herman Lubin had the idea to tear down the old car barns at 50th Street and 7th Avenue and erect the world's largest theater on the site. As Lubin's plans took shape, he began thinking about staffing the great hall. One man's name rose to the top of the list— S. L. ("ROXY") ROTHAFEL, the greatest motion-picture showman in the world, who virtually invented the idea of the deluxe motion-picture house. Roxy was firmly ensconced at the CAPITOL THEATER, site of his latest triumphs, and from which he broadcast his popular radio show. Roxy was happy at the Capitol, so it took some ingenious negotiation by Lubin to attract his services. Lubin offered Roxy a large salary, a percentage of the theater's profits, as well as stock options. To clinch the deal, Lubin offered to name the new theater after the showman.

With Roxy secured, plans for the theater began. Roxy explained his ideas for the new theater in the August 1926 issue of *Metronome Magazine*:

> The matter of personality is the most important thing in the world dealing with the public. I am going to keep it in mind in my new theater. I have often said in discussing it that we should not call it a theater at all, but rather an institution which receives its stamp of individuality from the man who runs it. I cannot tell you of the many activities which it is going to represent, but the theater will be one part of it.

Naturally, with Roxy at the helm, the plans for the theater grew more and more extravagant and, as a result, more and more expensive. Lubin realized he could

The Roxy Theater.

not handle the immense financial commitment, so he sold the control of the theater to William Fox for $5 million and managed to reap a $3,000 profit.

When the theater was completed in 1927, it was indeed the largest in the world. The auditorium seated almost 6,000 patrons, and there was standing room for 500 more at the rear of the audience. While the audience watched the show, there was room for 2,500 more people to wait patiently in the lobby for the next show. Backstage, the numbers were also impressive. More than a hundred musicians played in the symphony orchestra, and a staff of 300 saw that the show ran smoothly both behind the stage and in the office. The ballet corps had 100 dancers in its ranks. On a sold-out night, there might be as many as 10,000 people in the theater.

The audience entered the theater through an outer foyer, which was part of the Taft Hotel. The foyer space was rented from the hotel, which opened as the Manger in 1926. From the foyer, the audience entered the great rotunda. Roxy would fire his ushers if they called the rotunda simply "the lobby." The great space featured 12 green antique marble columns soaring 5 stories to the ceiling. The floor of the rotunda was covered with an enormous circular carpet. The 2-ton carpet was billed as "the largest oval rug in the world." The 70-foot-wide rotunda led to the seating area. Patrons could either enter the orchestra area through gigantic bronze doors or rise to the balcony level by climbing the grand staircase. Although the theater was advertised as seating 6,000 patrons, there was actually room for 5,920 seated patrons. When pressed, the ushers were instructed by Roxy to state that the theater seated more then 6,000, but not all those seats were in the auditorium.

Also in the theater complex was a broadcasting studio from which Roxy could continue his radio broadcasts. The studio was large enough to contain a 2-manual Kimball pipe organ, usually played by Lew White, plus the 110-piece symphony orchestra, conducted by Erno Rapee, and the chorus and soloists who appeared on the Roxy stage. Immense as this studio was, the building still had room for dressing rooms, a costume department, 3 floors of chorus dressing rooms, dry-cleaning and laundry rooms, a hairdresser and a barbershop, a dining room, a ballet room big enough to rehearse in, and a menagerie for the productions' animals. The theater complex also had a hospital, an immense engine room, the offices, and the rehearsal room, almost as big as the stage itself. There were 2 stories of private dressing rooms, each containing a complete bath, closet, desk, bed, and makeup table. In addition, there were rehearsal rooms for the chorus, a private screening room that seated 100, a publicity shop, the ushers' dressing rooms and lounge, and the accounting department. For the staff's relaxation, there was a gymnasium, billiard room, cafeteria, nap room, library, and showers.

The first movie to play the Roxy was Gloria Swanson's *The Love of Sunya*. It was accompanied by a "presentation show," which featured an overture, a ballet, a newsreel, and a line of 16 dancers. The troupe's leader was Russell Markert, a dancer and Broadway choreographer who admired the English group, the Tiller Girls. In 1927 Markert put together a line of dancers and played the Missouri Theater in St. Louis. They became a hit in St. Louis and were brought to the Roxy in November 1927. Four months later their number was doubled, and they were officially dubbed the Roxyettes. In 1932 Roxy, now at Radio City Music Hall, brought the dancers with him and redubbed them the Rockettes.

Following the Roxyettes came a cut-down ("tab") version of a popular operetta or opera. It featured the chorus and perhaps a specially hired soloist. Following the tab show came a finale, featuring the entire cast, and finally the feature production.

Author Nunnally Johnson described the Roxy's opening night:

> Samuel L. Rothafel, described in the elaborate program as Roxy the Maestro and by the boys along the Rialto as just plain Roxy, opened his theater—"the world's largest and greatest"—at Seventh Avenue and Fiftieth Street last night, thus discommoding the lads who ordinarily foregather there of an evening to play "craps," shoot each other, stab one another and otherwise make merry.
>
> It is only fair to mention in passing, however, that there were 6,500 men and women, ranging from James J. Walker, once of City Hall, later of Havana, and now again of City Hall, to my very favorite barber, Jo, who seemed to have quite a pleasant evening of it, the discomfiture of the crap-shooters notwithstanding. They, of course, were the people who possessed what looked something like pasteboard (but which I guess was something else entirely) tickets entitling them to fight their way through a frenzied throng and pass solemnly into Mr. Rothafel's "lasting monument to the greatest force for wholesome amusement the world has ever known."

Orchestra, mezzanine, and balcony of the Roxy Theater.

> "The first impression on entering the Roxy is that of agreeable surprise," said a line in my program. It wasn't mine, however, for I found I had forgotten my ticket and had to come way home again for it.

The New Yorker also covered the theater's opening:

> It was good to discover that the theatre is quite a beautiful thing in spots; it goes in for awfulness with far greater dignity than its closest rival, the little Paramount. The seats were comfortable—more so than any others in town that we can think of.
>
> Tickets were $11, and for this consideration the buyer received (according to our private tabulation) the following boons: allegory, patriotism, symphony, clairvoyance, grand opera, terpischore and Mayor Walker. The whole show was typically Rothafellian—or so we are told by those who have followed his career—from the very start when a gentleman who looked like a monk said, in an awful voice: "let there be light!" and by gum there *was* light.
>
> Practically everything that happened was unexpected, including, probably, the somewhat dim applause which finally cropped up here and there at the conclusion of the motion picture. It was distinctly an evening of surprises, and there was just a trace of boyish prankishness in the way Roxy played now-you-see-it-and-now-you-don't with his hundred-piece orchestra and his wondering organ.

The Roxy, owned by William Fox, was naturally the flagship of the magnificent Fox chain of theaters. As such, it premiered all the first-class Fox output. The box-office record was held by an otherwise forgotten film, *The Cock-eyed World*. It had 208,785 paid admissions during one week in August 1929.

After Roxy's contract ran out on March 29, 1931, he resigned and later left to join the new Radio City Music Hall. Art director Clark Robinson assumed Roxy's post until a new director could be found. The Fox Corporation decided to install the producing team of Fanchon and Marco, who had produced shows for the Fox chain. Fred Waring was chosen to replace Erno Rapee. However, with Roxy gone, the theater lost some of its glamor. When the Depression descended, the Fox Film and Theater Company was hard hit. In April 1932 the company was forced to default on a $200,000 mortgage payment. The stockholders voted out the Fox Corporation and closed the theater for eight weeks. During that time the stage area was extended over the orchestra pit. This meant that the orchestra lift could not be used. The organ was also made inoperable, and the three consoles were moved to the basement.

Howard Cullman, a president of the Port Authority and owner of an apothecary firm, was put in charge of the space. Despite his lack of theatrical experience, he did manage to reopen the theater. Wisely, Cullman decided to pare down the expensive operation. The 80-person ushering staff was cut down to a mere 18. The presentation shows were discarded and replaced with a vaudeville-style stage show. In order to attract an audience, the admission was reduced to 35 cents, which would enable a patron to sit in any seat in the house. The theater featured other incentives for attendance. A free massage service was offered in the ladies' lounge, the men's smoking room gave out free tobacco, and the grand lounge dispensed free coffee. There were also advertising tie-ins, and a couple of boxes of toothpaste or detergent could get one free admission.

After the Fox organization had been voted out, the quality of the films fell. The other movie companies had their own first-run theaters on Broadway, so the Roxy was reduced to playing B pictures or the products of independents like Monogram. Attendance suffered. Ironically, a Fox picture saved the theater. Shirley Temple's *Baby Take a Bow* opened in June 1934. Instead of the usual 1-week run, the picture was held over and eventually played 4 weeks. It actually sold out its engagement and gave the theater a much-needed shot in the arm. However, with *Baby Take a Bow* gone, the theater again went into a slump.

In 1937 the new Twentieth Century–Fox corporation signed a 20-year lease on the theater. The new owners made changes in the decoration to "modernize" the look. Unfortunately, the new designs were much inferior to the originals. They hung giant, red-and-white candy-striped draperies over the proscenium and along the sides of the audience. A new neon marquee replaced the old one. The original wrought-iron lighting fixtures were replaced with garish fluorescent lights. The marble floors were completely covered with checkered linoleum tiles. The owners also decided to reinstate the organ. They placed it in one of the side boxes, only to discover that the pipes had been sealed behind concrete. Not to be thwarted, the management decided to pipe the organ music over the public-address system.

Following the Depression, in 1942, A. J. Balaban of the Balaban and Katz chain took over the theater's operation. The new producing director hired top names to head the stage shows. Milton Berle, Jack Benny, Cab Calloway, and the New York Philharmonic all played the Roxy. A better class of films was booked, and the theater's fortunes improved. The all-time box-office-champion movie, *Forever Amber*, was booked during this period. However, that policy lasted only six years. Its next transformation was astounding. The stage area was covered with a 30-foot-by-30-foot ice floor for ice shows. The theater's seating capacity was reduced to 5,886. The Center Theater on 6th Avenue was also converted to ice, and both theaters did successful business.

In 1952 Congress legislated that the movie companies were to divest their theater ownership. Metro-Goldwyn-Mayer spun off its Loew's chain, and Twentieth Century-Fox sold their chain to its exhibitor, National Theaters. Finally, the Roxy's curtains were removed from the auditorium, and the ice stage was almost doubled, to 60 feet. The orchestra pit was made larger, and black-light effects were installed.

Another major change was undertaken in September 1953. With the advent of television, the movie companies searched for ways to make their films a viable alternative to the free entertainment. They returned to an old idea, wide-screen pictures. Fox had already experimented with and discarded its Grandeur process, which played the Roxy in 1930. A new screen was put into the theater, and the wide-screen process, renamed Cinemascope, was introduced again. The first Cinemascope feature to play the Roxy was *The Robe*. Because of the size of the new screen, the stage show was eliminated, along with part of the proscenium. When the engagement of *The Robe* was over, the 70-foot-wide screen was removed and the damaged proscenium was covered with turquoise curtains. In October 1955, Robert C. Rothafel, Roxy's nephew, took control of the theater and two months later reinstated the ice shows.

Rockefeller Center to the east was expanding, and the Roxy Theater stood in the way. In September 1956 the Rockefeller Center interests bought the Roxy and its land. They intended to hold on to the land until the time was right to tear down the theater and build a new headquarters for the Time-Life Building. However, the Roxy underwent yet another transformation in 1958. An even larger screen, 100 feet across, was installed, and more of the proscenium was destroyed. The Cinemiracle process opened with *Windjammer*. The balcony and loge were closed off, and the theater's capacity was reduced to 2,710. Few of those seats were sold, and children's rides were installed in the grand lounge. The rotunda's snack bars featured clam chowder in tribute to the nautical attraction on the big screen, but business did not increase and the film was pulled.

With *Windjammer* out of the theater, more draperies were hung to cover the additional damage to the theater. Russell V. Downing, president of Radio City Music Hall, was put in charge of the theater's operations in November 1959, and he tried to revitalize the theater. A year later he decided to stop the stage show once and for all. In the end, it wasn't the Rockefellers who caused the Roxy's demolition. The Taft Hotel, from which the Roxy leased its foyer space, was owned by Bing and Bing Realtors, whose head was William Zeckendorf. The company bought the Roxy from the Rockefellers with the intent of expanding the Taft's room space. When the plans for the enlarged Taft fell through, Zeckendorf became the owner of a theater that was losing thousands of dollars a week. The theater also cost $20,000 a month in taxes. Zeckendorf decided to cut his losses by razing the Roxy.

On March 19, 1960, the Roxy closed its doors following the last showing of its last feature, *The Wind Cannot Read*. An auction of the theater's fixtures raised only $10,000. The 30 pairs of bronze exit doors were scrapped, along with anything else that was unsold. The two-story French crystal Rotunda chandelier was offered to Cardinal Spellman, but he turned it down. The Roxy's 3,000-piece costume collection was given away, as was the huge music library. Long Island University received the antiques and oil paintings. In August 1960 the Roxy was demolished.

ROYALE THEATRE. 242 W. 45th Street. Architect: Herbert J. Krapp. Opening: January 11, 1927; *Piggy*.

The Chanin Brothers built the Royale Theater in 1927 on what is considered the most important of all Broadway cross streets. Because of its high concentration of theaters, 45th Street is the one street in the Times Square area where foot traffic is thought to affect box office. The Chanins purchased a large plot of land on 8th Avenue between 44th and 45th Streets. On the land they built the Golden Theater and Theater Masque (*see* JOHN GOLDEN THEATER [2]), the MAJESTIC THEATRE, and the Lincoln Hotel (currently the Milford Plaza Hotel).

The first offering at the 1,058-seat theater was *Piggy* (1/11/27; 79 performances), a musical comedy by Cliff Friend and Lew Brown (*see* DE SYLVA, BROWN, AND HENDERSON). *Piggy* never caught on with the public. Producer William B. Friedlander even changed the name of the show to *I Told You So* during the run. The STUNT didn't work, and *Piggy*, or rather *I Told You So*, closed quickly. The Royale's next production, *Judy* (2/8/27; 104 performances), had a score by Charles Rosoff and Leo Robin. Queenie Smith starred with Charles Purcell and George Meeker. *Judy* made way for a musicalization of *The Importance of Being Earnest*, called *Oh, Earnest!* (5/9/27; 56 performances). The musical had a score by Robert Hood Bowers and Francis DeWitt. The next offering, *Rang-Tang* (7/12/27; 119 performances), starred the popular black performers Aubrey Lyles and Flournoy Miller. The show's songs, written by Ford Dabney and Jo Trent, included "Come to Africa," "Sambo's Banjo,"

Royale Theatre, right before its opening in 1927, featuring Sam Bernard in *Piggy*.

"Sammy and Topsy," "Tramps of the Desert," and "Harlem." The titles indicate the general state of black musicals at the time. Only the songwriting team of Noble Sissle and Eubie Blake (*see* SISSLE AND BLAKE) were able to begin to overcome the popular prejudices and stereotypes. *The Madcap* (1/31/28; 103 performances) starred Mitzi, Harry Puck, and Arthur Treacher. Although old fashioned, the show caught on and played a respectable run. Following it was the theater's first straight play, the mystery *Sh! The Octopus* (2/21/28; 47 performances).

The first smash hit for the theater was the Mae West vehicle *Diamond Lil* (4/9/28; 323 performances). West had written a script similar to another by Mark Linder, so the two joined forces, and *Diamond Lil* was born. Half of the show was owned by Owney Madden, a GANGSTER best known as proprietor of the Cotton Club. The play caused a sensation following its opening. It was among a group of plays of the 1920s, including *Burlesque* and *Broadway*, that owed their success in part to their settings: the world of gangsters, prostitutes, and drugs. These shows gave audiences, accustomed to the more-refined drawing room comedies or clichéd melodramas, a chance to see what they thought was real life. CRITIC Percy Hammond described the audience of *Diamond Lil* as "persons anxious to encourage a conscience-smitten transgressor in her desire to be meritricious [*sic*]. Miss West, its star and author, recently under lock and key, is now more admired by her public than is Jane Cowl, Lynn Fontanne [*see* LUNT AND FONTANNE], HELEN HAYES or Eva Le Gallienne." West had been arrested as a result of a previous Broadway offering, *Sex*.

Robert Garland, writing in the *Evening Telegram*, was the most vociferous admirer of the star. "So regal is Miss West's manner, so assured is her artistry, so devastating are her charms in the eyes of all red-blooded men, so blonde, so beautiful, so buxom is she that she makes Miss Ethel Barrymore [*see* BARRYMORE FAMILY] look like the late lamented Mr. Bert Savoy." Savoy was a female impersonator. Naturally, the script was loaded with typical Mae West lines. These included "When a girl goes wrong, men usually go right after her" and "I'm one of the finest women who ever walked the streets." West later revived the show on Broadway in 1949 for 181 performances and in 1951 for 67 performances. *Diamond Lil* was followed by a failure, the musical *Woof, Woof* (12/25/29; 45 performances).

The SHUBERT BROTHERS began management of the Royale in 1930. A big success was the review *Second Little Show* (9/2/30; 63 performances). DIETZ AND SCHWARTZ wrote the songs. However, the show's hit tune, "Sing Something Simple," was written by Herman Hupfeld. Mae West returned to the Royale in *The*

Constant Sinner (9/14/31; 64 performances). Her previous Broadway offering, *The Pleasure Man*, was raided by the police and closed after only two performances. *The Constant Sinner* was set in Harlem, and West played a woman married to a prizefighter. On the side, she has two lovers, one black and one a millionaire. The millionaire kills the black lover (played by George Givot in blackface). The West character, who incidently has been selling dope on the side, allows her husband to be framed for the murder. In the end, the millionaire puts up the money for a first-class lawyer, and the husband is freed. She ends up with both men. West insisted on casting a real black man as Givot's understudy, to the chagrin of the producers (the Shuberts).

Howard Barnes, writing in the *Herald Tribune*, described the play as "a melodrama nicely calculated to offend public taste and attract paying customers." Not everyone was a fan of the actress. Percy Hammond didn't mince words when he wrote: "She is so different from anything you have seen outside the zoo that you decide her impersonation is deliberately outlandish. When her various heroes ply her with jewels and admiration you suspect that they should be feeding her peanuts." After the play's closing, West moved to Hollywood and the movies. She continued to push back the boundaries of subject matter and to buck the critics and censors. West returned to Broadway in 1944 with her play *Catherine Was Great*. JOHN CHAPMAN, writing in the *Daily News*, opined, "I'm afraid *Catherine Was Great* will be a bust—which is one more than Mae West needs."

A more subdued play, *When Ladies Meet* (10/6/32; 187 performances), opened next at the Royale. Maxwell Anderson's *Both Your Houses* (3/6/33; 72 performances), was an exposé of political morality. The play won the PULITZER PRIZE. After a few more inconsequential shows, the theater's name was changed. When producer John Golden lost his John Golden Theater on 54th Street, he leased the Royale, renaming it the Golden Theater. GEORGE ABBOTT directed the first offering, Norman Krasna's *Small Miracle* (9/26/34; 188 performances). It featured Ilka Chase and Myron McCormick. *Rain from Heaven* (12/24/34; 99 performances) by S. N. Behrman opened with Jane Cowl and John Halliday.

During the Depression, the theater's fortunes fell along with Broadway's, and in December 1936 it was taken over by CBS as a radio theater. Golden moved operations to the Masque Theater next door, and he renamed it the John Golden Theater. In 1940 CBS relinquished its lease, and the theater's name reverted to the Royale. After housing a series of plays that moved from other houses, the Royale housed popular comedienne ZaSu Pitts in *Ramshackle Inn* (1/5/44; 216 performances). *School for Brides* (8/1/44; 375 performances), its title a takeoff on Molière's *School for Wives*, enjoyed a long run. Mae West then returned to the Royale in *Catharine Was Great*, which had originally opened at the Shubert Theater (*see* SAM S. SHUBERT THEATRE).

Louis Calhern and Dorothy Gish starred in *The Magnificent Yankee* (1/22/46; 160 performances) by Emmet Lavery, a play that was much respected by critics. Ina Claire appeared at the Royale in *The Fatal Weakness* (11/19/46; 119 performances), by George Kelly. Moss Hart's (*see* KAUFMAN AND HART) *Light up the Sky* (11/18/48; 214 performances) was an affectionate and sometimes barbed spoof of the Broadway theater in the same style as his and George S. Kaufman's *Once in a Lifetime*. The satirical comedy opened with Sam Levene and Audrey Christie. To begin a new decade, Christopher Fry's London hit, *The Lady's Not for Burning* (11/8/50; 151 performances), opened at the Royale with Richard Burton, John Gielgud, and Pamela Brown.

Leonard Sillman opened the biggest hit in his series of *New Faces* revues at the Royale on May 16, 1952. The show introduced such future stars as Carol Lawrence, Alice Ghostley, Robert Clary, Eartha Kitt, Paul Lynde, and Ronny Graham. The terrific songs, written by Arthur Siegel and June Carroll, included the standard "Love Is a Simple Thing." Other well-received songs in the show were "Penny Candy" and "Monotonous" by Siegel and Carroll, "Guess Who I Saw Today?" by Murray Grand and Elisse Boyd, and "Lizzie Borden" by Michael Brown. *New Faces of 1952*, with its 365-performance run, was the last successful popular Broadway revue for years. In the early 1950s audiences could see the same type of show in the comfort of their living rooms through the miracle of television; there was no need to go to Broadway.

André Gide's play *The Immoralist* (2/8/54; 96 performances), based on his novel, explored the theme of homosexuality. Geraldine Page, Louis Jourdan, and James Dean were the stars of the Billy Rose production. The chancy subject matter limited the play to a 96-performance run.

More popular was Sandy Wilson's affectionate parody of 1920s musicals, *The Boy Friend* (9/30/54; 485 performances). The musical introduced a new star to Broadway, Julie Andrews, and was the first of the musical parodies. Thornton Wilder's *The Matchmaker* (12/5/55; 486 performances) was a rewrite of his early failure *The Merchant of Yonkers*. The German play on which *The Merchant of Yonkers* was based was later adapted into *On the Razzle*, by Tom Stoppard. The stars were Ruth Gordon, Loring Smith, Eileen Herlie, and Robert Morse. Not all the critics appreciated the comedy, complaining that it lacked Wilder's personal stamp. The playwright, who had contributed such classics as *Our Town* and *The Skin of Our Teeth* to the American theater, was reduced, some thought, to writing a standard Broadway farce. They were right, but audiences were amused anyway. Later *The Matchmaker* was transformed into *Hello, Dolly!* which critic Brooks Atkinson called "interminable."

Another comedy, *The Tunnel of Love* (2/13/57; 417 performances), by Joseph Fields (*see* FIELDS FAMILY) and Peter DeVries, starred Tom Ewell. *The Entertainer* (2/12/58; 96 performances), by John Osborne, was hailed for its performance by Laurence Olivier. The play also starred Joan Plowright and Brenda de Banzie. Producer DAVID MERRICK ignored critics' carping about the play but couldn't keep it running. Robert Dhery's revue *La Plume de Ma Tante* (11/11/58; 835 performances) did not have any hit songs or any stars, but audiences were entranced by the Gallic entertainment. Another revue, *From the Second City* (9/26/61; 87 performances), introduced stars from the Chicago-based improv company, including Barbara Harris, Alan Arkin, and Paul Sand, to New York.

Bette Davis appeared at the Royale with Patrick O'Neal, Margaret Leighton, and Alan Webb in TENNESSEE WILLIAMS' *The Night of the Iguana* (12/28/61; 316 performances). Williams' play opened to mixed reviews. Some felt he had become a parody of himself, and others found the bizarre play to be the apotheosis of the Williams style. *Lord Pengo* (11/19/62; 175 performances), by S. N. Behrman, opened with Charles Boyer, Agnes Moorehead, Brian Bedford, and Henry Daniell. The next hit at the Royale, *The Subject Was Roses* (5/25/64; 832 performances) by Frank D. Gilroy, won the Pulitzer prize. The play was Gilroy's first Broadway production. His prior play, *Who'll Save the Plowboy?*, opened in 1962 at the Phoenix Theater. *The Subject Was Roses* opened with critics hailing Gilroy's tight dialogue and detailed realism, in great contrast to the work of the best-known Broadway dramatists of the day. Like his contemporary playwrights, Gilroy filled his drama with empathy for his characters, but he differed from them in his interest in the rituals of daily life. Jack Albertson, Martin Sheen, and Irene Dailey made up the entire cast.

One of the biggest hits of the 1960s was the French farce *Cactus Flower* (12/8/65; 1,234 performances). Lauren Bacall made her Broadway debut in the comedy, supported by Barry Nelson, Robert Moore, and Brenda Vaccaro. Abe Burrows adapted the show for American audiences and directed the proceedings. The 1960s was the last decade in which audiences were willing to be charmed on Broadway. Later audiences wanted to be wowed by Broadway, but in the 1960s they were still content to sit back and watch a star go through his or her paces.

A notable booking at the Royale was the musical *Grease*, which moved to the theater from the

Martin Sheen, Irene Dailey, and Jack Albertson in *The Subject Was Roses*, 1964.

BROADHURST in 1972 and remained for eight years. By the time *Grease* closed, the set was actually peeling and the cast was less than prime, but it had racked up 3,388 performances, a record at the time.

Whose Life Is It Anyway? (4/17/79; 223 performances) was a British import with Tom Conti. Brian Clark's play was a success on Broadway. Conti played a paralyzed man who wants to gain control of his life by getting the right to die. When Conti left the cast, the producers, faced with the problem of finding a replacement, made the unlikely choice of television star Mary Tyler Moore. Clark adapted the script for a female lead, and Moore received excellent reviews.

Alexander Cohen presented the American version of a British revue, *A Day in Hollywood/A Night in the Ukraine* (5/1/80; 558 performances), at the Royale. The revue was directed and choreographed by Tommy Tune and featured David Garrison, Peggy Hewett, Frank Lazarus, and Priscilla Lopez. The show was reinforced with three songs by JERRY HERMAN.

Tim Rice and ANDREW LLOYD WEBBER's third Broadway success, *Joseph and the Amazing Techni-*

color Dreamcoat, moved from off Broadway on January 27, 1982, to the Royale. The show was a failure with the critics but a hit with audiences, playing 751 performances. Lloyd Webber returned to the Royale with his show *Song and Dance* (9/18/85; 474 performances). The musical featured Bernadette Peters in the first act, a one-woman musical. The second act featured dancer Christopher d'Amboise and a small chorus. The two acts were linked by a tenuous story line.

George Abbott directed a revival of his play *Broadway*, written in collaboration with Philip Dunning. The show opened on Abbott's 100th birthday, June 25, 1987. Unfortunately, the poorly produced production was not a success, running for only four performances. The Royale was dark for a long period until the New York Shakespeare Festival's production of Caryl Churchill's English play *Serious Money* opened in January 1988. The play was not a success in its transfer from off Broadway.

On May 3, 1988, theatergoers were treated to the premiere of David Mamet's *Speed-the-Plow* (279 performances). The comedy, a production of the Lincoln

Center Theater Company, featured brilliant performances by Joe Mantegna and Ron Silver. The third cast member, making her Broadway debut, was the rock star Madonna. Unfortunately, her talents proved insufficient to the play's needs. She did, however, sell tickets, and the show soon sold out. Madonna's appearance confused many theatergoers. Many patrons waited patiently for their idol to break into song. Japanese tourists were especially confused by the play, with its heavy reliance on rapid-fire dialogue and little action.

The next success to play the Royale was Herb Gardner's comedy drama *Conversations with My Father* (3/22/92; 402 performances). Judd Hirsch starred in the show, ably supported by Tony Shalhoub, Marilyn Sokol, William Biff McGuire, and Jason Biggs (later of *American Pie* fame).

J. B. Priestley's traditional mystery *An Inspector Calls* (4/27/1994; 454 performances) received a decidedly nontraditional mounting at the Royale. Director Stephen Daldry and designer Ian MacNeil came up with a surrealistic and naturalistic setting that expanded the depth of the playwriting and allowed it to attain a universalist symbolism. The show was originally produced in London at the Royal National Theatre to great acclaim.

Another English transfer, David Hare's *Skylight* (9/19/96; 116 performances), never achieved its potential with Broadway audiences. It was followed by an ill-conceived musical revue, *Dream* (4/3/97; 109 performances), spotlighting the lyrics of Johnny Mercer. John Pizzarelli and Margaret Whiting were among the only highlights in an otherwise cruise-ship-friendly production.

The next British import, *Art* (3/1/98; 600 performances) was a deserved smash at the Royale. Yasmin Reza's comedy drama, first produced by the Royal National Theatre, explored the relationship of three men. On opening night these characters were portrayed by Alan Alda, Victor Garber, and Alfred Molina. The show might have run longer but the producers grew tired of replacing the cast every six months.

The next hit was also a British transfer, also from the Royal National Theatre, Michael Frayn's *Copenhagen* (4/11/2000; 326 performances). The deftly written dense drama explored speculations surrounding an actual meeting between physicists Niels Bohr and Werner Heisenberg on the eve of World War II. Michael Cumpsty, Philip Bosco, and Blair Brown made up the cast.

The theater's next hit was a limited engagement of John Leguizamo's one-man show, *Sexaholic . . . a Love Story* (12/2/2001; 67 performances). The theater's next tenant was a poorly received (although well acted) revival of Bernard Pomerance's only play, *The*

Elephant Man (4/14/2002; 57 performances). Billy Crudup, Kate Burton, and Rupert Graves headed the cast.

RUNYON, DAMON. Famed newspaper and short-story writer whose characters were drawn from the netherworld of Times Square; b. Alfred Damon Runyon, Manhattan, Kansas, October 4, 1884; d. New York, New York, December 10, 1946.

Damon Runyon was a newspaper columnist, short-story writer, and inventor and recorder of SLANG who used Broadway and Times Square as the backdrop for many of his works. Runyon was a regular fixture at various Times Square haunts, particularly LINDY's, which he immortalized as Mindy's. He achieved some of his greatest success posthumously through the production of the Broadway musical *Guys and Dolls*, which was based on several of his short stories.

Runyon inherited his interests in things literary from his father, Alfred Lee Runyon, a printer who also established newspapers. Runyon also inherited his father's strong political beliefs in the rights of the common person. When he was just 18, he enlisted in the Spanish-American War. Runyon was accepted as a member of the 13th Minnesota Volunteers. He was sent to the Philippines, arriving on July 31, 1898, two

Damon Runyon, his wife, and their dog, Silk.

days before Manila surrendered. Later Runyon would embellish the truth and claim to have joined at the age of 14 and to have participated in the battle of Manila; both stories were untrue.

After Runyon returned home, he joined the *Pueblo Chieftain* as a reporter. He moved up to newspapers in Denver and, later, San Francisco. Like other great journalists of his generation, such as A. J. LIEBLING, Runyon first became acquainted with the characters inhabiting Times Square through his love of sports. He moved to New York in 1911 and found employment as a sports reporter on the *American*. His byline originally read "Alfred Damon Runyon." Since brevity was a hallmark of many papers, editors shortened his name to Damon Runyon.

In those more freewheeling times, newspaper reporters were often hired for their journalistic talents rather than for their expertise in any one particular field. The young Runyon was assigned to cover murders, trials, and politics as well as sports. Among the more celebrated trials that he covered were the Hall Mills Case in 1926, the Snyder-Gray trial in 1927, and Bruno Richard Hauptmann's trial for the kidnapping of the Lindbergh baby. In 1916 the Hearst empire sent him to Mexico to follow General John Pershing in his quest for Pancho Villa: the Pershing Punitive Expedition. In 1916–17 Runyon went overseas with the 1st Army. He expanded his audience when he was appointed as a columnist and feature writer with King Features and the International News Service.

Runyon eventually wrote three columns for the Hearst papers. The first began in 1926 and was titled "Both Barrels." The next year he began "As I See It." "As I See It" was originally Arthur Brisbane's column, but Brisbane was a serious writer who wrote about solemn themes. Runyon didn't see the world in quite the same way as Brisbane. Two months later Runyon began a column called, "The Brighter Side." His column made him a minimum of $20,000 a year during the 1920s.

Like many of his fellow writers, Runyon answered a call from Hollywood. He joined RKO in 1941, and in that same year signed on with Twentieth Century-Fox as a producer and writer. His first picture was *The Big Street*. Runyon's many short stories appeared in the *Saturday Evening Post, Collier's, Liberty,* and *Cosmopolitan*. The magazines payed $1,500 for his stories in the beginning, but that rate soon escalated until Runyon was getting $5,000 a yarn. His stories covered a wide range of subjects and locales, but it was for his New York stories that Runyon received his greatest renown. He captured the characters and locations that made Times Square almost legendary to many of his readers.

Runyon was adept at giving the flavor of the street life through his descriptions and his characters' dialogue. For this, he invented or recorded many slang terms that later became a part of the language. This "Broadwayese" included several of his most famous terms, such as "guys" for men and "dolls" for women. Free tickets to shows he dubbed "Chinee" because the tickets had holes punched in them and so resembled Chinese coins. Money was called "potatoes," and one "tore a herring" in one's favorite deli.

Runyon covered the night beat, when the city really came alive. His headquarters was Lindy's Restaurant, where he would down dozens of cups of coffee. He would keep an ear peeled for the latest dialogue and would weave many local characters and incidents into his writing. BUGS BAER described Runyon as "harder to approach than a rodeo bull in a chute. There wasn't a time when he wouldn't throw a drowning man both ends of the rope."

Runyon's characters were the prizefighters, gangsters, theatrical agents, gamblers, producers, show girls, molls, bootleggers, and beggars whose whole universe revolved around the intersection of Broadway and 7th Avenue. His characters were a unique blend of hard edges and soft hearts. Harry the Horse, Spanish John, Wilbur Willard, Big Butch, Frankie Ferocious, Big Nig, Madame La Gimp (formerly Apple Annie), Waldo Winchester, Dream Street Rose, Lily of St. Pierre, Light Finger Moe, Sorrowful Jones, Little Isadore, Little Miss Marker, Dave the Dude, and Joe the Joker all became well known through his stories and later film adaptations. Hollywood found in Runyon a gold mine of plot and characters. Among the 16 films based on his stories (a record for one author) were *Lady for a Day, Little Miss Marker,* and *A Pocketful of Miracles* (a remake of *Lady for a Day*). During the Depression, he made as much as $30,000 in options on his stories.

Damon Runyon died in New York on December 10, 1946. He had suffered a long battle against cancer. Colonel Eddie Rickenbacker, following Runyon's will, flew over Times Square spreading Runyon's ashes over the streets of Broadway. The Damon Runyon Cancer Fund was established in the building that Owney Madden ran as the Club Napoleon.

In 1950 the Frank Loesser musical *Guys and Dolls* opened on Broadway. The show incorporated many of Runyon's characters and was based on his story *The Idyll of Miss Sarah Brown*. Runyon's character Sky Masterson was based on Broadway gambler Titanic Thompson. *Guys and Dolls* ran for 1,200 performances in New York and played more than 500 performances in London. It was later made into a successful motion picture starring Marlon Brando and Frank Sinatra.

ST. JAMES THEATRE. 246 W. 44th Street. Architects: Warren & Wetmore—F. Richard Anderson. Original name: Erlanger's Theatre. Opening: September 26, 1927; *The Merry Malones.*

In 1929 Abraham Erlanger, head of the monopolistic Theatrical Syndicate and among the most hated men in show business, built Erlanger's Theatre as the flagship of his nationwide chain. Erlanger chose the telling name Caesar Theatre Corporation as the purchasing agent. He chose 44th Street as a challenge to his rivals the SHUBERT BROTHERS who already had several theaters on 44th Street. Erlanger spent more than $1.5 million on the 1,600-seat theater, whose architects had Grand Central Terminal to their credit. His money was apparently well spent. The *New York Times* described the John Singraldi–designed auditorium: "There has been a studied attempt to create an intimate rather than a theatrical atmosphere. The interior design is Georgian, the color scheme coral and antique gold. Murals decorate the side walls and the proscenium arch."

With 1,600 seats to fill, Erlanger planned to present large-scale musicals. Not really a producer but a booker of shows through his United Booking Office, Erlanger chose GEORGE M. COHAN's musical *The Merry Malones* (216 performances) as the first show for the new theater. The musical starred Cohan, and he also composed the score, wrote the lyrics and libretto, and produced the proceedings. Historians have not recorded why Cohan did not direct the show; Edward Royce and Sam Forrest both were credited as directors. Of course, any George M. Cohan production really had Cohan as director, and *The Merry Malones* was no different. Cohan had an odd way of directing; he would slump down in a theater seat with his feet on the back of the seat in front of him, swinging a foot back and forth to indicate how he wanted actors to move.

Cohan wasn't supposed to star in the play, but at the final dress rehearsal veteran actor Arthur Deagon died after doing a series of handsprings across the stage. The company was concerned that the opening would have to be canceled because of the 56-year-old actor's death. But Cohan, in the best show-must-go-on tradition, declared that he would play the part. Cohan had not performed in a musical in 13 years, but he never lost his touch. *The Merry Malones* opened the next day out of town in Boston and was a smash. At Erlanger's it repeated the Boston success. Richard Watts summed up the proceedings, which contained "all of the materials that have made the Cohan name eminent—the flags, the sentiment, the hokum, the persistent kidding of the plot, the Irish-American family humor, all managed with the most skilled of showmanship."

The next hit at Erlanger's was the last musical that Cohan wrote: *Billie* (10/1/28; 112 performances). The show, although written only one year after *The Merry Malones*, seemed dated. Between the two shows, Broadway audiences had been introduced to *Show Boat*, the great musical that marked the direction in which musical comedy was heading. The critics enjoyed the show, but they did proclaim it as terribly old-fashioned.

Fine and Dandy (9/23/30; 246 performances) boasted a good score by one of Broadway's few female composers, Kay Swift, and her husband, Paul James. It included two hits, the title tune and "Can This Be Love." The cast included comedian Joe Cook, dancer Eleanor Powell, and future Hollywood restauranteur Dave Chasen.

Erlanger's empire began to crumble during the Depression, and he lost the theater. The Astor estate, owner of the land on which the Erlanger stood, took over the theater's operations and put in Lodewick Vroom as manager. On December 7, 1932, the theater's name was changed to the St. James, after a fa-

Erlanger's Theatre just prior to its opening in 1927.

supplied the lyrics. The show's other hit was James F. Hanley's "Zing Went the Strings of My Heart."

Operetta made a rare return to the New York stage with SIGMUND ROMBERG and OSCAR HAMMERSTEIN II's *May Wine* (12/5/35; 212 performances). Reviews were mixed, although all the CRITICS found something nice to say. John Anderson, writing in the *New York Journal*, summed up the response: "I found it somewhat dry, with too much body, as the vintners say, and not enough alcoholic content—nothing, in fact, to get intoxicated over or on. Though some of Prof. Romberg's tunes are gracefully stimulating, and it is all sung, said and dressed up in Mr. [Laurence] Schwab's accustomed lavish manner, *May Wine* crushes more than the grape."

John Gielgud's production of *Hamlet* moved to the St. James in January 1937 from the historic EMPIRE THEATER, where it concluded its 132-performance run. William Shakespeare continued to hold the St. James stage with the Margaret Webster production of *Richard II* (2/15/37; 132 performances), starring Maurice Evans. The drama opened 37 years after the previous American production. Surprisingly, audiences during the Depression were overjoyed to spend their evenings with *Richard II*, but the summer heat forced the production to close. Evans then undertook a nationwide tour of the play, but it was not as successful. Evans quoted one candy butcher (candy salesman) saying to

mous London theater. The first attraction under the new name was the revue *Walk a Little Faster* (12/7/32; 121 performances). Beatrice Lillie, Penny Singleton (Blondie in the movies), and the comedy team Bobby Clark and Paul McCullough appeared in the revue. The show's fine score was written by composer VERNON DUKE and lyricist E. Y. HARBURG. The smash hit from the show was "April in Paris." However, opening night at the St. James was a disaster. During the overture, the front curtain began its rise to the flies, but unfortunately the bottom of the drape caught on something on the stage floor. Still, the batten holding the curtain kept rising, pulling the curtain taut. The amazed audience watched the curtain stretch until a ripping sound was heard, the great swag of material tore away from the batten, and fell to the stage and over the orchestra pit. Still the band played on, despite the darkness of the muffled pit.

After short seasons of Gilbert and Sullivan and the Ballet Russe de Monte Carlo, Clark and McCullough returned to the St. James. Their new show was *Thumbs Up!* (12/27/34; 156 performances), with a score by a variety of songwriters. Again Vernon Duke came up with a hit, along the same lines as "April in Paris." The song was "Autumn in New York," and Duke also

St. James Theatre, early 1950s.

another, "Put away the Baby Ruths and Love Nests—this is a class show." Evans brought the play back to New York on April 1, 1940, for an additional 32 performances.

Before the return of *Richard II*, Evans essayed *Hamlet* (10/12/38; 96 performances) in another Margaret Webster–directed production. The play opened with Mady Christians, Katherine Locke, and Alexander Scourby completing the leads. The production was the first complete and uncut version of *Hamlet* to play in the United States. The curtain rose for the first act at 6:30 P.M. The act ran two hours, and the audiences had an hour intermission for dinner. The curtain rose again at 9:30 for acts 2 and 3, and finally fell for good at 11:15. The actual production took 3 hours and 38 minutes to perform. Still, the show was a success.

Two events surrounding this production surprised and even shocked Broadway regulars. In the first week a more traditional cut-down version of *Hamlet* was performed, but the uncut version was much more popular and the shorter version was no longer produced. The second surprise was the discovery that audiences would rather sit through the entire play without having a dinner break, so that break was taken out. The production was hailed by critics and audiences, but there was an understandably limited audience for Shakespeare, no matter how well presented. Margaret Webster suggested, with tongue in cheek, that the play be advertised as "Shakespeare's *Hamlet* in its entirety. Eight minutes shorter than *Gone with the Wind*." Evans would repeat the role on three successive occasions.

Evans continued his dominance of the St. James stage with Shakespeare's *Henry IV Part I* (1/30/39; 74 performances). The play received excellent reviews. Margaret Webster again directed, Edmund O'Brien starred in the title role, and Mady Christians appeared as Lady Percy. The production was successful for Shakespeare. Evans felt it would have run longer, but audiences didn't want to see him in bravura character roles but "in black silk tights." While Evans and company toured, the last edition of EARL CARROLL'S VANITIES (1/13/40; 25 performances) opened at the St. James. The show was a decided failure, supposedly marking the introduction of microphones to the Broadway stage.

Shakespeare returned with Maurice Evans in the THEATRE GUILD and Gilbert Miller production of *Twelfth Night* (11/19/40; 129 performances). Margaret Webster directed a distinguished cast, including Evans, Wesley Addy, HELEN HAYES, June Walker, and Sophie Stewart. Helen Hayes was by now 40 but was playing a teenage girl. Critics were unconcerned; they preferred to spar over her interpretation. Past Violas (her character) had emphasized the poetry in Shakespeare's writing, but Hayes decided to speak the lines in a conversational manner. The arguments over this interpretation continued until the play closed.

Richard Wright adapted his novel *Native Son* (3/24/41; 114 performances) for the stage, with the help of Paul Green. Orson Welles and John Houseman produced the venture. The production divided critics and theatergoers. The story is about the events following a black man's accidental murder of a white woman. William Randolph Hearst's *Journal American* labeled the play Communistic. *Time* magazine, the bastion of Henry Luce, dubbed it "the strongest play of the season." Welles received his fair share of accolades by the press. BROOKS ATKINSON wrote of Welles:

> When he applies the theatricalism of his personal nature to a stage problem something exciting comes into existence. The space and the sound of the theater, which are only partly used in ordinary productions, yield a fresh sensation. It is as if the theater had been shaken up and recharged with life.

The "boy wonder" was at once brilliant and mischievous. Although no one could figure out why, Welles insisted that among the stage props be a boy's sled upon which was written the word *Rosebud*. The play was produced in the same year that Welles' cinematic masterpiece *Citizen Kane* was released.

The Shubert brothers took over the St. James late in 1941 and presented as their first productions a repertory offering of the Boston Comic Opera Company and the Jooss Ballet Dance Theater. The offerings included a revival of *H.M.S. Pinafore* on January 21, 1942; *The Mikado* on February 3; *The Green Table* on February 10, followed by *The Big City* later that month; *Pirates of Penzance* and *The Prodigal Son* on February 17; *Iolanthe* on February 23; *Trial by Jury* on February 28; and finally *The Gondoliers* on March 3.

Next, the Theatre Guild presented the premiere of Philip Barry's play *Without Love* (11/10/42; 110 performances), which featured Katharine Hepburn, Elliott Nugent, and Audrey Christie. Its departure opened the way for the theater's most important production, *Oklahoma!* (3/31/43; 2,248 performances). The RODGERS AND HAMMERSTEIN musical, considered the apex of the art form at its opening, saved the Theatre Guild, which had had little luck with recent offerings. Hammerstein, too, was considered washed up until the premiere of *Oklahoma!*. The show also marked a turning point in the American musical theater. Its construction was followed zealously by lesser talents, and for a while it seemed that every Broadway show had to have two couples—one the love interest and one the comic relief—a dream ballet, a nontraditional chorus, and a homey, bucolic American setting. *Oklahoma!* became the model to which almost every musical aimed.

FRANK LOESSER, the brilliant composer and lyricist, adapted Brandon Thomas's *Charley's Aunt* into the musical comedy *Where's Charley?* (10/11/48; 792 performances). GEORGE ABBOTT, a champion of new talents, wrote the libretto and directed Loesser's first Broadway show. *Where's Charley?* opened with Broadway and Hollywood star Ray Bolger. Loesser gave him the evening's big hit song, "Once in Love with Amy," with which Bolger would forever be linked. Byron Palmer, Allyn Ann McLerie, and Doretta Morrow costarred in the delightful show. *Where's Charley?* proved an auspicious debut for Loesser, Broadway's most ambitious songwriter.

Richard Rodgers and Oscar Hammerstein returned to the St. James with their great musical, *The King and I* (3/29/51; 1,246 performances). Gertrude Lawrence starred as Anna, and Yul Brynner played the King. Doretta Morrow, previously in *Where's Charley?*, Dorothy Sarnoff, Larry Douglas, and Johnny Stewart were featured. The superb production was directed by John Van Druten, with choreography by the brilliant Jerome Robbins. The critics were nearly unanimous in their praise, although they felt that Rodgers and Hammerstein had broken no new ground. Actually, they had taken many risks in *The King and I*. Brooks Atkinson, writing in the *New York Times*, opined, "It is an original and beautiful excursion into the rich splendors of the Far East, done with impeccable taste by two artists and brought to life with a warm, romantic score, idiomatic lyrics and some exquisite dancing." Tragedy struck the production when Gertrude Lawrence died during the show's run.

George Abbott continued his introduction of new talents to Broadway with the musical comedy, *The Pajama Game* (5/13/54; 1,061 performances). Abbott co-authored the libretto with Broadway newcomer Richard Bissell. The charming, enthusiastic score was written by Richard Adler and Jerry Ross, marking their first collaboration on a book show. The show also marked the choreographic debut of Bob Fosse, one of the Broadway musical's most unique talents. The score contained two smash hits: "Hey There," which leading man John Raitt sang as a duet with himself (he accomplished this feat by singing the song into a Dictaphone), and the tango "Hernando's Hideaway." Janis Paige, Reta Shaw, Eddie Foy Jr., Carol Haney, Shirley MacLaine, and Peter Gennaro were also featured in the fine cast. The show was also producer HAROLD PRINCE's first production, in association with Frederick Brisson and Robert E. Griffith. *The Pajama Game* had the unique distinction of having a musical written about it, *Say, Darling*.

Johnny Mercer, one of Hollywood's best lyricists, collaborated with Gene de Paul on the score of the St. James' next show, *Li'l Abner* (11/15/56; 693 performances), based on the comic strip by Al Capp. Edith Adams and Peter Palmer starred as Daisy Mae and Abner, Stubby Kaye as Marryin' Sam, and Howard St. John as General Bullmoose. The score was one of the funniest and most high-spirited in Broadway history. The lyrics successfully straddled the line between satire and sincerity. The denizens of Dogpatch were really just disguised characters out of black vaudeville. Michael Kidd's choreography was among the most athletic ever seen on Broadway.

The Shuberts were forced by the federal government to divest themselves of many of their Broadway holdings, and the St. James was included in the judgment. The Jujamcyn Organization bought the theater's lease, as well as those of several other former Shubert properties. The new owners of the building, Scarborough House, Inc., hired designer Frederick Fox to completely redo the theater. The interior was reduced to a shell, and the public areas were completely redesigned.

The theater reopened on December 1, 1958, with a hit show, Rodgers and Hammerstein's *Flower Drum Song* (600 performances). Hollywood star Gene Kelly directed the proceedings, with Hammerstein and Joseph Fields (*see* FIELDS FAMILY) contributing the libretto. *Flower Drum Song*, starring Larry Blyden, Pat Suzuki, Miyoshi Umeki, Patrick Adiarte, Juanita Hall, Ed Kenney, and Keye Luke, was not as successful as some of the team's past offerings. However, even second-rate Rodgers and Hammerstein was better than most musicals.

On May 9, 1960, Carol Burnett and her star-making musical, *Once upon a Mattress*, moved to the St. James as a big hit. The score was written by lyricist Marshall Barer and Richard Rodgers' daughter, Mary Rodgers. The book was written by Jay Thompson and Dean Fuller. *Once upon a Mattress*, an alternately sweet and zany retelling of the fairy tale *The Princess and the Pea*, eventually ran for 460 performances. Next up at the St. James, Laurence Olivier and Anthony Quinn opened in Jean Anouilh's drama *Becket* (10/5/60; 193 performances) before it was made into a hit motion picture.

Composer JULE STYNE and lyricists COMDEN AND GREEN provided the scores for the next two shows at the St. James. The first was a Phil Silvers and Nancy Walker vehicle, *Do Re Mi* (1/26/60; 400 performances). The show opened with DAVID MERRICK producing and Garson Kanin directing and writing the libretto. The score was excellent and wide in scope. "Make Someone Happy" was the popular hit, but the rest of the score was more adventurous and much underrated. John Reardon and Nancy Dussault provided the love interest.

Sydney Chaplin (Charlie's son), Carol Lawrence, Phyllis Newman (Adolph Green's wife), and Orson

Bean starred in Styne, Comden, and Green's second show at the St. James, David Merrick's production of *Subways Are for Sleeping* (12/27/61; 205 performances). The show was a typically jovial romp in the best traditions of the team's work together. The fine score had its expected hit, "Comes Once in a Lifetime." The rest of the score was equally bright and witty and, most important, theatrical.

IRVING BERLIN, perhaps the greatest songwriter in American history, left Broadway with a lackluster show, *Mr. President* (10/20/62; 265 performances). Robert Ryan and Nanette Fabray tried to enliven the proceedings, but the show was clearly in trouble. The play owed more to television sitcoms than theater, and its sentimentality and patriotism seemed out of date. *Mr. President* opened with the largest advance in Broadway history until then, thanks to the Berlin name.

Hello, Dolly! (1/16/64; 2,844 performances) was the next show to open at the St. James, and it proved to be an amazing phenomenon. Carol Channing's miraculous performance and JERRY HERMAN's stirring score propelled the show forward in the best Broadway style. Professionalism and slickness were rampant on the stage, if depth and emotion were not—an apt appraisal of all Gower Champion–directed shows.

After a 40-year absence Shakespeare returned to the St. James. With *Two Gentlemen of Verona* (12/1/71; 614 performances), Galt MacDermot set Shakespeare's words to music, with lyrics by playwright John Guare. The musical starred Raul Julia, Clifton Davis, Jonelle Allen, Diana Davila, and John Bottoms. It proved to be a controversial show, beating out *Follies* for the best musical TONY AWARD.

A string of failures, including a 25th-anniversary revival of *My Fair Lady*, ran at the St. James through the mid-1970s. Comden and Green broke the jinx with *On the Twentieth Century* (2/19/78; 460 performances). Cy Coleman provided a complex score for this musical. The show joined STEPHEN SONDHEIM's *Follies* and *Company* as one of the best musicals of the 1970s. All three shows were directed by Harold Prince. *On the Twentieth Century* starred Madeline Kahn (replaced soon after the opening by Judy Kaye in a stunning debut), Kevin Kline, John Cullum, and Imogene Coca. Another important feature of the show was the exemplary production, especially Robin Wagner's superb set. Many theater historians consider *On the Twentieth Century* to be the last great American musical comedy.

Barnum (4/30/80; 854 performances), starring Jim Dale, enjoyed a 2-year run, with Cy Coleman and Michael Stewart's rousing score. However, more failures followed *Barnum*, until *My One and Only* (3/1/83; 767 performances) opened at the theater. Tommy Tune and

Twiggy starred in the new musical, which used songs by GEORGE AND IRA GERSHWIN. The whole affair was charming, stylish, and fun.

Tyne Daly, a well-known television actress, turned her attention and career toward the stage with a revival of *Gypsy* (11/16/89; 476 performances). The production moved to the MARQUIS THEATER to make room for *The Secret Garden* (4/25/91; 709 performances). Pop songwriter Lucy Simon provided the music, and playwright Marsha Norman wrote the lyrics and libretto. The show was a hit with the family crowd, due in large part to the performance of Mandy Patinkin. Another actor who received critical accolades was John Cameron Mitchell. He would later write and appear in the off-Broadway production *Hedwig and the Angry Inch*.

Des McAnuff directed a stage version of The Who's rock album *Tommy* (4/22/93; 899 performances) at the St. James. The show's stars were the score and the elaborate scenic effects by John Arnone. Baby boomers flocked to the theater to catch a bit of their youth, and Gen-Xers came to discover the roots of rock and roll when it still had a hint of anarchy.

A revival of Stephen Sondheim's *A Funny Thing Happened on the Way to the Forum* (4/18/96; 715 performances) opened at the St. James and kept audiences in stitches with its brilliant cast headed by Nathan Lane. Also noteworthy were the performances of Lewis J. Stadlen, Mark Linn-Baker, Ernie Sabella, and Jim Stanek. Even the understudies were equal to the comic demands—most noteworthy was Kenneth Kantor.

Three fast flops followed. *High Society* (4/27/98; 144 performances) was an inept theatricalization of the COLE PORTER film. *The Civil War* (4/22/99; 61 performances) was Frank Wildhorn's decidedly ersatz take on what could have been a moving reflection on an especially tragic period of American history. Instead, it was neither a real musical nor a concert. It was simply a bunch of songs strung together with minimal scenery, plot, or artistic merit. *Swing!* (12/9/99; 461 performances) might have fit more comfortably on a cruise ship, but it did boast the talents of Anne Hampton Callaway and Laura Benati. The extremely inventive (if emotionally bereft) choreography was by Lynn Taylor Corbett. The revue succeeded in what it tried to do—entertain with high energy—but Broadway audiences demanded more: a set and characters and style.

Mel Brooks and Thomas Meehan began the new millennium with a bang with their adaptation of Brooks' classic film comedy *The Producers* (4/19/2002). The show became almost legendary from its first performance, becoming the hottest ticket on Broadway. The exceptional cast included Nathan Lane, Matthew Broderick, Brad Oscar, Gary Beach,

Cady Huffman, and Roger Bart. Broadway audiences were more than ready to welcome old-fashioned musical comedy back to the Main Stem. And the show certainly delivered on all fronts. True, the score was a little simplistic, but it served its purpose.

SAM H. HARRIS THEATER. *See* **Harris Theater.**

SAM S. SHUBERT FOUNDATION AWARD. This award has been presented since 1954 by the Shubert Foundation "in recognition of the most outstanding individual contribution to the New York theatrical season." Past winners have included Victor Borge (the first recipient), DAVID MERRICK, GEORGE ABBOTT, and Roger L. Stevens.

SAM S. SHUBERT THEATRE. 225 W. 44th Street. Architect: Henry B. Herts. Opening: c. September 29, 1913; Forbes-Robertson Repertory Company.

When Sam Shubert died on May 12, 1905, as a result of injuries suffered in a train crash, his devoted brother Lee (*see* SHUBERT BROTHERS) vowed to build a theater in his honor in every city in the country. Each of the Sam Shubert theaters would have a picture of Sam hanging in its lobby. Lee fulfilled at least part of his vow when the Sam S. Shubert Theatre opened in New York with the Forbes-Robertson Repertory Company. There is some disagreement about the actual date of the opening: Louis Botto's *At This Theater* lists the opening as October 2, 1913; George Freedley's *Biographical Encyclopedia and Who's Who of the American Theatre* lists the opening as September 29, 1913; Jerry Stagg's *The Brothers Shubert* lists the opening as October 28, 1913; in the appendix of all Shubert productions, Stagg lists the opening as September 3, 1913. Whatever the opening date, the theater was a great success.

The Venetian Renaissance interior was designed by O. H. Bauer. Its 1,400 seats all afforded a clear view of the stage, and its paneled walls lent an air of refinement. Lee Shubert called the new theater "a temple of dramatic art" and "a place of beauty and dedication." He had offices built on the second floor overlooking 44th Street and the new Shubert Alley, as well as a private apartment. At the time that the Shubert and the BOOTH THEATRE were constructed, New York zoning regulations required all theaters to have alleys attached to their side exits. The shared sidewalls of the Shubert and Booth and the back of the ASTOR HOTEL formed Shubert Alley.

After their production of *A Thousand Years Ago* (1/6/14; 87 performances), the Shuberts opened their first

musical at the theater, *The Belle of Bond Street* (3/30/14; 48 performances), based on the English musical *The Girl from Kay's*. Interpolated into the score was the Fred Fisher and Alfred Bryan song "Who Paid the Rent for Mrs. Rip Van Winkle When Rip Van Winkle Was Away." Franz Lehar's *Alone at Last* (10/14/15; 180 performances) was the theater's first big hit. The show starred Jose Collins and John Charles Thomas. A bigger hit was JEROME KERN's *Love o' Mike* (1/15/17; 192 performances), with lyrics by HARRY B. SMITH; Clifton Webb and Peggy Wood starred.

Maytime (8/16/17; 492 performances) had music by SIGMUND ROMBERG and book and lyrics by Rida Johnson Young. The show starred William Norris, Peggy Wood, and Charles Purcell. For the first and last time in Broadway history, a second company of a hit musical was presented at the same time as the original. The second company played across the street from the Shubert at the 44TH STREET THEATRE. *Maytime* contained one of Romberg and Young's most enduring songs, "Will You Remember," known better as "Sweetheart."

Sometime (10/4/18; 283 performances), a RUDOLF FRIML and Rida Johnson Young musical, was produced by ARTHUR HAMMERSTEIN with the somewhat unlikely team of Mae West, Ed Wynn, and dramatic actress Francine Larrimore. West took the opportunity to introduce the shimmy to Broadway. *Good Morning, Judge* (2/6/19; 140 performances) was a British musical by Lionel Monckton and Howard Talbot. The show was Americanized, and two songs by GEORGE GERSHWIN and Irving Caesar were added. Romberg and Frederic Arnold Kummer wrote *The Magic Melody* (11/11/19; 143 performances), which starred Charles Purcell and Flavia Arcaro.

The Shubert hosted a number of revues in the 1920s at this theater. *The Greenwich Village Follies* (8/31/21; 167 performances), the first edition of the show appearing on Broadway, was staged by JOHN MURRAY ANDERSON. This third edition starred Ted Lewis, Irene Franklin, and Peggy Hope. The next edition opened on September 12, 1922, with Savoy and Brennan, John Hazzard, and Carl Randall. Two years later, after a sojourn at the WINTER GARDEN THEATRE, the *Greenwich Village Follies* returned to the Shubert, opening on September 16, 1924. This time, the score was written by COLE PORTER. None of the songs became standards. The Dolly Sisters, Georgie Hale, Moran and Mack, and Vincent Lopez and his orchestra were featured. The 1924 edition ran 131 performances. The final edition to appear at the Shubert Theatre opened on March 15, 1926, and played 180 performances. The show was a revision of the previous year's edition, which had wowed 'em at the Winter Garden.

More revues followed at the Shubert. *Artists and Models* (8/20/23; 312 performances) was a Shubert-produced revué series. The slightly risqué show was the first of the American revues to emulate the *Folies Bergère* (*see* HELEN HAYES THEATER), and it was also the first show on Broadway to feature topless chorines. Frank Fay starred in the show, along with Grace Hamilton and Harry Kelly. Five more editions of the series appeared on Broadway, although none at the Shubert. *Vogues of 1924* (3/27/24; 114 performances) starred Fred Allen, May Boley, Odette Myrtil, Jimmy Savo, and J. Harold Murray. The title indicates that the Shuberts hoped the show might prove popular enough to spin off into an annual series. Usually Lee attended to the brothers' finances (his office adjoined the vault) and J.J. stuck to the artistic slate. On this occasion J.J. was on an extended trip to Europe, so Lee decided to show his brother up and mount his own musical production, *Vogues of 1924*.

A musical, *The Magnolia Lady* (11/25/24; 49 performances), was not a success, despite the talents of Ruth Chatterton, Skeets Gallagher, and Ralph Forbes. The Shuberts presented *Gay Paree* (8/18/25; 181 performances) at the Shubert with Chic Sale, Jack Haley, and Winnie Lightner. As with many Shubert shows, the hit song was interpolated into the score. *Gay Paree's* hit was "I Can't Believe That You're in Love with Me," by Jimmy McHugh and Clarence Gaskill. The majority of the score was written by ALFRED GOODMAN, Clifford Grey, and Harold Atteridge. The next year a new edition opened at the Winter Garden.

The Shuberts were firm believers in the power of operettas. They insisted on producing them long after the form had gone out of favor. When *Countess Maritza* (9/18/26; 321 performances) opened, however, theatergoers found they could still enjoy this old-fashioned musical entertainment. The musical starred Harry K. Morton, Carl Randall, and Yvonne D'Arle. Emmerich Kalman and Harry B. Smith supplied the score, which featured the hit song "Play Gypsies, Dance Gypsies." Another musical, *A Night in Venice* (5/21/29; 175 performances), followed. It starred Ted Healy and not one but two troupes of dancing girls, the Allan K. Foster Girls and the Chester Hale Girls. Ranks of women dancing in unison were a staple of 1920s and '30s musicals. The choreographer of *A Night in Venice* later took the idea of a corps of synchronized dancers and translated his steps to Hollywood; he was Busby Berkeley.

Everybody's Welcome (10/13/31; 127 performances) starred Ann Pennington, Oscar Shaw, Ann Sothern (then named Harriette Lake), Frances Williams, and the band of Tommy and Jimmy Dorsey. Sammy Fain and Irving Kahal were responsible for most of the score, but again an interpolated song proved to be the classic. "As Time Goes By," composed by Herman Hupfeld, first appeared in the musical. Surprisingly, the song did not achieve much attention until it was used in the movie *Casablanca*.

Another revue, the last of 3 in a series, was *Americana* (10/5/32; 77 performances). The show contained a song that became the unofficial anthem of the Depression: "Brother Can You Spare a Dime?" composed by Jay Gorney and with lyrics by E. Y. HARBURG. *Americana* is also noteworthy as the first Broadway show to offer a serious ballet. Modern dancer Charles Weidman was the choreographer, but the show's lack of success (and the success of "Brother Can You Spare a Dime?") overshadowed his efforts. The score contained some other songs that later achieved some renown. These included "Satan's Li'l Lamb," by HAROLD ARLEN, Harburg, and Johnny Mercer; "Woud'ja for a Big Red Apple?" by Henry Souvaine and Mercer; and "Five Minutes of Spring," by Gorney and Harburg.

Suddenly a spate of straight plays opened at the Shubert. The first was Sidney Howard's *Dodsworth* (2/24/34; 147 performances). Walter Huston, Maria Ouspenskaya, Fay Bainter, and Nan Sunderland starred. *Dodsworth* closed and then reopened on August 20, 1934, for an additional 170 performances. Next came Robert E. Sherwood's antiwar drama *Idiot's Delight* (3/24/36; 120 performances). The play won the PULITZER PRIZE for drama. It reopened at the Shubert on August 31, 1936, and continued for an additional 179 performances. LUNT AND FONTANNE starred in the THEATER GUILD production. Dudley Digges, Margo, Henry Hull, and Leo G. Carroll opened in Maxwell Anderson's *The Masque of Kings* (2/8/37; 89 performances), a failure.

Musical comedy, and a lighter air, returned to the Shubert with RODGERS AND HART's smash hit musical *Babes in Arms* (4/14/37; 289 performances). Audiences heard for the first time such future classic songs as "I Wish I Were in Love Again," "Where or When," "The Lady Is a Tramp," "My Funny Valentine," and "Johnny One Note." George Balanchine contributed the choreography for a show in which dance played a role equal to the score. The young and able cast included Alfred Drake, Mitzi Green, Ray Heatherton, Wynn Murray, the Nicholas Brothers, and Robert Rounseville—all immensely talented performers.

S. N. Behrman's *Amphitryon 38* (11/1/37; 152 performances), based on French playwright Jean Giraudoux's original, starred the Lunts. The day after the Theater Guild production opened, Behrman took Giraudoux to the Shubert to see the play. The show had received raves, and the theater was packed. In Paris Giraudoux's play had played to an audience of 300. When Behrman took the playwright into the Shubert with its 697 orchestra seats, all full, Giradoux was thunderstruck. "Is there another room?" he asked. Behrman nodded and took the Frenchman upstairs to the balcony, where another 762 patrons sat. Giradoux seemed upset. Behrman asked why he seemed so distressed at seeing 1,300 seats packed with enthusiastic theatergoers. Giradoux asked the price of tickets, and Behrman figured that the weekly gross would come to $24,000. Giradoux looked even sadder and commented, "I shall have difficulty with my income tax." *Amphitryon 38* made Giradoux very wealthy. The play opened with Jupiter and Mercury looking down from the clouds onto the mortals below.

The next offering at the Shubert also had a celestial theme. The title *I Married an Angel* (5/11/38; 338 performances) was meant to be taken literally. The angel was played by ballerina Vera Zorina, ably supported by Audrey Christie, Charles Walters, Dennis King, Vivienne Segal, and Walter Slezak. The score was up to Rodgers and Hart's excellent standards, although only "I'll Tell the Man in the Street" and "Spring Is Here" achieved any renown.

The Theatre Guild had a huge hit with Philip Barry's *The Philadelphia Story* (3/28/39; 417 performances). Katharine Hepburn enjoyed her greatest stage success in the comedy of manners. *The Philadelphia Story* opened at the Shubert and saved the Theatre Guild, which was then $60,000 in debt. Barry's almost admiring denunciation of the shallowness of the rich illustrated that even the most limited person can have a soul if you dig deep enough. *The Philadelphia Story* also starred Joseph Cotten, Shirley Booth, and Van Heflin.

Rodgers and Hart returned to the Shubert with *Higher and Higher* (4/4/40; 84 performances). The elements for success all seemed to be in place: a cast including Shirley Ross (returning from Hollywood), Marta Eggerth, Jack Haley, Leif Erickson, Robert Rounseville, and Sharkey the Seal; a libretto by JOSHUA LOGAN and Gladys Hurlbut, and direction by Logan; and a hit tune in "It Never Entered My Mind." However, the show, an *Upstairs Downstairs* type of comedy, was a failure.

The Shuberts' next offering, *Hold on to Your Hats* (9/11/40; 158 performances), was also a failure, but for different reasons. It opened with AL JOLSON making a Broadway comeback, ably assisted by the hilarious Martha Raye. Jack Whiting, Gil Lamb, and Jinx Falkenburg were also in the cast. The score, by BURTON LANE and E. Y. Harburg, contained the hit "There's a Great Day Coming Mañana." The reviewers raved about the show. Brooks Atkinson said the show was "one of the funniest musical plays that have stumbled onto Broadway for years. Hold your sides as tightly as the title directs you to hold your hat." But Jolson

was unhappy. He was constrained by the libretto and frequently threw it away completely, to the delight of audiences and the chagrin of his fellow cast members. At one point during the proceedings, Jolson decided to give the audience an extra free show at the end of the curtain call, a favorite trick of his. The audience, of course, ate it up, and the cast stayed onstage and had a good time also. The only person in the theater not having a ball with the bonus concert was George Jessel, who had a date with one of the chorus girls. As Jolson continued running through his hits, Jessel grew more and more impatient. Finally he could stand it no more. Jessel bounded on stage, took his girlfriend by the hand, and left the theater. Jolson was also undergoing a messy divorce from Ruby Keeler, who had walked out of both the show and Jolson's life in Chicago, to be replaced by Eunice Healy. To top it all off, Jolson caught pneumonia. Without its star, *Hold on to Your Hats* had to close.

Two notable revivals next occupied the Shubert's stage. KATHARINE CORNELL, Raymond Massey, Bramwell Fletcher, and Clarence Derwent appeared in George Bernard Shaw's *The Doctor's Dilemma* (3/11/41; 112 performances). Richard Brinsley Sheridan's 18th-century comedy *The Rivals* (1/14/42; 54 performances) starred Mary Boland, Helen Ford, Bobby Clark, and Walter Hampden. Then Rodgers and Hart's *By Jupiter* (6/3/42; 427 performances), their last full score, opened with Ray Bolger, Ronald Graham, Benay Venuta, and Vera-Ellen. The musical, sadly, contains one of the team's most neglected scores. Ray Bolger left the show to join the armed services, and the show closed.

Mae West returned to Broadway in the Mike Todd and Shuberts' co-production of the actress' play *Catherine Was Great* (8/2/44; 191 performances). West opened to less-than-great reviews. Louis Kronenberger, writing in *P.M.*, reflected his colleagues' opinions when he titled his review "Mae West Slips on the Steppes." However, a later headline in *VARIETY*, during the show's national tour, summed up the New York run best: "Critics cold but b.o. hot."

Harold Arlen and E. Y. Harburg enjoyed one of their greatest successes with *Bloomer Girl* (10/5/44; 657 performances), a delightful musical comedy with serious overtones. The show told the story of a follower of early feminist Dolly Bloomer, with a subplot concerning the Underground Railroad. Celeste Holm starred along with David Brooks, Joan McCracken, Mabel Taliaferro, and Dooley Wilson as a runaway slave. *Bloomer Girl* made powerful statements about human rights in a most entertaining way. The Arlen and Harburg score contained one standard, "Right as the Rain." There was also a powerful song for Dooley Wilson, "The Eagle and Me." The rest of the score was equally rich and dynamic. Agnes de Mille choreographed a classic number, "The Civil War Ballet," for the production.

A revival of VICTOR HERBERT's operetta *Sweethearts* (1/21/47; 288 performances) was a surprise hit, with Marjorie Gateson and Bobby Clark in the leads. Revivals were relatively rare on Broadway (between *The Boy Friend* and *No, No Nanette*, 16 years would pass without one revival produced for Broadway). *Anne of the Thousand Days* (12/8/48; 288 performances), by Maxwell Anderson, was a drama about Anne Bolyn and King Henry VIII. It starred Joyce Redman and Rex Harrison.

The Lunts returned with playwright S. N. Behrman's *I Know My Love* (11/2/49; 246 performances). The plot followed the romantic life of a couple from their youth to their 80s. The Lunts, celebrating their 25th anniversary onstage, saw the play as a parable of their own lives. The production was an adaptation of Marcel Achard's *Auprès de Ma Blonde*.

LERNER AND LOEWE wrote *Paint Your Wagon* (11/12/51; 289 performances), a story set against the California gold rush. The score had two hits: "I Talk to the Trees" and "They Call the Wind Maria." James Barton, Tony Bavaar, and Olga San Juan starred. It would be the team's second hit show. Katharine Hepburn returned to Broadway and the Shuberts' stage in Shaw's *The Millionairess* (10/17/52; 84 performances), with Cyril Ritchard. Rex Harrison returned in *The Love of Four Colonels* (1/15/53; 141 performances), by Peter Ustinov; his co-star was his wife, Lilli Palmer.

RODGERS AND HAMMERSTEIN slipped with *Pipe Dream* (11/30/55; 246 performances), their musicalization of John Steinbeck's novel *Sweet Thursday*. The show opened with Mike Kellin, Helen Traubel, Louise Troy, Judy Tyler, and William Johnson. *Pipe Dream* had a disappointing run, and many critics wondered if the team had lost its touch.

The Shubert's next show, the Theatre Guild musical *Bells Are Ringing* (11/29/56; 924 performances), was a happy hit with its lead Judy Holliday. JULE STYNE and COMDEN AND GREEN concocted a delightful show with an alternately poignant and funny score. The hit songs included "Just in Time" and "The Party's Over." The strong, well-integrated score was well served by Holliday's co-stars Sydney Chaplin, Eddie Lawrence, and Jean Stapleton.

Bob Merrill wrote the music and lyrics to the musicalization of EUGENE O'NEILL's *Ah, Wilderness*, titled *Take Me Along* (10/22/59; 448 performances). DAVID MERRICK presented Jackie Gleason, Robert Morse, Eileen Herlie, Walter Pidgeon, and Una Merkel. *Take Me Along* had a small hit with its title song, although "Staying Young" was the best song in the score. The

show closed shortly after Gleason left and was replaced by William Bendix.

HAROLD ROME's last full-scale Broadway musical was *I Can Get It for You Wholesale* (3/22/62; 300 performances). The David Merrick production made history when, on opening night, a star was born. Her name was Barbra Streisand; although she had only a small role as Miss Marmelstein, a secretary, she stopped the show. Her co-stars included Marilyn Cooper, Harold Lang, Sheree North, and Lilian Roth. The nominal star of the show was Elliott Gould, whom Streisand soon married.

Anthony Newley starred in David Merrick's production *Stop the World—I Want to Get Off* (10/3/62; 556 performances), which he also wrote with Leslie Bricusse. The score contained the standards "Gonna Build a Mountain," "What Kind of Fool Am I," and "Once in a Lifetime." Newley and his co-star Anna Quayle handled the superior score well. Meredith Willson, author of *The Music Man*, fared less well with his musicalization of *Miracle on 34th Street*, which he entitled *Here's Love* (10/3/63; 334 performances). The show opened with Craig Stevens and Janis Paige in the leads.

The Apple Tree (10/18/66; 443 performances) was the name of BOCK AND HARNICK's evening of three one-act musicals. Jerome Coopersmith and the songwriters wrote the libretti based on Mark Twain's *The Diary of Adam and Eve*, Frank Stockton's *The Lady or the Tiger*, and Jules Feiffer's *Passionella*. The evening was wittily directed by Mike Nichols and brilliantly performed by Barbara Harris, Larry Blyden, and Alan Alda.

Golden Rainbow (2/4/68; 385 performances) was ostensibly a musicalization of Arnold Schulman's play *A Hole in the Head*, but the critics announced that it was more like a glorified nightclub show put on by its stars, Steve Lawrence and Eydie Gorme. Walter Marks wrote a good score with a smash hit song: "I've Got to Be Me." NEIL SIMON's musical *Promises, Promises* (12/1/68; 1,281 performances) boasted a score by Broadway newcomers Burt Bacharach and Hal David and was brilliantly orchestrated by Jonathan Tunick. David Merrick's production proved to be one of the greatest successes of the 1960s. Jerry Orbach, Jill O'Hara, Ken Howard, and Marian Mercer led the cast. The musical was based on Billy Wilder's film *The Apartment*. *Promises, Promises* contained a big hit song: "I'll Never Fall in Love Again."

Tunick again supplied excellent orchestrations to a very different score that consisted only of waltzes. The show was STEPHEN SONDHEIM's *A Little Night Music* (2/25/73; 601 performances), with one of the musical theater's greatest songs, "Send in the Clowns." Hugh Wheeler based his libretto on Ingmar Bergman's film

Smiles of a Summer Night. HAROLD PRINCE's adroit producing and directing, and the fine performances by Glynis Johns, Len Cariou, Laurence Guittard, Patricia Elliott, and Hermione Gingold, equaled one of the show's greatest assets, Boris Aronson's brilliant settings.

Two plays occupied the Shubert's stage in 1975. Edward Albee's *Seascape* (1/26/75; 65 performances) opened with Deborah Kerr, Barry Nelson, and Frank Langella. It won the Pulitzer prize a year after it closed. The second play of the year was a revival of Somerset Maugham's *The Constant Wife*, with Ingrid Bergman.

The next tenant at the Shubert Theatre made Broadway history, eventually becoming the longest-running show at that time. The show was *A Chorus Line*, a transfer from Joseph Papp's Public Theater. *A Chorus Line* moved to Broadway on July 25, 1975, with a cast that included Carole Bishop, Priscilla Lopez, Robert LuPone, Donna McKechnie, Thommie Walsh, and Sammy Williams. The show was an unusual success. Its score by Marvin Hamlisch and Edward Kleban contained but one hit song, "What I Did for Love." The book was by James Kirkwood and Nicholas Dante. The Pulitzer prize–winning show's tremendous success was laid at the feet of director-choreographer Michael Bennett, a true genius. Unfortunately, *A Chorus Line* outlived two of its creators, Bennett and Kleban. It closed on April 28, 1990, after 6,137 performances.

The Buddy Holly story was told in the appropriately titled *Buddy* (11/4/90; 225 performances). A smash hit in London, running for more than 10 years, the show closed on Broadway a flop. Paul Hipp repeated his West End performance for the American production.

George and Ira Gershwin's *Girl Crazy* was refashioned into the new musical *Crazy for You* (2/19/92; 1,622 performances). Ken Ludwig wrote a new book that was just as clunky as the original. Susan Stroman choreographed, and Mike Ockrent directed. Purists were mildly amused, but "hix from the stix" ate it up.

Big (4/28/96; 193 performances) was based on the beloved Tom Hanks film of the same name. Despite a winning score by Richard Maltby Jr. and David Shire, however, and fine performances by Daniel H. Jenkins, John Cypher, Patrick Levis, Brett Tabisel, Barbara Walsh, and Frank Vlastnik, *Big* was not so.

The Shubert's next tenant, *Chicago*, moved in on Februray 11, 1997, a transfer from the RICHARD RODGERS THEATER.

SARDI'S RESTAURANT. 234 W. 44th Street. Sardi's is the preeminent theater restaurant. It hosts most Broadway opening-night parties, a tradition that

Eugenia, Vincent Jr., and Vincent Sardi Sr. in their restaurant.

began with the opening of *Come Back Little Sheba* on February 15, 1950.

The restaurant was opened in May 1921 down the block from its present location. It moved to the new building in 1927. Vincent Sardi Sr. and his wife, Eugenia, worked at the Bartholdi Inn prior to opening the restaurant. As Vincent Sardi Jr. recalls,

> When my parents, who came from Italy, opened the first restaurant—where the St. James Theatre is now—this area was all theaters, and there were some theatrical hotels or boarding houses.
>
> "The Shuberts, who owned most of the theaters and produced most of the shows, built the building we're in. It was only supposed to be three stories high at first, but old J. J. Shubert wanted a penthouse for himself, so it became an 11-story building.

Sardi's interior is dominated by the hundreds of caricatures of famous theatrical persons that line the wall. Vincent Sardi Jr. explains,

> It started quite innocently. There was a group of men who used to meet here regularly for lunch. Called themselves the Cheese Club. Alex Gard was one of them, and he'd be drawing pictures of the other members as they talked or argued, or whatever. He'd give them out, or tack them to the wall when the meeting was over. Someone suggested to my father that he have them framed and hung—maybe get Alex to do some of the other patrons.

Alex agreed. His pay was two meals a day, six days a week, and Dad would own the pictures. Their contract said Gard was not allowed to complain about the food, and Dad would not complain about the pictures.

The contract was signed in 1929. When Sardi's became famous for the pictures and Gard's fame grew, the artist refused to change the agreement. He continued supplying the drawings in exchange for meals. Upon Gard's death, he was succeeded by Don Bevan, also known as the playwright of *Stalag 17*. Bevan was in turn replaced by Richard Baratz.

Vincent Sardi Jr. served as an apprentice in Sardi's kitchens following his graduation from Columbia University in 1937. After an 18-month apprenticeship he became the restaurant's host and captain. In 1946, following a stint in the Marine Corps, he took over the management of the restaurant. In 1937 James Molinski also began work at Sardi's, as a glass washer, and worked his way up to host and dining room manager. He remained at his post just inside Sardi's front door until he retired in 1980. Molinski was known for his good humor and paternal relationship with many of the actors whose careers he followed.

The late 1930s was Sardi's golden age. Hatcheck girl Renee Carroll worked in the restaurant from the late 1930s through the '40s. During slack times she would read scripts that had been checked by playwrights and producers. On presentation of their checks, they got not only their apparel but also a critique of their plays. Carroll's judgment was usually sound and was proved right by the box office once the plays were produced. Soon she began receiving scripts even in the summer, when there was nothing to check. Once an especially poor playwright wrote the amateur critic, asking if he could send her his script because he was too impoverished to eat at Sardi's. Carroll replied that the play, a Western, was probably not a good idea anyway. A far better idea would be a story about a hatcheck girl who reads scripts. She even offered to help in the research—for a third of the royalties.

In 1946 Vincent Sardi Sr. turned over control of Sardi's to his son, who recalled:

My father was really just burnt out. The restaurant never showed a profit during prohibition because we weren't a speakeasy, and then there was the Depression, and when the restaurant finally started coming around, so did the war, and trying to run a restaurant during the war was tough. It took its toll on him, so when I returned he offered to let me buy him out, which I did over a number of years. I replaced my father in the dining room, but it took three men to replace my mother, who ran the kitchen—a buyer, an issuing steward, and a kitchen manager. She was quite a gal.

Sardi's hasn't changed much since the son took over management of the restaurant. Two rooms, the Eugenia

on the fourth floor and the Belasco on the third floor, host receptions and special events. The ground-floor bar, once known as "the tiniest bar in town," has been expanded and is a popular meeting space. And upstairs, the second-floor dining room, once considered Siberia, has been enlivened by workers from the nearby *New York Times*.

Vincent Sardi has no plans to change the ambiance of the room. "It took us a long time to arrive at this scheme and there's no way I'm ever going to change it. The lighting is particularly amazing. It's very flattering."

In 1986 Sardi's was sold to Broadway speculators Harvey Klaris and Ivan Bloch and restaurateur Stuart Lichtenstein. The price of the sale was reputed to be $6 million. Vincent Sardi Jr. was to continue as a consultant for at least 5 years. But in 1991 Lichtenstein declared bankruptcy and Vincent Sardi Jr., who was owed more than $6 million, regained control of the family business along with his partner Max Klimavicius.

Although the food is mainly undistinguished, the prices are high, and most of Broadway's new generation prefer the more intimate theater restaurants like Joe Allen's, J.R.'s, Barrymore's, and Sam's, Sardi's remains in most people's minds as the quintessential theater restaurant. It even features a special actor's menu with reduced prices for members of the profession. RICHARD MANEY, the great publicist, called Sardi's "the club, mess hall, lounge, post office, saloon, and market place of the people of the theater."

SAVE THE THEATERS. Save the Theaters was an organization at the forefront of the movement to preserve the Broadway theater buildings, the companies that service the theater industry, as well as the unique atmosphere of the theater district. It was started in 1978–79 as a committee of ACTORS' EQUITY in response to the impending demolition of the MOROSCO, HELEN HAYES, and BIJOU theaters for what are now the Marriott Marquis Hotel and MARQUIS THEATER. After those theaters came down in March 1982, the community realized that the rest of the Broadway theaters were also in danger of city development policies. Those concerned realized that some organization was necessary to make sure that what happened to the Helen Hayes, Morosco, and Bijou theaters didn't happen again.

Save the Theaters had a variety of other programs concentrating on space problems off and off-off Broadway, including the rest of the country. Chris Hagedorn of Save the Theaters explains the organization's philosophy:

We're not trying to preserve theaters as empty artifacts. But I think theater is a cyclical business. Tearing them down is not an answer. There was a season maybe ten or fifteen years ago when there were only ten shows on Broadway. If we had torn all those empty theaters down, where would the shows we have today go? We're not here to subsidize theaters during bad seasons. If you're in the theater business you know that plays don't always succeed and your theaters may be dark. There are certain things that we've recommended that can be done for the theaters such as tax abatements during dark periods.

The battle to protect the remaining Broadway theaters pitted Save the Theaters against the three major Broadway theater owners: the Shubert Organization, the Nederlander Group, and Jujamcyn Theaters, which together own 31 of the 35 Broadway theaters. In December 1985 the first three theaters, the AMBASSADOR, the NEIL SIMON, and the VIRGINIA were approved for landmark designation by New York City's Preservation Commission. In an unusually united front, the theater owners tried to reverse the designations of the three theaters and to postpone any further action by the commission for a year. This last-ditch effort failed because the theater owners never had enough votes to bring it up as a resolution. The designation of the exterior of the Ambassador Theater was rejected unanimously, but the exteriors of the Virginia and the Neil Simon were approved unanimously, and the interiors of the Neil Simon and Ambassador were approved by a 10-to-1 vote. This dissenting vote was cast by Queens borough president Donald Manes, who later committed suicide after being removed from office and implicated in a major New York City scandal.

This, however, wasn't the only action on the theaters taken by the Preservation Commission. It also directed the Landmarks Commission to try to further define the landmark guidelines in regard to the special needs of individual productions to adapt the theaters' interiors to fit their requirements. It also directed the City Planning Commission to reconsider its policy of "buildovers" on designated theaters under the city's zoning laws.

This 1985 victory was heartening to Save the Theaters, but the board's attitude made it clear that more work was required. Chris Hagedorn said, "Between '82 and now we've participated in the Theater Advisory Council's processes, we've completed a study of the theater district, we testified on the Landmarks Commission's hearings, and got hundreds of actors and directors and producers and designers to go in and testify."

SCHWARTZ, ARTHUR. *See* **Dietz and Schwartz.**

SELWYN THEATER. *See* **American Airlines Theatre.**

SHAKESPEARE'S THEATER. *See* **Jolson's 59th Street Theater.**

SHUBERT BROTHERS. The most prolific of all Broadway producers, concentrating on productions aimed at the widest possible audience; Lee, b. Levi Shubert, Syracuse, New York, March 15, 1875, d. New York, New York, December 25, 1953; Sam S., b. Syracuse, New York, 1875, d. Harrisburg, Pennsylvania, May 12, 1905; and J.J., b. Jacob J. Shubert, Syracuse, New York, August 15, 1877, d. New York, New York, December 26, 1963.

The Shuberts were ruthless moguls who at one time owned 31 theaters in New York and 63 others across the United States, and they were at least part owners of 5 theaters in London. From their first production, *Brixton Burglary*, presented at the Herald Square Theater on May 20, 1901, through the last production under the brothers' control, *The Starcross Story*, presented at the ROYALE THEATRE on January 13, 1954, they presented more than 520 productions on Broadway. They also were responsible for countless touring shows and even some London productions. It was estimated that fully one-fourth of the productions presented on Broadway were Shubert productions, and these shows accounted for two-thirds of the total ticket sales for Broadway. After the brothers' deaths, the Shubert Organization was formed, and it continues today.

The Shuberts' long history of play production was not marked by many high points in the American theater. They left experimental and high-minded dramas to producers with a conscience, like WILLIAM A. BRADY, DAVID BELASCO, the THEATRE GUILD, and others. Great musical productions were left to FLORENZ ZIEGFELD, Max Gordon, Sam H. Harris, AARONS AND FREEDLEY, RODGERS AND HAMMERSTEIN, and others. Although they did present some notable productions, the Shuberts catered mostly to the broadest possible audience, concentrating on shows to please the tired businessman. Despite the small percentage of Shubert shows that have weathered the years, the brothers did produce some near classics. SIGMUND ROMBERG and Dorothy Donnelly's *Blossom Time*, and the same team's *The Student Prince*; Olsen and Johnson's *Hellzapoppin!*; Vincente Minnelli's *The Show Is On*; DIETZ AND SCHWARTZ's *At Home Abroad*; and two productions of the ZIEGFELD FOLLIES following the great showman's death were highlights of their musical offerings. None of the Shuberts' straight plays have entered the American repertoire.

The Shubert brothers, specifically J.J. (or Jake) and Lee, were known for their lack of humor and their secretiveness. They would firmly deny rumors about productions, and then turn around and make an announcement when they were ready. The two brothers were also noted for their frugality and their abhorrence of refunding ticket money, no matter what the circumstances. Once, when the scenery and costumes of a Shubert production were lost in a blizzard, J.J. explained to the audience that the show would go on and made a disaster into a triumph. He managed to avoid refunds in the bargain.

Channing Pollock, a playwright and lyricist as well as a Shubert PRESS AGENT, said of the brothers: "They knew little more of literature and drama than a cow knows of the albuminous content of milk, but that was equally true of almost every manager in New York. Any of the brothers might have been mistaken for an office boy, as I mistook Sam when I applied for a position with the firm."

J.J. was in charge of the musical productions, including the negotiations with composers, musical directors, and choreographers; the operation of the WINTER GARDEN THEATRE; the regional theater holdings; theater upkeep; and construction and personnel matters. Lee was in charge of booking the Shuberts' vast holdings, the New York theaters except for the Winter Garden, real-estate transactions, straight-play productions, and the company's finances. His office was conveniently located next to the vault.

The Shuberts were the first producers to hire women as ushers. They set this historic precedent in 1908 at the CASINO THEATRE. They were also the first to charge for paper cups near the water fountain and the first to mix up what was called "orange drink." The liquid was made in a basement and then meted out to the various theaters. The Shuberts always had money on their minds, and that might be why they refused to supply hot water in their rest rooms. They did have hot-water taps on the sinks, but no hot water came out of them. In a more serious vein, the Shuberts were the first to hold tickets in racks on the wall of the box offices and also the first to provide special "count up" rooms to reconcile the books.

David Szemanski, the patriarch of the Shubert family, fled Lithuania for England and finally arrived in Syracuse, New York. He sent for his wife, Catharine, and their 6 children in 1882. Sam was the first introduced to the world of the theater. He and his brother Levi (Lee) sold papers outside the Wieting Theatre in Syracuse. One fateful day Sam was invited to come in out of the cold by John Kerr, manager of the theater. Sam took a seat in the rear, and his life was forever changed. When David Belasco brought his production of May Blossom to the theater in 1885, he hired Sam to play a small part. Sam undertook a series of increasingly important jobs in Syracuse theaters, ending up with a post as treasurer of the Wieting Theatre.

In 1894 Sam decided to go into producing. He bought the touring rights to Charles Hoyt's A Texas Steer. Sam's brothers Lee and Jake joined him in the venture. The success of the abbreviated tour of the northeast was followed by another tour of a play by Hoyt. This successful second tour led Sam to risk another step forward in his career. He bought the Bastable Theatre and set himself up as manager. Soon thereafter a group of speculators agreed to build the Baker Theatre for Sam to manage. Sam was contacted by Abraham Erlanger, head of the Theatrical Syndicate, which was trying to gain a monopoly on all the important American theaters. The Syndicate, operated by Hayman and Frohman, Nixon and Zimmerman, and Klaw and Erlanger, controlled the plays, and if a theater owner wanted to be able to book plays, he had to deal with the Syndicate or lose the show to a rival theater. Once Erlanger gained control of all the important theaters in a region, he took up to 50 percent of each theater's profits. Soon Erlanger lost interest in the little fiefdom the Shuberts had set up, but the Shuberts had learned from him the Erlanger method of operation.

The brothers purchased more theaters, including the Grand Opera House in Syracuse, thus giving them control of all Syracuse theaters, and then they branched out into nearby Utica. Sam was now ready for the big move. He took a lease on the Herald Square Theater in New York City from its owner, Charles Evans. The brothers were warned that the Herald Square, on the east side of 35th Street, was a surefire failure. They ignored the warnings and contracted with the celebrated actor Richard Mansfield to present his productions at the Herald Square Theater.

The Shuberts brought Erlanger into the operation of the Herald Square to ensure product and to be able to get a closer look at the despot's methods. At the same time the Shuberts bought the rights to tour one of the biggest hits of the 1890s, The Belle of New York. This time the Shuberts acquired rights for the entire country, not just the northeast.

The first attraction at the Herald Square Theater was a western play, Arizona (9/10/00; 140 performances), but it was presented by Kirke La Shelle, not the Shuberts. The supposedly jinxed Herald Square Theater was now a success, but the Shuberts had to wait out two more successful productions after Arizona before they became Broadway producers. In the meantime Sam was gaining experience as a producer by presenting special matinee productions of new plays at the Herald Square. The first two plays were abject failures, slammed by the press and scorned by the public. Sam decided that the lesson here was that he should never present a play by an unknown author (one of the plays was by George Bernard Shaw, but he was unknown at the time). Sam learned his lesson well and taught

485

his brothers. They would never again take a chance with a new playwright.

Finally, on May 20, 1901, with *Brixton Burglary* (48 performances), Sam Shubert had his name above the title as producer at the Herald Square. The Shuberts continued their acquisition of new theaters, both in the provinces and in New York. With the Herald Square booked with other people's productions, Sam found a new outlet for his producing efforts. He bought the Casino Theatre on 39th Street. The Shuberts opened their first bona-fide smash hit, *A Chinese Honeymoon* (6/2/02; 376 performances), at the Casino. The show, presented in association with producers Nixon and Zimmerman, solidified the Shuberts' prestige in the minds of the theater community. The success gave the Shuberts enough cash to acquire their first piece of New York property—a plot of land across from the Casino on West 39th Street.

Erlanger, concerned about the burgeoning Shubert empire, tried to force the brothers out of business. The leading theatrical paper of the day, the *Morning Telegraph*, was a mouthpiece for the Syndicate. It promptly began a campaign of rumor and invective against the Shubert family. Lee retaliated in the only way he knew how, financially. He pulled all advertisements for Shubert shows and thus began a lifelong battle with the press.

Virtually every newspaper in New York felt the wrath of the Shuberts. The most famous incident concerned the Shuberts and *New York Times* critic ALEXANDER WOOLLCOTT. In 1915 the journalist had panned a Shubert production, *Taking Chances*, and was banned from future Shubert opening nights. Woollcott, a fighter at heart, simply purchased tickets for the next Shubert show, but he was met at the door to the theater by J.J. and refused entry. This charade was repeated 22 times. The *Times* brought the Shuberts to court and won an injunction against the producers. The *Times*, meanwhile, turned the tables on the Shuberts by not accepting their advertising. The Shuberts picked their fight with the *Times* because at the time it was a minor New York paper and posed no real threat. But the lawsuit and the battle gave the *Times* and Woollcott inestimable publicity, and the *Times* became one of the most widely read New York dailies. Other producers refused to do business with the Shuberts, because a *Times* review was now important. The Shuberts relented, and after a year the feud was settled.

Other CRITICS were banned from reviewing Shubert productions. These included Goodman Ace in Kansas, Philip Hale of Boston, and George Holland, who got himself appointed a fire marshal and "inspected" the Shubert Boston theaters on every opening night. In New York, Lee barred gossip columnists Leonard Lyons and WALTER WINCHELL. The latter commented,

"I do not mind missing Shubert openings. I can always go the second night and see the closing." Also barred were critics Heywood Broun from the *World*, Louis Kronenberger of the newspaper *P.M.*, Gilbert Gabriel from the *Sun*, Percy Hammond of the *Post*, and his successor Charles Collins, who was barred simply to maintain the tradition of barring the *Post* critic. Even Channing Pollock (formerly a Shubert employee) was forbidden entry. Pollock wore a series of disguises to Shubert productions until it almost became a game.

Pollock, in addition to acting as press agent, also screened plays for the brothers. In his role of play screener, he was given a copy of Richard Walton Tully's *Rose of the Rancho*. When Tully brought the play to Pollock for his consideration, he added the caveat that the two previous producers who were asked to read the play, Kirke La Shelle and Fred Hamlin, died before they were able to pass judgment. Pollock was not a superstitious man and so gave the matter no thought. When, Tully asked for his script a few months later, Pollock found it missing. It finally turned up in the bag that Sam Shubert was carrying on his fatal train ride.

This tragedy struck while the Shuberts were still battling with Erlanger over control of the American theater. A night train to Pittsburgh, carrying Sam and two members of his staff, collided with a parked work train. On May 11, 1905, Sam died. The blow almost made Lee give up the business, and he went so far as to meet with Erlanger with the intent of selling out the Shubert holdings to the Syndicate. The meeting collapsed, and Lee became even more resolved to keep the business. Sam's will caused an irreparable rift in the surviving brothers' relationship. Sam gave all his holdings to brother Lee; Jake was not mentioned at all in the document. Lee effectively took control and embarked on a massive expansion. Producers Harrison Fiske and David Belasco signed agreements with the Shuberts, and Lee invited other producers to join in the fight against Erlanger. Then he announced the signing of Sarah Bernhardt, the greatest actress of her day. Other producers rallied around Lee, determined to join the "trust busters." Actually, the Shuberts were building their own monopoly, but at the time they were still the underdogs.

Erlanger ran into trouble with the beginnings of the movie industry. It was clear that the new art form was gaining favor, and vaudeville was the hardest-hit popular entertainment. Erlanger was the owner of several vaudeville theaters and found his holdings threatened. He finally sold his vaudeville interests to B. F. Keith and E. F. ALBEE, the owners of a vast vaudeville empire. Erlanger was given $500,000 to stay out of vaudeville for 10 years. Erlanger, in turn, gave half the money to the Shuberts so that they would also stay out of the vaudeville business. Lee was only too happy to concur, because the Shuberts had no interest in anything but the legitimate theater.

In July 1917 the Shuberts achieved their greatest triumph. They purchased the estate of George Cox, the largest theater holder in the United States. By buying Cox's holdings for an 8-figure fee, they put the final pieces in place for a Shubert empire. Now the Shuberts could guarantee producers the pick of American cities for their tours. Forty of the greatest producers in the country booked their shows into Shubert houses, bypassing the Syndicate. Of course, the Shuberts continued to build and buy more theaters, but their immediate problem was in supplying their chain with product. The brothers made sure that they put out a practically endless stream of shows. Those that were profitable were kept on Broadway long enough to establish a name and then were sent on the road. The brothers found that audiences never tired of some shows, like *Blossom Time*. The Romberg operetta toured almost indefinitely. The same costumes and sets were reused over and over again for each additional company. The brothers would book each tour for one performance at the AMBASSADOR THEATRE. After the one performance, the show would be sent on the road advertised as "direct from Broadway." *Blossom Time* opened in 1921; only 3 years later, it showed a profit of $700,000.

In 1918 the Shuberts presented 15 shows on Broadway. The straight plays were most often flops, but the musicals, especially the operettas, were hits. The Shubert factory operated in much the same way as the motion picture industry at the height of the studio system. Among the Shubert contractees were composer Sigmund Romberg, who wrote 34 scores for the brothers; lyricist-librettist Harold Atteridge; director J. C. Huffman; set designer Watson Barratt; choreographer Allan K. Foster; and jack-of-all-trades Melville Ellis. Performers under contract to the Shuberts included AL JOLSON, who appeared in 11 Shubert productions, and Willie and Eugene Howard. Because the Shuberts owned the largest collection of costumes, sets, and equipment in the country, they often asked their writers to compose shows around the current stock.

There seemed to be no stopping the Shuberts' dominance of the American theater scene. In 1920, however, they began implementing one of their first unsuccessful policies. Lee announced that they would enter the vaudeville field. Almost immediately, the policy was a failure. The Shuberts were forced to pay too much to lure stars from their rivals Keith and Albee. Also, the Shubert theaters were too small to turn a profit, even if they were sold out. Jake, whose operettas and musical revues made money, was angry. After all, the profits his shows made simply went to offset the losses of Lee's vaudeville policy. The Shuberts even

went so far as to invest in Keith's operations under the name Mr. Diamond. The fictitious Mr. Diamond was well hidden from Keith and Albee. Because Diamond was a stockholder in the Keith-Albee syndicate operation, his lawyers were able to take periodic looks at the Keith-Albee books. In this way, the Shuberts could find out exactly how their rival was doing. They learned that their vaudeville enterprise wasn't affecting the Keith-Albee dominance in the least, but at least they were making money off the Keith-Albee profits.

By 1924 the Shubert empire consisted of 86 theaters in New York, Boston, Philadelphia, and Chicago. Thirty of these theaters were in New York City. They owned an additional 27 in other cities. They also controlled the booking of 750 other theaters. During some weeks they earned $1 million at the box office. The Shuberts kept their juggernaut rolling, despite the fact that the relationship between the brothers was constantly deteriorating. Each liked the success that the other's productions brought to the firm, but each was also jealous of the other. By 1927 their relationship had soured to the point that Lee kept his offices in the Shubert Theatre (*see* SAM S. SHUBERT THEATRE), and Jake moved across the street to the new Sardi Building (which the brothers owned).

The Depression hit the entertainment industry hard, and the Shuberts lost $1 million in its first year. As the Depression deepened, Broadway suffered. Audiences would not be wooed by lower ticket prices; they were becoming more and more choosy. The days when patrons would decide to go to the theater without having a particular show in mind were over. Attendance and profits were declining at a prodigious rate. The Shuberts, never known for the artistry of their productions, were in trouble. The company lost $3 million in both 1930 and 1931. At the end of 1931, the Shuberts went into receivership. The Irving Trust Company and Lee Shubert were named coreceivers.

The Shuberts were hit with a number of lawsuits, and their stockholders insisted that the books be reviewed. During the 1932–33 season, the company produced only 5 plays. On January 1, 1933, a judge announced that the assets of the Shubert Theatre Corporation would be sold at auction, which took place on April 7, 1933. Because the theater business was failing, however, there were not too many interested bidders. In fact, there was only 1: Lee Shubert. He bought the assets of the Shuberts for $400,000 under the name Select Theatres Incorporated. After all the bookkeeping was done, with bond holders repaid, it turned out that Lee had bought his own company for $100,000. He was certainly rich enough to retire, but he knew only the theater business. He had no close friendships or relationships, and his work was his life.

The Shuberts weathered the duration of the Depression by booking their theaters for nothing in return for a piece of the box office. Thus they "produced" shows without investing a dime. They figured rightly that every producer was undergoing bad times and would need the brothers' help. This way, the producers wouldn't have to raise the money for theater rentals, and the Shuberts would have attractions in their houses that just might turn a profit.

Jake's son John was brought into the Shubert fold and began producing shows for the brothers. He picked up where his father had left off, with operettas and musical revues. Jake was nursing wounds he had suffered when Lee wouldn't let him have anything to do with the ZIEGFELD FOLLIES, which the Shuberts produced after Ziegfeld's death. Jake prided himself on his revues, and his *Passing Show*, series had rivaled Ziegfeld's. But Lee held all the aces, and in 1934 he even booked the *Follies*, the first since Ziegfeld's death, at Jake's Winter Garden Theatre. The show was a hit, and that rankled Jake even more. Then, too, his own son had joined the enemy's side. Jake left for an extended trip to Europe.

More than 60 percent of the plays on Broadway during the worst of the Depression were either produced by the Shuberts or involved Shubert houses, for which the Shuberts received a part of the proceeds. By 1937 it seemed the worst was over. Lee had put more than $5 million of his own money into the Shubert Organization to keep it alive, and therefore he was largely responsible for keeping Broadway theater alive. Jake spent most of the Depression in Europe. He produced his first show in years, *Frederika*, in 1937, but the operetta closed after only 94 performances.

In 1939 Lee began buying more theaters, many of which the Shuberts had lost due to the bankruptcy. Although the Depression was almost over, the Shuberts did not increase their producing; they didn't have to. They managed to own pieces in 75 percent of the shows playing on Broadway. They either put up the additional capital needed by a rival producer or leased their 17 Broadway theaters in exchange for a piece of the box office. Even if they didn't have any money in a show, they still owned 90 percent of the Broadway theaters, so in effect they *were* Broadway.

In 1948 the Shuberts started the Sam S. Shubert Foundation with $500,000. It was planned that eventually all the Shubert assets would go to the foundation. The establishment of the foundation was the beginning of a plan devised by Lee and J.J. to take care of the organization when they retired. The brothers consolidated their empire through the second-largest real-estate transaction in contemporary New York history (the first was Rockefeller Center). On November 10,

1948, the Shuberts purchased the BOOTH, Shubert, BROADHURST, and PLYMOUTH theaters, and the Shubert Alley property. The deal cost almost $4 million. The transaction gave them the entire square block between Broadway and 8th Avenue and 44th and 45th Streets, except for the plots on which the ASTOR and Manhattan hotels stood. However, the federal government dealt the Shuberts a serious blow when chairman of the House Judiciary Committee, Emanuel Celler, began a probe of the Shubert operations, charging that the brothers held an unfair monopoly on American theater. Celler stated:

> The Shubert interests have clamped a strangle hold on the theater. Theatrical people are afraid to testify. I have checked and I have found a malodorous picture. The Shuberts control 60 percent of New York and 90 percent of legitimate theatre elsewhere. They have allocated tickets to hit shows to "pet" brokers, using kickbacks of all kinds.

Celler also attacked the Shuberts' house-seat policy. Every show had a certain number of the prime seats set aside for the Shuberts' use. The brothers took these tickets and sold them through speculators and ticket brokers for a huge markup. They didn't claim the profit on their taxes, only the actual price of the tickets. The press discovered, for example, that the Shuberts had held back tickets for the first 19 rows of the Philadelphia production of ANNIE GET YOUR GUN in 1946. If each of the tickets cost a top price of $6.60, they would be worth $46,200. But the Shuberts planned to sell them to illegitimate brokers, who would scalp the tickets for as much as $75 each. This would bring the Shuberts $525,000. They had only to pay the amusement tax on the actual cost of the tickets: $46,200. Thus, they netted a tax-free profit of $478,800. The Shuberts instructed their box offices to play other games with ticket sales. If the brothers had another producer's show booked into one of their theaters and they wanted the theater for one of their own productions, they could legally kick out the competition's show only if the box office receipts fell below a certain level. The Shuberts made sure the show didn't reach its minimum by instructing their box office personnel simply to tell all potential ticket buyers that the show was sold out. They then effectively sold no tickets. The converse applied when the Shuberts had a show that was not doing good business but that they wanted to appear to be a success. They simply took their own money and bought out all the remaining tickets. True, there were no bodies in the seats, but the tickets were sold.

Publicity from the *Annie Get Your Gun* affair spurred the government's interest in Shubert practices. The attorney general of the United States held his own investigation, in addition to Representative Celler's. Independent producers who were unable to get bookings in cities where the Shuberts owned a monopoly of theaters brought suit against the brothers. The attorney general laid out his allegations against the Shuberts:

> The defendants for many years have been, and are now engaged in a combination and conspiracy in restraint of interstate trade in producing, booking, and presentation of legitimate attractions.
>
> They compel producers to book their legitimate attractions through defendants.
>
> They exclude others from booking legitimate attractions. They prevent competition in presentation of legitimate attractions. They combine their power to maintain and strengthen their domination in these fields.

The government began to gather witnesses to speak against the Shuberts. Naturally, the majority of actors, producers, and directors chose to remain anonymous, afraid of the all-powerful Shuberts. Lee Shubert was incensed at both what he thought was cowardice and the government's attacks. He reasoned that without the Shuberts the country's road business would collapse, because barely enough shows were produced to keep the Shubert-owned theaters open. Of course, he was right. Without the Shuberts there would be a vacuum with no others to fill it. In regard to the anonymous complainants, Lee wanted to know where they were when the Shuberts were keeping the American theater alive almost single-handedly during the Depression.

The government was unmoved. It demanded that the Shuberts get out of either the booking business or the theater-ownership business. The brothers were also told to unload a sufficient number of theaters so that whatever competition there was could be given a chance. Lee responded by buying a half interest in EARL CARROLL's theater in Hollywood.

Lee decided to fight the government in the courts and have the matter settled once and for all. While waiting for the government to put its case together, Lee kept up normal activities, even proposing a television series called *Shubert Alley*. Then on December 21, 1953, he suffered a series of strokes. He rallied for a while but died on Christmas Day. The last show to be produced by the Shubert brothers was *The Starcross Story*, which opened and closed on January 13, 1954.

Jake, always the Shubert in the background, would now have to assume control of the empire and fight the battles with the government. Jake had lawyer William Klein on his side. Klein had been with the brothers since 1901 and had brought about and defended thousands of suits. The government faced a temporary setback when a federal district court ruled that the Shuberts were exempt from antitrust laws. The government appealed to the U.S. Supreme Court.

Meanwhile, Jake was feuding with Lee's family over control of the empire. He systematically fired every staff member who owed any allegiance to Lee and replaced them with his own handpicked successors. His son, John, had come over to Jake's side before Lee's death. As it was, Lee had always seen to the daily operation of the vast empire; Jake was a producer, not an administrator, and he knew nothing of the Shubert holdings. Not only was he in the dark as to the company's operation, but he also didn't have the necessary education to administer the vast company. Unable to grasp the big picture, Jake concentrated on the more trivial aspects of the organization.

On February 16, 1958, the government ordered the Shubert organization to sell 12 of its theaters in 6 cities in 2 years and to stop entirely their booking business. Jake issued a statement in response to the government's order:

> I will live up to the decree, although I have my doubts as to whether some of its provisions will not hurt rather than benefit the legitimate theater. The decree requires us to sell a number of theaters which were assembled over half a century. Whether these theaters in other hands will continue to be operated as legitimate houses only time will tell.
>
> If we have been financially successful, the legitimate theater and the public will someday benefit from the fruits of our labor through the means of the Sam S. Shubert Foundation.

As Jake slipped into senility, John took over the reins of the Shubert Organization, but John was able to produce only one play, *Jules, Jake and Uncle Joe*, that opened and closed on January 28, 1961. On November 17, 1962, John died of a heart attack. Jake died on December 26, 1963, at the age of 86. The Shubert empire continued with Lawrence Shubert Jr. in charge, but the organization no longer produced shows. It merely managed theaters and the vast real-estate holdings, and little by little the organization lost its connection to the theater and became a typical bureaucratic company.

One of the lawyers involved in defending the Shuberts against the government's antitrust suit was Gerald Schoenfeld. He brought his friend Bernard Jacobs into the business, and soon they took over operation of the Shubert Organization. Schoenfeld became the chairman, and Jacobs the president. Extremely savvy attorneys, they brought the Shubert Organization back to life. They began producing, and they reestablished the organization's dominance of the American theater. The two men, known collectively as the Shuberts even though they were not part of the family, used their great power to bring some of the greatest hits of the London stage to New York. These included the blockbusters *Cats* and *Phantom of the Opera*. The two men also professed an interest in art, and they have at times put the Shubert resources behind chancier plays by some of the top playwrights writing in English, including Tom Stoppard, Simon Gray, Harold Pinter, and David Mamet. Of course, the Shuberts did not originate any of these playwrights' productions; they were either London imports or tried out in American regional theaters. The so-called Shuberts, like the brothers who preceded them, loathe taking chances with unproven talents. Jacobs died on August 27, 1996.

The Shubert Organization is a subsidiary of the non-profit Shubert Foundation, which gives it certain tax advantages that its competition resents. The Shubert Organization, being the dominant power in American theater, receives its due share of complaints. Some are well founded, some are just sour grapes. The organization controls 17 theaters in New York and either owns or operates others in Boston, Washington, Philadelphia, Chicago, and Los Angeles. Many of the Shubert-owned theaters outside New York have been demolished and replaced with office buildings. Some view the Shuberts as real-estate operators, not really producers.

Many of the smaller Shubert houses like the BELASCO THEATRE in New York sit dark for long periods. Instead of booking the theaters, or making them available to local groups, the Shuberts would rather let them sit empty. They do not like to take chances. Also, by letting the theaters sit, they prove their point that the buildings are unprofitable and local governments should allow them to be destroyed. Even the larger Shubert houses, like the National in Washington, D.C., sit empty for long periods, until a big blockbuster like *Cats* or *A Chorus Line* can be booked for a six-month run. In between engagements they remain dark in lonely downtowns.

Critics also point out that the Shuberts always lead the way with higher ticket prices. True, costs have risen dramatically and the Shuberts are, some critics say, responsible for that, too. After all, because their conservative producing style, booking only proven hits guarantees they'll make money, they can afford to pay stagehands and musicians more. At the same time, their competitors, who take greater chances and don't have the financial resources of the Shubert Organization behind them, can ill afford the high guarantees and inflated salaries.

To the Shuberts' credit, they have generally kept up their theater holdings admirably, although with a certain lack of taste in choice of color scheme. They also revolutionized box office procedures through computerization and the acceptance of credit-card sales. Also to their credit are the many charitable activities they support through free leases on their theaters for special events and donations to worthy causes through the Shubert Foundation. However, even now,

more than 100 years since its founding, the Shubert empire is still creating controversy.

SHUBERT THEATER. *See* **Sam S. Shubert Theatre.**

SIGNAGE. Nothing represents the popular view of Times Square so much as the giant signs that line the canyons of Broadway and 7th Avenue. Tama Starr of ARTKRAFT STRAUSS says of the lights:

[They] create an atmosphere which is a real large part of setting the mood. And it's obvious to say but I'll say it anyway, it's unique, it's irreplaceable. What makes Times Square unique is the long sight lines and the fact that the buildings are set way back so even in the middle of the crowded city (and Times Square is one of the most crowded places in a crowded city) you still have a sense of openness and you can see the sky. You don't feel hemmed in like on Madison Avenue.

The first signs were illuminated with gas. Mel Starr of Artkraft Strauss explained their construction:

They had a gas mantle—a pipe with a string of jets, and they covered the facade with a metal sheet with the name of the attraction punched out. Each hole was covered with a little glass cap. Those were inserted into the holes. The twinkling of the lights came from the flickering of the gas flames and the color from the glass caps. Later on, bulbs emulated the twinkling of the lights.

In 1897, down Broadway at Madison Square, a sign for the "ocean breezes" of Coney Island was the first to be electrified. The first Broadway show to feature a moving electric sign was VICTOR HERBERT's operetta, *The Red Mill*. Carbon bulbs outlined the mill's sails, which appeared to spin around. *Florodora*, famous for its beautiful sextette of dancers, had another notable moving sign. The facade of the CASINO THEATRE, at 38th and Broadway, was marked by an outline of the six lovelies dancing from side to side. The first Broadway star to have her name in lights was Maxine Elliott.

Tama Starr explained the change to electricity. "It was inevitable. What you traded off by having this archaic looking twinkling you get back by having more brightness." As the years passed, the signs grew larger and larger and more and more elaborate. The introduction of neon around 1927 introduced a whole spectrum of brilliant colors, and slowly the Great White Way resembled a rainbow. The neon changed the look of signs because the old lightbulbs were only points of light. Neon allowed designers to work with another dimension: lines.

Surprisingly, the signs for Broadway shows were often just billboards, while the signs for commercial products began to dominate the square. Among the most famous were those for Wrigley's gum (first erected in 1917 and revised in 1935), the Pepsi-Cola waterfall, Coca-Cola, Maxwell House coffee, Anheuser-Busch, Johnnie Walker, Admiral television, and Kleenex. Some signs were simple billboards with a gimmick of one kind or another. Typical of these were Camel cigarettes, with its smoke rings, and later, in the same location, Right Guard antiperspirant. Most of the more dramatic signs were designed by DOUGLAS LEIGH.

Also dominant were the huge "spectaculars" built by Artkraft Strauss for the many movie palaces that lined the streets. The ASTOR and VICTORIA theaters shared facades and exhibited the fanciest presentations. Each week the massive signs would be changed to advertise the current picture. Artkraft Strauss owned an inventory of letters in different styles and fonts that could be plugged into the existing outlets to spell out the picture's title and the names of the leading players. Artkraft Strauss used reflective material on wood bases that would catch the headlights of passing cars. Color was provided by nail polish. During World War II the lights on Broadway were dimmed. It was discovered that the bright lights of Times Square could be seen from the ocean, and American ships were neatly outlined against the shore.

Artkraft Strauss leases the space for the sign from the owner of the building. Artkraft, in turn, leases the rights to an advertiser. The sign company fabricates the sign, installs it, and supplies the space and operation, and, if there is a running message, the teletypes. Once a company decides to have a sign built, it meets with Artkraft's designers and engineers. Usually a scale model is built. After the model is approved, a single element, like one letter, is constructed in a full-size model. The letter is made to perform exactly as required on the actual sign. Sometimes a computer simulation is made, indicating how the sign will look in the context of the entire square.

Each of the large signs has carefully programmed animation. The change of lights is orchestrated much like a music score. Each element or portion of an element is noted. The elements may include the color, whether a sign "moves" in a spiral or blinks on and off, and how the lights are programmed. Every two or three years the patterns are changed. The change catches peoples' eyes in a different way, and the sign appears new. The signs' patterns can be quite intricate. The Kleenex sign at the northeast corner of Broadway and 43rd Street featured the character Little Lulu as she skipped from one to another of the 16-foot letters spelling *Kleenex*—lighting each letter when she passed by. When she reached the *X*, she jumped down onto a sheet of pop-up Kleenex and slid down onto the 50-foot-long Kleenex box. A giant neon hand then reached down, grasped a sheet of Kleenex, and pulled it out to

demonstrate the pop-up feature of the product. There were 32 different Lulus in the operation and 8 hands, all electronically superimposed to give the illusion of a single action. In addition, the sign was wired for neon tubing, enabling the sign to repeat the entire operation in five different colors. A final feature on the Kleenex sign was the addition of a motograph message in moving lights in letters one story high. Operated by remote control, it permitted messages of any length, which could be changed in seconds.

Each sign is divided into individual light boxes that are individually wired. They are hoisted into place with giant cranes. The boxes usually measure 6 by 8 feet. The neon is already placed on the light boxes. The engineer has allowed for wind resistance, the sign's weight, and the supports necessary according to physics and New York City codes. The Kleenex sign boasted 1,000 transformers, 25,000 feet of neon tubing, 4,600 incandescent lamps, and 500,000 feet of wire, enough to stretch from New York to Philadelphia.

Painted billboards are painted by artists using 4-inch brushes directly on the billboard. The artist takes a drawing or a piece of art and squares it off, and then duplicates the grid on the billboard or wall. The artist then draws the outline of the artwork on the wall in indelible pencil. Then he or she gives the board a coat of shellac to protect the cartoon. This turns the pencil marks purple and makes them easier to see. Then the artist paints by the numbers. Skin tones and portraits of products and human beings are especially difficult. Some billboards look flat and two-dimensional, but a good billboard artist can create a three-dimensional look, spending a whole day on just a mouth or cheek. To make the face, often 30 or more feet tall, appear not to be distorted is difficult. Sometimes the artists use a kind of pointillism for the pictures, because the drawings are seen from so far away.

The advertiser's costs include rent, maintenance, insurance, electricity, and the operation and construction of the sign. Some of the large signs cost up to half a million dollars. The best-known signs, such as Coca Cola or Fuji, would cost over $1.5 million if built today. Each sign also costs a couple of thousand dollars a month in electricity bills. The price to the companies (now mostly Japanese) is cost-effective, however. After all, nearly 13 million people pass through the square each week. As Tama Starr explains, "The medium is unique. Elsewhere, in a magazine for example, you skip the ads or on television you go out of the room during commercials. But here people come just to see the ads."

She further states, "In the old days there was an opening for every sign and sign lighting ceremonies." The Kleenex sign was illuminated for the frist time on Wednesday, January 30, 1957, in support of Heart

Month and the New York Heart Fund. Perry Como, dubbed "King of Hearts" of the 1957 national drive, and Ann Marie Christie, Heart Fund poster girl of 1957, flipped the switch illuminating the 80-by-180-foot sign. In addition to the lighting, the occasion included models wearing ski costumes in the five shades of Kleenex (white, blue, pink, yellow, and green). The models staged a winter fashion show at the base of the sign.

Most signs aren't constructed to advertise a specific product but rather to enhance the image of a whole company. For example, Panasonic's huge sign contained only the word *Panasonic* without mentioning any of the company's products. The company was making its corporate image part of the landscape. Artkraft Strauss has a slogan, "Make your trademark a landmark." As Starr explains, "By having this confident, large-scale appearance they are becoming more of a presence. They're looking for an architectural fantasy that makes their corporate image a permanent and bright part of civilization." The signs are also seen around the world through movies and photographs. Because the signs are in Times Square, they may have a greater impact outside New York than in the city itself.

Unfortunately, the many great sign locations are being replaced by skyscrapers. The Astor/Victoria site, once home to the largest billboard in the world, was replaced by the Marriott Marquis Hotel. At one time the location boasted the famous Budweiser sign, a billboard made up of 48 separate drawings. The National Theatre's skyscraper replaced the site of the great Kleenex sign. Up Broadway at 51st Street, the CAPITOL THEATER, home of the Anheuser-Busch eagle, is gone. The Nathan's site, originally intended to be a skyscraper, supported the TWA sign and the Budweiser bottle. Today an office building occupies the site. Another building intended to be a skyscraper was the MARK HELLINGER THEATER. That skyscraper was finally built as the Novotel Hotel, and another site was lost. More sites have been lost due to the 42nd Street Redevelopment project. However, because of improved zoning laws, new buildings are required to provide signage on their facades.

Tama Starr explained the problem when the designers decided to forgo signage and remove the theaters' marquees:

> They were taking the position that marquees cause crime because they allow criminals to get out of the rain. Everybody knows the primary function of light is to make streets safer. They may have taken an extreme position knowing they would have to make a compromise. The environmental impact statement, around 2,000 pages, never addressed the subject of light. They tried to brush it under the rug entirely. Now people like the Municipal Art Society say don't take away all the light. Now they're

talking about putting some little bitsy neon stuff, shoe shine parlor kind of things, on the ground level of the buildings.

In February 1987, those responsible for the project's zoning required all developers to allow for signage on their buildings. According to Robert A. Mayers, president of Mayers and Schiff Associates, a consultant on the 42nd Street project, lighting colors will be limited to white. He also would like to see the entire Times Square area surfaced with sidewalks of black granite. Mayers also suggested that 80-foot tubular steel pylons be erected at street corners. These would hold cantilevered advertising signage. Jules Fisher, a noted Broadway lighting designer, and Paul Marantz also consulted on the project. They envisioned huge interactive billboards placed on separate buildings.

Other spectacular effects were also considered, including laser light shows, phosphorescent special effects, holographic effects in sidewalks, walls of glass, and huge mirrored walls. Many of these new spectaculars were being designed by artists for strictly artistic purposes. Starr believes the insistently commercial aspects of current signage is important: "The huge signs are expensive and only a commercial advertiser can pay for it. I'd be opposed to the National Endowment for the Arts paying for this kind of thing, it's not appropriate but it is appropriate for the Canon company." Despite all the artistic planning of the consultants, none of their artistic ideas were adopted; the new signage has no elements of the spectacular and often relies on flat billboards with exterior lighting.

Noteworthy Broadway Signs of the Past

Canadian Club Spectacular
A good example of the complexity and dimension of the giant signs above Times Square is the Canadian Club spectacular. The sign stood on 47th Street above the present-day Coca-Cola spectacular. The 3 signs at the site are certainly the most visible in the area. The Coca Cola spectacular, which occupied a site directly below the Canadian Club sign's old spot, is perhaps the most famous sign in the world. Both were dismantled in June 1990 to allow the razing of the building upon which they stood. The signs were replaced once the building was finished.

The original Canadian Club spectacular, built by Artkraft Strauss, was 48 feet by 62 feet. The background of the sign was 3,000 square feet of yellow vitreous porcelain-enameled steel. The same material is used for refrigerators and stoves, which speaks well of its ability to accommodate considerable fluctuations in temperature. Approximately 25,000 lightbulbs were used in the display. More than 2 miles of neon tubing covered the face of the sign. All these bulbs and tubes required more than a hundred miles of wire to connect them to the 1,000 separate circuits that controlled the sign. If all the elements of the sign were lit simultaneously, it would have consumed more than 750,000 watts of electricity. It delivered more than 2.5 million candlepower—two candlepower for every visitor to Times Square per day.

The uppercase letters in the words *Canadian Club* were 22 feet, 6 inches high, and the lowercase letters were 12 feet high. The words *Imported Whisky* were 6 feet high. The sign was capable of 42 different animation changes. This included the colors of the sign, the pattern of the neon lights behind the letters, and the order of the patterns of lights.

Vikings Spectacular

The shared roofs of the Astor and Victoria (*see* GAIETY THEATER) theaters was one of the greatest of the Times Square sign locations. The block-long Astor/Victoria site was the longest sign locale in the world. Today the Marriott Marquis Hotel and its theater take their place. Any sign erected there was bound to dominate the square. In later years the location was used for giant paintings without special construction or lights. The most famous of these is probably the Budweiser sign.

When Times Square was the movie premiere capital of the world, the location was used to its best advantage. Of all the great spectaculars on the site, the sign for the film *The Vikings* was the most impressive. At the time it was the world's largest and costliest outdoor advertising piece ever constructed for a motion picture. Because the movie opened at both the Astor and the Victoria theaters, the sign and the marquee below ran for the entire block. The sign was dedicated on June 11, 1958, by Kirk Douglas, the star and producer of the film. He was swung from the top of the sign in a bosun's chair to the boat built into the sign. He then christened the boat with seawater brought from Hardangerfjord, Norway. Hardangerfjord was the home port of the real Vikings and also served as a location for the picture.

The sign was 270 feet long and 59 feet high. Across the bottom was the message "Sail the seas of passion and violence with the boldest warriors the world has ever known." The 73 letters were each 7 feet high. The title of the picture was written in letters 10 feet tall and mounted on shields. The letters on the sign were delineated in lightbulbs, more than 4,500 of them, each of which was expected to last only 30 hours. The boat itself was 214 feet long, almost three times larger than the real Viking ships. The sail of the ship was mounted on a mast 50 feet tall. It was constructed of canvas,

and the press release claimed that it was the largest single sail made for a vessel in New York. The boat was fitted with 16-foot oars, which actually moved over a sea of simulated moving waves. The oars were propelled by an elaborate series of cams and walking beams powered by a 5-horsepower motor. On both sides of the sail were 28-foot-tall portraits of the picture's stars, Kirk Douglas, Tony Curtis, Ernest Borgnine, and Janet Leigh. The letters in their names were 8.5 feet high and illuminated with 6,150 bulbs.

Kodak Sign

The original Eastman Kodak sign, on the Marriott Marquis Hotel, was the largest backlighted sign in the world. It was the first built into the facade of a building in an attempt to mollify critics of the new architecture in Times Square. The Marriott agreed to put four signs on the hotel's facade to help retain the flavor of the square. Unfortunately the signs were not integrated into the building's architecture, nor can they replace the huge sign that formerly occupied what was called the Astor/Victoria site. In recent years, additional signage was added to the hotel's facade.

The Kodak sign was a 30-by-50-foot light box. The photograph that constituted the major element of design was made of Kodak Duratrans and was essentially a huge fabric slide hung on the frame. Eight hundred eighty fluorescent lights glowed behind the sign. Huge exhaust fans carried the heat from behind the sign and also served to hold the giant picture against its frame and keep it from flapping in the air. Artkraft Strauss built the huge box and the electronic crawl (letters defined in light bulbs) similar to the MOTOGRAM on the TIMES TOWER. The crawl advertised Kodak products for the company, which has a long-term lease on the location. The sign was officially inaugurated on November 26, 1985, with a photo advertising *Santa Claus, the Movie.* Subsequent photos have not advertised a specific product but rather show greeting-card-type scenes of barns, skiers, puppies, and so forth.

SIMON, NEIL. The most successful American playwright of the 20th century; b. Bronx, New York, July 4, 1927.

Simon has written nearly a play a year since his first Broadway production, *Come Blow Your Horn,* in 1961. Simon's output surpasses even that of TENNESSEE WILLIAMS, one of the most prolific modern playwrights. Simon's dramatic language is not as poetic as Williams', nor is he as politically motivated as ARTHUR MILLER or as psychologically provoking as EUGENE O'NEILL. Simon's style relies mainly on jokes and humorous situations. Simon does have his serious side, however, and more recently his plays have become increasingly emotional in content. Simon has managed to improve his artistry while achieving popular acclaim with almost every play he has written. Some critics have ascribed Simon's success not to any special talent but to his choice of white, middle-class characters—an exact mirror of the average Broadway audience. His detractors distrust his facility in eliciting laughs, and the funnier his plays are the more he sinks in their estimation. A chronological list of Simon's plays reveals, better than anything else, his maturation and continued growth. His early comedies are the closest to sitcoms, and his later works have real, honest, uncontrived emotional punch.

He recalled that when he was still a young boy he clambered on a stone ledge to see a Charlie Chaplin movie that was being screened outdoors. "I laughed so hard I fell off, cut my head open and was taken to the doctor, bleeding and laughing. . . . My idea of the ultimate achievement in a comedy is to make a whole audience fall onto the floor, writhing and laughing so hard that some of them pass out."

Simon began his career as a television writer. He contributed material for the *Phil Silvers Show* (*You'll Never Get Rich*) as well as the *Tallulah Bankhead Show*, the *Sid Caesar Show*, the *Garry Moore Show*, and others. These programs, running mostly in the late 1950s, enabled Simon to build his comic muscle. He had earlier provided sketches for shows presented at a popular summer camp, Tamiment. Simon's first Broadway work was written in collaboration with his brother Danny, considered one of the great comic technicians in the business. The Simon brothers wrote some sketches for the musical revue, *Catch a Star!* (9/6/55; 23 performances). They also contributed material to Leonard Sillman's *New Faces of 1956* (6/14/56).

Neil Simon had his first Broadway success with *Come Blow Your Horn* (2/22/61; 677 performances), the slightly autobiographical story of two brothers learning to grow up. Simon's next project was a libretto for the Cy Coleman and Carolyn Leigh musical *Little Me* (11/17/62; 257 performances). Simon's hilarious script was based on the well-known novel by Patrick Dennis. The show, which starred Sid Caesar, Nancy Andrews, Virginia Martin, and Swen Swenson, deserved a much longer run: It remains the funniest musical produced in recent times. Simon's many innovations were overlooked because the show was not "serious." Nancy Andrews played Belle Poitrine, a successful actress dictating her memoirs. Her character enjoys a series of husbands, who all die in mysterious and sometimes hilarious ways. Caesar played all the husbands; Martin played the young Belle. Simon's book not only is innovative in construction, but it also lampoons musical-comedy techniques and keeps its tongue firmly implanted in its cheek.

Simon's next play was *Barefoot in the Park* (10/23/63; 1,530 performances), one of the most successful productions of the 1960s. *Barefoot in the Park* seemed to take up where his earlier play left off. The new piece examined a young couple's first days of marriage. Robert Redford co-starred with Elizabeth Ashley. It was followed by *The Odd Couple* (3/10/65; 964 performances), one of Simon's best-known plays, mainly because of the popularity of the hit television series based on it. The original play opened at the PLYMOUTH THEATRE, with Art Carney and Walter Matthau as Felix Unger and Oscar Madison. With *The Odd Couple*, Simon went from exploring a young marriage to a tale of two divorced and very mismatched men trying to share an apartment.

A musical, *Sweet Charity* (1/29/66; 608 performances), came next. Simon based his book on an earlier draft by director-choreographer Bob Fosse. *Sweet Charity* boasted a jazzy score by Cy Coleman and Dorothy Fields (*see* FIELDS FAMILY). The show's big song, "Big Spender," was the flashiest but not the best. The book never really took shape, although many of the scenes were funny and individual pieces of stage business were excellent. The show's primary asset, after the score, was Gwen Verdon's touching, vibrant performance as Charity. Helen Gallagher, Thelma Oliver, and John McMartin co-starred. Despite its flaws, *Sweet Charity* was stylish and contained some of Fosse's best choreography.

The Star-Spangled Girl (12/21/66; 261 performances) was one of Simon's few failures. The play opened with Anthony Perkins, Richard Benjamin, and Connie Stevens making up the cast. At the time of its opening, Simon was the first playwright to have four shows running simultaneously on Broadway. Simon bounced back with *Plaza Suite* (2/14/68; 1,097 performances), consisting of 3 one-act plays, all of which take place in the same suite in the Plaza Hotel. The show opened at the Plymouth Theater (which seemed to house only Neil Simon shows), with George C. Scott and Maureen Stapleton in the leads. Later that same year, the Burt Bacharach and Hal David musical *Promises, Promises* (12/1/68; 1,281 performances) opened with Jerry Orbach and Jill O'Hara in the leads. The show, a hip musicalization of Billy Wilder's film, *The Apartment*, gave librettist Simon ample opportunity to examine the mating habits of the white-collar worker.

In *The Last of the Red Hot Lovers* (12/28/69; 706 performances), Simon again experimented with the one-act form. The play opened at the EUGENE O'NEILL THEATER with James Coco, Linda Lavin, Marcia Rodd, and Doris Roberts. Coco's character, Barney Cashman, was seen in 3 acts trying to overcome the sexual and emotional frustration of his middle age by conquering 3 women. *The Gingerbread Lady* (12/13/70; 193 performances) was only the second failure of Simon's decade-long career. Maureen Stapleton starred as an alcoholic singer. Audiences did not want a Neil Simon who examined loneliness, but nonetheless the play was named one of the 10 best of the year by the *Best Plays* series.

In *The Prisoner of Second Avenue* (11/11/71; 780 performances), Simon was somewhat lighter in mood but still trying to expand his range. The play opened with Peter Falk and Lee Grant. Falk's character finds his life collapsing around him. The play ended on a decidedly downbeat note, but Simon sweetened the message with humor. Another popular Simon vehicle was *The Sunshine Boys* (12/20/72; 538 performances). Some critics considered it a geriatric *Odd Couple*. It actually told of 2 vaudevillians, played by Jack Albertson and Sam Levene, who, after 11 years of feuding, try to reconcile their differences. *The Good Doctor* (11/27/73; 125 performances) was Simon's third failure. He adapted several stories of Chekhov and added his own twists, but the play (also recognized by *Best Plays)* failed to find an audience. Another less popular offering followed; *God's Favorite* (12/11/74; 119 performances) opened at the Eugene O'Neill Theater with Vincent Gardenia and Maria Karnilova. The play was a contemporary retelling of the story of Job.

With *California Suite* (7/2/77; 445 performances), Simon began to reverse his downward spiral. The West Coast variation of *Plaza Suite* starred Jack Weston, Tammy Grimes, Barbara Barrie, and George Grizzard in the four one-act plays. *Chapter Two* (12/4/77; 857 performances) opened at the IMPERIAL THEATRE with Judd Hirsch, Cliff Gorman, Anita Gillette, and Ann Wedgeworth making up the cast. The four-character comedy explored the attempts of a recent widower (as Simon was) to reconnect with his own emotions and those of a new woman in his life. By the end of the play it's clear the couple will get married, and in fact Simon also remarried in real life. *Chapter Two*'s run broke Simon's string of failures—for a while. Critics observed that, when the author had personal problems, his plays suffered, too.

They're Playing Our Song (2/11/79; 1,082 performances), although a big hit, was a lackluster musical and didn't represent Simon or his collaborators, Marvin Hamlisch and Carole Bayer Sager, at their best. *I Ought to Be in Pictures* (4/3/80; 324 performances) opened at Simon's own Eugene O'Neill Theater with Ron Liebman, Dinah Manoff, and Joyce Van Patten. The play was the story of a Hollywood screenwriter who is visited by the estranged daughter he hasn't seen in 16 years. Two failures followed: *Fools* (4/6/81; 40 performances), starring John Rubenstein, was Simon's shortest run to date. It was followed by an unsuccessful

revival of *Little Me*, which premiered the following year.

Simon again hit his stride with an autobiographical trilogy beginning with *Brighton Beach Memoirs* (3/27/83; 1,530 performances). Matthew Broderick made an impressive Broadway debut as Eugene Jerome (the Simon character), winning a TONY AWARD in the bargain. Joyce Van Patten, Elizabeth Franz, and Zeljko Ivanek costarred. By the time the play closed, its sequel, *Biloxi Blues* (2/28/85; 524 performances), had opened. Matthew Broderick was again the star. *Biloxi Blues* was the story of Eugene's induction into the U.S. Army and exposure to a different world. In the third play of the trilogy, *Broadway Bound* (12/4/86; 756 performances), Eugene is back in Brighton Beach and breaking into radio. *Broadway Bound* featured Jonathan Silverman as Eugene, Linda Lavin as his mother, and Phyllis Newman as his aunt. However, Simon's next show, *Rumors* (11/17/88; 535 performances), received less than raves. The play was a throwback to his early farces. Ron Leibman, Jessica Walter, Ken Howard, Christine Baranski, and Joyce Van Patten were featured in the comedy.

The playwright bounced back with *Lost in Yonkers* (2/21/91; 780 performances) at the RICHARD RODGERS THEATER. The memory play of Simon's adolescence starred Mercedes Reuhl, Irene Worth, Danny Gerard, and Kevin Spacey. The remainder of the decade saw no letup in Simon's output, but none of his subsequent productions were successes.

He followed *Lost in Yonkers* with the musical version of his play *The Goodbye Girl*. Marvin Hamlisch and David Zippel provided the score and Simon the libretto. Bernadette Peters and Martin Short headed the cast on opening night, March 4, 1993. Reviews were tepid, as was audience reaction. What should have been a major success had had troubles on the road, and a few key production staff were replaced prior to Broadway. *The Goodbye Girl* closed after only 188 performances.

Laughter on the 23rd Floor (11/22/93; 320 performances) was a look back at the playwright's early career writing for the Sid Caesar show. An excellent cast including Nathan Lane, Lewis J. Stadlen, Mark Linn-Baker, and Randy Graff gave it their all, but audiences found the play lacked heart.

Proposals (11/6/97; 77 performances) didn't have a big name to sell tickets. When the reviews were mixed to negative, audiences found other ways to occupy their time. The Simon name wasn't enough to guarantee a hit. With his new plays exhibiting unimpressive runs, Simon revisited a past hit, *The Sunshine Boys* (12/8/97; 230 performances). Tony Randall's National Actors Theatre produced the revival, which starred the television version's stars, Tony Randall and

Jack Klugman. Klugman made a brave return to legitimate theater after suffering a bout with throat cancer.

Martin Short returned to Broadway in another Simon musical, this time Broadway's second revival of *Little Me* (11/12/98; 99 performances) produced by the Roundabout Theatre. Faith Prince costarred as both younger and older Belle Poitrine, two roles that were played by separate actresses originally. Cy Coleman and Carolyn Leigh's brilliant score held up its end of the bargain, but the show was frantically directed without wit and, for the third time, *Little Me* was a Broadway failure.

Simon greeted the new millennium with another new play, *The Dinner Party* (10/19/200; 364 performances). But his luck hadn't changed, and the reviews were mostly negative. However, the play managed a moderate run because the appearance of two television performers, John Ritter and Henry Winkler, drew in the suburban crowd for a while. They were ably abetted by established Broadway performers Len Cariou, Veanne Cox, Penny Fuller, and Jan Maxwell.

The playwright's most recent offering, *45 Seconds from Broadway* (11/11/2001; 73 performances), took place at the so-called Polish Tea Room, the coffee shop of the Edison Hotel a few doors down from the Richard Rodgers Theater in which *45 Seconds* briefly appeared. Simon, beset with reported health problems, never was able to attend rehearsals or the opening night.

Despite his recent failures, Neil Simon has proved to be America's most successful playwright, with an astounding output of which an equally impressive number have been great hits that have become a permanent part of the theater's canon.

SISSLE AND BLAKE. The first major black songwriters to break the Broadway color barrier; Noble Lee Sissle, b. Indianapolis, Indiana, July 10, 1889, d. Tampa, Florida, December 17, 1975; James Hubert "Eubie" Blake, b. Baltimore, Maryland, February 7, 1883; d. Brooklyn, New York, February 12, 1983.

Sissle (lyrics) and Blake's (music) Broadway shows were the first to employ blacks in the theater with a minimum of stereotyping and without resorting to weak imitations of European operettas. During the team's heyday in the 1920s, their successful shows included *Shuffle Along*, which was the first all-black musical to enjoy a long run and be treated as more than an oddity.

Eubie Blake was the youngest of 11 children, all of whom had died before he was born. His parents, former slaves, were strict disciplinarians. When their son was six, the Blakes bought an organ. During an earlier visit to a department store, Blake surprised everyone by picking out tunes on the instrument. He took lessons from a neighbor, Margaret Marshall. Despite her warnings and those of his mother, Blake began to pick up the new ragtime syncopations. The only places to practice the new rhythms were saloons and bawdy houses. Blake got his first professional job at Aggie Sheldon's sporting house at the age of 15. In 1901, after 3 years at Aggie Sheldon's, Blake joined Dr. Frazier's Medicine Show. Just 2 years earlier, Scott Joplin's "Maple Leaf Rag" swept the country. Blake was already composing, waiting for a big break and soaking up the new music and new techniques.

A succession of jobs followed. Minstrel shows, hotels, whorehouses, and saloons were Blake's places of employment. He finally settled in Atlantic City, playing with other classic ragtime pianists during the summer months. Blake continued writing, influenced mostly by his co-pioneers in the ragtime field and popular composers of the day, like the English composer Leslie Stuart.

Noble Sissle's father was a pastor in the Methodist Episcopal Church. Sissle's parents raised him strictly, fully expecting him to follow in his father's footsteps. In 1906 the family moved to Cleveland, Ohio, where Sissle was lucky enough to attend a high school where race was not an issue. While in school Sissle joined the glee club and soon became chief soloist and leader. He began his professional career as a member of Ed-

Eubie Blake. Photo by George Maillard Kesslere.

ward Thomas' Male Quartet, which toured the Chautauqua circuit.

Sissle attended De Pauw University in Greencastle, Indiana, and Butler University in Indianapolis. While at the latter school, he wrote song parodies that were sung during football games. At about this time, new dance crazes began to take the country by storm. VERNON AND IRENE CASTLE's musical director was James Reese Europe, a distinguished black musician. There was a demand for black entertainers as the syncopations of jazz replaced European rhythms. In 1915 Sissle was asked to put together an all-black orchestra for the Severin Hotel in Indianapolis. That led to a job as vocalist for Joe Porter's Serenaders. The Serenaders were booked into River View Park in Baltimore, Maryland, for the 1915 summer season. It was then that Sissle met Eubie Blake. Sissle went on to Palm Beach as part of Bob Young's Sextet, which entertained the elite at the Royal Poinciana Hotel. The next year they were picked to play the PALACE THEATER in New York.

Later that same year Sissle and Blake worked together in the New York area. They began collaborating on songs and formed a vaudeville act, the Dixie Duo. They played throughout the country, polishing the act until it became one of the best on the circuits. During an NAACP benefit in Philadelphia, they met Aubrey Lyles and Flournoy Miller, another black vaudeville team. Miller and Lyles wanted to write and star in a Broadway musical comedy. They were tired of the treatment afforded black entertainers on the road, and they aspired to Broadway for both professional and political reasons.

The two teams got together to write a show based on the Miller and Lyles act, *The Mayor of Dixie*. The result was *Shuffle Along* (5/23/21; 504 performances). It was almost impossible to mount a black show on Broadway, so *Shuffle Along* endured a long, grueling tryout. The company played 1-night stands in all manner of buildings in all sizes of towns. Finally the show reached New York under the auspices of producer John Cort. It opened at the 63rd Street Theater (a run-down lecture hall). Sissle and Blake were worried about the show's reception because it was not a typical black entertainment. The cast didn't wear blackface, nor were they portraying the racist stereotypes common in that era. Whether they would be taken seriously when presenting love songs was a big concern. Because of lack of proper financing, the show was somewhat slapdash, but despite this the audiences went wild for the show.

Shuffle Along introduced a score that incorporated all the new syncopations then in vogue. The biggest hit from the show, and a future standard, was "I'm Just Wild About Harry," which was presented in waltz time. The closest song to a ragtime hit was "If You've

Never Been Vamped by a Brownskin." Other fine songs included, "Honeysuckle Time" and "Love Will Find a Way." The cast included some of the greatest black performers of the time: Sissle and Blake, Lottie Gee, Roger Matthews, and Miller and Lyles. The chorus and succeeding casts also featured artists who received their first important exposure through *Shuffle Along*, including Florence Mills, Josephine Baker, and Paul Robeson. The show established a new era of regard and respect for black performers. Unfortunately, it was an era that quickly passed.

The team's next Broadway attempt, *Elsie* (4/2/23; 40 performances), wasn't a success. The show had additional songs written by Alma Sanders and Monte Carlo. *The Chocolate Dandies* (9/1/24; 96 performances) was the team's next show, and this time they contributed the complete score. The cast at the Colonial Theater included Sissle and Blake, Josephine Baker, Ivan Harold Browning, Lottie Gee, Lew Payton, Valaida Snow, and Elisabeth Welch.

Blake and Andy Razaf contributed songs to producer Lew Leslie's *Blackbirds of 1930* (10/22/30; 61 performances) at the ROYALE THEATRE. The show featured Buck and Bubbles, Minto Cato, Flournoy Miller, Mantan Moreland, The Cecil Mack Choir, and the great Ethel Waters. "My Handy Man's Not Handy Any More" and "You're Lucky to Me" were the two future standards to emerge from the score.

Shuffle Along of 1933 (12/26/32; 17 performances) was an attempt to recapture the success of *Shuffle Along*. It opened at the Mansfield Theater (*see* BROOKS ATKINSON THEATER), with Sissle and Blake, Flournoy Miller, Mantan Moreland, and Edith Wilson. The team then split for a while. Noble Sissle formed a band in 1933 and played long dates at the Park Central Hotel in New York City and at Billy Rose's Diamond Horseshoe (*see* CENTURY THEATER [1]). Eubie Blake wrote *Swing It* (7/22/37; 60 performances) in collaboration with Joshua Milton Reddie. It was produced by the WPA Variety Theater and Frank Merlin.

In 1940, Blake teamed with Andy Razaf (lyricist of the song "Ain't Misbehavin") to write the nightclub show *Tan Manhattan*, which starred Nina Mae McKinney.

In 1948 when Harry Truman ran against Thomas Dewey for the presidency, Truman chose the Sissle and Blake song "I'm Just Wild About Harry" for his campaign song. The song again became a top-10 standard, and the team of Sissle and Blake was again in demand. The new success of "I'm Just Wild About Harry" and the team's new fame led to their first Broadway collaboration since *Shuffle Along of 1933*. For *Shuffle Along of 1952* (5/8/52; 4 performances), Sissle and Blake were reunited with Flournoy Miller. The show was in trouble from the beginning of rehearsals, however, and never could recover from its many problems.

The songwriters went into virtual retirement until rediscovered by musicologist Robert Kimball and musician William Bolcom. Their book, *Reminiscing with Sissle and Blake* (1973), revived interest in the two men's careers

Blake returned to public acclaim through Kimball and Bolcom's efforts. He recorded a two LP set, "86 Years of Eubie Blake" for Columbia Records, with Noble Sissle accompanying Blake on vocals. Blake then founded Eubie Blake Records, which included reissues of early recordings as well as new recordings by Blake and his contemporaries. A Broadway revue, *Eubie* (9/20/78; 439 performances), opened to mixed reviews.

SLANG. Broadway was a hotbed of slang, especially in the 1920s and '30s. The slang words and sayings were picked up and trumpeted by Broadway's columnists and PRESS AGENTS. Those most directly responsible for the invention of slang were columnist WALTER WINCHELL and the entertainment world's "bible," *VARIETY*.

Winchell was named as among the 10 most fertile contributors to American slang by lexicographer W. J. Funk. H. L. Mencken claimed that "Winchell if he did not actually invent 'whoopee,' at least gave it the popularity it enjoyed." Among Winchell's most ingenious contributions were slang words for marriage. The euphemisms included "welded," "merged," "middle-aisled," and "Lohengrined." For divorce, Winchell used "telling it to a judge," "wilted," "this-and-that-way," "Reno-vating," "straining at the handcuffs," and "have phfft." In the event that the marriage was a happy one, Winchell announced the birth of a baby with "blessed event," "getting storked," "blessed expense," "bundle from heaven," "preparing a bassinet," "infanticipating," and "baby-bound." Two people in love were said to be "that way," "blazing," "on the verge," "uh-huh," "Adam-and-Eveing it," "man-and-womanizing it," and "cupiding."

Other Winchellisms include "sextress," "intelligentleman," "messer of ceremonies," "debutramp" (debutante), "pash" (passion), "shafts" (legs), "Chicagorilla" (gangster), "revusical" (musical revue), "phewd" (feud), "Wildeman" (homosexual), "fooff" (pest), "dotter" (daughter), "giggle-water" (liquor), and "heheheh" (mocking laugh). Times Square was dubbed the "Hardened Artery," "Baloney Blvd.," "the Bulb Belt," and "Hard Times Square." Winchell dubbed movies "moom pictures" and "phlickers" or "flickers."

Variety was just as verbally rich and inventive as Winchell. As George Bernard Shaw commented to Ben-

nett Cerf in 1938, "I thought I knew the English language until one day I saw *Variety* in a friend's home. Upon my soul, I didn't understand a word of it."

Many of the words coined by *Variety's* "muggs" (writers) entered the English language even far from the "Main Stem" (Broadway). These words include "cliffhanger," "soap opera," "boffo," "payoff," "freeloader," "bimbo," "platter," "tie-in," "hoofer," "smash," "scram," "wowed," "hick," "pushover," "gams," "discjockey," "brush-off," "chiseler," "corny," "screwy," "nix," "click," "whodunit," "payola," "baloney," "palooka," "nuts," and "emcee."

Other Varietyisms that never caught on to quite the same degree were "yawner" (a boring show), "femme du pave" (prostitute), "oats opera" and "oater" (western film), "hoofologist" (dancer), "mitting" (applauding), "leerics" (suggestive lyrics), "ozoner" and "passion pit" (drive-in movie), "hardtop" (indoor movie theater), "inked" (signed—especially contracts), and "authored" (written).

Variety's headlines are famous for being loaded with "slanguage." Among the best known are "Wall Street Lays an Egg" and "Sticks Nix Hick Pix." Among those less well known were "Bliz Boffs Buff" when a snowstorm knocked out Buffalo, New York.

Other words, not attributable to Winchell or *Variety*, were recorded by Times Square journalist DAMON RUNYON. Runyon frequently coined his own terms but mostly recorded the slang terms used by his characters, who themselves had names that were based in slang. Characters like Spider McCoy, Brandy Bottle Bates, Nathan Detroit, Madame La Gimp, and Dave the Dude used slang terms that included "guys" for men and "dolls" for women. Other nicknames for men and women included "John" and "Jane" and "bum" and "broad."

Many words revolved around the horse race betters who were regulars in Times Square. "Can do," for example, meant that a horse could win a race. The "morning line" was the well-known newspaper the *Racing Form*. "Shooters" were men who played craps with their "bundle"—the amount they had to bet with.

In fact, the unofficial nickname of Manhattan itself, "the Big Apple," was a term first used by the horsemen. *Morning Telegraph* horse racing columnist John J. FitzGerald titled his columns "Around the Big Apple" and "On the Big Apple." FitzGerald had overheard a conversation between two stablehands after a race in New Orleans. One told the other that he was heading for "the Big Apple," where the big racing money was. He was referring to New York.

FitzGerald lived at Broadway and 54th Street, on the northern edge of Times Square. The city has put up a sign at the corner commemorating FitzGerald's contribution, dubbing the intersection as Big Apple Corner.

The *Morning Telegram* was also responsible for another well-known slang term, "The Great White Way." This was coined by *Morning Telegraph* writer Shep Friedman in 1901. He borrowed the term from a contemporary book about the Arctic. Friedman used Great White Way to describe Broadway after a particularly heavy snowfall, but the saying soon referred to the street's bright lights.

"Turkey" referred to a show that was produced between Thanksgiving and New Year's because there were so many people attending the theater that even lousy shows succeeded at the box office. Originally, turkeys made money and were put up intentionally, although the producers knew they were bad.

With the decline of Times Square in the 1950s and especially the 1960s, the old Broadwayites left for the West Coast or Miami and stopped patronizing their haunts. Newspapers had become more respectable and stopped accepting the overblown hype of flacks (press agents). With only three daily papers left in New York and with the decline of radio, the gossip columnist became less important, and those who remained imagined themselves serious journalists. Today's two main columnists, Liz Smith and Cindy Adams, don't associate themselves exclusively with Broadway, because Broadway and Times Square are no longer the center of the world's entertainment. As Broadway has been homogenized, it has lost its flash and show biz razzmatazz. Even *Variety* moved its offices from the heart of Times Square to a modern office tower on Park Avenue South.

Many of the words coined along the Great White Way or the Main Stem have entered the English language. Others have passed through the language and are now almost meaningless. But Broadway is certainly the poorer for the lack of slang, which gave the street so much of its unique flair.

SMITH, HARRY B. The most prolific of all turn-of-the-century Broadway lyricist-librettists, although his work is practically unknown today; b. Harry Bache Smith, Buffalo, New York, December 28, 1860; d. Atlantic City, New Jersey, January 2, 1936.

Smith was the author of 123 musicals produced in a 45-year career. Including adaptations and straight plays, Smith, by his own count, claimed authorship to more than 300 shows. Smith had no special style or flair for lyric writing; instead, although he obviously had talent, perhaps his greatest asset was his speed and satisfactory work. His greatest musical successes— *Robin Hood, The Spring Maid, Sweethearts, Watch Your Step, Countess Maritza, The Girl from Utah,* and

The Rich Mr. Hoggenheimer—were written in collaboration with such composers as Ludwig Englander, Reginald De Koven, VICTOR HERBERT, John Philip Sousa, Robert Hood Bowers, Gus Edwards, JEROME KERN, Franz Lehar, Leo Fall, Ivan Caryll, A. Baldwin Sloane, SIGMUND ROMBERG, and Emmerich Kalman. Smith also estimated that he contributed lyrics to more than 3,000 songs. His greatest success as a lyricist came with the songs "The Sheik of Araby" (from *Make It Snappy*), "Gypsy Love Song" (from *The Serenade*), and "Yours Is My Heart Alone" (from *Yours Is My Heart*). Smith's brother, Robert B. Smith, was also a successful librettist.

Smith attempted to become an operatic performer, but, meeting with little interest or enthusiasm, he found a job on the *Chicago Daily News* as music critic. Smith began to write humorous verse and stories for a variety of magazines and newspapers. His verses gained the attention of a major star, Fay Templeton. She commissioned Smith to write the libretto for her production of *Rosita, or Cupid and Cupidity*. George Schleiffarth composed the music for the operetta, which opened in Chicago in 1883. The success of that show led to another commission for *Amaryllis or Mammon and Gammon*, with music by H. H. Thiele. That show was mounted in Milwaukee in 1884 and was also a success.

Fay Templeton next convinced Smith to abandon journalism and to move to Boston to write full time for the musical theater. She introduced the writer to Colonel John C. McCaull, a leading Boston producer. He, in turn, brought Smith together with composer Reginald De Koven. They collaborated on *The Bugun* (1887). Two years later came the team's next show, *Don Quixote*, produced by the Bostonians, a successful producing organization. However, Henry Clay Barnabee, the star, was not strong enough for the role, and it closed after only a few months.

Smith and De Koven's greatest success, one of the biggest hits of the turn of the 20th century, was *Robin Hood* (1891). The success of that show, written in only three weeks, convinced Smith to become a full-time writer for the theater. He moved to New York and began his career in earnest. *Robin Hood* was the first truly successful American operetta. Smith received royalties on it for more than 25 years before wisely deciding to sell out his interests for a substantial sum.

In 1895, after 5 more collaborations with De Koven as well as two other shows, Smith teamed up with Victor Herbert. Herbert had composed a poorly received operetta produced by the Bostonians called *Prince Ananias*. The show's failure didn't deter Smith from approaching Herbert and suggesting they collaborate. Smith added new lyrics to the Herbert score as well as a new libretto. The result was *The Wizard of the Nile* (11/4/1895), which opened at the CASINO THE-

ATRE. In 1899, Smith had 8 shows produced, including *Papa's Wife*, which starred ANNA HELD. *Papa's Wife* was thought by many to be the precursor of the intimate shows that later developed into the modern musical comedy. In 1911 Smith contributed nine shows to Broadway.

Smith's prolific career continued, although little of his work has lasted beyond his lifetime. His later Broadway shows and their composers included *The Girl from Utah* (Jerome Kern; 8/24/14; 120 performances), *90 in the Shade* (Jerome Kern; 1/25/15; 40 performances), *Sybil* (Victor Jacobi; 1/10/16; 168 performances), *Caroline* (Edward Kunneke, ALFRED GOODMAN; 1/31/23; 151 performances), *Princess Flavia* (Sigmund Romberg; 11/2/25; 152 performances), *Countess Maritza* (Emmerich Kalman; 9/18/26; 321 performances), *The Circus Princess* (Emmerich Kalman; 4/25/27; 192 performances), and *The Red Robe* (Jean Gilbert; 12/25/28; 167 performances).

Smith's last Broadway musical was the 1932 *Marching By*. By then, the operetta was going out of favor and Smith's output slowed to only one or two shows a season. By the time of his death on January 2, 1936, Smith was overshadowed by such modern lyricists as IRA GERSHWIN Howard Dietz (*see* DIETZ AND SCHWARTZ), and E. Y. HARBURG. But he certainly had been hugely popular at the height of his career. Carl Van Vechten flattered Smith when he dubbed the lyricist "the Sarah Bernhardt of librettists." The *New York Times* commented in 1926 that "The name Harry B. Smith in fact became such a byword in these productions that if they were not signed by him, they just weren't comic operas." Smith himself wrote in his 1931 autobiography, *First Nights and First Editions*:

Often my life seems all of the theater, a Chinese play lasting not through many nights but through many years. In other moods, I feel that the theater has been just a shop where I worked at a trade, and that my real life has belonged to my own people and my friends. Life is for most of us a long walk uphill against the wind, with now and then a pleasant place to rest, perhaps to laugh a little before plodding on.

The quote illustrates just how much his style was mired in the florid, operatic style of the turn of the 20th century. Smith was unable to keep pace with the changing styles of the American musical theater, in which romanticism was replaced with sophistication.

SONDHEIM, STEPHEN. Considered the leading composer/lyricist of the modern musical theater; b. New York, New York, March 22, 1930.

Sondheim's shows, usually with HAROLD PRINCE as producer and director, have expanded the art of the musical as have those of few of his contemporaries.

Sondheim's style is unmistakably his own. The hallmarks of his work are intricate rhythms and melodies composed without concern about Tin Pan Alley. These tunes exist solely for the exigencies of the plot and characters. Sondheim's lyrics are laced with witty, intellectual rhymes and an abundance of ideas. This high level of intelligence sometimes puts off his critics, who find his work coldly intellectual and somewhat emotionally uninvolving. The offbeat subjects of many of his shows and his lack of widely popular songs have sometimes kept Sondheim from achieving widespread fame among middle-class theatergoers.

Sondheim was born on March 22, 1930. An early friend was James Hammerstein, son of OSCAR HAMMERSTEIN II. Oscar became the 15-year-old Sondheim's mentor. While at Williams College Sondheim wrote musicals and prepared for a professional career on Broadway. His first effort, *Saturday Night*, was optioned by producer Lemuel Ayers. Unfortunately, Ayers died before the production could be mounted, and it was not to be produced for almost 50 years. Among the Broadway professionals who had heard Sondheim's work was librettist Arthur Laurents, who was working on a new musical with LEONARD BERNSTEIN. Laurents introduced Sondheim to Bernstein, who was suitably impressed with the 25-year-old's work. Sondheim was hired to provide the lyrics for *West Side Story* (9/26/57; 734 performances). Among the Sondheim/Bernstein songs were "Tonight," "Maria," " America," "I Feel Pretty," and "Something's Coming." The show starred Larry Kert and Carol Lawrence as Tony and Maria, and Chita Rivera, Art Smith, Mickey Calin, Harvey Evans, and Grover Dale in supporting roles.

Sondheim's goal was to contribute both music and lyrics for his next Broadway show. But friends convinced him that working on *Gypsy* would afford him the opportunity to work with an established Broadway composer, Jule Styne, and to give him experience writing for a star, ETHEL MERMAN. *Gypsy* (4/21/59; 702 performances) was a musicalization of the memoirs of Gypsy Rose Lee. Arthur Laurents again contributed the libretto. The excellent Sondheim and Styne songs included the standards "Everything's Coming Up Roses," "Together," "Let Me Entertain You," and "Small World." Ethel Merman was ably assisted by Jack Klugman, Sandra Church, Paul Walker, Maria Karnilova, and Jacqueline Mayro.

Although Sondheim's initial Broadway works were successes, he was still determined to supply the music as well as lyrics for his next show. The opportunity came when Burt Shevelove approached him with the idea of musicalizing the comedies of the Roman playwright Plautus. The result was *A Funny Thing Happened on the Way to the Forum* (5/8/62; 967 performances), with a libretto also by Larry Gelbart. Zero

Mostel played Pseudolus, a Roman slave with aspirations for freedom. His compatriot was played by Jack Gilford. GEORGE ABBOTT and Jerome Robbins directed the show and Harold Prince produced.

The success of *A Funny Thing Happened on the Way to the Forum* led to Sondheim's next show, a failure. Arthur Laurents contributed the original idea for *Anyone Can Whistle* (4/4/64; 9 performances). Angela Lansbury, Lee Remick, and Harry Guardino made their Broadway musical debuts in the show. The plot concerned escapees from an asylum who find themselves in the midst of a town ruled by a crooked mayor. The failure of *Anyone Can Whistle* led to Sondheim's teaming with Richard Rodgers (*see* RODGERS AND HAMMERSTEIN and RODGERS AND HART) on *Do I Hear a Waltz* (3/18/65; 220 performances). The show was a musical version of Arthur Laurents' play *Time of the Cuckoo*. Elizabeth Allen and Sergio Franchi starred. Sondheim and Rodgers had a stormy relationship but contributed a good score.

Playwright George Furth approached Harold Prince about producing a script he had written. Prince suggested the material might be more successful as a musical, and Sondheim was brought in to complete the production team. The resulting show, *Company* (4/26/70; 706 performances), opened at the Alvin Theater (*see* NEIL SIMON THEATER). Prince also directed the show which starred Dean Jones, Barbara Barrie, Donna McKechnie, and Elaine Stritch. *Company*, a ruthless examination of marriage set against an aggressively urban setting, was an immediate success.

Sondheim was by then firmly established as a superior and innovative talent. His next project was *Follies* (4/4/71; 522 performances), one of the greatest of all musicals. Harold Prince codirected and produced the show, which had a book by James Goldman. Michael Bennett codirected with Prince and supplied the choreography. *Follies* boasted an impressive physical production. The set was designed by Boris Aronson, the costumes by Florence Klotz, and the lighting by Tharon Musser. The show was about a reunion of a group of former Follies performers. The action took place on two levels, the party itself and the ghosts of the past who haunt the celebrants' present. The brilliant staging perfectly joined the two worlds. The show, however, was more than an examination of the characters' past and present lives. It succeeded in presenting a psychological examination of their feelings and thoughts. The final sequence takes place in Loveland, which is actually a physical realization of the characters' problems. Their psyches are illustrated as acts in a performance of the ZIEGFELD FOLLIES. The show starred Dorothy Collins, Alexis Smith, John McMartin, Gene Nelson, and Yvonne DeCarlo. It opened at the WINTER GARDEN THEATRE. Audiences, unaccus-

tomed to actually thinking during a musical comedy, sometimes found the show confusing and disorienting, but for many the evening was stimulating and moving.

The glamour and immensity of *Follies* led to the more intimate *A Little Night Music* (2/25/73; 601 performances), an elegant rendering of Ingmar Bergman's romantic film *Smiles of a Summer Night*. Hugh Wheeler supplied his first libretto for a Sondheim show, with Prince in his usual dual role as producer and director. The show opened at the SAM S. SHUBERT THEATRE, with Glynis Johns, Len Cariou, Hermione Gingold, and Patricia Elliott. *A Little Night Music* contained a rich and varied score all in three-quarter time. Surprisingly, one of the songs, "Send in the Clowns," attained popular status.

For his next show, Sondheim was drawn to an unlikely subject, the opening of relations between Japan and the United States in the 19th century. *Pacific Overtures* (1/11/75; 193 performances) opened at the Winter Garden Theatre. A play by John Weidman was the source, which Weidman and Hugh Wheeler adapted. Prince again produced and directed the production, which featured an all-Japanese cast. The show, attempted to show great events through the examination of the lives of a few common people.

The next Prince/Sondheim collaboration was the thriller *Sweeney Todd* (3/1/79; 558 performances). The story was set against England's Industrial Revolution. Sweeney Todd, the lead character, is a barber who returns home from jail to seek vengeance on those who had ruined his life. His act of vengeance soon turns into full-fledged insanity, and Todd finds an accomplice in Mrs. Lovett, a baker of meat pies. As Todd dispatched friend and foe, Mrs. Lovett obligingly incorporates their corpses into her baked goods. This Grand Guignol production opened at the Uris Theatre (*see* GERSHWIN THEATER). Audiences were delighted to be scared out of their wits. Angela Lansbury and Len Cariou starred as the partners in crime.

Sondheim's next project was his last collaboration with Harold Prince. George Furth, of *Company* fame, supplied the book for *Merrily We Roll Along* (11/16/81; 16 performances), an adaptation of the Kaufman and Hart play. The show was told in reverse order. The cast was composed entirely of teenagers and performers in their early 20s. This was a limitation that, when coupled with a misguided design and badly written book, added up to failure, although Sondheim's score was typically brilliant. The show opened at the Alvin Theater.

Sondheim might have been discouraged by the failure of *Merrily We Roll Along*, but he was not about to pander to popular taste or let his work sink to the lowest common denominator. His next undertaking, *Sunday in the Park with George* (5/2/84; 604 perfor-

mances), proved to be one of his most experimental outings. James Lapine contributed the book and direction to the show, which used French painter Georges Seurat as a springboard for the examination of what it means to be an artist. The first act of the musical concernes Seurat's life and takes place while he is painting his masterpiece, *A Sunday Afternoon on the Island of La Grande Jatte*. The second act takes place 100 years later with the story of Seurat's great-grandson, a modern artist. The show starred Bernadette Peters and Mandy Patinkin. It won the PULITZER PRIZE.

For his next excursion, Sondheim again chose an unlikely subject. *Into the Woods* tells the story of three fairy tales, "Little Red Riding Hood," "The Baker and His Wife," and "Jack and the Beanstalk," and what happens after "they lived happily ever after." James Lapine supplied the book as well as the direction. *Into the Woods* (11/5/87; 764 performances) opened at the MARTIN BECK THEATRE. It boasted a score sung by a superior cast, including Bernadette Peters, Joanna Gleason, Chip Zien, Kim Crosby, Tom Aldredge, Ben Wright, Barbara Bryne, Daniele Ferland, and Robert Westenberg. The TONY voters chose Sondheim's score over that of Andrew Lloyd Webber's *Phantom of the Opera*.

By this time Sondheim had been writing long enough for revivals of his works to make it to Broadway. The Circle in the Square produced a new production of *Sweeney Todd* (9/14/89; 188 performances). *Gypsy* (11/16/89; 476 performances) was next, with Tyne Daly starring as Rose. It was followed by a concert version of *Company* on April 11 and 12, featuring a reunion of the show's original cast.

Passion (5/9/94; 280 performances) was Sondheim's next original musical. Based on an obsure Italian film, *Passione d'Amore*, it tells the story of a handsome soldier who leaves his beautiful mistress when he is assigned to a remote outpost. When he arrives, he is introduced to Fosca, the sickly, ugly daughter of the head of the regiment. She develops an infatuation with the soldier, who is repelled by her. As time goes on, he begins to see beneath her façade and to glimpse the beauty within. His mistress writes him to say that their affair is over, and he is devastated. Slowly the soldier warms to Fosca, but as he learns the lessons of vanity and inner beauty Fosca dies. For *Passion* Sondheim developed a score with recurring themes rather than specific breaks for songs. Librettist James Lapine helped Sondheim weave the score through the show. Audiences used to Broadway pablum didn't warm to Sondheim and Lapine's themes, and Lapine's direction veered in the direction of melodrama and operetta.

After a special concert version of *Sunday in the Park with George* in March 1995, *Company* (10/5/95; 60

performances) was revived by the Roundabout Theatre. Although Roundabout kept trying to present revivals, including *Little Me, 1776, She Loves Me,* and *Boys from Syracuse*, among others, none was successful either artistically or financially. Their one musical revival that proved wildly successful, *Cabaret*, was essentially a remounting of a London hit. *Company* would prove to be no more successful than Roundabout's other attempts.

Sondheim made his Broadway playwriting debut (along with co-author George Furth) with the comic thriller *Getting Away with Murder* (3/17/96; 17 performances). The show was ably constructed and scripted, but the direction played against it, and it lasted barely 2 weeks.

Revivals of Sondheim's works continued apace. *A Funny Thing Happened on the Way to the Forum* (4/18/96; 715 performances) was well produced by Dodger Theatricals, leading producers of Broadway revivals. Unlike many Dodger productions, *Funny Thing* looked expensively produced and respected the original source material. The show, ably directed by Jerry Zaks, boasted an excellent cast including Nathan Lane, Lewis J. Stadlen, Mark Linn-Baker, and Jim Stanek. The revivals continued with *Putting It Together* (11/21/99; 101 performances) starring Carol Burnett and George Hearn. Burnett's name carried what was otherwise a disastrous production with atrocious direction by Eric Schaeffer.

The next Sondheim revival was the much anticipated revival of the legendary *Follies* (4/5/2001; 117 performances). Unfortunately, every aspect of this production, except the casting, was far below Broadway standards. The Roundabout Theatre did manage to round up some interesting performers for the subsidiary roles, including Joan Roberts (the original Laurie in *Oklahoma!*), Betty Garrett, Polly Bergen, Marge Champion, Donald Saddler, and Jane White. But the leads were mostly incompetent at best. Judith Ivey and Blythe Danner, while fine dramatic actors, couldn't meet the rigors of singing and dancing. Treat Williams came across the best of the leads, with Gregory Harrison providing competent if unexciting support. The direction and choreography matched the ugliness of the physical production, and if there's one thing *Follies* needs, it's a good production.

The next Sondheim revival was *Into the Woods* (5/20/2002; 279 performances) at the BROADHURST THEATER. James Lapine, author of the libretto, also directed the moderately well-received production.

Broadway is avidly waiting for a new Sondheim musical. He had one new show, titled *Wise Guys*, which was commissioned by the Kennedy Center. A workshop was held in New York, but legal and artistic problems slowed a full production. The retitled *Bounce* opened at the Goodman Theatre in Chicago in the summer of 2003.

In the meantime, a new revival of *Gypsy*, starring Bernadette Peters, opened on Broadway on May 1, 2003.

Stephen Sondheim has proven himself to be the greatest of the composer-lyricists in the Broadway tradition. The fact that he has seen fit to expand those traditions and not simply work within their confines is both his chief asset and perhaps one of his faults. His shows have contained mostly brilliant scores that have a somewhat limited appeal to the average Broadway audience. However, each of his shows has proven, sometimes in retrospect, to be an important part of the history of the American musical theater.

STAGE DOOR CANTEEN. *See* **American Theatre Wing.**

STAIRCASE THEATER. *See* **Century Theater (1).**

STARR, JACOB. *See* **Artkraft Strauss.**

STARR, MELVIN. *See* **Artkraft Strauss.**

STRAND THEATER. 47th Street and Broadway. Architect: Thomas W. Lamb. Opening: April 11, 1914; *The Spoilers.*

The Strand was the first great movie palace in the world. It began a progression of increasingly lavish theaters, culminating in the opening of the ROXY THEATER.

Since the early years of the 20th century, Times Square has had the reputation as the place to make one's mark in the world of entertainment. Thousands have come to Broadway to rise to the top of their professions. Two of these were Mitchell and Moe Mark, brothers who owned nickelodeons. They came to Times Square to erect a theater, and chose a site at 47th Street and Broadway, the location of the Brewster Carriage Factory. They leased the land and announced their plan to build a "million dollar theater." Mitchell Mark stated, "From the first moment we conceived of erecting the Strand we made studies of all the best theaters in Europe and America."

The problem of what to put in the theater seemingly stumped the brothers. Their original plan was to build a 50-cent-admission vaudeville theater. Four months before the completion of the theater, the policy still wasn't determined. At one point almost every possible type of theatrical presentation was considered. The Marks even stated that the Metropolitan Opera would

move to the new house. Finally, Mitchell Mark made the announcement that the Strand Theater would be a "national institution that would stand for all time as the model of moving picture palaces," and thus ended the speculation. Once the decision was made to use the Strand for movies, the Marks hired the greatest motion picture impresario in the world, S. L. ("ROXY") ROTHAFEL. He was then running the Regent Theater on 116th Street, designed by Thomas W. Lamb, who also designed the Strand. Roxy moved to the Strand and prepared for the grand opening.

Lamb, who became one of the greatest motion-picture-palace architects, designed a magnificent theater. With 2,985 seats, the Strand had a shallow stage and perfect sight lines. J. Victor Wilson, writing in *The American Architect*, wrote, "The evolution from the converted store building and other makeshifts, to the specially designed moving picture theatre, finds in a sense a culmination in the Strand Theatre." Another publication described the Strand as a theater full of "gilt and marble and deep pile rugs, crystal chandeliers hanging from the ceiling and original art works on the walls, with luxurious lounges and comfortable chairs, a thirty piece symphony orchestra . . . and a mighty Wurlitzer."

The organ was an important part of any movie palace. Carl Edouarde, the Strand's musical director, commented that:

If an exhibitor should be forced to choose between a poor orchestra and a good organist, he should consider it his duty to give the organist the preference. After all, it is quality and not quantity that really counts. Besides, it has been my experience that audiences would rather hear music played extremely well than extremely loud.

The new theater opened on April 11, 1914. The event was reported by Victor Watson in the following day's *New York Times*:

Going to the new Strand Theater last night was very much like going to a Presidential reception, a first night at the opera or the opening of the horse show. It seemed like everyone in town had simultaneously arrived at the conclusion that a visit to the magnificent new movie playhouse was necessary.

I have always tried to keep abreast of the times and be able to look ahead a little way, but I must confess that when I saw the wonderful audience last night in all its costly togs, the one thought that came to my mind was that if anyone had told me two years ago that the time would come when the finest-looking people in town would be going to the biggest and newest theater on Broadway for the purpose of seeing motion pictures I would have sent them down to visit my friend, Dr. Minas Gregory at Bellevue Hospital. The doctor runs the city's bughouse, you know.

Strand Theatre just prior to opening.

William Farnum, the star of the theater's first presentation, *The Spoilers*, was present, as were GEORGE M. COHAN, Vincent Astor, and producers Daniel Frohman, Sam Harris, and Abe Erlanger. The gala opening ceremony began with an artillery salute of three shots. Then came the 50-member Strand Concert Orchestra playing the "Star Spangled Banner" under the direction of Carl Edouarde.

The *Moving Picture World* reported on the stirring opening of the evening's entertainment:

We saw in lightning rapidity the scenes which inspired the deathless hymn of glory. In the roar and sweat of battle the starry flag still breezed in eloquent triumph over the brave hearts of the country's defenders. With the swiftness of thought the audience recognized the happy inspiration of sending the new theater on its career to the strains of patriotic music with the rare glimpse of American glory visualized and, as we all stood up in loving homage, no one failed to congratulate the man-

agement on its inspiration. At the same time Rothapfel unmasked his artillery, the darkness in and about the screen was converted into a flood of light and the splendid decorations, the flowers, the hedges of green, the graceful fountains of changing color, and the pretty effects in the wings stood revealed as if by magic.

The orchestra then played the Hungarian Rhapsody No. 2. Following the concert, the screen was lit up by *The Strand Topical Review*, an up-to-the-minute newsreel featuring scenes from that afternoon's Brooklyn Federal League baseball game. A travelogue of Italy entitled *A Neapolitan Incident* came next, and, since this was still the era of the silent film, a tenor hidden behind the screen sang "O Sole Mio." The Mutual Film Corporation's star, the Mutual Girl, appeared in a one-reel comedy and then made a personal appearance alongside Roxy. Another musical interlude followed, with the Strand Quartet singing a selection from *Rigoletto*.

STRAND THEATER

Roxy came up with another first for the new picture palace. He had 4 projectors put into the booth so that the 9-reel feature could be presented without interruption. This was a surprise to the audience. The *New York Times* reporter commented that the audience "absorbed the story without an effort and its interest never lagged—at 11:30 we were more interested in the fate of Glenister and all the rest than at 9:15 though we had been looking intently at the screen for more than two hours." The opening was a tremendous success, although VARIETY erroneously stated that the theater would cease its motion picture policy and present musical comedy.

The Strand changed its program every Sunday. Each consisted of "a fine picture, and an hour and a quarter's entertainment, and a first-class orchestra to boot for the same price," as described by Roxy. Those shows beginning at 2:00, 7:30, and 9:30 were called "deluxe" and contained the entire program. The other shows, at noon, 4:15, and 6:00, omitted the orchestral portion, substituting the Wurlitzer organ for the musical program. Roxy kept the admissions low. During the afternoon performances, the balcony seats were 15 cents, seats in the orchestra were 25 cents, and loge and box seats were 50 cents. On weekends, the balcony seats were 25 cents, and the orchestra was split into two price ranges, 35 cents and 50 cents.

Within two years, with the Strand Theater firmly established, Roxy left to open the RIALTO THEATER on Broadway at 42nd Street. The Strand later became the Warner Theater and after many renovations was twinned. It finally succumbed to the wrecker's ball in 1987.

STROUSE AND ADAMS. Successful Broadway songwriters of the 1960s and '70s; Charles Strouse, b. New York, New York, June 7, 1928; and Lee Adams, b. Mansfield, Ohio, August 14, 1924.

Charles Strouse was one of the leading musical comedy composers throughout the 1960s and 1970s. During his most successful period, he collaborated with lyricist Lee Adams. They supplied a string of lighthearted scores to entertaining musicals. Strouse's music contains catchy themes with a dramatic flair. Adams lyrics seem simple, yet they perfectly complement the theatricality of Strouse's tunes.

Strouse's interest in music began in his early teens. Later he studied at the Eastman School of Music and under Aaron Copland and Nadia Boulanger. Adams had a lifelong fascination with words and worked as a staff member of *Pageant* magazine and as editor of *This Week* magazine. The two met in 1949 and began writing songs at Green Mansions summer camp. Their revue songs were transferred from the camp setting to

off Broadway and a series of shows for Ben Bagley. *The Shoestring Revue* (2/28/55; 95 performances), *The Littlest Revue* (5/22/56; 32 performances), and *Shoestring '57* (11/5/56; 110 performances) gave the team more time to hone their skills.

Strouse and Adams were ready to attempt a full-fledged musical comedy by the late 1950s. Their first effort, *Bye Bye Birdie* (4/14/60; 607 performances), was a true sleeper and an immediate smash. The show, a satire on the newly emergent rock industry, starred Dick Van Dyke and Chita Rivera, with Paul Lynde, Susan Watson, and Kay Medford in supporting roles. Dick Gautier played a thinly veiled parody of Elvis Presley. The score contained the team's greatest success, the jaunty "Put on a Happy Face." Their first Broadway show was also the first full musical directed by Gower Champion, and the first for which Michael Stewart supplied a libretto.

For their second project, the team turned once again to satire. Mel Brooks provided the libretto for *All American* (2/19/62; 80 performances). Despite the talents of Ray Bolger and Eileen Herlie and JOSHUA LOGAN's direction, the show was a failure. The score, which was almost as good as that of *Bye Bye Birdie*, did contain one standard, "Once upon a Time."

The next show for which Strouse and Adams supplied a score was a departure from their usual light satire. *Golden Boy* (10/20/64; 569 performances) was a powerful drama by Clifford Odets. It wasn't an obvious choice for musical comedy, but producer Hillard Elkins convinced the team to take it on. Certainly, the score was excellent, combining Broadway razzmatazz with the serious subject matter. Another remarkable aspect of the production was the casting of Sammy Davis Jr. as the prizefighter. Odets had died while writing the libretto, and William Gibson took over the task. The show proved controversial with the casting of a black lead along with a white woman. People actually shot bullets into the marquee of the MAJESTIC THEATRE.

For their next project, Strouse and Adams attempted *It's a Bird . . . It's a Plane . . . It's Superman* (3/29/66; 129 performances). The show was a pop-art depiction of the famous comic-book character. It was a tongue-in-cheek attempt to bring to the stage what *Batman* would later bring to television. The show enjoyed a superior score and production under the direction of HAROLD PRINCE. David Newman, coauthor of the libretto with Robert Benton, would have better luck with the same subject when he scripted *Superman*, the movie. Jack Cassidy, Linda Lavin, Patricia Marand, and Bob Holiday starred in the musical.

After the failure of *It's a Bird . . . It's a Plane . . . It's Superman* came the success of *Applause* (3/30/70; 896 performances). The show was an adaptation of the

506

Danny Daniels, Eileen Herlie, and Ray Bolger in rehearsal for *All American*, 1962.

movie *All About Eve*. In the lead was a newcomer to musical comedy, Lauren Bacall. COMDEN AND GREEN supplied the libretto. Although none of the creative contributions were particularly outstanding, the show was their longest run as a team. Next, Strouse wrote the book and lyrics to his own music for an off-Broadway show, *Six* (4/12/71; 8 performances), which opened to negative reviews, although it boasted excellent choreography by Denny Martin Flinn. The following year the team had a failure with *I and Albert*, a musical about Queen Victoria that was staged in London.

Seven years after *Applause* Strouse opened a new Broadway musical, his second based on a comic strip character. The show was *Annie* (4/21/77; 2,377 performances), with lyrics by Martin Charnin. Andrea McArdle played the title character, assisted by Sandy Faison, Dorothy Loudon, Reid Shelton, and Raymond Thorne. The song "Tomorrow" became an anthem of prepubescent girls everywhere. The show was directed by Charnin and had a libretto by Thomas Meehan.

Strouse and Adams reunited for *A Broadway Musical* but to little result; the show opened and closed on December 21, 1978. William F. Brown supplied the book and Gower Champion the direction. After that failure, Strouse undertook another London assignment. *Flowers for Algernon* was based on the movie *Charly*, and for its American opening was retitled *Charlie and Algernon* (9/14/80; 17 performances).

Strouse and Adams's last Broadway collaboration, was a sequel to their first show, *Bye Bye Birdie*. Its name was *Bring Back Birdie* (3/5/81; 4 performances), and again Michael Stewart contributed the book and Chita Rivera starred. She was assisted by Donald O'Connor.

Strouse wrote a children's opera, *Nightingale*, in 1982, contributing book, music, and lyrics. His next Broadway outing was *Dance a Little Closer*, for which he teamed with Alan Jay Lerner (*see* LERNER AND LOEWE). Lerner also contributed the libretto and direction to *Dance a Little Closer*, an updating of Robert

Bob Holiday flies over Metropolis in *It's a Bird . . . It's a Plane . . . It's Superman*, 1966.

Sherwood's *Idiot's Delight*. The show, which opened on May 11, 1983, at the MINSKOFF THEATRE, unfortunately fared as badly as Lerner's previous Broadway show, closing after only one performance. Despite the show's poor record, the score is considered a good one. The title song gained some small amount of recognition among cabaret artists.

Strouse's next Broadway score contained some of his best tunes. Unfortunately, the other elements of *Rags* (8/21/86; 4 performances) were not as well written. *Rags* had a book by Joseph Stein and lyrics by Stephen Schwartz. It starred opera diva Teresa Stratas and featured Larry Kert, Terence Mann, Marcia Lewis, Dick Latessa, and Lonny Price in a sprawling tale of American immigration.

Nick & Nora (12/8/91; 9 performances), the Thin Man musical had a book by Arthur Laurents and lyrics by Richard Maltby Jr. The creative staff was at odds throughout the creative process; despite a seasoned cast, including Barry Bostwick, Joanna Gleason,

Christine Baranski and Faith Prince, the show never jelled. However, several of the Strouse-Maltby songs have continued to be performed by pop and cabaret singers. Lee Adams saw his musical *Ain't Broadway Grand* (4/18/93), written with Mitch Leigh, close after 25 performances. It was a musical biography of producer Mike Todd.

Strouse and Adams began collaborating again in the 1990s with adaptations of *An American Tragedy* and *Marty*. Strouse also collaborated on a musical version of *The Night They Raided Minsky's*. The original Strouse and Adams songs were tossed out in favor of a new score. Mike Ockrent was set to direct, with Susan Stroman, Ockrent's wife, supplying the choreography. But Ockrent's death and Stroman's success with *The Producers* scotched the project.

At the high points of his career, Strouse has shown a rare ability to time the subjects of his projects to popular taste. *Annie* and *Bye Bye Birdie* both profited by their perfect convergence with what the public was looking for in a Broadway musical. *Bye Bye Birdie* dealt with the timely, up-to-date subject of Elvis Presley's recent induction into the U.S. Army and rock and roll's popularity at a time when other teams were contributing old-fashioned scores like *The Sound of Music* and *Camelot*. Marilyn Stasio of *Cue* attributed *Annie's* success to "an uncanny insight into what people need right now." Of course, Strouse's timing hasn't always been so strong. *Superman* suffered by being ahead of its time. Musical-comedy audiences are not always at the forefront of trends.

All of Strouse's shows, and especially those written with Lee Adams, show an exuberance and emotional fullness. The early shows, even when wedded to ungainly books or weak productions, maintained a high level of technique and professionalism.

STUDIO 54. 254 W. 54th Street. Architect: Eugene DeRosa. Opening: as an opera house, the Gallo Theater, November 7, 1927, *La Bohème*; as a legitimate theater, May 12, 1930, *The Vikings*.

Opera impresario Fortune Gallo had his Gallo Theater built to house the San Carlo Opera Company. The house was not a success, and his building was sold in foreclosure for $1,045,000 6 weeks after the crash of 1929. The new owners named the theater the New Yorker Theater with their production of *The Vikings*. The Depression hurt the theater, and it was also unsuccessful.

The theater was redesigned as one of the first theater restaurants in New York, the Casino de Paree, on December 13, 1933. It seated 1,100 diners at tables. The club, owned by the Continental Music Halls, Inc., was originally called Billy Rose's Casino de Paree, but the bantam producer Billy Rose soon sold out his interest.

The man who ran the Casino was Lew Brown, best known as a member of the songwriting team DE SYLVA, BROWN, AND HENDERSON. But Brown wasn't the owner; that distinction went to Tommy Lucchese. Milton Berle played the Casino and recalled his first impression of Lucchese: "[He] struck me as sort of naive, a nice quiet gentleman who must have been in an accident—I thought because he only had three fingers on one hand." Berle later wised up to the fact that Lucchese was the notorious gangster Three-Fingers Brown.

Lucchese, like most GANGSTERS, was paranoid. He wouldn't accept a cigar from anyone. Instead, he'd jump in a cab and go to a cigar store where he was not known. Lucchese's caution paid off. He was never arrested and lived a quiet life until he died of cancer in 1967.

Like many mob-operated clubs, the Casino de Paree was successful, but it couldn't survive the effects of the

Depression despite talents like Berle, Bill "Bojangles" Robinson, and Smith and Dale. On January 16, 1936, the theater was renamed the Palladium. The Palladium lasted only 3 weeks (better than the one-week run of *The Vikings*), and in 1937 the FEDERAL THEATRE PROJECT leased it and renamed it the Federal Music Theater. The theater's name was changed again, once again to the New Yorker Theater, and returned to legitimate theater productions on March 21, 1939, with *The Swing Mikado* (86 performances). After 8 weeks, the show transferred to the 44TH STREET THEATRE, where it completed its run. The first public display of theater television premiered at the theater in 1941. A boxing match at Madison Square Garden down 8th Avenue on 50th Street was projected on a large 15-by-20-foot screen on the stage. Television would return to the theater in 1943 when CBS turned the theater into the CBS Radio Playhouse Number 4 and later Studio No. 52.

The building achieved perhaps its greatest success in 1976 when Steve Rubell and Ian Schrager bought the theater and transformed it into Studio 54. They were forced to sell the theater in 1980, although it remained a disco, cabaret, and nightclub. In 1989 the theater became a rock concert hall, and the name was changed to the Ritz. It became a legitimate theater again in November 1998 with the Roundabout Theatre's revival of *Cabaret*, which moved from the Kit Kat Klub (*see* HENRY MILLER'S THEATRE).

STUNTS. Times Square, the heart of Manhattan and the center of the entertainment industry, is seldom out of the papers. Because of its proximity to the limelight, and to the offices of the *New York Times*, Times Square is the location of most of the great publicity stunts of modern times.

A publicity stunt is an unusual event designed to call attention to a performer, product, or show. Broadway columnist Bernard Sobel recalled the days when newspapers and magazines went along with the joke:

In those mellow times editors were generous and warm hearted; they regarded theatrical stories and photographs as a legitimate form of news of the day, amusing to the reader, and entitled to the space no matter how crazy the copy, especially when that copy combined a mixture of smooth writing, good humor and pseudo-truth. But that was a time for pure tomfoolery, and space was made available for it. This was true especially for pictures; there were gracious sepia-toned rotogravure supplements, a newspaper section now forgotten and almost quite unknown to many newcomers in our trade.

Stunts in particular were the press agents'—and the editors'—delight; among others of my craft, I turned them out almost daily, sometimes talking over two telephones at the same time, while shouting instructions to my assistants.

The *Sunny* Dairy Room stunt.

Most of the early stunts following the turn of the 20th century involved the beautiful girls who graced the early musical comedies. A pretty girl with an ankle or leg showing could always be counted on to draw a paper's reporters and photographers. Stunts, called "fakes" in the old days, often became very elaborate so that editors would swallow them more easily. Stunts have also been known to backfire. Mrs. Patrick Campbell was involved in a stunt in which it was claimed that the noted actress had won much money while playing bridge with society ladies. However, the backlash from moral-minded readers and religious leaders made the publicity all the more damning.

As the new century got under way, newspapers and radio were coming into their own. There was plenty of space to fill, and PRESS AGENTS were there to see to it that their clients received their fair share of column inches. The most famous and most exploited performer in her time was ANNA HELD. FLORENZ ZIEGFELD had met her in Paris in 1895. He immediately imported her and drummed up interest in her meager talents through a series of outrageous stunts, the most famous of which was her milk baths. During the run of the *ZIEGFELD FOLLIES*, Mae Daw, an unknown at the time, decided to challenge dancing star Ann Pennington to a cow-milking contest. She had no reason to do so except to get her name in the papers. It worked; papers the next day pictured the two women at the Long Island home of James J. Corbett. *Follies* girls were forever being trotted out for one grand scheme or another. Mae Daw also spent months practicing the saxophone for a "surf jazz" party of the *Follies* girls. Jean Stewart traveled with a baby lamb to combat her loneliness. Pearl Eaton almost drowned the entire line when she crashed her team's boat into another during a Central Park boat race. Fortunately, the stage-door Johnnies who lined the shore could swim and pulled the soaking girls from the lake.

Gilda Gray, best known for her shimmy, became a star when an enterprising press agent arranged for a suitably handsome man to wrap a $100,000 diamond necklace around a bouquet and toss it onstage during her number. The same exact stunt was used for actress Julia Sanderson. This time the bouquet, thrown by a "German baron," contained an $18,000 necklace. The press bought the story again.

Press agent Will A. Page was the mastermind behind many of these stunts, but his personal favorite was the "Strip Golf Game." The idea grew out of an argument between chorus girls Shirley Vernon and Nellie Savage. At a party after the argument, the girls' dates insisted on their naming a date for the unusual match. The men were so insistent that plans were made to drive to Long Island and play that very next day. Before leaving, Miss Vernon had the foresight to phone Will Page and ask him to serve as referee. He agreed and made some phone calls himself, ensuring press coverage. The rules of the game were simple. If the hole was halved or tied, the girls would remain as they were. If the hole was lost, however, the loser would remove one piece of clothing. All 18 holes were to be played. Midway through the match, quite a crowd had gathered and the women were reduced to their underthings. Fortunately, someone came to the aid of Miss Vernon at the last minute and supplied her with a barrel. It did nothing for her game, but it did make her a star. The photo of her strange garb was printed all over the world, and offers for Miss Vernon's services came from Hollywood and Broadway. Ziegfeld was forced to raise her salary again and again until she replaced Marilyn Miller in *Sally*.

Page also managed to make Alice Delysia a huge star through a series of stunts. As luck would have it, the performer had a well-developed sense of humor and the desire to see her name exploited. When Page and producer Morris Gest decided to bring Delysia from the Continent during Prohibition, they wrote an unusual clause in her contract. It stated that she was to have available 1 bottle of wine at every meal. The reason given for this request was that the actress needed the liquor to keep up her joie de vivre and "without which Mlle. Delysia will pine away and her audience-value diminish."

When Delysia arrived in the United States, she was outfitted in a flaming-red leather dress and an ankle watch encrusted with huge diamonds. Following that, Page kept the heat on her career by a variety of ploys. A dog was trained to attack her during a luncheon. It was planned that she would then divest herself of the canine and exclaim, "More muzzles or foreign artistes will never visit these shores again." Unfortunately, the dog didn't quite understand its part, and the actress was nearly mauled, resulting in the closing of her show for 3 nights.

Page also cooked up a scheme for Delysia that took its leading participant by surprise. Delysia had been receiving love notes from a millionaire suitor. She wasn't interested in the man and wanted him to go away. Consulting Page, she happened to show him one of the missives, in which the young man stated, "You doubt my love but you are wrong. Merely to kiss your hand, I would crawl over broken glass on my hands and knees." Page arranged the press to be present in the actress' dressing room when the young man arrived. Little did the suitor expect to find the floor strewn with broken glass. At the other end of the trail of glass was his adored one, Delysia. She challenged him, "You said you would crawl over broken glass on your hands and knees to get me. Let me see you crawl." This was meant to be the end of the stunt, but the young man quickly dropped to his knees and actually crept across the room to the velvet-clad Delysia. The actress and the other guests stared in horror as the man slowly crossed the room. When at her feet, he rose and stated, "I've made good, now what about yourself?" Delysia changed her mind about the man, and they enjoyed a long relationship.

The 1910s and '20s were filled with stunts, usually built around famous actresses: Valeska Suratt's Fourth of July Christmas tree; Olga Nethersole's "Sappho" kiss; and Ruth Urban's banquet for 30, which featured a pig as the guest of honor. Harry Reichenbach put a live lion in a midtown hotel room in order to publicize the 1921 production of *Tarzan of the Apes*; however, the play managed only 13 performances.

EARL CARROLL, producer of EARL CARROLL'S VANITIES, produced the unsuccessful *The Lady of the Lamp* in 1920. Carroll was desperate for the show to succeed, because it was his first producing venture. "I Am Gambling My Last Thousand Dollars," claimed headlines over the articles in which Carroll begged the public to support his show, which he had written. Carroll asserted that if audience members were unsatisfied, he personally would meet them in the lobby after the show and refund their money. True to his word, Carroll was in the lobby at the end of every performance. However, most people admired the producer's pluck and left after shaking his hand. The show closed after a respectable, although not profitable, 111 performances. Carroll managed to make the event a success anyway, because, following one of the performances, a distinguished gentleman named William R. Edrington handed Carroll his card and asked to see him. Carroll made an appointment with the banker, which resulted in Carroll becoming owner of the EARL CARROLL THEATRE.

Bernard Sobol, an author and press agent who represented both Ziegfeld and Carroll, recalled one of his stunts produced while in Carroll's employ:

I was working for Earl Carroll, exploiting *The Blue Kitten*, and sent out a story that Lillian Lorraine, star of the show, did her own washing. Of course, down in the second or third paragraph I qualified this plebian statement by saying she didn't exactly stand over a washtub doing the heavy work, such as bath towels or pillow cases and bed sheets. She confined her "washing" only to those dainty bits of personal apparel . . . negligees, gloves or light lacy handkerchiefs, the things that surely could not be entrusted to the indignity of a common laundry.

Sobel also remembered a series of stunts on Ziegfeld's behalf:

When I moved into the Ziegfeld office I learned that the great Flo, as a press agent, was always one step ahead of me. The battle was violent, pleasurable, and long. He taunted me, reprimanded me and seldom praised me, but the joy of working for him, and with him, was praise enough.

Stunts made news, and each day I planned something new. I had the chorus girls from *Louis the 14th* parade in bathing suits at City Hall, as a military recruiting drive. Ziegfeld gently asked me to refrain from this kind of publicity. Inwardly he rejoiced, since the stunt helped prolong the show's life on Broadway and launch its road tour.

Ziegfeld girls staged a monster Maypole Dance on Michigan Boulevard in Chicago, twirling long ropes of brilliantly colored ribbons. Equally successful was the stunt we staged in Central Park to herald the advent of spring in New York, an early March 21st. A bevy of showgirls shivered in bikinis of the day, to be chased by the cops: we had forgotten to get a permit for the party. I wrote a feature column for Yale students and used the Ziegfeld byline, but he never knew about it; later it was reprinted in the *Herald-Tribune*. In Ziegfeld's name I also wrote a preface to a Kenyon Nicholson book—"Revues." He placed so little emphasis on authorship—he had bought and sold so many authors, Ring Lardner included—that he pitched the volume into a waste basket, from which I very gratefully rescued the tome once he left the room.

But the most surprising stunt I ever arranged occurred at the time "Gentlemen Prefer Blondes" was a literary best seller. Latching on to a topic that suggested a stunt was always a good tactic. In this instance, I planned a "strike."

The idea was that Ziegfeld became annoyed at the popularity of blondes created by the book's eminence, and was showing great preference for brunettes in the company. I didn't write a story, but coached Paulette Goddard, then a dream of a teen-age blonde, to lead a group of blondes to strike.

The "strikers" wound up in the editorial room of the *New York Times* to air their complaint against Ziegfeld; the first day there was a half-column story, then another the following day. We could have had plenty more, except for Ziegfeld.

I had, of course, neglected to tell him about the stunt; when the *Times* telephoned him about the strike, he had to reveal his own ignorance of the subject. He laughed about it later, admitting he had been fooled by the stunt. Later I talked it over with a *Times* reporter and expressed my own surprise that the staid newspaper had printed anything about the hoax. He said: "We knew it was a stunt, but we enjoy a bit of it when it's properly mixed with humor."

Howard Dietz (*see* DIETZ AND SCHWARTZ), Broadway lyricist and head of publicity for MGM, got lots of space when he put live women in flesh-colored tights on the huge sign advertising the *Hollywood Revue of 1929*, which was then playing at the ASTOR THEATRE.

Another famed fake was the bet by Margaret Mayo that she could write a play in one day. The actress was appearing in *Pretty Peggy*, and press agent Channing Pollock needed an idea to drum up business. The scheme worked in this way. Mayo made a bet with playwright Theodore Burt Sayre that she could write a play in 24 hours. To prove that the wager was on the up and up, it was decided that Sayre would himself provide the synopsis, which would be delivered in a sealed envelope at the start of the day.

Pollock arranged for his stenographer to aide the actress in finishing the 4-act work. The night before, a finished play of Mayo's was hidden around the room where the writing was to take place. All through the day, Pollock and Mayo pretended to be in the throes of creativity. Between visits by reporters, they enjoyed leisurely meals. Sayre, who happened to be a close friend of Pollock, assured the press that he himself wrote the synopsis. That he did, while Pollock dictated it to him over the telephone. The newspapermen were suitably impressed when, at 6 o'clock the next morning, an exhausted Mayo delivered the manuscript, entitled *The Mart*. Mayo became an author in her own right with successes such as *Baby Mine* and *Polly of the Circus*.

Many stunts were instigated in order to disguise the shoddiness of a production. Edward L. Bernays was a fledgling producer in 1913 with his production, *Damaged Goods*. The play's title seemed entirely too apt, so a plan was hatched. Bernays happened also to be the co-editor of the *Medical Review of Reviews*. The play was somewhat racy for its time, and the producer decided to open it only to members of the newly formed Medical Review of Reviews Sociological Fund. Membership cost exactly the same as a theater ticket. Newly enrolled members of the fund kept the play running for 66 performances.

Stunts have often taken the form of legal action. Performers were continually suing management and vice versa. Marion Alexander might have started the idea when she sued Sam S. Shubert (*see* SHUBERT

BROTHERS) for $10,000 because he stated she was not beautiful.

During the run of *Fantana* in 1905, Channing Pollock hatched a stunt in which a chorus girl's dog wore expensive diamond earrings. Neither the dog nor the chorus girl owned a pair of earrings, so Pollock was happy to supply a pair of cheap fakes and the bubble gum needed to make them adhere. The press looked askance at such an obvious fraud, and the reporter from the *World* had the nerve to refuse to use the photo. Pollock was forced to defend his honor and have the dog's ears pierced, and Tiffany's was asked to supply a pair of earrings suitable for canine use. This time, all the papers used the photo.

Pollock drummed up business for the 1906 production *Happyland* at the CASINO THEATRE by announcing a matinee "for women only." To ensure coverage of the nonevent, Pollock arranged for a man to crash the theater dressed in ladies' garments. There was also a husband who insisted that his wife exit the theater immediately if he was not allowed to attend. Pollock's window dressing was unnecessary because the event turned out to be tremendously popular, and the performance was sold out.

In the days before photocopy machines, scripts had to be hand-typed with crude carbon-paper copies. In order to cut down on secretarial work, actors received "sides," which contained only their lines and a few cues. Thus in the latter part of 1905, when producer Henry Miller claimed that his play *Grierson's Way* had to be postponed because the only complete script had been lost, the press bought into the lie. A $500 reward was announced to sweeten the story while the rehearsals continued. The press agent on the show was surprised to learn that Miller subsequently did lose the script and was panicked at the thought of having to pay the $500. A stagehand found the script and accepted a small reward.

Pollock thought up many other stunts to please his producers. Nena Blake, a chorus girl with *The Royal Chef* (9/1/04), was kidnapped in costume and sent halfway across the country. Her sister, Bertha, kissed a man who had never been kissed before. Actor Adele Ritchie's niece had her name legally changed to Adele Ritchie Jr., and the namesake was wooed by a "Siamese millionaire."

Times Square has also had its share of flagpole sitters and marathon dances (*see* ROSELAND) and other physical feats. One of the most famous flagpole sitter was Shipwreck Kelly, who lasted 13 days atop the Paramount Hotel in 1930. He was also found on Friday the 13th atop the Chanin Building on 42nd Street. For this stunt, in October 1939, Kelly ate 13 donuts while standing on his head.

Fakes have passed into disfavor. Show business is more a business than a show, and newspapers pride themselves on reporting the truth. On the other hand, publicist RICHARD MANEY doted on fakes that were obviously fake and, in fact, too ridiculous to pass up. Maney created most of his stunts while under the employ of the master showman DAVID MERRICK. Facing an embarrassing failure with his first outing, *Clutterbuck* (12/3/49; 218 performances), Merrick arranged to have a Mr. Clutterbuck paged throughout Manhattan. Every hotel and restaurant resounded with the name Mr. Clutterbuck. Although the show was not a success, Merrick saw the value of a good stunt.

When Grace Kelly got married in Monaco, a plane circled overhead trailing a banner exhorting the wedding party to come and see the Merrick production *Fanny* (11/4/54; 888 performances). Closer to home, Merrick was seen in Manhattan walking an ostrich named Fanny. *Fanny* featured a belly dancer, so Merrick placed a statue of her in Poet's Corner in Central Park; the statue was nude. This enraged the sculptor, who saw his art on perhaps a higher plane, and again the newspapers reveled in Merrick's mischievousness. Even this wasn't enough to satisfy the indefatigable Merrick. He found names of suburbanites listed in the phone book and called them to invite them to see *Fanny* for free, provided they brought one paying customer. When *Fanny* finally closed after 888 performances, the ledger books showed a handsome profit of almost $1 million.

Other Merrick-Maney stunts were just as colorful as those for *Fanny*. When *The Good Soup* (3/2/60; 21 performances) opened, someone circulated the rumor that the playwright, Félicien Marceau, was a Nazi collaborator. Much newspaper coverage ensued. When Merrick's production of *The World of Suzi Wong* and the RODGERS AND HAMMERSTEIN musical *Flower Drum Song* were both about to open in 1958, Merrick sent Asian-Americans to picket the *Flower Drum Song* box office with signs proclaiming Wong as "the only authentic Chinese show." Richard Rodgers was not amused.

The Matchmaker (12/5/55; 486 performances) was given the Merrick treatment when he arranged to have a chimpanzee drive a taxi around town carrying the sign "I am driving my master to see *The Matchmaker*." Merrick's fondness for animals again became evident when, for no apparent reason, a platypus showed up at the first press conference announcing *Romanoff and Juliet*. History was made during a performance of the explosive drama *Look Back In Anger* (10/1/57; 407 performances), when a woman burst from her seat, jumped onstage, and slapped actor Kenneth Haigh. This was reported in all the papers. It received attention again when Merrick admitted that the $250 he had paid

the woman just might have had something to do with her outburst.

And as a remedy for a bad critical reception, Merrick was known to prescribe some strong medicine. At the beginning of a live broadcast from outside the theater of one of his flops, Merrick gleefully assigned a press agent to take an ax to the television cable, thereby literally cutting off the bad review. When faced with less-than-positive reviews of his musical *Subways Are for Sleeping* (12/27/61; 205 performances), Merrick simply went to the phone book and called people whose names matched those of New York's leading dramatic CRITICS. The critics were Howard Taubman (*New York Times*), WALTER KERR (*Herald Tribune*), John Chapman (*Daily News*), Robert Coleman (*Daily Mirror*), Norman Nadel (*World Telegram*), John McLain (*Journal-American*), and Richard Watts (*Post*). He then brought these people to the city, wined and dined them at the Plaza Hotel's Oak Room, and transported them to the theater. After, he asked them what they thought of the show and suggested they lend their names to quotes that he composed. Advertising manager Fred Golden, a Merrick favorite, made up a full-page ad to be run in all the New York papers, which reprinted the erstwhile quotes, names, and pictures. The *New York Times* discovered the stunt after its first edition and pulled it. However, the attendant publicity became so enormous that the *Times* was forced to run the ad when reporting the hoax. The other dailies did not catch the fraud.

More recently, stunts have been used sparingly and with little of the panache that earlier practitioners brought to the art. When *Grease* celebrated its fourth birthday on St. Valentine's Day 1976, a couple was married onstage. For *Knockout* (5/6/79), a staged bout between star Danny Aiello and heavyweight Larry Holmes was held. Wilbur the pig, a cast member of *King of Hearts* (10/22/78; 48 performances), was treated to a limousine ride and lunch at SARDI'S. For the first anniversary of *Deathtrap* on February 26, 1979, press agent Jeffrey Richards gave a party for psychics who predicted the future of the show and its cast. Larry Blyden, who co-produced and starred in the 1972 revival of *A Funny Thing Happened on the Way to the Forum* with Phil Silvers, decided to give a free Fourth of July performance. By 11 A.M. all the tickets were gone. Josh Ellis of Solters/Roskin and Freedman had a unit of the New York Blood Program in the lobby of *Dracula* (10/20/77; 925 performances). For every year of its long run, *Big River* hosted a jumping-frog contest outside its theater under the auspices of publicist Adrian Bryan-Brown. But for the most part, stunts and fakes have lost their appeal. Richard Maney once bemoaned the fact that today the authors of stunts would be "drummed out of the regi-

Carol Lawrence and Sydney Chaplin in *Subways Are for Sleeping*, 1961.

ment. Hyperbole and deception no longer are effective weapons."

John Golden produced a show called *Pigs*, which played in the halcyon year of 1924. In those days, a person could pull a stunt and be proud of it. For the show, a dozen of the title characters were shuttled between a stable and the theater. Harry Kline was the enterprising press agent for the show and saw to it that every day the pigs were transported in a straw-covered wagon. The driver took his squealing load up and down the streets of Times Square. On the wagon was a sign with the message: "These Pigs Perform Nightly at the Little Theater."

STUYVESANT THEATER. *See* **Belasco Theatre.**

STYNE, JULE. Among the most successful and prolific of all Broadway composers, primarily active in

the 1960s and '70s; b. Julius Kerwin Stein, London, England, December 31, 1905; d. New York, New York, September 20, 1994.

Many consider Styne the ultimate composer when it comes to writing to suit the talents of stars. He tailored *Gentlemen Prefer Blondes* for Carol Channing, *Gypsy* for ETHEL MERMAN, *Funny Girl* for Barbra Streisand, and *Bells Are Ringing* for Judy Holliday. Although these shows remain indelibly associated with their stars, they also exist as perfect examples of cohesive, well-integrated scores that serve their theatrical needs as fully as they serve the needs of their performers. It is this versatility and superb artistry that led many to consider Styne our greatest living composer.

Styne's family emigrated from England to the United States in 1913 and settled in Chicago. By the time the youngster was a teenager, Chicago was becoming more and more of an influence in the development of jazz and popular song. The early jazz groups

Michael Kidd, Mark Breaux, and Jule Styne during rehearsals for *Subways Are For Sleeping*, 1961.

known as the Chicagoans did not escape the notice of the young prodigy. Despite a solid classical background (he made his debut at the age of 9 as a solo pianist with the Chicago Symphony), Styne felt more and more drawn to the music of the back-room bars and nightclubs.

A scholarship to the Chicago College of Music enabled Styne to perfect his technique and to study composition, theory, and harmony. He formed his own dance band, for which he played the piano and contributed arrangements. He joined some of the smaller bands then touring the country, most notably that of Art Jarrett. Styne's early days in Chicago were an important influence in his career. He was aware of all the great musicians playing at the time and called Chicago at the time "a feast."

In 1934 Styne moved to New York, where he earned his living as a vocal coach and then accompanist for

Harry Richman, a top Broadway and nightclub performer. Styne received an offer from Twentieth Century–Fox asking him to come to Hollywood a year later to coach Alice Faye, Tony Martin, Shirley Temple, and other Fox stars.

Styne previously had a big hit with his first song, "Sunday," written in 1927, and it didn't take the studio long to move Styne into the composers' stable. Styne moved from Fox to Republic and then to Paramount and Columbia. Among the movies for which he contributed music were *Anchors Aweigh*, *Tonight and Every Night*, *Tars and Spars*, *The Kid from Brooklyn*, *It Happened in Brooklyn*, *Romance on the High Seas*, *Two Guys from Texas*, *It's a Great Feeling*, *The West Point Story*, *Two Tickets to Broadway*, *My Sister Eileen*, and *Meet Me After the Show*.

Styne's principal collaborators during his Hollywood years were FRANK LOESSER and Sammy Cahn.

They collaborated with Styne on such songs as "I Don't Want to Walk Without You, Baby," "I've Heard that Song Before," "I Said No," "Victory Polka," "I'll Walk Alone," "Anywhere," "It's a Great Feeling," "Saturday Night Is the Loneliest Night in the Week," "Poor Little Rhode Island," "The Charm of You," "I Fall in Love Too Easily," "What Makes the Sunset," "It's Been a Long, Long, Time," "Let It Snow, Let It Snow, Let It Snow," "The Things We Did Last Summer," "Five Minutes More," "Time After Time," "Three Coins in the Fountain" (which received an Academy Award in 1954), and "It's Magic."

After success in Hollywood, Cahn and Styne attempted to write a Broadway musical. The result, *Glad to See You* (1944), was planned as a vehicle for Phil Silvers. His unavailability and other problems forced the show to close out of town. However, a standard did emerge from the score, "Guess I'll Hang My Tears out to Dry." The team had much better luck with their next attempt, *High Button Shoes* (10/9/47; 727 performances). This time they got their man, Phil Silvers, and he and Nanette Fabray opened the show at the CENTURY THEATER. The Styne–Cahn score contributed at least 1 song to the hit parade, the polka "Poppa Won't You Dance with Me." Other standouts were "Can't You Just See Yourself?" and "I Still Get Jealous."

Two years later Styne again opened a show on Broadway, this time with Leo Robin as lyricist. It was just as big a success as *High Button Shoes*. The show was *Gentlemen Prefer Blondes* (12/8/49; 740 performances), an adaptation of Anita Loos' popular novel. It was noteworthy for several reasons, the most important being the debut of Carol Channing as Lorelei Lee. Styne and Robin provided Channing with the first song that would become her trademark, "Diamonds Are a Girl's Best Friend." The show also featured such hits as "Bye Bye Baby," "A Little Girl from Little Rock," and "You Say You Care."

Styne's next show wasn't as successful, but it was important as the first meeting between Styne and his longtime collaborators COMDEN AND GREEN. *Two on the Aisle* (7/19/51; 281 performances) was Styne's only Broadway revue and was written to fit the talents of Bert Lahr and Dolores Gray. Styne's third collaborator in as many shows was Bob Hilliard, with whom he worked on *Hazel Flagg* (2/11/53; 190 performances), a musicalization of Ben Hecht's movie *Nothing Sacred*. The show was a disappointment despite a fine performance by Helen Gallagher. "Every Street's a Boulevard (in Old New York)" achieved some fame.

Director/choreographer Jerome Robbins was out of town working on a musical version of *Peter Pan*, starring MARY MARTIN. The show was having trouble, and

the writing team of Jule Styne and Comden and Green was called in to bolster the Moose Charlap–Carolyn Leigh score. The principal Styne, Comden, and Green songs were "Never Never Land," "Distant Melody," and "Captain Hook's Waltz." *Peter Pan* (10/20/54; 152 performances) played at the WINTER GARDEN THEATRE before a commitment to televise the show forced the Broadway production to close. It became a perennial favorite on NBC, with Martin and Cyril Ritchard having the time of their lives in the J. M. Barrie fantasy.

Next, Styne, Comden, and Green collaborated on *Bells Are Ringing* (11/29/56; 924 performances), written as a vehicle for Judy Holliday. Comden and Green had cut their teeth performing with Holliday as members of the Revuers, an early musical comedy act that played Greenwich Village clubs. For the new show, the songwriters gave their star two great hits, "The Party's Over" and "Just In Time." *Say, Darling* (4/3/58; 332 performances), the trio's next Broadway offering, was a play about a musical. The source was a thinly disguised novel by Richard Bissel that told of his experiences working as co-librettist on *The Pajama Game*. The show starred Vivian Blaine, David Wayne, Johnny Desmond, and brash Robert Morse as a spoof on HAROLD PRINCE. The show unfortunately never achieved its due. The problem was that the show was more of a play with songs than a full-fledged musical. Audiences were disappointed not to find the typical musical-comedy trappings. The one hit from the score was "Dance Only with Me."

Styne then collaborated with STEPHEN SONDHEIM on what some consider the greatest musical of all time, *Gypsy* (5/21/59; 702 performances); Arthur Laurents wrote the libretto. Rose was the ultimate stage mother; to play her, the producers, DAVID MERRICK and Leland Hayward, chose the ultimate musical-comedy star, Ethel Merman. Jerome Robbins was the director and choreographer. Styne and Sondheim perfectly tailored their bravura score to Merman's talents, and they also served the dramatic needs of the script. The brassy, challenging score contained several hit songs, "Let Me Entertain You," "Some People," "Together," and "Everything's Coming Up Roses." All the elements of the production fused in Ethel Merman's last number, the thrilling "Rose's Turn," a high point in the actor's career and in the history of musical theater.

Styne next moved on to another collaboration with Comden and Green, *Do Re Mi* (12/26/60; 400 performances). Styne again fashioned a score for Phil Silvers. His co-star in this was Nancy Walker with John Reardon, David Burns, and Nancy Dussault rounding out the leads. *Do Re Mi* was the story of the mob's control of the jukebox industry and Phil Silvers' quest to make a quick buck. The show's run was based mainly on

Adolph Green, Betty Comden, Judy Holliday, and Jule Styne in a publicity shot for *Bells Are Ringing*, 1956.

the comic inventiveness of the stars and the hit song, "Make Someone Happy." *Subways Are for Sleeping* (12/27/61; 205 performances) was the threesome's next offering. Sydney Chaplin, Carol Lawrence, Orson Bean, and Phyllis Newman starred. The score was well received, with "Comes Once in a Lifetime" achieving the most notice. The show is best remembered for a series of publicity STUNTS engineered by producer David Merrick.

Styne's next production was his biggest hit. *Funny Girl* (3/26/64; 1,348 performances), starring Barbra Streisand, opened at the Winter Garden Theatre. Bob Merrill provided the lyrics to Styne's music. Garson Kanin and Jerome Robbins whipped the show into shape after a particularly stormy tryout. By opening night it was clear that Broadway had a major hit and a major star on its hands. Regrettably, *Funny Girl* was Streisand's last Broadway appearance. The story of FANNY BRICE had the same show-business ambiance that had inspired *Gypsy*. The score provided another star with a Styne signature tune. Streisand introduced "People," and the song became hers alone. Other numbers in the score also received airplay, includ-ing "Don't Rain on My Parade" and "Who Are You Now?"

Styne's next show also featured another young star, Carol Burnett. However, *Fade Out—Fade In* (5/26/64; 271 performances) didn't achieve the fame of *Funny Girl*. None of the Styne, Comden, and Green songs clicked with the hit parade, and Burnett's problems with the show forced it to close, reopen, then close for good. *Hallelujah, Baby!* (4/26/67; 293 performances) reteamed Styne with his *Gypsy* librettist, Arthur Laurents. The score, with lyrics by Comden and Green, was exceptional, but the book, purporting to follow the progress made by blacks in the 20th century, proved unwieldy. The show won the TONY AWARD as Best Musical after it had closed. Leslie Uggams, Robert Hooks, and Allen Case starred.

Darling of the Day (1/27/68; 32 performances) was another show with a fine Styne score that achieved little success. This time, the lyrics were by master lyricist E. Y. HARBURG. Although the show wasn't a success, the score was wonderfully witty and tuneful and deserves rediscovery. Styne teamed up with his old partner Sammy Cahn for *Look to the Lilies* (3/29/70;

STYNE, JULE

25 performances). The adaptation of *Lilies of the Field* wasn't very strong despite the best efforts of the star, Shirley Booth. That failure was followed by *Prettybelle*, which starred Angela Lansbury and closed out of town.

Bob Merrill, who provided Styne with such strong lyrics for *Funny Girl* and not such strong ones for *Prettybelle*, was unable to repeat his popular success with *Sugar* (4/9/72; 505 performances), a musical adaptation of the Billy Wilder movie *Some Like It Hot*. Cyril Ritchard and Robert Morse made their second appearances in Styne musicals along with co-stars Tony Roberts and Elaine Joyce. The show's long run was due more to the work of producer David Merrick rather than the worthiness of the material.

One Night Stand proved not even equal to its title, closing on October 25, 1980, after eight previews. Herb Gardner provided the lyrics.

With Broadway's fitful success with musical productions in the 1980s and 90s, Styne was relegated to the wings. His attempt at musicalizing *Treasure Island* with lyricist Susan Birkenhead got no further than Edmonton, Canada. Jule Styne's final score also had lyrics by Susan Birkenhead. However, *The Red Shoes* (12/16/93; 5 performances) was in trouble from the first preview. Styne's frequent collaborator, Bob Merrill, was brought in to work on new songs. Merrill chose to work under the pseudonym Paul Stryker. That name was chosen because, when he was a staff writer at Republic Pictures, the executives wanted Styne to change his name to Paul Stryker. Despite some wonderful songs and good performances, *The Red Shoes* couldn't overcome a weak book, bad direction, and poor producing. It was to be Jule Styne's last Broadway show.

SULLIVAN, ED. Broadway columnist who became a famed TV variety-show host; b. New York, New York, September 28, 1902; d. New York, New York; October 13, 1974.

In the 1930s and 1940s Walter Winchell, Louis Sobol, Earl Wilson, Ed Sullivan, Mark Hellinger, and Damon Runyon were the men who ruled Broadway with their newspaper columns. Each of them could make or break careers and shows with a stroke of their pens. They were night people who scoured the speakeasies and clubs for tales of those who gave Broadway and Times Square its energy. Sullivan wasn't the most famous of the group, but he turned out to be the most influential when he began his weekly variety show on CBS in the late 1940s.

Sullivan, like the others, believed in Broadway as a phenomenon that mattered more than any other acreage in the world. He treated it with the respect and

Ed Sullivan.

scorn he felt it deserved. Hollywood and the capitals of Europe were viewed as distant kingdoms whose inhabitants really mattered only when on the streets of Times Square. In those days, all the great gossip columns came from New York. Hedda Hopper and Louella Parsons were important only to the movie industry. Hollywood was simply a remote outpost that existed to serve Broadway's needs. Surprisingly, residents of Hollywood agreed with the Great White Way's ethnocentrism. The goal of many of the great movie actors was to star in a Broadway play. Columnists like Sullivan and Winchell fed that feeling with their somewhat myopic view of the world.

Ed Sullivan's first New York newspaper job was at the *Evening Mail* as a sports writer. He thereafter held a succession of short-term jobs, first at the *Philadelphia Ledger*, then the *Morning World*, the *Bulletin*, the *Leader*, and the *Morning Telegraph*. He finally settled at the *Graphic* in 1927. He soon found himself elevated to the post of sports editor. The *Graphic* was considered a yellow-journalism rag by its contemporaries. Publisher Bernarr Macfadden's daily was even described by Sullivan as "a step removed from pornography." Winchell, then the paper's gossip columnist, wrote a column headed "Broadway Hearsay." He often fought with his editors and was soon lured to the *Daily Mirror*. Louis Sobol took Winchell's place and shortly thereafter moved to the *Journal-American*. In looking around for a replacement, the editors chose Sullivan. The reluctant reporter accepted the job, because the only alternative was looking for work on another paper.

On June 1, 1931, "Ed Sullivan Sees Broadway" was printed for the first time. Sullivan was resolved not to emulate his predecessors. He believed he had a higher mission. In his first column, he attacked his forerunner's style:

> I charge the Broadway columnists with defaming the street. I have entered a field of writing that ranks so low that it is difficult to distinguish anyone columnist from his road companions. I have entered a field which offers scant competition. The Broadway columnists have lifted themselves to distinction by borrowed gags, gossip that is not always kindly and keyholes that too often reveal what might better be hidden. Phonies will receive no comfort in this space. To get into this particular column will be a badge of merit and a citation—divorces will not be propagated in this column. . . . In my capacity as drama critic I pledge you of the theater that if I like the show I will say so without any ambiguities of phrasing that might protect my *VARIETY* box score. . . . With the theater in the doldrums, it means a decisive voice and I promise to supply it.

Naturally, Sobol and Winchell took exception to his inferences. Sobol, in his column, labeled Sullivan's diatribe "The Ennui of His Contempt-oraries." Sobol claimed that "empty vessels make the most sound." Sullivan didn't always keep his word, but he tried as best he could to keep his high ideals. When the *Graphic* folded on July 7, 1932, Sullivan moved to Joseph Patterson's *Daily News* for $200 a week. By this time Sullivan had already gone into radio, starting with a sports show sponsored by Adam Hats. CBS picked him up two years later in 1932 with a program entitled "Broadway's Greatest Thrills." The sponsor was American Safety Razor, and the salary was $1,000 a week. Because he had been forced to take a $175-a-week pay cut to join the *News*, the radio salary became his major means of support. It was later called *Ed Sullivan Entertains* and was broadcast live from the 21 Club. Sullivan opened his show with the sound of a typewriter.

A reviewer wrote: "The clackety-clack of the Remington, with the carriage moved back intermittently, is a switch on the Winchellian telegraphic staccato. . . . Although Sullivan's voice does not have the weight and authority for this type of work, it's no drawback. Different type pipes are welcome."

Boris Morros persuaded Sullivan to follow in Winchell's footsteps once again, and he moved into live entertainment as a producer of variety shows at the PARAMOUNT THEATER. The shows were entitled *Gems*

of the Town. Sullivan demurred until the $3,750-per-show salary was mentioned. The first *Gems of the Town* premiered with the film *Take a Chance*. With the success at the Paramount behind him, Sullivan moved to LOEW'S STATE THEATER for a series of revues featuring Harry Rose, "the Broadway Jester," as emcee. Sullivan soon took over the hosting chores of his *Dawn Patrol* shows. At this time Sullivan began introducing celebrities sitting in the audience, a practice he continued on television. Sullivan's tenure at the State brought other revues to the stage. The revue of July 6, 1934, was typical. *The All-Star All-American Nightclub Revue of 1934* featured Georgie Tapps, Ken Harvey, Joan Abbott, and ballroom dancers, Mr. and Mrs. Paul Mears.

It seemed natural for Sullivan to tackle Broadway next, but his offering, a revue entitled *Crazy with the Heat* (1/14/41), lasted only 99 performances. Not willing to lose everything, he moved the second act of the show into Loew's State for a two-week run. Sullivan's next stab at Broadway was an all-black revue, *Harlem Cavalcade*, which opened on May 1, 1942. It fared no better than his first try and folded after only 49 performances. Sullivan also hosted the annual *Daily News* amateur ballroom dance competition, the Harvest Moon Ball. He began his duties in 1936 and continued for 12 years thereafter. At the 12th edition of the contest, CBS had set up a live remote from Madison Square Garden. Sullivan was unaware of the cameras until the next day, when Jack Benny called to congratulate him on his work. Thus did Ed Sullivan make his television debut on September 3, 1947.

Worthington Miner was CBS's director of programming. He was impressed with Sullivan and offered him the chance to do a weekly variety series to be titled *You're the Top*. The series, retitled *The Toast of the Town*, premiered at 9 o'clock on Sunday, June 20, 1948. The MAXINE ELLIOTT'S THEATRE was used as the studio. Among the guests on that first show were the phenomenally successful songwriting team RODGERS AND HAMMERSTEIN. In their portion of the show they talked about *Oklahoma!* and *South Pacific*. *Oklahoma!* had just closed on May 29, 1948; *South Pacific* was to open on April 7, 1949. Their third Broadway musical, *Allegro*, was then currently at the end of its run and received a boost at the box office from the team's appearance.

Sullivan continued plugging Broadway shows on his program, giving them the national recognition that only television could bring. Hit shows tended not to need the Sullivan show for publicity, although there were some notable exceptions. Julie Andrews appeared many times on the show, singing songs from *My Fair Lady*. She appeared during the Broadway run and subsequent London engagement. Andrews reappeared on the show, along with co-star Richard Burton, to plug *Camelot*. Often the Sullivan tapes offer the only glimpses of legendary performances. Some shows like *Fanny* and *Do Re Mi* enjoyed extended exposure on the show, over 40 minutes total. The Sullivan show archives are an invaluable record of Broadway over two decades.

Sullivan wrote his newspaper column for the entire time his show was on the air. The Sullivan show moved operations to the Hammerstein Theater, on Broadway between 53rd and 54th Street. As a tribute to the showman, CBS renamed the theater the ED SULLIVAN THEATER in 1967. CBS finally canceled the show in 1971.

TAUBMAN, HOWARD. Critic; b. New York, New York, July 5, 1907; d. Fairfield, Connecticut, January 8, 1996.

Howard Taubman's career was associated more with music than with theater, but he was the drama CRITIC of the *New York Times* for a brief period. While at Cornell University he held a part-time job at the *New York Post* copy desk. In 1929, after his graduation, he moved to the *Times*. A year later he started work in the music division. In 1935 he became music editor for the *Times* and remained in that position until 1955, with a brief sojourn during World War II writing for *Stars and Stripes* in the Mediterranean. From 1955 to 1960 Taubman served as the *Times'* music critic, and for the next 5 years he held the post of drama critic. In 1966 Taubman became a critic at large at the *Times*. Taubman wrote many books on music including *The Maestro: The Life of Arturo Toscanini* and *Music on My Beat*.

THANATOPSIS. In the 1920s and early 1930s Thanatopsis, or, more properly, The Young Men's Upper West Side Thanatopsis Literary and Inside Straight Club, was the late-night adjunct of the ALGONQUIN ROUND TABLE.

The organization was, to put it bluntly, a nightly poker session. Frank Case, the owner of the Algonquin Hotel, was the host of the club. Case, realizing that the Round Table, as well as Thanatopsis, was an important publicity tool, provided a second-floor suite as well as refreshments. People would often go to the hotel merely to gape at the celebrities. They still go to see where all the history was made.

John Peter Toohey came up with the prolix title of the group, which included at one time or another most of the famous names in theater and particularly vaudeville, including Howard Dietz, (*see* DIETZ AND SCHWARTZ),

Brock Pemberton, Margalo Gillmore, Harpo Marx, Ina Claire, Peggy Wood, George S. Kaufman (*see* KAUFMAN AND HART), and Marc Connelly. In addition to the stage notables attending the party, men from the world of letters also attended. ALEXANDER WOOLLCOTT and his boss Herbert Bayard Swope, both of the *World*; Harold Ross, the editor of *The New Yorker*; E. Haldeman-Julius, who invented the first paperbacks (Little Blue Books); Dorothy Parker; ROBERT BENCHLEY; John V. A. Weaver; Peggy Leech; Jane Grant; David Wallace; Herman J. Mankiewicz; Neysa McMein; Murdock Pemberton; Deems Taylor; Donald Ogden Stewart; and Corey Ford all sat in on the party. Other members at one time or another included Douglas Fairbanks and Jascha Heifetz. Swope once brought in an outside caterer from the Colony Restaurant uptown, so Case put a sign on the door of the suite stating, "Basket Parties Not Welcome. Frank Case, Proprietor." The members of the club, wishing to teach Case a lesson, moved the game to the Colony for two weeks.

Swope sometimes bet as high as $10,000. Harpo Marx entered the game in 1924, invited by Woollcott. Marx's delight in gambling forced the stakes higher and higher, and many players became disillusioned as the stakes grew. Woollcott, Marc Connelly, and Heywood Broun decided they couldn't afford the higher stakes. They were in the club for entertainment, not to win money. Woollcott wrote to the other club members on behalf of his associates: "The persistent rumors that we resigned from pique at our losses are unworthy of those who circulate them. It just happens to be true that Mr. Connelly (as always) and Mr. Broun and myself, for a change, did suffer some rather severe misfortunes; but as we always say, it all evens up in the course of a year." When Woollcott, Connelly, and Broun left the group, much of its soul did too. Thanatopsis lasted, with gradual changes in membership, until the mid-1930s.

THEATER DEVELOPMENT FUND. No other single organization has had as great an impact on the Broadway theater as the nonprofit Theater Development Fund (TDF). Since its inception in 1968, TDF has served both the Broadway theater community and its audiences through projects designed to increase theater attendance and to introduce new audiences to theatergoing. TDF also subsidizes important productions that might not otherwise be presented due to the brutally commercial climate of Broadway today.

The best known of TDF's activities is the TKTS BOOTH in Duffy Square. The TKTS Booth at Times Square annually sells more than 1.5 million tickets at half price. This translates into more than $30 million in receipts paid to theaters. For a show about to close, the added revenues from the TKTS Booth could mean the difference between a profitable run and a failure. Shows such as *A Chorus Line* and *42nd Street* received more than $2 million of TKTS Booth sales in only one year.

Through its theater subsidy program, TDF attempts to provide financial support to commercially produced plays, on and off Broadway, of artistic merit. TDF makes a commitment to a producer to buy a specified number of tickets (the average is 1,000) to a show for resale at a lower, or subsidized, price to patrons on the TDF mailing list. In the 2001–2002 season, for example, TDF subsidized 14 Broadway shows, including *Urinetown*, *Dance of Death*, and *Thou Shalt Not*. In total, 76,861 tickets were sold, resulting in $1,959,472 spent on subsidized tickets. The sale of these tickets is designed to foster an expansion of the Broadway audience.

TDF also posts an ACTORS' EQUITY bond for certain productions. This bond is held in escrow against the production's salaries for the cast. Some productions have difficulty raising the funds to meet their budgets, so TDF's posting helps them put the money they have raised into actual expenses incurred by the mounting of the show.

Long-running shows may also use TDF to fill up houses without using subsidies to cover ticket costs. The producers offer the tickets to TDF's 100,000-name mailing list at a discount price. This is simply an alternative to the TKTS Booth in making discount tickets available. A producer using this service knows how many tickets are sold well in advance of the actual performance date and thus can better gauge his or her budgetary needs.

TDF's Group Sales Program has been in existence since 1971. Not-for-profit groups (of residents of adult communities, high schools, university students, teachers, senior citizens, and unions) can all avail themselves of this service. The tickets are allotted by producers and are used to encourage attendance by people who could not otherwise afford to enjoy theater or those for whom the performing arts are a new experience.

The Theater Access Project was inaugurated in 1979 to "encourage and facilitate the theatergoing of persons who are deaf or hearing impaired, blind or partially sighted, physically impaired or confined to a wheelchair." The tickets are made available to those whose handicaps would prevent them from attending theater under normal circumstances. In the 2001–2002 season, 12,682 tickets were sold to disabled persons, their families, friends, or teachers through TDF's Theater Access Project. Deaf persons were offered special sign-interpreted performances of shows like *Thoroughly Modern Millie*, *Vagina Monologues*, *Aida*, *42nd Street*, *Noises Off*, and *The Goat* through this program.

TDF has other programs not directly connected with the Broadway theater. Through its Musical Instrument Revolving Fund, it enables small orchestras in New York State to purchase instruments. The Commercial Theater Institute holds two seminars each year to encourage fledgling producers. During the 3-day conference, they are taught legal, financial, and management aspects of production, and a 14-week seminar on producing also is offered. The organization also administers the Costume Collection. A warehouse contains more than 100,000 donated costumes that are rented for a nominal fee to arts groups across the country. Tickets are also offered to qualified theatergoers through a voucher program aimed mainly at increasing attendance of off Broadway and off off Broadway events.

Altogether, TDF handled 2,239,446 tickets to theater, dance, and music events in the 2001–2002 season. The revenue received came to $76,272,920. Because of TDF support, many shows were able to weather slow periods or to run longer than would have been otherwise possible.

Although TDF cannot actually save a failure from closing, it has been instrumental in keeping more shows alive on Broadway and giving others a larger return on their investments. It has also introduced new audiences to the live theater and has enabled other not-so-wealthy theater lovers to attend Broadway productions, despite the constantly rising price of tickets.

THEATRE GUILD. The Theatre Guild, the oldest producing organization in the United States, has been producing Broadway shows since its inception in 1919. Although it has been fairly inactive in recent years, its amazingly long history has been marked by incredible highs and incredible lows. All producing organizations of note have presented great plays, and all have produced flops, but the Theatre Guild has had many close calls when its existence has depended on the success or failure of a single production.

The Guild's often shaky finances were the result of an ambitious producing schedule and its choice of plays that did not conform to the public's expectations. Many of the playwrights whom the Guild championed are ranked with the greatest dramatists of our time, including such luminaries as Maxwell Anderson, Robert Emmett Sherwood, S. N. Behrman, Philip Barry, William Saroyan, and Sidney Howard. These American dramatists were joined by many great British and European talents, chief among them George Bernard Shaw. The Guild produced 18 of Shaw's plays. The other playwright represented by the Guild through most of his career was EUGENE O'NEILL, considered by many to be the greatest American playwright.

The Guild branched into operating subscription programs for many theaters and also produced movies.

The organization also operated the Theatre Guild Abroad program, which sent Americans to European theaters. The Guild's activity slowed in the 1960s, and by the 1980s it was practically moribund. However, the Guild has been pronounced dead before only to emerge triumphant time and time again.

The Guild was born at a time when a wave of experimentation was surging through all the arts. The Armory Show of 1913 introduced America to the new masters of European post-impressionism. Poets, musicians, and playwrights were also experimenting. Many little theaters sprang up across the country, and these often produced the works of experimental dramatists who were breaking away from more traditional plays. One of these organizations was the Washington Square Players, a group that produced such progressive playwrights as Arthur Schnitzler, Oscar Wilde, John Reed, O'Neill, Maurice Maeterlinck, Elmer Rice, Henrik Ibsen, Shaw, Anton Chekhov, and Basil Lawrence.

Board of Directors of the Theater Guild: Lee Simonson, Helen Westley, Philop Moeller, Maurice Wertheim, Lawrence Langner and Theresa Helburn.

Lawrence was a pseudonym for Lawrence Langner, who, with Theresa Helburn, later administrated the Guild. Among the actors who began their careers with the Players were Frank Conroy, KATHARINE CORNELL, Glenn Hunter, and José Ruben. Theresa Helburn was cast in a Washington Square Players production, but her parents made her withdraw.

On May 13, 1918, with increasing debt and the country involved in World War I, the group disbanded. The closing of the Washington Square Players led the way to the Theatre Guild. Helen Westley, Lawrence Langner, and Philip Moeller formed a new organization described as "a little theater grown up, and should be governed entirely by a Board of Managers, to which its director should be responsible. It should be a professional theater, employ professional actors and produce only long plays, 'which should be great plays.' " The first board members of the new Theater Guild included the 3 founders, as well as Josephine A. Meyer, Lee Simonson, Edna Kenton, Helen Freeman, and Rollo Peters. Theresa Helburn, although not a member of the board, was named play representative. Peters and Freeman left within the first year.

The Guild's roller-coaster financial status began with its first productions. Financier Otto Kahn helped the Guild mount its first production. Kahn, the owner of the Garrick Theater, liked the Guild and allowed them to lease the theater rent free. Langner himself put $1,610 into the new organization, and an additional $474 was raised by selling subscriptions. With $1,000 more from various sources, the Guild was ready to begin production. When the first play opened, the Guild had exactly $19.50 to its credit.

The Guild's first offering was a commedia dell'arte by Jacinto Benavente, which John Garrett Underhill translated and titled *The Bonds of Interest* (4/14/19; 32 performances). The show opened at the Garrick Theater on West 35th Street. It was a quick failure with a loss of $500 per week. One reason why the play ran past its opening night was the Guild's 150 subscribers. These optimistic theatergoers had paid for a 2-play series, so the Guild looked for another play to present. The second Guild presentation at the Garrick was St. John Ervine's play *John Ferguson* (5/13/19; 177 performances). This time the Guild hit pay dirt. Augustin Duncan, the brother of dancer Isadora Duncan, starred in the melodrama and also directed. The success of *John Ferguson* was due to circumstances other than its questionable dramatic merits. When the ACTORS' STRIKE OF 1919 hit Broadway, the newly formed ACTORS' EQUITY closed down all Broadway productions. The Guild was spared because of its unique democratic structuring. Therefore, theatergoers who longed to see theater were faced with only 2 alternatives: *John Ferguson* or nothing.

Its success and popularity was almost embarrassing to the Guild, because it was not a "great play." The Guild was certainly not prepared for its success. A business manager was hastily hired; he was future Hollywood director Walter Wanger. The Guild decided to move the play to the larger Fulton Theater, later named the HELEN HAYES THEATER. The play's success led to a dramatic increase in the Guild's subscribers: 500 avid theatergoers signed up for the second season, which began with a series of failures. St. John Ervine was called on to save the Guild. His play *Jane Clegg* (2/23/20; 112 performances), starring Margaret Wycherly, was well received by audiences and critics.

The next season found the Guild's subscription base increased to 1,300 patrons. For its first production of its third season, it presented the American premiere of George Bernard Shaw's *Heartbreak House* (11/10/20; 128 performances). Albert Perry had the leading role at the Garrick Theater, where lines formed to see the 3 1/2-hour play. The production was important as the first directed for the Guild by Dudley Digges, a mainstay of the Guild from then on. The third season proved very popular. A. A. Milne's *Mr. Pim Passes By* (2/28/21; 210 performances) starred Laura Hope Crews. Ferenc Molnár's *Liliom* (4/20/21; 311 performances) proved to be an even bigger success. *Liliom* starred Eva Le Gallienne, Dudley Digges, Helen Westley, and Edgar Stehli. *Liliom* later served the Guild well as the basis for RODGERS AND HAMMERSTEIN's *Carousel*.

Highlights of the next season included Leonid Andreyev's *He Who Gets Slapped* (1/9/22; 308 performances) and Shaw's *Back to Methuselah* (2/27/22; 25 performance cycles). The Shaw play was subtitled a *Gospel of Creative Evolution*. It almost took as long as evolution itself. The Guild broke the play into sections and presented it over 3 separate evenings in repertory over 3 weeks. Four directors were called on to stage the massive undertaking. Dennis King, Margaret Wycherly, Walter Abel, and A. P. Kaye starred, each playing a variety of roles. The Guild endeared itself to Shaw by this bold production. When contract negotiations were announced, Shaw responded, "A contract is unnecessary. It isn't likely that any other lunatics will want to produce it." Shaw was correct, and even fewer people wanted to see it.

The Guild was broke at the beginning of its fifth season, but it did have 6,000 subscribers. Karel Capek's *R.U.R.* (10/9/22; 182 performances) opened the season at the Garrick. It was hailed as one of the decade's best plays and introduced the world to the word *robot*. Elmer Rice's expressionistic drama *The Adding Machine* (3/19/23; 72 performances) was another highlight of the season.

During the next season, the Guild produced Shaw's *Saint Joan* (12/23/23; 214 performances). The play, like many of Shaw's, was long and the Guild implored the playwright to let them make cuts because suburbanites could not get to their trains by the time the play was over. Shaw responded, "The old, old story. Begin at eight, or run later trains."

History was made again with the opening of the seventh season. Molnár's play *Where Ignorance Is Bliss* was retitled *The Guardsman* (10/13/24; 274 performances), and the comedy marked the beginning of LUNT AND FONTANNE's long and prosperous association with the Guild. The production also marked the first success of designer Jo Mielziner. With *The Guardsman*, the Guild hit its stride and entered into its most productive period. It next presented Sidney Howard's *They Knew What They Wanted* (11/24/24; 192 performances), with Pauline Lord, Richard Bennett, and Glenn Anders. *They Knew What They Wanted* won the PULITZER PRIZE.

The success of the Guild's productions was hampered by the Garrick's small capacity and off-the-beaten-track location. The theater district had moved from Herald Square to Times Square, and the Guild was determined to move with it. They commissioned C. Howard Crane to design a new theater that would be named the Guild Theater (*see* VIRGINIA THEATER). On April 13, 1925, President Calvin Coolidge threw a switch from the White House, which illuminated the new theater. The theater's first production was Shaw's *Caesar and Cleopatra*, with HELEN HAYES and Lionel Atwill. The production received mixed notices.

A special fund-raising event was planned for a Sunday night at the Garrick Theater. The show, a musical revue, was titled *The Garrick Gaieties*. The evening of May 17, 1925, was the date set for the opening. The show was so successful that it was presented on several occasions until a full run was inaugurated on June 8, 1925. Songs for the *Garrick Gaieties* were provided by a virtually unknown RODGERS AND HART. They wrote a delightfully witty score, which included one standard, "Manhattan." The evening also featured satires on Guild plays. For example, *They Knew What They Wanted* was satirized as *They Didn't Know What They Were Getting*.

The Guild was now firmly ensconced on Broadway, although its finances were, as usual, in a precarious state due to the expense of running its own theater. Another drain on the Guild's coffers was the permanent repertory theater it launched in New York in 1926. The public did not jump on the repertory bandwagon, and two years later the repertory idea was dropped. Among the Guild's most successful productions of its middle years were Du Bose and Dorothy Heyward's *Porgy* (10/11/27; 367 performances); Eugene O'Neill's *Marco Millions* (1/9/28; 102 performances) and *Strange Interlude* (1/23/28; 426 performances); Shaw's *Major Barbara* (11/20/28;

73 performances), with Helen Westley, Gale Sondergaard, Dudley Digges, and Winifred Lenihan; and Philip Moeller's adaptation of Sil-Vara's *Caprice* (12/31/28; 178 performances), with Lunt and Fontanne.

By the end of the 1920s, discord began to arise in the Guild's ranks. It seemed, throughout its history, that success bred failure. Perhaps the Guild needed to be lean and hungry to work well. The Guild's artistic success from 1926 to 1928 led to infighting among the board. There were other upheavals as well. Some of the Guild's most prominent playwrights left and formed THE PLAYWRIGHTS' COMPANY. Some of the Guild's best actors left and created the GROUP THEATER. Even the Lunts eventually left the Guild, although they later returned to act in several productions.

Despite the fighting and upheavals, the Guild still had many successes in the late 1920s and early '30s, including S. N. Behrman's *Meteor* (12/23/29; 92 performances); Shaw's *The Apple Cart* (2/24/30; 88 performances), with Tom Powers, Claude Rains, Morris Carnovsky, Helen Westley, and Violet Kemble Cooper; Glenn Anders, Ruth Gordon, Morris Carnovsky, and Franchot Tone in Philip Barry's *Hotel Universe* (4/14/30; 81 performances); and Maxwell Anderson's *Elizabeth the Queen* (11/3/30; 135 performances), with Lunt and Fontanne.

The Group Theater presented Paul Green's *The House of Connelly* (9/28/31; 72 performances) under the Guild's auspices at the MARTIN BECK THEATRE. O'Neill's *Mourning Becomes Electra* (10/26/31; 150 performances) starred Alla Nazimova and Alice Brady. Hits of the 1930s also included Robert Emmett Sherwood's *Reunion in Vienna* (11/16/31; 280 performances), with the Lunts; Ina Claire in S. N. Behrman's *Biography* (12/12/32; 210 performances); O'Neill's comedy *Ah, Wilderness!* (10/2/33; 285 performances), with veteran Broadway player GEORGE M. COHAN, Elisha Cook Jr., Gene Lockhart, and Marjorie Marquis; and Helen Hayes, Philip Merivale, and Helen Menken in Maxwell Anderson's *Mary of Scotland* (11/27/33; 236 performances).

After an acclaimed production of William Shakespeare's *The Taming of the Shrew* (9/30/35; 128 performances), with Lunt and Fontanne, came one of the Guild's most ambitious offerings, *Porgy and Bess* (10/10/35; 124 performances) starring Todd Duncan and Anne Brown. GEORGE GERSHWIN composed the music for the black folk opera. His brother Ira and Du Bose Heyward wrote the lyrics. Heyward's libretto was directed by Rouben Mamoulian. The opening at the Alvin Theater (*see* NEIL SIMON THEATER) met with mixed reviews. Critics differed on whether the show was an opera or a musical, and instead of concentrating on the play they engaged in a war of semantics, trying to neatly pigeonhole the proceedings. The failure was a major disappointment to the Guild, which had been having its usual financial difficulties.

Porgy was followed by three successes. Tyrone Guthrie's production of Dody Smith's comedy *Call It a Day* (1/28/36; 194 performances) starred Gladys Cooper and Philip Merivale. S. N. Behrman's *End of Summer* (2/17/36; 153 performances), starring Ina Claire and Osgood Perkins, was also a success. *Idiot's Delight* (3/24/36; 300 performances), one of the Guild's greatest successes, opened at the SAM S. SHU-BERT THEATRE. Robert Emmett Sherwood's play starred the Lunts, Sydney Greenstreet, director Bretaigne Windust, George Meader, and Richard Whorf.

After this last hit, the Guild again faced difficulties. Behrman's *Amphitryon 38* (11/1/37; 153 performances) opened with the Lunts, Richard Whorf, and Sydney Greenstreet. The play's run was an oasis in a desert of failures. One such failure was the American premiere of Anton Chekhov's *The Sea Gull* (3/28/38; 40 performances), translated by Stark Young. The limited engagement featured excellent sets by Robert Edmond Jones. Between the success of *Amphitryon 38* and its next hit, Philip Barry's *The Philadelphia Story*, the Guild mounted 9 productions, all failures. In 1936, the Guild's debts totaled $60,000. However, *The Philadelphia Story* (3/28/39; 417 performances) revived the Guild. The play opened at the Shubert with Shirley Booth, Vera Allen, Lenore Lonergan, Katharine Hepburn, Van Heflin, and Joseph Cotten. The play saved the Guild from bankruptcy. As Theresa Helburn remarked, "There's no money in producing anymore. The money's in authorship."

The Guild's next hit came with William Saroyan's *The Time of Your Life* (10/25/39; 185 performances). Gene Kelly, William Bendix, Celeste Holm, Will Lee, Julie Haydon, and Edward Andrews were featured, as was Eddie Dowling, who co-produced with the Guild and co-directed with Saroyan. The small role of the newsboy was played by Ross Bagdasarian, better known as the creator of the Chipmunks; *The Time of Your Life* returned for an additional 32 performances. The Lunts appeared with Alan Reed, Estelle Winwood, Juanita Hall, James O'Neill, and Muriel Rahn in Behrman's *The Pirate* (11/27/42; 177 performances), which was presented in association with The Playwrights' Company.

The Guild was at another low when Richard Rodgers again stepped in to replenish the Guild's coffers. The event was one of the milestones of the American theater: Rodgers and Hammerstein's *Oklahoma!* (3/31/43; 2,248 performances). The musical ran for 5 years, in addition to having touring companies and foreign productions. The Guild then had a plentiful cash flow, but, surprisingly, its output fell. It did not even have the succès d'estime it had enjoyed in the

1920s and '30s. There were other hits, but the huge success of *Oklahoma!* seemed to take the starch out of Theresa Helburn and Lawrence Langner's artistic manifesto.

A production of *Othello* (10/19/43; 295 performances), with Paul Robeson, José Ferrer, and Uta Hagen, opened to generally favorable reviews. Its run seemed to indicate that for the Guild nothing had changed. But success seemed mostly out of the producers' reach. The failures were forgettable, without the raw energy and political fervor of past flops. Blame was laid at the feet of Langner and Helburn, who were described by one director as "gifted amateurs." They were accused of paying too much attention to the small concerns of the organization without being able to grasp the big picture or to make educated decisions. A former staff member said they were incapable of delegating responsibility. The Guild Theater was becoming a burden because the Guild did not have enough productions to keep it occupied, and the theater didn't have enough seats to attract other producers. In 1944 the Guild sold the theater.

The Guild's next success came with Rodgers and Hammerstein's *Carousel* (4/19/45; 890 performances) at the MAJESTIC THEATRE. *Oklahoma!* was based on a previous Guild presentation, Lynn Riggs' *Green Grow the Lilacs* (1/26/31; 64 performances); *Carousel* was also based on a play that the Guild had originally presented, *Liliom*. The success of *Carousel* and the failure of most other Guild offerings led the Guild's supporters to ask, "Where is the commitment to drama? Why aren't more chances being taken?"

The Guild branched out into radio and began broadcasting its show *The Theatre Guild of the Air* in 1945. Although the producing organization presented more successful dramas on the stage, these became less and less frequent. O'Neill's *The Iceman Cometh* (10/9/46; 136 performances) premiered at the Martin Beck Theatre. By this time Armina Marshall (Mrs. Lawrence Langner) had joined Langner and Helburn in running the Guild. The other board members had long since left in disgust. Later hits for the Guild included William Inge's *Come Back Little Sheba* (2/15/50; 190 performances), with Shirley Booth, at the BOOTH THEATRE; *The Lady's Not for Burning* (11/8/50; 151 performances), by Christopher Fry, at the ROYALE THEATRE; and *Picnic* (2/19/53; 477 performances) at the MUSIC BOX THEATER.

During the 1950s the Guild, without much theater activity to keep itself busy, turned to television. In 1953 *The Theatre Guild of the Air* transferred to television. Its name was changed to honor its sponsor, United States Steel. The *United States Steel Hour* ran until 1963. The show was among the best of the anthology series to introduce new American writers. The

1950s also saw the Guild branch out into motion pictures. Among the notable movies produced by the Guild were *The Pawnbroker*, *Judgment at Nuremberg*, and *A Child Is Waiting*.

Although the 1950s and 1960s were slow decades for the Guild, the organization did mount a few notable productions. JULE STYNE, Betty Comden, and Adolph Green (*see* COMDEN AND GREEN), wrote the Judy Holliday musical *Bells Are Ringing* (11/29/56; 924 performances). The show introduced such standards as "The Party's Over" and "Just in Time." Dore Schary's *Sunrise at Campobello* (1/30/58; 556 performances), with Ralph Bellamy, opened at the CORT THEATRE. Peter Shaffer's *The Royal Hunt of the Sun* (10/26/65; 261 performances) opened at the ANTA Theatre (the former Guild Theater; *see* VIRGINIA THEATER) with George Rose, Christopher Plummer, John Vernon, and David Carradine. Harold Pinter's *The Homecoming* (1/5/67; 324 performances) opened at the Music Box Theater, and Allan Ayckbourn's *Absurd Person Singular* was also a success.

Since then, the Guild has concentrated on managing a subscription series in other cities. Its producing days are over.

THEATER WORLD AWARD. *See* **Daniel Blum Theatre World Award.**

THEATRE ARTS MAGAZINE. Many attempts have been made to publish a theater-oriented magazine for the theatergoer. *VARIETY*, *BILLBOARD*, and others were written for professionals. Fans of the theater needed their own organ.

In November 1916 *Theatre Arts Magazine*, an illustrated quarterly published out of Detroit, Michigan, began, with Sheldon Chaney as editor. The magazine sought to cover the gamut of theater interests in the country. It contained articles on Broadway, regional companies, the road, and the burgeoning little-theater movement. Early contributors included such luminaries as Ruth St. Denis, Winthrop Ames, Percy Mackaye, and Thomas Wood Stevens. The tone of the magazine was serious, and it considered itself a progressive voice in the theater community.

A short time later, motion pictures took hold of the nation, and fan magazines like *Photoplay* became huge sellers. *Theatre Arts* hung on with a small but loyal readership as the nation's theater scene became smaller and smaller. Soon the focus of the magazine was almost totally the Broadway theater, with occasional forays into London's West End.

Edith J. R. Isaacs and later Rosamond Gilder were editors of what became a monthly magazine. Their co-editors were Stark Young, Ashley Dukes, Norris

Houghton, Hermine Rich Isaacs, and Kenneth Macgowan. Many theater luminaries contributed articles to the magazine, including Norman Bel Geddes, HELEN HAYES, Vincente Minnelli, John Mason Brown, Jean-Paul Sartre, Jo Mielziner, and Margaret Webster. Illustrations were also important, and most issues featured photographs of stage and costume designs as well as serious studies of actors in their current roles.

Although an excellent magazine, *Theatre Arts* could not compete with the movie fan magazines, and as Broadway shrank so did its readership. In February 1948 the magazine folded. But in the spring of that same year, a new *Theatre Arts Magazine* was born (now merged with its rival, *Stage*). Charles MacArthur was the editor; although the tone was still serious, there was more of a lighthearted air to the proceedings. The new magazine featured a more theatrical spirit and boasted new departments dedicated to reviews, theater news, calendar and recordings, and a dining-out column. The focal point of the magazine was the complete play script included in each issue.

The new magazine was certainly more in the spirit of the new Broadway. But as Broadway continued its decline, so did *Theatre Arts*. Several new editors tried to keep the magazine alive, but the spring 1964 issue was its last.

THEATRE MASQUE. *See* **John Golden Theatre.**

THEATRE REPUBLIC. *See* **New Victory Theatre.**

TIMES SQUARE THEATER. 219 W. 42nd Street. Architects: Eugene DeRosa and Pereira. Opening: September 30, 1920; *The Mirage*.

The Times Square Theater had a short but noteworthy life as a legitimate theater. Built by Arch and Edgar Selwyn, the Times Square became the third of their 3 Broadway theaters, the others being The Selwyn (*see* AMERICAN AIRLINES THEATRE) and the APOLLO. The Times Square and the Apollo were the last new theaters to be built on Times Square. The Times Square boasted a 1,057-seat auditorium designed in the Adam style; it was decorated in silver, black, and a green that almost became gray. The black velvet stage curtain separated the audience from the large, 40-foot-wide stage. Its layout was similar to that of the MUSIC BOX THEATER.

The *New York Review* wrote, "In the Times Square, located just west of the LYRIC THEATRE, on 42nd Street, New York has one of the handsomest playhouses in America, simple, dignified, and luxurious in every detail. It is an ideal theatre for high class drama and musical attractions." *New York Evening World* called the theater "a beautiful thing of gray and green and silver." The theater's facade was shared with the Apollo Theatre next door, although the two theaters each had separate marquees. The theater opened with a hit, *The Mirage* (192 performances). Theater owner Edgar Selwyn was the author, and Florence Reed starred. The *New York Globe Commerical* reported on the social aspects of the evening:

1) the crowds on the sidewalk
2) the movie fans standing at the back applauding Miss Reed and staring at Mae Murray
3) the girl in the upper box who had the largest green fan we have ever seen.

The theater's next offering was the musical comedy *The Right Girl* (3/15/21; 98 performances), written by Percy Wenrich and Raymond W. Peck and starring Tom Lewis and Robert Woolsey. The revue, *The Broadway Whirl* (6/8/21; 85 performances), soon followed. Blanche Ring, Richard Carle, and Charles Winninger starred. Three plays followed in quick succession: *The Demi Virgin* (10/18/21; 268 performances); *Honors Are Even* (8/10/21; 70 performances); and *Love Dreams*, a "melody drama" by Anne Nichols, the author of *Abie's Irish Rose*.

The great American actress KATHARINE CORNELL opened in *A Bill of Divorcement* (10/10/21; 173 performance) at the Times Square. The play was one of her earliest successes. *The Charlatan* (4/24/22; 64 performances) followed. Tallulah Bankhead appeared at the Times Square Theater in *The Exciters* (9/22/22; 35 performances). Writing in the *Tribune*, CRITIC Percy Hammond commented, "Few actresses can portray more convincingly than Miss Bankhead the difficult part of a pretty girl."

The next play at the Times Square was Channing Pollock's *The Fool* (10/23/22; 373 performances), which was lambasted by the critics. Business was terrible, with less than $300 in advance sales. Nonetheless, Pollock received many letters from prominent citizens praising the play and congratulating him on writing it. The author took a quarter-page ad in papers the next day with the headline, "Are All These Wise Men Fools?" Under that banner Pollock reprinted excerpts of the letters he had received. In two weeks, the box office take increased to $1,000. Apparently, clergymen had preached sermons about the play. The box office receipts for the third week totaled $14,000, enough to break even. By the fourth week the theater was sold out, and matinees were added. By Christmas, the theater had added matinees to handle the crowd, bringing the total performances for the week to 12. Seven road companies were touring the country, playing to 85,000 people each week. The companies employed almost 300 actors, with a weekly payroll of

nearly $40,000. In all, *The Fool* showed a $1 million profit.

The next hit to play the Times Square was *Andre Charlot's Revue of 1924* (1/9/24; 298 performances). On opening night, American audiences were introduced to 3 great British talents: Gertrude Lawrence, Jack Buchanan, and Beatrice Lillie. *Charlot's Revue* also featured a hit song, "Limehouse Blues," by Philip Braham and Douglas Furber. Theatergoers used to a 4-hour Ziegfeld extravaganza were surprised at the revue's fast clip and modern theatricality. JEROME KERN and Howard Dietz (see DIETZ AND SCHWARTZ) provided the score for *Dear Sir* (9/23/24; 15 performances), the next show to originate at the Times Square. FLORENZ ZIEGFELD mounted *Annie Dear* (11/4/24; 103 performances) at the Times Square as a vehicle for his wife, Billie Burke. SIGMUND ROMBERG, Clare Kummer, and Clifford Grey contributed the score. A third musical, *Kosher Kitty Kelly* (6/15/25; 1 performance) was an ill-disguised ripoff of *Abie's Irish Rose*.

Channing Pollock's antiwar play *The Enemy* (10/20/25; 202 performances), like *The Fool*, garnered mostly negative reviews but was enjoyed by the public. At the end of its run Pollock was told by the theater's ladies'-room attendant that she was never sorrier to see a play close. Pollock was moved, until the woman explained that she had never before enjoyed such a booming business of powder-rags. Apparently the pacifist play was so moving that ladies retired to the lounge to cry their eyes out.

The Selwyns' partnership broke up in 1925; following the closing of *The Enemy*, there was an ominous portent. The Times Square was used to show motion pictures. The policy didn't last long; on May 31, 1926, the play *Love 'Em and Leave 'Em* moved from the Apollo Theater to the Times Square. The next hit to play the Times Square was Anita Loos' *Gentlemen Prefer Blondes* (9/28/26; 201 performances), the story of gold-digger Lorelei Lee and her friend Dorothy. The theater then returned for a season to a motion picture policy. While Warner Brothers was premiering its talking picture *The Jazz Singer* to the world, the Times Square was hosting the silent film *Sunrise*, by F. W. Murnau. The classic played practically the entire 1927–28 season.

The next season was taken up with Ben Hecht and Charles MacArthur's smash hit play *The Front Page* (8/14/28; 281 performances). The comedy of the rough-and-tumble world of Chicago newspapers became one of the most enduring plays of the decade. The Depression heralded a slowdown in the number of productions presented on Broadway. The Times Square was home to the pacifist musical *Strike up the Band* (1/14/30; 191 performances), with a score by GEORGE AND IRA GERSHWIN and a satirical libretto by

Morrie Ryskind and George S. Kaufman (*see* KAUF-MAN AND HART).

The Times Square hosted 6 productions during the 1930–31 season. The last of these, Noël Coward's *Private Lives* (1/27/31; 248 performances), was the only success. Coward, Gertrude Lawrence, Laurence Olivier, Jill Esmond, and Therese Quadri comprised the cast. Coward wrote one song for the play, "Some Day I'll Find You." When the show opened the Apollo Theatre next door was empty, so the producers featured Coward's name above the title on one marquee and Lawrence's on the other.

The 1931–32 season was a complete washout for the Times Square. None of the 4 plays that managed to open lasted longer than a month. The next season, the last for legitimate production at the theater, was barely better. It started with the Bella and Samuel Spewack comedy *Clear All Wires* (9/14/32; 91 performances), starring Thomas Mitchell. It was followed by *Foolscap* (1/11/33; 13 performances). The last play to open at the Times Square was *Forsaking All Others* (3/1/33; 101 performances), starring Tallulah Bankhead with Thomas Mitchell directing. The drawing room comedy had the misfortune to open on the day that the federal government closed all the banks. As usual, the actress received glowing notices, although the play did not.

The Times Square Theater was then leased to the Brandts, owners or leasees of most of the 42nd Street theaters. The Brandts began a movie policy for the theater, and so it remained. In 1939 the Brandts developed the Times Square's stage area into retail space. When the renovation of 42nd Street began in the late 1980s, the Brandts were stripped of their theaters (in spite of the fact that they agreed to renovate them all and begin a legitimate theater policy). Since then, the Times Square has stood empty. When Garth Drabinsky gained control of the LYRIC and Apollo Theatres, demolishing them and creating the FORD CENTER FOR THE PERFORMING ARTS, he got the 42nd Street Redevelopment people to agree to exclude a theater use for the Times Square.

TIMES TOWER. West 42nd Street and 7th Avenue. Architects: Cyrus L. W. Eidlitz and Andrew C. McKenzie, 1904; remodeled by Smith, Smith, Haines, Lundbert, & Wheeler, 1966.

The Times Tower is the most significant building on Times Square and the focal point of the southern end of the square. It is the scene of the annual New Year's Eve celebration. The building is a symbol of the changes the square has undergone and perhaps a guide to its future.

In what was then called Longacre Square, a quiet crossroads housing primarily carriage factories, the *New York Times* chose to build its new headquarters. The *Herald* had previously chosen a similar site on what became Herald Square, then the center of New York. Adolph Ochs, owner of the *New York Times*, wished for the same visibility. After considering a downtown site at Broadway and Barclay Street, where the Woolworth Building now stands, he realized the uptown flow of the city would make Longacre Square preeminent.

The building, completed in 1904, was the second tallest structure in the city. The triangular site, formed by the convergence of Broadway and 7th Avenue, led to comparisons with the Flatiron Building at the intersection of Broadway, 5th Avenue, and 23rd Street. However, the Flatiron Building, considered New York's first skyscraper, addressed its location with more success. The Times Tower, though called "the second Flatiron Building," was a rectangular building on a triangular piece of land.

The new skyscraper, inspired by Giotto's campanile, was built on the site of the Pabst Hotel. The hotel and previous buildings occupying the site had faced south, toward the city proper. But Ochs and his architects realized that the growing city would surround the tower, and so they pointed its front uptown. The completion of the Italian Rennaisance–style tower on December 31, 1904, was celebrated with a fireworks display, the forerunner to the annual New Year's Eve celebrations. The 375-foot-tall tower dwarfed its neighbors, none of which rose more than 6 stories in height. It also extended down 55 feet below the street, under the new IRT subway, for which Ochs had lobbied. At one time the building could be entered directly from the subway, a novel idea at the time.

As the area around the tower grew, so did the newspaper. By 1913 it had grown too large for its building and constructed a new headquarters down the block on 43rd Street. However, the *Times* retained an office for classified-ad placement in the tower. As news of elections and sports results came into the paper, makeshift banners were hung outside the building. This increased the public's perception of the paper as an important news source. The impromptu celebrations following such announcements made the square a gathering place for important events. In 1928, on the eve of the presidential elections, the MOTOGRAM moving sign was inaugurated. The Motogram's lights wrapped around the building, spelling out the news. Perhaps the most important news flashed by the sign was the announcement of the Japanese surrender, marking the end to World War II. The V-J DAY celebration was the most impressive demonstration surrounding the tower.

The *Times* retained ownership of the building until 1961, when the newspaper sold the building to DOUGLAS LEIGH, the designer of many of Times Square's most fabulous "spectaculars" (*see* SIGNAGE). Leigh eventually sold the building to the Allied Chemical company, and the outside was stripped of its terra-cotta facade. It reopened in 1966, featuring a continuous marble skin. The stark exterior on street level encouraged gatherings by undesirable characters. As the area declined, the Times Tower, now dubbed the Allied Chemical Tower, turned a blind eye to its surroundings.

In 1974 Allied Chemical sold the building to real estate magnate Alex Parker. He already had leased 23 floors from Allied Chemical before buying the building for a little more than $6 million. Parker decided to call the building Expo America, but soon simply called the building One Times Square. Parker sold the building to Lawrence Linksman and his TSNY Realty Company for more than $12 million in 1981. The new ownership was marked by the appearance in 1982 of the Spectacolor Sign. In July 1984, the building was again sold. A partnership bought the building for $16.5 million and then, one year later, sold it for $20 million.

TKTS BOOTH. W. 47th Street between 7th Avenue and Broadway. Architects: Meyers & Schiff, 1973.

The TKTS Booth is the Times Square location most sought out by the thousands of tourists who flock to the square each year. More than 1.5 million people pass through the TKTS Booth and buy half-price, same-day tickets to Broadway and off-Broadway shows. There is one other booth in lower Manhattan.

One precedent for the half-price ticket policy was Joe Leblang's discount ticket counter in the basement of Gray's Drugstore during the 1940s. The THEATER DEVELOPMENT FUND used the idea to create the TKTS Booth.

The producers of Broadway's shows were initially wary of the booth. The idea for a half-price ticket grew out of the nature of the theater business. If the owner of a clothing store has unsold inventory at the end of the day, he can always sell it the next day. But the theater owner has a perishable inventory: the theater seat. Each performance brings a new inventory that must be sold or lost. This concept was difficult to explain to many of the producers, who knew that a show running at 70 percent capacity could break even. Proponents of the booth explained to them that the 30 percent of tickets remaining unsold might mean thousands of dollars of profit for the show. They also pointed out that shows needing 50 percent of capacity to break even but running at only 40 percent might make up the needed revenues by selling an additional 20 percent of their seats through half-price ticket sales. The public, complaining about rising prices, was quick to discover the booth and flocked to buy the cut-rate tickets. Top shows like *Cats* and *Me and My Girl* seldom used the TKTS Booth more than once or twice a year, but other, less popular shows relied on daily TKTS Booth sales to stay open.

As time went by, more and more producers saw the usefulness of the booth, and it became firmly entrenched in the financing and planning of shows. Ticket prices continue to rise to the point where the half-price ticket of today costs as much as the full-price ticket of yesterday. This constant inflation of prices has led some producers to question the usefulness of the booth. Some claim that big-ticket shows like *Cats* become expense-account shows, attended primarily by businesspeople and their spouses. Others attend such high-priced entertainments as a special event for which they save up over the course of a year. This change in attitude has drastically affected the theater. The public no longer attends the theater as it would a movie; rather, it's a special, expensive night out.

Critics of the booth claim that it actually serves to raise the average price of Broadway shows. They argue that the producer, when making up a budget, must compare the cost of mounting and operating the show against the number of seats in the theater and the ticket price of each seat. The half-price booth is accounted for, and the producer depends on a certain number of half price tickets to be sold for the show to stay on. Because no show can run only on a half-price policy, the producer raises regular prices to force up the half-price numbers. Therefore, if the producer needs to sell each ticket at $20 to break even, the producer sets the ticket price at $40, knowing that all the seats won't sell at half price and that those ticket buyers who can afford the full price will make up the difference—a classic example of the tail wagging the dog. Furthermore, critics complain that if ticket prices were kept low, more people would attend the theater more regularly and more shows would do better and run longer. They claim that the public perceives those shows that sell half-price tickets at the booth as second-rate.

Whether the booth is a solution to a problem or a cause of the problem may be debatable, but the success of the operation is not. The architectural design of the booth is successful as well. It features canvas banners stretched on metal scaffolding surrounding and disguising the ordinary trailer that serves as a box office. As a result of this design, the architects received a commission to design the building across 47th Street where the Coca-Cola spectacular stood.

TONY AWARD. The Tony Awards, or, more properly, the Antoinette Perry Awards, are Broadway's equivalent to the Oscars, Emmys, and Grammys. Like any such awards, the Tonys have their share of detractors, and these naysayers have a point: the system and its choices aren't perfect. Despite the carping and the competition from many other annual theater awards, the Tonys are the most important of Broadway's awards and have been since their inception in 1947. Dore Schary once wrote:

> There are two types of people. One type asserts that awards mean nothing to them. The second type breaks out into tears upon receiving an award, and thanks their mother, father, children, the producer, the director and, if they can crowd it in—the American Baseball League.
>
> However, I believe that people in the theater who receive this award have a special feeling that makes them cherish the winning of a Tony. It prevents them from going on effusively. The Tony has a special value. It was created to award distinguished achievement in the theater.

Antoinette Perry was a producer, director, actress, and active member of the AMERICAN THEATRE WING. The Wing is the sponsor of the awards named for the woman who gave herself selflessly to its activities. She was chairperson and secretary of the Wing during its most active period, World War II.

Perry began her theatrical career at the age of 18, in 1906. Her first appearance was in the David Warfield vehicle *Music Master*. The next year she starred in DAVID BELASCO's production of *A Grand Army Man*. In 1909 she retired from acting to raise her family, but in 1922 she returned to the theater following her husband's death. She acted and later directed many plays. Among her best-known directorial efforts were Preston Sturges' *Strictly Dishonorable* (9/18/29) and Mary Chase's PULITZER PRIZE–winning comedy, *Harvey* (11/1/44).

After Perry's death on June 28, 1946, Jacob Wilk, a story editor who worked at Warner Brothers, talked to producer John Golden about establishing a memorial in her name. Golden approached the American Theatre Wing, which took up the motion. Brock Pemberton was made chairperson of a committee formed to explore the possibilities of the memorial. They decided to honor her with an annual series of awards. A panel of theater professionals was entrusted with selecting the first recipients of the newly erected honor. The first members of that committee were Vera Allen, BROOKS ATKINSON, Louise Beck, Kermit Bloomgarden, Clayton Collyer, Jane Cowl, HELEN HAYES, George Heller, Rudy Karnolt, Burns Mantle, Gilbert Miller, Warren P. Munsell, Solly Pernick, James E. Sauter, and Oliver Sayler.

On Easter Sunday, April 6, 1947, the first Tony Awards were handed out. Mickey Rooney, Herb Shriner, Ethel Waters, and David Wayne entertained in the Grand Ballroom of the Waldorf-Astoria. During the initial years of the Tony Awards, the winners were announced without any mention of the competition. In these first years the award went to "distinguished" performers, designers, directors, and so on. Later they went to the "best" in each category. The earliest recipients of the Tony Award were José Ferrer and Fredric March for dramatic actor, Ingrid Bergman and Helen Hayes for dramatic actress, Patricia Neal for supporting actress (dramatic), and David Wayne for supporting actor (musical). A technical award went to David Folkes for his costumes for *Henry VIII*, and Lucinda Ballard won in the same category for her work on *Happy Birthday*, *Another Part of the Forest*, *Street Scene*, *John Loves Mary*, and *The Chocolate Soldier*. Elia Kazan won for his work as director of *All My Sons*, and the talents of choreographers Michael Kidd and Agnes de Mille were also noted. Special awards went to Dora Chamberlain, Mr. and Mrs. Ira Katzenberg, Jules Leventhal, Burns Mantle, P. A. MacDonald, ARTHUR MILLER, Vincent Sardi Sr. (*see* SARDI'S), and KURT WEILL. That was the extent of the first year's honorees.

The first winners of the Tony Awards received a scroll documenting their honor. In addition, the men were presented with a cigarette case and the women a compact. Two years later the United Scenic Artists held a contest for a new design. The winner was Herman Rosse, who fashioned a medallion featuring the masks of comedy and tragedy on one side and a portrait of Antoinette Perry on the other. The new award was first issued in 1949. The Tony nominations, usually 4 in each category, were announced for the first time in 1956, and usually only 1 winner was announced in each category.

In later years, various award categories came and went. Stage technicians had their own category in 1948 and from 1950 through 1964. At one time there was an award for conductors. Producers had their own category once, but now they share the award for best play or musical. Music and lyrics received separate awards for a few years in the late 1960s and early '70s.

The Tony Awards have always had media exposure. The first ceremonies, held in hotel ballrooms including the Plaza, Waldorf-Astoria, and the ASTOR HOTEL, were broadcast locally on WOR radio and carried on the Mutual Radio Network. In 1956 the awards were televised locally for the first time. Channel 5, a member of the old DuMont network, broadcast the awards. The hosts were Brock Pemberton, Mrs. Martin Beck, Helen Hayes, and Ilka Chase.

The sudden death of actress Helen Menken, then chair of the Theater Wing, changed the tone of the 1966 awards, which were presented at the Rainbow Room. The award ceremony was held in the afternoon without entertainment or public attendance.

In 1967 the Tony Awards were broadcast nationally for the first time. The Wing allowed the League of New York Theatres (now the LEAGUE OF AMERICAN THEATRES AND PRODUCERS) to co-present the awards. Alexander Cohen, a Broadway producer, was in charge of the television broadcast as well as the ball and dinner dance following the awards. Playwright and NBC executive Alvin Cooperman suggested moving the show from a hotel ballroom to a theater.

The ceremony has been carried on television ever since. Beginning in 1979, CBS agreed to carry the show on its network. Their agreement was to continue into the 2004 season, at least.

The 51st annual presentation in 1997 saw changes in the Tony format. Because the show was a victim of low ratings and also consistently ran over schedule, it was decided that the first hour of the awards would be shown on PBS and the second part would be broadcast on CBS. The PBS segment generally carried the presentation of 10 awards and also presented mini-documentaries on costumes, sets, and so on.

1979 was a milestone for another reason. The venue for the awards was permanently changed to the 6,000-seat Radio City Music Hall. Tickets were made available to the general public. The awards have been held at Radio City every year since, with the exception of 1999, when the auditorium was closed for renovation. The GERSHWIN THEATER acted as the venue for that season.

The Tony television broadcast has always been considered the most entertaining and sophisticated of the many show-business award shows. In recent years, however, the ceremony has received a fair share of criticism. Critics charged the show with poor writing, inclusion of television stars as hosts rather than Broadway personalities, and a second-rate variety-show feel to the proceedings. In 1987 the television ceremony was broadcast for the first time without producer Alexander Cohen at the helm. The 1988 Tony Award broadcast received the lowest ratings in its history. Many have claimed that the Tonys have sold out to the needs of television and have just become a poorly produced advertisement for current Broadway hits. Most musical numbers are not even presented live. Rather, they are pretaped. In the 1988 awards not only was the *Phantom of the Opera* segment pretaped, but the actors were lip-syncing to a sound track. (In the theater, many of Sarah Brightman's high notes were taped while she pretended to sing.)

The Tony procedures have also come under attack on occasion. An Eligibility Committee decides on possible nominees. In recent years, some leading performers have been nominated in the supporting category. This was arranged sometimes so that they would have less fierce competition. The Eligibility Committee sends its list to the Nominating Committee, which decides on the actual nominations. Unfortunately, this committee is made up of members who are removed from the Broadway scene. Because the Theater Wing doesn't want the committee to be accused of favoritism, the Nominating Committee is composed of members who are academicians, ex-critics, theater curators, and former theater professionals. Because many of these committee members live outside the New York area, and because some shows play only a limited number of performances, the rules read, "each eligible production and performer shall have been seen by as many members as possible." Because some shows are never seen by any members of the committee, or by only a few, the nominations are skewed toward the long-run hits. Because of the current scarcity of quality musicals and the general decline in the number of productions, some categories have less-than-qualified nominees simply to make up the required 4 nominations in each category. On occasion, the committee has decided to limit the nominations to 3 or even 2 in each category.

The voters are made up of selected members of ACTORS' EQUITY, the DRAMATISTS GUILD, the Society of Stage Directors and Choreographers, and the United Scene Artists. Members of the press on the first- or second-night press lists and producers who are members of the New York Theater and Producers, Inc., and the board of directors of the American Theatre Wing are also allowed to vote. The Wing feels they would not be able to overcome their urge to vote only for shows on which they have worked. The voters must certify that they have seen all performances in each category. This is, of course, impossible. Obviously all 560 or so voters can't have seen all the nominated shows, especially those that closed after only 1 performance.

There have been a few major gaffes. One such mistake occurred in 1972 when STEPHEN SONDHEIM and James Goldman's musical *Follies* won 7 Tony Awards, including those for Best Actress, Best Director, Best Score, Best Scenic Designer, Best Costume Designer, Best Choreographer, and Best Lighting Designer. Nonetheless, *Two Gentlemen of Verona*, winner of the book award, carried off the award for Best Musical. Mistakes have been made in at least two instances when the wrong performer was nominated because the committee mistook the actor for another who should have been the actual nominee.

The Tony Award can mean life or death to a marginally successful play. Winning a Tony Award is a powerful publicity tool and can result in thousands of dollars in additional revenues. The Tonys have also had an impact on the theater season proper. It's no surprise that a majority of productions open in the spring, at the end of the season, so they'll be fresh in Tony

The Town Hall.

voters' minds. In fact, the week before the nomination cutoff date sees a flurry of activity. Some shows have postponed their opening nights until after the Tony cutoff date so that they would not look bad by receiving no nominations.

The Tony Award may not be perfect, but it is recognized as the leading theatrical award, and its impact on the theater is enormous. As JULE STYNE once commented, "The curious thing about awards is that one receives them for work one does not expect to receive them for, and does not receive them for work one does. For instance, I received the Tony for *Hallelujah, Baby!*—and not for *Gypsy!* But, the Tony, which stands for excellence in the theater is an honor whenever it comes!"

TOWN HALL. 123 W. 43rd Street. Architect: McKim, Mead, & White. Town Hall, a 1,498-seat concert/lecture hall, has enjoyed a long history of distinguished offerings, including political meetings, readings, film showings, concerts, and radio broadcasts.

Town Hall opened in 1921 as a lecture hall operated by the League for Political Education. The League rented out the hall to other political organizations that hosted speakers and conventions. According to the *New York Times*, the hall was conceived as "a kind of uptown Cooper Union, on the theory that efficient democratic government and healthy democratic life require a suitable meeting place for the public discussion of subjects related to the common welfare." Speakers in the hall's early history included Booker T. Washington, William Jennings Bryan, and Theodore Roosevelt. Margaret Sanger, lecturing on birth control, was arrested on the stage of Town Hall and taken to the 47th Street police station. The hall, which also presented silent films, hosted readings by such authors as Thomas Mann, Henry James, John Galsworthy, W. H. Auden, and William Butler Yeats.

Almost from the start, the hall was regarded as a top-flight concert hall. Jascha Heifetz, Fritz Kreisler, Wanda Landowska, Béla Bartók, Sergei Rachmaninoff, Mischa Elman, and Kirsten Flagstad all performed on its stage. Such notable classical singers and musicians as Lotte Lehman, Gina Bachauer, Joan Sutherland, Marian Anderson, Andres Segovia, and Elisabeth Schwarzkopf made their debuts there. A number of jazz musicians, including Eddie Condon, made Town Hall their home when playing for large audiences. From 1935 to 1956 the theater hosted "America's Town Meetings of the Air," a series of public forums, lectures, speeches, and debates. Among the notables who spoke on national radio were Eleanor Roosevelt, Winston Churchill, and Richard Nixon.

When Lincoln Center was built, Town Hall lost much of its cachet. Today, after a total renovation that was completed in 1984, the hall books a variety of ethnic theater and dance companies that could not otherwise afford to perform in New York. An especially successful series at the theater is the semiannual production of New York's only Yiddish theater company. Other companies that account for Town Hall's 90-percent-capacity record include the Philharmonia Virtuosi, the annual jazz festival, the Mabel Mercer Foundation Cabaret Convention, the People's Symphony, and a children's theater series that entertains 100,000 youngsters annually.

TRAFALGAR THEATER. *See* **Nederlander Theatre.**

URIS THEATRE. *See* **Gershwin Theater.**

VARIETY. "The show business bible," *Variety* has served the entertainment community with honesty and impartiality since its founding nearly 100 years ago. The success of the newspaper is all the more remarkable in view of the changes in the entertainment field since its inception. The paper has recognized these changes and has modified its viewpoint and content in order to remain the top show-business publication.

Variety was founded on December 16, 1905, by a young editor, Sime Silverman, who was in love with vaudeville in all its many forms. He was equally enthralled with seal acts, plate spinners, and the top comics. He had the rare fortune to be stage-struck without the conceit that he might one day succeed as a performer. Silverman realized that his talent was writing, so he wrote about his first love, vaudeville. His first break came when George Graham Rice published the first edition of the *Daily American* in 1899. Rice's paper was designed as a competitor to the *Morning Telegraph*. To achieve success, Rice followed the example of many of his contemporaries by simply hiring the best staff members off his rival's paper. One of these, Joshua Lowitke, secretary to editor Leander Richardson, urged Silverman to begin writing for the new paper. Silverman accepted the job and, under the byname "The Man in the Third Row," began publishing reviews.

The *American* was a success for a brief while until the post office closed it down. It seems that the owner wanted the paper only as a means to advertise his bookie joints. This didn't sit well with the government, and soon the staff was unemployed. Richardson and Lowitke returned to the *Telegraph* and found an opening for Silverman when the vaudeville critic Epes W. Sargent quit. This job proved only slightly more profitable than his last. After two weeks Silverman, writing under the pseudonym "Robert Spear," was fired for writing unduly harsh criticism. What the paper was actually worried about was losing the advertising of the acts Silverman panned, which happened when the comedy team Redford and Winchester canceled a Christmas ad because of a bad Silverman review. So, Silverman was unemployed again.

While at Pabst's Columbus Circle Restaurant, Silverman drew the logo of *Variety* on a tablecloth. Some report that it was his wife, Hattie, who drew the logo at the West End Beer Garden on West 125th Street. His idea was to form his own paper that would report honestly without regard for advertising dollars or the power of the great vaudeville empires of Keith and Albee (*see* E. F. ALBEE), Pantages, or Loew's. Silverman picked the name *Variety* after the English word for music-hall entertainments. To Silverman, it was a better reflection of the whole scope of entertainment than the term *vaudeville*. Even at this time, he envisioned coverage of a wider spectrum of entertainment than simply the stage, although cinema was in its infancy and radio and television were not yet on the horizon.

Silverman borrowed $1,500 from his father-in-law (his father was against vaudeville reviews) and proceeded to gather a staff. The first two employees were John J. O'Connor, a onetime usher at the Alhambra Theater, and Alfred "Al" Greason. Silverman set up a 1-room office with $40 worth of used furniture at the Knickerbocker Building on Broadway and 38th Street.

The first issue of the paper was published on December 16, 1905, for the grand price of 5 cents. The front cover contained photographs of the 4-man editorial staff, with their faces framed by an oval and the ovals mounted on Grecian pillars. These men were Silverman, Greason, Epes W. Sargeant, and Joshua Lowe.

Sargeant, born in the West Indies, was well known in vaudeville circles for his reviews, which he signed, "Chicot." Silverman would later shorten that to "Chic." Sargeant was, in fact, chic, choosing to dress in a stylish, natty black impresario hat and a loose Windsor tie around his neck.

Greason was a sometime alcoholic, like Sargeant and other staffers, and later was mad about golf. He had a special interest in the stock market, contributing financial articles to *Variety*. When he was off the staff, which he was occasionally, he would cover the coffee, cotton, and other commodity markets.

Lowe made his mark in *Variety* in his review of a trained mule, "Giddyap, Napoleon, small time bound." Lowe was assigned the London beat, in which he served through the Blitz; he was killed when struck by a taxi during a blackout.

The paper closed on Wednesday and appeared on Friday. On Thursday the staff played baseball with the Show Biz League.

Variety began slowly to make a name for itself, and in 1906 Silverman increased the staff. Joe Raymond was appointed associate to O'Connor, who had been appointed advertising solicitor. Sam Mitnick was hired as circulation manager. The new staff went after their tasks enthusiastically. After all, the ad reps received a 25-percent commission on sales. O'Connor went to the scene of his most recent job, the Alhambra, but neither Matt Keefe, a singer, nor Tony Pearl, a harpist, opted for ads. O'Connor was luckier at Proctor's Fifth Avenue. Grace Cameron, a leading entertainer, bought the first full-page ad for $50. She received a bonus for her support: Silverman threw in the front cover as thanks. Joe Cook, the monologist and comedian, bought the cover for $25 in one of those early issues. *Variety*'s success, as well as Cook's, can be gauged by the fact that only a few years later Cook bought the cover for $25,000.

By 1907 Silverman was ready to expand *Variety*'s field. On January 19, the paper published its first film review, for the 7-minute comedy *An Exciting Honeymoon*. Later in the year O'Connor was dispatched on a 14-month voyage from vaudeville house to vaudeville house, drumming up business. He would talk up the newspaper to dealers who previously had carried only the *Clipper*. He then went to the theaters and described *Variety*'s success to the actors and tried to drum up advertising and subscriptions. In order to expand the paper's coverage, O'Connor put a number of correspondents on retainer. In return for submitting news and reviews to the home office, the lucky reporters received free passes to their local theaters. Because *Variety* couldn't afford to pay, these early contributors were vaudeville buffs and other neophytes. As the paper's fortunes rose, Silverman replaced his early

stringers with real reporters. He still didn't pay them, but at least they were professionals in the field. O'Connor opened branch offices in San Francisco and Chicago before he returned to New York to gather the fruits of his labors. Little by little *Variety* grew, and advertising rates increased with the circulation.

In 1910 the paper moved to a second-floor office on 45th Street and Broadway. The building was later the site of the LOEW'S STATE THEATER.

Ed Reynard, a well-known ventriloquist, was the first to buy a long-term advertisement. He paid $145 for a 2-inch ad that was included in the paper for a full year. Reynard proved lucky when Silverman flipped him double or nothing and lost. Silverman didn't stop there. He proposed to Reynard another flip of a coin. If Silverman won, Reynard would pay $500. If Reynard won, he would receive free advertising for the life of the paper. The coin was tossed and Silverman lost. So Reynard received a free ad for life, and Silverman received nothing for his first long-term advertisement. Reynard's ad continued to run, until he begged Silverman to discontinue it when *Variety* was blacklisted by vaudeville kingpin Edward Albee of the Keith-Albee chain in 1913. Albee, who expected only good reviews befitting his position as the major vaudeville mogul in the country, resented *Variety*'s impartial attitude. He vowed to blacklist any performers advertising in the paper. Reynard was caught in the middle. On one hand he was receiving hundreds of dollars in free publicity, but on the other hand the ad wasn't doing him much good because he couldn't work in the majority of vaudeville houses.

Albee turned up the heat on *Variety* by convincing music publishers that if they retained their advertising in *Variety* they would never hear their numbers performed in an Albee theater. This was a major setback to Silverman, who depended on the publishers to take out half- and full-page ads. Silverman refused to give up the battle. Albee's competitors advanced Silverman credit, and he barely managed to keep the paper afloat. By 1914 both sides were exhausted, and the feud was clearly doing neither side any good. Albee had his assistant J. J. Murdock sign an agreement that allowed advertising in *Variety* by Albee artists and that allowed the *Variety* reporters into Albee's theaters.

In 1918 *Variety* changed printers. A strike was called against the commercial print shops in Manhattan, including the C. J. O'Brien shop, which printed the glossy magazine. O'Brien warned Silverman of the impending strike and advised him to find another printer who could put out the paper during the strike. Silverman chose the Rogowski Company on Pearl Street in lower Manhattan, and the paper was printed for the first time in a newspaper format. Rogowski could get out the paper overnight, which pleased Silverman greatly. After the strike Silverman returned for a time to O'Brien, but a few years later he moved permanently to Rogowski and the newspaper format.

Variety moved again when Silverman bought a building at 154 West 46th Street from Mrs. Nate Spingold (better known as Madame Frances, the couturier). The 5-story building was a 16-foot-wide brownstone walk-up. The paper would remain there for 68 years.

Silverman again expanded the staff, known as "muggs." Joshua Lowitke, who got Silverman started in the first place, joined the paper. The staff called him Joe Lowe because he signed his articles "Jolo." Silverman had insisted that his employees adopt abbreviations for their bylines. Because Silverman signed his work "Sime," all others opted for short pseudonyms out of respect for the boss. Abel Green, who eventually took over for Silverman, became "Abel"; Arthur Unger, West Coast bureau chief, became "Ung"; and Jack Pulaski, the legitimate-theater editor, became "Ibee," although the office staff dubbed him "the Man in the Iron Mask" because of his disfigured face: his nose had been bashed in during a college football game. Other "sigs" were "Hyho" for Hy Hollinger, "Ammo" for Jack Ammon, and "Drek" for Derek Elley. Silverman's wife, Hattie, was dubbed "Skirt," and their son, Sid, who began writing vaudeville reviews for the paper at age 7, was known as "Skigie." More modern sobriquets were "Remy" for Jeremy Girard, "Cart" for Todd McCarthy, "Daws" for Amy Dawes, "Erjo" for Christopher Jones, "Evan" for Greg Evans, "Harv" for Dennis Harvey, "Mart" for Markland Taylor, and "Bril" for Brian Lowry.

It was thus that the *Variety* critics signed their reviews. In part this was because of Silverman's wars with enemies such as the White Rats agents syndicate and the SHUBERT BROTHERS. However, on the week of August 5, 1991, history was made again at the newspaper. For the first time, bylines appeared with the reviewers' actual names.

Variety was also noted for its contributions to the English language. Its SLANG gave the paper its special flavor. Jack Conway, a white-haired, red-faced former catcher for the Brooklyn ball team in the old Federal League, was the king of slanguage. Conway used many newly coined words in his reportage. Conway later married Silverman's secretary, Betty Brown, only to die on his honeymoon in Bermuda. Conway and *Variety*'s contributions to the English language were immortalized in H. L. Mencken's classic book, *The American Language*.

Variety's two best-known headlines have won almost legendary status. Silverman wrote the first when the stock market crashed in October 1929. The *Variety* headline blared "Wall St. Lays an Egg." (Surprisingly,

the year that the stock market crashed and America entered the Depression was the first year *Variety* showed a profit.) When the stock market fell again in 1962, *Variety*'s headline was "Wall Street, Son of Egg." In 1987, when Wall Street made its biggest fall, *Variety* headlined, "Wall Street Lays an Egg: The Sequel." After Silverman's death, *Variety* kept up the tradition with a headline describing how farmers rejected Hollywood's attempts to woo them with rural movies. The classic banner read "Sticks Nix Hick Pix."

Silverman was a strong personality and a strong editor, and for a man so loquacious he was sometimes amazingly quiet. Before his death in 1933, he asked Abel Green into his office. Silverman stood up and motioned for Green to sit in his chair. Silverman said, "You sit here, Abel," and left the room. And that is how Green became the second editor of *Variety*, shortly before Silverman's death, just one month after he established *Daily Variety* in Hollywood under the leadership of Arthur Ungar.

Abel Green brought to the editor's desk a style different from Silverman's but just as unique. Green wasn't a particularly good reporter, nor was he especially good on facts. Once, the gossip column, dubbed "Chatter," was forced to admit, "The attorneys for Mrs. Johnathan Bell Small announce that she did not give birth to a baby last week in Doctor's Hospital." Mr. Small was the father, so Green assumed his wife was the happy mother. However, it was his mistress who had given birth. When the *Mona Lisa* was lent by the Vatican to the United States, the "Europe to US" column listed Mona Lisa among the celebrities making the trans-Atlantic crossing. Green didn't recognize the name and wondered if she was "some stripper." But Green was a crackerjack editor, and his writing had all the flavor of his predecessor. Someone once remarked, "He writes faster than I can read." The paper flourished under Green's leadership, with Harold Erichs acting as business manager. Green was described by Les Brown, the television critic, as "not exactly forward looking. He was wedded to a show biz that was—and when that changed, he was wedded to nostalgia."

In 1929 Silverman had announced gratefully, "For the first time in 24 years *Variety* got out of debt in 1929. May it keep out. Some years ago it was said on this page that when *Variety* paid off, if ever, it would be told. Here 'tis."

But then the Depression began and *Variety* saw its profits disappear. In 1935 the Rogowski Company was nearing bankruptcy. Sid Silverman and business manager Erichs took over the company's operation in order to ensure the continued printing of the paper. Of course, running a printing company had its own headaches.

In 1950, Sid Silverman and Arthur Ungar died within 6 months of each other. Harold Erichs succeeded to the presidency of the parent company, while Joe Schoenfeld replaced Ungar as editor of *Daily Variety*. The paper continued to be managed by Abel Green and Harold Erichs.

Silverman's grandson Syd inherited the paper when Hattie Silverman, Sime's wife, died at age 100. Although only 19 and a sophomore at Princeton University, he assumed ownership with a watchful eye. In 1956, following two years of military service, Syd returned to 46th Street and was named publisher.

In 1957 the Rogowski plant in lower Manhattan was condemned to make way for a housing project. *Variety* purchased the *Bronx Home News* plant in the South Bronx, on 148th Street. The plant had been owned by the *Post* to print its Bronx editions.

In 1970 the paper switched to web offset printing, a job that was handled by the Balan Printing Company in Brooklyn. Typesetting was still done at the plant in the South Bronx. After an 18-month labor action by the printers union, the Bronx plant was closed for good. At that time, Balan switched printing methods to photocomposition and brought *Variety* to its Valley Stream, Long Island, plant.

Green died on May 10, 1973, and his monicker, "Abel," died with him. It had been in continuous use at *Variety* for 55 years, since 1918. When Green died, Les Brown believed himself to be heir to the throne, but Syd Silverman—a quiet, introspective man whose personality couldn't be further removed from his grandfather's or Abel Green's—took over operations.

In the first 78 years of its existence, *Variety* had only 3 legit editors. First was Jack Pulaski ("Ibee"), who served till his death in 1948; then Hobe Morrison ("Hobe"); and finally Richard Hummler ("Humm").

History was made when *Variety* was sold to a European conglomerate, Cahners Publishing Company, in July 1987. The organization moved to the Cahners offices at 32nd Street and Park Avenue South on November 10, 1987, with former film mogul Peter Bart acting as editor. The staff thought up the headline "Variety Ankles Great White Way." And in 1988, printing the paper was undertaken by the *Times-Journal* plant in Springfield, Virginia.

On December 7, 1988, another chapter was begun. *Variety* upgraded its paper to a glossy stock (Mando Bright), and 4-color printing was available for the first time. The page length was shortened, and a new graphic look was adopted. The original masthead became a 2- and 3-column headline. What had originally been in Franklin Gothic type was replaced by 72-point Cheltenham Bold Extra Condensed, capitalized. The 3-column advertising space was replaced by a 5-column "ad strip" running across the bottom of the page.

Variety also accepted full-page cover advertising with the editorial pages beginning on page 3. And for the first time, the paper printed photographs as part of its editorial space.

Not everyone liked the new look. Harvey Sabinson, executive director of the LEAGUE OF AMERICAN THEATRES AND PRODUCERS, was quoted in the *New York Times* as saying, "If Coca-Cola could admit a mistake when it came out with New Coke, than so could *Variety*. There's less of it, and some of the pictures look like yearbook pictures."

Arthur L. Anderman, corporate supervisor of *Variety* for Cahners, defended the new look. "We wanted *Variety* to become more reader-friendly, and to take out some of the things appropriate to the time of vaudeville. It was time to bring *Variety* into the 20th Century, without adversely affecting this venerable publication we love."

With the October 1989 issue of the paper, Peter Bart, a Hollywood heavyweight, assumed the editor's chair. In 1990 Syd Silverman was named chaiman and Gerard Bryne became publisher. Michael Silverman, Syd's son, became publisher of *Daily Variety*. Reed Business now publishes *Variety*.

Variety has lost some of its snap and spit, but it continues to prosper. Like show business itself, *Variety* has become blander and more fiscally oriented, which is both good and bad for the industry and *Variety*.

VARIETY NEW YORK DRAMA CRITICS POLL. Beginning in 1939, the theater trade newspaper *VARIETY* has published the results of a poll of New York–based newspaper and magazine critics. The categories include best performance by a male in a straight play, best performance by a female lead in a straight play, best performance by a male lead in a musical, best performance by a female lead in a musical, best performance by an actor in a supporting part, and best performance by an actress in a supporting part. Awards are also given to the most promising new actor and most promising new actress. Additional awards include those for best director, best scenic designer, best costume designer, best composer, best lyricist, best librettist, and most promising playwright.

VENETIAN TERRACE GARDEN. *See* **Victoria Theater (1).**

VENICE THEATER. *See* **Jolson's 59th Street Theater.**

VICTORIA THEATER (1). 42nd Street and 7th Avenue. Architect: J. B. McElfatrick and Co. Opening: March 2, 1899; *The Reign of Error*.

Oscar Hammerstein I was the true pioneer of Times Square. His Olympia theater complex was the first entertainment attraction in what was then Longacre Square. Hammerstein's decision to build the Victoria was just another example of the amazing recuperative powers and self-confidence that allowed him to rise from the ashes of his past failures again and again. Just the year before, Hammerstein had lost the Olympia to the New York Life Insurance Company. After this setback, Hammerstein, then more than $1 million in debt, passed an acquaintance on Broadway and offered him a cigar. Hammerstein commented, "I have lost my theaters, my home and everything else. My fortune consists of two cigars. I will share it with you."

Undaunted by his losses, Hammerstein summoned his energy and convinced the owner of the Market Livery Company, which owned Gilley Moore's Market Stables on the corner of 7th Avenue and 42nd Street, to lease it to him for 20 years with no money down. Terms of the lease were reported to be $10,000 for the first year and $7,000 each succeeding year. Hammerstein saw the huge potential of the site: "The finest site in New York for a theatre. I am going to build one there and I have only ten cents in my pocket."

He probably wasn't exagerating when he said he only had 10 cents in his pocket. He knew that having the lease on the property didn't mean he had a theater. Hammerstein sold patents on his inventions to raise capital for the theater building. His brother Arthur Hammerstein, a successful building contractor, oversaw the construction of the theater, which was scheduled to open in early 1899. Friends and associates were skeptical. One bet Oscar Hammerstein a suit of clothes that the building would be a year late in opening. Oscar had no problem naming the theater. As he said, "I call my theatre The Victoria because I have been victorious over mine enemies, those bloodsuckers at New York Life!"

As construction continued, the question of what to put in the theater became increasingly important. Hammerstein had already demonstrated his penchant for opera, with the opening of his Harlem Opera House in 1889 and the first Manhattan Opera House (where Macy's now stands). But his forays into lighter fare had always been more successful than his operatic endeavors, notwithstanding the spectacular failure of the Olympia.

Hammerstein sent a letter to the superintendent of buildings stating that:

the premises to be erected are not intended for theatrical or operatic performances, that there will be no excavation, room or cellar underneath a stage platform, that there will be no fly galleries, scene rooms, carpenter shop, or paint frame, . . . that we shall not provide or keep what is known as theatrical scenery on the premises, nor

erect or provide stationary appurtenances necessary for performances or theatrical or operatic character; also, that no application for theatrical license will be made and that the premises when completed are to be devoted to attractions only, permitted under the existing concert licenses.

Hammerstein wanted a license for a concert hall, since a theater license was much more demanding and would require a greater outlay of cash.

It was decided to open the 1,350-seat house with a variety policy. Despite what Hammerstein told the Building Department, he planned on presenting vaudeville and musical comedy, both just coming into their own. The first show, *The Reign of Error*, featured a pair of Dutch comics, the Rogers Brothers. A poor man's Weber and Fields, the Rogers Brothers were nevertheless successful, and their offering proved popular with audiences.

Although the paint was still wet on the walls, the theater opened on schedule and Hammerstein arrived for opening night wearing the new suit won in his bet. For the opening-night performance, Hammerstein composed a "Victoria Festival March." At the curtain call, the impresario told the gathered throng, "I believe I shall carry the memory of this night to my grave."

Arthur Hammerstein, responsible for the interior decoration, described the Hammersteins' unique way of theater design:

The reason the coloring was white and gold was that we had no money for paint—the "white" was only the unpainted plaster. We covered the supporting beams with cast cornices, which I made in my shop, and highlighted the ornament with gilt. We modeled the cornices with a leaf encircling a hole for electric light bulbs to be inserted, thereby eliminating the expense of electrical fixtures.

Reportedly Arthur had his workers save every brick and board from the demolished building that had stood on the site previously for use in constructing the Victoria. The carpeting was purchased for 25 cents a yard from an ocean liner that was being refitted with new carpeting. The seats were also secondhand. The previous building's hayloft served backstage as the fly loft.

The *Dramatic Mirror* reported:

The features which attract attention first are the wide, roomy promenades, which run all around the house at the rear of the orchestra boxes and balcony seats. Although the house seats only 1,200, there is room for 2,000 standees who have the privilege of sitting at small tables if they choose. . . . The proscenium is square, the opening being 38 feet wide and 42 feet high. The decorations are in white and canary, with a little gold here and there. The effect is pretty and the house has a very bright, cheery look, which is emphasized by the warm, red colors in the chairs, carpets and hangings.

Referring to Hammerstein's love of red decorations, Arthur was once quoted as saying, "If father could buy enough red plush for a theater curtain, there would be a theater built around it."

Venetian Terrace Garden

Above the Victoria, Hammerstein built a roof garden, which he named the Venetian Terrace Garden. The space, decorated with greenery and more than 2,000 electric lights, contained a small stage surrounded on all sides by the audience. The Venetian Terrace Garden opened on June 26, 1899. The theater-in-the-round concept made hearing the acts difficult, so the theater usually booked silent acts like acrobats and jugglers. The next year Hammerstein built the Republic Theater next to the Victoria, and in 1901 he built the Paradise Gardens on their shared roofs. Usually, the Victoria would be closed in the summer and the Paradise Gardens would open. Seldom were both theaters open at the same time.

The Paradise Gardens theater proper was on the Victoria's roof, with a glass-enclosed auditorium allowing for an open-air feeling to the hall. On nice nights the windows were opened to allow breezes to ventilate the hall. The Gardens offered a "Swiss farm" with live barnyard animals on the Republic's roof and the first singing waiters in New York. The Paradise also featured, at one time or another, New York's first flea circus, ice-skating exhibitions, a sort of freak show including "the Girl with the Longest Eyelashes in the World," "the Girl with the Smallest Waist in the World," and swimming demonstrations. The Paradise Gardens also predated the Victoria downstairs in presenting vaudeville acts. In 1908 the Paradise Gardens was renamed Hammerstein's Roof Garden.

The *New York Dramatic Mirror* described the Paradise Gardens as having:

> a spacious platform that has tables and chairs set about, and a little pond of real water wherein disport sundry truly live ducks, not to mention a couple of property boats, one labeled "Shamrock III." Also there is a real water wheel that works, and a beautiful more or less arabesque arch with illuminated panels of stained glass that artistically disguises the customarily uninspiring institution known as a fire escape. Over the duck pond there is a pretty rustic bridge that takes one up to a still higher platform that boasts a Hollandish village with a little cottage, a practicable windmill, a cow-shed with property cow peering out at the window, and a vegetable garden containing sprouting cabbages, potatoes, and all that sort of thing.

The following year Hammerstein leased the Republic to DAVID BELASCO, who promptly renamed it the BELASCO THEATRE. The Victoria offered a musical,

Sweet Marie, which premiered on October 10, 1901. The show was ascribed to R. Jackson and W. Brown, but Broadway wags felt that it had actually been written by Hammerstein. The *Dramatic Mirror* stated that "there was scarcely a chance for a doubt that the managerial genius had himself written and composed the new offering just as the programme confessed that he had staged it." In any event, he had contributed a song to the proceedings. *Sweet Marie* closed after only 28 performances.

The theater presented the great actress Eleonora Duse for two weeks in November 1902. Hammerstein next presented Blanche Walsh in Tolstoy's *Resurrection* (2/17/03). The production was a huge success, despite a review in the *New York Times* that called it "a tinned soupy Siberio-religious melodrama, with only a squint of Tolstoi." *Resurrection* ran for 88 performances at the Victoria and for more than a year and a half on the road. Hammerstein made more than $100,000 in profit.

The Paradise Gardens was still doing great business. The *New York Dramatic Mirror* reviewed the proceedings in the Swiss farm:

> The simple minded citizens of the great metropolis are more than eager to expend their good money for the glimpse of pastoral life that the Paradise Gardens afford and to contemplate in almost childish glee the crops that are propagated on the roof. Mr. Hammerstein's agricultural exhibition is now bigger, brighter, and better than ever, the corn belt is particularly prolific, and the prospects are excellent for the potatoes and cabbages. The ducks are even more blasé than last year, but the chickens are most condescending and communicative. The cow's demeanor continues to be very "up-stage," and the windmill and the water wheel squeak on joyously. The attendance is enormous all the time.

In 1904, after a series of short runs by unimportant musical comedies, Hammerstein decided to change gears yet again, to a strict vaudeville policy. He had always been successful with vaudeville, and he preferred to direct his attention to his opera productions. He engaged his son Willie (*see* WILLIAM HAMMERSTEIN) to put the bills together. Willie, taught by vaudeville booker William Morris, proved a genius at this, and the theater continued to be financially successful. The Hammersteins ensured their success and ability to weather dry periods at the box office through a slightly shady policy: They never printed the price of admission on tickets. Thus, for an act that was a big draw, the box office could command high prices. When the weather was good and patrons tended to stay outdoors in the fresh air, the ticket prices could be reduced as a draw.

Initially, the Victoria presented only high-class vaudeville. The *Dramatic Mirror* opined that "Mr.

Hammerstein is providing bills of extraordinary merit, using more big headliners, than any other house in the country." Each show at the Victoria concluded with the showing of a newsreel. As time passed, Willie turned the Victoria into a unique vaudeville house. Instead of offering top acts of the day, he created his own attractions with a combination of brilliant showmanship and sheer gall. In 1904 the Victoria began to present sensational acts right off the pages of the yellow press. The father-son team continually filled all 1,200 seats and 30 boxes with acts like Conrad and Graham, two women who had been convicted of shooting W. E. D. Stokes in the Ansonia Hotel. The two women had never appeared before the public and had to be coached on how to walk, talk, and stand in front of an audience. The duo was billed as "The Shooting Stars." Unfortunately, the pair proved to have no stage ability whatsoever. But this didn't daunt the resourceful Hammersteins. They simply had Loney Haskell lecture about them while the two murderers stood by uncomfortably. The $300 they each received no doubt helped ease any of the embarrassment that they may have felt. After Willie presented one murderer, he was asked by a newspaperman whether she was to be held over for another week. Hammerstein responded, "Not unless she shoots somebody else."

In 1905 Willie Hammerstein presented the Cherry Sisters, proudly billed as "America's Worst Act." The audience was urged to throw fruit and vegetables at the two midwesterners. To protect them, Willie had a net lowered between the audience and the hapless stars. Although it slightly dampened the fun, it saved them from concussion by legumes. It was never decided whether the sisters, Addie, Effie, Ella, Jessie, and Ella, (two appeared at any one time) were serious or putting the audience on. *The World* on November 21, 1900, admitted such when it printed, "Opinion was divided as to whether they were fooled or were fooling in New York. At any rate they had a capable press agent, got lots of advertising and went back West with enough money to build a fine house and make a big splash in Cedar Rapids."

Another paper, on October 20, 1901, concurred,

The average theatregoer still is at a loss to know whether the Cherry Sisters really were sincere in their efforts or whether they appreciated the fact that their act was the most ludicrous thing ever attempted on the stage. Hammerstein declares they really believe they are embryo Bernhardts and Melbas. At any rate, their act did much to increase the attendance at the Olympia when it was under Oscar Hammerstein's management and created as much talk as perhaps any act that ever came into the metropolis.

Their efforts frequently were greeted with jeers, cat calls and hisses, but to all appearances the young women were deaf to adverse criticism. They continued their one act drama, recited poems and sang ballads with all the enthusiasm of the artist. Moreover, at the end of the week they received a comfortable salary.

That same year Willie presented "Captain Bloom's Demonstration of Marconi's Wireless Telegraphy" on the Paradise Gardens stage. This was the first demonstration of radio in vaudeville. He also presented "Abdul Kadar and His Three Wives in an Exhibition of Rapid Painting." Kadar was actually a Swiss artist, and his "three wives" were his wife, daughter, and sister-in-law. They arrived in the United States but were briefly denied entry when Willie anonymously tipped off authorities that they were not who they seemed. Willie also alerted the newspapers. Once in the country, the trio made the rounds of the New York hotels but were refused entry, another part of the elaborate STUNT. Finally they ended up at the apartment that Willie had booked for them.

Willie, in a constant search for the unusual person or circumstance to book for the Victoria's stage, found "Sober Sue." The billing this time was "Sober Sue— You Can't Make Her Laugh." Top comedians of the day, Willie Collier, Sam Bernard, Eddie Leonard, and Louis Mann, all took the stage of the Victoria and tried to convulse the deadpan woman. But none of them could win the $1,000 reward Willie had posted. Willie paid Sue only $25 a week, but he did throw in a few $30 dresses for her costumes. At the end of her engagement, Willie confessed that Sue would never smile because her facial muscles were paralyzed. Another typical act at the Victoria was Dorando, the Italian runner. The winner of the 1908 Olympic marathon stood on stage while Loney Haskell lectured. A song, "Run, Run, Run, You Son of a Gun, Dorando," was written in his honor.

Victoria Theater emcee Lonny Haskell described Willie's genius in securing acts:

A stately, very handsome girl named Gertrude Van Dyke came along, telling him that she was the victim of managerial oppression, that although everyone knew she had a beautiful voice no one would give her an engagement. Willie Hammerstein said to her, "All right, Gertrude, you go out and get your name in the papers and I'll book you at the Victoria."

Gertrude went, and we gave her a hand. She got hold of a cowgirl costume and a very imposing pure white horse with something of a fancy gait. On this animal she rode up and down Broadway. The horse alone would probably have been sufficient to draw a crowd in these days, but it wasn't then. Gertrude had to add something of her own. She did. When she reached Times Square she opened her mouth and burst into song. As that was a time when anyone bursting into song was not drowned out by the sound of taxis, trucks, buses, and compressed-air drills, Gertrude attracted a crowd. First it was a little sidewalk crowd, then it was a big Avenue crowd overflowing into the car tracks. That was where we came in. We had fixed it with the nearest traffic cop (for the consideration of two passes to the Victoria) to arrest Miss Van Dyke and her horse for obstructing the traffic. When the crowd had become unruly and was surging back and forth from the building line to the horse's flanks, the cop walked up and did his duty, which included seeing that Gertrude was headed for the lock-up. That meant appearing in the Night Court, to which unhappy place a large portion of the crowd followed.

Those who got inside the courtroom were delighted at the ensuing scene. The magistrate asked Miss Van Dyke: "What's the idea?" Miss Van Dyke answered that the idea was to get a job. She came of decent, respectable folks in Denver, she said. Everyone told her, and she knew they were right, that she had a marvelous voice, that she ought to go to New York, where they could use marvelous voices. But what did her talent do for her when she got to New York? Nothing except humiliate her. It had come to seem to her, she said, that no virtuous girl could get a job in the theatres of New York. But Gertrude was not going to yield. She had made up her mind that she would be the first to get a job without succumbing to the importunities of the devilish impresarios. How was she doing to do it? Why, by going out in to the center of the most crowded part of Manhattan's amusement district and letting the crowds hear her voice until they shouted for her. Then the managers would have to give in.

That scene in the Night Court was a front-page story for a week. The sob-sisters of the Sunday supplements interviewed Gertrude till she was exhausted. They printed her story in thousands of words. They printed pictures of her and her family and her home and her horse and everything connected with her. They praised her courage and her womanly integrity.

In the midst of this ballyhoo Willie Hammerstein played his trump card: He posted in front of the Victoria an enormous four-sheet billboard, which read in great letters: "Special Engagement—Gertrude Van Dyke. Mr. Hammerstein is not a Hard Hearted Cold Blooded Manager. He is Willing to Give Any Girl a Chance." The following week Gertrude opened to an unprecedented house. Unfortunately for this story, Gertrude did not live up to her publicity. She had managed to get her audience but she couldn't hold it. She lasted for one week only.

By 1906 Willie had decided to pepper the attractions with stars of real talent. Will Rogers, the Four Keatons (including the youngster, Buster), AL JOLSON, Weber and Fields (see FIELDS FAMILY), FANNY BRICE, Harry Houdini, and Fred Karno's comedy troupe (featuring Stan Laurel and Charlie Chaplin) all appeared on the Victoria's stage. Willie also instituted the policy of presenting top New York cartoonists at the Victoria. Winsor McCay, Bud Fisher, Rube Goldberg, and Tad Dorgan presented "chalk talks" that were great flops but did result in great publicity. Willie also presented, for the first time in New York, the new motion picture,

The Great Train Robbery. The film, shot in nearby Fort Lee, New Jersey, ran for 3 weeks. Another film shown on the Victoria stage was the beginning of the 1908 New York–to–Paris auto race. Naturally, the start of the race took place directly in front of the Victoria Theater.

Of course, not all the acts were made up of talented performers. Upstairs at the Paradise Gardens, Willie had La Belle Baigneuse, Lalla Selbini, juggle while riding a bicycle. The gimmick was that she performed the act in a bathing suit. *VARIETY* reported the act was "frankly indecent." Willie later presented A. Z. Marino, the "Auto Defier," who lay down upon the Victoria stage while an automobile containing 4 men ran over him. And when temperatures rose outside, Willie convinced patrons that the Victoria's auditorium was 10 degrees cooler by exhibiting a thermometer resting on an artfully concealed block of ice.

The most successful act to play the Victoria was Gertrude Hoffman, a popular dancer and choreographer who performed Salome's dance. The risqué attraction earned $20,000 in ticket sales in its first week. Hoffman, whose specialty was dancing with the head of John the Baptist, remained at the Victoria for 22 weeks. This marked the beginning of a long fascination with Salome, which resulted in the writing of several popular songs ("Sadie Salome Go Home," by IRVING BERLIN, among them).

Willie quit the Victoria in 1912 (the year Houdini appeared on the roof along with a real skating rink) when he discovered that, behind his back, his father was negotiating the future of the Victoria. By 1913 Hammerstein had sold their exclusive vaudeville booking rights to the Times Square area. This mistake would signal the beginning of the end for the Victoria.

At Arthur's insistence, Willie rejoined the Victoria and, before its final fall, presented one of its most infamous attractions. The act featured Evelyn Nesbitt, the wife of Harry K. Thaw, who had killed architect Stanford White in a jealous rage. Willie billed her as "the Girl on the Red Velvet Swing." Nesbitt also danced with her partner, Jack Clifford, but it wasn't her terpsichorean talents that brought in the crowds. During their theatrical engagement in 1913, a miracle occurred: Thaw escaped from jail. The resultant publicity was stupendous. Willie even got credit for masterminding the escape to coincide with Nesbitt's opening. Nesbitt earned the theater $175,000.

A series of events brought an end to the Hammerstein dynasty. The PALACE THEATER was quickly taking the leading role in vaudeville presentation in Times Square. On June 10, 1914, Willie Hammerstein died. That same year, two of Oscar Hammerstein's other sons, Abe and Harry, also passed away. Arthur took over the management of the Victoria but did not have

Willie's showmanship. Meanwhile, Hammerstein entered into an agreement with the Metropolitan Opera, which refused him the right to produce opera in New York. He was forced to convert his Lexington Opera House to a movie theater. The next year, 1915, Hammerstein was through; at the age of 68, he sold the Lexington and Victoria Theaters. Morose over his forced retirement, he died only 4 years later.

Hammerstein sold the Victoria to the man who would take over his mantle as the premier showman in New York: S. L. ("ROXY") ROTHAFEL. On Sunday May 2, 1915, the Victoria Theater closed following a week of vaudeville dedicated to Willie Hammerstein. In its 17 years as the premier vaudeville house in New York, the Victoria grossed $20 million and netted $5 million. Buster Keaton once wrote that the Victoria was "America's greatest vaudeville theater. That grand old showcase was in its day everything—and perhaps a little more—than the Palace became later. Any old timer will tell you, Hammerstein's Victoria was vaudeville at its all-time best." George Jessel and Will Rogers concurred with Keaton's opinion.

Roxy gutted the theater and created the RIALTO movie theater, designed by Thomas W. Lamb. In 1935 the theater was again redesigned and became the New Rialto. This Brandt Theater specialized in the usual kung fu and second-run attractions found on 42nd Street. The Brandts remodeled it again in 1980, opened a Broadway entrance, and attempted to present legitimate attractions at the theater. But none caught on, and the theater returned to showing kung fu movies. In 1987, the Cineplex Odeon chain took over the theater's operations and remodeled the interior. The theater reopened as the Cineplex Odeon Warner. It was torn down in 2000 to make way for an office building.

VICTORIA THEATER (2). *See* **Gaiety Theater.**

VICTORY THEATRE. *See* **New Victory Theatre.**

VIRGINIA THEATER. 245 W. 52nd Street. Architect: C. Howard Crane. Opening: as Guild Theater, April 13, 1925; *Caesar and Cleopatra*.

The THEATRE GUILD, the most important producing entity of the 1920s and '30s, was using the Garrick Theater to present its shows. The Guild decided it needed its own building to house its productions and provide space for its school, so it commissioned C. Howard Crane, Kenneth Franzheim, and Charles Bettis to design a new theater. Set designers Norman Bel Geddes and Lee Simonson consulted on the project, which resulted in the Guild Theater.

At its opening, the theater was called "Home for All the Arts of the Theater." It existed "for drama, for beauty, for ideas." Strangely, the architects decided to build the theater on the second floor of the Italian-style building with a Spanish-tile roof. Despite the design talents involved, the Guild was judged as less than a success by artists and audiences. Lawrence Langner, a founder of the Theatre Guild, wrote, "We made the ghastly mistake of providing a theater with all the stage space necessary for a repertory of plays without enough seating capacity to provide the income necessary to support the repertory." The design of the auditorium was also deemed boring by audiences, who were used to the European-style interior decorations of most Broadway theaters.

The Theatre Guild opened the new house with a production of George Bernard Shaw's *Caesar and Cleopatra*, starring HELEN HAYES. President Calvin Coolidge, in Washington, threw a switch that illuminated the theater on opening night. The theater housed some of the finest work on Broadway. The Guild's eighth season began with LUNT AND FONTANNE in Shaw's *Arms and the Man* (9/14/25; 181 performances). Ferenc Molnár's *The Glass Slipper* (10/19/25; 65 performances) was the next attraction, but, after playing to the Theatre Guild's 15,000 subscribers, it closed. During this time, the Theatre Guild continued to present works at other theaters, while hits played the Guild.

The Lunts were the Theatre Guild's chief acting asset. They appeared together and separately in several productions at the Guild Theater, including *Goat Song* (1/25/26; 58 performances), *At Mrs. Beam's* (4/26/26; 222 performances), *Juarez and Maximilian* (10/11/26; 42 performances), *The Brothers Karamazov* (1/3/27; 56 performances), S. N. Behrman's *The Second Man* (4/11/27; 178 performances), Shaw's *The Doctor's Dilemma* (11/21/27; 115 performances), *Caprice* (12/31/28; 178 performances), and Behrman's *Meteor* (12/23/29; 92 performances). Lunt was featured in Eugene O'Neill's *Marco Millions* (1/9/28; 102 performances), and Fontanne starred in *Pygmalion* (11/15/26; 143 performances).

While the Lunts were in rehearsal, other actors were featured on the Guild's stage. Edward G. Robinson was featured in Pirandello's *Right You Are if You Think You Are* (2/23/27; 58 performances). Dudley Digges played Mephistopheles in Goethe's *Faust* (10/8/28; 48 performances). In November 1928 Winifred Lenihan, Helen Westley, Gale Sondergaard, and Dudley Digges were in Shaw's *Major Barbara* (11/19/28; 73 performances), directed by Philip Moeller. Otto Kruger, Claude Rains, Alice Brady, and Gale Sondergaard opened the 12th season at the Guild with *Karl and Anna* (10/17/29; 49 performances). Rouben Mamou-

Jane Wheatley as Catherine Petkoff and Lynn Fontanne as Raina in Shaw's *Arms and the Man*, 1925.

lian directed the next production, *The Game of Love and Death* (11/25/29; 48 performances), with Alice Brady, Otto Kruger, and Claude Rains. Turgenev's *A Month in the Country* (7/17/30; 72 performances) starred Alla Nazimova, Dudley Digges, and Douglas Dumbrille. Katia the maid was played by Hortense Alden, better known as Katharine Hepburn. The 12th season of the Theatre Guild was brought to a close with the third edition of *The Garrick Gaieties* (10/16/30; 12 performances), a musical revue. It featured Sterling Holloway, Hildegarde Halliday, Imogene Coca, and, later in the run, Rosalind Russell.

Lunt and Fontanne returned to the Guild stage in Maxwell Anderson's *Elizabeth the Queen* (11/3/30; 145 performances). The next production, *Midnight* (12/29/30; 48 performances), was undistinguished except for the inclusion in the cast of Clifford Odets. Franchot Tone, Helen Westley, June Walker, Lee Strasberg, and Woodward (Tex) Ritter were among the cast in *Green Grow the Lilacs* (1/26/31; 64 performances). The play gained notice again when it was later adapted for the musical *Oklahoma!* (1943).

Most of the Theatre Guild's larger and more ambitious productions were staged at the MARTIN BECK THEATRE. One of its finest productions, however,

opened at the Guild Theater on October 26, 1931. This was Eugene O'Neill's *Mourning Becomes Electra* (158 performances). The 5-hour production starred Alla Nazimova and Alice Brady. Shaw's *Too True to Be Good* (4/4/32; 56 performances) was not a hit, despite a cast including Beatrice Lillie, Hope Williams, Leo G. Carroll, and Claude Rains. The next play was a dramatization of Pearl Buck's *The Good Earth* (10/17/32; 56 performances) with Alla Nazimova, Sydney Greenstreet, Jessie Ralph, Claude Rains, and Henry Travers. Ina Claire followed next in S. N. Behrman's comedy *Biography* (12/12/32; 210 performances). Shirley Booth, Leo G. Carroll, Judith Anderson, and Humphrey Bogart appeared in Somerset Maugham's translation of *The Mask and the Face* (5/8/33; 40 performances), which closed the 15th season.

The opening of the 1933 season on October 2 marked GEORGE M. COHAN's next-to-last Broadway appearance and EUGENE O'NEILL's only comedy. *Ah, Wilderness!* (285 performances) also featured Elisha Cook Jr. and Gene Lockhart. Its success meant that the Theatre Guild had to mount the rest of the season's productions at other theaters.

The 17th season opened with Ruth Gordon and Glenn Anders in *A Sleeping Clergyman* (10/8/34; 40 performances), which was followed by an epic, *Valley Forge* (12/10/34; 58 performances) by Maxwell Anderson. This production starred Philip Merivale and Margalo Gilmore. The next production of note was a revue, *Parade* (5/20/35; 40 performances), starring Ralph Riggs, Eve Arden, Jimmy Savo, Charles Walters, and Ezra Stone. Lunt and Fontanne opened with *The Taming of the Shrew* (9/30/35; 128 performances), co-starring Bretaigne Windust, Richard Whorf, Le Roi Operti, and Sydney Greenstreet. The 1930s ended with highlights including Behrman's *End of Summer* (12/17/36; 152 performances) starring Ina Claire, Osgood Perkins, Shepperd Strudwick, Mildred Natwick, and Van Heflin; and Ben Hecht's *To Quito and Back* (10/6/37; 46 performances), with Sylvia Sidney, Leslie Banks, and Joseph Buloff.

As fine as these productions were, the Theatre Guild was losing money because of the relatively small seating capacity of the theater and the scale of its productions. The Guild also was at the forefront of those productions mounted by people willing to take chances, so many of the typical Broadway audiences weren't ready for Guild productions. As a result, the Theatre Guild found it necessary to lease the theater to other producers. The best of these outside productions was William Saroyan's *The Time of Your Life*, which moved to the Guild in 1940. Because other producers were no more successful than the Theatre Guild in paying the bills, the Theatre Guild leased the theater as a radio theater in 1943.

The theater was renamed the WOR Mutual Theater on March 19, 1943. In 1950 the AMERICAN NATIONAL THEATRE AND ACADEMY (ANTA) bought the theater and renamed it the ANTA Playhouse. ANTA renovated the theater and opened its first production on November 26, 1950. This was Robinson Jeffers' *The Tower Beyond Tragedy* (32 performances), with Judith Anderson. Next came a hit, Gloria Swanson and José Ferrer in a revival of Ben Hecht and Charles MacArthur's *Twentieth Century* (12/24/50; 218 performances). Because it was a hit, it moved to the Fulton Theater (*see* HELEN HAYES THEATER [1]). Revivals at the playhouse included *Desire Under the Elms* (1/16/52; 48 performances), with Karl Malden, and *Golden Boy* (3/12/52; 55 performances), with John Garfield and Lee J. Cobb. The next big hit was *Mrs. McThing* (2/20/52; 350 performances), featuring Helen Hayes, Ernest Borgnine, Jules Munshin, and Brandon de Wilde. It was such a big hit that it moved to the MOROSCO THEATRE. Helen Hayes was also in the theater's next hit, a revival of Thornton Wilder's *The Skin of Our Teeth* (8/17/55; 22 performances). It also starred Mary Martin, GEORGE ABBOTT, and Don Murray. The Lunts returned in *The Great Sebastians* (1/4/56; 174 performances), by Lindsay and Crouse.

The theater was renamed the American Academy of Dramatic Arts in 1953 and renamed again the ANTA Theater on December 21, 1954, with the opening of *Portrait of a Lady* (7 performances). A hit that actually stayed in the theater was Paddy Chayefsky's *Middle of the Night* (2/8/56; 477 performances), starring Edward G. Robinson. *Say, Darling* (4/3/58; 332 performances) starred Vivian Blaine, Johnny Desmond, and Robert Morse. It was a surprise hit with a score by JULE STYNE and COMDEN AND GREEN. Next came the PULITZER PRIZE–winning play, *J.B.* (12/11/58; 364 performances). The Archibald MacLeish drama starred Raymond Massey, Pat Hingle, and Christopher Plummer.

The 1960s were good years for the theater. A musical revue based on the writings of James Thurber was aptly named *A Thurber Carnival* (2/26/60; 127 performances). Hugh Wheeler's *Big Fish, Little Fish* (3/15/61; 101 performances) was directed by Sir John Gielgud. Later that year, *A Man for All Seasons* (11/22/61; 640 performances), by Robert Bolt, starred Paul Scofield and became the longest run at the theater. On October 13, 1963, history was made when Robert Noah's play *The Advocate* opened on Broadway and was broadcast on 5 Westinghouse stations. The company invested $60,000 in the William Hammerstein and Michael Ellis production, which was bankrolled for $100,000. Robert Noah's play was taped in a television studio in Mineola, Long Island. Live pickups of the ANTA's audience were broadcast before the opening, during the intermission, and after the show.

James Baldwin's *Blues for Mister Charlie* (4/23/64; 148 performances), with Rip Torn, Diana Sands, Pat Hingle, and Rosetta Le Noire, was followed by *The Owl and the Pussycat* (11/18/64; 421 performances), a light comedy with Diana Sands and Alan Alda. Producer Philip Rose bravely cast the two as lovers in spite of one being black and the other white. This was among the first instances of nontraditional casting in the theater. The last big hit of the 1960s at this theater was *The Royal Hunt of the Sun* (10/26/65; 261 performances), starring Christopher Plummer and George Rose.

The 1970s reflected the decline in Broadway's offerings. Helen Hayes, James Stewart, and Jesse White started the decade off right in a revival of *Harvey* (1970). A revival of Tennessee Williams' *Cat on a Hot Tin Roof* was a hit in 1974 with Elizabeth Ashley, Keir Dullea, Kate Reid, and Fred Gwynne. The revue *Bubbling Brown Sugar* (3/2/76; 766 performances) was a surprise hit. Another was the Goodspeed Opera Company's revival of *Whoopee!* (1979), which starred Charles Repole. It ran until Tom Stoppard's *Night and Day* (11/27/79; 95 performances) with Maggie Smith replaced it later that year.

The 1980s saw even less of merit at the theater. *Oh, Brother!* (11/10/81; 16 performances) with a score by Michael Valenti was an undeserved failure. In August 1981, the theater was bought by the Jujamcyn chain. The name was changed to the Virginia Theater, after Virginia M. Binger, who owned the theater with her husband, James. The theater was renovated again, but still it was not considered a top Broadway house. Nonetheless, two successful musicals played the house: an excellent revival of RODGERS AND HART's *On Your Toes* (3/6/83; 505 performances); *City of Angels* (12/11/89; 879 performances), a musical by Cy Coleman, Larry Gelbart, and David Zippel was another success.

Jelly's Last Jam (4/26/92; 569 performances) was a musicalization of the life of Jelly Roll Morton, self-proclaimed inventor of jazz. The show marked Gregory Hines' welcome return to Broadway; Savion Glover, the remarkable tap dancer, was his co-star. *Smokey Joe's Café* (3/2/95; 2,037 performances) was the the theater's next hit. The show, built around the songs of Lieber and Stoller, received lukewarm reviews from the critics, but canny marketing to the suburban audiences kept the show running. It eventually became the longest running revue in Broadway history.

The 1999–2000 season saw not one but two musicals based on Joseph Moncure Marsh's epic poem *The Wild Party*. One opened at Manhattan Theatre Club off Broadway, with music and lyrics by Jason Robert Brown. The second opened at the Virginia Theater on April 13, 2000, with a score by Michael John

LaChiusa. It was produced by the New York Shakespeare Festival, and the Festival's artistic director, George Wolfe, directed. Mandy Patinkin starred along with Toni Collette and Eartha Kitt. Both *Wild Party*s were failures; the Broadway production closed after only 68 performances.

Following an all-star revival of Gore Vidal's *The Best Man* (9/17/2000; 121 performances), August Wilson's most recent play to appear on Broadway, *King Hedley II*, opened at the Virginia on May 1, 2001. Brian Stokes Mitchell, Leslie Uggams, and Charles Brown were featured. The show closed after only 72 performances.

Laura Linney, Liam Neeson, and Brian Murray starred in a revival of Arthur Miller's *The Crucible* (3/7/2002; 101 performances). RODGERS AND HAMMERSTEIN's *The Flower Drum Song*, with a new libretto by David Henry Hwang opened on October 17, 2002, and ran 169 performances.

The exterior of the Virginia has been designated a historic landmark by the New York City Landmarks Preservation Commission.

VITAGRAPH THEATER. *See* **Olympia.**

V-J DAY. Times Square has, throughout most of its history, served as a gathering place where New Yorkers have celebrated events ranging from prizefight outcomes to election results to the annual New Year's Eve celebration. Although the V-E Day celebration on May 9, 1945, was enormous, by far the largest and most flamboyant outpouring of shared emotion was the V-J Day celebration, marking the Japanese surrender and the end of the World War II.

For most of these mass gatherings, the focal point has been the TIMES TOWER and the moving sign, the MOTOGRAM, that runs around the tower. Before the advent of television and the invention of the portable transistor radio, the Motogram was the fastest way for people who were not at home or in an office to get news. When important events were imminent, great crowds gathered at the base of the Times Tower.

On August 14, 1945, rumors had circulated all day that Japan was about to surrender. The population of New York knew that both the first announcement and the festivities to follow would take place in Times Square. When people left work they headed for Times Square. By 5 P.M. more than 200,000 people had gathered facing the Motogram. Streets were blocked off from 40th to 49th Streets to accommodate the growing crowds, which spilled beyond Times Square south to Herald Square and north to Columbus Circle. At 7:03 P.M. the light bulbs on the sign spelled out the message, "Official Truman announces Japanese surrender." The crowd, which had grown to 750,000, gasped in disbelief and then a roar went up, echoing up and down the streets of the city.

As the evening progressed, jubilant New Yorkers continued to gather in the square. By 10 P.M. more than 2 million people were jammed together in a sea of laughing, shrieking humanity. From the PARAMOUNT BUILDING and the other surrounding structures, a spontaneous ticker-tape celebration took place. People threw paper, boxes, confetti, hats, and newspapers into the square. Flags were prominently displayed in windows and on flagpoles, and people brought small handheld flags from their homes and waved them furiously. Sailors, soldiers, secretaries, and survivors kissed strangers and danced together under the artificial moonlight of the advertising spectaculars (*see* SIGNAGE) ringing the square.

The *New York Times* reported, "The victory roar beat upon the eardrums until it numbed the senses." The huge crowd could be heard inside the many theaters up and down the avenues and side streets. Broadway shows were halted and movies interrupted as audiences left to join the celebration. Afterward Times Square was filled with a record amount of trash. Altogether, 5,438 tons of paper were picked up from Manhattan streets.

Although President Truman officially claimed September 2 as V-J Day, because that was the actual date of the signing of the surrender papers, most Americans think of the Times Square celebration on August 14 as V-J Day.

WALLACK'S THEATER. *See* **Anco Theater.**

WALTER KERR THEATRE. *See* **Ritz Theatre (1).**

WALTERS, LOU. A master of the nightclub, and one of Broadway's most successful entrepreneurs; b. London, England, 1896; d. Miami, Florida, August 15, 1977.

Walters was born in London and came with his family to New York when he was 15. One of his first jobs was as an office boy in a vaudeville office. Within a few months he was earning $4 a week for scouting acts. At the tender age of 17 he entered the world of the nightclub. He began booking acts for one club, and within 3 years he was responsible for hiring 200 acts per week. This early success motivated him to set up a business for himself in Boston. He started the concern with only $75, the cost of rent and phone hookup.

Nightclubs continued thriving even as other forms of variety were drying up. Vaudeville was all but dead, replaced by radio and sound pictures. Walters concentrated on booking clubs. In 1932 he received a piece of the profits of a nightclub in Boston's Bradford Hotel, a taste of ownership that gave him the idea to start his own club. He saved his money, and in 1937 spent all but 63 cents to open his first Latin Quarter in Boston. As Walters later wrote, "I threw the 63 cents into a cuspidor. I thought I might as well start broke." The club was an immediate success. Only 3 years later, in 1940, the club was earning $500,000 a year. Walters plowed those profits into more ventures. He bought EARL CARROLL's Palm Island Club in 1940. That Miami Beach supper club was also successful (entertaining more than 7,000 patrons a week) and gave Walters the capital to open his greatest nightclub.

In 1942 he opened the Latin Quarter in Times Square, on 48th Street between Broadway and 7th Avenue. With the war on, the Broadway cognoscenti proclaimed the new venture a flop even before it opened. But Walters remembered, "I had no feeling this was a gamble, no thought of the possibility of failure. I thought then, and still do, that the American public will go where they get a run for their money." The new club was an immediate hit, grossing more than $1.5 million in its first year. The newest Walters club capitalized on Times Square's central location and attracted a wide range of clientele. Tourists, East Siders, society members, and celebrities from movies and theater all flocked there.

Indeed, once the club opened, the press was enthusiastic. Danton Walker wrote, "Lou Walters' new Latin Quarter is just what the doctor ordered for an ailing Broadway—a big, lively show featuring spectacular vaudeville acts and a lineup of pretty and talented girls, with a minimum charge that isn't above the reach of Mr. and Mrs. John Q. Taxpayers!"

Walters explained his success through his theory of nightclub management: "I throw the book at them. I try to give them the nightclub of their dreams. Cut pile carpets, velvet on the walls, satin draperies, fountains with colored water, mirrors on the balustrade. Fill them full of food and take their breath away. Let them feel all the time they are shooting the works."

Walters' early experiences as a talent agent served him well. He drew on established stars like Sophie Tucker, Milton Berle, and Ted Lewis, as well as up-and-coming faces like Patti Page and Johnny Ray. Mae West, Frank Sinatra, Mickey Rooney, and Dorothy Lamour were other notables Walters presented at his club.

In 1954 the Latin Quarter earned 3 million. Of that, 6 or 7 percent was profit—around $200,000 that year. The club's overhead cost about $45,000 a week, including paying a staff of 200. Each of the Quarter's shows cost between $75,000 and $80,000.

Unlike many club owners, Walters insisted on a first-rate kitchen. Others felt that as long as the drinks were strong and the lights low the food didn't matter, but Walters disagreed with that philosophy: "It's a popular fallacy in this business to say that your money is made or lost in the kitchen. The man who goes to a nightclub goes in a spirit of splurging, and you've got to splurge right along with him. My motto used to be when the customer does not leave something on his plate, it's bad. I am always urging my stewards and chefs to give the customers more food than they expect."

In the first 13 years of its existence the club was closed for only 2 days. Walters explained in the *World Telegram and Sun*:

> We rebuilt the front and stayed open through it. We rebuilt the stage twice and didn't miss a show. We took out the air-conditioning and put in a new system. We melted, but we stayed open.
>
> The only time we closed we did so voluntarily for two days after President Roosevelt died in 1945. People just didn't want to laugh then.

In the first 10 years of its existence the Latin Quarter earned more than $10 million and served more than 5 million people. Through it all, Walters remained calm and collected. "I'm probably the calmest one around here in a bad spot. Since my early days in Boston I told my staff not to call me at night. If the place is on fire, I can't put it out. If someone runs off with the money, I can't catch him. Even if there's an earthquake, I told them, let me get a night's sleep."

The success of the Latin Quarter led Walters to further ventures. The theater beckoned, and his first attempt at producing was the ZIEGFELD FOLLIES OF 1943 (4/14/43; 553 performances). The show was co-produced by the SHUBERT BROTHERS. The score was by Ray Henderson and Jack Yellen. The lavish revue starred Milton Berle, Eric Blore, Arthur Treacher, and the Bil Baird Marionettes. It was an immediate success. Unfortunately, his later theatrical ventures, *Artists and Models* (11/5/43) and *Star Time* (9/12/44), were failures. In 1953, he began Lou Walters Enterprises, a management firm, at 1576 Broadway. He sold his interest in the Latin Quarter in 1957 and began producing shows in Las Vegas. There he introduced the *Folies Bergère* (see HELEN HAYES THEATER [1]). In July 1957 the *Latin Quarter Follies* was the final revue Walters presented at the Latin Quarter. In May 1958 he opened the Café de Paris at the corner of Broadway and 53rd Street, on the site of the old Arcadia Ballroom. It lasted barely 2 years.

Walters returned to the Latin Quarter in 1965, but times had changed. Costs were escalating, and the cho-

rus line demanded union representation. Walters retired after closing the club in 1967. Another notable achievement was his daughter, Barbara, today a successful television journalist. Lou Walters died in Miami on August 15, 1977.

WARNER BROTHERS THEATER. *See* **Mark Hellinger Theater.**

WATTS, RICHARD, JR. Critic; b. Parkersburg, West Virginia, January 12, 1898; d. New York, New York, January 2, 1981.

From 1922 to 1923 Watts worked at the *Brooklyn Times*. He moved to the *Herald-Sun Syndicate*, where he was assistant night editor from 1923 to 1924. In 1924 he joined the *Herald Tribune* where he became movie CRITIC. He held the post until 1936, when he became drama critic, replacing the late Percy Hammond. Watts stayed at the *Herald Tribune* until 1942 and World War II. During the war, he was posted in Dublin, Ireland, and Chungking, China. In 1946 he became the drama critic for the *New York Post*. He held that position until Clive Barnes moved to the *Post*. Watts continued to contribute to the paper until his death.

WEBBER, ANDREW LLOYD. English composer and producer of some of the 20th century's biggest hit musicals; b. March 22, 1948.

Composer Andrew Lloyd Webber is the greatest figure in British theater in the second half of the 20th century, and his reign on Broadway has lasted almost 30 years, a time when he came to dominate musical theater.

He was raised in a musical atmosphere. His father, William Southcombe Lloyd Webber, taught music theory and composition at the Royal College of Music, and his mother was a violinist and singer. They encouraged young Andrew to learn to play the violin when he was only 3 years old. By the time he was 6 he was writing original compositions, and he actually had one published in *Music Teacher* magazine at age 9.

He developed an interest in the theater after having been taken to the hits of the day by his parents and his Aunt Vi. She encouraged his musical abilities, and soon thereafter he built a small, makeshift theater in his parents' house. He wrote simple musicals and put them on for family and friends.

In 1956 he began composing music for his school's plays. While at Westminster, he continued his music education, winning a Challenge Scholarship in 1962. Two years later another scholarship allowed him to transfer to Oxford University.

On April 21, 1965, while attending Oxford, he received a letter from a young lyric writer, Tim Rice: "I've been told you're looking for a 'with it' writer of lyrics for your songs, and as I've been writing pop songs for a while and particularly enjoy writing the lyrics I wonder if you consider it worth your while meeting me." The two met and hit it off, beginning an especially fruitful collaboration. Lloyd Webber dropped out of Oxford and concentrated on writing music full time. The team's first show, *The Likes of Us*, was not a success, but their second was to make theater history.

Alan Doggett, the head of music at Colet Court preparatory school in London, who was well acquainted with Lloyd Webber, suggested that he and Rice present the school with a presentation for an end-of-term concert, preferably something religious. The songwriters looked through the Bible and found the story of Joseph and his father, Jacob. They devised a 15-minute musical based on the story. It was titled *Joseph and the Amazing Technicolor Dreamcoat*. It premiered on March 1, 1968, at the school. A second performance was held on May 12 of that year at the Central Hall, Westminster, featuring David Daltrey and the Mixed Bag.

The piece was expanded, and in May 1969, ever the businessman, Lloyd Webber—along with his partner, Tim Rice, their manager, Sefton Myers, and their adviser, David Land—began a new company, New Ventures Theatrical Management Ltd.

The American premiere of *Joseph* took place in May 1970 at the School of the Immaculate Conception in Douglastown, New York. In October of that year, a concept album was released featuring Ian Gillan, Yvonne Elliman, and Murray Head. A month later, producer Robert Stigwood purchased Myers' half interest in New Ventures. In May 1971 Stigwood bought the other half of the company from Land and became the sole owner of *Joseph*. The company was renamed Superstar Ventures Ltd.

At the end of that year Broadway saw the opening of *Jesus Christ Superstar* (10/12/71; 711 performances) at the MARK HELLINGER THEATER. Yvonne Elliman starred as Mary Magdalene, alongside Jeff Fenholt as Jesus and Ben Vereen as Judas. Also in the cast in chorus and supporting parts were Samuel E. Wright, Ted Neeley (who would apear in the film version) and Anita Morris. Robert Stigwood produced, and Tom O'Horgan, who had made a splash with *Hair*, directed, or rather "conceived for the stage," as the program credited. The show would also be the next Lloyd Webber and Rice musical on Broadway, when a revival opened at the LONGACRE THEATER on November 23, 1977.

On August 9, 1972, the duo's *Jesus Christ Superstar* opened at the Palace Theatre in London, where it ran an astonishing 3,358 performances. On February 17, 1973, *Joseph* opened on the West End at the Albery Theatre following a transfer from the Roundhouse Theatre (11/8/72). Later that year the film version of *Superstar* was released.

Lloyd Webber and playwright Alan Ayckbourn saw their musical *Jeeves* open in London on April 22, 1975. It was not a success, running for only 38 performances. Based on P. G. Wodehouse's Jeeves novels, the musical would finally make it to Broadway almost 25 years later (and would also fail there).

MCA released the *Evita* concept album in November 1976. Julie Covington, Colm Wilkinson, and Paul Jones were featured. The show itself opened in London at the Prince Edward Theatre on June 21, 1978, with Elaine Paige as Eva, David Essex as Che, and Joss Ackland as Peron. It would eventually run 2,900 performances. *Evita* opened at the BROADWAY THEATRE on September 25, 1979, under HAROLD PRINCE's direction. Patti LuPone starred as Eva Peron, along with Mandy Patinkin as Che and Bob Gunton as Peron.

In May 1979 Lloyd Webber and Rice's contract with Robert Stigwood came to an end. They were now free agents, with the ability to find their own producers. But Lloyd Webber had bigger ideas. Later that year he formed the Really Useful Company, Ltd., a solely owned production company dedicated to producing and exploiting his own shows and shows of other writers.

Lloyd Webber and Rice's next project was a one-act/one-person musical written for the BBC, *Tell Me on a Sunday*. The show was taped live at the Royalty Theatre in London on January 28, 1980, with Marti Webb starring, and was broadcast February 12.

Lloyd Webber and Rice's partnership took a break with the next Lloyd Webber show to open in London. A surprising choice of subject matter, T. S. Eliot's *Old Possum's Book of Cats*, formed the basis of the musical *Cats*. Furthermore, the production was booked into a new, out-of-the-way theater in London's West End. Pundits predicted a quick failure. But *Cats*, crediting the late T. S. Eliot as lyricist, opened to mainly enthusiastic reviews at the New London Theatre on May 11, 1981. It featured Elaine Paige as Grizabella and Brian Blessed as Old Deuteronomy. Seasoned critics frowned on it, but audiences were entranced.

On January 27, 1982, *Joseph and the Amazing Technicolor Dreamcoat* (747 performances) finally opened on Broadway at the ROYALE THEATRE. The production transferred from off-Broadway's Entermedia Theatre, where it opened on November 18, 1981. It starred Bill Hutton as Joseph and Laurie Beechman as the Narrator.

Tell Me on a Sunday was paired with an orchestral piece of Lloyd Webber's *Variations* to make up the show *Song and Dance*. It opened at London's Palace

Theatre on April 7, 1982. It starred Marti Webb (song) and Wayne Sleep (dance), and it ran for 781 performances.

Then it was back to New York and the opening at the WINTER GARDEN THEATRE of *Cats* (10/7/82). Betty Buckley starred as Grizabella, along with Ken Page as Old Deuteronomy. Critics were not kind, but *Cats* went on to become the longest-running musical in Broadway history, closing on September 10, 2000, after 7,485 performances. The big hit song, written by Lloyd Webber and director Trevor Nunn, was "Memory." To the astonishment of theaterphiles, T. S. Eliot won the TONY AWARD for his "lyrics."

Back in London, another audacious idea for a musical, racing trains, became transformed into *Starlight Express*. The entire cast was on roller skates, whizzing around London's Apollo Victoria Theatre. Ray Shell played Rusty, Lon Satton was Poppa, and Stephanie Lawrence starred as Pearl. Adults dutifully took their children, and thousands of Japanese tourists attended, and *Starlight Express* became the little show that could, closing after 7,406 performances.

Song & Dance opened at the Royale Theatre on Broadway on September 18, 1985, to moderate critical notices. Bernadette Peters played the first act (song), and Christopher d'Amboise played the second act (dance). The production ran for 474 performances.

On January 6, 1986, Lloyd Webber took his Really Useful Company public on the London Stock Exchange. Hundreds of investors bet on the success of the composer's future shows. They would not be disappointed, because Lloyd Webber's next show was one of his greatest successes, *Phantom of the Opera*. Michael Crawford starred as the Phantom, and Lloyd Webber's new wife, Sarah Brightman, played Christine. The production opened in London at Her Majesty's Theatre on October 6, 1986.

Starlight Express (3/15/87) was the composer's next Broadway show. It opened at the GERSHWIN THEATER, with Greg Mowry as Rusty, Steve Fowler as Poppa, and Reva Rice as Pearl. The show was not a success, closing after 761 performances.

But Lloyd Webber's next Broadway show was another smash hit. *Phantom of the Opera* (1/26/88) opened at the MAJESTIC THEATRE, with Michael Crawford, Sarah Brightman, and Steve Barton repeating their London roles.

From the spectacular to the sublime: Lloyd Webber's next show was *Aspects of Love* at the Prince of Wales Theatre in London. The chamber musical opened on April 17, 1989, with Michael Ball, Ann Crumb, and Kevin Colson starring. It was a big success, running for 1,325 performances. But it was a feat not to be duplicated on Broadway. The show opened at the BROADHURST THEATER, with the West End stars

along with Brad Oscar. The Broadway production lasted only one season, closing after 376 performances. It would, at the time, be the most expensive failure in Broadway history.

With pressures on his company due to the failure of the Broadway version of *Aspects*, Lloyd Webber bought out his shareholders in the Really Useful holdings company for £77.5 million in December of 1990.

Right after that came a successful revival of *Joseph* at the London Palladium, with Jason Donovan starring as Joseph and Linzi Hateley as the Narrator. The show opened on June 12, 1991, and ran for 1,095 performances.

With successes in London and Broadway, Lloyd Webber bought the New London Theatre where *Cats* was enjoying its run. One month later, in August of 1991, Lloyd Webber sold a 30 percent share of Really Useful holdings to Polygram for £78 million.

With the unlikely concept of presenting *Jesus Christ Superstar* as a Japanese Kabuki-style production at London's Dominion Theatre, Lloyd Webber had 6 shows playing simultaneously in the West End.

In June 1992, Queen Elizabeth II, granted a knighthood to Lloyd Webber, and he became Sir Andrew Lloyd Webber.

Another audacious concept followed. Bored with the long run of *Starlight Express*, Sir Andrew decided to revamp the show. Five new songs were added, and the script was altered. The show reopened on November 23, 1992. That same year, he increased his hold on British theater with his purchase of 50 percent interest in London's Adelphi Theatre.

He promptly made plans for his next musical, *Sunset Boulevard*, to play the Adelphi in London. Patti LuPone opened in the troubled show on July 12, 1993, along with Kevin Anderson and Daniel Benzali. The show was not a success, but Sir Andrew kept it running until April 5, 1997.

A new revival of *Joseph* began life at Los Angeles' Pantages Theatre, with Michael Damian as Joseph. It moved to Broadway's MINSKOFF THEATRE, where it opened on November 10, 1993. It closed after only 231 performances.

A revamped *Sunset Boulevard* opened in December 1993 at Los Angeles' Shubert Theatre, with Glenn Close as Norma, Alan Campbell as Joe, and George Hearn as Max. It received mixed reviews. That version of the show was then duplicated in the still-running London production, but the changes would not help the show artistically. The Los Angeles production moved to the Minskoff Theatre on November 17, 1994. It closed on March 29, 1997, to apathetic houses, after 977 performances. A decent run, but a money loser.

Webber and playwright Alan Ayckbourn had produced a musical in London in 1975 titled *Jeeves*. It had been a quick failure, but the idea still appealed to Sir Andrew, and he mounted a revival in London's West End on July 2, 1996, under a slightly revamped title, *By Jeeves*. It played only until late February 1997. America's Goodspeed Opera House in East Haddam, Connecticut, hosted the American premiere of *By Jeeves* in November 1996.

Sir Andrew's next American show, *Whistle Down the Wind*, opened at Washington, D.C.'s National Theatre in December 1996. It received terrible reviews, and the production closed after the Washington engagement.

Sir Andrew received good news on February 26, 1997, when he was inducted into the House of Lords as Lord Lloyd Webber of Sydmonton, but failure was to follow. The English version of *Whistle Down the Wind* played 6 months after its opening on July 7, 1998. A year later, Lloyd Webber bought back the 30 percent share of Really Useful from Polygram (then Universal).

In January 2000 he purchased the Lyric, Apollo, Gielgud, Queen's, Duchess, Theatre Royal Drury Lane, Cambridge, Garrick, and Her Majesty's theaters, as well as the London Palladium, making him the largest theater owner in London's West End.

Still another failure was to follow. A Broadway revival of *Jesus Christ Superstar* (4/16/2000) opened at the FORD CENTER FOR THE PERFORMING ARTS, to horrible reviews. It starred Glenn Carter as Jesus, Maya Days as Mary, and Tony Vincent as Judas. It closed after a dismal 161 performances. More failures followed. The West End production of *The Beautiful Game*, a soccer musical, proved a quick flop. The American version of *By Jeeves* (10/28/2001) finally opened at the HELEN HAYES THEATER, with John Scherer as Bertie and Martin Jarvis as Jeeves. It closed after only 73 performances.

But Broadway refuses to count out Lloyd Webber. His new musical, *Bombay Dreams*, the first he's produced without writing the music, became a hit in London and is poised to transfer to the United States. And, as the theater's most audacious composer, who knows what new ideas might come along.

WEBER AND FIELDS' MUSIC HALL. *See* **44th Street Theatre.**

WEILL, KURT. Urbane composer of the 1930s and '40s, famous for his collaborations with Bertolt Brecht in Germany and later with Ira Gershwin in the United States; b. Dessau, Germany, March 2, 1900; d. New York, New York, April 3, 1950.

Weill's early career was associated primarily with Bertolt Brecht. Their most famous collaboration was *Die Dreigroschenoper (The Threepenny Opera)*. Another of their works, *Mahagonny*, has also endured through many productions throughout the world. When Adolf Hitler came into power, Weill emigrated to the United States. He brought with him his belief in the power of the musical theater, a power not yet fully realized in the United States. Weill felt, correctly, that he could entertain audiences and still tackle major themes and ideas. Because of his work with Brecht, Weill had a high regard for authors, especially poets. A hallmark of his career was the collaborations he enjoyed with many great authors whose work in the musical theater was otherwise negligible.

Weill's first Broadway production was an unsuccessful mounting of *The Threepenny Opera* (4/13/33; 12 performances). The translation was by Gifford Cochran and Jerrold Krimsky. Broadway audiences weren't ready for the serious musical theater that *The Threepenny Opera* typified. In 1935 Weill had a production of *A Kingdom for a Cow* in London with Desmond Carter's lyrics. The play was originally written as *Der Kubbandel* by Robert Vambery, but a production in Germany was out of the question. The show opened on June 28, 1935, at the Savoy Theater. It was Weill's second failure.

Weill returned to the United States and wrote the music for the antiwar musical *Johnny Johnson* (11/19/36; 68 performances). Playwright Paul Green contributed the book and lyrics to the show. The GROUP THEATER produced the piece. Besides the score, the most impressive of *Johnny Johnson*'s elements was its cast. It included such greats as Luther Adler, Morris Carnovsky, Lee J. Cobb, John Garfield, Elia Kazan, Will Lee, Robert Lewis, Sanford Meisner, Art Smith, and Albert Dekker. But the United States wasn't ready for *Johnny Johnson*'s cautionary messages.

Maxwell Anderson, Lotte Lenya, and Kurt Weill at the time of *Knickerbocker Holiday*.

Weill achieved somewhat more fame with a more successful production, *Knickerbocker Holiday* (10/19/38; 168 performances) at the ETHEL BARRYMORE THEATRE. The show, the story of Peter Stuyvesant in early Manhattan, also had political overtones, but they were put across in a more palatable manner. Walter Huston, Richard Kollmar, Ray Middleton, Robert Rounseville, and Jeanne Madden headed the cast. Huston made an especially strong impression in the leading role. He was lucky enough to have Weill's first popular standard to sing, "September Song." For this show Weill again chose a prominent playwright as his collaborator: Maxwell Anderson wrote the book and lyrics. THE PLAYWRIGHTS' COMPANY produced the show, and JOSHUA LOGAN directed.

Lady in the Dark (1/23/41; 467 performances), at the Alvin Theater (*see* NEIL SIMON THEATER), was Weill's first Broadway success. Weill's collaborator was Broadway veteran IRA GERSHWIN. The show fit Weill's requirement of an adult theme. This time it was psychoanalysis. Gertrude Lawrence played the lead, a magazine editor who simply couldn't make up her mind. Through a series of spectacular dreams, Lawrence discovered the root of her problems. The Weill and Gershwin score was among the best written for any musical. "My Ship" and "The Saga of Jenny" received the most notice. Also in the cast was Danny Kaye making his second Broadway appearance. For the comic singer, Gershwin concocted an especially difficult tongue twister, "Tchaikowsky." The song was a long list of actual names of Russian composers. Macdonald Carey, Natalie Schafer, and Victor Mature also had featured roles.

Weill's next big production was *One Touch of Venus* (10/7/43; 567 performances). Poet Ogden Nash supplied the lyrics to Weill's music. Nash and satirist

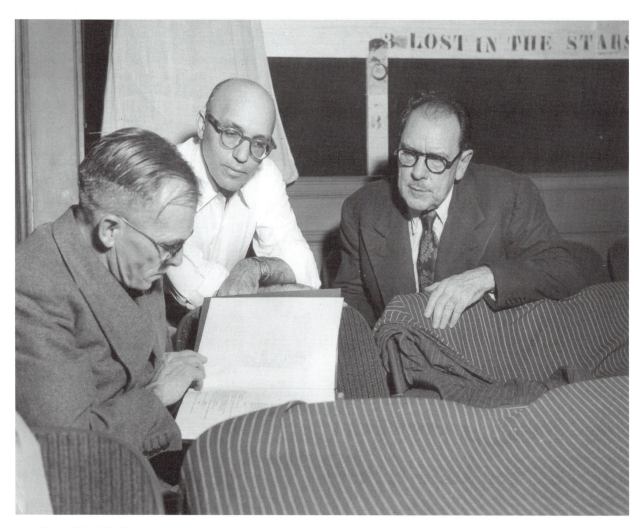

Alan Paton, Kurt Weill and Maxwell Anderson at the time of their collaboration on *Lost in the Stars*, 1949.

S. J. Perelman wrote the book. Elia Kazan directed, with Cheryl Crawford and John Wildberg producing. The story of a statue that comes to life was written for Marlene Dietrich but played by MARY MARTIN. Kenny Baker was her bedeviled suitor, with John Boles, Teddy Hart, and Paula Laurence rounding out the cast. The Weill and Nash score yielded many gems. "Foolish Heart" and "Speak Low" were the popular hits, and other songs in the score were equally good. "That's Him," "West Wind," and "The Trouble with Women" all had their partisans.

Weill and Gershwin reteamed for the unsuccessful *The Firebrand of Florence* (3/22/45; 43 performances). The show starred Melville Cooper, Earl Wrightson, and Weill's wife, Lotte Lenya. Weill again enlisted an unusual collaborator for his next production, *Street Scene* (1/9/47; 148 performances). Elmer Rice adapted his classic play for the musical. Anne Jeffreys, Polyna Stoska, Brian Sullivan, Hope Emerson, Sheila Bond, and Danny Daniels starred. "Moon-Faced, Starry-Eyed" achieved some success, but for the most part this exceptional score remains largely unknown. It certainly wasn't well appreciated at the time. Next, Weill tried another experiment, this time with Alan Jay Lerner (*see* LERNER AND LOEWE). *Love Life* (10/7/48; 252 performances) followed a marriage against the background of changing history. The couple never aged, although time marched on. The show began in colonial times and ended at the time of the show. Nanette Fabray and Ray Middleton starred as the hapless couple. They and the rest of the cast were afforded some fine songs, including "Here I'll Stay."

Weill's last Broadway show was one of his most impassioned. *Lost in the Stars* (10/30/49; 281 performances) featured lyrics by Weill's past collaborator, Maxwell Anderson. It was based on Alan Paton's novel about black citizens in South Africa *Cry the Beloved Country*. The tragic story was well captured through Weill and Anderson's powerful and dramatic score. Todd Duncan, the original Porgy in Gershwin's *Porgy and Bess*, Herbert Coleman, Inez Matthews, and Julian Mayfield headed the excellent cast. *Lost in the Stars* has won high regard as the years have passed.

Kurt Weill's final project was a musicalization of *Huckleberry Finn*, written with Maxwell Anderson. Unfortunately, Weill died before the project could be finished. Weill's most successful production occurred 4 years after his death. It was an off-Broadway revival of *The Threepenny Opera*. Lotte Lenya starred in the remounting of one of Weill's earliest successes. The opening at the Theater De Lys took place on September 10, 1954. It played for 94 performances. The Marc Blitzstein translation reopened on September 30, 1955. This time it ran for 2,611 performances. Other cast members were Charlotte Rae, Scott Merrill, Martin Wolfson, Jo Sullivan, Gerald Price, and Beatrice Arthur. The hit parade success of "Mack the Knife" accounted for much of the success of the show.

Weill's early death at age 50 was a blow to the Broadway community. His scores stand equal to those of Broadway's finest composers. Weill's themes pointed up the possiblities for the American musical theater—possibilities that still have not been fully realized.

WHITE, GEORGE. Actor, dancer, producer, director, choreographer, composer, lyricist, librettist, and the force behind the *Ziegfeld Follies'* biggest rival, *George White's Scandals*; b. Toronto, Canada, 1890; d. Hollywood, California, October 11, 1968.

As producer of the *Scandals*, White nurtured many young talents. These included GEORGE GERSHWIN, DE SYLVA, BROWN, AND HENDERSON, and Alice Faye.

White was born in Toronto, Canada, in 1890. Soon thereafter his parents moved to New York City. He learned to dance while standing on Third Avenue hawking newspapers. His first stage appearance was at the age of 12. When he was about 16, he teamed up with Ben Ryan, and together they toured on the vaudeville circuit in a dancing act. A scout for producer Charles Dillingham spotted White and introduced him to Dillingham, who promptly hired White for his next show. White made his New York debut at the Globe Theatre (*see* LUNT-FONTANNE THEATER) in *The Echo* on August 17, 1910. He next appeared at the WINTER GARDEN THEATRE in *The Pleasure Seekers* (11/3/13). This led to his joining the cast of *The Midnight Girl* at the 44TH STREET THEATRE in the middle of its run.

George White.

By then, he was starting to make his reputation and was hired by FLORENZ ZIEGFELD for the 1915 edition of his *Follies*. After the *Follies*, Ziegfeld hired White for the JEROME KERN and P. G. Wodehouse revue *Miss 1917* (11/5/17; 40 performances). The show was a financial failure, although it played to standing-room-only houses.

White became convinced that he could outdo Ziegfeld by producing his own revues. He raised the money and opened the first GEORGE WHITE'S SCANDALS on June 2, 1919. The show featured a score by Richard Whiting and Herbert Spencer, composers, and Arthur Jackson and White himself as lyricists. This was the first instance of a team creating the entire score for a revue. Until then, revue producers would receive entries from a variety of songwriters and pick the songs they liked from the samples submitted. White performed in the show, as well as choreographing it. Also appearing in the first *Scandals* was White's former dance partner from the *Follies*, Ann Pennington. She became the first in a series of regulars who starred in succeeding *Scandals*, eventually appearing in 5 of the annual revues. Other performers who were part of the informal company were Willie and Eugene Howard (6 editions), Florence Williams (4 occasions), and Lou Holtz and Winnie Lightner (each appeared 3 times). Apart from the regulars, White brought in many top stars from the stage and radio. These performers included ETHEL MERMAN, Rudy Vallee (twice), Alice Faye, Everett Marshall, Charles King, Paul Whiteman and his orchestra, Dolores Costello (twice), Ray Bolger, Ethel Barrymore Colt, Cliff Edwards, Bert Lahr, Ben Blue, Harry Richman (twice), Ella Logan, and Ann Miller.

White's shows were fast and snappy, with a youthful exuberance. This was due in large part to the songs that were written for the series. George Gershwin contributed 5 scores for the series. Among the best known of the Gershwin songs are "The Scandal Walk," "Drifting Along with the Tide," "I'll Build a Stairway to Paradise," and "Somebody Loves Me." The lyrics for the Gershwin tunes were written by Arthur Jackson, IRA GERSHWIN, Ballard Macdonald, and B. G. De Sylva. De Sylva also contributed to 3 other *Scandals* with his partners Lew Brown and Ray Henderson. They contributed some of the greatest songs to come out of the Broadway theater. Together they wrote "Birth of the Blues," "This Is My Lucky Day," and "Black Bottom." Henderson and Brown contributed one more score to the series, but without De Sylva. The score was probably the *Scandals'* best, and it included "Ladies and Gentlemen, That's Love," "That's Why Darkies Were Born," "This Is the Missus," "My Song," "The Thrill Is Gone," and "Life Is Just a Bowl of Cherries."

Although best known for the *Scandals*, White also produced book musicals. The first was *Runnin' Wild* (10/29/23; 167 performances). This was an all-black musical, featuring Elisabeth Welch, Adelaide Hall, Flournoy Miller, and Aubrey Lyles. The show was typical of White's works. It was fast paced and up-to-the-minute. In fact, it was in *Runnin' Wild* that audiences first heard and saw the Charleston. Elisabeth Welch sang the James P. Johnson and Cecil Mack song as a bevy of beauties illustrated the dance steps. The Charleston swept through the nation and became the hottest dance craze of the 1920s.

White's next non-*Scandals* show was *Manhattan Mary* (9/26/27; 264 performances). The score was composed by *Scandals* regulars De Sylva, Brown, and Henderson. White co-authored the book with William K. Wells, in addition to producing, directing, and starring in the show. Ed Wynn, Harland Dixon, and Ona Munson were also in the cast, as were *Scandals* regulars Lou Holtz and Paul Frawley. Although the show wasn't one of the *Scandals*, it was a close relation. At the end, the heroine attains her fondest dream: joining the *Scandals*. White played himself. White's next musical, *Flying High* (3/3/30; 355 performances), also by De Sylva, Brown, and Henderson, featured Kate Smith, Bert Lahr, and Oscar Shaw.

By 1932 the country was deep into the Depression, and money was hard to come by for both the populace and producers. Instead of mounting an expensive *Scandals*, White presented *George White's Music Hall Varieties* (11/22/32; 71 performances), a simpler version of the same formula. Eleanor Powell, Harry Richman, and Bert Lahr headlined, but the show wasn't a success. Perhaps when the curtain rose on its opening night, audiences were expecting a more lavish evening's entertainment. The songs were written by a variety of songwriting teams, including HAROLD ARLEN and Irving Caesar, Cliff Friend and Herb Magidson, and Carmen Lombardo. But the hit of the show, and a future standard, was Herman Hupfeld's "Let's Turn out the Lights and Go to Bed."

The next year White presented his last non-*Scandals* Broadway show, *Melody* (2/14/33; 80 performances). He produced and directed the show, which was a distinct change from his usual offerings. It was written by SIGMUND ROMBERG, noted mostly for his operettas, and Irving Caesar. The show proved to be a failure, despite the talents of Gypsy Rose Lee, Everett Marshall, and Ina Ray Hutton. Following his last *Scandals* in 1939, White toured with a tab edition called *George White's Scandals Cavalcade*. White brought the show to LOEW'S STATE THEATER in June 1941.

In addition to his stage chores, White ran several nightclubs. The first was the Gay White Way, where he presented and directed a revue, *Midnight Scandals*, in 1941. He also produced and directed an original nightclub revue, *Nice to See You*, at the Versailles in April 1953. White's final nightclub show was presented in Jack Silverman's International Theater-Restaurant. The show *George White's Scandals* opened on October 9, 1963. The *Scandals* were also filmed by Hollywood several times. Fox presented *George White's Scandals* in 1934 and *George White's 1935 Scandals* the following year. White wrote, produced, directed, and appeared in the two films. *George White's Scandals* was an RKO picture that debuted in 1945. He also appeared as himself in the Warner Brothers picture *Rhapsody in Blue*, also in 1945.

White died in Hollywood on October 11, 1968. He certainly helped define the 1920s through his shows, which featured such revolutionary dance crazes as the Charleston and the Black Bottom. In addition to helping the careers of many artists, he also brought Broadway's glamour to millions of people through movies and nightclub entertainments. Close friends remember him as a shy, introverted man whose greatest pleasure was sneaking into his box offices and selling tickets. When friends would come to the box office expecting free seats, White would insist on selling them tickets at full price. It was said that his greatest ambition was to sell a ticket to one of his shows to rival producer Florenz Ziegfeld. But Ziegfeld was shrewd and bought his *Scandals* tickets through a speculator.

WIENNIG AND SBERBER'S. At the turn of the 20th century, many new restaurants were established. RECTOR'S and Shanley's attracted the upper classes, who would dine after attending an operetta or melodrama. Times Square also had its share of restaurants that catered to the actors who appeared on the stages of Broadway and vaudeville. Chief among these was LINDY'S. Another earlier example of the genre was Wiennig and Sberber's on 45th Street. The two restaurants were alike in many ways. Foremost was the presence of a real character as owner, one who was patient with the rambunctious performers and who was also sympathetic and extended credit in lean times. Whereas Lindy's had only one such person at the helm (not to ignore the contribution of Clara Lindemann), Wiennig and Sberber's had two.

Sberber was described by George Burns as the kind of man who "smelt everything before he bought it." Sberber began the habit when offered cigars; soon the habit extended to anything offered. Napkin salesmen would find their goods held up to Sberber's nose and given a good strong sniff. If it passed muster, an order was placed. Sberber was also the world's expert authority on every subject, whether he knew what he was talking about or not. No conversation could be held

without Sberber butting in and making an ironclad proclamation.

Wiennig had more to do with the clientele than Sberber. This motley group mainly consisted of vaudeville performers. Wiennig couldn't seem to remember anyone's name; he preferred to associate the performers with one of their hit songs. When AL JOLSON arrived, Wiennig would greet him with a hearty "Hello, 'April Showers.' " A waiter serving FANNY BRICE would be instructed to "give the roast beef special to 'My Man.' " Wiennig also had the strange habit of answering any question with the answer to a previous query. For example if George Burns said, "Hello, Mr. Wiennig. Have you seen Manny Mannishaw?," Wiennig would reply "Look on the floor, maybe it fell down there."

The waiters were also eccentrics. Burns remembered them as being extremely harried. Once when a customer asked where the rest room was, the waiter impatiently replied "Please! I've only got two hands!" The waiters also distrusted each other. They always thought their coworkers were stealing their tips when their backs were turned, so they walked backward to the kitchen and yelled their orders over their shoulders.

Wiennig and Sberber's also had traditions. Whenever Wiennig and Sberber went to answer the wall-mounted phone and turned their backs to speak into the mouthpiece, they would be pelted with sugar cubes. The owners learned to talk quickly and briefly to their callers, trying to keep their backs turned as little as possible. When they grew tired of ducking sugar cubes, they switched to putting only granulated sugar on the tables (after Sberber smelled it first). But business fell off—the customers were apparently let down by the elimination of ammunition. To bring back their customers, Wiennig and Sberber brought back the sugar cubes.

WILLIAMS, TENNESSEE. One of America's greatest dramatists; b. Thomas Lanier Williams, Columbus, Mississippi, March 26, 1911; d. New York, New York, February 25, 1983.

Williams' mother, much like Blanche in his masterwork, *A Streetcar Named Desire*, adhered to largely irrelevant mores and a somewhat unreal idea of then-current social convention. Williams' father called his son "Miss Nancy" and relentlessly expressed his disgust for the youngster. The family moved to St. Louis when Williams was 8. After college Williams finally found the strength to escape his family, but no matter how far he fled the memories and scars of those years stayed with him.

The Glass Menagerie (3/31/45; 561 performances), at THE PLAYHOUSE THEATRE, was his first Broadway

Tennessee Williams at the time of *The Glass Menagerie*, 1945.

success. A previous play, *Battle of Angels*, was closed by its producers, the THEATRE GUILD, in Boston. The Guild actually apologized to audiences for presenting an obscene play. Of course, standards in Boston were different from those in the rest of the country.

The Glass Menagerie introduced one of Williams' major themes. The "memory play" juxtaposed the rebellious son Tom, played by Eddie Dowling, with the crippled daughter Laura, played by Julie Haydon. Both long to escape from Laurette Taylor's character, Amanda, the domineering mother, but the girl does so only through her withdrawal into fantasy. Anthony Ross played the Gentleman Caller, who reveals the possibility of escape to the brother and sister.

Williams' next work was perhaps his greatest achievement. *A Streetcar Named Desire* (12/3/47; 855 performances) opened at the Barrymore Theater (*see* ETHEL BARRYMORE THEATRE). The drama was a milestone in the American theater, firmly demonstrating that Williams was a major playwright. It starred Jessica Tandy as Blanche DuBois, Karl Malden as Mitch, and Kim Hunter as Stella. It also introduced a new star to Broadway, Marlon Brando as Stanley Kowalski. The character Blanche DuBois finds herself in an unstable world of violence and brutality. She can never achieve her dreams, nor can Stanley Kowalski, who wants re-

spect as well as the good, secure life that seems always out of reach. Both characters, denied what they most want, fall prey to desire. Their impulses rule their actions as they lash out at each other in their own ways. Williams explores the dichotomy between Stanley's intense physicality and Blanche's soulfulness. Each character's yearnings for the qualities they admire in each other take hold and destroy them. The puritanical Williams examines the pain of the two lost souls, who can achieve catharsis only through violence or madness. *A Streetcar Named Desire* won the NEW YORK DRAMA CRITICS' CIRCLE AWARD, as well as the PULITZER PRIZE.

Williams's next play, *Summer and Smoke* (10/6/48; 102 performances), was unsuccessful at the time, perhaps because it paled in comparison with *Streetcar*. The play opened at the MUSIC BOX THEATER. It has since been reevaluated and enjoys many revivals. Next came another classic, *Cat on a Hot Tin Roof* (3/24/55; 694 performances), which opened at the MOROSCO THEATRE. The play examines the breakdown in relationships among members of a Southern plantation family who find that the only way they can communicate is through lies.

BROOKS ATKINSON's review in the *New York Times* of March 25, 1955, was perceptive in its evalution of Williams' craft:

> *Cat on a Hot Tin Roof* is the work of a mature observer of men and women and a gifted craftsman. To say that it is the drama of people who refuse to face the truth of life is to suggest a whole school of problem dramatists. But one of its great achievements is the honesty and simplicity of the craftsmanship. It seems not to have been written. It is the quintessence of life. It is the basic truth. Always a seeker after honesty in his writing, Mr. Williams has not only found a solid part of the truth but found the way to say it with complete honesty. It is not only part of the truth of life; it is the absolute truth of the theatre.

Sweet Bird of Youth (3/10/59; 375 performances), at the MARTIN BECK THEATRE, featured powerful performances by Geraldine Page and Paul Newman. *Period of Adjustment* (11/10/60; 132 performances), Williams' attempt to write a somewhat traditional sex comedy, opened at the HELEN HAYES THEATER.

Night of the Iguana (12/28/61; 316 performances), produced at the ROYALE THEATRE, was perhaps Williams' most eccentric play. It was widely parodied at the time. In *Night of the Iguana* Williams again explored the theme of the human desire to attain peace. The sexuality and violence of Williams' earlier works are still present, but they are tempered and relegated to the sidelines. In a way, it is Williams' most optimistic work; *Night of the Iguana* shows that peace, however impermanent, can be achieved. Although CRITICS were divided on the play's merits, all agreed that the

Anthony Ross, Laurette Taylor, Eddie Dowling and Julie Hayden in *The Glass Menagerie*, 1945.

cast, led by Margaret Leighton, Bette Davis, and Alan Webb, was superb.

Williams did not have another success on Broadway. His later plays all showed a marked change in his abilities. Although his dialogue sometimes remained as trenchant and poetic, his plays became muddled in style and insubstantial at their core. Still, Williams continued writing until his death in 1983 and in the end almost seemed like a character in one of his own plays.

WINCHELL, WALTER. The most powerful and most controversial of all Broadway columnists; b. New York, New York, April 7, 1897; d. Los Angeles, California, February 20, 1972.

Columnist Walter Winchell's colorful vocabulary was as well known as his opinions. Lexicographer W. J. Funk included Winchell among a list of the 10 major contributors of American SLANG. Fellow columnist ALEXANDER WOOLLCOTT once noted: "With a

punch line at the end of a column, his own or judiciously quoted, he is capable of ending a career, or beginning a new chapter of history."

Winchell had his defenders and enemies. St. Claire McKelway, an ardent detractor of gossip, stated in a *New Yorker* magazine article that gossip's "presence in American journalism is almost entirely due to the peculiar personality of one man. This man is Walter Winchell." *Time* covered Winchell in 1931 and reported that he was

> no ordinary scandal-snooper. Famed is he in theater lobbies, speakeasies, nightclubs. From one gossip center to another he travels to get column material. Alert, the Winchell ear hears all. Amiable, the Winchell disposition makes friendly, easily, elicits scandal scraps. Then, at three or four in the morning, he goes back to his typewriter and two-fingers what he has learned, adding here and there the result of an imaginative mind.

Winchell's city editor at the *New York Herald Tribune*, Stanley Walker, explained Winchell's great success:

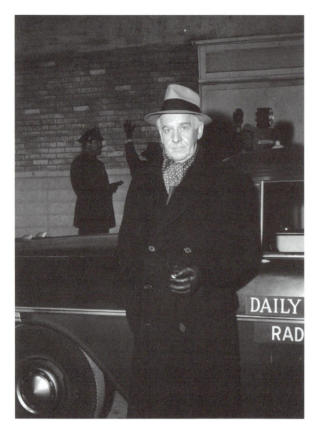

Walter Winchell.

Winchell did much for journalism, for which journalism has been slow to thank him. He helped change the dreary, ponderous impersonality which was pervading the whole press. Do newspapers today print twice, or ten times, as many items about people—what they are like, what their crotchets are, what they eat and drink and wear—as they did ten years ago? Some of that credit belongs to Winchell. . . . Winchell brought to his job the perfect equipment—great energy, an eager desire to know what was going on, a lack of learning and an unquenchable desire to be a newspaperman. If his background had been different, he would have been so befuddled by canons of what some people call good taste that he would have been revolted at some of his best stuff. If he had been better educated he might have been dull. As it was, everything he saw was news to him. . . .

Janet and Jacob Winchel (the added "l" was accidently added on a theater marquee and soon adopted by young Walter) were Russian immigrants who came to New York's Harlem in 1893. Walter escaped the harsh conditions of the Harlem streets by skipping school and attending vaudeville performances. While fooling around for his school friends, Winchell discovered a talent for dancing. Since he himself admitted that, "I was the school's prize dunce," he decided at the age of 13 to try his luck on the vaudeville stage. Winchell had worked as a ticket taker and usher in

Harlem's Imperial Theatre, along with boyhood friend George Jessel. They soon earned $4 a week leading audiences in sing-alongs during intermission. The duo added another member, Jack Weiner, and billed themselves as Lawrence, Stanley, and McKinley: the Little Men with the Big Voices. The act wasn't very successful, but it brought them to the attention of Gus Edwards, a vaudevillian who toured with a kiddie act then titled the "Newsboy Sextette."

In December 1914 Winchell quit Gus Edwards' troupe and mainly hung around in front of the PALACE THEATER along with other out-of-work vaudevillians. When the United States entered World War I, Winchell brought his vaudeville career to a close and enlisted in the U.S. Navy. After his discharge Winchell rejoined his sometime vaudeville partner Rita Greene and married her. The duo played around the country in 1919, during which time Walter began a hobby. He typed a 1-page vaudeville news sheet entitled "Newsense" and distributed it to his fellow vaudevillians. The gossip sheet soon expanded to 2 pages and, much to Winchell's amazement, achieved some popularity. Soon Winchell began reporting newsier features in addition to the usual births, deaths, marriages, and bookings, and he even began putting some of his own opinions in the paper. Winchell began using his trademark style while writing "Newsense." He would separate items with three dots. Winchell later told his assistant Herman Klurfeld that he created the style when the dash key on his typewriter was stuck. Others attribute it to playwright and speaker Rennold Wolf in his *Morning Telegraph* column. It is clear that Winchell began his unique use of the English language from the beginning.

Emile Gavreau, later Winchell's editor on the *New York Evening Graphic* and the *Mirror*, explained how Winchell's style emerged:

His lack of newspaper experience . . . his refreshing insouciance about the difference between a subject and a predicate, became an ironical asset which preserved his personality and may have had the virtue of saving him years of learning to be like everyone else. In his pate rattled more than a grain of genius which was to produce a "slanguage" often too puzzling for the venerable gentlemen of the courts who were not permitted to go beyond old man Webster.

While Winchell was in Chicago, the *Herald* and *Examiner* asked him to cover comings and goings at the train station. Late in 1919, he began to submit items to BILLBOARD. After returning to New York, Winchell's career was stalled until he landed a job with the *New York Vaudeville News*, a house organ of the E. F. ALBEE vaudeville empire. Albee began the paper in order to crush VARIETY, a paper that supported Albee's enemy, the White Rats actors union. Winchell began writing for Albee in November of 1920 and promptly drew a close to his vaudeville career and his recent marriage. Winchell's column in the *New York Vaudeville News* was titled "Merciless Truth" and later "Broadway Hearsay," for which he was paid $25 a week. Winchell supplemented his salary by selling advertising space in the paper. He made sure that the advertisers also featured prominently in his column.

While at the *Vaudeville News*, Winchell met his second wife, June, a woman who had little interest in show business or show people. In 1924, he moved to a $100-a-week job on the *New York Evening Graphic* under the auspices of its owners, Bernarr Macfadden and Fulton Oursler. Winchell's column, entitled "Broadway Hearsay" and "Your Broadway and Mine," was featured each Monday. It developed into a true gossip column, with the writer putting in more and more items about personalities. Winchell's gossip was at first frowned on by Emile Gavreau, but, when the column's gossip quotient rose, so did circulation. While at the *Graphic*, Winchell enjoyed his first major feud. The antagonists were the SHUBERT BROTHERS, the most powerful producers in the history of Broadway. Winchell had given several of the Shubert shows bad reviews, so the Shuberts banned him from their theaters. The battle drew to a close when Shubert star AL JOLSON refused to open his latest show unless Winchell was allowed to attend.

Winning the battle with the Shuberts signified to Broadwayites and especially *Graphic* readers that Winchell was a powerful force along the Great White Way. He was lured away from the *Graphic* by publisher William Randolph Hearst, not personally a Winchell fan. On June 10, 1929, Winchell's column first appeared in Hearst's paper, the *Mirror*. He soon became the *Mirror*'s leading feature, responsible for one-third of the paper's circulation. The *Graphic*'s demise 3 years later was certainly hastened by Winchell's departure. Winchell remained at the *Mirror* until the paper folded in 1963. The *Mirror* wasn't much better than the scandal sheet that was the *Graphic*. In fact, 2 months after Winchell joined the *Mirror*, Emile Gavreau left the *Graphic* and became Winchell's managing editor at the *Mirror*. Gavreau and Winchell by this time were barely speaking and carried their feud throughout their careers.

Winchell made his radio debut on January 18, 1929, over a 42-station network. The show was called "New York by a Representative New Yorker." The success of that series led Winchell to CBS in 1932. Winchell had also made a triumphant return to vaudeville in 1931 with a booking at the Palace along with fellow columnist MARK HELLINGER. Winchell earned $3,500 a week for his stint at the Palace. Winchell also made a brief stab at the movies in a Vitaphone short titled *The Bard of Broadway*. Winchell himself was the thinly disguised subject of a play entitled *Blessed Event* that opened on February 12, 1932, at Broadway's LONGACRE THEATER.

Like many of his contemporaries, especially DAMON RUNYON, Winchell was fascinated with GANGSTERS and organized crime. He called the crimelords the "UN," for "underworld nobility." Winchell seemed to glorify their lives and deaths. He became a tool of some of the hoods themselves, but he was also a patriot who numbered J. Edgar Hoover among his friends. During the Lindburgh trial Hoover used Winchell's column to leak information that proved damaging to Bruno Hauptmann's case. Louis "Lepke" Buchalter, the godfather of Murder, Inc., surrendered to Winchell, who then handed the gangster over to the police. Winchell staunchly opposed Hitler and Nazi activities in the United States and urged America's entry into World War II. Winchell's power extended to the White House. President Franklin Roosevelt was elected to a third term with Winchell's help.

Winchell attempted television several times but to no great success. His best-remembered television assignment was as narrator for *The Untouchables*. Winchell's lack of success on television was due in part to his dwindling influence through his column. By 1960 his national domain had been reduced to 150 papers. Winchell's haunts, primarily the Stork Club, went out of favor. Time seemed to pass Winchell by, and old age was slowing down his spirit.

On October 15, 1963, the *Mirror* folded. A 115-day printers' strike forced the paper to close, and it never recovered. Hearst's other New York paper, the afternoon *Journal-American*, picked up the *Mirror's* features. However, the *Journal-American's* editorial staff wasn't keen on Winchell's column. An executive was later quoted in the *New York Times* as saying, "Frankly our general feeling is that Winchell was passé. In his genre I think he was the best but I don't think he has substantial reader appeal anymore." But the *Journal-American* was having its own problems. The New York newspaper scene was shrinking drastically. Another strike, this one for 140 days in 1965, led to the merging of the *Herald Tribune*, the *Sun*, and the *World Telegram* into the *World Journal Tribune*. A few months later, the paper folded for good. Winchell continued to write for the Hearst syndicate but was denied a New York outlet.

The closing of the Stork Club in October 1965 seemed to symbolize the end of an era. Winchell sank into self-pity. He simply could not handle the changes in the Broadway scene and his slide into near obscurity. *Variety* offered Winchell a weekly column, but it was unsatisfying to the newsman. He debased himself by taking out a full-page ad in *Variety* begging for a New York paper to carry his column. In 1968 Winchell found a job with the *Daily Column*, a small paper that picked up the flotsam and jetsam from New York's many newspaper closings. The new post didn't last long. Winchell retired on February 5, 1968. Despite failing health, he fought the need to slow down. When a new *Daily Mirror* began publication in 1971, Winchell was there with 3 columns a week. However, within a year Winchell's worsening health forced him to leave the paper.

WINDSOR THEATER. *See* **48th Street Theatre.**

WINTER GARDEN THEATRE. 1634 Broadway between 50th and 51st Streets. Architect: William A. Swasey. Opening: March 20. 1911; *Bow Sing* and *La Belle Paree*.

The Winter Garden Theatre was built by the SHUBERT BROTHERS on the site of William K. Vanderbilt's American Horse Exchange (1885). In fact, when flop shows were presented on its stage, the CRITICS would say they could still smell the stables. The Shuberts leased the space from Vanderbilt and named their theater after an English theater, and the new theater "devoted to novel, international, spectacular and musical entertainments" was designed to resemble an English garden. An earlier Winter Garden Theatre stood on lower Broadway near Bond Street during the mid-19th century.

The opening evening was a gala one, and scalpers were getting as much as $19 for a $2.50 ticket. A newspaper described the evening:

> Crowds began to arrive at the Winter Garden long before eight o'clock until the sidewalk was almost blocked and the lobby filled to overflowing. The line of carriages and automobiles extended for two blocks when the first nighters were coming more plentifully. . . .
>
> Once inside the theater, the people seemed disinclined to go at once to their seats, but filled all of the wide promenade space back of the orchestra seats until the overture began.

Winter Garden Theater postcard.

Not the least attractive part of the Winter Garden is the simplicity and harmony of the decorations of the auditorium. The walls and balcony front are in old ivory and gold and the ceiling marked off in latticed squares in old ivory behind which is an artificial sky of blue. . . .

The audience last night found the seats wide and comfortably spaced, with a receptacle for cigar ashes attached to the back of each chair.

The building followed the general layout of the Horse Exchange. The exterior was clad in graystone, with a roof-topped cupola. The theater's entrance was placed in the middle of the block, allowing the Shuberts to make money from retail-store rentals. The corner of 50th Street and Broadway featured a triplex nightclub that went under several names, including Palais de Danse, Montmartre, and Singapore.

The theater itself, built for musical presentations, opened with *La Belle Paree*, a show that included a "one-act Chinese fantasy opera" called *Bow Sing*. The Shuberts tried to pack too much into the evening. By the time AL JOLSON, making his Broadway debut, took the stage, the show had already run for $3\frac{1}{2}$ hours. Jolson was not yet well known, and when he sang "Paris Is a Paradise for Coons" in blackface, the audience was unimpressed. Jolson's Broadway debut did not go unnoticed by the critics, however. Adolph Klauber wrote in the *New York Times*, "Among the very best features were those provided by the two unctuous ragtime comedians, Miss Stella Mayhew and Mr. Al Jolson, both of whom had good songs and the dialects and the acting ability to deliver every bit of good that was in them."

Despite its problems, the show was not a failure. The Shuberts cut portions and rearranged the lineup to bring Jolson into the show earlier. The critics returned to *La Belle Paree* to see what Jolson had wrought and were pleased. *La Belle Paree* played 104 performances, passing what *VARIETY* called the century mark: 100 performances. At that time, shows were judged to be successful after only 100 performances. *Variety* had previously dubbed the show a "double sockeroo," another example of the paper's marvelous SLANG. Jolson certainly earned the $250 a week he was paid by the Shuberts. After the show closed, he convinced them to tour the show, complete with its Broadway cast and production. The Shuberts agreed, and *La Belle Paree* became the first show to tour the country following its Broadway run. *The Revue of Revues* (9/27/11; 55 performances) with Gaby Deslys, Harry Jolson (Al's brother), and Ernest Hare opened next.

Vera Violetta (11/20/11; 112 performances) again featured Al Jolson, who starred along with Gaby Deslys, Ernest Hare, Stella Mayhew, and Annette Kellerman; Mae West had a small part in the production but almost stole the show from Deslys. During the show's run in New Haven, Connecticut, Yale students rioted because parts of the show had been cleaned up by order of the police. One account claimed that West was "in the middle of the fray, if, indeed, she did not start it." The opening at the Winter Garden went much more smoothly, probably because West was not on stage. Management claimed she was stricken with pneumonia. The show, even without West, was greeted with general acclaim by the critics. *Vera Violetta* was billed as the "largest, most elaborate production in North America."

The Shuberts then inaugurated a series of Sunday evening concerts in the theater, taking advantage of its dark night. The concert series was a great success, because there was little other entertainment in New York on Sundays. The biggest star of the series was Jolson, who preferred to perform rather than have a day off. *Variety* proclaimed that "the Shuberts may run the Winter Garden, but Al Jolson owns it. That dandy performer does as he will with the audience, whether Sunday or on weekdays."

Jolson, Stella Mayhew, and Gaby Deslys returned to the Winter Garden in *The Whirl of Society* (3/5/12; 136 performances). The show also featured a future rival of the Shuberts: GEORGE WHITE, who later mounted the *Scandals*, one of the top yearly revue series. *The Whirl of Society* is best-remembered today as the first show that featured a runway down the center of the auditorium. It was a great device for Jolson, who was used to jumping off the stage and performing in the aisles. Max Reinhardt, the brilliant German director, had developed a thrust stage that broke the proscenium's "fourth wall." The Shuberts and Jolson went him one better. The runway was later dubbed "the bridge of thighs" because of the showgirls who paraded up and down its length.

When Jolson was on the road, the Shuberts had to come up with an attraction for the Winter Garden. The theater was the personal responsibility of J.J. (Jake) Shubert; he controlled all the Shuberts' musical productions. His brother Lee controlled the plays and the empire's finances. Jake was angry at FLORENZ ZIEGFELD, whom he considered an archrival, so Jake decided to outdo Ziegfeld, whose ZIEGFELD FOLLIES were such a success. J.J. settled on an annual revue series, *The Passing Show*, so titled because the Shuberts planned them to run on Broadway for a short time and then tour the country. The shows often parodied current Broadway offerings, but their main feature was seminude chorines. The material was usually secondrate. The Shuberts even insisted that their contract writers supply songs to fit already existing scenery.

The first *Passing Show* (7/22/12; 136 performances) included songs by Louis A. Hirsch and Harold At-teridge, both Shubert contract employees. Songs were also contributed by IRVING BERLIN and EARL CARROLL, whose *EARL CARROLL'S VANITIES* later rivaled the Shuberts' revues and Ziegfeld's famous *Follies*. The *Passing Show* starred Adelaide and Hughes, Trixie Friganza, Charlotte Greenwood, Eugene and Willie Howard, and Anna Wheaton.

Paris and all things French were big draws on Broadway in the early years of the 20th century. After all, the French had the raciest of cultures, and nude showgirls were guaranteed to increase ticket sales. So naturally the Shuberts' next offering at the Winter Garden was titled *Broadway to Paris* (11/20/12; 77 performances). The show had little to do with anything French, but composers Max Hoffman and Anatole Friedland came up with some suitably French-sounding numbers.

The Honeymoon Express (2/6/13; 156 performances) featured FANNY BRICE, Gaby Deslys, and Yancsi Dolly (of the Dolly Sisters), as well as Al Jolson. As usual, the show was overly long on opening night. So Jolson simply broke character, came down to the front of the stage, and asked the audience whether they would prefer to see the remainder of the show or sit back and hear an impromptu concert by Jolson. The question was hypothetical, because Jolson had already stopped the show cold and nothing could keep him from taking over the stage.

The Passing Show of 1913 (7/24/13; 116 performances) was typically undistinguished, but it did contain one hit song, "You Made Me Love You," by James V. Monaco and Joseph McCarthy. Usually, the only hits in early Shubert shows were interpolations of popular songs of the day. The second edition of the *Passing Show* series starred Charlotte Greenwood, May Boley, Bessie Clayton, John Charles Thomas, and Carter De Haven. *The Pleasure Seekers* (11/3/13; 72 performances) was produced by Lew Fields (*see* FIELDS FAMILY) and Marcus Loew of the Loew's chain of movie theaters. Loew had a unique idea for promoting his musical. The *New York Times* reported on November 9, 1914:

> If "The Pleasure Seekers" proves to be a success, or if it is good enough to be sent on tour, moving pictures of the piece in its various stages will be shown in all of the Loew theatres. Films have already been made of the rehearsals of the musical comedy and of scenes at railroad stations while the piece was on its short preliminary tour, and these will displayed in the twenty or more theatres controlled by Loew in Greater New York to-night, together with announcements that the original itself can be seen at the Winter Garden. If the show is sent "on the road" the films will go in advance and take the place of much of the billboard advertising commonly used.

Next came *The Whirl of the World* (1/10/14; 161 performances), which introduced Broadway to one of its greatest composers, SIGMUND ROMBERG. Romberg became a Shubert contract employee and was forced to churn out shows on demand. Writing under such circumstances did not inspire Romberg, and few of his contract shows for the Shuberts contained successful songs.

The Passing Show of 1914 (6/10/14; 133 performances) also had a score by Romberg and lyricist Harold Atteridge. The show was no better than any of the Shubert offerings. However, it did mark the Broadway debut of Marilyn Miller, a delightful dancer, who became a particular favorite with Broadway audiences. Lee Shubert discovered Miller, but he wasn't told that she was only 15 years old. Although the nominal stars of the show were Jose Collins and George Monroe, it was Miller who got the lion's share of the notices. The *Herald* proclaimed, "A hitherto unknown young woman named Marilyn Miller—an exceedingly clever person who will be much better known before long—made one of the hits of the piece. She looked well, danced well and did some capital imitations." The finale was a fanciful re-creation of the San Francisco earthquake of 1906. After the magnificent earthquake, a new, sparkling, modern city rose from the ruins. Modernity was typified by a landing strip for zeppelins. The huge blimps picked up the chorus and took them across the ocean to Paris, where the girls danced the Eagle Rock.

Dancing Around (10/10/14; 145 performances) starred Al Jolson, Georgia O'Ramey, and Harland Dixon. Jolson again conquered Broadway despite lackluster material. The Sigmund Romberg, Harry Carroll, and Harold Atteridge score failed to yield a single hit. The *Passing Show* series continued with the 1915 edition (5/29/15; 145 performances). It opened with Marilyn Miller starring, along with Willie and Eugene Howard, John Charles Thomas, and John Boles. This edition also introduced dances new to Broadway: the hula and pan-Pacific drag. The next year's edition opened on June 22, 1916, with Florence Moore and Ed Wynn. It ran 140 performances. The *Passing Show of 1917* (4/26/17; 196 performances) was the most successful edition yet. It starred Irene Franklin, DeWolf Hopper, and Zeke Colvin.

Jolson returned in *Sinbad* (2/14/18; 164 performances). The musical opened with a score by Sigmund Romberg and Harold Atteridge. As usual, the best songs were interpolated. These included some of Jolson's greatest hits: "My Mammy" by Walter Donaldson, Sam Lewis, and Joe Young; "Rock-a-Bye Your Baby with a Dixie Melody" by Jean Schwartz, Joe Young, and Sam Lewis; and "Swanee" by GEORGE GERSHWIN and Irving Caesar. In *Sinbad*, Jolson introduced one of his best-loved characters, Gus. The musical director of this edition, ALFRED GOODMAN, was responsible for at least some of the success of the show. "Swanee" had been premiered at the CAPITOL THEATER to little notice, but with Goodman's arrangement and Jolson's delivery the song became a standard.

The Passing Show of 1918 (7/25/18; 124 performances) featured the dance team of FRED AND ADELE ASTAIRE. This was the Astaires' second Broadway appearance. Also on the bill were Lou Clayton, Willie and Eugene Howard, Nita Naldi, Charles Ruggles, and Frank Fay. Critic Heywood Broun singled out the Astaires for special praise: "In an evening in which there was an abundance of good dancing, Fred Astaire stood out. He and his partner Adele Astaire made the show pause early in the evening with a beautiful loose-limbed dance. It almost seemed as if the two young persons had been poured into the dance." In 1918 there was a surfeit of talent on Broadway, and the excellence of the Astaires wasn't anything out of the ordinary.

The next attraction at the Winter Garden was *Monte Cristo, Jr.* (2/12/19; 254 performances), a big hit. The show starred Jack Squire, Adelaide and Hughes, and Tom Lewis. *The Passing Show of 1919* (10/23/19; 280 performances) topped all the previous editions. The show featured James Barton, Dick and George Raft, Blanche Ring, Charles Winninger, Reginald Denny, and Walter Woolf. It was followed by *Cinderella on Broadway* (6/24/20; 126 performances), starring George Price, Al Sexton, Shirley Royce, and Flo Burt.

The title *Broadway Brevities of 1920* (9/29/20; 105 performances) indicated that its creators were hoping the show would develop into an annual revue, but that didn't happen. Eddie Cantor, Bert Williams, and George LeMaire starred. There was no *Passing Show of 1920*; the 1921 edition (12/29/20; 191 performances) starred Marie Dressler and J. Harold Murray. One of the songs was titled "Beautiful Girls Are Like Opium."

The Whirl of New York (6/13/21; 124 performances) opened with J. Harold Murray, Mlle. Adelaide, and Smith and Dale. *Make It Snappy* (4/13/22; 96 performances) opened with Eddie Cantor, Georgie Hale, J. Harold Murray, and Tot Qualters in the leads. "The Sheik of Araby" by Ted Snyder, HARRY B. SMITH, and Francis Wheeler was the big hit. Cantor satirized Jolson with the tune "My Yiddish Mammy."

In 1922 noted theater architect Herbert Krapp was hired to modernize the Winter Garden. The old auditorium was never popular, considered cold and with bad acoustics. Krapp lowered the ceiling, eliminating the exposed beams (outlined in bare bulbs), and decreased the width of the proscenium. Krapp also eliminated the famous Winter Garden runway, filling it in with an extra 100 seats.

The *Passing Show of 1922* (9/20/22; 95 performances) starred Fred Allen, George Hassell, Ethel

Shutta, and Willie and Eugene Howard. This edition of the *Passing Show* cost the Shuberts $36,000, a lot for a show at the time but not near what Ziegfeld spent on his *Follies*. The sets and costumes were mainly from other Shubert productions. Fred Allen introduced one of his most inspired ideas in this show. This was the Old Joke Cemetery: a backdrop painted with tombstones upon which were written such hoary old jokes as "The church is on fire: holy smoke" or "A husband is something no respectable family should be without." The worse the jokes, the bigger the laughs. The backdrop was featured for a full 5 minutes with no one on stage.

The Dancing Girl (1/24/23; 142 performances) was noteworthy in that the Romberg, Atteridge, and Irving Caesar score was supplemented by songs by George Gershwin and COLE PORTER. However, their contribution was no better than Romberg's uninspired melodies. *The Dancing Girl* was followed by the *Passing Show of 1923* (6/14/23; 118 performances), which opened with George Jessel leading the cast. The *Greenwich Village Follies* (9/20/23; 131 performances), another revue series, was followed by *Innocent Eyes* (5/20/24; 119 performances). It starred Cecil Lean and Cleo Mayfield along with Mistinguett and Frances Williams. The last of the long-running *Passing Show* series came in autumn 1924 (9/3/24; 106 performances); Romberg, Jean Schwartz, and Atteridge supplied the score. Direction was by J. C. Huffman, and sets were by Watson Barrett—all Shubert contractees. The song "Nothing Naughty in a Nightie" pretty much summed up the show. In 1932 the Shuberts tried to revive the series, but the show closed out of town. A 1945 edition also closed before coming to New York.

The *Passing Shows* were over, and the Winter Garden's next show, *Big Boy* (1/7/25; 48 performances) marked the last time Jolson appeared at the theater. He interpolated such hits as "California, Here I Come, " "If You Knew Susie," and "Keep Smiling at Trouble." But Jolson developed an acute case of laryngitis during the run and had to leave the show. In addition to the *Passing Shows*, the Shuberts ran a revue series called *Artists and Models*. The 1925 edition (6/24/25; 416 performances) boasted the number "The Rotisserie." It featured the chorus girls spinning on a giant spit. The scene was a big hit. The Clifford Grey and Maurie Rubens musical *The Great Temptations* (5/18/26; 197 performances) was notable only in its casting of Jack Benny, fresh from vaudeville. In 1925, the Shuberts presented a show called *Gay Paree*. They used the title again the following year. The second *Gay Paree* (11/9/26; 175 performances) was followed by the operetta, *The Circus Princess* (4/25/27; 192 performances). *Artists and Models of 1927* (11/15/27; 151 performances) opened with Ted Lewis, Jack Pearl, Jack Squire, and

Gladys Wheaton. One hit song from the score, "Here Am I—Broken Hearted," was by DE SYLVA, HENDERSON, AND LEW BROWN. Ted Lewis wove his signature phrase—"Is everybody happy?"—into a song with Maurie Rubens and Jack Osterman.

The revue series *Greenwich Village Follies* returned to the theater on April 19, 1926, for its last edition. When it closed after 158 performances, it also marked the end of an era at the Winter Garden. After this legitimate booking, Warner Brothers leased the theater and converted it into a talkie movie theater. The first movie to play the Winter Garden was *The Singing Fool*, starring who else but Al Jolson. It remained a motion picture house until 1933.

The Winter Garden resumed a legitimate policy with the opening of *Hold Your Horses* (9/25/33; 88 performances). Orchestrator ROBERT RUSSELL BENNETT, best known for his work on RODGERS AND HAMMERSTEIN musicals, tried his hand as a Broadway composer. Owen Murphy and Robert A. Simon provided the lyrics. Comedian Joe Cook, future Hollywood restauranteur Dave Chasen, Ona Munson, Tom Patricola, and Harriet Hoctor starred.

Jake Shubert believed he would have the last laugh, albeit posthumously, with his archrival Florenz Ziegfeld. Shubert bought the *Ziegfeld Follies* title from Ziegfeld's widow, Billie Burke. The Shubert-produced *Ziegfeld Follies of 1934* (1/4/34; 182 performances) had a score by VERNON DUKE and E. Y. HARBURG. They contributed at least two standards: "I Like the Likes of You" and "What Is There to Say?" The fine cast included Eve Arden, Everett Marshall, Ziegfeld alumnus FANNY BRICE, Buddy and Vilma Ebsen, *Passing Show* favorites Willie and Eugene Howard, Robert Cummings, and Jane Froman.

Life Begins at 8:40 (8/27/34; 238 performances) was the clever title of the next Winter Garden tenant. HAROLD ARLEN, E. Y. Harburg, and IRA GERSHWIN contributed a fine score that included such hits as "Fun to Be Fooled," "Let's Take a Walk Around the Block," and "You're a Builder Upper." In *Life Begins at 8:40*, Arlen and Harburg discovered a new, more sophisticated facet of the talents of Bert Lahr, the comic previously known for his BURLESQUE-style grotesqueries. Lahr, in turn, gave Arlen his first opportunities to compose out-and-out comedy songs. Previously Arlen had composed his well-known ballads upbeat production numbers, and racy, risqué songs for the Cotton Club. But with Lahr, Arlen was able to break new ground in his career. Arlen and Harburg went on to create Lahr's most beloved character, the Cowardly Lion in the film *The Wizard of Oz*. The successful 238 performance run of *Life Begins at 8:40* was also due to the talents of Ray Bolger and Frances Williams.

Earl Carroll rented the Winter Garden to present *Earl Carroll's Sketch Book*. The show opened on June 4, 1935, with Ken Murray and Sunnie O'Dea starring. The score, written mostly by Murray Mencher, Charles Newman, and Charles Tobias, was passable. It was Carroll's way with beautiful women that accounted for the 207-performance run. Another revue, *At Home Abroad*, more sophisticated than *Earl Carroll's Sketch Book*, opened at the Winter Garden on September 19, 1935, with a fine score by Arthur Schwartz and Howard Dietz (*see* DIETZ AND SCHWARTZ). Their songs, "O What a Wonderful World," "Love Is a Dancing Thing," and "Get Yourself a Geisha," were well handled by the talented cast, which included Beatrice Lillie, Reginald Gardner, Ethel Waters, Eleanor Powell, and Eddie Foy Jr. During rehearsals for *At Home Abroad*, Howard Dietz had a disagreement with director Vincente Minnelli. Their argument was not getting resolved through reasonable means, so Dietz went to his contract with the Shuberts and pointed out the clause that gave him complete control over all aspects of the production. Minnelli pulled out the contract he had negotiated with Lee Shubert and found the same exact clause. With a common enemy to hate, Dietz and Minnelli decided to resolve their problems to their mutual satisfaction.

Minnelli returned to the Winter Garden to design the sets for its next offering, the *Ziegfeld Follies of 1936* (1/30/36; 115 performances). JOHN MURRAY ANDERSON, responsible for the previous *Follies* and the *Greenwich Village Follies*, directed. Vernon Duke repeated his past *Follies* assignment, but this time the lyricist was Ira Gershwin. They came up with a great song, "I Can't Get Started." It was sung by Bob Hope and Eve Arden in the production. The show also starred Bobby Clark, Josephine Baker, Fanny Brice as Baby Snooks, Gypsy Rose Lee, the Nicholas Brothers, Jane Pickens, and Gertrude Neisen—a stupendous cast.

Minnelli returned to his directorial chores with *The Show Is On* (12/25/36; 236 performances). He also designed the sets and costumes for the all-star revue. *The Show Is On* brought Bert Lahr, Beatrice Lillie, and Reginald Gardiner back to the stage of the Winter Garden. Lahr arranged for Arlen and Harburg to write him a song, "The Song of the Woodman," that again perfectly captured his brilliant talents. Beatrice Lillie scattered garters, while floating out over the audience on a moon. She also made "Rhythm" by Richard Rodgers and Lorenz Hart (*see* RODGERS AND HART) totally her own. George and Ira Gershwin provided a sprightly waltz, "By Strauss," and Vernon Duke and Ted Fetter contributed the haunting tune "Now." Hoagy Carmichael and Stanley Adams had a hit with "Little Old Lady." Schwartz and Dietz and Herman Hupfeld also had songs in the score.

E. Y. Harburg, never one to shrink from airing his political and moral beliefs on stage, wrote lyrics with Harold Arlen for the antiwar musical *Hooray for What!* (12/1/37; 199 performances). Harburg chose Howard Lindsay and Russel Crouse to script his story, with Lindsay also directing. *Hooray for What!* tells the story of a meek horticulturist who invents a gas that kills insects. One of its side effects is that it also kills humans. Naturally, it then becomes a valuable commodity, with the nations of the world vying for the formula. Ed Wynn, Vivian Vance, Jack Whiting, and June Clyde starred. The cast also included Kay Thompson, who handled the vocal arranging along with Hugh Martin. Among the hopefuls trying out for the chorus was Ralph Blane. After being rejected, Blane, who would have given anything to be in an Arlen musical, simply got on line to audition for choreographer AGNES DE MILLE. Blane had no training as a dancer and was quickly dismissed, but he did not give up. He arranged for an agent to pester Thompson until she agreed to give Blane an audition. Exasperated, she told Blane to come to her apartment, where she was rehearsing the already assembled Kay Thompson Singers. Thompson ignored Blane while she rehearsed the group, and finally it was time to go to the theater to show the number to Shubert henchman Harry Kaufman. Kaufman was much hated by the entire company, because he continually tried to quash any attempts at art in favor of cheesecake. At the theater, Blane, who had learned the song's vocal arrangement while sitting in Thompson's apartment, simply joined in with the assembled group. He tried to make himself invisible in the last row, but Kaufman spotted him. "Didn't I throw you out of here twice already?" asked Kaufman. Blane, thinking fast, told Kaufman he had been hired by Thompson. This was news to her, but her annoyance with Blane was nowhere near her hatred of Kaufman. She stuck up for Blane, and Arlen, Minnelli, and Harburg concurred that Blane was indeed a member of the cast. Because of Blane's persistence and the company's antipathy for Harry Kaufman, Blane met Hugh Martin, and the two went on to write the score for *Best Foot Forward*, and other musicals on stage and screen.

Hooray for What! traveled a rocky road to its Broadway opening. While out of town in Boston, Thompson was fired. De Mille's choreography was "helped" by a choreographer whom Kaufman had hired to juice up her classically inspired steps. Two leads were fired, and Harburg's trenchant story became more and more emasculated by Kaufman's orders. Before she was canned by Kaufman, Thompson telephoned de Mille. The choreographer was shocked to be awakened at 2:30 in the morning and asked what could be so important. Thompson enthusiastically reported that Kaufman had fallen into the orchestra pit and had broken his back. De Mille replied, "You're just telling me this to make me feel good." Surprisingly, despite its hazardous preopening experiences, *Hooray for What!* was a success. Critics especially praised Ed Wynn's return to the legitimate stage after a protracted run on radio. Richard Watts exclaimed that "gone and happily forgotten are those unfortunate nights when the furious but feeble antics of the Fire Chief were demonstrating what terrible things the wanton wireless can do to a great comedian."

You Never Know (9/31/38; 78 performances) was a Cole Porter failure that contained one hit song, "At Long Last Love." Porter had a good excuse for the show's uninspired score. While working on the show, he was critically injured in a horseback-riding accident. Porter's legs were crushed by the horse, and he never fully recovered from the accident. The story, perhaps apocryphal, was that Porter worked on the lyrics to "At Long Last Love" while waiting for help.

Ole Olsen and Chic Johnson's phenomenally successful revue *Hellzapoppin'* had moved to the Winter Garden from the 46th Street Theatre (*see* RICHARD RODGERS THEATER) on November 26, 1938. It would remain at the Winter Garden until almost the completion of its 1,404-performance run. The show moved on November 25, 1941, to the MAJESTIC THEATRE, where it closed on December 17. The Shuberts quickly capitalized on Olsen and Johnson's great popularity by creating the show *Sons o' Fun* (12/1/41; 742 performances) for them. The musical comedy opened with Joe Besser, Ella Logan, and Carmen Miranda completing the cast. Sammy Fain and Jack Yellen wrote a mostly forgettable score.

A last Shubert-produced *Ziegfeld Follies* (4/14/43; 553 performances) opened at the Winter Garden the day after the opening of *Oklahoma!* It ran longer than any other edition of the show. Contributing were the talents of songwriters Ray Henderson and Jack Yellen, cast members Milton Berle, Eric Blore, Ilona Massey, and Arthur Treacher, and the puppetry of Bil and Cora Baird. Berle was the first performer in *Follies* history to be advertised above the title.

Cole Porter returned to the Winter Garden with *Mexican Hayride* (1/28/44; 479 performances). The Mike Todd production opened with a book by Herbert and Dorothy Fields (*see* FIELDS FAMILY). Bobby Clark, Wilbur Evans, June Havoc, and George Givot starred. Porter's score wasn't one of his best, but it did have one hit song, "I Love You." Olsen and Johnson returned to the Winter Garden in *Laffing Room Only* (12/13/44; 232 performances). The revue had music and lyrics by BURTON LANE. Olsen and Johnson were joined on the stage by Betty Garrett and Fred Waring's Glee Club. *Marinka* (7/18/45; 165 performances) was an attempt to bring operetta back to Broadway, but the Emmerich

Kalman music failed to catch on with audiences. Following *Marinka*, the Winter Garden abandoned legitimate production and returned to showing movies.

Three years later, a new musical comedy, *As the Girls Go* (11/13/48; 414 performances), opened at the theater. Michael Todd was the producer, Bobby Clark was the star, and Jimmy McHugh and Harold Adamson wrote the score. Todd presented his *Michael Todd's Peep Show* (6/28/50; 278 performances) at the Winter Garden. This time Bobby Clark did not appear onstage but wrote some of the sketches. HAROLD ROME, JULE STYNE, and Bob Hilliard and Sammy Stept all wrote songs for the show. Several songs were written by Bhumibol, the king of Thailand. This was certainly the only time that royalty contributed songs to a girlie show.

By the time *Top Banana* (11/1/51; 350 performances) opened at the Winter Garden, television had taken hold of the nation's imagination. Broadway was afraid of the impact of the "boob tube," as its detractors dubbed it. *Top Banana*, a satire on television with a jaunty score by Johnny Mercer, was reputedly a takeoff on Milton Berle's early adventures in the new medium. Phil Silvers, Jack Albertson, Rose Marie, and Judy Lynn starred. The show was dotted with vaudeville and burlesque turns, along with a stock musical-comedy plot line. It had the distinction of being filmed during an actual performance. The film was released in movie theaters to little notice.

The theater's next hit was a major one. *Wonderful Town* (2/25/53; 559 performances) reunited LEONARD BERNSTEIN with COMDEN AND GREEN, and they came up with what can only be described as a brilliant score. Joseph Fields and Jerome Chodorov based their libretto on their play *My Sister Eileen*. Rosalind Russell made her musical comedy debut, with Edith Adams as her sister Eileen. Cris Alexander, Jordan Bentley, and George Gaynes were also featured. Director GEORGE ABBOTT kept the show moving, and the entire proceedings were hailed by critics. On March 1, 1957, the final edition of the *Ziegfeld Follies* (123 performances) opened at the Winter Garden Theatre. Beatrice Lillie, Billy DeWolfe, Carol Lawrence, Harold Lang, and Jane Morgan starred.

Leonard Bernstein collaborated with STEPHEN SONDHEIM (in his first Broadway assignment) on the score for *West Side Story* (9/26/57; 732 performances). Robert E. Griffith and HAROLD PRINCE produced; Arthur Laurents wrote the libretto, which was loosely based on William Shakespeare's *Romeo and Juliet*, updated to contemporary New York. Jerome Robbins directed and choreographed with his usual genius. The show starred Larry Kert and Carol Lawrence (late of the *Ziegfeld Follies of 1957*) as the star-crossed lovers Tony and Maria. The cast also featured Chita Rivera (who became a star due to her fiery performance as Anita), future Broadway lyricist Martin Charnin, and Marilyn Cooper. "Tonight," "Something's Coming," "Somewhere," "Maria," and "I Feel Pretty" all became standards. *West Side Story* returned to Broadway on April 27, 1960, for an additional 249 performances.

Meredith Willson tried to repeat his success of *The Music Man* with his next musical, *The Unsinkable Molly Brown* (11/3/60; 532 performances). Tammy Grimes and Harve Presnell starred. Willson ably captured the optimistic exuberance of the turn of the 20th century. Tammy Grimes' energetic performance helped the show along. "I Ain't Down Yet" was the show's hit and became a popular standard. *The Unsinkable Molly Brown* was one of the last successes for the THEATRE GUILD, which co-produced the evening with playwright Dore Schary.

Jerome Robbins had a hand in the Winter Garden's next smash hit, *Funny Girl* (3/26/64; 1,348 performances). Barbra Streisand played the Winter Garden star Fanny Brice with Danny Meehan, Kay Medford, Sydney Chaplin, and Jean Stapleton in supporting roles. Jule Styne and Bob Merrill wrote a great score, full of theatrically exciting melodies and rhythms. "People" became the hit of the show as well as Streisand's signature tune. "Don't Rain on My Parade" was also much performed outside the show.

A strong central performance and catchy score was also responsible for the success of the Winter Garden's next hit, *Mame* (5/24/66; 1,508 performances). The JERRY HERMAN show had an enjoyable libretto by playwrights Jerome Lawrence and Robert E. Lee, as well as an excellent performance by Angela Lansbury as the title character. Beatrice Arthur, Sab Shimono, Jane Connell, Jerry Lanning, and Frankie Michaels made up the supporting cast. *Mame* was a smash hit at a time when the general consensus was that Broadway was dead.

A brilliant musical, the greatest production to play the Great White Way in decades, was Stephen Sondheim and James Goldman's *Follies* (4/4/71; 522 performances). Sondheim's score was in part a pastiche of the accomplishments of his predecessors in the musical theater, and it also contained sharp, scathing original numbers. Goldman's libretto broke open the traditional confines of the musical comedy. Through co-directors Harold Prince and Michael Bennett's genius, the show kept the past and present in constant juxtaposition. Boris Aronson's set design, Florence Klotz's costumes, and Tharon Musser's lighting added up to make the most spectacular physical production Broadway had seen since the days of the original *Ziegfeld Follies*. The show had a complex concept in which ghosts from past *Follies* haunt the memories of the present-day performers, who are gathered together to remember their youthful days

on Broadway. The occasion is the impending demolition of the theater that hosted the revues. By the end of the show, the audience had entered the psyches of the leading characters through a series of *Follies*-style numbers. Audiences either left the Winter Garden literally speechless, stunned by the force of this powerful show, or emerged onto Broadway bewildered. For the sophisticated theatergoer, *Follies* was an unforgettable experience. *Follies* had enough theatricality and ideas to fuel 20 ordinary Broadway musicals. The *Follies* cast—Dorothy Collins, Alexis Smith, Gene Nelson, John McMartin, Ethel Shutta, Yvonne De Carlo, Kurt Peterson, Marti Rolph, Virginia Sandifur, Harvey Evans, and Mary McCarty—brought a resonance to the show that no other musical has come close to capturing. The show won seven TONY AWARDS but failed to win Best Musical, which went to Galt McDermot's rock musicalization of *Two Gentlemen of Verona*. The failure of *Follies* to win for Best Musical stands as an indictment of the entire awards process and the Tony Awards in particular. *Follies* became a legendary production itself.

The New York Shakespeare Festival, responsible for the production of *Two Gentlemen of Verona*, which won the Tony Award over *Follies*, produced the next hit at the Winter Garden, Shakespeare's *Much Ado About Nothing* (11/11/72; 116 performances). Critics hailed Kathleen Widdoes' and Sam Waterston's performances, as well as A. J. Antoon's direction. Angela Lansbury returned to the Winter Garden in *Gypsy* (9/23/74; 120 performances), with its masterful score by Jule Styne and Stephen Sondheim. The revival was originally mounted in London. Lansbury received a Tony Award for Best Actress for her portrayal of Rose, the ultimate stage mother.

The theater again resounded with the music of Stephen Sondheim when his *Pacific Overtures* (1/11/76; 193 performances) opened. The rather unconventional basis of *Pacific Overtures* was Commodore Perry's forays into feudal Japan. The show explored the different perceptions of life by the two cultures and the unavoidable changes in Japanese traditions. *Pacific Overtures* was a tragedy, with a scope seldom attempted on Broadway. However, the score, which included songs like the masterpiece "Someone in a Tree," was not easily appreciated by the average theatergoer.

A revival of *Fiddler on the Roof* with its original star, Zero Mostel, played the Winter Garden for 167 performances in 1976. Unfortunately, Mostel, a mercurial actor with an amazing range, could not contain himself and constantly mugged his way through the show. A concert performance by Beatles look-alikes, *Beatlemania* (920 performances), began previews at the Winter Garden on May 26, 1977. The producers, knowing that the Broadway critics would slaughter the show, refused to hold an official opening night. The expected bad reviews appeared anyway. But *Beatlemania's* audiences didn't care what the *New York Times* thought. The younger set from New Jersey and Long Island jammed the theater and kept *Beatlemania* running.

A historic opening night occurred at DAVID MERRICK's production, *42nd Street* (8/24/80; 3,486 performances). After the curtain rang down on what most critics called a stunning success, Merrick took center stage. He announced to the assemblage that the show's director and choreographer, Gower Champion, had died that afternoon. The Broadway community was stunned; Champion was considered a fine talent, and the fact that he died on the eve of what would be his greatest triumph was especially painful.

After *42nd Street* moved to the Majestic Theatre (and then moved to the ST. JAMES THEATRE to make way for *The Phantom of the Opera)*, the Shuberts closed the Winter Garden for renovation. It reopened with the blockbuster musical *Cats* (10/7/82). *Cats*, the brainchild of ANDREW LLOYD WEBBER and director Trevor Nunn, received mixed reviews. But the musicalization of T. S. Eliot's children's poetry was presold because of its great success in London. One wag accounted for the play's great success by claiming that everyone was interested in watching physically fit performers jumping up and down in skintight leotards. It had a hit song, "Memory," which many people felt owed much to Puccini. Broadwayites were astonished when Eliot, who had been dead for years and who never would have dreamed that his simple poems would become the basis for an overblown spectacle, won the Tony Award for Best Lyrics. Through the courtesy of Japanese tourists, *Cats* went on to run 7,485 performances to become the longest-running musical in Broadway history.

When *Cats* finally closed on September 10, 2000, the Winter Garden was renovated and refurbished to make way for the opening of *Mamma Mia* (10/18/2001). Louise Pitre, Karen Mason, and Judy Kaye headed the cast. *Mamma Mia*, a smash hit in London and Toronto, is based on the songs of the rock group ABBA, written by Bjorn Ulvaeus and Benny Andersson. In May 2002, during the run of *Mamma Mia*, the Winter Garden's name was officially changed to the Cadillac Winter Garden Theatre.

WINTHROP AMES THEATER. *See* **Little Theatre.**

WOOLLCOTT, ALEXANDER. Noted theatrical critic, wit, and essayist of the first half of the 20th century; b. Phalanx, New Jersey, January 19, 1887; d. New York, New York, January 23, 1943.

Today Alexander Woollcott is perhaps best remembered as the model for the character Sheridan Whiteside in KAUFMAN AND HART's comedy *The Man Who Came to Dinner*. In the play, he was depicted as a vain, vituperative sentimentalist. In real life, he was all those things and more. Woollcott was among the most important voices in the publishing world as both CRITIC and essayist.

At the turn of the 20th century the theater was the primary source of entertainment, and the newspapers were the primary source of news. Stagestruck since his teens, Woollcott managed to influence both worlds with his acerbic, witty writing and boosterism. He castigated those he considered hacks and championed those he considered geniuses. His influence extended beyond the printed page to radio and to society. He was the majordomo of the ALGONQUIN ROUND TABLE, and from his vantage point passed judgment on the men and women of the theater and letters.

Woollcott was born on January 19, 1887, in Phalanx, New Jersey, but he spent most of his early years in Kansas City. There he met Roswell M. Field, a newspaperman on the *Kansas City Star*. Woollcott took an immediate liking to Field, who informed him that journalists often received free tickets to the local theatrical attractions. In fact, Field's niece took Woollcott to his first live performance. Woollcott was hooked on the theater and journalism at the age of 8 and vowed to become a reporter. After moving back to New Jersey and attending a succession of private schools, Woollcott received his first professional assignments, writing book reviews for the *Philadelphia Telegraph*. His pay was ownership of the books he reviewed and his name on the reviews. He contributed to the *Telegraph* throughout his senior year of high school.

Hamilton then enrolled at Hamilton College. Toward the end of his days at the school, Woollcott ran across Samuel Hopkins Adams. Adams later described Woollcott as

> an odd figure. . . . The youth was clad in excessively wrinkled and baggy trousers, a misshapen corduroy coat, grimy sneakers, and a red fez with a gilt tassel. . . . I was struck with the owlish gravity of the eyes behind the large lenses, and an air not so much cocky as confident, suggesting the trustfulness of a tenderly reared baby.

Adams introduced Woollcott to Carr Van Anda, managing editor of the *New York Times*. Van Anda hired Woollcott, assigning him to the city room where he eventually worked his way up from cub reporter and gofer to full-fledged reporter and feature writer. When *Times* drama critic Adolph Klauber retired, Van Anda hired Woollcott as critic. Although only 27, Woollcott had firm opinions, and he set about his job with a sense of mission. Woollcott wouldn't knuckle under to the influence of any producer or associate.

Most reviewers at the time were simply paid pawns of the producers. Neither reviewers nor their editors regarded the theater as an art, and most of the reviews were not really criticism but rather extended press releases. Woollcott, however, saw himself as an independent. He did not consider himself an outsider looking in from afar, but rather he believed the critic was an important part of the creative force of the theater. He had been a prop boy and actor in amateur theatricals and so regarded himself better qualified than most in voicing his opinion. He soon convinced Van Anda to give him space in the Sunday edition of the *Times*. He used this space for reflective essays under the banner "Second Thoughts on First Nights." This was the first instance of reflective journalism in the drama pages and set a precedent for essays that continue to be published even today in the *Times* and other newspapers.

Woollcott's attempts at performing left a soft spot in his heart for actors, and he tended to be kind to them. But he was not afraid of his opinions and felt that his writing should reflect the atmosphere of Times Square and the theater community. Woollcott's attitude took hold, and soon the drama pages became among the most important of the paper's sections. Critic Burns Mantle wrote in 1915 that Woollcott had "become the most talked-of and the widest-read dramatic critic in town." Woollcott, the talk of the theater community, won the appreciation of most actors because he took their work seriously. But the producers found Woollcott and his thoughtful criticism an increasingly powerful nuisance.

The SHUBERT BROTHERS in particular took offense at the young reporter's refusal to write puff pieces. When they opened an insignificant play, *Taking Chances*, at the 39th Street Theater on March 17, 1915, Woollcott disliked the play and said so in print, writing that there were "moments when a puzzled audience wonders what it is all about." The Shuberts, expecting the negative notice, took out an ad in the same issue as Woollcott's review, admonishing: "Do not believe everything you see in the notices today." Next they banned Woollcott from their theaters. *Times* owner Adolph Ochs stood by Woollcott, and on April 1 he banned all Shubert advertising from his paper until his critic was allowed to attend Shubert openings.

Thus, the battle lines were drawn, with both parties backed into a corner. The *Times* took the Shuberts to court in order to obtain an injunction. When the newspaper succeeded, the Shuberts dragged the matter back before a judge. The Shuberts lost this appeal and immediately went to a higher court. The higher court sided with the Shuberts and held that they were allowed to admit anyone they desired, because, after all, they owned the theaters. This Shubert victory only served to alienate the Broadway community, who considered Woollcott their champion and were inclined to root for the underdog. As the battle raged, more and more readers were introduced to Woollcott, and circulation increased; so did advertising revenue, based on increased readership. Woollcott was given more space on Sundays and a raise from $60 a week to $100 a week.

The battle was resolved late in 1915 through pressure put on the Shuberts by producer Oliver Morosco. Morosco was the leading West Coast producer and allowed the Shuberts rights to present his plays in New York. Morosco was an intelligent man and realized his productions were being harmed through the Shubert-*Times* feud. It didn't matter to Morosco whether he went with the Shuberts or another management, and he told the Shuberts that he needed the *Times* advertising and so would sever ties with their organization. The Shuberts saw the wisdom in his position and approached the *Times* to settle the feud. The *Times* agreed, and Woollcott once more was allowed access to Shubert theaters. With this success, the job of theatrical reviewer was regarded in a new light. The reviewer was considered a real journalist, and the arts section of the newspaper was deemed as important as the sports or front pages. The *Times* became the leading newspaper in coverage of the arts. People felt the *Times* critic, right or wrong, had integrity, and they read Woollcott and listened to his opinions in increasing numbers.

Woollcott, by this time a great force in society and journalism, was unhappy with his pay at the *Times* and so was lured to the *New York Herald* by its publisher, Frank Munsey. His Sunday column was titled "In the Wake of the Plays." The *Herald* merged with the *Tribune* in the spring of 1924, and Woollcott was transferred to the other Munsey-owned paper, the *New York Sun*. The *Sun* was an afternoon paper of little importance, and Woollcott could hardly wait until August 1925, when his contract expired and he could join the *World*. He replaced journalist and critic Heywood Broun, who became a news columnist.

Although Woollcott was prone to overenthusiasm in his reviews, he was also noted for his caustic comments. Producers were especially upset when Woollcott used their hard work as an opportunity for a witty phrase or bon mot, but Woollcott couldn't resist. His best friends were the members of the Algonquin Round Table, a group of writers and performers known for their rapier wit. This influence rubbed off on him, and he could not help showing off in his reviews. One example is in Woollcott's review of a play that concerned a pilot whose plane crashes near an Indian reservation, The pilot, badly hurt, is adopted by an Indian family. There he is nursed back to health by the warrior's daughter, who develops a crush on the airman. The mother discovers the pilot and girl in a passionate embrace and tells the father, who threatens to kill the white man. The second act opens with the pilot proclaiming his innocence. The parents accuse him of having sex with their daughter and declare he must die. The pilot denies the accusation. At the end of the play, the pilot reveals that it was impossible for him to have made love to the girl because he had been castrated in the plane crash. Woollcott commented: "In the first act she becomes a lady. In the second act, he becomes a lady." However, those who feared Woollcott's barbed reviews didn't have to worry long. Woollcott was tired of the *World* and resented the interference of his editor, Herbert Bayard Swope, and his publisher, Joseph Pulitzer. When his contract ran out in May of 1928, Woollcott quit the newspaper business.

A collection of his writing, *Going to Pieces*, contained his thoughts on reviewing:

> I find myself engaged in the business—the business, mind you—of going to the theater. I do not write plays. I do not act plays. I do not even produce plays. I merely go to see them. By contracts between the party of the first part, the party of the second part and all that sort of thing my life is actually so arranged that in the past dozen years I have not only attended two thousand first nights in New York, London, Paris and Berlin, but far from paying for the privilege, am myself paid for the inconvenience. Professional playgoing seems to me hardly a career which a decent man would deliberately map out for himself any more than one would plan an exclusive diet of macaroons or lemon meringue pie.

Woollcott went on to write many pieces for magazines such as the *New Yorker, Collier's*, and the *Saturday Evening Post*. He published anthologies of his magazine works, many of which were on the theater. He attempted playwriting by collaborating with George S. Kaufman (*see* KAUFMAN AND HART) on *The Channel Road*, which premiered on November 17, 1929. The play received decidedly mixed reviews, with most of the critics making comments about drama critics attempting to write drama. The play lasted 60 performances at the PLYMOUTH THEATER. It might have run longer but for an unfortunate bit of timing; in November 1929, right after the stock market crash, most people's minds weren't on the theater.

Despite heavy losses in the stock market, Woollcott was able to weather the storm with his talents. He continued contributing magazine pieces, and in the fall of 1929 he found himself on the radio for the Mutual Broadcasting Network. After his 13-week run on WOR, he moved to CBS while continuing his weekly

contributions to the *New Yorker* and articles for *Collier's* and other magazines.

Despite his abdication as the theater's finest critic, Woollcott continued to influence the drama through his writing and radio broadcasts, which often revolved around luminaries of the drama and their works. But no one was ready for Woollcott's next foray into the theaters of Times Square. After trying his hand at playwriting, he decided to try acting.

Woollcott opened at the BELASCO THEATRE on November 9, 1931, in S. N. Behrman's *Brief Moment*. The played was presented by KATHARINE CORNELL and Guthrie McClintic and starred Frances Larrimore. Woollcott played Harold Sigrift, a character described in the script as "very fat, about thirty years old, and lies down whenever possible. He somewhat resembles Alexander Woollcott, who conceivably might play him." The play was a flop, but Woollcott received glowing notices. After all, he had been playing the character all his adult life! BROOKS ATKINSON commented in the *New York Times*, "Mr. Woollcott tosses it across the footlights with a relish that the audience shares. If he enjoyed himself as much as the audience last night enjoyed him, he must have been having a very good time."

The play lasted 129 performances, mostly on the basis of Woollcott's performance. The play was selected by Burns Mantle as one of the year's 10 best. Although Woollcott played a character based on himself, he did differ from Harold Sigrift in some ways. In the first act, the character states, "Let me tell you something about vitality, my chuck. It's fatiguing to live with. I lived with a girl once who had vitality. She wore me out. Nowadays I go in for languor." Woollcott certainly never lived with a girl, considering himself a confirmed bachelor. And he definitely did not go in for languor. At this point, he was as busy as could be.

Two years later Woollcott increased his schedule, beginning another stint on CBS Radio. This was even more successful than his first forays on the airwaves, and Woollcott again extended his influence. Later in 1933, he premiered his second dramatic collaboration with George S. Kaufman. *The Dark Tower* opened on November 25 at the MOROSCO THEATRE. The play was a failure, running only 57 performances. S. N. Behrman used Woollcott in another of his plays, *Wine of Choice*. This opened at the Guild Theater (*see* VIRGINIA THEATER) on February 21, 1938. It fared no better than *Brief Moment* and closed after only 43 performances.

Woollcott continued his advocacy of writers whom he believed did not get their due, including Ernest Hemingway, Clarence Day, and James Hilton. All owed much of their early success to Woollcott's efforts. He convinced Little, Brown to publish Hilton's *Goodbye Mr. Chips*, which became a huge success. He also trumpeted the talents of John Steinbeck and his sometime collaborator George S. Kaufman. Kaufman repaid the compliment by making Woollcott the main character in his and Moss Hart's comedy *The Man Who Came to Dinner*. In 1934 Woollcott had become the Town Crier in a series of broadcasts for Cream of Wheat. When the sponsor objected to Woollcott's damnation of Hitler and Mussolini, Woollcott chose to drop the show. In 1937 he returned to the airwaves for the Granger Pipe Tobacco Company. In *The Man Who Came to Dinner*, Kaufman and Hart made Sheridan Whiteside (the character based on Woollcott) a radio personality who was sponsored by Cream of Mush. The play opened on October 16, 1939. Although there was some talk of Woollcott himself playing the lead, it was given to Monty Woolley, with Woollcott's blessing.

The critics were unanimous in their raves. Naturally, much was made of Woollcott's reactions to being made the "irascible, not to say insulting hero of the play," as Burns Mantle put it. Woollcott, with tongue in cheek, denied everything: "Of course this is a libelous caricature. It is not true that the role of the obnoxious Sheridan Whiteside ... was patterned after me. Whiteside is merely a composite of the better qualities of the play's two authors." Woollcott finally played the role in stock at the Pasadena Civic Auditorium on March 6, 1940. The next month, when Woollcott was playing the part in San Francisco, he was stricken with a heart attack. Woollcott recovered relatively quickly and resumed his hectic schedule. In March 1942, after a trip to England, he returned home and was stricken again. His recuperation was only partially successful, and a long period of rest followed. During a broadcast at CBS on January 23, 1943, he collapsed and died soon after.

Woollcott was both the obnoxious, literary snob and the florid sentimentalist. He was a crusader for causes and a supporter of worthy charities. He had the nerve to stake his job and reputation against the powerful Shuberts, and he had a penchant for indulging himself in witticisms at others' expense. He adored *Goodbye Mr. Chips* and was a lifelong collector of true murder stories. In all, he was a complex man who, at his most powerful, lived an uncompromising life with himself as the star. Edna Ferber said that Woollcott was a New Jersey Nero who mistook his pinafore for a toga. Howard Dietz (*see* DIETZ AND SCHWARTZ) dubbed him "Louisa M. Woollcott". George S. Kaufman, one of Woollcott's closest friends, told Moss Hart, "Life without Aleck is like a play with a crucial scene dropped. It still plays, but something good has gone out of it."

WORLD THEATER. *See* **Charles Hopkins Theater.**

YIDDISH ART THEATER. *See* **George Abbott Theater** and **Jolson's 59th Street Theater.**

YOUMANS, VINCENT. The quintessential 1920s composer; b. New York, New York, September 27, 1898; d. Denver, Colorado, April 5, 1946.

Vincent Youmans' shows dominated the Roaring Twenties. His closest competitor was GEORGE GERSHWIN who was born one day before Youmans. JEROME KERN also provided scores to many fine shows in the 1920s, including the greatest of his career, *Show Boat*. But Youmans imbued his music with a drive and rhythm that seems to define the decade, its spirit, its speed, and its humor. Zelda Fitzgerald even gave him a nod in her novel *Save Me the Waltz*. Youmans' hits, all of which came in the 1920s, included *No, No, Nanette*; *Hit the Deck*; and *Wildflower*. Although these shows were wonderfully popular, Youmans' career as a whole was not as impressive as those of some of his contemporaries, for two reasons. First, with only 93 published songs to his credit, he wasn't that prolific. Gershwin sometimes was represented by 4 shows in a single season; Youmans had two or more shows in a single year on only two occasions. Second, he was hampered by a constant battle with tuberculosis and alcoholism.

The composer began writing songs while at the Army's Great Lakes Training Station. The camp shows gave Youmans enough of a taste for show business so that after his discharge he was committed to a composing career. Like many of his contemporaries, he broke into the business as a song plugger for Remick's music publishers, his second choice, having been turned down by Max Dreyfus of T. B. Harms publishing. Remick's published Youmans' first popular song, "The Country Cousin," written with lyricist Al Bryan. Youmans landed his first theater job as a rehearsal

pianist for producer Alex Aarons' (*see* AARONS AND FREEDLEY) show *Oui Madame*. VICTOR HERBERT was the composer. Later, composer HAROLD ARLEN got his start in the theater as a rehearsal pianist for Youmans' *Great Day!* Youmans had his first song written for the stage interpolated into a Charlotte Greenwood vehicle, *Linger Longer Letty*. The song was "Maid-to-Order Maid" but it was in for only one performance while the show played Stamford, Connecticut. Youmans next had two songs interpolated into the show *Piccadilly to Broadway* in Atlantic City, New Jersey, but the show closed out of town.

Youmans decided to see Dreyfus again and ask for a job. The music publisher was a sort of father figure for his employees, and he took pains to give them every opportunity to develop their talents. Dreyfus hired Youmans as a song plugger. Alex Aarons paired Youmans with composer Paul Lannin (fated to be Youmans' lifelong friend and drinking buddy) and brought in George Gershwin's brother Ira to supply the lyrics. At that time Ira was writing under the name Arthur Francis. The resulting show was *Two Little Girls in Blue* (5/3/21; 135 performances), starring the Fairbanks sisters, Madeline and Marion. The show marked the Broadway debuts of both Youmans and IRA GERSHWIN. Aarons had sold his interest in the show to producer Abraham Erlanger, head of the despised Theatrical Trust. Erlanger was among the most powerful men in the business and held the first near monopoly in the American theater. The show was a hit, which made Dreyfus happy, because the songs "Who's Who with You," "Dolly," and "Oh, Me! Oh, My" were all successful.

Although Youmans had passed his first test, he was not happy. He was unable to get another Broadway assignment and found himself again behind the piano working rehearsals of Victor Herbert's *Orange Blos-*

Vincent Youmans' *Great Day!*, 1929.

soms. Youmans' drinking increased, despite the fact that his second show, *Wildflower* (2/7/23; 477 performances), proved to be a great success and solidified his place in the musical theater. ARTHUR HAMMERSTEIN produced *Wildflower*, which had book and lyrics by OSCAR HAMMERSTEIN II and OTTO HARBACH. Herbert Stothart also composed music for some of the songs. The show opened with Edith Day, Olin Howland, and Charles Judels leading the cast. The show received mostly excellent reviews, although Youmans and Stothart must have been taken aback when they read in the *New York Times* that the show "contains the most tuneful score that RUDOLF FRIML has written in a number of seasons." Charles Darnton, writing in the *New York Evening World*, stated, "at first the music seemed too good to last, but this fear proved groundless as the score offered one gay, youthful, charming melody after another." ALEXANDER WOOLLCOTT, writing in the *New York Herald*, was one of the dissenters. He was concerned that the show contained "an entirely

unobjectionable mixture of songs and dances which we are going to have a mighty hard time remembering when someone asks us next September what show followed Sally, Irene and Mary at the Casino." Several of the critics predicted that the hit song would be "Bambalina."

Mary Jane McKane (12/25/23; 151 performances) opened at the IMPERIAL THEATRE. Mary Hay starred in the show, along with Stanley Ridges and Eva Clark. Youmans collaborated with lyricists William Cary Duncan and Oscar Hammerstein II; Herbert Stothart also composed some songs for this show. The show received good reviews, although none of the songs achieved much success. Laurence Stallings of the *New York World* was pleased that "someone at last has staged a production number that doesn't present girls as soft drinks or popular race horses."

Youmans composed his first score without a co-composer for *Lollipop* (1/21/24; 145 performances). He was teamed with Zelda Sears, one of the few women lyricists writing for Broadway. Youmans now had three shows running on Broadway simultaneously, because *Wildflower* and *Mary Jane McKane* were still in the theaters. *Lollipop* was another success for Youmans. However, the show didn't contain any hit songs and didn't break any new ground. It certainly didn't prepare Broadway for his next triumph.

Youmans's next assignment, *No, No, Nanette* (9/16/25; 239 performances), proved to be an even bigger hit, although it did not run as long as *Wildflower*. *No, No, Nanette* was produced and directed by H. H. Frazee, past owner of the Boston Red Sox. Frazee worked out a precedent-setting deal with his star, Louise Groody, who played the title character. She was the first star in Broadway history to receive a percentage of the box office in addition to a salary. *No, No, Nanette* provided Youmans with a modern setting, and his talents exploded. He seemed made to compose up-to-the-minute tunes that perfectly captured the syncopation and drive of the era. Irving Caesar's fine lyrics perfectly complemented Youmans' music. The show contained one of the greatest hit songs of the 1920s: "Tea for Two." Caesar claimed the lyric was a dummy lyric, used to set rhythms in his mind before writing the actual words. But the dummy lyric proved so popular that he kept it. The other smash hit from the score was "I Want to Be Happy," a title that seemed to express the mood of the entire country in the giddy years before the Depression. *No, No, Nanette* toured successfully and enjoyed a long life in both professional and amateur theaters for years to come. *Nanette* might have run longer on Broadway, but prior to its New York engagement Frazee ran the show for a year in Chicago, set up three national companies, and even sent a company to Europe.

A Night Out was the name of Youmans' next show, written at the behest of producer Alex Aarons. Irving Caesar and Clifford Grey collaborated on the lyrics. The show opened in Philadelphia and closed before coming to New York. *No, No, Nanette* actually opened after *A Night Out* because its pre-Broadway tour went on for so long. Next, Youmans paired up with lyricist Anne Caldwell for *Oh, Please!* (12/17/26; 79 performances). Caldwell wrote the libretto with Otto Harbach. The show was produced by Charles Dillingham, a gentleman producer. The cast was excellent, featuring Beatrice Lillie, Helen Broderick, Charles Purcell, and Charles Winninger, but the score and libretto were lackluster.

Youmans was unhappy with the way his shows were produced, so he produced *Hit the Deck* (4/25/27; 352 performances) himself, in collaboration with veteran producer Lew Fields (*see* FIELDS FAMILY). He stated: "For the first time in my life I am able to select my own singers and my own cast to interpret my music

and to play the parts as I would like to have them played. For the past six or seven years, I have been completely at the mercy of the managers and of the actors." Leo Robin and Clifford Grey provided the lyrics and Herbert Fields (*see* FIELDS FAMILY) wrote the libretto. *Hit the Deck* contained two smash hit songs, "Hallelujah" and "Sometimes I'm Happy." Louise Groody, the star of *No, No, Nanette*, was also the star here, along with Stella Mayhew and Charles King.

Although Youmans continued his producing career after the success of *Hit the Deck*, he provided only the score for his next show, *Rainbow* (11/21/28; 29 performances). It reunited Youmans with Oscar Hammerstein II, who directed and collaborated on the libretto with Laurence Stallings (the one-time critic who once reviewed Youmans). Hammerstein had just enjoyed a success with his previous show, *The New Moon*, but his luck did not hold with *Rainbow*. Youmans also went from a great hit to a great failure, repeating the pattern he established with *No, No, Nanette* and *Oh, Please! Rainbow* had a particularly disastrous opening night. Gilbert Gabriel commented: "One intermission was so long and lapsy that the orchestra played everything but Dixie to fill it up." Critics weren't totally unkind, and several found things to admire. Howard Barnes commented in the *New York Herald Tribune*, "Youmans maintains his place as one of our first jazz composers in the piece, which boasts not so much a nosegay of song hits as a coordinated score."

Youmans bounced back to form, but a poor libretto, and history, would doom his next show, *Great Day* (10/17/29; 37 performances). He was so sure of his producing talents that he bought the Cosmopolitan Theatre, long considered a jinxed house. Billy Rose and Edward Eliscu wrote the lyrics for what was one of Youmans' best scores. It contained four big hits, "Happy Because I'm in Love," "More Than You Know," "Without a Song," and the title tune. Despite the great score, the show was a mess. It suffered a particularly painful out-of-town tryout, leading Broadway wags to dub it *Great Delay*. A week after the show opened, the stock market crashed, and Youmans, producer as well as composer, was forced to close the show. With *Great Day* a failure, Youmans was left with an empty theater. The Depression hurt Broadway terribly, and there were no producers looking for theaters. So Youmans put a play, *Damn Your Honor* (12/30/29; 8 performances), into the house. The play opened to dreadful reviews. Youmans was unable to raise money for any further productions at the theater.

Youmans then fled New York for the more hospitable clime of Hollywood. He saw several of his stage musicals adapted for the screen, and he wrote an original movie musical, *What a Widow!* It was a flop, and Youmans returned to New York. Youmans had borrowed money from FLORENZ ZIEGFELD to bring *Great Day* into New York, and in return he promised to supply a score for Ziegfeld. The result, *Smiles* (11/18/30; 63 performances), opened at the ZIEGFELD THEATER, with lyrics by Clifford Grey and Harold Adamson. The cast was fine—with FRED AND ADELE ASTAIRE, Larry Adler, Virginia Bruce, Marilyn Miller, Bob Hope, and Eddie Foy, Jr.—but the show was a failure. Youmans and Ziegfeld fought incessantly and Ziegfeld went so far as to get a court injunction barring Youmans from the out-of-town theater. The hit from *Smiles* was the standard "Time on My Hands" with lyrics by Adamson and Mack Gordon.

Youmans' career was clearly on the skids. His work wasn't bad, but personal problems prevented him from realizing his potential. He had determined that his failures were due to bad management. He produced *Through the Years* (1/28/31; 20 performances), his next Broadway offering, but the show was another huge failure. Again, Youmans handed in a fine score, with lyrics by Edward Heyman. "Drums in My Heart" and the title song received the most notice, but the show didn't work. Youmans's last Broadway show was *Take a Chance* (11/26/32; 243 performances). He was asked to come in to bolster the score by Richard Whiting, Nacio Herb Brown, and B. G. De Sylva. They were the authors of the hit songs "You're an Old Smoothie" and "Eadie Was a Lady." The show had a good cast, including ETHEL MERMAN, Jack Haley, June Knight, Mitzi Mayfair, and Sid Silvers. *Take a Chance* closed Youmans' Broadway career with a hit.

The composer's last assignment was for the movie *Flying Down to Rio*. Youmans tried to come to an agreement with RKO for more movies. While negotiations slowly proceeded, he discovered he had tuberculosis. Although his health improved, his relationship with RKO did not. He gave up on movies and decided to tackle classical composing, as George Gershwin had done. Youmans' health wavered as he moved from location to location, trying vainly to settle down. He was nearly broke, which was all the harder on him because he was used to living well. He was unemployable on Broadway, and Hollywood rejected his demands.

Youmans continued his classical lessons and occupied his last years readying a revue that would feature Latin rhythms. The show was titled *Vincent Youmans's Revue*, although there were no songs by Youmans. There was a little ballet and a few Cuban numbers by Ernesto Lecuona. Leonide Massine choreographed the ballet, and Eugene van Grona staged the Cuban numbers. The show was terribly disjointed and closed in Baltimore shortly after its January 27, 1944, opening. After that, the composer suffered personal disappointments, and another stab at Hollywood proved fruitless.

YOUNG, STARK. Critic; b. Como, Mississippi, October 11, 1881; d. Fairfield, Connecticut, January 6, 1962.

Young became an English teacher at the University of Mississippi in 1904 and later moved to the University of Texas and Amherst College, where he remained until 1922. He became associate editor of *THEATRE ARTS MAGAZINE* in 1921, and in 1922 was hired by the *New Republic*. In 1924, on leaving his post at *Theater Arts*, he was named drama critic of the *New York Times*. After two years at the *Times*, he returned to the *New Republic*, where he served as drama editor. Young was a lecturer at the New School for Social Research in New York from 1925 to 1928. In addition to his newspaper work, he wrote plays and novels (including *So Red the Rose*) and dabbled in painting.

ZIEGFELD, FLORENZ. Famed Broadway producer of the early 20th century who created the long-running *Ziegfeld Follies* revue; b. Chicago, March 15 or 21, 1867 or 1869; d. Santa Monica, California, July 22, 1932.

Just as S. L. ("ROXY") ROTHAFEL's name signifies the apex of motion picture showmanship, Florenz Ziegfeld's name forever stands as a symbol of lavish showmanship in the musical theater. He was a man of superlatives, for whom the show was everything. The most renowned producer of his time, he was not a good businessman; he was often broke, and he preferred to plow the fortunes he made into the highly speculative world of theatrical producing. Ziegfeld's organization and methods (although not his financial practices) were the precursors to the famous Hollywood studio star system of the 1930s and '40s. His monument, the ZIEGFELD FOLLIES revue series, has become a legend while his competitors' shows—the SHUBERT BROTHERS' *Passing Shows*, *EARL CARROLL'S VANITIES*, and *GEORGE WHITE'S SCANDALS*—are practically forgotten. Ziegfeld also produced many book musicals. These included some of the greatest hits of the 1920s: *Sally*, *Kid Boots*, *Rio Rita*, *The Three Musketeers*, *Whoopee*, and his masterwork, *Show Boat*. Ziegfeld gave these musicals and others the sumptuous physical production that was his hallmark.

Ziegfeld's accomplishments go beyond his astuteness as a manager. Ziegfeld admitted to Eddie Cantor: "You know I don't have a very quick sense of humor. Half the great comedians I've had in my shows and that I paid a lot of money to and who made my customers shriek were not only not funny to me, but I couldn't understand why they were funny to anybody." Despite this, he made many of the biggest stars of Broadway, paid them stars' salaries, and surrounded them with a publicity machine that kept their careers in the ascendancy. He was instrumental in introducing the American public to such stars as ANNA HELD, FANNY BRICE, Eddie Cantor, W. C. Fields, Will Rogers, and Bert Williams. He was equally influential in his championing of such songwriters as IRVING BERLIN, GEORGE GERSHWIN, VICTOR HERBERT (late in Herbert's career), RODGERS AND HART, SIGMUND ROMBERG, and RUDOLF FRIML. Ziegfeld's unerring sense of design led to a long collaboration with architect/scenic designer Joseph Urban. However, Ziegfeld himself became his greatest creation. He had the reputation of being a flamboyant showman, Casanova, artist, magician, dictator, and arbiter of popular taste. Ziegfeld represented the Broadway mogul to hundreds who sought to emulate him without success. One sign of his genius and celebrity is the fact that his personal traits and practices have become stereotypes themselves.

Ziegfeld was born on either March 15 or 21 in 1867 or 1869, the son of Florenz Ziegfeld Sr., president of the Chicago Musical College. The Chicago World's Fair of 1893 gave the young Ziegfeld his first taste of show business. He worked beside his father, who was in charge of supplying classical bands for the fair. The two seldom saw eye to eye, as Ziegfeld junior was more drawn to the flamboyant. The younger Ziegfeld brought a strongman, Sandow the Great, to Chicago and the fair. Sandow became a huge hit when Ziegfeld, with an unerring sense of publicity, invited two of the doyennes of Chicago society, Mrs. Potter Palmer and Mrs. George Pullman, to step up and examine Sandow's muscles. The ladies were overwhelmed by the strongman, and soon all society lined up to feel the mighty Sandow's muscles. It was quite daring and more than a little naughty. Ziegfeld took the muscle man to New York and another conquest of society. In 1895, after visiting Paris, Berlin, and Monte Carlo with Sandow, Ziegfeld ran out of money and became

Florenz Ziegfeld.

stranded in London. It was the first time he was broke, but it wasn't the last.

Ziegfeld simply couldn't save money. Nothing was too good for him or his productions. He spent thousands of dollars on his shows not because he felt that the added expense would pay off at the box office, but rather because he felt that anything with his name attached must mean the best. Fortunately, most of the time he was successful enough to keep himself and his shows well appointed. Charles Evans, late of the comedy team Evans and Hoey, brought the broke Ziegfeld to a music hall. There Ziegfeld discovered Anna Held a French chanteuse with an hourglass figure and sparkling eyes. Ziegfeld was struck by the woman's presence and immediately begged Evans for an introduction. Evans knew that the 27-year-old showman would get nowhere with Held, because many American producers with greater credits and more capital had offered her their services. But Ziegfeld was adamant, and he even got Evans to agree to reteam with Hoey if he could convince Held to come to the United

States with him. Ziegfeld wooed Held and came away with a contract. That he was broke was secondary, for he now had Held and Evans and Hoey for a Broadway show. Ziegfeld cabled DIAMOND JIM BRADY for sufficient funds for the entourage to sail to New York.

Ziegfeld was an astute enough publicist to realize that it would be a mistake for Anna Held to burst onto the Broadway scene. Instead, he opened his production, *A Parlor Match* (10/21/1896), with Evans and Hoey featured and Held relegated to a small singing part during the entr'acte. Audiences were captivated by the beauty and felt they had discovered a star. Ziegfeld stoked the publicity machine with his famous milk-bath stunt, perhaps the greatest of all publicity STUNTS. A Brooklyn milkman (paid by Ziegfeld) "sued" Ziegfeld for the money for milk that he had supposedly delivered to the Hotel Marlborough each day for a month. Reporters became curious, and one traced the young actress to the hotel and discovered the "secret" that Held bathed in milk every day. The stunt was the idea of playwright Max Marcin, who was inspired while reading Edward Gibbon's *Decline and Fall of the Roman Empire*. The *Sun* exposed the stunt (bringing even more publicity), but the other papers preferred to ignore the truth.

A year after *The Parlor Match* opened, Held and Ziegfeld were married. For the next few years, Ziegfeld concentrated on Held's career. By the end of 1906 he was simultaneously broke and on the eve of his greatest triumph. Held is credited with coming up with the idea for the *Follies*. She suggested that Ziegfeld could outdo the famed Paris *Folies Bergère* if he gathered together his own bevy of beauties. Ziegfeld, along with Held, producer-director Frank McKee, producer and theater owner A. L. Erlanger, and Ziegfeld's assistant Jerry Siegel, auditioned the performers who would become the Anna Held Girls. McKee and Erlanger each owned a one-third interest in the *Follies*. Siegel, a man-about-Broadway, held down the fort when Ziegfeld went overseas. A popular newspaper column, "Follies of the Day," supplied the title for the revue series. Held suggested that Ziegfeld call the show "Follies of the Year," but the superstitious Ziegfeld wanted a title with 13 letters: hence *Follies of 1907*.

The *Follies* was announced at the bottom of an advertisement for the Jardin de Paris atop the New York Theatre (*see* OLYMPIA) on Broadway and 44th Street. The ad stated: "Very soon the Ziegfeld Revue Follies of 1907." It was the first time that the French spelling, *revue*, was used in the United States. The Jardin de Paris was a highly uncomfortable theater. It was topped by a glass dome that acted as a huge magnifying lens for the sun's rays. In the days before air conditioning, it was hot; when it rained, the audience held umbrellas over their heads because the dome leaked.

Klaw and Erlanger footed the entire bill for the *Follies*: $16,800. The show opened on July 9, 1907, and received mostly rave reviews, although CRITICS could still be shocked at the 50 Anna Held Girls, who actually showed their bloomers. One critic opined: "In seeking to reproduce some of the audacities of the French capital, Mr. Ziegfeld has come occasionally into collusion with a sense of propriety which still distinguishes a large portion of the public over here." Another newspaper's critic observed,

> Mr. Florenz Ziegfeld, Jr., has given New York quite the best melange of mirth, music and pretty young women that has been seen here in many summers. There is not a dull moment in the entire show. The many ensembles, songs and dances and the costuming of the principals and chorus carried the new review to success and assured it a long residence on Broadway.

Despite the heat in the Jardin de Paris, Ziegfeld kept the show running through the summer. Most other shows closed on May 31 and reopened on Labor Day.

After the *Follies of 1907*, the series became a tradition for the next 25 years. Ziegfeld advertised his *Follies* as "an American institution," and stated their goal as "glorifying the American girl." The 20th and last *Follies* under Ziegfeld's auspices opened on July 1, 1931. The Shuberts and Ziegfeld's widow Billie Burke presented two more *Follies* in 1934 and 1936, and the Shuberts alone presented a *Follies* in 1956. It was ironic that the Shuberts ended up presenting the *Follies*, because the Shuberts and Ziegfeld were mortal enemies.

During their quarter of a century under Ziegfeld's stewardship, the *Follies* featured such performers as Nora Bayes, Mae Murray, Fanny Brice, the Dolly Sisters, Leon Errol, Bessie McCoy, Bert Williams, Ed Wynn, W. C. Fields, Ina Claire, Marion Davies, Eddie Cantor, Joe Frisco, Marilyn Miller, Gus Van and Joe Schenck, John Steel, Gallagher and Shean, Olsen and Johnson, Paul Whiteman, Will Rogers, Ruth Etting, and Harry Richman. The *Follies* introduced such great songs to the canon of American standards as "Shine on Harvest Moon," "The Dance of the Grizzly Bear," "Be My Little Baby Bumble Bee," "Row, Row, Row," "Hello, Frisco, Hello," "A Pretty Girl Is Like a Melody," "My Man," "Second-Hand Rose," "Strut Miss Lizzy," "Mr. Gallagher and Mr. Shean," "Half Caste Woman," and "You Made Me Love You."

Ziegfeld presented other revues tied into the *Follies*. On the roof of the NEW AMSTERDAM THEATRE, he presented a series of *Ziegfeld Midnight Frolics*. Material would be tried out in the *Midnight Frolics*, and would feature some of the stars appearing in the *Follies*, before being introduced on the large stage below. The Roof Garden above the New Amsterdam was part cabaret and part supper club. It had a $5 cover charge, which usually narrowed the audience down to members of the Four Hundred. The *Frolics* were usually directed by Ned Waybum, and they had music and lyrics by Dave Stamper and Gene Buck. Buck is also credited with much of the success of the *Follies*. It was he who usually whipped Ziegfeld's ideas into shape and who discovered such stars as W. C. Fields and Eddie Cantor.

Ziegfeld contributed more to the theater than just the *Follies*. In 1908, in addition to the annual *Follies* edition, Ziegfeld presented two shows: *The Soul Kiss* (1/28/08; 122 performances) starred Adeline Genee, Cecil Lean, and Florence Holbrook, and was followed by *Miss Innocence* (11/30/08; 176 performances). At the time, anything running more than 100 performances was considered a hit.

In 1912 Ziegfeld produced two forgettable shows. The first was *Over the River* (1/8/12; 120 performances), a musical with music and lyrics by John Golden, in which co-producer Charles Dillingham introduced ballroom dancing to the legitimate stage. Peggy Wood, Eddie Foy Sr., and Lillian Lorraine starred. Foy starred as Madison Parke, a gay rogue who is sentenced to 30 days on Blackwell's Island for cutting too much of a rug on Broadway. After his release, he tries to convince his wife he was in Mexico. The musical marked Foy's retirement from the legitimate theater. Thereafter he played only in vaudeville. *A Winsome Widow* (4/11/12; 172 performances), based on Charles Hoyt's *A Trip to Chinatown*, opened at the Moulin Rouge (formerly the Jardin de Paris), and contained one smash hit song, "Be My Little Baby Bumble Bee," which was originally in the *Follies of 1911*. Raymond Hubbell wrote the majority of the show's songs, with an interpolation by JEROME KERN. The show starred the Dolly Sisters, Elizabeth Brice, Leon Errol, Charles King, Frank Tinney, and Mae West.

In 1913 Ziegfeld and Held were divorced. Nevertheless, she continued to appear under Ziegfeld's auspices in vaudeville. On New Year's Eve 1913 Ziegfeld, attending a ball at the ASTOR HOTEL, ran into actress Billie Burke. Burke was later quoted by a newspaperman as saying, "I have no intention of marrying Mr. Ziegfeld or anyone else although Mr. Ziegfeld is a very charming man." The couple were married on April 11, 1914, after a matinee of Burke's show, *Jerry*. Anna Held died on August 12, 1918.

The next non-*Follies* show that Ziegfeld presented was *The Century Girl* (11/6/16; 200 performances). Irving Berlin composed the music and lyrics, with some instrumental pieces composed by Victor Herbert. *The Century Girl* opened with Sam Bernard, Hazel Dawn, Marie Dressler, Leon Errol, Elsie Janis, Van and Schenck, Frank Tinney, and Lilyan Tashman. Of Frank Tinney, PERCY HAMMOND later wrote, "He fertilizes the most sterile wheeze with the persuasive manures of his unctuous manner, and makes it blossom with laughter unabashed."

The following year, *Miss 1917* (11/5/17; 40 performances), one of the most expensive productions of its time, opened with a score by Jerome Kern and P.G. Wodehouse. George Gershwin was the rehearsal pianist for the show. Even with sold-out houses, the show could not recoup its cost. Ziegfeld and Dillingham were forced to close it despite its smash hit status.

Ziegfeld's next musical-comedy production, *Sally* (12/21/20; 570 performances), was a happier experience. Kern and Wodehouse collaborated on the score along with co-lyricist Clifford Grey. The score contained several hits, including "Whip-Poor-Will" and "Look for the Silver Lining." Both songs featured lyrics by B. G. De Sylva. Marilyn Miller starred in the production, along with Walter Catlett and Leon Errol. Eddie Cantor, who got his start with Ziegfeld, was

given his first book show, *Kid Boots* (12/13/23; 479 performances). Cantor, bandleader George Olsen, Harland Dixon, and Mary Eaton introduced a score by Harry Tierney and Joseph McCarthy. *Kid Boots* had a $16 top ticket price at its opening. Although it was a smash hit, Ziegfeld couldn't stop trying to improve the show. He spent $20,000 on new costumes for the first-act finale. It was no surprise to Eddie Cantor when he received the following telegram from Ziegfeld on Christmas Day: "Merry Christmas to you and yours. May we remain together as long as both of us remain in show business, although profits on *Kid Boots* have been far less than *Sally*."

The Sigmund Romberg, Clare Kummer, and Clifford Grey show *Annie Dear* (11/4/24; 103 performances) opened as a vehicle for Billie Burke. Romberg wrote his second book show for Ziegfeld, *Louie the 14th* (3/3/25; 319 performances), with Englishman Arthur Wimperis. Ziegfeld favorite Leon Errol co-starred with Ethel Shutta. In 1926 Ziegfeld quarrelled with Erlanger over the name *Follies*. He was forced to title his 1926 edition *No Foolin'*. Later that year, the producer opened *Betsy* (12/28/26; 39 performances), by Richard Rodgers and Lorenz Hart.

In 1927 Ziegfeld produced two of his biggest successes. *Rio Rita* (2/2/27; 494 performances) opened with a score by Harry Tierney and Joseph McCarthy. The songwriters composed their finest score, one that contained many hits. The title tune, "The Rangers' Song," and "If You're in Love You'll Waltz" were recorded countless times and sold thousands of copies of sheet music. Ada May, Ethelind Terry, Bert Wheeler, J. Harold Murray, and Walter Catlett starred in what was one of the last great operettas. *Rio Rita* had a top ticket price of $5.50, which was high for the time.

Ziegfeld's greatest contribution to musical-theater history came on December 27, 1927, the opening night of *Show Boat* (575 performances). The Jerome Kern and OSCAR HAMMERSTEIN II musical contained what some consider to be the best musical-theater score ever written. Ziegfeld mounted a brilliant production. He did not just produce a spectacle for the eye and ear but used his unerring taste to make *Show Boat* a spectacle for the heart and mind. The musical starred Norma Terris, Helen Morgan, Jules Bledsoe, Edna May Oliver, Charles Winninger, Howard Marsh, and Eva Puck. The musical, considered quite daring for its time, is still performed in major productions on Broadway and around the world.

Where others might produce a single show each year, Ziegfeld produced two or three. *Rosalie* (1/10/28; 327 performances) continued Ziegfeld's amazing output. It had a score by George and Ira Gershwin, Sigmund Romberg, and P. G. Wodehouse. The Gershwins accounted for the show's hit "How Long Has

Show Boat, 1927, Ziegfeld's greatest contribution to musical theater.

This Been Going On." The classic "The Man I Love" was cut from the score prior to the show's opening (already having been deleted from the score of *Lady Be Good*). Marilyn Miller was the star, ably supported by Frank Morgan, Jack Donahue, and Gladys Glad.

The Three Musketeers (3/13/28; 319 performances) was Ziegfeld's second production in 1928. Rudolf Friml, P. G. Wodehouse, and Clifford Grey supplied the hit score, which contained such great songs as "Ma Belle," "March of the Musketeers," "One Kiss," and "Gascony." The show was Friml's last great achievement. Operettas were on the decline, as popular taste shifted to the more modern rhythms of Gershwin, Rodgers, and Berlin. Dennis King, Douglas Dumbrille, Harriet Hoctor, and Vivienne Segal starred. Critic Percy Hammond's review of the performance in the *New York Herald Tribune* included a summation of Ziegfeld's recent hit productions: "His enterprises were swamp lilies of the theatre, beauty arising from stagnant pools. But all of a sudden he has changed, ventured into fields more healthful, with the result that he is now the happy maestro of four pure and undefiled successes, *Rio Rita, Rosalie, Show Boat* and *The Three Musketeers*."

Whoopee (12/4/28; 255 performances), another big hit for Ziegfeld, was written as a vehicle for former *Follies* headliner Eddie Cantor. The show has a surprisingly strong book and score, although it was written to suit Cantor's varied talents. The hit songs by Walter Donaldson and Gus Kahn included the title tune, "My Baby Just Cares for Me," "I'm Bringing a Red, Red Rose," and the classic torch song "Love Me or Leave Me." Ruth Etting, Ethel Shutta, Frances Upton, and Jack Shaw starred. Another telegram to Cantor, on the day after *Whoopee*'s opening, illustrates

Ziegfeld's taste in theater as well as his reputation (or at least his self-image) as a roué. Ziegfeld wrote,

My dear Eddie: I want to extend to you my heartiest congratulations. I knew you could do it and you did do it. You gave them an artistic, clean and enjoyable performance from start to finish. I was with sixty of the representative women of New York and they were simply enchanted.

The Gershwins and Gus Kahn contributed the score to *Show Girl* (7/2/29; 111 performances), which included the song "Liza (All the Clouds'll Roll Away)." Jimmy Durante, featured in the show with his partners Eddie Jackson and Lou Clayton, wrote his own numbers. *Show Girl* also featured Ruby Keeler, Duke Ellington and his orchestra, Eddie Foy Jr., Harriet Hoctor, and Nick Lucas.

A definite departure for Ziegfeld was his co-production with Arch Selwyn of Noël Coward's *Bittersweet* (11/5/29; 159 performances). The English operetta boasted such hits as "I'll See You Again" and "If Love Were All." However, the stock market crash on October 29 of that year wiped Ziegfeld out. Although he produced more shows, he never regained his fortune.

Rodgers and Hart provided a fantasy for Ed Wynn in *Simple Simon* (2/18/30; 135 performances). The showstopper was Ruth Etting's performance of the Rodgers and Hart classic, "Ten Cents a Dance." *Smiles* (11/18/30; 63 performances) also contained a smash hit tune: "Time on My Hands" by VINCENT YOUMANS, Harold Adamson, and Mack Gordon. Walter Donaldson's "You're Driving Me Crazy" was added after the Marilyn Miller starrer opened. FRED AND ADELE ASTAIRE co-starred, along with Larry Adler, Bob Hope, Eddie Foy Jr., and Virginia Bruce.

In 1932 Ziegfeld presented a revival of his greatest hit, *Show Boat*. His last Broadway musical, *Hot-Cha!* (3/8/32; 118 performances), opened with a score by Ray Henderson and Lew Brown (*see* DE SYLVA, BROWN, AND HENDERSON). They also contributed the libretto, along with columnist MARK HELLINGER. Eleanor Powell, Buddy Rogers, Bert Lahr, June Knight, and Gypsy Rose Lee starred. Ziegfeld financed the production with the assistance of GANGSTERS like Dutch Schultz.

Ziegfeld had other accomplishments to his credit besides shows. He hosted a weekly radio series and produced a color movie of *Whoopee* with Samuel Goldwyn. He was also responsible for erecting the magnificent ZIEGFELD THEATER, with a stunning design by Joseph Urban.

Ziegfeld's health, hurt by the pressures of business and avoiding creditors, quickly deteriorated in the 1930s. Bill collectors took Ziegfeld's office furniture in lieu of payment. Broadway sign makers ARTKRAFT

STRAUSS owned his desk for years. Ziegfeld was stricken with pleurisy, and although he rallied for a time (he sent $6,000 worth of telegrams from the hospital) he died in July 1932.

Will Rogers delivered Ziegfeld's eulogy. He commented,

> He picked us from all walks of life and led us into what little fame we achieved. . . . He brought beauty into the entertainment world. To have been the master amusement provider of your generation, surely a life's work has been accomplished. . . . He left something that hundreds of us will treasure till our final curtains fall, and that is a badge, a badge of which we are proud and want to read the lettering: "I worked for Ziegfeld."

ZIEGFELD DANSE DE FOLLIES. *See* **New Amsterdam Theatre.**

ZIEGFELD FOLLIES. The *Ziegfeld Follies* was the first great revue series in the American theater, and the series that defined class and entertainment when it ran during the first decades of the 20th century and for decades afterward. FLORENZ ZIEGFELD, the genius behind the *Follies*, saw to it that the series exhibited the best talents available in the American musical theater. Ziegfeld hired the top stars, created even more, hired great designers to create sumptuous costumes and lavish settings, commissioned the top songwriting talents from Tin Pan Alley, and wove the whole proceedings together with girls, hundreds of beautiful girls.

According to Ziegfeld's publicist, Will Page, in the beginning the name Ziegfeld, The Great Glorifier, "meant a musical entertainment for tired business men which should represent almost the possible limit of what could decently be done upon the stage." Later, said Page, "the atmosphere of the *Follies* . . . changed so that naughtiness is not tolerated and more attention is paid to beauty of scenes and to gorgeousness of gowns with, of course, the finest flowers that could be collected in the garden of girls."

The *Follies* showgirls were quite celebrated. It was the great couturier Lady Duff-Gordon who introduced Ziegfeld to the concept of the showgirl. They were not the chorus: They did not sing or dance. They existed simply to be beautiful. Among the famous showgirls were Olive Thomas, Dolores, Drucilla Strain, Imogene Wilson, Katherine Burke, Jessie Reed, Merle Finlay, and Hazel Forbes. Some—like Irene Dunne, Peggy Hopkins Joyce, Mae Murray, Marion Davies, Billie Dove, Justine Johnstone, Paulette Goddard, Lilyan Tashman, Barbara Stanwyck, and Vera Maxwell—

went on to become stars in their own right. For other showgirls, their beauty was their primary talent. It was enough for Ziegfeld. The showman's favorite words were *glorification*, *femininity*, and *pulchritude*. All three applied to his showgirls. Where other producers paid their girls $30 a week, Ziegfeld paid his $125. The women were never presented in the nude, and Ziegfeld insisted that they be treated with respect. Sex was the byword of Ziegfeld's rivals EARL CARROLL, GEORGE WHITE, and the SHUBERT BROTHERS, but Ziegfeld stressed sensuality, admiring women simply for their statuesque beauty.

Ziegfeld had his favorite performers, most of whom he discovered. FANNY BRICE, comedian Bert Williams, Ann Pennington, W. C. Fields, Will Rogers, Leon Errol, Ray Dooley, Lillian Lorraine, Nora Bayes, Eddie Cantor, and Van and Schenck all appeared in multiple editions of the *Follies*.

The *Follies* also boasted a long relationship with its production staff. Many of the *Follies* cost as much as $200,000 to produce. A huge part of the budget was taken up with sets and costumes. Although Ziegfeld was extravagant with money, he had the good taste and design sense to make sure every dime was visible on the stage. Ziegfeld would get his inspiration for *Follies* numbers from the day's headlines, pictures in magazines, postcards, and idle comments. He would jot down his ideas and then tell his staff to put together a scene around a specific design element.

Joseph Urban, a noted architect, designed many of the great drops and set pieces for the *Follies*. Ben Ali Haggin designed the scenes called *tableaux vivants*, or living pictures, for the *Follies* from 1917 to 1925. The *tableaux* were artfully posed groupings of seminude showgirls draped in fine fabrics. Ziegfeld's costumers included such noted couturiers as Lady Duff-Gordon (Lucile), Cora McGeachy, and Alice O'Neil. Gene Buck wrote lyrics for many of the shows, and he is generally credited with fulfilling Ziegfeld's visions on stage. Ned Wayburn, a noted choreographer, staged the dances and directed most of the proceedings. The contribution of Albert Cheney Johnston should not be overlooked. The great photographer was the official portraitist for all the *Follies* girls. Because only a limited number of people could see the *Follies* in any one year, Johnston's photos were the only glimpse many people had of the magical Ziegfeld touch.

Ziegfeld didn't put as much stock in the songs. He was happy as long as the shows were sumptuous and the girls beautiful. However, many great songs were introduced in the *Follies*, either written specifically for Ziegfeld or as popular songs interpolated into the shows. These included "My Man," "By the Light of the Silvery Moon," "Be My Little Baby Bumble Bee," "Row, Row, Row," "Hello, Frisco, Hello," "A Pretty

Gene Buck with the *Ziegfeld Follies* girls, 1911.

Girl Is Like a Melody," "Second Hand Rose," and "Shaking the Blues Away." Favorite songwriters of Ziegfeld were IRVING BERLIN (the first to write an entire *Follies* score by himself), VICTOR HERBERT, Dave Stamper and Gene Buck, Louis A. Hirsch, and Raymond Hubbell. Sketches were contributed by HARRY B. SMITH, George V. Hobart, Rennold Wolf, and Channing Pollock.

Eddie Cantor and Dave Freedman, in their Ziegfeld biography entitled *The Great Glorifyer*, described the *Follies* atmosphere:

> Girls from every part of the country stood backstage on the threshold of glorification. The dressing-rooms were filled with so many stars that the skies looked deserted. Forty-second Street was a bobbing black sea of high-powered imported cars. The lobby of the New Amsterdam Theatre glittered with aristocracy.

The *Follies* did not begin on quite such a prestigious note. Credit for originating the idea for the *Follies* goes to Ziegfeld's then-wife, ANNA HELD, who suggested

Ziegfeld model a revue on the French *Folies Bergère*. Librettist-lyricist Harry B. Smith suggested the showman name his show after an old newspaper column of Smith's, "Follies of the Day." But Ziegfeld, who was superstitious, wanted the name of the show to contain 13 letters. He settled on *Follies of 1907*. The first *Follies* took place on a rooftop theater, the Jardin de Paris, on July 9, 1907. The revue (Ziegfeld was the first to use the French spelling of "review") starred Emma Carus, Grace La Rue, and Lillian Lee. The first *Follies* was an immediate hit, following a move to the LIBERTY THEATRE, and became the first Broadway show to run through the hot summer months.

The show's success led Ziegfeld to announce a new edition of the *Follies*, and thereafter the revue became an annual Broadway event. Ziegfeld's partner in the *Follies* was Abraham Erlanger, one of the most hated producers in theater history. Erlanger owned and operated a string of theaters, practically a monopoly, across the country. If the producer of a show or act wanted to play an Erlanger house, the producer would be forced to join Erlanger's Syndicate. Erlanger tried to dictate to Ziegfeld the content of the *Follies*, but Ziegfeld would have none of it.

In 1911 Ziegfeld joined his name to the *Follies* for the first time. In 1913, after 6 editions, Ziegfeld finally had enough faith in the series to move it to a large legitimate theater, the NEW AMSTERDAM. The *Follies* remained at the New Amsterdam (with one exception) until the last edition under Ziegfeld in 1931, which opened at the new ZIEGFELD THEATER. In all, Ziegfeld presented 21 *Follies*, some of which had more than one edition. By the time Ziegfeld died in 1932, the *Follies* truly lived up to their reputation as "a national institution glorifying the American girl."

After the showman's death, Ziegfeld's rivals, the Shuberts, bought the rights to produce their own edition of the *Follies* from Ziegfeld's widow, Billie Burke, for $1,000. Ziegfeld's estate received 3 percent of the gross. The Shuberts presented 3 *Follies*, in 1934, 1936, and 1943. There also was one revue using the *Follies* name in 1957. But no *Follies* following the master's death could truly lay claim to the title *Follies*. For one thing, no post-Ziegfeld *Follies* were as lavish because other producers, particularly the Shuberts, were fiscally more responsible and placed a higher priority on making money than on sumptuous productions. Ziegfeld himself, although notoriously heedless of the bottom line, never lost money on a *Follies*, and they often realized a profit after Broadway while touring. Ziegfeld made sure that the annual series that bore his name reflected the pride he had in himself. Hollywood, television, and the literary world all used the example of the *Follies* to portray the glamour, romance, and extravagance of Broadway, when in fact few other shows exhibited these qualities in such quantity. Today the *Follies* and Ziegfeld are still considered the epitome of Broadway's art.

ZIEGFELD THEATER. Northwest corner of 6th Avenue and 54th Street. Architects: Joseph Urban and Thomas A. Lamb. Opening: February 2, 1927; *Rio Rita*.

Until the mid-1920s, 6th Avenue was a street of 3-story brownstones under a permanent shadow of the elevated train. When the 6th Avenue El was torn down in 1927, the real-estate market, driven by a bearish Wall Street, boomed. Speculators abounded, and parcels of the thoroughfare were acquired quickly in the new land rush.

Producer FLORENZ ZIEGFELD had long considered the NEW AMSTERDAM THEATRE his home base. But this magnificent 42nd Street theater was owned by Abe Erlanger, a man of quick temper with as ruthless a business sense as Ziegfeld himself. So Ziegfeld was not averse to a move. The owner of the property at 6th Avenue and 54th Street was none other than media mogul William Randolph Hearst. The newspaper giant owned several large plots of land surrounding the future site of the Ziegfeld Theater, and in fact he had just constructed the Warwick Hotel on an adjacent block. Hearst recognized that a theater across the street from the Warwick would drive up the value of his as-yet-undeveloped plots. When plans to dismantle the el were announced, Hearst and his partner, Arthur Brisbane, approached Ziegfeld.

The producer hired one of the premiere movie palace architects, Thomas Lamb, to design his new theater. Lamb's traditional neo-Georgian design just didn't make the dramatic statement that the great showman wanted, so he turned to his brilliant scenic designer, Joseph Urban (who practiced architecture in his native Vienna), to design the theater of his dreams. Ziegfeld's daughter Patricia cemented the cornerstone that contained a program from Ziegfeld's musical *Sally*, photos of the Ziegfeld family, a program from the original *Follies of 1907*, and a brick from an ancient Greek theater. The cornerstone was laid with appropriate Ziegfeldian fanfare on December 9, 1926, at 2:47 P.M. More than 800 people, including stars of past and future Ziegfeld productions, watched, while a huge audience followed the proceedings on the radio.

The theater's façade featured tan limestone, and it curved to reflect the oval auditorium inside. The oval interior eschewed right angles and the typically baroque decoration of most New York theaters. The walls were covered with a modernistic mural by Lillian Gaertner, one of Urban's pupils. This painting, entitled *The Joy of Living*, was said to be the largest oil painting in the world. Urban described his theater as "a modern playhouse for musical shows animated by gay detail to unite actor and audience."

Architectural Forum described the exterior of the theater:

> Considered from without, the playhouse is unlike any other in New York. The façade clearly expresses the purpose of the building. The auditorium is indicated by the bow on the avenue side, and the stage is represented by the ornamentation of the false proscenium. Two large masks, the conventional dramatic symbols of comedy and tragedy, are used at the sides of this proscenium opening. Thus the intent of the building is apparent to the passerby, marking the structure clearly as a temple devoted exclusively to the drama.

The *New York Times* described the interior for its readers on February 1, 1927:

> The decorations, walls, and ceilings are specially designed to tune the mood of the audience to the gay, youthful, and beautiful *scenes* which the stage unfolds. One enters what seems a hall of gold, the richness of

Crowds lining up after the opening of *Kismet* at the Ziegfeld Theatre, 1953.

the golden curtain, proscenium, carpets, chairs, lights, affording a setting of ineffable luxury. As the eye wanders from the stage to the walls and ceilings there is a blend from the stark rich gold of the stage to a mural painting of gold, delicately blended with pastel shades of blue and green, which at first seem splashed all over the walls and ceilings like a cubist version of anything at all, but finally take shape in quaint lovely figures like those on a Gobelin tapestry.

What does all this mean? One asks Mr. Urban. Why, nothing at all. He composed these gay figures of young lovers, some kissing, some running and dancing, some hunting, simply to go with the stage settings. A question of atmosphere. The idea is to throw the audience into the spirit of the thing.

The new theater was opened on February 2, 1927, with *Rio Rita* (504 performances), an operetta boasting a score by Harry Tierney and Joseph McCarthy. The top ticket price for the new show was $5.50. The production transferred to the LYRIC THEATRE to make

room for Ziegfeld's last masterpiece, *Show Boat* (12/27/27; 575 performances), which opened next at the theater. The JEROME KERN and OSCAR HAMMERSTEIN II adaptation of Edna Ferber's novel became one of the seminal works of the American musical theater. Hammerstein's treatment of serious social issues and the superior score made *Show Boat* an almost legendary musical. The cast included Norma Terris, Tess Gardella, Edna May Oliver, Charles Winninger, Eva Puck, Sammy White, Helen Morgan, Howard Marsh, and Jules Bledsoe.

GEORGE AND IRA GERSHWIN's musical *Show Girl* (7/2/29; 111 performances) followed. The production might have run longer but for the stock market crash on October 29, 1929. Ziegfeld was practically wiped out by the crash, and his landlord, William Randolph Hearst, was badly shaken too.

Meanwhile, the theater was leased to other managements, who presented a string of successes on its stage.

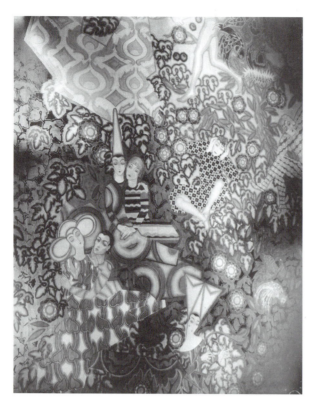

Joseph Urban mural in the Ziegfeld Theatre.

The first was Noël Coward's London import, *Bittersweet* (11/5/29; 159 performances). It was followed by a Ziegfeld production, *Simple Simon* (2/24/30; 135 performances), starring Ed Wynn and Ruth Etting. The RODGERS AND HART score contained the hit "Ten Cents a Dance."

Ziegfeld's last *Follies* opened at his theater on July 21, 1931. The score was by Mack Gordon and Harry Revel. The show played for 165 performances before closing. The next Ziegfeld production at his theater, *Hot-Cha!* (3/14/32; 118 performances), boasted a score by Ray Henderson and Lew Brown (*see* DE SYLVA, BROWN, AND HENDERSON). Ziegfeld was forced to raise the capital for the production from mobster Dutch Schultz. Despite the talents of Bert Lahr, Gypsy Rose Lee, Lupe Velez, and Eleanor Powell, the show was a failure.

Ziegfeld died on July 22, 1932, and management of the theater reverted to the Hearst Company. After the dismal run of *Hot-Cha!*, the theater was converted to motion picture presentations. Loew's Theatrical Enterprises took over the management for Hearst. Movies were doing slightly better than theater during the Depression, and the Loew's chain eyed the site. Hearst was having his own financial problems and was forced to sell off vast sections of his financial empire. Obviously, the theater was high on the list of expendable

properties. Just before Hearst signed over the deed to the movie chain, in stepped showman extraordinaire Billy Rose.

Rose had long admired the beautiful theater and especially coveted the huge private apartment that Urban had included. Rose saw himself as equal to or better than Ziegfeld, so it seemed logical that as Ziegfeld's natural successor, he should also possess the late showman's prize asset. Rose acquired the theater for only $630,000 in 1944. Ziegfeld's spectaculars had been marked by his own great taste; Rose may have equaled Ziegfeld in his vision, but his taste was more vulgar and more populist than his predecessor's. Rose did, however, appreciate the beauty of the theater and hired Gretl Urban, daughter of the late architect, to restore the Ziegfeld to its former glory. To Rose's credit, he always kept the theater in top condition.

Rose reestablished the legitimate policy and presented his production of *The Seven Lively Arts* (12/17/44; 182 performances). Cole Porter contributed the

Brigadoon, 1947.

score that featured "Ev'rytime We Say Goodbye" as its hit. The show starred Beatrice Lillie, Bert Lahr, Benny Goodman, Helen Gallagher, and Dolores Gray. Following a short-lived show, *Concert Varieties* (6/1/45), came one of the theater's biggest successes, a revival of *The Red Mill* (11/4/45; 531 performances), which ran almost twice as long as the original 1906 production. This unexpected success was followed with a revival of *Show Boat* (1/5/46; 418 performances).

These two smash-hit revivals led to another classic musical attraction, *Brigadoon* (3/13/47; 581 performances). The LERNER AND LOEWE score contained an overabundance of marvelous songs, including "Come to Me, Bend to Me," "Almost Like Being in Love," and "The Heather on the Hill."

The theater's next big success came with the hit show *Gentlemen Prefer Blondes* (12/8/49; 740 performances). Carol Channing and Yvonne Adair starred as Anita Loos' classic gold diggers. The JULE STYNE and Leo Robin musical comedy included Channing's signature song, "Diamonds Are a Girl's Best Friend."

Laurence Olivier and Vivian Leigh played the Ziegfeld in a revival of *Caesar and Cleopatra* (12/20/51; 67 performances) by George Bernard Shaw. The drama was followed by a revival of the Gershwins' *Of Thee I Sing* on May 5, 1952, which played a few months. The next hit for the theater was another Gershwin revival. *Porgy and Bess* enjoyed a 305-performance run commencing March 10, 1953. This made way for another huge success, *Kismet* (12/3/53; 583 performances), with songs based on melodies by Borodin. The Wright and Forrest score included such standards as "Baubles, Bangles and Beads" and "Stranger in Paradise." Alfred Drake and Joan Diener starred in the Arabian fantasy.

Following *Kismet*, the theater was rented by NBC, beginning in 1955. Television occupied its stage until 1963, when live entertainment was again featured. Jack Benny and Danny Kaye presented solo appearances in that year. A flop musical, *Foxy* (2/16/64; 72 performances), with Bert Lahr, briefly played the theater and was replaced by another Wright and Forrest show, *Anya* (11/29/65; 16 performances). But *Anya* was not to follow the success of *Kismet*, the team's previous offering.

With *Anya*'s closing also came the closing of the Ziegfeld Theater. Billy Rose had passed away, and his estate sold the theater for $17 million. The *World Journal Tribune* of Sunday, March 19, 1967, carried the following story:

> A STONE FOR THE ZIEGFELD The Ziegfeld Theater, or what is left of it, is due for one last show next month. There will be ceremonies when the demolition crew gets down to the corner stone. Patricia Ziegfeld, daughter of the late illustrious impresario, will fly in from Los Angeles. She is now Mrs. William Stephenson, married to a California architect. The memorabilia in the corner stone will be presented to the Smithsonian Institute.

Incidentally, the two enormous reclining figures above the Ziegfeld entrance have already been claimed by souvenir hunters. One entire figure, weighing a ton, will go to the East Hampton estate of theater angel, Evan Frankel. The head of the second statue is earmarked for the Sutton Place Terrace of Zachary Fisher who is building a new skyscraper on the site.

Preservationists tried to save the theater, but to no avail. Burlington House, a generic office building, was constructed on the site. The Loew's Corporation built a new movie theater immediately to the west and named it the Ziegfeld. Showcases with memorabilia from Ziegfeld's career were set in the lower lobby.

INDEX

Gillette, Anita, 259, 351, 358, 495
Gillette, Priscilla, 417, 432
Gillette, William, 51, 76, 148, 322, 377
Gilley Moore's Market Stables, 541
Gillmore, Frank, 6, 7
Gilmore, Margalo, 11, 152, 224, 234, 322, 337, 435, 521, 546
Gilmour, J.H., 84
Gilroy, Frank D., 303, 312, 468
Gilsey House, 207
Gimbel, Norman, 306
Gin Game, The, 264, 324
Gingerbread Lady, The, 413, 494
Gingham Girl, The, 139
Gingold, Hermione, 257, 422, 482, 501
Ginsberg, Al, 460
Girard, Jeremy, 539
Giraudoux, Jean, 19, 321, 333, 409, 479
Girl and the Wizard, The, 100
Girl Behind the Counter, The, 100
Girl Behind the Gun, The, 74, 377
Girl Crazy, 2, 191, 345, 371, 482
Girl form Utah, The, 276
Girl Friend, The, 165, 447
"Girl Friend, The," 447
Girl from Brazil, The, 452
Girl from Kay's, The, 478
Girl from Maxim's, The, 383, 387, 388
Girl from Rector's, The, 428
Girl from Utah, The, 500
Girl I Left Behind Me, The, 59, 147, 149
Girl in Pink Tights, The, 127, 169, 333, 455
Girl in the Spotlight, The, 239
Girl in the Taxi, The, 39
Girl of My Dreams, The, 217
Girl of the Golden West, The, 58, 60, 381
Girl on the Film, The, 171
"Girl on the Magazine Cover, The," 315
"Girl on the Prow, The," 211", 253, 453
"Girl That I Marry, The," 25, 67
Girls of Gottenberg, The, 276
Girofle-Girofla, 99
Gish, Lillian, 61, 104, 118, 149, 312, 381, 468
Give a Girl a Break, 193
"Give a Little, Get a Little Love," 332
Give and Take, 172
"Give It Back to the Indians," 255
"Give Me the Moonlight, Give Me the Girl," 128
"Give My Regards to Broadway," 108, 296, 400
Give Us This Night, 212
Givot, George, 467, 567
Glad, Gladys, 233, 581
Glad of It, 53
Glad Tidings, 323
Glad Tidings Tabernacle, 199
"Glad to Be Unhappy," 448
Glad to See You, 516
Glaser, Lulu, 99
Glaser, Milton, 418
Glass Menagerie, The, 104, 224, 364, 406, 557

Glass Slipper, The, 418, 545
Glass, Joanna M., 423
Glass, Julia, 96
Gleason, Bernadette, 503
Gleason, Jackie, 91, 185, 269, 350, 392, 481
Gleason, James, 3, 338
Gleason, Joanna, 335, 342, 508
Glengarry Glen Ross, 264
Glenn, Scott, 407
Gliere, Reinhold, 136
Globe Theatre, 190, 280, 312, 320, 447, 555
Gloriana, 174
Glorifying the American Girl, 201
Glover, Danny, 323
Glover, Savion, 16, 354, 547
Gluck, Alma, 321
Gluck, Morris, 72
Glyn, Elinor, 96
Go to It, 425
Goat, The, 522
Goat, or Who Is Sylvia? The, 264
Goat Song, 545
"God Bless America," 66, 67, 106
God Gave Me Twenty Cents, 400
Goddard, Paulette, 511, 582
Godreau, Miguel, 333
God's Favorite, 157, 495
Gods of the Lightning, 339
Godsol, F.J., 95
Godspell, 82
Goelet, Robert, xiv
Goethe, 545
Goetz, Augustus, 71, 120
Goetz, E. Ray, 85, 188, 190, 316, 416, 451, 452
Goetz, Ruth, 71, 120
Goetzl, Anselm, 14, 221
Goggle's Dollhouse, 106
Going Greek, 74
Going Places, 74, 287
Going to Pieces, 571
Going Up, 108, 109, 217
Going Up (play), 271
Gold Bug, The, 236
Gold Diggers, The, 322
Gold Eagle Guy, 61
Golda, 358
Goldberg, Rube, 544
Goldberg, Whoopi, 323
Goldberger, Paul, 289
Golden, Annie, 15
Golden, Fred, 513
Golden, Grace, 20, 99
Golden, John, 6, 8, 14, 32, 180, 247, 264, 298, 299, 311, 388, 467, 514, 531, 579
Golden Barge, The, 247
Golden Boy, 19, 61, 198, 329, 421, 506, 547
Golden Child, 312
Golden Dawn, 143, 145, 205, 211, 218
"Golden Days," 268, 453
Golden Rainbow, 481

Hanks, Tom, 482
Hanky Panky, 85
Hanley, Ellen, 72
Hanley, James F., 474
Hanneford, Poodles, 248
Hans Christian Andersen, 304
Hansberry, Lorraine, 155, 311, 433
Happiest Girl in the World, The, 220
Happiest Millionaire, The, 323
"Happiness Is a Thing Called Joe," 29
"Happy As the Day Is Long," 28, 30
"Happy Because I'm in Love," 575
Happy Birthday, 82, 224, 309, 531
Happy Birthday, Wanda June, 143
Happy Days, 248
Happy Go Lucky, 41, 336
Happy Hunting, 347
"Happy Talk," 329
Happy Time, The, 86, 352, 412
Happyland, 512
Harbach, Otto, 16, 65, 136, 145, 171, 172, 174, 190, 196,
    203, 204, 210, **216**, 229, 253, 278, 279, 280, 281, 316,
    317, 324, 327, 379, 453, 454, 574
Harburg, E.Y., 17, 29, 74, 127, 132, 137, 172, 185, 186, 190,
    191, 196, **219**, 257, 268, 285, 286, 292, 349, 432, 474,
    479, 480, 500, 517, 565, 566
Harcourt, Cyril, 109
Harcourt, William, 6
Hard Rock Hotel, 360
Hardart, Frank, 43
Harding, Ann, 63, 369
Harding, President, 299
Hardwicke, Sir Cedric, 21, 263, 370
Hardy Holzman Pfeiffer, 379
Hare, David, 77, 156, 413, 470
Hare, Ernest, 562
Harem, The, 60
Harlan, Otis, 386
"Harlem," 467
Harlem Cavalcade, 519
Harlem Club, 286
Harlem Nocturne, 288
Harlem on Broadway, 180
"Harlem on My Mind," 67, 363
Harlem Opera House, 207, 208
Harlem Opera House, 541
Harling, Frank, 286
Harlow, 398
Harman, Barry, 303
Harney, Ben, 259
Harnick, Sheldon, 3, 5, 72, 82, 88, 137, 157, 318, 419, 420,
    424, 445
Harp of Life, The, 315, 320
Harriet, 234
"Harrigan," 108
Harrigan, Ned, 229
Harrigan, Nedda, 229
Harrigan, William, 149
Harrigan and Hart, 89, 90
Harrington, John Carbox, 12

Harrington, Pat, 257, 364
Harris, Barbara, 73, 74, 286, 293, 333, 468, 481
Harris, Elmer, 355
Harris, Henry B., 251, 227
Harris, Jed, 17, 71, 81, 118, 223, 330, 339, 419
Harris, Julie, 76, 125, 149, 151, 311, 318, 324, 358
Harris, Rene, 251
Harris, Richard, 293
Harris, Rosemary, 231, 414, 437
Harris, Sam H., 7, 12, 27, 67, 108, 109, 110, 185, 191, 220,
    274, 282, 355, 356, 360, 361, 363, 364, 484, 505
Harris, William, 147
Harris, William B., 23, 242, 434
Harris Theatre, 23, 39, 185, **220**, 319, 379
Harrison, Gregory, 62, 503
Harrison, Ray, 68
Harrison, Rex, 15, 104, 152, 194, 292, 333, 481
Harrold, Orville, 203, 387
Hart, Charles, 82, 423
Hart, Frieda, 445
Hart, Kitty Carlisle, 405
Hart, Lorenz (*See also* Rodgers and Hart), xii, 132, 135, 185,
    212, 307, 452, 580
Hart, Max, 445
Hart, Moss (*See also* Kaufman and Hart), 21, 76, 169, 172,
    193, 234, 255, **271**, 292, 322, 329, 333, 363, 364, 372,
    378, 448, 455, 468, 572
Hart, Teddy, 118, 256, 337, 406, 449, 555
Hart, William S., 386
Hartley, Dr., 12
Hartman, Grace, 156, 172, 332
Hartman, Louis, 60
Hartman, Paul, 156, 172, 332
Harvard Dramatic Club, 3
"Harvest According, The," 128
Harvest Moon Ball, 519
Harvey, 171, 224, 225, 531, 547
Harvey, Dennis, 539
Harvey, Ken, 519
Harvey, Laurence, 125, 293
Haskell, Loney, 543
Hassard Short's Ritz Revue, 435
Hassell, George, 564
Hastings, Thomas, 147
Hasty Pudding shows, 290, 363
Hatcher, Mary, 332
Hateley, Linzi, 552
Hatful of Rain, A, 323
Hauerbach, Otto (*See* Otto Harbach)
Haunted, The, 391
"Haunted Heart," 135
Haunted House, The, 186
Hauptmann, Bruno Richard, 471, 561
Havana, 100
Have a Heart, 74, 277, 296
"Have You Met Miss Jones?," 372, 448
Having Our Say, 77
Having Wonderful Time, 322, 419, 455
Havoc, June, 133, 152, 168, 347, 417, 567
Hawkins, June, 340